The Seattle School
2510 Elliott Ave.

D0046680

DRAWN

The Seattle School

10033022

THE NEW WESTMINSTER DICTIONARY
OF LITURGY AND WORSHIP

THE NEW WESTMINSTER DICTIONARY OF LITURGY AND WORSHIP

EDITED BY

PAUL BRADSHAW

Westminster John Knox Press

LOUISVILLE • LONDON

© SCM Press 2002

First published in Great Britain in 2002 under the title The New SCM Dictionary of Liturgy and Worship

All rights reserved. No part of this book may be reproduced or transmitted in any form or by any means, electronic or mechanical, including photocopying, recording, or by any information storage or retrieval system, without permission in writing from the publisher. For information, address Westminster John Knox Press, 100 Witherspoon Street, Louisville, Kentucky 40202-1396.

First American edition
Published by Westminster John Knox Press
Louisville, Kentucky

This book is printed on acid-free paper that meets the American National Standards Institute Z39.48 standard.∞

PRINTED IN GREAT BRITAIN

02 03 04 05 06 07 08 09 10 11 — 10 9 8 7 6 5 4 3 2 1

Library of Congress Cataloging-in-Publication Data is on file at the Library of Congress, Washington, D.C.

ISBN 0-664-22655-8

PREFACE

Although this dictionary is very obviously closely related to the *Dictionary of Liturgy and Worship* edited by J. G. Davies (SCM Press, London 1972, 2nd edn 1986), it is not merely a further edition of that work, but rather its successor. While the vast majority of the headings used in that earlier volume have been adopted here, some have been deleted, new ones added, and other subjects rearranged. For example, 'experimental forms of worship' has been eliminated because it now seems an outdated category, and for a similar reason 'feminist liturgical movement' subsumed within the wider category of 'women and worship'; while entries referring to more recent developments, like 'praise and worship movement', have been inserted. The broad entry on 'liturgies' has been replaced by two separate entries, on 'eucharist' and on 'word, services of the'. In some cases entries have been placed under new headings that would be more commonly used today. Thus, for instance, 'year, liturgical' has been substituted for 'calendar'; 'daily prayer' for 'canonical hours'; 'eucharistic prayer' for 'anaphora'; 'inculturation' for 'indigenization'; and so on.

All entries have been entirely rewritten, and in nearly every case by a new contributor. Contributors have been chosen on the basis of their expertise in the particular subject, in some instances from within the particular worship tradition under discussion, in others from outside, since both views shed valuable and complementary light. All the entries, except the shortest, have been broken up into numbered sections with sub-headings for ease of use and provided with bibliographical resources for further study. Where appropriate, the literature listed has been divided into selected texts and studies, with works containing a more extensive bibliography indicated by the symbol (bib.). It is the editor's earnest hope that with these changes and improvements the volume will serve as a comprehensive guide to the subject for future years as well as Davies' work has done for the last thirty years.

PAUL BRADSHAW

CONTRIBUTORS

Dr Daniel Albrecht, *Professor of Christian History and Spirituality, Bethany College, Scotts Valley, California, USA*. **Assemblies of God Churches' Worship**

The Rt Revd Dr J. Neil Alexander, *Bishop of the Episcopal Diocese of Atlanta, and formerly Professor of Liturgics and Norma and Olan Mills Professor of Divinity in the School of Theology of the University of the South, Sewanee, Tennessee, USA*. **Advent; Advent Wreath; Creeds in Liturgy**

The Revd Stefanos Alexopoulos, *Orthodox deacon and doctoral candidate in liturgical studies, University of Notre Dame, Notre Dame, Indiana, USA*. **Fan; Incense; Litany**

The Revd Dr Horace T. Allen, Jr, *Professor of Worship and Preaching, Boston University School of Theology, Boston, Massachusetts, USA*. **Lectionaries**

Dr Ronald J. Allen, *Nettie Sweeney and Hugh Th. Miller Professor of Preaching and New Testament, Christian Theological Seminary, Indianapolis, Indiana, USA*. **Funerals 6: Christian Church; Marriage 6: Christian Church**

Dr Paul N. Anderson, *Professor of Biblical and Quaker Studies, George Fox University, Newberg, Oregon, USA*. **Quaker Worship**

The Revd Dr S. Wesley Ariarajah, *Methodist minister from Sri Lanka, currently Professor of Ecumenical Theology, Drew University School of Theology, Madison, New Jersey, USA*. **Sri Lanka, Worship in the Church in**

The Revd Dr John F. Baldovin, SJ, *Professor of Historical and Liturgical Theology, Weston Jesuit School of Theology, Cambridge, Massachusetts, USA*. **Eucharistic Prayer; Roman Catholic Worship**

Dr George Bebawi, *Director of Studies, Institute for Orthodox Christian Studies, Cambridge*. **Coptic Worship**

Dr Mary Berry, *Director of the Schola Gregoriana of Cambridge and a member of the Faculty of Music, Cambridge University*. **Chants of the Proper of the Mass; Church Modes; Gregorian Chant; Hymns 1: Latin; Motet; Music in the Mass of the Roman Rite; Notation and Rhythm; Polyphony; Psalm-Tones**

The Revd Dr Thomas F. Best, *Executive Secretary for Faith and Order, World Council of Churches, and an ordained minister of the Christian Church (Disciples of Christ)*. **Baptism 6: Christian Church; Books, Liturgical 6: Christian Church; Christian Church (Disciples of Christ) Worship; Eucharist 6: Christian Church; Ordination 6: Christian Church; Word, Services of the, 6: Christian Church**

Dr Kathleen M. Black, *Gerald Kennedy Professor of Homiletics and Liturgics, Claremont School of Theology, Claremont, California, USA*. **Deaf Persons and Worship; Disabilities, Worship and Persons with**

The Revd Dr Paul F. Bradshaw, *Professor of Liturgy, University of Notre Dame, Indiana, USA*. **Acolyte; Anamnesis; Anointing; Benedictus; Bishop; Blessing; Books, Liturgical 1: Early Christianity; Confession; Consecration, Prayer of; Coronation Services; Crucifer; Daily Prayer 1: Early Christianity; Deacon; Deaconess;**

Dedication; Dismissal; Easter; Easter Garden or Sepulchre; Easter Vigil; Ecu-
menical Co-operation in Liturgical Revision; Elder; Epiclesis; Eucharist 1: Early
Christianity; Fast Days; Grace; Harvest Thanksgiving; Host; Institution Narra-
tive; Last Rites; Lector; Low Sunday; *Lucernarium*; Mass; Minor Orders; Mixed
Chalice; Office Hymn; Ordinary Time; Ordination 1: Early Christianity;
Ordination 2: Eastern Churches; Ordination 4: Anglican; Preface; Presbyter;
Reader; Sanctus; Sentences; Server; Subdeacon; Superintendent; Synaxis;
Viaticum; Vigil; Western Rites; Whitsunday; Word, Services of the, 1: Early
Christianity

The Rt Revd Colin O. Buchanan, *Bishop of Woolwich.* **Books, Liturgical 4: Anglican;
Charismatic Worship; Eucharist 4: Anglican; Funerals 4: Anglican; House
Church Worship**

The Revd Dr Richard F. Buxton, *sometime Lecturer in Liturgy, University of Manchester.*
**Octave; Quinquagesima; Sanctification of Time, The; Sunday; Transfiguration;
Trinity Sunday**

The Revd Dr Andrew Cameron-Mowat, SJ, *Lecturer, Department of Pastoral Studies,
Heythrop College, University of London.* **All Saints; All Souls; Annunciation;
Common of Saints; Marian Feasts; Saints, Cult of the**

The Revd Dr Stanislaus Campbell, FSC, *Auxiliary Provincial, De La Salle Christian
Brothers, Napa, California, USA.* **Daily Prayer 3: Medieval and Roman Catholic;
Word, Services of the, 3: Medieval and Roman Catholic**

The Revd Anscar J. Chupungco, OSB, *Director, Paul VI Institute of Liturgy, The
Philippines.* **Inculturation**

The Revd Dr Richard Cleaves, *Minister, Highbury Congregational Church, Cheltenham,
and Tutor, Congregational Federation Integrated Training Course.* **Baptism 7: Congregationalist; Congregationalist Worship; Funerals 7: Congregationalist**

The Revd Francis X. Clooney, SJ, *Professor of Comparative Theology, Boston College,
Chestnut Hill, Massachusetts, USA.* **Hindu Worship**

Dr Martin F. Connell, *Assistant Professor of Liturgical Studies, School of Theology,
St John's University, Collegeville, Minnesota, USA.* **Ascension Day; Christmas;
Christmas Crib; Ember Days; Epiphany; Foot-Washing; Pentecost; Year,
Liturgical**

Dr Dimitri Conomos, *Oxford.* **Byzantine Chant**

Dr Melva Wilson Costen, *Helmar Emil Nielsen Professor of Worship and Music,
Interdenominational Theological Center, Atlanta, Georgia, USA.* **Black Churches
Worship 2: USA; Spirituals**

The Revd Dr Mary Cotes, *Baptist minister, Pontypridd, Wales.* **Word, Services of the, 5:
Baptist**

The Revd Dr Anthony R. Cross, *Research Fellow, Centre for Advanced Theological
Research, University of Surrey Roehampton, London.* **Baptism 5: Baptist**

The Venerable Dr Mark Dalby, *Archdeacon emeritus of Rochdale, Lancashire.* **Children
and Worship**

The Revd Dr James Dallen, *Professor of Sacramental and Liturgical Theology, Religious
Studies Department, Gonzaga University, Spokane, Washington, USA.* **Penance**

The Revd Dr Anne Dawtry, *Principal of Ordained Local Ministry and Integrated
Education, Diocese of Salisbury.* **Art and Worship; Laity and Worship; Lay
Ministries; Word, Service of the 4: Anglican**

The Revd Dr Michael S. Driscoll, *Associate Professor of Liturgy, University of Notre Dame, Indiana, USA.* **Books, Liturgical 3: Medieval and Roman Catholic; Eucharist 3: Medieval and Roman Catholic; Funerals 3: Medieval and Roman Catholic**

The Revd Dr Martin Dudley, *Rector of St Bartholomew the Great, Smithfield, London.* **Absolution; Absolution Prayer; Absolutions of the Dead; Altar; Altar Hangings; Altar Rails; Baldachin; Baptistery; Catechism; Ceremonial; Collect; Colours, Liturgical; Consecration of Churches; Frontal; Movements in Worship; Procession; Reredos; Riddel, Ridle; Rogation Days; Rubrics; Three Hours Devotion**

The Revd Michael Durber, *Training Co-ordinator, Congregational Federation.* **Eucharist 7: Congregationalist; Marriage 7: Congregationalist**

The Revd Christopher J. Ellis, *Principal, Bristol Baptist College, Bristol.* **Baptist Worship**

The Revd Dr M. Daniel Findikyan, *Archbishop Tiran Nersoyan Professor of Liturgy, St Nersess Armenian Seminary, New Rochelle, New York, USA.* **Funerals 2: Eastern Churches; Marriage 2: Eastern Churches**

Dr Kathleen Flake, *Assistant Professor of American Religious History, Vanderbilt University Divinity School, Nashville, Tennessee, USA.* **Church of Jesus Christ of Latter-day Saints Worship**

The Revd Dr Peter Galadza, *Kule Family Professor of Liturgy, Sheptytsky Institute of Eastern Christian Studies, Saint Paul University, Ottawa, Canada.* **Books, Liturgical 2: Eastern Churches**

The Revd Jonathan Goodall, *Chaplain and Research Assistant to the Bishop in Europe, formerly Chaplain and Sacrist, Westminster Abbey.* **Ambo; Aumbry; Chalice and Paten; Chrismatory; Cross, Crucifix; Martyrium; Orientation; Pulpit; Veil**

The Revd Hugh F. Graham, OCC, *Minister of Stepney Meeting House United Reformed Church, London.* **United Reformed Church Worship**

The Revd Dr Donald Gray, *Canon emeritus of Westminster.* **Alms; Alms Dish; Anglican Worship; Ante-Communion; Bells; Communion; Fraction; Lavabo; Law and Worship 2: Church of England; Remembrance Sunday; Words of Administration**

The Revd Dr Robert W. Gribben, *Professor of Worship and Mission, Uniting Church Theological Hall, Ormond College, University of Melbourne, Australia.* **Australia, Worship in the Uniting Church in**

Mr W. Jardine Grisbrooke, *Orthodox layperson and formerly Lecturer in Liturgical Studies at the Queen's College, Birmingham.* **Agnus Dei; Doxology; Kyrie; Lord's Prayer, The; Ordinary; Proper; Silent Prayer; Suffrages; *Super Oblata***

The Revd George Guiver, CR, *Vice-Principal, The College of the Resurrection, Mirfield, West Yorkshire.* **Daily Prayer 4: Anglican; Intercession; Prayer**

The Revd Dr Stanley R. Hall, *Associate Professor of Liturgics, Austin Presbyterian Theological Seminary, Austin, Texas, USA.* **Books, Liturgical 12: Reformed; Presbyterian Worship 2: USA**

Dr John Harper, *Director General, Royal School of Church Music, and Research Professor, University of Wales, Bangor.* **Anthem; Antiphon; Carol; Chants; Choir (Musical); Hymns 2: Vernacular; Metrical Psalms; Organ; Psalmody; Responsorial Psalm; Responsory or Respond**

The Revd Jeremy Haselock, *Canon Precentor, Norwich Cathedral.* **Cathedra; Cathedral; Gestures; Posture**

The Revd Dr Brian Haymes, *Minister, Bloomsbury Central Baptist Church, London.*
Ordination 5: Baptist
The Revd Dr Dagmar Heller, *Secretary for Ecumenism and Relations with the Orthodox
Churches of the Evangelical Church in Germany.* **Ecumenical Worship; Inter-
communion**
Mr Stephen Hodge, *Buddhist translator and author.* **Buddhist Worship**
Dr Lawrence A. Hoffman, *Professor of Liturgy, Hebrew Union College–Jewish Institute
of Religion, New York, USA.* **Jewish Worship**
The Revd Canon David R. Holeton, *Professor of Liturgy, Charles University, Prague,
Czech Republic.* **Bohemian Liturgy; Infant Communion; Vestments**
Brother Tristam Holland, SSF, *Hilfield Friary, Dorchester, Dorset.* **Advent Antiphons;
Censer; Ciborium; Credence Table; Corporal; Cruet; Monstrance; Pall;
Passiontide; Purificator; Pyx; Tabernacle; Thurible; Thurifer**
The Revd John M. Huels, OSM, *Professor of Canon Law, Saint Paul University, Ottawa,
Canada.* **Law and Worship 1: Roman Catholic**
Professor John M. Hull, *School of Education, University of Birmingham, Edgbaston,
Birmingham.* **School Worship (England and Wales)**
Information Office of Jehovah's Witnesses, London. **Jehovah's Witnesses Worship**
The Revd Dr Gordon Jeanes, *Vicar of St Anne's Church, Wandsworth, London.*
**Bidding Prayer; Canticles; Cantor; Commination; Feria; Last Gospel; Readings,
Eucharistic**
The Revd Dr Philip Jenson, *Lecturer in Old Testament and Hebrew, Trinity College,
Bristol.* **Old Testament Worship**
Dr Calvin M. Johansson, *Professor of Church Music, Evangel University, Springfield,
Missouri, USA.* **Pentecostal Worship**
The Revd Dr Maxwell E. Johnson, *Associate Professor of Liturgy, University of Notre
Dame, Indiana, USA.* **Baptism 1: Early Christianity; Catechumen, Catechumen-
ate; Confirmation; Godparents; Insufflation; Lent; Mystagogy; Scrutinies,
Baptismal**
The Revd Dr Jan Michael Joncas, *Associate Professor of Theology and Teaching Fellow
in Catholic Studies, University of St Thomas, St Paul, Minnesota, USA.* **Music as
Worship; Ordination 3: Medieval and Roman Catholic**
The Revd Dr Thomas A. Kane, CSP, *Associate Professor of Homiletics and Liturgical
Practice, Weston Jesuit School of Theology, Cambridge, Massachusetts, USA.* **Dance,
Liturgical**
Dr William S. Kervin, *Assistant Professor of Public Worship, Emmanuel College,
Toronto, Canada.* **Canada, Worship in the United Church of**
Habtemichael Kidane, *former Lecturer in Liturgy at the Joint Seminaries of Addis Ababa
(Ethiopia) and Asmara (Eritrea).* **Ethiopian (or Ge'ez) Worship**
Dr John Klentos, *Assistant Professor of Eastern Orthodox Studies, Graduate Theological
Union, Berkeley, California, USA.* **Antidoron; Diptychs; Enarxis; Eucharist 2:
Eastern Churches; Great Entrance; Little Entrance; Orthodox Worship;
Prothesis**
The Revd Canon Dr Christopher Lamb, *Rector of Warmington, South Warwickshire and
formerly Secretary for Inter-Faith Relations for the General Synod of the Church of
England and for Churches Together in Britain and Ireland.* **Inter-Faith Worship**
Dr Lizette Larson-Miller, *Associate Professor of Liturgical Studies, Church Divinity*

School of the Pacific/Graduate Theological Union, Berkeley, California, USA. **Liberation and Worship**

The Revd Dr Gordon Lathrop, *Charles A. Schieren Professor of Liturgy, Lutheran Theological Seminary, Philadelphia, Pennsylvania, USA.* **Bible, Use of in Worship; Daily Prayer 5: Lutheran; Eucharist 8: Lutheran; Word, Services of the, 8: Lutheran**

The Venerable Trevor Lloyd, *Archdeacon of Barnstaple, Devon.* **Lectern; Mission and Worship; Pews**

Dr Thomas G. Long, *Bandy Professor of Preaching, Candler School of Theology, Emory University, Atlanta, Georgia, USA.* **Funerals 12: Reformed; Marriage 12: Reformed**

The Revd Dr Richard D. McCall, *Associate Professor of Liturgy and Church Music, Episcopal Divinity School, Cambridge, Massachusetts, USA.* **Drama and Worship**

The Revd Dr Andrew McGowan, *Associate Professor of Early Christian History, Episcopal Divinity School, Cambridge, Massachusetts, USA.* **Agape; Alleluia; Amen; Lord's Supper, The; New Testament Worship.**

Dr A. J. MacGregor, *Librarian, Ushaw College, Durham.* **Candles, Lamps, and Lights; Easter Candle; New Fire**

The Revd Dr Frank D. Macchia, *Associate Professor of Theology, Vanguard University, Costa Mesa, California, USA.* **Baptism 11: Pentecostal; Eucharist 11: Pentecostal; Ordination 11: Pentecostal; Word, Services of the, 11: Pentecostal**

The Revd Michael D. Macchia, *Senior Pastor, Christian Assembly Church, Hobart, Indiana, USA.* **Books, Liturgical 11: Pentecostal; Funerals 11: Pentecostal; Marriage 11: Pentecostal**

The Revd Dr Pauly Maniyattu, *Lecturer in Liturgical Theology, St Ephrem's Theological College, Satna, M.P., India.* **East Syrian Worship**

The Revd Dr George Mathew, *Lecturer, Mar Thoma Theological Seminary, Kottayam, Kerala, India.* **Mar Thoma Church Worship**

Dr Marchita B. Mauck, *Professor of Art History, Louisiana State University, USA.* **Aisle; Architectural Setting; Apse; Atrium; Basilica; Centralized Building; Chancel; Chantry; Chapel; Gallery; Narthex; Nave; Choir (Architectural); Communion Table; Rostrum; Sacristy; Sanctuary; Sedilia; Tower; Transept; Vestry**

The Revd Dr Daniel J. Meeter, *Senior Pastor, Central Reformed Church, Grand Rapids, Michigan, USA.* **Baptism 12: Reformed**

The Revd Dr John A. Melloh, SM, *Director of the John S. Marten Program in Homiletics and Liturgics, University of Notre Dame, Indiana, USA.* **Preaching and Worship**

The Revd Dr Ruth A. Meyers, *Associate Professor of Liturgics, Seabury-Western Theological Seminary, Evanston, Illinois, USA.* **Baptism 4: Anglican; Baptismal Vows, Renewal of; Ordination of Women**

The Revd John A. Midgley, *Minister of Cross Street Unitarian Chapel, Manchester.* **Unitarian Worship**

Dr Nathan Mitchell, *Associate Director, Institute for Church Life, University of Notre Dame, Indiana, USA.* **Cult, Cultus; Eucharistic Theologies 1: Historical; Rite, Ritual; Sacrament 1: Historical; Secularization and Worship; Sign, Symbol**

The Revd Dr Douglas M. Murray, *Principal of Trinity College and Senior Lecturer in Ecclesiastical History, University of Glasgow.* **Presbyterian Worship 1: United Kingdom; Reformed Worship**

Dr John Nelson, *Assistant Professor, Department of Theology and Religious Studies, University of San Francisco, California, USA.* **Shinto Worship**

The Revd Dr Paul R. Nelson (deceased), *former Director for Worship, Evangelical Lutheran Church in America.* **Lutheran Worship; Ordination 8: Lutheran**

The Revd Stephen Oliver, *Canon Precentor, St Paul's Cathedral, London.* **Media, Worship on the; Pastoral Care and Worship**

The Revd Kenan B. Osborne, OFM, *Professor of Systematic Theology, Franciscan School of Theology, Berkeley, California, USA.* **Eucharistic Theologies 2: Modern; Mystery; Sacrament 2: Modern; Sacramentals**

The Revd Dr John M. Parry, *Tutor in Missiology and World Faiths, Partnership for Theological Education, Manchester.* **Sikh Worship**

The Revd Dr Keith F. Pecklers, SJ, *Professor of Liturgical History, Pontifical Liturgical Institute, Rome, Italy.* **Liturgical Movement, The 1: Europe; Liturgical Movement, The 3: USA**

The Revd Dr Philip H. Pfatteicher, *Associate Pastor, First Lutheran Church, Pittsburgh, Pennsylvania, USA, and Adjunct Professor of Sacred Music, Duquesne University.* **Funerals 8: Lutheran; Marriage 8: Lutheran**

The Revd Dr L. Edward Phillips, *Associate Professor of Historical Theology, Garrett-Evangelical Theological Seminary, Evanston, Illinois, USA.* **Ethics and Worship; Funerals 1: Early Christianity; Kiss, Ritual; Thanksgiving (USA)**

Dr Joanne M. Pierce, *Associate Professor, Department of Religious Studies, College of the Holy Cross, Worcester, Massachusetts, USA.* **Altar, Stripping of; Altar, Washing of; Ash Wednesday; Ashes; Churching of Women; Good Friday; Holy Saturday; Holy Week; Maundy Thursday; Palm Sunday; Tenebrae; Veneration of the Cross**

The Very Revd Stephen Platten, *Dean of Norwich.* **Pilgrimage**

Dr Colin Podmore, *London.* **Advent Star; Candle Service, Moravian; Christingle; Moravian Worship**

Dr Marjorie Procter-Smith, *LeVan Professor of Christian Worship, Perkins School of Theology, Southern Methodist University, Dallas, Texas, USA.* **Women and Worship**

Dr Gail Ramshaw, *scholar of liturgical language, Philadelphia, Pennsylvania, USA.* **Inclusive Language; Language, Liturgical**

The Revd Kathy N. Reeves, *Pastor, Euclid Avenue United Methodist Church, Oak Park, Illinois, USA.* **Blind Persons and Worship**

The Revd Dr John Rempel, *Mennonite Central Committee Liaison to the United Nations in New York City, USA.* **Mennonite Worship**

Dr R. David Rightmire, *Professor of Bible and Theology, Asbury College, Wilmore, Kentucky, USA.* **Salvation Army Worship**

The Revd Dr Lester Ruth, *Assistant Professor of Worship and Liturgy, Asbury Theological Seminary, Wilmore, Kentucky, USA.* **Extempore Prayer; Independent Evangelical Church Worship; Praise-and-Worship Movement**

Dr Don E. Saliers, *William R. Cannon Distinguished Professor of Theology and Worship, Emory University, Atlanta, Georgia, USA.* **Spirituality, Liturgical**

The Revd Dr Thaddeus A. Schnitker, *former Professor of Liturgy, Diocesan Seminary, Catholic Diocese of the Old Catholics in Germany.* **Baptism 10: Old Catholic; Books, Liturgical 10: Old Catholic; Eucharist 10: Old Catholic; Funerals 10: Old Catholic; Marriage 10: Old Catholic; Old Catholic Worship; Ordination 10: Old Catholic; Word, Services of the, 10: Old Catholic**

The Revd Dr Frank C. Senn, *Pastor, Immanuel Lutheran Church, Evanston, Illinois, USA.* **Books, Liturgical 8: Lutheran**

The Revd Dr Paul Sheppy, *Baptist Minister and Secretary of the Joint Liturgical Group of Great Britain.* **Books, Liturgical 5: Baptist; Eucharist 5: Baptist; Funerals 5: Baptist; Marriage 5: Baptist**

Dr Ataullah Siddiqui, *Senior Research Fellow, The Islamic Foundation, Leicester.* **Islamic Worship**

The Revd Dr Godwin R. Singh, *Principal, Leonard Theological College, Jabalpur, M.P., India.* **North India, Worship in the Church of**

The Revd Dr William David Spencer, *Ranked Adjunct Associate Professor of Theology and the Arts, Gordon-Conwell Theological Seminary, South Hamilton, Massachusetts, USA.* **Rastafarian Worship**

The Revd Dr Bryan D. Spinks, *Professor of Liturgical Studies, Yale University Institute of Sacred Music and Yale Divinity School, New Haven, Connecticut, USA.* **Liturgical Movement, The 2: United Kingdom**

The Revd S. Anita Stauffer, *Lutheran Pastor, USA, and formerly Study Secretary for Worship and Congregational Life, Lutheran World Federation.* **Font**

Dr Stephen J. Stein, *Chancellors' Professor of Religious Studies, Indiana University, Bloomington, Indiana, USA.* **Shaker Worship**

The Rt Revd Dr Kenneth W. Stevenson, *Bishop of Portsmouth.* **Candlemas; Family Services; Offertory; Marriage 1: Early Christianity; Marriage 3: Medieval and Roman Catholic; Marriage 4: Anglican**

Dr Kenneth B. Stout, *Professor of Preaching and Christian Ministry, Seventh-Day Adventist Theological Seminary, Andrews University, Berrien Springs, Michigan, USA.* **Seventh-Day Adventist Worship**

Dr Martin Stringer, *Lecturer in Anthropology/Sociology of Religion, Department of Theology, University of Birmingham.* **Social Sciences and the Study of Liturgy**

The Revd Mark Sturge, *General Director, African and Caribbean Evangelical Alliance, London.* **Black Churches' Worship 1**

The Revd Dr M. Thomas Thangaraj, *D. W. and Ruth Brooks Associate Professor of World Christianity, Candler School of Theology, Emory University, Atlanta, Georgia, USA.* **South India, Worship in the Church of**

The Revd Michael Thompson, *Rector of St Mary and St Martin, Stamford, Lincolnshire.* **Ablutions; Commixture; Disposal of the Eucharistic Remains; Piscina; Screen; Stoup**

The Revd Dr Stewart Todd, *retired minister of the Church of Scotland, formerly incumbent of the Cathedral Church of St Machar, Aberdeen.* **Ordination 12: Reformed**

The Revd Dr David Tripp, *Pastor, North Indiana Conference, United Methodist Church, and Adjunct Professor, Associated Mennonite Biblical Seminary, Elkhart, Indiana, USA.* **Covenant Service; Love-Feast; Plymouth Brethren/Christian Brethren Worship; Watch-Night**

The Revd Diane Karay Tripp, *Minister, Presbyterian Church, USA.* **Daily Prayer 6: Reformed**

The Revd Dr Jeffrey A. Truscott, *Instructor in Liturgics, Japan Lutheran College and Theological Seminary, Tokyo, Japan.* **Baptism 8: Lutheran**

The Revd Dr Karen B. Westerfield Tucker, *Associate Professor of Christian Worship, Duke University, Durham, North Carolina, USA.* **Baptism 9: Methodist; Books, Liturgical 9: Methodist; Camp Meeting; Funerals 9: Methodist; Marriage 9: Methodist; Methodist Worship 2: USA; Ordination 9: Methodist; Sick, Liturgical**

Ministry to the; Word, Services of the, 9: Methodist

The Revd Dr Baby Varghese, *Professor of Liturgy, Orthodox Theological Seminary, Kottayam, Kerala, India.* **West Syrian Worship**

The Revd Dr Geoffrey Wainwright, *Cushman Professor of Christian Theology, Duke University, Durham, North Carolina, USA.* **Eucharist 9: Methodist; Theology of Worship**

The Revd C. Norman R. Wallwork, *Associate Lecturer in Liturgy, Wesley College, Bristol.* **Anniversary; Chairman of District; Class Leader/Class Meeting; Lay Preacher; Local Preacher; Methodist Worship 1: United Kingdom; Prayer Meeting**

The Revd Canon Christopher Walsh, *formerly Director of the Institute for Liturgy and Mission, Sarum College, Salisbury.* **Benediction; Catechist; Celebrant; Concelebration; Corpus Christi; Exposition; Forty Hours' Devotion; Reservation; Rosary; Sacred Heart; Stations of the Cross; Votive Mass**

The Revd Dr Joseph Weiss, SJ, *Administrative Director, Institute for Church Life, University of Notre Dame, Indiana, USA.* **Angelus; Asperges; Exorcism, Exorcist; Papal Rites; Requiem Mass**

Dr Gabriele Winkler, *Professor of Liturgical Studies, University of Tübingen, Germany.* **Armenian Worship; Baptism 2: Eastern Churches**

Dr John Witvliet, *Director, Calvin Institute of Christian Worship, and Assistant Professor of Worship, Calvin College and Theological Seminary, Grand Rapids, Michigan, USA.* **Eucharist 12: Reformed; Word, Services of the, 12: Reformed**

The Revd Dr Gregory Woolfenden, *Lecturer in Liturgy and Worship, Ripon College, Cuddesdon, Oxford.* **Daily Prayer 2: Eastern Churches; Icon; Iconostasis; Presanctified, Liturgy of the; *Trisagion*; Word, Services of the, 2: Eastern Churches**

The Revd Dr Janet H. Wootton, *Minister, Union Chapel, Islington, London, and Tutor, Congregational Federation Integrated Training Course.* **Books, Liturgical 7: Congregationalist; Ordination 7: Congregationalist; Word, Services of the, 7: Congregationalist**

The Revd Dr Edward J. Yarnold, SJ, *Research Lecturer, Campion Hall, Oxford University.* **Baptism 3: Medieval and Roman Catholic**

ABBREVIATIONS

BCE	Before the Common Era
BCP	*Book of Common Prayer*
(bib.)	A work containing extensive bibliography
CE	Common Era
Horton Davies, *WTE*	Horton Davies, *Worship and Theology in England*, 6 vols, Princeton/London 1961–96
NG2	Stanley Sadie and John Tyrrell (eds), *The New Grove Dictionary of Music and Musicians*, 2nd edn, London 2001 (also on-line at www.grove.com), which includes extensive bibliography, with ongoing on-line updating.
NT	New Testament
OT	Old Testament
RC	Roman Catholic

* An asterisk before a word indicates a separate entry under that or a similar heading.

References to Psalms follow the Hebrew rather than the Septuagint/Latin numbering.

Ablutions

The purifications of the sacred vessels following the consumption of the bread and wine at
the *eucharist. In early centuries the water (also
at times wine) used for the ablution of the
vessels was poured away into the *sacrarium* or
*piscina. By the eleventh century it was con-
sumed by the minister performing the ablutions
(the *deacon, *acolyte or other minister in the
Western liturgy or the deacon or priest in
Eastern rites). It is now common for water
alone to be used. Present RC instructions make
plain that the preferred place for such rituals is
a side table. If used at all, the end rather than
centre of the *altar is employed. RC instructions permit deferring the ablutions until after
the eucharist, as was the earliest known practice of the church. All such cleansing formerly
took place in the *sacristy. Under present rules
the bread and wine may be suitably covered
until after the departure of the faithful when the
ablutions are performed. This practice is similar to that ordered in the 1662 *BCP*, a custom
known from Elizabethan times.

See also **Disposal of the Eucharistic
Remains**.

MICHAEL THOMPSON

Absolution

A declaration of God's forgiveness pronounced
either in response to a general *confession
made during the liturgy or following individual
confession of sin as part of the ministry of
*penance and reconciliation. The ministerial
authority to forgive is understood to derive
from Christ's gift of the Spirit in John 20.23 ('If
you forgive the sins of any, they are forgiven')
and from the power of binding and loosing
given in Matt. 16.19; 18.18, and is specifically
conferred in priestly *ordination in the Roman
Pontifical and the Anglican *BCP*.

The penitential discipline of the church has
involved public and private strands. The former
included the *Ash Wednesday expulsion from
the community of grave sinners and their
reconciliation by the bishop on *Maundy
Thursday. Public penitence generally gave way
to the Celtic practice of private confession
and absolution. Penitential prayers appear in
eighth-century texts of eucharistic liturgies in
the East and confession of sin enters Western
eucharistic rites around 1000. Declaratory and
precatory forms of absolution, i.e., praying for
and declaring God's forgiveness, have been
used alongside the indicative form, 'I absolve
you'.

The most frequently used form of confession
and absolution in Anglican churches is that
contained within the eucharistic celebration. It
is made by the whole assembly as a preparation
for receiving *communion, and absolution is
pronounced by the president. Although there is
now wide provision for individual confession,
Anglican theology holds that such general
confession and absolution is efficacious for the
forgiveness of all types of sin. In the RC
Church, while a deprecatory form of absolution
concludes the penitential rite in the eucharist,
sacramental absolution is pronounced only in
the rite of penance.

MARTIN DUDLEY

Absolution Prayer

This short prayer, in three forms, was found in
the Roman Breviary after the psalms and before
the readings of each nocturn at matins (*see*
Daily Prayer 3). One form was used at the end
of each. The prayer ended a section of the office
and invoked the loving-kindness and mercy of
God.

MARTIN DUDLEY

Absolutions of the Dead

Absolutio defunctorum, an RC rite which once
concluded the *funeral liturgy in church. It
consisted of a chant asking that the dead person
might be freed from all sins (often *Libera me,
Domine*) sung while the coffin was sprinkled
and censed. The modern rite has replaced this
with a final commendation.

MARTIN DUDLEY

Acolyte

The office of acolyte (from a Greek word meaning 'follower' or 'attendant') is first referred to at Rome in the middle of the third century, and remained an exclusively Western phenomenon until very much later in history. It came to be regarded as one of the *minor orders, and the oldest evidence for a liturgical rite in connection with its conferral dates from the sixth century: the candidate was given the linen bag which held consecrated bread at the *eucharist as a symbol of his office, accompanied by a short blessing. The acolyte's functions were similar to those of the modern *server. When the RC Church abolished the minor orders in 1972, the acolyte survived as a 'ministry' to be conferred by 'institution' rather than 'ordination'. This institution takes place after the ministry of the word in the eucharist, or during a service of the *word, and consists of a bidding, a prayer and handing over of a vessel intended to contain the bread or wine for the eucharist. The term 'acolyte' is also often used more generally for those who serve in liturgical rites, and especially those who carry candles in processions.

EDITOR

Adaptation, Liturgical

see Inculturation

Advent

Derived from the Latin *adventus*, 'coming', the term designates the period in *Western rites beginning on the fourth Sunday before 25 December and continuing until the first celebration of *Christmas. In Eastern rites, preparatory rites for Christmas exist, but nothing that is historically or ritually parallel to Advent in the West.

Advent was the last season of the liturgical *year to develop and its origins remain obscure. Fifth- and sixth-century evidence shows a variety of penitential observances in Gaul and Spain lasting as many as six weeks. Some have sought the origin of Advent in the practice of *Epiphany baptism by noting parallels to the shape of *Lent. Others have called attention to sixth-century synodical documents and episcopal decrees that enjoin the faithful to penitence from the feast of Martin of Tours (11 November) to the feast of Epiphany (6 January). Still others have taken note of the fast of the tenth month (December) of pagan Rome and suggest that Advent may have begun as a response of the church to the continuing memory of the pagan winter fast. Each hypothesis is of continuing interest, but all contain serious flaws that make it impossible to claim with confidence a credible explanation of the origin of Advent.

Roman *lectionary lists of the seventh century continued to preserve Christmas as the beginning of the liturgical year, the readings for Advent being found at the end of the lists. This has led some to speculate that Rome itself resisted the emergence of Advent and that it was the church in Gaul and Spain that was largely responsible for the season's penitential quality. This stands in contrast to the more purely Roman preparation for Christmas that was less penitential and more focused on the joyful anticipation of Christ's coming.

In current practice, churches that follow a liturgical year understand it to begin on the first Sunday of Advent. The year concludes on the last Sunday after *Pentecost, often designated as the feast of Christ the King. The readings for the first two Sundays of Advent usually continue themes related to the eternal reign of Christ and the promise of his second advent. The readings of the third and fourth Sundays more clearly anticipate the coming celebration of Christmas.

J. Neil Alexander, *Waiting for the Coming: The Liturgical Meaning of Advent, Christmas, and Epiphany*, Washington, DC 1993; Thomas J. Talley, *The Origins of the Liturgical Year*, 2nd edn, Collegeville 1991, 147–53.

J. NEIL ALEXANDER

Advent Antiphons

The *antiphons traditionally sung in the West before and after the Magnificat at evening prayer on the seven days before *Christmas Eve. As they all begin with the word 'O', they are often called the Great 'O's. Each draws on an OT title of God, goes on to allude to a story linked with that title, and concludes with imploring God to come: come and save us, come and deliver us, come and redeem us, etc. Deliberately associated with the principal *canticle, namely Mary's great acclamation of her Saviour God in willing response to the angel Gabriel's announcement that she would bear the 'Son of the Most High' to the world, the antiphons create the climax to the imminent fulfilment of the OT prophecies of God's complete and unreserved participation in his creation. They are entitled: 17 December, *O Wisdom*; 18 December, *O Adonai*; 19 December, *O Root of Jesse*; 20 December, *O Key of David*; 21 December, *O Dayspring*; 22 December, *O King of the nations*; 23 December, *O Emmanuel*. An additional antiphon was included on 23 December in medieval England, namely *O Virgin of virgins*, thus pushing the others a day earlier, and its use was continued in some Anglican liturgical texts, including the 1549 *BCP*. Assumed to be addressed to the Virgin Mary and therefore inappropriate in connection with the other Great 'O's, all of which are addressed to God, it is now rarely used.

TRISTAM HOLLAND

Advent Star

From the first Sunday in *Advent until *Epiphany three-dimensional paper Advent stars, illuminated from within, hang in *Moravian homes and churches. This tradition originated in the Moravian school at Niesky, Germany; an illuminated star with 110 points hung in the courtyard during its fiftieth anniversary celebrations from 4 to 6 January 1821. These dates suggest that the reference was originally to the star of Bethlehem (Matt. 2). However, star symbols had been used by the Moravian Church since the 1730s (for example, a flat star replacing the cock on weathervanes) to point to Christ as 'the bright morning star' (Rev. 22.16). The illuminated star became an 'Advent Star' – festal decoration for what in the Moravian Church is not a penitential season but a time of joyful anticipation. By the mid-nineteenth century Advent stars were being made in other German Moravian schools, as they still are in the *Zinzendorfschulen*, Königsfeld im Schwarzwald. Between 20 and 110 3- to 8-sided paper points (depending on the geometrical pattern used) are glued to a card framework, into which a light bulb is inserted. The most common design has 26 points.

Advent stars came to be used in homes. Their use in worship halls (churches) began in Berlin and spread to Herrnhut and other congregations from 1925. Advent stars have been manufactured commercially in Herrnhut (Saxony) since 1897. Originally, the points were affixed to a solid metal core; since 1924 they have been joined together using paper fasteners. Since the 1980s, all sizes (rays 13–130 cm long) have also been available in plastic; these are found as street decorations in Moravian settlements.

Stars are also produced commercially by the Moravian Church in Edmonton, Alberta, Canada.

COLIN PODMORE

Advent Wreath

The Advent wreath is a popular accompaniment to domestic devotion and public liturgy on the Sundays of *Advent. The wreath consists of a circle of evergreens to which are added four candles, one to be lighted on each of the Sundays to mark the passage of the season. Although the completion of Advent is sometimes marked by the addition of a fifth 'Christ candle', the disappearance of the wreath and its replacement by decorations appropriate to *Christmas is more widely observed.

The precise origin of the Advent wreath is obscure. Its roots are surely in the pagan practices surrounding the keeping of the winter solstice. As the days of the solar year grew shorter, an increase in the number of lights that were brought indoors ritualized the longed-for return of the sun. Evergreens were shaped into wreaths – circles of green – and adorned with candles to symbolize the return of light and life. The pattern was reversed by the approach of the spring equinox as candles were extinguished, a phenomenon perhaps related to the extinguishing of candles at *tenebrae that originally extended over several weeks in *Lent.

The current appropriation of the Advent wreath first developed in Germany in the seventeenth century. It was a domestic devotion, which served as the focus for family prayer, candle lighting and fellowship during the weeks leading up to Christmas. The liturgical use of the Advent wreath was occasional and did not become widespread until the middle of the twentieth century. Its introduction into liturgical practice seems also to have grown out of its use in family and personal devotions.

The attachment of names and stories to the candles is of quite recent vintage and obscures the power of the symbol. The Advent wreath is perhaps best thought of as the church's clock that marks the passage of weeks during that season in which the church is most conscious of the passage of time as it awaits the coming of the redeemer. The use of coloured candles is an anachronism that is no longer congruent with the liturgical calendars of most churches. The use of plain white candles is to be preferred.

J. NEIL ALEXANDER

Adventist Worship

see **Seventh-Day Adventist Worship**

African-American Worship

see **Black Worship** 2

Agape

This Greek word for love or charity (or in this case 'love-feast') has been a prominent theme in much Christian thought and practice (see 1 Cor. 13). Agape, or translations of it, has also been used as the name for some communal meals in both ancient and modern times.

1. *Earliest Traditions*. Agape may originally have been a term used locally, perhaps in Asia Minor, for the Christian meal gathering. Along with '*eucharist', '*Lord's supper', 'the breaking of the bread' and others, its use represents an unsurprising original diversity of terminology, as of practice, in early Christian communal or eucharistic meals. None of the earliest uses of agape imply that this 'love-feast' exists separately from the eucharist. Either it is the only meal mentioned (Jude 12; 2 Peter 2.13; *Epistula Apostolorum* 15), or it is synonymous with the eucharist, at least with the occasion if not the food itself (Ignatius, *Romans* 7). Other early writers treat the agape with suspicion (Clement of Alexandria, *Paedagogus* 2.1). Tertullian provides the one reasonably detailed description of a meal called agape: prayer is offered before reclining; food and drink are taken in moderation; hands are washed; after the bringing of lights, participants sing biblical or other hymns; the whole closes with prayer (*Apology* 39). This is simply a Christian version of the Graeco-Roman banquet; the precise form, as well as the level of ethical success, may well have varied according to local custom.

Modern scholars of ancient Christianity have often identified the agape as a meal with a distinctive form or function, including both a meal within which the eucharistic actions are placed (1 Cor. 10—11), and also various Christian meals somehow unlike the normative eucharist commemorating Jesus' death (*Didache* 9–10; *Apostolic Tradition* 25–7). Such uses are at best speculative, since none of these examples is termed agape in the original sources. It has also been suggested that agape indicates a meal with charitable purposes (and vice versa; see Ignatius, *Smyrneans*; Tertullian, *1 Apology*).

Charity is characteristic, but this can also be true of meals called 'eucharist' (Justin Martyr, *First Apology* 65–7) and others. The agape may therefore not have been an especially distinctive meal in form or function at the earliest point, beyond its Christian milieu and the implied ethical imperative of the name.

2. *Later Developments*. Over time, the term agape does become more clearly associated with communal meals distinct from the eucharist. In the fourth century it refers to meals held in homes (Council of Gangra, Canon 11), and to some monastic gatherings (Palladius, *Lausiac History* 16); these are comparable to some of the earlier meals, but the terminology has emerged more clearly, over and against definitive eucharistic rites. Monastic meals may be one setting where a survival of the agape beyond the ancient church can be claimed, although the terminology has not been retained. Some paintings from the Roman catacombs (Sts Peter and Marcellinus) do have meal scenes with captions including agape; some would therefore see a link between the 'love-feast' and funerary meal customs. These meals, however, seem better described by the term *refrigerium*; there are points in common with other communal meals, but no specific reason to call these scenes, or the meals they refer to, by the name agape. Agape-meals are mentioned as late as the seventh century but really seem to have faded in prominence after the fourth.

3. *Modern Revivals*. Meals called agape, *love-feast, and similar have been held in a number of Protestant traditions from the eighteenth century onwards, apparently based on readings of the ancient sources mentioned above. More recently, parishes and communities of RC, Anglican and other traditions, as well as *ecumenical gatherings, have used the term agape for various shared meals. The *Book of Occasional Services* of the American Episcopal Church includes a form of agape for use on *Maundy Thursday after the eucharist.

Adalbert Hamman, *Vie liturgique et vie sociale*, Paris 1968; Hans Lietzmann, *Mass and Lord's Supper: A Study in the History of Liturgy*, Leiden 1979; Gene Outka, *Agape: An Ethical Analysis*, New Haven 1972; Michael J. Townsend, 'Exit the Agape?', *The Expository Times* XC, 1979, 356–61.

ANDREW MCGOWAN

Agnus Dei

This *anthem, 'Lamb of God', originally sung to accompany the *fraction in the Roman *mass, was for many centuries displaced and sung between the fraction and *communion, and was only restored to its former purpose in the twentieth-century revision of the RC rite. It seems to be of Eastern origin, as the word 'lamb' is commonly used in the Eastern liturgies to designate both Christ and the consecrated bread of the eucharist. The *West Syrian rite also contains fraction anthems which speak of 'the Lamb of God who takes away the sins of the world'. It was probably introduced into the Roman rite in the seventh century, perhaps during the pontificate of Sergius I (687–701), since this was a period of considerable Eastern, and especially Syrian, influence at Rome: Syria had recently been overrun by the Muslims, and many Syrian clergy found their way to Rome, among them Pope Theodore I (642–9), while Sergius I was a Syrian by descent.

It is addressed specifically to Christ present in the eucharist as a sacrificial offering, and originally consisted of as many repetitions as necessary of the sentence, 'Lamb of God, who take away the sins of the world, have mercy on us'. When time needed for the fraction was reduced as a result of the introduction of the use of unleavened bread, the number of repetitions was fixed at three, probably about the middle of the ninth century. During the tenth and eleventh centuries, when the fraction had become so brief that in practice the anthem accompanied the *kiss of peace immediately afterwards, the third clause was given the appropriately variant ending, 'grant us peace', instead of 'have mercy on us'. As early as the eleventh century, a further variant appeared: at *requiem masses the first and second petitions ended 'grant them rest', and the third, 'grant them rest everlasting'. The present RC rite has suppressed this variant. Provision has also been made for additional repetitions of the opening sentence when the fraction is more prolonged than usual.

The Agnus Dei was retained in the 1549 Anglican *BCP* as a communion anthem, but suppressed in that of 1552, as in most of the reformed liturgies of the sixteenth and later centuries. However, in varying translations or paraphrases, it has been incorporated in many twentieth-century revisions of eucharistic rites, either as a *confractorium* or as a communion anthem.

See also **Music in the Mass of the Roman Rite; Ordinary**.

———

J. A. Jungmann, *The Mass of the Roman Rite*, New York 1951, II, 332–40.

W. JARDINE GRISBROOKE

Aisle

A longitudinal passage or walkway flanking the *nave, the *transept or *choir of a church. There can be one or more aisles. The aisle is usually separated from its adjacent space by an arcade of columns or piers.

MARCHITA B. MAUCK

Alb *see* **Vestments** 3(a)

All Saints

The feast of All Saints originates from a feast for all known and unknown martyrs, of which we have evidence from Syria around the beginning of the fifth century. This was on the Friday after *Easter, but it is observed on the octave day of *Pentecost in the Byzantine liturgy. The first mention of All Saints is found in a feast commemorating the transfer of relics of martyrs from the catacombs to the Pantheon in Rome by Pope Boniface IV and the consecration of that building on 13 May 609. The date seems to have moved to 1 November after the dedication on this day of a chapel to the Saviour, Mary, the apostles, martyrs and confessors in St Peter's. Pope Gregory III (731–41) instructed that a short office of all the saints be recited there each evening. The feast of All Martyrs and All Saints and of Our Lady was renamed the feast of All Saints in 835. The Eastern church maintains the link of this feast with the Easter season. The liturgy of the feast is designed to emphasize the presence of holy men and women in the church (gospel reading: Matt. 5, the Beatitudes) and presents them as examples of faithful and joy-filled service for the living members of the church to emulate on their journey to the new Jerusalem. In a return to the possible origins of the feast, many Christians on this day think of departed brothers and sisters of inspirational faith and life-giving witness whom they trustfully believe are in heaven, among the unknown saints.

See also **Saints, Cult of the.**

———

Adolf Adam, *The Liturgical Year*, New York

1981, 228–30; Michael Witczak, 'All Saints, Feast of', *New Dictionary of Liturgy and Sacramental Worship*, ed. Peter Fink, Collegeville 1990, 41.

ANDREW CAMERON-MOWAT

All Souls

Many Christian denominations include memorials of the dead and prayers for the faithful departed in their liturgies. Prayers of *intercession, prayers included within the *eucharistic prayers and other petitions and prayers during liturgies point to the ongoing practice of Christians of remembering the dead and praying for their union with God. In the Byzantine tradition the departed are commemorated every Saturday in the year, except when it is a major festival. In the West, this feast, celebrated on 2 November, comes the day after the feast of *All Saints, and so is deliberately linked to it in theology and tradition. It owes its origin to Isidore of Seville (d. 636), who included a celebration of the liturgy for the dead on the day after *Pentecost in his rule, and to Odilo of Cluny who fixed the date as 2 November in 998. The tradition of allowing priests to celebrate three masses on this day seems to have arisen during the period of the growth of mass stipends in the fifteenth and sixteenth centuries, and became particularly important after the devastation caused by the First World War. The theology of the feast mirrors that for all commemorations of the dead, particularly at funerals, with this important difference: rather than remembering individual people and offering their lives to God for mercy during funeral rites, the church as a whole is linked to all those who are awaiting eternal life with God, confident in God's mercy, and sure of the power of the resurrection.

Adolf Adam, *The Liturgical Year,* New York 1981, 237–40; Michael Witczak, 'All Souls, Feast of', *New Dictionary of Liturgy and Sacramental Worship*, ed. Peter Fink, Collegeville 1990, 42–3.

ANDREW CAMERON-MOWAT

Alleluia

A Latinized version of the Hebrew *hallelujah*, 'praise Yah(weh)'. In the Hebrew Bible it occurs at the beginning and/or end of certain psalms, implying a call to communal praise. In such individual *hallel* psalms and the Book of Psalms as a whole, *Hallelujah* exemplifies one pole of a movement from lament to praise. *Hallelujah* was simply transliterated in the Septuagint, and is attested (*c.* 100 BCE) as an independent cry of deliverance (3 Macc. 7.13). The *hallel* psalms (such as Pss 146–150) were associated with Jewish festivals and probably moved from Temple to synagogue (Mishnah, *Pesachim* 5), although patterns of Jewish use continued to develop. Early Christians envisioned the heavenly chorus singing '*hallelujah*' (Rev. 19). The *Odes of Solomon* (second century) use *hallelujah* as a frame or refrain, like the biblical Psalms. Alleluia was used freely in conjunction with psalms in communal prayer (Tertullian, *De oratione* 27).

In the West, alleluia was associated with *Easter by Augustine's time, and it was omitted in *Lent and from *funeral rites. In the East, however, alleluia has been retained for the whole year, and is especially emphasized in Lent and at funerals. At the *eucharist, both Eastern and Western liturgies have used a chanted alleluia before the gospel; Eastern liturgies also include it at the *Great Entrance and elsewhere. The RC rites have now provided for use of alleluia at funerals. Although Anglican and Protestant liturgies had often lost these characteristic uses, hymnody and new liturgical books have reintroduced them to some extent. In evangelical and *charismatic worship, the use of 'Hallelujah' as a spontaneous cry of praise or approval recalls something of the original sense.

See also **Chants of the Proper of the Mass; Music in the Mass of the Roman Rite**.

N. Alldrit, 'The Song of an Easter People', *Theology* CIII, 2000, 97–107; Walter Brueggemann, *The Psalms and the Life of Faith*, Minneapolis 1995; J. A. Jungmann, *The Mass of the Roman Rite*, New York 1951, I, 421–36; Stefan Reif, *Judaism and Hebrew Prayer*, Cambridge 1993; R. Weakland, 'Alleluia', *New Catholic Encyclopedia*, New York 1967, I, 321–3.

ANDREW McGOWAN

Alms

That which is given out of compassion, ultimately derived from the Greek word *eleemosune*. Jesus recognized almsgiving as a duty in the Sermon on the Mount (Matt. 6.2); Peter and John were asked for alms as they left the Temple (Acts 3.3); Paul regularly collected alms and admonished others to generosity (1 Cor. 16.2); and early Christian writings, from Justin Martyr onwards, mention almsgiving as a basic duty. In the West the offerings were generally divided into four: for the *bishop, for the clergy, for the poor and for church repairs; but this division is no longer observed. In the ancient church gifts were often made in kind, and this custom continues in some parts of the world.

Modern concepts of 'stewardship' have emphasized the importance of allocating time, talents and money to the service of the church and the world. The 'collection' (of alms) in services has been increasingly associated, in the *eucharist, with the presentation of the bread and wine at the laying of the table, but this close identification has not been without its critics.

DONALD GRAY

Alms Dish

The receptacle used for receiving the monetary collection at church services. This collection ought not be called 'the *offertory'; that title belongs to the ceremonial presentation of the bread and wine for the eucharist. The confusion in Anglicanism (followed by others) derives from the Prayer Book direction that such moneys should be collected during the singing (or saying) of the 'offertory *sentences'. In 1549 and 1552 the money was placed in 'the poor man's box', but in 1662 the parish was directed to provide 'a decent bason' for the purpose, which should then be placed on the holy table. Some of the ceremonies accompanying the presentation of the alms have been criticized as being almost idolatrous: the dish solemnly elevated and then carried out with utmost reverence at the end of the service.

DONALD GRAY

Almuce *see* Vestments 3(d)

Altar

In Christian liturgy the altar, at its simplest, is the table-like structure of wood, stone or other material on which the elements of bread and wine are placed for the *eucharist. It stands, however, at the centre of a complex symbolic matrix combining the OT tradition of altars of sacrifice as focuses of divine communication and the NT stress on table-fellowship and the breaking of bread. In addition, the altar has

been seen as representative of Christ's presence in the church building.

1. *History.* The earliest Christian altars were wooden tables set in the midst of the community. The cult of the martyrs led to a number of changes including a clear link between the altar and the tombs of martyrs and other saints. The eucharist was not celebrated on the tombs, but the table was put in proximity to the tomb for the celebration of the martyr-cult, and when the martyrs' remains were moved out of the cemeteries of Rome and into the churches in the fifth and sixth centuries, the tomb was either incorporated into the altar or put in the open space, called the *confessio*, beneath it. Free-standing altars were increasingly of stone, square in shape, and surmounted by a canopy called a *ciborium (*see* **Baldachin**). The tendency to link shrine and altar continued in the Frankish church, and altars came to be built beside shrines. Around 1000 the *cross came to be put on the altar, and then one or two, later six, lights (*see* **Candles, Lamps, and Lights**). The altar lengthened, the ciborium was abandoned, and the retable and *reredos grew in height and complexity. Dwarfed by these ever more elaborate structures, the altar frequently looked insignificant.

The earliest churches had, as Orthodox churches still do, a single altar. With the growth in the Latin West of the so-called private *mass, said daily by a priest with only a *server, the number of altars in a church building multiplied. They were *dedicated to particular saints or mysteries, or endowed as *chantry or guild altars, and festal *processions went from altar to altar in the greater, monastic and cathedral churches. The multiplication of altars reduced the significance of the main altar of the church, now called the High Altar.

2. *Roman Catholic Practice.* The liturgical reforms of the late twentieth century sought to restore to the altar the dignity and simplicity it was thought to have had in earlier ages. The *General Instruction on the Roman Missal* (1970) called it 'the centre from which thanksgiving is offered to God through the celebration of the Eucharist', and required the main altar of any church to be free standing, away from any wall, so that the priest can walk around it and can celebrate facing the people. The table-top or *mensa* is to be made of natural stone and consecrated. The *Instruction* also allowed for lesser movable altars; but their multiplication,

and inferior nature, has detracted from the original symbolic conception. In the USA the bishops offered further instructions: the altar should be the most noble and most beautifully designed and constructed table the community can provide. It is never to be used as a table of convenience or a resting place for anything. It is to stand free, approachable and uncluttered. It should not be elongated but square or slightly rectangular, constructed of solid and beautiful materials, with pure and simple proportions. In any liturgical space there should only be one altar.

Fixed altars must be consecrated by a *bishop. According to RC canon *law, the ancient practice of putting relics of the saints (and not necessarily only of martyrs) within the structure of an altar is to be continued where possible but with 'relics of a size sufficient for them to be recognized as parts of human bodies' properly authenticated. An altar is dedicated in the context of the eucharist. The present rite is a simplified version of that contained in the 1595–6 Roman Pontifical. First, the altar is sprinkled with blessed water; then, after the liturgy of the word and the *litany of the saints, the relics are deposited. Chrism (see **Anointing**) is poured on the table, at the centre and four corners, and spread across it. Then *incense is burned on the altar, either in a brazier or in a heap mixed with small candles, and the altar is also censed using a *thurible. The altar table is wiped clean and covered if necessary with a waterproof covering to protect the altar cloth (now spread on it) from oil and water. The candles are set in place for the eucharist, and festive lighting takes place. The bishop then *kisses the altar and uses a prayer over the gifts calling upon God to send his Spirit upon the altar. The eucharist then proceeds as usual.

3. *Anglican Practice.* At the Reformation in England the practice of radical reformers ran ahead of the law. In May 1550 Bishop Ridley ordered the abolition of altars in his diocese. The Privy Council extended this to the whole country in November. Under Queen Mary the stone altars were restored and those that, having been taken down, had been set into the ground were raised and reused. Under Queen Elizabeth I, they were again taken down and wooden tables were installed instead. Wooden tables were usual even when, in Georgian times, there were few objections to stone-topped tables. Further controversy raged dur-

ing the Ritualist Controversy in the nineteenth century, but stone was increasingly used for new altars.

There are no regulations in Anglican churches equivalent to the modern RC ones, but the celebrated case before the Church of England Court of Ecclesiastical Causes Reserved (1987) of the Henry Moore altar in St Stephen Walbrook in the City of London – a large round stone structure beneath the central dome of a Wren church, likened to a Camembert cheese – clarified the altar–table relationship, defining a table as a 'horizontal surface raised above the ground', and effectively closed the Reformation debate over the nature, structure and placing of the holy table. Although there is no requirement to dedicate the altar in an Anglican church, this is often done.

The definitive work is J. Braun, *Der christliche Altar*, 2 vols, Munich 1914 and 1924. Other studies include: P. F. Anson, *Churches: Their Plan and Furnishing*, Milwaukee 1948; J. N. Comper, *On the Christian Altar and the buildings which contain it*, London 1950; C. E. Pocknee, *The Christian Altar*, London 1963. On medieval altars: Percy Dearmer, *Fifty Pictures of Gothic Altars*, London 1910, reprinted 1922. On modern altars: Charles Davis, 'The Christian Altar', *The Modern Architectural Setting of the Liturgy*, ed. William Lockett, London 1964, 13–31; Frédéric Debuyst, *L'Art chrétien contemporain*, Paris 1988.

MARTIN DUDLEY

Altar Hangings

When the ancient *altar stood beneath its *ciborium (see **Baldachin**), curtains hung around it, either from the architraves or from rods attached to the pillars. These hangings hid the altar on all four sides – the term *tetravela* is used – during the most solemn moments of the *eucharist. The *Liber Pontificalis* provides evidence for veiling in the Roman *basilicas. Pope Sergius (687–701) gave a set of eight *veils to St Peter's, four of white and four of scarlet. Pope John VI (701–5) gave several sets in various colours to St John Lateran and St Paul's Outside the Walls.

In the West the veil in front of the altar was given up except in *Lent, when a special veil hung right across the *sanctuary. As the altar changed its shape, from a cube to an elongated rectangle, so the ciborium also disappeared, but the idea of enclosing and enshrining the altar was retained. The altar itself was concealed by the *frontal and the table-top (*mensa*) by the altar cloths – normally three in number – which hung right down to the floor at each end. It was then hung around with curtains, called dorsal or dossal behind the altar and *riddels at either end, hanging from rods. The dorsal was sometimes replaced by a *reredos. Later dossals and riddels were often very elaborate, embroidered silks and damasks, sometimes decorated with jewels. Most medieval illustrations show the curtains at little more than head height but the *requiem mass illustrated in the Spinola Hours of *c*. 1520 shows a tall solid altarpiece with a curtain behind it and riddels hanging from rods more than two metres above the altar *mensa*. There is little evidence for the use of curtains later in the sixteenth century and the practice was reintroduced in England in the nineteenth century by conscious imitation of medieval practice.

Hangings were sometimes used in liturgical ceremonies. In the papal chapel on *Passion Sunday (now *Lent 5), at the words, *Jesus autem abscondit se* ('But Jesus hid himself') at the end of the gospel, a system of ropes enabled the clergy to pull up a veil that covered all the painted images. In other churches the veiling of crosses, images, etc., took place before first vespers of Passion Sunday. The veils were removed again during the Gloria in excelsis at the *Easter vigil. Altarpieces, especially important ones, seem to have been veiled at other times. The curtains themselves were sometimes painted with religious images. The hangings were described as *pro conservatione picture*, but there may have originally been a liturgical purpose in only revealing the main image on feast days.

For bibliography, *see* **Altar**.

MARTIN DUDLEY

Altar Rails (also called Communion Rails)

There were *cancelli* or low *screens around the *altar in the earliest churches; these were not, however, used for receiving *communion. Nor were there altar rails in the Middle Ages. Rails may have been initially introduced in England in the Elizabethan period to protect the holy table from profanation, especially by stray dogs, after the removal of medieval screens. In

1559 Queen Elizabeth I required that new, movable wooden holy tables were to be introduced into churches and that they were to be placed in the *chancel for the eucharist and to stand at the east end, where the altar stood, at all other times. Opponents of the Elizabethan settlement wanted the holy table kept out in the chancel. From 1627 onwards Charles I pursued an active policy of returning altars to the east end and at this point rails were generally introduced. There was considerable Puritan opposition. The first example of a requirement to rail the altar is in the Archdeaconry of Derby in 1630. In 1636 Bishop Wren of Norwich required that a rail be made in accordance with Archbishop Laud's injunctions of the previous year 'reachinge crosse from the north walle to the south walle, neere one yard in hight, and so thicke with pillars, that doggs may not get in'. Bishop Montagu of Norwich (1639) refers to the practice of 'comeing upp to the rayles as they called it in tyme of the holy communion'. Some clergy clearly refused to give communion to those who did not come to the rails. Seventeenth- and eighteenth-century prints show communicants kneeling at the rails to receive communion but not resting on them. The removal of the rails was ordered by Parliament in 1641, but they were again required after 1660. Later church *law held them to be merely 'legal and usual' and their use is no longer required by law. Altar rails were made in wood, and then, in the eighteenth century, in wrought iron. The rails sometimes extend across the chancel or else enclose the altar on three sides, or even four sides, with entry gates. In the RC Church altar rails came into use in Italy in the sixteenth century, and were in general use in eighteenth-century France; they remained almost universally until after the Second Vatican Council.

K. Fincham (ed.), *Visitation Articles and Injunctions of the Early Stuart Church* II, Woodbridge 1998; Gerald Randall, *Church Furnishings in England and Wales*, London 1980.

MARTIN DUDLEY

Altar, Stripping of

The ritual stripping of the *altar became part of the medieval ritual of *Maundy Thursday. First, the reserved sacrament was removed from the *tabernacle (or other place of *reservation) in the main church, and carried to its place of deposition, where it would remain for the remainder of the Triduum (*see* **Easter**). Then the altars of the church would be stripped; the altar linens and *candles would be removed, as well as other decoration (if any). The main altar would then also be ritually washed with water and wine, a symbol, as some have suggested, of creation washed with the blood of Christ (*see* **Altar, Washing of**). Other interpretations focused on the altar as a symbol of Christ; thus, the act could be connected to various moments during the passion of Christ, e.g. the division of his clothing at the crucifixion, the ripping of the Temple altar veil at his death, or the stripping of Christ before he was scourged. The altar would remain bare until re-vested with linens and candles during the *Easter vigil. Some Christian traditions (e.g. RC) still retain the practice of stripping (but not washing) the altar at this time.

For bibliography, *see* **Holy Week**.

JOANNE M. PIERCE

Altar, Washing of

The ritual washing of an *altar was a component of two major liturgical celebrations in the medieval period: the liturgy for the *consecration of a church, and the liturgy of *Maundy Thursday. In the latter, all altars in the church were stripped of linens, *candles, and other ornaments after the celebration of the *eucharist and the ritual procession with the reserved sacrament from the main church and *tabernacle (*see* **Altar, Stripping of**). The altar was then washed with water and with wine. Originally a utilitarian rite, it came to be invested with a variety of symbolic explanations, among them that it symbolized the cleansing power of the blood of Christ. Today, only the high altar at St Peter's in Rome is ritually washed in this way.

JOANNE M. PIERCE

Ambo

An elevated platform for reading or preaching. Canon 15 of Laodicea (late fourth century), implies the ascent of steps, and restricts access to those in orders above *lector. Classically, the platform has a parapet often incorporating a reading desk, is approached by steps (on one or both sides) and is often of sufficient size to accommodate a reader and several attendants. The ambo was a focal point of early Christian liturgy, proper to the proclamation of the word of God, the declamations of the *deacons, and occasionally the teaching of the *bishop. Sometimes made of wood, but more often of marble or stone, the dignity of the ambo attracted embellishment with inset marbles or porphyries, and carved or tessellated surfaces.

The earliest form of ambo (from the fourth century) in Syria and Mesopotamia, known as a bema, comprised a dais in the centre of the *nave with an apsidal bench for the clergy. The architectural complexity of the ambo developed with the liturgy, maintaining a central position on the main axis, often with access from the *apse by a raised walkway (*solea*). It seems likely that this arrangement was introduced into the West during the 530s, and rubrics in sixth- and seventh-century ordos mention the use of ambos. Here the ambo (occasionally two, for gospel and epistle, north and south, e.g. S. Clemente in Rome) developed into a raised promontory extending into the nave from the chord of the apse. The presence of an elaborate fixed candle stand (e.g. St Lawrence outside the Walls, Rome) and thematic iconography indicates the ambo's use for the deacon's proclamation of the *Exultet* at the *Easter vigil (*see* **Easter Candle**). Ambos have enjoyed a revival, of which that in Westminster Cathedral is a good example.

D. Hickley, 'The Ambo in Early Liturgical Planning', *Heythrop Journal* VII, 1966, 407–27; Robert Taft, 'Some Notes on the *Bema* in the East and West Syrian Traditions', *Orientalia Christiana Periodica* XXXIV, 1968, 326–59; 'Ambo' and 'Early Christian and Byzantine Art', *The Grove Dictionary of Art*, London 1996.

JONATHAN GOODALL

Ambrosian Rite *see* Western Rites

Amen

The Hebrew word *Amen* can be translated by 'surely' or 'so be it'. It confirms preceding statements, both in formal and liturgical settings of prayer, *blessing, curse and *doxology (Deut. 27.15–26; Jer. 11.5 etc.), and in other speech (1 Kings 1.36). It is prominent in the Psalms (41.13; 72.19 etc.), and in Ps. 106 appears explicitly as a response. The fact that Amen was sometimes simply transliterated into Greek in the Septuagint reflects that it was a technical term before the time of Jesus.

Jesus' use of Amen introducing statements

(in all the Gospels; 'Amen, Amen' in John; cf. Num. 5.22) asserts the truth of what follows. For the Revelation to John, Jesus himself is 'the Amen' (3.14). Use as an end of prayer or doxology is reflected in the letters of Paul (Rom. 1.25; Gal. 1.5; Phil. 4.20), as is more spontaneous use in early Christian worship, responding to praise and thanksgiving (1 Cor. 14.16).

Amen comes to characterize communal participation in prayer in general, and *eucharistic prayer in particular (Justin Martyr, *First Apology* 65; *Didache* 10.6); it was a response to receiving communion at least from the third century (*see* **Words of Administration**). Augustine and Jerome acknowledged that as a foreign word it had special impact on the worshipper. Protestant practice has contributed to a diversity of usage, such as the sung (e.g. 'threefold') Amen concluding worship, and spontaneous use of Amen as an affirmation or response by individuals to preaching and prayer.

Bruce Chilton, 'Amen', *Anchor Bible Dictionary*, New York 1992, I, 184–6; Bernhard Lang, *Sacred Games: A History of Christian Worship,* New Haven 1997, 111–20; J. M. Ross, 'Amen', *The Expository Times* CII, 1991, 166–71.

ANDREW MCGOWAN

Amice *see* Vestments 3(a)

Anabaptist Worship

see **Mennonite Worship**

Anamnesis

A Greek word meaning 'remembrance', as in 'Do this in remembrance of me' (Luke 22.19; 1 Cor. 11.24–25). As a theological concept with Jewish roots, it has featured prominently in modern ecumenical discussions in relation to the connection between the saving death of Christ on the cross and the celebration of the eucharist. In a liturgical context, it can refer to any act or text in which the mighty works of God are recounted, but is also used in a narrower sense to denote the section of many *eucharistic prayers following the *institution narrative in which the church fulfils the above dominical command by recalling the redemptive acts of Christ, usually his death and resurrection, but sometimes other aspects, most commonly his ascension into heaven and/or his sitting in glory. In ancient eucharistic prayers this anamnesis led into a statement of what the church understood itself to be doing in the rite: 'having in remembrance . . . we offer'. While this pattern is retained in some ecclesiastical traditions today, Reformation churches have generally been reluctant to understand the eucharistic action in terms of offering (*see* **Offertory; Eucharistic Theologies**).

EDITOR

Anaphora *see* Eucharistic Prayer

Angelus

A devotion, in the Western Catholic tradition, which honours the incarnation three times a day (early morning, noon and evening) at the tolling of the church bell. The name derives from the Latin phrase *Angelus Domini* ('Angel of the Lord'), which introduces the devotion: 'The angel of the Lord declared to Mary/and she conceived of the Holy Spirit.' This versicle and response is followed by the Hail Mary, then two more versicles and responses: 'Behold the handmaid of the Lord/be it done unto me according to your word'; 'The Word was made flesh/and dwelt among us.' A Hail Mary also follows each of these biblical texts. The devotion is completed by prayer addressed to God that recalls the 'incarnation, made known by the message of an angel'.

The origin of this devotion is obscure. However, historians seem to agree that the custom began with the practice of the evening tolling of the bell for compline (*see* **Daily Prayer**) in monasteries or the tolling of the bell for curfew. The practice may go back as far as the tenth century in England and the thirteenth century in Germany. The morning Angelus first appears in the fourteenth century while the earliest evidence for the midday Angelus is from the fifteenth century. The devotion was finalized, as it is known today, during the sixteenth century but did not come into general use until the seventeenth century. During the Easter season, the Angelus is replaced by a similar devotion, the *Regina coeli* ('Queen of heaven').

F. Courth, 'Marianische Gebetsformen', *Handbuch der Marienkunde*, ed. W. Beinert and H. Petri, Regensburg 1996, 548–50; H. Graef, *Mary, A History of Doctrine and Devotion*, Westminster, MD 1963–65, 308; G. Alastruey Sánchez, *The Blessed Virgin Mary* II, St Louis,

MO 1964, 270–1; H. Thurston, 'The Angelus', *The Month* XCVII, 1901, 483–99, 607–16; XCIX, 1902, 61–73, 518–32.

JOSEPH WEISS

Anglican Worship

Anglicans maintain their worship reflects a basic claim of their denomination to be an integral part of the Catholic church; their liturgy is not sui generis, being never more than a local and contemporary adaptation of what has been handed down from apostolic times.

1. *The Book of Common Prayer*. Acknowledging that in the process of transmission traditions had been 'altered, broken and neglected', in 1549 the Church of England took the opportunity of the break with Rome to produce 'an order of prayer much agreeable to the mind and purpose of the old fathers, and a great deal more profitable and commodious, than that which of late was used' (Preface, 1549 *BCP*). While much of the Prayer Book contents were clearly in continuity with the immediate past, there were detailed changes that allied it to the concerns of the sixteenth-century European continental Reformation. These included fundamental matters that have continued to be marks of all Anglican worship. In the first place the services were now in English in contrast to the Latin used previously. Second, the rules for ordering the service were much simplified; third, there was to be a nationwide uniformity; and fourth, *rubrics were introduced to guarantee that the scriptures and other parts of the service were read 'distinctly and in a loud voice that people may hear'. The reading of the Bible and the place of the sermon in worship are of paramount importance in Anglican worship. The congregational singing of psalms has always been important in parish churches and was integral to services long before the introduction of hymns. Hymns were at first viewed with considerable suspicion, as part of the enthusiasm normally associated in England with the Dissenting and Nonconformist sects, in contrast to the present-day scene where no major act of worship would be believed to be complete without its ration of hymns.

Subsequent English revisions between 1552 and 1662 did not deviate from these principles, but later some provinces of the Anglican Communion were slower to shed their 'colonial' origins and *inculturate their worship. The problem was that it had come to be understood that the Prayer Book of 1662 was 'a strong band of unity throughout the whole Anglican Communion' (1948 Lambeth Conference, Resolution 78a). The monolithic status accorded to the Prayer Book (and to a lesser extent to English hymn books and gothic architecture) began to diminish soon after, with the result that the 1995 meeting of the International Anglican Liturgical Consultation could report that it had 'effectively disappeared from the on-going life of many parts of the Communion' (David R. Holeton, ed., *Our Thanks and Praise*, Toronto 1998, 7).

2. *The Nineteenth Century*. Although the early Tractarians and leaders of the Oxford Movement (such as Keble, Newman and Pusey), continuing in the tradition of their high-church heritage, celebrated the rites of the *BCP* 'decently and in order' and defended them against threats of dilution or alteration, they were not concerned about rubrical details and ceremonial niceties. However, for their successors in the 1860s, influenced originally by John Mason Neale (1816–66) and the ecclesiological movement, a rebirth of liturgical studies and later by often slavish imitation of current RC fashions, external, ceremonial and ritual aspects of the liturgy came to be a major concern. This resulted in considerable controversy and a polarization in forms of worship throughout Anglicanism, along with a striving to remain within one Communion. Outside England in many places the extent of the influence of the 'High Churchmen' or 'Ritualists' was usually determined by the churchmanship of the missionary society that had supplied the original missionaries in that part of the world. In the USA, although there had always been a strong evangelical party, reflecting the 'puritan' origins of the earliest settlers, 'the general liturgical trend throughout the [nineteenth] century was in the high-church direction' (Robert T. Handy, *The History of the Churches in the United States and Canada*, London 1976, 205).

3. *The Twentieth Century*. The twentieth-century *Liturgical Movement had a profound influence on Anglican liturgy, in both its performance and its setting, as well as in the consequential liturgical reforms. Building on its tradition of liturgical scholarship, the Communion provided a number of scholars whose studies influenced these developments: W. H. Frere (1863–1938), W. P. Ladd (1876–1941), Gregory Dix (1901–52), A. G. Hebert (1886–

1963), Massey Shepherd (1913–90). Though Anglicans could claim that some of the aims of the movement, notably simplification of rites and the use of the vernacular, had been anticipated by their sixteenth- and seventeenth-century reforms, the centrality of the *eucharist in Christian worship which had been implicit in Anglican Prayer Books was reaffirmed, and parochial worship patterns were modified to affirm this. Equally, pastoral policies encouraged by such organizations as Parish and People in Britain and Associated Parishes in North America were adapted to emphasize its social and political consequences.

A commitment to the Ecumenical Movement from its earliest days has guaranteed enthusiastic Anglican involvement in the search for common liturgical texts. In all its provinces modern liturgical revisions incorporate the result of the work of the International Consultation on English Texts and its successor the English Language Liturgical Consultation, and there has been almost universal acceptance of the ecumenical *Revised Common Lectionary* (*see* **Ecumenical Co-operation in Liturgical Revision**).

One aspect of definitive Anglican worship has remained substantially unchanged, and that is choral evensong, often sung daily in cathedrals, collegiate churches and college chapels in England and other places worldwide. This particular, and peculiar, service has survived any attempts at liturgical revision mainly in order that its large repertoire of fine music is regularly performed.

Throughout the Anglican Communion the externals of worship may vary enormously; in one place it may be accompanied by all the impedimenta of 'Catholic' worship (*vestments, *candles, 'bells and smells' [i.e., *incense]), while in another there will be either a much plainer, more austere, 'low-church' approach; or perhaps it may consist of a more extravagant, multi-media, *charismatic, evangelical celebration. It is into such a 'pick-and-mix' situation that currently Anglican authorities, no less than other churches, are attempting to preserve a discipline of set and authorized services based on traditional patterns, which nonetheless provide a flexibility that was not hitherto officially encouraged.

See also **Books, Liturgical** 4.

G. J. Cuming, *A History of Anglican Liturgy*, 2nd edn, London 1982 (bib.); Marion J. Hatchett, *Commentary on the American Prayer Book*, New York 1980; R. C. D. Jasper, *The Development of the Anglican Liturgy 1662–1980*, London 1989; Christopher Irvine (ed.), *They Shaped Our Worship*, London 1998; D. E. W. Harrison and Michael C. Sansom, *Worship in the Church of England*, London 1982; Horton Davies, *WTE*; Donald Gray, *Earth and Altar*, Norwich 1986; Michael Moriarty, *The Liturgical Revolution*, New York 1996; Kenneth Stevenson and Bryan Spinks (eds), *The Identity of Anglican Worship*, London 1991.

DONALD GRAY

Anniversary

In Methodism and the other British Free Churches an annual celebration of the founding of a congregation or the erection of a building, the latter corresponding to a feast of *dedication. It is often marked by the invitation to a visiting preacher and will include special hymns, *anthems, solos and readings. Before the rediscovery of the Christian *year the highlights in the Free Church calendar were marked by a series of anniversaries such as Women's Sunday, Men's Sunday, Guild Sunday, Youth Sunday and choir anniversary. In the heyday of Sunday schools the Sunday School Anniversary was the high festival of spring or early summer. The *sanctuary was overlaid with a tiered platform on which the scholars sat in serried ranks and performed musical items interspersed with recitations and solos. The Sunday School Anniversary was often the best-attended event in the congregation. In Lancashire, and other industrial towns of northern England, the Sunday School Anniversary was known as 'Sermons' and was accompanied by 'Whit-walks' with banners and processions. Such anniversary celebrations often overshadowed the major Christian festival on which they were being held, including *Good Friday, *Easter Day or *Pentecost. In many places only the church or chapel anniversary now survives, and quite often the original foundation dates have been forgotten and the church anniversary has become a moveable feast. There is sometimes a serious tension as to whether it is the living community or the building that is the source of the celebration, with attendant theological and liturgical confusion.

C. NORMAN R. WALLWORK

Annunciation

The feast commemorating the story of the message of the Angel Gabriel to Mary (Luke

1.26–38). Traditionally there were two celebrations of the story of the annunciation, one during *Advent on the 20 December (now often celebrated on the fourth Sunday of Advent), the other on 25 March, exactly nine months before the celebration of the Nativity of Christ on 25 December. Both commemorations seem to have become regular events during the seventh century. The latter, the feast proper, was called the 'Annunciation of the Blessed Virgin Mary' until 1969 in the RC Church, when it was given the more correct title, 'Annunciation of Our Lord'. In early Christianity 25 March was also counted as the date of the creation and the end of the world, and of the conception and death of Christ.

Brian Daley, 'Mary, Feasts of', *New Dictionary of Liturgy and Sacramental Worship*, ed. Peter Fink, Collegeville 1990, 818–22; A. G. Martimort et al., *The Church at Prayer* IV, Collegeville 1986, 95–6 (bib.); Thomas J. Talley, *The Origins of the Liturgical Year*, 2nd edn, Collegeville 1991, 91–103 (bib.).

ANDREW CAMERON-MOWAT

Anointing

The practice of anointing persons or things in sacred rites, most often with oil but also with other substances, has been a feature of very many religions throughout human history. Its chief uses have been either to bring about the healing and restoration of someone who was sick or suffering in some way or to effect the consecration or sanctification of a person or an object, their setting apart for holy purposes. Thus, for example, in the OT Jacob anoints the stone at Bethel (Gen. 28.28), and the tent of meeting and all its furniture and utensils are consecrated with a special blend of oil, myrrh and spices (Exod. 30.22–29). Anointing is also associated with the appointment of both kings (e.g. 2 Sam. 10.1; 16.13) and priests (e.g. Ex. 8.30; Lev. 8.12, 30) as a symbolic expression that the person had been chosen by God for that office. From that practice developed the image of the one whom God was expected to send to lead and redeem his people as being his anointed one, in Hebrew 'Messiah'.

In the NT Jesus is understood as the Anointed One (Greek, *Christos*), anointed with God's Spirit to bring good news to his people (Luke 4.18–21), and the one through whom the same Spirit is poured out on those who believe in him (Acts 2.33). Whether references to the anointing of Christians (e.g. 1 John 2.20, 27) and their being sealed with the Holy Spirit (2 Cor. 1.22; Eph. 1.13; 4.30) are just metaphorical at this stage or whether they had already given rise to an actual use of oil in the initiation of converts cannot be determined, but certainly by the beginning of the third century, if not sooner, anointing is regularly used in connection with *baptism, where it either is understood as symbolizing affiliation with Jesus the Anointed One and entry into the royal priesthood of the church (1 Peter 2.5, 9), what might be called a 'christic' anointing, or is associated with the bestowal of the Holy Spirit, as a 'pneumatic' anointing. The NT also refers to the use of oil for healing purposes (Mark 6.13; James 5.14), and this aspect also comes to be incorporated into both baptismal anointing and also the church's ministry to the *sick. Although baptismal rites from later periods show considerable variation from region to region, they generally distinguish between a pre-baptismal anointing with oil, often associated with *exorcism and (at least at first) poured over the entire body, and a post-baptismal anointing with chrism (*myron* in Greek, olive oil mixed with a fragrant oil such as balsam and other aromatic substances) related to the gift of the Spirit. All three oils – for the sick, for exorcism, and chrism – came to be consecrated annually by bishops just before Easter, often on *Maundy Thursday, so that the baptismal oils might be used at the *Easter vigil.

In the West, at least from the eighth century onwards, anointing began to be used in connection with *ordination, first of new presbyters' hands, and later of a new bishop's hands and then of his head, in imitation of the OT practice for the high priest. On the same scriptural basis, Christian emperors and kings came to be anointed at their *coronation. Oil has also been used in the *consecration of churches and for other similar purposes.

The sixteenth-century Reformers abolished anointing along with many other ritual acts as being superstitious ceremonies, but the twentieth century has seen a growing appreciation within many Reformation churches of the value of visible signs, particularly those that can claim a biblical precedent. Thus, some Anglican and Lutheran churches now make optional provision for anointing in relation to both baptism and the ministry to the sick, and in a few cases even for ordination.

G. Ellard, *Ordination Anointings in the West-*

ern Church before 1000 AD, Cambridge, MA 1933; Gabriele Winkler, 'The Original Meaning of the Prebaptismal Anointing and its Implications', *Living Water, Sealing Spirit: Readings on Christian Initiation*, ed. Maxwell E. Johnson, Collegeville 1995, 58–81.

EDITOR

Ante-Communion

This term, of comparatively recent use in Anglicanism and subsequently copied by some other denominations, is now practically obsolete as a description of a liturgical rite. From the seventeenth to the nineteenth century, when there was implementation of the *rubrical provision in the *BCP* that 'if there is no communion' the *communion service should be said up to the end of the prayer for the church and then concluded with a *collect and *blessing, it was usually referred to as 'the second service', that is, the service which followed morning prayer and the *litany every Sunday morning. In 1967 the term 'ante-communion' achieved official currency in England for a short time during the period of experimental liturgy, the *eucharistic rite being divided into 'The Ante-Communion' and 'The Communion', but this nomenclature did not survive further revision.

It is a term that can be said to demonstrate the patristic division into the liturgy of the catechumens (*missa catechumenorum*) and the liturgy of the faithful (*missa fidelium*). It also recalls the less commendable medieval dry mass (*missa sicca*, or sometimes *nudum officium*). This rite, which included most of the mass except the *eucharistic prayer and carefully avoided the presence of both bread and wine and vessels, was 'tainted by some admixture, at least of superstitious motive and sometimes of superstitious practice' (W. E. Scudamore, *Notitia Eucharistica*, London 1872, 719) and therefore much suspected by the Reformers for pretending to be more than it was.

From 1892 onwards American Episcopalians were permitted to say morning prayer on Sundays without requiring the ante-communion to follow and to have the eucharist without a preceding service of morning prayer. Equal freedom from the prescriptions of the 1662 *BCP*, together with the influence of the *Liturgical Movement, have allowed other parts of the Anglican Communion to develop various other patterns of Sunday worship. In England the last vestiges of the ante-communion can be found in the resources provided in *Patterns*

for Worship (1995) in an attempt to bring some order into the ubiquitous, non-eucharistic *family service, and in *Common Worship* (2000), where directions for 'A Service without Communion' are provided (334).

W. C. Bishop, 'Ante-Communion', *The Prayer Book Dictionary*, ed. George Harford and Morley Stevenson, London 1912, 27–9.

DONALD GRAY

Anthem

The anthem is sung by the choir after the third *collect at morning or evening prayer according to the 1662 *BCP* of the Church of England. In directing its use 'in quires and places where they sing', the 1662 *BCP* formalized a practice established before the Commonwealth, and first allowed by the Injunctions of Queen Elizabeth I (1559). It is characteristic of the Anglican Church (and the Church of England in particular), with a large repertory dating from the mid-sixteenth century to the present day. Although sung before the prayers and conclusion of morning and evening prayer, it stands outside the liturgy, since the formal pattern of these services ends at the collects, and no anthem texts are prescribed.

The antecedent of the English anthem is found in the Latin *antiphon sung most often after the end of vespers (or vespers and compline) in the pre-Reformation liturgy. The antiphon sung at this point is properly part of a truncated office (Magnificat antiphon, with related versicle and response, and collect). The texts are frequently in honour of the Blessed Virgin Mary, sung to plainsong melodies, but during the fifteenth and early sixteenth century in Britain it became customary for special singers to be designated to sing the antiphon in 'pricksong' (i.e., written-down *polyphony). Often these singers, normally consisting of both boys and men, constituted a separate Lady Chapel choir in a *cathedral, college or monastery, which sang the *mass and office (*see* **Daily Prayer** 3) in honour of the Blessed Virgin Mary each day, and joined the main body of priest-singers in choir on Sundays and feast days. Part of this pre-Reformation repertory is extant in the Caius, Eton and Lambeth choirbooks. These include a wide variety of devotional texts, often set in elaborate, florid polyphony.

The earliest vernacular anthems probably date from the 1540s. Often it is hard to distinguish sacred polyphonic songs sung devotionally in the home from anthems intended for use in church. Since the royal court was a central force in post-Reformation music, and composers often worked both in the Chapel Royal and in secular court music, this distinction may be less significant. Certainly the earliest composers of English anthems (including Tye, Tallis and Sheppard) drew on the form of the secular partsong, with its repeated second half, syllabic word-setting, and cautious imitative polyphony. The next generation (Farrant, Byrd and Morley) also drew on the secular consort song (for voices and instruments) in devising the so-called 'verse anthem', an anthem with alternating sections for solo singers and full choir, accompanied by the organ, or in some cases by instrumental ensemble. A majority of the Tudor anthem texts are collects or psalms.

The foundations of the English anthem were well established by 1600, and the two basic types of full anthem and verse anthem persisted until the nineteenth century. Because Elizabeth I, James I and Charles I engaged musicians in the Chapel Royal who also held posts in provincial cathedrals they ensured a link between court and cathedral practice. Much of the finest music of the period 1580–1640 survives in MSS from cathedral collections but may have originated in the Chapel Royal. These include a cycle of Caroline verse anthems by Thomas Tomkins for the principal feasts of the Chapel Royal year: *Christmas Day, *Easter Day, *Ascension Day, the King's Accession (May 31), *Pentecost, and *All Saints' Day.

Two printed collections have contributed to the continuity of the English anthem repertory. Barnard's *Selected Church Musick* (1641) was much used in the choral revival after the Restoration, and even informed Boyce's *Cathedral Music* (1760–73), which appeared in three volumes. As a result of these publications some sixteenth- and seventeenth-century anthems have never left the cathedral repertory. However, each generation of composers has responded to current fashion. The most striking change occurred when Charles II encouraged the use of contemporary French (and Italian) styles in the anthems with string orchestra of the Chapel Royal in the 1660s, an idiom taken up by Purcell in his verse anthems. The death of Queen Mary (1695) marked the end of the significance and influence of the Chapel Royal. However, the anthem continued to be influenced by the styles of foreign opera, cantata

and oratorio performed in British cities in the eighteenth and nineteenth centuries, though tempered by the limitations of cathedral singers, lack of rehearsal, and the organist-composers. Some occasional works, e.g., Handel's Coronation Anthems (1727), remain outstanding examples of first-class, large-scale composition. Less magnificent, but original in their own way, are the large-scale anthems of the reforming church musician, S. S. Wesley, including 'The Wilderness' and 'Blessed be the God and Father'.

Until the nineteenth century anthems were largely the preserve of fewer than one hundred British cathedral and college choirs. The advent of cheap music printing and the rise of parish choirs resulted in a larger output of easy and often indifferent anthems from the mid-nineteenth century. Since the late nineteenth century, composers of church music have been less overtly influenced by secular vocal genres. Some have adopted Austro-Germanic styles (e.g. Stanford and Parry), others have looked to earlier English and Continental models of church music, notably the music of the late sixteenth and early seventeenth century (e.g. Vaughan Williams and Charles Wood). Since 1900, as in previous times, anthems have been composed by church musicians (especially cathedral organists), including Bairstow, Harris and Philip Moore, but there have been significant contributions from mainstream British composers, including Finzi, Howells, Britten, Mathias, Leighton and Judith Weir.

'Anthem', *NG2* I, 719–28; E. H. Fellowes, revised J. A. Westrup, *English Cathedral Music*, London 1969; Frank Ll. Harrison, *Music in Medieval Britain*, London 1958, 4th edn, Beuren 1984; Peter le Huray, *Music and the Reformation in England*, London 1967.

JOHN HARPER

Anthropology and Liturgy

see **Social Sciences and the Study of Liturgy**

Antidoron

Literally 'instead of the gift', this Greek term refers to the portion of bread not prepared during the *prothesis and consecrated in the eucharistic liturgy, but cut into small pieces, blessed during the *eucharist, and distributed at the end of the service. Originating in Byzantium, it has also become part of Armenian and Syrian rites. In present usage, the pieces of non-eucharistic bread are presented to the celebrant immediately after the consecration to be blessed above the sanctified gifts. At the end of the liturgy the antidoron is distributed to all who are present either by the *bishop at the throne or by the priest at the front of the church. Practically, this disposes of any extra bread not used for *communion. Some see this as a remnant of the primitive *agape, but this seems to be a very late explanation. Commenting on Canon 2 of the Regional Council of Antioch, Theodore Balsamon (d. after 1195) states that antidoron imparts a blessing to those who, for whatever reason, did not receive the eucharist. Nicholas Cabasilas (*Commentary on the Divine Liturgy* 53) echoes this in saying that it is a means by which all can glorify God by partaking in something that has been in close proximity to the consecrated gifts. In a modern context where only Orthodox faithful who are adequately prepared are allowed to receive the eucharist, this is a way of including all who attend. Although most consume the antidoron on the spot, some take it home, consuming a portion daily as part of their private prayer.

JOHN KLENTOS

Antiphon

In the Latin *daily prayer office, a *proper, seasonal, common or *ferial text, sung before and after a psalm or *canticle; in the Latin *mass, a proper text sung at the introit or *communion. In the early church the whole psalm was sung, and the antiphon was repeated after each verse. Vestiges of this practice survive in some later introit chants, where only a single psalm verse and Gloria Patri were sung, while the communion was normally sung without any verse. Some of the most important antiphons are those that were sung at the *Benedictus in the morning office and the Magnificat in the evening office, some taking their text from the gospel reading of the day. Some Latin antiphons are sung as independent chants, as a devotional '*anthem' at the end of the office or as part of the repertory of chants sung during a liturgical *procession. However, a number of these originated as antiphons to the Benedictus and Magnificat.

See also **Chants of the Proper of the Mass; Psalmody.**

'Antiphon', *NG2* I, 735–48; David Hiley,

Western Plainchant: A Handbook, Oxford 1993.

JOHN HARPER

Antiphonal Psalmody *see* Psalmody 1

Apse

A semi-circular or polygonal (sometimes square or rectangular in monastic churches) culmination of the central *aisle (*nave) of a church. The apse usually contains the main *altar.

MARCHITA B. MAUCK

Architectural Setting (Historical)

The buildings for Christian worship provide a panorama over time of the way the community understands itself and conducts its worship. There is an ebb and flow of initiatives emanating from the lay community at some periods, and from the ecclesiastical hierarchy and even imperial courts at others. More than the story of evolving architectural forms, we discover in the places they have designed to house their worship the presumptions, politics and passions of the Christian community.

1. *Early House Churches.* The story begins with small neighbourhood groups of believers who gathered first in each other's homes, and by the late second and early third centuries had begun renovating domestic spaces throughout the Roman Empire to meet the community's needs. The archaeological remains of a number of these house churches have been discovered in Rome, with evidence of others a little later in England. The best preserved house church is that in Dura-Europos, eastern Syria, dating from the early third century. In this prosperous and rather cosmopolitan town on the Euphrates River, along a major trade route to the east, the Christians renovated a modest private home along the same street as a richly decorated Jewish synagogue. The community took out one wall to provide a large hall in which to gather some 50–70 people. There is evidence of a small platform, probably for the presider, but no fixed place for the *altar. A small separate room was converted into a *baptistery, incorporating a tomb-shaped *font with a vaulted canopy overhead.

2. *The Basilica.* With the accession of Constantine as emperor in 312 CE and his subse-

quent proclamation of Christianity as the state religion, the domestic gathering of the faithful for the *eucharist gave way to public celebrations requiring large physical spaces. The intimacy of the house church gradually disappeared in the face of a *processional liturgy whose pageantry and scale, derived from the ceremonies of the imperial court, now befitted the dignity and splendour of a state religion.

The secular Roman *basilica emerged as the logical choice for a suitable building-type to house the rituals of a vastly enlarged Christian community. These buildings were rectangular, with a large central *aisle usually flanked by one or more side aisles. *Apses projected from one or more sides of the building. The main entrance customarily lay on one of the long sides, opening onto a civic forum. The *nave, or central aisle, typically stood taller than the side aisles, allowing light to pour into the interior from the clerestory windows. Basilicas served a number of purposes throughout the empire, such as imperial audience halls, law courts, military administrative offices, and even as cover for merchants in inclement weather. They provided a familiar model for large spaces, and unlike the old temples, did not have any objectionable symbolic associations with pagan religion. The imperial connotations of the audience hall were suitable for the image of Christ as the 'King of heaven'.

The generic character of the basilica plan lent itself to modification for a variety of needs. The earliest churches in the West, built under the patronage of the emperor Constantine, adopted the longitudinal basilican plan of a wide centre aisle flanked by other aisles, terminating in an apse. The main entry shifted from the side of the building to the short end opposite the apse. An *atrium or open courtyard preceded the main entry porch or *narthex. The first Constantinian church was the congregational church of St John Lateran begun in about about 313, on an east–west axis within the city walls, as the seat of the *Bishop of Rome. On land donated by the emperor, this basilica included short wings that projected from the side aisles near the apse, possibly for storage of the gifts brought for the poor of the city. The funerary basilica of St Peter, built outside the walls in the cemetery over the traditional site of the burial of St Peter, includes an entirely new architectural element inserted into the basilica plan. A tall transverse hall, a *transept, standing at a right angle to the central nave, separates the nave from the apse. This transept provides

circulation space around the tomb of St Peter, and demarcates the area as symbolically important. The church of St John Lateran had no transept as there were no burials in the church, no tomb to revere. In both of these churches the space around the altar in the apse was reserved for the clergy, and separated from the rest of the church by elaborate *screens. Basilicas for funerary banquets and commemorative services in the cemeteries exhibit yet another basilican variation. In these churches the outermost aisles wrapped around the apse to provide a continuous walkway surrounding the interior of the building. The floor was filled with numerous tombs of the faithful who wished to be buried near the graves of martyrs.

In the eastern empire, Constantine and his mother occupied themselves with building churches at the sites significant in the life of Christ. There is a different emphasis architecturally in these buildings. Rotundas appended to basilican structures mark the sacred sites, central-plan forms that carry the legacy of imperial funerary architecture. A rotunda stood over the site of the tomb of Christ at Golgotha in Jerusalem as well as over the supposed site of the nativity in Bethlehem. The round or polygonal funerary building, designed often with an opening to the sky to allow for the apotheosis of the divine majesty of the emperor, was reserved in the early centuries for the sites connected to Christ. Even St Peter did not merit the same architectural form over his tomb. Christianity further appropriated the imperial tomb structure as the model for baptisteries, a metaphor for the death and rebirth experienced in the *sacrament of *baptism. Only later did the central plan appear for *martyria in the West, such as the fifth-century church of S. Stefano Rotondo in Rome, housing relics of St Stephen brought from the Holy Land.

3. *Early Medieval Developments*. In the Roman West the basilica plan remained throughout the early Middle Ages the preferred form for church architecture, with the exception of *centralized structures serving as baptisteries or martyria. The longitudinal axis well served the needs of a processional liturgy. Although the basilica plan is not unknown in the Christian East, there the central plan predominated. The most common form was a cross within a square, often surmounted with a dome.

Roman customs and practices impressed

emissaries of Frankish courts north of the Alps as early as the eighth century. After his early ninth-century visit to Rome, Bishop Chrodegang of Metz introduced Roman liturgy and chant into his northern European see. He was also instrumental in obtaining relics for monasteries at Gorze and Lorsch. His efforts heralded a flurry of activity throughout the Carolingian era that showed a preference for early Christian building-types, in which Roman liturgical practices and the Roman cult of *saints contributed to major shifts in the design of churches. Prominent among the new elements was a multiplication of altars, intruding into the nave as well as side aisles of the relatively unencumbered early Christian basilica plan. The monastic church of St Riquier in Centula, France, built with the financial and imperial patronage of Charlemagne in the 790s, demonstrates the influence of the Roman stational liturgy. It was customary in Rome, particularly during *Holy Week, to process from one church to another in imitation of Jesus' journey to Golgotha. At St Riquier altars with separate dedications served as the 'stations' – these being readily available in Rome, with its proliferation of churches, but not in rural northern France where churches were not within walking distance of each other. The introduction of multiple altars during Carolingian times reflects other liturgical developments as well. The custom of having *masses said for the dead (see **Requiem Mass**), in addition to the new custom of offering masses for penitential purposes, required numerous altars in order for priests to fulfil all the mass requests. Church architecture responded to the new needs by breaking up spaces earlier reserved for the gathered assembly so that private masses could be celebrated simultaneously.

The church of St Riquier may represent the earliest example of another Carolingian innovation, the massing of towers flanking a porch at the western entrance, creating a facade or *westwork* that would eventually evolve into the familiar twin-spired facades of the Gothic *cathedrals. At St Riquier, as (a few years later) at Charlemagne's own palace chapel in Aachen, the towers flanking the entry provided stairs to an upper story. The space at St Riquier was an ample chapel dedicated to the Saviour that served as an additional station for the liturgy. The Ottonian dynasty from Saxony that succeeded Charlemagne's grandsons delighted in the geometry and profiles of these stair turrets, increasing their height and complexity, and integrating them into the porch designs.

4. *Later Medieval Developments.* The two hundred and fifty years' dominance of imperial court patronage and reform efforts throughout the Carolingian and Ottonian eras reversed abruptly at the turn of the first millennium. Throughout Europe a new spiritual authority replaced that of the imperial courts, and the age of the Romanesque arrived. Europe breathed a sigh of relief that the world did not end at the turn into the year 1000, and faced the future with enormous energy. An eleventh-century monk, Raoul Glaber, was moved to describe Europe as clothed in a 'white mantle of churches', a poetic image for an enormous surge in church-building. The cult of relics encouraged in Carolingian times and the identification of the supposed relics of the Apostle James in a remote corner of north-west Spain loosed a frenzy of popular religiosity. Europe was at peace, commerce increased, new towns grew and cities prospered, a merchant class emerged, and people got caught up in the desire to travel, to go on religious *pilgrimage. The commerce and competition for relics among towns along the routes to the shrine of St James in Santiago de Compostela, along with the increasing hordes of foot pilgrims desiring to venerate the relics, led to the introduction of continuous aisles (ambulatories) along the outer perimeter of the nave, transepts and apses of churches and the introduction of multiple *chapels along the transepts and apse. These plan alterations provided a traffic pattern to keep the pilgrims moving around the church to the various chapels and out of the way of the clergy in the nave and choir.

An additional practical innovation was the introduction of Roman-style masonry barrel or groin vaults. Though more complex and expensive than the traditional timber roofs, masonry vaults provided fire protection and offered a more acoustically live space for chant and singing. These pilgrimage churches introduced lavish exterior sculptural programmes at the portals, and rich interior carvings. In England and the north of France, following William's conquest of England in 1066, the dukes of Normandy embarked on experiments in vaulting of another sort, the masonry ribbed groin vault. The cathedral at Durham, England, provides an early extant example of Norman ribbed vaulting. The vaulting of rectangular bays with a skeletal structure of ribs and pointed arches considerably lightened the weight of the vault, enabling it to extend to greater heights and safely accommodate windows at the upper level.

This new structural form provided a foundation for the Gothic builders to interpret theological ideas coming from the royal abbey at St Denis near Paris at the beginning of the twelfth century. The royal abbey housed the tombs of the Frankish kings and the relics of St Denis, first Bishop of Paris and patron of France. Abbot Suger, a powerful adviser to both Kings Louis VI and VII, embarked upon the rebuilding of the abbey church. The *choir of the building, dedicated in 1144, expressed a new mode of luxury and theological ideas, defining the basic vocabulary of the Gothic style. The abbot was influenced by Neoplatonic ideas about light and by Augustinian notions concerning the relationship of geometry and proportion to divinity. The introduction of immense stained-glass windows in the radiating chapels surrounding the apse transformed ordinary light into a royal purple evocation of the divine presence. The splendour of the primarily ruby-red and bright blue glass overwhelmed the viewer for whom walls dissolved into curtains of jewel-like light. Unlike the sturdy, satisfying gravity of the Romanesque pilgrimage churches, Gothic cathedrals became dematerialized, spiritualized structures lifting spirits to mystical heights. As the scale of the buildings increased to lengths over 200 feet, and the height to ten or twelve storeys, the significance of the assembly decreased. The assembly watched in wonder as the clergy performed liturgies at a distance, celebrating mysteries too holy for participation by the faithful.

The Gothic visual vocabulary of linearity, dematerialization, pierced twin-spired facades, jewel-toned stained glass, and soaring vaults came to birth in the ether of twelfth-century French monarchical aspirations and heady theological and philosophical speculation. Beyond France, delight in the aesthetic elements of the style resulted in adaptations that were decidedly non-French. A good example is Salisbury Cathedral in England, begun in the early thirteenth century. All the elements are present, but the emphasis (with the exception of the crossing tower added later) is horizontal rather than vertical.

5. *The Renaissance and After.* While the Gothic style continued to feed the imagination of northern European architects as late as the sixteenth century, a stirring of nostalgia for the classical past erupted in Italy by the late fourteenth century. Petrarch and other humanists opened a new era by their shift in emphasis to classical literature, art and architecture as models for human achievement, perfection and virtue. For early Renaissance architects, particularly the architect and theorist Leon Battista Alberti, the central plan was the ideal plan, for the circle is the image of perfection. Alberti's ideas are best represented in the work of Giuliano da Sangallo at the Church of Santa Maria delle Carceri in Prato, begun in 1485. A circular dome rests above a square flanked by four short arms. The circular dome within a square whose side arms form a cross could all be inscribed within a circle. Sixty-five years later Michelangelo's 1546 plan for the new St Peter's similarly provided a central plan, appropriate for the martyrium of the saint.

The political and religious upheavals of the sixteenth century provoked contrasting RC and Protestant images for churches for the following four hundred years. Architectural examples illustrate the duel between the austere Protestant Reformation in the north and an ebullient and triumphant Counter-Reformation Roman Catholicism in Rome. Bernini's colonnade at St Peter's that reaches out to embrace the faithful, the ten-storey-tall baldachino topped with the orb of the universe over the tomb of St Peter, and the assertion of the authority of bishops from St Peter to the present pope in the majestic shrine of the Chair of Peter in the apse at St Peter's celebrated Roman Catholicism.

Roman Catholicism's embrace of the mystical and supernatural in clouds of angels and dramatic, theatrical light contrasted with the cool simplicity of the whitewashed interiors of former RC churches in the Protestant north whose paintings and images of saints had been removed. The Protestant insistence on the priesthood of all believers dismantled the medieval separation of the clergy from the laity at worship. All worshipped in the same room, necessitating gathering all the people with the clergy in the same place for the proclamation of scripture and preaching, and for *communion. Both preaching and communion might occur in the nave of a formerly RC church, or the whole congregation might experience the service of the word in the nave and move to the *chancel (from which the screen had been removed) around the altar table for communion. A high value was placed on services being both audible and visible. The size and height of *pulpits increased dramatically, often with large soundboards behind and above them. The pulpit was relocated to a place along the side midway down the nave, with seats for ministers flanking it. The assembly stood or was seated facing the pulpit. The Reformers' rejection of the sacrificial nature of the eucharist required an altar table (or *communion table) rather than the immovable solid stone altars customary in the RC tradition. The Reformers felt a table was more in accord with their understanding of the customs of the early Christian community. Further, a movable table allowed the minister to stand behind the table facing the congregation.

Although denominational customs and preferences that distinguish them developed over time among Calvinists, Lutherans, Anglicans and others, they all emphasized the prominence of the pulpit and insisted that the congregation be able to hear and see. In some traditions elaborate *organs supported congregational singing, becoming focal points in the space. Stacked *galleries brought people closer to the pulpit. Baptismal bowls were often attached to pulpits, though in the Anglican tradition fonts generally remained near the entrance. A seventeenth-century Anglican innovation was Archbishop Laud's relocating the altar to the east wall with a rail around it (*see* **Altar Rails**). Christopher Wren's rebuilding of numerous churches in London after the great fire of 1666 established a liturgical one-room norm for Anglican churches that persisted until the mid-nineteenth century.

The Oxford Movement, begun in 1833 by a group of Anglican clergy at Oxford University intent on reforming the Church of England by reclaiming pre-Reformation Catholic traditions and doctrines, substantially subverted in England the architectural developments celebrated in the work of Christopher Wren. The centralized one-room church gave way once more to a longitudinal church plan with nave, transept and chancel. In 1841 the architect and theorist Augustus Welby Pugin published his *True Principles of Pointed Architecture*, arguing that authentic Gothic style of the fourteenth century was the only appropriate and moral style for Christian churches. Nineteenth-century Romanticism's preference for all things medieval prevailed in the style of Protestant and RC churches in England and the USA until the middle of the twentieth century.

The emergence of the *Liturgical Movement in both Europe and the USA in the early twentieth century, and the promulgation of the 1963 Constitution on the Liturgy as the initial proceeding of the Second Vatican Council, provide the foundation for the story of modern church architecture.

M. Camille, *Gothic Art: Glorious Visions*, New York 1997; K. Conant, *Carolingian and Romanesque Architecture, 800–1200*, 4th edn, New Haven, CT 1992; P. Frankl, *Gothic Architecture*, Harmondsworth 1962; R. Krautheimer and S. Ćurčić, *Early Christian and Byzantine Architecture*, 4th edn, New Haven, CT 1986; R. Milburn, *Early Christian Art and Architecture*, Berkeley, CA 1988; O. von Simson, *The Gothic Cathedral: Origins of Gothic Architecture and the Medieval Concept of Order*, 3rd edn, Princeton 1988; W. Stoddard, *Art and Architecture in Medieval France*, New York 1972; J. F. White, *Protestant Worship and Church Architecture*, New York 1964; R. Wittkower, *Art and Architecture in Italy, 1600 to 1750*, 3 vols, 6th edn, New Haven, CT 1999; N. Yates, *Buildings, Faith, and Worship*, Oxford 1991.

MARCHITA B. MAUCK

Architectural Setting (Modern)

1. *Beginnings*. Church architecture of the twentieth and twenty-first centuries has its origins in several distinct stories. One was the post-war necessity of rebuilding thousands of European churches destroyed during World War II. Another story is that of the modern *Liturgical Movement, begun in the second half of the nineteenth century. The use of expressive new building materials such as reinforced concrete and steel, combined with the design implications of an emerging conviction that participation in worship by the people is important, loosened the grip of a romantic medievalism demanding Gothic or Romanesque style churches.

Notable efforts at a modern architectural style for churches appear as early as the first two decades of the twentieth century in both Europe and the USA. In his 1922 church of Notre-Dame du Raincy, Auguste Perret demonstrated the beauty and utility of reinforced concrete as a dignified medium for building churches. In Germany the architect Dominikus Böhm experimented with new materials, especially reinforced concrete, but also with steel and glass to create unencumbered spaces. Long *basilica-shaped churches with *naves interrupted by the arcades of side *aisles and with remote eastern *chancels made it impossible to bring the assembly close to the *altar. Steel beams can span wide spaces, and cast concrete allows for sculpting and moulding spaces more appropriate for the reordering of the assembly.

Long before the Second Vatican Council, small shifts appeared in the role and expectations of the laity, prompting some architects and theologians to turn their attention to the arrangement of the assembly. Pope Pius X issued his decree 'On Frequent and even Daily Communion' in 1905. This Roman stirring of encouragement for increased participation in the *eucharist provoked theological reflection on the significance of the altar. Both Perret and Böhm attempted to make the altar more prominent by providing a raised platform. Böhm engaged in lengthy discussions about the importance of the liturgy for church design with Father I. van Acken, who had published in Germany a book on church design in 1923. Böhm went so far as to detach the *tabernacle from the altar in a Dutch Benedictine monastery he designed at Vaals in 1922. He advocated in his designs relocation of the baptismal *font to a more prominent position within the entry hall and placement of the altar in a more central place in the assembly.

Although not a liturgical space, Frank Lloyd Wright's Unity Temple in Chicago, built in 1906, stands as the earliest icon of American modern church architecture. Like his colleagues in Europe, Wright chose concrete as his medium, casting the forms on site. The church's lines are rectilinear and right angled in imitation of the powerful simplicity of ancient temples.

A rich fermentation of ideas and design possibilities filled the post-war decade between the early 1950s and the opening of the Second Vatican Council in 1962. The architect Le Corbusier challenged all notions of a traditional church in his 1950–55 pilgrimage church of Notre-Dame-du-Haut at Ronchamp, France. On an ancient pilgrimage site bombed in 1944, architecture became sculpture and poetry, evoking praying hands, or a crab shell, or the hull of a ship. The exterior walls range from some twelve feet thick at the base to four feet at the top. Mere slits on the exterior turn into large windows on the inside, throwing strong shafts of light into the womb-like interior. A narrow band of light seeps between the walls and the ceiling, creating an illusion that the slightly sagging concrete ceiling mysteriously hovers above the walls rather than rests upon them. A quiet calm prevails inside for the individual pilgrim, while the exterior is designed to provide for outdoor feast-day eucharists for thousands of visitors.

Perhaps emboldened by Le Corbusier's sculptural assertion of organic forms at Ronchamp, other architects experimented with new forms as well. The 1962 Benedictine Priory Chapel in St Louis, designed by Hellmuth, Obata and Kassabaum, utilizes concrete to construct three dramatic concentric rings of parabolic arches. The round shape allowed placement of the altar in the centre of the space. Marcel Breuer's massive church for St John's Abbey at Collegeville, Minnesota, built between 1953 and 1961, demonstrated the effectiveness once more of concrete cast on the site. The bell tower wedges into the sky, erupting dramatically from its base. The concrete and glass honeycomb facade renders the massive wall airy and light. The cube design provided for major emphasis on the altar located near the centre of the church in the midst of the monastic community.

In addition to the assimilation of new construction materials and technologies, in France in particular, a major initiative occurred in the commissioning of works of art by prominent artists for churches. The Dominican priest M. A. Coutourier collaborated in the designing of the church of Notre-Dame-de-Toute-Grace at Assy, and was responsible for commissioning works by famous artists including Richier, Matisse, Roualt, Lurcat and Chagall. Although not without controversy, the efforts at Assy raised the important question of the role of contemporary artists and modern art in churches. Conservative constituents raised howls of dismay and despair at the departure in the art works from the sentimental piety of the nineteenth century, but the Assy projects set the precedent for engaging modern artists for church work, and establishing that modern art has something to say to the faithful.

2. *The Effects of Vatican II*. The opening of the Second Vatican Council in 1962, convened by Pope John XXIII, marked a turning point for the direction of new church designs. It is not that the Constitution on the Sacred Liturgy (published in December of 1963) provided specific guidelines for building churches. It did

not. The Constitution articulated not so much a new vision of the church as the 'people of God' who together with the clergy celebrate the liturgy (paragraphs 7 and 48), but, as Romano Guardini phrased it, restored a forgotten way of doing things. In describing the liturgy as the summit toward which the activity of the church is directed and the font from which all her power flows, the document points out that by virtue of their baptism the faithful are called to full, active and conscious participation (paragraphs 10 and 14). The Constitution on the Sacred Liturgy was a watershed document and moment for RC liturgical reform and for the wider ecumenical community.

Foundations for the understanding of church in the Constitution had been laid much earlier. The serious study of liturgy begun by Dom Prosper Guéranger, OSB, in the second half of the nineteenth century at the monastery of Solesmes, France, had opened the way for developments that would culminate in deliberations on the liturgy by the Second Vatican Council. In 1909, at a conference in Malines, Belgium, Dom Lambert Beauduin, OSB, called for increased participation by the people in the liturgy, in effect calling for a declericalization of the celebration. Significant liturgical study was occurring at the monasteries of Maria Laach and Beuron in Germany, Klosterneuburg in Austria, and St John's in College-ville, Minnesota. By the mid 1940s pastoral liturgy institutes were established at Trier, Germany, and in Paris. Pope Pius XII's restoration of the ancient rites of *Holy Saturday in 1951 and his 1955 restoration of the whole of *Holy Week made available to the faithful the fullness of the liturgical *year and new possibilities for participation.

In mandating full, active and conscious participation by the faithful, the framers of the Constitution on the Sacred Liturgy perhaps unwittingly set in motion the theological and liturgical reflection leading inexorably to the revision of ideas about the arrangement of liturgical spaces. The position of the altar in relationship to the assembly, the restoration of *baptism by immersion instead of sprinkling, the restoration of emphasis on the liturgy of the *word, the location of the tabernacle, and the proper disposition of devotional images now mattered as elements of spiritual formation. Over time, as revisions of each of the sacramental rites were published, these questions became more and more focused. The liturgy and its celebration now became the basis for church design. Corporate worship involving the whole community took precedence over private devotion.

The Constitution's shift in emphasis from the strictly hierarchal clerical model to the image of the whole people of God celebrating liturgy, each according to his or her own roles, brought forth serious consideration of numerous new arrangements of worship spaces for the assembly. Full and active participation by the faithful required that the altar be located closer to the assembly, prompting throughout the late 1960s and 1970s explorations of round, fan-shaped, and antiphonal seating designs with altars thrust into the assembly on raised platforms.

The euphoric post-Conciliar rush to express architecturally what was essentially a new ecclesiology led at times to over-zealous responses. An effort to achieve eucharistic spaces of simplicity and beauty in churches the interiors of which had been richly decorated and primarily devotional led in some cases to the stripping of old churches or the building of new churches best described as resembling cold, barren warehouses. Those 1970s stripped-down, school-gym 'flexible' spaces proved untenable. They did not satisfy the need of the worshippers for beauty or for places dedicated for worship. They were barren of devotional opportunities and devoid of mystery.

Over the some forty years since the Second Vatican Council, all the RC sacramental rites have been revised. In 1978 the American Bishops' Committee on the Liturgy published their first document on art and architecture, *Environment and Art in Catholic Worship*. This document, written by Robert Hovda, renowned lover of the liturgy, focused on the actions of the assembly as the subject of liturgy and called for noble simplicity, beauty and authenticity of materials. Its tone was poetic, not prescriptive. Its language was God-centred, valuing the numinous and symbolic. It affirmed the appropriateness of contemporary styles of art and design articulated in Chapter VII of the Constitution on the Sacred Liturgy.

3. *The Ecumenical Dimension*. The document *Environment and Art in Catholic Worship*, as reflection on the Constitution on the Sacred Liturgy, has had great influence on the design of RC churches, but also a wide ecumenical effect. American Episcopalians and Lutherans as well as other Protestant denominations have entered the conversation about the ways in which worship spaces support and shape an

understanding of the Christian community. The Anglican Church in England has been seriously engaged in the same conversation, calling it the reordering of churches. Peter Hammond's book, *Liturgy and Architecture* (London 1960), followed by the volume edited by Gilbert Cope, *Making the Building Serve the Liturgy* (London 1962), early on recognized that buildings shape the vision of church that people hold, either for ill or for good. Reflection on the issues of the reordering of churches, in light of the wisdom gained since the Vatican Council and in light of the American experience, has most recently been taken up by Richard Giles in his book *Re-Pitching the Tent: Re-Ordering the Church Building for Worship and Mission in the New Millennium* (Norwich 1997).

4. *A Liturgically Designed Church*. What are the components of a liturgically designed church? They include attention to the spaces that support all the ritual actions of the community and its devotional needs. The place for the celebration of the eucharist, with altar, *ambo or *pulpit and presider's chair, occupies the central focus. Gathering the assembly around the altar facilitates participation in the offering made by the whole church, laity and their ministers together.

The RC *Rite of Christian Initiation of Adults*, as well as the *General Introduction to Christian Initiation*, calls for fonts large enough to accommodate the immersion of adults as the fuller, most expressive sign of the *sacrament. The candidates are baptized into the Christian community and into the paschal *mystery by passing through the waters of death into new life. Location of the font near the entry reminds worshippers of their entry into the faith, imaging the path of Christian life leading to the celebration of the eucharist.

Provision of a significant portal and an entry gathering-space provides the hospitality that is part of the community's identity, as well as a place for the greeting rites that are part of Sunday celebrations, such as for infant baptisms or the welcoming of *catechumens. In RC churches the role of private devotional piety is important. This includes ideally a *chapel for the *reserved sacrament, for providing *communion for those not able to participate in the assembly's eucharist, and for the private prayer of the faithful. The place for the tabernacle is to be beautiful, visible to the assembly, and suitable for private prayer.

Places for veneration of *saints with images of artistic quality, affording opportunities for the faithful to express popular piety and devotion, and yet not so intrusive as to interfere with ritual, are also appropriate. There is a hierarchy in which the places for the sacramental rites take precedence over those serving private devotional purposes. A liturgically designed church will visually express these priorities.

To design a church appropriately for today's liturgy and today's people is not an easy undertaking. Hiring a world-famous architect does not mean one will end up with a world-class liturgical space. In 1990 the Diocese of Rome began an initiative to build '50 churches for Rome 2000' for the Jubilee year. The American architect Richard Meier won the commission to design a church for the working-class neighbourhood of Tor Tre Teste. In his design three curved concrete shells rising like great sails connected by glass walls embrace the interior community centre and church spaces. A skylight fills the whole ceiling of the church area. Various technical problems prevented the completion of the building for the Jubilee year, and it is now scheduled to be completed in 2002. Openness and airiness dominate the design, with a dramatic luminosity in the church space, but liturgically the design is a great disappointment. The skin of the building is modern and sculptural, but the arrangement of the assembly in long rows facing a *sanctuary at the front offers nothing to inspire full, conscious and active participation in the liturgy. There are no provisions for the devotional life of the people.

In contrast the Archdiocese of Los Angeles, California, hired another prize-winning architect, the Spaniard Jose Rafael Moneo, to design its new *cathedral. In Moneo's design, the priority of the liturgical principles held sway over the simply sculptural. Mighty bronze doors three storeys tall mark the entry into the cathedral, opening from a plaza that can seat 6,000. *Iconography for the doors includes Our Lady of the Angels with images of the cultural diversity of the archdiocese. Within the worship space, the assembly gathers around the altar, with all within about one hundred feet of the altar for parochial services. The archbishop, Cardinal Mahoney, carefully differentiated the ritual axis from the devotional areas by locating the eucharistic chapel apart from the main nave. Devotional chapels along the ambulatory face the outer walls rather than into the worship space. Worshippers enter at the altar end of the cross-plan building, encountering the baptismal font along the way. Among the art works commissioned for the building will be 36 tapestries representing the communion of *saints, in 133 ten-foot-tall figures of holy men and women from the Americas and the world. Light, here filtered through alabaster-glazed windows, is a significant symbolic part of the palette of colours and materials.

Of his new cathedral Cardinal Mahoney has said: 'The eyes should be drawn gently but powerfully to the Sanctuary where the human community gathers to offer worship to our Creator. The progression of one's faith-life should become unmistakable: entry into the life of Christ at Baptism and the celebration of the Eucharist and the Church's Liturgy and Sacraments to sustain that spiritual journey. At the same time, the soul should seem to float upwards and about as the Cathedral structure itself entices each person to the grandeur of God and the irresistible longing to be with God. The limits of creation's "now" should be freed to allow the "eternal" of the Kingdom of God to be in some ways experienced.'

5. *Recent Developments*. The American bishops have published a new set of guidelines for the design of RC churches entitled *Built of Living Stones: Art, Architecture, and Worship* (Washington, DC 2000). The new document trades Robert Hovda's poetry and mystical theology of the assembly as the people of God doing *leiturgia* for a reassertion of the hierarchical distinction of the clergy and the laity. The document is preoccupied with the location and symbolism of the presider's chair, the separation of the sanctuary from the assembly, and an excessive concern about the location of the tabernacle. Although much in the new document cites the Constitution, the *General Introduction to the Roman Missal*, and various of the revised rites as its sources, the general tone is pedantic and ideological.

The retrenchment apparent in *Built of Living Stones* reflects what Nathan Mitchell describes as a clash of two Catholic cultures. One group sees Catholicism as 'inclusionist', the church big enough to embrace diversity while not sacrificing unity. The other group understands Catholicism as an identity system, one threatened by the vicissitudes of a modern culture whose liturgy erases their distinctiveness. The remedy for this group is a reassertion of rigour, discipline, ancient beliefs and devotional practices. The bishops' new document speaks to and for those who see Catholicism as an identity system.

The future of worship lies in the outcome of the clash of these two spiritualities. Much is at stake, because the design and arrangement of churches reflect what people believe and the priorities they choose to set forth. A yearning for a past in which 'churches looked like churches' and the hierarchy of power was satisfyingly manifest, leads some in their distaste for anything modern to call for a restoration of a 'classical' ecclesiastical architecture. There is certainly a place for the ongoing creative exploration of a suitable, dignified, majestic architecture for churches. Liturgical reform is compromised when 'classical' becomes a code-word for a pre-Vatican II spirituality and theology of the assembly.

Canadian Conference of Catholic Bishops, *Our Place of Worship*, Ottawa 1999; Walter C. Huffman and S. Anita Stauffer, *Where We Worship*, Minneapolis 1987; Richard Hurley and Wilfrid Cantwell, *Contemporary Irish Church Architecture*, Dublin 1985; Irish Episcopal Commission for Liturgy, *The Place of Worship*, Dublin 1991; Regina Kuehn, *A Place for Baptism*, Chicago 1992; Randall S. Lindstrom, *Creativity and Contradiction: European Churches since 1970*, Washington, DC 1987; Marchita B. Mauck, *Places for Worship: A Guide to Building and Renovation*, Collegeville 1995; Marchita B. Mauck, *Shaping a House for the Church*, Chicago 1990; E. A. Sovik, *Architecture for Worship*, Minneapolis 1973; James F. White, *Protestant Worship and Church Architecture*, New York 1964.

MARCHITA B. MAUCK

Armenian Worship

Armenia's geopolitical setting at the crossroad of Byzantium and Persia is reflected in the evolution of her liturgical practices. Moreover, one of the outstanding features of her rituals is a strong sense of symmetry, which can be observed in the structural outline of the prayers, and sometimes even in the prayers themselves, as well as in the *creed placed before the night office at the very beginning of the *horologion* (a feature shared with the Ethiopian office, where a very archaic creed is intertwined with the *trisagion*).

Another fascinating aspect of Armenian liturgy lies in the fact that it has preserved in many respects the oldest layers of Christian worship, reflecting in its various creeds, the initiation rites, the pattern of *daily prayer, and the older recension of the *eucharistic liturgy of St Basil either Syriac translation techniques (as e.g. in some of its creeds), Syrian thought-patterns (e.g. in some of its *troparia*), or Syriac liturgical practices (as in the original form of the rites of initiation). This undoubtedly can be traced back to the first missionaries to enter Armenian territory, probably from the south-west, bringing with them their liturgical customs, just as the initial attempts at creating an Armenian alphabet led the Armenians first and foremost to Edessa. Yet Jerusalem also has significantly contributed to the formation of the Armenian liturgy, as is clearly evident, for example, in the shape and content of the *lectionary. And with the crusades during the high Middle Ages the Armenian rite became to some extent Latinized.

1. *The *Eucharistic Prayer*. The various Armenian anaphoras were attributed to Gregory the Illuminator, to Sahak, Basil, Gregory of Nazianzus, Cyril and Athanasius. Although the oldest manuscripts of the so-called Liturgy of Athanasius stem from the high Middle Ages, it must have replaced the widely used formulary of Basil already some time before the ninth or tenth centuries. For the tenth-century commentary of Xosrov Anjewac'i, presenting the liturgical practice of the Armenian province of Vaspurakan, gives an interpretation of the Liturgy of Athanasius betraying at various points an older stage of the anaphora than that transmitted by the manuscripts. Today the Liturgy of Athanasius is the only one in use, but we know from fifth-century sources that the liturgy of Basil was celebrated at that time. In the manuscript tradition this anaphora of Basil is named after Gregory the Illuminator, but in reality it reflects not only the older Armenian redactions, but one of the oldest redactions altogether of this widely used anaphora associated with Basil. Since H. Engberding's seminal work on the various recensions of the Liturgy of Basil it is commonly assumed that the Egyptian redaction mirrors the oldest shape of this anaphora, even antedating Basil, and that all other recensions, including both Armenian versions, belong to a later period. Engberding's theory still holds. However, several passages of the first Armenian redaction indicate an earlier stage than the Egyptian redactions in Greek, Coptic and Ethiopian. Moreover this first Armenian version clearly points towards ties with Syria, not with Cappadocia. Another peculiarity of

several redactions of the Liturgy of Basil consists in the fact that the extended prayer after the *Sanctus was closely shaped according to the respective (baptismal) creeds, which in the case of the Armenian version can be shown conclusively. More recent detailed and critical examinations of the Armenian anaphoras have so far been restricted to the anaphora of Basil and the Liturgy of Athanasius, of which a critical edition and detailed commentary will be published shortly.

2. *The Rites of Initiation*. On the one hand, the evolution of the initiation rites shows the efforts of the Armenians to associate themselves with the Greek missionary activities from Cappadocia; on the other hand, a closer investigation of the earliest evidence reflected in the description of king Trdat's baptism in the river Euphrates clearly points toward Syria. Yet not only the Armenian patristic evidence but also the earliest manuscripts of the ninth century still mirror striking Syrian connections. Characteristic of the ninth- or tenth-century *baptismal ordo (and also the *textus receptus*) is the absence of verbal *exorcisms, in contrast to the eighth-century Constantinopolitan ordo (*Codex Barberini 336*), with its heavy emphasis on exorcistic elements. Although one prayer of the Armenian baptismal ordo has some exorcistic traits, there are no verbal exorcisms like those found in many other baptismal traditions, including that of Constantinople. Another striking feature is the preservation of the Johannine baptismal theology following the old Syrian model and still present in the Maronite rite. Only one Armenian *rubric (and none of the prayers) has absorbed a reference to Romans 6, reflecting the Pauline interpretation of baptism.

3. *The *Creeds*. The earliest credal statements follow the early Syriac evidence: like the Syrians, the Armenians altered in their creeds the expressions for the incarnation and the precise wording of the relationship between the Son and the Father during the fifth to sixth centuries by creating neologisms more closely conformed to the Greek vocabulary of *ousia* ('Being'), *homoousios* ('of one Being'), and *sarkothenta* ('incarnate'). One of the characteristics of the fifth- and sixth-century Armenian translations of the Nicene Creed is the striking absence of the *enanthropesanta* ('having become human'), which is also missing in several other versions. The so-called

'Armeniacum', used nowadays during the eucharist and baptism, must be associated with the sixth century, rather than with an earlier period, as was hitherto thought. During baptism another short creed is recited which derives from the baptismal interrogation. The most intriguing creed, however, is the one placed at the beginning of the *horologion*: it seems to have been the former baptismal creed. The basic features of this *symbolum* stem from an extremely early period, but its framework, including several passages of the creed, pertain to the sixth century. The archaic vocabulary of some parts of the *symbolum* shows a close affinity with Syrian models.

4. **Daily Prayer*. The Armenian *horologion* is decidedly 'cathedral' in character: the monastic psalmody in numerical order is restricted to the night office, as in the **East Syrian tradition. The oldest layers can be traced in the Sunday **vigil which commemorates the resurrection. This Sunday cathedral vigil has preserved more closely than any other rite the Jerusalem structure of this resurrection office, particularly with its three canticles, which derive from the **Easter vigil, its three psalms, and above all its reading of the burial and resurrection account, just as described by Egeria, who visited Jerusalem in 381–4. This resurrection vigil commemorates the three women who came to Jesus' tomb early on Easter morning.

The morning (*a'řawotean*) and evening (*erekoyean*) offices have preserved their original cathedral features, in contrast to the Byzantine *orthros* and *hesperinos*, which begin with the monastic psalmody recited in numerical order. The morning and evening cathedral offices experienced a duplication: 'the office of sunrise' (*arewagali*) was apparently developed out of the last part of *a'řawotean*; likewise the evening hour unfolded into the 'hour of peace' (*xałałakan*), concluding with the 'hour of rest' (*hangstean*). The evening hour comprises, it seems, a juxtaposition of two cathedral offices (each of which has the universal evening psalm, 141) with no traces of monastic influence. The first part of the office derives from elsewhere, whereas the second part seems to mirror the genuine Armenian tradition. The morning office, as in the East-Syrian office, opens with Ps. 51 (not Ps. 63, the universal morning psalm of Antioch, Palestine, perhaps also Cappadocia), followed by Pss 148–150 and the Gloria in excelsis.

The most intriguing office is that referred to as *času-žam* ('midday office'). Corresponding to the eighth-century 'third hour', it is nothing else but the 'Liturgy of the **Word'. Interestingly enough, the Georgian synaxis referred to as *samḫrad* ('midday') on feast days in the Georgian lectionary and the Georgian collection of *troparia* (*iadgari*) mirror the same structural outline as *času-žam*. This congruency probably points to a Jerusalem origin.

5. *The Liturgical Year*. The liturgical **year originally began with the feast of **Epiphany, as in Jerusalem. It is still disputed whether the leitmotif of Jesus' baptism in the river Jordan combined with his birth in Bethlehem, a characteristic of Armenian Epiphany, is due to monophysite tendencies, as is generally assumed, or whether it mirrors the earliest layer of the feast itself with its characteristic celebration of both Jesus' baptism and his birth. In addition to the oldest manuscripts of the lectionary, the oldest witnesses of the *synaxarion* (life of the saints) and the *šaraknoc'* (collection of *troparia*) also once began with the feast of Epiphany.

Recent studies or studies underway have also dealt with the Latinization of the Armenian rite during the Middle Ages, the burial liturgy, and the evolution of the *šaraknoc'*.

See also **Books, Liturgical** 2.1.

Athanase (Charles) Renoux, *Le codex arménien Jérusalem 121*, 2 vols, Turnhout, Belgium 1969, 1971; Gabriele Winkler, 'Der armenische Ritus: Bestandsaufnahme und neue Erkenntnisse', *The Christian East*, ed. Robert Taft, Rome 1996, 265–98 (bib.).

For 1: Hans-Jürgen Feulner, *Die armenische Athanasius-Anaphora. Krit. Edition, Übersetzung und liturgievergleichender Kommentar*, Rome 2001; Gabriele Winkler, 'Zur Erforschung orientalischer Anaphoren I', *Orientalia Christiana Periodica* LXIII, 1997, 363–420; Part II, R. Taft, G. Winkler (eds), *Comparative Liturgy Fifty Years after Anton Baumstark*, Rome 2001.

For 2: Ch. Renoux, *Initiation chrétienne* I, Paris 1997; Gabriele Winkler, *Das armenische Initiationsrituale*, Rome 1982.

For 3: Gabriele Winkler, *Über die Entwicklungsgeschichte des armenischen Symbolums. Ein Vergleich mit dem syrischen und griechischen Formelgut*, Rome 2000.

For 4–5: Michael Findikyan, *The Commentary on the Armenian Daily Office by Bishop Step'anos Siwnec'i († 735): Edition and Trans-*

lation, forthcoming; 'The Liturgical Expositions Attributed to Catholicos Yovhannēs
Ōjnecʻi: Problems and Inconsistency', *The
Armenian Christian Tradition*, Rome 1997,
125–73; Andrea B. Schmidt, *Kanon der
Entschlafenen*, Wiesbaden 1994; Gabriele
Winkler, 'The Armenian Night Office I–II',
*Studies in Early Christian Liturgy and its
Context*, ed. G. Winkler, Aldershot 1997,
93–113, 471–551; 'Über die Bedeutung einiger
liturgischer Begriffe im georgischen Lektionar
u. Iadgari sowie im armenischen Ritus', *Studi
sull Oriente Cristiano* IV, 2000.

GABRIELE WINKLER

Art and Worship

1. *Early Traditions*. The earliest Israelite tradition had no problem with decorating sacred
objects to be used in worship. The original ark
of the covenant, the ephod, teraphim and pole
were all lavishly embellished (Judg. 8.26–27;
18.14, 17–19; Num. 21.8–9). Yet from the time
of the Deuteronomic reforms of the seventh
century BCE the construction and use of sacred
images was expressly banned (Ex. 20.4–5).
Within Christianity there were also two
responses to the use of art in worship. Many
of the earliest *basilicas were furnished with
representations of Christ and the saints, a tradition that was later continued in the wall paintings and carved tympana of the medieval West.
Gregory the Great encouraged art in churches
because of its potential as a teaching aid. A different perspective, however, was put forward
by Tertullian, who argued that art distracted the
worshipper from the more important aspects of
worship, and by Jerome, who was concerned
that money spent on embellishing churches
could be better used for the relief of poverty.

2. *Icons and Iconoclasm*. In the East debate
centred around the use in worship of *icons,
which had early become closely associated
with both public and private devotion. This perspective was challenged in the eighth century
by the iconoclasts, who, moved by a strong
transcendentalism which despised any attempts
to represent the Godhead, called for a ban on
all religious images and for their wholesale
destruction. This situation was eventually
resolved at a Council of Nicaea in 787, which
ruled that the use of icons was in accordance
with scripture. In coming to this decision the
council was much influenced by the teachings
of John Damascene, who in his *Apologia*

argued that in the incarnation God had revealed
himself in the person and humanity of Christ
thus making it clear that he did not wish to
remain hidden any longer from his people.

3. *The Medieval West*. The medieval church
continued to be divided on the question of
the use of art in worship. In the twelfth and
thirteenth centuries there was an age of building fine churches with stained-glass windows,
wall paintings and carvings in stone. These
decorative elements served to pass on in picture
language the story of the incarnation of Christ
and the redemption of humanity. Yet they also
spoke to the soul, as at the abbey church of St
Denis, built by Abbot Suger between 1135 and
1144. This church was designed to translate
worshippers in their devotions from this world
to the next. As they passed through scenes of
the Last Judgement at the threshold, their eyes
were led to the east end of the church, bathed in
light, standing as a symbol of the heavenly city
for which they longed. Against such mysticism,
Bernard of Clairvaux argued that religious
art and decoration distracted the worshipper
from a proper concentration on God and upon
the centrality of the *eucharist. Cistercian
churches built under his influence during the
twelfth century were therefore essentially plain
and devoid of any coloured glass or carving.

4. *Renaissance and Reformation*. An even
fiercer debate arose during the sixteenth century. In the RC Church creativity took on a new
lease of life and artists such as Michelangelo
were now regarded not only as makers but also
as co-creators with God. New masterpieces
such as the ceiling of the Sistine Chapel were
painted with images of Christ, the Virgin Mary
and the saints. The church defended itself on
the grounds that reverence to religious paintings and images was not idolatry, since honour
was being shown not to the images themselves
but to the prototypes or realities that these
images represented. Counter to this argument,
the Protestant Reformers on the Continent of
Europe waged a strenuous battle against the
continued use of iconography within churches.
They stressed the importance of salvation
through faith and through the scriptures alone.
Representational art, they believed, detracted
from this focus on the word. In the Church of
England a compromise was initially reached
which stressed the primacy of the word but
which allowed for the presence of images and
paintings in churches so long as 'no Godly

honour is paid to them' (*The King's Book*, 1543). This by no means satisfied the Puritans and in the English Civil War of the seventeenth century a wholesale destruction of religious art took place.

5. *Twentieth-Century Perspectives.*
Twentieth-century theology did little to clarify the issue. While Hans Urs von Balthasar and Paul Tillich both devoted substantial portions of their writings to the study of aesthetics and beauty within the context of Christianity and Christian art, Rudolf Bultmann largely ignored the arts as unimportant to the task of 'breaking the word', while Karl Barth argued that images and symbol had no place at all in a building designed for Christian worship.

Papal policy towards the use of contemporary art in churches was equally mixed. In 1947 Pius XI was still speaking out strongly against modern art and its influence in *Mediator Dei*. By 1972, however, Paul VI had taken a different stance. In his encyclical *Le Nobili Espressioni* he apologized to artists for the way in which the church had limited their creativity down the centuries and expressed a hope that a new relationship between artists and the church might be built up. Much good work was done in this area in the first half of the twentieth century by the Liturgical Arts movement in the USA, which aimed to foster good practice and to create a dialogue between the RC Church and contemporary artists.

In practical terms much of the modern debate continues to centre around whether contemporary art has a place in the church. Pioneering work took place in England between 1940 and 1978 under the direction of Walter Hussey, first as parish priest of St Matthew's, Northampton and then as Dean of Chichester. In these two very different settings Hussey patronized the work of all the great British artists of his day, including Graham Sutherland, John Piper and Henry Moore. In Europe more recent work has been done by Friedhelm Mennekes at Cologne. Here the area behind the *altar has been painted white, thus providing a canvas for contemporary works of art in the form of triptychs. Each artist is invited to display his or her work for three months and is given a free hand in terms of style and treatment.

Interest is also being focused both in Europe and in the USA on the principles to be followed whenever a work of art is being commissioned for church use from an artist of national or local repute. The art must be capable of bearing the sacred and of serving the needs of the liturgy. The work must be designed so as to never take over the place or rhythm of worship. Any colour or texture present therefore must point to the spiritual reality of which they are signs and not focus attention on the work itself. Finally duplication of images (such as crosses) should also be avoided at all costs, since this has the effect of taking away the power of symbol.

David Brown and Ann Loades (eds), *The Sense of the Sacramental: Movement and Measure in Art and Music, Place and Time*, London 1995; John Dillenberger, *A Theology of Artistic Sensibilities*, London 1986; Eamon Duffy, *The Stripping of the Altars*, New Haven 1992; Umberto Eco, *Art and Beauty in the Middle Ages*, Yale 1986; K. Walker, *Images or Idols*, Norwich 1986; Janet Walton, *Art and Worship: A Vital Connection*, Collegeville 1988; Susan J. White, *Art, Architecture and Liturgical Reform*, New York 1990.

ANNE DAWTRY

Ascension Day

This day marks the remembrance and celebration of the ascension of the risen Christ to heaven. Of the four evangelists, only Luke narrates the ascension, in two places, concisely at the end of the Gospel (24.50–51) and with more detail at the beginning of the Acts of the Apostles (1.1–12). Here it is said to have happened 'forty days after he had suffered' (Acts 1.3), after the period in the gospel narratives during which he appeared to the apostles and spoke of the kingdom. The theology of the Lucan narrative reflects the exaltation of the risen Christ and is associated with the gift of the Holy Spirit at Pentecost (Acts 1.8). The appearance of two white-robed witnesses might suggest an association of the narrative of the ascension with *baptism rites and with the white garments that would later clothe the initiated at *Easter and in the Easter season.

First celebrated in the fourth century, the temporal placement of the celebration of the ascension in the liturgical *year has traditionally been during the fifty days of the Easter season, but it was at first variously positioned there in different geographical regions: at the mid-point of the span (on the twenty-fifth day, Mid-Pentecost), at the end (on the fiftieth day, *Pentecost) and, increasingly, in the late fourth century, on the fortieth day. This result was possible only after the fixing of the NT canon and the subsequent tendency of Christian communities to have the chronology of the liturgical year follow the narrative of the life of Jesus as known from intermittent chronological clues in the Gospels.

Even today, as in the early church, the temporal locus of Ascension Day is arranged differently by different Christian communities. Some celebrate 'Ascension Thursday', the fortieth day after Easter Day, while others observe it on the Sunday closest to the fortieth day, i.e., the sixth Sunday of the Easter season, the Sunday before Pentecost.

MARTIN F. CONNELL

Ash Wednesday

In the early medieval period in the West, as *Lent developed and its observance became more elaborate, the ceremonial distribution of *ashes to the clergy and faithful was observed on the fortieth day before Easter to begin this penitential season. Thus that fortieth day became known as Ash Wednesday. While this practice was abandoned in many of the Reformation churches, some Christian traditions (e.g. RC) still retain the ritual. After a prayer of blessing over the ashes, the members of the congregation may line up in single file, as in a *communion procession, and proceed to the steps of the *sanctuary area. The priest or minister dips his/her thumb in the small bowl of ashes, and marks the recipient with them on the forehead (often in the shape of a cross). A distribution formula accompanies this action, e.g. 'Repent and believe the Good News', or the older 'Remember man that you are dust and unto dust you shall return'. Along with *Good Friday, Ash Wednesday is observed as an official *fast day in the RC Church: traditionally, only one full meal is permitted, as well as two smaller 'snacks', which, if combined, would be less than a second full meal.

See also **Commination**.

JOANNE M. PIERCE

Ashes

In biblical tradition, and later in early and medieval Christian tradition, covering the head with ashes (or indeed sitting in ashes) is considered a sign of repentance, sorrow and mourning (*see* **Penance**). Thus, the distribution of ashes is understood in many Christian churches to be an appropriate way to mark the beginning of the penitential season of *Lent. It

is from this custom that the name *Ash Wednesday is given to the first day of the season. Traditionally, the ashes are made by burning the palm leaves that have been blessed the previous year on *Palm Sunday to mark the beginning of *Holy Week. Ashes can also be used as a symbol of purification, and were mixed into special blessed water called 'Gregorian water' to be used at the *consecration of churches in the Middle Ages.

JOANNE M. PIERCE

Asperges

The ceremony of sprinkling holy water over the *altar, the ministers and people before the principal *eucharist on Sundays in the Western Catholic tradition. The name (from the Latin *aspergere*, 'to sprinkle') echoes the words of Ps. 51.9: 'Cleanse me of sin with hyssop, that I may be purified; wash me, and I shall be whiter than snow'. Formerly other verses of the psalm were sung or said during the sprinkling, which took place usually in a *procession of *celebrant, ministers and *servers around the church.

The rite of the Sunday asperges probably had its origin in the monastic custom of sprinkling the monastery on that day but certainly goes back to the ninth century when it is referred to by Hincmar of Reims in his *Epistola synodica*. Originally, it would seem, an *exorcistic rite for the cleansing of a building or place where a liturgical service was to take place, the asperges became in the course of centuries connected with *baptism both as a reminder of the sacrament and as a means of renewing its grace. In the RC Tridentine liturgy this is indicated both by the sprinkling of the people after the renewal of their *baptismal promises at the *Easter vigil and by the change of text during the Easter season (Ezek. 47.1, 8, 9: 'I saw water coming out from the temple on the right side and all whom this water touched were saved . . .').

According to the liturgical reforms of the Second Vatican Council, the Sunday renewal of baptism has replaced the asperges in the order of the *mass. This revised rite of sprinkling is no longer restricted to the principal mass or to parish churches but may be used 'at all Sunday Masses, even those anticipated on Saturday evening in all churches and oratories' (Appendix I, *Missale Romanum*, 1975). To make this point clear, the rite is printed in the order of the mass as an alternative

to the penitential rite. The latter is simply omitted when holy water is blessed and sprinkled.
The prayer of blessing of the water, which
follows the priest's initial greeting, and the
selection of songs to accompany the sprinkling,
indicate the purpose of the rite: 'to express the
paschal character of Sunday and a memorial of
baptism'. After the rite of sprinkling, the mass
continues with the Gloria in excelsis or the
opening prayer.

Ludwig Eisenhofer, *Handbuch der katholis-
chen Liturgik* I, Freiburg 1932, 476–80; C.
Goeb, 'The Asperges', *Orate Fratres* II, 1927–
8, 338–42; J. A. Jungmann, *The Mass of the
Roman Rite*, New York 1951, 270–7; P.
LeFevre, 'La bénèdiction dominicale de l'eau,
l'aspersion des fidèles et des lieux', *Questions
liturgiques et paroissiales* LI, 1970, 29–36.

JOSEPH WEISS

Assemblies of God Churches' Worship

The Assemblies of God (A/G), formed by 300
pastors and laypeople in 1914 in Hot Springs,
Arkansas to help provide leadership within
certain branches of the emerging *Pentecostal
movement of the early twentieth century, now
consists of national organizations from 162
countries that together make up a worldwide
communion of some 35 million believers – perhaps one-tenth of the total global Pentecostal
population. The growth of the denomination,
its adherents believe, is linked to its Spirit-filled
worship and the life in the Spirit that proceeds
from that worship. Enthusiastic, congregational, participatory forms of prayer, praise,
preaching and worship often characterize an
A/G 'liturgy'. Worship within the A/G can be
considered in three categories: the rites as
structure and the acts of worship; the sensibilities, i.e., types of embodied attitudes worshippers experience; and the values that are implied
and fundamental to worship. Terms such as
'rites' and 'liturgy' are not native to A/G
congregants, but are used here to assist the
description.

1. *Rites: Structure and Acts of Worship.*
Fundamentally, A/G worship services (liturgies) are quite simple. The basic structure owes
much to the traditions of the Free Church and to
the American revivalist/frontier forms. Three
foundational rites proceed in a basic tripartite
service consisting of worship and praise,

sermon, and altar response. A closer look discloses a certain complexity to A/G worship.
Permeating the three foundational rites, a host
of worship acts and expressions, i.e., sub-rites,
function within A/G worship. These rites and
sub-rites of worship can be defined as those
acts, actions, dramas and performances that a
community creates, continues, recognizes and
sanctions as ways of behaving that express
appropriate attitudes, sensibilities, values and
beliefs as they signify worship. Examples of
such sub-rites in A/G worship include *extemporaneous prayer often in a 'concert' of united
audible prayer, extended singing with a variety
of musical instruments, personal testimonies,
gifts of the Holy Spirit, *anointing with oil and
prayer for the *sick, altar responses for conversion, raised hands, and other kinaesthetic
*gestures.

2. *Sensibilities: Attitudes of and in Worship.*
The sensibilities with which the rites are
enacted and experienced are important when
seeking to understand A/G worship. Each A/G
rite or act of worship in a liturgy is combined
with at least one mode of sensibility, i.e., a type
of embodied attitude, which is the result of
the ability to feel or perceive, to be receptive
and responsive to particular affections. These
embodied attitudes play a fundamental role
in helping to orient and animate each of the
various A/G worship practices. A dynamic
affect mediates between the acts of worship
(i.e., the rites) on the one hand, and the attitudes
of worship (i.e., the sensibilities) on the other.
A variety of worship sensibilities pervade and
breathe life into A/G liturgies. The following
are examples of modes of worship sensibilities.

The *celebrative mode* which embodies an
attitude characterized by expressiveness and
spontaneity roots in the actions and attitude
of playfulness. A/G praise rites frequently
demonstrate a celebrative sensibility. The
mode of transcendental efficacy occupies the
other end of the liturgical attitude spectrum. It
is an attitude that participates in pragmatic
ritual work particularly in relationship to God
and the power of God to produce an affect. This
efficacious sensibility functions with practical
goals, concerned more with consequence than
meaning. A/G prayers for healing and healing
services often embody this sensibility. The
contemplative mode in the A/G services reflects
a deep receptivity, a sense of openness to and
docility before God. Portions of the worship-
in-song rite or the concluding altar service can

be marked by a contemplative attitude. At other times, the altar service reflects a *penitent/ purgative mode* of sensibility – an attitude characterized by contrition, repentance, or even grieving. The *mode of ecstasy* is the sense that the worshipper is directly influenced by God, a sense of being inspired, moved to act, or even the sense of being overwhelmed by the Spirit. Spirit baptism may signify this mode. The *ceremonial mode* shows more intentionality than the other sensibilities in A/G worship; it requires some suppression of individuality in favour of a larger liturgical task. This sensibility often accompanies the *Lord's supper and *baptism, for example.

3. *Values at the Heart of A/G Worship*. At the heart of the A/G worship and spirituality lies a set of core values. These values permeate the worship service, its rites and sensibilities, informing and supporting the worship. A few values are foundational to A/G worship. Perhaps the most fundamental is *experience*. Personal spiritual experience of the presence of the Holy Spirit is not only central to A/G worship, it represents for A/G congregants the primary realm of authentic and vital religion. A/G people emphasize the role of the Holy Spirit in God's manifest presence and actions. Worship connotes encounter with God, an encounter that expects empowerment and transformation. Worship services work to provide a context and atmosphere in which people can recognize and respond to the moving of God, the manifestations of the Holy Spirit.

A second core value that complements and balances the focus on experience can be seen in the emphasis on the *Word of God*, and the sense of biblical authority. The belief that God has spoken and still speaks remains central to A/G worship and spirituality. Words of scripture are taken at face value, which helps to explain some of the unique practices and beliefs of A/G liturgy and life. 'Word of God' refers to the words of the Bible fundamentally, but it may also refer to how God yet speaks, especially within congregational narrative forms – sermons, testimonies, and charismatic words or utterances, for example. Such 'words' must be discerned as genuine and are measured against the Bible.

Another important value in A/G worship is *orality*. Walter Hollenweger has noted the significance of 'oral liturgy' among Pentecostals worldwide. He claims that orality makes their liturgy accessible to a wide range of people globally. Historically, the oral dimension has assisted congregants toward an active participation in liturgy. In many place, orality fuses with kinaesthetic movement in the liturgy. Such physical manifestations reflect a holistic understanding of the human person and of the worshipping person. Sacred *dance, for instance, in African A/G worship represents this understanding.

Accompanying orality and kinaesthetics is the value placed on *improvisation*. The sense of spontaneity has been stressed. This emphasis reflects the belief that the Holy Spirit is the ultimate leader and guide of the worship service. Since the Spirit may move unpredictably, A/G worship leaders and congregants must be open to a kind of liturgical improvisation. While there is an underlying liturgical 'script', the script anticipates improvisation, within the structure of the fundamental rites. Such flexibility furnishes the freedom to respond to the impulses of the Spirit with authentic heartfelt expressions of worship.

A/G worship services reflect a strong value placed on *ministry*. Ministry is to God, the church, and the world and it begins in the worship service itself. A/G congregants are taught to worship God as a ministry unto God, and to serve one another in various edifying ministries even during the liturgy itself. Fellowship within the community can be poignant and extend beyond the service or the sanctuary. Emerging from the liturgy, there is a movement outward into the world; a strong emphasis is placed on evangelistic outreach, foreign missions projects, and other services to humankind as ministry to the world. These ministries are recognized to be the responsibility and privilege of all the believers, not just the leaders. Shaping this value of ministry are certain pragmatic attitudes, entrepreneurialism, and desire to be relevant to the popular culture.

The exercising of *spiritual gifts* (especially the Pauline charismata) continues to be a core value for A/G worshippers. The gifts are linked in A/G understanding and experience to baptism in the Holy Spirit. Spirit baptism along with the charismata represent empowerment for life and service and a transformative, edifying power that builds up individuals and the believing community. This value also highlights an inherent egalitarian orientation, a democratic-participatory inclusiveness that is rooted in the belief that all bear the gift of the Spirit and may be used by the Spirit.

It should be noted that in recent years some

of the above values and practices are less obvious in A/G worship services, especially in the USA. The reasons for change might include: the growing size of many A/G congregations, upward social mobility and the acceptance of mainstream middle-class values, the emerging postmodern culture, the phenomenon of routinization of the charismata, the influence of non-charismatic, evangelical individuals and groups, and the borrowing of liturgical practices from mainline churches and from *charismatic groups.

Daniel E. Albrecht, *Rites in the Spirit: A Ritual Approach to Pentecostal/Charismatic Spirituality*, Sheffield 1999; Edith L. Blumhofer, *Restoring the Faith: The Assemblies of God, Pentecostalism, and American Culture*, Chicago 1993; Stanley M. Burgess, Gary B. McGee and Patrick H. Alexander (eds), *Dictionary of Pentecostal and Charismatic Movements*, Grand Rapids, MI 1988; Walter Hollenweger, *Pentecostalism: Origins and Development Worldwide*, Peabody, MA 1997; Margaret M. Poloma, *The Assemblies of God at the Crossroads: Charisma and Institutional Dilemmas*, Knoxville, TN 1989.

DANIEL E. ALBRECHT

Assumption *see* Marian Feasts

Atrium

The open, entry courtyard to a church. Historically, this courtyard was often defined by a colonnade or arches. Church atriums were probably derived from the open courtyards with basins to catch rainwater that formed the centre of Roman houses in antiquity. A good example is the atrium of Old St Peter's Church in Rome.

MARCHITA B. MAUCK

Aumbry

An aumbry or ambry (from the old French *almerie*, Latin *armarium*, a chest, safe) is a niche (with doors or grille) in the wall of a church or *sacristy of sufficient size to store artefacts for the liturgy (vessels, scriptures, liturgical *books), holy oils, and sometimes either reliquaries and/or the consecrated bread from the *eucharist.

From the Constantinian era the *sanctuaries of churches or their annexes, rather than as before the homes of the faithful, became the standard place for the *reservation of the consecrated bread for the *communion of the *sick between celebrations of the eucharist. The location was most often out of view of the faithful, the *altar itself remaining the focus of a church as a place of prayer outside liturgical celebrations. However, from the ninth century a preference developed to set the box (*capsa*) on, or suspended above, the altar. As the blessed sacrament thus became the object of a cult, a diversity of pedestal- or wall-mounted sacrament houses, caskets or hanging *pyxes developed with elaborate architectural or iconographic decoration. Glass- and grille-fronted containers facilitated permanent *exposition. The importance of the contents required secure storage, and an order of the Fourth Lateran Council (1215) – that the reserved sacrament be kept under lock and key – affected fixed aumbries, so-called 'propitiatory' chests, and hanging pyxes. Wall-aumbries remained most consistently used as sacrament houses in Scotland, Sweden, Germany and Italy, though in the last case, following the Council of Trent and the *Rituale Romanum* of 1614, practice changed. The fixing of a *tabernacle on the altar became standard RC practice by the mid-nineteenth century, and in the East the tabernacle, often elaborately cast in the form of a church building, stands on the altar.

From an early date the holy oils (*see* **Chrismatory**) appear consistently to be stored in wall-aumbries, which (especially following the removal of the sacrament to another receptacle) were sometimes inscribed *olea sancta* or *oleum infirmorum*.

Despite the medieval preference in England for hanging pyxes, many abandoned aumbries in medieval English churches (on which hinges and locks often remain) have been expertly refurbished during the last 150 years for reservation.

Gregory Dix, *A Detection of Aumbries*, London 1942; and its critique: S. J. P. van Dijk and J. H. Walker, *The Myth of the Aumbry*, London 1957; Archdale King and C. E. Pocknee, *Eucharistic Reservation in the Western Church*, London 1965.

JONATHAN GOODALL

Australia, Worship in the Uniting Church in

The Uniting Church was formed in 1977 by a union of *Congregationalist, *Methodist and

*Presbyterian churches. Each used the authorized liturgical and hymn book of its British counterpart or an Australian adaptation, but Sunday services, apart from the sacraments which were more formally observed, allowed for *extempore prayer and free adaptation of other sources within a basic pattern, according to Free Church custom. The ferment of the 1960s meant that there were many experiments with modern language and music, especially for youth services. The denominational services were authorized for continued use, but after union it became clear that congregations wanted liturgies which belonged to an Australian and united context.

A series of paperback booklets was published between 1980 and 1984, providing for the *eucharist, *baptism and related services, *marriage, *funeral, *ordination and a series of commissioning services for *elders and various lay office-bearers. *Uniting in Worship* (Melbourne 1988) appeared in two volumes, the *People's Book* with outlines of services and essential responses, a psalter and an anthology of prayers, and the *Leader's Book* with full services and much alternative material. The *People's Book* did not sell well, perhaps because its bound cover raised fears of imposed and formal liturgy. In fact the opposite was intended: to allow the congregation full participation in a variety of words and an understanding of the structure of each service. There is an increased preference for a weekly photocopied service sheet which allows greater flexibility of choice in words and music. An official commentary was prepared to introduce the new services (Robert Gribben, *A Guide to Uniting in Worship*, Melbourne 1990). The *Australian Hymn Book* (Sydney 1977), an ecumenical compilation, providentially offered a new hymn book in the right spirit, and was adopted almost universally by Uniting congregations.

The eucharistic rites show the results of modern ecumenical liturgical scholarship: the 'Service of the Lord's Day' provides for word and sacrament as the norm, but the structure allows for the same pattern to be followed on non-sacramental celebrations (i.e., the ministry of the word remains central, with intercessions and offering following). There is a standard Great Prayer of Thanksgiving written for this book, plus eight alternatives from a variety of sources. Some require the *institution narrative to be read as a 'warrant'; most incorporate it in the prayer itself. This reflects the two traditions

from Methodist and Calvinist forebears. One alternative prayer is shared with the Anglican Church of Australia. These provisions are regarded as models, and in practice many ministers adopt prayers from other sources which express a similar theological understanding.

There are two main baptismal services, the first for adult candidates or families, the second (largely identical) for children. The Apostles' *Creed in interrogative form follows a renunciation of evil. A more generous use of water is encouraged, including immersion. A lighted candle is given in the dismissal rite. These elaborations suggest a greater attention to the power of symbol in recent revision. There are three services of reaffirmation of baptism, the first being *confirmation, then one for congregational use and one for individuals. These are partly in response to a *charismatic and neo-evangelical critique of paedo-baptism, which the Assembly answered with a desire to give greater value to baptism whenever it occurs. There is also a form of the (Methodist) *Covenant Service.

There are signs that pastors and people favour a more informal approach to both the content and the conduct of worship on Sundays than these liturgical resources imply. Preaching has become less formal and briefer; readings and intercessions are often led by laypeople; musical preference is for songs and choruses rather than hymns. There is a concomitant loss of liturgical tradition, of a 'high' sense of worship and address to God, and of the teaching aspect of worship. Many congregations, however, resist these trends.

A new national worship resource is in preparation. It will need to allow for a wide variety of cultural and theological conviction. It is likely to appear in book form (though less likely in two volumes) and on CD-ROM and the Internet for access by congregations preparing their own service sheet. There is a challenge ahead to maintain theological standards and liturgical consistency in the Uniting Church. The distances involved in Australia make any educational process difficult and expensive, and the present mood of individualism militates against it. The church shows signs of a general move from classical Reformed and Wesleyan forms to Free Church (and neo-evangelical) liberty. With reduced numbers and income affecting all denominations, not least outside major cities, it is difficult to predict what kind of church will emerge in Australia in the next decades, or what kind of liturgy will characterize it, though the necessary ecumenical co-operation will play a role.

———

Robert W. Gribben, '*Uniting in Worship*: The Uniting Church in Australia', and H. D'Arcy Wood, 'Text and Context in a Newly United Denomination: The Liturgical Experience in Australia', *The Sunday Service of the Methodists: Twentieth-Century Worship in Worldwide Methodism*, ed. Karen B. Westerfield Tucker, Nashville 1996, 67–79, 81–93.

ROBERT W. GRIBBEN

Baldachin

A general term for a canopy or overhanging used as a mark of honour. The name is derived from Baghdad, the source of the rich cloth originally used for the purpose. Three types of canopy come under this heading. First, a *ciborium (the same word is applied to a container, like a *chalice with a lid, used to contain the consecrated bread at the *eucharist) which is a substantial structure made in stone, wood or metal, with columns, arches and a roof, covering an *altar. The papal altar in St Peter's Basilica in Rome is covered by a ciborium but it tends to be referred to as Bernini's great baldachino. English examples include those at Peterborough Cathedral (1894), Westminster Cathedral (1901) and St Paul's Cathedral (1960s). Second, a baldachin or baldachino, which is a form of tester, a simpler structure that hangs from the roof and over the altar or is attached to the wall or to two pillars at the rear of the altar like a bracket. Third, any other sort of canopy used for honour, whether it is fixed, such as that over an episcopal throne, or portable, such as the canopy of cloth supported on poles that is carried over the Blessed Sacrament in procession. Canopies of honour are not limited to ecclesiastical functions and were frequently found in royal palaces, e.g. the canopy of state over the King's throne at Hampton Court Palace. The canopy defines an area beneath which only those who are authorized, by order or office, are permitted to stand.

MARTIN DUDLEY

Baptism

From the Greek verb, *baptizein*, to dip, the water rite of initiation into Christianity practised by nearly all ecclesiastical traditions and based on NT precedent and precept. In some traditions baptism forms the complete rite of initiation, while others also include a rite of *confirmation. Most denominations administer it to both adults and children, but some restrict baptism to those able to make a personal profession of faith.

———

General bibliography: Maxwell E. Johnson, *The Rites of Christian Initiation: Their Evolution and Interpretation*, Collegeville 1999; (ed.), *Living Water, Sealing Spirit: Readings on Christian Initiation*, Collegeville 1995; Aidan Kavanagh, *The Shape of Baptism*, New York 1976; E. C. Whitaker, *Documents of the Baptismal Liturgy*, London 1970.

1. Early Christianity; 2. Eastern Churches; 3. Medieval and Roman Catholic; 4. Anglican; 5. Baptist; 6. Christian Church; 7. Congregationalist; 8. Lutheran; 9. Methodist; 10. Old Catholic; 11. Pentecostal; 12. Reformed.

1. *Early Christianity*. Based on the baptismal practice of John the Baptist, and in general continuity with the ritual washings and bathing customs in first-century Judaism, new converts to Christianity were initiated into Christ and the church by baptism, a ritual bath or washing that eventually was based in the command of the risen Jesus himself (Matt. 28.19). Unfortunately, the NT itself records little detail about baptismal rites. Rather, it provides several images and possible allusions to baptismal practice, two of which will stand out with particular emphasis in patristic theology: baptism as new birth through water and the Holy Spirit (John 3.5ff.); and baptism as being united with Christ in his death, burial and resurrection (Rom. 6.3–11). Around these, several other NT images will eventually cluster in the form of accompanying rites.

1.1. *The Second Century*. *Didache* 7 directs that, after *catechesis, and one or two days of fasting on the part of the candidates, baptizers, and community alike, baptism is to be conferred in 'living' (i.e., cold running) water or, lacking that, water is to be poured over the head of the candidate, accompanied by the trinitarian formula of Matt. 28.19. Only the baptized were admitted to the *eucharist. In mid-second-century Rome, chapters 61 and 65 of the *First Apology* of Justin Martyr corroborate this and add a few other details, e.g., pre-baptismal catechesis, baptism administered at a place where there is water, and immediate sharing in the prayers and eucharist of the community as the culmination of baptism. In addition, Justin refers to baptism as 'new birth' and 'enlightenment', and to credal language accompanying its administration.

1.2. *The Third Century.* In the Syrian *Didascalia apostolorum* and the apocryphal *Acts of the Apostles* a pattern appears wherein the baptism of Jesus is seen as the paradigm for Christian baptism and its theology flows from the new-birth theology of John 3. Although minimal stress is placed on catechesis, there is a strong emphasis on a pre-baptismal *anointing of the head (and, eventually, the whole body), interpreted as a 'royal' anointing by which the Holy Spirit assimilates the candidate to the kingship and priesthood of Christ; baptism is accompanied by the trinitarian formula, and the eucharist concludes the rite. It is also possible that baptisms took place on 6 January, the feast of the *Epiphany, as the feast of Jesus' baptism. Early Egyptian practice may have been similar, although in Egypt it appears that candidates for baptism were enrolled *on* Epiphany and then baptized forty days later, with catechesis given during a fast associated with Jesus' own fast in the wilderness.

Western sources display alternative patterns. In North Africa, Tertullian's *De baptismo* (*c.* 200) describes a ritual process which included 'frequent' *vigils and fasts, a renunciation of Satan, a threefold credal profession of faith in the context of the conferral of baptism, a post-baptismal 'christic' anointing, a hand-laying prayer associated with the gift of the Holy Spirit, and participation in the eucharist, which also included the reception of milk and honey, as symbols of entering into the 'promised land'. Tertullian is also the first author to express a preference for baptism taking place either at *Easter or during *Pentecost. Tertullian's description is corroborated generally a little later in North Africa by Cyprian of Carthage, and for perhaps Rome in the so-called *Apostolic Tradition*, attributed to Hippolytus of Rome (*c.* 215).

According to the *Apostolic Tradition*, pre-baptismal catechesis was to last for three years and included frequent prayer, fasting and *exorcism, with entrance into the *catechumenate accompanied by a detailed interrogation of the motives and lifestyles of those seeking admittance, on whose behalf 'sponsors' testified (*see* **Godparents**). For the *elecți* who passed this test, baptism took place at a vigil (we do not know if this was the *Easter vigil), and consisted of a renunciation of Satan, a full

body anointing with the 'oil of exorcism', a threefold credal interrogation accompanying the baptismal immersions, an anointing by a *presbyter with the 'oil of thanksgiving', an entrance into the assembly, where the *bishop performed a hand-laying with prayer and a second anointing, and, after a *kiss, the sharing of the eucharist, including the cup(s) of milk and honey. Given current scholarly debate on this document, the details provided by it must be received with due caution, and several of these elements may well reflect later (fourth-century) additions. Nevertheless, the bishop's hand-laying and anointing will come to be interpreted as giving the Holy Spirit, and, at least at Rome, will remain a characteristic emphasis (*see* **Confirmation**).

1.3. *Infant Baptism.* Third-century sources also show that infant baptism, including *infant communion, was being practised widely. Tertullian strongly cautions against it (*De baptismo* 18). Origen calls it an 'apostolic custom' (*In Rom. com.* 5.9). The *Apostolic Tradition* makes provision for those 'who cannot answer for themselves'. And Cyprian gives a theological defence based on the inheritance of the 'disease of death' from Adam (*Ep.* 64).

1.4. *The Fourth Century.* In the aftermath of Constantine's rise to power several changes occur in the baptismal rites. Thanks to the great 'mystagogues' (Cyril of Jerusalem, John Chrysostom and Theodore of Mopsuestia for the East, and Ambrose of Milan for the West), as well as other writings (the Letter of Innocent I to Decentius of Gubbio and the Letter of John the Deacon to Senarius) baptismal practice is easily reconstructed for this period. The following came to characterize baptism in the Christian East: (a) the adoption of Easter baptism and the now forty-day season of *Lent as the time of pre-baptismal (daily) catechesis on scripture, Christian life and the *creed for the *photizomenoi* or *illuminandi* ('those to be enlightened'); (b) the use of *scrutinies and daily exorcisms throughout the period of final catechesis; (c) the development of rites called *apotaxis* (renunciation) and *syntaxis* (adherence) as demonstrating a change of ownership for the candidates; (d) the development of ceremonies like the solemn *traditio* and *redditio symboli* (the presentation and recitation of the Nicene Creed); (e) the reinterpretation of the pre-baptismal anointing as exorcism, purification, and/or preparation for combat against Satan; (f) the rediscovery and use of

Romans 6 as the paradigm for interpreting baptism as entrance into the 'tomb' with Christ with a passive formula employed in its administration ('N. is baptized . . .'); (g) the introduction of a post-baptismal anointing associated with the gift and 'seal' of the Holy Spirit (*see* **Confirmation**); and (h) the use of Easter week for *mystagogical catechesis.

Although a similar pattern existed in the West, sources there display some significant differences. Ambrose witnesses to a post-baptismal rite of *foot-washing (*pedilavium*). John the Deacon refers to three public scrutinies on the third, fourth and fifth Sundays of Lent. And Innocent I demonstrates that at Rome itself the pattern of episcopal hand-laying with prayer and anointing, noted already in the *Apostolic Tradition*, was understood as an essential aspect of the rite and was now associated explicitly with the bishop's 'giving' of the Holy Spirit. The West did not yet employ a baptismal formula but used the three credal questions and their responses instead.

The adoption of several dramatic ceremonies in this period was, undoubtedly, the result of the church seeking to ensure that its sacramental life would continue to have some kind of integrity when, in a changed social and cultural context, authentic conversion and properly motivated desire could no longer be assumed. Hence, as the rites themselves take on numerous elements which heightened dramatically the experience of those being baptized, the intent was surely to impress upon them the seriousness of the step they were taking.

Designed for adults, the baptismal process in these several sources was to be short-lived, owing, in part, to its success. The North African controversy over Pelagianism, and Augustine's rationale for infant initiation based on 'original sin', led to the catechumenate's further decline. Augustine's lengthy battle over the Donatist practice of 'rebaptizing' Catholics and their insistence on the moral character of the baptizer led also to an 'orthodox' sacramental theology based on the use of proper elements and words, with Christ himself underscored as the true sacramental minister. Augustine's own theological emphases would set the agenda for a later Western medieval sacramental minimalism focused on 'matter' and 'form', the *quamprimum* ('as soon as possible') baptism of infants, and an objective sacramental validity ensured by an *ex opere operato* understanding.

Edward Yarnold, *The Awe-Inspiring Rites of Initiation*, 2nd edn, Edinburgh/Collegeville 1994.

MAXWELL E. JOHNSON

2. *Eastern Churches.* Eastern baptismal rites show a variety of structural outlines and theological interpretations which are already present in the NT, for example the Johannine *pneumatic* emphasis in depicting the entry into the kingdom of heaven with the imagery of being born of water and spirit (John 3.5) in contrast to the Pauline *christocentric* death-mysticism of Romans 6, by which the baptized is assimilated to the death of Christ.

2.1. *Manuscripts and Studies.* Our knowledge about the manuscripts of the various rites, including the received traditions, varies greatly. Besides O. H. E. Burmester's 1945 study we have no monographs on the *Coptic rite. The scholarly information about the *Ethiopic rite goes back to 1878. We know even less about the historical development of the Georgian baptismal rites, which originally may have been related to the early *Armenian evidence. However, by looking through the oldest extant Georgian manuscripts, for example the still unpublished *Codex Sin. georg. 12* of the tenth century, it is clear that there is no direct resemblance to the oldest Armenian manuscripts of the same period. *Cod. Sin. georg 12* (fol. 101(a)–106(a)) of the Manuscript Library at Tbilissi shows the following intriguing contents: (a) the blessing of a new *candle; (b) the consecration of the baptismal *font by the *bishop, with a reference to the river Jordan and the second birth reflecting Syrian thought-patterns, as does the Armenian baptismal rite; (c) the simple *anointing of the head with the holy oil; (d) an allusion to the *eucharist; (e) a prayer for conversion to Christianity; (f) a prayer for those to be illuminated; (g) another prayer for the *catechumens with a reference to the second birth; (h) the enrolment, accompanied by signing the boy or girl, at the eastern door of the church, with the cross and the laying-on of the hand with a prayer (which mentions the second birth at baptism), followed by another prayer for the baptismal candidate; (i) the reference to the miraculous feeding of the crowd with the twelve baskets of bread (cf. Matt 14.20; Mark 6.43; Luke 9.17; John 6.13) concluding with an *epiclesis ('send the same blessing over this bread and wine, and give [them] to us, your

servants, unto our bliss and thanks . . .') which
seems to pertain to the eucharist. None of the
prayers contains any reference to the Pauline
baptismal theology of Romans 6. In contrast to
the Georgian, Coptic and Ethiopian baptismal
rites, the Syrian, Armenian and Byzantine rites
are quite well studied on the basis of the extant
manuscripts.

2.2. *Historical Overview.* The most important structural differences lie in the positioning
of the anointing(s), either before or after
baptism proper, and the interpretation given to
these anointings and to the initiation rites as a
whole. Despite claims to the contrary in recent
publications, the early Syriac evidence (e.g.
Acts of Thomas) clearly points towards an
anointing before baptism only. The East Syrian
epiclesis is recognizable by the verb 'come', in
contrast to the verb 'send' prevalent in Greek
and later West Syrian invocations of the Spirit.
The spectre of the early Syriac baptismal
liturgy and the evidence in the *Apostolic
Tradition* and other documents of the third to
fourth centuries have to be expanded by a study
of the evolving baptismal initiation rites of the
Greek-speaking coastline of fourth-century
Syro-Palestine. By the second half of the
century we are rather well informed by these
sources, which mirror the first thorough reshaping of the rites of initiation, parallel to the
evolving christological reflections, in the light
of which also the changes in the baptismal
rites, including the eucharist, have to be seen.
The pre-baptismal anointing serves now to
strengthen the baptismal candidate for combat,
the baptismal water is no longer interpreted as
the womb which gives birth, but is seen as the
tomb into which the candidate descends in
order to be assimilated with Christ's death
and burial, following the Pauline baptismal
theology of Romans 6. Thus cleansed, the
candidate receives conferral of the Spirit at the
anointing after baptism, attested for the first
time in fourth-century Jerusalem.

The oldest Byzantine baptismal rite (*Codex
Barberini 336*, eighth century) mirrors the
earlier Greek evidence, characterized above
all by repeated *exorcisms. In contrast, the
Armenian baptismal liturgy of *Codex 320*
(ninth century), as well as in the present ritual,
shows very archaic features not only in the
absence of verbal exorcisms in the highly trans-
parent structural outline of the entire rite, but
also in its affinity to the Syriac patristic evidence to which an anointing after baptism was
later added. The old Syriac baptismal theology

based on John 3 is best preserved in the
Maronite rite. Those baptismal liturgies which
remained firmly grounded in the creation
account (in particular Gen. 1.2, with the hover-
ing of the Spirit over the primordial waters) and
in Jesus' own baptism in the river Jordan (with
its centre of gravity in the descent of the Spirit
upon Jesus), combined with the inclusion of
being born through the Spirit (John 3.5), tend
not to favour the expansion of exorcisms.

2.3. *Current Practice.* In most Eastern
churches, a newborn baby is greeted with
prayers on the fortieth day, and in some cases
on the first and eighth as well. Since infant
baptism is standard in all the churches, the
baptismal rites follow very soon after birth.
Among Eastern churches the integral unity and
the sequence of the sacraments of initiation is
preserved and considered important. Thus,
even a baby receives baptism, chrismation and
the eucharist in one liturgical celebration. The
baptismal rites of the Eastern churches may be
divided into four parts:

(a) The first part, which we might call 'the
making of the catechumen', reflects the enrolment and the pre-baptismal preparation of the
catechumens in the ancient church. When
infant baptism became the norm, all these
preparatory rites came to be placed in the
beginning of the baptismal service itself. This
part may include enrolment, imposition of
hands, exorcisms, renunciation of the devil and
acceptance of Christ, and profession of faith.
The *godparent plays an important role not
only in responding to the questions asked in
this part of the rites, but also in taking responsibility for the spiritual upbringing of the baptized child.

(b) In the second part, which we might call
the baptism proper, the procession to the font,
the blessing of the baptismal waters, the
pouring of oil or chrism in the waters, the
anointing of the body of the baptizand (in some
traditions – highly developed by the Syrians but
suppressed by the Armenians), and the triple
immersion with the baptismal formula take
place. In all traditions other than the Coptic,
Ethiopic and Maronite, the baptismal formula
is the third person singular passive ('N is
baptized . . .').

(c) The administration of chrism (chrismation) constitutes the third part of the baptismal
rite. The formula of chrismation varies among
the Eastern churches, but since its adoption by
the RC Church, the formula 'the seal of the
gift of the Holy Spirit' of the Byzantine rite is

probably the best known. Chrism is applied to various parts of the body of the baptized, not just the forehead. Among Eastern churches, chrismation is not the prerogative of the bishop. The celebrant of the baptism, whether *presbyter or bishop, chrismates. The chrism, however, is always consecrated by the bishop, patriarch or catholicos at a special service. Chrismation in the Coptic and Ethiopic rite is followed by an imposition of hands. After the child is dressed, the crowning of the newly baptized takes place in some traditions.

(d) The fourth part is the administration of communion, preceded in the Byzantine tradition by the *trisagion and the readings. Because of the demise of adult baptism, the rites originally intended for the eighth day after baptism have also been appended at the end of the baptismal rites themselves.

For the Byzantine rite: Miguel Arranz, 'Les sacrements de l'ancien eucologe constantinopolitain I–VII', *Orientalia Christiana Periodica* XLVIII, 1982, 284–335; XLIX, 1983, 42–90, 284–302; L, 1984, 43–64, 372–97; LI, 1985, 60–86; LII, 1986, 145–78.

For the Coptic and Ethiopic rites: Heinzgerd Brakmann, 'Neue Funde und Forschungen zur Liturgie der Kopten 1992–1996', *Ägypten und Nubien in spätantiker und christlicher Zeit*, ed. Stephen Emmel et al., Wiesbaden 1999, I, 451–64; O. H. E. Burmester, 'The Baptismal Rite of the Coptic Church', *Bulletin de la Société d'Archéologie Copte* XI, 1945, 27–86; Georg Kretschmar, 'Beiträge zur Geschichte der Liturgie insbes. der Tauftheologie in Ägypten', *Jahrbuch für Liturgie und Hymnologie* VIII, 1963, 1–54; E. Trump, 'Das Taufbuch der äthiopischen Kirche. Äthiopisch und Deutsch', *Abhandlungen der philosophisch-philologischen Classe d. königl. Bayerischen Akademie der Wissenschaften* XIV, 1878, 147–83.

For Syria and Armenia: Sebastian Brock, 'The Epiklesis in the Antiochene Baptismal Ordines', *Symposium Syriacum 1972*, Rome 1974, 183–215; *The Holy Spirit in the Syrian Baptismal Tradition*, Poona 1979; 'Studies in the Early History of the Syrian Orthodox Baptismal Liturgy', *Journal of Theological Studies* XXIII, 1972, 16–64; Augustin Mouhanna, *Les rites de l'initiation dans l'Église maronite*, Rome 1980; Gabriele Winkler, *Das armenische Initiationsrituale*, Rome 1982; 'The Blessing of the Water in the Oriental Liturgies', *Concilium* 21, 1985, 53–61; *Studies*

in Early Christian Liturgy and its Context, Aldershot 1997.

GABRIELE WINKLER

3.1. *Medieval*. The early medieval period was an age of great missionary expansion within Europe so that baptism was often celebrated for adults; however, once Christianity was established and most baptisms were those of babies, the rite for their baptism remained little more than a compressed version of the rite for adults. *Godparents or ministers made the responses to the baptismal questions for children who were too young to make them for themselves: 'Does he/she renounce . . . ?' 'They renounce . . .', etc. (Ambrosian); the Spanish *Liber Ordinum* and the Sarum rites gave also the alternative form, 'Do you renounce . . . ?' 'I renounce', etc. Several ceremonies, such as the handing over of the *creed and the *Lord's Prayer, and the administration of milk and honey at the baptismal *eucharist were eventually discarded; others, such as the admission to the *catechumenate, the *exorcisms, the administration of salt and the clothing with a white garment remained. Others again were given a new meaning: e.g., in the Gelasian Sacramentary, the 'Opening', once a touching of the ears and nostrils recalling the cure of the deaf mute (Mark 7.32), became a symbolic reading of the beginning of each of the four Gospels; the *scrutinies, instead of being the verification by the *bishop that candidates had been freed from the devil's power as testified by their reaction to exorcism, became a test of their acceptance and retention of the creed, and eventually little more than another name for a solemn exorcism; by the time of *Ordo Romanus* XI the number had increased from three to seven. At first, *Easter and *Pentecost remained the preferred occasions for baptism, though the high rate of infant mortality led to the administration of the sacrament within a few days of the child's birth irrespective of the season. Consequently in the popular mind baptism became a name-giving ceremony, as indicated by the continued use of the verb 'to christen' in the sense of 'to name'.

Although in the East the three sacraments of baptism, chrismation and first communion were usually administered by a *presbyter on a single occasion soon after birth, various factors led to their separation in the West. In Rome, while baptism was administered by a presbyter within a few days of birth, what came to be known as *confirmation was reserved to the bishop, and therefore postponed to a later convenient occasion, though first *communion continued to be given at the time of baptism. Consequently the traditional sequence of baptism–confirmation–first communion was changed by the inversion of the order of the last two sacraments, until in the eleventh century the developing reverence for the sacramental species led to the postponement of first communion until the age of about seven or even later. Later the widespread neglect of confirmation made it necessary for Archbishop Peckham of Canterbury to insist at the Council of Lambeth (1281) that children in England were not to be given communion until they had been confirmed. Spain and southern Gaul, on the other hand, for a while followed the Eastern practice and thus the unity of initiation was preserved. Other regional variants persisted for a time: in Spain a single instead of a triple immersion, and in Gallican, Irish and Milanese usage a rite of *foot-washing after baptism.

Thus in the West, while chrismation of the forehead and hand-laying for the imparting of the Holy Spirit by the bishop generally took place on a later occasion, the presbyter anointed the child's head with chrism immediately after baptism to symbolize a share in Christ's royal and priestly *anointing. It consequently became necessary to define what confirmation added to the effects of these earlier rites: for Innocent I it was the delivering of the Holy Spirit; in a fifth-century homily attributed to Faustus of Riez in Gaul it was the provision of arms for the struggles of life; for Rabanus Maurus, the ninth-century abbot of Fulda, the baptismal chrismation signified sanctification and a share in Christ's kingdom, while confirmation imparted the sevenfold gift of the Spirit to equip the Christian for the proclamation of the gospel.

3.2. *Roman Catholic.* While the oriental rites of the RC Church maintain broadly the same liturgical traditions as the Orthodox churches, the Latin (Western) rites in the main continued the medieval practices described above until the Second Vatican Council (1962–5). In its Decree on the Sacred Liturgy, *Sacrosanctum concilium*, the Council ordered the revision of the rite for the baptism of babies so as to remove the illogical convention of putting questions to infants which their godparents answered in their place, to express the duties of parents and godparents more clearly and to modify the rite when a large number of children were to be baptized (nn. 67–9). A mass

for the conferring of baptism was to be inserted into the Roman missal (n. 66). In addition rites for the catechumenate leading up to the baptism of adults were to be restored (n. 64) – a measure intended primarily for missionary countries which has proved to be of great pastoral value also in established churches in the West.

These directives were put into effect in a series of revised rites: for the *Baptism of Children* (1969), for *Confirmation* (1971) and for the *Christian Initiation of Adults* (1972); a *General Introduction to Christian Initiation* (1969) had already set out the principles on which these revisions were to be based. This Introduction linked baptism, confirmation and first communion as the three 'sacraments of initiation', ideally to be received in that order, though most dioceses still choose to postpone confirmation until after first communion, as for pastoral reasons they are allowed to do. When the sacraments are administered to adults, confirmation and first communion are normally to follow immediately after baptism, even when the minister is not a bishop, and the presbyteral anointing of the head with chrism is omitted – a pity, because this is the only place at which the candidate's association with Christ's messianic anointing as priest, prophet and king is expressed. According to the new rites the whole community is responsible for the formation of the catechumens, and is required to vouch for their readiness to receive the sacraments. At the baptism of babies the parents and godparents do not make the responses on behalf of the child who is unable to make them him/herself, but as a profession of their own faith; the congregation into which the child is admitted also professes its faith.

Although Aidan Kavanagh has argued that adult baptism is now regarded as the 'norm', the Congregation for the Doctrine of the Faith in its 1980 document entitled *Pastoralis actio* defended the practice of infant baptism, explaining with St Augustine that, while reception of a sacrament requires faith, it is the faith of the Church not that of the infant which fulfils this condition; moreover the inability of the child to contribute anything to the process is witness to the 'gratuitous character' of God's love.

The 1993 *Ecumenical Directory* clarified the conditions for the recognition by RCs of other churches' baptisms. If the official liturgical books of a church prescribe the use of the trinitarian formula together with either immersion or the pouring of water, the baptisms are to be presumed to be valid and conditional (re)baptism is not required, unless there are grounds for thinking that these regulations have not been observed. Insufficient faith in the minister does not of itself invalidate the sacrament, provided there is the intention of doing what the church does.

Medieval: Peter Cramer, *Baptism and Change in the Early Middle Ages, c. 200–c. 1150*, Cambridge 1993 (bib.); J. D. C. Fisher, *Christian Initiation: Baptism in the Medieval West*, London 1965.

Modern: *The Rites of the Catholic Church*, vol. 1A, *Initiation*, New York 1976, 3–334; *The Rite of Christian Initiation of Adults: A Study Book*, London 1988; 'Pastoralis actio', *Vatican II: More Postconciliar Documents*, ed. Austin Flannery, Leominster/Grand Rapids 1982, 103–11; Kenan B. Osborne, *The Christian Sacraments of Initiation*, Mahwah, NJ 1987.

EDWARD J. YARNOLD

4. *Anglican*. The Anglican reformers continued the medieval practice of infant baptism. The first Anglican baptismal rite, in the 1549 *BCP*, was a conservative revision of the Sarum rite. Like its medieval predecessor, the first part of the service took place at the church door and included signing with the cross on forehead and breast and an *exorcism. Following the entrance to the church, the rite at the *font proceeded with renunciations and a credal affirmation, administration of water, bestowal of a white garment and *anointing. The rite included several exhortations drawn chiefly from Lutheran sources, and Lutheran influence is also evident in the inclusion of Luther's 'flood prayer'.

Reformation influences were much more evident in the baptismal rite in the 1552 *BCP*. The entire rite was to be administered at the font, and the traditional ceremonies of exorcism, bestowal of the white garment and unction were eliminated. Consignation on the forehead remained but was administered immediately following the water. The inclusion of consignation became a long-standing point of disagreement with Puritans, who viewed it as unscriptural. Nonetheless, the 1552 rite was retained essentially unchanged in the 1662 English *BCP*.

As the Anabaptist movement grew, Anglicans defended the practice of infant baptism. But the existence of this movement, along with the beginnings of colonialism which brought contact with native peoples and slaves who were unbaptized, led to the inclusion in the 1662 *BCP* of a rite of baptism for those 'of riper years', an adaptation of the rite for infant baptism. The 1662 rites for infants and adults became the source of subsequent Anglican rites throughout the world until the twentieth century.

4.1. *The Relation of Baptism and Confirmation*. In the late nineteenth century, Anglicans began what became a century-long debate about the meaning of confirmation in relation to baptism. One side, championed by A. J. Mason and Gregory Dix, argued that baptism was a preliminary rite that cleansed the baptizand from sin, while the indwelling gift of the Spirit was given only in *confirmation. Others, such as Geoffrey Lampe, asserted that the seal of the Spirit was an integral part of baptism. At issue is whether baptism constitutes full Christian initiation and, if so, whether confirmation should be required for admission to *communion. All Anglican Prayer Books, beginning in 1549, had included a 'confirmation rubric' setting confirmation as a prerequisite for communion. The 1968 Lambeth Conference invited member churches to experiment with admission to communion before confirmation. A new level of agreement was achieved at an International Anglican Liturgical Consultation in 1991, when participants affirmed that 'baptism is complete sacramental initiation', including the gift of the Holy Spirit, and 'leads to participation in *eucharist'.

4.2. *Modern Rites*. The principles affirmed at the 1991 Consultation are manifest in varying degrees in the contemporary rites and practices of churches of the Anglican Communion. Many modern Anglican books provide a single baptismal rite used for both children and adults. This was pioneered in the 1928 American *BCP*, which utilized the structure and texts of earlier Anglican books. More recent revisions have diverged significantly from the inherited 1662 rites, and there are also significant differences among the rites of the different Anglican provinces. In a growing number of provinces, including the USA, Canada, Brazil and New Zealand, baptism is understood as full initiation, leading to admission to communion. Many of the rites call for baptism to be administered in the context of eucharist, but some also provide for baptism as a separate service and/or in the context of a *daily office. Most emphasize the public nature of baptism. Although the historic rites had called for public baptism on a Sunday or holy day, in practice many baptisms took place apart from principal services. Contemporary rites make various provisions for participation of the congregation, for example joining the credal affirmation and declaring support for the candidates.

While most recent rites acknowledge the bestowal of the Spirit at baptism, the relation between baptism and confirmation continues to be unclear. A number of the rites provide for confirmation to be administered as part of the baptismal rite, and some urge that adults be baptized and confirmed in the same service. The American rite specifies that adults baptized by a *bishop need not be confirmed, while the Canadian rite can be interpreted as not requiring confirmation of anyone baptized as an adult, whether or not a bishop presided. These rites are unique among Anglican rites in including in the baptismal rite the prayer for the sevenfold gift of the Spirit that traditionally has been part of Anglican confirmation rites.

In a significant departure from earlier practice, many of the rites include, in addition to the central water act, symbolic actions such as anointing, giving a lighted *candle and clothing with a white garment, although frequently these are optional ceremonies. The significance of the oil (often, but not in all rites, called 'chrism') varies. Most of the rites associate chrism with the traditional post-baptismal consignation, using a formula referring to the 'sign of Christ'. A pneumatic formula is provided in the American rite ('you are sealed by the Holy Spirit . . .'), while the English rite permits use of pure olive oil with a pre-baptismal consignation and/or a post-baptismal anointing with chrism during a prayer referring to Christ's 'anointing Spirit'.

In response to concerns about 'indiscriminate baptism', many contemporary rites require pre-baptismal instruction of candidates or their parents and *godparents. Some provinces have implemented a *catechumenate which includes a process of formation and pre-baptismal rites for adult candidates.

Many of the new rites and accompanying interpretive materials emphasize the significance of baptism for Christian life. The traditional question asking whether the candidate would 'keep God's holy will and commandments' has been restated, in some rites taking the form of a series of questions. In the American and Canadian rites, these questions are joined with an interrogatory *creed in the 'baptismal covenant', while in the English rite similar questions are part of the 'commission' which follows the interrogatory creed and water action.

Paul F. Bradshaw (ed.), *A Companion to Common Worship* I, London 2001, 148–78; Marion J. Hatchett, *Commentary on the American Prayer Book*, New York 1981, 251–88; David R. Holeton (ed.), *Growing in Newness of Life: Christian Initiation in Anglicanism Today*, Toronto 1993; Ruth A. Meyers, *Continuing the Reformation: Re-Visioning Baptism in the Episcopal Church*, New York 1997 (bib.); Daniel B. Stevick, *Baptismal Moments; Baptismal Meanings*, New York 1987 (bib.).
RUTH A. MEYERS

5. *Baptist*. With their origins in the early seventeenth century as a development out of English separatism, the Baptists' most distinctive feature is their practice of believer's baptism, which is derived from their prior understanding of the authority of Christ revealed in scripture, the necessity of personal faith and the definition of the church as the fellowship of believers. While they reject infant baptism, Baptists do not overlook their infants, but have developed a service of infant presentation/*dedication in which God is thanked for the gift of the child, and the parents and church family commit themselves to raise the child in a Christian environment.

Among Baptists there is no single theology of baptism, neither is there a single practice of baptism, though many common patterns are discernible. Few of the issues involved in baptism have escaped some form of controversy and the present survey focuses on those Baptists in membership with the Baptist Union of Great Britain.

Pre-baptismal preparation usually includes some form of interview in which the genuineness of the person's faith-commitment is discerned. The preparation itself, usually though not necessarily led by the minister, often involves working through a series of studies, of varying duration, which use either published or privately prepared materials. These often combine material on baptism, membership and discipleship. While faith and not age is determinative, the norm is to baptize youths in their early to mid-teens, though some will baptize children at whatever age they make a commitment for themselves, while Southern Baptists have been known to baptize children at a much younger age.

By the late nineteenth century baptism and the *Lord's supper had become addenda to one of the main Sunday services, but this is no longer the case. Special baptismal services within the context of the church at worship are not unknown, but baptism normally takes place at Sunday worship. The *Liturgical Movement has influenced a growing number to incorporate baptism into a service of baptism–reception into membership–*communion, a pattern which can take place in a single service, be spread over a morning and evening service or over two successive Sundays, and this reflects the recognition that baptism is a part of the process of Christian initiation and the growing acceptance of the sacramental nature of baptism.

The act of baptism usually forms the climax of congregational worship in which the sermon focuses on a special word of exhortation, an evangelistic message, an exposition of the meaning of baptism or a combination of these. The increasing number of printed orders of service and ministers' manuals and the inroads of the Liturgical Movement have led to a more standardized and structured form of service, though Baptists are free to adapt such materials or follow their own patterns of service.

The central act of the baptismal service is the candidate's profession of faith in the gracious, saving work of Christ. This takes a number of forms: a personal testimony or a reply to formal questions put by the administrant, and not infrequently both, which can take place either before or after entering the baptistery. This is then followed by a spoken 'formula' immediately prior to the act of (single) immersion which incorporates reference to the Trinity (Matt. 28.19), e.g., 'On your profession of repentance toward God and of faith in our Lord Jesus Christ, I baptize you in the name of the Father and of the Son and of the Holy Spirit.' It is also the practice of some to give a promise to each candidate, often from scripture, intended to be a word of encouragement and guidance. As the church's representative, the minister is the normal administrant, and is often assisted in the actual act of immersion by another member of the congregation. Lay administration is practised and is an expression of the priesthood of all believers. The immersion itself is usually backwards, though some will get the candidate to kneel and be immersed forwards, or sometimes the head is gently pressed under the

water. Most baptisms occur within the church building, though many occur in other places – rivers, the sea, even swimming pools. On such occasions it is usual for the whole service to be conducted in that location. Immersion is the normal mode, adopted for its symbolism (of the believer's participation by faith in the death, burial and resurrection of Christ) and its biblical precedent (as the meaning of *baptizein*, also Matt. 3.16; Rom. 6.4, 9). However, the first Baptists practised affusion, and this mode is often employed in the case of age, infirmity or sickness. The laying-on of hands has become more common in recent years, encouraged by the Liturgical and *Charismatic Movements, and can take place before or after baptism, or as part of the act of baptism itself. It symbolizes and accompanies a prayer for the reception of the Spirit. Baptism is then followed by a prayer or *hymn/song, by an appeal for those who wish to be baptized or respond to the gospel, and a benediction (e.g. 2 Cor. 13.14).

Baptists have paid little attention to post-baptismal issues, and what they do has generally focused on receiving the candidate(s) into church membership, though in open membership churches this may already have happened, or may happen later or not at all (the latter a practice for which they have been rightly criticized).

Selected texts: Alec Gilmore, Edward Smalley and Michael J. Walker, *Praise God: A Collection of Source Material for Christian Worship*, London 1980; Ernest A. Payne and Stephen F. Winward, *Orders and Prayers for Church Worship: A Manual for Ministers*, London 1960; *Patterns and Prayers for Christian Worship: A Guidebook for Worship Leaders*, Oxford 1991.

Studies: Paul Beasley-Murray, *Faith and Festivity: A Guide for Today's Worship Leaders*, Eastbourne 1991; Raymond F. G. Burnish, *The Meaning of Baptism: A Comparison of the Teaching and Practice of the Fourth Century with the Present Day*, London 1985; Anthony R. Cross, *Baptism and the Baptists: Theology and Practice in Twentieth-Century Britain*, Carlisle 2000 (bib.); Horton Davies, *WTE*, esp. vols 5–6; Christopher J. Ellis, *Baptist Worship Today*, Didcot 1999; Michael J. Walker, 'Baptist Worship in the Twentieth Century', *Baptists in the Twentieth Century*, ed. Keith W. Clements, London 1983, 21–30; W. Morris S. West, 'The Child and the Church', *Pilgrim Pathways: Essays in Baptist*

History in Honour of B. R. White, ed. William
H. Brackney, Paul S. Fiddes and John H. Y.
Briggs, Macon, GA 1999, 75–110.

ANTHONY R. CROSS

6. *Christian Church*. For the Christian Church
(Disciples of Christ) baptism is a public act of
the church in which a believer, responding
by personal profession of faith to God's saving
initiative in Jesus Christ, is immersed in water
in the name of the Father, Son and Holy Spirit
and thereby incorporated into the church and
set on a path of lifelong growth into Christ.
Baptism is a *sacrament, an expression of
God's grace in the visible sign of water. It has
immediate social consequences, for the life
entered into is one of love of neighbour and
sacrificial service in the world.

Disciples' founders developed a coherent
understanding and practice of baptism from
their reading of the NT: the 'design' or purpose
of baptism is to give evidence of justification
by grace alone (thus Alexander Campbell's
comment that 'in baptism we are passive in
everything but in giving our consent'); it is to
be performed upon penitent adult believers;
and its 'mode' is immersion (Campbell in his
translation of the NT famously translated
baptizein as 'immerse'). In excluding infant
and other 'indiscriminate' baptism Disciples
sought to distinguish the church from the
surrounding culture and from the state. Barton
W. Stone did not insist upon immersion as the
only possible form of baptism but Campbell's
stricter position prevailed, and until at least
1900 Disciples' congregations were accustomed to 'complete one's obedience to Christ'
by immersing persons already baptized but in
other ways. (Strikingly, the logic of Disciples'
*eucharistic theology led to open admission to
the table – including for persons not baptized
by immersion.)

Baptism comes in response to a personal
profession of faith, usually made after a 'hymn
of invitation' sung at the conclusion of Sunday
worship. The candidate affirms Jesus as the
Christ, the Son of the Living God, and personal
Lord and Saviour. The rite of baptism is performed after instruction, normally during
Sunday worship and in a *baptistery in the
church building (often located directly behind
the *altar, and in any case visible to the congregation). The candidate is submerged once 'in
the name of the Father, and of the Son, and of
the Holy Spirit', and is then greeted by the
congregation on behalf of the wider church. For

children the typical age for baptism has been
about thirteen, though there are tendencies
towards an earlier age. Many congregations
celebrate a *blessing or *dedication of very
young children, anticipating their later personal
profession of faith and baptism, and committing their parents to raising them within the
community of faith.

Increasingly Disciples agree that the baptismal service should include the following elements: proclamation of scripture(s); repentance
and renunciation of evil; profession of faith in
Jesus Christ; invocation of the Holy Spirit; use
of water (normally full immersion); a declaration, following Matt. 28.19, that the baptism is
administered 'in the name of the Trinity'; welcome into the life of the church. Disciples'
understanding of baptism has been enriched by
the *Liturgical and Ecumenical Movements,
including the church's involvement in the
Consultation on Church Union. The World
Council of Churches' *Baptism, Eucharist and
Ministry* has been influential, especially in its
insistence that baptism has strong social as
well as personal dimensions, and that as a
sacrament of unity baptism is unrepeatable.
Since about 1900, congregations have increasingly accepted the baptism of persons transferring membership from 'non-immersion'
churches, and the Disciples' official response
to *Baptism, Eucharist and Ministry* may be
regarded as consolidating its rejection of 're'-
baptism.

Other developments include concern for a
more careful preparation for baptism, a new
awareness of the role of the Holy Spirit in
baptism, moves toward liturgical enrichment of
the service (for example by a blessing of the
water to emphasize God's initiative in the
event), and a new stress on the renewal of
*baptismal vows during various worship
events. The church's Commission on Theology
has proposed a new form of the profession of
faith indicating the ecclesial and social, as well
as personal, dimensions of baptism: 'Do you,
with Christians of every time and place, believe
that "Jesus is the Christ, the Son of the Living
God" (Matt. 16.16)?' Some interest has been
shown in developing the role of baptismal
sponsors. Questions persist about the proper
age for baptism and the relation of baptism to
church membership. As in many churches there
is discussion of the traditional trinitarian
baptismal formula, with parts of the church
raising thoughtful concerns about its masculine
imagery. However the traditional formula

remains normative for baptism, not least in view of the church's extensive ecumenical commitments.

'A Word to the Church on Baptism (1987), A Report of the Committee on Theology', *The Church for Disciples of Christ: Seeking to be Truly Church Today*, ed. Paul A. Crow, Jr and James O. Duke, St Louis 1998, 121–37; Colbert S. Cartwright and O. I. Cricket Harrison (eds), *Chalice Worship*, St Louis 1997; Keith Watkins (ed.), *Baptism and Belonging: A Resource for Christian Worship*, St Louis 1991 (bib.); Clark M. Williamson, *Baptism, Embodiment of the Gospel: Disciples Baptismal Theology*, St Louis 1987 (bib.).

THOMAS F. BEST

7. *Congregationalist*. With their emphasis on the gathered church meeting together in the presence of Christ often in the face of persecution, the first Congregational churches regarded baptism as a sign of belonging to the covenanted fellowship of the church. Following the teaching of John Calvin, it was for them a sign of the free gift of God's grace. It was a *sacrament of the church instituted by Christ to be conducted not in the home but in the meeting house or usual place of worship as part of the worship of the church. It was appropriate to share both with adult converts to the Christian faith and with the children of believing parents who were part of the covenant fellowship. Simplicity marked their services: at the baptism of seven children in 1592 the congregation 'had neither godfathers nor godmothers' – the fellowship of the church was all important. The minister 'took water and washed the faces of them that were baptised, . . . saying only in the administration of this sacrament, "I do baptise thee in the name of the Father of the Son and of the Holy Ghost" without using any other ceremony . . .' (Horton Davies, *WTE* I, 331).

Baptism continued to be seen as the sacrament of the Covenant of Grace through the eighteenth century. From two contemporary sources Horton Davies reconstructs the essential elements of a baptism service: 'an explanation of the meaning of the rite and its Biblical basis; the explicit or implicit requirement from the parents of assurances that they will instruct their child in the meaning of the covenant of grace and in the rudiments of Christian belief, behaviour, and worship; a prayer for the child that it may receive the blessings of the covenant and be empowered by the Holy Spirit; the

Baptism in the Triune Name and the declaration that the child is now received into Christ's Church; and a final exhortation to the parents to remember their duties and to the church members to be faithful to their Baptismal covenant' (*WTE* III, 104).

At the beginning of the nineteenth century Robert Halley argued from Matt. 28 that baptism should not be restricted to the children of believers who belonged to the church, but shared with any who were serious in their request to baptize their children. His views were adopted by many Congregationalists, most influentially by R. W. Dale in his *Manual of Congregational Principles*, 126ff. (He quotes Robert Halley extensively, 134f.)

By the beginning of the twentieth century baptism in Congregational churches had lost much of its significance. The link with the gift of God's grace had often been broken and the service itself had shifted its focus from the grace of God to the commitment of the parents. It had become little more than a *dedication of a child to God. In *The Church and the Sacraments*, P. T. Forsyth spoke of the debased treatment of baptism in many Congregational churches. He urged the rediscovery of baptism as a sacrament of the whole church, in which even when administered to infants, it was an opportunity for everyone present to relive their own baptism. The focus in baptism should not be on the individual, but on the grace of Christ and on the act of the church. 'It is the Church that does the sacramental act. Nay, more, they are the acts of Christ really present by His Holy Spirit in the Church' (177). Such a rediscovery of baptism as a sacrament of grace led to an attempt to breathe fresh life into the sacrament of baptism in subsequent orders of service books published by Congregationalists.

Bringing together the various strands of Congregational thinking on baptism, there are five main elements in the sacrament:

(a) baptism is first a celebration of the gift of God's grace: the drama of the baptism of an infant expresses to everyone sharing at that moment in the sacrament the truth that God takes the initiative to pour out his love before anyone has done anything to deserve it;

(b) it is accompanied by the prayer that the individual who is being baptized should make this gift of God's grace their own by responding in faith, in the case of an adult at that moment and on into the future, in the case of a child in a way that is appropriate at each stage of their development until in the fullness of time they make a personal commitment of faith for themselves;

(c) promises are made by the parents of the child being baptized to bring their child up in the security of a loving home, where the love of God can be experienced as a reality, and in the covenanted fellowship of the church, where the love of God can be shared with all God's people, in the teachings of the Christian faith and in the presence of Jesus Christ;

(d) baptism is a sign of belonging to the body of Christ, the church – and so the church too makes its promises to care for those who belong through childhood into adulthood;

(e) baptism is a challenge to all who participate in the sacrament: all are challenged to ask themselves whether they have responded to the gift of God's love celebrated in baptism by turning to God and believing in Jesus Christ as Lord and Saviour.

R. W. Dale, *Manual of Congregational Principles*, London 1884; P. T. Forsyth, *The Church and the Sacraments*, London 1917; Horton Davies, *WTE*; R. Tudur Jones, *Congregationalism in England 1662–1962*, London 1962.

RICHARD CLEAVES

8. *Lutheran*. Among his liturgical reforms, Martin Luther offered two revisions of the late-medieval baptismal rite. His *Taufbüchlein* ('little baptism book') of 1523, prepared for use in the church at Wittenberg, was based on the Latin Magdeburg rite of 1497. In order 'not to offend weak consciences', Luther retained the customary pre-baptismal ceremonies of *insufflation, the giving of salt, *exorcisms with signings of the cross (though reduced in number), a recitation of the *Lord's Prayer, the *effeta* (opening of the ears) with the use of spittle, the threefold renunciation of Satan and profession of faith, and an *anointing. Following the water rite using the customary trinitarian formula, Luther's rite included the traditional post-baptismal anointing and conferrals of the baptismal garment and lighted *candle. Unlike other Reformation era rites, Luther had no admonition to the *godparents concerning their responsibilities for the Christian formation of the child. Because he viewed the exorcisms, anointings, and the conferrals of garment and candle as embellishments that tended to obscure the importance and centrality of the washing rite, in his 1526 revision he further reduced the number of these accompanying ceremonies. Additionally, in the

1526 rite Luther used a form of the traditional post-baptismal anointing formula to accompany the conferral of the baptismal garment.

For Luther baptism was a significant event in which God saved a person from sin, death and the devil. In his *Small Catechism*, Luther stated that the saving effects derived not from the water itself, but from the connection of water with a divine word of promise. Although baptism was a decisive event in a person's life, it nevertheless had ongoing significance for the Christian life. According to the *Small Catechism* baptism signifies that 'the old Adam in us, together with all sins and evil lusts, should be drowned by daily sorrow and repentance and be put to death, and the righteous man should come forth daily and rise up, cleansed and righteous, to live forever in God's presence'. Because baptism constituted full and complete Christian initiation, Luther denied the sacramental legitimacy of *confirmation.

The Lutheran confessions of the sixteenth century insisted on the necessity of baptism for salvation. The *Augsburg Confession* (1530) stressed the importance of baptism for saving children from the damnatory effects of original sin (Art. II) and condemned the Anabaptists for their rejection of infant baptism (Art. IX). Among Lutherans the 'emergency' baptism of children near death arose out of these doctrinal concerns and became a sign of orthodoxy. Rites for 'emergency' baptism appeared in Lutheran worship books into the twentieth century.

8.1. *The Sixteenth-Century Church Orders*. The German church orders – documents that regulated the ecclesiastical and liturgical life of Lutheran churches in German provinces and towns – tended to incorporate baptismal rites based on Luther's 1526 *Taufbüchlein*, rather than the 1523 rite. Yet, these rites did not simply copy the 1526 *Taufbüchlein*, but reduced the number of accompanying ceremonies. The traditional Western post-baptismal anointing prayer, for example, separated from the anointing but connected to the bestowal of the garment in the 1526 rite, remained in subsequent Lutheran rites as a blessing or handlaying prayer with neither anointing nor garment attached. Some of the church orders also omitted certain pre-baptismal rites (e.g. the exorcisms and marking with the sign of the cross).

8.2. *Modern Rites*. The twentieth-century *Liturgical Movement and scholarly interest in ancient rites have had some influence on the shape of contemporary Lutheran baptismal rites. Notable is the baptismal rite in the American *Lutheran Book of Worship* (1978), which is intended for candidates of all ages. It views baptism as a complex of acts that together constitute the 'fullness' of baptism: presentation of the candidates, thanksgiving prayer over the baptismal water, baptism with water, the laying-on of hands, and signation (chrismation). Thus the rite is based on the early unitive pattern of baptism that knew of no separate confirmation rite. It is clearly a liturgical act, as evidenced by the suggestion for celebrating it within the Sunday (eucharistic) service, particularly on feasts with baptismal overtones (e.g. on the Baptism of Our Lord, at the *Easter vigil and at *Pentecost). It also gives a greater role to the liturgical assembly by including the intercessory prayers within the rite and by having the assembly welcome the neophyte(s) into the priesthood of all believers. The assembly also provides a baptismal garment and candle that are presented to the neophyte in the post-baptismal section. Ultimately, it envisions each celebration of baptism as an occasion for all members of the liturgical assembly to be renewed in their own baptisms.

Other Lutheran rites have taken a more conservative approach. *Lutheran Worship*, produced by the Lutheran Church–Missouri Synod (USA) in 1982, along with Danish, German and Australian rites, like Luther's 1526 rite, use the traditional post-baptismal prayer to accompany a hand-laying immediately following the washing, rather than placing confirmation elements (i.e., prayer for the sevenfold gifts and chrismation) after the washing, as in the *Lutheran Book of Worship*. Finnish, Swedish and Norwegian rites that contain post-baptismal hand-layings accompanied by other formulae are also somewhat more restrained. Yet like the *Lutheran Book of Worship*, *Lutheran Worship*, which is also a rite for candidates of all ages, does have optional conferrals of the baptismal garment and candle, as well as a congregational welcome to the neophyte.

Recently, Lutherans have begun to take an interest in the Christian initiation of adults. The Evangelical Lutheran Church in Canada and the Evangelical Lutheran Church in America have recovered the ancient baptismal *catechumenate by providing rites for important stages in the catechumen's Christian formation. This recovery is not based on a fascination with ancient rites but rather on a desire to focus the life and mission of the church on the gospel command to 'go and make disciples of all nations'. In the area of Christian initiation, the evangelization of unchurched adults and questions over the proper age for the *communion of children pose the greatest challenges for Lutheran churches in the years ahead.

Selected texts: Evangelical Lutheran Church in America, *Use of the Means of Grace: A Statement on the Practice of Word and Sacrament*, Minneapolis 1997; *Welcome to Christ: Lutheran Rites for the Catechumenate*, Minneapolis 1997; Evangelical Lutheran Church in Canada, *Living Witness: The Adult Catechumenate*, Winnipeg 1992.

Studies: Hans C. Boehringer, 'Baptism, Confirmation, and First Communion: Christian Initiation in the Contemporary Church', *Christian Initiation: Reborn of Water and the Spirit*, ed. Daniel C. Brockopp et al., Valparaiso, IN 1981, 73–98; Eugene L. Brand, *Baptism: A Pastoral Perspective*, Minneapolis 1975; Maxwell E. Johnson, 'The Shape of Christian Initiation in the Lutheran Churches: Liturgical Texts and Future Directions', *Studia Liturgica* XXVII, 1997, 33–60; Hughes Oliphant Old, *The Shaping of the Reformed Baptismal Rites in the Sixteenth Century*, Grand Rapids 1992; Edmund Schlink, *The Doctrine of Baptism*, St Louis 1972; Frank C. Senn, 'A New Baptismal Rite: Toward Revitalizing the Whole Community', *Currents in Theology and Mission* II, 1975, 206–14; 'The Shape and Content of Christian Initiation: An Exposition of the New Lutheran Liturgy of Holy Baptism', *Dialog* XIV, 1975, 97–107; Bryan D. Spinks, 'Luther's Timely Theology of Unilateral Baptism', *Lutheran Quarterly* IX, 1995, 23–45.

JEFFREY A. TRUSCOTT

9. *Methodist.* The first Methodist baptismal liturgies came from John Wesley's editing and shortening of the Church of England's 1662 *BCP* rites for infants and for those of 'riper years'. Wesley's *Sunday Service of the Methodists in North America* (1784) includes infant and adult offices, but omits rites for private baptism of infants and for *confirmation; the ecclesial aspect of baptism was thereby affirmed, as was the sufficiency of the sacrament of baptism alone for church membership.

Overall in the infant rite, rubrics are modified and exhortations expunged. In accordance with his long-standing objection to vows made on behalf of the child, Wesley eliminated all references and actions regarding *godparents, though unspecified 'Friends' still give the child's name. Consequently, no vows of renunciation and profession appear. Sprinkling joins dipping as a legitimate mode, and after Wesley's death a rubric for pouring was added. Some versions of the 1784 text allow for signing with the cross at the reception of the newly baptized, but not so the 1786 and subsequent editions. Wesley's abridgement in 1784 of the Anglican Articles of Religion called baptism 'a sign of regeneration or the new birth', yet references to baptismal regeneration are found only in prayers prior to the imposition of water, not afterward. In 1786, two prayers with allusions to regeneration were dropped and the phrase 'mystical washing away of sin' was altered in one prayer and struck from another; the paraphrase of John 3.5 in the opening address was retained.

Alterations to the 'riper years' service parallel many made to the infant rite. Godparents are absent, but here the renunciation and profession of faith remain, with Christ's 'descent into hell' deleted from the *creed in 1786. Dipping and pouring are specified modes, later supplemented with sprinkling; signation and reception never appear. Adjustments were made to the language of baptismal regeneration in 1784 and again in 1786; regeneration references survive in Wesley's editions of the adult rite, though eventually even they were modified.

Controversies over the regenerative nature of baptism continued in American and British Methodism, and in their offshoots abroad, with the revision or construction of baptismal texts shaped by current debates. Methodists have always tried to hold in tandem an objective baptismal grace with a subjective human response and experience of the Holy Spirit, which as a result yields a wide range of perspectives on the sacramentality of baptism. Holiness Methodists, in particular, emphasized the personal profession of faith, and kept a rite of infant baptism that essentially functioned as a type of dedication. Sprinkling generally has been the preferred mode for all candidates, though in the late twentieth century interest in immersion increased on account of a recovered emphasis on baptism providing remission of sins.

Wesley's texts as revised in America in 1792 were largely kept throughout the nineteenth century in all American Methodist branches despite some editing, the dropping of certain prayers, and the provision for substitute lessons. In keeping with a growing emphasis on the 'Christian nurture' of children, addresses to parents and their responses were introduced in some denominational rites from the 1860s. The Methodist Episcopal Church, South in 1866 allowed for the optional laying-on of hands in both services. Separate 'membership' rites with a personal profession of faith appeared from the 1860s, though none would be explicitly called 'confirmation' until 1964. During the twentieth century, revisions generally departed from the 1792 texts; the rites of the African Methodist Episcopal Church stayed closest to them. Alternative orders emerged, among them an office for children and youth who could speak for themselves and 'brief versions' of the infant rite. Allowances were made for sponsors. The services of the 'Baptismal Covenant' used by the United Methodist Church (1992) attempt to recover the early church's unified initiation process and use the same ritual sequence for infants and adults, but retain an order for confirmation.

In Great Britain during the nineteenth century, infant and adult baptism services in the various Methodist branches could come from the *BCP*, the 1792 British edition of *Sunday Service* or subsequent revisions of it, or (especially in the smaller denominations) newly created orders. 'Membership' rites appeared in the late nineteenth century. Shortly after union, the Methodist Church in 1936 produced infant and adults rites with strong affinities to the Wesley texts, along with a new form for the 'Public Recognition of New Members'. Rites for 'Entry into the Church' authorized in 1975 departed from Wesley and instead were indebted to emphases of the Ecumenical and *Liturgical Movements, even though the 'membership' rite was labelled 'confirmation': sponsors, thanksgiving at the font and signation are included. The 1999 *Worship Book* expands the 'entry' rites that now exhibit a more strongly paschal character.

Gayle Carlton Felton, *This Gift of Water*, Nashville 1992 (bib.); Bernard G. Holland, *Baptism in Early Methodism*, London 1970; Wesley F. Swift, ' "The Sunday Service of the Methodists": A Study of Nineteenth-Century Liturgy', *Proceedings of the Wesley Historical Society* XXXI, 1957–1958, 112–18,133–43; Karen B. Westerfield Tucker, *American Methodist Worship*, New York 2000, 82–117.

KAREN B. WESTERFIELD TUCKER

10. *Old Catholic*. All the Old Catholic churches of the Union of Utrecht administer baptism
with water in the name of the Father, the Son
and the Holy Spirit. The theology and practice
of this sacrament closely followed that of the
RC Church, and the liturgical rites today are
increasingly being renewed, partly in light of
the World Council of Churches' *Baptism,
Eucharist and Ministry*, which has been
accepted by all the churches. The baptism of
adults is taken as the theological norm and is
increasingly common at least in former
Communist areas, but the baptism of infants is
(still) the regular practice in most parishes.

The Old Catholic Church of the Netherlands
knows a *catechumenate for adults, normally
during the course of *Lent. In the Swiss Old
Catholic Church, a short catechumenate rite
for infants may take place sometime before
baptism, at home and in the presence of the
sponsors, presided at by the minister who has
prepared for the baptism with the family. Other
churches are in the process of developing a
catechumenate for adults, but over a shorter
period of time than in some other churches
where classical models of the catechumenate
have been restored.

10.1. *The Rite*. The setting of baptism is
either the parish Sunday *eucharist (either at
the beginning or after the homily) or a service
of the *word. A prayer for preservation from
the evil or some words of renunciation have
been included in all baptismal rites, either prior
to, or after, the blessing of baptismal water if
applicable. During Eastertide, the water used
for baptism is that blessed in the *Easter vigil.
Outside that period, water is blessed if fresh
water is used. This blessing always precedes
the confession of faith so as not to favour the
idea that baptism basically means simply the
application of holy water.

By way of example, the order of baptism of
infants as used in the Old Catholic Church in
Germany is described here. The setting is that
of the parish Sunday eucharist. Either the
Sunday readings or special lections are used. In
conjunction with the opening of the eucharist,
the parents, candidate(s) and family members
are welcomed. The parents or mother give the
name of the candidate. The candidate is signed
with the cross by the priest/*deacon and by the
parents, sponsors and representatives of the
parish. Two questions to the parents and sponsors about their responsibility are asked. A
prayer for protection follows, concluded with
the *anointing with the oil of catechumens, if

so desired. The *effeta* rite of opening the ears
and mouth of the candidate may be included
here. After the homily of the eucharist, baptismal water is blessed, if necessary, by a
berakah-style prayer with acclamations by the
congregation. The entire congregation professes its faith, and the candidate is then
baptized, either by affusion or infusion. The
Western formula, 'N., I baptize you in the
name . . .', has lost its exclusiveness. In the Old
Catholic Church of the Netherlands, the Eastern formula may also be used: 'N. is baptized in
the name . . .'; in the Old Catholic Church of
Switzerland, the priest or deacon says, 'N., you
are baptized in the name . . .' The newly baptized is then anointed with chrism (the accompanying prayer alluding to 1 Peter 2.9–10), the
white baptismal garment is presented and the
baptismal *candle handed over. The eucharist
continues with the *intercessions. Those baptized in this celebration as adults or older
children will receive *communion: communion of baptized infants is not practised in any
Old Catholic church. If the baptism has been
performed outside the eucharist, intercessions
and the *Lord's Prayer follow. A special blessing at the end concludes the celebration.

10.2. *Confirmation*. All Old Catholic
churches know a second rite with chrismation
sometime after baptism; the interpretation of
that rite and its relationship to baptism has
come under scrutiny. *Confirmation, as it is
normally called, is administered in most Old
Catholic churches by the *bishop to a candidate
who is at least fourteen years of age; adults and
older children receive the confirmation anointing immediately after the water rite. If separated from the water rite, the link to baptism
is created by the renewal of the *baptismal
promises preceding the actual laying-on of
hands and chrismation. In the Swiss Old
Catholic Church, this laying-on of hands and
chrismation as a sign of the gift of the Spirit is
done immediately after the water rite, even in
the case of infants. The latter are considered
fully initiated, except that they will not receive
communion immediately and they will receive
a laying-on of hands by the bishop as adolescents to strengthen them in their situation of
transition to mature Christian life and witness.

In some Old Catholic churches the bishop
can delegate the laying-on of hands and chrismation to a priest who is baptizing older children and adults. The theological thinking of the
Old Catholic churches on 'confirmation' is thus
somewhat inconsistent and allows for three

separate interpretations: (a) those baptized as adults or older children and anointed with the 'confirmation' anointing immediately after the water rite are 'fully initiated'; (b) those who as infants have undergone the water rite and the chrismation following are 'baptized' and – at least in practice – able to receive communion; (c) those who in the Swiss rite receive a laying-on of hands by the bishop as adolescents receive a rite which basically would be repeatable and has more in common with confirmation as a mature commitment.

THADDEUS A. SCHNITKER

11. *Pentecostal.* Water baptism is understood among the vast majority of Pentecostals as the first major act of faith and obedience in which one testifies of one's identification with Christ. Though there are Pentecostal churches in Chile and elsewhere that practise infant baptism and sprinkling, the vast majority of Pentecostal churches worldwide practise believer's baptism through submersion in water in order to stress the symbolism of dying to sin and rising with Christ to newness of life (Rom. 6.1–11). The baptismal candidate is questioned during the rite so that his or her commitment to following Christ is clearly stated. Typical are the following questions posed by a Swiss Pentecostal pastor in a baptismal service that occurred one Sunday morning in Lake Zurich, Switzerland: 'Do you believe in the Lord Jesus Christ as the Son of the living God? Have you broken every ungodly link with the world, and with every known sin . . . ? Will you also give yourself through baptism to be crucified to the world in the death of Jesus, and to die to sin? Will you place the interests of the Kingdom of God in all circumstances and in every place above your own interests?' (Walter Hollenweger, *The Pentecostals*, reprint, Peabody, MA 1988, 390–1).

The Pentecostal emphasis on baptism as a witness of one's obedience and lifelong commitment to Christ is commonly joined with the conviction that God has transformed the believer's life through the power of the gospel and the Spirit of God. Baptism is thus fundamentally a witness to the life-transforming power of God in the life of the baptismal candidate. In fact, many Pentecostal baptismal candidates have testified that God has blessed them, for example, with a revelation of truth or an experience of healing, at the moment of their baptism. Furthermore, baptism itself is understood as ideally a charismatic event that may

include congregational participation through speaking in tongues, prophesying, or the healing of someone's body from illness. Pentecostals are also convinced that God is present during the baptismal service to call sinners to repentance. The baptismal service is often cherished for its evangelistic appeal, since God may convict sinners during the rite, save them and bring them to the baptismal waters.

11.1. *The Baptismal Formula.* A major controversy broke out among Pentecostals in the early years of the US-based *Assemblies of God denomination (c. 1914) over whether or not baptism should be practised in Jesus' name only. Pentecostals from early on held to a Christocentric gospel that tended to be coupled with a devotion to prayer in Jesus' name as the means by which God's salvific and healing power could be invoked. A minority wing of the Assemblies of God decided in 1914 that baptism must be in Jesus' name only in order to be valid and effectual. Those of this conviction separated from the Assemblies of God and came to be known as Oneness or Apostolic Pentecostals. The trinitarian formula for baptism was rejected by this faction along with the doctrine of the Trinity itself. The devotion to Jesus' name in baptism soon evolved into a Christocentric modalism, whereby Jesus, as God's Son in his human nature only, was viewed as the incarnation of the one God who functions as 'Father' and 'Spirit' and who is now present and active, especially through the name of Jesus. Though Trinitarian Pentecostals generally held that prayer in Jesus' name is effectual and many would use Jesus' name in baptism, the devotion to the power of Jesus' name in baptism was developed and preserved in the Oneness (or Apostolic) Pentecostal churches, which represent a substantial minority movement within Pentecostalism.

In the early years of the Oneness controversy, the Oneness Pentecostals would appeal to the use of Jesus' name in baptism in the Acts of the Apostles, while the Trinitarian Pentecostals referred to Matthew 28.19 and the witness of the early church fathers and creeds. A Pentecostal movement committed originally to replace 'dead forms and creeds' with a 'living, practical Christianity' was soon caught up in a quarrel over whether or not the witness of the church fathers and Nicaea may be termed 'apostolic'. Pentecostals sought to do theology in part from the implications in their liturgical practice (i.e., the baptismal rite) with regard to the understanding of the nature of baptism and even of the very nature of God as 'Father, Son and Spirit'. At stake was whether or not a movement of Christian affirmation may be termed 'apostolic' if its worship is implicitly trinitarian but anti-trinitarian in its credal statements and doctrinal beliefs.

11.2. *Baptism in the Spirit.* The Oneness Pentecostal controversy also related to the relationship of baptism to conversion and to the baptism in the Holy Spirit. The vast majority of Pentecostals distinguish water baptism from the baptism in the Holy Spirit, the latter of which they understand as the free act of God that cannot be formalized by a church rite. Spirit baptism, especially as evidenced by speaking in tongues (Acts 2.4), is understood by most Pentecostals as the empowerment of Christians for witness in the world (Acts 1.8). Most of the Oneness Pentecostal churches, however, formed an integral relation between one's initial conversion to Christ, water baptism in Jesus' name, and Spirit baptism, all three steps being viewed as part of a complex event of initiation to Christ and the life of the Spirit. Trinitarian Pentecostals have tended to separate these steps from each other, though some are currently considering a more integral relation between them as well. Regardless of the diversity of viewpoints among Pentecostals on baptism, the mystery and power of the event and its significance for one's identification with Christ by the Spirit will occupy the Pentecostal theological imagination for years to come.

Gordon Anderson, 'Baptism in the Holy Spirit, Initial Evidence, and a New Model', *Paraclete*, Fall 1993, 1–10; E. N. Bell, 'Sad New Issue', *Weekly Evangel*, 5 June, 1915; D. K. Bernard, *The Oneness of God*, Hazelwood, MO 1983; H. D. Hunter, 'Ordinances, Pentecostal', *Dictionary of Pentecostal and Charismatic Movements*, ed. Stanley M. Burgess and Gary B. McGee, Grand Rapids 1988, 653–4; David Reed, 'Oneness Pentecostalism: Problems and Possibilities for Pentecostal Theology', *Journal of Pentecostal Theology* XI, 1997, 73–93; John Christopher Thomas, 'Ministering the Sacraments', *Ministry and Theology*, Cleveland, TN 1993, 161–79.

FRANK D. MACCHIA

12. *Reformed.* Baptism in the Reformed tradition is a 'sign and seal' of the covenant of grace in Jesus Christ. The water *signifies* cleansing in Christ's blood and Holy Spirit, and the sacrament *seals* the extension, application and confirmation of the covenantal promises which are announced in the gospel. The *font stands near the *pulpit and *communion table before the congregation. Baptism is therefore not primarily initiation nor participation in the paschal mystery, but these themes are subsumed under a more comprehensive trinitarian doctrine of the sacrament. Most Reformed churches maintain their confidence in the normativity of infant baptism.

12.1. *The Historic Pattern.* The liturgical values of the Reformed tradition are simplicity and clarity, biblical fidelity, apostolic integrity and congregational ownership. The various national churches freely developed their own rites, but there is a characteristic pattern: exposition, prayer, Apostles' *Creed, exhortation, baptism and prayer. The sacrament is normally celebrated by the pastor before the congregation on the Lord's Day, after the sermon and a hymn. The exposition in Calvin's French liturgy uses the theme of regeneration, while the German and Dutch liturgies explain baptism in terms of the persons of the Trinity. The exposition typically includes the institution from Matt. 28.19f., and ends with a defence of infant baptism. The prayer usually asks God, by the Spirit, to apply to the candidate the covenant promises in Christ. A widespread baptismal prayer is the Zurich version of the 'flood prayer'. This includes an *anamnesis of the OT covenants and an *epiclesis upon the action – not upon the water. The creed is followed by an exhortation to the parents (or adult candidate), which includes questions concerning intent, understanding and commitment. The minister baptizes with a trinitarian formula. The mode of application, whether single or triple sprinkling or pouring, is up to local custom (immersion is accepted in principle but rarely practised). The final prayer is a thanksgiving for the sacrament and an intercession for those involved. This pattern was adapted by the Dutch in 1603 for adult baptisms as well.

Admission to baptism is governed by the local consistory ('session') of pastors and *elders. Some measure of commitment is expected from the parents, though less so within 'established' Reformed churches. The role of the parents is to represent the congregation to the child. The tradition's regard for discipline is expressed through the catechetical training of baptized children, culminating in 'profession of faith' (*confirmation in some churches) and admission to *communion. The conviction is growing that baptism itself is admission to the table.

12.2. *Current Issues.* Under the influence of rationalism and pietism, the tradition's values have tended toward the devolution of the sacrament into a mere pastoral ordinance. Some churches do little more than the required minimum of the water act and the trinitarian formula. The last decades have seen attempts to revitalize the ritual with new forms. The baptismal prayer is being recast in a eucharistic pattern. While the practices of renunciation, *exorcism, signation and chrismation were regarded as distractions from the divinely instituted covenantal sign, some of these are being introduced. How far the Reformed churches will go with these remains to be seen. At issue are the form and content of the baptismal prayer, the meaning of the covenant, the significance of the water, and whether ceremonial elaboration serves the sacrament better than doctrinal exposition. The Reformers would not have thought to give thanks for the water, quite apart from lacking any scriptural warrant, since they saw the water as the sign of judgement and purification. The questions asked of the candidates have often been reformulated as vows, but this risks Pelagianism and alters their original purpose, which was simply disciplinary and catechetical. Some American churches have borrowed the Episcopalian 'baptismal covenant,' but this is a different use of the word 'covenant' than the historic Reformed one.

12.3. *Modern Rites.* The modern Hungarian rite maintains the emphasis on simplicity and clarity. After a baptismal hymn, the pastor recites the biblical institution and briefly addresses the parties and the congregation, after which the creed is recited. The pastor asks promises of the parents, godparents and congregation, administers the baptism, and gives a blessing, followed by another hymn (*Magyar Református Énekeskönyv,* Budapest 1996). At the other end of the spectrum are the relatively elaborate American Presbyterian rites for 'Baptism and Reaffirmation of the Baptismal Covenant'. They use such third-century models as the so-called *Apostolic Tradition* and Tertullian, and consider adult baptism as the norm from which infant baptism is derived. The first section of the rites, the presentation, opens with the institution plus other scriptures. The candidates are brought forward by sponsors, all of whom are asked questions. The

profession of faith includes a renunciation, the creed (optionally as three questions), and a further question. The prayer is a thanksgiving over the water, modelled on the *eucharistic prayer. There is a double *epiclesis upon the participants and the water, which the minister is invited to touch. The baptism is followed by the laying-on of hands, with optional signation and chrismation. The congregation welcomes the baptized and exchanges the peace (*Book of Common Worship,* Louisville 1993).

In the middle of the spectrum is the new rite of the Church of Scotland. The institution (both Matt. 28 and Acts 2.38f. plus optional texts) is followed by a short doctrinal statement. There is a single question of the parents, and the congregation recites the creed. The prayer is an anamnetic thanksgiving for water and the Spirit, and has the double epiclesis, but in this case the minister pours the water. The minister pronounces a declaration derived from the French Reformed liturgy, then baptizes, blesses and offers a further declaration. At this point come the baptismal promises of the parents and the congregation. The intent of this placement is to preserve the priority of God's initiative and to express the catechetical disciplines which follow baptism. A variation of the rite is offered for adults, which includes confirmation and the laying-on of hands (*Common Order,* Edinburgh 1994).

Hughes Oliphant Old, *The Shaping of the Reformed Baptismal Rite in the Sixteenth Century,* Grand Rapids 1992; Daniel James Meeter, *Bless the Lord, O My Soul,* Lanham, MD 1998.

DANIEL J. MEETER

Baptismal Vows, Renewal of

A renewal of *baptism developed among the *Bohemian Brethren during the fifteenth century and emerged more fully during the Reformation. Those reformed churches which retained infant baptism developed forms for ritual profession of faith by adolescents. Specifying this as 'renewal of baptismal vows' may have first appeared in the *confirmation rite in the 1662 *BCP* of the Church of England, which introduced this question: 'Do ye . . . renew the solemn promise and vow that was made in your name at your Baptism . . .?' A similar practice is evident in the *covenant renewal service introduced by John Wesley. However, this service did not connect the renewal to baptism but rather referred to the experience of conversion.

In churches today, renewal of baptismal vows is practised in one or more ways:

1. Many Reformation churches which historically provided an adolescent renewal of baptism, commonly called '*confirmation', have introduced a repeatable rite of reaffirmation. The RC Church, following the *Constitution on the Sacred Liturgy*, has revised its confirmation rite to include a renewal of baptismal promises.

2. The revised *Easter vigil introduced by the RC Church in 1951 provided a congregational renewal of baptismal vows preceding the traditional *asperges, which may also be used on Easter Day. Other churches also included a verbal renewal and/or asperges when they introduced the Easter vigil. In the American and Canadian Anglican rites, this renewal may also occur on the first Sunday after the *Epiphany (baptism of Jesus), *Pentecost and *All Saints' Day.

3. Some churches, including the American Presbyterian and United Methodist service books, the Anglican Church in Southern Africa, and the Church of England, provide separate rites for congregational renewal of baptismal vows.

4. Many new baptismal rites include a congregational reaffirmation of baptismal promises.

What is meant by 'baptismal vows' varies. In most instances they include the Apostles' *Creed or a paraphrase. Sometimes a renunciation of evil precedes the creed. In the American and Canadian Anglican books, credal questions are followed by questions ascertaining commitment to Christian life, and the entire set of questions is entitled the 'baptismal covenant'. Similar questions of commitment appear separate from the creed in rites of baptism and reaffirmation in the service books of other churches; sometimes these questions are addressed to candidates alone.

Colin Buchanan, 'The Renewal of Baptismal Vows', *Studia Liturgica* XVII, 1987, 47–51; Ruth A. Meyers, 'Christian Rites of Adolescence', *Life Cycles in Jewish and Christian Worship*, ed. Paul F. Bradshaw and Lawrence A. Hoffman, Notre Dame 1996, 55–80.

RUTH A. MEYERS

Baptist Worship

The world Baptist community originated in England, though its largest concentration is in the USA, and can be found in varying numbers in most countries. Congregationally governed, Baptists are usually evangelical in ethos and have a particular concern for freedom. In worship, this concern is expressed through each congregation having freedom to order its own worship, independent of any centralized control and, apart from some modern exceptions, a distrust of set written prayers and liturgical responses.

1. *Origins*. Baptists emerged in the early years of the seventeenth century as part of the Radical Reformation. Particular (Calvinistic) Baptists separated from Independents over the question of believer's baptism in the 1630s, but their worship resembled that of the Separatists they left, keeping in close fellowship with them.

The earlier General (Arminian) Baptists began about 1608 as a group of English emigrés in Holland. They were both more radical, through the rejection of most worship conventions, and more conservative, in resisting developments to be found among other Free Churches. An early service would include three or four extempore sermons and discussion on a given scripture passage, together with free prayer. They also practised *foot-washing and, like other Separatists and Puritans, only permitted in worship that which they could see commanded in scripture – what they called 'ordinances'.

In Britain, the Calvinistic Baptists became the main group. Most English General Baptists became *Unitarian in the eighteenth century, though those who remained orthodox were influenced in worship by the evangelical revival, including the increasing use of *hymns. In the USA the Arminian strand remained orthodox and the distinctions which developed were more to do with general Free Church polarities expressed by the so-called Charleston (or British) and Frontier traditions. In the rest of the world there are clear family resemblances, though there are regional cultural distinctives. For example, the worship of the large Baptist community in eastern Europe is strongly pietistic and self-consciously non-liturgical. Cultural influence from the sending churches of missionaries is still clear in Latin America, Africa and Asia, through some voices are now calling for greater *inculturation of forms of worship. Some African congregations will, for example, incorporate *dancing with the bringing forward of *offertory gifts.

2. *Features*. Despite the concern for freedom and local flexibility, Baptist worship has a number of distinctive features which are shared with many evangelical free churches, and there are discernible patterns even though the services do not use written liturgies.

2.1. *Preaching* is the most common and prominent feature. Until the mid-twentieth century, the sermon would dominate the rest of the service by its length and would usually be regarded as the climax of worship. The most famous preacher was Charles Haddon Spurgeon (1834–92) who preached to weekly congregations of 5,000. Some early Baptists debated whether sermons could be prepared in advance, let alone read like the Anglicans, reflecting a concern that the leader of worship be open to the Holy Spirit. Yet many Baptists did not see study as contrary to inspiration and the first seminary began to train an educated ministry in 1720. *Preaching is regarded as an event in which God encounters the congregation and requires a response.

2.2. *Free Prayer*. While some contemporary leaders of worship will use written prayers some of the time, for most of their history Baptists have prized *extempore prayer. In public worship this will usually mean representative prayer led by one person, with the congregation saying 'Amen'. This is not simply a reaction to the imposition of the *BCP* in the seventeenth century, but a concern that the person praying should be open to God and inspired by the Spirit, as suggested by Rom. 8.26–27. John Bunyan (1628–88), imprisoned for his persistence in leading free worship and his rejection of the *BCP*, made no significant distinction between public and private prayer and defined it as 'a sincere, sensible, affectionate pouring out of the heart or soul to God through Christ, in the strength and assistance of the Holy Spirit'. Extempore prayer remains the norm in Baptist worship, though leaders will often prepare in advance (what Isaac Watts called 'conceived prayer'). Written prayers and experimental responses are sometimes used in some parts of the world.

2.3. *Hymnody*. Particular Baptist churches were the first churches in England to introduce the congregational singing of hymns in Sunday worship, as a development from the more widely exercised singing of metrical psalms. Benjamin Keach (1640–1704) began by introducing a hymn after *communion (justified by Mark 14.26) and later at the close of each service. For much of the eighteenth century, most Baptists used Watt's *Psalms and Hymns*, though *The Bristol Collection* of Ash and Evans appeared in 1769 as the first hymn book for congregational use which comprised a collection of texts from different authors. This, and the more widespread *Selection* of John Rippon (1750–1836), contributed to the demise of 'lining out' the hymns with a cantor, and to the modern custom of each member of the congregation singing from their own hymn book. Hymn books became important repositories of spiritual writings and an occasional link between corporate worship and private devotion.

In the latter part of the twentieth century, *charismatic renewal has influenced the content and use of congregational songs in a number of ways. It has introduced the worship song, as distinct from the hymn, and in some churches the interspersing of hymns throughout the service has been replaced or supplemented by continuous sequences of worship songs, usually repeated and often concentrating on devotion and celebration. This has also led to an increased congregational participation, though through the use of more pre-composed texts in the form of those songs.

2.4. *The Culture of Informality*. A general concern for freedom from fixed forms is closely related to a culture in which informality is perceived as a virtue. This has several roots. Historically, Baptists have often identified ritual and formality with hypocrisy, or 'lip-worship', while informality has been seen as a sign of spontaneity and sincerity. In addition, the concern for mission leads to a desire that the worship of the local churches should be user-friendly and visitor-friendly, and informality is seen as an important way of achieving this. Such an ethos can result in a warm, relational experience, in which gathering for worship is an expression of genuine fellowship, but it can also lead to sloppy and ill-prepared worship.

2.5. *Patterns of Worship*. This informality and concern for freedom has meant a suspicion of liturgical forms, though in the twentieth century some Baptists have both used material from other traditions and self-consciously constructed worship on the basis of liturgical principles. Yet prayer, praise and preaching remain the building blocks of worship and the order in which they take place is seen to be of less importance than their sincerity and spiritual value.

3. *Spirituality*. Baptists have tended to be

influenced more by Pauline than by Johannine spiritualities. Stronger on salvation than incarnation, they have emphasized the word rather than embodied expressions in worship, such as images or ritual actions. They are usually very committed to evangelism and will often make provision for some kind of personal response within worship. This strong concern for mission leads to a desire for relevance and accessibility in worship, generally expressed through the culture of informality and the use of contemporary language.

Their traditional attitude to extempore prayer is based as much on pneumatological considerations as on a simple rejection of imposed or set structures and words. It is helpful to make a distinction between *expressive* prayer, as an outflowing of the heart, and *impressive* prayer, in which pre-composed words are used to shape and express the prayers of the worshippers. The emphasis on expressive prayer is an example of how Baptists, in worship, see the sincere attitude of the heart as more important than outward actions. Yet impressive dimensions are obviously evident in the use of hymnody and song as devotional aids.

_____

Christopher J. Ellis, *Baptist Worship Today*, Didcot 1999; Horton Davies, *WTE*; E. A. Payne, *The Fellowship of Believers*, London, enlarged edition 1952; S. F. Winward, *The Reformation of our Worship*, London 1964; R. P. Martin, *The Worship of God*, Grand Rapids 1982; James F. White, *Protestant Worship: Traditions in Transition*, Louisville, KY 1989.

CHRISTOPHER J. ELLIS

Baptistery

The building or part of a building in which *baptism is administered and which contains a bath, *font or fountain. In the *Baptist Church the term refers to the baptismal pool, which is usually below floor level and covered except when in use.

For the first two hundred years of Christianity, baptism was celebrated outdoors in natural bodies of water, following the example of Acts 8. Tertullian declared that 'it makes no difference at all whether a man is baptized in the sea or a pool, in a river or a spring, in a lake or a tub'. Because of persecution or inconvenience, baptism moved into private spaces, courtyard fountains or bathrooms providing the setting

and the water. The oldest known baptistery *chapel is that of the Christian church at Dura Europos in the Syrian desert near to the Euphrates, a Roman town abandoned in 257. The square baptistery contains a canopied font-basin, too small for the immersion of candidates.

From at least the third century onwards baptisteries were constructed, often as separate buildings. Among notable detached baptisteries are those at the Lateran in Rome, 'wholly exceptional in size and magnificence', and at Pisa, Ravenna, Florence, Nocera, Tebéssa, el-Kantara and Poitiers. Baptisteries were erected first only in episcopal cities as the *bishop was the ordinary minister of baptism. As baptism was increasingly delegated to priests in the Greek East, the number of baptisteries increased. J. G. Davies held that it was the nature of adult baptism, with disrobing, washing, *anointing, clothing in white robes, and a *procession to the main building for the *eucharist, that gave rise to the detached building provided, when space allowed, with rooms for the various rites. The baptistery itself took various symbolic shapes: square, cruciform, circular, hexagonal and octagonal, each shape being linked to some aspect of the baptismal mystery, e.g. the hexagon represents Friday, the day of Christ's death and the octagon Sunday, the day of his resurrection. Different shapes were often combined in the structure of the building and of the font and in the design on the floor.

In Ravenna there are two baptisteries dating from the fifth and sixth centuries, one Orthodox and the other Arian. Both are domed octagons with central, walled pools. That of the Orthodox, *c.* 458, has decoration of exceptional richness. The building is octagonal, as is the font. The decoration begins at arcade level with vine scrolls enclosing figures holding books; above the arcade there are windows flanked by stuccoed figures carrying books or scrolls; the dome is covered with mosaic in three concentric circles: architectural fantasies with alternating enthroned crosses and altars displaying gospel books; the twelve apostles bearing crowns; and at the summit a medallion showing the baptism of Christ. The baptistery of the Arians, *c.* 500–25, is less well preserved but the dome also has the twelve apostles with an enthroned cross in the thirteenth space and a summit medallion of Christ's baptism.

There are two rare examples of monumental baptisteries from the twelfth century at Pisa and

Parma. The circular baptistery at Pisa was designed by Diotisalvi – the scheme is like that of the rotunda of the Anastasis in Jerusalem. It was begun in 1153 and the exterior was remodelled in the Gothic style by Nicola Pisano (1250–65). The baptistery at Parma, octagonal externally and circular internally, was begun in 1196. Another baptistery, that of San Giovanni in Florence, though superficially of the eleventh and twelfth centuries, may in fact date from the fifth century.

In the later Middle Ages the detached type of baptistery ceased to be built and the font was placed in the church, often near the main door. Carlo Borromeo, in his instructions for the diocese of Milan, 1559, required the font to be in a separate chapel, close to the chief doorway and on the gospel (north) side of the church. This became the general pattern in RC churches until the Second World War. Baptisteries were not favoured in Protestant churches. Lutherans used a font located at the east end near to the *communion table and *pulpit; Calvinists used shallow basins either on the holy table or attached by a bracket to the pulpit. Anglicans continued the medieval practice of having the font by the church door.

In 1947 the German RC Liturgical Commission set out the principles to be used in constructing new churches. Of the font it said: 'In the ideal church this "spring of baptism" would be given a monumental treatment and be placed in a separate room near the entrance. According to venerable tradition this room should be circular or polygonal, with the font in the centre; and the inward meaning of the ritual of baptism leads to the same architectural solution. For at the core of this ritual man appears not as an actor, but merely as the passive recipient of the mysterious action of God, and accordingly the appropriate architectural form is not a long room, which in symbolic language expresses action, but a room which is centrally planned, and which, since its axis is vertical, has a passive character.' Post-war RC churches regularly had a separate baptistery but after Vatican II there was a growing tendency to put the font in the body of the church. The General Introduction to the new RC Rites of Initiation (1972) simply specified the baptistery as 'the area where the baptismal font flows or has been placed' in a chapel inside or outside the church or in some other part of the church 'easily seen by the faithful'. It stressed that the baptistery should be reserved for baptism. In 1977 the American bishops only required that the siting of the font should facilitate full congregational participation, especially at the *Easter vigil.

J. G. Davies, *The Architectural Setting of Baptism*, London 1962; Peter Hammond (ed.), *Towards a Church Architecture*, London 1962; Regina Kuehn, *A Place for Baptism*, Chicago 1992 (with excellent illustrations of a variety of fonts and baptisteries); Robert Milburn, *Early Christian Art and Architecture*, Berkeley, CA 1988.

MARTIN DUDLEY

Basilica

A long rectangular hall with one or more surrounding *aisles, one or more *apses (sometimes called *exedrae*), a lateral entrance on one of the long sides, and a high central aisle with clerestory windows for illumination. Despite their common elements, basilicas took a variety of forms. The apses, for example, could be enclosed within the rectangular hall as in the third-century basilica at Leptis Magna, Libya. The earliest basilicas are Roman secular buildings dating from as early as the second century BCE. Often located along one side of a civic forum, they served among other purposes as imperial audience halls, law courts, military administrative offices, and even as cover for merchants in inclement weather. Typically built of stone or concrete faced with stone or brick, most basilicas had wooden truss roofs. Superimposed colonnades separating the *nave from the side aisles provided the possibility for *galleries above the side aisles. An example of an imperial basilica in Rome is the Basilica Ulpia of the second century CE, opening directly onto the Forum of Trajan in Rome. The secular basilica's combination of a longitudinal axis, an unimpeded centre aisle for gathering a large assembly, and the absence of association with pagan religion proved irresistible for Christian architects in the early fourth century CE after the emperor Constantine's conversion, and his subsequent establishment of Christianity as the state religion. In appropriating the Roman basilica, architects of the first churches relocated the entry to one of the short sides to create a longitudinal axis, terminated the aisle or aisles with an apse, and added a *narthex (entry porch) preceded by an *atrium. A variety of forms of Christian basilicas emerged to meet differing needs of the Christian community. Among the most important types are:

1. Parish church, a simple basilican plan

with the entry on the longitudinal axis, and the *altar located in the apse, e.g. St John Lateran, Rome. The nave was flanked by double side aisles. Two rooms project from the side aisles, possibly for storage of the gifts brought by the congregation for distribution to the poor.

2. Martyrial church or *martyrium, e.g. Old St Peter's, Rome, built in the cemetery over the traditional site of the burial of St Peter. The revolutionary element of a *transept, or cross arm, was introduced to the basilican plan to mark the site of the burial architecturally. The transept creates the 'cross-shaped' church plan which persists to the present day.

3. Funerary church, a basilica which functioned as a covered cemetery, e.g. S. Lorenzo, Rome. Typically the floors were full of graves of the faithful and the side aisles continued around the apse to form a continuous ambulatory or walkway. In the earliest examples the martyr's tomb was outside the church in the adjacent catacomb. The buildings accommodated funeral banquets and commemorative services.

See also **Architectural Setting (Historical) 2.**

MARCHITA B. MAUCK

Bells

There has been the ringing of bells both inside and outside churches for much of its history. The external bell served to call folk to prayer, to punctuate the day, or to give news; while ringing within the church functioned to recall the faithful to concentration in their devotions. The earliest bells were handbells made of thin sheets of metal such as that preserved in the National Museum of Ireland and alleged to be the Bell of St Patrick. Hanging bells came into use by the eighth century. There was a peal of three bells at St Peter's, Rome in the time of Pope Stephen II (752–7) and an early depiction of Winchester Cathedral (*c*. 980) features bells.

The external bells of monasteries and cathedrals sounded the hours of *daily prayer, while those of the parish church reminded people of the *Angelus to be said daily. The Anglican Prayer Books enjoined the ringing of the bell before morning and evening prayer each day. The church bells served as the common bell of the parish or municipality: the passing bell calling them to pray for some departing soul; the death knell telling them it was all over; the muffled bells announced the *requiem; while wedding bells gave more joyful news. There

were other messages conveyed by the church bells: the market bell regulated hours of business; the gleaning bell ensured a fair start for all; the fire bell summoned help. Although most of these customs have died out, a revival since the later part of the nineteenth century of the skills of change-ringing has ensured the use and maintenance of the church's bells.

Inside church small bells (sacring or *Sanctus bell) have been used at the *altar (or occasionally in a Sanctus bell turret) to remind worshippers of the progress of the service. In the RC Church this was particularly necessary before the introduction of the vernacular. More recently the RC Church has been equivocal regarding the continuance of the custom, questioning the need for this signal 'to elicit joy and attention' at the central part of the *eucharist.

DONALD GRAY

Bema *see* **Ambo**

Benedicite *see* **Canticles**

Benediction

An RC service with the *reserved sacrament, benediction seems to have derived from two different liturgical sources, the hours of *daily prayer and the *Corpus Christi *procession. From at least the tenth century it had been customary to conclude the divine office with a Marian hymn or anthem, known as *laude* in Italy, *salut* in France. In the fourteenth century, solemnity was often added to these evening devotions by *exposing the blessed *sacrament in a *monstrance and *blessing the people with it at the end. This closely parallels a custom, first recorded in fourteenth-century Germany, of interrupting and concluding the Corpus Christi procession with a solemn blessing of the people with the monstrance. Later in that century, similar processions concluding with benediction were found on the occasion of other major feasts, civic celebrations and secular crises.

These origins suggest that benediction was not originally an independent ritual but served as a solemn conclusion to another liturgy. This situation is still reflected in the post-Tridentine Roman Ritual of 1614, where it is never referred to as an independent liturgy. The Sacred Congregation of Rites (established 1588 to regulate the liturgy) was constantly cautious and restrictive in its regulations and reluctant to provide official rites for it. The model (for Corpus Christi) in the 1614 Ritual consisted of an *incensation, the *Tantum ergo* stanzas from the hymn *Pange lingua*, the Corpus Christi *collect, and the blessing of the people with the monstrance in the form of a cross. From the seventeenth to the twentieth centuries this basic format was expanded in local publications and practice with further hymns (e.g. *O salutaris hostia*), prayers, *litanies and acclamations.

In the nineteenth and early twentieth centuries benediction, often with *rosary and sermon, reached the height of its popularity as a Sunday evening service, which allowed for participatory devotions, popular hymnody and vernacular prayers, which were excluded from the official liturgy. With the introduction and spread of evening *mass since the 1950s, however, the frequency and popularity of benediction, with or without other devotions, has declined sharply.

The revised Roman Ritual (1973) classifies and regulates benediction as a 'brief exposition', governed by the same principles and broad liturgical guidelines as exposition. The reformed rite allows for greater flexibility in the choice of hymns, collects and acclamations, and commends readings from scripture and periods of silent adoration. All prayer and reflection must centre on the person of Christ, and any Marian prayers or anthems may follow only after the sacrament has been returned to the *tabernacle.

Robert Cabié, 'Worship of the Eucharist Outside Mass', *The Church at Prayer* II, ed. A. G. Martimort, Collegeville 1986, 231–53; Nathan Mitchell, *Cult and Controversy: The Worship of the Eucharist outside Mass*, New York 1982.
CHRISTOPHER WALSH

Benedictus

This Latin title, 'Blessed', may refer either to the NT *canticle, 'Blessed be the Lord God of Israel' (Luke 1.68–79), or to the anthem, 'Blessed is he who comes in the name of the Lord', often found attached to the *Sanctus in the *eucharistic prayer (and sometimes designated as Benedictus qui venit to distinguish it from the former).

See also **Music in the Mass of the Roman Rite**; **Ordinary.**

EDITOR

Berakah *see* Blessing

Bible Services *see* Word, Services of the

Bible, Use of in Worship

1. *A Collection for Worship.* 'The Bible', as we call the collection into a single volume of the many diverse books of the OT and NT, is a book intended for use in Christian worship. The very history of the collection is a history of worship practice. Thus, there is evidence that many Christian communities early adopted those books that were read in the synagogues as books that were also to be read in their own meetings: the five 'books of Moses' and the many other writings collectively called 'the prophets'. So, in a passage which echoes the word-and-meal shape of the Christian Sunday meeting as it was known in some late first-century communities, Luke has the risen Christ begin 'with Moses and all the prophets' and interpret 'to them the things about himself in all the scriptures' (Luke 24.27).

As the NT books came to be written, many of them echoed this Christian use of 'the scriptures' by themselves also being intended for public reading in the assembly of the church (see 1 Thess. 5.27; Col. 4.16). The very salutations and conclusions of the Pauline letters may indicate that the writer assumed a setting in communal worship as the place where the letter would be read (e.g. 2 Cor. 13.12: 'Greet one another with a holy kiss'). Furthermore, the very shape of the 'gospel', the written genre developed to tell the story of Jesus, may have similarly assumed a communal, ecclesial setting, framed as it was with *baptism at the outset and *eucharist, the passion-resurrection account and sometimes images of the Sunday assembly itself (Luke 24.13–49; John 20.19–29) at the conclusion. In any case, when one ancient list of the NT books discussed why *The Shepherd of Hermas* ought indeed to be read but not 'read publicly in the church to the people', it made clear what the purpose of such lists were: agreement among churches on what books of 'the prophets' and of 'the apostles' were worthy of public reading in the assembly (*Muratorian Canon*, lines 78–80).

Disagreements continued concerning the actual contents of these lists. Marcion argued in the second century for reading only ten of the letters of Paul and an edited form of Luke, with nothing from the Hebrew scriptures. Most Greek-speaking Christian communities, however, adopted the old Jewish Septuagint translation for their reading of the Hebrew scriptures, and they thereby included several books not later found in the official lists of the synagogues. These books were then rejected by some Christian teachers of the fourth and fifth centuries, notably Jerome, and came to be disputed as 'apocrypha' or, at least, as 'deutero-canonical books', at the time of the Reformation. Among the New Testament books, conflicts continued over the appropriateness of Revelation and Jude, Hebrews and 2 Peter. But the very conflicts illustrate the point: the collection of books we call 'the Bible' was drawn together for the sake of reading in the church. Handheld volumes – *codices* – came to be favoured over scrolls by Christians of the early centuries, probably in order to enable this extensive public reading at meetings in the houses of the faithful.

2. *Reading in Worship.* The practice which became the dominant Christian pattern, then, can be represented by the mid-second-century Roman report of Justin: 'On the day named after the sun all, whether they live in the city or the countryside, are gathered together in unity. Then the records of the apostles or the writings of the prophets are read for as long as there is time. When the reader has concluded, the presider in a discourse admonishes and invites us into the pattern of these good things . . .' (*First Apology* 67). To the present day, the most obvious use of the Bible in the public worship of Christians remains its public reading and its homiletical interpretation in sermons. Diverse patterns of *what* passages are to be read grew up in East and West (*see* **Lectionaries**), but almost all of these patterns continued to make use of at least two *readings on Sundays, just as Justin already reported. The homily which followed these readings has frequently been a focus for Christian renewal: the scriptural readings need to be accompanied by a living voice making their mysteries accessible to contemporary hearers (*see* **Preaching and Worship**).

3. *Language for Worship.* But the use of the Bible for actual public reading has not been the only way in which the Bible has been present in Christian worship. Biblical texts have also provided the primary source for the actual language used in Christian prayers and *hymns. The biblical Psalter formed the first Christian hymnal. Biblical prayers furnished texts and models for Christian communal prayers. And biblical images lived on, reborn in Christian

preaching and song. So the historical liturgies have been much marked by a poetry which makes extensive use of biblical rhetoric and images, a poetry of which Ephrem of Edessa and Romanos the Melodist in the East were the classic masters. And more recent additions in various denominations – hymns and opening greetings, *eucharistic prayers and postcommunion songs – have frequently been enduringly successful to the extent that they too have taken up the creative use of direct biblical language or borrowed biblical imagery. Each of these particular uses has a history, but they all root in the deep Christian conviction that the Christian assembly continues to live in the presence of the biblical God and to experience the matters to which the biblical texts bear witness.

4. *Mandates for Worship.* Indeed, it may be, in the Christian sense that the assembly for worship has the same intention as does the Bible, that one finds the most important use of the Bible in worship. Christians have believed that they are engaging in an assembly in continuity with assemblies of both the OT and NT, that they are singing biblical praise and praying biblical thanksgivings and supplications, and, especially, that they are enacting a preaching, a baptizing and a meal-keeping both modelled and enjoined in the Bible. A fruitful way to study the history of Christian worship in the future would be to focus primarily upon the history of the use of the Bible in the assemblies of Christians.

The papers of the 1991 Congress of Societas Liturgica, *Studia Liturgica* XXII/2, 1992; Dietrich Bonhoeffer, *Life Together; Prayerbook of the Bible*, Minneapolis 1996; Jean Daniélou, *The Bible and the Liturgy*, Notre Dame 1956; Austin Farrer, *A Rebirth of Images*, London 1949; Northrop Frye, *The Great Code*, New York 1982.

GORDON LATHROP

Bidding Prayer

According to the earliest sources for the *intercessions in the *eucharist in the Roman rite it was common for each topic to be introduced by a bidding inviting the congregation's prayers. This would be followed by silent prayer and a *collect. Apart from the *Good Friday solemn prayers this pattern later fell into disuse, though it has been revived in recent years.

The early biddings and collects were replaced by *litany forms of intercession. After these disappeared from use, from the ninth century there grew up in English, French and German churches the custom of vernacular bidding prayers. These were a stable element in the eucharist through the Middle Ages, and along with a sermon, instruction and notices were known as the Prone and as such were an important feature of congregational participation and pastoral liturgy. In France and Germany the Prone achieved a formal structure and influenced the form and content of Lutheran and Reformed liturgies. In England the same elements were present. The prayers were known as 'bidding of the bedes' from the Anglo-Saxon meaning the 'praying of the prayers'. The structure of the bidding was similar in practice to the patristic model in that the invitation to pray was followed by congregational prayer. Originally this was the *Lord's Prayer said silently and a collect recited by the priest. Later the biddings were lengthy, covering the full range of church, state, the community and the departed, and they were divided into two or three sets followed by the Lord's Prayer and also psalms, *preces* and collects. The content of the bidding was always variable according to circumstance but governed by convention. The inclusion of the names of those presenting offerings or of the departed (the 'Bede-Roll') was very important. The bidding prayer carried on through the Reformation and was to be used before sermons. Its content was increasingly subject to government direction, but variation happened in practice and Canon 55 of the Canons of 1604, which sets out a text, directs the preacher to pray 'in this form or to this effect'. But with the vernacular liturgy the bidding prayer lost its central role and was more rarely used. It has been revived as a form in some modern services, such as the intercessions in 'traditional' carol services.

In the RC Church today the intercessions in the mass are known as the bidding prayers.

F. E. Brightman, *The English Rite*, London 1915, II, 1020–45.

GORDON JEANES

Bishop

Although the Greek word *episkopos* ('overseer') is found in the NT, many – but not all – scholars have concluded that it does not refer there to an order of ministry which is clearly distinct from that of a *presbyteros* ('*elder'). Some NT books mention elders but not bishops; Phil. 1.1 apparently mentions bishops and *deacons, but not elders; and in Acts 20.28 elders themselves are described as being *episkopoi*. The same is true of some other early Christian writings: *1 Clement* (usually dated *c*. 96 CE) implies that both the Roman and Corinthian churches were under the authority of a body of *presbyters, while an ancient church order, *The Didache*, speaks only of bishops and deacons. The letters of Ignatius of Antioch in the first half of the second century are the oldest witness to a threefold pattern of ministry (bishop, presbyters and deacons), which seems to be establishing itself only with difficulty; and many scholars believe that a separate office of bishop was not firmly in place at Rome or in a number of other cities until at least the middle of the second century.

Eventually, however, this threefold pattern became normative throughout the Christian church, and the bishop subsumed into himself the ministries earlier exercised by prophets and teachers. He also became the normal president of all liturgical assemblies, although as the church expanded, he found it increasingly necessary to delegate some of these responsibilities to presbyters, especially the *baptism of new converts and the presidency of the *eucharist. The *ordination of a bishop was probably performed by his own local church at first, but by the middle of the third century there is evidence in North Africa for the involvement of neighbouring bishops in the proceedings, and the Council of Nicaea required at least three bishops to be present and preside over the act, with the rest sending their approval in writing if unable to be there.

From the third century onwards, the bishop began to be described as a 'priest' (*hiereus* in Greek, *sacerdos* in Latin) or 'high priest', although later the term priest was attached to the presbyter instead as he became the more usual eucharistic president. Because in the medieval West ordained ministry came to be defined almost exclusively in terms of the concept of priesthood, doubts then arose as to whether the episcopate really constituted a distinct order from the presbyterate or was merely a higher degree within the presbyteral order. Most theologians inclined towards the latter view, and spoke of bishops being 'consecrated' rather than 'ordained'. It was not until the Second Vatican Council that the RC Church finally determined that the episcopate was a separate order (*Lumen gentium* 21).

At the Reformation the office of bishop was retained in the Church of England and by some, but not all, *Lutheran churches. The *Moravians also preserved the episcopal order, but they have not always regarded the imposition of a bishop's hands as necessary for ordination. The office of bishop was introduced in the *Methodist Church in the USA in the eighteenth century, and in the twentieth century the title was adopted in some Lutheran churches which had formerly had *superintendents, and in several united churches.

EDITOR

Black Churches' Worship

1. *United Kingdom*. The Second World War saw Britain extending an invitation to its colonies to aid it in its war effort, and after the war many workers stayed on to help rebuild the war-torn British industries and infrastructure. Additionally, 21 June 1948 saw the arrival of 496 workers from the Caribbean on *Empire Windrush* and the beginning of modern-day migration. With these immigrants came a new and fresh expression of faith and spirituality. Many migrants felt that British churches were not welcoming or that they were prohibited or inhibited in their worship of God who deserved the 'highest praise'. This was a cause of severe disillusionment and did not reflect or express the kinds of spirituality taught or promoted by the missionaries. Very soon Black Christians began to pray and worship in their homes – in what they called 'bed-sitter' churches. These 'bed-sitter' churches grew into denominations as early as 1951, the first being the Calvary Church of God in Christ. The 1980s saw the emergence of churches from the African continent. With over 3,000 churches and 250,000 regular attendees, churches from the African and Caribbean diaspora are the fastest growing in Britain.

1.1. *Black Majority Churches*. Today, congregations where the majority of attendees are Black can be found not only in churches of African and Caribbean diaspora but also in every major historical or 'mainstream' denomination. The spectrum of these denominations also reflects the variety of worship styles and customs. These styles are observed in at least five expressions of Black majority churches (BMCs): (a) churches of Caribbean diaspora, such as the New Testament Church of God, Church of God of Prophecy, New Testament Assembly; (b) churches of African diaspora, such as New Covenant Church, Redeemed Christian Church of God and Christ Apostolic Church; (c) BMCs within white majority Pentecostal churches, such as Kensington Temple (Elim), Emmanuel Christian Centre (Assemblies of God) and All Nations Centre (Apostolic); (d) BMCs in historical denominations such as the Church of England and Methodist, Baptist and United Reformed Churches; (e) African and Caribbean Instituted Spiritual Churches (ACISCs) such as Aladura, Cherubim and Seraphim, Mount Zion Spiritual Baptist, Brotherhood of the Cross and Star.

Worship in BMCs tends to follow the traditions of their parent denominations or the ones from which they have emerged. Often these are modified with cultural variations. The *charismatic and *Pentecostal traditions influence a significant number of BMCs. The majority of Caribbean churches are influenced by traditions emerging from the USA, and therefore share many common aspects. Many BMCs do not consider the ACISCs as belonging to orthodox Christianity because of issues of faith and practice. Some tend to be synchronistic, merging a high Anglican or Catholic tradition with cultural customs, prayers, visions, trances, dreams and prophecies on demand. Such practices are considered akin to divination rather than the biblical disciplines or arising from the gift of the Holy Spirit. In some ACISCs their leaders are treated as a deity.

1.2. *Worship as a Lifestyle*. To Black Christians worship is not seen merely as an act – the doing, but predominantly as a lifestyle – the being. It is not unusual for proclamations to be made by a speaker, either in the *pulpit or the *pew, that they did not attend church to worship, as their worship is ongoing and an integral part of their lives. Alternatively, as a protest or chastisement, the worship leader might say, 'I'm not going to prime or pump you to worship God, you should have started before you got here!' This continuum of worship is also seen in Gospel concerts and entertainment events, where the paying audience is admonished by artistes, 'I haven't come here to entertain you but to worship God.' Worship as a lifestyle reinforces the notion that we are constantly in the presence of a holy God who deserves to be worshipped at all times in every circumstance. Therefore, holiness codes and promises in scripture aid and abet this worship lifestyle.

1.3. *The Preacher and Worship*. The preacher is at the heart of worship in BMCs. This is depicted by the amount of time allocated to preaching, between 40 minutes and an hour, which excludes additional time 'when the Spirit moves'. Other aspects of the service tend to serve as a warm-up for the preacher, as there is a strong steering of worshippers towards the preached word. Therefore the onus is on the preacher to let the Holy Spirit 'fall' or to 'mash up the place', as on the day of Pentecost. This creates the worshipping preacher who cannot rely merely on expository preaching or exegeting a text, as he or she may be considered dead, dry or lacking the anointing. Consequently, sermons are punctuated with call and response interaction to ensure that the audience is 'feeling' the preacher. Calls like: 'Can I have a witness?' 'Is anyone there?' 'Hello?' 'Are you with me?' or 'Say praise the Lord somebody!' are responded to with shouts of: 'Amen!' 'Hallelujahs!' 'Preach it!' or 'Bless him/her Lord!'

1.4. *Elements in Worship*. Although BMCs outside the historical denominations do not have a written liturgy, there are predictable patterns which regular attendees will identify. Joel Edwards highlights the following:

(a) devotional service – includes a song, prayer and scripture reading. This period is often used as a settling-down time and functions in the same way as the chiming bell's call to worship;

(b) further singing and testimonies. Testimonies are normally given in the evening service, though not exclusively. They could set the tone of the service as they can uplift the congregation. Equally testimonies are sometimes used to test the depth of spirituality of individuals. On occasions they replace sermons, and visitors and members alike could be called on to give theirs. Very often members may choose to sing their testimony as a song may express better their sentiment;

(c) special prayer – for the sick or those needing ministry;

(d) offering. This is emphasized as an integral part of worship with the clarion call 'God loves a cheerful giver'. Additionally, the call may go out, 'It's offering time', followed by loud cheers, drum rolls and *dancing. Increasingly some churches tend to spend up to five minutes explaining a passage of scripture to establish the basis and virtue of giving. In churches of the African diaspora additional thanksgiving offerings are made to celebrate

success in a job, birthdays, anniversaries or the birth of a child;

(e) special singing. This can range from a soloist to the choir, and is often seen as the prelude to the preaching;

(f) the sermon. In some instances this used to be given by a member of the congregation, without prior notice. This is becoming less frequent;

(g) the altar call. This is the test whether the preacher has made an impact. Non-Christians are challenged to repent of their sins, while Christians are asked to respond to the preached word. This is also a time for individuals to place whatever burdens they may still have 'at the foot of the cross'.

1.5. *Additional Aspects of Worship*. (a) The *Lord's supper. Some churches still re-enact the Last Supper, including *foot-washing. These *communion services tend to be less frequent than in historical denominations. (b) Hand-clapping and dance before the Lord are actively encouraged as a sign of joy and thankfulness for good health and strength and as a means of celebration. More recently, classical dance and use of flags have been borrowed from the historical churches to add variety or to form focal points. (c) The use of spiritual gifts and disciplines such as prayer, fasting and personal devotion is actively encouraged. Not only are these seen as acts of worship but also means by which we effectively worship.

————

Many Winters On, formerly *Forty Winters On*, reprinted with permission by African and Caribbean Evangelical Alliance 1998; Joel Edwards, 'The Pulpit Response to Worship' and 'Pentecostal Distinctives' in *Let's Praise Him Again: An African-Caribbean Perspective on Worship*, Kingsway Publications 1992; R. David Muir, *A Mighty Long Way*, African and Caribbean Evangelical Alliance 1998.

MARK STURGE

2. *USA*. Worship in African American churches is a reflection of the rich diversity of a people of God whose religious heritage is rooted in African primal world views and ritual practices in traditional (West) African religions, religious practices in the West Indies (during the 'Middle Passage' for enslaved Africans), and encounters with Almighty God in an oppressive American slave system. During the earlier period as African Americans shaped worship, they transposed African world views, theology

and practices of spirituality, creative gifts of oral/aural traditions, uninhibited emotional expression and holistic involvement of body, soul and mind into new forms and styles of religious expression. Under the power of the Holy Spirit worshippers continue to gather as communities of faith to worship the Triune God and to affirm their identity and 'somebodiness' among folks of a kindred lineage and common needs. As an African people they continually create new rituals, new songs, new ways of preaching, singing and praying in the light of existential situations.

It must be noted at the outset that there is no one uniform 'Black manner of worship' to which all Black congregations must ascribe in order to be considered 'authentic'. That which authenticates Black worship is the creative freedom that a community exerts as ritual actions are shaped and reshaped to accommodate the *Sitz im Leben*. While differences in denominational polity and theology affect much of the content, flow, rites and ceremonial action as related to *baptism and the *Lord's supper, there are common practices that can be identified as African-American worship styles. Some African-American Christians prefer to continue to express their spirituality in forms more reflective of their earlier exposure to Euro-American worship. A common practice is to combine a number of forms, both old and 'contemporary', with a continual concern for God's word in Jesus the Christ made fresh every morning and in every generation. Thus, the diversity continues among historically Black denominations as well Black congregations in predominantly Euro-American and RC traditions.

2.1. *Historical Overview of Worship in 'Invisible Institutions'*. From the latter part of the seventeenth century, African Americans shaped worship in the context of their enslavement in secret places. The earliest sanctuaries for secret (clandestine) gatherings were actually improvised spaces in the wood, in gullies and swamps identified by ex-slaves as 'hush', 'brush' and 'bush' harbours. It was often necessary to surround the space with wet quilts and black pots to squelch the sound, and set guards to watch for possible intruders. Clandestine space was conducive to personal and communal expressions of hope for freedom in tones and rhythms that Africans in diaspora understood and appreciated. Through prayers, songs, sermons and testimonies, plans for escape routes for freedom via the 'underground railroad' were made. Worship services afforded opportunities for slaves to be the institutional church, and thus the Black Church at worship was later identified as 'invisible institutions'.

The elements of early worship and the manner (or style) in which the elements unfolded were naturally unique to the needs of a marginal people as they sought hope amid oppression. Although the sociological situation has changed, many of the rituals and manner of performance continue into the twenty-first century. Earliest elements included a call to worship or several notifications prior to worship. Announcements of secret meetings were made during the slave workday through songs or with signals directing worshippers to the meeting place. According to oral records of ex-slaves, other elements included a praise or devotional period, prayers, songs and preaching, with occasional testimonies and shouting.

2.2. *Current Worship Trends.* The concept of Black worship or African-American worship is grounded in an understanding of 'holistic expressiveness'. This is encompassed in the terms 'soul' or 'soulfulness', popularized *c.* 1958 as African Americans assumed the freedom to name and describe themselves. In worship one is made aware of certain aspects of African-rooted spirituality which permeate worship:

(a) a genuine depth of feeling which runs the spectrum of human emotions – from deepest gloom to the illimitable heights of exhilaration – and which bursts forth under the power of the Holy Spirit;

(b) uninhibited spontaneity which frees worshippers to engage in meaningful verbal and physical dialogue with the preacher and singers (call and response) throughout worship; under the power of the Holy Spirit, worshippers may sing, dance and shout;

(c) minimal concern for the length of time for worship, with a focus on the freedom, power and movement of the Holy Spirit;

(d) sermons deeply rooted in scripture, with interpretations based on needs of the local community. The Authorized (King James) Version is frequently used, with movement toward the New Revised Standard Version over the past ten years;

(e) music visibly and audibly present, constituting 80% of most services, with a recent focus on Black gospel music. Hammond organs, keyboard instruments, snare drum sets are frequently used. Some organists will occasionally provided rhythmic and harmonic accompaniment for the concluding 'celebration' by the preacher. Many congregations have multiple choirs according to age levels and music genres;

(f) a fundamental behaviour principle rooted in an African spirituality concept of 'rhythm of life', wherein there is a divine connection between all of God's created world. This serves as a basis for the concept of communal kinship, the unity of sacred and secular and the importance of holistic involvement in worship. It is the divine sense of rhythm that is paramount in a Black positive self-image which is imbedded in the good news of the gospel.

The latter aspect, perhaps the least discernible by one not familiar with Black life, is most important as a reminder of the holistic nature of humanity, in tune with God. In worship, the unity of sacred/secular is reflected in vocal and instrumental styles. The propensity for natural expressiveness keeps the individual and the community in tune with the rhythm of God and life, which is not dichotomized into sacred and secular. This has been and remains the foundation for Black survival in America.

Unique features of Black worship which continue into the twenty-first century include:

(a) song forms and styles: *spirituals, lined (metre) hymns; Black gospel songs; improvised (or 'blackenized') hymns;

(b) gospel songs (created by artists outside the church) often become music for the liturgy/ music for worship;

(c) keyboard style, with a preference for the 'Hammond' organ or synthesizers which lend themselves to a wide range of vibratos;

(d) use of drums, and other instruments reflective of jazz combos;

(e) musical call-and-response preaching style with preacher and congregation in dialogue;

(f) biblical messages that proclaim the good news of Jesus the Christ and offer words of protest where the divine message is blurred by human error.

MELVA WILSON COSTEN

Blessing

The authoritative pronouncement of God's favour on people, places, events or objects. Biblical examples of the practice are plentiful. For instance, in the account of creation God blesses all creatures of the sea and birds of the air (Gen. 1.22); Melchizedek blesses Abram (Gen. 14.19–20); and Isaac blesses Jacob (Gen.

27.27–30). In the NT Jesus blesses children (Mark 10.16) and his disciples at his Ascension (Luke 24.50). But many biblical references to blessing are instead to prayers in which God is praised for the gift of something, rather than the divine blessing being invoked directly upon the person or thing. Yet, in thus acknowledging God as the author of all creation and the giver of all good gifts, that for which God is blessed is also revealed as holy and thereby sanctified or consecrated. Known in Hebrew as a *berakah*, in Greek *eulogia*, its standard form began, 'Blessed be God, who has . . .', and went on to state the grounds for the blessing (see, e.g. Gen. 24.26–27; Ex. 18.10–11; Luke 1.68f.; 1 Peter 1.3). This was a common way in which blessings over food and drink were said, although later the use of the second person rather than the third became more usual: 'Blessed are you, Lord our God, who . . .' There was also an alternative form of prayer in use, which began, 'I/we give thanks to you, O Lord, because . . .', which seems to have been preferred by the early Christians (see the prayers of Jesus himself in Matt. 11.25–26//Luke 10.21 and John 11.41; and of the twenty-four elders in Rev. 11.17–18; and the use of 'thank' rather than 'bless' in relation to Jesus' prayer over the cup at the Last Supper in Matt. 26.27 and Mark 14.23, and over both bread and cup in Luke 22.17–19; 1 Cor. 11.24).

The latter seems to lie at the roots of later *eucharistic prayers and of some other solemn prayers of blessing, as for example over baptismal water and in the *ordination of ministers, but the Christian tradition also continued the practice of pronouncing blessings directly over persons and things. The blessing of the people was a standard part of the *dismissal rite at the end of services from early times, and was continued in most Reformation churches, using either the Aaronic blessing (Num. 6.24–26) or Phil. 4.7 followed by the medieval episcopal blessing: 'and the blessing of God almighty . . .' Similarly, blessings have been said over a wide range of objects, including church buildings (*see* **Consecration of Churches**), liturgical furnishings and *vestments, *incense, oil for *anointing, dwellings, cemeteries, fields and crops (*see* **Rogation Days**). Many Christian traditions restrict the saying of liturgical blessings to ordained ministers, and some the saying of certain blessings to specific orders of ministry, e.g. a *bishop; and they provide forms of blessing for a variety of purposes in their official service books (*see* **Books, Liturgical**).

The RC Church also has a substantial separate *Book of Blessings* (1989).

EDITOR

Blind Persons and Worship

Among people who are blind (no vision or the ability to distinguish between light and dark) and 'legally blind' (visual acuity is 20/200 or less in the better eye) there is a variety of vision loss. Making worship services and other ministries available for people who have low vision or no vision at all requires a variety of communication methods. Individuals have their preferred methods for obtaining access to worship based on the degree of their sight loss, forms of training in the usage of adaptive devices, as well as their ability to understand their particular vision loss. The most effective way to determine the most productive form of communication is to ask a person about their preferences.

1. *Oral Accommodation.* Persons who prefer oral communication may require worship materials in advance of the service. These materials may include bulletins, hymn selections and scripture lessons. These can be read directly or placed on audio-cassette tape. When reading materials that have been published, it is important to acknowledge the title, author, publisher and copyright date of the publication. It is recommended that a statement to the effect that this recording is solely for use for blind and physically disabled individuals should be read on the tape along with the name of the person preparing the recording.

2. *Printed Resources.* Some people who are blind or have low vision and who were trained to use Braille may prefer Braille as the method of choice for communication in order to read along with others during the worship service. Currently Bibles and a few hymnals are available in Braille. These publications usually consist of several volumes. It is most expedient to inform those using Braille about materials needed for the worship service in advance. This makes it possible for users of Braille to be unencumbered with access materials. Contracts with companies and persons who specialize in Braille can be used to ensure that worship materials such as bulletins, Bible studies, Christian education materials, newsletters and other publications that are used in the parish are also fully accessible.

3. *Large Print.* Developing materials in large print can be done using a photocopier machine. Type that is considered to be large print generally involves a point size of 16 or larger. This means that if a church publication normally uses 10-point size, it should be enlarged 160% on a photocopier. Another method for creating large print is to change the font size on a computer. Increasing the font to 16 or 18 point often allows a large-print reader to see the text. While there are Bibles and hymnals that are published in larger font sizes, often increase in print size is still required for visual access.

4. *Computers.* Computer technology has increased access to the printed word for persons who are blind and visually impaired. Both hardware and software packages for personal computers provide access to most publications that are available on disks. Braille computers and printers make it possible for the printed word to be transformed into Braille text. Speech synthesizers provide voice technology that reads print. Image enlarger systems increase the size of printed text that is presented on the computer screen. Any documents that can be placed on disks can be shared with those having access to these technologies.

5. *Visuals.* When worship includes visual activities and movement within the service, it is important to inform persons who are blind and partially sighted about what will occur. This is essential for understanding and sharing in these activities. If lighting is to be decreased with candle lighting or dimming the lights, it is imperative that persons know where exits are available for their safety. Verbal cues can increase understanding of visual activities within the worship service.

Among the most important forms of support is the ability to work towards full inclusion. When this becomes a high priority, access will follow.

See also **Disabilities, Worship and Persons with.**

KATHY N. REEVES

Bohemian Liturgy

Beginning in the third quarter of the fourteenth century, and continuing for almost three centuries, Bohemia witnessed a most remarkable sacramental and liturgical movement. Born in the 'Jerusalem' community of the reform-minded priest Jan Milíč, clergy, laity (both single and married) and a number of former prostitutes gathered for daily celebrations of the *eucharist at which there was vernacular *preaching and *communion was distributed to all who desired it. In an eschatologically charged society, this initiative kindled a renewed enthusiasm for the place of frequent communion in the lives of the laity as well as the role of communion in social transformation. By the end of the fourteenth century, the movement had won substantial theological support, most importantly from Matthias (Matěj) of Janov, the approbation of the Archbishop of Prague (Jan Jenštejn) and had become popularized throughout the Kingdom of Bohemia through the vernacular writings of the layman Tomáš Štítný of Štítné.

By the early years of the fifteenth century, frequent (at least weekly, best daily) communion was a widespread practice in Bohemia. Largely inspired by the extensive collections of texts (biblical, patristic, scholastic and canonical) favouring this practice, some theologians (notably Jakoubek of Stříbro and Nicholas of Dresden) began promoting the restoration of the lay *chalice, a practice instituted in Prague in 1414 while Jan Hus was in prison in Constance awaiting trial before the Council. Hus's death at the stake on 6 July 1415 served as the catalyst which popularly entrenched the lay chalice and made it the symbol of Bohemian resistance to the Roman authorities. (It is from their practice of communion under both species, *sub utraque specie*, that the reform movement came to be known as Utraquism and its members Utraquists – Hussite was a term used only by the movement's enemies.) Two years later, in 1417, using the same dossier of texts used to support frequent communion, supplemented by texts supporting the chalice, Jakoubek and others extended communicant status to all the baptized, including *infants. For over 200 years, the regular reception of communion by all the baptized, regardless of age, remained a fundamental premise of Utraquism.

When the Hussite Revolution broke out in 1419, more extreme groups within Utraquism began making more radical demands for liturgical reform. Groups centred in southern Bohemia, who came to be known as Taborites, abandoned the Roman rite and returned to what they believed to be a 'biblical' simplicity, abandoning liturgical practices for which they could find no scriptural justification. After the defeat of the Taborites at the Battle of Lipany in 1434, these radical initiatives were forced under-

ground but surfaced later in the century in the small reforming group that called itself the *Jednota Bratrská* (Unity of Brethren, *Unitas Fratrum*). This latter group developed a rite of *confirmation for adolescents that, through Erasmus, became the model for the reformed confirmation practices of the sixteenth-century Reformers.

More widely significant were initiatives undertaken in translating the whole Roman liturgy (eucharist, office and ritual) into Czech. The *Jistebnice Kancional* is an important witness to this initiative dating from around 1420, but at present scholars are not able to say how widespread this practice became before the second decade of the sixteenth century. (The Bible had existed in Czech translations since the fourteenth century and from at least the 1380s there had been some experiments reading the lections in Czech. From its inception in the same period, a large corpus of vernacular hymnody played an important role in Utraquist worship.)

The defeat of the Bohemian Estates at the Battle of the White Mountain (Bilá Hora) in 1620 saw at first the gradual, then absolute, imposition of the Counter-Reformation in the Bohemian Lands. Initially there was some accommodation to Utraquist liturgical practice (frequent communion *sub utraque specie* and vernacular lections), but soon absolute conformity to the norms of the post-Tridentine liturgical books was demanded and all religious practice other than Roman Catholicism and Judaism became a capital offence.

David R. Holeton, 'The Evolution of Utraquist Liturgy: A Precursor of Western Liturgical Reform', *Studia Liturgica* XXV, 1995, 51–67; 'The Bohemian Eucharistic Movement in its European Context', *The Bohemian Reformation and Religious Practice* I, 1996, 23–47; 'The Evolution of Utraquist Eucharistic Liturgy: A Textual Study', *The Bohemian Reformation and Religious Practice* II, 1998, 97–126; 'The Fifteenth Century Bohemian Origins of the Reformation Understanding of Confirmation', *With Ever Joyful Hearts: Essays on Liturgy and Music in Honor of Marion J. Hatchett*, ed. J. Neil Alexander, New York 1999, 82–102.

DAVID R. HOLETON

Books, Liturgical

Many ecclesiastical traditions have written or

printed texts containing the directions for the conduct of worship and the words of prayers and other formulae to be said. Even those which do not require such books to be used often have printed guidelines and suggested forms to be followed.

1. Early Christianity; 2. Eastern Churches; 3. Medieval and Roman Catholic; 4. Anglican; 5. Baptist; 6. Christian Church; 7. Congregationalist; 8. Lutheran; 9. Methodist; 10. Old Catholic; 11. Pentecostal; 12. Reformed.

1. *Early Christianity*. The earliest Christians did not possess any liturgical books as such. Like their Jewish predecessors, they preferred not to write down the prayers that they used but *extemporize afresh on each occasion, usually on the basis of a conventional outline or pattern. The oldest literary sources to include apparent liturgical texts are so-called apostolic church orders: the *Didache* or 'Teaching of the Twelve Apostles', probably dating from the end of the first century or the beginning of the second; the anonymous document usually known as the *Apostolic Tradition* and questionably attributed to Hippolytus of Rome in the early third century; and the fourth-century *Canons of Hippolytus*, *Apostolic Constitutions* and *Testamentum Domini*. However, these works are not the official manuals of any local church, but rather collections of material deriving from various sources, and perhaps various places and times, and generally showing the idiosyncratic hands of their compilers. They cannot, therefore, be safely used without other corroboration as firm evidence for the actual liturgical practices of any particular Christian group. Other fourth-century sources, however, do begin to quote extracts from liturgical texts, suggesting that by this time certain key prayers – especially the *eucharistic prayers – were being written down, and in North Africa at least ecclesiastical legislation began to require texts to receive official approval before they were used. The oldest complete collection of prayers that has survived is the *Sacramentary of Sarapion*, from Egypt and probably compiled around 350. Also from Egypt is a fragmentary text of a eucharistic prayer, Strasbourg papyrus 254, which appears to date from the fourth or fifth century, although the prayer itself may be older. All other extant liturgical texts, however, are of a later date. Nevertheless, it is often possible to distinguish earlier from later strata in them, and see where parts have been copied from one prayer to another, and so to attempt to reconstruct more ancient forms of the text.

Allan Bouley, *From Freedom to Formula: The Evolution of the Eucharistic Prayer from Oral Improvisation to Written Texts*, Washington, DC 1981; Paul F. Bradshaw, *The Search for the Origins of Christian Worship*, 2nd edn, London/New York 2002; Paul F. Bradshaw, Maxwell E. Johnson and L. Edward Phillips, *The Apostolic Tradition: A Commentary*, Minneapolis 2002; John R. K. Fenwick, *Fourth Century Anaphoral Construction Techniques*, Nottingham 1986; Maxwell E. Johnson, *The Prayers of Sarapion of Thmuis: A Literary, Liturgical, and Theological Analysis*, Rome 1995.

EDITOR

2. *Eastern Churches*. The official liturgical books of the various Eastern churches, whether *Orthodox or Catholic, are generally marked by a 'medieval' trait (indicative of the period when they were codified): they tend to be discrete – and sometimes large – tomes intended for use by a limited number of ministers (clergy and singers). Especially in the West, the need for diglot, or simply vernacular, anthologies, coupled with the desire to put (abridged) texts into the hands of the congregation, has spurred the proliferation of publications whose quantity prevents their being analysed here, even though in the West they often become de facto *the* liturgical books of a given church. Alongside this tendency, however, one also notes a more recent, though not yet widespread, movement to publish Western-language translations of the official ('medieval') service books in their entirety, though the average parish in the West will never use much of the material found therein.

The list below adheres to the following order: *lectionaries and compilations of biblical material; commentaries on the latter; books for the *eucharist and for other *sacraments and rites; books for *daily prayer and the *propers for that; and finally, 'directories'. These divisions can be fluid as some propers for daily prayer are sometimes also sung at the eucharist. Until Vatican II, many of the Eastern Catholic ('Uniate') Churches published books intended to facilitate private recitation, thus collating materials from different books to create Eastern 'missals' or 'breviaries'.

2.1. *Armenian.
(a) *Jashots* ('the book of the meal'), a lec-

tionary and ordo containing the *readings for the eucharist and for daily prayer, and some parts sung by the clergy and *servers.

(b) *Badarakamaduyts* ('the book of the sacrifice') contains the presbyteral prayers and abbreviated diaconal parts for the Liturgy attributed to St Athanasius, the usual formulary used today. Some editions include *ordination rites.

(c) *Mashdots* (named after the ninth-century catholicos, Mashdots Eghivardetsi) contains the sacraments; *funerals and related rites, hymns and prayers; the blessing of homes for *Epiphany and *Easter; and other lesser blessings.

(d) *Mayr Mashdots* ('mother mashdots'), an amplified version of the above with rites conducted by the *bishop, e.g. ordinations.

(e) *Zhamakirk* ('book of hours') also called *Zhamagarkutyun* ('order of the hours') contains the *ordinary (psalms and prayers) of the daily hours of prayer.

(f) *Sharagnots* (possibly from 'series', also called *Sharagan*) contains the *canticles and hymns for the daily hours of prayer.

(g) *Haysmavurk* ('this very day'), a martyrology containing abridged lives of the saints along with homilies read before vespers on major feasts.

(h) *Donatsuyts* ('indicator of feasts'), a calendar and detailed directory (analogous to the Byzantine typicon) with extensive prescriptions for the various cases of concurrence along with information regarding the appointed hymns, readings and psalms.

2.2. *Byzantine*. The use of anthologies (*Synekdemos* in Greek, *Sbornik* or *Izbornyk* in Slavonic) began earlier in some churches of the Byzantine tradition than among most other Eastern Christians. Thus these have acquired quasi-official status, though – along with countless more popular compilations – they comprise selections from the following official books (listed here in Greek, and also in Slavonic owing to the latter tradition's prominence).

(a) The *Evangelion* (Slavonic *Yevangelie*) contains the four Gospels with the text printed either continuously (the pericopes being noted in the margins and footnotes) or as extracts arranged for liturgical use.

(b) The *Apostolos* (Slavonic *Apostol*) contains the readings from the Acts of the Apostles and the Epistles, together with the *prokeimena* (responsorials) and their verses sung before the epistle at the eucharist, and the verses

farcing the *alleluia sung after it. Like the *evangelion*, it can be structured in two different ways. The OT readings (used predominantly at vespers) are normally included in the *Triodion*, *Pentekostarion* or *Menaion* (see below), though some traditions also have a separate book (Slavonic *Paremiinik*).

(c) The *Psalterion* (Slavonic *Psaltir*) contains the Psalms divided into twenty sections (*kathismata*) together with nine canticles from the OT and NT for *orthros* (morning prayer). It is rarely used in parishes because psalms of the ordinary are printed in the other books and the monastic psalmody called for by the tradition is usually omitted.

(d) The *Euchologion to mega* ('the great book of prayers') normally contains the following, distributed slightly differently and with different titles in the Slavic tradition (see below): (i) the ordinary of vespers, *orthros*, the eucharistic liturgies of Chrysostom and Basil, and the liturgy of the *presanctified, the priest's part being given in full, and those of *deacon, *lector and singers sometimes in abbreviated form; (ii) the remaining sacramental rites; (iii) other occasional services. Among the Slavs, the *Velikii Trebnik* ('the great book of prayers', usually mistakenly rendered as 'the great book of needs') contains the material found in the Great Euchologion, except for the ordinary of daily hours of prayer and the eucharist.

(e) The *Mikron Euchologion* or *Agiasmatarion* ('book of sanctifications', Slavonic *Malyi Trebnik*) omits the whole group of services listed under (i) above and those rites proper to the bishop, such as ordination and the *consecration of a church; it contains the remaining sacraments, funeral rites, and the most commonly required blessings. Some Greek editions add the priest's part of the major daily offices and the eucharist.

(f) The *Liturgikon* ('book of the liturgy') or *Hieratikon* ('book for the priest') or *Hierotelestikon* ('for the accomplishment of the sacred'; Slavonic *Sluzhebnik*, 'book of the service') contains the priest's – and in all Slavonic, though not all Greek editions the deacon's – part at vespers, *orthros* and the eucharist, together with related supplementary matter.

(g) The *Archieratikon* ('book for the hierarch', Slavonic *Chinovnik*, 'book of order', or *Sviatitel'skii Sluzhebnik*, 'the ordainer's service book') contains services and blessings either reserved to, or most commonly performed by, the bishop.

(h) The *Horologion* ('book of the hours', Slavonic *Chasoslov*) contains the ordinary and a very limited number of propers for the eight daily offices (the midnight service, *orthros*, the lesser hours – prime, terce, sext, none – vespers and compline); among the Greeks it is intended primarily for the readers and singers while among the Slavs all of the clergy's parts are also usually included. A fuller version, *Horologion to mega* (Slavonic, *Velikii Chasoslov*) adds short offices between the lesser hours, and brief accounts of the feast or life of the saint in the calendar section. All the lesser hours can be recited in full from the *Horologion*, which is why they usually include the two proper anthems of the day. However, other books are required for vespers and *orthros* (and frequently for compline), books containing the propers that change from day to day. These volumes (described next) contain the material of the three cycles of the Byzantine liturgical *year, the weekly cycle, the annual cycle of moveable feasts, and the annual cycle of fixed feasts.

(i) The *Oktoechos* ('book of the eight tones', Slavonic *Oktoikh*), also known as the *Parakletike* ('book of supplication') contains the variable parts of the daily offices for all seven days of the week divided into eight sections for each of the Byzantine chant tones. The eight tones are used in sequence throughout the year, beginning with the first tone at Easter. An edition of the *Oktoechos* for Sundays only also exists.

(j) The *Triodion* ('book of the three odes', Slavonic *Triod'*, so called from the fact that for most days it provides only three proper odes for *orthros*) contains the propers for *Lent.

(k) The *Pentekostarion* ('book of the fifty days', Slavonic *Triod' Tsvetnaia*) contains the services proper to the Easter season and *Pentecost.

(l) The *Menaia* ('books of the months', Slavonic *Minia*) contain the propers for fixed feasts throughout the year. Most full editions are divided into twelve volumes. The Festal Menaion is a popular version of these same propers for the more solemn fixed feasts, and the General Menaion provides generic propers for different categories of saints which are used when the twelve-volume version is unavailable.

(m) The *Eirmologion* ('book of the *eirmoi*') contains the texts and sometimes music for the anthems (*eirmoi*) sung at the beginning of each of the odes at *orthros*.

(n) The *Bohohlasnyk* ('of divine sound') contains chorales (usually banned from use in Orthodox Churches), published in this and similar books among Slavic Byzantine Catholics since at least 1790.

(o) The *Synaxarion* ('book of assembly') or *Menologion* ('book of remembrance') is analogous to the Western martyrology.

(p) The *Typikon* ('book of ordinances', Slavonic *Ustav*) is a general (not annually issued) directory (ordo) with prescriptions for the celebration of services throughout the year. Many churches, however, do issue an annual directory which simply applies the general prescriptions.

2.3. *Coptic*. Owing in part to the strong monastic current in Coptic Christianity, even smaller parishes will usually own all the books listed below, and will attempt to make the more important of them available to the congregation. The structure of many of the services and books is such that a frequent turning from one volume to another (as is required in some other Eastern traditions) is less pronounced. Thus, only the need for diglot texts with the vernacular has driven the publication of divers booklets based on the following official sources:

(a) *Katameros* (from the Greek for 'divided into parts'), a lectionary including readings from Paul, the Pastoral Epistles, Acts, Psalms and the Gospels divided into four sections – Sundays and feasts, weekdays, Lent, and Easter-Pentecost.

(b) *Al-Tafasir* ('expanded explanation'), an Arabic translation of the readings for the eucharist, with commentaries on these.

(c) *Al-Mawa'iza* ('sermon'), an anthology of patristic homiletic texts sometimes included in (b) above.

(d) *Synaxarion*, a martyrology with entries of varying length for every day of the year read at the eucharist after Acts to show the continuity of salvation history.

(e) *Kholagi* ('holy liturgy'), a book of prayers for the eucharist, including the three *eucharistic prayers in use (Basil, Gregory and Cyril) along with the ordinary of the evening and morning offices for the presider.

(f) *Khedmet al-shammas* ('service book for the deacon'), an expanded version of the above for the deacons and congregation.

(g) *Alhan al-Tawzee* ('hymns for communion'), either individual or collated booklets with festal communion chants sung also at the evening and morning offices as well as at non-liturgical gatherings. New compositions are constantly being added with the result that today the book sometimes appears in a binder format.

(h) *Al-Khadmat* ('service book'), a sacramentary including various blessings.

(i) *Office of Laqqan* ('basin'), book for blessing of water on Epiphany, *Maundy Thursday and feast of Peter and Paul.

(j) *Agpia* ('prayers of the hours'), ordinary parts for the seven hours of the daily office.

(k) *Al-Epsalmodia al Sanawia* ('annual psalmody'), the book for midnight praises with prayers for every day of the year.

(l) *Al-Tamagid* ('praises'), interpretive hymns and narrative doxologies for saints' feasts.

(m) *Al-Mayamir* ('extracts from the life'), a series of homilies for the evening and morning offices describing the feast being celebrated.

(n) *Difnar*, a menologion with brief notes about the saint being celebrated and hymns for the saints' feasts; used at the evening office.

(o) *Al-Sirah* ('biography'), lives of the saints read sometimes, though rarely, after the *Al-Mayamir* and sometimes included as part of (l) above. More frequently it is used for devotional reading.

(p) *Al-Pascha*, the prayers and readings for *Holy Week.

(q) *Al-Sagda* ('prostration'), prayers of kneeling for the service after the eucharist on the feast of Pentecost.

(r) *Al-Dawrah* ('procession'), the texts for the processions on the feasts of the Holy Cross (at vespers) and *Palm Sunday (at matins).

(s) *Al-Epsalmodia al-Kiahk*, propers for vespers and the midnight office for the month of Kiahk (before Christmas) dedicated to the Mother of God.

2.4. *East Syrian

(a) *Iwangaliyun* (from the Greek for 'gospel', though the text is the Peshita) contains the extracted pericopes arranged for liturgical use.

(b) *Qiryana* ('reading'), a lectionary containing either all of the readings for the eucharist including the gospel, or only those from the OT, Acts and the epistles.

(c) *Shlikha* ('apostle'), the epistle book when bound separately.

(d) *Davidha* (from 'David'), a psalter divided into twenty-one sections (*hulali*, from 'Alleluia') with interpolated verses and prayers throughout. The last *hulala* contains the canticles of Moses and Isaiah. *Litanies are sometimes appended.

(e) *Turgama* ('interpretation'), a book of explanatory hymns sung before the NT readings on Sundays and feasts.

(f) *Warda* (from the apparent twelfth/ thirteenth-century author George Warda) contains hymns describing the feasts, sung after the gospel and during communion.

(g) *Taksa d'Qudaša* (from the Greek for 'order') contains the eucharistic liturgies (sometimes with all three eucharistic prayers of the East Syrian tradition: Addai and Mari, Theodore, and Nestorius); the offices of preparation of the elements and – in varying combinations – *baptism and other sacraments; consecration of churches with and without oil; other lesser blessings; and the ordinary presbyteral prayers for the daily prayer services, especially *ramsha* (vespers), *lilia* (the midnight office) and *sapra* (the morning office).

(h) *Abukhalim(a)* (from the name of its twelfth-century compiler, patriarch Elias III Abu-Khalim) contains presbyteral prayers and sometimes occasional offices, e.g. for the preparation of the elements.

(i) *Khudra* ('cycle'), a large volume containing the parts of the eucharist and daily offices proper to Sundays, feasts of the Lord, and major saints' days. The readings are usually only indicated with incipits.

(j) *Shamashutha* ('diaconal') contains the deacon's parts of the eucharist.

(k) *Burakha* ('blessing'), the *marriage service book.

(l) *Siamidha* ('laying-on of hands') contains ordination rites.

(m) *Anidha* ('the dead') contains funeral rites for men, women and children.

(n) *Kurasta* (apparently derived from a word for clergy) contains funeral rites for the ordained.

(o) *Gaza* or *Geza* ('treasury'), a large volume containing the hymns and anthems proper to feasts, excluding Sundays.

(p) *Qdhamuwathar*, more fully *Kthawa daqdham wadhwathar it* ('book of before and after') contains anthems and other hymnography for ordinary weekdays and feasts that do not vary with the season; thus named because the weeks are designated 'before' or 'after' depending on whether the first or second choir begins the service.

(q) *Kashkul* ('containing all'), a large book with the evening anthems and the sessional chants at the night service for ordinary weekdays in the different seasons, or weekday propers in general.

2.5. *Ethiopian

(a) *Mäsehafä Gessawe*, containing the biblical readings for the eucharist.

(b) *Senkessar*, a *synaxarion* or martyrology, read during the eucharist or daily services.

(c) *Ta 'amrä Maryam*, the 'miracles of Mary', read during the eucharist or daily services.

(d) *Haymanotä Abäw*, the 'faith of the fathers', read during the eucharist or daily services.

(e) *Mäsehafä Qeddase*, containing the eucharistic rite and numerous eucharistic prayers.

(f) *Zemmare*, a collection of hymns now mostly used in the eucharistic liturgy.

(g) *Mäsehafä Krestenna*, containing the baptismal ritual.

(h) *Mäsehafä Täklil*, containing the marriage ritual.

(i) *Mäsehafä Nessheha*, containing the rites of *penance.

(j) *Mäsehafä Qändil*, containing the rite for the unction of the *sick.

(k) *Mäsehafä Genzät*, containing the funeral rite.

(l) *Mäwase't*, forms of antiphonal chants, nowadays used mainly in the funeral rite.

(m) *Mäsehafä Simät*, 'book of nomination', i.e., the ordination rites.

(n) *Mäsehafä Sä'atat zä-Gebs*, the Coptic *horologion* or daily prayer book reflecting a strictly monastic tradition.

(o) *Mäsehafä Sä'atat zä-Giyorgis*, the *horologion* of Giyorgis, a more popular version of the daily prayer tradition.

(p) *Mäsehafä Deggwa*, containing hymns for the daily services.

(q) *Mäsehafä Meœ'af*, the ordinary, containing the Psalter and presbyteral prayers for the daily services.

(r) *Gebrä Hemamat*, containing the Holy Week liturgies.

(s) *Ser'atä Menkwesenna*, the rituals for the investiture of a monk.

2.6. *West Syrian. In North America, one of the churches of the West Syrian tradition, the Maronite, has been publishing popular and at the same time semi-official vernacular anthologies since Vatican II. These are compiled from the following official books.

(a) *Eywanghelion* (from the Greek for 'gospel', though the text is the Peshita) provides extracted pericopes for the eucharist, vespers and matins for the whole year beginning (among the Orthodox) with the Feast of the Renewal of the Church (October). Earlier editions sometimes included patristic homilies after the pericope.

(b) *Kthobo d'Quryono* ('book of readings') combines readings from the OT with those from Acts, Paul and the Pastoral Epistles following the same system as the gospel book. Today the Syrian Orthodox usually proclaim only three readings (from Acts, the Epistles and Gospels), while previously there were six (still the case in Lent).

(c) *Khtobo d'Qurobo* ('book of the oblation') or *d'anafuras* contains the presbyteral prayers for the eucharist and any number of eucharistic prayers (from a repertory of almost eighty). Today approximately ten are regularly used among both the Syrian Orthodox and the Maronites, the choice being made by the priest, except on the most solemn feasts when the anaphora of James is always used.

(d) *Kthobo d'Teshmeshto* or *Tekhmet* ('book of the service') contains the deacon's parts and congregation's responses. Among the Maronites it was supplemented extensively during the eighteenth century with chants and prayers for lesser commemorations.

(e) *Kthobo d'Mamoditho* ('book of the immersion') for baptism-chrismation.

(f) *Kthobo d'Borokh Klilo* ('book of the blessing of the crowning') contains the three marriage rites (for those marrying the first, second or third time).

(g) *Kthobo d'Oufoyo* ('book of burial').

(h) *Shehimo* ('simple') contains the ordinary and propers for the seven daily hours of prayer on ordinary weekdays (which excludes Lent).

(i) *Penqitho* or *Fenqitho* ('treasure chest') contains the propers sung at the daily hours of prayer throughout the year and published in varying numbers of volumes, e.g. one for Saturday vespers, Sunday matins and terce; a second for Lent, etc.

(j) *Hasho*, usually published as a separate volume among the Maronites, contains the rites of Holy Week.

For all the traditions above except the Byzantine, the following contain bibliographies and further details: Julius Assfalg and Paul Krüger, *Kleines Wörterbuch des Christlichen Orients*, Wiesbaden 1975; Micheline Albert et al., *Christianismes orientaux: Introduction à l'étude des langues et des littératures*, Paris 1993. For the Byzantine tradition: Alexander P. Kazhdan (ed.), *The Oxford*

Dictionary of Byzantium, New York 1991; Elena Velkova Velkovska, 'Byzantine Liturgical Books', *Handbook for Liturgical Studies*, ed. Anscar J. Chupungco, I, Collegeville 1997, 225–40. For additional material on the Coptic tradition: Aziz S. Atiya (ed.), *The Coptic Encyclopedia*, New York 1991; for the East Syrian: C. Mousses, *Les livres liturgiques de l'Eglise Chaldéenne*, Beirut 1955.

PETER GALADZA

3.1. *Medieval*. The Middle Ages knew no liturgical uniformity, despite any attempts to impose it from the time of Charlemagne and after. Consequently the classification of liturgical books is difficult in the period between the sixth and thirteenth centuries, since each book was custom-made by a local *scriptorium* and met the needs of a local church. Yet, in spite of this difficulty in categorizing the great number of liturgical books that easily surpass a hundred kinds, one can distinguish between two general types: books for the *eucharist and books for the divine office (*see* **Daily Prayer** 3).

3.1.1. *The Eucharist*
(a) The sacramentary was the book that from the early Middle Ages supplied *bishops and *presbyters with the prayers they needed for the eucharist and other liturgical occasions. It contains all the orations and the canon of the mass (today called the *eucharistic prayer) needed by the presider for every day of the liturgical *year. While the orations vary according to the feast and season (the formularies of the temporal and sanctoral cycles, as well as *votive masses), the canon of the mass was unchangeable. The sacramentaries often have a calendar, an *ordo missae*, and the sacramental rites, such as *baptism, *funerals and public *penance.

The forerunner of the sacramentary was a small and incomplete collection of prayer texts in the form of independent booklets (*libelli missarum*) of liturgical formularies dating to the late fifth century. Known as the Leonine Sacramentary because it was thought that Pope Leo (440–61) was the author, it also goes under the name of the Verona Sacramentary because it is preserved in the Verona library. It is missing the masses from January to April.

The two main types of sacramentary are the Gelasian and the Gregorian named after Popes Gelasius I (492–6) and Gregory the Great (590–604). The Gelasian Sacramentary or Old Gelasian (as distinguished from a later group of Frankish Gelasians of the second half of the

eighth century) contains texts for the entire year beginning with the vigil of *Christmas and with the sanctoral cycle separate from the temporal cycle. This book represents the liturgy of a presbyteral church of seventh-century Rome. Because the surviving text is a Frankish copy, it reflects Frankish additions. The Gregorian Sacramentary is known from a copy sent by Pope Hadrian I to Charlemagne to be used as a template for liturgical reform. This edition is known also as the Hadrianum and reflects papal liturgical use around 630. It is deficient in prayers needed by priests outside of Rome, so a supplement of prayers was necessarily provided by Benedict of Aniane in addition to other elements derived from the Gelasian type. A second type of Gregorian Sacramentary is found in Padua, which is a papal sacramentary modified for presbyteral use. A characteristic of the Gregorian-type sacramentaries is that the temporal and sanctoral cycles are combined. The Gelasian and Gregorian sacramentaries represent the two main types of sacramentaries that are found in pure or mixed form in all other sacramentaries.

(b) The ritual *ordines romani*. The sacramentaries contain sparse directions for the implementation of the liturgy. As the liturgy became gradually more complex, separate documents, called *ordines*, were produced outside of Rome, mostly in Frankish territories. The *ordines* would have been used in conjunction with the sacramentaries and other sacramental rituals, providing more detailed instructions for liturgical celebrations.

(c) The *Liber pontificalis*. The Pontifical is a liturgical book containing rites for exclusive use of the bishop, for example the rite of *ordination, blessing of oils, and the *consecration of churches. Developed along similar lines to the *ordines*, the *Liber pontificalis* evolved from the ninth to the fifteenth centuries and reflects the gradual complexity of episcopal rituals.

(d) The *lectionary contains the *readings for the mass. The earliest form of lectionary, called a *comes, liber comitis* or *comicus*, was simply a list of the scriptural citations or the incipits (opening words) and explicits (closing words) of the scriptural passages. When the gospel readings are separated out from the other readings in a distinct book, it is called an *evangeliorum*.

(e) The missal is the fusion of all or most of the liturgical books of the mass combined into one volume for the use of the priest. This book developed gradually from the tenth century to the middle of the thirteenth century but with no standard format. The missal represents the general clericalizing of the mass, since the priest assumed all the roles that had previously been assigned to other liturgical ministers. After the Council of Trent (1540–65) the *Missale Romanum* was standardized, now made possible because of the printing press.

(f) The books of *chant. Chant manuscripts of various kinds proliferated for both the mass and the divine office. The books for the mass contained musical settings for both the *propers and *ordinary parts. The *antiphonale* made its appearance in the eighth century and contained *antiphons for both the mass and the office. When the antiphons were progressively sorted according to the two uses, those used for the mass (*antiphonale missarum*) were incorporated into a book sometimes called the *graduale*. Over time other books evolved, called *troparia*, *sequentiaria* and *cantatorium*, and they witness to the subsequent development of new musical forms for the liturgy.

3.1.2. *The Divine Office*

(a) The Psalter, the oldest book of the office, contains the one hundred and fifty Psalms, sometimes along with biblical *canticles used in the office.

(b) The homilary or sermonary contains patristic homilies to be read at various times of the day in addition to praying the office.

(c) The breviary is to the office as the missal is to the mass. All the distinct books are united into one.

(d) Musical books. As mentioned above under chants of the mass, the office also incorporated chant settings of the antiphons in a separate book called the antiphonal. A second musical book called the hymnal contained *hymns, non-biblical sung texts, which in many instances were translations from Greek.

3.2. *Roman Catholic.* The Roman liturgy today is dependent upon four major reform movements: those of Pope Gregory VII (1073–85); Pope Innocent III (1198–1216); the Council of Trent (1545–63); and the Second Vatican Council (1962–65). The Constitution on the Sacred Liturgy (*Sacrosanctum concilium*) of the Second Vatican Council (1963) mandated the complete revision of all Roman liturgical books. By 1973 the Latin edition (*editio typica*) of major books was introduced. These books can be grouped in four major divisions: missal, rituals, pontifical and office. The revised liturgical books appeared in the following chronological order: (a) missal: Order of Mass and Lectionary, 1960, Sacramentary, 1970; (b) rituals: Baptism of Children, 1969, Marriage, 1969, Funerals, 1969 revised 1985, Religious Profession, 1970, Adult Initiation, 1971, Pastoral Care of the Sick, 1972, Eucharistic Adoration, 1973, Penance, 1973, Blessings, 1984; (c) pontifical: Ordinations, 1968, Consecration of Virgins and Abbatial Blessings, 1970, Blessing of Oils, 1970, Confirmation, 1971, Institution of Readers and Acolytes, 1972, Church Dedication, 1972; (d) office: Liturgy of the Hours, 1971.

———

Eric Palazzo, *A History of Liturgical Books from the Beginning to the Thirteenth Century*, Collegeville 1998; Cyrille Vogel, revised by William Storey and Niels Rasmussen, *Medieval Liturgy: An Introduction to the Sources*, Washington, DC 1986.

MICHAEL S. DRISCOLL

4. *Anglican.* The Reformation was rooted in the spread of printing, and in England the provision of liturgical books not only exhibited the progress of the Reformation but actually effected it. The vernacular Bible (which in England dated from 1537) had a foundational role in this, being itself both the instrument of reform and the indispensable accompaniment of the reformed liturgical services.

Four liturgy-related books overlapped with the latter stages of the Latin service books: The *Litany* (1544) and *The King's Primer* (1545), both in Henry VIII's reign, and *The Book of Homilies* (1547) and *The Order of the Communion* (1548), both in Edward VI's reign. But the first book to provide a complete and distinct range of services in English was the 1549 *BCP*, and its authorization extinguished the use of the Latin services. It superseded the breviary, the missal, the processional and the manual, and its Preface claimed 'the curates shall need none other books . . . but this book and the Bible'. This very phrase indicated an often forgotten feature of the Prayer Book, that it was in fact supplied and purchased (at a cost somewhere near to a farm-labourer's wages for a week) simply for the minister. There was no expectation that lay worshippers would be holding a book in their own hands, not least because of widespread illiteracy; and where any part of the rites was to be said by the people, then they would repeat it after the minister. The 1549 book was followed by a 1550 Ordinal, which replaced the *ordination rites in the old pontifical.

In 1552 a second *BCP* was authorized, with a revision of the 1550 Ordinal also bound into it. The general character of the book was unchanged, but there were structural and verbal changes in several rites to make them more fully reformed. This book was banned when Mary succeeded to the throne, but was revived (with minute alterations) in 1559 under Elizabeth I, and was central to the Elizabethan Settlement. It provoked the criticism of the Puritans who thought it insufficiently reformed; and, when James I inherited the throne, they picketed him for further changes, and he in response convened the Hampton Court Conference in 1604. He made a few liturgical concessions, hardly touching their central points, though he did commission a new translation of the Bible, which in the next fifty years virtually drove out all other English versions and was categorized as the 'Authorized' Version (alias the 'King James Bible').

Under Charles I a separate Prayer Book, partly reverting to 1549, was prepared for Scotland in 1637. It provoked total confrontation with the Puritan Scots, never passed into use, and helped to bring about the Civil War. The ascendancy of Parliament through the war led in 1645 to the banning of the 1604 book in England, and the authorization of the *Directory of Public Worship* (also known as the 'Westminster Directory'). However, on the 'Restoration' of Charles II in 1660, steps were taken towards reviving the 1604 book and, after a very unsatisfactory 'Savoy Conference' in 1661 between bishops and Puritans, Convocation revised the 1604 text and submitted it with minute changes to Parliament, for its enforcement from 24 August 1662 by the Act of Uniformity. The Act required a Welsh translation, and a French one was also quickly provided.

The 1662 book, usually published with the Ordinal, the Psalter and the Thirty-Nine Articles all bound together, has been the generally accepted liturgical core of worldwide Anglicanism ever since it was authorized. The first separate full Prayer Book, in the USA in 1789, followed both its shape and its contents closely, though the *eucharistic rite owed part of its character to the earlier changes in Scotland (not then incorporated into a full book) dating from 1764. Small changes were found elsewhere from that time onwards; and, as Anglican missions and chaplaincies were established all over the world, 1662 rites were translated into many vernaculars, and

were sometimes bound into full Prayer Books, though often remaining in smaller format. In England and elsewhere the idea of the *BCP* as belonging to the congregation and being owned by laypeople also grew, until in the nineteenth century it was thought to be basic to 'Common' Prayer that all could follow the service holding a copy each. The text of the *BCP* was very minimally revised in Ireland in 1878 (following disestablishment); and the American book was also re-touched in 1892.

In the twentieth century new Prayer Books arose, partly reflecting provincial independence, partly reflecting a gentle (or even thorough) 'catholicizing' of 1662. The exceptions to this latter point were the very little changed books of Canada in 1922 and of Ireland (now post-partition) in 1926. More 'catholic' books were found in Scotland in 1912, in the USA in 1928, and, proposed but rejected by Parliament, in England in 1927–8. In South Africa, a eucharistic rite tried out from 1924 onwards became the heart of a whole provincial Prayer Book in 1954, and this was regularly used also in Central Africa. New books appeared also in Japan in 1959, in India, Pakistan, Burma and Ceylon in 1960, and in Canada (now slightly catholicized) in 1962.

From the mid-1960s onwards, there developed more and more of a 'booklet' style – single services being published cheaply in an interim form, sometimes with a view to being bound again in a full book, sometimes in an open-ended way. In English-speaking provinces the language moved from addressing God as 'thou' to 'you' in the late 1960s, which precipitated more experimentation. But the goal of a full book often remained, and even interim services were often bound together into substantial paperback publications, as in the USA (1970 and 1973), Melanesia (1973) and Southern Africa (1975). There has also been an element of Provincial identity attaching to the provision of a Provincial prayer book, and short-term experimentation has led back to more definitive publications in this form in Australia (1978), USA (1979), England (1980), Wales (1984), Ireland (1984), New Zealand (1989), Southern Africa (1989), Australia (again, 1995), England (again, 2000).

The large book has encountered growing difficulties, and the Church of England's *Common Worship* provision of 2000 illustrates it – for it is not one book, but several, and is not necessarily best understood in book form, and is even less useful to the worshipper in full book form. A great range of options in the rites makes it hard for the worshipper to follow the officiant; the habit of laypeople of owning their own book has greatly diminished; and the coming of new technology has made it easier to provide service sheets or booklets which contain only the forms which are actually going to be used. In the 'Western' world of the future the Anglican 'Book' may have to be sought on a computer disk or a website rather than on a study desk or vestry shelf; while in many developing countries the aim of having a Provincial Book may still be a goal to be achieved.

See also **Anglican Worship.**

—————

Selected texts: F. E. Brightman, *The English Rite*, 2 vols, London 1915; Bernard Wigan, *The Liturgy in English*, London 1962; Colin O. Buchanan (ed.), *Modern Anglican Liturgies 1958–1968*, London 1968; *Further Anglican Liturgies 1968–1975*, Nottingham 1975; *Latest Anglican Liturgies 1976–1984*, London 1985.

COLIN O. BUCHANAN

5. *Baptist.* Baptists generally speak of 'worship' rather than of 'liturgy' and generally expect worship to be celebrated without liturgical books. Such a view does not imply lack of form or of preparation, but rather an anticipation that, having prepared, the congregation will express its prayers (if not its praises) *extempore. It was not unknown for Baptist preachers of the seventeenth and eighteenth century to translate the scriptures in the congregation directly from the Hebrew and the Greek. The practice arose from an understanding of the inspiration of scripture in which the Holy Spirit was seen to be active contemporaneously (*ex tempore*) – even in the reading of the scriptures in worship. Such a view does not preclude rigorous, scholarly preparation. It does imply a suspicion of set forms.

Even if most ministers of the present day do not share their predecessors' linguistic skills or discipline, their congregations continue to prefer worship without books. When books are produced, they have no central authority for the shaping of either congregational worship or private devotion. The preface to the British book of Baptist worship published in 1991 as 'a guidebook for worship leaders' begins: 'Baptists have their roots deep within the Free Church tradition. Therefore the freedom of the Holy Spirit is a significant factor in their worship, and they do not have a fixed liturgy or prayer-book.' Observing these sensibilities, the

book was entitled *Patterns and Prayers for Christian Worship*. Its use is solely at the discretion of those responsible for the leading of worship. The present writer knows of no local church where the congregation holds copies for Sunday use by all the members.

The main liturgical book used by Baptists is the hymn book, supplemented increasingly by song collections either gathered in a bound form, or projected overhead on acetates, or downloaded from the World Wide Web. In former times, denominational hymn books were a very powerful form of liturgical glue for Free Church worshippers. With the explosion of hymn writing since the 1960s, it has been increasingly difficult to offer a book to meet the needs of large numbers of congregations. With the growth of ecumenical encounter following the RC Second Vatican Council, Christians have become accustomed to worshipping with one another and to learning one another's hymns and songs. Baptists have not been immune to this experience of cross-fertilization; often they have been at its heart. Baptist hymn books now are as likely to include *Kyries and Latin chants from Taizé as hymns by Watts and Wesley.

This widening engagement with Christians of other traditions, along with the collapse of rigid denominationalism in postmodernity, has meant that despite the traditional Baptist hesitancy about liturgical books, there has been a growing awareness of liturgical shape. This has manifested itself among some in their celebration of the *eucharist or Lord's supper, where written prayers may frequently be used by those presiding. It has certainly meant that the use of versicle and response or even of written prayers in *intercessions has become far more common. Indeed, contemporary Baptist hymn books include such material in their collections. Gradually, Baptists are being offered increasing access to written texts other than hymnody in their worship.

Written texts raise questions of *language – especially *inclusive language. Baptists generally are happier with inclusive language about human beings than they are with inclusive language about God. Yet even here there is no clear direction. One interesting case study is to compare how the hymn books of the *United Reformed Church (*Rejoice and Sing, 1991) and the Baptist Union of Great Britain (*Baptist Praise and Worship*, 1991) deal with Robert Bridges' hymn 'All my hope on God is founded'. *Rejoice and Sing*, employing a clear policy on inclusive language relating to humans, retains Bridges' archaisms ('Me through change and chance he guideth') but not his exclusive language ('*Human* pride and earthly glory'). *Baptist Praise and Worship* eschews archaism ('Through all change and chance *he guides me*') but keeps the exclusive language ('Pride of *man* and earthly glory').

Because Baptist congregations are not governed by central authorities but by their own church meetings, it is impossible to offer one single description of Baptist worship as it relates to liturgical books. Just as there are congregations who would never use liturgical books or written texts, others are to be found who gladly use both. What is profoundly interesting is Baptist use of scripture in worship.

The Bible is widely seen as a study text rather than as a liturgical book. In Sunday worship and at the midweek prayer meeting scripture is read as a preparation (sometimes almost as a preface) for the sermon or study address. It is rarely followed by a silence in which the scripture speaks without further comment. Even rarer is any liturgical framing of the reading of scripture, such as a gospel procession or an acclamation or response. Very few congregations sing the Psalms, unless it be occasionally in the Scottish metrical form. There are still many congregations where at a main Sunday service only one reading from scripture will be heard. More and more are using two readings, but very few use three (OT, epistle and gospel). However, by reason of the ecumenical encounter previously noted, there is a growing awareness of the customs in other Christian traditions – not least in the area of *lectionary. The *Revised Common Lectionary* has increasingly attracted notice and use. This is still not the common experience of congregations, but it is less rare than it was.

It may be that in the use of such ecumenical lectionaries Baptists will find deepening connections with those from other traditions, leading to an increased awareness of other liturgical books. It is highly unlikely that this will ever be a predominant form among us, but for some it will be a journey unimaginable to their predecessors of the Radical Reformation.

PAUL SHEPPY

6. *Christian Church.* The Christian Church (Disciples of Christ), which came into existence in the United States in the early decades of the nineteenth century, produced its first authorized liturgical book – and that for voluntary use – in 1953. This was due to the fact that local congregations were entrusted with the responsible ordering of their own worship, as well as to a reluctance to introduce anything other than the NT as authoritative in matters of faith and practice, including worship practice. The NT supplied the basis for understanding and administering the two sacraments (the *Lord's supper and *baptism) central to the church and its worship life, and in this sense itself served as the 'liturgical book' for the early Disciples' movement.

Until the mid-twentieth century it was the hymnals published by Disciples which (through widespread use rather than official prescription) provided a measure of common worship experience within the church. The tradition began notably with Alexander Campbell's early (Bethany, Virginia 1834) and widely used hymnal; prominent later on was *Hymns of the United Church* (Chicago 1924), co-edited by C. C. Morrison and Herbert L. Willett. The most widely used hymnals from the 1940s on were *Christian Worship: A Hymnal* (St Louis 1941) and *Hymnbook for Christian Worship* (St Louis/Valley Forge 1970), both published jointly by the denominational press and that of the American Baptist Convention. The last volume stressed the inclusion of modern hymns, including some from the Ecumenical Movement, while 'retiring' hymns considered overly sentimental or theologically simplistic. These hymnals also provided some music, biblical texts and prayers for use in worship. These books are now being superseded by the *Chalice Hymnal* (St Louis 1995), published by the church and introduced at its General Assembly in 1995 (see also *Chalice Hymnal: Worship Leader's Companion*, ed. Susan L. Adams, Colbert S. Cartwright, Daniel B. Merrick, St Louis 1998). This both retains material from the long Christian tradition of hymnody, and is thoroughly modern in its generous inclusion of hymns from churches around the world and from the Ecumenical Movement as well as from the African-American and Hispanic contexts, and in its sensitivity to issues of language. In keeping with Disciples' piety and tradition, the book includes probably more *communion hymns than any other currently available hymnal. A Psalter and worship materials are also included. The hymnal has been warmly received within the church.

Two worship books have been produced by the church and widely used in local congregations. *Christian Worship: A Service Book* (St Louis 1953) was largely due to G. Edwin Osborn (1897–1965). Osborn, a student of the psychology of worship, advocated a 'relevant' worship planned on themes selected by the minister. In keeping with Disciples' tradition this volume of more than 400 pages stressed scriptural materials for use in worship, and a vision of the worldwide church beyond denominational boundaries. It included a *lectionary and prayers as well as suggested orders of service for various occasions. The volume remained in print until the 1970s and was widely influential. Though not intending to offer standardized liturgical texts, it nevertheless encouraged a more positive attitude toward a degree of common practice in the church's worship life.

This worship book has recently been superseded by *Chalice Worship*, ed. Colbert S. Cartwright and O. I. Cricket Harrison (St Louis 1997). With this book the church has finally a rich collection of services and service material which both honours its own tradition and that of the wider church, and is thoroughly modern in its engagement with the *Liturgical and Ecumenical Movements (particularly the World Council of Churches' *Baptism, Eucharist and Ministry*) and in its attention to contemporary worship needs. Thus in addition to Lord's Day and *baptism services it offers such material as a service of 'recognition, commissioning or *ordination' of *elders, an *Easter vigil service, three examples of worship in ecumenical contexts (including one for use on Martin Luther King, Jr day), material for use during the Week of Prayer for Christian Unity, a prayer service for healing, and prayers 'for one who has been molested' or for those 'in a coma or unable to communicate'.

In addition to the hymnals and worship books produced by the church a wealth of worship material is being produced by individuals from within its midst. Of special importance is the publication of the first Disciples' set of lectionary-based communion and postcommunion prayers (Michael E. Dixon and Sandy Dixon, *Fed by God's Grace: Communion Prayers for Year B*, St Louis 1999 and *Fed by God's Grace: Communion Prayers for Year C*, St Louis 2000). Neither *Chalice Worship* nor the *Chalice Hymnal* establish a normative liturgy or body of hymns for the church; this would be inimical to Disciples' ecclesiology and ethos alike. Yet they reflect a significant official investment of time, energy and financial resources, and signal the commitment of the church to renew and deepen its worship life. These liturgical books, together with the worship material being produced by individuals within the church, are evidence of its new liturgical vitality.

THOMAS F. BEST

7. *Congregationalist.* Congregational worship is essentially an oral rather than a written tradition. It follows no set order of worship, nor do Congregationalists generally use a *lectionary, though most celebrate the major traditional Christian festivals. Books of services have appeared, largely in the twentieth century, but they are all offered as resources rather than replacements for the oral tradition, which itself has been fiercely guarded. The exception, of course, has been hymn books. These are quite clearly written resources for worship, and could in no way be seen as defined liturgical orders. But even the development of hymnody was greeted with suspicion in the earliest days of Congregationalism.

The imposition in England of the *BCP* in 1549 and onwards met resistance among ministers and congregations. Its rigid enforcement of uniformity and exclusion of opportunities for *extempore prayer and marginalization of *preaching were seen as the suppression of the gifts of the Holy Spirit. Resistance gained momentum until in 1645 the law requiring the use of the *BCP* was repealed, and then its use was proscribed on pain of fines or imprisonment. By 1662 the tide had turned, and the *BCP*, in revised form, was once again imposed. Nonconformist congregations, now illegal, held to the freedom of extempore prayer and a non-liturgical form of worship. Dr John Owen described worship in the 1660s and 1670s as very simple in form, including reading from the Bible, prayer, the singing of a psalm, and preaching. Only the words of scripture existed in written form. Controversy over written liturgies raged in the publication of pamphlets, Dr John Owen's *A Discourse concerning Liturgies and their Imposition* (London 1662) putting the case against the written form. Extempore prayer and preaching did not, however, imply a lack of scholarship or preparation. Prayer and preaching arose from the deep spiritual life and scholarship of the speaker. Many ministers were trained at Dissenting academies, which rivalled in discipline and learning the universities of Oxford and Cambridge, from which Dissenters were excluded.

7.1. *Written Resources*. In the mid-nine-teenth century, Congregationalism began to move towards greater form and dignity in all aspects of church life. The architecture and music of churches altered, and there was an attempt to recognize and learn from the liturgi-cal practices of other denominations. Thomas Binney's *A Chapter on Liturgies* (London 1856) not only caught the mood of the time, but presaged greater changes to come. Two small books of intercessory services were published. The first by P. T. Forsyth, *Intercessory Services* (London 1896), was offered rather tentatively as the fruit of experiment in worship, explicitly aimed at a new age: 'Whereas now the church is but the minority of the congregation, and a power so sympathetic to free prayer cannot do its mighty work because of unbelief.' The second book, *Intercession Services* by G. H. Russell (Matlock 1923), described itself with far greater confidence. It was specifically not experimental, and included services of *Baptism and Communion, Induction of Sun-day School Teachers and the Reception of Church Members. R. W. Dale was somewhat scathing of such written forms. In his *Manual of Congregational Principles* (London 1884, ed. Digby L James 1996), as in his *Nine Lectures on Preaching*, he sees the request for liturgy arising from the weakness and tempta-tions of ineffective ministers, to be resisted in favour of well-prepared extempore prayer. Written liturgy, while having its own attrac-tions and strengths, is 'out of harmony with the genius of Congregationalism' (p. 164) in which the presence of the living Christ and the indwelling of the Holy Spirit give rise to the highest order of extempore corporate worship.

The Book of Congregational Worship was published by the Congregational Union in 1920, so giving official blessing to printed litur-gies. This was followed in 1936 by the *Manual for Ministers*. In the latter, the foreword by the general secretary of the Congregational Union of England and Wales, Sidney Berry, claims the book as a rich resource for prayer, but not a set of prescribed services, for, 'it is in the blending of freedom and order that we shall find the best way for the conduct of the worship of our churches'. Here, for the first time, a service of *ordination is included, and a *lec-tionary based on the Christian *year, with a footnote about special services such as Hospital Sunday and Peace Sunday. Communion, or the Lord's supper, has become 'Holy Com-munion' and the material is far fuller and far more clearly based on liturgical traditions than in any previous collection. Later books generally followed the trend towards conform-ity of worship.

American Congregationalism embraced what it called 'liturgical renewal' to a far greater extent. The 1948 *Book of Worship for Free Churches* included an essay on sym-bolism, which recommended replacing the *communion table with an *altar, and the use of liturgical *colours. These were taken up in some American congregational churches.

7.2. *Hymn Books*. But the most widespread literary resource for Congregational worship is undoubtedly the hymn book. Isaac Watts, a Dissenting minister, was among the first to urge the use of other than scriptural words in worship through the use of hymns. His texts were at first rejected as 'mere human words', but eventually became extremely popular. His collection, *Hymns and Spiritual Songs* (1707), went through an enormous number of editions, and for a long time books of hymns for Congregational use, including *The Congrega-tional Hymn Book* of 1836, were seen as supplements to Watts' texts. The year 1887 saw the publication of a collection drawing on the new music of the Evangelical Revival, *The Congregational Church Hymnal*. This was followed in 1916 by *The Congregational Hymnary*, which attempted to meet the needs of evangelical and traditional congregations. *Congregational Praise*, begun before the Second World War but published in 1951, was a brilliant book of its time, including, in a far smaller collection, what its compilers con-sidered the best of the traditional material with some radical modern hymnody.

7.3. *The Present Day*. There is, at present, no hymn book published for, or generally used by, Congregational Churches in Britain, though churches in several countries are still using *Congregational Praise*. The Congregational Federation recently published a short resource, called *Peculiar Honours* (1998), containing 101 texts, which sought to gather hymns on the various themes of Congregational ecclesiology. Over the last thirty years, the churches of the Congregational Federation have regained some of their heritage of a radical style of oral worship, centred on preaching. The book, *Patterns for Worship* by Richard Cleaves and Michael Durber, published by the Congrega-tional Federation (Nottingham 1992), was greeted by the May Assembly at which it was introduced by a vigorous debate on oral and written forms. The book is widely used as a resource in the context of a worship style which remains free and true to its roots in an oral tradition.

See also **Congregationalist Worship**.

R. W. Dale, *History of English Congregationalism*, London 1907; R. Tudur Jones, *Congregationalism in England, 1662–1962*, London 1962; Geoffrey F. Nuttall, *Visible Saints: The Congregational Way, 1640–1660*, Oxford 1957; *Companion to Congregational Praise*, London 1953.

JANET H. WOOTTON

8. *Lutheran*. Martin Luther (1483–1546) bequeathed to Lutheranism two types of liturgy which have existed side by side or in some blended combination. The *Formula Missae et Communionis (Form of the Mass and Communion for the Church at Wittenberg*, 1523) was an evangelical 'correction' of the Latin *mass and assumed the continued use of *choirs to sing the Latin *ordinary and *propers. The *Deutsche Messe und Gottesdienst (German Mass and Order of Service*, 1526) provided vernacular versifications of the ordinary and vernacular *hymns in place of the introit and gradual set to music composed by Luther himself. This German mass 'arranged for the sake of the unlearned lay folk' would be sung by the congregation in places that lacked professional musical resources. These two styles of liturgy required two kinds of liturgical books: hymnals for the people, which proliferated from 1524 on, and *cantionales* for choirs, which began appearing in 1545. Hymnals and *cantionales*, which achieved enormous size by the middle of the sixteenth century, were published by entrepreneurs. The orders of service were regulated by official church orders (*Kirchenordnungen*) which were promulgated in each territory that implemented the Reformation. The principal Reformers were all involved as consultants in the compilation of the church orders and there was much borrowing among them. Thus, in spite of their proliferation, a standard Lutheran liturgy emerged which was based on the medieval orders of the mass, the divine office, and occasional services. The church orders, however, were not liturgical books that might be used at the *altar; they gave directions for doing the liturgy. Pre-Reformation missals and breviaries continued to be used as sources of Latin liturgical texts. Orders of service were also printed in the back pages of hymnals, thus beginning a tradition in which Lutheran worship books included a collection of hymns, liturgical orders and liturgical texts.

8.1. *Germany*. The Thirty Years' War had a disastrous affect on church life in Germany, including the destruction of pre-Reformation liturgical books. These were replaced by 'agendas' containing orders and texts of the mass, the prayer offices, and occasional services. Pietism and Rationalism in the eighteenth century contributed to the loss of the use of Latin, liturgical choir music, the celebration of Holy Communion every Sunday and festival, and daily matins and vespers. Liturgical restoration began with the Agenda prepared by King Friedrich Wilhelm III in 1822 for Lutheran and Reformed populations in the expanded Kingdom of Prussia. The Prussian return to the sixteenth-century church orders was followed in the Lutheran Churches of Bavaria, Hanover, Mecklenburg and Saxony. The formation of the United Evangelical Lutheran Church in Germany (VELKD) in 1948 led to the first common Agenda in the history of German Lutheranism (1958), although hymnals continued to be published by the territorial churches (*Landeskirchen*). *Erneuerte Agende* (Renewed Agenda, 1991) and the four volumes of the *Agende für evangelisch-lutherische Kirchen und Gemeinden* published during the 1990s culminated in *Evangelisches Gottesdienstbuch* (1999), used in both VELKD and the Evangelical Church in Germany (EKU), a union of Lutheran and Reformed Churches.

8.2. *Nordic Countries*. In the sixteenth century Denmark, Norway and Iceland were governed ecclesiastically and politically from Copenhagen. A church order for Denmark was prepared by the Wittenberg Reformer Johannes Bugenhagen in 1537. It was filled out with the Use of the Church of Our Lady in Copenhagen in 1540. A definitive Danish hymnal was compiled and published by Bishop Hans Tausen in 1544. These provisions remained in use until 1640 when a new church order was issued. The Danish liturgy has depended upon a copious use of hymns. The current Danish hymnal is the 1953 *Psalmbog*. Not until the 1963 *Ritualbog* (Ritual Book) was provision made for greater use of sung liturgical prose. The 1992 *Danske Alterbog* expanded the options of liturgical texts. The Norwegian Church received its own Church Ritual in 1683, which remained the basis of the Norwegian Mass of 1920. The current official worship book for the Church of

Norway is *Gudstjenestbog for den Norske Kirke* (1992). The current worship book of the Church of Iceland is *Handbók, Íslensku kirkjunnar* (1981).

In Sweden Olavus Petri's vernacular *Manual* (1529), a book of occasional services, and *Swedish Mass* (1531) were authorized for use only in Stockholm. While approved by a national synod in 1536, their use was not required in the rest of the realm where the Swedish mass made only slow inroads. In fact, the pre-Reformation Latin liturgical books remained in use well into the seventeenth century when they began to be replaced with vernacular hymnals. A definitive *Swedish Church Order*, prepared by Archbishop Laurentius Petri in 1561, was finally authorized and published in 1571. The Swedish–Latin 'Red Book' (1576) of King Johan III was in authorized use until his death in 1592. The Synod of Uppsala in 1593 restored the Church Order of Archbishop Petri and with it the Swedish Mass of 1557 and the Manual (*Handboken*) of Olavus Petri. The Manual was revised in 1599 and again in 1614. This version of the Manual remained in use until 1693, when a minor revision was made. It then remained in use until 1811, when a revised manual and hymnal were issued reflecting the rationalism of the time. *Den svenska handboken* (1942) and *Den svenska psalmboken* (1942) reflect liturgical restoration in texts and use of plainchant. The current books used in the Church of Sweden, which reflect the modern liturgical renewal more than the other European Lutheran Churches, are *Den svenska kyrkohandboken* I and II (1986, 1987), which has the liturgical texts for ministers, and *Den svenska psalmboken* (1986), the hymnal with orders of worship, prayers and readings for the congregation.

The Church of Finland acquired de facto independence from the Church of Sweden in 1809 when Sweden lost Finland to Russia, but the Swedish liturgical books remained in use until 1886 when they were superseded by Finnish language books. The component parts of the *Suomen Evankelis-Luterilaisen Kirkon Kirkkokäsikirja* (Finnish Evangelical Lutheran Church Church-Handbook) are I. The Lectionary (1958), II. The Liturgical Book (1968), III. Church Rites (1984), and IV. The Prayer Book (1968).

8.3. *North America*. Lutheran settlers in North America brought their own agendas and hymnals with them. In 1748 Henry Melchior

Muhlenberg prepared a handwritten liturgy based on the use of the German Lutheran congregation in London for use in congregations in the British colonies. Lutheran hymnals in the early American republic reflected the same rationalist trends as the European books, as well as the spirit of American revivalism. Beginning in 1860 an English-language liturgy was adopted by the Ministerium of Pennsylvania, included in the 1868 *Church Book*, that reflected the trend toward liturgical restoration in Europe. The Common Service of 1888 provided English-language services of holy communion, matins and vespers that were approved by and incorporated into the worship books of the General Council, the General Synod and the United Synod of the South. These three bodies joined together to produce the *Common Service Book* of 1917 and merged into the United Lutheran Church in America in 1918. Other synods and church bodies also began incorporating the Common Service into their English-language worship books. The *Service Book and Hymnal* of 1958, produced by eight church bodies, which in 1960 and 1962 merged into two, was the high-water mark of liturgical restoration. The *Lutheran Book of Worship* (1978) reflects the ecumenical liturgical renewal movement more than any other Lutheran liturgical book. It is used in the Evangelical Lutheran Church in America (formed in 1988), the Evangelical Lutheran Church in Canada (formed in 1987), and some congregations of the Lutheran Church–Missouri Synod. The *Lutheran Book of Worship* was followed by *Occasional Services* (1982). The Missouri Synod published its own version of The *Lutheran Book of Worship* in *Lutheran Worship* (1982). The Wisconsin Evangelical Lutheran Synod published its *Christian Worship* in 1993. Supplements to The *Lutheran Book of Worship* and *Lutheran Worship* have appeared respectively as *With One Voice* (1995) and *Hymnal Supplement 1998*. The *Lutheran Book of Worship* has served as the basis of the Spanish-language *Libro de Liturgia y Cántico* (1998) and, with *Lutheran Worship*, of the African American Lutheran worship book, *This Far by Faith* (1999), although both books also draw on culturally specific resources.

8.4. *Other Churches*. Lutheran churches in Latin America, Africa and Asia published their own liturgical books in the late twentieth century. Some churches and their books still reflect the dominance of the European tradition, such as *Celebracoes de Povo de Deus* (*Celebrations of the People of God*, 1991), published by The Evangelical Church of the Lutheran Confession in Brazil, and the *Lutheran Hymnal with Supplement* (1989) of the Lutheran Church in Australia. The latter also published *Church Rites*, the first compilation of occasional services in the history of that church. In other instances liturgical books reflect greater effort at *inculturation, especially in the use of indigenous music. Noteworthy are the English-language *Lutheran Service Book and Hymnal* of the Lutheran Church in Guyana, which includes a Caribbean Hymn Service of Holy Communion. The Kenya Evangelical Lutheran Church and the Evangelical Lutheran Church in Tanzania use *Mwimbieni Bwana* (*Sing for the Lord*, 1988), which provides African as well as Western songs. About 12% of the hymns in the hymnal of the Evangelical Lutheran Church in Hong Kong are indigenous Chinese music as well as two settings of the eucharistic liturgy. The Lutheran Church in Korea has been introducing both a historic Western liturgy and adapting it to Korean music.

Lutheran Churches in Eastern Europe have experienced a resurgence of spiritual life following the collapse of the Soviet Union. In 1991 a new hymnal and prayer book was published for use in Estonian-speaking congregations both in Estonia and in the diaspora. The same kind of work has been undertaken in Latvia and Lithuania. A Russian-language hymnal has also been approved by the Synod of the Evangelical Lutheran Church of Ingria. The Slovak Evangelical Church of the Augsburg Confession introduced a new hymnal in 1993, which for the first time was in the Slovak language.

Selected texts: *Luther's Works* LIII, Philadelphia 1965, 'Liturgy and Hymns'; Aemelius L. Richter (ed.), *Die evangelischen Kirchenordnungen des sechzehnten Jahrhunderts,* 2nd edn, Leipzig 1871; Emil Sehling (ed.), *Die evangelischen Kirchenordnungen des XVI Jahrhunderts* I–V, Leipzig 1902–13; VI–XV Tübingen 1955–77.
Studies: Luther D. Reed, *The Lutheran Liturgy*, Philadelphia 1959; Frank C. Senn, *Christian Liturgy – Catholic and Evangelical*, Minneapolis 1997.

FRANK C. SENN

9. *Methodist.* Because Methodism began as a society within the Church of England, at first liturgical books per se were not necessary. Yet the brothers John and Charles Wesley, founders of the Methodist movement, published books to support Methodist worship, public and private. Prayers to be used alongside the *BCP* were distributed in discrete collections for each day of the week, for families and for children; of course, Methodists were still expected to pray *extempore. Hymn tracts and books offered sacred poems on a single subject, as in the *Hymns for the Nativity of our Lord* (1744) and the *Hymns on the Lord's Supper* (1745), or on the entire range of themes encompassed within the Wesleyan *via salutis,* such as the *Collection of Hymns for the Use of the People called Methodists* (1780). Texts never were issued for the Methodist *watch-night or *love-feast, but in 1780 John Wesley brought out a pamphlet with *Directions for Renewing our Covenant with God*.

9.1. *The Sunday Service.* The first Methodist book containing Sunday, sacramental, pastoral (*marriage and *funeral) and *ordination rites was the *Sunday Service of the Methodists in North America. With other Occasional Services* (1784), a revision of the 1662 *BCP* made by John Wesley and accomplished primarily by abbreviation and omission rather than by addition. Some of Wesley's alterations corresponded with changes to the *BCP* suggested by Puritans or Nonconformists in his and previous generations; others were apparently unique. Wesley's *Collection of Psalms and Hymns for the Lord's Day* accompanied the *Sunday Service* to America in 1784. At least two more editions of *Sunday Service* were issued for Methodists in the USA until the Americans laid the book aside in 1792. The sacramental, pastoral and ordination orders in *Sunday Service* survived, with editing, in books of *Discipline* of the various branches of American Methodism in a section entitled 'Sacramental Services, etc.', later renamed the 'Ritual'. These services were generally followed, particularly those for the sacraments and ordination, but not mandated; such was and is the case in Methodist worship worldwide. In 1867 the Methodist Episcopal Church, South reprinted the *Sunday Service*, and several times in the twentieth century it was republished in full or in part, but it never had widespread use.

The *Sunday Service* arranged for Methodists throughout the British Empire went through numerous editions from 1786 until 1910. A shorter version containing selected rites, entitled *Order of Administration of the Sacraments and Other Services*, became available between 1839 and 1881. The largest Methodist body, the Wesleyan Methodists, brought out in 1882 the *Book of Public Prayers and Services* which was based more on the 1662 *BCP* than on Wesley's revision; this book and *Sunday Service* coexisted for a time. Collections of texts for public worship were also produced by the smaller Methodist denominations during the nineteenth century, but these usually bore little resemblance to Wesley's texts or the *BCP*. All the denominations produced separate books of hymn texts and hymn tunes until words and music were brought together into a single volume; some congregations, however, opted instead to sing from unauthorized hymnals.

9.2. *British Methodism*. The Methodist Church in Great Britain, created in 1932 from the union of most branches of British Methodism, in the following year published a *Methodist Hymn-Book* that contained more than two hundred hymns by Charles Wesley and was expected to be in every Methodist home. The Church in 1935 approved *Divine Worship* (versions of morning prayer, other services and numerous *collects) and in 1936 authorized the *Book of Offices* and, bound in with it, the *Order for Morning Prayer*: both still exhibited connections to the *BCP* and thus Wesley's orders, though the former showed a willingness to include newly composed prayers and those borrowed from other Free Church sources. *Hymns and Songs, a Supplement to the Methodist Hymn Book* appeared in 1960. Shortly thereafter, the denomination printed for trial use a series of services bearing the influence of the wider *Liturgical and Ecumenical Movements that then contributed to the *Methodist Service Book* (1975). A new hymnal, *Hymns and Psalms: A Methodist and Ecumenical Hymn Book* (1983), was the product of ecumenical co-operation, and though it reduced the number of Wesley hymns, it expanded the repertoire of twentieth-century compositions. The *Methodist Worship Book* (1999) continued the 1975 book's intention of preserving Methodist traditions while taking into account liturgical renewal, and also broadened the range of services offered.

Methodist churches throughout the world founded in the traditions of British Methodism continued to use British materials until they developed their own liturgical books, many of which still bore the imprint of the parent denomination. In a tribute to its liturgical ancestry, the Methodist Church in the Caribbean and the Americas selected the title *Prayer Book of the Methodist Church* (1992). Churches planted in Canada, Australia and India used British Methodist worship books until union with other Christian denominations created the United Church of *Canada, the Uniting Church in *Australia, and the Church of *South India. The liturgical texts developed by these new denominations – at least in the first generation – displayed some evidence of their Methodist roots; such was certainly the case in the selection of hymns for new hymnals. At the beginning of the twenty-first century, Methodist denominations in Africa and Asia are compiling liturgical books that acknowledge their Methodist heritage, but take into account the indigenous culture.

9.3. *USA*. In the United States, all branches of Methodism published hymnals for worship, some of which, by the late nineteenth century, began to include responsive readings and either outlines or full texts for Sunday use. Although the liturgical services were found in a section of the *Discipline*, some denominations also occasionally produced a separate volume with selected portions of the 'Ritual' as a pastoral aid. The Methodist Church's *Book of Worship* (1944) was the first official and separate book of worship texts to be authorized since the *Sunday Service*. The Methodist Church revised the book in 1964 and, after union with the Evangelical United Brethren Church in 1968, brought out the *United Methodist Book of Worship* (1992) with texts indebted to insights gained from the Liturgical Movement. Other American Methodist liturgical books include the *Book of Worship* of the African Methodist Episcopal Church (1984) and the African Methodist Episcopal Zion Church's *Book of Worship* (1996). American Methodist offshoots in other parts of the world have also produced liturgical books, among them the *Agende* of the Evangelisch-methodistische Kirche in Germany (1991), and the *Ang Imnaryo at Ritual* of the Iglesia Evangelica Metodista in the Philippines (1993).

Karen B. Westerfield Tucker, *American Methodist Worship*, New York 2000; (ed.), *The Sunday Service of the Methodists*, Nashville 1996.

KAREN B. WESTERFIELD TUCKER

10. *Old Catholic*. Each Old Catholic church belonging to the Union of Utrecht has its own

liturgical books. It is part of the ministry of the diocesan *bishop(s) of that church to order the liturgy (*ius liturgicum*), which includes publishing the books and making them the official version. The basis of the liturgy of the Old Catholic churches and therefore of the books has been the RC rite. Each church has at some point in its history translated the respective parts into the vernacular. The first editions of these books were sometimes more or less literal translations and sometimes free renderings of the texts. In the course of later revisions, sources from other churches, in particular the Anglican Communion and, in the case of the Old Catholic Church of Switzerland, the Orthodox churches, played a significant role. There are liturgical books in the following languages: Dutch (the Netherlands), German (Germany, Switzerland, Austria), French (Switzerland, France), Czech (the Czech Republic), English (USA, Canada), Polish (Poland, also in the Polish National Catholic Church in the USA and Canada), Italian (Italy), Croatian (Croatia).

The revision process, initiated in the beginning of the second half of the twentieth century, still continues in most churches. The liturgical texts are either published in booklet form or in other suitable ways to facilitate their reforms. Some churches resort to experimental versions of the respective liturgies so that pastoral experience with the provisions may yet change the ultimate form. The only Old Catholic church that has something similar to a *BCP* is the Old Catholic Church of the Netherlands. Its *Kerkboek van de Oud-Katholieke Kerk van Nederland* (1993) contains all the texts for the *eucharist (except the *readings, published in *Lectionarium bij het Kerkboek*, 1993), the texts and rites of the other sacraments, the liturgy for the departed, the celebration of lauds (morning praise) and vespers (evensong), a service of the *word, the Psalms, *canticles and *antiphons. This church also has an expansive hymnal, *Gezangboek van de Oud-Katholieke Kerk van Nederland* (1990), with 764 psalm versions, liturgical settings, hymns, mass settings and appendices.

The Old Catholic Church in Germany published *Die Feier der Eucharistie* in 1995. The other parts of the liturgy are still being revised and published in small booklets. The hymnal, printed in 1986, will in the years to come be subject to a major revision. The Old Catholic Church of Switzerland has its *Messliturgie und Gesangbuch der Christkatholischen Kirche*

(1978); this is being revised. The Old Catholic Church of Austria has four booklets containing four different forms of the eucharist; the *Feier der Eucharistie* of the German diocese has also been officially permitted. The other parts of the liturgy are printed in booklets as well. The Old Catholic Church in the Czech Republic has seen a major outburst of revising all parts of its liturgy recently. The Polish National Catholic Church in the USA published *The Celebration of the Holy Sacrifice of the Mass* in 1990. This book contains the order of the eucharist in three different versions. The Polish Catholic Church (Poland) has a missal; for the other sacraments and other parts of the liturgy, the RC books are used.

The International Old Catholic Liturgical Commission has been charged by the International Old Catholic Bishops' Conference of the Union of Utrecht to draft a Union-wide pontifical. *Ordination rites for the episcopate, presbyterate and diaconate were approved in 1985; but there has been no official publication, and the texts exist in photocopied form only. The rite of the *consecration of churches exists in draft form.

THADDEUS A. SCHNITKER

11. *Pentecostal.* Pentecostal churches have no official liturgical books as such, but there are a number of manuals which are popular among their ministers. Thus, the Gospel Publishing House of the Assemblies of God published a *Minister's Manual* in three volumes by William E. Pickthorn (Springfield, MO 1965). The first volume includes scripture references for calls to worship, *offertory references, *doxologies and benedictions. Orders of service are included for child *dedication, water *baptism, reception of members, and the *Lord's supper. Volume two includes sample ceremonies for *marriage, *funeral and burial services. Volume three contains liturgies for the installation of pastors and workers, and guidelines for various special church functions like ground-breaking and building-dedication services. These guidelines are brief and only serve as suggestions for the pastor to follow. The Church of God, Cleveland, Tennessee published a manual by Zeno C. Tharp, *The Ministers' Guide for Special Occasions* (Cleveland, TN 1953). It includes service formats and appropriate scripture references for special services, funerals and weddings, holidays and benedictions. It also includes liturgies for the Lord's supper and *foot-

washing. Another manual by Clyne W. Buxton, *Minister's Service Manual* (Cleveland, TN 1999) includes much of the same. All these manuals contain very few prayers. Usually, they will include short statements by the author suggesting certain important elements the pastor may include in a prayer. An exception to the rule is the *Church of God in Christ Official Manual* (ed. C. F. Range, Memphis, TN 1992), where the 'Prayers of Invocation' section contains actual written prayers that may be read publicly, and the call to Easter worship consists of a responsive reading. This general lack of written prayers points to the fact that Pentecostals generally prefer spontaneous and innovative prayers that are inspired at the appropriate moment by the Holy Spirit. It also reflects the tendency of many Pentecostal churches worldwide towards an oral liturgy. On the other hand, Pentecostal churches do not seem to be short on 'self-help' books concerning prayer that are geared to the individual devotional life or to small-group prayer meetings. The Gospel Publishing House of the Assemblies of God catalogue includes at least twenty books on prayer.

Music makes up a large part of most Pentecostal services, and Pentecostals are generally eclectic in their selection of music. Each denomination tends to have a favourite hymn book, but they usually select their music from a larger variety of sources and styles. Pentecostal hymn books generally contain a diverse selection of hymns from various sources, along with responsive readings of scriptures and other material that may be used in any order by congregations. The Church of God, Cleveland, Tennessee publishes a hymn book entitled *Hymns of the Spirit* (ed. Connor B. Hall, Cleveland, TN 1969), which includes many of the old-time revival hymns along with responsive readings for different themes, pledge to the American flag, Christian flag, and the Bible, the *Lord's Prayer, calls to worship, and benedictions. The Church of God in Christ publishes a hymn book entitled *Yes Lord!* (ed. Norman N. Quick, Memphis/Nashville, TN 1982), which includes an 'Aids to Worship' section containing the statement of faith, calls to worship, invocations, a thanksgiving prayer, the Lord's Prayer, the Ten Commandments, the Beatitudes and the Nicene and Apostles' *Creeds. There is another section entitled 'Topical Index of Scripture Readings', where the hymns are organized according to the various responsive reading themes at the back of the book. The

Gospel Publishing House of the Assemblies of God publishes a hymn book entitled *Sing His Praise* (Springfield, MO 1991), which differs from the others in that it contains a mix of old revival hymns along with a substantial list of contemporary praise choruses (praise choruses are choruses written to be sung many times over as the people of God wait on the Spirit of the Lord).

However, even with this wonderful mix of music, Pentecostals still rely on other sources for their worship needs. Some churches, like the well-known Assemblies of God church that hosts the Brownsville Revival, compose their own music and sell it on the market to other churches. Integrity, Hosanna, Hill Songs from Australia, Brownsville Revival and Maranatha music are popular among Assemblies of God churches in general. One music director of a large Church of God, Cleveland, Tennessee church would add to the above list Brooklyn Tabernacle Choir and Christ Church Choir music, the *Hymns of Spirit* hymn book, and various 'liturgical hymns' that might appeal to the RC and Episcopal adherents who attend his church.

Many Pentecostal churches project their hymns and praise choruses on a screen using a transparency or computer projector. Songs are stored not in church hymnals in the pews, but in binders or on computer hard drives. One large Pentecostal church compiled their favourite hymns and praise songs from a large variety of sources into their own hymn book. This seems to fit the eclectic style of Pentecostals in selecting their own worship music. The music is not selected by a publisher somewhere, but by music directors, pastors and church congregations according to their own context and their perception of the leading of the Spirit.

All of this is a sign that Pentecostals still wish to choose freely from a variety of written sources and innovative media for shaping the liturgy of a church service, and the decisions are finally made on the local level. The trend is for Pentecostals to borrow from other Evangelical prayers and hymns in an innovative and eclectic worship service that stresses emotional experiences of God and empowerment to serve God both in the church and in the world through a variety of spiritual gifts. The Pentecostal curiosity concerning how to pray expresses itself almost exclusively in 'self-help' books for individuals and small groups. Whether or not such a curiosity will be turned toward corporate and more standardized forms of prayer is unlikely. The same may be said of liturgical guidance for other aspects of the order of service. Though Pentecostals are gradually beginning to incorporate written liturgies into their oral worship tradition, they are far from using any standardized written liturgical guides. One may never see such standardized liturgies given the current trend toward diversity of liturgical forms and media.

MICHAEL D. MACCHIA

12. *Reformed.* The Psalter, with the Psalms and other biblical *canticles in the vernacular and *metred for singing, was the first book for worship developed in the Reformed tradition. Such books included liturgical texts for use by the minister, with directions and guidance for ordering worship. Worship served by these books stressed preaching, scriptural praises (biblical psalms, and also hymns), the corporate character of *sacrament and prayer, and a strong sense of the work of the Holy Spirit.

The most famous of the early Reformed documents are the *De canone missae epichiresis* (1523) and *Action oder Bruch des Nachtmals* (1525) of Ulrich Zwingli, and the *Genevan Psalter* of 1542 and 1545 (*La forme des prières ecclésiastiques*) from John Calvin's ministries in Strasbourg and Geneva. Zwingli among others first attempted a reform of the *mass. Soon he replaced it with a preaching service. The *Lord's supper (composed 1525) was celebrated quarterly (at *Christmas, *Easter, *Pentecost and September 11) and as a service distinct from the normal Sunday worship.

The Sunday service of the *Genevan Psalter* featured preaching on a 'lectio continua' basis of the Bible, thanksgiving and *intercessory prayers, and singing of psalms. The Lord's supper was part of the normal order, though it was never celebrated 'at least once every Sunday' as in Calvin's intention. While in Strasbourg after his flight from Geneva (1538–41), Calvin served the French-speaking church using a version of the liturgy strongly shaped by Martin Bucer. This 1539 Psalter was the basis of worship when Calvin returned to Geneva. The 1545 edition of the *Genevan Psalter* is a primary source for French-speaking Reformed worship, and the Scottish Reformed tradition through John Knox and others. An edition of 1556, entitled *The Forme of Prayers and ministration of the sacraments as used in the English Congregation*, also known as the *Genevan Service Book* of John Knox, was used

during his time in Frankfurt with the refugee congregation there. *The Forme of Prayers and Ministration of the Sacraments* (a 1562 edition) was printed in Scotland, and it became the *Book of Common Order* (1562, 1564) of the Church of Scotland.

The Swiss cantons produced their own versions of a Reformed Psalter or service book. Jean-Frédéric Ostervald (1663–1747), Guillaume Farel's successor at Neuchâtel, produced *La Liturgie ou La Maniere de celebrer le Service Divin* (1707–13), influenced by the *BCP*. Geneva revised the tradition of Calvin (*Les Prieres ecclésiastiques*, 1724, and *La Liturgie*, 1743). The 1945 *Liturgie de L'Église de Genève* in the Lord's supper displays twentieth-century efforts to recover Reformed sacramental theology, and benefit from studies of historic Christian worship.

In France the Reformed Church held to Calvin's Psalter as their heritage 'in the desert', from the Edict of Nantes until 1802. Eugene Bersier (1831–89), founding pastor of l'église de l'Etoile, Paris, composed *Liturgie à l'usage des Églises réformées* (1874) and *Project de Révision de la Liturgie* (1888), which show an appreciation for older Western tradition. The Reformed Church of France published a more familiar *Liturgie des Églises réformées de France* (1897) which served until 1945. In the twentieth century, Richard Paquier (1905–85) and 'Eglise et Liturgie' produced a *communion rite (1931) with supplement for feast days (1933), drawing from Calvin's sacramental theology and ecumenical liturgical practice. The *Liturgie de l'Église réformée de France* produced in 1950 (final version in 1963, without major changes) continued this trend. The French Reformed Church adopted a new service book in 1996.

Dutch and German Reformed churches were strongly influenced by the church order of Heidelberg and the *Palatinate Liturgy* (1563, Dutch translation by Peter Dathenius 1566). The American Dutch received this liturgy (revised by the Synod of Dort, 1618–19) in 1738 (English, 1767). The Reformed Church in America revised their *Liturgy* in 1907, and produced *Liturgy and Psalms* in 1968. *Worship the Lord* (1987) supplemented *Liturgy and Psalms*, and includes a *Directory for Worship* with equal constitutional authority. Three principal Protestant denominations in the Netherlands, two Reformed and one Lutheran, are currently developing a new shared service book, *Dienstboek, een proeve*.

The Church of Scotland used the *Book of Common Order* widely if irregularly from 1562 (seventy printings, 1564–1644) until it was replaced by *A Directory for the Public Worship of God* (1645), otherwise known as the 'Westminster Directory'. The Scots added *Directory for Family Worship* for *daily prayer (1647). The 'Westminster Directory' was a set of directions and guidance for the Lord's day, with instructions on sermons, outlines for sacraments and occasional rites (visitation of the *sick, *marriage, *funerals). Unofficial liturgical efforts were contributed through the later nineteenth century, especially by the Church Service Society. The United Free Church published its *Book of Common Order* in 1928, and a reunited Church of Scotland produced the *Book of Common Order* (1940), which had influence in most English-speaking *Presbyterian traditions, including those of the USA. The *Book of Common Order* (1979), with a normative Sunday *eucharist in three orders, was a radical model for the Church of Scotland. The *Book of Common Order* (1994, revised 1996) is cast in the model of the 1940 rather than the 1979 book.

Metrical psalters and the *Directory for Worship* were brought by Presbyterians to North America. The General Assembly of the Presbyterian Church in the USA adopted a new version of the latter in 1788, with permissive *rubrics and few models. The Associate-Reformed Church Synod in 1799 approved a conservative adaptation of the two Scottish directories, for public worship and family worship. Little official attention was given to worship until after private efforts in the nineteenth century at service books and other publications, such as a collection of sixteenth-century Reformed liturgies, *Eutaxia, or The Presbyterian Liturgies*, by Charles W. Baird (1855, 1857).

The *Book of Common Worship* (1906) of the Presbyterian Church in the USA., largely the work of Henry van Dyke and Louis Benson, was a service book with rubrics of the *Directory*. The 1906 book and an expanded 1932 edition provided Sunday services, sacraments and some of the first prayers of a liturgical *year. The *Book of Common Worship* (1946) owed much to the Scottish 1940 *Book of Common Order*. A new and theologically substantial *Directory for Worship* (1961) preceded a fourth edition, *The Worshipbook* (1970, with hymns 1972) for the United Presbyterian Church in the USA. A normative Sunday eucharist and the

first version of the new RC *lectionary were its most radical features. The *Book of Common Worship* (1993) is a model of the liturgical renewal movement of the later twentieth century, serving the Presbyterian Church (USA) together with the expanded *Directory for Worship* (1989). The Cumberland Presbyterian Church use the 1993 *Book of Common Worship*, but adopted a new *Directory* (1984).

Smaller Reformed and Presbyterian churches have produced liturgical books. *A Book of Services* (1980) of the *United Reformed Church in Great Britain is to be succeeded by a service book in 2001 (draft orders for communion and baptism, 2000). The Uniting Church in *Australia has *Uniting in Worship* (1988).The United Church of Christ in the USA has *Book of Worship* (1986). The Presbyterian Church in Canada published *The Book of Common Worship* (1991). All these Reformed books of the last quarter of the twentieth century offer a Sunday eucharist, a form of ecumenical lectionary and other similar features. More conservative bodies fashion liturgical materials more closely on sixteenth-century models; examples include the Christian Reformed Church in North America (*Psalter Hymnal* 1987, fourth edn), and the Canadian Reformed Churches (*Book of Praise: Anglo-Genevan Psalter*, 1980, revised edn 1984). In its *Orden de Culto y Liturgia* (n.d.), the National Presbyterian Church of Mexico preserves a version of a 'directory-with-texts' model.

———

Historic texts in Bruno Bürki, *Cène du Seigneur – Eucharistie de l'Église*, Fribourg 1985; R. C. D. Jasper and G. J. Cuming (eds), *Prayers of the Eucharist: Early and Reformed*, 3rd edn, New York 1987; Irmgard Pahl (ed.), *Coena Domini I. Die Abendmahlsliturgie der Reformationskirchen im 16/17 Jahrhundert*, Fribourg 1983; Bard Thompson (ed.), *Liturgies of the Western Church*, Cleveland 1961.

Studies of current liturgies by Stewart Todd, K. H. W. Klaassens and Stuart Ludbrook in *Studia Liturgica* XXXI, 2001, 38–48, 101–18.

STANLEY R. HALL

Bowing *see* **Gestures** 7

Breviary *see* **Books, Liturgical** 3.1.2.c

Buddhist Worship

1. *Overview*. Since Buddhism is formally a

non-theistic religion, many conventional forms of worship and prayer were absent both during the lifetime of its founder, the Buddha Gautama Siddhārtha (fifth century BCE), and also in the schools of Buddhism which adhere most literally to his original teachings. Initially, the Buddha was thought to be a person who had fully realized the ultimate spiritual potentiality with which all living beings are endowed. According to the earliest scriptures that survive in Pāli and Chinese, the Buddha is not known to have advocated any form of worship, prayer or ritual – indeed, on occasions, he speaks of the futility of such activities. While the Buddha accepted the existence of various traditional Indian gods, their powers were considered to be limited as they were not endowed with immortality. Hence, though they were perhaps worthy of some respect and could be the objects of petitionary prayer, they were only able to assist humans in mundane matters. Since the goal of Buddhism is liberation from the cycle of repeated life and death with its concomitant suffering and ignorance, the ideal form of spiritual practice is morality and meditation which are the only means to accomplish this aim.

2. *Cultic Ritual during the Buddha's Lifetime.* Though he was not considered to be divine, it was common for people to express their respect towards the Buddha during his lifetime through various devotional acts. In themselves, these acts were not specifically Buddhist in nature but were common Indian ways of showing respect to holy men. These various elements were to be retained as the core of many future modes of Buddhist worship as they developed, and include: prostration, offerings of flowers and foodstuffs, confession of personal failings, praise, requesting teachings and so forth. Although there seems to have been some use of verse praises in memory of the Buddha in the first centuries after his passing, he was never considered as divine and the only focal points that acted as cultic centres were the various *stupas* erected over portions of his ashes, since it was felt by some that there was a kind of residual presence of the Buddha there. The custom of *pilgrimage began to develop around these *stupas* and other later holy sites, and attracted many pilgrims from many parts of the Buddhist world. Apart from such *stupas*, only simple symbols such as a wheel or footprints carved into stone initially served as representations of the Buddha. Iconic forms of

the Buddha such as statues began to be created in the Gandhara region of north-west India through Hellenic influence and these would have attracted more elaborate rituals of commemorative worship.

3. *The Standard Structure of Buddhist Devotion.* Even today in the Theravāda Buddhism of south-east Asia, which retains many features of early Buddhism, petitionary and *intercessory types of prayer and worship are not found. A typical devotional act (*pūja*) by laypeople will include prostrations, offerings of flowers, *incense and candles, a recitation of the refuge formula by which one affirms one's reliance upon the Buddha as teacher, the Dharma as his guiding teachings and the Sangha as the community of the monks and nuns who are living embodiments of those teachings. Also commonly included will be a recitation of the basic set of five moral precepts, some form of praise for the Buddha's life and achievement, a meditation on loving-kindness and some short scriptural recitation. Other present-day Asian forms of Buddhism also utilize this general structure of worship with certain additions that will be mentioned below.

4. *Mahāyāna Buddhalogical Innovations.* Around the first century BCE onwards, a new form of Buddhism known as Mahāyāna developed, both as a culmination of certain earlier sectarian developments and also as a reaction to various trends that were thought to betray the spirit of the Buddha's life and teachings. A complete description of this movement within Buddhism would be extremely lengthy but we may note here the emergence of a new religious ideal, that of the Bodhisattva, according to which a person compassionately devotes their life to the benefiting of others as well as developing their own purity and spiritual insight. This ideal took various accounts of the past and final lives of the Buddha as a model for emulation. At the same time, Mahāyāna also introduced a number of innovative Buddhalogical concepts. Whereas in earlier times the Buddha had been viewed merely as an extraordinary human being, his presence in the world was now seen as an embodiment (*nirmāna-kāya*) of a pre-existing or even eternal perfect mode of existence (*dharma-kāya*). This latter mode of existence shares some features with theistic concepts with the exclusion of being a creator. An additional, intermediary form was also posited as a subtle mode of embodiment

(*saṃbhoga-kāya*) of a Buddha which was accessible only to beings of high spiritual attainments. The introduction of these new Buddhalogical ideas, coupled with the Bodhisattva ideal, was to have a profound influence upon Buddhist forms of worship.

5. *Pure Lands*. Since the idea of the Buddha or rather Buddhas, as a multitude of Buddhas were now considered to be present in the universe, had acquired various transcendental features, it was thought that they were able to interact with the human world in other ways beyond teaching a path to liberation. By virtue of their vows made prior to achieving enlightenment, beings were guaranteed various benefits by recollecting the names or various other aspects of these Buddhas. Most typically, such Buddhas are thought to dwell in specially privileged abodes known as Pure Lands where conditions for rapid liberation are ideal. Faith in the power of the Buddha Amitābha to ensure rebirth in his Pure Land of Sukhāvatī became extremely popular in northern and eastern Asia and remains so even today, especially in Japan where the two large Pure Land sects promote the recitation of Amitābha's name (*nembutsu*) as their primary devotional act. Likewise, certain highly advanced Bodhisattvas who no longer abide in human form are considered to have salvific abilities although these relate more to a short-term relief from suffering rather than liberation from rebirth. Such Bodhisattvas include Avalokiteśvara, known in his feminized Chinese form as Guan-yin, and Tārā, the female saving Bodhisattva who is especially revered in Tibetan Buddhist circles. Devotional cults focused on these Buddhas and Bodhisattvas include, apart from the standard acts of worship mentioned above, the recitation of lengthy songs of praise, their names and titles, and meditational visualization of their appearance.

6. *The Seven-Branched Prayer*. Mahāyāna also saw the development of a standardized form of worship known as the Seven-Branched Prayer which comprises the following elements, usually expressed in verse form: salutation to the Buddhas, offerings, confessing one's faults, rejoicing in the good fortune of others, requesting the Buddhas to make the Dharma available, entreating the Buddhas not to abandon beings, and dedication of the merit which accrues through these acts of devotion for the welfare of others. As the main successors

of pure Indian Mahāyāna Buddhism, this practice still flourishes in Tibetan communities, although east-Asian forms of Mahāyāna Buddhism utilize similar formats of prayer.

7. *Shrines*. Though not corroborated by archaeological evidence, it can be assumed that the construction and use of household shrines or altars developed in early medieval India and their use spread to all other Buddhist lands where they are still much in evidence today. Their specific layout varies from country to country and according to the Buddhist school with which the devotee is affiliated. However, the centre of focus is always an image, painted or sculpted, of the Buddha, flanked by fresh flower offerings and candles and a receptacle for burning incense in front. Some schools of Buddhism make use of a small handbell during devotional rites and this may be placed on the shrine when not in use. East Asians will also place memorial tablets inscribed with names of dead family members in the shrine. Tibetan family shrines are fairly elaborate and will additionally have a number of statues of other Buddhist sacred beings such as Tārā, pictures of their religious teachers (including the Dalai Lama) and a larger range of offering materials, including foodstuffs, drinks, precious objects, relics and scriptures suitably arranged.

8. *Tantric Buddhism*. From the seventh century CE, a new form of Buddhism developed from Mahāyāna which makes great use of meditative visualization, the recitation of mantras and the use of hand gestures (*mudrā*) to invoke Buddhas and Bodhisattvas for the purpose of devotion and self-identification. This form of Buddhism is typical of Tibetan religious practice but also is found in a variant form in Japan and some parts of China. Prior to engaging in such practices, the devotee needs to receive the appropriate initiation from a teacher (*guru*) as certain aspects of the practices are regarded as being secret. Many ritual handbooks (*sādhana*) exist which detail the necessary instructions for invoking one of a wide range of sacred beings who are seen as aspects of the totality of enlightenment. The ritual begins with most of the standard elements of Buddhist worship. The devotee then proceeds to visualize in detail the image of the subject of the meditation according to the liturgical description given in the handbook. This may be undertaken in two manners: the devotee may visualize that Buddha to be in front of him or he may visual-

ize himself in that form. The first method is more associated with devotional rituals while the second is connected with techniques of self-transformation. In either case, having generated this image, the devotee then calls upon the actual being concerned to merge with the image – thus becoming truly present. The devotional type of ritual proceeds with the presentation of offerings and praises, as well as requests for assistance and spiritual gifts. As with the self-transformational ritual, the devotee will also recite the particular mantra associated with that divine being, usually using a *rosary (*mālā*) comprising one hundred and eight beads. In both types of ritual, the departure of the divine being is requested and the devotee concludes the ritual with prayers for the welfare of others such as parents and teachers, and then dedicates all the merit accrued for the benefit of others.

STEPHEN HODGE

Burial *see* Funerals

Byzantine Chant

The medieval sacred music of Christian churches following the Eastern rite. This tradition, principally encompassing the Greek-speaking world, developed in Constantinople from its foundation in 330 until the conquest of 1453. It is undeniably of composite origin, drawing on the artistic and technical productions of the classical age and on Jewish music, and inspired by the plainsong that evolved in the early Christian cities of Alexandria, Antioch and Ephesus. Byzantine chant manuscripts date from the ninth century, while *lectionaries of biblical readings with recitative symbols (ecphonetic notation) begin about a century earlier.

In common with other musical dialects in the East and West, Byzantine chant is purely vocal and exclusively monodic. The most ancient evidence suggests that the hymns and psalms were originally syllabic or quasi-syllabic in style, stemming as they did from congregational recitatives. Later, with the development of monasticism, at first in Palestine and then in Constantinople, and with the augmentation of rites and ceremonies in new and magnificent edifices (such as Hagia Sophia), trained choirs, each with its own leader (the *protopsaltes* for the right choir; the *lampadarios* for the left) and soloist (the *domestikos* or *kanonarch*), assumed full musical responsibilities.

Byzantine chants were systematically assigned to the eight ecclesiastical modes that, from about the eighth century, provided the compositional framework for Eastern and Western musical practices. Research has demonstrated that for all practical purposes, the oktoechos, as the system is called, was the same for Latins, Greeks and Slavs in the Middle Ages.

Both psalmody and hymnody are represented by florid and simple musical repertories in the manuscript tradition. A special position was accorded to non-biblical hymnody within which the generic term *troparion* came to signify a monostrophic stanza, or one of a series of stanzas, in poetic prose of irregular length and accentuated patterns. The earliest *troparia* may have been interpolated after psalm verses or biblical *canticles, while others act as invitatory prefaces to liturgical chants. At first restricted to the *daily office, they are in later times found in all Byzantine services. Two venerable examples, still used, are the vesperal *Phos hilaron* (O Gladsome Light) and *Ho Monogenes Huios* (Only-begotten Son) from the Divine Liturgy.

The development of larger forms began in the fifth century with the rise of the *kontakion*, a long and elaborate metrical poem, reputedly of Syriac origin, which finds its acme in the work of St Romanos the Melodist (sixth century). This was sung during *orthros* (the morning office) in a simple and direct syllabic style. In the second half of the seventh century a new type of hymn, the *kanon*, was initiated by St Andrew of Crete (*c.* 660–*c.* 740) and developed by Sts John of Damascus and Kosmas of Jerusalem (both eighth century). Essentially, the *kanon* is a hymnodic complex comprising nine odes that were attached to the nine biblical canticles and related to these by means of corresponding poetic allusion or textual quotation. Its musical style is quasi-syllabic. After *c.* 850 composers began to elaborate and to ornament, and this produced a radically new melismatic and ultimately *kalophonic* style whose chants were collected in large anthologies. This final phase of musical activity provided the main thrust that was to survive throughout the Ottoman period (1453–1821) and that continues to dominate the current tradition of Greek church singing.

Dimitri Conomos, *Byzantine Hymnography and Byzantine Chant*, Boston 1985; *Byzantine Trisagia and Cheroubika of the Fourteenth and*

Fifteenth Centuries, Thessaloniki 1974 (bib.); *The Late Byzantine and Slavonic Communion Cycle*, Washington, DC 1985 (bib.); Kenneth Levy, 'The Byzantine Sanctus and its Modal Tradition in East and West', *Annales Musicologiques* VI, 1958–63, 7–67; Oliver Strunk, *Essays on Music in the Byzantine World*, New York 1977 (bib.); Egon Wellesz, *Eastern Elements in Western Chant*, Boston 1947; *A History of Byzantine Music and Hymnography*, Oxford 1962 (bib.).

DIMITRI CONOMOS

Byzantine Rite *see* Orthodox Worship

Calendar *see* Year, Liturgical

Camp Meeting

The camp meetings that flourished in the USA during the first half of the nineteenth century have as antecedents the Scottish *Presbyterian 'sacramental seasons', the outdoor preaching services of certain Separate *Baptists, and the quarterly meetings of the *Methodists. Because these events could last several days and since lodgings could not accommodate the numbers in attendance, participants who came a distance carried their own provisions and slept on site.

The extended open-air revivals in Kentucky at Gasper River (1800) and Cane Ridge (1801) that sparked fires of religious enthusiasm have long been heralded as catalysts for the Second Great Awakening. Camp meetings multiplied rapidly and were a significant social institution on the sparsely inhabited frontier, but were also widespread in settled areas. Languages other than English could be heard at these gatherings, where white people with ancestry in various parts of Europe, black and native people might be found together at prayer.

Assemblies were characterized by several preaching services each day during which impassioned leaders and preachers implored sinners to repent and admonished the converted to deepen their faith. Hymns, songs and choruses, some improvised and sung to familiar secular melodies, spoke of judgement, repentance, grace and forgiveness. Prayer meetings, sometimes delimited by gender or age and held late into the night, stoked the spiritual fervour. Pleas and cries for mercy echoed throughout the camp as 'mourners' sought pardon; assurances of salvation brought shouts for joy. The emotional intensity occasionally evoked uncontrolled physical responses such as barking, jerking or dancing; while some denounced these activities, others declared them to be a visible manifestation of the Holy Spirit.

More recognizably ecclesiastical rites also found a place in the camp. The newly converted could be *baptized in the nearby creek used as the water source. Couples who had come from remote regions seeking an ordained minister might be united in *marriage. The *Lord's supper typically was celebrated on the final evening or on the day of departure.

Although Baptists generally disapproved of the camp meetings, individual preachers participated fully in them, but at multi-denominational gatherings would withdraw to perform their own baptism and *communion services. Presbyterians eventually abandoned the meetings, whereas the Methodists cultivated them. The American Methodist Lorenzo Dow exported the camp format to Britain, where the first meeting was held at Mow Cop, Staffordshire, in 1807. British Methodist reception was mixed: the majority deemed the meetings too disorderly and denounced them; a few Methodists who embraced the form established the Primitive Methodist Church in 1811.

By the mid-nineteenth century, camp meetings in America had become more structured and organized with such features as established designs for the layout of the camp, printed regulations for participants and sentinels to prevent disruption. Permanent cabins or cottages were built in some campgrounds, which then slowly evolved into denominational resorts or Chautauqua centres.

From the late nineteenth century to the present, some Methodist congregations, Holiness churches and *Pentecostal groups have kept alive the camp meeting as a summertime social and liturgical event.

———

Kenneth O. Brown, *Holy Ground: A Study of the American Camp Meeting*, New York 1992; Dickson D. Bruce, Jr, *And They All Sang Hallelujah*, Knoxville, TN 1974; Ellen Eslinger, *Citizens of Zion*, Knoxville, TN 1999.

KAREN B. WESTERFIELD TUCKER

Canada, Worship in the United Church of

The United Church of Canada was formed in

1925 from the union of Canadian *Methodists, *Congregationalists, 70% of *Presbyterians and a number of 'union' congregations, making it the first union of its kind in the world. Others joined later, including Wesleyan Methodists of Bermuda (1930), Evangelical United Brethren (1968) and numerous congregations from other communions. The 'Basis of Union' states that 'the freedom of worship . . . in the negotiating Churches shall not be interfered with . . .' There are no prescribed liturgies with the exception of part of the *ordination rite. While authority for worship resides in the congregation, resources are produced at the national level to support and reform worship. Such material is both a response to and source of developing practices.

Sunday worship in the founding traditions consisted primarily of preaching services with, at most, quarterly communion. *Forms of Service for the Offices of the Church* (1926) included orders for sacraments and occasional services drawn from the uniting denominations. *The Hymnary of The United Church of Canada* (1930) and *The Book of Common Order of the United Church of Canada* (1932) shifted the focus from denominational particularity to greater catholicity. The legacy of the *Hymnary* was its gospel and children's hymns, social gospel texts, prose psalms and select pieces of service music. *The Book of Common Order* defined the ethos of United Church worship as 'ordered liberty', an effort to embrace both 'the experience of many ages of devotion' and 'the leading of the Spirit'. In the tradition of John Knox's service books, United Church worship is a synthesis of 'prayer book' and 'directory' in which orders of service offer models of structure and content.

The 'First Directory for Public Worship' in *The Book of Common Order* was a hybrid of Anglican *daily prayer and the *Westminster Directory* with the sermon as the climax. The 'Second Directory' offered the *eucharistic pattern as normative. Orders for the Lord's supper suggest influence of the Church of England's *Prayer Book as Proposed in 1928*. BCP material dominates the language of *baptism, '*confirmation', *marriage, *funeral and ordination rites. The first woman was ordained in 1938. The 'Treasury of Prayers' was a favourite section, while the 'Table of Lessons' with seasonal *collects was seldom used.

As the stability of the 1950s gave way to the turmoil of the 1960s, calls for the revision of *The Book of Common Order* gathered around

issues of *language, theology and liturgical experimentation. This was complicated by the early stages of the ecumenical *Liturgical Movement and union negotiations with the Anglican Church of Canada. *Service Book for the Use of Ministers Conducting Public Worship* (1969) asserted the principle of the 'unity of word and sacrament', placing the order for the Lord's supper first and basing those of initiation, public worship and occasional services on it. 'Contemporary' orders accompanied many of the rites. An emerging consciousness of *lectionary and calendar is evident in the rubrics and 'Table of Lessons'. Unison prayers and litanies and the responsive Psalms in the *Service Book for the use of the people* (1969) point to more active congregational participation.

The Hymn Book of the Anglican Church of Canada and the United Church of Canada (1971) was produced with the Anglicans in anticipation of a union which was never consummated. While its organization owed much to *Service Book*, its sophisticated musical sensibilities and the loss of gospel hymns alienated many United Church persons. Nevertheless, it supported growing calendar observance and contributed new texts and tunes to United Church hymnody. Equally significant during this period was the emergence of liturgical periodicals, one descendant of which, *Gathering*, continues. *Service Book*, *Hymn Book* and *Gathering* helped prepare the way for some of the features of ecumenical liturgical convergence.

The 1980s saw the publication of a series of booklets 'for optional use' which introduced the resources of liturgical convergence to United Church worship. *A Sunday Liturgy* (1984), *The Celebration of Marriage* (1985), *Baptism and Renewal of Baptismal Faith* (1986), *Services for Death and Burial* (1987), *Pastoral Liturgies and Prayers for Special Occasions* (1990) grew out of a vision of the 'word-and-table' shape of worship, renewed attention to Christian initiation and a greater awareness of the language of symbol and sacrament. Common lectionary and calendar became widely accepted with the introduction of the lectionary-based Christian educational curriculum, *Whole People of God*. *Inclusive language, lay leadership and 'intergenerational worship' has become more mainstream. White albs, seasonal stoles and architectural renovations are common. *Songs for a Gospel People* (Winfield 1987), a western

Canada initiative to supplement *Hymn Book*, was an instant best-seller and important precursor to the next generation of resources.

The new hymn book, *Voices United* (1996), filters the musical resources of liturgical convergence through a United Church lens. Its popular success suggests a significant impact on United Church worship. It is marked by a breadth of classic and contemporary texts and tunes, a variety of musical and cultural styles and diverse local and global contributions. Service music from Russia to Iona supports increasing sacramentality in United Church worship. The structure of the book is calendar-based and lectionary-indexed. Resources for prayer model orthodox and radical theologies. Inclusive language is the norm, balance is the goal, diversity is the result.

The latest service book is *Celebrate God's Presence* (2000). Nearly every section contains noteworthy if not controversial innovations. 'General' and 'seasonal' resources can be adapted to any order of service, though a word-and-table structure set within the Christian calendar is presupposed. *Eucharistic prayers range from that attributed to Hippolytus to those reflecting feminist Christologies and resources for original compositions. Services of initiation provide options for promises and blessings in inclusive language. Orders for 'Marriage and Life Partnership' permit same-sex covenants. Funeral materials include prayers for 'When a pregnancy is terminated' and 'On the death of a pet'. The second half of the book is given to pastoral occasions, including seasonal prayers beyond the scope of the traditional liturgical calendar, orders for the blessing of homes, fields, fisheries and animals, as well as ritual resources for 'healing,' 'closure' and daily prayer. *Celebrate God's Presence* is perhaps the first effort at a postmodern liturgical style that is post-ecumenical convergence. Notable, finally, is its title and several chapter headings, taken from the United Church's 'A New Creed'. Introduced in 1968, it is now widely used as an affirmation of faith and is increasingly definitive of United Church worship and theology.

Each generation of United Church worship resources reflects and contributes to the dialectic of order and liberty that is its liturgical ethos. Liturgical freedom continues to be prized; regional, theological and stylistic diversity persist; ecumenism, liberalism and activism converge. From the contributions of the founding traditions to the catholicity of an increasingly established church, the experimentation of the 1960s, the ecumenical convergence of the 1980s and the postmodernity of the turn of the millennium, worship in the United Church continues to strive for both the ordered wisdom of the 'many ages of devotion' and the freeing liberty of 'the leading of the Spirit'.

Alan Barthel, David R. Newman, Paul Scott Wilson (eds), *A Guide to Sunday Worship in The United Church of Canada*, Toronto 1988; Thomas Harding, 'Ordered Liberty: Sunday Worship in the United Church of Canada', *The Sunday Service of the Methodists: Twentieth-Century Worship in Worldwide Methodism*, ed. Karen B. Westerfield Tucker, Nashville, TN 1996, 95–116; Thomas Harding, *Presbyterian, Methodist and Congregational Worship in Canada Prior to 1925*, Toronto 1995 (bib.); Thomas Harding and Bruce Harding, *Patterns of Worship in The United Church of Canada 1925–1987*, Toronto 1996 (bib.).

WILLIAM S. KERVIN

Candle Service, Moravian

The *Moravian *Christnachtfeier* (Christmas Eve celebration) dates from 1732, and the distribution of candles at it from a children's *watch-night service held in Marienborn, Germany on Christmas Eve 1747 by Bishop Johannes von Watteville. After an opening hymn-verse, he catechized the children about the Christmas story. There were sung and said dialogues between bishop and children and solo hymn verses. Verses by the children were read. The bishop 'made it quite lively and fresh to them what unspeakable happiness accrues to us from our Saviour's being born'; Christ had 'kindled in each happy little heart a blood-red flame, which keeps ever burning to their joy and to our happiness; for an impressing memorial of which, each child shall now have a little lighted wax candle with a red ribbon, which was done accordingly and occasioned in great and small a happy children's joy.' During concluding responses, the children held their candles over their heads. After a final hymn verse they 'went out full of joy with their little lighted candles'.

At least until the 1970s, in German Moravian churches children sang or recited songs, verses or prayers individually at the *Kleine Christnacht*; they are still catechized about the Christmas story and may sing or perform a nativity play collectively. The Christmas story

(Luke 2) is read, punctuated with hymns, and the service culminates in the distribution of lighted candles to symbolize Christ's incarnation (cf. John 12.46). The candles have ruffs of paper strips – originally (and in America still) red, to symbolize the blood of Christ, but now also green, gold or white.

The first recorded Christmas Eve candle service in America was at Bethlehem, Pennsylvania in 1752. In 1756 the service concluded thus: 'Each [child] received a wax candle. These were lit during [two hymn-verses], and all of a sudden more than 250 candles were burning, producing a charming sight and a very lovely odour . . . Finally, Brother Petrus [Peter Boehler, the minister] dismissed the children with the wish that their hearts might burn as brightly toward the Child Jesus, as the candles now did. So they went home heartily content with burning candles in their hands.'

In most North American Moravian churches the candle service is for adults as well as children. In some, it takes the form of a *love-feast with coffee or chocolate milk and a biscuit or love-feast bun. The candles, handmade from beeswax, are distributed to all the worshippers during the singing of hymns. 'Morning star, O cheering sight!' – a translation of *Morgenstern auf finstre Nacht* by Johannes Scheffler (Angelus Silesius) – is sung antiphonally by a child soloist and the congregation. In Britain and Ireland, candles have been replaced by *Christingles.

COLIN PODMORE

Candlemas

Towards the end of the birth narrative of Jesus in Luke's Gospel, Jesus is presented in the Temple by his parents at the age of forty days, according to Jewish custom for all males; Luke conflates this with Mary's purification, then required after childbirth. The aged Simeon and Anna are there to greet Jesus, the former uttering the Nunc dimittis, and prophesying about the contradictions of Jesus' future ministry (Luke 2.22–40). This gospel event is celebrated in a festival forty days after the celebration of the Nativity (*see* **Christmas**), on 2 February in the Western calendar. In the East, where it originated in the fourth century, it is invariably called *Hypapante*, the 'meeting' of the five, a sign of the new community. In the West, it has been variously called 'The Purification of the Blessed Virgin Mary' and treated as a *Marian feast, or 'The Presentation

of the Lord', as nowadays in both Anglican and RC books. 'Candlemas' is a medieval nickname, of North European origin, referring to the ancient custom of a procession with lighted *candles before the *eucharist on this day (see Luke 2.32).

A. G. Martimort et al., *The Church at Prayer* IV, Collegeville 1986, 88–90; Kenneth W. Stevenson, 'The Origins and Development of Candlemas: A Struggle for Identity and Coherence?', *Time and Community*, ed. J. Neil Alexander, Washington, DC 1990, 43–80.

KENNETH W. STEVENSON

Candles, Lamps and Lights

The prominence of light in Christian theology perhaps made it inevitable that the use of lights at divine worship should be interpreted in a symbolic way. For in the early history of the church, services held either during the hours of darkness or in badly lit rooms and buildings necessitated artificial illumination. It was perhaps also inevitable that the early church borrowed some use of light both from the practices of the secular world in which it existed and from pagan religious ceremonies.

Lights may be divided into three types: functional, symbolic and honorific, or those lit in honour of a person. However, there is considerable overlap in their use; and from very early times a lamp or candle could serve all three purposes. Moreover, at times it is difficult to differentiate between their symbolic and honorific use, and it must be stressed that throughout the history of divine worship there has always been great diversity in the use of liturgical illumination.

The earliest evidence for the use of liturgical light, discounting the inconclusive mention of 'many lights' in Acts 20.8, is to be found in the document known as the *Apostolic Tradition* and conventionally dated *c.* 215, where a lamp is used symbolically at an evening service of prayer, known in later sources as the *lucernarium*. From the first part of the fourth century come references to the symbolic use of seven lamps and seven candlesticks in churches at Cirta in North Africa and at St John Lateran in Rome. That the functional use of light was given a symbolic interpretation is also apparent from the statement in the fourth-century church order, *Testamentum Domini*: 'Let all places be lighted, for a type and for the readings' (I.19). This would suggest that lights were used liturgically in all churches (if 'places' refers to buildings), and that their use had been extended to all Christian services.

1. *Baptism.* The use of lights at *baptism was almost certainly due to the influence of so-called mystery religions. As early as the fourth century the newly baptized received a candle both for symbolic reasons – baptism was termed 'illumination' – and for practical reasons: the ceremony took place during the dark hours of the *Easter vigil and could involve a procession. In earlier centuries it is not always clear at what point the baptizands received their candle. In later centuries, however, in the West it became usual to present the candidates – or more usually, with the increase of infant baptism, the sponsors – with a lighted candle after the administration of the sacrament, a practice which survives to this day. In some churches during the Middle Ages the candles were dipped into the blessed water of the *font either lit or unlit – practice varied – prior to distribution, symbolizing the descent of the Holy Spirit at Jesus' baptism.

2. *Eucharist.* Jerome in the fourth century attests the use of lights at the reading of the gospel during the *eucharist. Originally to provide light for reading, they came to symbolize the presence of Christ in the written word, and are still used in this way both in the Western and Orthodox traditions. In the Roman rite the *Easter candle is used for this purpose at the gospel during the Easter vigil. In the early Middle Ages seven candles were borne in procession at the introit by *acolytes when the Bishop of Rome presided at the eucharist. They symbolized both his temporal power in that city and also the unity of the Roman Church. By the sixteenth century their number had been reduced to two; and today their processional use is closely associated with the book of the Gospels. In the later Middle Ages it became common to light a candle at the consecration, a practice which subsequently became optional. From at least the fourth century seven lights were placed in front of the altar in symbolic imitation of the seven lamps which burned before the throne of God in Revelation 4.5. In later centuries these lamps were replaced in many churches by a seven-branch candlestick introduced into western Europe in the wake of the Crusades in imitation of the menorah of Solomon's Temple. Some examples survive in parts of central Europe and Scandinavia.

3. *Altar Lights.* The placing of candles on the *altar both at the eucharist and at the offices dates from the eleventh century. For practical reasons two was the usual number; but with the extension in the length of altars in the West in the eleventh century larger numbers became possible. Their number has varied from diocese to diocese and from monastery to monastery depending on the type of service or the rank of the president or the feast day. Two are still usual at most of the services in the Roman, Anglican and Lutheran traditions; but at high *mass and at *benediction in the Roman Tridentine rite six and twelve lights respectively are used. Among the Eastern churches altar candles are lit only during the eucharist.

4. *Other Uses.* Lights have been used extensively throughout Christendom to honour both the living and the dead, and the presence of God, and many of the usages derive ultimately from pre-Christian rites and practices. Inherited from paganism are the perpetual lights at tombs, and later by extension those lit to honour the relics of Christian *saints both in churches and at the *consecration of churches which involved the use of relics. In some liturgical traditions candles are placed next to the coffin at *funerals in honour of the deceased. The use of honorific lights is more prominent in Eastern churches, where lights burn in church before the *icons on the chancel screen, known as the *iconostasis, and before icons in private homes. From *c.* 1000 in the West the reserved sacrament has been honoured with its own light whether in a *tabernacle in RC churches or in the *aumbry often used in Anglican churches; and also during the sacrament's repose in the *Easter sepulchre from *Maundy Thursday to *Holy Saturday.

Among other symbolic uses of lights in Christian liturgy are the Easter candle and in more recent times the Christmas candle, which represent respectively the resurrection and nativity of Christ. The latter is surrounded by four red or purple candles which, lit one each week, themselves stand for the four Sundays of Advent (*see* **Advent Wreath**). Formerly candles were extinguished one by one at the night office of the last three days of *Holy Week, known as *tenebrae, 'darkness'. The varying number used from church to church may have symbolized the desertion or the weariness of the disciples in the Garden of Gethsemane. The triple candle, formerly used to light the Easter candle, came to symbolize the Trinity, as does still the *trikiri*, or three-pronged light, held by the bishop at the blessing in the Byzantine tradition; the *dikiri*, or double candle held in the bishop's other hand, stands for the two natures of Christ.

The provision and number of lights, whether for functional or for liturgical purposes, has throughout the liturgical history of the church been to a large extent determined by the cost of both containers (lamps, candlesticks) and fuel (wax, oil), and their use or not, as the case may be, has usually reflected the wealth of individual churches. In most traditions of the church there is still a preference or even obligation to use either oil lamps or candles for all ritual or liturgical action; although for reasons of safety the use of electric light for the sanctuary lamp is not unknown. The high cost of beeswax has meant that altar candles and the Easter candle now contain only a percentage of this substance; and other ornamental and hand-held candles are usually made of paraffin wax or tallow.

Active congregational participation in the liturgical use of light includes the carrying of a lighted candle in procession at the Presentation of our Lord (*Candlemas) on 2 February – a ceremony inherited from the pagan Roman rites of Ceres; the holding of a candle at the renewal of *baptismal vows during the Easter vigil; and in more recent years the use of a small candle symbolizing Christ the light of the world at the *Christingle service.

The use of lights in the East has never been uniform, each church being independent in this matter. Attempts to enforce uniformity in the Catholic West were made in the sixteenth century when Rome made mandatory the use of the new Roman Missal following the Council of Trent. However, many of the dioceses of France continued to observe their traditional practices until well into the nineteenth century. At the Reformation the Lutheran, but not the Calvinist, churches continued to use lights at the eucharist; and it is only in the twentieth century that opposition to their use in churches of the Anglican Communion has by and large disappeared.

Adrian Fortescue and J. B. O'Connell (eds), *The Ceremonies of the Roman Rite*, 11th edn, London 1960; D. R. Dendy, *The Use of Lights in Christian Worship*, London 1959; A. J. MacGregor, *Fire and Light in the Western Triduum*, Collegeville 1992.

A. J. MACGREGOR

Canon *see* **Eucharistic Prayer**

Canonical Hours *see* **Daily Prayer**

Canticles

From the Latin *canticulum*, a small song. Canticles are songs (and other passages used as songs) from the Bible other than from the Book of Psalms. The four canticles most widely used in Christian worship are the *Benedictus (Luke 1.68–79; not to be confused with the Benedictus qui venit which follows the *Sanctus in most *eucharistic prayers), the Magnificat (Luke 1.46–55), the Nunc dimittis (Luke 2.29–32) and the Benedicite (verses 35–66a of the Song of the Three Holy Children in the Apocrypha). These are to be found used in the daily office of traditions in both East and West (*see* **Daily Prayer**). The present RC daily office as well as other present and past liturgies use some fifty or more different canticles. In addition there are a number of ancient Christian *hymns used or referred to as canticles, among them the Te Deum laudamus. The Church of England Franciscan office, *Celebrating Common Prayer*, includes as canticles passages composed up to the last century.

Canticles are generally used in two different ways in the daily office. The first is as a supplement to the psalms, making use of poetic passages of scripture. The second is to mark the particular hour of the day. In the Eastern Orthodox Church the Magnificat is the canticle for *orthros* (morning prayer). Originally it was paired with the Benedictus and came as the last of a series of nine canticles (now recited only in Lent). The West originally had a similar pattern but the Magnificat was moved to become the canticle for the evening office and the Nunc dimittis used at compline.

At the Reformation the Church of England abandoned compline with most of the other medieval hours of prayer, and had a canticle after each of the two readings in morning and evening prayer, with a psalm as an alternative. The three Lucan canticles were employed along with the Te Deum and the Benedicite. With more complex offices in the last generation this Anglican pattern has to some extent dissolved.

Robert F. Taft, *The Liturgy of the Hours in East and West*, 2nd edn, Collegeville 1993.

GORDON JEANES

Cantor

The person, clerical or lay, who sets the pitch and leads the singing – especially unaccompanied singing. In *Jewish synagogue worship the cantor is a minister of considerable importance, and the office has also existed in both Eastern and Western Christendom. In the former the cantor is a minor cleric. With the elaboration of psalmody and its accompanying *antiphons in the monastic and cathedral services of the medieval West, the cantor became essential for the proper performance of the *eucharist and daily offices (see **Daily Prayer** 3). Elaborate rules were laid down to govern the number of cantors proper to the various feasts and seasons. The titles of precentor and succentor borne by some clergy in *cathedral and collegiate churches are derived from the term, as is the custom of describing the northern side of the *choir as 'cantoris'.

GORDON JEANES

Carol

Normally a popular religious song associated with a season of the church *year, and especially with *Christmas. There is a small number of non-religious carol texts. Although similar songs can be found in France, Germany, Italy and Spain, the carol is distinct to the English language. The term 'carol' may derive from the French carole and from dancing, but most English carols are not dance songs. Over at least eight centuries 'carol' has come to be applied to many songs. Only in the fourteenth to sixteenth centuries does it relate to a specific genre, Thereafter it encompasses folk song, part song and *hymn, or a mixture of the three. Six significant periods of carol composition and compilation can be delineated in England: the fourteenth and fifteenth centuries, the sixteenth century, the eighteenth century, the nineteenth century, the early twentieth century, and the late twentieth century.

Medieval English carols are found in six main manuscript sources dating from the fifteenth and early sixteenth century (though some were composed in the fourteenth century). They are distinct in form and language. The form consists of a burden (or refrain) and verses. The burden is sung before the first verse and after each verse. The text is usually vernacular or macaronic (Latin and English). Most are *polyphonic, normally for three voices, but sometimes only two, especially in the verse sections. Some carols (e.g. 'There is no rose') reveal the influence of contemporary improvised polyphony (faburden and discant). Some have courtly associations, others may be monastic in origin, though they seem to be non-liturgical. However, the frequent use of the refrain Benedicamus Domino may indicate some relation to worship, either as a substitute for a liturgical item, or perhaps for use outside the church in cloister or hall. At least two come from the Coventry cycle of mystery plays, and others may have had associations with medieval *drama.

Sixteenth-century carols are polyphonic songs with five or more voices, often following the formal burden and verse pattern of the medieval carol. Among them are Byrd's 'Lullaby, An earthly tree' and 'This day Christ was born'. These are part of the domestic repertory of polyphonic part songs and consort songs sung at court and in the houses of the aristocracy and educated merchants. An anonymous setting of 'Swete was the song the virgin sang' is known in versions for voices and lute, voice and bass viol, and voice and four instruments, indicative of the adaptation of such pieces to suit different circumstances.

By contrast with the high culture of earlier carols, the eighteenth-century gallery carols are unsophisticated, more closely related to folk tradition melded with the burgeoning genre of English hymnody. Sung in parish church *galleries at Christmas, especially in the West Country, their verse is straightforward and their musical technique primitive. Here, perhaps more than elsewhere, the associations of the oral traditions of folk song and folk poetry, and the written idioms of *metrical psalm and vernacular hymn come closest. Many of the folk carols collected in the nineteenth century have far earlier origins: 'The Boar's Head Carol' dates at least to the sixteenth century, and both 'The St Day Carol' and 'The Cherry Carol' may have even earlier roots.

The decline of the carol was noted in 1822 by William Hone and Davies Gilbert. The revival was led by scholars and antiquarians, and among the most significant collections are those made by Sandys (1833), Rimbault (1846), and Neale and Helmore (1853 and 1854). The Victorian construction of Christmas celebration may have encouraged Stainer and Bramley's popular volume, Christmas Carols New and Old (1871), whose use was widespread well into the second half of the twentieth century. This collection includes many of what are now the most popular traditional texts and melodies as well as newly composed carols, often sentimental in mood and musical style, though not unattractive (e.g. Barnby's 'The virgin stills the crying').

Far more robust is the classic collection of *The Oxford Book of Carols* (1928), edited by Percy Dearmer, Ralph Vaughan Williams and Martin Shaw. It followed on from *The Cowley Carol Book* (1901) and *The Cambridge Carol Book* (1924), which each introduced texts and melodies from Continental Europe, as well as traditional English carols. *The Oxford Book of Carols* is systematically ordered. At its core are the texts and melodies of English Christian folksong, many of them sensitively harmonized by Vaughan Williams, including 'This is the truth' and 'The Sussex Carol'. There are also foreign and new carols, including Holst's 'Lullay, my liking', Warlock's 'Adam lay ybounden', and Rubbra's 'Dormi Jesu'.

The annual Festival of Nine Lessons and Carols from King's College, Cambridge, first broadcast on radio in 1929, has been influential internationally, not only in the promulgation of carol services but also of the repertory. One of the most significant broadcasts included new arrangements and descants by David Willcocks in 1958. Here the world of carol concert and carol service came together stylistically. The related volume, *Carols for Choirs* (1961), has led the way to a proliferation of new and newly arranged carols for choir, choir and organ, and choir and orchestra, with John Rutter as the doyen of the idiom. Set against this trend is *The New Oxford Book of Carols* (1992), edited by Andrew Parrott and Hugh Keyte, an even wider anthology than its predecessor, well researched and intended to recover something of the strength of a genre which has its roots in popular religious tradition. It also includes some of the more striking, and strikingly simple, later twentieth-century carols composed by Boris Ord, John Joubert, Richard Rodney Bennett and Peter Maxwell Davies.

'Carol', *NG2*, V, 162–73; Hugh Keyte and Andrew Parrott (eds), *The New Oxford Book of Carols*, Oxford 1992; Erik Routley, *The English Carol*, London 1958; John Stevens (ed.), *Mediaeval Carols*, London 1952, 2nd edn 1958, revised 1970.

JOHN HARPER

Cassock *see* **Vestments** 3(d)

Catechesis *see* **Catechumen**

Catechism

A manual of Christian doctrine intended either to be used by those teaching the faith or as a simple summary for those learning about it. Catechisms were actively used before the Reformation but after the publication of Luther's *Kleiner Katechismus*, 'Small Catechism' (1529), they multiplied. Other Protestant catechisms include those of Geneva (Calvinist), Heidelberg (Calvinist/Lutheran) and Westminster (Presbyterian).

The Anglican Catechism was not published separately but included in the 1549 *BCP*. It provided a series of questions and answers 'to be learned of every person before he be brought to be confirmed by the Bishop'. It included the *Lord's Prayer, Apostles' *Creed and Ten Commandments with teaching about the *sacraments. Since 1661 there has been a requirement to give instruction in the catechism after the second lesson at evensong but this has almost certainly never happened. An extended version called *The Revised Catechism* was published in 1961 but no catechism was bound into the *Alternative Service Book 1980*. The American Episcopal Church produced a new catechism for its 1979 *BCP* and this has been widely followed by other Anglican provinces.

The RC Catechism of 1566 was intended as a guide for clergy and propagated the teachings of the Council of Trent. The RC Church in England produced *A Catechism of Christian Doctrine* in 1898 which was widely used and popularly known as the 'Penny Catechism'. In 1992 the RC Church produced an extensive *Catechism of the Catholic Church* which expresses traditional teaching in the terms used at and after the Second Vatican Council.

MARTIN DUDLEY

Catechist

A term with distinct but related meanings in religious education, missionary organization and the liturgical rites of initiation. *Catechumens in the early church were interviewed, instructed and supervised by persons described variously as 'teachers' or 'doctors', who led them in prayer, laid hands on them and delivered instruction, as well as sharing in the weekday ministry of the word to the baptized faithful. In recent centuries the ministry was revived in missionary churches, and catechists assumed the important role of religious educators, prayer leaders and local pastoral deputies to an often itinerant clergy.

The twentieth-century *Liturgical Movement was accompanied by a catechetical movement which saw Christian formation of both adults and children more in the context of the life and worship of the parish community than in the schoolroom, and led to a developing ministry of lay volunteers and specialists. With the restoration of a formal catechumenate after the Second Vatican Council and the issue of the revised Roman rites of infant baptism (1969) and adult initiation (1972), as well as rites for the catechumenate in the US Episcopal Church (1979), the role of the catechist was given formal liturgical recognition. In infant *baptism, catechists assist in the preparation of parents and *godparents and, in the Roman rite, may be deputed to celebrate the baptism in the absence of a priest. In adult initiation, catechists assist in the formation and discernment of candidates, and may be deputed to conduct minor rites such as *exorcisms and *blessings.

———

David Power, *Gifts that Differ: Lay Ministries Established and Unestablished*, New York 1980.

CHRISTOPHER WALSH

Catechumen, Catechumenate

From the Greek verb *catecheo*, meaning 'to instruct' or 'to resound or echo in the ear', catechumens are adult converts preparing for *baptism, after having been enrolled in the catechumenate, a period of formation, prayer and discernment in the Christian life. In current RC practice, the catechumenate is to last for at least one year, following a period of unspecified length called Inquiry or Precatechumenate. At the end of this period, catechumens are 'elected' for baptism, usually at the *cathedral on the first Sunday of *Lent, and then, as *electi*, *illuminandi* or *photizomenoi* (those to be 'enlightened') enter a more intense period of preparation throughout Lent ('Purification and Enlightenment'), during which various rites, including *scrutinies, are celebrated on the third, fourth and fifth Sundays. After the rites of initiation at the *Easter vigil, those now designated neophytes enter yet another period called 'Mystagogy' during which '*mystagogical catechesis' on the sacraments is provided.

The practice just described for the contemporary RC rite and for many other Christian traditions today is a modern attempt at restoring early Christian catechumenal processes for adult converts. Sources from the late first (*Didache*) and mid-second century (Justin Martyr) refer to the pre-baptismal moral formation of converts, including the requirement of fasting, and in the early third century Tertullian describes frequent prayer, fasting and *vigils for this period. The so-called *Apostolic Tradition*, attributed to Hippolytus of Rome (*c*. 215), divides the catechumenate into a three-year period for *audientes* ('hearers') and the period of more intense preparation after their 'election', without indicating when during the liturgical year this was to take place. The 'Golden Age' of the catechumenate was during the fourth and fifth centuries, as indicated in the catechetical sermons of Cyril of Jerusalem, Theodore of Mopsuestia and John Chrysostom for the East, and Ambrose of Milan, Augustine of Hippo as well as others for the West. By this time the period of final preparation for baptism coincided with Lent. Ceremonies like the giving of salt and signings with the cross accompanied enrolment, catechesis focused also on the contents of the *creed in addition to moral formation, several *exorcisms and scrutinies accompanied the process at various intervals, and additional ceremonies, such as the solemn *traditio symboli* (the delivery of the creed) and the *redditio symboli* (the recitation of the creed by memory before baptism), the introduction to the Gospels, or the giving and return of the 'Our Father', were added before baptism ultimately took place at the Easter vigil. Catechumens, both *audientes* and *electi*, were regularly dismissed from the liturgical assembly prior to the celebration of the *eucharist, and sponsors or *godparents were called upon not only to assist the catechumens in their formation but to testify on their behalf both prior to election and prior to baptism itself.

Until its modern restoration, and with the exception of some relatively successful attempts at restoration by Catholic missionaries in the sixteenth century, the success of the catechumenate and the widespread practice of infant initiation from Augustine onwards led to its disappearance. Although in the early Middle Ages it seems that parents still brought their infants for 'catechesis' during Lent, what appears to have taken place were some of the ceremonies previously associated with catechesis in the early period. Eventually, the catechumenate itself was compressed into a series of multiple pre-baptismal ceremonies for the making of catechumens (e.g. exorcisms, compressed scrutinies and other rites) done at the beginning of the baptismal rite at the door of the church building. Hence, what in early Christianity may have taken years to accomplish was reduced to a few minutes.

Michel Dujarier, *A History of the Catechumenate: The First Six Centuries*, New York 1979; Maxwell E. Johnson, *The Rites of Christian Initiation: Their Evolution and Interpretation*, Collegeville 1999; E. C. Whitaker, *Documents of the Baptismal Liturgy*, London 1970; Edward Yarnold, *The Awe-Inspiring Rites of Initiation*, 2nd edn, Edinburgh/Collegeville 1994.

MAXWELL E. JOHNSON

Cathedra

The principal seat of the *bishop in the mother church of his diocese, named from the Greek, signifying 'a thing sat upon', and hence giving the name '*cathedral' to the bishop's church. The model of monarchical episcopacy saw this seat as a throne, a symbol of rule, and from this came the term 'enthronement' for the official inauguration of a bishop's ministry. The Syrian author of the late fourth-century *Apostolic Constitutions* (8.5) writes: 'And early in the morning let him be placed in this throne in a place set apart for him among the bishops, they all giving him the kiss in the Lord.' This was the sign that the bishop was invested with authority to oversee the affairs of the local church in a designated territorial area or diocese. From this rite the cathedra came to be seen as the principal symbol of the bishop's authority, long before bishops took to wearing mitres (*see* **Vestments** 3.d) or rings or even to carrying the pastoral staff or crozier. Other early authorities understand the chair to be the *protokathedra* or seat of the first *elder of the church. The chair of the bishop flanked by the seats of the *presbyters (*synthronos*) around the *apse can be seen as an expression of the collegiality of the bishop with his priests.

The *Testamentum Domini* (a fifth-century Greek text, surviving only in a seventh-century Syrian translation), giving precise instructions concerning the liturgical ordering of church buildings, dictates that the cathedra should be placed in the centre of the apse, behind the *altar and elevated upon three steps. From here the bishop both presided at the *eucharist and gave instruction. This arrangement survives in a number of early cathedral buildings on the European continent. In northern Europe after 1200 the apsidal east ends of cathedral churches were either squared off, as generally the case in England, or developed into a series of radiating chapels, as in France, and so the bishop's chair had to be located to one side of the *sanctuary, west of the high altar.

New models of episcopacy would see the cathedra as less of a throne and more of the chair of a teacher, much as a university professor today is still said to 'hold the chair' of his or her discipline. It is the pre-eminent sign of the teaching authority belonging to the bishop in his own church. The monarchical idea of enthronement has been rightly abandoned in favour of the more presidential suggestion of installation. Today the siting of the bishop's chair is crucial in the ordering of a new cathedral building. The chair anchors the place from which the bishop exercises presidency, providing a visual assurance of order in the assembly. Its position should suggest neither domination nor remoteness. By analogy the chair of the presiding priest, who represents the bishop at the eucharist in the local context, should occupy a similar position in a parish church building.

Richard Krautheimer, *Early Christian and Byzantine Architecture*, Harmondsworth 1975; National Conference of Catholic Bishops (USA), *Environment and Art in Catholic Worship*, Washington, DC 1978; Mark G. Boyer, *The Liturgical Environment – What the Documents Say*, Collegeville 1990.

JEREMY HASELOCK

Cathedral

The principal church building of a diocese, housing the bishop's *cathedra, and from which the *bishop exercises spiritual and teaching authority and liturgical presidency. It should be the principal diocesan centre of worship and mission and, as such, the naturally appropriate place for the bishop to *baptize and *confirm, to preside at the *eucharist, to perform *ordinations, to teach, and to officiate at diocesan services.

The significant architectural features of cathedrals built in the West before the *Liturgical Movement extended its influence into the environment of worship can be traced directly back to the secular *basilica of Roman times. The *aisled, columnar hall with clerestory and wooden roof required remarkably little change to suit religious purposes, designed as it was for the performance of a variety of rituals in the presence of a large assembly. The bishop's chair, replacing that of the magistrate, was placed at the head of the major axis of the building and the *altar on the chord of the *apse. This utilitarian approach to architecture was initially appropriate to a body of believers who could worship anywhere, for whom the building was merely a 'house for the Church'. However, it was soon replaced by a view, originating in the OT and developed after 312 under imperial patronage, which saw the building more as the house of God on the model of Solomon's Temple. Eusebius's account of his own cathedral at Tyre (*Ecclesiastical History* X. iv. 37–63) treats the building as a distinctive holy place and draws close parallels with the Jerusalem Temple. The increasingly political role of the bishop in the early Middle Ages saw his church aggrandized as scale and magnificence were equated with power and wealth.

The adapted basilican plan was sustained throughout the Middle Ages remarkably unchanged, as for example at Norwich, even when developing liturgical customs required the accommodation of enclosed *choirs for the clergy; shrines for saintly relics (often in a 'feretory' at the east end) and the consequent provision of circulation space for *pilgrims; and extra altars as private *masses became the norm and *chantry foundations proliferated. The rediscovery of classical architecture in the Renaissance for the most part reaffirmed the basilican plan (as in Michelangelo's St Peter's basilica in the Vatican), which then remained the norm either in classical or Gothic-revival dress until the twentieth century.

A renewed understanding of liturgy and of the role of the assembly in worship since the Second Vatican Council has led to a radical rethink in cathedral design. The continuing requirement for wide open spaces for impressive ceremonies and the contrasting need to form the eucharistic community more closely *around* the altar and the bishop's chair have combined to result in centrally planned designs such as Liverpool Metropolitan Cathedral, consecrated in 1967, and St Mary's Roman Catholic Cathedral, San Francisco.

Cathedral organization has developed far further from its primitive origins than has its basic architecture. Originally served by the bishop and his household clergy, the administration of the cathedral was soon delegated to a group of specialist clerics who were also charged with running the increasingly more elaborate cathedral worship. This body developed into a distinct ecclesiastical corporation or chapter with privileges and rights granted by the bishop. Uniquely in England, eight of the medieval cathedrals were staffed by monastic communities ruled by a prior (the bishop being titular abbot), while the other nine followed the more normal model of a chapter of secular canons presided over by a dean. At the Reformation in England the religious communities were suppressed and the monastic cathedrals refounded – hence cathedrals of the New Foundation – with secular deans, chapters and new statutes. Six former abbey churches were raised to cathedral status to serve the new dioceses created by Henry VIII and provided with deans and chapters. Today, since the *Cathedrals Measure* of 1999, all English cathedrals are governed by new statutes whereby the considerable freedoms hitherto enjoyed by deans and chapters are curtailed and the capitular body made answerable to a Cathedral Council on which there is substantial lay representation.

The role of the cathedral in today's church and society has been much debated. Throughout the twentieth century there was a move away from the inward-looking, quasi-monastic model of a capitular body dedicated exclusively to daily worship, the encouragement of scholarship and the preservation of privilege, to an active view of the cathedral as the mother church of its diocese, seeking both a wider role in the local community and to be a sign of the church within the life of the world. Today, extending logically from the primary functions associated with being the bishop's church, English cathedrals try to keep up daily worship of a greater beauty and degree of elaboration than is generally possible in the parishes, using their resources to maintain professional standards of music-making and to safeguard five centuries of a choral tradition that is the envy of the world. Key figures like Walter Hussey, Dean of Chichester from 1955 to 1977, pushed cathedrals into the forefront of the movement to revive Christian art. As liturgical laboratories, cathedrals are privileged to lead the way in the renewal of core forms of worship, to pioneer new forms of service and to model good practice. Cathedrals can generally keep open all day to admit tourists, schoolchildren, pilgrims and those who come to pray in times of need, and in the popular mind they are the natural venues for great services of rejoicing or national mourning.

Heritage and Renewal: The Report of the Arch-bishops' Commission on Cathedrals, London 1994; M. Kitchen, J. Halliburton and K. Walker (eds), *Cathedrals in Society*, London 1995; I. M. Mackenzie (ed.), *Cathedrals Now*, London 1996; Stephen Platten and Christopher Lewis (eds), *Flagships of the Spirit*, London 1998.

JEREMY HASELOCK

Cathedral Office *see* **Daily Prayer 1**

Celebrant

A term which has been commonly used for the leader of a liturgical service, though less widely employed in the *rubrics of recently revised liturgical books. A recovered appreciation of the entire worshipping assembly as the agent or celebrant, in Christ, of the liturgical action is implicit in most contemporary liturgical books and not infrequently explicitly affirmed. All baptized believers are celebrants or concelebrants of the liturgy. In consequence, those who lead are now more usually described by reference to their differentiating rank or ordained status (e.g. minister, priest, *bishop) or to their functional role within the celebrating assembly (e.g. president, presiding minister).

The term is retained most prominently in the rites of North American Anglicans (USA 1979, Canada 1985) and in the RC rite of adult initiation (1972). Except in the case of *concelebration, it is no longer employed in the rubrics of the Roman Missal, but only in the attached General Instruction where it is qualified as 'priest celebrant' and balanced by reference to the active role of the entire assembly (no. 95) and to the presiding role of the bishop or priest (nos 93, 310). The Church of England's *Common Worship* (2000) uses 'minister' and 'priest' but most commonly 'president', a usage going back as far as the second century.

The presiding celebrant acts not so much for, or on behalf of, a passive congregation, but with them. He or she leads the people in prayer, in listening to and assimilating the word, in response and offering, encourages the participation of all and co-ordinates it into one harmonious action. Presiding skills have emerged as a distinct discipline in formation for all levels of ministry.

Robert Hovda, *Strong, Loving and Wise: Presiding in Liturgy*, Collegeville 1976; Lucien Deiss, *Persons in Liturgical Celebrations*, Chicago 1978; H. G. Hardin, *The Leadership*

of Worship, Nashville, TN 1980; Aidan Kavanagh, *Elements of Rite: A Handbook of Liturgical Style*, New York 1982; Kathleen Hughes, *Lay Presidency: The Art of Leading Prayer*, Washington 1988.

CHRISTOPHER WALSH

Celtic Rite *see* **Western Rites**

Censer

The generic title for all containers in which *incense is burned. Although it is normally burned in a *thurible, and thus able to be carried about during worship and swung ceremonially, it may also be burned in a stationary bowl, made of pottery or of metal in varying degrees of ornateness. Such bowls are usually placed before an *altar or an *icon, or sometimes in close proximity to the *Easter candle, and although they may be re-charged with either charcoal or incense during the liturgy, they are not normally carried about.

TRISTAM HOLLAND

Centralized Building

A symmetrical plan, radiating in equal distances from a centre core. Examples include a square, circle, hexagon, octagon, or Greek cross (with all the arms the same length). Early Christian examples were primarily polygonal *baptisteries and round *martyria (built over a saint's tomb or a holy place such as the Church of the Nativity in Bethlehem). Baptisteries adopted central-plan funerary structures as appropriate for the experience of dying with Christ in baptism. They were often octagonal, symbolizing the eighth day, the day of the resurrection of Christ and new life. Parish churches were generally not built on a central plan as the *basilica was better suited to a processional liturgy. Although efforts were made to reintroduce the central plan during the Renaissance and later, it is only since Vatican II that a central plan with the assembly gathered around an *altar in the middle became widespread for RC parish churches.

See also **Architectural Setting.**

MARCHITA B. MAUCK

Ceremonial

The ceremonies of the church are intended to give glory to God and to lift the hearts and minds of worshippers to heavenly realities, using a system of signs, *movements and actions. Ceremony concerns action rather than words and ceremonial includes actions of all sorts, e.g. bowing, genuflecting, processing, making the sign of the cross, sprinkling water, *anointing, censing persons and things (*see also* **Gestures**). The Council of Trent (Sess. XXII, cap. v) included in ceremonial not only the actions but also the things over which or with which prayers are pronounced, e.g. *candles, *incense, *vestments, etc. In Anglican terms these latter objects count as 'ornaments'. *Ritual, in ecclesiastical terminology, generally refers to the words spoken, but contemporary ritual studies are concerned with the human ability to perform a wide range of ritual actions and would view liturgical ceremonies as instances of ritual. In general, therefore, we may say that the sum total of the ceremonies of an individual function makes a rite (*ritus*), e.g. the rite of baptism, and the ceremonies common to a given church or communion create a Rite or Use, e.g. the Roman Rite, the Ambrosian Rite, the Use of Sarum. The volume called a Ceremonial sets out the details of the ceremonies appropriate to a given church or group of people. Thus, a monastic ceremonial (*Caeremoniale monasticon*) prescribes the way in which the members of the community enter and leave the choir, bow, prostrate, sit, etc., to establish a conformity of use. The RC Ceremonial of Bishops provides for all the ceremonies at which a *bishop presides.

MARTIN DUDLEY

Chair or Chairman of District

In British Methodism this office dates from 1792. Each Chair of District has pastoral and disciplinary responsibility for the *presbyters and *deacons within the circuits of his or her district. They are involved in ministerial appointments, have a leadership and worship role within their districts and preside over their own synods. Each works ecumenically with the *bishops and regional leaders of other Christian traditions, but none at present has any ex officio role in *ordinations.

C. NORMAN R. WALLWORK

Chaldean Church

see **East Syrian Worship**

Chalice and Paten

Liturgical vessels used to hold the wine and bread respectively at the *eucharist. From the Middle Ages in the West the paten normally rested on the chalice when not in use. In addition to a chalice and paten, the Byzantine rite requires an *asteriskos* (literally meaning 'star' in Greek: a metal frame used to hold a *veil up above the eucharistic loaf); a small knife (used during the preparation of the eucharistic bread, and symbolizing the centurion's lance at the crucifixion); and a spoon (used for administering *communion to the laity). Since they were viewed as being characteristic of the ministry of priests, chalice and paten also became the symbols of office solemnly given to newly ordained priests by the *bishop at their *ordination in the medieval West, a practice continued down to the present in the RC Church and in some Anglican churches.

1. *Chalice* (from the Latin *calix*, 'drinking vessel'). In the Christian centuries before the Carolingian period (late eighth century), in the absence of formal restrictions, chalices were made of the same variety of materials as secular cups: glass, wood, horn, ivory and costly and base metals. Repeated attempts were made in following centuries to ensure that only silver, silver-gilt and gold were used for eucharistic vessels; but a certain amount of variety persisted especially in the chalice-foot rather than the bowl itself. These regulations did not apply to funerary vessels.

The dimensions and form have, however, evolved without regulation. Surviving early examples and iconography attest to the widespread use of a deep goblet (often double-handled), with a shallow foot, for so long as the faithful received in both kinds, and especially in the East. However, from the late twelfth century new forms emerged, comprising several parts: wide circular foot, knop, possibly a cylindrical stem, and the *cuppa* itself. By the end of the following century the process of elongation in the profile was widespread, not least because the chalice's function had, with the near total disappearance of communion in both kinds, changed into a sacrificial vessel partaken only by the clergy. The decision of the Council of Constance (1414–18) to withhold the chalice from the faithful consolidated this development. The foot developed a polygonal lobed outline, either convex or concave, and the knop was increasingly decorated with architectural devices or ornaments. In the more elaborate examples the whole stem receives architectural and figurative treatment. This shape was standard throughout the sixteenth century, though a parallel development had been under way in Italy since the mid-Renaissance (1450s). Here a simple, small, lipped beaker-bowl nestles amid ornamental decoration atop an even further elongated and decorated stem; the knop often resembled a pear, and together with an often large semi-ovoid base was covered in beaten and chased (typically foliage) decoration. This form served the enterprise of Baroque artists without much further development. Designers in the nineteenth and twentieth centuries have developed revival interpretations of both traditions.

The restoration of communion in both kinds at the Reformation in England prompted the development in the mid-seventeenth to early nineteenth century of a significantly larger, deep, straight-sided form. A *tazza* or shallow cup mounted on a foot (similar to the paten in the East) served as a paten in use, and lid when not. Apart from engravings they are often quite plain.

Stylized period ornamentation was often added to chalices, but various aspects of the sacrifice of the cross evolved into a complex design tradition of symbol and inscription. There is a rich interplay in Christian iconography between the wounds of Christ, especially his pierced side (a primary theme in the gospel crucifixion and resurrection narratives), and the chalice. Either angels are depicted at Calvary collecting the Saviour's blood in chalices, or the Saviour (typically the entombed 'man of sorrows' form) appears above the *altar during the eucharist, blood flowing into the chalice. In either direction the dogmatic relationship between Calvary and the eucharistic chalice is highlighted. Occasionally the 'man of sorrows' is shown in a chalice.

2. *Paten* (from the Greek, *patene*, 'basin'). The paten shared with its companion, the chalice, the initial lack of restriction on material for manufacture. Its dimensions and form were heavily influenced by its use, not least because of the liturgically crucial action of the 'breaking of the bread'. The *fraction retained its significance until the twelfth century, and increasingly widespread use of pre-cut *hosts and irregular communion. The earliest patens are often rectangular (a circular form only coming to dominate when a handle-less chalice was in general use) and feature enamels. The proportions were much reduced once it came to be used for the *celebrant's host alone. A standard disk form developed, sometimes

incorporating a shallow, bevelled central dish and wide brim to make the paten more practical in use. Its wide flat surface is often used for images of sacrifice, particularly in the East, where it was also usually mounted on a foot. Increasingly today, larger dish patens (and *ciboria) are used in the West to accommodate the pattern of more frequent communion.

V. H. Elbern, 'Der eucharistiche Kelch im frühen Mittelalter', *Zeitschrift des Deutschen Vereins für Kunstwissenschaft* XVII, 1953, 1–67, 117–88; 'Kelch', *Lexikon des Mittelalters* V, Munich 1991; W. Watts, *Catalogue of Chalices*, London 1922; 'Chalice', *The Grove Dictionary of Art*, London 1996 (bib.).

JONATHAN GOODALL

Chancel

The entire end of the church beyond the crossing where the main altar is located. An elaborate arch sometimes marks the transition from the rest of the church into the chancel. Also called the presbytery, historically this was the space in which assisting clergy (*deacons and *subdeacons) gathered with the presiding priest, and was ordinarily separated from the rest of the church by lattice-like *screens or *cancelli*. The name chancel derives from the Latin word *cancellus* or dividing screen. Eventually the word for the screen came to designate the area for the clergy set apart by the screen. Chancel screens were of stone or elaborately carved wood. Particularly in English churches complex screen designs could include *galleries with stairs as well as vaulting, paintings and intricate tracery. Chancel screens often supported a rood (or cross) that could include images of John and Mary flanking the crucified Christ. Such chancel screens were called rood screens.

MARCHITA B. MAUCK

Chant, Byzantine *see* Byzantine Chant

Chant, Gregorian *see* Gregorian Chant

Chantry

An endowment to pay for *masses offered for the souls of particular deceased persons. Chantry *chapels were endowed for the masses offered on behalf of the founder or the founder's relatives. A small chapel attached to a church can also be called a chantry.

MARCHITA B. MAUCK

Chants

One of the particularities of the reformed English church is the chanting of psalms to a harmonized melodic formula, normally repeated every one or two verses. The practice was formalized in the late seventeenth and eighteenth centuries, but its origins can be traced back to the Middle Ages. Latin psalms and *canticles were chanted to one of the plainsong *psalm-tones, chosen to match the *antiphon. It became customary to elaborate on these tones in *polyphony in alternate verses. Some of this elaboration was recorded in written-down polyphony, but most was improvised. Forms of this improvised practice were widespread throughout Europe, known variously as faburden, fauxbourdon or falsobordone. There are examples of falsobordone in the psalm and canticle settings of Palestrina, Victoria and Monteverdi, for instance, and in Allegri's famous *Miserere*.

The practice of singing psalms to the old plainsong tones continued in England after the Reformation. So too did the practice of embellishing them with polyphony, and there are examples of this practice in the vernacular festal psalm-settings of Tallis and Byrd, though here all the text is set polyphonically. Although the music is written out in full, the same musical formula is used for each verse. This is the basis for the practice of harmonized chanting of psalms. By the time of Gibbons, the use of the plainsong tone had been abandoned, but the formulaic approach continues. The revival of chanting psalms after the Restoration marks the beginning of more widespread composition of harmonized chants for choral recitation of the psalms. Unlike their pre-Restoration models (most often scored for five voices), these are scored for four voices. Most early chants provide a musical formula repeated for every verse of the psalm (single chant). The earliest examples of a musical formula repeated every two verses (double chant) date from the end of the seventeenth century, written by William Turner and Bartholomew Isaack. However, this practice is prefigured in some of the festal psalms of John Amner, composed before the Commonwealth.

The classic pattern of the Anglican chant follows the bipartite structure of the psalm verse. The first part consists of a reciting chord followed by a progression of three chords forming a cadence; the second part begins with a reciting chord followed by five chords leading to the final cadence. This pattern is repeated verse by verse in a single chant. In a double chant the harmonic formula consists of the pattern repeated, so that the chant extends over two verses: v. 1: reciting chord + 3 chords, reciting chord + 5 chords; v. 2: reciting chord + 3 chords, reciting chord + 5 chords. This allows for greater harmonic range, especially in the choice of cadences. It is this pattern of double chant that has been used most often by the profusion of organists and other minor composers of the nineteenth and twentieth centuries who have contributed to the repertory of Anglican chant, together with a smaller number of single chants, and a sprinkling of triple and quadruple chants.

Evidence from the sources suggests that early chanting was measured, and allowed time for embellishment by the singers. From the late nineteenth century, there has been a tendency to encourage freer recitation, based on 'speech rhythm'. This has coincided with the publication of pointed psalters – editions where signs and symbols in the text of the psalms and canticles indicate the points at which the chords of the chant are to be changed. An influential model was *The Cathedral Psalter* (1874), complemented and contrasted by *The Parish Psalter* (1928) and *The Oxford Psalter* (1929). In practice each choir and congregation adopts its own nuances and mannerisms in the sung recitation of the psalms.

Other forms of chanting have been explored in the twentieth century. *The Grail Psalter* (1966) is a translation which takes special account of rhythmic stress and flexible chant patterns, following the French vernacular pattern for which Père Joseph Gelineau first devised the chanting system a decade before. Examples of simplified forms of harmonized chant for parish singing may be found in the Royal School of Church Music's *Music for Common Worship I* (2000).

'Anglican Chant', NG2 I, 672–3; Ruth M. Wilson, *Anglican Chant and Chanting in England, Scotland, and America, 1660–1820*, Oxford 1996.

JOHN HARPER

Chants of the Proper of the Mass

The chants of the *mass fall into two categories: 1. those of the *ordinary, with texts that are fixed, the *Kyrie, Gloria in excelsis, Credo, *Sanctus (with Benedictus) and *Agnus Dei; 2.

those of the *proper, with texts that change from one mass to another, the introit, gradual, alleluia, tract, sequence, *offertory and *communion. The function of each of these chants determines the form of the music. The introit and the communion both accompany *processions. The introit accompanies the entry of the clergy at the beginning of the *eucharist, the communion the procession of the faithful to receive communion. The chant takes the form of an *antiphon sung with one or more verses of a psalm. For many centuries only one psalm-verse was sung at the introit and the antiphon was repeated after the Gloria Patri. Recently attempts have been made to restore several verses, using the antiphon as a refrain. Over the centuries the communion psalm also came to be omitted: eventually nothing was left but the antiphon. Here, too, there has been a move to reintroduce the missing psalm-verses.

The gradual (named after the steps, *gradus*, of the *ambo on or near which it was sung) was originally a psalm sung by a solo *cantor to which the congregation responded with a brief interjection, such as 'Alleluia', or a verse from the psalm itself. Later the gradual assumed its present form: a respond for the choir, made up of one or two verses, followed by a florid verse for the cantor. Today the gradual presents an overall form of ABA, with the choir repeating the original respond after the verse. The usual form of the alleluia is AABA, with the alleluia and its *jubilus* – a wordless vocalization on the last syllable – sung first by the cantors, then repeated by the choir. This is followed by a solo verse, and the alleluia is repeated after the verse. Both the gradual and the alleluia are chants of meditation and they follow the first and second readings. In the *Easter season two alleluias are sung, the first one replacing the gradual. During *Lent a tract replaces the alleluia. The tract may be either a group of selected verses from a psalm or, more rarely, a complete psalm, sung straight through without antiphon or respond. The melodies of tracts are ancient and extremely elaborate psalm-tones.

The sequence was a new form of chant growing out of the alleluia and associated with it: an addition of either melody or text, or both. It has been suggested that it came about because of the difficulty of memorizing the florid vocalizations of the alleluia. Its development is said to owe much to Notker Balbulus, a monk of St Gall (*c.* 840–912), whose master instructed him to set every note of the *jubilus* to a separate syllable – suggesting that Notker did not invent

the sequence himself. Sequences became very popular during the Middle Ages, many being written in rhyming verse. The Council of Trent discarded all but a handful of them. The modern Roman *Graduale* has retained four: *Victimae paschali laudes* (for Easter), *Veni Sancte Spiritus* (for *Pentecost), *Lauda Sion* (for Corpus Christi) and *Stabat mater* (for the Seven Dolours of the Blessed Virgin Mary). The best-known of all sequences, the *Dies irae* (from the *requiem mass), no longer figures among the proper chants for the mass, but is sung as a hymn during the office of the dead.

The offertory was originally a psalm sung antiphonally by the two halves of the choir. In its present form it is a fully developed semi-florid chant, more suitable for a solo cantor than for the choir. The chants of the offertory are the only ones that repeat words or whole phrases; this may be due to the fact that the chant would have continued until a sign was given by the celebrant for the cantors to cease.

René-Jean Hesbert (ed.), *Antiphonale Missarum Sextuplex*, Rome 1935; Ferdinand Haberl, *Das Graduale Romanum, liturgische und musikalische Aspekte*, Erster Band, Bonn 1976; *Graduale Triplex*, Solesmes 1979; *Offertoriale Monasticum*, Solesmes 1985.

MARY BERRY

Chapel

A small building used for worship, or a small space with its own *altar used for private or small group worship within a larger church. A chapel dedicated to the Virgin Mary, ordinarily extending from the centre of the *apse, is called a Lady Chapel. The proliferation of chapels occurred with the late-eleventh-century passion for the collection of relics that then required places for display and veneration. Chapels radiated from the exterior of the apse and *transepts of a church, and in later eras appeared enclosed within the bays of the side *aisles.

MARCHITA B. MAUCK

Charismatic Worship

The qualifying adjective 'charismatic' is usually applied to Pentecostal-like programmes, performances or people, when they are to be found in the historic or 'mainline' denominations. Until the late 1950s virtually all distinctively *Pentecostalist ways of worship were to be found exclusively within the various

Pentecostalist denominations, themselves a product of the early twentieth century. These were strongly separatist, and they declined ecumenical or other shared forms of partnership with the historic churches, prizing their high-profile spiritual life and extroverted forms of participatory worship far above any external relationships with local churches or larger national networks. The first hints of change came in the ministry between 1940 and 1975 within international Pentecostalism of David Du Plessis, who called upon Pentecostalists to work closely with other Christians. This was matched coincidentally by the prophetic call of Lesslie Newbigin in *The Household of God* (London 1952) for the Ecumenical Movement to recognize and welcome this 'third strand' – a strand of the Spirit (over and above Protestantism and Catholicism) – in the world church.

From the late 1950s onwards, Pentecostalism broke out across the world in the historic churches and, for the first time, did not necessarily lead to secession among those so touched. The first generation were usually existing worshippers whose lives were then suddenly affected by the swamping experience often dubbed 'baptism in the Holy Spirit', and frequently accompanied by 'speaking in tongues'. RCs in particular made great, and largely successful, attempts to bring an understanding of these phenomena within their existing theological framework; other denominations have not always managed it so easily. While the title 'neo-pentecostalist' has at times been used of the spirituality of people thus affected, 'charismatic' has passed into the widest currency, and is in use throughout the world and across the denominations. The word usually connotes a great emphasis upon the experiential, both in private spirituality and in the corporate gatherings for worship. The Charismatic Movement in the historic churches has been characterized by an emphasis on the gifts of each worshipper which are to be exercised, and charismatic worship has often given vast responsibility to 'worship-leaders' who, by running a highly flexible programme, have enabled this development of gifts. Classic liturgical ground plans have often been overthrown or severely dented in this radical new atmosphere; but severely word-based believers have found a rich three-dimensional world of ceremonial and symbolism; and sacramentalists have found new life in the word coursing through them.

The initial 'baptism in the Spirit' has become both open to theological enquiry on the one hand, and yet not always a requisite for people to be recognized as charismatics on the other. The major continuing defining feature has been the experiential test. But a whole culture of worship has arisen, harmonizing comfortably or uncomfortably with existing liturgical traditions. This culture includes: an explosion of chorus-style songs, often led by 'singing groups' and guitars; bodily participation such as raising arms in the air, *dancing, clapping, laying hands on others, and hugging; *extemporary and fervent prayer; 'tongues' and 'interpretation'; prophesying; ministries of healing; ministries of deliverance; prayer counselling; and the 'Toronto blessing' (or being 'slain in the Spirit'). The experiential immediacy of desired and felt direct encounter with God has often given rise to an unrooted existentialism, which has counted history and tradition and even doctrinal norms for little. Conversely, a second generation of charismatics may be found to return to a higher valuing of classic liturgical forms, without thereby abandoning the principles of being charismatic.

While a distinct new worshipping tradition has arisen as described, it is incorrect to see it as sealed off in a separate compartment from the rest of church life in the different denominations. Rather, there has been a broad effect touching the worship of denominations and congregations on a much wider scale than simply in the congregations known as charismatic. Informality and openness, extemporary prayer and testimony, choruses and healing ministry alike have all flowed over into this wider church life.

COLIN O. BUCHANAN

Chasuble see **Vestments** 3(b)

Children and Worship

1. *Early Practice*. Jewish children were born into the covenant people, and their presence was assumed at the Passover celebration. The NT epistles indicate that the children of Christians were regarded as church members, and there are occasional references to their instruction and nurture. But there is no hint of any special worship provisions for them, and they seem simply to have taken their place with their parents in the ordinary assembly. Cyprian (d. 258) indicates that even infants received

*communion, and this is still the case in the East, although the practice was discontinued in the West at the end of the twelfth century. Even when infants rather than adults were the usual recipients of *baptism, the rites used were essentially the adult ones. There was continuing concern for their subsequent instruction, which was the shared responsibility of parish priest, parents and *godparents, but there was no distinctive worship provision until the Reformation, and even then it was minimal.

2. *The Reformation.* New baptismal rites were now designed specifically for infants, and *confirmation rites (where used) envisaged that the recipients were adolescents. Luther and Calvin both issued *catechisms for children, who could not now be admitted to communion until they had been adequately instructed and examined, but the regular services were still designed with adults in mind and as in other spheres, including family or household prayers, children were expected to participate as 'young adults' in an essentially adult activity. In England the *BCP* provided for the instruction and examination of children on Sundays and holy days immediately before evensong. In 1662 these were to take place within evensong itself, after the second lesson and in the presence of the ordinary congregation, but no liturgical concessions were made to the presence of the children.

3. *The Sunday School Movement.* Martin Luther wrote his hymn *Von Himmel hoch* possibly for his children, then aged nine and six, or possibly for a children's nativity pageant. In 1715 Isaac Watts published his *Divine and Moral Songs for Children*, and in 1763 John and Charles Wesley followed suit with their *Hymns for Children*. But distinctive children's worship seems to have begun only after the rise of the Sunday school movement towards the end of the eighteenth century. Initially the emphasis of Sunday schools was on the education and instruction of the poor, and they were officially regarded as supplementary to regular congregational worship rather than as substitutes for it. Gradually some of them assumed a more evangelistic purpose: 'that children may be habituated to a regular and devout attendance upon the public worship of Almighty God'. Special worship material was produced for them, and this included prayers, hymns and sometimes quasi-liturgical forms. This material usually reflected the theology of the sponsoring churches, and in Anglican churches the catechism and the *collects often held a prominent place. There was always a stress on duty and morality, but in more liberal churches children were also given an emphasis on the beauties of creation, on human brotherhood and on personal endeavour. In more evangelical churches they were quickly exposed to the themes of sin and atonement.

Sunday school numbers increased rapidly and by 1900 there were at least five million children attending them in Britain. In the early and mid-twentieth century they usually met in the afternoon, and some of them developed a life of their own almost as para-churches. Indeed, the ideal of some teachers – themselves the product of Sunday schools – was that children who continued attending into their teens should also become Sunday school teachers rather than members of the regular congregation. This illustrates an essential defect of the movement. Religion was seen primarily in terms of biblical knowledge and conventional morality. Worship, church membership and even sacraments were often optional extras.

4. *The Twentieth Century.* The RC Church was unaffected by the Sunday school movement, and children came into their own with the elaborate first communion ceremonies which developed first in France. The formative element for RC children was invariably the *eucharist, but though the essential (silent) rite was the same everywhere, the accompanying devotions in a school mass were particularly geared to children. The 1910 decree *Quam singulari* urged first communion at an early age, usually around seven, and communion before confirmation became the norm for most RC children. After the Second Vatican Council special *eucharistic prayers were issued for use at childrens' masses.

In England, the Sunday school movement declined in the twentieth century – at first slowly and then from the 1960s more rapidly. Non-churchgoing parents ceased to 'send' their children to the afternoon Sunday schools, and churchgoing parents preferred to bring their children with them to the morning service. In some Free Churches, Sunday schools had met in the morning as well as or instead of the afternoon, and there had developed the custom of a children's address at an early point in the service, after which children withdrew to their separate classes. Some Anglican churches have now adopted the same pattern, though where the church is eucharistically centred, children usually meet initially in their own groups and then join the adult congregation either at the *Offertory or at the administration of communion where they receive a blessing at the *altar rail. Although these children's groups or classes are still known as Sunday schools in some churches, in others they are known as 'Junior Church', 'Children's Church' or something more imaginative.

Meanwhile many churches are experimenting – usually monthly, though sometimes weekly – with what were called first '*family services' and later 'all-age worship', and in the Church of England what is now called 'A Service of the *Word' was originally designed to give legal status to such services. But while some all-age worship is excellent, in many areas it is creating problems which have not yet been resolved. This is especially the case where the idea that 'children should be seen but not heard' has been replaced by the slogan 'children first'. At its worst, worship orientated primarily to younger children is often more akin to entertainment. It appeals to the lowest common factor, is inadequate for adults and embarrassing to teenagers, and deprives the children themselves of an exposure to traditional liturgy and hymnody with their stress on the praise and grandeur of God and their ability to draw children in worship to the One who is both with them and yet beyond them.

These problems are particularly acute in churches whose worship and architecture has traditionally reflected the Reformation emphasis on the verbal and the cerebral, and for whom a service is a formal occasion with a defined beginning and end. To some extent this emphasis is now apparent in much RC worship, but it is absent in the East. Here the participation of all ages in a traditional liturgical setting seems least self-conscious. People of all ages come and go as seems appropriate, they participate in different ways and at different levels, and there is plenty of opportunity for movement. The East has been unaffected by the Western *Liturgical Movement with its implication that the participation of the laity should be at the same level, whatever the age or understanding of the participant. Apart from the appearance of Sunday schools in the twentieth century, it has also been unaffected by the Reformation and Counter-Reformation emphasis on instruction. Here the East can learn from the West, but the

West can learn from the East in its refusal to dilute the liturgy, its allowing space for individuals of all ages within this liturgy, and its stress on belonging as much as on understanding. That worship should be deliberately incomprehensible would be absurd. But if God himself is beyond our understanding, to aim at worship which removes the element of mystery is self-defeating even for adults, let alone for children. But the children who know that they belong by virtue of their baptism, who experience a genuine sense of welcome and acceptance and whose participation is encouraged can cope with – and even welcome – much that is beyond their present understanding. This is especially the case when they are not merely blessed but communicated.

5. *The Admission of Children to Communion.* The growth of eucharistic worship, new understandings of 'faith development', the ecumenical emphasis on baptism and the persistence of theological questions about confirmation has now led in many churches to demands for the admission of children to communion at an early age, and before confirmation where that exists. This is already common practice in North America and is now gaining ground in England, but while some advocate admission around seven as in the RC Church, i.e., after basic instruction, others see the right to communion as implicit in baptism and argue for *infant communion, as has always been the practice of Eastern churches.

––––––

Philippe Ariès, *Centuries of Childhood*, New York 1962; *Directory for Masses with Children*, London 1974; Ronald C. D. Jasper (ed.), *Worship and the Child*, London 1975; Ruth A. Meyers (ed.), *Children at the Table: A Collection of Essays on Children and the Eucharist*, New York 1995; Diana Wood (ed.), *The Church and Childhood*, Oxford 1994.

MARK DALBY

Chimere *see* **Vestments** 3(d)

Choir (Architectural)

The place reserved for the use of monks in a monastery or canons in a secular *cathedral celebrating the daily office (*see* **Daily Prayer** 3). Throughout the early Middle Ages the choir usually occupied the area of the *chancel or *sanctuary closest to the crossing, between the *apse and the *nave. By the twelfth century the choir had migrated to a position in front of the *altar, and could be separated from the nave by a *screen, arcade, steps or a railing. Because those praying the daily office in the choir stood throughout much of the service, the choir stall, a characteristic ecclesiastical furniture style, developed to accommodate both standing and sitting. Made usually of wood, the stalls included a tall back, a folding seat, tall sides with elbow rests for leaning, and a book rest in front of them. Choir stalls were often elaborately carved.

MARCHITA B. MAUCK

Choir (Musical)

Two principal musical meanings of this term persist: (a) a group of designated singers, and (b) the body of clergy, monks or religious gathered in that part of the church known as the choir to sing the *daily office and *mass. Although the first meaning has come to dominate modern use of the term, the second was more prevalent in the Western church influenced by monastic practice between the sixth and the sixteenth centuries.

The norm of singing all the texts heard in the liturgy meant that all who voiced a text did so in song, whether prayer, reading or psalm sung principally on a single note with simple formulaic embellishment to mark punctuation, or with the elaborate melody of a great *antiphon or *responsory. Knowledge of liturgical chant and competence in singing it were standard requirements of all *cathedral, collegiate and household chapel clergy, and of monks, nuns and other religious. In the later Middle Ages, senior cathedral and collegiate clergy delegated the conduct of the daily mass and office to substitutes, often known as vicars choral, working alongside minor canons (who had day-to-day responsibility in choir) and juniors (clerks and boys). Effectively there was a professional liturgical clergy skilled in the singing and ceremony of the daily services. Specified *cantors and soloists began the chant, and sang specific sections; and in some places these sections were on occasion embellished in *polyphony. But the bulk of the singing was chant sung by all present in choir.

In the early church there were designated singers, most often cantors, who were responsible for singing the gradual (*see* **Chants of the Proper of the Mass**). The establishment of the choir as a group of designated singers seems to date from the fourteenth and fifteenth centuries.

A specific group was assigned special duties in a Lady Chapel, and in some instances these were singers who were not part of the main body of clergy, but additional chaplains with comparable liturgical and musical skills. In fifteenth-century England, boys began to play a more significant musical part in the Lady Chapel music (and in other devotions), and lay musicians were engaged to train and teach them, and to sing. By 1500 most great churches in England had a Lady Chapel choir, or equivalent, perhaps with five or six boys and a comparable number of adult singers (predominantly clergy); so too did an increasing number of parish churches. It was these small choirs which promulgated polyphonic singing of both mass and office, joining the main body of the choir on Sundays and feast days.

With the removal of much of the funding to support a professional liturgical clergy, and the demise of all monastic and most collegiate institutions during the English Reformation, it was the small Lady Chapel choir which was effectively redeployed as the English cathedral choir. What had been their duty in choir on Sundays and feast days now became their daily duty: responsibility for maintaining services in choir now rested on an increasing number of lay singers (lay vicars or lay clerks) directed by the musician formerly in charge of the Lady Chapel choir (now often known as Organist and Master of the Choristers).

In Continental Europe the change was different. First, with the influence of friars, preaching and the mass became dominant. In many Italian churches built after 1250 the liturgical choir is placed in an *apse behind the *altar, so that the view of *pulpit and *sanctuary could be open to all present. The delegation of the singing of both mass and vespers to skilled musicians resulted in their performance not from the liturgical choir, but from a *gallery or platform. Since they took the musical part of those formerly in choir they became known as *coro*, the choir. In Spain, where the carved liturgical choir with its great *lectern for the chant books often complements the sanctuary at the opposite end of the church, polyphonic singers were also normally located in the gallery with the *organ. Throughout Europe the physical separation of the musical choir from the conduct of the liturgy is normative, even in Lutheran churches. Where the choir included girls (e.g. the Ospedali in Venice), they sang unseen behind a grille. Only in the Anglican tradition are the singers constituting the musical choir located in the part of the church known liturgically as the choir.

The tradition of cathedral choirs in England and Wales consisting of boy and adult singers has remained unbroken since before the Reformation, except for the interruption of the Commonwealth (1649–60) when liturgical worship was suspended. Music in parish churches has been less continuous. Although many town parish churches established small choirs competent to sing polyphony with boys, chaplains and lay singers in the late fifteenth century and early sixteenth century, these lost their funding and were dispersed at the Edwardian Reformation (1548–52). In the eighteenth century there were groups of singers assembled in the gallery, often with instruments. Only in the nineteenth century, following the influence of the Oxford and the ecclesiological movements, did robed choirs in parish churches start to be established. There has always been a tension between the function of a parish choir leading simple music, and the desire to emulate cathedral musical practices. This is even more prevalent in an age of pastoral liturgy, and many parishes abandoned a robed choir in the last quarter of the twentieth century, a move often accelerated by the decline in numbers and the shortage of competent choir trainers. By contrast, in the United States, many larger churches support a range of different choirs under the direction of a professional church musician.

With recording and broadcasting, liturgical choirs of boys and men in the English cathedral tradition have established a unique international reputation. There have been two significant developments, begun in the late twentieth century: the introduction of a second choir of girls in over half of the English cathedrals, and the rise of chapel choirs of male and female choral scholars in some English university colleges, the best of which can match or surpass the standards of the traditional cathedral choirs.

John Morehen (ed.), *English Choral Practice, 1400–1650*, Cambridge 1995.

JOHN HARPER

Chrism *see* Anointing

Chrismatory

A container designed to store the three sacramental oils that have been in Christian litur-

gical use since the early centuries. The three-lobed or sectioned container, which is often highly decorated, may be a flat-based casket or raised on a pedestal-foot. It takes its name from the oil of chrism (in Greek *myron*), which is distinguished from the other oils – for the *anointing(s) of the *sick or dying, and for the pre-baptismal anointing of the *catechumens – by the addition of perfume (normally balsam), and is the subject of much patristic interpretation. Chrism has several uses, chief among them the 'completion' of baptism (*confirmation or chrismation), the anointing of Christian ministers at their *ordination and of sovereigns at their *coronation, and the *dedication of churches and *altars.

Martin Dudley and Geoffrey Rowell (eds), *Oil of Gladness*, London 1993.

JONATHAN GOODALL

Christian Church (Disciples of Christ) Worship

1. *Origin and Character of the Church*. The Christian Church (Disciples of Christ) began on the US 'frontier' (western Pennsylvania, western Virginia, Kentucky and Ohio) in the early decades of the nineteenth century. Scottish/Irish Presbyterian immigrants Thomas Campbell (1763–1854) and son Alexander (1788–1866), together with Barton W. Stone (1772–1844), sought a unity of Christians through restoring the 'clear picture' of the church found in the NT. Combining Enlightenment rationalism and evangelistic zeal, the movement was characterized by the observance of the *Lord's supper on each Lord's day (Sunday), following a broadly Reformed pattern but with *elders delivering *extempore prayers over the elements; *baptism by full immersion of penitent adult believers; a congregational polity; and an emphasis upon Christian unity (which Thomas Campbell described as the church's 'polar star').

As this 'Restorationist' movement developed, more conservative positions coalesced around the refusal to use instrumental music in worship and to form co-operative institutions which might threaten congregational autonomy. By the early twentieth century these forces were forming separate churches, such as the Church of Christ. Restorationist movements emerged in many other countries around the world; in these the division between the Christian Church (Disciples of Christ) and more conservative bodies such as the Church of Christ is less clear.

While a robust sense of local autonomy remains, the Disciples' 'Restructure' process in the 1960s established clearer structures of oversight at national and regional levels. The commitment to unity has led to active participation in the Ecumenical Movement and to Disciples-related churches entering into church unions around the world. Practice in these churches follows local patterns, and we concentrate here on worship in the Christian Church (Disciples of Christ) in the USA.

2. *Character of Disciples' Worship*. For early Disciples each Lord's day (Sunday) worship should include proclamation of the word and the Lord's supper. Since no detailed rite is prescribed in the NT it was incumbent upon congregations and their ordained elders, exercising reason and in the maturity of faith, to order the supper. Typical practice involved scripture readings and hymns, extempore prayers for the bread and wine, distribution of the elements, preaching, more hymns and a concluding collection. The supper was understood as the experience and visible sign of the unity of Christ's church. Both the supper and baptism had strong social as well as personal dimensions, linking believers to one another as well as to Christ. Early Disciples understood both of them as a visible sign and seal of God's grace. For historical and theological reasons they shied away from the term *sacrament and preferred 'ordinance', meaning one of several practices 'ordained' by Christ as a means of making God's saving action evident in the world. Each ordinance has its particular grace: for baptism, it is the remission of sin unto newness of life in Christ; for the supper, nourishing the faith and unity of believers.

By the mid-twentieth century most Disciples' congregations had settled into comfortable patterns of worship, varied but always respecting the weekly observance of the Lord's supper (including prayers by the elders, even as the ordained minister gained an increasing role at the table) and the restriction of baptism to penitent adult believers. The liberal theology of the first half of the century, together with a cultural insensitivity to representational thought, tended to diminish the sense of the sacred in worship, to elevate the sermon over the supper, and to encourage a purely commemorative understanding of the supper.

3. *Recovery and Renewal of the Tradition*. Significant renewal of the church's worship life has occurred in the second half of the twentieth century. Three persons have been central to this process. G. Edwin Osborn (1897–1965) produced the church's first 'semi-official' worship book in 1953, stressing biblical and ecumenical resources for worship. William Robinson (1888–1963) helped recover the centrality of the Lord's supper. Keith Watkins has more recently led in recovering Disciples' own worship heritage and engaging with the Liturgical and Ecumenical Movements. Liturgical renewal is reflected in recent Disciples' worship materials. Engagement in the Ecumenical Movement (in particular with the Faith and Order text *Baptism, Eucharist and Ministry*, the Consultation on Church Union, and the international dialogue with the RC Church) has clarified and enriched the church's thought on baptism and the table.

Two recent processes, one theological and one liturgical, have been central to the renewal of Disciples' worship. First is the study on the church begun by the Commission on Theology in 1978. Three of its texts touch directly on worship (ministry, 1985; baptism, 1987; the Lord's supper, 1993), and the overall report (1997) affirms (in language new for many Disciples) that in worship the church makes 'defining signs of its true identity' as it listens to scripture, proclaims the word, confesses sin and receives God's forgiving grace, celebrates the sacramental acts of baptism and holy *communion, and communicates in prayer with God.

Second is a series of liturgical studies aimed at renewing worship practice. *Thankful Praise: A Resource for Christian Worship*, ed. Keith Watkins (St Louis 1987), sought 'to strengthen Christian public worship and especially the celebration of the Lord's Supper'. Its goals summarize Disciples' thinking on worship at the end of the twentieth century: to connect Disciples' worship with the great tradition of Christian worship; to reflect liturgically the results of ecumenical convergence; to be faithful to the crucial features of traditional Disciples' worship; to be sensitive to social injustice, especially anti-Jewish and sexist; to enhance the beauty and diversity of worship through vivid, biblical and felicitous language, and by encouraging variety within services. This volume was followed in 1991 by *Baptism and Belonging: A Resource for Christian Worship*, ed. Keith Watkins (St Louis 1991), seeking a parallel renewal in Disciples' understanding and practice of baptism.

These processes have been supported by a wide range of worship materials and books, notably by Colbert S. Cartwright, interpreting these new worship perspectives to the church. The renewal has culminated in the recently issued *Chalice Hymnal* (St Louis 1995) and *Chalice Worship*, ed. Colbert S. Cartwright and O. I. Cricket Harrison (St Louis 1997), both fresh and creative works which reflect the mind – and heart – of the church as it enters the twenty-first century.

Alexander Campbell, *The Christian System*, 2nd edn, Cincinnati 1839; Colbert S. Cartwright, *Candles of Grace: Disciples Worship in Perspective*, St Louis 1992; Paul A. Crow, Jr and James O. Duke (eds), *The Church for Disciples of Christ: Seeking to be Truly Church Today*, St Louis 1998 (bib.); G. Edwin Osborn, *The Glory of Christian Worship*, St Louis 1953; William E. Tucker and Lester G. McAllister, *Journey in Faith: A History of the Christian Church (Disciples of Christ)*, St Louis 1975 (bib.); Keith Watkins, *The Great Thanksgiving*, St Louis 1995; D. Newell Williams (ed.), *A Case Study of Mainstream Protestantism: The Disciples' Relation to American Culture, 1880–1989*, Grand Rapids/St Louis 1991.

THOMAS F. BEST

Christingle

In British and Irish *Moravian churches a lighted Christingle is given to children in the Christingle service held on the Sunday before *Christmas, Christmas Eve or Christmas Day. The Christingle is an orange with a hole bored in the top. A cleansed goose quill, from which the feathered portion has been removed, is wrapped in a white or red paper frill and inserted in the hole. The end of the quill is cut into half a dozen sharp 'points', to which are affixed blanched almonds, raisins and small jellied sweets of different colours. A small Christmas tree candle is pushed down into the heart of the quill. The orange symbolizes the world and the candle Christ, the light of the world; a white paper frill represents purity, red Christ's passion; the nuts, raisins and sweets signify God's good gifts to his children. The Christingle's origins are obscure. They were given to children in West Yorkshire Moravian homes in the 1870s and perhaps a generation earlier. The term 'Christingle' could mean 'Christ fire'

(from 'ingle', as in 'ingle-nook'), or may derive from the German *Christ-Kindl* (Christ-child) or *Christ-Engel* (Christ-angel).

The Moravian custom of distributing lighted candles to children at a service on Christmas Eve dates from 1747 (*see* **Candle Service, Moravian**). Christingles seem first to have been used at such a service instead of candles at Fairfield, Manchester in the later 1890s. They were used at school services in Fulneck, Yorkshire from the early 1920s and spread to other Moravian churches in the later 1920s. After readings, recitations and carols, each child receives a lighted candle. The children process with them round the darkened church, and the service ends with the hymn 'Morning star, O cheering sight!'

Since 1968 the Anglican charity, The Children's Society, has popularized the Christingle service as a money-raising initiative. Cocktail sticks usually replace the goose quills, and a length of red ribbon is often tied round the orange. A liturgy for a Christingle Service is included in the Church of England service book, *The Promise of His Glory* (1991).

D. A. Connor, 'Christingles', *Moravian Messenger* XLIII, 1951, 179–80; J. Cooper, 'Christingles', *Moravian Historical Magazine* I, 1991, 10–12.

COLIN PODMORE

Christmas

The annual liturgical remembrance and celebration of the birth of Jesus. Its location in the calendar on 25 December was originally an observance of the churches of Rome in the fourth century. In the earliest evidence from Rome, the date of Jesus' birth begins the dates of the feasts of martyrs, *depositio martyrum*, part of the Roman Chronograph of the year 354, with internal data indicating that the list was put together in the year 336. Some have conjectured that the observance is even older, but this is not established with certainty. The feast of 25 December was rapidly taken up by many communities outside Rome and north Africa (which zealously followed Roman liturgical custom), and by the middle of the fifth century its observance was nearly universal, if perhaps as much for political as theological or liturgical reasons. It was eventually adopted by the churches in Constantinople and Antioch, though resisted until the seventh century by the churches in Palestine. Constantinople, Antioch and Jerusalem were all churches that had earlier marked the birth of Jesus on 6 January, as one of a variety of epiphanies or 'manifestations' celebrated on that day (*see* **Epiphany**). The date of 25 December for celebrating the birth of Jesus is still not observed by the Armenian Orthodox Church.

In late antiquity there was some epistolary exchange about whether or not this feast was a day of remembering the birth of Jesus only, or if it was indeed a feast marking the incarnation as a mystery integrated into the experience of the risen Christ in the present. Over time the feast has popularly reflected the piety of remembrance, yet the prayers of the day clearly mark it as reflecting a unique aspect of the paschal mystery. In the East, the feast includes the theme of the visit of the Magi (Matt. 2.1–12), celebrated in the West on 6 January.

There are two major hypotheses regarding the choice of the date for the feast. For a long time the ascendant scholarly hypothesis was that of the 'history of religions' school, according to which the placement of Jesus' birth, which is not assigned a date in the NT narratives of Jesus' infancy, was on a date chosen to oppose the pagan cult of the birthday of the invincible sun, *Natalis solis invicti*, established on that date in 274 by the Roman emperor Aurelian. It is thought that the Christian observance adopted the biblical text from Malachi 4.2, 'and the sun of justice will rise for you who fear my name', as part of its rhetoric of the feast, in order to make use of the image of the sun from the earlier pagan rite and shift attention away from the pagan observance to the newly appointed Christian day of the calendar. The image of the sun connected to the feast of Christmas in the early church was maintained in the later euchology of the day.

The second theory about the origin of 25 December as the date of the birth of Jesus is known as the 'calculation' hypothesis, and has gained favour more recently through the work of Thomas Talley. According to this hypothesis, some early Christians calculated that the date of Jesus' death would have been 25 March in the Julian calendar. Perhaps adapting a rabbinic idea that the deaths of patriarchs would have fallen exactly on the anniversary of their birth, they would have come to believe that 25 March was also the date of Christ's conception, and counting forward nine months arrived at 25 December as the date of his birth.

In late antiquity in Rome the feast was appointed with unique liturgical texts for three eucharistic celebrations at midnight, at dawn and on the day itself, and these are retained in the RC Church and some other traditions today.

———

Susan K. Roll, *Toward the Origins of Christmas*, Kampen, Netherlands 1995; Thomas J. Talley, *The Origins of the Liturgical Year*, 2nd edn, Collegeville 1991, 79–162.

MARTIN F. CONNELL

Christmas Crib

The word for the crib of Jesus in the Greek of the NT, *phatne*, literally means a 'feeding trough' for animals, and it reflects the Christology of the only NT book in which the term is used, the Gospel of Luke. Before Jerome wrote, after his visit to Palestine in 385, that some of the desert fathers venerated the manger, there is virtually no testimony to the veneration, or even the existence, of the crib (in Latin, *praesepe*) into which the baby Jesus was delivered from Mary. Later in his life, Jerome himself laments that he did not see the crib. Although the travel diary of the pilgrim Egeria mentions in detail the devotions and liturgies taking place at Bethlehem while she visited, she does not mention the crib.

The medieval liturgical dramas of the nativity begin to emerge in the twelfth and thirteenth century, and they focus attention on the place of the birth of Jesus and on the Christmas crib. The devotions of Francis of Assisi and his followers to the feast of Christmas and to the replica of the manger, *presepio* in the Italian vernacular of the time, occasion the veneration of the manger as a significant devotional object in the history of Christian salvation. Such devotion to the crib has continued unabated since that time. The crafting of elaborate cribs and scenes of the birth of Jesus, the devotion of the shepherds and the visit of the Magi has had a large place in popular piety, especially in southern Italy and Germany, and the manger's association with the Christian tree in the homes of believers has remained a staple of popular piety from Francis of Assisi to today.

MARTIN F. CONNELL

Church of Jesus Christ of Latter-day Saints Worship

Founded in 1830 in Fayette, New York, the Church of Jesus Christ of Latter-day Saints (LDS) has been from its beginnings a priestly organization which places equal emphasis upon sacrament and word. Believing their origins independent of both Protestant and Catholic history and authority, the Latter-day Saints consider themselves a 'restored' church of Christ. Since the restoration is a 'fullness' of all biblical promises, it is not limited to NT forms, nor to the Christian Bible. Joseph Smith (1805–44), founder and prophet of the church, reconfigured the traditions of both Christians and Jews. From his theological merger of OT tribe and covenant with NT discipleship and grace has arisen a religious community whose liturgy is located not only in its churches, but homes and temples. This is possible because all male members of the LDS Church, if found worthy and at least twelve years old, are ordained to priestly authority for the purpose of administering church ordinances. These ordinances are: blessing and naming of infants at birth; *baptism by immersion for those eight years and older; *confirmation for the gift of the Holy Ghost; the sacrament of the *Lord's supper; *ordination; *marriage; healing through *anointing with consecrated oil and by the laying-on of hands; and the dedication of graves for the burial of the dead. The Church's prophetic and priestly tradition, coupled with a belief in an open canon and the necessity of sacraments, has created a rich corpus of LDS scripture and complex ritual practice that orders both communal and personal life.

1. *The LDS Liturgy of the Church*. The commemoration of the Lord's supper is the definitive liturgical action of LDS public worship each Sunday and, for it, the word 'sacrament' is reserved. All other rituals are called ordinances. Hence, in LDS usage, the Sunday meeting which all members are required to attend is the 'sacrament meeting' where they partake of 'the sacrament'. This Sunday service consists of set components, with only minor variations from week to week, even on such traditional holy days as *Christmas and *Easter. The meeting is opened and closed with prayer and hymn and centres on the performance of the sacrament of the Lord's supper and the presentation of sermons by members of the congregation.

The prayers spoken during the blessing of the sacrament are scripturally prescribed and are unique for their being read verbatim from the text. First recorded in *The Book of Mormon*, published in 1830, the year of the church's incorporation, these prayers are virtually identical to the prayers used today. The only change is the substitution, also in 1830, of 'water' for 'wine' to reflect concern for impurities. The sacrament obliges its partakers to 'witness . . . that they are willing to take upon them the name of [Christ], and always remember him, and keep his commandments . . . that they may always have his Spirit to be with them'.

The sacrament's covenant obligation is understood in terms of ministry and is acted out communally in a service performed on the first Sunday of each month. On this Sunday, the congregation brings money offerings for the poor based on meals they sacrificed through fasting, and they testify by description (as opposed to scriptural exegesis) to God's grace manifest in their individual lives. These offerings, as well as all other monetary gifts to the church, are not gathered as part of the service. Rather, they are given privately in a separate envelope and only to the bishopric, the three-member lay leadership of the congregation. Other gifts include a 10% tithe and a period of full-time missionary service at one's own expense.

Canonical texts related to the sacrament identify its partakers with those disciples who associated with Christ in Jerusalem and the Americas, before and after his death and resurrection. Ritually partaking of the emblems of Christ's body and blood becomes the sine qua non of discipleship; others may not partake. Participation imposes obligations of discipleship which require a response in daily living. This response is expressed in terms of ethical relations to others: ministry by witness and service to those within and without the community defined by covenant. Finally, the sacrament expresses the hope of actual physical communion, figured by the ritual communion, with Christ.

In the order of Sunday services, the sacrament is followed by two to three sermons or 'talks' given by previously invited members of the congregation, who are expected to base their remarks on canon. The best known of the Saints' multi-volume canon is *The Book of Mormon*, a nearly 600-page narrative of a family's flight from sixth-century BCE Jerusalem and establishment of a civilization in the western hemisphere where, later, the resurrected Christ appeared. Smith also published *The Book of Abraham* describing Abram's struggle against idolatry in Ur and his later vision of the heavens which would make him Pharaoh's great astronomer. Smith rewrote other significant passages of the King James Version of the Bible to create what is called *The Joseph Smith Translation of the Bible*. Today, the church uses the King James Version with Smith's emendations contained in footnotes and appendices. The church's fourth and final canon is *The Book of Doctrine and Covenants*, which contains an account of Smith's revelations guiding the organization of the church and a few revelations of later prophets concerning church doctrine.

2. *The Liturgy of the LDS Home*. The LDS denominate their homes 'the fundamental unit of the Church'. This reflects their understanding that all the sacramental powers at work in the congregation are also present in the family. Indeed, many of the sacraments are performed by family members, even when conducted in congregational settings. This is especially true of blessing infants and baptizing and confirming children. In addition, anointing the sick and blessing those in need of guidance and comfort is performed routinely in the home. Doctrinal instruction is considered the responsibility of the parents and has been formalized by the incorporation of a specific liturgy to be conducted by all church families. Called 'Family Home Evening', the programme is to be conducted each Monday night, and includes prayer, hymn singing, and both catechetical and social activities which strengthen family bonds and church devotion. To ensure that those without priesthood authority in their homes have access to all ordinances, each member of the congregation is assigned male 'Home Teachers', who are to visit regularly to provide such aid and instruction as is desired. Women visit other women as 'Visiting Teachers' to provide assistance of a non-sacramental nature.

The status of women within the LDS Church is ambiguous at best. While they are not formally ordained, the lay nature of LDS organization means that women perform virtually all aspects of traditional Protestant ministry, except explicitly sacramental acts, such as baptizing or blessing the sacrament of the Lord's supper. They give sermons; organize and preside over a wide range of official church gatherings, as well as routinely offering prayers of invocation and benediction; teach doctrinal classes; minister to the sick; prepare the dead for burial; and serve proselytizing missions. In the temple, they actually officiate in ordinances. Nevertheless, there are a number of aspects of church leadership and sacramental practice which they explicitly cannot do. This includes serving in the policy-making offices of the church and performing any ordinances outside of the temple. While historically women did perform ordinances of healing and blessing, especially in connection with childbirth and local church stewardship, they were discouraged from doing so in the early twentieth century, as the church entered the mainstream of American culture.

3. *The Liturgy of the LDS Temple*. For the Latter-day Saints, the temple represents a means of being 'endued' or 'clothed with power from on high' (Luke 24.49). Thus, the temple ritual is called 'the endowment'. Because the church does not publish its temple liturgy, even for members, the only authoritative description of the endowment is contained in *The Encyclopedia of Mormonism*, published by Macmillan with the church's co-operation and defining four aspects of the rite. First, the candidate is ritually washed, anointed and dressed in white clothing. Second, he or she receives a series of 'lectures and representations', including 'a recital of the most prominent events of the Creation, a figurative depiction of the advent of Adam and Eve and of every man and every woman, the entry of Adam and Eve into the Garden of Eden, the consequent expulsion from the garden, their condition in the world, and their receiving of the Plan of Salvation leading to the return to the presence of God'. Third, the candidate makes covenants which are considered 'the unfolding or culmination of' the baptismal covenant. Finally, the ritual cultivates 'a sense of divine presence' for the purpose of receiving revelation necessary to return to God.

In addition, the Saints go to their temples to be married. This ceremony is called a 'sealing' and makes of the couple and their progeny an 'eternal family'. This is understood in two senses. Most obviously, it means that by death they do *not* part. Second, it places the members of the family in a salvific relationship, giving them power to bless each other's lives, even assisting in each other's salvation. Thus, 'eternal marriage', as it is called in the church, partakes of the same elements as the scripturally familiar 'eternal life'. All temple ordinances, as well as those performed in the church, such as baptism and confirmation, are performed in the temple on behalf of the deceased also,

The Church's genealogical resources enable members to identify ancestors who have died without benefit of saving ordinances in order that these ordinances may be performed by proxy in the temple. In sum, the LDS temple hosts those ordinances which are designed to sanctify individuals and make their extended family relationships eternal.

As it functions in their churches, homes and temples, the worship practices of the Latter-day Saints order them within a sacred cosmology and give meaning to their daily lives. Their complex liturgy of word and sacrament moulds them into forms of Christian discipleship and covenant-based tribal bonds that extend to those who came before and those who are still to come.

————

Primary sources: James B. Allen, Ronald W. Walker and David J. Whittaker (eds), *Studies in Mormon History, 1830–1997: An Indexed Bibliography*, Urbana, IL 2000 (bib.); David J. Whittaker (ed.), *Mormon Americana: A Guide to Sources and Collections in the United States*, 1995 (bib.). Both primary and secondary materials are available on CD-ROM, including *New Mormon Studies CD-ROM: A Comprehensive Resource Library*, Salt Lake City 1998, and *Infobases LDS Collectors' Library*, Provo, UT 1998. The church's canon, as well as other documentation of its beliefs and practices, are available at the church's official website, http://www.lds.org. Other significant primary sources include a multi-volume project to publish Smith's original writings, which has yielded to date: *The Papers of Joseph Smith*, vols I–II, ed. Dean C. Jessee, Salt Lake City 1989–92.

Studies: Richard L. Bushman, *Joseph Smith and the Beginnings of Mormonism*, Urbana, IL 1984; Jill Mulvay Derr, Janath Russell Cannon and Maureen Ursenbach Beecher, *Woman of Covenant: The Story of the Relief Society*, Salt Lake City 1992; Sterling M. McMurrin, *The Philosophical Foundations of Mormon Theology*, Salt Lake City, reprint 1979; Jan Shipps, *Mormonism: The Story of a New Religious Tradition*, Urbana, IL 1985; Susan Buhler Taber, *Mormon Lives: A Year in the Elkton Ward*, Urbana, IL 1993.

KATHLEEN FLAKE

Church Modes

During the eighth and ninth centuries the melodies of the Western chant repertoire came to be classified according to a system of eight modes comparable to that already practised in Eastern Christianity. The Western system post-dated by many centuries the bulk of these melodies, which had already existed in a living oral tradition, obeying its own rules of melodic structure as regards opening phrases, passages of recitation on pre-selected degrees of the scale, and typical cadences. In dealing with this ancient repertoire, the new Carolingian modal theory achieved a brilliant synthesis, though the musical facts occasionally belie the logic of such systematization.

The eight modes may be reduced to four, as each pair shares a portion of the same modal scale and returns to the same final, or 'home' note. Using the white notes of the piano as a convenient way of illustrating the modal scales, the four finals are d, e, f and g. This is summarized in the simple diagram below, which avoids the misleading, if picturesque, Greek names, Dorian, Phrygian, Lydian, etc., of the textbooks, in use for many years.

Mode		Final (or 'home' note)	Range	Dominant (or reciting -note)
I	1	d	d–d'	a
	2	d	A–a	f
II	3	e	e–e'	c'
	4	e	B–b	a
III	5	f	f–f'	c'
	6	f	c–c'	a
IV	7	g	g–g'	d'
	8	g	d–d'	c'

The dominant, or reciting-note, of each of the four *authentic* modes, 1, 3, 5 and 7, is normally found five degrees above the final, with the exception of Mode 3, because the b (the fifth note up from e) was an unsatisfactory note for recitation as it could be sung either as a b natural or a b flat. So it came to be raised to the more stable c'. The even-numbered modes, 2, 4, 6 and 8 (named *plagal*, or 'changed') start their scale four degrees below the final of the odd-numbered *authentic* ones. The dominants of the plagal modes are found a third below those of their corresponding authentic partners. By analogy, in Mode 4 the g was raised to a. In Mode 8 the reciting note is again c', not b, because of the instability of the b. In certain cases a mode might be transposed up a fifth in order to avoid an f sharp or an e flat, or if the b flat (the fourth degree of the modal scale) was to be used constantly throughout the piece.

Thus Mode 5 could occasionally have c as its final, as in the *Alleluia Te martyrum*.

The medieval modal system, like its faraway ancestor, was both more complex and more subtle than our modern system of two modes, major and minor, which superseded it from about the seventeenth century. The chant owes much of its beauty to its ancient modality. The melodies gravitate around other centres than those of the customary major and minor modes; semitones are found in unexpected places and familiar leading-notes have little or no part to play. All this contributes to the extraordinary richness and variety of the music. Modal composition was not extinguished by the development of the classical scale system, but lived on to provide welcome variety and contrast to diatonic melody and harmony. One has only to look at works by Vaughan Williams or Bartok, for example, and by many others, from the eighteenth century to the present day.

Juan Carlos Asensio, Louis Hage, Marie-Noël Colette, 'La composition modale avant l'Octo-échos', *Etudes Grégoriennes* XXVII, 1999, 144–84; John Caldwell, *Medieval Music*, London 1978; Jean Claire, 'Les répertoires liturgiques latins avant l'Octoéchos', *Etudes Grégoriennes* XV, 1975; Michel Huglo, *Les Tonaires*, Paris 1971; Alberto Turco, 'Les répertoires liturgiques latins en marche vers l'Octoéchos', *Etudes Grégoriennes* XVIII, 1979, 177–223.

MARY BERRY

Churches of Christ Worship

see **Christian Church Worship**

Churching of Women

The Christian rite for the 'churching' of women after childbirth was widely used in the West during the medieval period and through the Reformation era to the eve of the Second Vatican Council. The service functioned as a ritual 'reintroduction' of the new mother into the church (and wider society) and had, over the centuries, a variety of meanings, including purification, thanksgiving and celebration.

1. *Biblical Background.* Early Christian attitudes toward the impurity of childbirth can be traced to the Christian 'rediscovery' of the OT in the second century. The book of Leviticus prescribed a time of ritual impurity for a new mother after the birth of a child: forty days after the birth of a boy, and eighty days after the birth of a girl. The mother would then go through a ceremony of ritual purification, judged to be similar to those prescribed for any involuntary bodily pollution (e.g. nocturnal emission).

2. *Early Christian Sources.* Present scholarship has discovered no actual rites for the purification or churching of women after childbirth in the West that pre-date the eleventh century. However, there are other indications of their special, ambiguous status in late antiquity and the early medieval period. Canon 18 of the *Canons of Hippolytus* (*c.* 340) specifies that both new mothers and midwives are to take a place among the *catechumens, if they enter the church at all before their time of purification is up. For new mothers, the period is forty days after the birth of a boy, eighty days after the birth of a girl (as in Leviticus); for midwives, the period is twenty days and forty days, respectively. Other early sources to discuss a period of purification after childbirth include a letter of Gregory the Great (d. 604) to Augustine of Canterbury, preserved in Bede's *History of the English Church and People*, and several early medieval Irish penitentials from the late sixth and seventh centuries. None of these early sources contain actual ritual texts. But comparable prescriptions, together with rites of purification to mark the end of the period, also occur in later Eastern liturgical books. So, for example, the Eastern Orthodox Church has a set of three prayers for the mother to be said by the priest in the home on the day of the birth itself, and also a rite for use on the fortieth day after birth when she returns to church with her child.

3. *The Medieval West.* Rituals for the churching of women show some variety in the medieval period. An eleventh-century Salzburg rite appears to be the earliest extant rite for the ceremony. It is fairly complex: the woman is met at the door of the church by the priest and assisting ministers; two psalms (113 and 128) and a series of versicles and responses follow. The prologue to the Gospel of John is read, and then the priest, holding the woman by the right hand, leads her into the church with a prayer. The woman lies prostrate on the floor while another psalm is recited (51), followed by the *Lord's Prayer, a blessing and a *collect. The woman is then sprinkled with holy water and the priest recites a second collect; and the

service is concluded in the act of censing the woman with *incense.

Arguably the most studied of all the medieval rites is that from the Sarum manual. This fourteenth-century rite was in use in most of England by the mid-fifteenth century. It is quite simple: the woman is met by the priest and assisting minister at the door of the church; two psalms are recited (121 and 128), followed by a series of versicles and responses (including the Lord's Prayer) and a collect. The woman is then sprinkled with holy water, and is led into the church by the priest (who grasps her right hand) with this formula: 'Enter into the temple of God that you might have eternal life and that you might live for ever and ever. Amen.' Another late medieval English rite, from the York manual, contains many of the same components, but begins with the ritual entrance into the church. Two psalms (67 and 128), versicles and responses, and a different collect are recited at the *altar. After mass, the woman receives blessed bread and a final blessing.

4. *Reformation and Post-Reformation Trends*. The Reformation era produced a number of changes in the rite. The texts found in the earliest versions of the *BCP* differ only slightly from one another in terms of texts (though Ps. 128 from the Sarum rite is dropped); however, the earlier title ('Order for the Purification of Women') is changed significantly in the 1552 *BCP* ('The Thanksgiving of Women after Childbirth'). The location for the start of the rite changes as well: in 1549 the woman stands at the 'quire door', while in 1552 she begins the service near the 'table'. Later disputes among various political and theological parties over the English rite centred on the issues of the obligation of the new mother to wear a veil for the service, and whether she should be required to carry a lighted *candle.

The revised *Rituale Romanum* (1614) also contained a rite; however, even after this book appeared, there appears to have still been great variety among RC rites for churching. Some of these are currently being collected and analysed. On the eve of the Second Vatican Council, the rite had been re-titled 'The Blessing of a Woman after Childbirth, and of her Child'. The woman and child, with other women, met the priest and assisting ministers at the entrance to the church. The woman held a lighted candle. All were sprinkled with holy water and greeted with 'Pax vobiscum'. The woman and her party were led to the altar by the priest, where she placed her candle into a stand and knelt. All recited together the Magnificat, followed by the *Kyrie and other versicles. The service concluded with a prayer of blessing over the mother and a second over the child; both were then sprinkled with holy water. A second, shorter form of the rite was provided for a woman whose infant had died.

5. *Modern Practice*. The American *BCP* (1979) contains an order of service called 'A Thanksgiving for the Birth or Adoption of a Child'. The service is held 'before the altar' and includes both parents and other family members. An opening collect (followed by a dialogue and ritual 'handing over' for an older adopted child) precedes the group recitation of the Magnificat (Pss 116 and 23 are listed as options), a second collect, a series of optional prayers (e.g. for the parents), a final blessing, and an optional greeting of peace. Similar provision also occurs in the English *Common Worship* (2000).

In the RC Church, the primary blessing for a woman after childbirth is now a part of the revised rite of baptism itself (1969), which concludes with a series of blessings for the mother, the father and the entire assembly. The *Book of Blessings* (1989) lists a number of orders for blessings of mothers before and, if she did not attend the child's baptism, after childbirth. The rite may be led by a priest, *deacon or lay person, and begins with a greeting and words of welcome. Next comes a reading from scripture (1 Sam. 1.20–28; 1 Sam. 2.1–10; or Luke 1.67–79), followed by Ps. 128 and opportunity for a brief homily. The service closes with an intercessory thanksgiving prayer, a blessing (collect) of the mother, and a final blessing. A concluding song is recommended. A series of alternative blessings follow, including a short form of the blessing of a new mother, a blessing of parents after a miscarriage (a long and short form) and a service for the blessing of parents on the adoption of a child.

Selected texts in Adolf Franz, *Die kirchlichen Benediktionen im Mittelalter*, Freiburg 1909, Graz 1960, II, 213–40.

Studies: Walter von Arx, 'The Churching of Women after Childbirth', *Liturgy and Human Passage* (*Concilium* 112), ed. David Power and Luis Maldonado, New York 1979, 62–72; David Cressy, *Birth, Marriage and Death: Ritual, Religion and the Life-Cycle in Tudor and Stuart England*, New York 1997 (bib.);

Natalie Knödel, 'Reconsidering an Obsolete Rite: The Churching of Women and Feminist Liturgical Theology', *Feminist Theology* XIV, 1997, 106–25; Joanne M. Pierce, '"Green Women" and Blood Pollution: Some Medieval Rituals for the Churching of Women', *Studia Liturgica* XXIX, 1999, 191–215 (bib.); Susan Roll, 'The Churching of Women after Childbirth: An Old Rite Raising New Issues', *Questions liturgiques* LXXVI, 1995, 206–29.

JOANNE M. PIERCE

Ciborium

Probably deriving from the Hellenized word for the hollow seed-case of the Egyptian water lily, ciborium now has two meanings in Christian liturgy.

1. A cup-shaped container used to hold the bread at the *eucharist; the ciborium may have developed either from the *pyx or from the paten (*see* **Chalice and Paten**), as it is used both to reserve the consecrated *host (when it is normally housed in a *tabernacle or *aumbry) and to carry it to each communicant during the eucharist. It now closely resembles a chalice, though it differs by always having a removable lid to act as a cover during *reservation. It only came into general use in the Middle Ages, with the development of reservation.

2. A fixed canopy or cover over an *altar; as such, a ciborium would have been made of stone, metal or wood and would normally be supported by columns, the whole edifice becoming more elaborate through the centuries. It is more often known today as a *baldachino, though it differs in that the latter derived its name from the silken hangings that were imported from Baghdad, which would imply a more transient structure.

TRISTAM HOLLAND

Cincture see Vestments 3(a)

Class Leader/Class Meeting

Beginning in Bristol in 1742 the early *Methodist societies were subdivided into 'little companies' or classes of twelve or more members. The local class leaders were first appointed to collect a penny a week to offset the debt on the preaching house, but they were soon pastorally involved with their members. Wesley declared 'this was the very thing we wanted' and charged the class leaders 'to watch over the souls of their brethren'. Classes were expected to meet for fellowship in the society's headquarters or the class leader's home. The 'class system' was part of the genius of original Methodism and has continued in the form of pastoral visitors or Class Leaders even though only a minority of Methodists still meet 'in class' for study and mutual support.

C. NORMAN R. WALLWORK

Collect

The collect (Latin, *oratio*, also *collecta*) is a short form of prayer, originally marked by simplicity and conciseness, and is a characteristic item in the Western liturgy. Already in use in the fifth century, collects are to be found in a developed form in the earliest Latin sacramentaries in sets of prayers for particular days. The collect forms a discrete liturgical unit and frequently migrates from its original association with a feast or Sunday to reappear in another place in subsequent liturgical books. Introduced in Latin by *Oremus* ('Let us pray'), it immediately precedes the *readings in the *eucharist. In the English version of the RC missal it is now called the 'opening prayer'. Though short, it divides into a number of parts: the invocation of God, the reason why God should hear and answer the prayer, and the actual petition, followed by a conclusion. A similar form is taken by the prayer over the gifts (*Super oblata) and the post-communion prayer.

Medieval missals provided a collect for every Sunday and feast day, but a number of additional commemorations could be added. On a major feast day there would be only one collect but at a *votive mass there could be as many as five or seven. Only a single collect is now used. The Latin collects of the Roman Missal of Paul VI were put into English in 1971–4 and another freer set was also written; a further revision of these opening prayers was initiated in the 1980s.

The Latin collects of the medieval missals were translated and adapted by Lutheran reformers and then for the 1549 *BCP* in England. Two-thirds of the 1549 collects followed the terse Latin originals; one-third were new. Nearly all the saints' days collects were new because the originals involved invocation of the *saints. A few new collects were added in 1662 but the greatest period for writing new collects in English has been the time of liturgical revision, 1880–2000. Late Victorian collects tended to be rather florid and over-rich in imagery. After 1950 there is a marked change in language as contemporary English begins to be used and becomes normative after 1972 with the South African *Modern Collects*. The Church of England collects of 1997 show a marked return to the Prayer Book idiom. With new writing and the many variants and adaptations, there are about one thousand collects in use in worldwide Anglican worship compared to 120 in the 1662 Prayer Book.

The collect was not an original part of the daily office (*see* **Daily Prayer**) and probably only found a place there in the eighth century, when the collect from the eucharist was used to provided a conclusion to vespers. In the Sarum Breviary it was used at lauds and vespers on Sundays, station days and festivals. The *BCP* introduced the collect into daily morning and evening prayer. The 1662 office normally had three collects, and four in *Lent and *Advent when the seasonal collect was added to the collect for the day, the other unchanging collects being appropriate to morning or evening. A collect is used as the concluding prayer in the current RC offices of morning and evening prayer. It has never been part of compline.

M. R. Dudley, *The Collect in Anglican Liturgy, Texts and Sources 1549–1989*, Collegeville 1994; J. A. Jungmann, *The Mass of the Roman Rite*, New York 1950, I, 359–90. On origins: G. G. Willis, *Further Essays in Early Roman Liturgy*, London 1968. On modern collects: Kathleen Hughes, 'Original Texts: Beginnings, Present Projects, Guidelines', *Shaping English Liturgy*, ed. Peter C. Finn and James M. Schellmann, Washington, DC 1990, 219–55.

MARTIN DUDLEY

Colours, Liturgical

1. *Medieval*. For over a thousand years varying colours have been used for liturgical *vestments and hangings in order to enhance the sense of worship. The first recorded use of a sequence of liturgical colours is that of the Augustinian Canons of the Holy Sepulchre in Jerusalem early in the twelfth century. It is, however, already a fully developed pattern and it seems likely that it may have derived from the rites of one of the French dioceses. The sequence is similar to that found in general use in western Europe during the Middle Ages. Black, violet and blue seem to be interchangeable in the medieval palette, and black was used

in Jerusalem in *Advent and on Christmas Eve instead of violet and was also assigned to feasts of the Blessed Virgin Mary (*see* **Marian feasts**). This is perhaps part of the development of blue as Mary's colour, as found in Cologne. This use developed further so that during the nineteenth century permission was given to the church in Spain and some churches in Naples to use blue vestments on the feast of the Immaculate Conception of the Blessed Virgin Mary. This is known as the 'Spanish privilege' and does not apply elsewhere. The first mass of *Christmas was celebrated in black in Jerusalem, the second in red and the third in white. This again was a common medieval custom, mentioned by Durandus, and still current in Paris and in Lyons in the nineteenth century. Blue was used for the *Epiphany and the *Ascension (which is unusual) and for Michaelmas; black from Septuagesima to *Passion Sunday and red from then until *Easter, which is usual. The ferial colour, which in the Roman sequence is green, is not given but seems likely to have been red.

Innocent III in the treatise *De sacro altaris mysterio*, written before his election as Pope in 1198, describes the ceremonies current in the Roman church at that time and the colour sequence employed there, but he is only recording the use and not modifying or promulgating it. White was worn for feasts other than those of martyrs, when red was worn; red for *Pentecost, black in penitential seasons and green for days without a festal character. The Premonstratensian *Liber ordinarius* of the same time pays no attention to rules about colours. It is clear, therefore, that there was not a standard sequence in the Latin church and that individual cathedrals, monasteries and greater churches followed their own patterns. The liturgical colours were applied to the eucharistic vestments (maniple, stole, chasuble), to the dalmatic and tunicle and to copes worn in procession and at the office, to the apparels on albs and amices, to the chalice veil and burse, and, if these were variable, to the frontal and altar hangings. Variations were not unusual even with a sequence and so we find that any colour could be used on the Epiphany in some places as long as the vestments were covered in stars! Latin names for the colours found in medieval inventories include *albus* and *candidus* for white; *rubeus*, *sub-rubeus* and *coccineus* for various shades of red; *purpureus* for red-purple and *violaceus* for blue-purple; *viridis* for green and *croceus* for yellow, which was interchangeable with green in England.

2. *Roman Catholic*. After 1570 the Roman sequence was set out in the rubrics of the missal. There were six colours: four main colours – white, red, green and violet – and two supplementary colours, black and rose-colour. White (*albus*) was used for all feasts of the Lord except of his cross and passion, for *Trinity Sunday, all feasts of the Blessed Virgin Mary, of the angels and of all saints who were not martyrs. It was also the seasonal colour from the first vespers of Christmas to the octave-day of the Epiphany and from Easter to the vigil of Pentecost. Red (*ruber*) was used for the *eucharist from the eve of Pentecost to the end of its *octave, for feasts of the Precious Blood and of the Cross, and for martyrs. It was also used for the blessing of the palms and procession on *Palm Sunday but not for the eucharist. Green (*viridis*) was the neutral colour and was used on Sundays and weekdays from the end of the Epiphany octave to Septuagesima and on Sundays and weekdays in the season after Pentecost (excluding Trinity Sunday). Violet was used as the colour of *penance on the Sundays and weekdays of Advent and from Septuagesima to the Wednesday of *Holy Week, except where rose-coloured vestments were worn. On *Holy Saturday and the eve of Pentecost the lessons and *collects and *litanies were said in violet and then white or red respectively used for the eucharist. Black (*niger*) was used for *Good Friday, *requiem masses and *funerals. Rose-colour (*color rosaceus*) was permitted on the third Sunday of Advent (called *Gaudete* Sunday) and the fourth Sunday of Lent (*Laetare* Sunday). For processions and *benediction of the blessed sacrament the colour was white.

The post-Vatican II *General Instruction on the Roman Missal* states that the colours in vestments 'give an effective expression to the celebration of the mysteries of the faith and, in the course of the year, a sense of progress in the Christian life'. It requires that the traditional four-colour sequence should be retained, with black and rose as optional extras, but also provides, in line with medieval practice, that 'on special occasions more noble vestments may be used, even if not the colour of the day'. Green is used throughout *Ordinary Time. Although white has been widely used for funerals, following the example of the funeral of Pope Paul VI, violet or black can still be used. The variation in the colour of cloth is considerable and there are no general prohibitions so long as the main colour conforms to the liturgical sequence. There is, however, a classical Roman tradition which, for example, uses a 'reddish' purple for violet rather than a 'bluish' purple.

3. *Anglican*. Colour sequences were abandoned in England at the Reformation. There is no instruction in the *BCP* as to the colour of the 'carpet of silke or other decent stuffe' covering the holy table. The ministers were 'in saying the publicke prayers and administering the sacraments' to wear 'a decent surplesse with sleeves' and the hood of their degree. Eucharistic vestments did not return to use until the catholic sacramental revivalism of the Oxford Movement and the Gothic revival in art and architecture brought a new appreciation of medieval liturgical practice during the nineteenth century. There were numerous controversies over vestments before the canons in the twentieth century permitted traditional vesture to be worn at the eucharist.

The Church of England *Alternative Service Book 1980* suggested appropriate liturgical colours but they were not mandatory and it was permissible to follow a local use. Festal vestments and hangings were white or gold with a simpler white set for lesser feasts. For Advent and Lent violet was commended, varying in colour from 'dark blue through true violet to "roman" *purple'. A Lenten array of unbleached linen could also be used. Rose was noted as an alternative for Lent 4 and Advent 3 and both black and white as alternatives to violet for funerals. In 1997 the Church of England made further suggestions, retaining and developing this basic pattern but expanding the detail and adapting to the developments in the revised liturgical calendar: white is used from Christmas until *Candlemas (and so continues for nearly a month longer than in the RC use); red is used in Holy Week but not for the eucharist on *Maundy Thursday, on the feast of Pentecost but not on the weekdays following, on the feasts of martyrs, and is commended for the period from *All Saints' Day to Advent 1. A number of contemporary Anglican liturgical books give no indication of colour sequence and leave it to local use. *Inculturation of the RC and Anglican churches in Africa and Asia has led to the adoption of colour schemes appropriate to local sensibilities that differ from the European use.

4. *Eastern Rites*. In the Byzantine tradition three liturgical colours were used: black for the Liturgy of the *Presanctified, purple for Lent, and white for all other occasions. In modern times this tradition has not been strictly maintained and for the normal celebration of the liturgy any colour that would not shock is counted as admissible.

W. H. St J. Hope and E. G. C. F. Atchley, *English Liturgical Colours*, London 1918.

MARTIN DUDLEY

Commination

The commination service in the *BCP* is a peculiarly Anglican observance. It would seem to combine two medieval practices. The 1549 Prayer Book gives no title for the service, but specifies that it is to be held on *Ash Wednesday after the *litany and before the *communion service. Thus it takes the place of the imposition of *ashes, a ceremony banned in January 1548. The second half of the Prayer Book devotion is a simplified form of this medieval original. Ps. 51 is recited (rather than all seven penitential psalms), followed by the *preces (see **Intercession**), and two *collects for penitence and forgiveness based on the original seven. However, the solemn *absolution is omitted, and also the blessing and imposition of ashes, though the *antiphons accompanying this rite are represented by an anthem in the Prayer Book. Like the medieval ceremony it leads immediately into the *eucharist.

The first half is composed of an introduction referring to the ancient discipline of public penance, with the hope expressed that it might be revived; a series of curses of evildoers based on Deuteronomy; and a homily composed of a catena of biblical verses on judgement and repentance. This first part of the service leading into the conservative second half would seem to be inspired by the medieval 'Greater Excommunication', a general denunciation of sinners read three or four times a year. There the faults are condemned by ecclesiastical rather than scriptural authority, and the Prayer Book rite presents more a contrast than a borrowing.

In the 1552 *BCP* the service is first called the commination (explained in 1662 as the 'Denouncing of God's Anger and Judgement'). It is also to be used at 'divers times in the year' and there is no mention of Ash Wednesday,

though in practice the connection was probably maintained, and in 1662 the explicit link restored.

Early-twentieth-century liturgical revisions have attempted various versions and simplifications, often using the Decalogue rather than the verses from Deuteronomy. But later Anglican services of the imposition of ashes have not used the commination as a model.

GORDON JEANES

Commixture

The commingling of a portion of the consecrated bread with the sacramental wine after the *fraction in the *eucharist. Long associated with the idea of unity and the exchange of the peace, the commixture shares its origins and development with the mixture of the *fermentum*. By this in the eucharists of early Christian Rome portions of the consecrated bread were sent after the *eucharistic prayer at the papal liturgy by the hands of inferior ministers to the various churches of the city. Receipt of the *fermentum* by the presiding local *presbyter was an expression not only of unity but of delegation. The portion of bread which was thus sent was added to the *chalice after the eucharistic prayer.

Later developments find the principal *host broken into three, of which one section communicated the priest and the ministers, another was mixed in the chalice and a third remained on the *altar throughout. The Eastern churches receive *communion by commixture on a spoon. The Western tradition continues to make the commixture following the breaking of the bread at the *Agnus Dei.

MICHAEL THOMPSON

Common of Saints

A liturgical source designed to supply texts, of both scripture and prayer, for the celebrations of those saints who have not been assigned their own set or *proper texts. These are to be used during times of *daily prayer and also at the *eucharist. A variety of texts are often offered, reflecting various themes, of which one or more will be characteristic of that saint or group of saints. For the RC Church the Common is composed of martyr, pastor or missionary, teacher or 'doctor' of the church, virgin, and holy man or woman. The latest provision in the Church of England supplies a Common for martyrs, teachers of the faith, bishops and other pastors, members of religious communities, missionaries and any saint without a proper.

ANDREW CAMERON-MOWAT

Communion

The act of reception of bread and wine within the *eucharist, and by extension and usually with the prefix 'Holy', the title used by many reformed and Protestant churches (including Anglican) for the whole eucharistic service. Among Orthodox and RCs 'communion service' would denote an order of worship in which consecrated bread and wine are distributed but the eucharist is not celebrated (*see* **Presanctified, Liturgy of the**). The term communion can also denote one of the *chants of the proper of the mass sung during the administration of the bread and wine.

The place and manner of receiving communion by the faithful has varied down the ages. In the patristic period the communicants received in their hands (see Cyril of Jerusalem, *Mystagogic Catecheses* 5.21–2). By the end of the sixth century women had come to be forbidden to receive the bread on the naked hand, and in the West worries about possible superstitious misuse of the sacrament and a growing respect for the eucharist led from around the ninth century to the practice of placing the *host directly into the mouth. This manner of distributing the sacrament removed anxiety that small particles might be dropped, and any scruples about the need to purify the communicant's fingers after communion, as had become the custom for the priest (*see* **Ablutions**).

The giving of the *chalice lasted longer than receiving the eucharistic bread into the hands. In the seventh century communion by intinction, that is, the dipping of the bread into the consecrated wine (*intinctio panis*) gained popularity. Forbidden in the West by the Third Council of Braga (675), it regained popularity in the eleventh century, only to be forbidden again in the thirteenth. By this time the reception of wine at communion by the laity had almost universally disappeared in the West, allegedly for fear of spillage. The development in eucharistic teaching that the entire Christ was present under either species (concomitance) was decisive in bringing it to an end. While the Council of Trent reaffirmed this doctrine, and restricted the chalice to the officiating priest, the Reformers maintained that communion under one form alone was contrary to the scriptural norm and the chalice was restored to the laity from the sixteenth century in the churches of the Reformation. Vatican II saw a (at first somewhat restrictive) restoration in the RC Church, and although communion in both kinds is still not the universal practice at every RC eucharist, it is becoming more general. In some Reformation churches hygienic concerns later led to the abandonment of the common cup and the adoption of small individual glasses, and more recently the custom of intinction has appeared in other places. In Eastern churches communion is given from particles which have been dropped into the chalice and taken out by means of a spoon and placed directly into the mouth.

The ancient practice was for communicants to receive standing, as is still the case in Eastern churches. That custom only gradually changed to kneeling in the West between the eleventh and sixteenth centuries. The kneeling *posture became a point of controversy in the Church of England in the sixteenth century and provoked the last-minute insertion into the 1552 *BCP* of the Declaration on Kneeling (commonly called 'the Black Rubric'), which asserted no adoration of the sacramental bread and wine was thus intended. In some Protestant traditions communicants leave their places to sit around a table, a process which may entail a number of successive 'tables'; in others communion is brought to the congregation, who receive sitting.

Although the Synod of Tours (567) affirmed the right of the faithful to ascend the steps to the *altar and receive communion there, in the Carolingian period they were usually communicated at a side altar. From the thirteenth century onwards there was a custom in some places of spreading a long white cloth before those kneeling at the altar. Its medieval English name was houselling cloth. It became obsolete in the RC Church after 1929 and replaced by a small metal plate. In England *altar rails were introduced after the Reformation, and from the seventeenth century onwards communion was generally administered to communicants kneeling at the rails.

See also **Words of Administration**.

───────

J. A. Jungmann, *The Mass of the Roman Rite*, New York 1951, II, 498–516; Robert Cabié, *The Church at Prayer* II, ed. A. G. Martimort, Collegeville 1986.

DONALD GRAY

Communion Rails *see* **Altar Rails**

Communion Table

The table used in Protestant churches instead of an *altar. The table is usually made of wood, of ordinary table height, and of relatively small scale. The communion table represents effort by the Reformers of the sixteenth century to disassociate themselves from the sacrificial connotations of the fixed stone altars used in the RC tradition. Martin Luther's insistence that the priest or minister stand behind the table and face the congregation required that it be brought forward toward the congregation. Thus the *apse became less important as it no longer housed the altar. Typically in a reformed church arrangement, a *pulpit stood at the front of the *nave, with the communion table between it and the congregation. Placing the communion table on the same floor (in the same room) as the assembly served to emphasize the priesthood of all believers gathered in the unity of communion.

MARCHITA B. MAUCK

Compline *see* Daily Prayer

Concelebration

A form of rite in which several ministers jointly celebrate the *eucharist or other *sacrament.

1. *Origins and Development*. At the close of the first century, Clement of Rome described the organic yet hierarchical nature of the church celebrating the eucharist, each order (*bishop, *presbyters, *deacons, laity) with its own contribution or place. At the beginning of the second century, Ignatius of Antioch insisted on the unity of the eucharistic celebration at one *altar, presided over by one bishop with his *presbyterium* or college of presbyters, and the deacons. A century or so later we have explicit directions for the participation by presbyters in the bishop's eucharist at Rome in the *Apostolic Tradition* attributed to Hippolytus: the deacons present the oblation over which the *presbyterium* extends hands, while the bishop alone gives thanks. From a very different community in third-century Syria, the *Didascalia* has a bishop welcoming a visiting colleague by inviting him not only to preach but also to say the *eucharistic prayer, or at the very least to pronounce the words over the cup. In this way both the unity of the sacrament and communion of faith and ministry were expressed. As yet there

could be no question of joint recitation, as *celebrants still improvised.

Even when texts were fixed, from the fourth century, this mode of concelebration did not change. Both Cyril of Jerusalem and Pseudo-Dionysius the Areopagite describe presbyters celebrating with the bishop, and as late as the Council of Constantinople (680) and the Photian Synod (880) Latin legates were invited to concelebrate with the Greeks without knowing enough of the language to recite the eucharistic prayer. But already by the eighth century a different practice was developing at Rome. While *Ordo* I directs the concelebrating bishops and priests to bow their heads during the pope's recitation of the eucharistic prayer, *Ordo* III has the cardinal priests recite the prayer together with the pope, while each holds bread in his hands.

In the West, the diffusion of the church in rural areas and the development of 'private *mass' led to the abandonment of the tradition of only one celebration. Traces of the older custom survived here and there only on *Maundy Thursday at the *blessing of oils during the eucharistic prayer and in the *ordination mass of bishops and priests (at least according to the pontificals of the twelfth and thirteenth centuries). According to their *rubrics, all the concelebrants recited sotto voce all the prayers from the *offertory onwards, or even, in some cases, from the beginning of mass, including the choir chants. At *communion, however, they received kneeling and in one kind only, like the rest of the congregation. St Thomas Aquinas (d. 1274) testifies that the practice was disappearing in his time, but justifies concelebration theologically on the grounds of the unity of all the priesthood in Christ.

A great variety of traditions has survived in the Eastern churches. With the *East Syrians, *Copts and *Ethiopians, the presiding bishop asks one of the presbyters to recite the eucharistic prayer; the other presbyters flank him without any active contribution. The *West Syrians and Ethiopians on certain occasions have synchronized celebrations by several priests who consecrate simultaneously, sometimes at the same altar. In the Byzantine rite the bishop remains the principal celebrant. In the Russian church the concelebrants recite together the most important parts of the eucharistic prayer, including the *institution narrative and the *epiclesis; some have thought this to be due to Western influences in the seventeenth century. Similar practices are to be found among the Greek Catholics, the Maronites and the Uniate Copts. But in the rest of the Orthodox churches the current practice is to share out only the *ekphoneses* (vocalized conclusions of the otherwise silent eucharistic prayer) and other prayers outside the anaphora, but this too seems to be a relatively late development. Other rites are also concelebrated in several Eastern traditions, most notably the *anointing of the *sick in the Byzantine, Coptic and *Armenian rites, though more commonly this entails a distribution of parts rather than joint recitation of the same parts.

2. *Restoration.* In Roman Catholicism the twentieth-century *Liturgical Movement led in some quarters to the demand for a revival of concelebration, at least as an alternative to the entrenched practice of multiple 'private' masses. In 1956 Pius XII ruled that 'in the proper sense of the term' concelebration meant the recitation by all the concelebrants of the institution narrative, all else being only 'ceremonial' concelebration; and it was in the light of this judgement that the Second Vatican Council discussed the question, decided upon a restoration, and commissioned the preparation of a new rite, which was issued in 1965. In the discussions, and in the ensuing rite, restored emphasis is given to the organic yet hierarchical nature of the church, to the unity of the eucharist, and to the collegial character of the ministry.

According to this restored rite, it is the prerogative of the bishop to preside over his own *presbyterium* (or a representative part of it) as principal celebrant, thus manifesting the original unity of the local church. In *cathedral liturgies, stational celebrations at deanery level, and major diocesan gatherings this is now general. In the absence of the bishop, the presidency could be said to be collective: any priest can take the role of principal celebrant. However, it is required that this essentially collegial ministry be represented by a single person who alone pronounces the greetings, dialogues, blessings and presidential prayers. The participation of the remaining concelebrants could in principle be expressed in various ways. According to this rite it is expressed in both word and gesture as follows: all sing or recite in unison the core of the eucharistic prayer (first epiclesis, institution narrative, *anamnesis, second epiclesis) and the concluding *doxology, with the principal celebrant's voice prevailing. The *intercessions of the

eucharistic prayer may be allocated to individual concelebrants. The concelebrants gather round the altar after the preparation of the gifts, taking care not to obscure the view of the congregation. During the first epiclesis they extend their hand(s) over or towards the elements (as indicated by Hippolytus), and during the words of institution they may extend their right hands towards the elements in an indicative sense. At communion they receive in both kinds according to a variety of methods: being served by bishop or deacon, passing the vessels among themselves, or serving themselves directly from the altar. One of the concelebrants may give the homily, proclaim the gospel in the absence of a deacon, and distribute communion. All wear the usual mass *vestments, but for a sufficient reason may adopt simply an alb and stole.

Not all have been happy with the form of concelebration adopted, feeling that the unity of eucharist and priesthood is expressed only at the cost of separating the 'power' of consecration from the role of presidency and unduly isolating the role of 'co-consecrating' presbyters from the rest of the celebrating church. For this reason many presbyters have preferred to join the celebration as members of the congregation.

It should be pointed out that the current attitude of the RC Church is not simply permissive but positively encourages concelebration 'whenever pastoral needs or other reasonable motives do not prevent it'. This is in line with the stated preference of the Second Vatican Council for 'celebration in common rather than by an individual and quasi-privately'. Thus, in the revised rites for the other sacraments a form of concelebration is now encouraged, in which Pius XII's distinction between 'sacramental' and 'ceremonial' concelebration is much less clear cut. Not only in the ordination of bishops and presbyters do other members of the respective order (as in Hippolytus) lay hands on the candidate together with the ordaining bishop, but in the rite of *confirmation, too, presbyters who have a special pastoral relationship with the candidates may actually confer the sacrament alongside the bishop, and in the rites of *baptism, anointing of the sick, and the reconciliation of several penitents (*see* **Penance**), several ministers may share the texts and secondary rituals between them and baptize, anoint or absolve concurrently within the one corporate celebration.

In Anglican rites of ordination likewise,

bishops and presbyters join the presiding bishop in laying hands on candidates for the episcopate and presbyterate respectively. In the accompanying eucharist, the Episcopal Church of the United States in its 1979 *BCP* makes explicit rubrical provision for concelebration, as it does for all celebrations of the eucharist, whereas the Church of England envisages no more than a 'ceremonial' concelebration. Some other churches also prescribe a collective laying-on of hands for ordination (e.g. the British *Methodist Worship Book*, 1999).

———

J. C. McGowan, *Concelebration: Sign of Unity in the Church*, New York 1964; Archdale King, *Concelebration in the Christian Church*, London 1966; Pierre Jounel, *The Rite of Concelebration of the Mass*, New York 1967; J. R. K. Fenwick, *Eucharistic Concelebration*, Nottingham 1982; Robert Taft, *Beyond East and West: Problems in Liturgical Understanding*, Washington, DC 1984, 81–99; John Baldovin, 'Concelebration: A Problem of Symbolic Roles in the Church', *Worship* LIX, 1985, 32–47; John Huels, *Disputed Questions in Liturgy Today*, Chicago 1988, 39–46; Gilbert Ostdiek, 'Concelebration Revisited', *Shaping English Liturgy*, ed. Peter Finn and James Schellman, Washington, DC 1990, 139–71.

CHRISTOPHER WALSH

Confession

The acknowledgement of sin, which usually includes the expression of contrition for past misdeeds, petition for God's forgiveness and often also the articulation of the intention for amendment of life. It may take the form of a corporate or general confession within a service, acknowledging either the sinful condition of human life in general or particular sins committed by individuals, or both. Alternatively, it may be a personal act, made by someone in their private prayer or as part of the sacrament of *penance. Both general and sacramental confession may be followed by an *absolution, but the RC Church holds that only the latter form is efficacious for the forgiveness of a penitent's sins.

EDITOR

Confirmation

Confirmation is the second of the three sacraments of Christian initiation in the RC Church, the 'seal of the Holy Spirit' completing *baptism and connected to a hand-laying prayer for the sevenfold gifts of the Holy Spirit and an *anointing with chrism, both usually performed by a *bishop (or by *presbyters in the case of adult initiation), leading to the fullness of Christian initiation signified by participation for the first time in the *eucharist. Although in the case of infant initiation, confirmation may be separated from baptism by an interval of several years (from the canonical age of 7 all the way to age 18 in the USA), confirmation follows baptism immediately for adults in the modern RC *Rite of Christian Initiation of Adults*. Post-baptismal 'chrismation', for both infants and adults, in the Eastern Orthodox and Eastern Catholic churches is often viewed as the equivalent to confirmation. In various Protestant traditions, however, the rite of confirmation is not part of 'initiation', properly speaking, but is, rather, a rite having to do with a public affirmation of one's baptism after catechesis, usually during adolescence, with baptism itself understood as constituting the fullness of initiation into Christ and the church. In both RC and Protestant practice, at least with regard to infant initiation, first communion itself often precedes this 'confirmation' rite. And, like chrismation in the Eastern rites, so confirmation in the RC rite is also used as part of the rites of reception into full communion with the church for those baptized in other Christian traditions.

1. *Origins*. The origins of what became confirmation are obscure and complex. Although traditional scholarship saw its origins in Acts 8 and 19, where an apostolic post-baptismal hand-laying rite associated with the gift of the Holy Spirit appears in the initiation of some Samaritan converts (Acts 8) and of others who had received only the baptism of John the Baptist (Acts 19), most scholars today would find reading confirmation into these texts to be anachronistic. Recent scholarship underscores their exceptional contexts and situations rather than interpreting them as indicative of a regular or normative practice in the apostolic churches. Similarly, while we do find reference to post-baptismal hand-laying in relationship to the gift of the Holy Spirit in *some* early Christian sources in North Africa (Tertullian and Cyprian), but *never* separated from baptism itself, other models of initiation abound elsewhere in the geographically and liturgically diverse churches of the early period. Early Syria, for example (as demon-

strated in the *Didadascalia Apostolorum* and apocryphal *Acts of the Apostles*), knew a pre-baptismal anointing associated with the gift of the Holy Spirit and no post-baptismal rites, with the exception of the eucharist.

The key Western document from the first three centuries which contains both a hand-laying rite and second anointing assigned to the bishop following a presbyteral post-baptismal anointing is the so-called *Apostolic Tradition*, attributed to Hippolytus of Rome (c. 215). This pattern reflected here is precisely that of the post-baptismal rites as they developed later in Rome. But the actual content of this rite in the *Apostolic Tradition* is difficult to interpret, especially because neither the hand-laying prayer nor the second anointing appears in the earliest extant version (fifth-century Latin) to be associated with the conferral of the Holy Spirit. Instead, the prayer assumes that baptism itself constitutes regeneration in water *and* the Holy Spirit and asks for 'grace' so that the newly baptized might serve God. The formula for the bishop's anointing is trinitarian and not pneumatic in nature.

Aidan Kavanagh has argued that these episcopal rites reflect only the traditional structure of what may be termed an episcopal *missa*, that is, a *dismissal of various categories of people from the liturgical assembly (e.g. *catechumens and penitents) as was known to happen frequently in Christian antiquity. Various groups of people, before leaving the liturgical assembly, would go before the bishop and receive, often by a hand-laying rite, his blessing. In the case of the *Apostolic Tradition*, just as these newly baptized had often been dismissed from both catechetical instruction and from liturgical gatherings by a rite which included the laying-on of hands, so now they are again dismissed by means of a similar ritual structure, but this time the dismissal is *from* the baptismal bath *to* the eucharistic table. Paul Turner has questioned whether these episcopal acts were an actual dismissal, and has suggested, alternatively, that they should be viewed as 'the first public gesture of ratification for the bishop and the faithful who did not witness the pouring of water' (P. Turner, 'The Origins of Confirmation: An Analysis of Aidan Kavanagh's Hypothesis', *Living Water, Sealing Spirit*, ed. Maxwell Johnson, Collegeville 1995, 255), as it is quite clear that both baptism and the presbyteral anointing happened at a place outside of the assembly itself. In other words, this unit constitutes a rite of 'welcome'

rather than dismissal, a rite by which those newly born of water and the Holy Spirit are now welcomed officially into the eucharistic communion of the church. And they are welcomed there by the chief pastor of the community, the bishop, who now prays for God's grace to guide them in order that they may be faithful to what their baptism has already made them to be.

By the time of the famous letter of Pope Innocent I to Decentius of Gubbio (416), however, it is clear that at Rome this episcopal unit has become associated with the gift of the Holy Spirit and was to be reserved to the ministry of bishops alone on the 'apostolic precedent' of Acts 8, either immediately if a bishop were present at baptism or at some time after baptism and first communion when a bishop could be present. Only bishops could anoint the baptized *in frontem* (on the forehead). Jerome also refers to a practice he has encountered at Rome of bishops completing baptisms by a hand-laying rite during episcopal visitations, a practice he says has more to do with the honour of the episcopacy than actual need. Even so, as late as the early seventh century, Pope Gregory I (590–604), actually permitted presbyters to do this rite in the absence of bishops.

2. *Medieval Practice*. It was not until 1971 that the Roman rite for confirmation began to use the language of 'N., be sealed with the Gift of the Holy Spirit' for the confirmation anointing, a deliberate borrowing from the single *presbyteral* post-baptismal chrismation of the Byzantine Rite. In early medieval documents (the Gelasian Sacramentary and *Ordo Romanus* XI), in addition to the hand-laying prayer for the sevenfold gift of the Spirit, the formula for the bishop's anointing *in frontem* was 'the sign of Christ for eternal life . . . Peace be with you', or 'in the name of the Father and of the Son and of the Holy Spirit'. Gradually, as the various medieval Pontificals indicate, this formula was to become 'I sign you with the sign of the cross and I confirm you with the chrism of salvation. In the name of the Father and of the Son and of the Holy Spirit . . . Peace be with you.' In addition, a light blow (*alapa*) on the cheek was given to the candidate by the bishop during the words 'Peace be with you' as a sign of the sufferings to be endured in the Christian life, and actual hand-laying during the prayer became either a collective imposition of hands by the bishop at the beginning of the prayer or a laying-on of the right hand on

the head of the candidate during the actual anointing of the forehead. Such remained the overall ritual of confirmation experienced by countless Roman Catholics from the end of the thirteenth century until the 1971 reform of the rite.

The necessity of completing emergency baptisms (e.g. sick catechumens) or irregular situations (e.g. the reconciliation of those baptized by schismatics or heretics, or the lack of chrism on hand during baptism), as evidenced in various local non-Roman Western councils in the fourth and fifth centuries, contributed to confirmation's development as a separate rite, and the terminology of *perficere* (to perfect or complete) or *confirmare* (to confirm) emerges to describe these rites of baptismal completion. It is important to note, however, that in places like Spain and Gaul, the terminology of 'confirmation' may also have referred simply to regular practices of episcopal visitation, episcopal oversight, and supervision of baptismal practices, and not to any 'rite' properly speaking. In addition, although all rites, both East and West, did now contain a post-baptismal (usually presbyteral) chrismation associated with the Spirit gift, using chrism consecrated by the bishop, and some also contained a concluding hand-laying rite, only the Roman Rite contained the unique episcopal unit of an additional hand-laying *and* anointing.

A famous, and possibly fifth-century, *Pentecost homily, attributed to Faustus of Riez, a semi-Pelagian bishop in southern Gaul, also contributed to confirmation's development. An important statement in this homily, based on a distinction between baptism and 'confirmation' as an *imposition of hands* by the bishop (*not* an anointing), is that the Holy Spirit 'in confirmation' gives 'an increase for grace', and that 'we are reborn in baptism for life, and we are confirmed after baptism for the strife. In baptism we are washed; after baptism we are strengthened.' In the Middle Ages, Faustus' words were attributed to a fictitious pope and cited as such in a collection of forged papal documents known as the *False Decretals.* From there they passed into what is known as the *Decretum* of Gratian, from which Peter Lombard incorporated them into his famous *Sentences*, and where Thomas Aquinas read them and repeated them in his own *Summa Theologiae*, as well as using language about the Holy Spirit imparting a spiritual maturity to the baptized. In such a way, confirmation emerged in the West as a distinct rite, separate from

baptism, as a special sacrament of the Holy Spirit for an increase of grace, strength to live and fight the battles of the Christian life, and as related to maturity.

When throughout the Middle Ages the Roman rite was adopted elsewhere in Europe, it was often the case that the Roman post-baptismal 'confirmation' rites did not occur in their traditional Roman position between baptism and first communion but were added at some point *after* both baptism and first communion had already been administered. In other words, it was not so much the case, as traditional scholarship asserted, that 'confirmation' became *separated* from baptism but that the Roman post-baptismal rites became an *addition* to what had been understood as complete rites of Christian initiation elsewhere. Further, there is no question but that this rite was often delayed outside of Rome (Rome itself, owing to the abundance of bishops, was able to maintain the primitive unity and fullness of Christian initiation, even for infants, through at least the twelfth century), and because of this the interval between baptism and confirmation grew longer, in part because of the rarity of episcopal visits to parishes throughout the vast dioceses of western Europe. It would also be incorrect to conclude that either the rite or its theological interpretations ('increase in grace' or 'strengthening' by the gift of the Holy Spirit) were readily accepted by clergy and/or laity alike throughout Europe. The exact opposite, in fact, was more likely to be the case, as the Western Middle Ages abound with repeated attempts on the part of bishops and conciliar legislation to impress upon people the necessity of confirmation. So much so was this the case that confirmation became, in the words of Gerard Austin, the 'neglected sacrament' in the medieval Western church. Equally important to note is that this same legislation also demonstrates that a concern for the age at which confirmation was to be administered has its origins in various attempts to set not a *minimal* age for its reception but a *maximal* age (varying from one, three, seven, or even ten years) by which confirmation was to have been received! What became the minimal 'canonical age' of seven for the reception of confirmation in the RC Church, the so-called 'age of reason' or 'discretion', became such on account of clerical and parental negligence and delay!

3. *Reformation Churches.* The Protestant Reformers of the sixteenth century reacted

quite negatively to confirmation in general. Only the 1549 *BCP* provided what amounted to a translation of the medieval rite (as it appeared in the liturgical books of the Sarum rite), though without anointing. Almost all Reformers denied that confirmation was a 'sacrament' instituted by Christ, a position subsequently defended with anathemas, but not clarified, by the Council of Trent. According to Luther, the sacrament and rite of confirmation as it existed in the late medieval church was nothing more than *Affenspiel* ('monkey business'), *Lügentand* ('fanciful deception'), and *Gaukelwerk* ('mumbo jumbo'). John Calvin's assault was even stronger ('one of the most deadly wiles of [and 'oil polluted by'] Satan'), arguing that if the Roman Church wanted the Reformers to take confirmation seriously then the Roman Church itself should take it seriously. At the same time, most of the Reformers were open to the possibility of some kind of reformed, but non-sacramental, rite, done in relationship to an examination of the faith of children after a period of catechetical instruction. The biblical gesture of hand-laying rather than anointing was to be the ceremony used in this rite. Calvin himself actually thought that such was the original practice of confirmation in the early church, a practice which had degenerated into episcopal chrismation only after this earlier practice died out. Thanks especially to the Reformer Martin Bucer, various Reformed rites of confirmation were produced, usually a hand-laying rite celebrated at some time in adolescence after extensive catechesis and often serving as a preparatory rite for the reception of first communion.

Among several contemporary Protestant rites, that which constituted confirmation historically in the West, the hand-laying prayer for the sevenfold gift of the Holy Spirit and a consignation with the cross (often even with chrism), has been restored to baptism itself, as in the RC rite. But consistent with the concerns of the sixteenth-century Protestant Reformers, specific 'confirmation' rites still called 'confirmation' or 'affirmation of baptism' have been prepared for those baptized in infancy who have completed a course of catechetical instruction. These rites generally contain a hand-laying prayer but, with the exception of some Anglican experimentation, do not contain an anointing. Consistently with the restoration of complete baptismal rites which underscore the fullness of Christian initiation in water and the Holy Spirit, recent developments in several

contemporary Protestant traditions also include the possibility of the communion of all the baptized, with first communion increasingly being restored even to infant baptism. Thus, the primitive Roman unity and sequence of baptism, 'confirmation' and first eucharist now restored for adult converts in the RC Church is increasingly being adapted for *all* the baptized within other Christian traditions.

4. *Unresolved Issues*. Several issues remain with regard to confirmation today. First, when separated from infant baptism by an interval of several years, confirmation still tends to be a rite in search of a meaning. It is interesting that contemporary RC educational thought often appeals in this context to Protestant Reformation-sounding models of adolescent baptismal affirmation or ratification, when it is clear in Catholic sacramental theology that confirmation belongs *with* baptism as its concluding 'seal' leading to eucharistic participation, which is itself defined as constituting the 'fullness' of initiation. This disordered sequence with regard to infant initiation, disrupted further by the requirement for first confession (*see* **Penance**) in relationship to first communion, tends to make confirmation rather than eucharist this completion.

Second, in spite of the ecumenical popularity of 'seal of the Holy Spirit' language used for the confirmation anointing in the RC rite or the post-baptismal consignation or anointing in various Protestant baptismal rites, the question of whether Western confirmation *is* the equivalent of Byzantine post-baptismal chrismation needs further attention. Along with this, the limited attention to the biblical gesture of hand-laying and the long pneumatic associations with this in the West would seem to call for a re-evaluation as well. Aidan Kavanagh's charge that the RC rite of confirmation (and, by implication, modern post-baptismal rites in general) has been 'Byzantinized' strongly speaks to this need for further attention to pneumatology in the Western liturgical tradition. In other words, in spite of official definitions, does hand-laying or chrismation actually constitute the rite itself?

Third, agreement on the age for confirmation has not yet been reached, although several RC dioceses have restored confirmation prior to first communion at the age of seven. It may be that, ultimately, what the RC rites restored for adults, and what several Protestant traditions have been able to do, will finally be restored in all cases within RC initiatory practice. But this will happen only when the unity and fullness of Christian initiation is seen as a more important value than the physical presence of bishops at confirmation. Fourth, if ecumenical recognition of baptism is common, similar recognition of confirmation is not, with confirmation still serving as part of reception into full communion with the RC Church, in spite of the fact that rites equivalent to confirmation are used precisely as the post-baptismal rites themselves in several contemporary Protestant worship books. And, finally, in spite of the general denial of the sacramentality of confirmation within Protestantism, several contemporary Protestant traditions, ironically, regularly practise *double* confirmation: once liturgically as part of baptism itself; and, once, catechetically in adolescence with a rite consistent with the sixteenth-century Protestant reinterpretation of confirmation as baptismal affirmation.

Gerard Austin, *The Rite of Confirmation: Anointing with the Spirit*, Collegeville 1985; Aidan Kavanagh, *Confirmation: Origins and Reform*, Collegeville 1988; Paul Turner, *Confirmation: The Baby in Solomon's Court*, Mahwah, NJ 1993; Gabriele Winkler, 'The Original Meaning of the Prebaptismal Anointing and its Implications', and 'Confirmation or Chrismation? A Study in Comparative Liturgy', *Living Water, Sealing Spirit: Readings on Christian Initiation*, ed. Maxwell E. Johnson, Collegeville 1995, 58–81, 202–18.

MAXWELL E. JOHNSON

Congregationalist Worship

1. *Origins*. In *A Discourse concerning Liturgies, and their Imposition* (1662) John Owen maintained that properly appointed public worship should include 'preaching of the word, administration of the sacraments, and the exercise of discipline; all to be performed with prayer and thanksgiving'. He held that there are two ways by which the worth of worship can be assured: by entrusting its leadership to those who are endowed with the spiritual gifts referred to by Paul in Eph. 4.7, 8, 11–13; or by the prescription of a form of words. Those who supported the Act of Uniformity and the 1662 *BCP* chose the second option. Owen and those Dissenters called Independents or Congregationalists were keen advocates of the first.

A century before, Robert Browne and Robert Harrison had arranged the order of their serv-

ices and permitted not only church officers but others who had 'the gift' to teach and to preach in accordance with the will of Christ. For those in the early seventeenth century exiled to Amsterdam and to New England, worship true to the NT was to be 'spiritual, proceeding originally out of the heart'. Independents insisted on the simplest kind of worship, often including only a Bible reading, a psalm, a scholarly, doctrinal sermon which 'did not study so much to please ye ear, as to prick ye conscience' and lengthy *extempore prayer.

2. *Later History*. This simple pattern of free worship continued into the eighteenth century: a typical morning service at Isaac Watts' church began with psalm-singing, was followed by a short prayer seeking the presence of God, a half-hour scripture exposition, the singing of a hymn or a psalm from his own innovative *Hymns and Spiritual Songs* (1707), a prayer, a sermon, another prayer and the blessing. The Evangelical Revival halted a decline towards dullness as vibrant preaching and passionate hymn-singing touched the emotions and revitalized worship. As churches from an Anglican background, some under the patronage of the Countess of Huntingdon, became Congregational, they also introduced to Congregationalists the use of a written liturgy touched with an evangelical warmth.

The beginning of the nineteenth century saw the dawn of the day of the popular preacher. By 1830, however, the sometimes over-wordy evangelical style gave way to more homely preaching, which in turn led to increasingly lengthy services made up of long extempore prayers and even longer sermons. Some Congregational churches were dissatisfied with this kind of worship and introduced more formal liturgies, influenced by Thomas Binney of King's Weigh House. Along with more disciplined singing, the publication of new denominational hymn books and the replacement of a variety of instruments with a single organ, worship in Congregational churches began to change and become more formal.

As the twentieth century began, P. T. Forsyth wondered whether 'the conditions for the sole use of free prayer may have ceased to exist' and went on to suggest that 'intercessory prayer offers a fit opening for a liturgical element, to the great enrichment, freshness and enlargement of heart in our devotion' (*Intercession Services for Congregational Use in Public Worship*, London 1923). Liturgical books and studies helped to shape more formal worship in many churches. John Hunter's *Devotional Services for Public Worship* (1882 and 1901) was followed by *The Book of Congregational Worship* published by the Congregational Union in 1920 and *A Manual for Ministers* in 1936. That same year saw the publication of *Christian Worship*, a collection of essays by members of Mansfield College and edited by Nathaniel Micklem, quickly followed in 1941 by Micklem's *Prayers and Praises*, a daily office, and by *A Book of Public Worship* in 1948, edited by John Marsh and others. *A Book of Services and Prayers* was published in 1959 by the Congregational Union of England and Wales and revised in 1969 by the Congregational Church in England and Wales. As the last named stated, however, such books were not intended to be 'used as a book of common prayer'; they were 'to provide guidance in the ordering and conduct of worship'.

3. *Modern.* By the second half of the twentieth century it seemed that, to ensure the worth of worship, John Owen's preferred option of dependence on the spiritual gifts of those leading worship was an ideal which could no longer be sustained. In its place was an increasing dependence on set forms of words. This espousal of Owen's 'second option' led some to pursue the quest for common forms of worship and liturgy as an expression of Christian unity through such bodies as the Joint Liturgical Group.

The *Charismatic Movement's rediscovery of the primacy of spiritual gifts and the postmodernism of the last quarter of the twentieth century prompted another major change of direction in the worship of Congregational churches. The early-twentieth-century confidence in set forms and prescribed words no longer has the same appeal. With the explosion of new ways of worshipping, new songwriting, *inclusive language, all-age worship, alternative worship among young people and a new spirituality, it is more important to guard the worth of worship by nurturing the spiritual gifts of those leading worship. The Congregational Federation's *Patterns for Worship* (1992) arose out of the Federation's Integrated Training Course: its aim is to enrich those with spiritual gifts in their leadership of worship. A good pattern for worship is more important than precise words. It might be a threefold pattern of praise, the word and prayer; it might be a pattern built around the dialogue at the

heart of worship between God and his people; it might be a pattern which reflects the biblical drama of salvation from creation through fall to the declaration of salvation and lasting praise and glory.

The search for unity can never be a quest for a common set of words. John Owen's words still ring true: 'To imagine that there should be a uniformity in words and phrases of speech, and the like, is an impracticable figment, which never was obtained, nor ever will be to the end of the world.' Instead it should affirm the rich diversity which goes back to the earliest Christian worship. In the very earliest days Christians worshipped in such diverse settings as the Temple, the synagogue and the charismatic *house-church. Today Congregationalists and others who find their roots in the synagogue worship of Jesus and his first followers should learn to appreciate those who find their roots in the ritual and ceremonial of the Temple worship he also valued, and both should rejoice in the third dimension of worship treasured by those who find their roots in the charismatic house-churches of the NT. The unity of the church will be seen wherever Christ is present among his worshipping people.

See also **Books, Liturgical** 7.

R. W. Dale, *History of Congregationalism*, London 1907; Horton Davies, *Christian Worship*, Wallington 1946; R. Tudur Jones, *Congregationalism in England*, London 1962.
RICHARD CLEAVES

Consecration *see* Dedication

Consecration of Bishops
see Ordination

Consecration of Churches

1. *Early Practices.* The *dedication of the Jerusalem Temple (1 Kings 8.63) provided a model for the consecration of places of Christian worship. Eusebius describes the dedication of the cathedral of Tyre in 314, but this did not involve any special ritual. From the simple celebration of a *eucharist of dedication the rite developed, between the sixth and eighth centuries, by (a) the incorporation of relics into the building with a solemn deposition, and (b) sprinkling with blessed water. The deposition of relics was a major part of the Roman

rite for consecrating a church: the *depositio reliquiarum* was much like a Christian *funeral and used perfumed ointments that gave rise to later *anointing of the *altar as the tomb of the saint. To these elements were added a series of other entrances and *processions, and the Gallican rite introduced the washing of parts of the building and anointing of walls and altar with chrism. Among the Roman *Ordines*, *Ordo* XLI gives a rite which combines Roman and Frankish elements and is the result of the Romanizing liturgical reforms of Pepin and Charlemagne. It can be dated between 775 and 825. The rite includes (a) an initial entry procession, (b) the great *litany, (c) prostration, (d) the tracing of the alphabet on the floor, (e) preparation of holy water, (f) mingling of water, salt, *ashes and wine, (g) the repeated tracing of crosses with holy water, (h) consecration of the altar, (i) blessing of altar linens, vessels and *vestments, (j) deposition of relics, (k) vesting of the altar, and (l) the eucharist. The alphabet was traced in Latin and Greek in ashes or sand along two diagonal lines, representing the Greek *X* for Χριστος, crossing the floor of the church. The rite was called dedication or consecration and there is no difference in meaning between the words.

2. *Medieval Rites*. Explaining the medieval rite, Hugh of St Victor (d. 1142), describes the church building as being like a soul to be sanctified and meaning is given to each of the actions of the *bishop, who here represents Christ. Water is *penance; salt the divine word stirring the soul; the threefold external sprinkling is the baptismal washing; the crosses with their lights are the Apostles, illuminating the church; the threefold striking of the lintel of the main door represents Christ's dominion over heaven, earth and hell; the writing of the alphabet is the teaching of the faith; the pavement is the human heart; the X shape the gathering of Jews and Gentiles, and so on. In a sermon on the dedication of a church Bernard of Clairvaux (d. 1153) stresses the fivefold symbolism of sprinkling, writing, anointing, illuminating and blessing. Neither Hugh nor Bernard, surprisingly, make anything of the deposition of relics. The very full account of the consecration in 1144 of the rebuilt abbey church of St Denis given by Abbot Suger shows how striking the medieval ceremonies could be.

The provision of a service is not, however, an indication of whether it was used and, if it was, then how frequently. In 1237 Otho the cardinal legate to the English church declared that he had found that many churches and even some *cathedrals had not been dedicated or consecrated with the oil of sanctification, despite having been built a long time previously. He ordered that all cathedral, conventual and parochial churches were to be consecrated within two years. Thirty years later the cardinal legate Othobon (Odduobuono) repeated this instruction.

The editio princeps of the *Pontificale Romanum*, 1595–6, contained a further developed rite, which placed equal stress on washing, anointing, the alphabet and deposition of relics, and which is extensively illustrated in the liturgical text. It included the anointing of twelve crosses marked on the walls of the church above candle prickets. The candles placed there are lit on the feast of dedication, the anniversary of this rite, each year. The mass used for the feast of dedication has the introit *Terribilis est locus iste* that links the church back to Jacob's rock in Genesis 28 as the house of God, and for the *communion anthem the text from the cleansing of the Temple in Matthew 21: *Domus mea domus orationis vocabitur* (My house shall be called a house of prayer). In the Roman calendar each church observed its own feast of dedication as well as those of its cathedral and of a number of Roman churches, namely the archbasilica of the Most Holy Saviour (St John Lateran), the basilicas of St Peter and St Paul, Our Lady of the Snow (S. Maria Maggiore) and St Michael the Archangel.

3. *Liturgical Revision*. In the RC Church the Codes of Canon Law of 1917 and 1983 required that a church be dedicated or at least blessed as soon as possible after the building was completed. The complex rites of the sixteenth-century Pontifical were revised in 1961 and again by Paul VI in 1977. The church is described in the revised rite as a visible building standing as 'a special sign of the pilgrim Church on earth' and reflecting 'the Church dwelling in heaven'. When it is a building 'destined solely and permanently for assembling the people of God and for carrying out sacred functions, it is fitting that it be dedicated to God with a solemn rite'. Every church to be dedicated must have a titular, and the 'feast of title' is then observed annually. Titulars range from the Blessed Trinity through the mysteries of Christ's life and titles, the Holy

Spirit and the Blessed Virgin Mary, to an angel or a saint inscribed in the Roman Martyrology. A church should also, if possible, contain authentic relics of such size that they may be recognized as parts of human bodies. The 1977 rite ideally begins with a procession to the new building with the unlocking and opening of the door and entry. Water is blessed and sprinkled on the people and the walls before the opening prayer and liturgy of the *word. The litany of the saints begins the dedication, the relics are deposited, the prayer of dedication is said, the altar and consecration crosses on the walls are anointed, and the altar and church are censed. A festive lighting of candles precedes the liturgy of the eucharist and the Blessed Sacrament Chapel is inaugurated after communion. The rite of blessing a church is used for buildings that are temporarily to be used for divine worship, oratories and *chapels, and consists of a eucharist in which the building is sprinkled with blessed water and the altar is also blessed.

4. *Anglican Practice*. In English law a building does not become a church until it is consecrated. Consecration may be accompanied by such religious ceremonies as the bishop thinks appropriate but it is effected by an act or sentence of consecration signed by the bishop setting aside the building for sacred purposes. During the ceremony the sentence is read by the diocesan chancellor or registrar. Dedication, no matter what religious ceremonies accompany it, is not legal consecration. The Church of England, unlike a number of other Anglican provinces, does not have a form for the consecration of churches and it is left to the discretion of individual bishops. William Laud, as Bishop of London, is reported to have used a very detailed and ceremonious form for consecrating. In 1661 a form for consecration was drawn up by Convocation but not authorized or published. In 1712 the bishops produced a form agreed by Convocation with some alterations but not given the royal assent. It was, however, widely and generally used. Bishop John Wordsworth of Salisbury made a detailed study of consecration rites and the version he compiled in 1886 for the consecration of Marlborough College Chapel was revised for the consecration of St George's in Jerusalem in 1898 and subsequently adopted in a number of dioceses. Wordsworth held that the stress on martyr-relics had deformed the medieval service and led to superstition. He endorsed the view of a number of medieval writers that the consecration of a church was a *sacrament and possibly the greatest of all sacraments. Bishop Leslie Hunter of Sheffield provided an updated form in *A Diocesan Service Book* (1965), which included the alphabet ceremony. The order used at the consecration of the new Coventry Cathedral has been influential. In 1536 Convocation ordered the feast of dedication to kept throughout England on the first Sunday of October. Though not included in the Prayer Book it became usual to observe it on this day when the date of consecration was not known. The revised calendar 1997 allows it to be observed on the first Sunday in October, the last Sunday after *Trinity, or on another date chosen locally. The practice in other Anglican provinces has varied widely.

5. *Other Churches*. Lutheran churches in the United States and Canada use an order which includes reception of the keys from the builder and dedication of the *font, *pulpit and altar, followed by the celebration of the eucharist. Many other Christian communities accompany the opening of a new church building with special prayers and lessons and an anniversary service is often celebrated, though without any suggestion that the building constitutes a holy place.

Brian Repsher, *The Rite of Church Dedication in the Early Medieval Era*, Lewiston/ Queenston/Lampeter 1998; C. Vogel, *Medieval Liturgy: An Introduction to the Sources*, Washington, DC 1986.

MARTIN DUDLEY

Consecration, Prayer of

The name given in the Scottish *BCP* of 1637 and the English *BCP* of 1662 to the *eucharistic prayer. More recent Anglican liturgies have tended to revert to the latter term instead, partly because it is more ancient and partly out of a recognition that the function of the prayer is more than merely to 'consecrate'.

EDITOR

Cope *see* Vestments 3(b)

Coptic Worship

1. *Eucharist*. The Coptic Church at the present time uses three *eucharistic liturgies, those of St Basil, St Gregory of Nazianzus and St Cyril of Alexandria, which was originally known as

the liturgy of St Mark. St Basil's Liturgy, being the shortest, has become the one most commonly used in modern times. Many parishes still have the Liturgy of St Gregory from *Easter to *Pentecost, and the Liturgy of St Cyril during *Lent, but this is not an absolute rule. The Coptic liturgy differs from the Byzantine in three significant ways: (a) all the prayers said by the *celebrant are recited aloud and followed by responses sung by both the *deacon and the congregation; (b) the whole celebration takes place inside the *sanctuary, and the doors of the sanctuary remain open throughout; (c) there are five readings, from the Pauline and the Catholic epistles, the Acts of the Apostles, the lives of the saints, and the gospel. The three Coptic liturgies contain almost identical intercessions for peace, the clergy and the meetings of the church.

A traditional (medieval) Coptic church has a solid sanctuary *screen, with a central door flanked by windows and side doors, and lighter screens to mark off the *choir and the men's and women's sections of the *nave. But the latter divisions are now omitted in modern churches, and often removed from old ones. Music has been preserved by oral tradition, but is now also studied formally. The blind are often trained as church singers and ordained as deacons.

2. *Other Rites*. Baptismal and other sacramental rites resemble those of the Greek Orthodox Church. *Baptism begins with *exorcisms which assume that the candidates are converts from idolatry, and *anointing. Four readings follow, further anointings, and the actual baptism, for which the active form, 'I baptize you . . .', is used, as in the West; and finally chrismation for the gift of the Spirit with chrism consecrated by the patriarch. Unction of the *sick calls for the lighting of seven lamps by seven priests, if available. It is often administered as a public healing service on the Friday before *Palm Sunday. *Funeral offices, varying for adults, children, clergy and monastics, each consist of a psalm, epistle, gospel and prayers. The Coptic Church has retained until the present time the prayer of general *absolution at the end of both vespers and matins. This same prayer is also used for absolution at private *confession, a fact which has caused many questions to be raised regarding the practice of private confession in the Coptic Church. It is known that it was abandoned in the Middle Ages and not restored until the present Coptic revival, which gathered momentum in the 1940s.

3. *Daily Prayer*. The *daily cycle appoints prayers to be said at dawn, and at 9.00 a.m., noon, 3.00 p.m., 5.00 p.m. and 6.00 p.m. (that is, the first, third, sixth, ninth, eleventh and twelfth hours), and at midnight. The resurrection of Christ is celebrated at dawn, the coming of the Holy Spirit upon the apostles at 9.00 a.m., the crucifixion at noon, and the death and burial of Christ at 3.00 p.m. Historically, no link has been established between the daily office and the celebration of the eucharist, but in modern times, whenever a eucharistic celebration takes place, the daily office is said first. The Coptic celebration of the eucharist on Sundays begins with vespers on Saturday evening, which is followed by the midnight office. In most parish churches today, these two services of prayer have in fact been joined together. Matins is said on Sunday morning immediately before the liturgy, and has become part of the eucharistic celebration. Both vespers and matins are traditionally known in Coptic and Arabic as 'the raising of incense', since *incense is offered at the beginning of every *litany. The highly symbolic meaning of the incense can be seen in Coptic hymns, where the *censer is seen to be a symbol of the Virgin Mary, the coal a symbol of the humanity of Christ and the fire his divinity. This image of fire united to the coal is used by Cyril of Alexandria as a type of the mystery of the incarnation. The incense is then seen as the fragrance of the life of Christ offered to God the Father on behalf of the church. This accompanies the litanies to signify that the life of Christ mediates between us and God.

4. *Liturgical Year*. The three cycles, daily, weekly and *yearly, are an important feature of Coptic worship. During the first thousand years of Christianity, the weekly and yearly cycles were blended together and then the daily office was overlaid, until a complex was created within which the overall pattern is difficult to discern. The weekly cycle from the very beginning of Christianity has centred on the liturgical celebration of Sunday. Sunday clearly remains a day of celebration of the joy of Easter: it cannot be designated a day of *fasting, and every Sunday throughout the year at dawn, before the main eucharistic celebration of the week takes place, there is a gospel reading of part of the account of the resurrection. *Holy

Week is marked by long readings from the OT and NT, terminating with Revelation and the Gospel of John on Easter Eve. An impressive ceremony is the procession of the entombment on *Good Friday afternoon. Water is blessed at *Epiphany and there are *foot-washing ceremonies on *Maundy Thursday and the feast of St Peter and St Paul. The temporale is arranged by the ancient Egyptian calendar, with twelve thirty-day months beginning on 29 August and five or six extra days at the end.

See also **Books, Liturgical** 2.3.

O. H. E. Burmester, 'The Canonical Hours of the Coptic Church', *Orientalia Christiana Periodica* II, 1936, 78–100; *The Egyptian or Coptic Church: A Detailed Description of Her Liturgical Services*, Cairo 1967; John, Marquis of Bute, *The Coptic Morning Service for the Lord's Day*, London 1882; G. Viaud, *La liturgie des coptes d'Egypte*, Paris 1978; L. Villecourt, 'Les observances liturgiques et la discipline du jêune dans l'Eglise copte', *Le Muséon* XXXVI, 1923, 149–92; XXXVII, 1924, 201–82; XXXVIII, 1925, 261–320.

GEORGE BEBAWI

Coronation Services

After the advent of Christendom from the fourth century onwards and the growing influence that the church then came to exercise over the peoples of very many countries, it was inevitable that in time rulers would find it politically advantageous to seek from the church some expression of the divine approval of the legitimacy of their reign, and that the church would welcome the power which this role gave to them to secure a position of privilege within the state. It is not surprising, therefore, to see coronation rites begin to emerge in various countries of Europe in the early Middle Ages. The details of such rites vary considerably from place to place, and the English rite described here is just one example among many.

The oldest rite known in England is that which appears in the 'Egbert Pontifical' and seems to have been used at the coronation of Queen Judith of Wessex in 856. It took place after the gospel at a *eucharist and consists simply of consecratory prayers, the *anointing of the monarch, a series of *blessings, and the delivery of the sceptre, rod and crown. After the eucharist there was a short charge on the chief duties of the monarch, which in subsequent rites would develop into a coronation

oath. A later version, used in 973 at the coronation of King Edgar and in 979 at the coronation of King Ethelred, adds other features drawn from Roman and French sources. It now takes place before the eucharist begins, and commences with the election of the king by *bishops and people, followed by the oath, and ends with his enthronement. Later forms introduce other changes. In particular, the consecratory prayers are multiplied, the anointing becomes more elaborate, and additional robes and symbols of office are blessed and bestowed. If there was a royal consort, she too was usually (but not always) also anointed and crowned (although male consorts were not). All this made the service very lengthy. Revisions in the late-seventeenth and eighteenth centuries did little to shorten it, the deletion of certain items to that end being largely offset by the addition of new musical compositions, but some abbreviations were made at coronations in the twentieth century.

It is important to note that this rite is not referred to as a 'coronation' in the medieval texts but as a 'consecration' or 'hallowing' of the monarch, and its central liturgical act is not the crowning (which is simply the last item of regalia to be bestowed) but the consecratory prayers and anointing, for which chrism rather than oil was used from the twelfth century onwards. It thus in a sense parallels baptismal anointing, which appears to have been the ultimate source of the Christian practice, although obviously also strongly influenced by the OT anointing of kings. The principal theological significance of the rite lies, therefore, in the sovereign's act of self-dedication to the service of God on the one hand and the symbolized promise of the outpouring of God's grace for the task which lies ahead on the other.

J. M. Bak (ed.), *Coronations: Medieval and Early Monarchic Ritual*, Berkeley 1990; C. A. Bouman, *Sacring and Crowning: The Development of the Latin Ritual for the Anointing of Kings and the Coronation of an Emperor before the Eleventh Century*, Groningen 1957; Paul F. Bradshaw (ed.), *Coronations Past, Present, and Future*, Cambridge 1997.

EDITOR

Corporal

In Western liturgical use, a small piece of cloth laid centrally on the altar cloth, on which sit the *chalice and the paten (and sometimes a *ciborium). It probably obtained its name because it 'hosted' the eucharistic body (*corpus*) and blood of Christ. Measuring about twenty inches square, the corporal developed out of one of the altar cloths, and at one point was large enough both to sit underneath the sacred vessels and also to cover them. Such a cloth is referred to in texts dating from the fourth century but seems not to be clearly distinguished from one of the altar cloths before the ninth century. Embroidered ornamentation of the corporal with elaborate crosses (as with the *pall and the *purificator) militates against its practical use, but the prevention of decoration has proved nearly impossible.

TRISTAM HOLLAND

Corpus Christi

A solemnity in the RC calendar, the Thursday after *Trinity Sunday, celebrating the sacramental body and blood of Christ. It originated in the diocese of Liège (Belgium) at a time of burgeoning devotion to the *reserved sacrament and theological concentration on the real presence. The visions of the nun, Juliana of Mont Cornillon, led her to campaign for such a feast. Bishop Robert established it in the diocese of Liège in 1246, the Dominicans spread it through France, Germany and Eastern Europe, and when Archdeacon Pantaleon from Liège became Pope Urban IV, he decreed its extension to the universal church in the bull *Transiturus*, 1264. However, he died within two months and the bull was ignored in Rome for the rest of the century. It was finally promulgated more successfully in 1317 by the efficient Avignon administration of John XXII.

The texts for the *mass and office, unusual in their biblical and theological richness, have traditionally been attributed to Aquinas, but scholars are more cautious. The *procession with the reserved sacrament, long associated with this feast, is first recorded at Cologne in 1279; its precedents are seen in the *Maundy Thursday procession to the 'altar of repose', in processions with *viaticum to the bedside of the dying, and in the *Palm Sunday procession in medieval England which, from the eleventh century, included the carrying of the sacrament. In the later Middle Ages the procession became an elaborate affair, often sponsored by fraternities and craft guilds, drawing in the whole of civic society and providing the context for the mystery plays and other dramas.

In the secularized culture of recent times the procession, at least outside the church precincts, has become much less common, and the liturgical reform has attempted to refocus the celebration in the action of the *eucharist itself, retitling the feast as Corpus *et Sanguis* Christi, and highlighting the theme of eating and drinking so profoundly treated in the traditional texts for the day.

In Reformation churches, for obvious theological and historical reasons, the feast was not retained. However, it has been restored as a 'thanksgiving for holy communion' in most recent Anglican calendars (England 1980, Scotland 1982, Wales 1984, South Africa 1989, New Zealand 1989, Australia 1995).

Nathan Mitchell, *Cult and Controversy: The Worship of the Eucharist outside Mass*, New York 1982; Miri Rubin, *Corpus Christi: The Eucharist in Late Medieval Culture*, Cambridge 1991; Martin Dudley, 'Liturgy and Doctrine: Corpus Christi', *Worship* LXVI, 1992, 417–26.

CHRISTOPHER WALSH

Covenant Service

Liturgical reaffirmation of the gracious bond between God and God's people (e.g. Ex. 24; Jer. 31, 50; Luke 1.72), or of the bonds uniting church members. (There is no essential link with 'federal theology'.) Reaffirmation of *baptismal vows appears in medieval and later exposition of monastic profession, and it functioned as a distinct rite of personal discipline in RC, *Reformed and Anglican devotion (e.g. *Country Parson's Advice to his Parishioners*, 1690; Dr Samuel Johnson, *Private Devotions*), and specifically in English Puritan guides to personal conversion (e.g. by Joseph and Richard Alleine, Philip Doddridge). Many *Congregationalist and *Baptist churches since the late sixteenth century have been established by covenants between members, uniting in a confession of faith, and corporately between each church and God, solemnly made and renewed in God's presence. This usage was prominent in eighteenth-century New England, and was revived in the late twentieth century.

In the Renewed (*Moravian) Church of the United Brethren, the Choir of Single Brethren introduced (1729) the 'Cup of Covenant,' cementing the bonds between partners embarking upon a new mission enterprise. It was probably this practice which John Wesley witnessed in August 1738, as a regular observance of the separate choirs, immediately after leaving a celebration of the *Lord's supper. The rite is carefully distinct from the *eucharist, but emphasizes the church as Christ's body. In British Moravianism, the structure is framed around these texts: John 15.1a, 5b (1 Cor. 12.27, when individual cups are used); Matt. 23.8b.

In his *Christian Library* (1749–55) John Wesley included slightly edited versions of Joseph Alleine's *Alarm to the Unconverted* (1671) and Richard Alleine's *Vindiciae pietatis* (1663–6), both of which gave readers directions for committing themselves to God in Christ in terms of 'the substantials of our baptismal covenant'. In 1755, Wesley began regularly to use these directions in a special service of covenant renewal, for which in 1780 he printed an excerpt from the *Vindiciae*: a long exhortation, and a long covenant prayer. This excerpt, with minor adaptations, remained in use, linked with holy *communion and observed on the first Sunday of the New Year, among British Wesleyans until 1936. Combination with the eucharist was based on the covenantal nature of the eucharist, which also encouraged Wesleyans to describe the *BCP* post-communion prayer of oblation as 'the covenant prayer'. The smaller British Methodist churches all produced their own versions, with new wording but the same intention. No later than 1922, the Wesleyan minister George B. Robson created a new form, centring on John 15, replacing most of the exhortation with prayers of adoration, thanksgiving and *confession, and replacing most of the prayer with another, itself derived from the Alleine exhortation. Emphasis now fell on the image of God as our employer. Robson's service, after years of use in parallel with the older text, was revised and made official in the now united British Methodist Church's *Book of Offices* (1936). Further revisions, strengthening the link with the eucharist and with *intercession for the entire church and the world, appeared in *Methodist Service Book* (1975) and *Methodist Worship Book* (1999). Since 1762, Charles Wesley's hymn, 'Come, let us use the grace divine' (based on Jer. 50.5, not specifically on the Covenant Service) has been regularly used at this celebration.

In US Methodism, the service has not yet established itself, despite occasionally revived interest. Charles Wesley's 'Covenant Hymn' was often sung at New Year's Eve *watchnight immediately after the midnight chimes.

Robson's revision (in the 1935 version, but with communion optional) appeared in *Book of Worship for Church and Home . . . for Voluntary and Optional Use* (1944), for the first Sunday of the year or watch-night, and for those 'or Other Occasions' among 'Services in the Methodist Tradition' in the 1964 *Book of Worship for Church and Home*. The 1992 *United Methodist Book of Worship*, reversing the Robson trend that emphasized the image of God as our employer, reintroduced major elements of Wesley's (i.e., Alleine's) exhortation and covenant prayer, within a eucharistic framework, for use in the *Christmas/New Year cycle. For most congregations, the accessible equivalents are the services for Reaffirmation of the Baptismal Covenant, included in the 1989 *United Methodist Hymnal* as well as in the *Book of Worship*. In a church seeking renewal, further liturgical revision and catechesis in covenant spirituality and celebration may prefer that starting point rather than the Covenant Service.

M. A. Jackson 'An Analysis of the Source of John Wesley's "Directions for Renewing Our Covenant with God"', *Methodist History* XXX, 1992, 176–84; William Parkes, 'Watchnight, Covenant Service, and the Love-Feast in Early British Methodism', *Wesleyan Theological Journal* XXXII/2, 1997, 35–58; D. H. Tripp, *The Renewal of the Covenant in the Methodist Tradition*, London 1969; 'Some Vicissitudes of "The Covenant Hymn"', *Proceedings of the Wesley Historical Society*, XLIX, 1993, 18–21.

DAVID TRIPP

Credence Table

A small table to the side of the *altar or *communion table, but in close proximity to it. It is usually covered with a fair linen cloth, and on it before the *eucharist may be placed containers for the bread and wine, the 'dressed' *chalice and paten, sometimes a *ciborium, and also the *lavabo bowl and towel, used for the washing of hands of the eucharistic president after the *offertory. Its name seems to be derived from the Latin *credo* (I believe or trust), which may relate to the side table in patrician homes from which food was tasted and tested prior to being served.

TRISTAM HOLLAND

Credo

see **Creeds in Liturgy; Music in the Mass of the Roman Rite; Ordinary**

Creeds in Liturgy

Credal statements attesting to aspects of the faith embraced by early Christians are already visible in the NT (e.g. Rom. 10.8–10; 1 Cor. 12.3; 2 Cor. 4.13). It is likely that such statements made their way into early Christian worship, but their precise use is impossible to verify. In the second and third centuries, credal statements developed gradually into longer declarations of the faith. These declarations were generally trinitarian in structure and are regularly found (in various stages of development) in descriptions of *baptism practice and in the fragments of baptismal rites available to us. In liturgical usage, sometimes referred to as the profession of faith, such texts were often cast in interrogatory form to which the baptismal candidate replied, 'I believe', during, or in close association with, the water bath. As the initiatory rites became more complex, the *traditio* (handing over), the *explanatio* (commentary), and *redditio symboli* (repetition of the creed) became the basis of baptismal catechesis and central components of the preparatory rites of initiation. By the end of the fourth century, the declaratory form of the baptismal creed came to be known as the Apostles' Creed (*Symbolum apostolicum*). In addition to its baptismal associations, the Apostles' Creed became a regular feature of the *daily office in the ninth century, although sporadic use can be found somewhat earlier. In the sixteenth century, some Reformers established the use of the Apostles' Creed in various *word services and as an alternative to the Nicene Creed at celebrations of the *eucharist.

The Nicene Creed (or Niceno-Constantinopolitan Creed) is a declaratory formula that developed in the course of the fourth century against the backdrop of the christological controversies of the period, particularly in response to Arianism. First drafted at the Council of Nicaea in 325, the text underwent expansion and revision at the Council of Constantinople in 381, and was cited by the Council of Chalcedon in 451. Although not by origin or intent a baptismal creed, a version of the Nicene Creed was incorporated by Cyril of Jerusalem (*c*. 350) into his instruction of those preparing for baptism, and it is probable that a variety of local baptismal creeds were known to the drafters of the Creed at Nicaea.

In the third to the fifth centuries, the need for a confession of faith at the eucharist was fulfilled by the exposition of the scriptures in preaching and by the form and content of the *eucharistic prayer. The use of the creed in the eucharistic liturgy originated in Antioch late in the fifth century and was regularized by the patriarch of Constantinople early in the sixth century. The use of the creed in the West originated in Spain in the late sixth century at the direction of the Council of Toledo (589). These early uses of the creed in both East and West were continuing responses to the ongoing challenge of Arianism to the orthodox faith of the church.

The widespread use of the creed in the West was slow in coming and developed over several centuries. Its use received further impetus at the end of the eighth century when the emperor Charlemagne and his theological advisors strongly reiterated the insertion of the Latin *Filioque* (and the Son) in the third article of the text, an emendation first commended by the Council of Toledo (589), but with little effect. Pope Leo III (795–816) resisted Charlemagne's insistence on the insertion of *Filioque* in the text, and held the view that the purpose of the creed was for the purpose of teaching doctrine and was not intended for use at the eucharist. In the eleventh century, the use of the creed was regularized in the Roman rite on Sundays (*Symbolum dominicale*), but was never required for use at every celebration. The impetus for its use again came from civil authority, and was at first resisted by Pope Benedict VIII (1012–24), but he finally relented to its regular liturgical use on Sundays.

The position of the creed within the structure of the liturgy suggests a variety of understandings of its ritual use. In the early occurrences in the fifth and sixth centuries, the creed was recited in close association with the eucharistic prayer as a further means of preparation for receiving *communion. As the Byzantine rite developed, the creed (and the *kiss of peace) retained a position between the *Great Entrance and the eucharistic prayer with similar intent. When the use of the creed gradually increased in the West, it was inserted after the reading of the gospel. In this position the creed was understood to be a response to the proclamation of the readings. The Reformers generally maintained the Western position of the creed following the readings and made its recitation mandatory for all celebrations of the eucharist.

Recent reforms have moved the creed after the sermon to emphasize the unity of the readings and the *preaching. In many traditions the mandatory use of the creed at all celebrations of the eucharist has been relaxed on weekdays, and provision has been made for occasional use of the Apostles' Creed or other professions of faith in its stead.

J. NEIL ALEXANDER

Cremation *see* Funerals

Cross, Crucifix

The cross is the most ubiquitous sign of Christian faith, and has a complex history of representation from the monumental to the most intimately devotional. Although its imagery is fully worked through in the NT and later writers, not until the fifth or sixth centuries did it become established in Christian iconography. Like the *chi-rho* monogram, it originated exclusively as a sign of victory, the banner of Christ and an object of veneration.

In the liturgy its forms are principally portable: *processional, *altar and pectoral (and many include a depiction of the *corpus* of the Saviour). Iconographically processional and altar crosses have been interchangeable, and sometimes literally. The use of processional crosses was permitted by the Edict of Milan (313) and thus entered use in the liturgy. The earliest use of altar crosses is attested in sixth-century Syria; and other crosses (such as the Sinai 'Moses cross') may have been used as a focus of prayer above an *iconastasis or *chancel beam. Although large crosses (and, later, roods) appear near altars from the seventh century, not until the eleventh are accounts of altar-mounted crosses frequent in the West, which may reflect contemporary changes in *eucharistic theology. There were few regulations as to materials; most surviving examples are of precious, enamelled or gilded metals.

The earliest forms of crucifix (painted or in relief) portray Christ alive and clothed in a full-length (often sleeveless) *colobium*. The form developed as a near-naked *suffering* figure in traditions of carved work (see Gero crucifix, Cologne, *c*. 950), and of panel-painting (notably in Italy where the crucified figure is supported by other figures or scenes in the frame or terminals of the cross outline). Such images were positioned behind the altar or suspended from a chancel arch.

The subsequent history of the form – in liturgical use as in more general Christian iconography – is one of response, by artist and believer alike, to the human passion of Christ's body. Portrayed in varying states of suffering or strength, each nuanced by varying inflexions of the head and gaze, limbs and joints, central abdomen and loincloth, and influenced by the limitations and possibilities of the materials being used, the emotion and humanity of the figure, both dying and dead, became increasingly intense.

Pectoral crosses (not required in the liturgy) survive from as early as the fifth century and were often prized for the relics they sometimes contained. They are first mentioned liturgically in the mid-twelfth century, and in later centuries explicitly as episcopal insignia, being established as obligatory in the 1570 Roman missal. Eastern bishops wear a circular *enkolpion* (literally meaning 'on the breast') often bearing an image of the Virgin Mary. Precious and hard materials and cast metals were predominantly used for pectoral crosses.

R. Schneider Barrenberg, *Kreuz, Kruzifix: eine Bibliographie*, Munich 1973 (bib.); C. E. Pocknee, *Cross and Crucifix*, London 1962; 'Cross', 'Crucifix', *The Grove Dictionary of Art*, London 1996 (bib.).

JONATHAN GOODALL

Cross, Sign of *see* Gestures 2

Crucifer

The name given to the person who carries a *processional *cross or crucifix.

EDITOR

Crucifix *see* Cross

Cruet

The word *cruette* means little jug, from the medieval French, but liturgically cruets refer to the vessels of precious metal, pottery or glass which hold the wine and water for the *eucharist, prior to their being poured into the *chalice. Such cruets would normally reside on the *credence table, but the English *BCP* refers to a flagon, when the wine it holds might also be consecrated in the flagon itself and presumably later used to replenish the chalice (canon law stipulating that 'a convenient cruet or flagon for bringing the wine to the *communion table' shall be provided).

TRISTAM HOLLAND

Cult, Cultus

The origins of the English word 'cult' are

domestic and agricultural, derived from the classical Latin verb *colere* ('to dwell' in a place and, hence, by metonymy, 'to till' the soil there). Branching figuratively from these fundamental roots, *colere* came to mean (1) 'to bestow care upon', (2) 'to polish or improve by care', and thus (3) 'to regard with care', 'to show worship, reverence, honour'. Cult therefore signifies the care with which highly valued persons, places or objects are ritually recognized and revered. By extension, 'cultus' refers to an organized system of worship: all the ritual actions by which communities and individuals outwardly express their religious beliefs, and so seek contact and communion with God.

The ancient Hebrew word for cult was *abodah*, which (like its English translation, 'service') could signify the ministry that serves a monarch, God, or God's 'house' (tent, dwelling, temple). Ancient Israelite worship shared many practices with other Middle Eastern peoples (e.g. grain and animal sacrifices), yet even prior to the Davidic dynasty's centralization of the national cult in Jerusalem, Israel's rites were distinguishable from those of its neighbours. During the period when cult was still conducted at several local sanctuaries (e.g. Bethel, Shiloh, Gilgal), monotheistic reformers insisted that one God alone – the *same* God – be worshipped at all sites (see Ex. 20.3; Deut. 5.7; 6.13). Israel's Lord, moreover, was the God of the Covenant, one who actively intervenes in human history rather than a divinity tied to extra-temporal myths. Finally, Israel permitted no 'graven images' in its cultus – a recognition that, since no image is adequate, the God 'of' history is utterly unique and transcendent. Thus, in the both First and Second Temples, the 'Holy of Holies' and the altars expressed worship of a God whose presence could not be represented by statue or symbol.

As an observant Jewish layman, Jesus would surely have participated in the worship of both synagogue and Temple, though he appears to have been critical of both (Luke 4.16–30; Mark 11.15–19). According to the synoptic Gospels, his own ministry was characterized by itinerant preaching, healings, *exorcisms, and an inclusive, open table-fellowship that welcomed marginalized persons (sinners, tax collectors, the troubled woman of Luke 7.36–50) and survived, to some extent, in the meal practices of early Christians. Paul provides the earliest description of one such practice among the household churches in Corinth – the '*Lord's

supper', which already resembles a distinctive ritual event distinguished from ordinary meals (1 Cor 11.17–34). It is thus possible that from the beginning Christians practised their own distinctive 'cult', though its largely domestic settings and apparent lack of traditional cultic personnel and paraphernalia (priests, temples, altars, sacrifices) made it a kind of oddity in the ancient world. Later, Christian cult came to be strictly regulated by authoritative documents (church orders), persons (*bishops), and meetings (synods, councils). RC tradition distinguishes between *public cult* (acts directed toward God or canonized saints and performed by authorized persons in the name of the church) and *private cult* (ritual acts that do not meet the aforementioned criteria).

Gordon W. Lathrop, *Holy Things: A Liturgical Theology*, Minneapolis 1993, 1–53; Roland de Vaux, *Ancient Israel,* New York 1961, II; James F. White, *Introduction to Christian Worship*, revised edn, Nashville, TN 1990, 21–51.

NATHAN MITCHELL

Culture and Worship

see **Inculturation**

Daily Prayer

Many ecclesiastical traditions encourage a fixed pattern of daily prayer among their members or even mandate their ministers to observe specific hours of prayer and to invite their people to do likewise. This practice is often called the daily office, the divine office, the canonical hours or (among RCs today) the liturgy of the hours.

———

General bibliography: George Guiver, *Company of Voices: Daily Prayer and the People of God*, 2nd edn, Norwich 2001; Robert F. Taft, *The Liturgy of the Hours in East and West*, 2nd edn, Collegeville 1993 (bib.).

1. Early Christianity; 2. Eastern Churches; 3. Medieval and Roman Catholic; 4. Anglican; 5. Lutheran; 6. Reformed.

1. *The Early Church.* Although it is often claimed that the early Christians prayed twice each day, morning and evening, the evidence appears to suggest that the oldest practice was rather to pray three times a day (*Didache* 8.3), which has a parallel in a threefold practice of

daily prayer in Judaism that may well be its origin, even if the precise hours ended up being a little different in each case. At least from the second century onwards, Jews were instructed to pray in the morning, in the afternoon, and again in the evening (the first two being understood as commemorating the times of the daily sacrifices in the former Jerusalem Temple). While for some Christian communities the times of daily prayer may have been morning, midday and evening, for others they appear to have been the third, sixth and ninth hours instead (approximately 9 a.m., 12 noon and 3 p.m.: Clement of Alexandria, *Strom.* 7.7.40.3; Origen, *De oratione* 12.2), while some third-century sources present a fivefold pattern of daily prayer – in the morning, at the third, sixth and ninth hours, and in the evening (together with prayer during the night) – which seems to be the result of a coalescence of the two earlier traditions of threefold prayer (Tertullian, *De oratione* 25; Cyprian, *De dominica oratione* 34–5).

In the fourth century, however, morning and evening do emerge as the pre-eminent hours of daily prayer, being seen as the Christian fulfilment of the OT morning and evening sacrifices, and they come to be celebrated publicly in churches everywhere, while the other times of prayer remain as the practice of pious individuals or religious communities. Scholars have assigned the designation 'cathedral offices' to these ecclesiastical celebrations. Their form was quite simple and comprised two principal elements: praise and *intercession. There were usually no readings, which belonged instead to separate services of the *word. The core of the praise in the morning was made up of Pss. 148–150, repeated daily, to which local traditions might add other elements, such as Ps. 63 or the canticle Gloria in excelsis. In the evening, many places began with a thanksgiving for light known as the *lucernarium, for which the hymn *Phos hilaron*, 'Hail, gladdening light', was widely used, and then there followed, at least in the East if not everywhere in the West, Ps. 141, with its second verse referring to 'the lifting up of my hands as an evening sacrifice'. The intercessions were often in the form of a wide-ranging *litany.

In the ascetic and early monastic communities that were forming themselves in the deserts of Egypt and Syria at this time, on the other hand, specific hours of prayer were shunned in favour of ceaseless prayer every waking hour.

Hence, while some of these communities did assemble for communal worship at the beginning and end of their day (the former in some cases being as early as cockcrow), their members were expected to continue that prayer individually for the rest of the day as they engaged in their labours. In contrast to the 'cathedral' office, the content of both communal and individual prayer centred around meditation on the word of God in the scriptures, and especially the Psalms, which were interpreted christologically – either as speaking about Christ, as the voice of Christ, or as the voice of the church to Christ. It soon became expected that novices would learn the whole psalter by heart and recite it constantly, and it is not surprising that in many communities communal worship consisted of the recitation of the Psalms in their biblical order by a solo voice, to which the rest of the community listened, each psalm being followed by a period of silent prayer and meditation.

By contrast, the monastic communities that grew up instead in the towns and cities throughout the Christian world at this time took as the foundation of their daily prayer all the hours originally observed by all Christians in the third century: morning, the third, sixth and ninth hours (later known as terce, sext and none in the West), evening, and in the night, to which was appended prayer at bedtime (later called compline in the West) to fulfil the biblical saying, 'seven times a day do I praise you' (Ps. 119.164). To the morning and evening hours were added some of the elements which formed part of the 'cathedral' offices of the church around them, and to the night hour was added a *vigil of psalmody, in imitation of the desert monastic practice. As this vigil lasted until the morning, when it concluded with morning prayer, it thus resulted in their 'day' actually beginning at midnight or cockcrow. Because there was a tendency for monks to return to bed after morning prayer for a 'second sleep', a further service at the first hour (prime) gradually began to be included in the daily cycle in many communities. It was this hybrid 'urban' monastic cycle of prayer that became the pattern for the later daily offices of the church in both East and West.

Paul F. Bradshaw, *Daily Prayer in the Early Church*, London 1981/New York 1982.

EDITOR

2. *Eastern Churches.* There is a family resem-

blance between most of the rites of daily prayer used in Eastern churches, and in these churches the celebration of the offices remains a popular communal celebration, as well as part of the discipline of monastic life.

2.1. *The Byzantine Tradition.* Down to the sack of Constantinople in 1204, Hagia Sofia celebrated what became known as the 'sung office' (*asmatiki akolouthia*). The round of worship comprised matins (*orthros*) and vespers (*lychnikon*) in the morning and evening, with short services at the third, sixth and ninth hours. In *Lent there was a special office (*tritoekti*) in the late morning, and on certain days a night *vigil (*pannychis*) and/or a midnight service. Psalms were sung *responsorially, and the Psalter in course (divided into sixty-eight *antiphons) was accomplished in the evening and the morning – more psalms being sung before light in the winter, vice versa in the summer. There were relatively few poetic pieces but many prayers and *litanies, and an impressive ceremonial movement from the *narthex to the *ambo in the centre of the church, and to the *altar on Sunday mornings. Relics of this service, especially presidential prayers, have survived into the modern office.

From the eighth/ninth century monasteries, and then other churches, began to use an office imported from Palestine that was characterized by the recitation of the Psalms by a single reader, but also had a great wealth of poetry interspersed among the fixed psalms and *canticles, and associated with the names of such as Andrew of Crete, John Damascene and Cosmas of Maium. This office, combined with elements of the 'sung office', is what is now used in all Byzantine Orthodox and Catholic churches. The services are ordered by the book known as the *Typikon*.

The office is dominated by the major services of vespers (*hesperinos*) and matins (*orthros*), the liturgical day starting in the evening. The Psalter is divided into twenty *kathismata*, each *kathisma* (session) comprising three *staseis*. The most straightforward arrangement is to allow for two *kathismata* each morning and one each evening (no continuous psalmody on Sunday night). Vespers begins with Ps. 104, then a litany, the reading from the Psalms and a short litany. The core of the evening office is Pss. 141, 142, 130 and 117, with poetic verses called *stichera* intercalated. The hymn 'Hail gladdening light' is followed by some psalm verses (the *prokeimenon*) and readings on feasts and in *Lent. There are another two

litanies with an ancient prayer between them and a prayer over the people. The third part begins with more *stichera* (relics of an ancient procession) and the Nunc dimittis, then come final prayers including the *Lord's Prayer and the *troparion* of the day (*see* **Byzantine Chant**).

Matins has a brief office of two psalms and some prayers prefaced to it, then the night part of the office begins with six fixed psalms (3, 38, 63, 88, 103, 143), a litany and some psalm verses with the *troparia* of the day. After the reading of the Psalter, on Sundays and Feasts, is the *polyeleos* (Pss. 135–136) and other chants to introduce a gospel reading, on Sundays one of eleven resurrection gospels. The morning part of the office begins with Ps. 51, followed by the canon of matins – eight sets of *troparia* (originally nine scriptural canticles); between the eighth and the ninth the Magnificat is normally sung. Now follows the *exaposteilarion* (to greet the rising sun, a symbol of the risen Christ), and Pss 148–150 with *stichera* on festal days. The festal office is concluded by the Great *Doxology ('Glory to God in the highest'), two litanies and prayer.

There are day hours at the first, third, sixth and ninth hours, normally comprising three fixed psalms, various poetic pieces and some prayers. The office after supper, compline, has two forms, one being quite similar to the day hours, the other much longer. Matins should be preceded by the largely fixed midnight office, usually comprising Ps. 119. Except in Lent when they are longer, these lesser offices are largely read by one voice. They are also normally combined with one another or with other services.

The offices are rarely celebrated in full outside of monasteries but daily vespers and matins are common in many Orthodox countries, Russian churches usually combining these services into a vigil on Saturday nights and the eves of feasts, while Greek churches celebrate vespers the evening before, and matins immediately before the *eucharist. The offices are very important at solemn periods such as *Holy Week, most of the characteristic observances of these days being attached to them.

2.2. *Other Eastern Offices.* A strong family resemblance may be found between the services of vespers in the *West Syrian, Maronite (*ramsho*), *Armenian and *East Syrian or Chaldean (*ramsha*) rites. In each case the services may be divided into three parts: a preparatory/meditative section, the central ceremonial and intercessory core, and a processional/devotional appendix. Psalmody in course has largely disappeared from the first part, except in the East Syrian service; the Armenians retain Ps. 86 as an introduction, as in the old Constantinople rite. All the Syrian rites have a core group of fixed psalms, 141, 142, 119.105–17 and 117, with an *incense rite following in the West Syrian services. The incense rite precedes these psalms in the Chaldean as it once accompanied a procession to the bema in the centre of the church. The Armenians use Pss 140–142, a light ceremony with 'Hail gladdening light' and then the incense rite, repeating verses of Ps. 141. Proper psalms and hymnody may well follow here and any readings (West Syrian and Maronite only). The central core concludes with intercessory prayers/litanies. The third part is much more varied but usually includes the *Trisagion and Lord's Prayer. The Chaldean service contains possible relics of a compline service in Lent.

The night to morning offices that parallel Byzantine *orthros* have a night section (*lilyo* or *lelya* in Syriac), which, after introductory material, was the traditional vehicle for the Psalter in course. The West Syrian/Maronite rites have lost the psalmody but retain three 'stations' or 'periods' of hymnody and prayer. In the East Syrian and Armenian rites the lengthy psalmody is followed by hymnody and prayer. At this point the East Syrian rite inserts a festal vigil of three psalms, hymnody and prayer. The morning offices (*safro* or *sapra*) are centred round the praise psalms, 148–150 (with 117 as a doxology in all the Syrian rites). In the West Syrian, Maronite and Armenian services these psalms are preceded by canticles, especially paschal ones like Benedicite. Hymnody extolling the light follows the psalms in all these rites, e.g. the Great Doxology in the Armenian. They all conclude with prayers of various kinds and, in some cases, a devotional appendix. As may be seen, the three parts of vespers and the movement from night to morning at matins are closely parallelled by what we have seen of Byzantine practices.

The West Syrian tradition has forms of prayer for the third, sixth and ninth hours that are normally attached to the morning prayer, and *suttoro* (compline) to follow vespers. Only the last has any psalms; hymnody has taken over completely. The East Syrian rite may never have possessed minor hours or compline except in a monastic use of which we know

nothing. The Armenians have orders for first, third, sixth and ninth hours, but except at the first, appropriate psalmody is not so important as poetic material and prayer. After supper the 'hour of peace' (*ałałakan*) and the 'hour of rest' (*hangstean*) employ a good deal of psalmody.

The Coptic tradition is now dominated by a monastic rite largely composed of the same psalms each day at eight services of more or less the same shape (except that the midnight one is longer and divided into watches). Some relics of a non-monastic form may survive in the offerings of evening and morning incense that precede the eucharist in all churches. Ethiopian offices are a very complex area involving several different uses, but in the ancient cathedral office vespers (*wazema*) is structurally simple: three appropriate psalms, supplications, reading and prayer. The night vigil (*mawaddes*) is the place for the Psalter in course, and the morning office (*sebhata nagh*) contains elements such as the canticles from Dan. 3 and Pss 148–150 together with hymnody, reading and prayer. Third, sixth and ninth hours exist only on certain days in this rite, and there is a complex vigil (*kestata aryam*) that replaces the normal daily vigil and morning prayer on great feasts.

Nicholas Uspensky, *Evening Worship in the Orthodox Church*, Crestwood, NY 1985; Oliver Strunk, 'The Byzantine Office at Hagia Sophia', *Dumbarton Oaks Papers* IX–X, 1956, 175–202; Alexander Lingas, 'Festal Vespers in Late Byzantium', *Orientalia Christiana Periodica* LXIII, 1997, 421–59.

                                        GREGORY WOOLFENDEN

3.1. *Medieval*. Following the testimony of the sixth-century *Rule* of St Benedict to the nature of one strain of urban monastic office in the environs of Rome, the first major witness to the shape and content of the early medieval, Romano-Frankish office is Amalarius of Metz (*c.* 780–850). The basic form of this office endured throughout the medieval, Renaissance and modern eras until its revision after the Second Vatican Council in the late twentieth century. From Amalarius' *Liber Officialis* IV, 1–2 and *Liber de ordine antiphonarii* 1–7 as well as from a contemporary Roman ordo, *Ordo XII*, the basic structure and content of the locally variable, daily prayer of the church in a great part of the West can be discerned. The night office known as nocturns or vigils, later called matins, began with the invitatory Ps. 95 with *antiphon. On Sundays there followed three nocturns of twelve psalms each, all without antiphons, and three readings, each followed by a *responsory, except in the third nocturn where the hymn Te Deum replaced the final responsory. On feasts each nocturn had only three psalms, and on weekdays there was only one nocturn of twelve psalms with antiphons. Morning prayer or matins, later called lauds, included Ps. 51 on weekdays or Ps. 93 on Sundays, followed by Pss 63, 66, a variable psalm, biblical *canticle, the *laudes* (Pss 148–150), *capitulum* (short reading), *Benedictus (gospel canticle), and *intercessions. Ps. 54, two sections (octonaries) of Ps. 119, versicle, *Kyrie, *Lord's Prayer, Apostles' *Creed, Ps. 51, versicle and *collect constituted prime. Terce, sext and none – the minor hours – consisted of three octonaries from Psalm 119 without antiphons, *capitulum*, response, and *preces* (intercessions). Evening prayer or vespers began with five variable psalms drawn from Pss 110–147. *Capitulum*, responsory, versicle, Magnificat (gospel canticle), intercessions and collect followed. Night prayer or compline consisted invariably of Pss 4, 31.1–6, 91 and 134, all without antiphons, and Nunc dimittis (gospel canticle).

Before the eighth century the Romano-Frankish office was often distributed among churches of a given region in western Europe so that no one church celebrated all the hours. Throughout the Carolingian reform in the eighth and ninth centuries, however, all clergy gradually assumed the obligation to celebrate all the hours in every church. The maintenance of Latin as the language of worship and accretions to the office, especially between the eleventh and the fifteenth centuries, contributed to a demise in participation by laypeople and the view by clergy and monks that the office was an obligatory burden. The situation was somewhat different on the Iberian Peninsula. Here popular matins (lauds) and vespers persisted according to local rites until Pope Gregory VII (1073–85) imposed the Roman rite in that area.

Especially from the latter part of the thirteenth century, laypeople turned to devotional practices among which was the use of primers or books of hours. These richly illuminated and illustrated books, used privately and in groups, often contained the recent accretions to the office: office of the Blessed Virgin, office of the dead, seven penitential psalms, gradual psalms,

litany of the saints, and prayers including other thematic offices (e.g. the cross, the Holy Spirit, John the Baptist). In the early fourteenth century these books began to appear in the vernacular languages of Europe. After the invention of printing in the mid-fifteenth century, their number increased tremendously. Most of the vernacular primers, however, lacked the rich illumination or illustration of the Latin books. Production of books of hours both by hand and by printing essentially ceased with the Reformation in the sixteenth century.

For many clergy of the thirteenth century, some relief from the burden of the office came with the adoption of the office of the Roman Curia. While not significantly different in content from that of the full Roman office, the curial office lacked many of the accretions that had made the office so burdensome to most clergy. This modification of the Roman office for the pope and his staff gained popularity through the Franciscans who had adopted it for their use and spread it in their travels.

The full Roman office was never completely replaced by the curial office, however, and continued to undergo change. Scriptural and patristic readings in the night office were shortened or eliminated while often legendary hagiographical readings were expanded. Clergy increasingly sought dispensation from the communal praying of this office because of educational obligations and pastoral responsibilities, replacing it with private recitation from a single book, the breviary. This book eventually contained all the elements of the office but was originally designed to be a kind of ordo or guide for using the various books necessary for the choral celebration of the office, i.e., psalter, antiphonary, lectionary and collectary.

Not until Pope Clement VII (1523–34) directed Francisco Cardinal Quiñones (1485–1540) to reform the office was there any significant and popular relief provided for those who were obliged to use it. Quiñones' *Breviary of the Holy Cross* went through two editions and over one hundred printings, attesting to its popularity. But it was designed for private recitation and thus earned the ire of some theologians who insisted on the choral, communal nature of the prayer of the hours. When Pope Pius V issued a new version of the traditional Roman office ordered by the Council of Trent (1545–63), he forbade any further use of Quiñones' breviary.

3.2. *Roman Catholic*. Between Quiñones' reform and that of Pope Pius X (1903–14), the most outstanding development in the office throughout western Europe was the creation of the diocesan neo-Gallican breviaries in France during the seventeenth and eighteenth centuries, which used some of Quiñones' principles. In these books there was more extensive use of scripture, a redistribution of the psalms so that there was relatively the same amount of psalmody at each hour, a shortened form of nocturns (matins), the use of only one of the *laudes* (Pss 148–150) at lauds, and the use of the ferial (weekday) psalms on all days except major feasts. Intended for private recitation by the clergy, these breviaries did not supplant the choral office in most cathedrals and parishes where at least Sunday vespers continued to attract the laity.

The privatization and clericalization of the office continued through the nineteenth and early twentieth centuries, even during a comprehensive reform begun by Pope Pius X and completed only after the Second Vatican Council. In 1911 Pius X decreed that there should be a redistribution and division, where necessary, of the psalms, a reduction in the number of them used daily, the omission of Pss 148–150 from daily lauds, the restoration of the use of the entire Psalter weekly, and the reduction in the number of psalms at matins and lauds. For matins, however, scriptural readings were not lengthened, and the unhistorical hagiographical readings were left intact. Pope Pius XI (1922–39) created needed historical perspective for the reform process by establishing in 1930 the historical section of the Sacred Congregation of Rites. With the assistance of this group, Pope Pius XII (1939–58) established in 1948 the Pontifical Commission for the Reform of the Liturgy. This commission devoted major effort to a study of the reform of the office. With the publication of the *Codex rubricarum* in 1960, however, the actual reform was minimal: the reduction of matins to one nocturn on most days. But with the establishment in 1960 by Pope John XXIII (1958–63) of the Pontifical Preparatory Commission on the Liturgy in preparation for the Second Vatican Council, the way was set for a genuinely comprehensive reform of the office.

In addition to the papal initiatives for reform throughout the twentieth century there were grass-roots efforts to restore communal, ecclesial prayer to the laity. Most significant among these efforts was the publication and widespread dissemination of the so-called short breviaries. Most of these appeared following Pope Pius XII's encyclical *Mediator Dei* (1947), in which the pope promoted the office as 'the prayer of the Mystical Body of Jesus Christ'. These short breviaries often combined hours, reduced the amount of psalmody at individual hours and the total number of psalms used, distributed the Psalms over a period of time longer than a week, and included more extensive biblical reading.

Among the propositions for a reformed office drafted by the Pontifical Preparatory Commission on the Liturgy to be included in its proposed schema for a conciliar document on the liturgy were: the distribution of the Psalms over an extended period of time (as was the case in many of the short breviaries), restoration of the traditional sequence of the hours to be prayed at proper times (referred to often as *veritas horarum*), designation of lauds and vespers as the principal hours of the day, and reshaping matins into an office of readings for use at any time of the day. All of these proposals became part of Chapter IV of the *Constitution on the Liturgy* adopted by the Second Vatican Council in 1963.

The post-conciliar commission established to implement the Constitution carefully adhered to the principles of Chapter IV in its reform of the office, but went beyond the Constitution by advocating in its *General Instruction on the Liturgy of the Hours* (nn. 20–7) that the office, especially morning and evening prayers, be celebrated communally by as many members of the church as possible and not just privately or communally by clerics, monks, and other religious alone. The reformers gave all the hours a similar structure – hymn, psalmody, reading, intercessions; they distributed the psalms over a four-week cycle and increased the number of biblical canticles, even adding some new selections from the NT. Matins became an office of readings to be prayed at any hour and even expanded, optionally, on Saturday nights and vigils of solemn feasts, into a substantial vigil office (texts in English in *The Divine Office,* Glasgow 1974/ *The Liturgy of the Hours*, New York 1975).

Despite the wholesale reform of the office, very few parishes adopted any of the hours for communal prayer. If they did, they often shortened an hour, usually morning or evening prayer, and included elements (e.g. *lucernarium* in evening prayer) common in the ancient cathedral office. Religious communities were more likely to adopt the communal use of the reformed office, but often prayed it unimaginatively and routinely. The vision of the *General Instruction* that 'the Liturgy of the Hours, like other liturgical actions, is not something private but belongs to the whole body of the Church' and that the most important of the 'groups of the faithful' who should celebrate the liturgy of the hours 'are the local parishes' (nn. 20 and 21) is still far from full realization.

The Benedictine Confederation, however, representing the majority of monastic communities in the West, provided with Vatican approval the *Thesaurus Liturgiae Horarum Monasticae* in 1976 to its monastaries as a source for shaping the monastic office to suit local circumstances. While providing for the essential structure of the monastic office, the *Thesaurus*, including its introduction (entitled in its English translation, *The Directory for the Celebration of the Work of God*, ed. Anne Field, Riverdale, MD 1981), allows for needed diversity. Some have wished that the Roman Liturgy of the Hours had provision for similar diversity.

Stanislaus Campbell, *From Breviary to Liturgy of the Hours: The Structural Reform of the Roman Office, 1964–1971*, Collegeville 1995; J. A. Jungmann, *Christian Prayer through the Centuries*, New York 1978; A. G. Martimort et al., *The Church at Prayer* IV, Collegeville 1986, 151–275; Pierre Salmon, *The Breviary through the Centuries,* Collegeville 1962.

STANISLAUS CAMPBELL

4. *Anglican.* For a variety of reasons the story of daily prayer in Anglicanism is unique. In the first *BCP* of 1549 Thomas Cranmer provided orders for morning and evening prayer (often known as matins and evensong) which remained little changed through subsequent revisions. Cranmer was partly influenced by German Lutheran reforms, partly by the drastic breviary reform of Cardinal Quiñones, but his main source was the Sarum use: elements from Sarum vigils, lauds and prime went to make up morning prayer, while the evening office drew on vespers and compline. Both have as a basic outline: penitential rite/psalmody/OT reading/*canticle/NT reading/canticle/*creed/ *Kyries/*Lord's Prayer/*preces/*collects. In addition on Sundays, Wednesdays and Fridays morning prayer was to be followed by the *litany (a long general supplication with over forty petitions falling into several sections). The whole Psalter was to be recited in numeri-

cal order each month, the whole Bible in a year. Apart from the collect of the day and four alternative canticles, the office was fixed and invariable. *Antiphons, *hymns and *responsories were abolished. *Gesture and *ceremony were reduced: choir dress for the clergy was retained, and there are directions for kneeling, standing and sitting. Other common usages, such as facing east to say the creed, are not in the rubrics.

In cathedrals and collegiate churches celebration of the daily offices has been sustained up to our own day, often drawing on music from a rich and unique repertoire. The resident choirs of cathedrals came in practice to take over the corporate recitation, while the canons simply process in and provide officiant and reader. The medieval arrangement of two antiphonal groups facing in parallel choir stalls has continued in such institutions until today. In the ancient cathedrals evensong is normally sung every day, while matins is nowadays more commonly said. A famous passage from Louis Bouyer's *Life and Liturgy* (London 1956, 47) is often quoted: 'the offices of Morning Prayer and of Evensong, as they are performed even today in St Paul's, Westminster Abbey, York Minster, or Canterbury Cathedral, are not only one of the most impressive, but also one of the purest forms of Christian common prayer to be found anywhere in the world.'

The *BCP* assumes their daily celebration in parish churches and the Canons of 1604 direct the church bell to be rung daily before each office. Little research has yet been done into parish practice in the sixteenth and seventeenth centuries, but in the eighteenth we have abundant evidence of regular daily public prayer. In some country parishes the priest recited some or all of the offices at home with his household, but in larger villages and towns they were public services often with high attendance. These parish daily offices gradually fell into desuetude in many places as part of the general church decline from the latter part of the eighteenth century. Tractarianism brought a revival in the nineteenth together with a rejuvenation of the cathedral tradition. At the time of writing it is relatively common for clergy to celebrate the daily offices in church, sometimes ringing the bell. Often alone, they are joined in some places by small groups of lay folk. This practice is most common in Britain, less so in other parts of the Anglican Communion.

Particularly characteristic has been the use of the offices on Sundays: matins, litany and *ante-communion in the morning, evensong in the evening. An Act of Parliament of 1872 allowed for the litany and ante-communion to be dropped, just when a weekly early celebration of the eucharist at 8 a.m. was beginning to become common, followed later the same morning either by sung matins or a sung eucharist. Until recent years, evensong has been a well-loved part of the Sunday round, amplified by hymns, a sermon and additional prayers.

Parallel with this history were unofficial experiments with the fuller course of six or seven offices, of which John Cosin's *Collection of Private Devotions* (1627) is a famous example. From the 1840s onwards this thread was picked up by the renascent religious orders, in varying ways adapting or replacing the Prayer Book offices within a framework expanded by the little hours and in some cases vigils.

The American *BCP* of 1979 made moves back towards the richer pre-Reformation tradition, and produced a fine translation of the Psalter, while the Canadian *Book of Alternative Services* (1985) was particularly influential in encouraging more imaginative approaches. In England the *The Alternative Service Book 1980* merely adapted the *BCP* offices, introducing a little diversification, and more manageable psalmody and readings. It served some well, but on the whole failed to satisfy. Frustration led to repeated pleas for better provision until in 1992 a semi-official group in partnership with the Society of St Francis produced *Celebrating Common Prayer*, whose extraordinary success marked a turning point in the fortunes of daily prayer in the Church of England. This book provides two forms: (a) a full breviary-type office restoring many of the riches of ancient tradition but in an imaginative and contemporary way and adding optional midday prayer and compline plus various other devotional exercises; (b) a much simpler form aiming to move beyond recitation of texts to an all-embracing celebration which nevertheless can easily be laid on with the simplest resources. Provision for a *lucernarium* happily coincides with a growing vogue in the use of *candles. There are parish churches in some places in Britain and various parts of the Anglican Communion where daily prayer has returned to being a communal, liturgical daily celebration. There is also much experimenting with prayer in small groups, either together or by aiming to pray offices at a mutually agreed time while going about the daily round. It is yet to be seen how this time of experiment and discovery will settle down, but there is clear movement towards the daily offices becoming a significant part of the daily prayer of the whole people of God.

G. J. Cuming, *A History of Anglican Liturgy*, 2nd edn, London 1982.

GEORGE GUIVER

5. *Lutheran*. In the *Formula Missae et communionis* of 1523, the most important of the actual liturgical proposals of Martin Luther, the reformer reported that matins, vespers and compline – filled as they were with *biblical* texts – were being continued on weekdays in the churches of Wittenberg. In the *Deutsche Messe* of 1526, he further outlined the actual practice of Sunday matins and Sunday vespers as two of the three liturgies (the other being the parish mass) in which he expected popular participation. Thus, it is no surprise that the subsequent Lutheran church orders (*Kirchenordnungen*) of the sixteenth century largely maintained a simple form of classic Western daily prayer, especially for use in the schools and in the principal city churches. With the closing of the monasteries, the daily office was once again seen as the responsibility of congregations, but the patterns for this prayer were largely the traditional ones and, at first, the books that were used were the traditional books. It was frequently envisioned – for example in the church orders written by Johannes Bugenhagen – that especially the churches which possessed scholars and/or a choir would still be celebrating daily morning and evening prayer, and that there would be congregational vespers on Saturdays and Sundays. In characteristically conservative fashion, the Brandenburg-Nuremberg Church Order of 1533 proposes that vespers should be celebrated 'at the usual time and in the usual manner'. Indeed, such celebration continued in places like Nuremberg or Leipzig for a very long time, yielding only centuries later to the ravages of war.

In a manner consistent with other contemporary proposals for the reform of the office, the office prescribed by the church orders followed the usual outline: psalmody, *hymn, scripture (sometimes followed by a sermon, here or after the *canticle), gospel canticle, prayers. Ps. 95 was drawn from ancient vigils to become the fixed 'invitatory' of morning prayer, now routinely called matins. The canticles (*Benedictus, Magnificat, Nunc dimittis, and sometimes Te Deum or the Athanasian Creed) were used (assigned to matins, vespers, vespers or compline, and matins respectively). In addition, many of the church orders printed psalm tones, and many local churches created *cantionales* which contained new and old music for the office.

Except in city centres which knew a long established office use, this heritage came to be ignored and neglected in the period of rationalism and pietism. The nineteenth-century recovery of Lutheran liturgical resources thus also included a recovery of the classic patterns of daily prayer. Wilhelm Löhe of Bavaria, for example, included orders for matins and vespers in his *Agende für christliche Gemeinden* (1844) as did the North American Common Service of 1888. Communities of *deaconesses, northern European cathedrals and city churches, and some seminaries became places for the recovery of frequent daily prayer on the old models. Saturday and Sunday evenings and Wednesday evenings in *Lent returned as common times for congregationally celebrated vespers. Most twentieth-century Lutheran liturgical books, in whatever language, include resources for the celebration of matins, vespers and sometimes compline.

The twentieth century witnessed yet further developments. Some churches participated in ecumenical efforts at daily prayer. The Church of Sweden, for example, joined in the publication of an ecumenical breviary (*Tidegården*) intended for wide use in the diverse churches. And the Lutheran churches of North America were influenced by the 'cathedral office' movement centred at the University of Notre Dame to include in the *Lutheran Book of Worship* (1978) a fixed psalm in vespers (Ps. 141) as well as matins, to introduce vespers with a *lucernarium*, to conclude vespers with a long sung *litany, and to add a 'little office of the resurrection' to Sunday matins.

See also **Books, Liturgical** 8.

Edward T. Horn, 'The Lutheran Sources of the Common Service', *Lutheran Quarterly* XXI, 1891, 239–68; Luther D. Reed, *The Lutheran Liturgy*, Philadelphia 1947; Frank Senn, *Christian Worship: Catholic and Reformed*, Minneapolis 1997, 338–42.

GORDON LATHROP

6. *Reformed*. Reformed daily prayer at church and home traditionally was corporate, liturgical

and sacramental with both baptismal and eucharistic dimensions. Regular prayer times derived from scripture. Calvin's widely observed counsel to pray on rising and at bedtime, before work, and before and after meals seems adapted from Ambrose (*On Virgins*). The tradition affirms that prayer in church and at home strengthen and support each other. Praying only at home 'breaketh in sunder the unity of faith and teareth in pieces the body of our Lord Jesus Christ' (Calvin, *Sermons on Deuteronomy*, Oxford 1987 edn, 920).

6.1. *Common Prayers*. (a) Europe. Adaptation to revolutionized worship was difficult for the first generation in Geneva and other places, but by 1685 great numbers worshipped together morning and evening all over Switzerland. Daily service with or without sermons, some with psalm-singing, others without music, according to a service-book or directory, became a fixture of religious life in European cities, towns and many villages, from Hungary/Transylvania, Lithuania, Poland, Germany, France and the Netherlands to Scotland. Common prayers thrived for almost two centuries, where not suppressed, with notable exceptions of uninterrupted observance to the present. Some early English Puritans attended parish weekday services, but all were later forced to worship clandestinely. The persecuted of France, Hungary and the Palatinate were driven from common prayers, worshipping instead in households and secret locations.

(b) Mission Settings and New Churches. Missionaries established common prayers among indigenous populations led by indigenous leaders where possible. Morning and evening prayers are plentifully documented in the nineteenth and twentieth centuries in Botswana, Congo, Ghana, Malawi, Sudan and South Africa, India, China, Hawaii, Tahiti and Vanuatu.

(c) USA. Occasional evidence exists of weekday common prayers. The *Presbyterian church in Chelsea, Massachusetts had daily prayers at 6 a.m. and 7 p.m. in 1842. In Lexington, Virginia Presbyterian Margaret Preston remarked that prayer meetings were held daily at 4 p.m. during the Civil War and very well attended. She presumed these were general throughout the country (the Confederacy?). While mid-nineteenth-century revival gave rise to well-attended daily prayer meetings in urban areas for a time, for most Americans ministers were too scarce and the populace too scattered to support weekday services.

(d) Present. Daily prayers are held in Hungary (usually in the morning); in Scottish cities such as Aberdeen, Edinburgh and Glasgow, and at the Fourth Presbyterian Church, Chicago, USA (9 a.m. each weekday). There is a wider American practice of liturgical prayer on Wednesday morning, noon or evening. In South Korea, Presbyterians pour into church by the thousands from Monday to Saturday at 5.30 a.m.

6.2. *Family Worship*. Morning and evening family worship was a regular feature of Reformed life in Great Britain, Europe and America; among Reformed immigrants to Australia, New Zealand and Canada, and among Hawaiian, South Pacific and African families. There was often a close intentional correspondence between household prayers and worship at church. In addition, the home was the locus of much sacramental catechesis. Household worship was the spiritual support of persecuted Reformed peoples – the Huguenots, English Puritans, the Palatines and Hungarians. In isolated rural or frontier regions of North America and South Africa, for example, pastorless faithful depended on 'church in the house'. Traditional standard practice was singing psalms or hymns, scripture reading and prayer. The head of the household also sometimes read a sermon from a book or briefly interpreted scripture. Uniformity in practice can be traced, in part, to the popularity of certain prayer books and devotional manuals. Lewis Bayly's *Practice of Piety* 'flew the Puritan flag everywhere' (W. R. Ward, *Protestant Evangelical Awakening*, Cambridge 1992, 12). Although evangelical revival periodically strengthened observance, the practice has gradually declined in frequency and content since around 1775, particularly in the West, reaching a low ebb in the late twentieth century. Family worship has faded from the Church of Scotland in general, but survives in remote areas and in the Free Church of Scotland. In 1991 only 3% of American Presbyterians polled by the Presbyterian Panel read the Bible regularly with family or friends. In the same year 30% of Reformed Church in America members surveyed had daily family devotions. Hungarian-American Reformed families are encouraged to worship together at home but find this almost impossible. Grace at mealtime is more widely observed within all churches.

6.3. *Devotions of Couples*. Common prayers of husband and wife were observed from at least the late sixteenth century in Great Britain, France, Hungary, North America and elsewhere and survive to the present. Puritan sources mention devotions shared morning and evening, contemporary accounts indicate once a day. The informal practice incorporates one or more of the following: scripture reading, reading from spiritual books, prayer, psalm or hymn singing, spiritual review of the day and contemplative silence.

6.4. *'Secret' Worship*. From the sixteenth into the nineteenth century devout individuals in the West worshipped morning and evening, as a minimum. Standard content was scripture reading, meditation, prayer (often concluding with the *Lord's Prayer and Apostles' *Creed), psalm/hymn singing and self-examination (evening). Spiritual memoirs and sacramental treatises for laypeople document the importance of renewal of the baptismal *covenant and preparation for the *Lord's supper, especially in the seventeenth and eighteenth centuries. 'Secret' devotions were also practised in Africa, Asia, the South Pacific and Hawaii. Into the eighteenth century a prayer for illumination was often used before reading scripture, based on the counsel of St Augustine (*Homily* II on 1 John). Since the risen Jesus opened up scripture for disciples on the road to Emmaus, the devout prayed for understanding of the word. Reading 'godly authors' was common in Great Britain, America, Europe and elsewhere. Some of the most widely read books were by (Lutheran) Johann Arndt, Richard Baxter, Lewis Bayly, Willem à Brakel, Heinrich Bullinger and Gerhard Tersteegen. From the late eighteenth century onwards, private devotional practice has eroded in frequency and content. In 1991 80% of Reformed Church in America members surveyed reported praying daily, but only 31% read the Bible each day. In the 1990s from one-half to two-thirds of American Presbyterians prayed daily, but only around 16% regularly read the Bible. Daily Bible reading is also a minority observance in Germany.

Texts: John H. Leith (ed.), *John Calvin: The Christian Life*, San Francisco 1984, 78–92 (Calvin's prayers); John Joseph Stoudt, *Private Devotions for Home and Church*, Philadelphia 1956, esp. 29–42, 48–9 (Huguenot family worship); Theology and Worship Ministry Unit for the Presbyterian Church (USA) and the Cumberland Presbyterian Church, *Book of Common Worship: Daily Prayer*, Louisville

1993; *Book of Common Order of the Church of Scotland*, Edinburgh 1994.

Studies: Harold Daniels, 'Every Day I Will Bless You', *Reformed Liturgy and Music* XXXIII/4, 1999, 3–12; Jonathan Neil Gerstner, *The Thousand Generation Covenant: Dutch Reformed Covenant Theology and Group Identity in Colonial South Africa, 1652–1814*, Leiden 1991 (bib.); Charles E. Hambrick-Stowe, *The Practice of Piety: Puritan Devotional Disciplines in Seventeenth-Century New England*, Chapel Hill 1982; Diane Karay Tripp, *Daily Prayer in the Reformed Tradition: An Initial Survey*, Cambridge 1996 (bib.); Tessa Watt, *Cheap Print and Popular Piety, 1550–1640*, Cambridge 1991; John D. Witvliet, 'The Spirituality of the Psalter: Metrical Psalms in Liturgy and Life in Calvin's Geneva', *Calvin Theological Journal* XXXII, 1997, 273–97 (bib.).

DIANE KARAY TRIPP

Dalmatic *see* Vestments 3(a)

Dance, Liturgical

The liturgy of the synagogue and church has been rich in a tradition of bodily *movement and *gestures. As *ritual activity, liturgy has always used different qualities of movement in its *ceremonies, such as *processing, bowing, kneeling and standing. Liturgical dance is a special type of sacred dance, employing movement, attitude and shaping by an individual dancer, a group of dancers or the entire assembly. Liturgical dance is not performance, but connects to the prayer of the assembly, enriching and deepening the service by creating a prayerful environment.

Liturgical dance serves the worship by drawing the community into the mysteries of God, by revealing new dimensions of the scriptures, by witnessing to the beauty of God, and by eliciting a faith response from the community. At the service of the assembly, liturgical dance bridges the visible and the invisible world of the spirit. By its unique, non-verbal interaction of spirit and body, liturgical dance can capture the non-verbal movements of the Holy Spirit, interacting with the assembly, moving through scripture and being manifest in the mysteries of the liturgy. Dance can externalize these movements and make them visible through the vehicle of the human body. Dance draws people in through the use of basic, non-literal materials, which include rhythms, dynamics

and shapes that stir subtle and heightened moods and feelings.

The style and shape of liturgical movement for worship is open to a variety of different dance traditions, such as modern dance, ballet, yoga, folk dancing and popular dancing, and can draw upon the movements of various world cultures. The movement aims to express the faith of the assembly in a genuine way.

Liturgical dance presupposes a prayer life and a faith commitment or relationship to a spiritual force on the part of those involved. Because dance is a performance art, training and discipline for the art form are required of the solo dancer or group. Inexperienced dancers are to be discouraged from performing since they may detract from the prayer of the assembly; however, simple gestures can enhance the community prayer when the entire assembly is involved.

Because liturgical dance takes place within the worship service, dance types can be determined according to their placement and function within the liturgy, providing a descriptive liturgical dance language. There are five types of liturgical dance.

1. *Procession dance* is the purest form of religious dance. A latent awareness of the rhythms of life and the movement of a group attains a fixed form in processions. Processions with interpretative movement can become meaningful parts of the liturgical celebration that benefits the total liturgical action. Though primarily functional movement, processions should move from one place to another with a sense of purpose. All processions, whether danced or not, possess a dance-like quality. Within the *eucharist, there are four occasions that involve procession-like movement.

(a) The entrance procession gathers all those assembled into a liturgical community, sets the seasonal theme of the celebration and accompanies the ministers to the celebration space.

(b) The gospel or scripture procession highlights the proclamation of the good news of salvation from the Bible. The *Alleluia chant accompanies the procession to the *ambo where the scripture is proclaimed. This procession solemnizes the scripture reading and may involve the reader, *acolytes with *candles, and *incense bearers. The book of scriptures is ordinarily held high with sustained, graceful movement.

(c) The gifts procession highlights the preparation of the table and the bringing forth the elements of bread and wine from the community. The *aisle(s) can be used to emphasize the movement of gifts from the gathered community to the table.

(d) The closing procession signals the end of the liturgy and accompanies the ministers from the celebration space. Artistically, it is suggested that the opening and closing processions be of a similar quality or tone.

2. *Proclamation dance* forms the core of the liturgy of the word, involving the proclamation of the scriptures and the *creed. The word instructs and nourishes the faithful in the continuing work of salvation while the creed underscores faith as the basis for the community gathering. The scriptures lend themselves to a dramatic presentation, enhancing the spoken text. In this way, reader and dancer jointly proclaim the message. To dramatize the scriptures is to embody them. Thus, the dancer heightens the word in a dramatic way, witnesses to the good news and reveals new dimensions of the word.

Even though the nature of liturgical dance is prayer, there remains movement that expresses the prayer of the assembly. Acclamation and invocation form two kinds of *prayer dance*, usually addressed to the Creator God. Acclamations are shouts of joy arising from the assembly as rousing assents of God's word and action and the dance may include the *Kyrie, *Sanctus, memorial acclamation and Great Amen. Invocations are prayers of praise and thanksgiving, including the Gloria in excelsis and the *Lord's Prayer.

3. *Meditation dance* is reflective by nature – a response to a reading, a commentary on a group of thematic readings or a thanksgiving. The psalm-dance can be a meditative response to the reading of the day, using communal gestures along with solo or group movement; the homily or sermon may also employ movement. This dance may inspire, challenge or proclaim the message of salvation in a special way and draws the assembly into reflecting on the impact of the message in their daily lives. Meditation dance is most popularly associated with the quiet time at the end of a service. As the ritual draws to a close, this contemplative time can reinforce the theme of the celebration, draw the community together in a spirit of thanksgiving or help provide insight into the celebration.

4. *Celebration dance* may be considered liturgical dance, although it is not formally connected to the ritual structure of the liturgy. More akin to the prelude and postlude of a worship service, celebration dance sets the tone for the gathering or brings it to a festive close. These dances tend to involve the entire assembly with simple gesture or movement. Circle dances that encompass the entire space at the end of a liturgy exemplify this type.

In conclusion, liturgical dance is determined by the ritual structure in which it is performed. Liturgical dance must clearly be prayer and not performance, involving all the participants in the ritual action. Liturgical dance may include solo or group dances, or congregational movement. Liturgical dance is communal, drawing the assembly together; inspirational, uplifting the spirit to God; evangelical, witnessing to the message of salvation, and prophetic, challenging the participants to live the gospel message.

J. G. Davies, *Liturgical Dance: An Historical, Theological and Practical Handbook*, London 1984; Carla De Sola, *The Spirit Moves: A Handbook of Dance and Prayer*, Washington, DC 1977; Ronald Gagne, Thomas Kane, Robert VerEecke, *Introducing Dance in Christian Worship*, Portland, OR 2000; *Liturgical Ministry* VI, 'Movement and Gesture', Collegeville 1997.

THOMAS A. KANE

Deacon

The Greek word *diakonos* ('servant') is used a number of times in the NT, but it appears more often to be in the more general sense of someone who serves the church in some way rather than as a reference to a distinct office as such (e.g. Col. 1.7, 25; 4.7; Eph. 6.21). Only in 1 Tim. 3.8–13 (and perhaps Phil. 1.1) is the diaconate clearly a ministerial office, one which may have included women (see Rom. 16.1, and perhaps 1 Tim. 3.11). What is clear is that there is no specific connection between deacons and the Seven who were appointed in Acts 6. By the beginning of the second century several sources refer to deacons as a recognizable group of ministers who are distinct from *elders/*presbyters, and also from *bishops when they too emerge as a separate ministry. But though deacons are plainly subordinate to these other offices, it is less obvious what their precise functions are. Ignatius of Antioch sees the service (*diakonia*) of Jesus Christ himself as the model for the diaconate (*Magnesians* 6.1; *Trallians* 2.3; 3.1), an image which is repeated in later writings. In Irenaeus towards the end of the second century we first encounter the use of St Stephen and his companions in Acts 6 as the biblical 'type' for the office of the deacon, and this alternative image continues in later texts alongside the servanthood of Christ. In the third century, a further biblical 'type', that of the OT Levite, also emerges as a way of defining the liturgical dimension of the office. While some sources (including the later Eastern tradition) see the diaconate as constituting part of the priesthood possessed by bishops and presbyters, others (including the later Western tradition) exclude deacons from the priesthood as such. Like bishops and presbyters, however, their *ordination was by prayer and the imposition of hands. Some early Syrian sources refer to women deacons, but by the fourth century they have been replaced with *deaconesses, whose functions differ from those of the male deacons.

Early texts do not elaborate much on what a deacon was supposed to do, either liturgically or pastorally. But general administrative assistance to the bishop, and especially responsibility for the church's finances and for its care for the poor and sick, emerge as the main pastoral duties, with the liturgical functions also being in terms of assisting the bishop, especially at the *eucharist (specifically in preparing the eucharistic elements of bread and wine and helping distribute *communion) and at *baptism. In some, but not all, ancient ecclesiastical traditions, the reading of the gospel at the eucharist also became the prerogative of a deacon, and he was the usual minister to recite the various biddings to prayer in *litanies and other forms of *intercession.

Although continuing to exist as a permanent office in Eastern traditions, the diaconate in the Middle Ages in the West became no more than a probationary period for candidates for the priesthood, increasingly of brief duration, and the deacon's traditional pastoral and liturgical functions were more commonly exercised by presbyters. (The medieval church, however, did grant to deacons the right to preach, which they had not had before.) This continued to be the case in the RC and Anglican churches in the post-Reformation period, but since the Second Vatican Council the RC Church has permitted married men to be ordained as deacons, thus restoring it as a permanent office. Anglican churches in the latter half of the twentieth century began to admit women to the diaconate (rather than just as deaconesses), but their subsequent admission to the presbyterate in many

Anglican provinces has returned the office to being just a stepping-stone to the presbyterate for both men and women in most, but not all, cases.

John Calvin included the office of deacon, along with pastors, teachers and elders, in the fourfold ministry which he believed reflected the pattern of the apostolic church. In the Reformed tradition, deacons are administrative and pastoral officers with care of the sick and the poor, rather than liturgical ministers. Deacons in Baptist and Congregational churches, however, have a role in the distribution of communion, as well as administrative responsibilities and pastoral duties, especially towards the sick and needy.

James M. Barnett, *The Diaconate: A Full and Equal Order*, Minneapolis 1979; Edward P. Echlin, *The Deacon in the Church*, New York 1971.

EDITOR

Deaconess

Female *deacons are first clearly mentioned in the third-century Syrian *Didascalia Apostolorum*, where they are assigned duties that propriety prevented a male deacon from performing – visiting women in their homes and *anointing the bodies of female baptismal candidates. From the fourth century onwards, however, the term 'deaconess' came into use instead throughout the East, and she was appointed by prayer and the imposition of hands for a ministry that also included supervising women in the liturgical assembly. The office later declined almost to the point of extinction in Eastern churches. The existence of female deacons was condemned by a succession of councils in France, and seems otherwise unknown in the West. Although the word 'deaconess' is sometimes found in Italian sources from the seventh century onwards, it refers there to a category of women religious rather than an ecclesiastical ministry as such. However, from about the middle of the nineteenth century onwards, the office began to be revived in German Lutheran, Anglican, Methodist and Presbyterian churches, where the duties were usually those of a general pastoral assistant in a congregation. In some cases the office remains down to the present day; in other cases it has now become a part of the diaconate itself. Orders of deaconesses are also found in several Baptist Unions.

Roger Gryson, *The Ministry of Women in the Early Church*, Collegeville 1976; A. G. Martimort, *Deaconesses: An Historical Study*, San Francisco 1986.

EDITOR

Deaf Persons and Worship

The individual needs of persons who are deaf, deafened and hard of hearing are based on a number of factors: the age that the person's hearing loss occurred, the culture with which the person identifies (deaf or hearing culture), and preferred method of communication (speaking and speech-reading, American Sign Language or British Sign Language, or an English-based sign language). The common experience of hearing loss, however, requires persons designing worship to be more visually oriented. Any printed material is always helpful: words to the choir anthem printed in the weekly bulletin, an outline or copy of the sermon, or the page number from the pew Bible so that they can read the scripture texts themselves. Beyond printed materials, there are several general guidelines for each of these three different groups of people.

1. *Designing Worship for Those who are Hard of Hearing*. An assistive listening system helps make the worship accessible. The three most common wireless systems for worship spaces are: a) infra-red, b) FM, and c) audio-loop. Each system requires a transmitter connected to the church's sound system and a receiver for each hard-of-hearing person using the system.

2. *Designing Worship for Those who are Deafened*. Persons who become deaf later in life often depend on written communication and speech-reading (lipreading). Printed materials can be supplemented by computer-assisted note-taking. Someone types everything that is said in worship but not printed in the bulletin into a computer, and this is then projected onto a 'screen' (slide screen, white wall, or computer monitor). Oral interpreters can be used for those who speech-read well. The deafened members watch the oral interpreter, who sits opposite them and repeats without voice (lipsynchs) everything that is presented orally in worship.

3. *Designing Worship for Persons who are Deaf*. Persons who communicate primarily in one or more forms of sign language require interpreters to make worship fully accessible. Since there is a native sign language unique to every country as well as manual codes of spoken languages (e.g. signed supported speech; seeing essential English), it is important that the deaf constituency determine which sign language they prefer the interpreter to use. Which sign language a person prefers depends upon their upbringing, education and exposure to the native sign language of their country. While certified interpreters are the most qualified, it is essential to make sure they are trained in religious and theological vocabulary as well.

The use of *drama, liturgical *dance, mime, signed poetry, slides, etc. visually enhances the worship experience. Certain musical aspects can be supplemented by visual modes of communication (the musical prelude can be accompanied by a visual procession or the choir anthem can be supplemented by a sign-language choir). Since deaf persons cannot sign with their hands while holding a hymnal or bulletin, responsive calls to worship, psalm texts and corporate prayers and hymns can be projected onto a screen by means of an overhead projector or a computer. In this way, persons can see the words and sign collectively with the rest of the congregation.

See also **Disabilities, Worship and Persons with**.

KATHLEEN M. BLACK

Dedication

The act of formally making over something or someone to another person or, in religious usage, to God. The term is used to refer to the action of setting apart or blessing of people or objects for the service of God, for which many churches provide fixed forms. *Baptism has often functioned as little more than a rite of infant dedication in some traditions, but those churches which do not practise infant baptism have often introduced a specific rite of infant dedication, and even some churches which do practise infant baptism have in the latter part of the twentieth century begun to adopt in addition similar rites of thanksgiving/blessing for the gift of a child. Eastern traditions have known such a rite since at least medieval times, if not considerably earlier. This takes place on the eighth day after birth, when the child is brought to church, given a name, and prayed over.

The word 'dedication' has often been employed interchangeably with 'consecration' in the Christian tradition, so that one may speak either of the *consecration of a church or of its dedication. (There is, however, a legal distinction in England between the two, consecration being understood as setting apart a building irrevocably from unhallowed uses, dedication as merely a blessing.) The 'dedication' of a church can also refer to the name by which it is known, e.g. St Mary's or St Peter's, although strictly speaking, the church is not dedicated to the saint but to God in honour of the saint. Dedication festivals, being the annual commemoration of the day of the consecration of a church building, are found as early as the fourth century, and are to be distinguished from patronal festivals, which are held on the feast day of the saint to whom the church is dedicated. When the actual day of the original consecration is unknown, some ecclesiastical traditions provide for a particular Sunday in the year to be observed as the dedication festival.

EDITOR

Diptychs

Literally 'double-folded, doubled', the Greek term came to signify 'writing tablet'. In liturgical use, reference is to the two lists of names (one for the living and the other for the departed) that the *deacon reads for liturgical remembrance at certain *eucharistic celebrations. By extension, 'the diptychs' is often applied to the commemoration itself. In Eastern liturgical traditions, the diptychs are generally read within the context of the *eucharistic prayer; the Antiochene structure places them after the *epiclesis, while in Alexandrian prayers the diptychs are found before the *Sanctus. Traditionally, diptychs of the living list first the ranking hierarch of a local church, followed by select hierarchs commemorated by name, concluding with more general commemorations of groups of people (ordained and lay). Diptychs of the departed begin by commemorating the Virgin Mary, and go on to remember others individually and as groups. Within the climate of doctrinal controversy, diptychs became powerful tools in identifying ally and enemy, victor and defeated.

The earliest explicit reference occurs in the homilies of Theodore, Bishop of Mopsuestia (392–428). Probably originating as ad hoc parochial lists of people making the offering and those to be remembered, diptychs evolved into standardized, official lists falling into four general categories: (1) hierarchical diptychs

contained the names of area bishops officially recognized by the local church; (2) *communion diptychs included distant hierarchs and churches as a means of signifying a bond of communion; (3) confessional diptychs are distinguished by the names of figures or councils that represent confessional identity; (4) mixed diptychs blend characteristics of the first three.

———

Robert F. Taft, *The Diptychs*, Rome 1991.

JOHN KLENTOS

Directions, Liturgical *see* Orientation

Disabilities, Worship and Persons with

Designing worship for persons with disabilities requires an attitude of openness and a conviction that all persons are children of God, and members of the community of faith. There are so many physical, mental and emotional disabilities in our world today, both visible and invisible, that it is virtually impossible for any pastor or congregation to be familiar with the needs of each person who lives with a disability. Despite the tremendous diversity, however, there are three basic categories of access that should be considered when designing worship for persons with disabilities.

1. *Physical Access.* The first obstacle for congregations with older buildings is designing an accessible entrance into the church building for worship. Once that has been accomplished, there are several factors to consider within the church itself. When deciding where persons who use wheelchairs will 'sit' in the church, instead of removing an entire *pew at the front and/or the back, it is worth considering removing one-third of a pew in several places throughout the church. In that way, persons who use wheelchairs have a choice where to sit and can sit next to friends or family (who sit in the pew) and not be left alone in an empty space. Those who use walkers can sit in the shortened pew and leave their walker in the empty space, out of the aisle. In addition to accessible seating, it is important to make the *chancel area, *altar/table, choir loft and *pulpit accessible as well. Persons with disabilities should not be further limited in the ways they can serve God as a choir member, scripture reader, communion server, liturgist, preacher or ordained minister.

2. *Communication Access.* Persons who are blind depend on oral cues and communication to be an active participant in worship (*see* **Blind Persons and Worship**). Deaf and hard-of-hearing persons require visual communication and often additional printed materials, sign language interpreters or oral interpreters (*see* **Deaf Persons and Worship**). Communication access also requires those designing worship to be sensitive to language in liturgies, preaching and prayers that equates with sin the lived realities of persons with disabilities. When the terms 'deaf', 'blind' or 'paralysed' are metaphorically used to describe one's broken relationship with God ('deaf' to God's call on our lives, 'blind' to God's will, 'paralysed' to act), we intentionally or unintentionally equate the physical condition of some with the wilful disobedience or sin of others. This reinforces society's negative attitudes towards persons who physically are deaf, blind or paralysed.

3. *Attitudinal Access.* The fear of vulnerability and fragility and theological notions of 'holiness' still cause some to believe that the presence of persons with disabilities profanes the church or is somehow an insult to God. An open attitude of acceptance and inclusion is necessary for persons with disabilities to feel as if they are welcomed participants in worship.

KATHLEEN M. BLACK

Disciples of Christ Worship

see **Christian Church Worship**

Dismissal

In early Christianity it was the practice for people to be formally dismissed when they left an act of worship. Thus, at Sunday worship *catechumens would be dismissed after the ministry of the word was over and before the prayers of the faithful and the celebration of the *eucharist itself, and the faithful would similarly be dismissed at very the end of the rite. From the fourth century onwards, however, with the emergence of the custom of many of the faithful choosing not to communicate but to leave before *communion was distributed, a pre-communion blessing began to appear in many rites.

The dismissal rite at both daily and Sunday services, known in Latin as a *missa* (and hence the word *mass), seems at first to have been quite lengthy. Those being dismissed bowed their heads while the *bishop (or other pre-siding minister) said a prayer of blessing over them all, and then each went in turn to receive an individual laying-on of hands from him. Some have thought that this was the origin of the rite of *confirmation. Later practice, however, was to be much briefer. In the East, the usual formula of dismissal, said by the *deacon, was 'Depart in peace'. At Rome, while the Leonine Sacramentary provided a prayer over the people (*super populum*) for use at every mass, the later Gregorian Sacramentary restricted its use to *Lent, and the normal formula said by the deacon was, *Ite, missa est* (literally, 'Go, it is the dismissal'), to which were added a greeting ('The Lord be with you', 'And with your spirit') and a response, *Deo gratias* ('Thanks be to God'). During the *Easter season 'Alleluia' was added to both formula and response. The Gallican tradition, however, seems to have used *Benedicamus Domino* ('Let us bless the Lord') as the dismissal formula, and from the eleventh century onwards both were used in the Western tradition, the Roman text on those occasions when the Gloria in excelsis was sung in the mass and the Gallican one at other times. Modern rites in many churches offer a choice of formulas, often expressing in one way or another the desire for Christianity to be carried out into the world.

EDITOR

Disposal of Eucharistic Remains

Although the earliest *eucharistic theology may remain ambiguous, it is evident that from the first the bread and wine of the *eucharist commanded reverence. Indeed, even that part of the elements not ultimately taken for thanksgiving was deemed in some way hallowed. From the writings of Origen in the third century we can discern an association beginning to be made between the eucharistic sacrifice and the sacrifices of the Mosaic dispensation. This informed the attitude of the church towards the consecrated elements, which, like the sacrifices of the Old Covenant, might remain to the following day but must be disposed of after that. Following Jewish precedents, the remains might be burnt, reverently buried or consumed by the innocent. The prevailing usage was for the remains to be carried to the *sacristy, that required for the *communion of the *sick being *reserved and the residue consumed – a practice close to that followed by the Eastern churches to this day. From the ninth century the Gallican practice of a minister cleansing the vessels at the conclusion of communion gained currency (*see* **Ablutions**). Roman custom required that a part of the host remained upon the *corporal so that the *altar be never without the sacrifice. The adoption, at Avignon, of the Gallican custom of reservation at the altar obviated this. While RC and Anglican churches continue the practice of reverent consumption after communion or at the end of the rite, some other traditions which take a different view of eucharistic consecration often throw away what remains or reuse it at a subsequent celebration of the eucharist.

William Lockton, *The Treatment of the Remains at the Eucharist*, Cambridge 1920.
                                    MICHAEL THOMPSON

Divine Office *see* Daily Prayer

Doctrine and Liturgy
see **Theology of Worship**

Dorsal, Dossal *see* Altar Hangings

Doxology

An ascription of praise (Greek *doxologia*, literally 'words of glory'), in Christian usage usually trinitarian in form, and often beginning with, or including, the word 'glory'. The term is used to refer to four principal forms.

1. From the fact that early Jewish and Christian prayers regularly ended with an ascription of praise to God, any trinitarian conclusion to a prayer came to be referred to as its doxology.

2. What is sometimes called the 'lesser doxology' or Gloria Patri is the ascription of praise beginning, 'Glory be to the Father, and to the Son, and to the Holy Spirit . . .', added to the end of psalms and *canticles in most Christian liturgies. The practice can be found from the late fourth century onwards, and replaced older forms, which spoke of 'through' the Son and 'in' the Holy Spirit', because they seemed to lend support to Arianism. Its ending varied from region to region, and still differs between Eastern and Western traditions. Protestant churches are familiar with a metrical version by Bishop Ken, sung to the tune, 'Old Hundredth'.

3. What is known as the 'greater doxology' is the hymn Gloria in excelsis, 'Glory to God in the highest', which exists in a number of versions, and is known from the third quarter of the fourth century. In the fifth-century Codex Alexandrinus it is entitled 'morning hymn', and it features as such in the morning office of a number of the historic liturgies, notably the Byzantine rite, in which it is the climax of the morning office of *orthros* or matins (*see* **Daily Prayer** 2). The use of this hymn at the *eucharist is peculiar to the West. By the beginning of the sixth century it had already an established place in the *mass at Rome, after the entrance and before the *collect of the day, although at first only when a *bishop was the president. It was not until the eleventh century that the rule was finally settled that it was to be used at all masses on Sundays and feasts, except in *Advent and *Lent. This tradition is followed in a number of churches today.

4. The title 'great doxology' is also sometimes used to denote the doxology at the end of the *eucharistic prayer.

J. A. Jungmann, *The Mass of the Roman Rite*, New York 1951, I, 346–59.
                              W. JARDINE GRISBROOKE

Drama and Worship

Speculation about the relationship between drama and worship focuses on two questions: first, what is and has been the place of dramatic performance within the context of worship and, second, is worship itself somehow a dramatic form? The first question can be addressed historically; the second has been the subject of theological and anthropological speculation and, recently, of the relatively new discipline called performance theory. The history both of worship and of drama reveals signs of the collaboration, antipathy and confusion between the two forms from the earliest period of human ritual enactment. It will be necessary to examine first the relationship between worship and drama at their purported origins, second, to trace the history of specific dramatic forms arising out of the liturgy of the medieval Christian church, and finally, to ask if postmodern performance theory can shed any light on the relationship between worship and drama in the present context.

Theatre historians have long noted the origins of Western dramatic forms in the religious festivals of fifth-century BCE Greece. These festivals (especially the Greater Dionysia, dedicated to the god Dionysus) included contests for the best dramatic rendering of religious narrative and were the setting for the tragedies of Aeschylus, Sophocles and Euripides, the comedies of Aristophanes and, by extension, the dramatic theory of Aristotle. Early-twentieth-century ritual theorists speculated that all drama arises from such religious rituals and that, in fact, the enactment of ritual precedes the mythological stories that develop later in order to explain the meaning of the enactment. This theory, though no longer universally subscribed to, set the terms for later speculation on the relationship between text or narrative and ritual or dramatic enactment.

Christian worship is rooted in the practices and texts of Jewish worship and shares with it the use of words and texts to bless, thank, remember and petition God. Since words are used as 'speech-acts', to use J. L. Austin's term (*How to Do Things with Words*, Cambridge 1962), they are often accompanied by a variety of gestures – body *postures, hand *gestures, *processions, touching, holding objects, throwing, breaking, lifting up – even, at the Temple in Jerusalem, the sacrifice of animals. These liturgical actions, to use Augustine's analysis in *On Christian Doctrine*, are symbolic acts, constituted as such by their juxtaposition with words, words that place the gestures in the context of an ongoing narrative about God and the world. Despite its use of such seemingly dramatic elements in its liturgy, the early church saw theatrical performance, because of the often sexual and violent content of Roman theatrical events, as sinful, and refused *baptism to actors who would not renounce their profession.

Given its symbolic and enacted character, it is understandable that some commentators, in both the East and the West, should by the fourth century have viewed the liturgy as a divine drama. Theodore of Mopsuestia in the East is perhaps the first to describe the sequence of acts and gestures of the *eucharist as a series of episodes representing scriptural events. In the West, Amalarius of Metz in the ninth century applied such an allegorical interpretation to the eucharist and, though condemned for it in his own day, began a trend toward such interpretation that would continue into the last century. Modern theatre historians, notably Carl Young (*The Drama of the Medieval Church*, Oxford 1933) and O. B. Hardison (*Christian Rite and Christian Drama in the Middle Ages*, Baltimore 1965), attribute the rise of medieval theatre in the bosom of the church to this 'dramatic' view of the liturgy.

Most historians would trace the development of Latin liturgical drama to the advent, somewhere in the eighth century, of the liturgical dialogue known as the *Quem quaeritis*. Having begun as a trope either on the Gloria in excelsis or on the *antiphon to the Magnificat for first vespers of *Easter Day, the *Quem quaeritis* consists of three lines sung responsively by the choir: 'Whom do you seek in the sepulchre, O followers of Christ? We seek Christ who was crucified, O heavenly ones. He is not here. He is risen! Go and tell the disciples, Alleluia!' Variants on this dialogue appeared in Europe and in England where, by the tenth century, the *Regularis Concordia* of St Ethelwald contains a detailed description of the dress and mimetic movements of the 'characters' – monks 'portraying' the three Marys and the angels – who enact the Easter morning scene at the entrance to the church's crypt. During the Middle Ages a number of liturgical dramas called 'Visits to the Sepulchre' were joined by others portraying the visit of the shepherds to the manger, the procession of prophets foretelling the birth of the Messiah, and the events surrounding Christ's passion.

By the fourteenth century, the feast of Corpus Christi, especially in England, was the occasion for the presentation of lengthy cycle plays dramatizing the scriptural narrative from creation to Last Judgement. Often mounted on pageant wagons drawn through the city streets (the forerunners of parade floats) these plays were acted in a mixture of the vernacular and Latin by members of the various trade guilds. In Europe, similar sweeping dramatic cycles called passion plays were performed on stages set up around the town square, each representing a different biblical location. Such so-called 'mansion staging' derived from similar, though less extensive, presentations of biblical dramas within the *nave of the church.

The vernacular cycle and passion plays were too elaborate, too lengthy, and often too irreverent for performance in the church in the context of the eucharist. They were, nevertheless, both tolerated and encouraged by the medieval church as a means of educating the populace and as a means for popular involvement with the Feast of Corpus Christi. The sixteenth-century Reformers, however, universally condemned these dramatic endeavours and caused performances to be suppressed in countries where they held sway. In England under the Puritan regime such a ban extended to all dramatic performances. It was not until the mid-twentieth century that revivals of the medieval plays were performed in churches in England. Music dramas, such as the *Play of Daniel*, were popularized in the USA by such early-music groups as Noah Greenberg's New York Pro Musica. In Germany, the passion play was revived in Oberammergau. These medieval revivals, although at times sponsored by churches, are not a regular part of the worship of most churches.

Perhaps the nearest surviving relatives to the medieval liturgical drama remain the *saints' days and *Holy Week processions still popular in countries that were less affected by the anti-dramatic prejudice of the Reformation. Following a late medieval practice, the reading of the passion narrative during Holy Week in many churches is divided into parts, including lines for the congregation. In addition, many churches incorporate simple dramatic readings or plays into their worship in the form of children's Christmas pageants and enacted biblical stories usually performed by children. Recently, the so-called 'seeker services' in large American mega-churches have sought to involve the unchurched by the use of live pop music and religious skits modelled on familiar television comedy forms.

The liturgical renewal of the twentieth century as exemplified in Gregory Dix's *The Shape of the Liturgy* (London 1945) began to focus more attention on the structure and enactment of liturgical forms as opposed to earlier scholars' concern with texts and origins. The relationship among worship, theatre and other types of performance has been re-evaluated during the second half of the twentieth century using the tools of *ritual studies, especially the relatively new discipline of performance theory. Drawing upon the methods of anthropology, *sociology, psychology, semiotics, and literary and dramatic criticism, performance theory attempts to examine the similarities and differences among a number of cultural forms all of which involve some sort of performance or enactment. Many of these forms, including religious ritual, theatre, political performance and sporting events, have historically been intertwined and often confused.

Drawing on Kenneth Burke's 'dramatistic' analysis (*A Grammar of Motives*, New York 1945/Berkeley 1969) and Victor Turner's understanding of 'social drama' (*Dramas, Fields, and Metaphors*, Ithaca, NY 1974) as well as Peter Berger and Thomas Luckman's theories of the 'social construction of reality'

(*The Social Construction of Reality*, New York 1966), this approach (exemplified in Richard Schechner's *Performance Theory*, New York 1988) understands performance as a basic human social way of being. To whatever end, human beings enact both their presence to each other and their relationships to the natural, social and spiritual world. Worship, then, becomes neither theatre nor political praxis, but a form of symbolic action through which the community performs itself in its relationship with God. The gestures of the rite take on equal importance with the texts of the prayers, the words of which are understood not as statements but as 'speech-acts', vocal gestures by which the worshipping community enacts its relationship with each other and with God. Performance in this sense is not the theatrical performance of the virtuoso for an audience, but rather the enactment of a community by its members playing various roles according to the particular ordering of each church.

Such an analysis can make an account of the clearly demarcated ritual acts of the so-called liturgical churches; but it is equally applicable for discovering the less formal ritualizations in the performance of worship in 'non-liturgical' traditions. Because it takes into account the 'dramatic' elements of worship, including vocal gesture, *movement, *music, space, the senses, and the *structure* of the enacted rite, regarding worship as a species of performance can serve as a place to stand when engaging questions of liturgical *inculturation, multicultural worship, and the use of inclusive/expansive *language in worship.

Catherine Bell, *Ritual: Perspectives and Dimensions*, New York 1997; Oscar G. Brockett, *History of the Theatre*, Boston 1967; Marvin Carlson, *Performance: A Critical Introduction*, New York 1996; E. K. Chambers, *The Medieval Stage*, Oxford 1903; Hardin Craig, *English Religious Drama*, Oxford 1955; Anselm Hughes (ed.), *Early Medieval Music up to 1300*, 2nd edn, Oxford 1990; Lynette R. Muir, *The Biblical Drama of Medieval Europe*, Cambridge 1995; A. M. Nagler, *The Medieval Religious Stage*, New Haven/London 1976 (bib.); Miri Rubin, *Corpus Christi: The Eucharist in Late Medieval Culture*, Cambridge 1991; Glynne Wickham, *The Medieval Theatre*, Cambridge 1987.

RICHARD D. MCCALL

Dry Mass *see* **Ante-Communion**

East Syrian Worship

East Syrian worship is one of the most ancient forms of Christian worship, retaining many of the Semitic traits of the early Jewish-Christian liturgical tradition. The East Syrian tradition is known also as the Edessan, Mesopotamian, Nestorian, Persian, Assyrian, Babylonian or Chaldean, and is shared by the Assyrian Church of the East, the Catholic Chaldean Church and the Syro-Malabar Church of the St Thomas Christians. Syriac is the traditional language of East Syrian worship; however, today the vernacular languages are also used.

1. *History.* This liturgical tradition had its origin in Edessa, the intellectual home of the Syriac language and Semitic culture, most probably in the second century. Christianity in Edessa, more than anywhere else, kept the Semitic traits of early Jewish-Christianity. This centre, blessed by the presence of great theologians, especially St Ephrem, gave shape to the characteristic features of the East Syrian liturgy. Later, Seleucia-Ctesiphon, the ecclesiastical centre of the ancient Mesopotamian church, became the milieu for the development of the liturgical tradition. The Synod of Seleucia Ctesiphon in 410 attempted to unify and fix the liturgical customs of the Mesopotamian church. The final codification of this liturgical tradition is attributed to Patriarch Išo'yahb III (650–8). In this regard, remarkable contributions were made by the Upper Monastery at Mosul as well.

The political and ecclesiastical isolation of the East Syrian church helped it to maintain its ancient Semitic characteristics, without much interference from the churches in the Roman empire. The typical *eucharistic prayer of this tradition, the anaphora of the Apostles Addai and Mari, is the Christian eucharistic prayer which is the closest to the Jewish *berakah*. The presence of numerous prayers addressed to Christ, repetition of prayers, and lengthy diaconal proclamations are some characteristic features of the East Syrian liturgy. The East Syrian tradition also has certain features in common with the *West Syrian rite. This does not mean that the Mesopotamian rite originated from the Antiochene rite. These common features are either shared by all Oriental rites or are to be explained as direct borrowings.

The St Thomas Christians of Malabar (in India), who had close contact with the Mesopotamian church from the early centuries, shared the same East Syrian liturgy. The so-called 'Synod of Diamper' in 1599 marked the beginning of the Latinization of this liturgy in Malabar. The Chaldeans, who have been in union with Rome since 1552, have adopted a number of Latin elements into their liturgical tradition.

2. *Sacraments.* The sacraments of initiation (*baptism, chrismation and *eucharist) are celebrated together. The baptismal rite is modelled after the eucharistic liturgy. The oil and water are blessed solemnly with prayers resembling the thanksgiving prayers of the anaphora. The oil is transferred to the altar in the manner of the transfer of the gifts in the eucharistic celebration. Emphasizing the completion and perfection of the Christian initiation, the East Syrian liturgy prefers the name chrismation to *confirmation.

Eucharistic celebration is known by different names. *Qurbana* (offering), *qudaša* (sanctification) and *raza* (mystery) are the common terms used. The liturgy of the word, noted for its similarity to the Jewish synagogue liturgy, has two readings each from the OT and from the NT. The psalms between the readings and the *turgama* (interpretation) are Jewish traits retained in the East Syrian liturgy. The eucharistic liturgy emphasizes the aspect of the commemoration of the paschal mystery. Two other anaphoras are also used, namely the anaphora of Theodore and the anaphora of Nestorius. These have been thought to be translations of the Greek anaphoras brought by Catholicos Mar Aba I (540–52). However, recent textual studies show them to be East Syrian in origin. The anaphora of Addai and Mari, the primitive form of which might be dated back to the second century, is remarkable for the absence of the *institution narrative in all the ancient manuscripts. The *epiclesis of this anaphora emphasizes the sanctification of the assembly more than the sanctification of the eucharistic elements.

The East Syrian tradition had different forms of celebrating the sacrament of *penance. Only penitents with grave sins like apostasy and homicide are required to go for individual confession. For all other penitents the *absolution of sins is granted within the eucharistic celebration itself, in the rite of absolution (*taksa d'hussaya*). In the celebration of *marriage, there are the special rites of the blessing of the ring and coronation. Malabar tradition has the blessing of *minnu* (a small cross) and *mantrakodi* (the wedding garment of the bride). *Anointing of the *sick is a communal celebration, with great emphasis on the physical cure of the sick.

3. **Daily Prayer*. East Syrian liturgy gives great importance to the communal celebration of the liturgy of hours. There are three major hours called *ramša* (evening office), *lelya* (night prayer) and *sapra* (morning prayer). There are other minor hours like *subbah* (compline), and *qala d-Sahra* (*vigil), *quttah* (terce) and *eddana* (sext). The East Syrian liturgy of hours evolved and reached its final shape in both cathedrals and monasteries. *Ramša* and *sapra* retain more of the elements of the cathedral system, whereas *lelya* retains more of the elements of the monastic system.

4. *Liturgical *Year*. The East Syrian liturgical year consists of nine seasons: *Subbara-Yalda* (Annunciation-Nativity), *Denha* (*Epiphany), *Sauma Rabba* (Great *Lent), *Qyamta* (*Easter), *Sliha* (*Pentecost), *Kaitta* (Summer), *Eliah-Sliba* (Elijah and Cross), *Moses*, and *Qudaš Etta* (*Dedication of the Church). Each season consists ideally of seven weeks, except *Subbara-Yalda* (4+2 weeks) and *Qudaš Etta* (four weeks). However, the number of weeks of other seasons may vary according to the date of Easter. One remarkable feature of the East Syrian calendar is that it is mainly centred on the mystery of the Christ-event. The commemoration of the *saints, generally made on the Fridays of the seasons of *Denha* and *Kaitta*, is in relation to the commemoration of the paschal mystery of Christ.

5. *Liturgical Architecture*. The church building, usually rectangular, is divided into three parts: *madbaha* (*sanctuary), *qestroma* (*choir), and *haykla* (*nave). In the middle of the *haykla*, there is an elevated platform called the bema with an *altar for the cross and gospel, two *lecterns for the readings, the chair of the *bishop and chairs for other ministers. The liturgy of the word and the liturgy of the hours are celebrated at the bema. A low walled pathway named *šqaqona* connects the *madbaha* to the bema. The main altar is attached to the eastern wall. There is the *diaqonikon* (*sacristy) on the north side of the *madbaha*, and on the south side of it, the *baptistery. The bread and wine are prepared at the two niches – *beth gazze* – on the eastern wall (sometimes on the northern and southern walls of the *madbaha*).

See also **Books, Liturgical** 2.4.

G. P. Badger, *The Nestorians and their Rituals*, 2 vols, London 1852; A. J. Maclean, *East Syrian Daily Offices*, London 1894; A. Gelston, *The Eucharistic Prayer of Addai and Mari*, Oxford 1992; P. Kannookadan, *The East Syrian Lectionary: An Historico-Liturgical Study*, Rome 1991; P. Maniyattu, *Heaven on Earth: Theology of the Liturgical Spacetime in the East Syrian Qurbana*, Rome 1995; T. Mannooramparampil, *The Anaphora and Post Anaphora of the Syro-Malabar Qurbana*, Kottayam 1984; P. Yousif, 'The Divine Liturgy according to the Rite of the Assyro-Chaldean Church', *The Eucharistic Liturgy in the Christian East*, ed. J. Madey, Kottayam/Paderborn 1983, 173–237; (ed.), *A Classified Bibliography on the East Syrian Liturgy*, Rome 1990 (bib.).

PAULY MANIYATTU

East, Turning *see* **Orientation**

Easter

Early Christian sources reveal two quite distinct modes of celebrating Easter. The one which ultimately became universal was to keep the feast on the Sunday following the Jewish Passover; the other, attested chiefly in second-century sources deriving from Asia Minor, was to locate it at the time of the Jewish Passover itself, during the night of 14 to 15 Nisan. Because of their attachment to the fourteenth day of the Jewish month, those who followed this latter custom were called 'Quartodecimans' by other Christians. The traditional scholarly consensus tended to be that the Sunday celebration was the older of the two, and the Quartodeciman no more than a local aberration from this norm. But many scholars would now see the Quartodeciman practice as an early Jewish-Christian adaptation of the Passover, and judge that other Christian communities may not have an annual Easter observance until sometime in the second century, when they introduced a Sunday celebration of the feast, especially as both traditions at first centred their understanding of the feast on 'Christ, the Passover lamb, sacrificed for us' (1 Cor. 5.7). The original form of the Easter celebration in both versions seems to have been to keep the preceding day as a *fast, which was extended into the night with a *vigil of readings and prayers and culminated in the celebration of the *eucharist at cockcrow (*see* **Easter Vigil**). Later the fast before the Sunday celebration was extended to two days, taking in the regular weekly Friday fast, and by the third century Christians in Syria and Egypt were fasting for the whole week beforehand, from Monday onwards, the roots of the later *Holy Week, or 'Great Week' as it is called in Eastern traditions. The feast was also by now being extended forwards, into a continuous fifty-day season of rejoicing (*see* **Pentecost**).

Already by the end of the second century in Alexandria a new interpretation of the feast had begun to emerge, not as 'passion' but 'passage' – the passage from death to life, no doubt influenced in part by its celebration on a Sunday, the day of resurrection, and this, coupled with the concept of Easter as a triduum, a three-day observance from Friday to Sunday (two days of fasting followed by the feast), slowly gave rise to seeing *Good Friday as the memorial of the death of Jesus, *Holy Saturday as commemorating his burial and/or descent into hell and Easter Day as celebrating his resurrection, which we find in many places by the end of the fourth century and which later became standard throughout the church. In later centuries, when the Easter vigil came to be celebrated during Holy Saturday, the Triduum was thought of as comprising *Maundy Thursday, Good Friday and Holy Saturday.

At first the calculation of when Easter should fall was made by local Christian communities, which produced considerable divergence of practice. Even after the Council of Nicaea in 325 when the Emperor directed that all churches should observe the same date, regional variations still persisted and it took many centuries for standardization to be realized. Today Eastern churches still follow the older Julian calendar and consequently keep Easter on a different day from the West, although discussions about adopting a common date have taken place in recent years.

Although originally the eucharist at the conclusion of the vigil constituted *the* Easter eucharist, other eucharistic celebrations came to be added on the morning of Easter Day in the medieval West, especially after the vigil had faded in prominence. Moreover, the medieval morning office (matins) on that day came to be the setting of a liturgical *dramatic piece called the 'Visit to the Sepulchre', which originated as a short liturgical dialogue between the three women and the angel at the tomb (known in Latin as the *Quem quaeritis*). In addition,

evening prayer (vespers) was marked in a particular way in a number of places, and at Rome a special eucharist was held at a separate time for those who had been baptized the previous year at Easter (the *pascha annotina*). In some areas, the exchange of decorated eggs became popular, since the egg was both a pagan symbol of spring and a Christian symbol of the new life of the resurrection.

Paul Bradshaw and Lawrence Hoffman (eds), *Passover and Easter: Origin and History to Modern Times*, Notre Dame 1999; Raniero Cantalamessa, *Easter in the Early Church*, Collegeville 1993; Anscar Chupungco, *Shaping the Easter Feast*, Washington, DC 1992.

EDITOR

Easter Candle

The Easter candle is lit at the *Easter vigil, from the *new fire which has just been kindled. This ceremony, which developed out of the daily lighting of the evening lamp at the *lucernarium*, dates back to at least the fourth century. In the East it was later moved from the beginning of the vigil to form part of its climax, but in the West it remained at the start. Surviving evidence points to a northern Italian provenance for its adoption in the West, and its use spread to all Western churches, reaching Rome in the tenth century, where it replaced the two massive candles used in that church's Easter vigil. The hymns of praise composed in its honour and sung by a *deacon suggest that the blessing of the candle was originally linked to a celebration of God's creation. References to bees and beeswax in these early versions of the *Exultet*, the hymn of praise and blessing still used and sung by a deacon in the Latin rites, suggest a celebration of the natural world; and the very composition of the candle – wax (earth), a papyrus wick (water) and fire – was seen to symbolize the whole of creation: 'universe of three in one' (Prudentius). The traditional use of flowers to decorate the paschal candlestick is a vivid reminder of its links with nature and creation.

Its use at the Easter vigil quickly lent itself to symbolizing the resurrection, which in turn resulted in an increase in the candle's size and height. This was also achieved by placing it on a huge or lofty candlestick. And it stood in a prominent place near the altar. In the early Middle Ages the candle was borne into church either lit or unlit, or placed in position before the start of the Easter vigil. Subsequently the latter practice became the norm because of the candle's size, and a single or triple candle was carried in procession to provide the flame for its lighting.

Inscribing the date *anno Domini* on the candle was borrowed from the Roman rite, and subsequently other chronological information was included either on the wax itself or on a plaque made of wood or parchment and known as a 'chart'. The chart was fastened to the candle itself or to the candlestick. In 1678 the chart at Rouen contained 48 items of information. Other markings, still used but now regarded as optional, were the incising of a cross into the wax, and the insertion of five grains of *incense, both actions seen as corresponding to benediction and censing.

Because of the high cost of beeswax the candle is today of modest proportions and portable, and now usually contains only a percentage of beeswax. Now lit directly from the new fire, it is seen to symbolize the Word of God and creation. As it is borne into church it represents the incarnation, and at the conclusion of the *Exultet* becomes a powerful symbol of the resurrection. In some churches the candle is lit after the vigil readings. This emphasizes Christ the Light of the World, but obscures the symbolism of Christ's existence before time. The candle also provides a visible link between *baptism and the resurrection, in that it is plunged into the water at the blessing of the *font in the vigil. Thereafter it is lit throughout the season of Easter, and at baptisms and (in many churches) at *funerals during the rest of the year.

Adrian Fortescue and J. B. O'Connell (eds), *The Ceremonies of the Roman Rite*, 11th edn, London 1960; A. J. MacGregor, *Fire and Light in the Western Triduum*, Collegeville 1992.

A. J. MACGREGOR

Easter Garden or Sepulchre

A representation of the garden tomb of Christ, which was set up in churches in *Holy Week from the early Middle Ages onwards. On *Good Friday, after vespers a *cross was deposited in the sepulchre to symbolize the burial of Christ and a candle was lit before it. In the late Middle Ages exclusively in England and Normandy, a special *host reserved from the *eucharist on *Maundy Thursday was also placed there. On Easter Day the cross and/or

host was removed to symbolize the resurrection. This custom fell out of use at the time of the Reformation, but the Easter garden itself can still be found in many English churches.

EDITOR

Easter Vigil

The oldest attested *vigil in the history of Christianity. The earliest Christians who observed *Easter apparently did so with a *eucharist at cockcrow, and preceded their celebration with a day of fasting, which was extended into the night with a vigil of readings and prayers, apparently in expectation of Christ's return at the feast. From the third century onwards, however, there was a tendency to shorten the vigil so that the celebration of the resurrection began at midnight. The practice of the *baptism of new converts to the faith at Easter is first mentioned in third-century sources from Rome and North Africa, but does not seem to have become a universal part of the Easter vigil until at least the middle of the fourth century. Later, the regular daily custom of lighting of the evening lamp was also given special significance within the vigil, and in the East eventually moved from its position at the beginning of the vigil to its climax (*see* **Easter Candle**).

Later sources give more precise details of the readings used. There is considerable variation from place to place both in the number of readings prescribed (although twelve is the most common) and in the particular biblical texts appointed to be read, although some passages – among them particularly the account of the creation and fall in Genesis, the binding of Isaac in the same book, and the narrative of the Exodus – occur with great regularity.

From the seventh century onwards in the West, the vigil liturgy began to be celebrated earlier and earlier for the sake of convenience, until by the late Middle Ages it took place in the morning of *Holy Saturday, thus destroying its dramatic effect and making the references to 'night' in the prayer texts nonsensical. As a consequence of the *Liturgical Movement in the twentieth century, Pius XII in 1951 authorized the restoration of the proper hour of celebration and an experimental revision of the rite itself, including a reduction in the number of readings and the introduction of a renewal of *baptismal vows. This assumed definitive form in the RC Church from 1955 onwards. A further revision took place in the wake of the

Second Vatican Council, and similar vigil rites were also adopted in other churches in the second half of the twentieth century. In some cases the RC pattern has been closely followed; in others the lighting of the candle has been moved to the climax of the rite, as in the East, and sometimes a real vigil rather than just an extended set of OT readings has been encouraged. Other churches have established the tradition of holding sunrise services at dawn.

Gabriel Bertonière, *The Historical Development of the Easter Vigil and Related Services in the Greek Church*, Rome 1972.

EDITOR

Eastern Rites *see* Orthodox Worship

Ecumenical Co-operation in Liturgical Revision

In the process of liturgical revision in which many churches engaged in the second half of the twentieth century, ecumenical co-operation played an increasingly larger part. Not only were individual churches aware of what was going on in other churches, and often drew on liturgical material from one another's compositions, but formal links became established between many of them. Some liturgical commissions invited other churches to send official observers to their deliberations, and regional organizations composed of representatives from a number of churches were established in different parts of the world. Thus in the UK the Joint Liturgical Group came into existence in 1963 and over the years has produced a large number of liturgical texts which have been taken up and incorporated into the liturgies of its member churches to a greater or lesser extent. In North America the Consultation on Common Texts was responsible for the creation in 1983 of the *Common Lectionary*, an ecumenical adaptation of the RC Sunday eucharistic lectionary, and of its amended version, the *Revised Common Lectionary*, which has come into widespread use throughout the English-speaking world (*see* **Lectionaries** 3).

There are also broader-based international bodies, including the worldwide organization of liturgical scholars, Societas Liturgica, founded in 1967, which facilitated the interchange of news and views about liturgical revision; and in the English-speaking world the International Consultation on English Texts (ICET, 1969–74), which grew out of the RC

International Commission on English in the Liturgy (ICEL), and which was succeeded by the English Language Liturgical Consultation (ELLC) in 1983. These two bodies have produced and then revised modern translations of central liturgical texts, including the Nicene *Creed and *Lord's Prayer, which have been widely adopted (*Prayers We Have in Common*, several editions from 1970 onwards).

See also **Liturgical Movement**.

EDITOR

Ecumenical Worship

1. *Definition*. One characteristic of Christian worship is its ecumenical nature, because its central message aims at the salvation of the whole world and the whole creation. But since Christians are divided in different churches, ecumenical worship has been developed as an event in which Christians from different traditions join together in celebrating, praying and praising God. Such worship services happen at different levels: locally, regionally and internationally. In each case there are basically two possibilities: (a) a worship service is held according to the liturgical order of one of the traditions represented, and everyone participates; or (b) an attempt is made to bring the various traditions together by combining different liturgical and cultural elements, so that all persons can find something of their own in the worship service.

2. *Development*. The second form has been developed especially since the end of the nineteenth and the beginning of the twentieth century with the rise of the Ecumenical Movement. Its development can be most clearly shown in the international ecumenical conferences from the beginnings, in the World Student Christian Federation, the World Missionary Conference, and the Faith and Order and Life and Work movements, to the assemblies of the World Council of Churches. Common worship played a central role in all these events, sometimes according to confessional forms and at other times with new forms which participants planned together. The pattern for commonly prepared worship services emerging at the first World Conferences on Life and Work (1925) and on Faith and Order (1927) united in a simple and straightforward way the liturgical elements common to the churches represented. In recent assemblies and conferences of the World Council of Churches the intention to be

as inclusive as possible has made ecumenical worship enriching and inspiring.

An increasing concern to have a simple order for daily worship services, following a liturgical structure which is common to most Christian traditions, has emerged over time, while using a variety of traditional and cultural elements such as music, symbolic actions and decoration from all over the world. Forms have been found uniting the different confessional and cultural traditions. There is a clear movement away from the strictly Protestant emphasis on the word, partly because of the language problem in international and regional meetings. Thus in recent years it has no longer been felt necessary to have a sermon in each service during a conference. More space was given to free prayer, and to *Orthodox elements. Elements which emphasize community, such as the exchange of the peace (*see* **Kiss, Ritual**), or elements which create a reverential atmosphere, such as a *procession with *icons, are more frequently included.

3. *Problems*. The main difficulty in ecumenical worship is the fact that a common *eucharist is not possible between RCs and Protestants/Anglicans and between Orthodox and non-Orthodox. At several international conferences though, there have been eucharistic services in the official conference programme. They were celebrated according to the so-called Lima-liturgy – a liturgy which was written for the Faith and Order Commission meeting 1982 in Lima/Peru, and which aimed at expressing the convergences found in the World Council of Churches' document *Baptism, Eucharist and Ministry*. But while all traditions were present in the service, not all of them were able to take *communion. As long as the question of mutual recognition of ministries, and hence the ecclesiology question, has not been resolved, common celebration of the eucharist will not be possible.

In recent years some other problems of ecumenical worship have been raised. One has to do with a psychological phenomenon. In a newly created liturgy it is hard to get one's bearings, to let oneself be carried along the way one does when the structure is familiar. Second, from a liturgical point of view, jointly planned ecumenical liturgies are sometimes in danger of having no unifying thread of meaning. A third problem concerns the fundamental differences in the understanding of liturgy. Protestant churches generally allow the possibility

for orders of worship to be freely created, while Orthodox worship, for example, stays with traditional forms. Worship is centred on the mystery of God and serves to unite human beings with God. Thus it has a deeply mystical component. Furthermore, for the Orthodox, in contrast to Protestantism, the centre of a worship service is the Divine Liturgy, that is, the celebration of the eucharist, which cannot be shared with separated churches. Protestants regard a service of the word as a complete and fully valid worship service. There is a fundamental imbalance in the way in which ecumenical worship is experienced and in the ability to share in worship with others.

4. *Principles*. There are various possibilities for common worship, each of which has advantages and disadvantages. Just as the Ecumenical Movement is not about one unified church, so neither can there be one unified form of worship.

Ecumenical worship therefore has to be prepared according to the context in which it is taking place. Recent work of the Faith and Order Commission points to the fact that there is an 'ordo' of worship common to all Christian traditions. It is the undergirding structure 'which is to be perceived in the ordering and scheduling of the most primary elements of Christian worship. This "ordo" . . . roots in word and sacrament held together' (Best and Heller, *So We Believe, So We Pray*, 6). This structure is characterized by three elements, which are related to each other in such a way that the first two belong closely together and lead, if they are held together, to the third: scripture reading and preaching together yield intercessions; the thanksgiving over bread and wine and eating/drinking together yield a collection for the poor and mission in the world.

The specific liturgical elements which are used in these three parts do not always have to occur in a specific order. But they can be assigned to the three fundamental parts on the basis of their function. Therefore, what makes a worship service ecumenical seems above all to be this common basic pattern, which can then be developed according to the needs of each situation by traditional and cultural elements, taking into account the specific possibilities and sensitivities depending on the churches represented.

It has to be taken seriously that different expressions do not make liturgies mutually exclusive, especially if it is taken into consideration that there is a common foundation. Ecumenical worship should express our differences in confessional traditions and cultures, but at the same time show our unity despite these differences.

See also **Love-Feast**; **Australia, Worship in the Uniting Church in; Canada, Worship in the United Church of; North India, Worship in the Church of; South India, Worship in the Church of**.

Thomas F. Best and Dagmar Heller (eds), *Eucharistic Worship in Ecumenical Contexts: The Lima Liturgy – and Beyond*, Geneva 1998; Thomas F. Best and Dagmar Heller (eds), *So We Believe, So We Pray: Towards Koinonia in Worship*, Geneva 1995; Janet Crawford and Thomas Best, 'Praise the Lord with the Lyre . . . and the Gamelan? Towards Koinonia in Worship', *Ecumenical Review* XLVI, 1994, 78–96; Per Harling (ed.), *Worshipping Ecumenically: Orders of Service from Global Meetings with Suggestions for Local Use*, Geneva 1995; S. Anita Stauffer (ed.), *Christian Worship: Unity in Cultural Diversity*, Geneva 1996 (bib.).

DAGMAR HELLER

Ektene see **Litany**

Elder

The Anglo-Saxon word used to translate the Greek term *presbyteros* and its Latin rendering *presbyter*. For its NT origins and its use to designate ordained ministers in early Christianity, see **Presbyter**. In the sixteenth century, however, John Calvin believed that the NT distinguished between ordained ministers of the word and elders who shared with them in the government of the church but had no liturgical functions. This distinction between presbyter/ minister and elder has been continued in almost all churches of the *Reformed tradition. Elders belong to the board or session which governs the local congregation, and may be elected to serve in the higher courts of the church. They may also have certain pastoral responsibilities in the congregation, and stand or be seated with the minister during church services. Early *Methodism also revived the used of the term 'elder', but to denote an ordained minister of the word, and the office is found in some other Christian traditions.

EDITOR

Elevation *see* Exposition

Ember Days

The name given to four groups of three days each – Wednesday, Friday and Saturday (the first two being customary weekly *fast days in early Christianity) – located near the beginning of each of the seasons of the year: spring, summer, autumn, winter. The spring group was located during the week between the first and second Sundays of *Lent; the summer group during the week following *Pentecost; the autumn group during the week after the festal celebration of the 'invention' (finding) of the true cross (14 September); and the winter group after the feast of Saint Lucy (13 December), usually between the third and fourth Sundays of *Advent. Leo the Great (Bishop of Rome, 441–60) referred to the fasts of the Ember Days in a few sermons of his episcopate, and there are suggestions of their observance in other witnesses in the early period, but universal reception in the West was not achieved until the ninth or tenth centuries, coincident with the growing influence of the church of Rome at that time.

The seasonal links of the days suggest that the name 'ember' may be a remnant of the word for 'seasons' in the Latin designation *quattuor tempora*, meaning 'four seasons', though this is not clearly established. The days were, most likely, agricultural festivals brought into Christian liturgical observance through *inculturation, and the issue of human labour in planting, growing and harvesting has stuck to the rhetoric and euchology of these days until today.

The character of the days was maintained by periods of prayer, fasting and penitence. For centuries and until recently, the Ember Days were the traditional time for the celebration of rites of *ordination in both Anglican and RC churches, because of the ancient rule which required fasting before ordination. In keeping with the fixed days of the week for the Ember Days, candidates for ordination were presented and examined on Wednesday and Friday, and the ordination itself celebrated on Saturday. In the *BCP* the Ember Days are still counted among the 'Days of Fasting or Abstinence'. The reform of the liturgical calendar in other Christian churches has occasioned the occlusion of the Ember Days. The RC Church, for example, advocates that, though no longer observed universally, they might be maintained by local churches. In churches where the fasting for the Ember Days is still observed, it is usually recommended that observers eat only one full meal and that they not eat meat.

G. G. Willis, *Essays in Early Roman Liturgy*, London 1964, 49–97.

MARTIN F. CONNELL

Enarxis

Generally, the beginning of any liturgical service, analogous to its *dismissal (*apolysis*). It is also a technical term referring to the initial elements of the Byzantine *eucharistic liturgy: (1) initial *doxology, (2) great *synapte* and *collect, (3) first *antiphon, (4) small *synapte* and collect, (5) second antiphon, (6) small *synapte* and collect, (7) third antiphon, (8) *little entrance with prayer and variable hymnody, (9) prayer and *Trisagion* chant (including enthronement rites at hierarchical celebrations), and (10) the greeting 'Peace be to all'.

The received configuration combines elements of popular stational services with entrance rituals and a fairly standard *litany (great *synapte*) originally placed after the readings. By the time Germanos, Patriarch of Constantinople, wrote his commentary *On the Divine Liturgy* in 730 and the production of the earliest extant euchologion (the eighth-century *Codex Barberini gr. 336*), an enarxis very similar to today's had been introduced. One century earlier, judging by the *Mystagogy* of Maximos the Confessor (*c.* 630), there was no enarxis and the eucharist began with a simple entrance of clergy and laity. As late as the tenth century, however, the *Typikon of the Great Church* indicates that the enarxis was not yet a permanent part of the eucharistic liturgy. The enarxis is still suppressed when the eucharist is celebrated in conjunction with vespers.

Originally each antiphon consisted of psalm verses between which a simple, popular hymn was chanted, with variations emphasizing important feasts. Over time the scriptural material was suppressed, leaving only the refrain. In the twelfth century, some monasteries replaced the usual antiphons with a selection of psalms from a Palestinian rite for *communion outside of the eucharistic liturgy (*typika*); these are still present in some Slavic and Greek communities.

John Baldovin, *The Urban Character of Christian Worship*, Rome 1987, 205–26; Juan Mateos, *La célébration de la parole dans la*

liturgie byzantine, Rome 1971, 1–126; Robert F. Taft, 'How Liturgies Grow: The Evolution of the Byzantine Divine Liturgy', *Beyond East and West*, 2nd edn, Rome 1997, 203–32, esp. 207–17.

JOHN KLENTOS

Enthronement of Bishops

see **Cathedra**

Epiclesis

A Greek word meaning 'invocation', which can be used in a general sense to refer to any prayer invoking God to act, but is more often restricted to a specific calling upon the Holy Spirit, especially within the *eucharistic prayer. Very early forms of epiclesis were addressed directly to the Spirit (or sometimes to the Logos) in the imperative: 'Come'. But as trinitarian doctrine was gradually refined in the fourth century, this simple form came to be replaced in eucharistic prayers by one in which God was asked to 'send' the Holy Spirit upon the bread and wine as well as upon the communicants, often with the addition of an explicit request for the bread and wine to be transformed into the body and blood of Christ. In the Alexandrian tradition, this epicletic material was divided into two separate parts in the prayer. Although the classic Roman eucharistic prayer did not include an epiclesis as such in this narrow sense, it did contain a petition for the consecration of the eucharistic elements, but even this tended to disappear in the prayers used in Reformation churches. However, modern eucharistic prayers in many Western ecclesiastical traditions have reintroduced an explicit epiclesis of the Holy Spirit in one form or another, sometimes before the institution narrative, sometimes after it (as in most Eastern prayers), and sometimes distributed between the two positions.

EDITOR

Epigonaton, Epimanikia

see **Vestments** 4(f–g)

Epiphany

Originating in Eastern Christianity and later appropriated also in the West, the feast of Epiphany has traditionally been celebrated on 6 January, although in the RC Church it is presently observed on the Sunday falling in the period 2–8 January. Unlike *Christmas, its seasonal counterpart in the West, which has grown in solemnity and pastoral importance over time, Epiphany has diminished in liturgical grandeur and pastoral gravity in the churches of Western Christianity, in spite of having a rich tradition in the early centuries. The word 'epiphany' signifies, in religious contexts, an appearance of God or gods, or, in civic contexts of former times, the birth or visit of a king.

The earliest evidence for the feast is in the writings of Clement of Alexandria in Egypt (around 215). He witnesses to its observance among the Basilidians, who commemorated the baptism of Jesus on that day (*Stromata* 1.21). By the fourth century, if not sooner, it was being celebrated by orthodox Christians, and the focus of the celebration had extended from the baptism (Mark 1.9–11) to the nativity of Christ (Luke 2.1–14) and beyond that to include among his manifestations the visit of the magi (Matt. 2.1–12) and the wedding feast at Cana, where Jesus turned water into wine (John 2.1–12). However, why this particular date was chosen for the feast remains something of a mystery. The 'history of religions' hypothesis maintained that, like the feast of Christmas on 25 December, it was in order to oppose a pagan epiphany feast celebrated on this day, but Thomas Talley has argued that there never was a widespread pagan feast on the day, and posited instead that it arose out of a Quartodeciman practice of keeping *Easter on the equivalent of the 14–15 of the first month of spring in Asia Minor, which would have been 6 April in the Julian calendar. Perhaps adapting a rabbinic idea that the deaths of patriarchs would have fallen exactly on the anniversary of their birth, Christians would have come to believe that 6 April was also the date of Christ's conception, and counting forward nine months arrived at 6 January as the date of his birth. This then would have functioned as the beginning of the liturgical year, when Christian communities would have commenced the reading of the gospel narratives, leading to the reading of Mark 1 on 6 January in Egypt, where Mark was highly regarded. In the absence of a more compelling theory, this remains the most likely hypothesis. A recent alternative proposal by Merja Merras, that it was a Christianization of the Jewish feast of Tabernacles, has not so far won acceptance.

In the earliest sermons for the feast in Western churches, the day was commonly tagged *dies epiphaniarum*, the 'day of the manifestations', and in these sermons too the 'manifestations' encompassed all four gospel events listed above. However, the churches at Rome and in North Africa were an exception, and at first only observed 25 December as the feast of Christ's incarnation. When they later adopted 6 January as well, in spite of the rich multiplicity of this feast in other churches the visit of the magi became established as the only narrative used at Rome on this occasion, although the narratives of the baptism and wedding at Cana were assigned to nearby Sundays. When Eastern churches in turn adopted 25 December in the late fourth century, the themes of the nativity and the magi both became assigned to that occasion, leaving the baptism and wedding at Cana as the focus of 6 January. Elsewhere in the West, practice evolved to bring other churches into line with Rome.

Merja Merras, *The Origins of the Celebration of the Christian Feast of Epiphany*, Joensuu, Finland 1995; Thomas J. Talley, *The Origins of the Liturgical Year*, 2nd edn, Collegeville 1991, 103–47; Gabriele Winkler, 'The Appearance of the Light at the Baptism of Jesus and the Origins of the Feast of the Epiphany: An Investigation of Greek, Syriac, Armenian, and Latin Sources', *Between Memory and Hope: Readings on the Liturgical Year*, ed. Maxwell E. Johnson, Collegeville 2000, 291–347.

MARTIN F. CONNELL

Epistle *see* **Readings, Eucharistic**

Epitrachelion *see* **Vestments** 4(c)

Ethics and Worship

In ordinary usage, 'liturgy' can refer to the discipline of liturgical studies or to the worship practice of a particular religious tradition or community. Similarly 'ethics' can refer to a discipline of study or to the practices of right living. In this latter sense, the connection of liturgical practice to ethical practice can be found in the OT prophets, who address the fruitlessness of worship without social justice, and in the Apostle Paul, who addresses the care for the poor in relationship to the *Lord's supper. On the level of discipline, however, the relationship of liturgy and ethics is much more recent, since ethics as a separate discipline is a development of the Enlightenment. In the late twentieth century, particularly in response to the liturgical renewal of the Western churches following Vatican II, there has been an increased interest in the relationship of liturgy and ethics. Generally the connection has been explored one of four ways: (1) liturgy is a source for ethics; (2) liturgy is a tool for ethical motivation; (3) liturgy is an object of ethical critique; and (4) liturgy and ethics are fundamentally related perspectives on the life of faith.

1. Liturgy can be understood to function as a source for ethical reflection. In the case of liturgical texts having an obvious ethical content, such as prayers of *confession, the text can function, much like scripture, as a basis for the formulation of an argument for a particular ethical concern. Likewise, liturgical rites can function as a normative source for constructing ethical arguments. William Willimon cites the action of the *eucharist as a demonstration of how Christians should deal with world hunger, and William Cavanagh argues that the eucharist provides a means for Christians living under oppressive regimes to resist the use of torture.

2. Liturgy can be said to function as a tool for ethics when it motivates worshippers to acts of justice and mercy as, for example, through the rites of Christian *baptism, which contain renunciation of sin and the powers of evil. Liturgy obviously functions as a tool when liturgical services are specifically constructed to advocate ethical reflection and action through occasional events which address various social justice issues, such as eucharists for world peace. Furthermore, para-liturgical or quasi-liturgical actions such as singing liberation songs during acts of civil disobedience or holding '*exorcisms' at nuclear weapons facilities could be construed as liturgy used as an instrument to promote ethical concerns.

3. Liturgy may also be the object of ethical critique. The various liberation theologies, typically employing the methods of sociological analysis, have pointed to ways that the practice of liturgy can perpetuate oppression by endorsing the status quo. Thus, Latin American theologian Gustavo Gutiérrez has suggested that the eucharist celebrated in the context of social oppression is mere 'make believe' unless it can serve as a radical critique of that oppression. Feminist liturgical theologians, such as Marjorie Procter-Smith, point to the preponderance of masculine language, imagery and leadership in worship as legitimating patriarchy. Other liberationists critique the Eurocentric aspects of the liturgy, which have pushed aside local language, art and custom, as

a form of colonialism. Common to the liberation approach is the assumption that the experiences of oppression and longing for personal freedom and flourishing are prior to the experience and practice of liturgy, which ideally should express these deeper longings.

4. Approaching liturgy as a source, tool or object for ethics may imply that liturgy and ethics occupy distinct spheres. Theologians working in a post-liberal vein challenge this implication. Rather, they see ethics and liturgy as fundamentally related perspectives on the life of faith. Consequently, the connection between liturgy and ethics is understood to be essential and prior to any discussion.

A starting point for this approach is Karl Barth's 1938 Gifford Lectures. There Barth uses the German word for 'worship', *Gottesdienst* (literally, 'service of God'), as a description of the Christian life. Liturgy, or the church's service of sacrament and preaching, Barth asserts, is the 'concrete centre' of the service that is the whole of Christian life. In the sense that ethics refers to the standards by which one conducts one's life, therefore, liturgy would be the core of that life. John Howard Yoder illustrates how this worked for early Christians in a discussion of 1 Cor. 11. For this Pauline community, the Lord's supper was not merely a ritually symbolic demonstration of economic sharing, but was the actual extension of the concept of family meal practice to include the entire church, so that in this case the practice of worship and ethics concretely coincide. In a similar way, but on a more theoretical level, Stanley Hauerwas argues that, while the discipline of ethics conventionally addresses various dilemmas that confront the individual or community, worship is a set of normative practices that gives shape and content to the way Christians understand all aspects of life, such as marriage, child bearing, and dying. Thus, an ethical dilemma, such as whether to allow physician-assisted suicide, becomes situated, not in a decision per se, but in relationship to a community that acknowledges baptism as dying with Christ.

This approach firmly denies that liturgy should be submitted to ethical or sociological critique from outside the liturgy itself. Rather, as Catherine Pickstock suggests, any ethical critique of liturgy must be an intensification of what is already given in liturgy, even if it is not fully realized. Indeed, from this perspective, liturgy is fundamentally the enactment of a comprehensive world view, which provides the critical principle for all of life, including ethics and morals.

Nevertheless, while these four approaches are discernibly different, they are not necessarily exclusive of each other. Advocates of type four may employ the tactics of type one, while advocates of type two often use the tactics of type three. In conclusion, to the degree that all four approaches to the question accede to a connection between liturgy and ethics, perhaps, as Yoder has suggested, it is most helpful to think of the relationship as two sides of a coin. Liturgy and ethics describe the life of faith from different perspectives, but, whether heads or tails, it is the same coin.

Rafael Avila, *Worship and Politics*, New York 1981; William T. Cavanaugh, *Torture and Eucharist*, Oxford 1998; Stanley M. Hauerwas, 'Worship, Evangelism, Ethics: On Eliminating the "And"', *Liturgy and the Moral Self: Humanity at Full Stretch before God*, ed. E. Byron Anderson and Bruce T. Morrille, Collegeville 1998, 95–106; L. Edward Phillips, 'Liturgy and Ethics', *Liturgy in Dialogue*, ed. Paul F. Bradshaw and Bryan Spinks, London 1994, 86–99; Catherine Pickstock, 'Liturgy, Art and Politics', *Modern Theology* XVI, 2000, 159–80; Marjorie Procter-Smith, *In Her Own Rite: Constructing Feminist Liturgical Tradition*, Nashville 1990; Mark Searle, *Liturgy and Social Justice*, Collegeville 1980; William H. Willimon, *The Service of God: How Worship and Ethics are Related*, Nashville 1983; John Howard Yoder, *Body Politics: Five Practices of the Christian Community before the Watching World*, Nashville 1992.

L. EDWARD PHILLIPS

Ethiopian (or Ge'ez) Worship

Since the political separation of Ethiopia and Eritrea, Ethiopian liturgy is more appropriately described as Ethio-Eritrean or Ge'ez liturgy, the latter from the name of the ancient language which it employs. The history of the liturgy is little explored and consequently poorly known. However, editions of a few liturgical books and a few publications concerning its *eucharistic prayers, *lectionary, *daily prayer offices, etc. in the last four decades give hope to scholars of liturgy.

1. *Origins*. A few decades after the council of Nicaea (325), the kingdom of Aksum adopted Christianity as the official state religion. Following the consecration of Frumentius as first *Bishop of Aksum by St Athanasius of Alexandria (before 356 CE), we can presume the existence of an ecclesiastical community with a well-organized liturgy. Indeed, according to the local tradition, Frumentius returned to Aksum carrying with him all of the liturgy. During the Aksumite period (fourth to ninth centuries), remarkable efforts were made not only to translate from external sources, but to create something new, more suitable to the Aksumite people. For example, tradition attributes to Yared (sixth century) the invention of the *zema* (sacred chant) and the initial composition of the books of hymnody. The introduction of liturgical song and *dance and the use of musical instruments may very well have started during the Aksumite period and subsequently developed.

2. *Influences*. The Ge'ez liturgy appears to be one of the most diverse and eclectic of ancient liturgical traditions. Possible contact with various other traditions needs further investigation. Pilgrims from Eritrea and Ethiopia travelling to and from Jerusalem were the main medium of contact between Ge'ez liturgy and other Eastern liturgies. Although the Ethio-Eritrean church remained hierarchically dependent on the Coptic church until 1951, it enriched its liturgy by elements gathered from other sources. The major influences were:

(a) Syrian. It is quite evident that the Ge'ez liturgical structure derives from the Syrian tradition. Some influences on the language, religious literature, liturgical structure, architecture, art, etc. go back to the sixth century, during which the monastic movement spread throughout the country and propagated the gospel. Most of the monks involved in evangelization are believed to have come from Syria.

(b) Coptic. From the thirteenth century the Coptic tradition started to exert a strong influence on the Ge'ez liturgy, and became the most important source of inspiration for major aspects of the Ge'ez liturgical tradition. This Coptic influence is evident because various liturgical texts, among them the Miracles of Mary, some eucharistic prayers, and the *Gebrä Hemamat* (liturgy for *Holy Week), are translated directly from Arabic. Even the observance of the Sabbath, the personification of Sunday, and the *tabot* are taken from the use of the Coptic church. The *tabot* is a piece of wood on which are written the name of the Trinity, Mary, the title of the church and the also the names of the founders of the village. Every church must have one. It is consecrated with chrism by the bishop and on it the eucharist is celebrated.

(c) Jewish. The presence of Judaic elements is evident in the Ge'ez liturgy, but their provenance is a matter of debate. They could have been derived from the Bible and/or from direct contact. Examples include the structure of the church building and the *tabot* (representing the ark of the covenant). The songs, chants and ritual dance in front of the *tabot* are strongly reminiscent of the ark of the covenant.

3. *The Process of Adaptation.* The Ethio-Eritrean church has always been open to other horizons in order to be nearer to the Oriental traditions. So it would be erroneous to think that the complex Ge'ez liturgy is a pure replica of the Coptic liturgy. Though many liturgical elements, in form and structure, remained very close to those of the mother church, we cannot speak of a total conformity of the Ge'ez liturgy to that of the church of Alexandria. Very early in its history, in fact, the Ethio-Eritrean church exhibited its capacity for enriching translated theological and liturgical books with local elements.

The fifteenth and seventeenth centuries were marked by liturgical renewal. Abba Giyorgis (d. 1426) was a prolific writer, and composed a *sä'atat* (*horologion*, or *daily prayer book) to substitute for the Egyptian one, which is still in use. Liturgical renewal was also part of the programme of Emperor Zär'a Ya'qob (1434–8). His period is characterized not only by the production of apologetic works and by a fight against paganism, dissidents and superstitious practices, but by the reformation and enrichment brought to the liturgy, the liturgical *year and liturgical books. The Gonder era (seventeenth and eighteenth centuries) could be considered one of the most important periods because it gave the liturgy the opportunity to become richer and more indigenous. Several important elements such as *mälk'* (hymn which describes and praises each organ of a saint), *aqwaqwam* (choreographic aspect of the divine office), *andemta* (commentaries, very significant because they help in the understanding of liturgical texts) belong to this period. The capacity to assimilate external sources and to use many local elements gives to the Ge'ez liturgy a definitely local character.

4. *Structure and Content of the *Eucharist.* As

in all rites, the Ge'ez liturgy is composed of variable and invariable parts. The variable parts are readings (from the NT), *mesbak* (a short extract from the Psalms to be chanted before the gospel), some special prayers which may be chanted at some liturgical period or solemnity, and the eucharistic prayers, used according to the liturgical circumstances. The pre-anaphora comprises: (a) prayers over the sacred vessels and *altar, (b) preparation of the gifts, (c) preparation of the *celebrant, (d) *offertory, (e) thanksgiving, (f) *absolution to the Son, (g) *intercessions, (h) *incense, (i) liturgy of the word, (j) other pre-anaphoral rites. The basic pattern of the eucharistic prayers is as follows: (a) dialogue, (b) preface, (c) *Sanctus, (d) anaphoral intercessions and *diptychs, (e) *epiclesis, (f) *institution narrative, (g) *anamnesis and doxology, (h) *Lord's Prayer, (i) *communion, (j) post-communion, (k) thanksgiving and dismissal. The structure of the eucharistic prayer can vary depending on the one in use.

5. *Akwätetä Qwerban (Eucharistic Prayers).* Characteristic of the Ge'ez liturgy is the use of a great number of eucharistic prayers. Most of them are not translations of other liturgies, but are a genuine local literature. Many of these locally composed anaphoras are named after Apostles or church fathers: the Apostles; Our Lord Jesus Christ; James, Brother of Our Lord; Basil; Jacob of Sarug; The 318 Orthodox Fathers; Cyril I; John, Son of Thunder; Our Lady by Cyriacus of Behensa; Athanasius; Gregory of Nyssa; Epiphanius; John Chrysostom; and Dioscorus.

The anaphoras of the Apostles (belonging to the ancient church order, the *Apostolic Tradition*), of Our Lord (from the *Testamentum Domini*), of St Mark (used *ab antiquo*) and of James, Brother of Our Lord (based on a Syriac text) are considered among those that have been used since the Aksumite period. The two anaphoras of Mary, one by Gregory and the other by Giyorgis Zä-Gassiccia, as well as the second anaphora attributed to Cyril, are found only in scholarly editions or in manuscripts. Some of them, however, are not included in the present Orthodox church missal. The Ge'ez missal edited by the Vatican in 1945 and used by the Ethio-Eritrean Catholics has inserted three of them: the anaphoras of Mary by Giyorgis Zä-Gassiccia, of St Mark, and of James, Brother of Our Lord.

The Ge'ez liturgy is known for the use of

Marian anaphoras in which the prayer exalts Mary directly. For this reason, although having a good thematic content, they are considered anomalous. On the basis of their structure, the Ge'ez anaphoras could be classified in three main groups: Alexandrine, *East Syrian and *West Syrian type. Others follow a free structure. To the latter belong mostly anaphoras which are considered of local composition and reflect Ethio-Eritrean theological debate of the Middle Ages.

6. *Daily Prayer. The Ethiopian tradition has kept a magnificent form of daily office which follows the traditional structure used in all ancient churches. It has parallel cathedral and monastic hours that remain separate and have not been fused into one office. The daily offices are made up of: mäwäddes (Sunday office); sebhatä nägh, (matins, with various forms); vespers, daily and festive forms, designated as mähatew (*lucernarium), wazema (*vigil) or sälotä särk (evening prayer); little hours (appearing mostly in Lent); kästetä aryam, a special office for feasts of saints; and mehella, stational office, celebrated ten times during the year. In addition to the cathedral services, the Ethiopian church has different types of sä'atat (horologion) and several other types of daily prayer preserved in office books.

7. Liturgical Year. The churches of Ethiopia and Eritrea follow the Julian calendar, with 13 months (12 months of thirty days each and one with five days, or six days in a year following a leap year). The year starts on 1 September, which corresponds to 11 or 12 September in the Gregorian calendar. The liturgical year is divided into four seasons of variable duration: Season of John, Season of Astämhero (supplication), Season of the Fast and the Paschal Season. There are a great number of feasts, the major ones being those of Our Lord, of Mary, of the angels, and of the saints (both OT and NT). There are nine major feasts of Our Lord: Incarnation; *Christmas; Baptism (*Epiphany); *Palm Sunday; Passion; *Easter; *Ascension; *Pentecost; *Transfiguration; and nine minor ones: Sebkät (Preaching), Berhan (Light) and Nolawi (Good Shepherd) on the first, second and third Sundays respectively before Christmas; Christmas Eve; Circumcision; Presentation in the Temple; Miracle of Cana; Sunday of Däbrä Zäyt (Mount of Olives); and Invention of the Cross. In addition to feasts of Ethio-Eritrean origin (which in-

clude numerous saints, mainly kings, founders of monasteries, monks and nuns), certain days of each month are dedicated to a fixed liturgical commemoration: the Nativity of Mary (1st of each month); Presentation of Mary in the Temple (3rd); Gäbrä Mänfäs Qeddus (5th); Qwesqwam (6th); Trinity (7th); St Michael (12th); Arägawi (14th); Kidanä Mehrät (the Covenant of Mercy, 16th); St Gabriel (19th); the Holy Virgin's Assumption (21st); Täklä Haymanot (24th); Death of Our Lord (27th); and Incarnation (29th). About 250 days during the year are observed as *fasts, of which about 180 are more obligatory. During fasting periods the eucharistic liturgy is celebrated in the afternoon, because communion breaks the fast.

8. Liturgical Music. The Ethio-Eritrean church has its own music, dance and instruments (drum, systrum), which reflect its tradition. The three modes of Ethio-Eritrean church music, which are considered to have been invented by divine inspiration, are called Ge'ez, 'Ezel and Araray. They symbolize the Father, the Son and the Holy Spirit respectively. The different modes are used according to the particular types of religious ceremonies (eucharist, divine office, *funeral rite, etc.) and the various occasions of the liturgical year.

9. Places of Worship. The eucharist is ordinarily celebrated in a consecrated church, but on the feast of the Baptism of Our Lord it is celebrated near a pool or river. In this case the tabot is taken in procession from the church to the river and it is placed in an appropriate place. Ethio-Eritrean church buildings have a rectangular, square or circular form. The place of worship, whatever its shape, is divided into three parts: (a) mäqdäs (the *sanctuary, the central part of the building), where the tabot is kept and the celebration of the divine liturgy takes place; access is allowed to the celebrants only; (b) qeddest (the holy), where those who will communicate (men: right side; women: left side) and the priests who are not on duty stand, also called enda tä'amer (place of miracles), because it is the place where the Book of Miracles is read; (c) qene mahlet (*choir), where daily prayer is celebrated and the däbtäras (cantor) stands. A church building has three (rarely four) doors: one towards the north, called muba'a gebr (the entrance of the offerings) and the other two towards the west and the south. On the east side of the church is

a small house, called *betä lehem* or *betä mestir* (house of the mystery), where the eucharistic elements are prepared immediately before the eucharist.

See also **Books, Liturgical** 2.5.

Selected texts: F. E. Brightman, *Liturgies Eastern and Western*, Oxford 1896, lxxii–lxxvi, 194–244; Marcos Daoud, *The Liturgy of the Ethiopian Church*, Cairo 1954; Habtemichael Kidane, *L'Ufficio divino della Chiesa etiopica: Studio storico-critico con particolare riferimento alle ore cattedrali*, Rome 1998; E. Hammerschmidt, *Studies in the Ethiopic Anaphoras*, 2nd edn, Wiesbaden 1987.

Studies: W. Macomber, 'Ethiopian Liturgy', *The Coptic Encyclopedia*, ed. Aziz S. Atiya, New York 1991, III, 987–90; Paulos Tzadua, 'The Divine Liturgy According to the Rite of the Ethiopian Church', *The Eucharistic Liturgy in the Christian East*, ed. J. Madey, Paderborn 1982, 35–68; M. Powne, *Ethiopian Music, An Introduction*, London 1968.

HABTEMICHAEL KIDANE

Eucharist

The principal ritual practice of most Christian denominations, attributed to its institution by Jesus Christ, but known under a variety of names, among them the Lord's Supper, Holy Communion, the Mass (the traditional title among RCs) and the Divine Liturgy (the term usual among Eastern Christians). The name eucharist, from the Greek word *eucharistia*, 'thanksgiving', has been used since at least the second century and is becoming increasingly common again today.

See also **Communion; Eucharistic Prayer; Eucharistic Theologies; Exposition; Intercommunion; Lord's Supper; Love-Feast; Mass; Offertory; Presanctified, Liturgy of the; Votive Mass.**

General bibliography: Anscar J. Chupungo (ed.), *Handbook for Liturgical Studies III: The Eucharist*, Collegeville 1999; Cheslyn Jones, Geoffrey Wainwright, Edward Yarnold and Paul Bradshaw (eds), *The Study of Liturgy*, 2nd edn, London/New York 1992, 184–338; Frank Senn, *Christian Worship: Catholic and Reformed*, Minneapolis 1997.

1. Early Christianity; 2. Eastern Churches; 3. Medieval and Roman Catholic; 4. Anglican; 5. Baptist; 6. Christian Church; 7. Congregationalist; 8. Lutheran; 9. Methodist; 10. Old Catholic; 11. Pentecostal; 12. Reformed.

1. *Early Christianity*. It is customary to trace the origins of the Christian eucharist to the Last Supper held by Jesus with his disciples before his death, and to see the fourfold shape of later eucharistic rites – taking bread and wine, giving thanks over them, breaking the bread, and sharing the bread and wine – as a subsequent conflation of the original sevenfold action of Jesus at the supper: taking bread, saying the blessing, breaking the bread, and sharing it at the beginning of the meal; taking the cup, saying the blessing, and sharing the wine at the end. But it is probably more accurate to see its roots in the various meals that Jesus shared with his followers and others throughout his life, and to recognize that different early Christian communities seem to have had their own form of communal meal practice, with a standardized form emerging only considerably later. There is, for example, evidence of a Christian meal in which the cup ritual seems to have preceded rather than followed the bread ritual, and of other traditions in which water rather than wine was used (perhaps giving rise later to the emphasis on the *mixed chalice). While some communities certainly linked their practice directly with the Last Supper, others appear at first not to have done so, but to have focused instead simply on continuing table-fellowship with their risen Lord and their expectation of its imminent fulfilment in the banquet in God's kingdom. The latter seems to be the case with the prayer texts for a Christian ritual meal which occur in the early church order known as the *Didache*, where brief prayers over cup and bread (in that order) precede the meal and a longer prayer follows it. The document also explicitly restricts participation in this meal to those who are baptized.

Gradually a normative practice began to emerge: meal and eucharist eventually became separated from one another everywhere (*see* **Agape**); the latter assumed the fourfold shape described above, and was celebrated every Sunday (and at first on no other day), preceded by a service of the *word, with *readings, *preaching and *intercessory prayer, concluded with the exchange of a *kiss, as the 'seal' of their prayers and an expression of their unity. The first indication of this is in the writings of Justin Martyr at Rome in the middle of the second century, but it may not have become universal until some time later. Here we see the importance attached to a communal celebration in which all Christians come together and share, with the result that *deacons take the 'eucharistized' (Justin's word) bread and wine to any unable to be there; and we also see the link between sacramental sharing and charitable giving to those in need: the wealthy deposit money with the 'president' (again Justin's word) of the community to distribute as he sees fit. Evidence from North Africa in the third century (Tertullian and Cyprian) confirms the testimony of the *Didache* that only the baptized could be present for both the community's prayers and the eucharistic action, others being dismissed after the ministry of the word, and that the bread and wine were brought from home by the participants, who were also allowed to take some home afterwards for ritual consumption during the week.

In the changed world of the fourth century, however, when Christians ceased to be liable to occasional persecution and became instead the favoured cult of the Roman empire, the character of their eucharistic worship also changed. Celebrated now in large public buildings, it took on the style of imperial court ceremonial and incorporated features drawn from the pagan religions around, of which it saw itself as the true fulfilment. Fixed prayers with elevated language began to replace the simpler *extempore compositions of earlier times, and these together with such things as music, *processions and *vesture were used to enhance the solemnity of the rite in the eyes and ears of the worshippers, who did not always seem to understand the significance of what was going on, and whose behaviour in church left much to be desired, according to the preachers of the age. The preachers also tried to exhort their congregations to amend their lives and come worthily to receive the sacrament, but this had the opposite effect from that intended: many people then preferred to come to church and not receive *communion rather than undertake the moral reformation asked of them in order to be communicants. This increased the tendency that was already forming for the eucharist to be viewed as something done by the clergy for the people rather than, as before, an action of the whole people of God. For those who now began to receive communion only infrequently, the eucharist not only ceased to be a communal action but was not even seen as food to be eaten. Instead, it became principally an object of devotion, to be gazed on. It is not surprising, therefore, that ancient liturgical commentators

then began to interpret the rite in terms of a drama that unfolded before the eyes of the spectators.

———

Paul F. Bradshaw, *The Search for the Origins of Christian Worship*, 2nd edn, London/New York 2002 (bib.).

EDITOR

2. *Eastern Churches*. Liturgical scholarship now agrees that in the first centuries of Christianity each local church had its own way of celebrating the eucharist. Beginning with the Peace of Constantine, diverse local practices were brought together and unified in the most important regional centres. With this movement the various Eastern families became distinct and developed independently (*see* **Orthodox Worship**), reaching final stability in relatively modern liturgical books. While all rites share common elements and structures, each has handled them in slightly different ways.

2.1. *Variety of Eucharistic Prayers*. In *East Syrian practice, three *eucharistic prayers are traditional: Addai and Mari, Nestorius and Theodore of Mopsuestia. Among the *West Syrian traditions, Syrian Orthodox generally use the liturgies of the Twelve Apostles and (Syriac) James, although the tradition preserves some eighty formularies. Indian churches commonly use James, Dionysius Bar Salibhi, Chrysostom and John the Evangelist. Most Eastern Christians belong to churches celebrating one of the four eucharistic prayers of the Byzantine rite. The Byzantine redaction of Basil is celebrated ten times a year, those of Gregory the Theologian (Nazianzus) and (Byzantine) James are traditionally used only on each saint's feast; the anaphora of John Chrysostom is prescribed on all other days Divine Liturgy is allowed. On days when eucharist is prohibited, the presanctified liturgy takes place in the evening; this is not technically a eucharistic rite. *Armenians have preserved five anaphoras, including a very early translation of Basil, later bearing attribution to Gregory the Illuminator. Of these, only the anaphora attributed to Athanasius is celebrated. Part of the Alexandrian family, *Coptic practice is primarily limited to a Coptic version of Basil, although the anaphoras of Gregory and Cyril (a redaction of Alexandrian Mark) are occasionally used. Although the *Ethiopian Church – another Alexandrian representative – knows at least 20 eucharistic prayers (eleven of which are local productions), only 14 are used.

2.2. *Characteristics*. Guests immediately notice the length and splendour of Eastern eucharistic celebrations. Apart from prayers rich in biblical allusion and theological meditation, over the centuries these rites developed several layers of liturgical accretions. During the period of liturgical formation, frequent contact between cultural centres resulted in a good deal of shared material; comparative analysis of texts reveals where particular units originated and how they were adapted by other traditions. While this process often resulted in the suppression of older elements, it ultimately led to the expansion of the service. The proclivity to commemorate saints by name, over time, lengthened liturgy considerably. As some rites developed the practice of clergy saying prayers inaudibly, diaconal *litanies and chanted pieces were introduced to fill the gap; on the one hand, this allowed all members of the worshipping community to participate; on the other, it hampered intelligibility. In the very recent past, most Eastern churches have embarked on the process of restoring their rites by recovering suppressed traditions and eliminating intrusive interpolations.

The popular roots of eucharistic celebration are obvious. Music plays a major role in all the rites, providing (ideally) for all the faithful an opportunity to glorify God and to reinforce theological truths. The worship space is generally open (*pews being a modern, western addition) allowing people to move about freely. *Processions bring sacred objects into the midst of the faithful. Frequent diaconal instructions to attend, arise and pray indicate that this activity sometimes needed to be controlled.

2.3. *Structure*. Eastern eucharistic rites can generally be understood as having a six-part structure: (a) preparatory rites in which the clergy vest and prepare the gifts; (b) the liturgy of the *word, which usually ends with a dismissal of *catechumens, justifying the appellation 'Liturgy of the Catechumens'; (c) pre-anaphoral rites, including elements for spiritual preparation of clergy and laity for the eucharistic offering as well as situating the bread and cup on the *altar; (d) the anaphora itself, (e) communion, and (f) concluding rites. Since catechumens were not present, parts (c) to (f) are sometimes called the 'Liturgy of the Faithful'. Robert Taft has deduced that certain 'soft points' in the liturgy are most susceptible

to radical differences between traditions; in this schema they are (a), (c), (e) and (f).

(a) Preparatory rites are often performed apart from the congregation. Armenian and Byzantine liturgies begin with an elaborate vesting ritual, with a psalm verse or prayer accompanying each vestment. Vesting is sometimes complemented with lengthy prayers and a ritual hand washing. Selection and initial preparation of the gifts is also elaborate, though some traditions such as the Chaldean and Maronite employ a simple rite as part of pre-anaphora. In Alexandrian traditions, priests wrap the selected bread in a silk veil and process around the altar. Byzantines cut portions in different shapes and sizes, arranging them on the paten to represent the whole church: Christ, the Mother of God, angels, saints, the living and departed. For Oriental Orthodox, preparation of the gifts begins even before leaving home: priests traditionally bake the bread themselves on the day of the liturgy. Coptic and Ethiopian prayers over the gifts employ epicletic, consecratory language.

(b) The liturgy of the word consistently includes the *Trisagion*; most traditions chant it at the beginning of this unit, but Alexandrian usage situates it before the gospel. Scripture readings are punctuated by psalmic material and always include a passage from the epistles or Acts as well as a gospel reading. Some rites also prescribe the reading of additional scriptural passages taken from the OT. Readings are preceded by at least one prayer asking that the people be enabled to receive the divine truths proclaimed. It is a uniquely Armenian practice to recite the Nicene *Creed immediately after the gospel. Today it is more common for a homily to follow the readings. The ancient practice of blessing and dismissing catechumens has fallen into disuse almost universally.

(c) Pre-anaphoral elements combine a ritual 'approach to the altar' with spiritual and physical preparation for the eucharistic offering. All traditions contain prayers (some rather lengthy) intended for the *celebrant, confessing personal unworthiness and requesting the mercy and blessing necessary to function as minister. Coptic and Ethiopian texts pay special attention to the congregation's spiritual purification. The rites move from spiritual to physical concerns. Armenian clergy and Byzantine hierarchs signify a spiritual change by removing some of their *vestments. If the bread and wine have been prepared before the liturgy, they are now transferred to the altar; some rites place the actual preparation here. The most elaborate transfer is the Byzantine *great entrance, which begins with an *incensation of altar and gifts to ready them, a grand procession of clergy bearing the *chalice and paten and depositing them on the altar with accompanying hymn texts, and another honorific incensation. Included among pre-anaphoral rites are recitation of the Nicene Creed and the *kiss of peace, indicating pure faith and love of others.

(d) The anaphora is hard to describe, given the number of discrete prayers discussed above, not to mention the various redactions of the major anaphoras. Generally speaking, Eastern anaphoras follow the standard West Syrian pattern: (i) dialogue; (ii) thanksgiving for creation, incarnation and redemption, incorporating (iii) the *Sanctus; (iv) *institution narrative; (v) *anamnesis; (vi) Spirit *epiclesis; (vii) intercessions and commemorations, often prefaced by praying for specific fruits of communion. Two particular items are of note: the East Syrian structure and the Alexandrian form of the Sanctus. The East Syrian anaphora of Addai and Mari does not incorporate an institution narrative. This striking absence caused some religious leaders to question the soundness of a eucharistic prayer lacking the words of institution. Consequently some editions have inserted the narrative and words into a prayer of thanksgiving and praise. Most traditions blend a slightly embellished form of Isa. 6.3 as the Sanctus, with the *Benedictus of Matt. 21.9, but Coptic and Ethiopian texts have preserved the indigenous Egyptian tradition of chanting only the Isaiah acclamation without the Benedictus qui venit.

(e) Communion rites function on two levels: spiritual and physical. As during the pre-anaphoral rites, the ministers recite psalm verses, fervently confess their unworthiness, ask forgiveness, and pray to be allowed to receive communion. As well as these non-scriptural texts, the *Lord's Prayer was also added to the preparatory regime, probably because of the petition 'forgive us our trespasses'. Physically, the celebrant must break the bread into appropriately sized pieces. In some rites – most notably East and West Syrian families – the fraction and arrangement are quite elaborate. All traditions dispense communion in both kinds, with the Copts and Chaldeans preserving the more ancient practice of administering the consecrated bread and cup separately. Only the Armenians and Maronites use unleavened bread.

(f) *Dismissal rites also vary widely. Their basic elements are a thanksgiving, final blessing (often with bowed heads), and dismissal. It is not unusual to find appropriate psalms chanted as part of this unit. Armenians conclude with a final gospel reading. Parallel to the preparatory rites conducted before the liturgy began, there are often ritualized ways of consuming leftover eucharistic elements, cleaning the vessels, washing hands and removing vestments.

2.4. *Theology.* Eastern liturgies are very much focused on praising and glorifying God for creation and salvation. Sometimes this concern with the history of salvation gives the impression that the eucharist has very little connection with the events of the present day. Because of the awe associated with standing before God's altar and the extreme reverence given to the body and blood present in the Liturgy, the texts are full of references to unworthiness and pleas for restoration. Any affirmation comes from God's implicit acceptance of self-confessed sinners. Although the Eastern eucharist is thoroughly centred on praise, glory and interaction with God, its complexity has sometimes distanced people, fostering allegorical 'Life of Christ' explanations.

Peter E. Fink, 'Worship in the Eastern Orthodox Tradition', *The Complete Library of Christian Worship, Volume 2: Twenty Centuries of Christian Worship*, ed. Robert E. Webber, Nashville 1994, 44–60; Grant Sperry-White, 'Eucharist, History of, in the East', *The New Dictionary of Sacramental Worship*, ed. Peter Fink, Collegeville 1990, 410–16.

JOHN KLENTOS

3. *Medieval and Roman Catholic.*

3.1. *Medieval.* Rather than 'eucharist', in the Middle Ages the preferred term was the mass or the sacrifice of the mass. The book that eventually governed the performance of the rite was therefore called the missal. Throughout the Middle Ages, beginning with the Carolingian period (eighth and ninth centuries), there was a great proliferation of new and diverse prayers. Popular devotional elements as well as prayers to accompany the feasts of different *saints found their place in the Roman Missal. Medieval piety was nourished heavily by liturgical allegory, whereby concocted and fanciful meanings were overlaid upon the liturgical actions and words. New prayers and hymns were composed and incorporated into prayer books to be recited and sung during mass. The Middle Ages witnessed the development of a eucharistic theology strongly sacrificial in nature, which determined the role of the presider as the sacerdotal mediator of the sacrifice. The mass was more an exercise of private devotion of the priest and the eucharistic theology stressed that each mass was in itself a good and holy work, a new act of Christ himself through which he applied his sacrifice of redemption.

Pope Gregory VII (1073–85) attempted to correct a lamentable ecclesial situation marked by gross illiteracy of the clergy by instituting a reform that included the liturgy. His ambitious programme tried to restore the clerical mores as well as ecclesiastical discipline. The Gregorian Reform, rather than truly reforming the liturgy, turned out to be a type of instruction given to the clergy so that they would know and recognize better the parts of the mass, most especially the canonical and liturgical rules. The final result of this reform was a movement of unification of the liturgy.

Despite the Gregorian Reform, there was not absolute uniformity in matters liturgical (*see* **Western Rites**). In Spain, for example, the liturgy of the Latin rite entered with great difficulty, gradually supplanting the old Mozarabic rites. The Spanish bishops in the northern dioceses of Spain found a solution allowing them a way to implant the official Roman rite (*more romano*), using monks from foreign lands. Little by little the Roman rite gained ground in the Ibernian peninsula, first in Aragon in 1071, moving towards Castille in 1078. At the Council of Burgos in 1085, the local rite disappeared in favour of the official Latin rite, except for the cities of Valencia and Toledo where special indult was granted to preserve the old Mozarabic rite.

Elsewhere in Italy an independent rite associated with St Ambrose flourished in the city of Milan. All attempts to suppress this rite in favour of religious and political unity and liturgical uniformity in the West were thwarted. The success of the Gregorian Reform, however, is attributed to two principle causes: the work of Franciscan mendicants in the thirteenth century and the influence of the printing press in the fifteenth century.

In the thirteenth century the Franciscan order was responsible for two liturgical consequences: abbreviation and unification. Former-

ly in Rome two kinds of liturgies coexisted: basilica liturgy and the liturgy of the papal court. Basilica liturgy was known for its conservative and traditional quality while the curial liturgy, which had been adapted to the needs of the papal chapel, was much less traditional. The papal chapel adopted the missal, containing all the readings and prayers in one consolidated book, because this could be transported more easily. This later led to the adoption of the missal in an abbreviated form in preference to the use of many different liturgical books. At the beginning of the thirteenth century, Innocent III officially established the Office of the Curia. The mendicant friars of St Francis diffused its use throughout Europe. In a papal decree of the Franciscan Pope Nicholas III, the abbreviated and simplified mass supplanted the ancient basilica liturgy. In spite of the resistance at the basilicas of St Peter and St John Lateran, the new missal was rapidly adopted with only minor adaptations of the local churches that maintained the celebrations of local saints within the liturgical *year. Shortly thereafter by another official decree, the calendar of the saints was made universal for the church, unifying the Roman liturgy even more.

A few notable exceptions to the liturgical simplification and uniformity can be found among the different monastic and religious orders. The Dominicans, heavily influenced by the basilica-style liturgy, launched their own reform of the liturgy between 1228 and 1238. The Cistercian Order for their part had derived their liturgy from the important reformed Benedictine Abbey of Cluny, which seemed to conserve Franco-Roman usages. In 1618 however they abandoned their ritual for the newly adopted Missal of Pius V. Other orders, such as the Premonstratensians and the Carmelites, blended the ancient liturgies of the early church with later liturgical customs.

The need for liturgical reform, especially of the Roman Missal, was recognized from the time of Pope Pius II (1458–64). During the pontificate of Sixtus IV, several feeble attempts at reform were enacted, especially in the area of chant at the celebrated Sistine Chapel (1473). He was formerly the Superior General of the Franciscan Order and favoured Franciscan liturgical usage. For many historical reasons, it was necessary to wait for the Council of Trent in the sixteenth century for the long needed liturgical reform.

3.2. *Roman Catholic.* Although the mass

text was fixed by the Council of Trent, the liturgical art and architecture, music and vessels continued to develop and change throughout the centuries. Yet in spite of these subtle changes, many RCs had the impression that the Roman rite was invariable and timeless. The fact that the execution was limited to the priests and *servers rendered the faithful mere spectators and fostered the idea that the mass was a fixed monument.

The Second Vatican Council (1963–5), after four hundred years of Tridentine theology and practice, assumed the mantle of liturgical renewal, giving special attention to the practice and the theology of the eucharist. Liturgical reform found expression in the first document of the council, the Constitution on the Sacred Liturgy (*Sacrosanctum Concilium*) promulgated in 1963. A principle aim of the Constitution was 'full, conscious and active participation' of the faithful which would restore to all the baptized a more active role in the eucharist as the 'source and summit' of the Christian life. The council mandated that all the sacraments, beginning with the mass, be revised so that extraneous liturgical material would be removed in conformity with the tradition and the rubrics would be simplified in order that the meaning of the rite would be more immediately accessible. As a result of Vatican II, the revised celebration has led to a renewal of study of the eucharist. New theological approaches are employed to give renewed understanding to classical theological notions of real presence and sacrifice. The eucharistic presence has greater appreciation within the context of the other presences of Christ in the word, in liturgical prayer, and especially within the liturgical assembly which gathers to pray, and sacrifice has been enriched by biblical studies and greater existential understanding. After four hundred years of liturgical conformity, there is renewed interest in liturgical *inculturation that respects the ongoing mystery of the incarnation through time and space and allows for greater diversity without sacrificing unity. Vernacular translations from the Latin have facilitated greater participation of the faithful for whom Latin was an obstacle. The liturgical practice gives rise to ongoing theological meditation that in turn calls for renewed practice. Although the liturgical reform of Vatican II has been implemented, the renewal is constantly before the church.

See also **Books, Liturgical** 3.

Gary Macy, *Treasures from the Storeroom: Medieval Religion and the Eucharist*, Collegeville 1999; Nathan Mitchell, *Cult and Controversy: The Worship of the Eucharist Outside Mass*, Collegeville 1982; David Power, *The Eucharistic Mystery: Revitalizing the Tradition*, New York 1992.

MICHAEL S. DRISCOLL

4. *Anglican*. The roots of Anglican eucharistic liturgy lie in the reforming work of Thomas Cranmer in the reign of Edward VI (1547–53). Cranmer's aims were: a wholly vernacular liturgy, a simplified ceremonial, participation by the people (partly by their receiving *communion regularly – and in both kinds), and elimination of transubstantiation, mass-sacrifice and other unreformed doctrines. His purpose, where holy communion was concerned, was to write a liturgy embodying receptionism.

Reform came by stages: in 1547 the epistle and gospel were read in English for the first time; in 1548 a brief insert into the Latin *mass, The Order of the Communion, written in English, implemented reception in both kinds, by providing after the priest's communion a penitential approach to the table and distribution; and then in 1549 came the first full English *BCP* with a complete communion service in English. This service followed the mass-plus-Order shape, but subtly changed its contents. The *ante-communion gained a homily after the *creed (with a long exhortation from 1548 following that), and the *offertory – a collecting of money – concluded it, whereby the worshippers put their alms in the new 'poor men's box' near the high *altar, and left, except that intending communicants remained in the *choir or *chancel for the sacramental part of the rite. For this the elements were made ready and the *eucharistic prayer followed. In it the Roman block of *intercessions remained, but prayers – not oblations – were offered. The saints were honoured, but not expected to help, and petition for the departed was grouped with that for the living. The sacramental theme began abruptly: God has given his Son to make on the cross 'a full, perfect, and sufficient sacrifice, oblation and satisfaction' for our sins – words serving devotional, didactic and polemical purposes. A petition (sometimes called an *epiclesis, but in the Western position) then asked God to bless and sanctify the gifts by his 'Holy Spirit and word'. The *institution narrative retained two manual acts, but no other ceremonial. The *anamnesis responding to the narrative's 'Do this in remembrance of me' then gave the key to Cranmer's staged reform. The Roman canon's 'Therefore . . . we offer a pure victim' was replaced by 'Wherefore . . . we . . . celebrate and make here . . . the memorial which thy Son hath willed us to make.' Whatever he meant, we mean! The prayer continued with self-oblation, petition for fruitful reception, some wisps of the old canon and a *doxology. After it came the *Lord's Prayer, the peace, and virtually the whole 1548 Order, concluded with a brief post-communion. The *rubrics ordered 'something more larger and thicker' than the previous wafers, to be divided during the distribution.

The 1552 rite may well have been already in preparation. The shape of the whole rite was altered, slightly in the ante-communion, drastically around the anamnesis. The response to the Lord's command 'Do this' was now understood as 'We are to eat the bread and drink the wine' and this was implemented straight after the command by *the actual eating and drinking*. The doctrinal background was the end of 'consecration' – name or thing. The epiclesis located consecration *in reception* (and there was thus no 'supplementary consecration'). The bringing forward of the distribution left much material to be relocated; so the end of the 1549 eucharistic prayer became an alternative post-communion 'prayer of oblation'; the Lord's Prayer opened the post-communion; the peace was lost; and most of the 1548 Order preceded the Sursum corda. The Prayer of Humble Access, however, moved to replace the 1549 intercessions after the *Sanctus (possibly through the influence of Isa. 6). The intercessions now went into the ante-communion to be read each week, even when, as often, there was no communion. They were explicitly labelled for the 'church militant here on earth'. So the 'eucharistic prayer' now had three paragraphs only: the 'one oblation' paragraph; the receptionist epiclesis; and the institution narrative – followed by the distribution. Gloria in excelsis went to the end of the rite, and closing rubrics provided for the bread to be such as is 'usual to be eaten', i.e., leavened, ordinary bread, and for any left over to be taken home for the minister's own use.

Queen Mary (1553–8) brought back the mass, but Elizabeth (1558–1603) revived the 1552 rite. Small changes then and in 1604 re-introduced 1549 *words of administration and

again located a moment of consecration back in the institution narrative, but a larger change came in the ill-fated 1637 Scottish rite, a half-reversion to 1549. After the Sanctus what was now called 'The Prayer of Consecration' went on immediately to the sacramental prayer remembering the death and sacrifice of Christ and included the 1549 epiclesis and the manual acts during the institution narrative, and added the 'Prayer of Oblation' after the narrative. The Lord's Prayer and Humble Access, moved from their 1552 positions, came after this long prayer and led into the distribution.

In 1645 the English rite was banned by Parliament, and the *Directory for Public Worship* was enforced. Charles II was 'restored' in 1660 and the 1662 rite kept the 1552 text and structure, but with the concept of 'consecration' (and *fraction) in the narrative fixed by rubrics. A discreet (non-petitionary) mention of the departed came into the intercessions. The 1662 rite remains an official liturgy of the Church of England, and lives on also in some other Anglican provinces, notably in vernacular languages in 'third world' countries.

Variants began in eighteenth-century Scotland, where the 1637 text was moved in an Eastern direction by the re-location of the epiclesis after the anamnesis in the years leading to 1764. It was also strengthened in its petition for a change in the elements; and the anamnesis gained an explicit oblation of the elements to God. The intercessions came back into the eucharistic prayer, at the end as in the East, and the whole of the 1548 Order went back to its 1549 position. Later Scottish rites of 1890, 1912, 1928 and 1966/1970 largely continued the same pattern.

In the USA, through Samuel Seabury's concordat signed with the Scottish bishops when they consecrated him as the first American bishop in 1784, the Scottish 1764 text strongly influenced the rite of 1789. This generally retained the pattern of an Eastern eucharistic prayer, and was continued in the American rites of 1892, 1928 and 1979, thus affecting rites in Brazil and those in other places where Americans went as missionaries.

The rise of anglo-catholicism in the nineteenth century led to varying rites in overseas parts of the Anglican Communion in the first half of the twentieth century. In some a direct borrowing from Rome occurred; but in others the Eastern-type epiclesis as in Scotland and the USA had its advocates, and this was introduced in South Africa (1924), in England (the abortive 1927/1928 proposals) and in the 1930s in Ceylon, China, Madagascar and elsewhere. Anglo-catholics desired a more primitive pattern for the eucharistic prayer, petitions for the departed, and a Godward 'memorial' in the anamnesis. But they disagreed about the propriety, position and form of an epiclesis, which contributed to the defeat of the 1927/1928 proposals twice in the House of Commons in England, though the main factor was the permitting of permanent *reservation of eucharistic elements even under strict conditions. In the late 1940s the Church of India, Pakistan, Burma and Ceylon tried a 1928-type rite, which went into their 1960 Prayer Book. In 1959 Japan and the West Indies provided rites with a more Roman-cum-1549 basis; and the 1959 Canadian text stood between 1662 and the Indian rite.

A turning point was Gregory Dix's *The Shape of the Liturgy* (London 1945), focusing attention on eucharistic *action* rather than *words*. The newly united Church of *South India authorized a rite based on this in 1950; and through the 1958 Lambeth Conference, when liturgical revision was first commended to the Anglican Communion, these South Indian principles prevailed and were found in the proposed *A Liturgy for Africa* (London 1964), and in other draft rites which drew on it. Features of this were: penitence (and Gloria in excelsis) at the beginning; a full ministry of the word, including OT reading; creed following the sermon; responsive forms of intercession; embryonic restoration of the peace; and a sacramental action broadly following Dix's 'four-action shape'. The eucharistic prayer recovered its full length and shape, but consecration was viewed as effected by the whole prayer, and not just by highlighted words. An emphasis upon the cross remained, but the other 'mighty works' of God in Christ were set alongside it; congregational acclamations followed the narrative – and the question arose as to whether offering the elements to God was a true response to Jesus' command to 'do this in remembrance of me'.

In the years following *A Liturgy for Africa*, new experimental rites with varying degrees of dependence on it appeared in several English-speaking parts of the Anglican Communion, most notably in New Zealand (1966), Australia (1966), the American *Prayer Book Studies XVII* (1967) and the Church of England's Series 2 (1967). Modern English was making its first appearance, but provincial innovation

and variation from one province to another was also evident. Some common trends can also be discerned, in which the needs of a main-service 'parish communion' have been paramount. A widely agreed ground plan undergirds considerable flexibility, with a great range of options, seasonal propers, and (apart usually from the eucharistic prayer) provision for *extemporary or local texts. There is increased congregational participation, stronger emphasis upon the corporate and ecclesial significance of the rite, and a persistent note of joy, praise and celebration. Even the most daring rites tend to be theologically conservative, and thus truly convey the faith to following generations. The *Revised Common Lectionary*, deriving from the RC three-year *lectionary, has enriched the reading of the word in most recent revisions.

Many texts are embodied in larger, definitive prayer books, such as Australia (1978), USA (1979), England (1980), Ireland (1984), Wales (1984), Canada (1985), Southern Africa (1989), New Zealand (1989), Australia again (1995), and the Church of England again (2000). But alongside these there has been the writing of a host of texts in Swahili, Spanish, Korean and other vernacular tongues, often in little booklets. Signs of real *inculturation and creativity are found in the Kenyan rite of 1989, used to open the 1998 Lambeth Conference, the first occasion to give full airing to rites from every part of the Communion.

Provincial autonomy in matters liturgical may be actually reinforced by a proper emphasis on inculturation. While two 'structure' documents were produced for the Anglican Communion in the 1960s, more help has come from the International Anglican Liturgical Consultation, first formed in 1985. Its public statements bearing upon the eucharist are those of 1985 (Boston, USA) on *children as recipients of communion, of 1989 (York, England) on inculturation, and of 1995 (at Dublin) on the renewal of the eucharist.

For bibliography, *see* **Anglican Worship; Books, Liturgical** 4.

COLIN O. BUCHANAN

5. *Baptist.* Few Baptist congregations would speak of 'the eucharist'. Most would talk of 'the Lord's supper' or of 'communion'. Nonetheless, the note of thanksgiving is a central feature of the way in which Baptists remember the death and resurrection of Christ at the

Lord's table. The celebration of the Lord's supper is regular, but not usually weekly. For some it will be once or twice a month, for others one a quarter. For a few it will occur every Sunday. The old practice of a separate service after the main preaching service continues in some quarters, but it is increasingly common to find an integration of the proclamation of the word and the eucharist into one service.

In their thanksgiving and remembrance, Baptists are frequently described as 'memorialists' with a Zwinglian eucharistic theology. In part this arises from the Baptist rejection of the doctrine of transubstantiation. It is presumed that such a stance necessarily implies a rejection of any sense of the Real Presence. In practice, the situation is not quite as clear-cut as this. Few Baptists (if any) would suggest that Christ is not present at the Lord's supper. The contention would be how that presence is manifested. For some, it will be a case of inward apprehension: Christ is present as we remember him. For others, it will be a question of the nature of Christ in the church gathered with his people: Christ present in the midst of those gathered in his name. For very few indeed would Christ be perceived as being present in the elements of bread and wine. Zwingli himself appears at times to have argued for what we might call 'trans-signification'. For Baptists, who want to say that the bread and wine are important signs and reminders of the body and blood of Christ, such a theology may be more congenial. Certainly, remembrance is not simply the private recall of the past; it is the congregational appropriation of the fruits of Christ's death and resurrection. To this extent there is a greater willingness to speak sacramentally of the eucharist than in former times, although the language of ordinance is still widespread.

A single prayer of thanksgiving may be spoken by the minister or two prayers of thanksgiving (one for the bread, one for the cup) may be uttered by appointed *deacons who will normally superintend the administration (following a pattern of diaconal service derived from that described in Acts 6). The two-prayer pattern is based upon the account of eucharistic celebration in 1 Cor. 11.23, a text which is frequently used as an anamnetic introduction to the observance of the Lord's supper. There is among some congregations a growing awareness and use of forms of *epiclesis. Any prayer for the descent of the Spirit is unlikely to be made over the gifts of bread and wine. Where such an invocation is used, it will normally be made for the people. This will either be in a petition that those who receive may know the Spirit's power in their lives so as to perceive the presence of Christ signified by the elements, or in a post-communion prayer of mission to the world.

For the administration of the elements the congregation remains seated, rather than moving to the table, and is served usually by deacons. The reception of individual pieces of bread (usually cut) and individual glasses is still widespread and probably the prevailing practice among the majority of Baptist congregations. However, a common loaf and cup are increasingly used.

For most Baptists the offertory at the communion service signifies not the bringing of the eucharistic elements to the table but the collection of money for the needs of others. The Communion Fund is frequently entrusted to the minister of the congregation to use at her or his discretion. In this way the Lord's supper is marked as an occasion to respond to the call of Christ's love in the ancient work of charity and the kingdom nature of the meal is demonstrated by a commitment to the values of justice, mercy and peace.

There are variations of custom among Baptists about who may receive at the Lord's supper reflecting varying degrees of openness of admission. The widest eucharistic hospitality is expressed in the invitation, 'Whosoever will may come'. Such an invitation presumes that the table belongs not to the church but to Christ and that he issues the invitation to which all may freely respond. Some (though not all) who use this formula are happy to exercise hospitality without asking questions about Christian faith and practice in those who receive. A less open position invites 'those who know and love the Lord Jesus as Saviour'. Here, living faith in Christ is presumed as the only qualification for admission: no requirement is made about *baptism or membership of any Christian tradition. Yet others invite 'those who are baptized and who are in good standing with their own congregation or church tradition'. Clearly, for those who exercise this form of hospitality the Lord's supper is seen as a church meal for which the church has responsibility in the sense of regulating those admitted. Admission is effectively open to the baptized alone, a position closer to most other main Christian traditions. The strictest admission policy is practised by those who 'fence the table'. In such congregations, communion is reserved to those baptized by immersion upon profession of faith and known or recommended to the local congregation, such a recommendation coming often initially by letter from a minister or congregation known to the receiving church. Among this last group it is likely that the Lord's supper would be observed in a separate service. Those not qualified to receive might remain to observe but would not be offered the elements.

Some recent Baptist practice at the Lord's supper has been influenced by ecumenical encounter. Signs of this change include: a growing willingness to use sacramental language; the wider experience of the weekly Sunday celebration of the eucharist; the greater use of a common loaf and cup; and attention in some quarters to the prayer of thanksgiving as an expression of praise for creation, redemption and the future hope. Despite the practice of the closed table in some congregations, there is generally a wide eucharistic hospitality extending to all believers. Nonetheless, for Christians from other traditions Baptist observance of the Lord's supper will commonly mark one of the clearer external differences in liturgical practice from that of their sisters and brothers in Christ.

See also **Baptist Worship**; **Books, Liturgical 5.**

PAUL SHEPPY

6. *Christian Church.* For the Christian Church (Disciples of Christ) the eucharist (more commonly called the *Lord's supper) is a public act in which the church, having heard the proclamation of the word, partakes of Christ's body and blood, thereby remembering God's reconciling initiative in Jesus Christ, celebrating the gift of the Spirit upon the church, and anticipating the coming reign of God. The Lord's supper is a *sacrament, an expression of Christ's body and blood in the visible signs of bread and wine. The host is the Lord, and the whole church is invited to his table. The supper has immediate social consequences; sharing at Christ's table compels the church to work in order that all may have 'bread and enough' to eat. The Lord's supper is central to the faith and piety of Disciples, who refer to themselves as 'people of the chalice'.

6.1. *The Early Disciples' Heritage.* Disciples' founders developed a coherent understanding and practice of the Lord's supper from

their reading of the NT: gathering at the table was 'the one essential act of Sunday worship', to be celebrated each and every Lord's Day. Originally *elders ordained by the local congregation to oversight of its life administered the supper; usually one offered an *extempore prayer for the loaf and another for the cup. For Alexander Campbell in *The Christian System* (2nd edn, Cincinnati 1839, 273) the supper was both profoundly personal ('the Lord says to each disciple, when he receives the symbols into his hand . . . "For *you* my body was wounded; for *you* my life was taken"') and profoundly social ('Each disciple in handing the symbols to his fellow-disciples, says in effect, "You, my brother . . . are now a citizen of heaven . . . Under Jesus the Messiah we are one. Mutually embraced in the everlasting arms, I embrace you in mind: thy sorrows shall be my sorrows, and thy joys my joys"').

Since Christ and not the church is host, all baptized Christians were – and continue to be – welcome at the table. Cultural factors led to an aversion to alcohol and thus to the tradition, still widespread today, of using unfermented grape juice rather than wine. Originally the sermon was placed at the end of the service where it might more easily be dispensed with if no elder present was 'suitable', and no itinerant evangelist available, to proclaim the word. The sermon remained at the conclusion of the service until the mid-twentieth century, but increasingly for a different reason: as a powerful evangelistic message reinforcing or calling out belief, the sermon, rather than the supper, came to be regarded as the climax of the service.

6.2. *Developments in Understanding and Practice.* The typical pattern which emerged by the mid-twentieth century included an active role for the ordained ministry. Typically elders, *deacons and the ordained minister would gather at the table. Elders would offer free prayers for the bread and wine. The ordained minister would recite the *institution narrative from the gospels or 1 Cor. 11, sometimes preceded by a brief meditation. The deacons distributed the elements to the congregation, whose members, remaining seated in the pews, passed the elements to one another. At best such a service conveyed the reality of Christ's sacrifice, and presence at the table. The sharing of leadership by laity and ordained ministry showed forth the ministry of all the people of God, and some elders' prayers reflected in simple and beautiful language a lifetime of growth into Christ. But the prayers sometimes lacked theological understanding or spiritual depth. And there was a tendency to think of the supper as purely commemorative, evoking the memory but not the presence of Christ.

6.3. *Renewal in Understanding and Practice*. In response to these problems, and through engagement with the *Liturgical and Ecumenical Movements, a renewed Disciples' eucharistic practice and theology emerged in the latter decades of the twentieth century. Thus a recent suggested order of service published by the church (in *Thankful Praise: A Resource for Christian Worship*, ed. Keith Watkins, St Louis 1987, and in *Chalice Worship*, ed. Colbert S. Cartwright and O. I. Cricket Harrison, St Louis 1997) includes the following dimensions: (a) gathering (greeting, opening prayer, music); (b) proclamation of the word (prayer, readings, response, sermon); (c) response to the word (call to discipleship, hymn of invitation, affirmation of faith, prayers of the people); (d) coming together around the Lord's table (invitation 'upon Christ's behalf for all baptized believers', offering, elders' prayers at the table, responsive prayers by pastor and congregation, institution narrative, breaking of bread; the *Lord's Prayer; the peace, *communion, final prayer); (e) going forth to serve God in mission (hymn, closing words, music).

Theological developments include the recovery – through engagement with the World Council of Churches' *Baptism, Eucharist and Ministry* – of the biblical notion of *anamnesis. It is recognized increasingly that Christ's command to 'do this in remembrance of me' – carved across the front of the communion table in many Disciples' churches – refers not merely to the commemoration of past events, but to an active remembering which invokes the true presence of Christ. There is also a strong desire for renewal of the theological content of the elders' prayers.

In its practice the church has aligned itself with the great tradition of Christian worship, as most congregations have moved the supper to its ancient place at the conclusion and climax of the service, with the sermon seen as a preparation for the table. In many congregations worshippers hold their cups after distribution, and then partake together. There are also moves toward bolder use of symbols and gestures. While some innovations have not been welcomed in some parts of the church, in others there is an openness to other methods of receiving communion (for example a common cup),

particularly on special occasions. Differences remain over the role of elders and ordained ministers at the table, and the admission of *children to the table before *baptism.

See also **Books, Liturgical** 6.

'A Word to the Church on the Lord's Supper (1991), A Report of the Committee on Theology', *The Church for Disciples of Christ: Seeking to be Truly Church Today*, ed. Paul A. Crow, Jr and James O. Duke, St Louis 1998, 139–52; James O. Duke and Richard L. Harrison, Jr, *The Lord's Supper*, St Louis 1993 (bib.); Keith Watkins, 'Breaking the Bread of Life: The Eucharistic Piety of the Christian Church (Disciples of Christ)', *Mid-Stream* XXXVI, 1997, 293–307; *Celebrate with Thanksgiving: Patterns of Prayer at the Communion Table*, St Louis 1991; 'The Lima Liturgy: When Theology Becomes Liturgy', *Mid-Stream* XXIII, 1984, 285–9.

THOMAS F. BEST

7. *Congregationalist*. The *Lord's supper as historically celebrated by Congregationalists offers a radical challenge to today's growing liturgical consensus. The early Independents took their lead from the Puritans in using scripture as their sole authority, and therefore abjured fixed liturgical forms. Their determination to rely on *extempore prayer and the Spirit's inspiration at the table was increased by persecution, with the ejections of 1660–2, and the imposition of set forms in the Anglican *BCP*.

7.1. *History*. The early Separatists, including the Brownists (early 1580s) and the Barrowists, (1587–93), took as their guide 1 Cor. 11.23ff., and in a simple service with much prayer and preaching, included two separate thanksgivings, for the bread and the cup. This continued into eighteenth-century Congregationalism. For example, it was customary at Isaac Watts's church in Bury Street, London. During the Commonwealth, the Independents, though involved in small measure with the Presbyterians in preparing *A Directory for the Publique Worship of God* in 1645 (the 'Westminster Directory'), were unhappy at the inclusion of a single blessing, and hesitated to endorse the idea of a directory at all. At the same time in New England, John Cotton said of the settlement churches, 'The prayers we use at the administration of the seals, are not any set forms prescribed to us, but conceived by the Minister, according to the present occasion and the nature of the duties in hand. Ceremonies we use none, but are careful to administer all things according to the primitive institution . . .' (*The Way of the Churches of Christ in New England*, London 1645, 68). In England and New England alike, the elements were administered to the people and minister sitting, the bread and wine 'not blessed together, but either of them apart' (*The Way*, 69). There was no *chancel or *altar rail, simply a table beneath the *pulpit without cross or candles, but only a white cloth and the vessels.

In keeping with their ecclesiology, Congregationalists restricted communion to covenanted members of gathered churches. The unworthy were excluded, and a period of preparation, redress of wrongs, and examination of conscience was normal. The *Westminster Directory* maintained that 'The ignorant and scandalous are not fit to receive this sacrament of the Lord's Supper.' However, the Congregationalists seemed less concerned to fence the table than the *Presbyterians. Robert Baillie, writing of the preparation of the *Directory*, commented, 'The Independents' way of celebration, seems to be very irreverent. They have communion every Sabbath without any preparation before or thanksgiving after; little examination of the people . . .' (*Letters and Journals* II, ed. David Laing, Edinburgh 1842, 148–9).

The connection between word and *sacrament, or ordinance, was considered essential. Robert Browne commented: 'How is the supper rightly ministered? The word must be duly preached. And the sign or sacrament must be rightly applied thereto' (*Life and Manners*, 280). Congregational eucharistic theology has been criticized for being memorialist. Without a set form of words, theology has been fluid, but the high theology of Calvin has been influential from the beginning. John Owen in his *Sacramental Discourses* (1669) notes that communion is (a) commemorative, in recognition of the death of Christ, (b) professional, in that the church professes and shows Christ's death, (c) eucharistic, in that there is a particular thanksgiving for Christ, and (d) federal, 'wherein God confirms the covenant with us, and wherein he calls us to make a recognition of the covenant unto God'. The sacrament was, alongside scripture and preaching, the way in which God represents Christ to the faith of believers. Christ 'comes to seal the covenant with his own blood in the administration of the ordinance'. This emphasis on the covenant is distinctive of Congregational celebrations of communion.

The significance of the meal remained strong in the eighteenth century. W. H. Davies, commenting on worship in Northampton led by Philip Doddridge and in London by Isaac Watts, observes that the sacrament was the climax of worship and a significant source of the spiritual nourishment. Watts's hymn, 'When I survey the wondrous cross', was written for use at communion. It demonstrates the continuing focus at the table on the work of Christ in the life of the believer. It was common practice for the pastor or teacher, later minister, to preside at communion, and early evidence suggests that a church might not celebrate the sacrament if it had no pastor. By 1884, however, R. W. Dale could write in his *Manual of Congregational Principles* (London 1884, ed. Digby L. James 1996, 151), 'An "ordained minister" is not necessary to give validity to the service.'

Certain elements remained common – the *institution narrative, the *fraction and the pouring with their separate prayers, the distribution of the elements, and a collection for the poor. However, there was a trend towards memorialism and didacticism on both sides of the Atlantic in the nineteenth century. The *Declaration of the Faith, Church Order and Discipline of the Congregational or Independent Dissenters* (1883), issued by the Congregational Union of England and Wales, stated that communion should be 'celebrated by Christian Churches as a token of faith in the Saviour and of brotherly love'. R. W. Dale reminded his contemporaries that although there was no mystical effect in the blessing of the bread, in the symbol of the bread, Christ's body was 'actually given', when met with gratitude and faith (*Manual*, 146, 150–1). P. T. Forsyth (*The Church and the Sacraments*, London 1917, 2nd edn 1947, xvi) thought 'a mere memorialism to be a more fatal error than the Mass, and far less lovely'.

7.2. *Recent practice*. During the twentieth century it became common for the invitation to be to 'all who love the Lord,' and the seriousness with which the sacrament was treated diminished. Less time was given to self-examination. Some sought greater formality and adopted an order reflecting the Anglican pattern. The 1920 *Book of Congregational Worship* included the Sursum corda and Sanctus, though with a rather brief thanksgiving and no *epiclesis. For others, communion became simply a fellowship meal at which Jesus was remembered as a brother. The 1936 Congregational *Manual for Ministers* evinced a greater sentimentality, for example through the inclusion of John Hunter's prayer, 'Come not because you must, but because you may . . . Come not to express an opinion, but to seek a presence.' The emphasis was on the congregation's approach to God, rather than God's activity.

In response to these trends, W. J. F. Huxtable's *A Book of Public Worship* (Oxford 1948) sought to recover the Puritan tradition, and adopted a 'High Genevan' style. The words of the institution remained separate from a prayer of 'consecration', but a prayer for the Spirit (an epiclesis) was included. The *Book of Services and Prayers* (London 1959) stressed that thanksgiving should always be included at communion, as should an awareness of the communion of saints. The trend was continued by the *Order for Public Worship* (London 1970) which included six 'eucharistic' prayers, all with the Sursum corda and Sanctus and set thanksgivings. Gone was the offertory for the poor, and the invitation was expunged.

In the USA, Henry David Gray's *Congregational Worshipbook* (Phoenix, AZ 1978) adopted an eclectic approach, with one order including no thanksgiving. It also contained a catechism demonstrating a low view of communion: 'The Lord's Supper is a sacrament in which . . . we remember his life and death, and become better Christians.'

A more robust approach is found in *Evangelical and Congregational* (1981), from the Evangelical Fellowship of Congregational Churches in Britain: 'the good news of saving grace is set forth visibly' in the sacrament (40). While formal liturgy may be a guard against theological aberration, so too may be education in sacramental theology, so since 1972 some in the Congregational Federation in Britain have encouraged the proper use of extempore prayer and a return to simplicity. Admission of children to communion is now common. Debate continues as to whether communion might only be celebrated by a (local) church, and not at, for example, a conference. The general pattern now is that communion is shared once or twice a month, as an integral part of a service in which preaching is also important. Although there is great variety in actual practice, the freedom from set forms and simplicity of order are characteristic.

See also **Books, Liturgical** 7.

Stephen Mayor, *The Lord's Supper in Early English Dissent*, London 1972; Nathaniel Micklem, 'The Sacraments', *Christian Worship: Studies in Its History and Meaning*, ed. Nathaniel Micklem, Oxford 1936, 243–56; John von Rohr, *The Shaping of American Congregationalism: 1620–1957*, Cleveland, OH 1992; Bryan D. Spinks, *Freedom or Order: The Eucharistic Liturgy in English Congregationalism*, Allison Park, PA 1984 (bib.).

MICHAEL DURBER

8. *Lutheran.* The first eucharistic liturgies which could be called 'Lutheran' had pre-Lutheran sources. These included the various local uses of the *Western rite that were known in the areas where the Lutheran reformation arose. But the later Lutheran liturgies were also influenced by a variety of early sixteenth-century attempts at reform of the mass. All of these patterns, in turn, had been influenced by Martin Luther's own discussions of the meanings and the perversions of the mass in his essays on 'The Blessed Sacrament of the Holy and True Body of Christ' (1519), 'The Babylonian Captivity of the Church' (1520), and 'The New Testament, that is the Holy Mass' (1520). While these essays urged some reformed practices – communion in both kinds for the laity and the audible proclamation of the words of *institution, for example – they were not primarily concerned with practical liturgical solutions but with the central theological distinction between what is given by God's mercy as constitutive of the sacrament and what is added by the church in thankful response. Indeed, Luther himself resisted publishing extensive liturgical materials lest they should become some new, 'evangelical' constraint. In contrast, Thomas Müntzer's 1524 publication was a thoroughgoing presentation of all the texts for a reformed mass, in German, with chant notation and with five seasonal variations.

8.1. *Luther.* But in December of 1523, in response to continued appeals that he himself might make a liturgical proposal to help with the chaos which could be found in congregations and towns which were embracing the doctrines of the Reformation, Luther at last relented. The resultant essay, 'An Order of Mass and Communion for the Church at Wittenberg' (*Formula missae et communionis pro ecclesia Wittembergensi*) was not a full liturgical book in the manner of Müntzer. Nor was it a universal prescription. It was rather an essay on the evangelical use of the received tradition, requiring the continuing but critical use of the current liturgical books. And it was an essay on the way things were being done in Wittenberg. It remained open to use or correction by others in other places. Of course, precisely because it was from Luther, it was of enormous influence.

The eucharistic liturgy envisioned in the *Formula missae* was conservative in shape and basic character. It presumed a *celebrant and a *choir. It presumed Latin intermixed with vernacular hymnody and vernacular preaching. And it followed this classic order: introit or full psalm, ninefold *Kyrie, Gloria, *collect, epistle, gradual and vernacular congregational hymn, gospel, sung *creed, sermon, preparation of the table, sung dialogue and preface newly edited to lead into the sung words of the institution, sung *Sanctus or vernacular hymn together with elevation, *Lord's Prayer, pax, communion of priest and people (in both kinds) during the singing of *Agnus Dei and other vernacular hymnody, proper communion chant, post-communion collect, Benedicamus, *blessing (either in the usual wording or in wording drawn from Num. 6.24–27 or Ps. 67.6–7). At the same time, the clear effort of this work was to make the received traditional order into a congregational service and to rework it critically into an evangelical one by eliminating the offertory prayers and the post-Sanctus prayers of the Roman canon.

All three of these motifs – traditional, communal, critical – then had a further, somewhat more radical expression in the second of Luther's primary liturgical works, the 'German Mass' (*Deutsche Messe*) of 1526. This work, too, was an essay, a discussion of liturgical practice and critical liturgical choices, including now choices among the burgeoning new hymns. It was not intended to replace but to supplement the earlier *Formula missae*. And it was accompanied by a fierce insistence that it not be made a new law, binding on consciences. Here, the traditional mass-order was still maintained, but with all of the texts (except the Kyrie) in German. The communal interest was served now by the increasing hymnody, some of it replacing the classic Latin texts of the *ordinary, and by the use of the vernacular throughout. Luther provided adaptations of classic chant tones for the collect, the readings, and the words of the institution in German. Evangelical criticism still fell most heavily on

the 'consecration' of the bread and wine: here the sermon was followed by Lord's Prayer or Lord's Prayer paraphrased as an exhortation; by the intoned *verba testamenti* (as the words of the institution were called) followed by the hymnic Sanctus with the elevation and the hymnic Agnus Dei during the communion. Luther actually recommended that the distribution of the consecrated bread should follow immediately the word concerning the bread, with the communicants then waiting for a similar consecration and distribution of the cup, but it is not clear how widely this awkward counsel was followed.

It is clear, from various reports of contemporary eyewitnesses, that these essays did not remain only written proposals. Liturgies which were something like both *Formula missae* and *Deutsche Messe* were enacted in Wittenberg and other cities of the Reformation, though both of the patterns remained works-in-progress. The patterns for thanksgiving at table, for example, received continually new treatment, as in the Swedish Mass of Olavus Petri (1531) restoring much that belongs to a eucharistic prayer to the long preface as it runs into the words of the institution, the Sanctus and the Lord's Prayer.

8.2. *Church Orders.* While Luther's formative proposals could be considered as essays on how to use the received liturgical books in an evangelical way, it was not long before Lutherans began to need and to produce books of their own. For the purposes of a rough outline, it can be observed that the eucharist continued to be celebrated in Lutheran churches in ways that can be categorized according to their use of the pattern of the *Formula missae* (now put into the vernacular, though sometimes, as in Nuremberg for centuries, still in both Latin and German) or their adoption of the largely hymnic scheme and more radical eucharistic solution of the *Deutsche Messe*. The many church orders influenced by the Brandenburg-Nuremberg *Kirchenordnung* of 1533 and the patterns adopted in Sweden and Finland, for example, followed the former. The church orders written by Johannes Bugenhagen (1485–1558) and the patterns adopted in Denmark, Norway and Iceland were more inclined to the latter. In each case, however, some continuation of local medieval uses could also be detected.

8.3. *Loss, Recovery and Renewal.* Regular Sunday eucharist and frequent communion continued to be the Lutheran norm in most places for at least two centuries. The usual Lutheran practice, however, was to encourage communicants to announce their communion to the pastor prior to Sunday and, at this announcement, to be catechized and *absolved. The intellectual and emotional climate of the eighteenth century was bound to break through these customs. Rationalism, with its anti-sacramentalism, brought about a greater infrequency of celebration in places that did not consciously resist. Liturgies, including liturgies of the eucharist, were turned into long, didactic texts, largely recited by the minister. And pietism placed a massive accent on the unworthiness of the individual, making appropriate preparation for communion into a wrenching and unusual undertaking. Even in orthodox Lutheran congregations, given the strictures against 'private masses', the mass could not continue to its conclusion if only the pastor was to be a communicant.

Nonetheless, orthodox Lutherans did continue their interest in evangelical and communal celebrations of the mass. Bach's Leipzig knew such celebrations in the mid-eighteenth century. And so did the small Lutheran communities on the Atlantic coast of North America served by Pastor Henry Melchior Muhlenberg (1711–87) and his successors. Muhlenberg's Liturgy (1748) was – like its great Lutheran forebears – also not an actual service book but a circulated essay about how pastors and congregations could make use of currently available hymnals and received Lutheran texts in order to enact the old order of the mass.

As in many other communions, the nineteenth century witnessed among Lutherans in the many lands where they now lived strong movements for the recovery of older patterns. The church orders of the sixteenth century frequently served as models for liturgical reform, even when eucharistic frequency was not yet recovered. The Bavarian *Agende* of Wilhelm Löhe (1844) and the Common Service of North America (1888) stand as high points in these efforts at liturgical recovery.

Among twentieth-century Lutherans a new consensus on the shape of the eucharist and a new openness to the fruits of the ecumenical *Liturgical Movement brought about a continued reform of the local liturgical books, now combined with a great growth in the frequency of celebration. Lutheran liturgies of the holy communion continue to be marked by *tradition* (now, in the reception of what is seen to

be early Christian as well as sixteenth-century patterns, as in the increasing use of full eucharistic prayers, for example), by *evangelical criticism* (in the continued centrality of preaching, for example, or the resistance to the language of 'sacrifice'), and by *communal action* (in the continuing liturgical importance of congregational hymnody, for example). It remains true that eucharistic rites can still be found with a closer connection to Martin Luther's 1523 essay on the Latin mass (e.g. the North American *Service Book and Hymnal*, 1958), and others can still be found as inheritors of his 1526 essay on mass in the vernacular (e.g. the sixth setting in the North American *With One Voice*, 1995). It can be argued that the current Lutheran interest in the shape or ordo of the eucharist as a tool for local liturgical planning (see the German *Erneuerte Agende*, 1990) is rooted in the interest of both essays in maintaining and reinterpreting the classic order of mass.

———

Selected Texts: *Luther's Works* XXXV, Philadelphia 1960, 'Word and Sacrament'; Irmgard Pahl, *Coena Domini* I, Freiburg 1983. *See also* **Books, Liturgical** 8.

Studies: Luther D. Reed, *The Lutheran Liturgy*, Philadelphia 1947; Günther Stiller, *Johann Sebastian Bach and Liturgical Life in Leipzig*, St Louis 1984.

GORDON LATHROP

9. *Methodist.* In its Wesleyan form, the evangelical revival of the eighteenth century was marked by increased use of the eucharist. At a time when many parishes in the Church of England were content with at best a quarterly observance of the Lord's supper, John Wesley himself typically celebrated or received the holy communion, according to his own records, at least seventy or eighty times a year. He encouraged the Methodists to press the Anglican clergy for more frequent eucharistic opportunities in their local churches; he included the sacrament in Methodist gatherings when priests were available; he made use of the *BCP* provision for family and friends to partake during the communion of the *sick and the dying. In contrast to the 'stillness' doctrine of the *Moravians, Wesley viewed the Lord's supper not only as a 'confirming' but also as a 'converting' ordinance, numbering it together with Bible reading and prayer among the 'means of grace' that were to be used by the baptized who already had some measure of

faith but were seeking full assurance. It was for the sake of sacramental ministry among the 'poor sheep in the wilderness' that Wesley took the irregular step of ordaining men for the newly independent USA and, in a letter of 10 September 1784 to the brethren in North America, 'advise[d] the elders to administer the Supper of the Lord on every Lord's Day'.

9.1. *The USA*. With *presbyters Coke, Whatcoat and Vasey, Wesley sent across the Atlantic the sheets of *The Sunday Service of the Methodists in North America*, 'a liturgy little differing from that of the Church of England'. In the Order for the Lord's Supper, Wesley's revisions took account of the changed political situation (the king disappeared from the opening *collects); '*elder' replaced 'priest' as the term for presbyter; and the habitual abbreviator cut out the Nicene *Creed (the Apostles' Creed would already have been said during morning prayer), the exhortations, and the second postcommunion prayer. A new rubric before the final *blessing allowed that 'the Elder, if he see it expedient, may put up an Extempore Prayer'. In American practice (codified already in the 1792 *Discipline* of the Methodist Episcopal Church), the *ante-communion was quickly abandoned in favour of the preaching service familiar from the more usual non-eucharistic occasions (*see* **Word, Service of the** 9); but Wesley's sacramental rite continued to provide the backbone for official orders of the Lord's supper itself in the largest Methodist denominations, even if some vertebrae were removed and others displaced. At one stage in the *Ritual* of the Methodist Episcopal Church, the preface and *Sanctus were located between the communion of the ministers and the communion of the people; and there was a long-standing permission – dating from the *Discipline* of 1792 – that 'if the Elder be straitened for time, he may omit any part of the service except the Prayer of Consecration'. After the reunion of the Methodist Episcopal Church, the Methodist Episcopal Church, South, and the Methodist Protestant Church as 'The Methodist Church' in 1939, the 1964 *Book of Worship* embodied what proved to be a final effort at a closer approximation to Wesley's eucharistic order. Among the historically black Methodist churches in the United States, the African Methodist Episcopal Church consistently remained nearest to Wesley's original as revised in 1792.

9.2. *Britain*. In Britain, the Wesleyan Methodists stuck quite tightly to the sacramental order provided by their founder in the version of his *Sunday Service* intended for use in the home country; some indeed reverted to employment of the Communion order in the *BCP*, a fact recognized when the Wesleyan Methodist Conference in its 1882 *Book of Public Prayers and Services* realigned the inherited Wesley text with the Anglican at some points. The 'Cranmer-Wesley' service figured as the first order of Holy Communion in the 1936 *Book of Offices*, which also included, however, a second order that was conceived as respecting more the practices of the smaller Methodist bodies that had joined with the Wesleyans to constitute the Methodist Church of Great Britain in 1932.

9.3. *Modern practice*. In the last third of the twentieth century, Methodist churches within both the British and the American ambits participated in the widespread revision of service books prompted by the ecumenically oriented *Liturgical Movement, although it is Methodist practice only to 'authorize' official books, not mandate them. Among eucharistic rites, the most important were the 1972 American 'Sacrament of the Lord's Supper: An Alternate Text', produced by the United Methodist Church following the 1968 merger of the Methodist Church and the Evangelical United Brethren, and the first order in the British *Methodist Service Book* of 1975. In both, the Word and the Table were proposed as the twin foci for regular worship on the Lord's Day. The first part of the service was to contain *readings from scripture (normally Old Testament, epistle, and gospel), sermon and prayers of *intercession; the second part of the service was structured by the four actions of (to use the British terminology) 'the setting of the table', 'the thanksgiving', 'the breaking of the bread' and 'the sharing of the bread and wine'. In constructing their 'great thanksgivings' or 'anaphoras', both the United Methodists and the British Methodists adopted in rather chaste form and style the 'West Syrian' pattern that had found greatest favour among contemporary liturgists.

Undergoing various revisions and developments, the 1972 order was taken up into the United Methodist *Book of Services* (1984), *Hymnal* (1989), and *Book of Worship* (1992); and a host of further eucharistic prayers of standard construction was provided for general, seasonal or occasional use in *At the Lord's Table* (1981) and then in the *Book of Worship*. In the British *Methodist Worship Book* of

1999, the 1975 structure of the Sunday service was largely maintained, although entire seasonal orders were now supplied for *Advent, *Christmas and *Epiphany, *Lent and *Passiontide, *Easter and *Pentecost.

Neither in North America nor in Britain did later Methodist observance of the Lord's supper ever meet the frequency that would have matched John Wesley's recommendation of 'constant communion' (the title of a sermon he published in 1787). The latter half of the twentieth century saw perhaps a modest increase of eucharistic practice in some regions, but Methodists have been much slower in this regard than (say) Anglicans or Lutherans.

A contribution to eucharistic life that has found some ecumenical acceptance are certain choice texts from the 166 items in the *Hymns on the Lord's Supper* published by John and Charles Wesley in 1745.

John C. Bowmer, *The Sacrament of the Lord's Supper in Early Methodism*, London 1951; *The Lord's Supper in Methodism 1791–1960*, London 1961; J. Ernest Rattenbury, *The Eucharistic Hymns of John and Charles Wesley*, London 1948; Karen B. Westerfield Tucker, *American Methodist Worship*, New York 2001, chapter 5; (ed.), *The Sunday Service of the Methodists: Twentieth-Century Worship in Worldwide Methodism*, Nashville 1996.

GEOFFREY WAINWRIGHT

10. *Old Catholic*. The eucharist is the central worship of the Old Catholic churches. All the Old Catholic churches of the Union of Utrecht maintain that without the regular celebration of the eucharist each Sunday, the church has lost its claim to catholicity and apostolicity. The shape of the eucharist is that common to all the Western catholic churches, differing only in details from that of the RC and Anglican churches. According to the catholic understanding of the ministry, it is only the *bishop or priest who can preside at the eucharist, but in all the Old Catholic churches all ministries carried out in the eucharist, save those of the presider and *deacon, are open to both men and women. The International Old Catholic Bishops' Conference has in 1985 made the diaconate available to women as well; the western European churches have also opened up the episcopate and *presbyterate to women and have ordained women priests.

The eucharist is nowadays always celebrated in the vernacular (sometimes still in Polish in the Polish National Catholic Church in the USA and Canada). The Old Catholic Church of the Netherlands switched from Latin to Dutch in 1909. All the other Old Catholic churches began to celebrate the eucharist in the vernacular from the beginning or as soon as there were translations or adaptations of the Latin texts.

The basic document of the Union of Utrecht, the 1889 Declaration of the Old Catholic bishops to the Catholic Church, in paragraph 6 calls the eucharist 'the perpetual commemoration of the sacrifice offered upon the Cross' and 'a sacrificial feast, by means of which the faithful, in receiving the Body and Blood of our Saviour, enter into communion with one another'. This double focus of the eucharist as being both a memorial of God's saving deeds in and through Christ, especially in the paschal mystery, and a holy meal has determined the texts and rites of the eucharist. Special emphasis is laid in the eucharistic prayer upon the action of God's Holy Spirit; it is the Holy Spirit and not the word of the bishop or priest reciting Christ's words who makes the bread the body of Christ and the wine the blood of Christ. All the modern versions of the eucharistic prayer speak of 'bread' and 'wine' until after the *epiclesis. Communion is always available with both bread and wine and open to all those believing Christ to be really present in the bread of life and the cup of salvation.

The most recent revisions of the shape of the eucharist have also resulted in a much greater appreciation of the word of God. All the Old Catholic churches have a *lectionary system which distributes the OT and NT readings among several years. The most common system is the RC three-year lectionary. The Dutch Church has adapted the lectionary of the Episcopal Church (USA), while the Old Catholic Church in the Czech Republic has adopted the *Revised Common Lectionary*.

Noteworthy are the number of versions of the eucharistic prayer in use in the different Old Catholic churches. For instance, the Old Catholic Church of the Netherlands has twelve texts, one of which to be sung in its entirety; the Catholic Diocese of the Old Catholics in Germany has twenty-three versions, the Old Catholic Church in the Czech Republic, basing its book upon the German altar book, has thirty-nine. The prayers vary in age in all the churches from the eucharistic prayer of the so-called *Apostolic Tradition* of Hippolytus to texts drafted in the 1980s and 1990s, including one 'Eucharistic Prayer of the Union of

Utrecht' common to all the member churches, and texts from the RC, Anglican and Lutheran traditions, Taizé and the Lima Liturgy. More than half of them follow the Antiochene pattern of praise (from the post-Sanctus through the words of *institution to the *anamnesis) followed by petition (the epiclesis over the gifts and those receiving them). Most of them also draw explicit attention to the catholic dimension of the celebration by naming the bishop, the fellowship of bishops and all men and women in the apostolic ministry, as well as the communion of saints.

Some peculiarities are worth mentioning. The Dutch and Swiss churches have retained a public preparatory rite (including the *confession of sin by both priest and congregation). The German church has *collects according to the three-year lectionary for the Sundays in *Ordinary Time. The Swiss church sings the Gloria after the collect as the first part of the liturgy of the word; they also sing the *Creed after the *intercessions. The Swiss order provides for a kind of *diptychs to be said by the deacon between the preparation of the altar and the holy gifts and the prayer over the gifts.

THADDEUS A. SCHNITKER

11. *Pentecostal.* The first General Council of the USA-based Pentecostal denomination, the *Assemblies of God, featured a gathering of the Council's participants in order to share the eucharist. An eye-witness report dated 28 October 1916, and entitled 'The Message of the Sacrament', stated that the Council's participants gathered 'to reverently partake of the emblems that spoke of the broken body and shed blood of Him who loved us and gave Himself for us'. That the emblems 'spoke' of Christ's crucifixion implies an understanding of the eucharist as a dramatization of the gospel that transforms those who partake in faith. Typical of the Pentecostal approaches to the Lord's supper, this report did not support a theoretical discussion of eucharistic doctrine but accented instead the obedient response to the eucharist as a life-transforming event. The report stated: 'we have no need to preach a doctrine of consubstantiation nor of transubstantiation; we receive Jesus' words and act on them.'

In the light of this report, Walter Hollenweger's insight that there is 'no fully developed eucharistic doctrine in the Pentecostal Movement', but that there is a 'clear and well-developed pattern of eucharistic devotion'

seems well founded. Of course, such eucharistic devotion requires theological reflection. Toward this end, Hollenweger describes three typical forms of Pentecostal eucharistic devotion, namely, an emphasis on the love of Jesus, 'that is, love for the faithful friend who is called Jesus'; a blood-and-wounds mysticism, 'that is, an absorption into the suffering and death of Jesus'; and a 'looking forward to the marriage feast of Jesus' at Christ's return. When discussing such devotion, one should not neglect the central Pentecostal conviction that Jesus is present through the Holy Spirit during the eucharistic meal to commune with believers, to transform them toward greater love and holiness, and to heal them in body and mind. Indeed, 'Pentecostals have long claimed transformations during their rites' (Daniel Albrecht). Thus, as Hollenweger noted, 'Pentecostals expect from their communion with the Son of God the strengthening of their inner being, strength in everyday temptations and the healing of sickness.'

The living Christ sanctifies through the implied 'Word' or message of the eucharist. The aforementioned report of the eucharistic meal shared by the first General Council of the Assemblies of God states that there is a 'message' in the Lord's supper which encourages 'the expulsion of every sign of sin, carnality and evil, so that we may keep the feast with the unleavened bread of sincerity and truth'. Supportive also of what may be termed a 'material' understanding of salvation (Miroslav Volf), the report stated further that the meal 'is involved not only for our spiritual but for our physical benefit. Here is good news for the sick. You are invited to a meal for your health.' There is potential here for developing the social significance of the eucharist for justice and reconciliation, though most Pentecostals have not traditionally expressed their eucharistic devotion explicitly in these terms. Yet, there is a growing recognition among Pentecostals of the social significance of the eucharist. For example, the first meeting of the Pentecostal/Charismatic Churches of North America (Memphis, TN, October 1994) which met to repudiate racism and to establish an interracial association of Pentecostal and *Charismatic denominations in the USA, Canada and Mexico, climaxed with a *footwashing ceremony and a eucharistic church service. The central theme of these rites was racial justice and reconciliation.

The communion with the living Christ that

sanctifies and heals in Pentecostal eucharistic devotion seems to connect the memorial of the past crucifixion and resurrection with the hope for the future coming of Christ. Many Pentecostals may state that they support a memorial (Zwinglian) understanding of the eucharist, but their actual eucharistic devotion is more complex. Notice how the afore-mentioned report of the Lord's supper of the first General Council of the Assemblies of God places the accent on communion with the living Christ during the Lord's supper: 'There is nothing old or stale about the memorial feast, the fruit of the vine is not old, the shed blood is not aged, the bread is not stale, the Lord's body is not a mere thing of the past, the way is *new and living*. The thing most striking about the character of the feast is its presentness and not its pastness or its futureness. It has a present aspect, there is a sign of warmth, the blood is ... flowing from the wounded side of Jesus ... The feast points back and is a memorial of the death of our Lord, and it points forward to his return, but there is also a distinct present aspect.'

Besides the accent on the ministry of the living Christ in the eucharist, Pentecostals also stress the faith and participation of believers during the meal. Everyone in a Pentecostal worship service is encouraged to enter and par-take of the divine life that flows from Jesus and the word of God proclaimed implicitly in the meal, inspiring a liturgy of 'common action' from which the gifts of the Holy Spirit such as healing, testimonies of God's grace, and tongues and prophecy (1 Cor. 12—14) may be exercised. The British Pentecostal Donald Gee complained that too many Pentecostal com-munion services were being dominated by the pastor's words or the prayers of certain select church leaders. The remedy, he suggested is not a silencing of those who typically speak but in a 'quicker response' by others. He warned that a failure to include others among the laity during the communion service could 'produce meet-ings so stereotyped that, for all their boasted freedom, they become more barren than the liturgical services they deprecate – and with less aesthetic appeal' (Hollenweger). Some Pentecostal churches in the USA (especially with a dominant ethnic identity) and in Europe and Latin America celebrate the eucharist with one loaf of bread and one cup of juice, implying the values of reconciliation and unity among diversely gifted individuals. Sometimes foot-washing is included and connected to the eucharist as an aspect of cleansing and to sym-bolize the call to serve one another in humility.

Perhaps Hollenweger exaggerates when he makes the general remark that 'the service of the Lord's Supper is the central point of Pente-costal worship', especially since the impor-tance of the meal varies from church to church, some observing it frequently while others only rarely. But when the meal is observed, it tends to hold a central place in that particular service because of its healing or transformative signifi-cance. Certainly, Pentecostals do not confine the event of Christ's self-giving to the preached word of God, but expand this event to include eucharistic and charismatic avenues of the Spirit's work. Typically sung at a communion service would be the following words:

For ev'ry contrite, wounded soul,
Calv'ry's stream is flowing,
step in just now, and be made whole,
Calv'ry's stream is flowing.
(L. H. Edmunds, *Hymns of Praise*, 1969, 98)

Daniel Albrecht, *Rites in the Spirit: A Ritual Approach to Pentecostal/Charismatic Spiritu-ality*, Sheffield 1999, 196–217; Walter Hollen-weger, *The Pentecostals*, reprint, Peabody, MA 1988, 385–7; H. D. Hunter, 'Ordinances, Pentecostal', *Dictionary of Pentecostal and Charismatic Movements*, ed. Stanley M. Burgess and Gary B. McGee, Grand Rapids, MI 1988, 653–4; John Christopher Thomas, 'Ministering the Sacraments,' *Ministry and Theology*, Cleveland, TN 1993, 161–79; Miro-slav Volf, 'Materiality of Salvation: An In-vestigation in the Soteriologies of Liberation and Pentecostal Theologies', *Journal of Ecu-menical Studies* XXVI, 1989, 447–67.

FRANK D. MACCHIA

12. *Reformed.* The Lord's supper has a central place in Reformed theology and polity, iden-tified by Reformed catechisms as one of 'the means of grace' and 'marks of the true church'.

12.1. *Reformation Practices.* Sixteenth-century Reformers abolished several Catholic practices, including private masses, the adora-tion of the elements, kneeling as a *posture for reception, reception of the bread alone for the laity, and anything that hinted that the sacra-ment was a propitiatory sacrifice (including the terms 'priest' and 'altar'). The key criterion for Reformed eucharistic practice was scriptural teaching; the most important models were the liturgical practices of the early church.

In Zurich, Ulrich Zwingli emphasized that the supper was an occasion for memorializing Jesus' death and a sign of unity and fellowship. For Zwingli, the phrase 'this is my body' meant that the bread symbolizes (not becomes) the body of Christ. His first liturgical revision, *De canone missae epicheiresis* (1523), was a theologically chastened version of the Roman mass. His second, *Action oder Bruch des Nachtmals* (1525), featured a much-simplified, vernacular liturgy, with an opening prayer, readings from 1 Cor. 11, John 6, Gloria in excelsis, Apostles' *Creed, *Lord's Prayer, a prayer of access, the words of *institution, communion, and post-communion thanksgiving. He mandated the use of simple, wooden communion cups and plates 'that pomp may not come back again', and the celebration of the supper four times a year, three of which, despite widespread disregard of the Christian calendar, were on Christian feast days (*Christmas, *Easter, *Pentecost). Later, in Dutch Reformed churches, the Lord's supper was celebrated on *Good Friday, in contrast to common practices elsewhere.

In Strasbourg, nearly twenty editions of the liturgy appeared in the first fifteen years of the Reformation. The resulting Strasbourg eucharistic rite consisted of an exhortation (which emphasized the real, spiritual presence of Christ), the Apostles' Creed, a prayer (which included a consecration of the participants rather than the elements), the Lord's Prayer, the words of institution (read as warrant for the sacrament), the communion, and a concluding prayer of thanksgiving and blessing.

In Geneva, Calvin's *La forme de prières* (1542) owes much to the Strasbourg rite. His exhortation features themes in his rich sacramental theology, including an emphasis on the Spirit's role in lifting up the heart of the believer to commune with Christ in heaven. Calvin's desire for weekly eucharist was denied by the more conservative town council.

Calvin's liturgy, as well as Knox's *Forme of Prayers* (1566), *The Book of Common Order of the Church of Scotland* (1562), the Dutch Reformed Liturgy of Dathenus (1566/1619), and the Palatinate liturgy of Ursinus and Oleivanus (1563), featured several common items: an invitation to the table and dismissal of unrepentant sinners, the creed, didactic exhortations, communion prayers (which included thanksgiving, an *epiclesis of the Holy Spirit, and a vow to live in covenant faithfulness to God), and the reading of the words of institu-

tion as warrant for the celebration. Many early liturgies called for the distribution to be accompanied by scripture reading and singing, and concluded with a post-communion thanksgiving. They consist almost exclusively of texts spoken by the presiding, ordained minister. The Lord's supper was always preceded by scripture reading and preaching and thus was organically linked with the liturgy of the word. Architecturally, the sacrament was celebrated around a table (not an *altar), located close to the congregation.

From the start, there has been a strong link between the Lord's supper and church discipline in Reformed churches. Concern about unworthy reception led to frequent excommunications in Calvin's Geneva, to solemn preparatory services in the Palatinate and Netherlands, to communion tokens given to all worthy participants in Scotland, and to a common requirement that all communicants make a public profession of faith. These practices have surrounded the table with an introspective, penitential ethos.

12.2. *Later Developments*. After the sixteenth century, Reformed practices diverged widely. Few congregations, until recently, ever lived up to Calvin's desire for weekly eucharist. Nevertheless, the Lord's supper has nearly always been experienced as a solemn and significant occasion, whether in quarterly celebrations or in the annual week-long 'sacramental seasons' in the Kirk of Scotland.

Perhaps the most influential post-Reformation movement was a reaction against set eucharistic liturgies. Among Presbyterians, the *Westminster Directory for Worship* (1644) and its successors have provided only basic parameters for worship, rather than prescribed liturgical texts. When authorized liturgical texts have been published, they have typically been issued for voluntary use, leaving much to ministerial discretion. This reaction against set forms was fuelled by a Puritan impulse which pressed for liturgical simplicity and for identifying explicit biblical mandates for all liturgical practices (the regulative principle). Equally significant was the influence of the Enlightenment thought, which undermined any sense of the sacrament as an occasion of divine action and served to desacralize the experience of the sacrament for worshippers.

Meanwhile, the tradition has also included a sacramental, ecumenical impulse that has led to liturgies that feature a balanced word–table structure, more frequent eucharistic celebrations, restored set prayers, and an openness to the Christian *year. Notable instances include the liturgy of the Swiss pastor Jean Frédéric Ostervald in the seventeenth century, and several nineteenth-century examples, including the Mercersburg liturgy of John W. Nevin and Philip Schaff, the French Reformed pastor Eugene Bersier's *Liturgie*, the Scottish Church Service Society's *Euchologion*, the work of the 'Liturgical Circle' in the Netherlands, and the historical work of the American Presbyterian Charles Baird.

In North America, this sacramental impulse has frequently been at odds with a revivalistic impulse that has viewed worship services as a means by which to produce conversions. North American *camp meetings, a direct descendant of Scottish sacramental seasons, featured a prominent place for the sacrament at the culmination of the meeting. Often a revivalistic view of worship coincided with less frequent celebrations of the Lord's supper, although the revivalism of the former Presbyterians Alexander Campbell and Barton Stone led to the birth of denominations that practise weekly communion (Churches of Christ and *Christian Churches–Disciples of Christ).

Often these various impulses have clashed. In nineteenth-century America, 'doctrinalist' Charles Hodge, 'sacramental' John W. Nevin, and 'revivalistic' Charles Finney all wrote treatises against each other, a pattern replicated in recent years with tensions among post-Vatican II liturgical ecumenists, confessional Reformed theologians, and church growth theorists.

Methods of reception have also varied widely. In some Dutch and Scottish communities, communicants sat at tables during the sacrament. In many North American Presbyterian congregations, dark-suited *elders process symmetrically from the table to distribute elements to communicants seated in *pews. In the North American temperance movement, grape juice became a common substitute for wine. A later concern for hygiene led to the use of small individual communion cups.

12.3. *Modern Practices*. Post-Vatican II ecumenical influence has led to a recovery of both the normative word–table pattern of Lord's Day worship and patristic patterns for eucharistic prayers, an emphasis on the multiple themes associated with the Lord's supper (thanksgiving, spiritual nourishment, remembrance, communion, eschatological hope), and a celebrative rather than penitential ethos

for the feast. Unlike their sixteenth-century counterparts, recent service books include multiple options for eucharistic prayers, including options for each season of the Christian year. There have been vigorous discussions among liturgically minded theologians about whether almsgiving should follow the sacrament or precede it as part of the traditional offertory, about whether the words of institution should be included within the eucharistic prayer or read as a warrant for the sacrament, and about ways to increase congregational participation in eucharistic celebrations. There has also been experimentation with many methods of reception, including intinction and a return to a common cup. Meanwhile, strong rationalistic, pietistic and revivalistic dimensions of the tradition persist, largely ignoring this recovery of eucharistic piety. In large North American mega-churches, for example, the sacrament is often practised quite infrequently, without use of traditional liturgical patterns or texts.

———

For texts, *see* **Books, Liturgical** 12.

Studies: Bruno Bürki, *Cène du Seigneur– Eucharistie de l'Eglise*, Fribourg 1985; Alasdair Heron, *Table and Tradition*, Edinburgh 1983; Daniel Meeter, '*Bless the Lord, O My Soul*': *The New-York Liturgy of the Dutch Reformed Church, 1767*, Lanham, MD 1998; H. O. Old, *Patristic Roots of Reformed Worship*, Zurich 1975; Leigh Eric Schmidt, *Holy Fairs: Scottish Communions and American Revivals in the Early Modern Period*, Princeton 1989; Bryan D. Spinks and Iain R. Torrance (eds), *To Glorify God: Essays on Modern Reformed Liturgy*, Edinburgh 1999.

JOHN WITVLIET

Eucharistic Prayer

1. Definition;   2. Origins;   3. Ante-Nicene Prayers;   4. Classic Traditions;   5. Reformation;   6. Modern Reforms;   7. Remaining Issues for the Churches.

1. *Definition*. The eucharistic prayer is the central prayer of the ritual of the *eucharist. It is fundamentally a prayer of praise and thanksgiving to God for what God has done in Christ. In many forms throughout the centuries, however, these prayers have included a number of other elements as well. The most common scholarly name given to them – anaphora – indicates that they were also considered a

prayer of offering (Greek, *anapherein,* 'to lift up, offer'). In Latin these prayers could likewise be named *actio sacrificii* ('making of the offering') or *oratio oblationis* ('prayer of offering'). The Latin tradition also uses the words *prex* ('prayer') and *praefatio* ('publicly declaimed oration') for such prayers. Eventually the sole eucharistic prayer of the Roman rite became known as the *Canon actionis* ('Rule' or 'standard of the [prayer of the] action'). The modern RC rite employs the term *Prex eucharistica* ('eucharistic prayer'). Some other churches use a title like 'The Great Thanksgiving'. The notion of giving thanks is rooted in the NT descriptions of Jesus' meal prayers (see Matt. 26.27; Mark 8.6; 14.23; Luke 22.19; John 6.11; 1 Cor. 11.24). The prayer-action of giving thanks eventually provided the name for the whole of the Sunday service of word and sacrament as well as to the elements of bread and wine over which the prayer was spoken and which were consumed in holy *communion.

2. *Origins.* It is more accurate to speak of the origins of the traditions of eucharistic praying than to speak of the origins of the eucharistic prayer. Today it seems clear that no single original eucharistic prayer existed as a prototype from which subsequent prayers diverged. Research in Jewish prayer forms has demonstrated that even these were not fixed in the time of Jesus. Therefore, when the NT accounts inform us that Jesus said the blessing or gave thanks in the course of a meal, we cannot know precisely what he said. On the other hand, it is possible to approximate the style of praying that Jesus might have used. Two forms of Jewish prayer have been suggested. The first is called the blessing (*berakah,* from the Hebrew verb *brk,* to bless or acknowledge); the second is called the thanksgiving (*hodayah* or *todah,* from the verb *ydh,* to know). Both types of prayer are known to us from biblical and deutero-canonical texts, and both combine acknowledgement of God (and what God has done) with petition, a commonsense structure found in the Psalms as well. It must be emphasized that reading back later prayers or theological concerns into early materials leads to a faulty understanding of them. For example, despite the importance of the *institution narrative for the later development of the tradition of eucharistic praying, the Last Supper accounts give no indication of the content of Jesus' prayer but rather a pattern (probably already

affected by liturgical practice) of eucharistic practice.

It is entirely probable that a number of meanings were attached to the early Christian meal practices that became known as eucharist and therefore that there are multiple factors (even some not from meal prayers) involved in the development of the tradition of eucharistic praying. In addition there is indisputable evidence that the content of such prayers was subject to improvisation (probably within set patterns) up to the fourth century.

At present two major theories have been proposed with regard to the development of the eucharistic prayer tradition. Cesare Giraudo has argued for a bipartite structure based on the model of the biblical *todah,* a prayer of thanksgiving accompanying the sacrifice of thanksgiving (*zebach todah*) and consisting of (a) recital of God's gracious deeds and (b) petition for further divine gifts (see, e.g., Ps. 9.1–12, 13–20; *Jubilees* 10.3–6). Giraudo names these parts (a) the anamnetic (recital, remembrance) and (b) epicletic (petitionary) elements. He categorizes prayers in the developed traditions by their placement of the institution narrative. Some prayers place the narrative within the anamnetic part, others within the *epicletic* part. In terms of the movement of the prayer, much will therefore depend on at what point God is asked to do something – either before or after the recital of the institution narrative.

A second theory has been put forward by Enrico Mazza, who finds a tripartite scheme in the early texts. For example, both chapters 9 and 10 of the *Didache* (late first century) contain two thanksgivings and a prayer of petition. In this structure, which indeed he finds in every example of eucharistic praying, Mazza finds the kernel of prayer (which he calls a paleoanaphora) that will later be filled in or added to with elements that make up a classic eucharistic prayer (institution narrative, *epiclesis, *anamnesis, *intercessions). Further, Mazza finds that the bulk of the prayer shifts from after the meal (as in the *Didache*) to before the elements are distributed and consumed (as in the so-called *Eucharistia mystica* of *Apostolic Constitutions* VII.25–6). This development had important consequences for a theology of consecration of the elements.

Both of these theories have considerable merit, although it can be pointed out that each author tries to force his preferred structure on certain texts. In any case both of these theories, and indeed the entire contemporary scholarly discussion, must deal with the absence and eventual insertion of the institution narrative into eucharistic prayer texts. The vast majority of prayers that precede the fourth century have no account of the words of Jesus at the Last Supper. These prayers include the *Didache*; the *East Syrian anaphora of Addai and Mari; the Egyptian Papyrus, Strasbourg Gk 254; *Apostolic Constitutions* VII.25–6; the *Acts of John* 85, 86, 109, 110; and the *Acts of Thomas* 27, 49, 50, 133, 158. Even the fourth-century prayers described by Cyril of Jerusalem (*Mystagogical Catechesis* 5) and Theodore of Mopsuestia (*Baptismal Homily* 4–5) arguably contain no institution narrative. On the other hand, even if it was not used liturgically, it is clear that Justin Martyr (in the second century, *First Apology* 66) and Cyril (*Mystagogical Catechesis* 4) do know the institution narrative, which of course is contained in the synoptic Gospels as well as 1 Cor. 11. The treatise known as the *Apostolic Tradition* and attributed to a third-century Roman presbyter, Hippolytus, has an anaphora which contains the institution narrative, but the dating of the text we now possess is at present far from certain. We must reckon with the possibility that the words of institution played a role in the distribution of the elements (their treatment by Justin Martyr and Cyril of Jerusalem might suggest that) but not the eucharistic prayer as such. Obviously the absence of an institution narrative within what would normally be considered a eucharistic prayer raises questions about late medieval and Reformation understandings of eucharistic consecration.

Even though the earliest eucharistic prayers might not have contained a narrative of institution derived from the Last Supper, Mazza has argued that they did possess a scriptural warrant for the celebration of the meal. In the case of the (admittedly retrojected) Jewish *birkat-ha-mazon* (blessing of the meal), it is a citation from Deut. 8.10. Mazza finds an allusion to the same verse in *Didache* 10.3. In the case of Papyrus Strasbourg Gk 254, the text is Mal. 1.11 (the perfect sacrifice offered among the nations). It is possible that such scriptural warrants grounded eucharistic praying. Mazza has also suggested that the earliest prayers may not have been single continuous compositions at all but rather combinations of brief, memorable prayer texts. The later development of the various traditions makes this a reasonable suggestion.

3. *Ante-Nicene Prayers*. A number of early texts pre-exist the flourishing of the genre in the fourth century. It must be kept in mind, however, that prior to the fourth century improvisation seems to have been the rule. In order to appreciate the diversity of traditions for eucharistic praying, we shall briefly survey five of these texts.

(a) *The Didache*. This proto-church order dates from at least the end of the first century. Chapters 9 and 10 each contain a set of three prayers that precede and follow a Christian meal. The first two prayers in each set are thanksgivings, the third a petition for the gathering of the church. Thus we find a tripartite structure which clearly has affinities with what later sources reveal to be a version of the Jewish *birkat-ha-mazon*. The thanksgivings before the meal are said over a sequence of cup, then bread. Together with the sequence in 1 Cor. 10 this has led Mazza to conclude that one early tradition had the sequence of praying over the cup before the bread. A doxology concludes each of the prayers in both chapters. In the Jewish *berakah* tradition the prayer was sealed (noun, *chatimah*) by a praise formula that recapitulated the opening phrase of the series.

(b) *Apostolic Constitutions VII*. This book in the fourth-century Syrian church order contains a revision of the prayers of *Didache* 9 and 10 that could well have been made in the third century. The two series of prayers in the *Didache* have now been linked more smoothly (i.e., the intervening doxologies have been eliminated). Also in contrast with the *Didache*, the prayer before partaking of the elements has been considerably expanded.

(c) *Acts of John 85, 109*. This apocryphal scripture, which is usually dated to the late second century, perhaps of Egyptian provenance, contains two prayers spoken by the apostle at eucharists with bread alone. These prayers are remarkable in that they consist solely of the praise of God addressed to Christ. They may bear witness to a tradition of eucharistic praying that consisted simply of praise and thanksgiving.

(d) *Strasbourg Papyrus Gk 254*. This text consists of a fragment which looks very much as though it was meant to be virtually a complete prayer. Although the prayer contains nothing specific about blessing a meal, it is a thanksgiving prayer of sacrifice with the structure: thanks – offering – intercessions. It has affinities with the first part of the later Alexandrian anaphora of St Mark. Its structure suggests a resemblance with the similar structure of the Jewish *todah*. In its allusion to the light which has come through Christ some have seen an origin to this prayer in the first blessing of Jewish morning prayer (*yotser*), a prayer which also contains the threefold 'Holy'. If so, it might support E. C. Ratcliff's contention that eucharistic praying might once have concluded with the singing of the *Sanctus, and the contention that eucharistic prayers may have incorporated material that came from sources other than praying at meals.

(e) *Apostolic Tradition*. This anaphora is found in the *ordination of a bishop in this church order conventionally attributed to the early-third-century Roman presbyter Hippolytus. It is clearly meant as a model rather than a set prayer. Its structure begins to approximate to what later become classic elements in the anaphoral tradition: dialogue; thanks for God's action in Christ culminating in an institution narrative; anamnesis of Christ's death and resurrection and offering of the bread and wine; invocation (epiclesis) of the Holy Spirit upon the gifts and for the gathering and strengthening of the church; doxology and Amen. The institution narrative is the final motive for thanksgiving in this prayer and lays out an elaborate warrant for the celebration of the eucharistic meal. Since the earliest manuscript of the *Apostolic Tradition* is a Latin translation from the late fourth century, Paul Bradshaw has questioned the commonly accepted attribution of this prayer as a whole (and therefore the inclusion of the institution narrative) to the early third century.

4. *Classic Traditions*. With the expansion and consolidation of the Christian church as well as a number of debates about doctrine, the fourth century was a fruitful period for the development of the eucharistic prayer traditions with which we are familiar today. The major ritual families of Christian faith and practice began to develop at this time and at least the basic framework of the classic anaphoras was in place.

There are five major 'families' of eucharistic prayers: Antiochene, East Syrian, Alexandrian, Roman and Gallican. The characteristic features of each tradition will be briefly summarized with an outline of the structure of a representative anaphora from each.

(a) *Antiochene (*West Syrian)*. In terms of influence (especially on the modern *Liturgical Movement) one of the most important traditions stems from West Syria. Major representatives of this tradition are the anaphora of St Basil (in both its Egyptian and Byzantine forms), the anaphora of St John Chrysostom and the anaphora of St James. All of the anaphoras in this family follow the same (rather logical) pattern: dialogue; series of thanksgivings (for creation or salvation history); Introduction to the Sanctus; Sanctus and *Benedictus; post-Sanctus thanksgiving (beginning with the word 'holy'); [thanksgiving for salvation history]; institution narrative; anamnesis of Christ's death and resurrection; oblation (offering); epiclesis (invocation) upon the gifts and communicants; intercessions for the living and the dead; doxology; Amen.

The logical progression of this prayer leads from praise and thanksgiving for creation and/or God's action in Christ through the acclamation of the Sanctus to the specific pattern for the eucharist, the institution narrative. From the institution narrative flows the focus of the memorial in the death and resurrection of Christ and the explicit offering of the gifts. At this point God is asked to do something, namely send the Holy Spirit upon the community and the gifts. From this basic petition follow the intercessions (and names of those to be prayed for, i.e., *diptychs) and finally the concluding doxology and Amen. It is probable that by the end of the fourth century theological and doctrinal considerations had led this tradition of prayer to be informed by a trinitarian structure (from Father to Son to Holy Spirit), even though the entire prayer was addressed to the Father. Like other fourth-century compositions these prayers were the result of the addition of several layers of prayer to various primitive traditions and in various combinations.

(b) *East Syrian*. Even though it has been argued that elements of the East Syrian Anaphora of Addai and Mari reach back to the third century, in its developed form this prayer is more appropriately described among compositions of the classic families. This prayer is still in use in the Church of the East (commonly called Nestorian) together with two other anaphoras, of Nestorius and Theodore the Interpreter (of Mopsuestia). Its structure differs significantly from that of the West Syrian tradition: dialogue; praise and thanks to the Trinity; introduction to the Sanctus; Sanctus; post-Sanctus thanksgiving (addressed to Christ); intercession for the dead and the living (addressed to the Father and with offering); anamnesis (memorial); epiclesis (invocation on offering and communicants); doxology; Amen.

The lack of clear logical progression of ideas has led some scholars to think that this text was originally configured differently. It certainly shows signs of various prayers being pieced together. The core of this prayer (which shares much with a Maronite anaphora – the third anaphora of St Peter) may well go back to the third century. It almost certainly precedes the separation of churches after the Council of Ephesus in 431. Most remarkable in this anaphora is the absence of an institution narrative, which we have seen is a common feature of ante-Nicene eucharistic prayers.

(c) *Alexandrian*. A third important family stems from Alexandria. The major representative outlined here is the anaphora of St Mark. This prayer has verbal and structural similarities with the Papyrus Strasbourg Gk 254 as well as a number of other fragments. It is also clearly related to a fourth-century prayer, that of Bishop Sarapion of Thmuis. The developed version of this prayer follows the following structure: dialogue; praise for creation; offering (on the basis of Mal. 1.11); intercessions (quite lengthy); introduction to Sanctus; Sanctus (with no Benedictus); post-Sanctus (beginning with the word 'full'); first epiclesis; institution narrative; anamnesis; second offering; second epiclesis; doxology; Amen.

The reduplication of both offering and epiclesis here lends credence to the theory that in the development of these prayer-traditions elements are regularly added to already existing prayers. It is thus possible to regard the first part of this prayer – up to the Sanctus – as a complete prayer in and of itself.

(d) *Roman*. Probably no single eucharistic prayer has ever been employed more than the prayer of the Roman rite. In contrast to the traditions we have surveyed above, this prayer-tradition always involves a variable first part of the prayer, i.e., up to the Sanctus. This part has been called the preface (although it is likely that *praefatio* originally referred to a publicly declaimed prayer, and thus the entire prayer). The Sanctus seems not to have been original to this prayer but rather added sometime during the fifth century. The form which this single rule of prayer (*canon*) achieved by the late sixth century is as follows: dialogue; variable thanksgiving (*Vere dignum*); introduction to Sanctus; Sanctus and Benedictus; prayer for acceptance of offering (*Te igitur*); memorial of the living (*Memento, Domine*); commemoration of saints (*Communicantes*); second prayer

for acceptance (*Hanc igitur*); prayer for consecration (*Quam oblationem*); institution narrative (*Qui pridie*); anamnesis and offering (*Unde et memores*); third prayer for acceptance (*Supra quae*); second prayer for consecration (*Supplices te*); memorial of the dead (*Memento etiam*); second commemoration of saints (*Nobis quoque*); blessing of other gifts (*Per quem*); doxology (*Per ipsum*); Amen.

From the late-fourth-century sermons of Ambrose of Milan we know that the Roman canon had by then assumed its basic shape in Latin. In its multiplication of the same kind of prayer (especially the prayer for consecration which functions like an epiclesis), the Roman canon is reminiscent of the anaphora of St Mark. Except for the preface, the prayer tends to read like a long plea for the acceptance of the eucharistic sacrifice. This gives the prayer a distinctly epicletic, as opposed to anamnetic, character.

(e) *Gallican*. The Latin church knew more than one tradition of eucharistic praying. Broadly termed Gallican, this tradition covers modern-day France and Germany as well as the Iberian peninsula (the so-called Visigothic or Mozarabic rites). This tradition employed yet another strategy in composing its prayers. Each prayer as a whole consisted of three variable prayers inserted into a structure of four fixed prayers (dialogue, Sanctus, institution narrative, and doxology) thus: dialogue; praise (*Contestatio, Immolatio*); introduction to Sanctus; Sanctus; post-Sanctus; institution narrative (*Secreta*); post-secreta (*Post pridie*); doxology; Amen.

Some of the Gallican or Visigothic prayers seem to predate the Roman canon even though they are all found in collections of later manuscripts. These prayers tend to be more florid and verbose than the style of prayer found in the Roman rite. In the fashion of Antiochene prayers, God is petitioned only after the institution narrative. Intercessions (in the form of the recital of names) took place before the dialogue.

By the end of late antiquity the various Christian rites had taken shape and with them traditions of eucharistic prayer. With the exception of the anaphora of Addai and Mari (which lacks the institution narrative), all of the major traditions included the following elements, though in different combinations and sequence: dialogue, praise and thanksgiving, Sanctus, institution narrative, Spirit epiclesis, intercessions, doxology and concluding Amen.

As we have seen, however, these elements came together from a variety of sources (some perhaps not even in the context of meal-prayer; e.g. Sanctus). There was no original eucharistic prayer nor most probably an original structure or pattern of eucharistic prayer.

5. *Reformation*. The sixteenth-century Reformers dealt with the eucharistic prayer in various ways, but all were heirs of a medieval theology that held the institution narrative to be consecratory and thus the centre of the prayer.

In his *Formula of Mass and Communion* (1523) Martin Luther retained the preface (at least the beginning of the preface) but omitted the entire Roman canon except for the institution narrative. His reasoning was that the canon was filled with works-righteousness. Only the institution narrative offered gospel forgiveness in the forms of Christ's own words. From what we have seen of the early tradition of eucharistic praying this move was ironic. At the end of the institution narrative the Sanctus and Benedictus were sung with the elements elevated during the Benedictus.

In the *German Mass* (1526) Luther eliminated the preface and further divided the institution narrative by encouraging the distribution of the consecrated bread and wine separately after each part of the institution narrative. They were accompanied by German versions of the Sanctus and *Agnus Dei or other German hymns. Luther was careful to couch his liturgical reforms in the language of recommendation rather than legislation. Therefore the various Lutheran German church orders adopted diverse approaches to the reform of the eucharistic prayer.

Ulrich Zwingli differed with Luther not only over eucharistic theology but also with regard to the shape and nature of eucharistic prayer. In his *Attack on the Roman Canon* (1523) he provided four extensive prayers following a preface and Sanctus. The first of these prayers was a memorial of God's action in Christ. The *Lord's Prayer followed and then three prayers that could loosely be characterized as epicletic, ending with an institution narrative and the distribution of the elements. These prayers were replaced two years later by a shorter prayer followed by recitation of the institution narrative and distribution.

One of the earliest Reformed theologians to develop a eucharistic rite was Martin Bucer of Strasbourg. In his service of 1539 he provided three sample prayers, each concluding with the Lord's Prayer and then the institution narrative. In all of these prayers many of the traditional elements (thanksgiving, anamnesis, epiclesis) were replaced by intercession and petition for worthy reception.

In John Calvin's *Geneva Service* (1542) intercessions were placed after the sermon and before the *creed. The institution narrative was then read after the elements had been placed on the table. There followed a rather long exhortation, the distribution of the elements and a postcommunion thanksgiving prayer. Therefore the eucharistic prayer, in the strict sense of the term, had been removed to a place after the reception of communion. John Knox's *Form of Prayers* (1556) followed Calvin's pattern up to the reading of the institution narrative. There followed an exhortation which effectively excommunicated the unworthy and a eucharistic prayer with thanks and praise for creation and redemption concluding with a doxology.

The sixteenth-century forms of the English *BCP* were more traditional in their approach. In the 1549 book Archbishop Cranmer retained a reformed version of the Roman canon. Reacting to the Catholic interpretation of this effort, Cranmer produced a more radical eucharistic prayer in 1552. The dialogue, preface and Sanctus were retained, but now the 'Prayer of Humble Access' was moved from a point immediately before communion to the end of the Sanctus. The consecratory epiclesis of 1549 was removed but Cranmer retained an element of petition before the institution. His most radical move was to introduce the distribution of communion immediately after the words of institution. After the elements were consumed the Lord's Prayer was said and then the oblationary part of the 1549 prayer concluding with the doxology and Amen. Thus Cranmer (unwittingly) restored a very primitive pattern of eucharistic prayer which placed the weight of prayer after, not before, the consumption of the sacred meal.

6. *Modern Reforms*. A revival of biblical and patristic studies in the twentieth century has had significant results in the reform of eucharistic prayers. At this point most Western Christian traditions have reformed their liturgical books. Perhaps the most significant change has been in the RC Church, which abandoned the fifteen-hundred-year tradition of having only one eucharistic prayer for a number of prayers. Currently ten prayers are approved for use and over one hundred prefaces may be used

in combination with the body of five of those prayers. Unlike a number of other communions which opted strongly for adoption of the Antiochene pattern of prayer, the RC rite employs prayers which have a 'consecratory' epiclesis before the institution narrative. (The first eucharistic prayer is the old Roman canon, and some may not be willing to regard its first prayer for consecration as epicletic.) In addition the Roman tradition has added an acclamation to Christ after the institution narrative. Two of the eucharistic prayers for use with children contain multiple acclamations throughout.

In the course of the past thirty years a number of churches have followed suit in reforming their eucharistic prayers. The Evangelical Lutheran Church of America, for example, has four eucharistic prayers in its 1978 *Lutheran Book of Worship*, thus reversing a long tradition of letting the words of institution stand free of a prayer context. This church adopted the Antiochene pattern of eucharistic prayer. In a similar fashion the United Methodist Church (USA) now has twenty-two eucharistic prayers on the Antiochene pattern in its book of worship. The Church of England has adopted eight new eucharistic prayers. These prayers follow diverse patterns. Three of them follow the pattern of *The Alternative Service Book 1980*. Like the Roman prayers they have an epiclesis before the institution narrative. Four of the other prayers follow the Antiochene pattern. One prayer was written with the presence of children in mind. Another is 'interactive', with about a third of the prayer said by the people. This prayer concludes with the Sanctus. One prayer is based on the Alexandrian form of the anaphora of St Basil; another is an adaptation of a prayer proposed by the RC International Commission on English in the Liturgy but never officially approved. Four of the prayers offer the opportunity for a number of acclamations throughout.

7. *Remaining Issues for the Churches.*

(a) The expression of eucharistic offering or sacrifice is an ongoing question. The twentieth-century theology of memorial (anamnesis) has greatly aided the search for ecumenical reconciliation on this subject but difficulties remain in the prayer texts. For example, the RC Eucharistic Prayer IV has a thoroughly untraditional expression of sacrifice in that it offers Christ's 'body and blood', instead of 'the gifts' or 'the cup and the bread'. Another solution

with a venerable tradition behind it (reaching back at least to Irenaeus in the second century) is the notion of a sacrifice of praise and thanksgiving. The United Methodist (USA) texts capture this well with their anamnesis and offering: 'And so, in remembrance of these your mighty acts in Jesus Christ, we offer ourselves as a holy and living sacrifice, in union with Christ's offering for us, as we proclaim the mystery of faith: Christ has died . . .'

(b) Most contemporary eucharistic prayers contain a memorial acclamation (e.g. 'Christ has died . . .') after the institution narrative. Some churches, including the United Methodist prayers noted above, place that acclamation after the anamnesis and offering, thus de-emphasizing a consecratory understanding of the institution narrative. In addition the employment of acclamations throughout the entire prayer might enhance a congregation's participation in what otherwise can become a dull monologue.

(c) Contemporary theology tends to affirm the entire eucharistic prayer (rather than a specific moment in it) as consecratory. Thus the longstanding debate between East and West as to whether the epiclesis or institution narrative is consecratory has been somewhat relativized. In terms of eucharistic prayers themselves, however, much will depend on the position of epiclesis and institution narrative vis-à-vis one another. The best solution might be for individual churches to employ several structures of eucharistic prayer. In addition experiment is called for with brief prayers consisting of blessing, thanksgiving and petition after some of the earliest patterns.

(d) The *posture of the assembly and the *gestures of its presiding minister have a significant effect on the perceived meaning of a eucharistic prayer. An assembly standing with arms raised and outstretched in the traditional *orans* position and a president of the assembly who does not diverge from that gesture suggests a different understanding than that of an assembly on its knees and a president at the altar imitating the (supposed) actions of Christ during the Last Supper.

(e) The most intractable problem with eucharistic praying may be the difficulty in encouraging members of the assembly to include their own thanksgivings in the church's great thanksgiving. Perhaps provision could be made for inviting them to include their own motives for gratitude to God either silently or aloud in the context of the prayer itself.

Eucharistic praying has had a rich and varied history from Christian beginnings to the present. Although consensus is developing among the churches as to the nature and function of the eucharistic prayer, it is to be hoped that the various communions will continue to produce varied and powerful texts for enabling God's people to express their praise and thanks for what has been done in Christ, for what is done at the holy table, and for its overflow to the rest of the world.

Selected texts: ancient prayers in their original languages in Anton Hänggi and Irmgard Pahl (eds), *Prex Eucharistica*, 3rd edn, Freibourg 1998; Reformation prayers in Irmgard Pahl (ed.), *Coena Domini*, Freiburg 1983; convenient collections in English in R. C. D. Jasper and G. J. Cuming (eds), *Prayers of the Eucharist: Early and Reformed*, 3rd edn, New York 1987; Bard Thompson, *Liturgies of the Western Church*, Cleveland 1961.

The secondary literature on this topic is enormous. Helpful guides with bibliography include Paul Bradshaw (ed.), *Essays on Early Eastern Eucharistic Prayers*, Collegeville 1997; Enrico Mazza, *The Eucharistic Prayers of the Roman Rite*, New York 1986; *The Origins of the Eucharistic Prayer*, Collegeville 1995; Frank Senn (ed.), *New Eucharistic Prayers*, New York 1987.

JOHN F. BALDOVIN

Eucharistic Theologies

1. *Historical.* Historical debates about the meaning of the *eucharist have centred around two principal themes: sacrifice and presence.

1.1. *Sacrifice.* Unquestionably, some NT writers had already begun to interpret Christ's death soteriologically, i.e., as a divinely willed salvific event, not merely a shameful miscarriage of justice or the murder of God's anointed, eschatological prophet (see Heb. 9; Phil. 2; Gal. 6.14). It was perhaps a short step from affirming the soteriological significance of Christ's cross to affirming a sacrificial understanding of the '*Lord's supper' which 'proclaims the Lord's death until he comes' (1 Cor. 11.26). The early church order known as the *Didache*, composed perhaps before the end of the first century CE, uses the Greek word *thusia* ('sacrifice') in relation to *eucharist, but it never directly links the community's liturgy on the 'Lord's Day' to Christ's death on the cross (14.1–3). Indeed, the table prayers of *Didache* 9–10 do not mention Christ's cross and passion at all. (Similarly, *Didache* 7 makes no attempt – as Paul does in Rom. 6.3–11 – to interpret baptism as union with Christ's death.) In contrast, the *eucharistic prayer found in the early-third-century church order known as the *Apostolic Tradition* speaks explicitly of Christ's saving cross and death, although it does not directly call the community's 'offering' a sacrifice. Thus, even though *Apostolic Tradition* 3–4 describes the *bishop's ministry as a 'high priesthood', it does not number sacrifice among his duties, but it does mention his offering 'the gifts' of the church. Neither of these church orders can be considered liturgically 'normative' in any modern sense, though they appear to have been widely translated and sometimes quoted (in whole or in part) in later church orders and canons.

Still, there do exist early Christian documents that link eucharist, sacrifice and Christian service understood as a 'priesthood'. The early Christians understood the whole of their lives, and consequently every act of worship and prayer, as a sacrificial offering to God (see Rom. 12.1; Heb. 13.15–16). Not surprisingly, therefore, they viewed the eucharist as their pre-eminent offering of the sacrifice of praise, and in their disputes with Jews claimed that it was the true fulfilment of the prophecy in Mal.1.11, the offering made in every place, because Jewish sacrifices had been restricted to the Temple (see Justin Martyr, *Dialogue with Trypho* 41). Alongside this idea they also began to interpret the bread and wine they brought from home for the service as being the fulfilment of the material elements which were offered to God in the OT (*Dialogue with Trypho* 41.3; 117.2), and because they also understood the eucharist as a memorial of the sacrificial death of Christ, it was not long before a connection began to be made between these various notions, so that the rite was viewed as what we might call a memorial sacrifice. Thus Justin notes that 'God accepts sacrifices from no one except through his priests. Therefore, God has in advance proclaimed that all sacrifices offered in his name are pleasing to him, as commanded by Jesus Christ, i.e., in the eucharist of the bread and the cup which is offered in every place throughout the world by Christians' (*Dialogue with Trypho* 116.3–117.1; the term 'priests' in this passage probably means 'the whole priestly family' of God, rather than the clergy.) Irenaeus of Lyons (*c.* 180 CE) explicitly calls the 'oblation offered

by the church' a 'pure sacrifice' (*Adv. haer.*
IV.18.1), and by the middle of the following
century (*c*. 250 CE), Latin Christianity in North
Africa, as represented by Bishop Cyprian of
Carthage, affirms the ministry of the bishop
(described as a priest, *sacerdos*) who acts 'in
the place of Christ' (*uice Christi*) and, at the
eucharist, 'offers in the church of God a real
and complete sacrifice' (*Letter* 63.14). Cyprian
also acknowledges that a 'valid hallowing' of
'the Lord's sacrifice' requires that 'oblation
and . . . sacrifice correspond to the passion',
because the eucharist is the '*sacrament of the
Lord's suffering and our redemption' (*Letter*
63.9, 14). Importing the OT language of priesthood and sacrifice, Cyprian thus interprets the
Christian eucharist as a sacrificial 'sacrament
of Christ's passion', presided over by the
bishop who acts in place of Christ.

In the East, sacrificial language applied to
the offering of the eucharist is also present: e.g.
the eucharistic prayer of *Apostolic Constitutions* (VIII.12.39) speaks of 'this sacrifice, a
witness to the sufferings of the Lord Jesus'; the
anaphora of James speaks of offering 'you,
Almighty One, this fearful and unbloody sacrifice'; and the anaphora of John Chrysostom
speaks of offering to God 'this rational,
unbloody worship'. Because the bread and
wine were believed to become the body and
blood of Christ, fourth-century writers use
language that identifies the offering of the
bread and wine very closely with the sacrifice
of Christ. For example, Cyril of Jerusalem
states that, 'we offer Christ who has been slain
for our sins' (*Mystagogical Catechesis* 5.10)
and Gregory Nazianzus says that 'you sacrifice
the Master's body and blood with bloodless
knife' (*Ep.* 171).

Medieval Latin theology's preoccupation
with the sacrificial aspects of eucharist developed in part from a tendency to separate
'sacrifice' from 'sacrament', and 'consecration' from the church's 'offering' and *communion. This trend reached a peak in the
thought of Gabriel Biel (d. 1495), who (following Duns Scotus) argued that the priest *conse-
crates* the gifts *in persona Chrsti* and *offers* the
sacrifice of the mass *in persona ecclesiae*.

1.2. *Real Presence*. Far more complex and
controverted, however, was the related sacramental question of Christ's presence in the
eucharist. Christian testimonies to the eucharistic presence of Christ's body and blood were
early and abundant. Ignatius of Antioch chided
those who do not confess that 'the eucharist

is the flesh of our Saviour Jesus Christ, who
suffered for our sins and whom the Father
raised up' (*Smyrn.* 7). Similarly Justin Martyr
calls the eucharist 'the flesh and blood of that
Jesus who was made flesh' (*First Apology* 66).
In a similarly realistic vein, Chrysostom writes
in his treatise *On the Priesthood* (III.4.176–7):
'When you see the Lord sacrificed and lying
[on the altar], and the high priest standing by
the victim and praying over it, and everyone
stained red with the precious blood . . . are you
not carried off to heaven?'

But what did such language mean, and how
was Christ's presence accomplished? For centuries in the West, theologians tried to maintain
the realism of Christ's somatic presence in the
sacrament without falling into the notion of a
purely natural, materialistic idea of eating and
drinking Christ's body and blood. As Augustine memorably expressed it, Christ's body and
blood are real meat and drink, but this food is
'not flesh torn in strips from a corpse, or as it is
sold in a butcher shop' (*On John* 27.5; cited
by Thomas Aquinas in *Summa Theologica*
IIIa.75.1, ad. 1).

In the ninth century, the first systematic
treatise on the eucharist resulted from a controversy between two monks from the monastery
of Corbie, Paschasius Radbertus (*c*. 785–*c*. 860)
and Ratramnus (died *c*. 868). Both monks
attempted to defend the notion of Christ's real
presence in the eucharist. Radbertus relied
upon extremely realistic and physical explanations, while Ratramnus favoured a more
spiritualized view. But church officials were
uncomfortable with the latter's subtle distinction between Christ's actual historical body and
the 'figure' of Christ's body and blood in the
eucharistic species. In the eleventh century the
controversy arose anew, again within a French
monastic context, owing to Berengarius of
Tours (*c*. 1000–88), who held that the relationship of Christ to the eucharist resembles the
relationship of smoke to fire. Although smoke
points to fire, the two remain distinct. Opposed
by Lanfranc of Bec (who seems to have coined
the term 'transubstantiation'), Berengarius was
summoned to a synod in Rome (1059), where
he was required to recant his views about
Christ's eucharistic presence through an oath,
in which he swore that Christ's body and
blood are 'sensually and not only sacramentally
present, touched and broken by the hands of the
priest and torn by the teeth of the faithful'.

Such controversies helped move the discussion of Christ's 'real presence' in new, more

philosophical directions. At the Fourth Lateran Council (1215), in response to the Cathars in the south of France who denied the goodness of anything physical in favour of the spiritual, the language of 'transubstantial change' (though not yet the noun *transubstantiatio*) first appears in an official church document. In the work of Thomas Aquinas (d. 1274), however, the noun *transubstantiatio* acquires more technical precision as an explanation for how the bread and wine could change without changing their outer perceptible form or accidents. As Aquinas understood it, transubstantiation does not mean that the 'substance' of bread is replaced by the (camouflaged) 'substance' of the flesh of Christ; it signifies, rather, a far more radical change – from 'non-existence' to 'existence' (on a parallel with God's act of creating ex nihilo). What is changed is not 'stuff', but the nature of change itself – at and by God's initiative at work in the sacramental signs. Despite its widespread use, the term 'transubstantiation' was not adopted officially by the Roman Church until the Council of Trent (Session 13, 1551). Trent's formula is quoted in the 1994 *Catechism of the Catholic Church* (sect. 1376), which, however, begins its discussion of real presence by noting that Christ is 'present in many ways to his Church: in his word, in his Church's prayer . . . in the poor, the sick, and the imprisoned, in the sacraments . . . in the sacrifice of the Mass . . . in the person of the minister . . . but . . . most especially in the Eucharistic species' (sect. 1373). The term 'real presence' is 'not intended to exclude the other types of presence' (sect. 1374).

1.3. *The Reformation*. While the Protestant Reformers of the sixteenth century were highly critical of the late medieval Roman mass (especially its interpretation as a 'propitiatory sacrifice'), they refused simply to reject all notions of 'sacrament' and 'presence'. Luther's early views on the eucharist (and on the need for liturgical reform) often read like a pastoral commentary on the Thomist principle, *sacramenta propter homines* ('sacraments exist for the sake of people'). Thus, for instance, Luther explicitly affirmed Christ's presence in the eucharist, but at the same time he protested the papal tyranny over the mass which denied lay people access to 'the complete sacrament' by withholding the cup from them. Luther was convinced that the communion of the people is an essential part of the eucharist as it was instituted by Christ. In this, Luther sought to reaffirm an early (and even medieval) Christian notion, that the eucharist is radically 'communitarian and corporate', and that this truth can be embodied only if the people actually receive communion at every eucharist (hence his hostility to 'private masses').

For Luther, moreover, 'communion' and 'sacrifice' were incompatible notions, when applied to eucharist. Even in Israel, Luther argued, the people did not 'sacrifice' God's covenant; they *received* it (as the Law on Mount Sinai). So too, the Christian covenant between God and humanity is not a 'sacrifice', but the gospel itself, preached in truth and heard in faith. The Christian offering is not 'sacrifice', but a call to faith and obedience in the word of God. Thus, the word – summarized in the eucharistic words of Jesus, proclaimed and preached at every mass – becomes the authentic centre of Christian worship.

John Calvin also affirmed that 'there is truly offered to us in the Supper a communion with [Christ's] body and blood – or (what amounts to the same thing) there is set before us a pledge, under the bread and wine, which makes us participants in the body and blood of Christ' (*Corpus reformatorum* IX, 519). While Luther and Calvin thus agreed that to eat and drink the eucharist is really to participate in Christ's body and blood, they reached this conclusion from different starting points. Luther had begun from the twin convictions (a) that Christ's words ('eat . . . drink') are a 'summary of the gospel', and hence constitute God's unfailing word of promise to sinful humanity, and (b) that the people's communion is essential to the sacramental action as instituted by Christ. Calvin's eucharistic doctrine, on the other hand, flowed from his conviction of God's absolute sovereignty (hence any theory of sacrament that might 'bind' or 'limit' God's action and presence must be rejected). Calvin wished to affirm that Christ is really present to people as they participate in the eucharist, but he opposed any view of 'presence' that would diminish God's freedom, make the Spirit 'captive' to the church's activity in the sacraments, or confine Christ (who has 'ascended' on high) locally to the species of bread and wine.

Still another view was championed by Ulrich Zwingli (died 1531), a popular Zurich pastor for whom the chief eucharistic question was not 'What happens to the elements?' but rather, 'What happens to the community?' when the eucharist is celebrated. Like Luther and (later) Calvin, Zwingli affirmed that 'the bread and wine become the body and blood of Christ to those who partake of them in faith'. This presence of Christ was not, however, the result of human intention or action, for the eucharist, Zwingli believed, was not an event where 'we sacrifice or offer to God', but one wherein 'God gives generously to us'. For that reason, the 'place' of eucharist is not an 'altar' (denoting sacrifice) but a 'table' (denoting God's act of feeding a hungry humanity).

In England, a similar emphasis on the communion of the people appeared in the *BCP*s of 1549 and 1552 drawn up by Archbishop Thomas Cranmer. Thus, Luther, Calvin, Zwingli and Cranmer all agreed on communion as essential to the eucharist as established by Christ. Less certain is how – or if – these Reformers agreed on the notion of Christ's 'real presence' in the sacrament. Cranmer's view, for instance, appears to have evolved over time. His mature position seems to have been that, while Christ is 'locally' (hence, corporally) seated at God's right hand in heaven, his presence in the Lord's supper, while 'true', must be spiritual. Such a view does not, of course, reduce the consecrated bread and wine of the eucharist to the status of 'nude signs' or 'bare tokens'. Rather, it suggests that Christ's presence is neither 'natural' nor 'carnal' (Augustine and Aquinas would probably have agreed), but precisely spiritual and supernatural – a reality that results not from human work or sacerdotal power but from God's faithful, loving care.

1.4. *Later Roman Catholicism*. In response to the Protestant Reformation, the Council of Trent (Session 22, 1562) insisted, in four canons, that: (a) the mass is a real and true sacrifice; (b) it was instituted by Christ, who also established a priesthood whose chief duty is to offer his body and blood; (c) the sacrifice of the mass is propitiatory, and so can bring to both the living and the dead pardon and satisfaction for sins; and (d) the mass in no way detracts from the sacrifice of the cross. Trent's assertions were clear, but they left many unanswered questions (e.g. *how* does all this happen?). The Second Vatican Council incorporated a passage from Trent's *Doctrina de ss. missae sacrificio* in its Constitution on the Liturgy (1963), noting that 'Christ is always present in his Church, especially in her liturgical celebrations. He is present in the Sacrifice of the Mass, not only in the person of his minister, "the same now offering, through the ministry of priests, who formerly offered himself on the cross" [Trent] but especially in the

eucharistic species' (7). In this way, Vatican II reaffirmed the sacrificial character of eucharist, but linked it much more closely (a) to the larger liturgical and sacramental life of Christians; (b) to Christ's many modes of presence within the Church; and (c) to Christ himself as the principal agent in all sacramental signs and celebrations.

Both Trent and Vatican II affirmed that the perfect, efficacious, once-for-all sacrifice of Christ on the cross can never be repeated, diminished, augmented or supplemented (see Heb. 9.11–18). It was thus their conviction that the eucharist is 'sacrificial' because it expresses, in the visible, sacramental signs of the church's liturgy, Christ's unique, historical self-offering on the cross. And since, in biblical and patristic perspectives, no sacrifice is complete without a meal, *communion* (and not only the 'consecration' of the gifts) is also integral to the notion of eucharistic sacrifice. Hence also, the eucharist may be understood as a *conclusive* sacrifice, which – through the act of communion – declares an end to the ancient human cycle of violence, victimization and appeasement.

Edward J. Kilmartin, *The Eucharist in the West*, Collegeville 1998; Gary Macy, *The Theologies of the Eucharist in the Early Scholastic Period*, New York 1984; *Treasures from the Storeroom: Medieval Religion and the Eucharist*, Collegeville 1999; Nathan Mitchell, *Real Presence: The Work of Eucharist*, 2nd edn, Chicago 2001; Miri Rubin, *Corpus Christi: The Eucharist in Late Medieval Culture*, New York 1991.

NATHAN MITCHELL

2. *Modern*. Seven key theological issues have structured much of eucharistic theology in recent decades.

2.1. The relationship of the eucharist as *sacrament to a theology of church as sacrament and to the humanity of Jesus as sacrament was developed by O. Semmelroth, K. Rahner and E. Schillebeeckx. Vatican II incorporated the understanding of church as a foundational sacrament into its own vision. Sacramentally, the theological relationship between church and eucharist as well as Jesus and eucharist both widen and deepen an understanding of the eucharist as sacrament. A deeper church–eucharist relationship is also stressed by the recent emphasis on the relationship of *baptism to eucharist. There can be no baptismal theology today which is not essentially related to eucharistic theology, and there can be no eucharistic theology today which is not essentially related to baptismal theology. Every theological presentation of a church–eucharist interconnection struggles today with the issue: which meaning of church is one talking about? An overarching universal church including all Christian communities is a theological abstraction. The same is true of a theology of a universal internal or spiritual church. The very term, church, is applied to *Anglican, Protestant, *RC and *Orthodox communities. Inter-church acceptance and toleration may be considerably greater today, but there is also an ecclesiological exclusivity in the theologies of many churches. The current reality of an inclusive–exclusive understanding of church decreases the clarity of the theological statement that the church is a foundational sacrament. Whose church is foundational? If eucharist and church are seen as intrinsically interrelated, the lack of clarity on church necessarily involves lack of clarity on eucharist.

2.2. The theology of the word and the theology of the eucharist are seen as intimately connected. The emphasis on the word has pleased Protestants and has at times confused Catholics. Today, theologians often speak of the eucharist of the word and the eucharist of the meal. Theologically, the key to this polar understanding is the meaning of presence, especially real presence. There is a real presence of Jesus and the Spirit in the word, and there is a real presence of Jesus and the Spirit in the eucharistic meal. How these two presences are theologically interrelated remains an open question.

2.3. The role of the Holy Spirit is more pronounced in Western theology of the eucharist than in the past. Virtually all new eucharistic rites, whether Protestant or Catholic, have a distinct *epiclesis in the central *eucharistic prayer. This theological emphasis on the role of the Holy Spirit is welcomed by those in the Calvinist (*Reformed) tradition and by those in the Orthodox tradition, since in both of these traditions the Holy Spirit is central to their theological presentation on the eucharist. This emphasis has christological ramifications as well, since only within a Spirit-Christology, not just within a word Christology, are both an understanding of Jesus and an understanding of eucharistic theology meaningful.

2.4. The gathered community is foundational to eucharistic theology. A Christian community celebrates eucharist, or as the *Catechism of the Catholic Church* remarkably states: eucharistic 'liturgy is an "action" of the whole Christ (*Christus totus*) . . . It is the whole community, the Body of Christ united to its head, that celebrates' (sect. 1136). Communion and fellowship in the bread and wine was one of the major eucharistic emphases of the Reformation. The emphasis on the common priesthood of all believers has, as yet, not been theologically presented in a way that is acceptable to both Protestant and Catholic. Still, the emphasis on community is a major component in developing today's eucharistic theology and has serious ramifications for the way in which one understands the ordained priesthood. *Koinonia* or sharing has been proposed as a starting point for eucharistic theology and spirituality. Sharing not only suggests the communal setting for the celebration of eucharist, but it also brings together two basic aspects of the entire mystery: the eucharist strengthens and deepens the bonds of community, but also eucharistic sharing means that one must divide, separate and give to another what is shared, and this denotes the self-giving of Christian life. In this self-giving of oneself to others in the eucharist there is as well a sacrament of the one sacrifice of Jesus, who gave himself for others. A Christian community includes *children and this involves a reconsideration of their exclusion from both baptism and eucharist. The role of *women in the eucharistic community is also profoundly important today.

2.5. The eucharist of the altar and the eucharist of the world are terms used in some contemporary eucharistic theologies. This cosmic dimension of the eucharist is not new, since some of the early fathers also wrote in this way, e.g. Maximus the Confessor. Today some authors have reclaimed the term 'cosmic eucharist'. There is a noteworthy renewed interest in the eschatological reality of eucharistic celebration, and every current eschatological movement leads to the final days when the entire world, the cosmos, is renewed. Eucharistic celebration is an anticipated celebration of this final cosmic transformation. The churches of the first three or four centuries had a deep sense of this eschatological dimension in the eucharist, but as time went by and the end of the world did not come, a focus on this dimension in the eucharist faded. In later years only a few Christian groups here and there, such as the Franciscan spirituals in the thirteenth and fourteenth centuries and the Anabaptists of the sixteenth century, maintained this eschatological centring of Christian faith and worship. The Reformation itself did not emphasize an eschatological eucharist. In modern times, however, a strong eschatological tone has entered into the eucharistic celebrations of Anglicans, *Lutherans, *Methodists and RCs. In these churches eucharistic celebration is an eschatological celebration of the 'now and not yet' presence of the divine.

2.6. Eucharistic liturgy today is being radically re-envisioned and practised by the multicultural dimensions of eucharistic Christians. The celebration of the eucharist in various languages is only a first step, and a small one at that, as far as a multicultural eucharist is concerned. The incorporation of cultural symbols and actions is more than a first step, and almost all contemporary Christian communities include cultural hymns, prayers and liturgical movements. In certain areas of the world, eucharistic liturgies are celebrated in an almost totally ethnic way. In the western world, eucharistic celebrations combine various ethnic musical elements, prayers and movements, leaving the eucharistic celebrations rather eclectic. A radical rethinking of both the theology and ritual of the eucharist within philosophies and world views other than the western Euro-American framework is slowly taking place. A radical inculturation of the eucharist did take place with the Hellenization of Christian life. A less radical inculturation of the eucharist took place during the Carolingian reformation. The many orthodox churches of early Christianity branched out into a number of dimensions. In today's *inculturation process the Euro-American framework continues to act as the benchmark for all other theological interpretations or ritual practices. This is an unhealthy situation and will not last. Rather, one must think through a theology of the eucharist, for example within Chinese philosophical and religious terms, and one must celebrate the eucharist in the context of these terms. This step is only beginning as we enter the new millennium, but the momentum to move in this direction is strong.

2.7. Postmodern thought has challenged Western sacramental theology in a major way. Not only are Aristotelian and scholastic thought categories called into question, but the entire world view of the Enlightenment has also been challenged. A slow but clear deconstruction of these thought forms has already begun in the West, and a slow reconstruction of Western ways of thinking has begun. This reconstruction is not only epistemological but it is also ontological. A new way of understanding human thought and, more profoundly, of human existence itself has been gradually developed by Husserl, Heidegger, Merleau-Ponty, Ricoeur and Gadamer, to mention only a few. Human experience is central to this new reconstruction. When this is applied to the sacraments, we see that only in the actual existential celebration of a sacrament is there sacramental reality. All writings on sacraments, including this one, are about sacraments. Each actual sacramental celebration is, however, unique and unrepeatable. The search for an essence of the eucharist is, in this view, meaningless. There are in actuality only a diverse multiplicity of eucharistic celebrations, each involving individual communities, individual persons, individual co-ordinates of space and time. In these actual celebrations, the divine enters into a deepening relationship with the Christian and each Christian responds in his or her unique way to the blessing of divine presence.

See also **Theology of Worship.**

Marcus Barth, *Rediscovering the Lord's Supper*, Atlanta 1988; William Crockett, *Eucharist: Symbol of Transformation*, New York 1989; Horton Davies, *Bread of Life and Cup of Joy: Newer Ecumenical Perspectives on the Eucharist*, Grand Rapids 1993; Regis Duffy, 'Sacraments in General', *Systematic Theology* II, ed. Francis Schüssler Fiorenza and John P. Galvin, Minneapolis 1991, 181–210; Dermot Lane, 'Eschatology', and Raymond Moloney, 'Eucharist', *The New Dictionary of Theology*, ed. Joseph A. Komonchak, Mary Collins and Dermot A. Lane, Wilmington, DE 1987, 329–55; Kenan B. Osborne, 'Eucharistic Theology Today', *Alternative Futures for Worship* III, ed. Bernard J. Lee, Collegeville 1987, 85–113; David Power, *The Eucharistic Mystery: Revitalizing the Tradition*, New York 1995; Laurence Stookey, *Eucharist: Christ's Feast with the Church*, Nashville 1993.

KENAN B. OSBORNE

Evangelical Church Worship

see **Independent Evangelical Church Worship**

Evensong see **Daily Prayer**

Exorcism, Exorcist

In Christian liturgy and theology an exorcism is the church's prayer in the name of Jesus Christ that a person or object be protected against the power of the evil one and withdrawn from his dominion. Exorcism was practised in many ancient cultures and is found in late Judaism (e.g. Tobit 6.8; 8.2; Mark 9.38; Luke 11.19; Acts 19.13). Jesus performed exorcisms and from him his disciples and the church received the power and office of exorcising (see Mark 1.25–26; 3.15; 6.7; 13; 16.17; Luke 11.14–23; Acts 16.18). In popular understanding exorcism generally refers to the driving out of a demon who has possessed a person. The RC Church however, according to the 1983 Code of Canon Law, is reluctant to admit supernatural possession in particular cases, since most apparent cases can be explained by pathological conditions (Canon 1172). Both modern biblical scholarship and current psychological theory and practice are inclined to admit a supernatural explanation only when a natural explanation has been proven impossible. A practical indication of this reluctance is the 1972 abolition of the office of exorcist with other *minor orders.

Historically, two basic types of exorcism developed in the church in the West. The first, solemn exorcism, called 'a major exorcism', involved freeing persons from obsessive spiritual conditions thought to derive from evil powers or diabolical spirits. Such solemn exorcisms came to be restricted, in time, to *bishops or to priests with explicit episcopal permission. Today in the RC Church, only a priest with the permission of the bishop can perform the solemn exorcism. The priest must proceed with prudence, strictly observing the rules established by the church. More common are exorcisms of the second type: ritual prayers for adult *catechumens, associated with the process of Christian initiation. Such exorcisms already are found in early Christian documents like the *Apostolic Tradition* attributed to Hippolytus, which directs the bishop to exorcise the catechumens on the day before their baptism. Similar prayers of exorcism were retained, even when increasingly, after the fourth century, the majority of candidates for baptism were infants.

Exorcisms in the form of prayers for protection from evil do remain in the RC *baptism rituals. The Rite of Baptism for Children contains two versions of the prayer of exorcism that accompanies the (optional) pre-baptismal *anointing. Both prayers acknowledge the power of Jesus, sent to the world 'to cast out the power of Satan' and 'to rescue us from the slavery of sin'. The intention of the prayer is that God will set the children 'free from original sin and to bring them out of the power of darkness'. Thus the *anamnetic formulas seek to acknowledge the power of Christ over the power of evil, and the petitionary formulas seek freedom from the power of evil.

More elaborate exorcisms are found in the Rite of Christian Initiation of Adults. Exorcism is there described as showing 'the true nature of the spiritual life as a battle between flesh and spirit' (RCIA 101) and the formulas (RCIA 113–18; 373) speak of preservation from sin and evil. The *scrutinies intended to purify and strengthen the candidate (RCIA 154) contain rites of exorcism whereby 'the church teaches the elect about the mystery of Christ who frees from sin. By exorcism they are freed from the effects of sin and from the influence of the devil, and they are strengthened in their spiritual journey and open their hearts to receive the gifts of the Saviour' (RCIA 156). The formulas themselves (RCIA 164, 171, 178, 379, 383, 387) reflect this understanding. Similarly, the blessing of baptismal water in the rituals and the blessing of water at the beginning of the *eucharist no longer contain an exorcism of water (or of salt, use of which is optional). Scepticism regarding demonic possession and de-emphasis of exorcism in no way imply denial of the power of evil customarily spoken of as the devil or Satan.

R. Béraudy, 'Scrutinies and Exorcisms', *Adult Baptism and the Catechumenate*, ed. J. Wagner [*Concilium* XXII], New York 1967, 57–61; J. Cortés and F. Gatti, *The Case against Possessions and Exorcisms*, New York 1975; J. Dallen, 'Exorcism', *New Catholic Encyclopedia*, ed. T. O'Brien, XVII, New York 1979, 220; L. Mitchell, *Baptismal Anointing*, London 1966; R. Wood, *The Occult Revolution*, New York 1971.

JOSEPH WEISS

Exposition

The earliest form of exposing the *sacrament to the people was, from the fourth century at least, at the invitation to *communion. Until the thirteenth century this was the only point in the Western *eucharist that the people were invited to gaze on the elements and reverence them. But from *c.* 1200, beginning in Paris, the elements were also elevated after the *institution narrative in the *eucharistic prayer, and this soon became in effect the ritual climax of the rite, and in many ways a substitute for communion for a people long deprived of aural and sacramental participation. It is recorded that people went from church to church to witness the elevation, fought each other for better vantage points, and besought priests to prolong the moment.

But exposition probably had other sources besides this, such as the custom of showing the consecrated elements to the dying, seemingly as a visual substitute for *viaticum, and above all in the development of the feast of *Corpus Christi and its *procession in the late thirteenth and early fourteenth centuries. Not until the close of the fourteenth century do we find evidence for the exposition of the sacrament independently of the liturgy in a *monstrance, and this may well have derived from the German manner of *reservation in a 'sacrament-house', which often had a glass window or open grille enabling the sacrament to be seen at all times. In the fourteenth centuries prominent churchmen and theologians like Nicholas of Cusa and Jean Gerson expressed serious reservations about these forms of extra-liturgical exposition, and provincial councils and synods warned repeatedly against excesses.

With the Counter-Reformation it became most popular in the two forms known as *Benediction and the *Forty Hours' Devotion, and in the Baroque and subsequent periods the principal *altars of churches were designed in such a way that a 'throne' for the monstrance, high above the altar and *tabernacle, often came to dominate the interior. Although in this period exposition was subjected to canonical regulation, it was not until the mid-twentieth century that the Roman authorities definitively accepted it into the official books of the liturgy.

In 1973 the Roman Ritual for the first time provided official guidelines for all forms of exposition and devotion to the eucharist, all of which, it insists, must be seen in clear and proper relation to the eucharist. They derive from it, must be in harmony with it, and should lead the faithful back to it. 'They prolong the union with Christ which the faithful have reached in communion, and invite us to the spiritual union with him which culminates in sacramental communion.' The arrangement and conduct of exposition should carefully exclude 'anything which might obscure the principal desire of Christ in instituting the eucharist, namely to be with us as food, medicine and comfort'. Accordingly, the celebration of the eucharist during exposition is forbidden, a single genuflection is made before the exposed sacrament, the monstrance should normally stand on the altar-table itself rather than on a distant pedestal, the same number of *candles are deployed as at the eucharist, and the *host used should have been consecrated at the most recent eucharist in the church. During the exposition there should be prayers, songs and readings; a homily may be given, and periods of silent prayer should be observed. Part of the liturgy of the hours (*see* **Daily Prayer** 3) may be celebrated. Exposition concludes with benediction. The normal minister is a priest or *deacon, but in their absence an *acolyte or special minister or designated religious may expose the sacrament but not offer the concluding *blessing with it.

––––––––

Robert Cabié, 'Worship of the Eucharist Outside Mass', *The Church at Prayer* II, ed. A. G. Martimort, Collegeville 1986, 231–53; Nathan Mitchell, *Cult and Controversy: The Worship of the Eucharist outside Mass*, New York 1982.
                                        CHRISTOPHER WALSH

Extempore Prayer

Extempore (or extemporaneous) prayer is address to God free-composed at the moment it is spoken. The term *ex tempore* in Latin literally means 'from/out of the time'. Thus the word itself highlights the acts of composing and praying as simultaneous. In this way extempore prayer should probably be distinguished from pre-composed prayer in which the prayer has been composed ahead of time, although the two types of prayer might share some common characteristics owing to their free-composed nature.

Recent oral-formulaic theory suggests several characteristics for extempore prayer. Typically, the one praying will draw upon several repertoires of formulas, phrases and clichés to create the prayer, especially biblical quotes and allusions, phrases central to the piety of the one who prays, and standardized indicators of internal structure and transition. These formulas will be organized by themes of some 'plot'. Immediate assessment of the moment and the congregation will guide the selection of material and how it is organized into its plot.

Thus every extempore prayer is both unique – in that the prayer has never existed precisely in that form before – and common – in that the prayer is based upon shared formulas, phrases and internal plots. Because of this dual nature, an extempore prayer can be both novel and familiar to a worshipping community.

As the main manner of liturgical praying, extempore prayer has been used in varying degrees throughout ecclesiastical history. Its use in the early patristic period is well attested. The *Didache*, Justin Martyr, and the *Apostolic Tradition* mention the use of extempore prayer by the presider. Justin and the *Apostolic Tradition* note that the one praying does so according to his 'ability'. The use of extempore prayer in worship waned in the fourth and fifth centuries as doctrinal controversy, growing theological sophistication and burgeoning liturgical complexity led to written improvisation and then written fixity. However, apart from the *eucharist, extempore prayer continued to be used in some important liturgical settings in the period, since Augustine once complained about the doctrinal errors made by some clergy in their improvising baptismal prayers.

Widespread extempore prayer as liturgical norm did not reappear until the Protestant reforms of the sixteenth and seventeenth centuries. Even then its adoption was not uniform among Protestants. Whereas Luther and Calvin, among others, prepared written liturgies, the more radical Reformers often preferred extempore prayer. Thus, it became a norm among Anabaptists. Likewise, in English-speaking Protestantism, the Church of England produced various liturgical books while Separatists, *Baptists and other Independents showed a strong preference for extempore prayer. The general Puritan sensibility, too, after a time of interest in various Reformed liturgies, was toward the use of extempore prayer. *Quakers, obviously, eschewed written prayers.

The Westminster Directory for the Public Worship of God (1645) solidified, in many ways, the position of these seventeenth-century Protestants. The views it contains highlight concerns typical of those who pray extempore, then and now. In critique of written prayers, the *Directory* complains that, ironically, using written prayers can actually be idolatrous since they objectify the worship of God, becoming an object of devotion themselves. Likewise, since no inner faith or character is needed to read a prayer, their use can be nothing more than hypocritical 'lip-labour'. In favour of extemporaneous praying, the *Directory* notes that the ability to pray extemporaneously is itself a gift of Jesus Christ bestowed on truly called ministers for the benefit of the church. The *Directory* also states what is obvious to those who regularly pray extemporaneously: that prayer can be used to get the congregation 'rightly affected'.

Similar sentiments have been expressed beyond the *Directory*. For the Lutheran pietist Philip Jacob Spener, for example, to pray with the mouth outwardly was not enough. The 'true' and 'best' prayer occurs in the inner person first and then breaks out into words. Likewise early *Methodists looked coldly upon 'formality' in worship that could not appeal to affections. Not surprisingly, John Wesley added a *rubric allowing extemporizing in the eucharist and once noted that he also constantly added extempore prayer to the *daily offices. Extempore prayer was the mainstay in early Methodist worship. From there, along with other similar populist religious movements in the early American Republic, the practice entered the mainstream of American Protestantism. In the last century, *Pentecostal and *Charismatic sensibilities about the immediacy of the Holy Spirit's activity in worship have reinforced the predilection for extempore prayer among some pieties.

In churches that use written liturgical resources, many recent revisions provide for greater extemporaneity in prayer. In some, the rubrics allow for introduction of spontaneous prayers as part of more structured prayer in both sacramental services and daily offices. In churches with deep connections to free prayer, the official resource (for example, the 1993 *Book of Common Worship* of the Presbyterian Church, USA) can grant the liberty to use extempore prayers, even offering its contents as guidelines for such prayers. Some resources take this approach a step further; one book describes the use of *Tongsung Kido*, a Korean practice in which all pray aloud simultaneously, perhaps on a common theme. Of course, official liturgical resources are sometimes ignored as presiders assume their own liberty in a complex liturgical world full of influences that cross denominations and spiritualities.

In predilections for extempore prayer, some traits, theological and otherwise, are typically found. One is a particular understanding of church that emphasizes liturgical assemblies as groups bound together by intimacy among themselves and God. Another is a particular sensibility about participation. Prayer should express the specific congregation's faith, allowing worshippers to recognize and own it. Sometimes the preference for extemporaneity is connected with an idea that all worshippers should be able to pray aloud in a congregation's worship and that, perhaps, all should do so simultaneously. In this way extempore prayer has been used to break down institutional markers of liturgical presidency. Another common trait is an emphasis upon affections or feelings in the piety: prayer should articulate interior communion with God, expressing this relationship's poignancy. Of course, this trait can vary, depending upon whether the piety's main appeal is to the head or the heart.

Attraction to extempore prayer can be fed by rejection of written prayers. Some have complained about the nature of written prayer itself. In this viewpoint, written prayer requires no faith in the one praying, only the ability to read. Thus, historically, some have been troubled by a discrepancy in the content of the prayer and the character of the liturgical presider. Others have argued that written prayer often has no relevance to specific contemporary liturgical situations. Others have charged that certain collections of written prayers are stilted, unmoving, not expressive of the faith of the people, or using language which has become unacceptable. In addition, some see the use of written prayer as unscriptural, since there is no specific biblical warrant for reading prayers and since scripture promises direct assistance of the Holy Spirit in praying.

For some, written prayers have broader associations. Rejection of reading prayers has been intended at times as rejection of dominant authority or values. This has occasionally occurred when certain liturgical books have close ties to an objectionable social milieu or centralized ecclesiastical authority. Not surprisingly, extempore prayer is often found in groups considered fledgling religious movements or with strong democratic sensibilities, a congregational polity in liturgical matters, or rejection of an established church. Of course, the possibility of illiteracy in some instances should not be overlooked.

Allan Bouley, *From Freedom to Formula*, Washington, DC 1981; John E. Skoglund, 'Free Prayer', *Studia Liturgica* X, 1974, 151–66.

LESTER RUTH

Exultet *see* **Easter Candle**

Family Services

There are two ways of describing family services; the first is (usually) non-eucharistic 'All-Age' Sunday worship of recent years; the second refers to new forms of domestic prayer. As far as the former are concerned, 'family services' are a development in Western Protestantism of the second half of the twentieth century which has two principal roots. The first was the need to respond to an adultist approach to regular public worship, whereby children had spent separate time 'learning' about the Christian faith, while everyone else worshipped; or else, in an earlier generation, they went to Sunday school on a Sunday afternoon, and the worship which they normally experienced was of a kind specially tailored to their needs. Another approach was thought necessary, namely to draw them fully into the main Sunday service, perhaps once a month. The second was particularly manifested in Church of England worship; the decline of evensong as a non-sacramental service with direct (and often evangelistic) preaching, together with the increase in the *eucharist as the main Sunday morning act of worship, replacing morning prayer, meant that many adults who were not *confirmed, and who were infrequent churchgoers, might be drawn into such a monthly service, alongside their children. Often referred to as 'All-Age Worship', these 'ad hoc' liturgies depend a great deal on the resources of a particular parish, and require careful monitoring. Their advantage is that they can have a great appeal to the unchurched, especially in suburban areas, and they can provide many of the increasing number of adult confirmation candidates of the post-Christendom scene. Their disadvantage is that they can become tired and facile; and one of the main criticisms is that they can leave people where they are, and not lead them on to greater participation, particularly in the eucharist. The new liturgies, e.g. of the Norwegian Church, bear witness to some of these questions, as also do the flexible forms of Sunday morning prayer and the responsorial eucharistic prayers in the Church of England's *Common Worship* (2000). The issues here are in some respects much older, and relate to the *catechumenate, and the extent to which people can be familiarized with the grammar and vocabulary of Christianity in its public form. Opinions continue to differ on

John Wesley's oft-quoted description of the eucharist as 'a converting ordinance'.

The other kind of 'family service' – domestic prayer – has been a regular feature of Christianity in one form or another from the beginning, persisting through the Middle Ages in the Books of Hours for the literate and moneyed. The daily offices of morning and evening prayer in the English *BCP* were an attempt to hand the daily services back to the laity, and subsequent simplifications of it, e.g. Edmund Gibson's *Family Prayers* (1706), proved influential on many households. Several modern service books provide forms for domestic prayer, and the American Episcopal *Book of Occasional Services* (1979) provides special domestic rites for the seasons, including the lighting of the *Advent wreath, blessing homes at *Epiphany, and blessing food at *Easter. Books like these represent a significant attempt to bring prayer back into the home, and they have themselves been fed by scholarly research into the origins of *daily prayer itself, liberating many from the (mistaken) convictions that the psalms can only be recited in sequence and that Bible readings have to be lengthy. They have also helped to provide an 'affective' and devotional counterbalance to some of the new public liturgies, which are often perceived to be well conceived but somewhat stark. There has also been a welcome recovery of older material which the era of liturgical revisions was in danger of losing.

See also **Children and Worship.**

―――――

Richard More, *Freedom in a Framework*, Nottingham 1975; Michael Perry (ed.), *The Family Service Book*, London 1985.

KENNETH W. STEVENSON

Fan

Rhipidion in Greek, *flabellum* in Latin, a liturgical object traditionally held by the *deacon. The earliest surviving liturgical fans are from the Kaper Koraon Treasure. They are made of silver, decorated with seraphim and cherubim, and are dated to 577. The liturgical use of fans is first attested in the fourth-century *Apostolic Constitutions*, after the transfer of the bread and wine to the *altar during the *eucharist: 'But let two of the deacons, on each side of the altar, each hold a fan, of thin membranes, or of feathers of the peacock, or of fine cloth, and let them silently drive away the flying insects, that they may not come near to the cups'

(VIII.12.3). Their use then was purely practical, and attested not only in Eastern but also in Western sources. Liturgical fans later took on the symbolism of the presence of the heavenly powers, and are still used in Eastern liturgical traditions. In the present Greek practice they are carried by *acolytes in *processions, and are called *hexapterigon* (six-winged), as the six-winged cherubim are depicted on them, stressing in this way their symbolism. When not in use, two are usually placed on the eastern side of the altar, one on each side of the *crucifix.

―――――

Marlia Mango, 'Rhipidion', *Oxford Dictionary of Byzantium*, ed. Alexander P. Kazhdan, Oxford 1991, III, 1790–1; Sévérien Salaville, *An Introduction to the Study of Eastern Liturgies*, London 1938, 148–9.

STEFANOS ALEXOPOULOS

Fast Days

It was apparently the custom among pious Jews in the first century to fast regularly on Mondays and Thursdays. In the early church Wednesdays and Fridays each week were adopted as the standard fast days, but whether Christians did this simply to differentiate themselves from Jews or were adhering to a variant Jewish custom is uncertain. The fast usually involved complete abstinence from food and drink until the ninth hour of the day (approximately 3 p.m.), when a service of the *word was held and then the fast was broken. This hour encouraged association of fasting with the death of Jesus. Communal fasting was also practised prior to the celebration of *baptism and *ordination, and on other days in the year, especially during *Lent and on *Ember and *Rogation days. Fasting was never allowed, however, on a Sunday or during the fifty days of Easter (*see* **Pentecost**), nor in Eastern traditions on Saturdays either, with the sole exception of *Holy Saturday. Additional times of fasting are also observed in the Orthodox tradition. Later in the West the regular weekly fast was restricted to Fridays, and generally required abstinence from meat rather than a complete fast. The RC Church now only designates *Ash Wednesday, *Good Friday and the Fridays of Lent as days of abstinence.

Fasting before the reception of *communion as a sign of reverence begins to be attested in the third century, was widespread in the fourth, and universal by the Middle Ages. The Orthodox rule is that the fast should be kept from the hour of rising; the RC Church formerly required fasting from midnight onwards, but it now need not be more than one hour before the time of reception.

EDITOR

Feminism and Worship

see **Women and Worship**

Feria

Christians, like the Jews, designated the days of the week by numbers, not by names. In the Latin West, a day was called a *feria*. Sunday, the first day of the week, became the 'Lord's Day', *dies dominica* (see Rev. 1.7), and Saturday retained its title of Sabbath, *sabbatum*, but the other days were known as *feria secunda*, *tertia*, etc. Liturgically a *feria* is a weekday which is not a feast day (ironically the exact opposite of the classical meaning of the word). Most ferial days are viewed as an extension of the preceding Sunday. In the Eastern Orthodox Church the *eucharist would not normally be celebrated, and in the West until recently eucharistic *readings would repeat those of the previous Sunday. But from the most ancient times certain days were celebrated with particular observance. The *Didache* early in the second century spoke of Wednesdays and Fridays as *fast days, adapting Jewish practice. The weekdays of *Lent including *Ash Wednesday, 17 to 24 December, the *Ember and *Rogation Days are also *ferias*, in that they are not feast days.

GORDON JEANES

Fermentum *see* Commixture

Font

A pool or container which holds the water for the administration of *baptism. Christian baptism is 'by water and the Spirit', and while the Spirit is always and everywhere present, the water needs a container to hold it. The water is the earthly element in this sacrament. Like baptism itself, it has three principal meanings: life (birth), and death (drowning), and bathing (purification). It both creates and destroys, both brings life and drowns it. It is God's instrument for both salvation and destruction. The font should be consistent in size and design with the meanings of the sacramental water.

1. *Early Fonts*. In the earliest centuries of Christianity, baptism was celebrated in natural bodies of water, such as rivers and lakes. In the second century, however, owing to the persecution of Christians, baptisms in North Africa and southern Europe may sometimes have occurred in bathing rooms and courtyard fountains of private homes, and in small public baths. The oldest font discovered (thus far) by archaeologists was in Dura Europos, in what is now Syria, found in an adapted house-church from the mid-third century. It resembled both basins in the Roman baths in Dura as well as Roman and Syrian tombs (sarcophagi) there. By the third and fourth centuries, especially after the persecutions were ended, special buildings (called *baptisteries) were constructed for the purpose of holding fonts. Adult baptism was the norm, and much evidence suggests that baptisms generally occurred during the *Easter vigil, although there is also evidence of infant baptisms and of the sacrament being celebrated at times other than the Easter vigil.

The design and symbolism of the font in the early church reflected the several layers of the meaning of water which are reflected in baptismal theology. Prior to the fourth century, when the paschal understanding of the sacrament gained prominence, birth imagery was predominant in the East, but there are also mentions of it in the West, probably based on John 3.5. In the late second century, Irenaeus of Lyons referred to the baptismal font as a womb. In the early third century, Tertullian of Carthage wrote extensively of baptism as birth. His imagery was echoed by Ambrose as well as by a number of North Africans, including Cyprian and Augustine. Some later theologians have suggested that the understanding of baptism as birth gave rise to the round shape of the font, but this cannot be proven. Baptism is also a washing, a sacramental purification from sinfulness (see 1 Cor. 6.11; Eph. 5.26; 2 Peter 1.9: tiny fonts of the late medieval and following ages contradict this meaning).

However, by the fourth century, especially in the West, the predominant understanding of baptism was paschal: to be baptized is to be joined to the death and resurrection of Christ (Rom. 6.3–5; Col. 2.12). These three meanings of birth, bath and burial are not unrelated. The baptismal bath is in fact a drowning flood, and the new birth must be preceded by the death of the 'old' person. Already in third-century Egypt, Origen had reflected Romans 6 in writing of baptism, and had referred to the font as a sepulchre, and the paschal understanding became the *cantus firmus* in the fourth-century mystagogical writings, e.g. of Cyril of Jerusalem and Ambrose of Milan. This led to the primary design of baptismal pools as cruciform or variations thereof (such as the quatrefoil), though shapes varied from place to place and from East to West.

It was not only the meaning of baptism that influenced the font shape; the mode of the sacrament (itself also influenced by and expressive of the meaning) was also highly influential in the designs and sizes of fonts. *Submersion* (sometimes called 'total immersion' or 'dipping') involves pushing the person's entire body under the water, and for this the water must be quite deep. In *immersion*, the adult candidate stands or kneels in the water (usually between ankle- and waist-deep) while water is poured over the head or the head is lowered partially into the water. *Affusion* involves pouring water over the candidate's head. It began to replace immersion and submersion in cold northern countries, as infant baptism became more common beginning in the medieval period in Europe. *Aspersion*, the most minimal mode, merely involves sprinkling water over the head. The more minimal the mode, the smaller the font required, so in-ground pools were gradually replaced by mere above ground containers, usually on one or more stone pedestals (often quite ornately carved). This became especially true as infant baptism became more common, and as *confirmation was separated from the baptismal rite.

Early fonts were usually pools in the ground, often of startlingly large proportions. The first (fourth-century) circular baptismal pool of the Lateran Baptistery in Rome was 8.5 metres in diameter, and sunk about one metre into the floor. The octagon was a very common early font shape. It was interpreted as representing the 'eighth day', the day of Christ's resurrection, into which we enter in baptism. In Milan, the baptistery constructed when Ambrose was bishop in the late fourth century contained an in-ground octagonal pool measuring almost five metres across and about 0.8 metres deep. Many other notable early pools were also octagonal, including those in Lyons, Fréjus, Aix-en-Provence and Riez, in France; Castelseprio, Varese and Cividale, in Italy.

Also common were hexagonal fonts, often understood to represent the 'sixth day', the day of the crucifixion (Rom. 6.3–5). Important hexagonal pools have been excavated in Aquileia, Grado, Lomello and Rome (San Marcello), in Italy; Cimiez, in France; and Carthage (Damous el-Karita), in Tunisia. Cruciform and quatrefoil/quadrilobe (a rounded-lobe variant of the cruciform shape) fonts are common in North Africa and in the East. These shapes, of course, represent the paschal understanding of baptism. A stunning mosaic-faced quadrilobe font from Kélibia, Tunisia, has been restored at the Bardo Museum in Tunis. Among the many cruciform pools are those in Tunisia, including Thuburbo Majus and Bulla Regia.

As already noted, the rectangle is the most ancient font shape (Dura Europos, mid-third century). The rectangle was the common shape of ancient sarcophagi and burial niches, and it remains the shape of coffins in the twenty-first century. Early font examples included the San Ponziano Catacomb in Rome, and the first stages of the fonts in Aquileia (Italy) and Geneva (Switzerland). A related shape is the square, of which Maktar (Tunisia) is a well-preserved example.

The round shape seems to have originated in fourth-century Rome, but was more common in the East than the West; in North Africa, ruins of more circular fonts can be found in Algeria than in Tunisia. The earliest font in the Orthodox Baptistery in Ravenna (Italy) was internally round, sunk about three metres below the present floor (the present medieval octagonal font was built on the foundations of the original circular plan). Other circular pools included the sixth-century font at Mustis, Tunisia, and certain stages of fonts in Aosta and Aquileia, both in Italy. There has been no clear agreement on the meaning of the circular pool; they may simply have derived from circular basins in Roman baths.

Most fonts were deep enough to require steps down into them, though the steps also were thought to serve a symbolic function of descending into death with Christ and then rising with him into new life.

2. *Later Developments.* In the late medieval period, in-ground pools were largely replaced by above-ground containers on pedestals, thus minimizing the significance and understanding of baptism. Originally they were large enough for infant submersion, but they grew smaller and smaller until finally they could accommodate only aspersion. Only in the late twentieth century were the larger in-ground pools begun to be recovered in liturgical churches in the West (they had been retained, usually in non-

symbolic shapes, in Baptist and Anabaptist churches), as the theology of baptism has regained prominence in many churches across the ecumenical spectrum, and the adult *catechumenate has been recovered in the RC Church around the world and in Lutheran and Episcopalian (Anglican) churches in North America. Stunning examples of new fonts large and deep enough to enable adult submersion include the cruciform pools at St Charles Borromeo and Guardian Angels churches in London, and the round pool at St Benedict the African church in Chicago.

Francis Bond, *Fonts and Font Covers*, London 1908 and 1985; J. G. Davies, *The Architectural Setting of Baptism*, London 1962; A. Khatchatrian, *Les baptistères paléochrétiens*, Paris 1962; Folke Nordström, *Mediaeval Baptismal Fonts: An Iconographical Study*, Stockholm 1984; S. Anita Stauffer, *On Baptismal Fonts: Ancient and Modern*, Cambridge 1994 (bib.).

S. ANITA STAUFFER

Foot-Washing

Though the rite of the washing of feet has come to be interpreted as a rite of humble service observed in many Christian churches only once a year, its meaning and its history are complex. The root of the complexity is apparent from the earliest stratum of the tradition, for the narrative of the foot-washing by Jesus is recorded in only one NT text, John 13.1–20. Even in the Gospel it is possible that the original narrative was the action alone, verses 5–11, with an initiation rite at its base, to which a layer of new interpretation was added as a teaching about service put on the lips of Jesus to recast the action, as evident in verses 13.12–20. The key to the initiation layer in the tradition depends on the meaning of verse 8, 'If I do not wash you, you have no part in me', suggesting perhaps that the foot-washing rite was the means by which members were brought into the community as members of Christ.

In the early church the initiation interpretation of the rite is confirmed intermittently in the writings of the fathers such as Ambrose of Milan, Chromatius of Aquileia, Ephraem of Syria, who describe it as a pre- or post-baptismal ceremony, and in canons of church councils, such as the Council of Elvira in 305, which forbade the initiation of infants by the washing of their feet. The same canon forbade the minister from accepting payment for the

initiation, and in both instances the canon testifies more likely to the certainty of the occurrence than to the absence of the practices.

Today the rite is observed annually by many Christian traditions on *Maundy Thursday. This location is ancient in itself, found, for example, as an option in a letter of Augustine to an inquirer (*Ep*. 55 to Januarius) and later in a canon of a synod that met in Toledo, Spain, in 694. The rite is sometimes referred to by the Latin word *mandatum*, meaning 'commandment', taken from the Latin translation of John 13.34, where Jesus says, 'I give you a new commandment', *mandatum novum*.

Although in the sixteenth century some Lutherans rejected the foot-washing as a Roman invention, other Protestant communities, the Anabaptists and *Mennonites in particular, have given prominence to it as a sign of unity and humility. Various communities within the *Baptist, *Moravian, *Pentecostal and *Seventh-Day Adventist traditions practise the foot-washing rite regularly, sometimes with gravity equal to the *eucharist, as an expression of service and unity.

Martin F. Connell, '*Nisi Pedes*, Except for the Feet: Footwashing in the Community of St John's Gospel', *Worship* LXX, 1996, 20–30; Peter Jeffery, '*Mandatum Novum Do Vobis*: Toward a Renewal of the Holy Thursday Footwashing Rite', *Worship* LXIV, 1990, 107–41. On Pentecostal Practice: Frank D. Macchia, 'Is Footwashing the Neglected Sacrament? A Theological Response to John Christopher Thomas', *Pneuma: The Journal of the Society for Pentecostal Studies* XIX, 1997, 239–49.

MARTIN F. CONNELL

Forty Hours' Devotion

Also known by its Italian name *Quarant' Ore*, this was an RC devotion in which the *reserved sacrament was *exposed for a continuous period of about forty hours, with the faithful in relays praying before it throughout.

The remote origins of the devotion may have been in the very popular medieval custom of keeping watch from *Good Friday to *Easter morning at the 'sepulchre' in which first the cross and later the eucharistic elements were 'buried'. Its immediate origins, however, were in sixteenth-century Milan as an intensive form of prayer during a national crisis. Soon this was organized in all the churches of the city in rotation. As early as 1534 St Anthony Mary Zaccaria was propagating the devotion further afield, and in 1550 St Philip Neri introduced it to the churches of Rome. In 1539 Pope Paul III gave approval to it as a form of reparation in time of severe social tension; in 1560 Pius V related it to Christ's forty-day fast and to the ancient Christian ideal of uninterrupted prayer. Clement XII in 1731 issued regulations for its conduct in the diocese of Rome which were widely adopted elsewhere. These show that the emphasis was by now less on reparation and more on piety towards the sacrament itself. The devotion was to open and close with a *votive mass of the blessed sacrament, and on the second day a mass of peace was to be celebrated at a separate *altar in the church. The 1917 *Code of Canon Law* ordered it be held annually in all churches where the sacrament was regularly reserved.

The revised Roman Ritual of 1973 makes no explicit mention of the devotion, but recommends that an 'extended period of exposition' should be observed each year in churches where the sacrament is regularly reserved, provided that suitable numbers can be present. It need no longer be strictly continuous, and indeed must be interrupted if the *eucharist is to be celebrated in the church or if the number of worshippers cannot be sustained. Otherwise the normal regulations for exposition apply.

J. A. Jungmann, *Pastoral Liturgy*, London/ New York 1962, 223–38; Nathan Mitchell, *Cult and Controversy: The Worship of the Eucharist outside Mass*, New York 1982.

CHRISTOPHER WALSH

Fraction

The now somewhat archaic term for the formal breaking of the bread which occurs in all *eucharistic liturgies. It is often replaced by the more direct term 'the breaking of the bread', which serves as a reminder of Christ's action at the Last Supper (Matt. 26.26 and parallels). This element, and its universal repetition, proved striking enough to make 'the breaking of the bread' (Acts 2.42; 20.7) the earliest designation given to the whole rite. Recently in modern liturgical revision (following Gregory Dix, *The Shape of the Liturgy*, London 1945, 48 and passim), this action was held to be one of the fundamental fourfold actions of the eucharist. This has now been challenged by some, but the utilitarian and scriptural aspects

of the ceremony – division of the consecrated bread so that all may share – have continued to be respected.

Many modern Anglican revisions provide words to be said at the breaking. In the revised RC rites the priest breaks a small portion from the *host and drops it into the *chalice (the *commixture) immediately after the *kiss of peace. During the *Agnus Dei, which follows, he divides the host into a number of portions which are used for the *communion of the people. The ceremony is considerably more elaborate in the Byzantine and other Eastern rites. Thus, in the Liturgy of St John Chrysostom, the host is divided into four portions, arranged on the paten in the form of a cross. Uniquely the 1662 *BCP* orders that the bread should be broken within the *institution narrative. Such a mnemonic tableau of an historic event was mistakenly adopted by some RCs after Vatican II, but has been censured.

DONALD GRAY

Frontal

A frontal or antependium is a panel of precious material, metal, wood or cloth, richly ornamented, used to cover the entire front of an *altar. It probably derives from the early Christian practice of covering the table altar with a coloured fabric. Frontals have been in general use in the East since the fourth century and in the West since the fifth. A very fine example of a metal antependium from the ninth century is to be found at Sant' Ambrogio, Milan. Fabric frontals could be very elaborate, e.g. that by Jacopo Cambi in Florence, dated 1336, 1 metre by 4 metres, celebrating the coronation of the Virgin and using coloured and painted silk and gold and silver thread. In the RC Church the *rubrics of the Roman Missal of 1570 required every altar to have a frontal and prescribed that it should be of the colour proper to the feast or season (*see* **Colours, Liturgical**). It was not however an absolute rule but one to be adhered to as far as possible. The post-Vatican II *General Instruction on the Roman Missal* omits all reference to frontals, and new fixed altars rarely have one. Modern portable altars, often little more than small tables placed in front of an older high altar, are frequently wrapped in cloth to conceal their inadequate structure. The frontal, though increasingly disused, is more likely to be found in Anglican churches where it takes one of three forms: a cloth hanging over the front of the altar, a stretched cloth on a frame attached to the front, or a throw-over which covers all sides of the altar and is sometimes known erroneously as a 'Laudian' or 'Jacobean' frontal.

MARTIN DUDLEY

Funerals

Nearly all Christian traditions have practised some rites or act of worship in relation to the death of a believer and the disposal of the body, whether by burial or cremation.

General bibliography: Bruce Gordon and Peter Marshall (eds), *The Place of the Dead: Death and Remembrance in Late Medieval and Early Modern Europe*, Cambridge 2000; Frederick S. Paxton, *Christianizing Death: The Creation of a Ritual Process in Early Medieval Europe*, Ithaca 1990 (bib.); Geoffrey Rowell, *The Liturgy of Christian Burial*, London 1977 (bib.).

1. Early Christianity; 2. Eastern Churches; 3. Medieval and Roman Catholic; 4. Anglican; 5. Baptist; 6. Christian Church; 7. Congregationalist; 8. Lutheran; 9. Methodist; 10. Old Catholic; 11. Pentecostal; 12. Reformed.

1. *Early Christianity*. The funeral rites of the early church drew upon local Jewish and pagan cultural traditions while reinterpreting and expanding them with distinctively Christian themes. Diversity of local custom and paucity of evidence make it difficult to construct a complete picture, especially in the pre-Constantinian period. Nevertheless, some common themes and practices do emerge.

Christian writers in this period encouraged an ascetic approach to death, avoiding the ostentatious mourning practices of pagan funerals. Among Christians of north Africa, Tertullian ridicules the pagan funeral banquet (*On the Resurrection of the Flesh* 1) and Commodian criticizes excessive displays of funeral pomp (*Instructions* 73–4). Nevertheless, Dionysius of Alexandria notes that Christians took care to give an appropriate preparation and burial to those who had died of a plague, while the pagans of Alexandria left corpses to rot (Eusebius, *Church History* 7.22.9). Some pagan authors remark that care for the dead helped to make Christianity appealing to the masses.

According to Pliny the Elder (*Natural History* 7.187), Romans preferred cremation, especially among the upper class. Christians, however, followed the Middle Eastern, and specifically Jewish, practice of inhumation (burial), in graves, tombs or catacombs. The preference for inhumation probably reflects Christian belief in the resurrection of the body as indicated by the Christian use of the Greek word *koimeterion* (literally, 'sleeping place') for a cemetery or catacomb (*Apostolic Tradition* 40). It was necessary for the wealthier members of the church to provide the burial space for the poor and slaves. Evidence of Christian burial sites, at least from the third century, indicate the importance of this ministry. In this respect, the churches functioned much like the Roman burial societies, which were common among the poor.

The funeral rites themselves are more difficult to establish. Tertullian alludes to an 'appointed office' for funerals, but does not describe the rite (*A Treatise on the Soul* 51). The earliest written evidence comes from a prayer in the collection attributed to Sarapion of Thmuis in Egypt (*c.* 350). This prayer, No. 30, employs mostly OT references. The *Apostolic Constitutions* (8.41) contains a prayer for the dead that likewise draws on OT themes. Funeral rites also included singing. Jerome refers to the singing of psalms done in the 'Christian manner' (*Ep.* 108), and John Chrysostom (*Homily on Hebrews* 4.7) indicates that Psalms 23, 32 and 126 were chanted at funerals in Constantinople.

While early Christians were urged to avoid the excesses of the pagan funeral banquet, or *refrigerium*, they did begin to associate the commemoration of the dead with the *euch*arist. Tertullian refers to a widow's yearly 'sacrifice' on behalf of her deceased husband, which suggests a eucharist (*On Monogamy* 10). The third-century *Didascalia Apostolorum* 6.22 calls for the eucharist in cemeteries without fear of ritual impurity, and by the late fourth century, *Apostolic Constitutions* 6.30 directs Christians to offer the eucharist in the church and in the 'sleeping places' and at funerals of the faithful. The Christian *refrigerium* could include an actual meal. Whereas the pagan custom was a private feast, Christians held a meal for the poor, similar to the *agape meal. *Apostolic Constitutions* 8.42 also commends the giving of alms from the estate of the deceased.

Following the burial, which took place within one day, *Apostolic Constitutions* 8.42 specifies commemorations on the third, ninth and fortieth days. The commemoration on the third day, which included 'psalms, lessons and prayers' may have its roots in Jewish mourning ritual, though a connection to the resurrection of Jesus justified the Christian practice.

James Stevenson, *The Catacombs: Life and Death in Early Christianity*, Nashville 1978; J. M. C. Toynbee, *Death and Burial in the Roman World*, London 1971.

L. EDWARD PHILLIPS

2. *Eastern Churches*. As in the West, funeral services in the Christian East are generally constructed around the three venues where the Christian community traditionally gathered for prayer while the deceased was prepared for interment: the home of the deceased, the church and the cemetery. Beyond this common matrix, funerals in the Christian East are remarkably diversified and complex because, more than other liturgical services, they are conditioned by local and cultural factors. Societal attitudes toward death and bereavement naturally inspired the theology and spirituality of funeral texts. Similarly, local geography and climate influenced how the body was prepared for burial, and how long the burial rites at the cemetery could reasonably last. Folk customs, some of them pre-Christian, also made their mark on the Eastern funeral orders. Such local factors mitigated against the normal forces of assimilation and unification witnessed in other liturgical orders, resulting in services of striking diversity and individuality. Moreover, the visceral human response to death fuelled an ongoing multiplication of liturgical texts, in which Christian cultures endeavoured to penetrate the mystery of death, exploring the scriptures for meaning and consolation. Characteristically for the Christian East, the theological weight of the services is within the rich and multiform hymns, which multiplied continuously in number and magnitude to accompany the *processions between the funeral stations, as well as the time-consuming actions associated with funerals: washing, dressing, *anointing, and laying out the body, processing to the church and cemetery, lowering the casket, filling in the grave, etc.

2.1. *Distinct Formularies*. This creative impulse resulted in the gradual differentiation of the funeral office into distinct services for various classes of faithful. A tenth-century *Armenian euchology already distinguishes separate orders for clergy, monks and lay.

Byzantine euchologies provide a separate office for monks after the thirteenth century, and distinct offices for priests and for children two centuries later. The *East Syrian, *Coptic and *Ethiopian rites carry the differentiation still further, furnishing separate formularies for adults and children of both sexes, while the *West Syrian rite has a single formula for all children. In general, the differences between these services are in the church *synaxis. Though it is changing in most Eastern rites, traditionally only the casket of a deceased clergyman was brought into the *sanctuary for the church service, while others were brought only as far as the church door or the *narthex. Clerical funerals tend to be much longer than lay funerals, the number of lections, prayers and hymns having greatly proliferated to incorporate scriptural references to, and poetic reflections on, the death of prominent figures in salvation history. The East Syrian rite limits lay funerals to passages from the OT and Acts of the Apostles, not out of any clericalism, but because lay deceased are brought directly from the home to the cemetery without a synaxis at church, and, according to the inner logic of this rite, the gospels and epistles must not be read publicly outside the sanctuary. Similarly, funerals for men and women differ not in ritual, but in the choice of lections, and in certain prayers and *litanies. These distinctions are not motivated by gender subordination, but out of a creative tendency, rooted in pastoral sensitivity, to adapt the services, as much as possible, to the exigencies of the situation. The Coptic funeral for women, for example, substitutes Matt. 26.6–13, Jesus' anointing by the woman at Bethany, for John 5.19–29 in the funeral for men. The principal prayer stresses the Mother of God's role in salvation history, and waxes on the soteriological value of the incarnation. In the Byzantine rite the differences between funerals for lay and ordained are all but erased for one week following *Easter, when a single, entirely different formulary is used, the liturgical texts of which are dominated by paschal themes.

2.2. *The Service at the Home*. St Gregory of Nyssa's fourth-century account of the death of his sister Macrina provides early evidence for an all-night *vigil with psalms and hymnody at the deathbed of the deceased. All Eastern rites preserve remnants of such a vigil, though generally today the 'wake' has been reduced to a token of what it once was. The extensive use of psalms in most of these rites corresponds to the fathers' insistence that psalmody replace the wailing lament of pagans. In their earliest forms the Eastern rites provide liturgical texts to accompany the washing of the body and veiling or dressing it. As in all phases of the funeral, *incense is used liberally, accompanied by prayers and hymns, especially in the greater Syrian rites. Scripture readings are also commonly found in this phase of the funeral.

2.3. *The Service at Church.* Only the Ethiopian rite celebrates the *eucharist at all funerals. A complete eucharistic liturgy of the word, and even some pre-anaphoral rites, take place in the home. In church a second complete liturgy of the word is followed by the same pre-anaphoral elements, a duplication that betrays the complicated evolution of this rite. The East Syrian and Armenian rites appoint the eucharist only for deceased clergy. The other rites offer various orders of psalmody, hymns, scripture readings and prayer, as well as a departure *kiss in the Byzantine and Coptic rites, and in the Armenian rite for priests. Some form of final *absolution is a standard component of the church service.

2.4. *Ancient Features.* Funeral unction has ancient roots in the Christian East. In the sixth-century environs of Antioch, Pseudo-Dionysius associates the anointing of the dead body with pre-baptismal anointing. If baptismal unction is the seal of fitness for Christian life, the unction of the dead prepares one for the life beyond. Although funeral unction has no connection with extreme unction, for centuries Western Crusaders and missionaries erroneously censured the Armenians and West Syrians for conferring the sacrament of the *sick on dead bodies. While some form of funeral unction was probably practised in all Eastern rites, today only the Armenians and Byzantines practise the rite, and that only for deceased clergy. Just before the kiss of peace in the funeral liturgy, the Armenians anoint the forehead and hands of the deceased cleric with chrism, whereupon the clergy kiss his anointed hands. In the Byzantine rite, at least since the fifteenth century, simple blessed oil is poured on the body at the cemetery. The West Syrians have preserved the prayer for anointing, but today this usually accompanies an offering of incense. The prayer asks that through the anointing the deceased 'may become slippery and unhindered by the adverse powers and the hosts of the enemies who lie in wait in the air to wage war against the souls of men'.

Another ancient element of Eastern funeral rites is the prayer that begins, 'God of spirits and of all flesh . . .' (Num. 16.22), traces of which are found in third-century Coptic and Nubian grave inscriptions, in the fourth-century Egyptian euchology of Sarapion of Thmuis, the *Apostolic Constitutions*, the eighth-century Greek euchology ms. Barberini gr. 336, and every Eastern rite. The prayer is repeated at each stage of the Byzantine funeral service, nine times during the priest's burial alone. The Armenians, whose version is more primitive than the Greek, offer the prayer at the home.

2.5. *The Service at the Grave and Memorials.* Graveside ceremonies vary greatly in length. The Copts do little more than lower the casket, recite a prayer and depart. The Armenians have a more extensive graveside ceremony that concludes with the 'sealing of the grave', a signation on four sides of the tomb to ward off grave-robbers. The protracted Ethiopian grave ceremony entails an inclination prayer, numerous *intercessions, two prayers for the imposition of hands, a litanic prayer attributed to Abba Sälama II (d. 1388), and a series of seven dismissal benedictions. Every Eastern rite includes a soil blessing recalling God's words to the fallen couple, that they would return to the dust from which they were taken (Gen. 3.19). Filling in the tomb often becomes a ritualized strewing of soil on the casket or body. Under late Latin influence, the Maronites sprinkle the casket with holy water.

Also of interest in the Eastern rites are the processions by which the body is conducted between the three stations of the funeral. The use of the *Trisagion* in funeral processions of the Coptic and Byzantine rites recalls its original function as a chant accompanying stational processions. Ps. 119 is used by several rites, including the elaborate Ethiopian procession to the church, where the psalm is said in seven sections. After each section the pall-bearers pause and lay down the casket for lections and prayers, a practice that appears to be a ritualization of the need for the pall-bearers to rest.

The Eastern rites provide supplemental memorial services that take place at the grave on certain days following the funeral, typically on the second, seventh and fortieth days, and on the anniversary, though patterns vary according to individual rites.

Hansjakob Becker and Hermann Ühlein (eds), *Liturgie im Angesicht des Todes*, St Ottilien

1997; O. H. E. Burmester, *The Egyptian or Coptic Church: A Detailed Description of her Liturgical Services and the Rites and Ceremonies Observed in the Administration of her Sacraments*, Cairo 1967, 201–13; W. Macomber, 'The Funeral Liturgy of the Chaldean Church', *Concilium* II, 1968, 19–22; Elena Velkova Velkovska, 'Funeral Rites in the East', *Handbook for Liturgical Studies*, ed. Anscar J. Chupungco, IV, Collegeville 2000, 345–54.

M. DANIEL FINDIKYAN

3. *Medieval and Roman Catholic.* The medieval rituals that surround the events of dying, death and burial indicate a substantial development and change over time.

3.1. *The Early Middle Ages.* The first rituals of death and burial draw from the patristic heritage marked by reassurance and hope as reflected in the early *ordo defunctorum.* Generally the rituals included the last rites for the dying, preparation of the body, *procession to and services in the church, procession to and rites at the cemetery, burial and post-burial rites. In the course of the ninth century the optimistic, hopeful attitude gave way to a more sober and penitential mood, which passed into the liturgical books of the Carolingian period and became the basis for later medieval development. On the theological level, there was a new emphasis on the grandeur of God as just judge and dispenser of mercy and indulgence.

Although synods exhorted pastors to play down the fear of death and emphasize divine mercy while ministering to the dying, they also stressed the final judgement and human sinfulness. Consequently, necessity of *confession and *absolution before death became more apparent. Intercessory prayers for the dead abounded. As for the body itself, there was a growing and almost macabre fascination, a phenomenon reflected in popular literature and art and certainly attested to by the charnel houses which housed the skeletal remains.

In the earliest Western liturgies the sequence of the last rites for the dying was constantly changing. Basically there was a reading of the passion of Christ, the recitation of psalms (normally the seven penitential psalms) and *litanies (sometimes immediately after death), and the administration of the last *communion, called *viaticum. From this simple early practice more elaborate forms developed, as additional ceremonies and prayers were added. From this evolved the *last rites, consisting of *anointing, and most importantly, confession and the absolution of sin. Since confession was administered privately, the last rites became a private affair, including the anointing and the reception of communion. The last rites were often referred to as Extreme Unction.

3.2. *Monastic Influence.* In Cluniac practice, after the dying monk confessed his sins and was anointed, he was brought before the monastic chapter and publicly confessed his faults and received absolution. Afterwards, the community processed to him, singing psalms. In the presence of the monastic community the dying monk was anointed and given viaticum. As death approached he was placed on a hair shirt (*cilicium*) sprinkled with *ashes. Then the community was summoned and they gathered outside the infirmary to say the *creed, litanies, responses and psalms. At the moment of death a prayer was recited commending the soul to God, while the community processed to the *chapel to pray the office of the dead.

In general, as a result of monastic influences, the rites of dying became longer and more elaborate, and as monastic influences were felt beyond the monasteries, laity copied and adapted those rites. A priest might make a preliminary visit to the dying person to hear the person's confession. He then returned to the church and rang the bells summoning the community to form a procession that would carry communion to the dying. At the bedside the role of the anointing gradually diminished in the later Middle Ages, because of the greater emphasis placed on confession, *penance and the reception of the last communion. The laity copied the monastic practice of reading the passion of Christ, but only if the dying person was literate.

When death occurred several prayers of commendation were recited along with psalms and antiphons, among which was the *Requiem aeternam* ('Rest eternal'), noted as early as the eighth century. Then the body was washed, accompanied by more psalms and antiphons, some with baptismal signification. Next, the body was clothed in dress appropriate to the station of the deceased, recalling the clothing in Christ at baptism. Finally the body was placed on a bier either to lie at home for the *vigil or to be carried in procession to the church. While the body was borne in procession to the church people of equal rank and dignity to the deceased sang or recited psalms and antiphons. In the monastic practice at Cluny there was a continuous recitation of psalms until burial.

The vigil was uninterrupted, except by the office of the dead and the *eucharist. Before the final procession of the body to the grave, numerous prayers could be said and accompanied with further psalms and antiphons. The body was carried to the grave preceded by lights and *incense. There prayers, psalms and antiphons were sung, and the grave was sprinkled with holy water and incensed to cover the stench of the body, and laurel was placed in it signifying the victory of those dying in Christ.

3.3. *Votive Masses*. From the ninth century onward, the sacramentaries witness the increase of votive masses. After the funeral people were encouraged to remember the dead in a variety of ways. For the literate who prayed the divine office (*see* **Daily Prayer** 3), the office of the dead was inserted. Progressively the office of the dead found its way into the illuminated Books of Hours along with an office patterned around the seven penitential psalms. Votive masses were celebrated for the deceased on the day of death and on the thirtieth day afterwards. The sacramentaries indicate that the names of the departed were inserted into the *Hanc igitur* and *Memento mortuorum* formulae of the canon of the mass. The names of the deceased could be inscribed on *diptychs along with benefactors, which were read at mass. Names of the deceased could also be listed on obituary roles (*rotuli*) arranged according to the months of the year, in order that prayers for the deceased might be said on the anniversaries of their deaths.

3.4. *More Recent Rites*. In 1614 in response to the Council of Trent the *Rituale Romanum* was promulgated as the first official and universal funeral rite. The ritual simplified the monastic burial rites, focusing on the transfer of the body to the church and to the cemetery, but the overall medieval tone of repentance and fear of judgement prevailed. This ritual remained in use until 1969 when the *Ordo Exequiarum* was promulgated as one of the liturgical reforms of the Second Vatican Council. The revised ritual presents a three-part complex of rites by which the church bids farewell to the dead: prayers at the time of death, eucharist of Christian burial, and the rite of committal. The revised ritual emphasizes the paschal mystery and attempts to retrieve the more hopeful attitude as found in the earliest rite, the *ordo defunctorum*.

———

Richard Rutherford, *The Death of a Christian:*

The Order of Christian Funerals, revised edn, Collegeville 1990.

MICHAEL S. DRISCOLL

4. *Anglican*. In medieval England, burial rites had two distinguishing features: their complicated and drawn-out structure and their purgatorial theology. Thus when Thomas Cranmer put the service into English in 1549, he simplified its structure and assimilated material from the previous vespers and matins into the 'office'. The rite now began with the churchyard *procession, and the office in church might come before or after the committal. Finally came *proper introit, *collect, epistle and gospel for the (presumably optional) *eucharist. Cautious petitions for the departed were retained, but, with the excision of mass-sacrifice (let alone the earlier confiscation of *chantries), *votive masses for the dead ceased. Purgatory might still have a fingerhold, but the atmosphere reflected a new emphasis on confidence in Christ's welcome to the departed and the assurance of resurrection to life. The service was generally directed to giving hope to the living, rather than seeking deliverance from sufferings for the departed.

The 1552 *BCP* worked out the logic of 1549 more exactly. The service was further truncated, and took place wholly at the graveside. The procession to the grave led almost immediately to the committal, and to an 'office' consisting solely of a reading from 1 Cor. 15, the lesser *litany, the *Lord's Prayer and two other prayers, one of which was the 1549 eucharistic collect (for there was now no eucharist). Petitions for the departed disappeared. For the living there was prayer that they should be joined with the departed in the general resurrection to life. (The 1552 *communion service simultaneously dropped all mention of the departed.) The 1552 rite, revived in 1559, remained unchanged till 1645 (though the 1637 Scottish eucharist reintroduced remembrance of the departed). In 1645 the Puritan *Directory of Public Worship* forbade all burial services, and bodies were to be interred without ceremony, prayer, scripture or preaching.

At the 1661 Savoy Conference the Puritans objected that the 1552 rite was too assured about the state of the departed. They gained the addition of a 'the' to the committal in the 1662 *BCP* – thus expressing hope less specifically of the deceased person's resurrection to life, but, more objectively, of *the* (general) resurrection of all at the last day. Among other changes made at this time were that the service could now be read in church; psalmody preceded the reading of 1 Cor. 15 straight after the entry procession with the coffin; the committal followed the reading; and the rest of the 1552 'office' completed the service; a new *rubric disallowed use of the rite over the unbaptized, the excommunicate and suicides; and the new provision of forms of prayer to be used at sea included a text for a committal 'to the deep'.

The last one hundred and fifty years have seen great changes in the ecclesiastical and social context within which funerals are conducted, and the following in particular have inevitably affected the liturgical evolution not only in England, but also in the Anglican Communion around the world.

First, in England a gulf has opened between church and society and it goes on widening; yet many who have shown no sign of Christian belief are brought to Christian funeral services, which sets up a tension for the church. This factor affects funerals in various other nations also.

Second, Christian funerals are very often now conducted elsewhere than in a church building – in a civic cemetery or crematorium *chapel. Even where there is a full service in church, with a committal to follow in a (perhaps distant) crematorium chapel, this can be both liturgically and pastorally unsatisfactory. The practice of cremation also calls in question the suitability of a committal 'to the ground' and 'earth to earth'. It also opens the possibility (and perhaps desirability) of a later interment (or scattering) of ashes, which, however dignified, means that the actual crematorium service loses some of its finality, and may arguably be diminished in its pastoral effectiveness.

Third, the funeral rites of the different provinces have naturally reflected changes in the style and culture of the more general liturgical provision. This is marked by flexibility, by scope for local creativity, by increased lay roles in leadership, and, in English-language rites, by a modernizing of Tudor English and a concern for *inclusive language. The pastoral situation has often required more relevant liturgical material (as, e.g., at the funeral of a child), and the rites have in many Anglican provinces been enriched with provision for short orders in the home or church prior to the funeral service itself, as well as for burial of ashes and memorial services subsequent to it. The liturgical range has been increased in many places by the re-emergence of communion services as the context for the funeral rite, or at least in close association with it.

Fourth, there has been a reintroduction of petitions for the departed. Partly this arose through the doctrinal convictions of the 'Catholic Revivalists' of the nineteenth century, partly through a growing national sentiment (one much fuelled by the agonies of the First World War) that wished to say *something* about the departed, while being hesitant to state that they were undoubtedly in bliss. These petitions usually have a rationale which is not dependent upon any belief in purgatory, and to that extent might have some show of primitive, and possibly even Anglican, precedent. In Scotland, America and other 'catholic' provinces of the Anglican Communion the reintroduction of such prayers has usually been unchallenged; but in provinces where evangelicals have had an influence such a change has been viewed as misleading and wrong. In England itself the petitions of the Series 1 Burial service very nearly led to the rite's defeat in 1966, and a more unitive approach has been found since then in the Doctrinal Commission's report, *Prayer and the Departed* (1971), in the *Alternative Service Book* funeral rites (1980), and in the *Common Worship* range (2000).

COLIN O. BUCHANAN

5. *Baptist.* For most Baptists the question, 'To whom do we minister in a funeral service?', would be answered without hesitation by the response, 'The bereaved'. For very few would there be any thought that the funeral had any effect upon the deceased apart from the reverent disposal of her or his mortal remains. Baptists share the view of the Protestant Reformation that prayers for the dead are ineffective. As to what happens beyond death, there is more division. Some would speak of immediate entry into heaven or hell. Others would speak of 'soul sleep' in which the departed await the general resurrection. There would be little suggestion of purgation. While these positions might indicate the 'official line', folk religion has its adherents among Baptists as among other Christians. Many bereaved people report conversations with the departed or a sense of their presence. Some are less certain about the doctrines of eternal life than the Christian tradition suggests. Increasingly, ministers are invited to take the funerals of those whose attachment to a Baptist congregation (or to any form of Christian faith and

practice) is at best tenuous. The old certainties have gone; yet many funeral services show few signs of this sea change.

One change from the severe practice of those Reformers who saw the occasion to warn the living of the suddenness of death and the certainty of judgement has been in a disinclination to speak as unequivocally about the fire of hell awaiting the unbeliever. This has probably arisen as much from the horrors of two world wars and the death camps across the world which have been shown on television screens, as from any other cause. There has been a theological shift, giving rise to a softened tone in ministry to the dying and the bereaved. There has also been a sociological shift in the rise of the funeral director (as distinct from the undertaker) who provides a funeral parlour and associated chapel. This has led to a reverence without God in which tributes to the deceased are expected rather than proclamation of the death and resurrection of Christ.

In facing these new pressures Baptists are no different from Christians of many other traditions. Where perhaps there has been a significant change is in the practice among some Baptists of having a private funeral service for families and close friends at the place of disposal, followed by a service of thanksgiving at church (often on the same day) for the wider congregation. There are difficulties with this arrangement. Some may feel excluded from the opportunity to lay the deceased to rest. Others may find the note of celebration too quickly sounded. Certainly, the wider congregation does not confront the darkness of death as it might in a traditional funeral service. Nonetheless, many find it preferable to a big funeral where hundreds attend at church but drift away before the family can return to greet them after the disposal of the body at a cemetery or crematorium.

Whether mourners choose a more traditional service or a private funeral followed by a large thanksgiving, the funeral rite itself will be predominantly a preaching service of the word. There is no sacramental dimension to the rites of death in Baptist faith and practice, and a eucharistic element is not a part of what occurs. Opening sentences and prayers speak of comfort and hope. Readings from the scripture are followed by preaching (sometimes with a tribute from a member of the family or a close friend). Prayers referring to the dead commit her or him to the mercy of God, or – where clear evidence of faith is present – may praise God for the experience of salvation now known by the departed. Prayers will also be made for comfort and consolation of the bereaved. Hymns will normally be sung where the funeral occurs in church. Such hymns will be as likely to refer to the glorious hope of the resurrection as to the darkness of death.

While the foregoing has referred to Baptists' Reformation roots, the ecumenical encounter has not been without influence. A number of congregations now offer additional services to mark death and bereavement. Some take the body into church overnight, so that the coffin stands before the *communion table as a reminder that Christ receives the one who has received him in earthly life. Some offer an annual remembrance service – often at the beginning of November. While resisting any notion of prayers for the dead, the connection with the feasts of *All Saints and *All Souls is not entirely a calendrical coincidence.

Such additional rites are in part a response to public dissatisfaction with a perceived impersonal nature of many funerals. Baptists are not alone in responding to consumerist pressures. The long-standing public silence about death is less a feature than it was. The death of Diana, Princess of Wales, the focus on death in television soap operas (particularly death arising from AIDS) and the placing of floral tributes at sites of disasters are each changing the ways in which people wish to mark death.

How Baptists and other Christian churches will adapt to personalization of funerals remains to be seen. Part of our funerary tradition is the conviction that death treats us all the same. As well as our particularity there is our common human lot. Alongside individual death, we place the story of Jesus, 'who was crucified, died, and was buried; he descended to the dead. On the third day he rose again.' Part of the strength of this Christian observance of death is a resistance to window-dressing the deceased to his or her best advantage. To those who say that they will have questions to ask of God when they die, we reply that it is God who will be asking the questions. Death, despite the increasing pressure to celebrate the life of the deceased, is yet an occasion to reflect that it is a fearful thing to fall into the hands of the living God.

PAUL SHEPPY

6. *Christian Church*. The Christian Church (Disciples of Christ) does not have a formal teaching magisterium nor an authorized book

of services of worship. Congregations are free to develop their own theologies of death and resurrection and to order burial services. However, this practice is heavily influenced by the theologies of the churches in the Ecumenical Movement. Congregations in the Christian Church do not hold unusual beliefs with respect to death and resurrection nor do they engage in atypical Christian burial practices.

Burial practices in this movement typically include three significant moments.

(a) The pastor, often accompanied by lay *elders, visits the bereaved for the reading of scripture, prayer, and initial grief counselling.

(b) A memorial service is usually held at the church building or funeral home. Although this denomination does not prescribe a service book, the denominational publishing house publishes worship resources that are widely used. *Chalice Worship* contains a 'Service of Grateful Memory'. This service usually lasts about thirty minutes: call to worship, music, greeting, opening prayer, prayer of illumination, readings from the Bible, sermon, statements of life in which persons present 'gratefully express the ways in which the deceased has graced their lives', general prayer and dismissal. Increasingly, the funeral service includes the breaking of the loaf. *Chalice Worship* also contains worship materials for the death of a stillborn or newly born child, for an older child, for a suicide, and for occasions of sudden tragedy.

(c) When the body is interred in the earth, a committal service is held at the graveside. The congregation commits the body to the ground, the dead to God, and the survivors to the loving care of the community. When the body is cremated, the pastor often accompanies the family to the crematorium for a committal service. The pastor and other members of the congregation often join the family in receiving the ashes and blessing the place(s) where the ashes will reside.

Colbert Cartwright and O. I. Harrison (eds), *Chalice Worship*, St. Louis 1997; David M. Greenhaw and Ronald J. Allen (eds), *Preaching in the Context of Worship*, St Louis 2000, 103–24; Clark M. Williamson and Ronald J. Allen, *Adventures of the Spirit: A Guide to Worship from the Perspective of Process Theology*, Lanham 1997, 240–53; Clark M. Williamson, *Way of Blessing, Way of Life: A Christian Theology*, St Louis 1999, 297–318.

RONALD J. ALLEN

7. *Congregationalist*. For the earliest Congregationalists there was no religious significance in burials or funerals: they were considered to be civil occasions. The sixteenth-century Separatist, Henry Barrow, found no authority 'in the booke of God, that it belonged to the ministers office to burie the dead'. He and his contemporaries were critical of prayers to the dead, elaborate tombstones (especially those in the shape of an *altar), mourning clothes, and the cost of funerals which was beyond the reach of the poor, not least in the custom of holding a wake afterwards. Barrow was most critical of the fulsome tributes which by the rhetoric of the preacher made the deceased 'a better Christian in his grave than ever he was in his life'. The opposition to ceremonies to accompany burial and to funeral sermons which tended 'to serve the humours only of rich people for a reward' continued through the period of the Commonwealth. In place of the ceremonial of a funeral and burial it seemed good that 'the Christian friends which accompany the dead body to the place appointed for public burial, do apply themselves to meditations and conferences suitable to the occasion: and that the minister, as upon other occasions, so at this time, if he be present, may put them in remembrance of their duty'.

By the eighteenth century the custom was to have a simple but dignified ceremony at the grave, though often attended by many people, and later to have a service in remembrance of that person at which the main focus was on the preaching of the word. With the advent of more formal liturgy and worship books at the end of the nineteenth century and on into the twentieth century came a form of worship with a focus on reading from the scripture and preaching of the word of God. The form of that service was simplified with the increasing popularity of cremation.

Some of the historic tensions have continued down to the present: to have a service in church or simply a ceremony at the graveside or in the crematorium, to deliver a tribute or to preach a sermon, to have a service in church prior to burial or cremation or to have a service of remembrance after burial or cremation. An interesting development has been awareness of the pastoral dimension of the funeral service. The preface to the 1948 *Book of Public Worship* highlights the three aims of a burial service: 'to give place for thanksgiving to God for the gift of a human life to men and for the gift of eternal life in Jesus Christ our Lord, as well as to bring to those who mourn the comforts and consolations of religion'.

Patterns for Worship, the most recent Congregational worship book, seeks to make a link between the funeral service and the recognized dimensions of grieving which are sometimes described sequentially as 'the grieving process'. The value of local customs associated with mourning, together with the centrality of the coffin to the funeral service in church, at the graveside or in the crematorium is a pastoral response to that dimension of grieving which can so easily give rise to denial. A primary function of the funeral is not to avoid, but rather to face the fact of bereavement. Anger is something not to be hidden but to be expressed. There is a flexibility in the Congregationalists' ordering of a funeral service in keeping with their openness to the immediacy of the guidance of the Spirit in worship and their reluctance to be tied to written services. It may be appropriate through the careful use of poetry or appropriate music to give voice to the anger that sometimes is very real.

Prayers of *confession celebrating the forgiving love of God create a context for the natural regret in bereavement, and the burden of guilt, which can weigh heavily. Most importantly the pastoral dimension is met by focusing on the one who has died, recalling their life in a spirit of thanksgiving. Through the pastoral care of the one leading the service, the funeral begins where those who mourn are, and leads them through thankful and personal remembrance of their loved one to an affirmation of the hope of the Christian gospel. This hope is then summed up in the words of committal and the final blessing of the worship. Through the service there is an attempt to respond to the various dimensions of grieving in such a way as to bring 'comfort and consolation'.

Selected texts: J. Huxtable, J. Marsh, R. Micklem, J. Todd, *A Book of Public Worship*, Oxford 1948; Richard Cleaves and Michael Durber, *Patterns for Worship*, Nottingham 1992.

Study: Horton Davies, *WTE* I–II.

RICHARD CLEAVES

8. *Lutheran*. As early as 1520 Luther vigorously attacked masses for the dead, and that attack persisted throughout his life. Because of what he perceived to be the use of the *requiem mass to influence and even manipulate God's dealing with the dead, Luther rejected the medieval rite

of burial but put nothing in its place except for a few hymns. Because Luther provided no order for burial, a great variety of forms and orders for burial existed in Lutheran churches and territories until well into the twentieth century. For a short while, especially in areas influenced by the *Reformed Church, the rejection of traditional rites was so radical that the church sometimes had nothing to do with funerals and left them to the family or to guilds.

The primary purpose of the funeral according to Luther and his followers is, in the face of death, to proclaim the resurrection of the dead. The use of church bells was generally retained at the moment of death or at the burial; the procession to the grave by pastor, verger, students, and a representative of each house in the community was retained to prevent secret burials, which were prohibited by sixteenth-century church orders. During the procession and at the grave hymns were sung to comfort mourners with the promise of forgiveness and the hope of the resurrection. Apparently the hymns were the principal, even the only form used at burial, but soon a sermon and prayers were added. Sometimes the prayers are for the departed. The sermon at first was usually preached only for members of the nobility as a memorial some days after the burial. Social stratification was long evident in burial practice. At Wittenberg (1533) bells were not rung for 'common people'; those of 'middle degree' were given music by school children; 'honourable people' were accompanied with the great bells and a procession.

Further decline is evident in the content of the funeral sermon. In the sixteenth century the sermons were generally biblical exposition and proclamation, but by the seventeenth century a eulogy for the departed was increasingly common with a summary of the person's life. As the eighteenth-century Enlightenment progressed, sermons moved further away from traditional biblical themes. The liturgical recovery of the mid-nineteenth century under the leadership in Germany of such pastors as Wilhelm Löhe provided for the first time complete funeral services, drawn principally from the medieval office of the dead with psalms, readings, *responsories, the Nunc dimittis and prayers. The committal was adapted from the 1552 *BCP*. This was the pattern in Germany and in North America until the *Lutheran Book of Worship* (1978).

The pattern of the present North American Lutheran burial rite is a significant departure from previous practice. It follows not the *daily office but the *eucharist (whether holy *communion is celebrated or not), based on the twentieth-century RC reforms and the American 1979 *BCP*. This change indicates a renewed appreciation of the centrality of the holy communion in Christian life and its appropriateness in a variety of circumstances, as well as being a return to the practice of the early church. The use of the requiem mass is not as widespread in North American Lutheran practice as is the nuptial eucharist, and many funerals are conducted in 'funeral homes'. For faithful church members who are buried from their parish church, however, the eucharist provides in word and action a pastorally desirable and a welcome proclamation of life and hope and strength.

Luther, who provided no burial rite, nonetheless gave the church a profound baptismal theology (*On the Holy and Blessed Sacrament of Baptism,* 1535), and this essay was of primary importance in the drafting of the present rite. Baptismal themes and allusions undergird the rite, for as Luther taught, death is the completion of *baptism. The Burial of the Dead is informed throughout by a paschal spirit. Liturgical provision for the commendation of the dying and a service with the family in the home before the funeral in the church (called Comforting the Bereaved) frees the liturgy of burial to proclaim the joy and confidence of the resurrection. The Burial of the Dead is thus properly understood as an Easter liturgy. The full rite is therefore a stational liturgy, beginning with the commendation of the dying, and continuing its progress with prayers in the home of the deceased, the liturgy in the church, and the interment. Prayers for use on the anniversary of a death are also provided.

Reflecting in part a modern spirit of cheerful optimism as well as the infrequency of funerals in the church, there is no section in the *Lutheran Book of Worship* hymnal with the title 'Death' or 'Burial'. The topical index suggests seven hymns under 'Burial' and sixteen under 'Death' drawn from other sections of the collection. The 1958 Book included six hymns under the heading 'Burial of the Dead'; the 1918 book had seven hymns under the heading 'Death'.

Selected texts: *Luther's Works* LIII, Philadelphia 1965, 'Preface to the Burial Hymns'; *see also* **Books, Liturgical** 8.
Studies: Philip H. Pfatteicher, 'The Burial

of the Dead: The Completion of Baptism', *Dialog* XXXII, 1993, 185–8; *Commentary on the Lutheran Book of Worship: Lutheran Litugy in Its Ecumenical Context*, Minneapolis 1990 (bib.); *Commentary on Occasional Services*, Philadelphia 1983, Chapter 5: 'Ministry at Time of Death'; *Liturgical Spirituality*, Valley Forge, PA 1997, Chapter 9: 'Baptism: Hallowing Life and Death'.

PHILIP H. PFATTEICHER

9. *Methodist.* Not only was brevity a concern for John Wesley in his revision of the 1662 *BCP* funeral liturgy for his *Sunday Service of the Methodists in North America* (1784), so was the removal of language that suggested foreknowledge or certainty of the deceased's eternal outcome. Thus, in the 'Order for the Burial of the Dead,' he omitted Ps. 39, the committal, the prayer 'Almighty God, with whom do live', and portions of the concluding *collect. Instructions about the service's location were left ambiguous in the first part of the rite; the second section was specified to be at the grave. Although Wesley deleted *rubrics denying the burial liturgy to the unbaptized, the excommunicate and suicides, many Methodists in the early years were loath to preside at the funerals of those who died by their own hand.

Methodist funerals were simple and solemn events intended to convey joy instead of hopeless grief. Understood also to be occasions for evangelism, Methodist funerals accentuated through sermons, *extemporary prayer and hymns – though none of these ritual components was mentioned in the official text – the belief that death, for faithful Christians, was the prelude to entry into the nearer presence of God. John Wesley and his brother Charles had published numerous hymns on funereal themes, and these were used at death-bed vigils, wakes, funeral processions, singing after the interment, funeral dinners, and services at which funeral sermons were preached, often weeks after burial. A note of Christian hope and triumph resounds in these hymns, e.g. 'Rejoice for a brother deceased/Our loss is his infinite gain.'

Whereas changes made in 1792 to the burial rite by the Americans further truncated Wesley's text and turned it essentially into a graveside service, nineteenth-century revisions in America – and in Britain – reversed previous efforts at abbreviation and even restored material that Wesley had deleted. The committal was introduced into rites on both sides of the

Atlantic: American Methodist branches were inspired by the form found in the burial rite of the Protestant Episcopal Church, while British Methodist denominations borrowed from the Church of England's *BCP*. Multiple scripture lessons were provided that proclaimed the resurrection promise and consoled the bereaved, with Psalms 39 and 90 and 1 Cor. 15 the principal texts. Prayers were printed in official and unofficial books that took into account the circumstances of death, the stage in life of the deceased (e.g. infant, youth or aged), and the contributions of the particularly godly. In America, the first part of service could take place at the home, the church or the grave, or, by the end of the nineteenth century, at the funeral home. Prior to 1880, English Methodists in rural areas were usually buried in the churchyard of the local Church of England parish, with the *BCP* rite performed by an Anglican clergyman; after that date, a change in law allowed churchyard burials without the *BCP* service and permitted a Methodist preacher to officiate.

By the twentieth century, some denominations had already developed separate orders for the burial of infants and children, and others then did so. The number of options within the rites continued to expand, prayers sensitive to modern concerns about death were composed, and new scripture lessons became standard, notably among them Ps. 23. Even with these changes, the imprint of the *Sunday Service* was still visible in rites produced up to mid-century: 'I heard a voice' (*Audivi vocem*), featuring the text from Rev. 14.13 that is traceable to funeral liturgies of the Sarum rite, still was said in many Methodist funeral services, though perhaps in a location different from that specified in 1784.

The United Methodist Church (1989, 1992) and the Methodist Church of Great Britain (1999) reformed their funeral liturgies and produced new texts along lines that emphasized the paschal character of Christian death and connected the last rite with *baptism. Both have services that assume the shape of the Sunday liturgy, though only the United Methodist rite encourages a (rarely practised) funeral *eucharist and has printed a distinctive thanksgiving prayer for such an occasion. A single United Methodist 'Service of Death and Resurrection' is provided for funerals and memorial services, with a separate liturgy for committal. The British book contains two patterns of funeral service, one leading from a

church service to the committal, the other from a cemetery or crematorium service to the church for a 'Service of Thanksgiving'. Additional resources are given in both denominational books for the time of death, for a wake or vigil, and for the death of a child or a stillbirth.

Karen B. Westerfield Tucker, *American Methodist Worship*, New York 2000, 199–223.
KAREN B. WESTERFIELD TUCKER

10. *Old Catholic.* As a general rule, the Old Catholic churches follow the habit of the catholic churches in the East and West of praying for the deceased and of burying the body or the cremated ashes with liturgical rites. Although they do not subscribe to the RC custom of indulgences for the dead, they do believe that even the dead are alive for God and not beyond the reach of his mercy and compassion. Old Catholics are not known for joining the speculation about the fate of the dead after death; the knowledge that God is greater than our hearts and that God's loving-kindness towards humans knows no limits is enough for them. They do not deny the sinfulness of humanity but do not dwell upon the sins of the deceased. The texts and prayers are therefore characterized more by the anticipation of life eternal with God than petition for forgiveness or fear of damnation.

The German Old Catholic funeral rite, taken as an example here, includes the following elements. In the cemetery chapel or hall: opening rite, including the recitation of a psalm (e.g. Ps. 130 or 23); prayer; a (short) reading (e.g. Isa. 46.4; Rom. 6.3–4, 8; Rom. 8.14–18; Rom. 14.7–9; Phil. 3.20–21; 1 Thess. 4.13–14, 17b–18); a homily; the commendation, including sprinkling with holy water and *incensing. At the gravesite: (blessing of the grave;) lowering of the coffin with John 11.25–26 and a formula; sign of the cross over the lowered coffin; *intercessions; the *Lord's Prayer; blessing of those present; dismissal. The burial of ashes follows more or less the same order. Usually the celebration of the *eucharist follows (or precedes) the funeral.

The official view on death and the dead is beautifully summarized in the following words, taken from the eucharistic prayer to be used in the German Old Catholic Church at the eucharist in conjunction with a funeral or as a memorial service: 'Holy, immortal God, Father of our Lord Jesus Christ and our Father, we praise and thank you because your mercy is infinite. For love you created us mortals and breathed in us life from your immortal life. You will not let grow cold forever the hands that were raised to you, the eyes that looked for your beauty, the hearts that longed for your rest. You will not let those perish in death whom you have called to eternal fellowship and communion with you, you give a share in the mystery of the death and resurrection of your Son . . . Raise us at the end of time when [your Son] comes and makes everything new; grant us then, (together with N. and) with all who have gone before us, the never-ending life in your glory . . . You are worthy to receive the blessing and the honour and the power, for you created all things and people. Through your will they are, and in your love they remain in Jesus, our living Lord.'

THADDEUS A. SCHNITKER

11. *Pentecostal.* Pentecostal funerals seek principally to draw attention to Jesus as the risen Lord and to the hope of the resurrection of the dead through him. Pentecostalism began at the beginning of the twentieth century as a movement of Christians convinced that they were riding the crest of the wave of history toward the consummation of the kingdom of God at the second coming of Jesus Christ. It is for this reason that Pentecostals have been more concerned with the end of the world and the resurrection of the dead than with life after death.

Consequently, Pentecostal funerals tend to draw from texts like John 11.25, in which Jesus is reported to have said of himself: 'I am the resurrection, and the life: he that believeth in me, though he were dead, yet shall he live: and whosoever liveth and believeth in me shall never die.' An examination of ministers' manuals for the Assemblies of God, Church of God, Cleveland, Tennessee and the Church of God in Christ (*see* **Books, Liturgical** 11) reveals the preference for the resurrection theme. Each section on funerals in these manuals is divided up into at least three subsections: scriptural references, sample funeral services, and burial or committal services. John 11.25–26 and 1 Cor. 15 are common to all the manuals, but verses concerning life after death are not. Though life after death in heaven is also used to comfort the grieving in these manuals, the emphasis in their orders of service is on the fulfilment of biblical prophecy in the coming of Christ and the bodily resurrection of the saints.

This emphasis on resurrection in Pentecostal funeral services is rooted in the Pentecostal preference for a literal interpretation of scripture and for what Miroslav Volf terms a 'material' understanding of salvation. Christ is believed to return to earth one day, at which time the saints will rise bodily from the grave. Even now, believers may experience physical healing in their bodies through faith in Jesus as a foretaste of the resurrection of the body yet to come. Resurrection is God's final victory over sickness and over humanity's greatest foe which is death. For Pentecostals, resurrection is the permanent healing of the body for all who believe in Jesus as their saviour. Healing miracles are signs of God's eschatological kingdom to come when all will receive healing. Eternal life and healing beyond the grave at the end of time are regarded as powerful assurances for the grieving family. Thus, in a funeral sermon, the minister will be prone to assure the grieving family that their loved one is safe in heaven with God and that, on the resurrection day, God will complete the healing in their loved one's body by giving him/her a new body that will never see corruption again.

Though comforting the grieving is important for Pentecostal preachers, they also desire to provide implicit witness to those who are unbelievers. The Pentecostal preacher will customarily attempt to convince the unbelieving that Jesus is the risen Christ, and that whoever believes in him will share in Christ's inheritance which is resurrection and life eternal in God's eschatological kingdom to come. Pentecostals have a passionate zeal for evangelism as Christ's great commission before his return. Consequently, Pentecostal preachers often direct the funeral message toward the unbelievers in an effort to evangelize them. 'If the minister can prove by his message, manner of approach, and sympathetic attitude that Christ is real even in the time of death, some of the hardhearted may come back to the church services. If there is no one led to Christ, it is the minister's duty to comfort the family as much as possible' (Zeno C. Tharp, *The Ministers' Guide for Special Occasions*, Cleveland, TN 1953, 143–4). Comforting the family and edifying believers at the funeral service are important, but there is a certain priority placed on converting the lost to Christ.

As with all Pentecostal services, the order of service tends to vary from place to place without a priority placed on a uniformity. But there are commonalties that may be detected in the orders of service across denominational and geographical boundaries. If the service eulogizes a believer and the funeral service is known to consist mostly of Christians, there might even be certain favoured spiritual gifts such as prophecy or speaking in tongues at the service. Ordinarily, however, such commonly experienced gifts are not in evidence at a funeral service. According to William Pickthorn (*Minister's Manual*, Springfield, MO 1965), a typical service would include an opening prayer or invocation, scripture reading, brief sermon and benediction. A solo or open chorus might immediately precede or follow the scripture reading. The pastor might also read a poem at the close of his/her sermon. Tharp recommends that the service begin with a song, then a scripture reading, prayer, sermon, and finally the benediction. Unlike the other ministers' manuals, Tharp includes actual sample sermons and a brief introductory section on pastoral practice. Tharp also includes special sections on heaven and future resurrection. Under each topic are included scripture references and a sermon. The *Church of God in Christ Official Manual* (ed. C. F. Range, Memphis, TN 1992) recommends the following service structure: processional, prayer, music, scripture lesson, condolences and resolutions, obituary, eulogy, recession, and graveside service. The prayer might include the words: 'Hear our prayer O Lord and comfort thy people and enable us to put our trust in thee who art mighty in life and triumphant in death.'

Miroslav Volf, 'Materiality of Salvation: An Investigation in the Soteriologies of Liberation and Pentecostal Theologies', *Journal of Ecumenical Studies* XXVI, 1989, 447–67.

MICHAEL D. MACCHIA

12. *Reformed*. In terms of funeral practices, the Reformed tradition began with what can only be described as a significant overreaction. Repulsed by the melancholy and wrathful tone of funerals in the medieval church and theologically offended by the prayers for the dead, the eulogies, the *absolutions, and other signs of what they viewed as 'popish superstitions', many of the early Reformed congregations did away with burial services altogether. Although Calvin did allow for the preaching of 'an appropriate sermon in the churchyard', the official Genevan church ordinances on record in Calvin's day provide for no burial rites and sternly warn those carrying the deceased to burial to avoid 'all superstitions contrary to the Word of God'. The English-language *Genevan Service Book* (1556) and, a century later, the *Westminster Directory for Public Worship* (1645) are but two examples of formative Reformed documents that call for the body of the deceased to be carried reverently to the grave and buried 'without any ceremony'.

It was more than just the tenets of Reformed theology that caused such severe pruning of the old church practices. Social forces were at work as well. Life expectancy was briefer than today, families larger, distances less easily travelled, and death more woven into the fabric of everyday existence. When someone died, the body was washed and dressed at home and carried within hours or a few days to the place of burial. Friends and neighbours would join the family to help and to share in the mourning, but death was essentially a home-centred event, and often no clergy would be present at any point to mark the passing. Since the medieval churchly funeral rites seemed to the Reformers to be thoroughly devoted to discredited ideas such as purgatory and interceding for the dead, it seemed quite unnecessary for the church to intercede liturgically in what was basically a domestic reality.

However, the elimination of all religious ritual in the circumstance of death, no matter how much this could be argued from Reformed theological principles, nevertheless violated a powerful human need to mark the passing of a human life. Indeed, protests against the prohibition of burial rites arose in Reformed circles as early as 1533 at the Synod of Strasbourg. Pointing both to early Christian practice and to the OT stories of the patriarchs as precedents for burial rites, advocates for a stronger church involvement at the time of death managed to convince the Synod to direct pastors to be present at all burials. Four years later, a Reformed order of service for burials in Strasbourg was created, which included scripture readings, sermon, prayers and the giving of alms. Moreover, there is some evidence that even in those places where official polity forbade burial ritual, actual practice was not always so severe. The *Westminster Directory*, for example, immediately after commanding a ceremony-less burial, hedges its position with a statement that gives a bit of room for an informal ritual: 'Howbeit, we judge it very convenient, that the Christian friends, which accompany the dead body to the place appointed for publick burial, do apply themselves to meditations and conferences suitable to the occasion and that the minister, as upon other occasions, so at this time, if he be present, may put them in remembrance of their duty.'

In the eighteenth and nineteenth centuries there gradually developed in the Reformed churches of Europe and America a fairly consistent funeral pattern. These services were strongly scriptural and more focused upon the promises of God found in the resurrection than upon the life and achievements of the deceased. Typically they involved a two-step ritual: first, a service at the church (or the home) with scripture readings from both Testaments, a sermon on the resurrection and the comfort of the gospel, and prayers of thanksgiving and intercession; and then, second, a brief graveside committal service with scripture sentences, prayer and blessing.

Liturgically these services embodied two powerful and complementary theological themes. First, they were a witness to the resurrection of Christ and to the promises of resurrection to the faithful, and, second, by virtue of involving movement with the body of the deceased from home to church to grave they were a dramatic symbolic enactment of the journey of a saint moving from this world to the next. In contemporary Reformed practice, the first theme has endured, while the second has weakened under a number of stresses. With urbanization and social mobility, the village church and cemetery, which formed the stage for the drama of the procession from church to grave, are for many only a nostalgic memory. With the rise of cremation and body donation and with criticisms of the excesses of the commercial funeral industry, there is less emphasis today on the presence of the body of the deceased in a funeral. With increased secularism of society and a heightened awareness of the psychological and therapeutic dimensions of the grief process, there is less focus on the theological identity of the deceased and more emphasis on the emotional state of the mourner.

Modern Reformed practice may have come full circle. The tradition began by reacting against the dirges of the medieval church and by banning all funerals. Today, once again Reformed churches are reacting against the sad and often expensive funerals of a previous generation, with their focus on the casket and the body. There is a significant trend away from funerals, this time not toward a vacuum, but in favour of 'memorial services', which typically are held after the disposition of the body and which tend to emphasize the joy of the resurrection, the gifts received in the life of the one who has died, and the movement of the mourners from grief to stability.

William D. Maxwell, *The Liturgical Portions of the Geneva Service Book*, London 1931; Richard Rutherford, *The Death of a Christian: The Rite of Funerals*, New York 1980; *The Funeral: A Service of Witness to the Resurrection*, Philadelphia 1986.

THOMAS G. LONG

Gallery

An open space or passage above a side *aisle or aisles and opening onto the *nave of a church. Galleries often have arcades or arched openings. If the opening is a triple arch, it is a *triforium*. This area can also be called a *tribune*. In the Western Christian tradition the assembly usually gathered in the nave of a church with the clergy occupying the *chancel or *sanctuary; thus the gallery seldom served as a place for the assembly. In the Eastern Christian tradition the nave was reserved for the clergy and the performance of the rites, with the congregation occupying both the side aisles and galleries.

MARCHITA B. MAUCK

Gallican Rite *see* Western Rites

Genuflexion *see* Gestures 7

Gestures

The language of gesture and the signals sent out by bodily *posture – body language – are both significant elements in the repertoire of means of communication at the disposal of liturgical worship. Humans of every culture use movements of the limbs, particularly hands and arms, as a means of expression. It is thus no accident that the language of love is a language of the hands nor that those who are deprived of speech or hearing converse so naturally through signing with the hands. For Christians there is another element: gestures affirm the incarnation, confirming the sanctity of our bodies, involving them in prayer and declaring them to be our primary instrument for worship. Stylized and circumscribed by carefully considered use over the ages, our instinctive gestures are harnessed to the rite to become the basis for the prescribed and formal actions that constitute recognizable worship. Most recently, therefore, in the Constitution on the Sacred Liturgy of the RC Church, official acknowledgement is made of the necessity of involving the whole person in liturgical worship: 'To promote active participation, the people should be encouraged to take part by means of . . . actions, gestures and bodily attitudes' (*Sacrosanctum concilium* 30).

Individuals in the congregation participate physically in the liturgy for their own sake, but a shared liturgical body-language also influences the worship experience of others. By the deliberate use of a common body-language in the worshipping assembly, unity in ritual, belief and community is affirmed and through the discipline of ceremonial action, minds are focused on the words and actions of the liturgy and people learn to pray with the totality of their being. Presidential gestures are perhaps even more important, enabling and supporting the prayer of the assembly and not distracting from it. To preside at an act of worship, therefore, requires skill and sensitivity in 'an art of great understatement'.

The wealth of expressive liturgical gestures, actions and movements used in our worship is derived from many sources. Some date back to early Christian times; others come from the medieval period; some have evolved more recently. They can be categorized as those actions that (1) express or embody an interior attitude; (2) serve a symbolic purpose; (3) express relationships on both horizontal – between members of the assembly – and vertical – between the worshipper and God – levels; and (4) are purely functional. Gestures with the hands are the most frequently employed by the presiding minister in liturgy: hands opened wide in prayer; folded in devotion; gracefully extended in welcome, invitation and inclusion; and tracing signs of indication and benediction. The following are currently still in use in various Christian traditions.

1. *Beating the Breast*. Striking the chest with a hand is a gesture of grief (Nahum 2.7) and so by extension of penitence or sorrow for sin. In the parable told by Jesus in Luke's Gospel concerning the Pharisee and the tax-collector, the latter beats his breast and says, 'God be merciful to me, a sinner' (Luke 18.13). The gesture is similarly used by the witnesses of the crucifixion (Luke 23.48). In the RC rite, the gesture is still prescribed in the *confession of sin at the opening of the *eucharist at the words *mea culpa* – 'my own fault' – where it is an expression of personal responsibility for sin and a sign of repentance. It is also used by some as an expression of unworthiness at the invitation to *communion.

2. *Signing with the Cross*. This specifically Christian gesture was certainly known as early as the end of the second century when Tertullian bears witness to its use in all the ordinary actions of daily life (*De corona* 3). It symbolizes a believer's unity with Christ, confessing the cross as central to the mystery of salvation and affirming baptismal identity. While multiple signings of the cross at every point in domestic life may never have become general outside Tertullian's circle, it certainly became widespread as a liturgical gesture and by the time of Augustine was prescribed at many points in the ceremonial for every kind of sacramental action: 'Only when the sign of the cross is made on the foreheads of the faithful, as on the water itself with which they are regenerated, or on the oil with which they are anointed with chrism, or on the sacrifice with which they are nourished, are any of these things duly performed' (*Tractatus in Joannem* 118). Such a claim led to the view that the sign of the cross was essential to the valid performance of sacramental acts and, because this appeared to reinforce an unacceptable *ex opere operato* system of sacramental operation, resulted in the rejection of the gesture by the Protestant Reformers. A little of the flavour of this controversy is preserved in the *rubrics of the *BCP* of the Church of England where the sign of the cross is retained only in *baptism but on the clear understanding that it 'is no part of the substance of the sacrament' but is 'a lawful outward ceremony and honourable badge, whereby the person who has been baptized is dedicated to the service of him that died upon the Cross'.

The signing of the forehead, lips and breast before the reading of the gospel at the eucharist dates from the eleventh century and, together with signing the page of the book, remains a ceremonial gesture for the one proclaiming and for the listening assembly in some traditions today. Signings proliferated in the *eucharistic prayer in the medieval rites – the Sarum rite prescribes twenty-six – but these have been reduced to one at the invocation of the Holy Spirit in the modern RC rite. Here it is both a gesture of *blessing or sanctification and a gesture of indication.

As can be seen from the above, the sign of the cross may be made over persons or things. It may be self-administered or directed towards others. As practicalities dictate, it can take several forms: with the thumb on the forehead – probably the original gesture noted by Tertullian – or on various parts of the body when associated with *anointing with oil; with the whole hand, or two fingers, touching forehead, breast, right shoulder and then left as is still done in the East (since the thirteenth century the Western tradition has made the sign from left to right). The sign of the cross may be made with a large, graceful gesture over the assembly in blessing. In so doing, *bishops may make three smaller signs of the cross over the congregation in the centre, to the left and then to the right. When it was first associated with the trinitarian formula, 'In the name of the Father, and of the Son, and of the Holy Spirit', the sign became a declaration of orthodoxy in the face of Arian error. Its continuing vitality as a gesture in common use has a clear baptismal reference, particularly explicit when associated with taking holy water on entering or leaving church.

3. *Laying-on of Hands.* Touching to show love, care and compassion is an instinctive gesture among human beings and so is a natural means of pastoral communication in the rites connected with ministries of healing, absolving, reconciling and blessing. This ritualized physical contact has also the acquired connotation of the transfer of power, grace or authority, making the gesture appropriate to ceremonies of *ordination, commissioning or *confirmation. The scriptural basis for this gesture in all the above areas is very wide (e.g. Gen. 48.14; Mark 6.5; 16.18; Acts 8.19; 13.3; 1 Tim. 4.14).

The laying-on of hands is sometimes combined with anointing with oil in rites of wholeness and healing, initiation (baptism and confirmation) and empowerment (ordination). When these rites are performed publicly in the worshipping community this provides them with additional visible expression. While generally in this gesture the hands are laid on the top of the head, in wholeness and healing rites the laying-on of hands – the gesture employed by Jesus himself – may be to another appropriate part of the body. Here care must always be taken to see that the touching is appropriate and not seen by the recipient as an invasion of privacy.

4. *Extension of the Hands in Blessing.* This gesture is related to the above, symbolizing the transmission of power from one person to another individual or to the assembly. Moses stretched out his hand over the Red Sea and it divided (Ex. 14.21). He also guided the fortunes of the Israelites in battle with the Amalekites by stretching out both his hands and empowering them for victory (Ex. 17.11–13). The Lord himself, 'with a mighty hand and an outstretched arm', gathers his people together and restores them (Ezek. 20.33). Thus at the end of eucharistic or other liturgies the presiding minister may bless the assembly with outstretched hands.

5. *Extension of the Hands in Prayer.* Associated with raising the eyes heavenward, the gesture of uplifting hands in prayer is ancient. Paul exhorts the community to pray 'lifting up holy hands' (1 Tim. 2.8) and Tertullian likened the gesture to the crucifixion of Christ (*De oratione* 14). Orant figures (Latin *orans*, praying) with such outstretched hands are to be found on Christian sarcophagi and in the frescos adorning the burial places in the Roman catacombs from the mid-third century. While this was the preferred posture for prayer for the early Christians, and is still often preserved in the gestures of the presiding minister during principal liturgical prayers, the widespread adoption of kneeling (*see* **Posture** 2) diminished its more general use. More convenient in this position is the now familiar gesture of folding the hands in prayer, the palms pressed lightly together. This seems to have been derived from a feudal gesture of homage by a vassal to his lord. Today, those influenced by the *Charismatic Movement in worship are often wont to pray and sing with hands upraised: a case where a spontaneous expression of rapture has recovered an ancient tradition.

6. *Extending the Hands for Communion.* The reception of the bread of the eucharist in the hand by the communicant was early given a symbolic meaning as can be seen in Cyril of Jerusalem's *Mystagogical Catecheses* 5.21: 'Do not approach with your wrists extended, or your fingers open; but make your left hand a throne for your right in which to receive your King. And, having made a hollow of your palm, receive the body of Christ and say, Amen.' This gesture, common in the Reformation churches since the sixteenth century owing to the widespread use of leavened bread, has been revived

in the RC Church since the liturgical reforms of the Second Vatican Council.

7. *Bending the Knee and Bowing the Head.* Both of these are vivid gestures of humility and reverence. The first is also known as genuflection and derives from a gesture of civil respect before imperial officials in antiquity. The action recalls Phil. 2.10, 'at the name of Jesus every knee should bend'. From the eleventh century in the West it was used at the words 'and was incarnate' in the Nicene *Creed at every Sunday eucharist and at the words 'and the Word became flesh' in the *Last Gospel daily, but where used today, the gesture is generally reserved only to the feasts of *Christmas and the *Annunciation. Since the fourteenth century the presence of the blessed *sacrament has been acknowledged by a genuflection and this reverence was extended to the *altar, the *crucifix and the bishop. A profound bow of the head and upper body is now more frequently used in these cases even when genuflection is prescribed in the rubrics, not least because it is a more graceful action and less awkward to perform. Such bows are an abbreviated form of the prostration once a regular feature of Christian worship (*see* **Posture 4**) but now a more recognizable characteristic of Muslim prayer. In the OT prostration or bowing is symbolic of the recognition of divine power and of the adoration due to the Almighty (Ps. 86.9). This symbolism undergirds the gesture in some liturgies where the *deacon bids the assembly be receptive to the divine blessing, 'Bow your heads and pray for God's blessing.' In the late medieval period it became the custom to bow the head at the mention of the name of Jesus, at the Gloria Patri at the end of each psalm (*see* **Doxology**), at the name of the *saint whose feast day it was and during the *Sanctus at the eucharist. The last of these is no longer prescribed in the RC rubrics.

See also **Kiss, Ritual.**

Gestes et paroles dans les diverses familles liturgiques, Conferences Saint Serge, Paris 1978; R. D. H. Bursell, *Liturgy, Order and the Law*, Oxford 1996; P. J. Elliott, *Ceremonies of the Modern Roman Rite*, San Francisco 1995; Balthasar Fischer, *Signs, Words and Gestures*, New York 1981; M. R. Francis and K. F. Pecklers (eds), *Liturgy for the New Millennium*, Collegeville 2000; J. A. Jungmann, *The Mass of the Roman Rite*, New York 1951; Aidan Kavanagh, *Elements of Rite*, New York 1982; A. G. Martimort et al., *The Church at Prayer* I, Collegeville 1987; M. P. Perham, *New Handbook of Pastoral Liturgy*, London 2000.

JEREMY HASELOCK

Girdle *see* **Vestments** 3(a)

Gloria in excelsis

see **Doxology**; **Music in the Mass of the Roman Rite**; **Ordinary**

Gloria Patri *see* Doxology

Godparents

Modern RC practice makes a canonical distinction between 'sponsors' and 'godparents'. In the case of adult initiation, sponsors are required to provide witness and guidance to each of the *catechumens from enrolment in the catechumenate until election for *baptism. At the rite of election either these sponsors or other persons may be chosen as 'godparents', properly speaking, to accompany the 'elect' during *Lent through the remainder of the catechumenal process leading to baptism. In the case of infants in the RC rite, godparents serve as sponsors as well, and at *confirmation for those baptized in infancy, either the godparents (ideally) or another sponsor is again required to accompany the candidates during catechesis and to present them to the *bishop or delegated *presbyter at the rite.

Other Christian traditions tend not to make a distinction between sponsors and godparents and treat the terms as equivalent. Historically, sponsors make their first clear appearance in the so-called *Apostolic Tradition*, attributed to Hippolytus of Rome, where, at the enrolment of catechumens, they testify to the worthiness of those seeking to enrol. Sponsors appear again during the catechumenal process itself, especially at the election to baptism, where they are again called on to bear witness to the catechumens' progress in conversion. And, during baptism itself, especially in the case of infants who cannot answer for themselves, sponsors (explicitly members of the candidate's family) respond on their behalf to the renunciation and three credal questions accompanying the baptismal immersions. Such roles and responsibilities continued through the early Middle Ages, even for infant candidates, with sponsors or godparents continuing to be present at various intervals during Lent: for enrolment or election, at the *scrutinies, and during the baptismal rite.

The special terminology of godparent may be first encountered in the late-fourth-century-pilgrimage-diary of Egeria, where sponsors for initiation in Jerusalem are identified as 'father' for male candidates and 'mother' for females. Although Egeria's own description may well have included biological parents of the candidates as sponsors, requirements are eventually set to exclude parents from this godparent role altogether in order to reinforce, undoubtedly, the ecclesial dimension of baptismal sponsorship. In the medieval West, however, especially in light of the dominance of infant baptism, the role of godparents became less ecclesial and much more familial in nature. That is, godparents were viewed as legal guardians who might provide for the support and welfare of their 'godchild' in the event of the parents' death. In addition, this relationship was solidified canonically and legally by various kinship bonds, restrictions and responsibilities.

Various regulations governing the selection of sponsors and godparents appear in the baptismal policies of most churches today. In some churches only those who are fully initiated and active members of the particular communion in which the baptism is to be celebrated are permitted to serve as godparents. In a modern ecumenical context, however, where the common and unifying sacramental bond of baptism is often highlighted, several churches do permit fully initiated and active persons from other Christian traditions to serve in this capacity, so long as their own communion accepts and supports the particular theology of baptism in the candidate's own church. That is, a sponsor or godparent from a church that teaches and practises only believer's baptism would normally be unacceptable as a godparent in a church that teaches and practises infant baptism.

Joseph H. Lynch, *Godparents and Kinship in Early Medieval Europe*, Princeton 1986.
MAXWELL E. JOHNSON

Good Friday

The Friday before *Easter Day is known as Good Friday in the Christian tradition. A pre-paschal *fast was observed on this day in earliest Christian practice. Later in antiquity, Friday became the day on which Christ's passion and death on the cross were primarily commemorated.

There are three main components to the Western medieval Christian service for Good Friday, a structure retained by some (e.g. RC) churches today. The earliest two components, part of the Jerusalem liturgy in the late fourth century, were the formal reading of the passion of Christ (from John), and the *veneration of a relic of the wood of the cross. This veneration essentially consisted of a *procession to the relic, held by the *bishop flanked by *deacons. The members of the congregation would approach the relic individually and ritually kiss it.

The early medieval Roman practice developed in two different liturgical 'circles': the *papal liturgy, and the *presbyteral liturgy of the smaller Roman 'parish' churches, or *tituli*. The papal liturgy stressed the formal reading of the passion (as on *Palm Sunday), and a series of 'solemn orations' (*orationes solemnes*), an elaborate set of intercessory prayers. The liturgy of the 'parishes', however, focused on the reading of the passion, the veneration of the cross, and the distribution of *communion from the sacrament reserved from the eucharist of *Maundy Thursday (the day before).

As the medieval period progressed, the shape of the Good Friday liturgy in Europe underwent several changes. The themes of sorrow and mourning associated with the day became even more intense, and took on additional overtones of anti-Semitism; the day itself began to be regarded as an 'unlucky' day for any number of activities. Some ritual elements became even more dominant, while others were less emphasized. The solemn orations came to number nine in all; the eighth prayer, for the conversion of the Jews, took on an anti-Semitic tone by referring to 'the perfidious Jews'. The rite of the veneration of the cross came to overshadow even the reading of the passion, and the ceremonial surrounding the act of veneration became more complex. An elaborate procession with a veiled cross and the sung *Trisagion* acclamation began the veneration rite, and the act of kissing the cross itself was augmented by a triple ritual genuflection and spoken versicles. A series of sung verses and responses, the *Improperia*, were sung during this veneration rite. These 'Reproaches' were understood to be Christ's reproaching the people of the Jews for causing his passion and crucifixion. Finally, the reception of communion gradually became restricted to the presider himself.

The liturgical reforms of Vatican II produced a Good Friday liturgy which maintained all three ritual elements – the reading of the passion, the procession with and veneration of the cross, and the distribution of communion from the reserved sacrament – celebrated in the mid-afternoon or early evening. Other churches have adopted similar patterns, though in some cases without communion from the reserved sacrament. Anti-Semitic overtones have been eliminated, both in the official liturgical structures and in the private devotional practices of the day. One of these private devotions, often celebrated by groups of clergy and laity in churches earlier in the day on Good Friday, is the *Stations of the Cross. Along with *Ash Wednesday, Good Friday is observed as an official fast day in the RC tradition: traditionally, only one full meal is permitted, as well as two smaller 'snacks', which, if combined, would be less than a second full meal.

For bibliography, *see* **Holy Week**.

JOANNE M. PIERCE

Gospel *see* **Readings, Eucharistic**

Gown *see* **Vestments** 3(d)

Grace

Derived from the Latin word *gratia* in the sense of gratefulness, the word grace is used to denote a short prayer of thanksgiving at the beginning or end of a meal. The practice of blessing God for the gift of food and drink at meals was established in Jewish circles at the time of Jesus, and lies behind many references to 'blessing' or 'giving thanks' in the NT (e.g. Mark 14.22–23; Acts 27.35; 1 Cor. 10.16). Out of this, the *eucharistic prayer developed. But Christians have also continued to say grace at other meals, and many traditional forms of this have survived in religious communities, colleges and schools.

The word grace also designates the scriptural verse 2 Cor. 13.14 ('The grace of our Lord Jesus Christ . . .'), which was being used as a liturgical greeting at least as early as the fourth century. In the English *BCP* of 1559, however, it was employed as the conclusion to morning and evening prayer, and its use for this purpose then spread to other churches, although many of them have also recently revived its employment as an initial greeting.

EDITOR

Gradual

see **Chants of the Proper of the Mass; Music in the Mass of the Roman Rite**

Great Entrance

The highly ritualized *procession transferring bread and wine from their place of preparation to the *altar during the *eucharistic liturgy in the East, the equivalent of the Western *offertory. Developed in the Byzantine church, the great entrance is also part of the *Armenian rite and was included in the Syrian eucharist until at least the thirteenth century.

Contrary to Western traditions, Eastern churches have always restricted the action to the clergy (although the emperor occasionally participated). People brought their gifts whenever they arrived at church and left them in the *skeuophylakion* with *deacons, who would often note who brought what and collect names to be commemorated. During the liturgy of the word, the deacons would prepare an appropriate quantity of bread and wine to be taken into the church just before the *eucharistic prayer.

Justin Martyr notes a transfer of gifts in the second century (*First Apology* 65), but it was simple and purely practical. The first reference of an elaborate entrance is by Patriarch Eutychios in sixth-century Constantinople (*Sermo de paschate et de ss. eucharistia*). Around this time the Cherubic Hymn (*Cheroubikon*) was introduced to cover the actions formerly performed in silence.

Today the people sing the *Cheroubikon* while the clergy prepare the area with prayers and *incensation. They take up the *chalice and paten, processing from the *prothesis through the nave and depositing the gifts on the altar. People often reach out to touch the celebrants or vessels. Its allegorical interpretation combines Christ's entrance into Jerusalem, his going to his passion and taking his body to the tomb.

Robert F. Taft, *The Great Entrance*, 2nd edn, Rome 1978.

JOHN KLENTOS

Gregorian Chant

The traditional monophonic music of Western Christianity has been variously described as: (1) *Cantus Romanus* (Roman chant); (2) *Cantus planus* (plainchant or plainsong); (3) *Can-*

tus Gregorianus (Gregorian chant). The term
'Roman chant' is misleading, as there exists
another repertoire, 'Old Roman chant', quite
distinct from what we now know as 'Gregorian
chant'. The term *Cantus planus* was originally
used to distinguish the traditional Latin chant of
Western Christianity from the various kinds of
measured music and *polyphony that developed from the tenth century onwards. The more
familiar term, Gregorian chant, refers back to
the legend which attributes the composition of
the basic repertoire to St Gregory the Great
(540–604) under divine inspiration. Gregory
may have had some part in the codification of
the chants of the *mass in the *Antiphonale
Missarum* that bears his name, but there is
uncertainty about the extent of his musical
activities, and claims for its authorship have
been made for others. This chant became official throughout the Carolingian empire under
Pépin le Bref (*c.* 715–68).

The chant has its roots firmly embedded in
the Temple and synagogue music of Judaism.
During the first centuries, as the Latin church
developed its own liturgy, the chant which
carried that liturgy grew and was passed on to
future generations by oral transmission. Musical notation only appeared much later, the earliest sources being found outside Rome, in St
Gall, Einsiedeln, Metz, Chartres and Laon. One
widely held theory is that at some stage, possibly in the mid-seventh century, an earlier form
of the chant repertoire, stemming from Rome,
underwent a fundamental revision somewhere
in Gaul, returning to Rome in its new guise,
thereafter recognized as standard. Bruno Stäblein has suggested that three reforming abbots
in Rome itself may have initiated this revision.
It is remarkable that, with few exceptions (such
as chants from the diocese of Milan, with its
own distinct Ambrosian chant), all the earliest
manuscripts with musical notation (ninth or
tenth century) bear witness to a surprising uniformity. One single, vigorous tradition appears
everywhere, from the British Isles to Switzerland and from the Alps to the Pyrenees.

The repertoire remained substantially intact
until late into the sixteenth century. Thereafter
the melodies suffered mutilation and distortion
at the hands of successive editors, who took
upon themselves to change the underlay of the
text to bring it into line with Renaissance theories of Latin prosody. They also drastically
reduced the number of notes in the florid
chants. These refurbished editions became the
received official versions and were used from

the end of the sixteenth century to the beginning of the twentieth. Towards the middle of
the nineteenth century, the Abbey of Solesmes
undertook the arduous task of preparing new
editions based on a comparative study of the
original manuscripts.

The principal official service books in use
today are largely the result of this study. The
Graduale contains the restored melodies of
the *eucharist, and the *Antiphonale* those of
the divine office (*see* **Daily Prayer** 3). These
books represent the largest assemblage of
monophonic music in existence, totalling about
three thousand melodies. They cover every
phase of liturgical worship from *baptism to
the *blessing of aircraft. Recent research into
the earliest notational signs provides a fuller
understanding than previously of the rhythm
and dynamics of the chant when it was still a
living oral tradition. Gregorian chant, to use
the now generally accepted term, is spiritually,
aesthetically and practically the ideal, as well
as being the only official church music of
Western Christianity. Firmly based on biblical
texts, mainly those of the OT, it is truly sung-
prayer and prayer-song.

Mary Berry, 'The Restoration of the Chant and
Seventy-five Years of Recording', *Early Music*
VII, 1979, 197–217; Eugène Cardine, *Grego-
rian Semiology*, Solesmes 1982; René-Jean
Hesbert (ed.), *Antiphonale Missarum Sextu-
plex*, Rome 1935; David Hiley, *Western Plain-
chant: A Handbook*, Oxford 1993; Bruno
Stäblein and Margareta LandWehr-Melnicki,
'Die Gesänge des altrömischen Graduale Vat.
lat. 5319', *Monumenta monodica medii aevi* II,
Kassel 1968, 54*–56*.

MARY BERRY

Harvest Thanksgiving

There is evidence in early Christianity for the
practice of offering of the first-fruits of the
harvest, which were then used for the support
of the community's ministers, following OT
prescription (Num. 18.8–32). This was the
beginning of the widespread Christian practice
of paying 'tithes'. The texts of the later liturgical rites of offering in both East and West lay
increasing stress on petition for benefits to
accrue to the offerer rather than on the earlier
thanksgiving for the gifts of creation. Although
in the patriarchal liturgy of Constantinople 15
August was designated as the day for offering
grapes, it was observed on 6 August or even

earlier in other places in both East and West, presumably because the climate brought grapes to maturity a little sooner there, and in regions where grapes were not grown, apples were offered instead. But the most common occasion for a harvest thanksgiving in the medieval West was 11 November, the feast of St Martin of Tours, and this was a public holiday in several countries. In some places this celebration continued down to the twentieth century. As is clear from its date, it marked the conclusion of the ingathering rather than the offering of first-fruits (although it did include within its festive meal the drinking of the first wine made from the grapes that had been harvested), and apart from attendance at mass it was largely secular in character. It was from this celebration, continued in the Netherlands even after the Reformation, that the Pilgrim Fathers inherited the *Thanksgiving observance which they introduced into North America.

In England 1 August was kept as a feast of thanksgiving for first-fruits of the wheat harvest and known as 'Lammas Day', the name being derived from the Anglo-Saxon 'Hlafmaesse', i.e., 'Loaf-mass', since on this day bread made from the new wheat was presented at the mass and solemnly blessed. The custom disappeared at the Reformation, and all that was left was the secular 'harvest home' – a festal meal held at the conclusion of the ingathering of the crops rather than at its inception. In 1843 the Revd R. S. Hawker revived the Lammas custom in his parish in Cornwall, and used bread made from the first ripe wheat as the sacramental bread of the *eucharist, but on the first Sunday in October instead of on 1 August, a date close to the usual time of the harvest home, as part of his purpose was to redeem the secular character of that celebration. Thereafter many local churches took it upon themselves to institute annual services of thanksgiving for the harvest and these became very popular, especially in rural areas. Eventually, in 1862 the Church of England made official provision for such a service, and similar forms have been included in many recent revisions of the *BCP* throughout the Anglican Communion and in other churches.

———

Paul F. Bradshaw, 'The Offering of the First-fruits of Creation: An Historical Study', *Creation and Liturgy: Studies in Honor of H. Boone Porter*, ed. Ralph McMichael, Jr, Washington, DC 1993, 29–41.

EDITOR

Healing, Services of
see **Sick, Liturgical Ministry to**

Hindu Worship

1. *Puja*. Hindu worship can be identified most simply as *puja*, which ordinarily and in its major forms is an encounter with a god or goddess embodied in an iconic or aniconic material form, and worshipped by a purified and ultimately transformed worshipper. Most Hindu worshippers are functionally henotheists, acknowledging many deities but confessing supreme devotion to some particular deity of personal or family choice. The deities worshipped vary greatly, from the ancient deities Agni and Soma, to widely popular deities such as Shiva, Vishnu, Rama, Krishna and Ganesha, local deities such as Aiyappan and Murukan and Swaminarayana, and goddesses such as Lakshmi, Kali and the great Goddess, Devi. Although worship varies according to situation and status, in its basic dynamic it mirrors the activities – purification, gift, food, rest – by which one might honour a guest of high rank or show gratitude to a patron and protector.

2. *Puja as Temple Worship and Home Worship*. Temples are the primary and paradigmatic location for this worship. Temples have often been dominant structures located centrally in villages or towns, though now they are found in many diverse urban and suburban locales. Classic temple architecture encodes the cosmos, enabling worshippers to make the gradual transition from an ordinary and dangerous world to a holy locale where encounter with the deity is possible and safe. Journeying through the porticoes of a large temple and inwards toward the central shrine replicates passage through personal and cosmic spaces towards the divine centre.

3. *The Calendar of Temple Worship*. Since most Hindus believe in the real presence of the deity, the temple priests carry out worship even in the absence of other worshippers. In theory at least, one can visit a temple deity at almost any time, but most worship locales operate by calendars which mark ordinary and extraordinary events. The daily schedule begins with the awakening of the deity in the early morning and concludes with the final preparations for sleep at night. Daytime is punctuated with prayers and acts of service in honour of the deity. The routine is observed daily, but Saturday is the

most popular day for worship by the wider community. There are also seasonal rites, marked by the lunar or solar calendar, the particular feasts of particular deities and saints, and other popular monthly or annual events. Other temple rituals occur according to the needs and desires of worshippers: particular rites in times of need, rites of passage, weddings and commemorations of the dead. Special rites of purification and penance occur periodically or when some particular emergency requires immediate rectification.

4. *Materials Used in Temple Worship.* Ancient rites presumed the presence of sacred fire as the authorizing witness for worship. Many rites also included animal sacrifice, although even in ancient times the shedding of blood was a secondary feature. Today, except in some Goddess temples, animals are rarely sacrificed. Even in ancient times vegetal offerings were acceptable substitutes for sacrificed animals in many rites; today the primary offering materials are water, melted butter, yogurt, honey and similar liquids customarily poured over the consecrated images in honorific cleansing. There are also food offerings of rice, fruit, nuts and raisins, etc., and these are subsequently shared with worshippers as tokens of divine favour (*prasad*). Incense and flowers, oil lamps and camphor, are also abundant. The consecrated images themselves can be simple or elaborate constructions made of clay, stone or metal; these can be iconic representations of divine forms, or aniconic symbols such as the bare column known as Shiva's lingam. When consecrated, these images are transformed by the (temporary or permanent) entrance of the divinity into them.

5. *Priests and Patrons.* Many rituals require the participation of brahmins, high-class religious agents, for proper recitation and purity, but two distinctions must be noted. First, not all brahmins function as public ritual practitioners, nor must all priests be brahmins; many come from other classes as well, including traditionally lower classes. Most priestly positions are a family affair, passed on from father to son. Second, the real enabler of a ritual is the patron, the householder (normally, a married man with property and in good health) who requests and pays for the performance. The priests are agents of the patron's intentions, and their reward is their stipend; the fruits of the performance itself accrue to the patron. Most

ritual descriptions and prescriptions have in mind male gods, priests and patrons. The oldest ritual texts mention women merely in relation to their husbands and as necessary though subordinate collaborators in male ritual activities. Even in Goddess temples priests are most often male, though female worshippers may predominate; today though, most believers and scholars readily admit that women possess diverse ritual traditions attuned specifically to their interests and values. So too, in contemporary popular religion and urban settings many traditional class barriers and distinctions are either modified or entirely discarded.

6. *Sacred Word.* Traditional worship required the recitation of metred verses (mantras) addressed to various deities, and this verbal enunciation of ritual meaning was considered essential to right performance, which always combined word and action. In more orthodox temples such verses are recited in the classical Sanskrit language. Since these are understood by few participants today, most temples also offer prayers in the vernacular, alongside Sanskrit recitation and not in replacement of it. While traditional recitation was not normally accompanied by musical instruments, at many popular rites and festivals singing is accompanied by stringed instruments, drums, cymbals, etc. Where heightened religious experience is a priority, ecstatic singing and dancing are not uncommon.

7. *Ritual Synthesis.* Although temple worship of divine images is vastly more popular today than Vedic fire rituals, those ancient rites are still performed, even if in elite specialist enclaves. More commonly, old fire rituals are incorporated into more popular temple rituals, as Vedic rites are used to adorn and enhance popular worship. Vedic rites are conceded their place, while newer rites are legitimated by a link to ancient traditions. Even transgressive tantric ritual is distinguished in part by its violation of the acknowledged boundaries of orthodox practice, as prohibited practices – e.g. the consumption of meat, alcohol and drugs, a preference for impure locales such as cremation grounds, sex acts – are deliberately ritualized by elite practitioners to signal a transition to a sacred realm.

8. *Worship at Home.* Although the temple context is normative, one can exaggerate its importance. Worshippers are not pressured to appear

regularly at temples. Rather, much Hindu worship takes place in homes, which usually have small prayer spaces or rooms, often near the kitchen. This worship is not private, however; often a senior male or female family member performs the worship for all and, as with other familial duties, this worship affects all even if it is the responsibility of only a few. Women are prominent participants in home worship; important rites are performed for women and by women, in the absence of males.

9. *Purposes and Effects of Worship.* In ancient times, ritual worship was usually aimed at the propitiation of individual deities, powerful beings able to harm or help. Since today's strongly monotheistic Hindu traditions continue to recognize the existence of multiple deities as worthy of worship, even today rituals may honour different deities side by side. So too, specific material goals can be stipulated, e.g. wealth, success in business, the birth of a son, and even (though frowned upon) the distress of enemies. Traditionally 'heaven', either a specific place or generalized state of happiness, was often stipulated the final cause of ritual performance. But many classical texts also highlighted the systemic preservation of cosmic and social order and warding off of chaos as central values dependent on correct performance.

Even the ancient Upanishads (before 500 BCE) emphasized the transformation of individual consciousness as a higher ritual goal. The aims of external ritual performance could in some cases be accomplished by interior mental performance sometimes as detailed and precise as exterior practice. Today, much Hindu worship aims at this personal transformation, and ritual practice is a means of discipline, purification and the enhancement of detachment and surrender; much worship aims at union or even identity with the deity through realization of one's own divine nature. Although this entire range of motives remains operative today, many worshippers aim simply at demonstrating their love toward the divine recipient of worship.

10. *Theology.* Much of the preceding has been explained and interpreted technically by indigenous liturgical theologians. Most notable is the liturgical science known as Mimamsa (from before 200 BCE). Mimamsa theologians so emphasized the sufficiency and autonomy of right performance – simple, economically

explained, in harmony with key texts and other rites – that they relegated to secondary status both the deities worshipped and the intentions of individual performers; ritual is intrinsically worthwhile, whatever the reality or force of external factors. Particularly after the fifth century CE one also finds other more theistic and temple-oriented liturgical theologies, e.g. the Vishnu-oriented Pancharatra and the Shiva-oriented Agamas. Today, temples commonly list their rituals on websites which blend the details of scheduling with theological explanations aimed at a wide audience inside and outside India.

11. *Other Areas.* Space allows only brief mention of other aspects of Hindu ritual practice and worship: personal vows and acts of purification; pilgrimages to holy places such as sacred mountains and rivers; seasonal community festivals and street processions; tantra and other ecstatic rites; the changing face of Hindu worship in urban India, and among immigrant Hindus outside of India and converts to Hinduism.

Gudrun Buhneman, *Puja: A Study in Smarta Ritual*, Vienna 1988; Francis X. Clooney, *Thinking Ritually: Rediscovering the Purva Mimamsa of Jaimini*, Vienna 1990; Diana Eck, *Darsan, Seeing the Divine Image in India*, New York 1996; Stella Kramisch, *The Hindu Temple*, Delhi 1996; Julia Leslie (ed.), *Roles and Rituals for Hindu Women*, Cranbury, NJ 1991; Vasudha Narayanan, *The Vernacular Veda: Revelation, Recitation, and Ritual*, Columbia, SC 1994; Sinclair Stevenson, *The Rites of the Twice-Born*, New Delhi 1971; Paul Younger. *The Home of Dancing Sivan*, Oxford 1995; David G. White (ed.), *Tantra in Practice*, Princeton 2000.

FRANCIS X. CLOONEY

Holy Saturday

The day before *Easter Day in Christian tradition, which became the locus of a number of different ritual practices during the ancient and medieval eras. The earliest form of observance was as part of a pre-paschal *fast, a day of quiet and prayer, mindful of Christ's entombment and 'descent into hell'. In addition, the celebration of Easter was marked by an all-night vigil of readings and prayer beginning on Saturday evening and culminating in the Easter eucharist (*see* **Easter Vigil**). This vigil also became the preferred time for conferring the sacraments of *baptism and *confirmation on *catechumens; and by the fifth century the morning and evening offices of Saturday became elaborated by liturgical ceremonies marking the final stages of their baptismal preparation. Today, the day of Holy Saturday remains a quiet time of preparation for the celebration of the vigil. The reserved sacrament in RC churches has been transferred to another location on *Maundy Thursday, so the *tabernacle of the parish church is empty, its door open and sanctuary light extinguished. The *altar and *sanctuary area have also been stripped of linens and other decorations on Maundy Thursday (*see* **Altar, Stripping of**).

———

For bibliography, *see* **Holy Week**.

JOANNE M. PIERCE

Holy Thursday *see* Maundy Thursday

Holy Week

The week immediately preceding *Easter in Western Christian traditions, known instead as 'Great Week' in the Christian East. It was formed first by the extension backwards in Syria and Egypt in the third century of the original one- or two-day *fast before Easter so as to include the entire week, beginning on the preceding Monday, and then by the creation of appropriate liturgies for various days of that week during the fourth century in Jerusalem, which had by that time become a great centre of *pilgrimage. This factor no doubt encouraged the emergence of liturgies at the sacred sites recalling particularly significant moments in the final days of Jesus' life and his death, burial and resurrection. These rites were subsequently imitated to greater or lesser extent throughout the East and West, and expanded with further subsidiary ceremonies which attempted to recreate the details of those events more fully, in response to a type of liturgical piety which Kenneth Stevenson has described as 'representational', in contrast to the earlier form which he designates as 'rememorative', where the events were recalled by liturgical action but no attempt was made to portray them literally or act them out. All this resulted in particular days of the week having certain very distinctive celebrations, especially *Palm Sunday (commemorating the triumphal entry of Christ into Jerusalem), *Maundy Thursday (commemorating the Last Supper), *Good Friday (commem-

orating Christ's death), *Holy Saturday (commemorating his entombment and/or descent into hell), and *Easter Day itself (commemorating his resurrection). Modern RC liturgical revision has pruned much of the medieval ceremonial excesses and restored a more primitive simplicity to the liturgies of the week. Many of these revised practices have also been re-appropriated by churches of the Reformation, which had usually rejected their medieval predecessors in the sixteenth century as corrupt and encouraging superstition.

———

John Baldovin, 'Holy Week, Liturgies of', *The New Dictionary of Sacramental Worship*, ed. Peter Fink, Collegeville 1990, 542–52 (bib.); J. D. Crichton, *The Liturgy of Holy Week*, Dublin 1983; J. G. Davies, *Holy Week: A Short History*, London/Richmond, VA 1963; Pierre Jounel, 'The Easter Cycle', *The Church at Prayer*, ed. A. G. Martimort, IV, Collegeville 1986, 46–56 (bib.); P. A. G. Kollamparampil (ed.), *Hebdomanae sanctae celebratio: Conspectus historicus comparativus. The Celebration of Holy Week in Ancient Jerusalem and its Development in the Rites of East and West*, Rome 1997 (bib.); Joanne M. Pierce, 'Holy Week and Easter in the Middle Ages', *Passover and Easter: Origin and History to Modern Times*, ed. Paul F. Bradshaw and Lawrence Λ. Hoffman, Notre Dame 1999, 161–85 (bib.); Roger E. Reynolds, 'Holy Week', *Dictionary of the Middle Ages*, ed. Joseph R. Strayer, VI, New York 1985, 276–80 (bib.); Kenneth Stevenson, *Jerusalem Revisited: The Liturgical Meaning of Holy Week,* Washington, DC 1988.

JOANNE M. PIERCE

Homily *see* Preaching and Worship

Hood *see* Vestments 3(d)

Host

A name given to the unleavened bread used for the *eucharist in the Western tradition, derived from the Latin *hostia*, 'victim', and referring to the body of Christ, the sacrificial offering on the cross. Although in the early centuries of Christianity, common leavened bread, brought by the people themselves, was customary for the eucharist, and leavened bread continues to be used in Eastern traditions, in the early medieval period in the West unleavened bread was substituted. Later small individual wafers were provided for the communion of the people rather than a sharing in one bread, and the *fraction became purely symbolic rather than utilitarian. The Reformation churches restored the use of leavened bread, and usually also a common loaf. In the RC Church today unleavened bread continues to be used but is required to have 'the consistency of bread', and hence the priest's host is generally larger and thicker than before. Several of these, broken into pieces, are sometimes now used for the communion of the people instead of individual wafers.

EDITOR

Hour Services *see* Daily Prayer

House-Church Worship

'House church' is a term which originated in England in the 1970s to characterize a growth of independent radical congregations, usually beginning in people's homes – and thus called 'house churches'. Many of these have grown enormously and tend to term themselves generically the 'new churches'. For, as they grow numerically, they no longer meet in houses, but in halls and schools hired for that purpose.

They are usually to be distinguished from the 'black-majority' *Pentecostalist churches in Britain, while not exclusive of ethnic minorities. By definition, they are not connected to historic denominations, though their style and culture tend to be Pentecostalist. They have often arisen through the spiritual energies of a single guru, so that their doctrinal and constitutional framework may be somewhat indefinite, as peripheral to their concerns. Similarly, while larger networks may arise, they have tended to stand aside from existing inter-church and ecumenical relationships; and have grown by a combination of 'associational' evangelism and attracting people from other churches. They are notable for the comparatively deep commitment of their members, for close pastoring by their leaders, and for spiritual self-sufficiency. They tend to lack historical perspectives, to be suspicious of heavyweight institutional life, to minimize financial overheads (but be generous to gospel and other needs where the world suffers), and to profess an openness to the leading of the Spirit.

Worship in these churches takes a variety of forms, and has tended to follow certain international 'fashions' (such as 'words of know-ledge' in the 1980s and the 'Toronto Blessing' in the 1990s). There is a strong emphasis upon music, usually provided by keyboard and guitars, though with other instruments contributing. Pipe organs would be not only unknown in most such assemblies, but would be regarded as relatively wooden and even unspiritual in their style of music. Songs and choruses tend towards the subjective and experiential, and 'worship leaders' (often with an instrument) provide continuity talk between sung items, go round again as they detect a readiness for repeating a particular sung item, and in many places facilitate 'singing in the Spirit', a deliberately unstructured set of chords enabling the congregation to sing or intone with any or no words (in any or no language) simultaneously. Prayer may be led from the front, or done in groups or pairs, or whole congregations may pray aloud extemporarily and even simultaneously. They frequently have no time-contract, explicit or implicit, in relation to the length of their services. In some the children are encouraged to participate as adults might, leading in prayer and giving encouragement by the word to others, being in the assembly throughout, rather than despatched to Sunday schools. The formal is eschewed, the spontaneous and informal is of God. Any ministry of the word may be lengthy and highly hortatory. As with Pentecostalists, preaching may be punctuated by audible and experienced responses. There are few ground rules or standard expectations.

*Baptism is usually administered to adults or adolescents only, in line with the experiential roots of the churches' formation. Those previously baptized as infants will be treated as unbaptized and urged towards baptism. The sacrament of *communion may be administered, but without a known liturgical framework.

In the second and third generation, a period starting to arrive in the year 2000, such churches, launched with the infectiousness of a forest fire in the 1970s, have to start grappling with issues of the settled continuity of their own institutions. Whether this coming in from the apogee has implications for their own worship is yet to be seen.

COLIN O. BUCHANAN

Houselling Cloth *see* Communion

Humeral Veil *see* Veil

Hymns

1. *Latin.* In his commentary on Ps. 148.14, Augustine (354–430) described a hymn as 'praise of God in song', adding that praise of God that is not sung is not a hymn. The earliest Christian hymn is probably the Gloria in excelsis Deo, and close on its heels came the *Te Deum laudamus*. Ambrose (*c.* 339–97) is named as the real father of Latin hymnody and four hymns are attributed to him by Augustine: *Aeterne rerum conditor*, *Deus creator omnium*, *Jam surgit hora tertia*, and *Veni redemptor gentium*. These early hymns with their simple iambic metre were easy to understand, to remember, and to sing. Tradition has it that these and other hymns were sung by the people in Ambrose's church in Milan to keep up their spirits during the Arian troubles. The names of other early Christian poets associated with hymn-writing include: Caelius Sedulius (fl. 450), famous for his *Christmas and *Epiphany hymns, e.g. the acrostic *A solis ortus cardine*; Prudentius (348–*c.* 410), who wrote the charming hymn *Salvete, flores martyrum* for Holy Innocents' Day; and Venantius Fortunatus (530–609), author of the processional hymn *Salve, festa dies* and the noble *Vexilla regis*. The best-known of all Latin hymns, the ninth-century *Veni creator Spiritus*, has been attributed to Rabanus Maurus (776 or 784–856), though his authorship is doubtful.

About three hundred and fifty hymn texts, ranging in date from the fourth century to the twentieth, occur in the various hours of the divine office (*see* **Daily Prayer** 3). Few hymn melodies, however, are to be found before the eleventh century. St Benedict (*c.* 480–550) made provision in his *Rule* for a hymn (which he termed 'the Ambrosian') to be sung by his monks at each hour of the divine office. The Roman Church did not admit hymns into the daily office of the secular clergy until the twelfth century, on account of the prejudice against importing other than biblical words into the liturgy. Indeed, the Psalms had in earlier centuries been regarded as songs of praise, in other words hymns, and tradition links the great *Hallel* group (113–118), which was recited or sung at the principal Jewish festivals, with the hymn sung at the Last Supper by Jesus and his disciples.

*Polyphonic settings of the Latin metrical hymns began to appear in the thirteenth century. There are hymn-settings by Dunstable, Dufay, Josquin des Prez, Tallis and Byrd, to mention only a handful of names. Palestrina published a fine collection of hymns founded on the chant melodies. Many Renaissance settings were intended for *alternatim* performance, one strophe in chant followed by the next in polyphony, and so on. Organ *alternatim* settings as well as improvisations based on the well-known tunes became extremely popular from the seventeenth century onwards, one late example being Marcel Dupré's set of *alternatim* organ *versets*, originally improvised for the *Ave maris stella* in 1919.

The *Liber Hymnarius* (Solesmes 1983) is an updated edition of the main Latin repertoire. See also Joseph Connelly, *Hymns of the Roman Liturgy*, London 1957; G. M. Dreves, C. Blume and H. M. Bannister (eds), *Analecta hymnica medii ævi*, Leipzig 1886–1922; J. Julian, *A Dictionary of Hymnology*, London, 1892, 2nd edn 1907; Bruno Stäblein (ed.), *Monumenta Monodica Medii Aevi* I, Basel 1970.

MARY BERRY

2. *Vernacular.* Whereas Latin hymns are intended primarily for the liturgical office, the nature and uses of vernacular hymns are more diverse, though they have in common their central purpose of song for all the people present. Specific textual and musical characteristics define a vernacular hymn: the text is strophic, metrical and often rhyming. The melody is generally syllabic, periodic and suitable for congregational singing. The harmony (where there is harmony) is generally diatonic and in four parts (whether intended for voices or keyboard accompaniment). Homophony predominates.

In the Western church, the earliest vernacular hymns date from 1505, a collection made by the *Bohemian Brethren for congregational singing. The sixteenth-century repertory of vernacular hymns includes translations of Latin hymns (especially in the Primers), *metrical translations of the psalms and other liturgical texts, and devotional songs. In the new Protestant denominations after the Reformation, there are distinct traditions of hymnody: chorales in the Lutheran Church, and metrical psalms in the Calvinist and Anglican Churches, for instance. However, there are also the *laudi spirituali*, vernacular sacred songs associated with the popular devotions of the oratories and confraternities established in Italy in the second half of the sixteenth century. The uses of these repertories differed. Chorales were central to

Lutheran worship, including translations and new texts. Metrical psalms alone were sung in Calvinist worship. In the Church of England, only the prose liturgical texts from the *BCP* were permitted, but other texts including metrical psalms were sung before and after the authorized services. Such songs also played an important part in religious life in the home. In Italy, *laudi* belonged to the devotional rather than the liturgical life of the church.

During the later seventeenth and eighteenth centuries, the rise of Dissenters in Britain and the missionary movement of Methodism encouraged new styles of hymn-writing with distinct theological and spiritual emphases in the texts. The hymns of Izaac Watts, a member of the dissenting Independents, mark the move from translation and scriptural paraphrase to creative writing. Of all the original writers, John and Charles Wesley must be singled out, not only for the large numbers of hymns they wrote, but for their use of the genre as a vehicle for engendering religious fervour. Hymn writing also burgeoned in the Church of England, and vernacular devotional hymns by Roman Catholics were also written. It was during the eighteenth century that the norm of hymnody was established, but it was in the nineteenth century that these hymns were codified and brought together in the substantial anthologies of hymn books that are now commonplace.

The most significant Church of England hymn book of the nineteenth century was *Hymns Ancient and Modern*, which first appeared in 1861. It has remained in print ever since, though in its latest manifestation it has been renamed *Common Praise* (2000). It was complemented and contrasted by *The English Hymnal*, first published in 1906, and substantially revised as *The New English Hymnal* in 1986. *The English Hymnal* is stronger in its liturgical emphasis (especially before revision), but both hymnals include a broad range of hymns for seasonal, devotional, evangelistic, missionary and didactic uses. The texts of both hymnals include early Greek, medieval Latin, and post-Reformation German texts, mostly in new translations, as well as a large selection of English texts drawn from a variety of theological and spiritual traditions from the sixteenth century onwards, including verse not originally intended for singing. Comparable eclecticism is evident in the musical materials: Latin plainsong melodies, chorale and metrical psalm melodies from abroad, traditional English psalm-tunes, tunes written for hymns,

and newly composed tunes. *The English Hymnal*, much influenced by Vaughan Williams, also includes folk melodies, Nonconformist Welsh hymn tunes, and melodies from seventeenth- and eighteenth-century Latin hymnals compiled in France. *The Church Hymnary*, with its Presbyterian usage and consequent emphasis on metrical psalms and scriptural paraphrases, charts a similar progress of taste in text and music since its first appearance in 1898.

With the emancipation of other denominations in England in the earlier nineteenth century, and the rapid expansion in the establishment of Nonconformist chapels and RC churches, hymn books have been compiled in all the main denominations. Each reflects a particular aesthetic, spirituality and theology that inform both text and music. There is also a small core of hymns which has become common to all traditions and denominations.

The issues that have informed twentieth-century liturgical reform have also affected hymnody, particularly its use and relevance as a vehicle for the song of the whole assembly since about 1960. The need for texts with accessible and *inclusive language has influenced the revision of established hymns and informed the writing of new verse, as have issues of social justice and race, together with new trends in spirituality and theology. In the English language, post-colonial trends have spurred new repertories of indigenous hymn-writing, for instance in Australia and New Zealand. Musically, the desire for accessibility has revived the tension between the hymn as a song of the people and the hymn as part of a formal pattern of worship. Music derived or adapted from the songs and hymns of the African-American and post-colonial North American traditions, of post-missionary Africa and South America, and of the American musical and other transatlantic popular traditions, features in modern hymn books, alongside old and new hymn tunes within the European tradition. The borderline between missionary or gospel song, song for worship and hymn is often blurred. Some hymn and song collections, such as *Mission Praise* (compiled between 1983 and 1990), have migrated across the denominations; others, such as the Scottish *Common Ground* (1998), have been conceived as ecumenical ventures. The uncertain, and sometimes uneasy, mixing of different aesthetics and spiritualities found in some recent books characterizes the cultural and spiritual diversity and uncertainty evident in some contemporary patterns and styles of worship. There is a particular tension between the hymn as a personal expression of religious feeling, and the hymn as a collective statement of prayer and praise of God's people. The resolution of this tension, which has both textual and musical implications, may determine the future directions of vernacular hymnody.

'Hymn IV', *NG2*, XII, 29–35; Nicholas Temperley, *The Hymn Index*, Oxford 1998; J. R. Wilson, *The English Hymn: A Critical and Historical Study*, Oxford 1997.

JOHN HARPER

Icon

A Greek term meaning 'image', applied to many religious images but normally to the form used commonly among the Byzantine Orthodox and Catholics. A reaction against the veneration of icons, the Iconoclast period (*c.* 725–842), led to the theological defence of icons by such figures as St John Damascene (*c.* 750) and St Theodore of Stoudios (826). Since that time the typical icon style has been strictly laid down, even though rendered with regional variations (e.g. Greek, Cretan, Serbian, Russian, etc.). The veneration paid to an icon is seen as passing over to the person or persons represented.

Orthodox churches, especially the *iconostasis, are decorated with icons according to a definite scheme. They play an important part in personal devotion and in defining the Orthodox worship space but are mentioned only seldom in liturgical books. There are *rubrics requiring certain preparatory prayers before the icons of the Saviour and the Mother of God, and also directing the *incensation of the icons and people. There is a service of prayer for the blessing of icons, which are often left on the *altar for a given number of celebrations of the *eucharist.

The Oriental Orthodox churches do not have as developed a theology of icons, not having suffered the iconoclast crisis. The Copts and Ethiopians have a strong continuing iconographic tradition, the Syrians and Armenians have tended in recent years to rely on a small number of western-style religious paintings, and the Church of the East on a plain cross.

John Baggley, *Doors of Perception*, London 1987; Christine Chaillot, *Rôle des images et vénération des icôns dans les églises ortho-*doxes orientales, Geneva 1993; Leonide Ouspensky and Georges Florovsky, *The Meaning of Icons*, Crestwood, NY 1982; Egon Sendler, *The Icon: Image of the Invisible*, Torrance, CA 1981.

GREGORY WOOLFENDEN

Iconostasis

This is the term normally applied to the screen dividing the *sanctuary from the rest of the church in Byzantine Orthodox and Catholic churches. More correctly called the *templon*, it was originally a low barrier, often of marble, enclosing the sanctuary and, at least in bigger churches, surmounted by columns bearing an architrave. Old illustrations, e.g. in the *Menologium of Basil II* (*c.* 1000), show this quite clearly. Old screens that still exist have usually had later *icons placed to fill the open spaces (an example in original condition is in the late-tenth-century church of the Holy Apostles in the Agora in Athens).

After the Iconoclast crises of the eighth and ninth centuries icons became more prominent in churches, often placed on the piers flanking the *templon,* as for example in Saint Saviour in Chora, Constantinople. From the fourteenth/fifteenth centuries, the screen became a solid wall of icons pierced by three doors, themselves carrying icons. This development was particularly strong in countries such as Russia and Romania, where later examples became very tall and grandiose.

It is common practice for icons of the Saviour and the Mother of God to flank the central (holy or royal) doors, to the right and left as one looks at the screen. The holy doors often carry depictions of the evangelists and/or the annunciation and the side doors ('deacons' doors'), holy *deacons or ministering angels. The patron saint of the church and other important saints are usually found on the same main row as the Saviour. Above this row are often found rows of the apostles, the major feasts, prophets and patriarchs, and frequently a Last Supper directly over the holy doors.

Except for the preparation prayers and the various *incensations, the iconostasis hardly figures in the liturgical *rubrics. However, liturgical commentators have reflected upon it. Pavel Florensky in 1922 saw it as the boundary between the visible and invisible worlds. It is not normally perceived as an obstacle to vision so much as an opening or bridge to the invisible worship of heaven in which the worshippers are taking part. However, in some places more open screens have become common, and at least one monastery in the USA (New Skete) has a form more like the old low barrier with architrave.

The side doors admit to the altar of preparation (*prothesis) and the *diaconicon* or *sacristy area respectively. Only *bishop, *presbyters and *deacons pass through the central holy doors to and from the *altar and that only when celebrating. Many larger churches and most central Russian parish churches have subsidiary altars with their own iconostases. The priestless old Ritualists in Russia have turned the whole east wall of their churches into a solid iconostasis since they have no *eucharist.

Maria Cheremeteff, 'The Transformation of the Russian Sanctuary Barrier and the Role of Theophanes the Greek', *The Millennium: Christianity and Russia*, ed. Albert Leong, Crestwood, NY 1990, 107–24; Pavel Florensky, *Iconostasis*, Crestwood, NY 1996; Peter Galadza, 'The Role of the Icons in Byzantine Worship', *Studia Liturgica* XXI, 1991, 113–35; Leonide Ouspensky, 'The Problem of the Iconostasis', *St Vladimir's Seminary Quarterly* VIII, 1964, 186–218; J. Walter, 'The Origins of the Iconostasis', *Eastern Churches Review* III, 1971, 251–67; Gregory Woolfenden, 'Is Seeing Necessarily Believing? Some Liturgical and Theological Reflections on the Templon Screen', *Studia Liturgica* XXIX, 1999, 84–99.

GREGORY WOOLFENDEN

Immaculate Conception

see **Marian Feasts**

Imposition of Hands *see* Gestures 3

Incense

From the Latin *incendere*, to burn, to kindle. Incense is made of substances from trees and plants which, when heated or burnt, give off a fragrant smell. Frankincense, that is, pure incense, otherwise known as olibanum, is the solidified resin yielded from trees of the Boswellia species.

1. *Use in the Non-Biblical World.* Incense played a significant role in the rites of the different cultures and religions of the ancient world. One might generally discern seven uses:

(a) as a sacrifice to the deity or deities – the incense could also be seen as representing the presence of the divine; (b) as a sacrifice to the soul of a deceased human being; (c) as an exorcism to drive away and protect against evil spirits; (d) as an honour to a living person; (e) as a means of purification or healing; (f) as a festive accompaniment to processions or other ceremonies; (g) as a personal cosmetic, and as a perfume at banquets or other occasions. The roots of its usage might be seen in the effort to do away with unpleasant odours on various occasions such as funerals. In the funeral rites of ancient Egypt incense was used as a means to preserve the dead, to prolong life and to aid the passage beyond death.

2. *Old Testament Use.* The use of incense is well attested in Israelite worship, as can be seen especially in the Books of Exodus, Leviticus and Numbers. For example, in Ex. 30 the use of incense is based on a divine commandment in which directions for the construction of the incense altar, the production of incense and its correct use are given. In Ex. 30.7–9 there is the distinction between lawful and unlawful worship, the former requiring Aaron to burn incense on the golden incense altar in front of the holy of holies every morning and evening. Moses is instructed by God to 'take sweet spices, stacte, and onycha, and galbanum, sweet spices with pure frankincense (an equal part of each), and make an incense blended as by the perfumer seasoned with salt, pure and holy' (Ex. 30.34). In Leviticus incense is seen as a protection against God's wrath (16.12–13). In addition, the cloud of smoke it produces is the symbol of the call upon the deity and the deity's appearance (16.2). In Num. 16.46–48 we see an apotropaic use of incense, in which Aaron stops the plague by placing himself with burning incense between the dead and the living. The use of incense as a cosmetic and medicine is also attested in the OT.

3. *New Testament Use.* In Luke 1.8–13 an angel of God appears to Zechariah while he is burning incense at the Temple, since incense brings the presence of God, as we have seen. Incense is brought to Christ by the magi (Matt. 2.11). In Rev. 5.8 incense is used to denote the prayers of the faithful, and in Rev. 8.3–4, 'another angel, having a golden *censer, came and stood at the altar. He was given much incense, that he should offer it with the prayers of all the saints upon the golden altar which

was before the throne. And the smoke of the incense, with the prayers of the saints, ascended before God from the angel's hand.' Finally, in 2 Cor. 2.14–16 the knowledge of Christ is described as a fragrant odour.

4. *Use in the Christian Church.* In the first three centuries there was no ceremonial use of incense in Christianity. In fact, early Christian writers denounced the use of incense, as they associated it with pagan religions and emperor worship. It is in the fourth century that the Christian view on incense starts to be modified. The earliest instance of a Christian use of incense is in the funeral procession of Peter of Alexandria in 311, and it is also mentioned by Egeria as forming part of the weekly Sunday *vigil at Jerusalem in the latter part of the fourth century. On the other hand, John Chrysostom in Antioch does not seem to know any ceremonial use of incense, and our first definite witness to the use of incense in Antioch is Theodoret of Cyr (*c.* 393–*c.* 466). After the fifth century the use of incense becomes general throughout the Christian church. One may discern three different usages of incense in the Christian tradition: (a) as honorific, to people, places and objects; (b) as exorcistic or apotropaic; and (c) as an oblation. In current RC practice one may use incense at any of the following moments in the *eucharist: in the entrance *procession to cense the *altar; in the gospel procession and during the reading of the gospel; at the preparation of the gifts to cense the offerings, the altar, the minister and the people; and at the elevation of the *host and *chalice during the *eucharistic prayer. In the current Byzantine practice the *celebrant or the *deacon censes the altar, the offerings on the *prothesis table, the *icons and the people, before the commencement of the service; further censing, with much variation depending on local custom, takes place before the reading of the gospel; additional censing takes place before, during and after the *great entrance, after the *epiclesis, and after *communion. Generally speaking, Eastern rites make abundant use of incense not only in the eucharist, but also in the celebration of the hours of *daily prayer and in any other service. It is the custom of many Eastern Christians to burn incense in their homes before icons and at times of prayer and devotion.

See also **Thurible**.

―――――

Cuthbert Atchley, *A History of the Use of*

Incense, London 1909; Kjeld Nielsen, *Incense in Ancient Israel*, Leiden 1986.

STEFANOS ALEXOPOULOS

Inclusive Language

During the second half of the twentieth century, many western societies began to revise their language toward greater inclusivity. This revision was based on several assumptions: that a language expresses the world view of its formulators; that use of a language perpetuates that world view among its contemporary speakers; that the world view behind western languages was androcentric, that is, assuming the male as the model for the species; that even so-called generic speech was in fact preferential toward white males; and that a social reform granting full and equal humanity to women requires changes in both the vocabulary and the grammar of speech. An example of the change of vocabulary in the English language is the abandoning of the traditional inclusive meaning of the word 'man'. Since whether 'man' includes women is often ambiguous, inclusive speech replaces 'man', when not synonymous with 'males', with 'human', as more clearly including other than men. A change in grammar is the replacement of 'he or she' for an assumed 'he' when the sex of the referent is unknown. The search for inclusive language has concerned itself not only with sex, but also with categories such as race, class and physical condition, so that normative speech would include all persons in equal and parallel fashion. For example, a sentence ought not mention one person's race or colour unless the race or colour of all persons is indicated. Pejorative designations for minority persons should be eliminated: for example, one would not state that an ignorant person is 'blind'.

In secular society, the move toward inclusive language has been controversial. Language that some people judge offensively exclusive is viewed as acceptable, even beloved, by others. Speakers of the language do not agree which words are offensive (e.g. 'black' as a symbol for evil); whether new terms (e.g. 'chairperson' for 'chairman') are felicitous; who is authorized to create new words (e.g. 'Ms', a title that, like 'Mr', is not indicative of marital status); and who is positioned to alter practice (e.g. changing the standard business address 'Dear Sir' to an inclusive address). Languages such as the Romance languages with systems of grammatical gender effect inclusivity in ways different from those languages with natural gender, such as American English, which increasingly avoids all gendered speech that does not refer to sexuality. In current usage in the USA, for example, a nation or the church is not a 'she'; non-gender-specific terms (e.g. 'flight attendant') are replacing sexually explicit terms (e.g. 'steward' and 'stewardess'); and use of the ending '-ess' (e.g. 'poetess') is declining.

In Christian churches, the move toward more inclusive language has been far more complicated than in the wider society because of complex religious issues.

1. *The gender of God.* Like Judaism and Islam, Christianity has denied that God is a sexual being; yet Christian texts, including the Hebrew and Greek of the Bible, have spoken as if God were of the masculine gender. Male terms for God, such as 'Father' and 'King', have predominated in many Christian pieties.

2. *The incarnation of God in Christ.* Christianity affirms that God became incarnate in a male. Thus christological speech is filled with masculine singular designations.

3. *Androcentric sacred texts.* Beloved biblical translations retain and sometimes even intensify the exclusive speech of the Hebrew and Greek originals. Translators do not agree how to translate androcentric speech, especially when its meaning is seen by the church as being inclusive. An example is how to render the masculine singular for the believer in John's Gospel.

4. *Androcentric liturgical language.* Many formulas used in public worship are cast in exclusive language. An example is the line 'And blessed be his kingdom now and forever', in which both *his* and *kingdom* are judged by some Christians to be exclusive words.

5. *Androcentric hymn texts.* Memorized hymns and the texts of classic church music are characterized by exclusive speech patterns, which because of the requirements of metre, rhyme and memory cannot readily be altered.

Currently the status of inclusive language in the speech of the Christian churches varies considerably. Some church bodies have attempted to mandate towards inclusive language; some have formally resisted any such changes; in some churches, authority for such decisions is vested locally, and thus the wide diversity in parish practice reflects the cultural, socio-economic and educational situation of the worshippers. What has been called *horizontal* inclusive language, that is, speech that refers to humankind, is more commonplace than what

has been called *vertical* language, that is, speech that refers to God, with some theologians claiming that any diminution of the biblical and traditional masculine designations for God introduces heresy. Yet an increasing number of Christians assert that the asexual being of God and the equality of the sexes in baptism demand use of inclusive language especially in the church. The importance of English usage within world Christianity suggests that the linguistic practices adopted by English speakers will have considerable effect on the Christian speech of future centuries.

Ruth C. Duck, *Finding Words for Worship: A Guide for Leaders*, Louisville 1995; Alvin F. Kimel, Jr, *Speaking the Christian God: The Holy Trinity and the Challenge of Feminism*, Grand Rapids 1992; Casey Miller and Kate Smith, *The Handbook of Nonsexist Writing*, 2nd edn, New York 1988; Gail Ramshaw, *God beyond Gender: Feminist Christian God-Talk*, Minneapolis 1995 (bib.); Brian Wren, *What Language Shall I Borrow? God-Talk in Worship: A Male Response to Feminist Theology*, London and New York 1989.

GAIL RAMSHAW

Inculturation

1. Definition; 2. History; 3. Areas of Inculturation; 4. Liturgical Texts; 5. Liturgical Rites.

1. *Definition.* The relationship between liturgy and culture has been expressed by the use of several different terms: *indigenization* was intended to indicate the process of conferring on liturgy a cultural form native to the local church; *contextualization* was introduced into ecclesiastical vocabulary by the World Council of Churches in 1972 to express the need for the church to be relevant to contemporary society; *adaptation* is the word used by the Constitution on the Sacred Liturgy of the RC Second Vatican Council; and *acculturation* describes the juxtaposition of two cultures, which interact but without mutual integration. *Inculturation*, however, is made up of three elements. The first is interaction or dialogue between the church's liturgical worship and the local culture with its components of values, rites, symbols, patterns and institutions. The second is the integration into the liturgy of such cultural elements as are pertinent and suitable. The third is the dynamic whereby the Christian form of worship is enriched by culture without

prejudice to its nature as a divine–human institution.

2. *History*. It can be claimed that liturgical inculturation is as old as the church. Different epochs deal differently with the question of inculturation. The church in the age of the fathers engaged with great fervour in the composition of original texts and ritual enhancement. It was a period of unparalleled liturgical creativity, which is one of the many forms of inculturation. The conversion of the emperor Constantine brought about a dramatic shift from the simplicity of homes to the splendour of imperial basilicas. When in the year 321 he decreed the observance of Sunday throughout the empire, the celebration of the *eucharist acquired a solemn character. Doctrinal controversies tapered textual creativity and led to mutual borrowings among the churches, especially in the East.

By the fifth century the primatial sees had developed their local rites, doubtless through inculturation. Of particular interest is the Roman liturgy that integrated the classical Roman patterns of sobriety, noble simplicity and practical sense into its prayer texts, rituals and liturgical space. In the eighth century the churches under the emperors Pepin the Short and Charlemagne performed another type of inculturation. They borrowed Roman liturgical books and adjusted their texts and rites to suit their Franco-Germanic cultural traditions. The result enriched the source liturgy in terms of ornate language and wealth of symbols. The work of 'adapting' the Roman rite to current theological thinking and popular practice continued unhampered until the Council of Trent put a halt to new liturgical developments in reaction to the Protestant Reformation.

The practice of liturgical inculturation has always been part of the church's missionary activities. Augustine of Canterbury received the blessing of Pope Gregory I to inculturate the liturgy to the culture of the English people. Cyril and Methodius did likewise among the Slavs. Though in a limited way, the sixteenth-century missionaries in Asia and Latin America dialogued with local cultures. The inculturation of the Chinese ancestral rites typifies some of the missionaries' wholesome attitude toward inculturation. It can be said that the churches in mission territories have been responsible for the revival of interest in liturgical inculturation.

The Second Vatican Council devoted four articles of its Constitution on the Liturgy (*Sacrosanctum concilium* 37–40) to the principles, criteria and practical norms covering the issue of liturgical adaptation. After the Council the RC Church was alarmed by uncontrolled liturgical experimentations, several of which were alien to the principles enunciated by the Constitution on the Liturgy. Initially, the reaction of the Vatican was characterized by prudent discretion, especially in the case of the mission churches. However, as inculturation progressed, the fear that the 'substantial unity of the Roman rite' was being undermined has led the Vatican to regard inculturation, especially in the area of translations and original compositions, with keen caution.

3. *Areas of Inculturation*. As a ritual action the liturgy is a confluence of texts, *gestures, material objects, music, time and space. Texts are either proclaimed or sung, and they can be classified as prayers, admonitions and homilies, greetings and responses, and song lyrics. Gestures, on the other hand, are bodily actions with ritual meaning and purpose. Such, for example, are the gestures of hand-laying, standing, kneeling, sitting, and exchange of peace. Bread, wine, water and oil are material objects that are commonly used in sacramental celebrations. To these we should add the *vestments, furnishings like the *altar, *lectern and chair, vessels, lighted *candle, wedding rings, and other such objects. Music is the preferred language of the liturgy. We do not only sing songs during the liturgy; we also sing the texts provided by the liturgy whenever singing is linguistically appropriate. The liturgy takes place in an appointed hour of the day, day of the week, and season of the year. Some liturgies, like the liturgy of the hours (*see* **Daily Prayer**), are tied to the hour of the day, while others, like the feast of *Easter, are bound to the months or seasons of the year. Finally, the liturgy requires a ritual environment that includes the physical space of a church or at times of an open-air location.

All of the above ritual elements originated and developed in cultural traditions, including the biblical. They are culturally bound and hence are the subject of inculturation. We ultimately trace our liturgical origins to the Jewish traditions and culture. In the West the Christian form of worship was subsequently influenced by Graeco-Roman cultural patterns of praying that persisted even after the Franco-Germanic culture dimmed the original Roman traits of sobriety, concision, noble simplicity and practical sense. The Western liturgies today still retain several of the Roman cultural patterns, even after medieval Europe had added its own contributions and the Reformation amended a number of them. Inculturation involves historical research. It requires that we examine closely the components of the liturgical ordo, namely its history, theology, structure, fundamental elements and cultural background. It is obvious that we should not modify or alter any system unless we are thoroughly informed about its nature and components.

4. *Liturgical Texts*. Liturgy communicates chiefly through a system that is both oral and aural. Presiders and ministers read, sing or speak, while the assembly listens and responds. Liturgical texts are dead letters, but they come alive when they are proclaimed and heard. That words are the principal components of Christian worship can be explained partly in the light of the incarnation of the Word of God. The incarnate Word is preached to us and dwells among us through human words. Liturgical texts preach Christ and render him sacramentally present in the worshipping assembly. But just as the Word of God became incarnate in the cultural milieu of the Jewish people, so the words of the liturgy need also to be incarnated, that is to say inculturated, among the people to whom they are proclaimed.

There are three ways of handling the question of inculturating liturgical texts. The first is by translation; the second is by the revision of existing texts; and the third is by original composition. To define translation it is useful to review its chief elements. Translation consists of re-expressing in the receptor language the message of the source language. The source language of the liturgy, which may be Hebrew, Greek or Latin among others, contains the original message. The receptor language is the language currently employed by the liturgy for a particular assembly. The message is the doctrine that the church intended to convey to the assembly through the text that had been originally prepared for it. In the tradition of the early Latin sacramentaries the *collects and prefaces for the eucharist often reflect the doctrinal and moral concerns of the *bishops for their flock. Liturgical texts can also mirror the traditions and culture of the people they address. For example, the prayers and rubrical directions of the Romano-Germanic Pontifical provide rich information about the world view

and way of life of the Franco-Germanic people in the tenth century.

'The purpose of liturgical translations is to communicate the message of salvation to believers and to express the prayer of the church to the Lord: "Liturgical translations have become the voice of the Church." It is not sufficient that a liturgical translation merely reproduces the expressions and ideas of the original text. Rather it must faithfully communicate to a given people, and in their own language, that which the Church by means of this given text originally intended to communicate to another people in another time' (Consilium for the Implementation of the Constitution on the Liturgy, 'Instruction on the Translation of Liturgical Texts'). This 1969 RC document discourages the use of the method of formal correspondence, which ignores the culture of the audience. Although it aims to be faithful to the original text, its fidelity centres almost exclusively on the surface level of the source language and on literal transference into the receptor language. Sometimes formal correspondence tries to recast the system of the receptor language in order to conform to the source language. This can do untold violence to the receptor language in a useless attempt to produce a word-for-word translation. The instruction notes that 'a faithful translation cannot be judged on the basis of individual words: the total context of this specific act of communication must be kept in mind, as well as the literary form proper to the respective language.'

What the instruction has in mind is clearly the method of dynamic equivalence whereby the original message is re-expressed in consonance with the values, traditions and linguistic patterns proper to the assembly. To achieve this fully the receptor language should possess equivalent rhetorical devices and patterns of speech that are found in the source language. Dynamic translation transmits to the audience of the receptor language the same message that the source language aims to transmit to its audience. 'Translation consists in the reproduction in the receptor language of the message of the source language in such a way that the receptors in the receptor language may be able to understand adequately how the original receptors in the source language understood the original message' (E. Nida, *Signs, Sense, Translation*, Cape Town 1984, 119). In short, the method of dynamic equivalence achieves the same purpose, as does the original text.

As much as possible, the message should be clothed, as it were, in equivalent linguistic vesture, so that the present audience can perceive how the original addressees understood the message. The Latin texts, for example, used heavily such rhetorical devices as *cursus*, binary succession, antithesis, and *concinnitas* or symmetry. The RC English Sacramentary revised by the International Commission on English in the Liturgy has, in some of its texts, remarkably captured the purpose for which the *cursus* had been used in Latin. In the alternative opening prayer for the eucharist on Christmas Day, we detect the English dynamic equivalent of *cursus*. The text is concise and moves quickly but gently. Its aural effect has a quality comparable to the Latin *cursus* that elicits a response of wonder and thanksgiving:

We praise you, gracious God,
for the glad tidings of peace,
the good news of salvation:
your Word became flesh,
and we have seen his glory.

Likewise, the revised Sacramentary has preserved the Latin binary succession in its translation of the second preface of the passion. After the solemn proem 'This is the hour', the text develops the theme of the paschal mystery using the binary succession introduced by 'when'.

This is the hour
when we celebrate his triumph over Satan's pride,
when we solemnly recall the mystery of our redemption.

The method of dynamic equivalence may in some circumstances require textual amplification or paraphrase. The translation of the triple *Sanctus proved particularly difficult in the Tagalog language, which is one of the liturgical languages in the Philippines. The Spanish missionaries introduced the word *santo* (holy), but for Filipinos it means 'saint' or 'sacred image'. Calling God *santo* can deliver the message that God is a saint or a sacred image. Furthermore the word *santo*, or for that matter any Tagalog word, sounds wooden and awkward when repeated thrice. The solution reached was to shift to *banal*, which is the Tagalog word for 'holy', and to amplify it: 'Holy are you, Almighty God; holy is your name; holy is your kingdom.'

Paraphrases are also helpful companions of dynamic equivalence. Some authors view paraphrases with disdain, dismissing them as unfaithful to the original message. In reality, paraphrasing is one of the many options to express the same thing. The weather prediction, for example, can be expressed in different ways. Instead of saying, 'heavy downpour is expected this afternoon', one can advise someone to bring along an umbrella. Paraphrases are often akin to idiomatic expressions. A proposed translation into the Igbo language of the Latin word *dignitas*, which is found in the Christmas collect, uses both paraphrase and idiomatic expression. The Latin text says that God created wondrously and reshaped even more wondrously the dignity of humans. The Igbo translation paraphrases this: 'From the beginning you [God] stuck the feather of an eagle on human beings.' This is a more picturesque way of conveying to the Igbo people what the Latin text proclaimed to the Roman assembly, but both say the same thing.

The second way to inculturate liturgical texts is to revise them. Periodic revision of existing translations is necessary in order to update the texts and make them contemporary. It is useful to remember that language, like the culture it expresses, constantly undergoes changes in structure and word usage. Today some old English favourites like 'we beseech' sound quaint, the word 'man' is no longer *inclusive of 'woman', and an overuse of gender language for God can paint the wrong image of God. Thus there is a need to revise older liturgical texts in light of linguistic developments. To insist, for example, on using the word 'man' to include women as well as men, fails to deliver the original message to an audience that understands 'man' as the male gender. The work of revision is one of inculturation, because it respects the cultural overtones of a language. In some instances revision will also take into consideration the shifts in theological perspectives.

The revised translation of the Roman Sacramentary by the International Commission on English in the Liturgy typifies such concern. The 1973 translation of the preface for the fourth eucharistic prayer is heavily masculine in its horizontal language: 'You formed man in your likeness and set him over the whole world to serve you, his creator, and to rule over all creatures. Even when he disobeyed you and lost your friendship you did not abandon him to the power of death, but helped all men to seek and find you. Again and again you offered a covenant to man . . .' The revised translation now reads: 'You formed man and woman in your own likeness and entrusted the whole world to their care, so that in serving you alone, their Creator, they might be stewards of all creation . . . Again and again you offered the human race a covenant . . .' Besides addressing the question of inclusive language, the revised translation, in consonance with the paradigm shift in theological thinking, has also significantly softened the power language 'rule over all creatures' by the use of the phrase 'be stewards of all creation'.

The third way of doing inculturation is by composing original texts. It is true that inculturation consists chiefly of dynamic translation, but not exclusively. As the 1969 instruction on liturgical translations admits, 'Texts translated from another language are clearly not sufficient for the celebration of a fully renewed liturgy. The creation of new texts will be necessary' ('Instruction on the Translation of Liturgical Texts'). Original composition is not one form that inculturation may conceivably take: it is a form to which that inculturation will often resort. The original messages in the source texts crafted in the early centuries and the Middle Ages could in no way foresee all the socio-cultural changes in the world as well as the challenges the church would meet in the future. Patristic and medieval liturgy could not be expected to deliver a message on popular religiosity, ecumenism, inter-religious dialogue, lay empowerment, ecological and environmental concerns, technological progress and the question of globalization, not to mention the changing patterns of family life and social relations. These concerns, arguably more than the doctrine on the Trinity and Christology, are the contexts in which the church lives today, and they strongly affect the faith and worship of the people. It would be an irresponsible act on the part of church authorities to deprive the worshipping community of prayers concerning current issues by minimizing the composition of original texts. The fear that there might come a time when there would be more original compositions than translations from original texts has no historical support. After all, the source texts we have today were once upon a time original compositions.

An example of how to incorporate popular religiosity into the liturgy is the revised RC Sacramentary's alternative opening prayer, an original composition, for the midnight mass of Christmas. The Latin focuses on light, but the popular perception of Christmas consists, among other things, of swaddling clothes, manger, angels' song and shepherds. The alternative text reads in part:

> Good and gracious God,
> on this holy night you gave us your Son,
> the Lord of the universe, wrapped in
> swaddling clothes,
> the Savior of all, lying in a manger . . .
> Join our voices with the heavenly host,
> that we may sing your glory on high.
> Give us a place among the shepherds . . .

The question of who should initiate and author original compositions needs to be addressed here. Should it be the local churches or can they delegate this to an international commission, like the International Commission on English in the Liturgy, of which they are members? Given the meagre resources of some local churches, the immense task of composing truly liturgical texts is often beyond their means. Consortia and mixed commissions, which are not foreign to church institutions, were conceived as helpful instruments for sharing resources. With such a situation in mind, the Liturgy Constitution of Vatican II envisions the establishment of regional and international commissions. Thus the member churches of the International Commission on English in the Liturgy can mandate the commission to produce original compositions that will in effect have the character of an English *editio typica* or source material. The idea is not a novelty in the liturgy. Several Latin prayers are modified forms of older ones or a conglomeration of elements borrowed from other texts. An English *editio typica* implies that the local churches can make the necessary adjustments to the text in order to make both its message and form respond more clearly to their particular situation. This option is, however, not as clear in the case of translations whose aim is to deliver the original message of the source text and hence are subject to local adjustments with some difficulty.

The opening prayer for Philippine Independence Day, which addresses the political and socio-economic reality of the nation, takes its inspiration from several original compositions of the International Commission on English in the Liturgy as from an *editio typica*:

> O God, author of freedom and source of
> unity,
> we recall the day when the Filipino people
> claimed their place among the family of
> nations.

Accept the prayers we offer for our country,
so that harmony and justice may be secured
by wise leaders and upright citizens,
and this country, the pearl of the orient seas,
may enjoy lasting prosperity and peace.

5. *Liturgical Rites*. The inculturation of liturgical rites can be brought about in two ways: first, by substituting an equivalent rite for the original, be it in the category of gesture, material thing, space or time; and second, by adding new elements to the existing rite. The first method is dynamic equivalence and works in the same way for rites as it does for texts. The second is similar to original compositions.

The following questions will illustrate how these two methods are applied. By way of example, let us focus our attention on the order of the eucharistic celebration. In the majority of traditions both Eastern and Western, it is made up of two principal parts: the liturgy of the word and the liturgy of the eucharist. Some traditions have developed secondary elements like the entrance and concluding rites, but these will not be considered here because of a great diversity in ritual practice.

In the traditional eucharistic ordo the structure of the liturgy of the word consists of biblical readings, chanting of psalms, homily and *intercessions. The liturgy of the word can be described as the word of God proclaimed in the readings, explained by the homily, and responded to through the intercessory prayer. In this part of the ordo the community leader occupies the presider's chair and breaks the word of God through the ministry of preaching. The assembly listens as the word of God is proclaimed and explained, and thereafter utters words of praise, thanksgiving and supplication.

The foregoing description of the liturgy of the word allows us to raise questions of inculturation. We can ask whether some local assemblies will need a more solemn, perhaps even dramatic, presentation of the book of scriptures. Unlike some Oriental rites, the Roman tradition, which is inherited by a number of Western churches, has no special introduction to the liturgy of the word; this begins abruptly with the first reading. There are cultural groups that feel uneasy about this system. It is a case where the addition of a new ritual element can be useful. We can also ask how the readers perform their task. Do they combine the qualities of liturgical reading with their people's cultural pattern of public proclamation, with attention to voice pitch, rhythmic cadence and public presence? Likewise the *posture of the assembly during the readings has cultural significance. Liturgical rubrics indicate the posture of sitting during the readings, except at the gospel when the assembly stands to listen in silent respect. However, in some cultural traditions the posture of standing while a person in authority speaks is considered disrespectful, an indication of boredom or eagerness to take leave. The practice in some African churches is to sit during the reading of the gospel. This is an interesting example of the type of dynamic equivalence where two opposing systems actually mean the same.

Biblical readings are orally proclaimed. Different people have different ways of proclaiming texts, and this should be carefully studied. The element of *drama is not alien to liturgical proclamation. Since the Middle Ages the Roman liturgy kept the practice of dramatizing the reading of the passion of Jesus Christ on *Palm Sunday and *Good Friday. Three readers take the roles of Christ, the narrator and the other passion characters. Sometimes visual aids accompanied the reading, when it was done in Latin, so that the assembly could have a clue of what was being read: the images, for example, of a human ear and a rooster on sticks to indicate the story about the ear of a servant and Peter's denial (Matt. 26.51, 75). Medieval liturgy produced the great dramas known as *Peregrinus* (the Pilgrim) and *Hortulanus* (the Gardener). They narrate respectively the apparitions of Christ to the disciples on the road to Emmaus (Luke 24.15–34) and to Mary Magdalene who mistook him as a gardener (John 20.15). The script for the *Peregrinus* directs the performers 'to walk about looking sad' as the gospel is proclaimed, while the one for the *Hortulanus* instructs the actor 'to walk slowly as if in search of something, in imitation of Mary Magdalene'. Dramatization can take the form of silent mimetic gestures performed by actors while the reading is proclaimed. If suited to the occasion, a full dramatic performance can fittingly follow the reading, similar to the washing of the feet in the RC Church after the gospel reading (John 13.1–15) of *Maundy Thursday. Because of the nature of the word of God in the liturgy as oral–aural communication, the drama should not replace the reading.

As regards the meal of thanksgiving, also called the liturgy of the eucharist, a question often raised is the use of local foodstuff in place of bread and wine. The issue is delicate, especially in those churches that recognize only wheat bread and grape wine as valid elements. Church discipline on such a complex matter should not be subverted by personal preferences or efforts to inculturate the eucharistic elements. It is a fact that the majority of people who receive *communion in the traditional form of bread and wine take it for granted that that is how things should be. One may add that, in a world heading speedily toward globalization, wheat bread and grape wine will probably no longer be unfamiliar to many across the world outside of the western hemisphere. The urgent call to inculturate the eucharistic elements has thus somewhat abated during the last decade. Nonetheless, it is not a futile exercise to address the question on a purely theoretical level. The church has the mission to incarnate itself among its people, in imitation of Christ who became Jewish in all things but sin. If Christ used bread and wine, should not the church in Asia use the people's staple food and drink? The question at hand is not merely christological; it is also and above all ecclesiological. The church must become, for example, Filipino in the same way as Christ became a Jew. The mystery of the incarnation subsists and continues to be operative in the church. The extent to which the church is inculturated in a particular people is the extent to which Christ and his gospel are present there. Inculturation 'expresses one of the elements of the great mystery of the incarnation' (John Paul II, 'Address to the Pontifical Biblical Commission', *Fede e cultura alla luce della Bibbia*, Turin 1981, 5).

If the Last Supper was a Passover meal, it was not an ordinary but a festive meal. Hence neither should the eucharist in the South Pacific, for example, be an ordinary meal, though it does not have to consist of foreign food and drink. Their kava, for instance, is ceremonially prepared and drunk for festive gatherings. The method of dynamic equivalence applies also to the type of foodstuff. The eucharist is a fellowship meal. Fellowship is expressed in the breaking and sharing of the one loaf of bread. Acts 2.46 calls the eucharist with a name that sums up what it is all about: 'breaking of bread'. Although in most cases today the eucharistic bread is pre-broken for practical reasons, the ritual gesture of breaking the bread continues to symbolize fellowship. Given the privileged position the breaking of bread has in eucharistic theology, the local foodstuff should be shared in a manner that is equivalent to the

breaking of bread and should be fully expressive of fellowship in Christ. The communal cup mentioned in 1 Cor. 10.16–17 also suggests fellowship among the members of the assembly. The principle of a communal cup would make us believe that before the age of the basilicas the size of the cup was determined by the size of the community. At the seventh-century *papal mass recorded by the Roman Ordo I a 'main cup' was used, thus implying that there were other cups, probably for the communion of the assembly. These practical solutions should not make us forget the basic value of community spirit expressed by the one bread that is broken and the single cup that is shared. Kava is normally passed around in one cup. Lastly, it is essential that the assembly is able to recognize in faith that the local foodstuff and drink are the sacraments of Christ's body and blood. This is a crucial point about true inculturation. Those who have been raised in the tradition of round wafer-like bread we call the 'sacred *host' will obviously need special assistance, while others will be warned not to make light of the local foodstuff and drink. Catechesis should always accompany the process of inculturation, especially when the people's concept of the sacred is confined to what a church traditionally celebrates in the liturgy.

The rite of communion presents various possibilities for the application of dynamic equivalence. In several eucharistic liturgies the sign of peace is exchanged at communion time. The appropriate manner of performing it is a matter that annoys both ecclesiastical authorities and liturgists alike. It will probably take several years before a suitable cultural sign can be found that satisfies the demand of the liturgy and the preferences of each member of the local community. For the inculturation of the rite of communion it would be useful to examine the ritual pattern of sharing food and drink in a given culture. Who offers them? How are they presented to the people? What words are used by the one who offers and what response is given by the one who receives? What gestures accompany the reception of food and drink? In passing it is important to note that the eucharistic communion, whether on the part of the recipient or of the minister, does not tolerate cultural patterns where a distinction is made between races, sexes, socio-economic classes and political alliances.

The *Misa ng Bayang Pilipino*, which is an inculturated form of the Roman mass for the dioceses in the Philippines, provides an example of dynamic equivalence for the rite of communion. The rubrics read: 'The priest and the special ministers of communion distribute communion to the people. After the communion of the people the priest distributes communion to the other ministers. He takes communion last.' The current liturgical practice is for the presider to receive communion first, perhaps as an expression of leadership in the church. The Filipino cultural pattern – and many other peoples in Asia share it – requires that the host eats after the guests have been served. While guests eat, the host moves about to entertain them. To behave otherwise is to forfeit one's role as host and assume the status of guest. At home the more traditional parents feed their children before they eat their meal. In short, according to this cultural pattern, eating last is a sign of hospitality, leadership and parents' care for their children. Incorporated into the communion rite, it signifies that leadership in the church consists of humble service, with possible allusion to Matt. 20.26–28. Far from contradicting the Roman practice, it supports the concept of eucharistic leadership through the use of dynamic equivalence.

———

Selected texts: Congregation for Divine Worship, *The Roman Liturgy and Inculturation*, 4th Instruction for the Right Application of the Conciliar Constitution on the Liturgy, Rome 1994; Consilium for the Implementation of the Constitution on the Liturgy, 'Instruction on the Translation of Liturgical Texts', *Documents on the Liturgy 1963–1979*, Collegeville 1982, 284–5.
     Studies: Anscar J. Chupungco, *Cultural Adaptation of the Liturgy*, New York 1982; A. J. Chupungco (ed.), *Handbook for Liturgical Studies* I, Collegeville 1997, 381–97; II, Collegeville 1998, 337–75; A. J. Chupungco, *Liturgical Inculturation: Sacramentals, Religiosity, Catechesis*, Collegeville 1992; *Liturgies of the Future: The Process and Methods of Inculturation*, New York 1989; *Worship: Progress and Tradition*, Washington, DC 1995; 'Two Methods of Liturgical Inculturation', *Christian Worship: Unity in Cultural Diversity*, ed. S. Anita Stauffer, Geneva 1996, 77–94; G. Ostdiek, 'Principles of Translation in the Revised Sacramentary', *Liturgy for the New Millennium*, ed. Mark R. Francis and Keith F. Pecklers, Collegeville 2000, 17–34; A. Shorter, *Toward a Theology of Inculturation*, London 1988.

                                    ANSCAR J. CHUPUNGCO

Independent Evangelical Church Worship

The term 'independent evangelical' describes a wide range of churches with respect to worship. Consequently, it is best to look at traits associated with the term rather than attempting to form a description applicable to all.

Evangelical churches share several characteristics that shape the nature of their worship. For one thing, evangelicals often emphasize the language of feeling: God is known by feeling; the operation of grace is sensed by feeling. Another characteristic is a congregational liturgical polity. There are no commonly received texts or liturgical norms, or, at least, written ones. While there might be a great degree of commonality between these churches in worship, it is a voluntary sharing which creates it. No central authority promulgates common worship. In addition, evangelical churches also have a high view of scripture and give great weight to it in personal piety. Thus they tend to grant a critical place to expository preaching in their worship. Evangelical churches also emphasize experiential and relational themes in their doctrine of salvation, all within a focus upon Christ as a distinctive Saviour. Their worship gives high value to personal religious experience (as in the use of testimonies), asking whether attendees have had a certain inward experience of grace while defining grace as intimate knowledge of Christ. Finally, the worship of evangelical churches is also often missionary, wanting to replicate saving experiences of grace and using worship as an opportunity to do so. To justify this missiological approach to worship, some evangelicals sharply divide the content of the gospel and its forms of proclamation, including worship. Worship is often a tool to proclaim the gospel and is subject to adaptation to increase that proclamation's perceived effectiveness. Historically, this missionary approach often emphasizes a climactic crisis in people's experience of grace in worship.

Within this broad term 'evangelical' are two smaller groups related to worship. One is *charismatic churches, whose worship is characterized by perceived guidance by the Holy Spirit, most clearly evidenced by use of biblical charismata. Within this charismatic grouping is the smaller group of *Pentecostals, whose piety classically has emphasized a second distinctive experience of baptism with the Holy Spirit evidenced by speaking in tongues. Classic Pentecostal worship, too, in comparison to general evangelical or charismatic worship, has tended to be more intense and exuberant. Recognizing these subdivisions within the broader 'evangelical' term reinforces the diversity within evangelical worship. Whereas all Pentecostals should be considered both charismatic and evangelical, the reverse is not true.

Liturgical diversity within independent evangelical churches also takes three different approaches in worship's basic sacramentality. Independent evangelical churches find three modes of God's presence in worship: in the word, in music, or in the sacraments. Churches which primarily stress God's presence in the word structure services around extensive reading of scripture as well as a detailed biblical preaching, perhaps as the climax to the service. Churches which emphasize sensing God's presence in music might use a *Praise-and-Worship order to the service, spending the first thirty minutes to an hour in extended congregational song. Evangelical churches which emphasize God's presence in the *sacraments are the fewest in number. They more frequently observe the *Lord's supper – as compared to other evangelical churches – and order worship in a way which balances Word and Table.

Diversity among independent evangelical churches is reinforced by congregations' economic, social and ethnic differences. Such varied cultural backgrounds can reflect wide levels of exuberance and sensibilities to length of services. Differences in congregational size, too, can affect the nature of evangelical worship.

Beyond these differences, independent evangelical churches often share particular practices and explanations of worship. For instance, it has become common to use Isa. 6.1–8 to explain the content of an ideal worship experience and sequence: praise and awe before the transcendence of God, *confession, forgiveness, divine call and personal commitment. In specific practices, evangelical churches share much common ground, too. Prayer tends to be *extempore, perhaps led by a variety of people. The liturgical *year is minimal, usually including only the most crucial feasts (*Christmas and *Easter) and a variety of other civic (e.g. Mother's Day) and ecclesiastical (e.g. Sunday School Promotion) days. Increasing use of common *lectionaries, however, has brought a fuller calendar to some churches. Sunday morning services can be supplemented by Sunday evening and weekday services. Sometimes these additional services are prayer services without preaching. Sacramental administration tends to be infrequent. Notions of sacraments as objectively efficacious instruments of grace are diminished. Often critical in this sensibility is the desire to link new birth to a definable personal moment rather than to *baptism. Many evangelical churches prefer immersion as the mode of baptism. Some evangelical churches, too, prefer to speak of 'ordinances' rather than 'sacraments'. The style of music shows great range, although some prefer more contemporary compositions and instrumentation. 'Special music' by soloists, a small team, or a choir is common. *Vestments tend to be minimal and spaces are visually straightforward. Some churches, however, are using increasingly sophisticated technology to project words to music and supplement preaching with visual images. *Chancels often seem like stages and *naves like auditoriums. The style of liturgical presidency can be rather informal, folksy and spontaneous. Liturgical ceremonial is often at a minimum. In addition to preaching, some churches use drama to proclaim the gospel.

With a congregational liturgical polity and pragmatic liturgical bent, independent evangelical churches often spontaneously create liturgical innovations, which soon gain widespread distribution. These innovations go through several standard stages of development, another shared quality in evangelical worship. Typically, these innovations emerge suddenly or coincidentally. A growing awareness of their usefulness follows. Then they are named, a step that allows promotion to other churches. After the innovation has become widespread, it is standardized and then institutionalized. Finally, there is decline as some churches remain committed to the practice as part of an evangelical tradition whereas others are attracted to a newer liturgical innovation.

Of particular note among independent evangelical churches are so-called mega-churches, deriving their name from the thousands or tens of thousands in worship attendance. These churches exert considerable influence upon evangelicalism through their publications, conferences and associations. Their innovations are the ones most intentionally imitated by other evangelical churches. Their worship is also characterized by performative excellence. Some mega-churches give great attention to making worship reflective of surrounding culture. Given the size of their congregations and the missiological bent to their worship, they typically rely upon small groups to provide intimate fellowship and to form their members.

_____

Paul Basden, *The Worship Maze: Finding a Style to Fit Your Church*, Downers Grove, IL 1999; Robert E. Webber (ed.), *The Complete Library of Christian Worship*, 7 vols, Nashville, TN 1994 (bib.); Robert E. Webber, *Signs of Wonder: The Phenomenon of Convergence in Modern Liturgical and Charismatic Churches*, Nashville, TN 1992; John D. Witvliet, 'The Blessing and Bane of the North American Megachurch: Implications for Twenty-first Century Congregational Song', *Hymn* L,1999, 6–14.

LESTER RUTH

Infant Communion

The origins of infant communion are inextricably bound up with the origins and development of the practice of infant *baptism. Ultimately, both remain obscure. When, by the third century, infant baptism had become a general practice in both the East and the West, one integral pattern of initiation had emerged consisting of a water bath (preceded or followed by an *anointing) and *communion. This pattern applied to all, regardless of age, and without all three elements the process was regarded as incomplete.

From at least the time of Cyprian, John 3.5 ('Unless one is born again of water and the Spirit') and 6.53 ('Unless you eat the flesh of the Son of Man') were used as a couplet in the *traditio fidei* and were establishing what was required of all for participation in the life of the Christian community. Patristic literature never questions the 'capacity' of infants to receive the benefits of communion any more than it questions their capacity to be baptized. The only questions about appropriate age that are raised are in the light of the common analogy between Jewish circumcision and Christian baptism when some asked if infant males could be initiated before the age for circumcision (eight days).

Throughout the patristic and early medieval periods, the baptismal communion of infants along with adult candidates was the regular practice of both Eastern and Western churches and, as the number of adult candidates diminished, came to constitute normative practice. In the East, it still remains the custom to communicate infants from the time of their initiation.

In the West, beginning in the eleventh century, infants were increasingly communicated only under the species of wine, on the grounds that they could not swallow or assimilate bread. But as at this time in the West it became the increasing practice to communicate the laity only under the species of bread, the practice of infant communion was generally abandoned. This was reinforced by some Scholastic theologians (e.g. Nicholas of Lyra) who argued the general principle that receiving the body and blood of Christ of themselves was of no value unless one received 'spiritually and with understanding', thus explicitly eliminating infants, who – they claimed – could only receive like animals and infidels! It was at this time that the Johannine couplet (3.5 and 6.53) that had been the principal biblical proof for the practice was replaced by 1 Cor. 11.28 ('Let a man examine himself before eating . . .') as the most frequently invoked biblical text on the question.

There was considerable debate over the question of infant communion at the Council of Basel, where the *Bohemian Utraquists, who had in 1417 restored the practice, argued that communion for all the baptized was one of the four 'Laws of God' and necessary for salvation. Basel rejected the notion and the Council's reservations became one of the anathematizations at the Council of Trent although no Reformation church, other than that in Bohemia, maintained the practice at that time. In seventeenth-century England, the question figured in the debates between paedo-baptists (Anglicans and Presbyterians) and those who practised believers' baptism ([Ana]baptists and more radical reformed groups). In the course of the debate, paedobaptists conceded that it was theologically inconsistent to maintain that infants could be baptized but not communicated.

In the last quarter of the twentieth century, the question became a lively discussion once again as churches reviewed their theology and practice of Christian initiation. As they examined the theological relationship between baptism and *eucharist and the historical evidence for communicating all the baptized, regardless of age, many churches pointed to the inconsistency of their practice and decided that children should be admitted to communion once again. Influential in this process was a consultation on children and communion held by the Faith and Order Commission of the WCC at Bad Segeberg in 1980. At first, many churches began to allow children to receive communion, but established minimum age limits (often five years). Soon, these restrictions were widely challenged on both pastoral and theological grounds so that, by the beginning of the twenty-first century, infant communion had once again become a common practice in many churches.

___

Colin O. Buchanan (ed.), *Nurturing Children in Communion*, Nottingham 1985; David R. Holeton, *Infant Communion – Then and Now*, Nottingham 1981; 'The Communion of Infants: the Basel Years,' *Communio Viatorum* XXIX/4, 1986, 15–40; Geiko Müller-Fahrenholz (ed.), . . . *And do not hinder them*, Geneva 1982; Ruth A. Meyers (ed.), *Children at the Table: A Collection of Essays on Children and the Eucharist*, New York 1995; Robert F. Taft, 'On the Question of Infant Communion in the Byzantine Catholic Churches of the USA', *Diakonia* XVII, 1982, 201–14.

DAVID R. HOLETON

Initiation, Christian *see* Baptism

Institution Narrative

An account of the Last Supper of Jesus, drawn from the NT narratives (Matt. 26.26–29; Mark 14.22–25; Luke 22.19–20; 1 Cor. 11.23–26) but usually not identical with any one of them, which began to be inserted into *eucharistic prayers in the fourth century, if not before. It can occur in ancient rites either as part of the thanksgiving/remembrance section of the prayer or within the petitionary section. In the West its recital came to be thought of as that which effected the consecration of the bread and wine. Most Reformation churches retained it within their eucharistic rites – though not always within a eucharistic prayer – as the warrant for the celebration of the eucharist, but modern liturgical revisions in those churches have increasingly placed it in a eucharistic prayer, at least optionally.

EDITOR

Insufflation

A breathing into the faces of baptismal candidates, in conjunction with either an *exorcism or the conferral of the Holy Spirit, is based, undoubtedly, on John 20.22, where the risen Christ 'breathes' the Holy Spirit upon the Apostles on Easter night. The rite is docu-mented in several early liturgical sources and other writings often in connection with exorcisms either during the final stages or *scrutinies of the *catechumenate (e.g. *Apostolic Tradition*, Cyril of Jerusalem, and Theodore of Mopsuestia) or in a more immediate pre-baptismal context (e.g. Augustine, Quodvultdeus of Carthage, John the Deacon, Isidore of Seville and Hildephonse of Toledo). The practice is further documented in Western medieval liturgical sources as well (e.g. the Mozarabic *Liber Ordinum*, *Ordo Romanus* L, and various sacramentaries and *rituales*), but here it is most often located as part of the immediate pre-baptismal rites for infant baptism since the catechumenate itself had disappeared. Although the exorcism of evil spirits and the conferral of the Holy Spirit are often closely associated in insufflation, the Gallican Bobbio Missal is clearly more pneumatic than exorcistic ('N., receive the Holy Spirit, mayest thou guard him in thy heart') and may well reflect the remnant of an earlier theological interpretation of pre-baptismal rites in some places of the early church. In other sources (Byzantine and Coptic) insufflation accompanies the pre-baptismal renunciation of Satan and in the Ambrosian rite (e.g. the Ambrosian *Manuale*) it accompanies the *Effeta* or *apertio*. And still in others (e.g. the Coptic Rite) insufflation is connected to the post-baptismal chrismation, interpreted pneumatically.

In addition to an insufflation upon catechumens and baptismal candidates, some Western medieval liturgical documents (e.g. Gregorian Sacramentary, Sarum Manual and the Gallican *Missale Gothicum*) and some Eastern sources (e.g. Maronite and West Syrian) include insufflation on the baptismal waters in connection to the *epiclesis of the Holy Spirit during their consecration. This practice, along with pouring or mixing chrism into the water, continued in the West in the RC baptismal rite until the recent liturgical reforms.

Although some of the early baptismal revisions of the Protestant Reformers kept this ceremony at the beginning of their rites (e.g. Martin Luther's 1523 *Taufbüchlein*, and in Strasbourg and Zurich), all Reformation liturgies, including the 1549 *BCP*, eventually omitted it as one of the unnecessary ceremonies which clouded the meaning of baptism. Insufflation is no longer present in most modern Western baptismal rites, though it still occurs as an option in some RC rites of exorcism associated with entrance into the catechumenate and in the RC rite for the consecration of chrism.

For bibliography, *see* **Baptism**.

MAXWELL E. JOHNSON

Intercession

A natural desire to ask God for things lies at the basis of the human motivation to intercede. Modern difficulties with intercession stem partly from a weakened sense of the objective reality of God and his prior initiative in all prayer. The main aspects of intercession include: (1) straightforward asking for something to be provided; (2) offering people or situations to God in thanksgiving, grief, concern, etc., without a clear picture of the optimum outcome; (3) offering our own prayer as individual or community in acknowledgement that we are bound together with others and the whole creation and they cannot be excluded from our prayer; (4) Christian service of others being naturally accompanied by prayer for God's assistance in that service; (5) the converse: intercession has to be accompanied where possible by action; (6) being called as members of Christ to participate in his heavenly intercession. Asking fellow-Christians to pray for us has never been seen as compromising the intermediary role of Christ. Asking the departed saints to intercede for us, a practice stemming from early church history, was challenged by the Reformation and remains a subject of controversy in ecumenical dialogue, something true also of prayer for the souls of the departed.

In Christian liturgy intercession takes many guises: (1) the whole worshipping life of the church is lived not only with the participants' profit in mind, but also that of the whole creation; as the kingdom will be assisted by our active co-operation, so worship contributes to the invisible working of God's grace for the good of the world simply by being offered; (2) worship is sprinkled with acts of intercession, e.g. in the *collects, *canticles, *Lord's Prayer, psalms and *hymns; (3) specific moments of intercession, traditionally the most common form being the *litany.

Intercession in the course of worship is mentioned in various places in the NT (e.g. 1 Tim. 2.1–4). In the *eucharist it always seems to have had a place. Justin Martyr in his *First Apology* (*c*. 150) tells us that the intercessions came between the sermon and the preparation of the gifts. These were often called the 'prayers of the faithful', frequently named also after the *diptychs – tablets on which names of importance in any particular local church were inscribed. There was a tendency to include some intercessions in the *eucharistic prayer, a practice already known in the Jewish table graces from which this prayer derives. In the Roman tradition, which became almost universal in the West, this led to the disappearance of the prayers of the faithful as such, and their transferral to the eucharistic prayer. The Byzantine rite on the other hand saw a proliferation of standardized litanies throughout all its liturgical forms. Both East and West knew the singing of long litanies through the streets of major cities as a prelude to the Sunday liturgy, a relic of which are the *Kyries at the beginning of the Western eucharist. Reformation liturgies tended to dismember the eucharistic prayer, and restore some form of specific intercession at another place in the rite. Cranmer in his *BCP* of 1552 restored the prayers of the faithful more or less to their ancient place. Modern liturgical reforms have gone further and restored the litany form.

*Daily prayer would naturally include intercession, and this is mentioned by early writers such as Tertullian. The public morning and evening services which became universal in the fourth century consisted fundamentally of psalmody followed by intercessions. By contrast the monastic prayer which emerged in the same period seems to have had little intercessory content. In the hands of the Celtic church in Britain the litany of intercession came to be replaced by *capitella*: psalm-verses which were used both for petition and response. These were eventually imported into Roman practice, where they were known as *preces*, replacing the earlier litany form. The sixfold form in the *BCP* is referred to in the Rule of Columbanus (sixth century). The litany form has been restored in the post-Vatican II RC liturgy of the hours. Current diversity of practice in various denominations includes traditional litanies, freshly composed *capitella* which give a more poetic and evocative framework to intercession, and scripture texts arranged in litanies of praise and thanksgiving, as in the current Ambrosian liturgy. Opportunity for *extempore prayer involving all those present is also increasingly encouraged. Some hold the view that intercession needs generous provision in the daily prayer of the secular church, as this is the typical task and bent of the priestly people of God. Others would caution that in a utilitarian age the gratuitous offering of worship is as important to our prayer for the world as specific intercession itself. In the end, acts of intercession are simply marking what is characteristic of all authentic Christian living and worship – a taking seriously both inside and outside worship of the call to love God and love our neighbour.

GEORGE GUIVER

Intercommunion

1. *The Problem*. 'Intercommunion' is the mutual sharing in the *eucharist between separated churches. In this sense it goes beyond the meaning of the other often-heard expression 'eucharistic hospitality', which does not necessarily include reciprocity. 'Intercommunion' is an ambiguous term. It expresses 'communion' *between* ('inter') different churches, which are not in (full) communion with each other. Some churches therefore would claim that 'intercommunion' does not make sense: it cannot exist before full ecclesial communion is established. Either churches are in full communion with each other and therefore have one eucharistic table, or there is no communion and therefore also no 'intercommunion'. Other churches would understand 'intercommunion' as a means towards full ecclesial communion and as a step on the way. What is at stake here is the understanding of a shared eucharist as means towards unity or as an expression of unity already achieved.

2. *The Present Situation*. The *RC Church and the *Orthodox churches especially consider the eucharist as an expression of existing unity, and therefore a common eucharist is only possible when ecclesial communion is already achieved. But for ecclesial communion full unity in faith is necessary, which includes, for example, the understanding of apostolic succession as episcopal succession or – on the RC side – the doctrine of the primacy of the pope. This is different in the Reformation churches: what is necessary for the unity of the church is the preaching of the gospel and the administration of the sacraments 'in accordance with the divine word', as it is expressed, for example, in the Augsburg Confession. Therefore, today an open communion, to which all baptized are invited, is practised in most of these churches.

In this sense we can distinguish two groups of churches: those which practise an open communion and those which practise a closed communion. Between those two groups, in principle, no intercommunion is possible. But within those groups we can speak of intercommunion taking place in cases where there is not yet full ecclesial communion: the RC Church would, since the Second Vatican Council, invite Orthodox to receive communion, although there is no ecclesial communion, while on the other hand Orthodox do not respond to this invitation, and on their side cannot invite Christians from any other church. Rome feels that there is greater unity in faith with the Orthodox than with other churches, which makes this invitation possible. Within the family of the Reformation churches (including the *Anglican churches) there exists a variety of agreements for ecclesial communion or intercommunion.

The situation becomes even more complex if the exceptions which exist between the two groups of churches described above are taken into account: The RC Church (*Decree on Ecumenism* and *Directory for the Application of Principles and Norms of Ecumenism*) opens up the possibility of exceptions, where other Christians can receive communion in the RC Church or where RCs are allowed to receive communion in other churches; but this must be distinguished from a general possibility for intercommunion. Also some Orthodox churches have known exceptions, as for example in Russia, where at the beginning of the twentieth century RCs were accepted to receive communion *kath' oikonomian* (on grounds of economy) for a certain time.

3. *Historical and Theological Background*. Historically the eucharistic table has become the sign of communion between different ecclesial bodies. Consequently 'excommunication' has been the sign of distorted community, or separation. The 'excommunication' between the Western and the Eastern church in 1054 had more to do with cultural differences and with power questions than with theological differences concerning the understanding of the eucharist. But in the Reformation, doctrinal differences over the understanding of the eucharist played a much more important role. The doctrine of justification, as it was developed by the Reformers and rejected at the Council of Trent, influenced the understanding of the eucharist. The point of disagreement between the Reformers and Rome was espe-

cially the question of the eucharist as a sacrifice. But also between the *Lutheran churches and the *Reformed churches the different understanding of the eucharist was a major point of disagreement. The fundamental issue here was the question of the presence of Christ in the eucharist. But in addition the understanding of ministry and episcopal succession became a problem in this context as some Reformation churches started to ordain pastors without the laying-on of hands by a *bishop in apostolic succession.

Only in the twentieth century has it been possible to come closer together again. One of the earliest agreements on intercommunion was the 'Bonn agreement on intercommunion' in 1931 between the *Old Catholic Church and the Anglican Communion. In 1954 the World Alliance of Reformed Churches recommended the admission to the Lord's table of 'any baptized person who loves and confesses Jesus Christ as Lord and Saviour', and most of the Reformation churches, including the Anglicans, followed this example. The next consequent step was the work towards full ecclesial communion. This was possible in 1973 between some Reformed, Lutheran and United Churches in Europe in the Leuenberg Concordat, which was joined later by some churches in Latin America and some *Methodist churches. In the USA the Evangelical Lutheran Church in America, the *Presbyterian Church (USA), the Reformed Church in America and the United Church of Christ declared in the 'Formula of Agreement' (1997/98) that they are in full communion with one another. This was more difficult between Lutheran and Anglican churches, because the recognition of ministries and the issue of the so-called episcopal succession is involved here. The first example for full communion between churches of these denominations is the so-called 'Porvoo agreement' (1992/98) between the British and Irish Anglican churches and Lutheran churches in the Nordic and Baltic States. In cases where ecclesial communion is not (yet) possible, there exist agreements on intercommunion, such as in the Meissen agreement (1988) between the Church of England and the Evangelical Church in Germany (EKD). In the USA the Episcopal Church and the Evangelical Lutheran Church in America voted for full ecclesial communion between the two churches in 1997 and 1999 respectively. In Canada the Anglican Church and the Lutherans adopted in 1989 an 'interim eucharistic shar-

ing' plan and planned to agree on full communion in 2001.

Influenced by the development of bilateral relationships between several churches, the convergence document on *Baptism, Eucharist and Ministry* of the Faith and Order Commission of the World Council of Churches (published in 1982) was a major step forward on the multilateral level. In turn it influenced especially the bilateral agreements between Anglican and Lutheran churches mentioned above.

On the liturgical level an effort was made to express these convergences in the so-called 'Lima liturgy', which was used in several assemblies of the World Council of Churches and in other circumstances as a way of celebrating the eucharist together. Nevertheless, it was clear that the liturgical expression of convergences does not solve the problem of intercommunion. This requires the solution of the deeper differences about the question of the ministry and hence ecclesiology as such. Therefore intercommunion is still not possible between the major Christian families such as Protestants, RCs and Orthodox.

See also **Ecumenical Worship.**

DAGMAR HELLER

Inter-Faith Worship

Inter-faith worship has caused much controversy, partly because many different things are meant by the term. Distinctions need to be made between: (1) Christians visiting places of worship of another faith community; (2) Christians observing the worship of another faith community; (3) Christians participating in the worship of another faith community; (4) visitors of another faith community being welcomed to Christian worship, which may be altered or added to in some way because of their presence; (5) an event in which representatives of different faiths contribute readings or songs from their own faith traditions one by one, but where there is no general expectation that those of different faiths will participate; (6) an event which has a common order and a common theme, but which draws upon the faith traditions of all present, and in which everyone present is invited to participate throughout. Of these different kinds of occasion only (5), often called 'serial inter-faith worship', and (6), often called 'common order inter-faith worship', can really be regarded as inter-faith worship, and some would exclude all but (6).

Some Christians have attempted to allay criticism by avoiding the word 'worship' and advertising an inter-faith worship event as an 'observance' or a 'celebration', rather than a 'service'. It is doubtful if the change in terminology helps, and the real theological question has been expressed as follows: 'We can come together to pray, but can we come to pray together?' Praying together implies a focus on the same divine being, which obviously creates difficulties for non-theistic Buddhists. Even among monotheists the differences in theological discourse about God may be felt so acutely that, for example, Orthodox Jews and many Muslims would find it impossible to participate. It is not only Christians who have difficulties of conscience with inter-faith worship. Yet attempts to remove all possible theological stumbling blocks are likely to produce language that is bland and unsatisfying. In support of inter-faith worship it may be said that no two believers of any faith hold exactly the same views, and Christians are assured that God has not left himself without witness (Acts 14.17). If there is only one God, we may surely intend to worship the same divine being even if there are radical differences in what we understand about that being. Can we meet friends of other faiths only in debate about what we hold most dear, and never in common prayer? Is God properly greeted only with debate about the divine nature and never with the common offering of heart and mind in worship?

At heart Christian anxieties are about the one to whom worship is offered, about the possibility of idolatry, and about the potential neglect or implicit denial of the person of Christ and the salvation offered through him alone. Particular Christian hostility has been expressed to interfaith services which claim to include a genuine Christian contribution, but in which the name of Christ is never mentioned. Inter-faith worship then raises fundamental questions about the character of any faith which does not place Christ at the centre of the understanding of God, and about the nature of salvation and the necessity of evangelism. In response one can say that in many faiths, especially in Judaism and Islam but also in Sikhism and other Indian traditions, there has long been a vigorous determination to focus on God alone and repudiate idolatry. The Hebrew scriptures condemn not only idolatrous worship but also formally correct worship carried out by people who practise injustice and deceit in their daily lives. The sayings of Jesus suggest that there will be

great astonishment about who will be saved and who will not.

Apart from theological difficulties there will be complications with the naming of any event, its location and its rationale. It is one thing to commemorate victims from different faith communities after a fire or aircraft disaster, in a secular venue like a city park, and after planning by the mayor with leaders of the city churches, synagogues, mosques and temples. It is obviously very different for members of a local inter-faith discussion group to experiment with a common order of service of their own in the church of one of their members. In the latter case it is likely that using English or the common language rather than the sacred language (Hebrew, Arabic, Sanskrit, etc.), sitting shod on chairs rather than barefoot on the floor, following a printed order of service rather than participating from memory – all these and other factors will mean that conventional Western Christian styles and practices in worship will predominate rather than a genuine mingling of faith traditions.

The Christian minister or leader faced with an occasion of inter-faith worship must ask these questions:

1. What kind of occasion is being proposed? Whose idea was it? Who will take responsibility for it? Who will support it and why? The most natural and successful occasions are those where the participants already know each other well.

2. Where will it be held, and who will make the decisions about what exactly is to happen? A neutral venue is often best.

3. How will a refusal to take part be understood? It should be possible to explain difficulties of conscience without giving offence.

4. What are the appropriate themes for such worship? Shared silence is often the most effective mode of prayer together, perhaps preceded by suggestions or bidding prayers. Peace, justice and ecological issues are often an appropriate focus.

5. What is the role of the Christian leader in the event? He or she will want to affirm the members of other faiths as valued fellow citizens without identifying the church with their beliefs and practices. It is possible to convey a common sense of the transcendent while giving a sensitive but distinctive Christian witness.

6. What will be the pastoral and spiritual impact of the event? This will depend on the preparation for the event, the care with which it

is publicized and explained, and on the local and national media reporting of it.

'Multi-Faith Worship'? Questions and Suggestions from the Inter-Faith Consultative Group, London 1992; Marcus Braybrooke, *A Wider Vision: A History of the World Congress of Faiths*, Oxford 1996, ch. 9.

CHRISTOPHER LAMB

Intinction *see* Communion

Introit

see **Chants of the Proper of the Mass; Music in the Mass of the Roman Rite**

Islamic Worship

The word in Arabic for worship is *'ibādah*, which literally means to 'lie flat and absolutely low', that is, to submit willingly. This submission stems from utmost adoration of God, who in Islam is seen as one who is full of love and affection. Ibn al-Qaiyyim, one of the scholars of Islam, emphasizes that there are two components of *'ibādah*: utmost love and utmost petition with humility. When the Qur'ān means the opposite of *'ibādah*, it uses the word *istıkbar* or arrogance.

Worship in Islam is a means for the purification of a person's soul and of his or her daily life. It is premised on the basic view that the true foundations of a successful life are soundness of belief and thought, purity of soul and righteousness of action. Islam aims to establish a direct link between the individual and Creator, and for this no intercession or intermediaries are necessary. Hence the concept of a priesthood is largely absent in Islam. The role of religious scholar or leader (*'ālim* or *imām*) is to guide the people in the right direction. Another significant point to note is that *'ibādah* or worship is not confined to specific places. A person can enter into a communion with his or her Lord wherever he or she wishes. The Prophet Muhammad once said that 'the [whole of the earth] has been rendered for me a Mosque: pure and clean'. Every virtuous action that a Muslim performs sincerely and with a clear objective to carry out God's commandment is considered an act of worship. This includes working for a living, rearing children, pursuing education or any worldly action performed with pure motives. Scholars agree that good intentions change acts of habit (*'ādah*)

into acts of worship (*'ibādah*). The duties of worship are summed up in the 'five pillars' of faith.

1. The *shahādah* or 'witnessing' is the first pillar of Islam. This confession of faith, also called the *kalimah*, or the word of belief, that is that 'there is no god but God; Muhammad is the messenger of God.' A Muslim is expected not simply to believe but also to declare this conviction verbally. These words also form part of the daily remembrance of God in a Muslim's life. The *kalimah* has two parts – one that reminds him or her of the Oneness of God and denies the existence of any other deities; the other recalls the example of the Prophet Muhammad, which is to be emulated by members of the community.

2. Worship is the renewal of faith (*īmān*) and the method of renewal is *salāt*, which means 'public worship' rather than 'prayers'. *salāt* is the second pillar and consists of various actions, such as standing, bowing and uttering appropriate praise of God; but the height of the *salāt* is the *sajdah*, or the touching of the ground with one's forehead. Therefore a place exclusively designated for Muslims to perform their *sajdah* is the *masjid* or mosque. This symbolizes the acknowledgement of the Supreme Being and absolute submission to him. Each unit of *salāt* consists of two *sajdahs* and there are slight variations in the number of units in five daily *salāts*. In normal circumstances a Muslim is expected to perform the *salāt* after due ablutions, and a congregational *salāt* is always encouraged. In a congregational *salāt* Muslims arrange themselves in parallel rows behind an *imām*, the person standing in front of them. The *salāt* ends with the utterance 'peace' (*salām*) to the right and left. In their *salāt* Muslims face towards Ka'bah (the cube-like structure covered with black brocade), which is in Makkah (former spelling, Mecca). The names of prayers are *fajar* or dawn, between dawn and sunrise; *zuhr* or midday; *'asr* or afternoon *salāt* before sunset; *maghrib* or sunset, soon after sunset, and finally *'ishā'* or evening *salāt*.

3. The Islamic vision of worship also provides for *zakāt* or 'poor due' as a part of worship. *Zakāt* is the third pillar of Islam. Literally it means 'purification and growth'. Next to *salāt* this act of giving is seen as one of the twin foundation stones of faith. It is obligatory upon those who have been able to save or are in a position to give a portion of their crops and herds to the poor. The amount to be given is left

to individual conscience, though different traditions have evolved, within various denominations of Islam, to fix the minimum. The purpose of *zakāt* is the purification of the soul and the condition of 'poor due' is that it should be paid out of the income earned only by fair and honest means. Furthermore, it is expected from a Muslim performing this act of worship that he or she will give what is of good quality and that the beneficiary's self-respect should not be hurt in any way.

4. Fasting for the whole month of Ramaḍān (the ninth month of the Islamic calendar) is another act of worship. *ṣaum* or *ṣiyām*, which literally means 'to be at rest', is the fourth pillar of Islam. While keeping fast or *ṣaum* he or she is expected to abstain from eating, drinking, smoking and sexual intercourse from dawn to dusk. The purpose of the *ṣaum* is to infuse piety into one's life. Al-Ghazālī remarks that 'the object of fasting is that man should produce within him a semblance of the Divine Attribute of *ṣamadīyah* (freedom from want).' The end of Ramaḍān is celebrated with '*Īd al-Fitr* or 'the festival of the breaking of the fast'. Along with *ṣalāt*, in many Muslim families keeping *ṣaum* is considered an important way of nurturing the young in Islam. During the month of Ramaḍān to mark the first Revelation of the Qur'ān special congregational *ṣalāts* are held in late evenings, in which the whole of the Qur'ān is recited.

5. *Hajj*, or the Pilgrimage, is the fifth pillar of Islam, and is obligatory on those able-bodied Muslims who can afford to travel to Makkah once in a lifetime. This act of *hajj* is associated with the Prophet Ibrāhīm or Abraham, who established the Ka'bah as the house of worship for the one and Only God. There are several references to this in the Qur'ān. For example: 'And when We made the House (at Makkah) a place of assembly for mankind and a place of safety (saying) take then the place whereon Abraham stood as your place of prayer' (Qur'ān 2.125). The *hajj* is performed in the eleventh month, in Dhu al-ḥijjah, which literally means the month of *hajj*. Pilgrims wear iḥrām or sanctity garb (men wearing two pieces of unsewn white cloth). Rituals begin in Makkah, where the pilgrims complete seven circuits (*ṭawāf*) of the Ka'bah and run briskly between Safā and Marwā, the two hills between which Hajar (Hagar), Ishma'il's mother, ran frantically in search of water. It takes three to four days to complete all the rituals of *hajj*. The '*umrah* is a lesser pilgrimage that can be performed any time of the year and takes only a few hours to complete.

These pillars are not ends in themselves but are meant, so to speak, to provide the structure and sustain the body of Islam. They are to promote, for example, '*adl* and *iḥsān*. '*Adl* means 'justice', 'fairness' and 'impartiality', which in the Qur'ānic vision has to be upheld even if close relatives suffer through it. *Iḥsān* means 'suitable', 'beautiful', 'proper' or 'fitting', and its essence is the love of God. An act performed with a sense of duty is one thing; the same act performed with a sense of love is another. *Iḥsān* represents the latter, serving as the inspiration for Muslim piety and spirituality. The five pillars of Islam shape the characteristics of Muslim faith and community life every day; but this does not mean that the devotional life of a Muslim ends here. Every act of the pillars ends or begins with *du'ā'*, which literally means 'calling' upon God. In the daily life of a Muslim *du'ā'* plays a significant role and it may be offered individually or collectively, softly or in silence. *Du'ā'* in Islam is the essence of worship. This calling upon God, as Prophet Muḥammad once remarked, 'is the weapon of the believer, the pillar of religion and the light of heaven and earth'. Muslims' supplication includes invoking the 'most beautiful names' of God. They are ninety-nine in number and by those names God is known and addressed. Closely related to *du'ā'* is *dhikr*, which means both to 'remember' and 'mention' God. The Qur'ān is also known as the book of remembrance (*dhikr*) and hence the reading and memorizing of the Qur'ān is considered as *dhikr*, which is part of a Muslim's devotional life. In *ṣūfī* or the mystic tradition great emphasis is laid on the denunciation of what is other than God. The utter devotion of the heart to the recollection of God and the absorption (*fanā'*) in God is the essence of the mystic way of life. However, the observance of the religious duties and bodily purification go hand in hand. In this process men and women aspire to and may manage to achieve the nearness (*qurb*) to God.

———

Hammudah Abdalati, *Islam in Focus*, Kuwait 1978; Edwin Elliot Calverley, *Worship in Islam* 1925, reprinted Westport, CT 1981 (translation of the 'Book of Worship' from Al-Ghazali's *Ihyā' 'ulūm al-dīn*; also published in Lahore 1977); Kenneth Cragg and R. Marston Speight (eds), *Islam from Within*, Belmont, CA 1980; Al-Ghazālī, *The Ninety-*

Nine Beautiful Names of God (translation of *al-Maqsad al-asnā fī sharh asmā' Allāh al-husnā* by David B. Burrell and Naziah Daher, with notes), Cambridge 1992; Al-Ghazālī, *Inner Dimensions of Islamic Worship* (translated by Muhtar Holland), Leicester 2000; Muhammad Al-Ghazali, *Remembrance and Prayer: The Way of the Prophet Muhammad* (translated by Yusuf Talal Delarenzo), Leicester 2000; Ahmad Zaki Hammad, *Lasting Prayers of the Qur'ān and the Prophet Muhammad*, Bridgeview, IL 1996; Abul Hasan Ali Nadwi, *The Four Pillars of Islam* (translated by M. Asif Kidwai), 2nd edn, Karachi 1975; Constance E. Padwick, *Muslim Devotions: A Study of Prayer-Manuals in Common Use*, London 1961.

ATAULLAH SIDDIQUI

Jacobite Church

see **West Syrian Worship**

Jehovah's Witnesses Worship

Jehovah's Witnesses are a body of ministers commissioned to proclaim the incoming kingdom of God as the only rightful government of the world (Matt. 24.14). They preach that this heavenly kingdom will soon bring an end to the present system of things and produce a world in which righteousness will prevail (2 Peter 3.13). They encourage others to study the Bible, to gain knowledge of God's purposes for the earth and mankind, and to live in harmony with the scriptures (Matt. 28.19, 20; 1 Tim. 2.4).

1. *Modern-Day Organization.* The modern-day activities of Jehovah's Witnesses began in the 1870s when Charles Taze Russell and a small group in Allegheny, Pennsylvania, USA, began a systematic study of the Bible. In 1884, Bible Students, as Jehovah's Witnesses were then known, formed Zion's Watch Tower Tract Society, a non-profit corporation in Pennsylvania, as a legal instrument to be used in carrying forward their Bible education work. To further the expansion of this work on an international scale, the Bible Students moved their headquarters to Brooklyn, New York, in 1909. There they formed an associate corporation now called the Watchtower Bible and Tract Society of New York, Inc. In 1914 they also formed the International Bible Students Association in London, England, to advance their activities throughout the British Commonwealth. The name Jehovah's Wit-

nesses (Isa. 43.10) was adopted in 1931. Today, Jehovah's Witnesses number six million, in more than 235 lands.

Since its inception, the Watch Tower Society has been active in the publishing of Bibles. As early as 1890, for example, it published Rotherham's New Testament in English. By the early 1940s, the Society was printing both the King James Version and the American Standard Version of the Bible. The *New World Translation of the Holy Scriptures* was published in one volume in 1961. And 1984 saw the release of the *New World Translation of the Holy Scriptures – With References,* which contains extensive marginal references, an index of Bible words, and appendix material.

A vast amount of Bible-based literature has also been published by the Watch Tower Society. *The Watchtower,* a semi-monthly magazine and the principal journal of Jehovah's Witnesses, had its start in 1879 and is now published in 140 languages. The average printing of each issue is more than twenty-three million. Their semi-monthly magazine *Awake!* which began in 1919 as *The Golden Age,* now has a circulation of over twenty million in more than eighty languages. Other Bible-based publications of the Watch Tower Society include the book *Knowledge That Leads to Everlasting Life* (1995) and the brochure *What Does God Require of Us?* (1996). Both of these are used extensively by Jehovah's Witnesses in helping others gain accurate knowledge of the basic teachings of the Bible.

The worldwide work of Jehovah's Witnesses is directed by the Governing Body – a central group of experienced *elders – located at the world headquarters of Jehovah's Witnesses in New York. Jehovah's Witnesses also have 110 branch offices worldwide, supervising the preaching work in various parts of the earth.

2. *Places of Worship.* Places of worship used by Jehovah's Witnesses are known as Kingdom Halls. These are modest buildings where more than ninety-one thousand congregations around the world meet to receive Bible instruction. Each congregation holds five Christian meetings every week: a 45-minute discourse on a Bible topic; a congregation discussion of a Bible article in *The Watchtower;* a school that provides training in presenting the Bible's message; a meeting that gives practical suggestions for the Christian ministry and for everyday life; and a smaller group Bible discussion usually held in private homes.

Elders, or overseers, in each congregation provide spiritual oversight. Their appointments are made on the basis of the scriptural requirements set out in 1 Tim. 3.1–10 and Titus 1.5–9. These men willingly take care of the spiritual needs of the congregation and provide comfort and guidance. They are not elevated above the rest of the congregation; neither are they given special titles, nor do they receive any remuneration. There is no class distinction or racial discrimination among them. They are assisted by ministerial servants.

Three times a year, Jehovah's Witnesses assemble in large gatherings where many congregations together enjoy a special programme of Bible education. *Baptism of new disciples by total immersion in water is a regular part of each such programme.

3. *Beliefs*. Jehovah's Witnesses accept the entire Bible as the inspired word of God. Hence, they hold to the Bible as the standard for all their beliefs.

(a) God: Jehovah's Witnesses are monotheistic. They worship the Creator, Jehovah, as the only true God (Ps. 83.18). They do not acknowledge the Trinity. That word does not appear in any translation of the Bible, and the teachings and creeds that proclaim it are part of human tradition that has built up over the centuries.

(b) Jesus Christ: they believe that Jesus is the Son of God and that he had been in heaven as a mighty spirit person before he was born on the earth as a human child. They acknowledge him as their Leader, Ransomer, Saviour and now-reigning King. In obedience to Jesus' command recorded in Luke 22.19, Jehovah's Witnesses hold a special meeting annually on the Jewish calendar date of Nisan 14 to commemorate the death of Jesus Christ. This is the only celebration they observe (Matt. 23.10; 20.28; John 17.5; Rev. 17.14; 19.11–16).

(c) Death: they believe that the dead are conscious of absolutely nothing and experience neither pain nor pleasure. The dead do not exist in some spirit realm but only in God's memory. Any prospect of future life for them lies in the resurrection hope (Eccles. 9.5, 10; John 5.28–29).

(d) Future life: they believe that 144,000 men and women, chosen from the first century down to our time, will share with Christ in his heavenly kingdom, ruling with him (Rev. 5.9–10; 14.1–3). Heavenly life is not viewed as the only reward for leading a good life. Witnesses look to the fulfilment of God's original purpose for the earth, when the earth will be a paradise inhabited by perfect humans, who will live for ever (Ps. 37.29; Isa. 45.18; Luke 23.43; Rev. 21.4). The dead will be resurrected and thereby receive an opportunity to share in these blessings (Acts 24.15). The human society on earth then will be governed by Christ's heavenly kingdom.

(e) Politics: they acknowledge secular governments as 'superior authorities' permitted by God to exercise authority. Therefore, they seek to be honest and law-abiding citizens (Rom. 13.1–4). However, they view human authority as relative, or secondary to obedience to God. When a conflict of loyalties arises, Jehovah's Witnesses follow the Christian precept: 'We must obey God as ruler rather than men' (Acts 5.29). They follow a course of strict neutrality in political matters, and they do not participate in the wars of any nation (John 15.19; 17.16). As a consequence, they have suffered persecution at the hands of various governments, including Nazi rule in Germany. In more recent years, they have been the object of hostility in a number of other countries. Even in more liberal lands, Jehovah's Witnesses have had to fight in courts for their rights of conscience and for the right to preach the good news. However, their actions have often led to the safeguarding of freedom of speech and religion for everyone.

(f) Marriage and family life: they regard marriage as a divine institution, authorized and established by the Creator himself in the garden of Eden when he brought Adam and Eve together (Gen. 2.22–24). In line with Heb. 13.4, they insist on fidelity and moral cleanness in marriage. Divorce is disapproved of except on the grounds of adultery (Matt. 19.9). Parents are expected to instruct and correct their children in a loving way and are urged to spend time with them, caring for their spiritual and emotional needs. Children are to be obedient to their parents (Eph. 6.1–4).

(g) Baptism: among Jehovah's Witnesses, baptism is a symbol of an individual's personal dedication to God and constitutes the *ordination of that person as one of God's ministers (Matt. 28.19). To qualify for baptism, a person must take in accurate knowledge of God's word (Rom. 10.13–15); put faith in God and have profound love for him (Matt. 22.37–40; Heb. 11.6); repent of past sins (Matt. 4.17); turn around, or convert (Acts 3.19); and then dedicate his or her life to God (Luke 9.23). Since babies and young children are not mature enough to take such steps, they are not baptized by Jehovah's Witnesses.

(h) Ministry: each baptized Christian is a minister and is commissioned to preach the good news of God's kingdom (Matt. 24.14). That being the case, Jehovah's Witnesses take their ministry seriously. They endeavour to contact people with their message by going from house to house, by approaching them in marketplaces and on the streets. Return visits are made when interest is shown, and home Bible studies are conducted free of charge with interested individuals.

Jehovah's Witnesses believe that the true worship of the Creator embraces every aspect of an individual's life (1 Cor. 10.31). So they concentrate on building up men, women and children spiritually through instruction in the Bible. Jehovah's Witnesses view one another as spiritual brothers and sisters. This 'entire association of brothers in the world' constitutes the worldwide preaching organization of Jehovah's Witnesses today (1 Peter 5.9).

_____

2001 Yearbook of Jehovah's Witnesses; *Jehovah's Witnesses – Proclaimers of God's Kingdom* (1993); *Jehovah's Witnesses – Unitedly Doing God's Will Worldwide* (1986); *Reasoning From the Scriptures* (1989); all published by the Watch Tower Bible and Tract Society of Pennsylvania.

INFORMATION OFFICE OF JEHOVAH'S
WITNESSES, LONDON

Jewish Worship

1. *Institutional Origins*. Jewish worship is a post-biblical innovation conceptualized and created by the leadership class called rabbis, largely in the first two centuries CE, though how the rabbis did so, and exactly what they did, is still debated. Scholars of the nineteenth and early twentieth centuries assumed the existence of single authoritative 'original' prayer texts from which later variations grew. One contemporary school of thought concurs, identifying the canonical activity with the 'chief' rabbinate of Gamaliel II (end of first century CE). The predominant opinion, however, assumes that despite agreement on general principles, variation of interpretation was the rule; consequently, no such authoritative 'original' prayers exist. Instead, worship for several centuries displayed variable texts, organized, however, in specific thematic order.

Rabbinic worship is intertwined with the Temple cult, the *chavurah* (or tableship group) and the synagogue. Even after the Temple's demise (70 CE), the biblically rooted sacrificial system remained the theoretical ideal, and so worship of the word was modelled after real or imaginary cultic blueprints, and the primary rabbinic prayer, the *Tefillah*, was regarded as a replacement for the defunct daily sacrifice.

More important was the *chavurah,* which emphasized worship around meals and produced the Passover *seder*, blessings over food, and the *grace after meals (Birkat Hamazon)*. Statutory public prayer (similar to the Christian *daily prayer) emerged from rabbinic study circles, and somehow – probably in the second or third century – was transferred to the already existent synagogue, which had arisen for other purposes, including public gathering and study. The synagogue and the *chavurah* (one's home) thus became twin liturgical focuses following the Temple's fall. Fixed worship is normally enacted at set times in these two locales.

2. *The Liturgical Text*.

2.1. *The Primacy of the Blessing*. Rabbinic prayer transcends biblical prototype by adopting, above all, a standardized prose style known as a *berakah* (a blessing or benediction). Stylistic rules for benedictions evolved slowly, but were largely fixed by the third century CE. Short blessings – one-line formulas that begin, 'Blessed art thou, Lord our God, Ruler of the Universe, who . . .', characterize individual piety (see below), but public liturgy usually comprises blessings of one or more paragraphs, and these are best conceptualized as liturgical essays on theological themes. They conclude with a *chatimah* ('seal') that sums up the blessing's theme ('Blessed art thou who . . .'). Worship services contain many kinds of texts, but feature clusters of blessings strung together. Of these, two stand out: the blessings that surround the *Shema*, and the *Tefillah* (see below). These 'blessing-essays' are often composite works reflecting centuries of oral transmission and editorial redaction. One major strand is Jewish gnosticism which emphasized word strings with rhythmic regularity and little cognitive enrichment beyond lavish praise of God, possibly with the goal of inducing a trance in which worshippers would join the heavenly angels seen by Isaiah (6.1ff.), there to praise God. Other rabbinic strands, however, stressed cognition, according to an agreed-upon thematic progression where each theme received its own blessing. Though the order was invariable, creative expressions of the blessings that it constituted were deemed desirable. By the fifth century, as verbal fixity increasingly crept in, lengthy and complex poetry known as *piyyutim* were adopted to ensure worship novelty.

2.2. *Codified Prayer Books*. By the eighth century, the various strands of prayer coalesced into fixed liturgies. These amalgams clustered into either the Palestinian or the Babylonian rite. The former retained poetic enrichment and eschewed verbal fixity. The latter limited poetry to a bare minimum, and established a fixed set of texts at the expense of creativity. In the mid-ninth century, Amram Gaon, the titular religious leader of Babylonian Jewry, created our first known comprehensive prayer book, *Seder Rav Amram* ('The *seder* [order of prayers according to] Rav Amram'), which became the basis for all subsequent rites.

2.3. *Outline of Services*. Following rabbinic models, *Seder Rav Amram* does not feature the Bible, though biblical citations abound. Three of them (Deut. 6.4–9; 11.13–21; Num. 15.37–41) constitute the well-known *Shema*, for instance, and entire psalms (called *hallels*) are recited as collections of praise. But biblical snippets are generally embedded transcontextually in blessings which redefine their meaning according to rabbinic interpretations. Even the *Shema* is bracketed by blessings. Implicitly, then, rabbinic worship reflects rabbinic theology, wherein the written Bible requires interpretation from oral tradition.

The most important worship units are the *Shema* and its blessings, and the *Tefillah*, 'The Prayer [par excellence]', which singly or together have constituted the bulk of every synagogue service since the first century. The *Shema* asserts God's unity while its accompanying blessings acknowledge God as the One who created the cosmos, chose Israel in love, and redeemed Israel from Egypt. Eschatologically, Egyptian redemption prefigures final deliverance at the end of time. Eschatological hope figures even more prominently in the *Tefillah*, a series of nineteen (originally eighteen) blessings, largely petitionary, organized at the end of the first century. The blessings follow the paradigmatic rabbinic doctrine of salvation, culminating in the coming of the messiah.

Early worship featured also the reading of *Torah* (the first five books of the Bible), on Mondays, Thursdays and holy days (Sabbaths, fasts and festivals). Sabbath mornings added a prophetic reading (called *haftarah*). The *lec-tionary was followed by an interpretive sermon that ended with a *nechemta* (expression of hope), and the *Kaddish*, a prayer akin to the *Lord's Prayer calling for the coming of God's reign. By the eighth century, the *Kaddish* was viewed as a prayer that benefits the dead, but it began as a conclusion to the study of *Torah*. An optional *hallel* (nowadays Pss. 145–150) preceded the official morning service, as did a private home rubric composed of study texts and blessings pertinent to arising. Amram moved this home devotion to the synagogue where it remains today. A final daily staple in antiquity was a confession following the *Tefillah*, but by the Middle Ages it was expanded and then replaced by a larger penitential rubric (the *Tachanun*), a set of supplications that acknowledge the lowliness of the human condition.

The daily morning service was thus mostly set by Amram's day: (a) morning blessings and text study; (b) *Hallel* (psalms of praise); (c) *Shema* and its blessings; (d) *Tefillah*; (e) the supplicatory *Tachanun*; (f) scripture reading with a sermon and *Kaddish*, calling for God's ultimate reign. The *Alenu*, which also anticipates God's final rule, is used by Amram as a prayer for *Rosh Hashanah* (the new year), but by the fourteenth century, it had been added as another concluding prayer for all services.

With slight alteration, the above outline of daily morning prayer (*shacharit*) characterizes also mandated afternoon (*minchah*) and evening (*arvit* or *ma'ariv*) services (usually held back-to-back at sunset). These daily occasions are suitably altered for holy days when, in addition, home worship predominates also. Passover, for example, calls for additional synagogue poetry on the theme of the Exodus; but also the home *seder* ritual. Holy-day home worship generally includes (a) the kindling of lights; (b) an introductory prayer called *Kiddush* that announces the onset of sacred time; and (c) *Havdalah* ('separation'), a concluding ritual that distinguishes sacred from secular time.

2.4. *Medieval European Developments*. Rites are very broadly classified as 'Sefardi' (Spanish) or 'Ashkenazi' (Northern European). In both places, the texts expanded poetically, forcing fourteenth-century Ashkenazi Jewry to divide their bulky liturgical corpus into separate volumes: (a) a *Siddur* for daily and Sabbath use; (b) a *Haggadah* for the Passover *seder*; and (c) a *Machzor* for festival prayers.

The most striking medieval enrichment came

from European mystics. Influenced by mendicant monastic piety, twelfth-century German pietists adopted a penitential, even ascetic, spirituality buttressed by an esoteric theology regarding God's glory and hidden meanings in liturgical wording. By the thirteenth century, Provençal Kabbalah reached Spain, and its Neoplatonic doctrine was carried throughout the Mediterranean by Spanish Jews expelled in 1492. In sixteenth-century Palestine, mystics experimented with such ecstatic practices as rote recitation of divine names, and self-hypnosis through music. Lurianic Kabbalists (named after Isaac Luria, their founder) composed a new introduction to Sabbath worship according to a theology which equated God with the universe, so that the human existential condition is also God's. The fractured state of being that God and humans share is reflected in the sexual metaphor of an androgynous deity, whose divided male and female elements are in search of sexual reunification. Worship conjoins God's male and female sides. The manifest content of prayer becomes unimportant. What matters is its esoteric meaning on which worshippers concentrate using introductory meditations. Eighteenth-century Polish/Russian Chasidism popularized Lurianic Kabbalah while simultaneously developing its esoteric theology for scholarly consideration. Worshippers saw prayer as almost sacramental activity that mends the fractured cosmos.

3. *Implicit Theology.* Worship's very form has theological and ecclesiological presuppositions. Private prayer may be desirable, but communal worship is obligatory in Judaism. The congregation must therefore include a quorum (*minyan*) of at least ten worshippers, representing the corporate People Israel. An implicit social contract underlies the prayer leader's function as *sheliach tzibbur*, an 'agent of the congregation', entrusted by the people to represent them on high.

Jewish worship depends, then, on this prayer leader, usually a trained *cantor (the *chazzan*) who is held accountable for the highest musical, vocal, textual and moral competence. In traditional worship, *chazzan* and congregation sing the service *antiphonally: first, the congregation reads quickly through a prayer, each worshipper at a somewhat different speed, and often, out loud as well – a custom called *davvening*; the *chazzan* then repeats it, all or in part, with the correct musical idiom (called *nusach*), and, especially in Ashkenazi tradition,

in extended melismatic form something akin to jazz improvisation. This 'dialogic' model, however, goes back to rabbinic attempts to replicate the angelic 'dialogue' in Isaiah's vision. The Sefardi tradition, which moved mostly to Mediterranean countries, eschews elaborate cantorial solos.

Judaism acknowledges the *Torah* as God's supreme gift of grace: Jewish liturgy is therefore suffused with *Torah* – not just the lectionary, but many scriptural and talmudic passages read both as prayer and as study. Jewish prayer represents covenantal partnership where God is praised for the *Torah* and its commandments, the *mitzvot*.

Private prayer enhances this theology of covenant by providing one-line blessings (see above) for performing commandments. Other, similar, blessings express radical awe as we enjoy God's world. Seeing a rainbow or eating fresh fruit, for instance, become sacred acts of enjoyment, evoking prayer. Jewish liturgical theology insists that it is a sin to walk through God's world unmoved.

4. *Modern Developments.* Jews newly released from medieval ghettos in the nineteenth century sought to modernize worship by replacing noisy *davvening* with decorum, adding a sermon in the vernacular, shortening the service, replacing cantors with operatic singers, and arranging old liturgical melodies for choirs. The rabbi now led services in theatre-style sanctuaries from truncated prayer books, translated from the Hebrew and purged of ancient but difficult-to-hold doctrines like the belief in bodily resurrection. Newly composed prayers emphasized nineteenth-century optimism and universalism. Of the two loci for Jewish worship, the home shrank in importance, as Judaism shifted to the synagogue, which modern Jews saw as their 'church'. Modern Orthodoxy too sought to dignify worship and joined reformers in some revisions, like admitting a sermon, but retained the entire traditional liturgy and its *davvening* style. Supported by the increasingly reactionary nature of nineteenth-century Europe, it polemicized against the Reformers' 'excessive' change. By the late nineteenth century, the fight for liturgical change had mostly moved to North America.

4.1. *Continuation in North America.* North American Jewish liturgy has gone through three stages: Classical Reform; Conservative Judaism; and late-twentieth-century liturgical renewal in all camps. Classical Reform was a reaction to the great eastern European immigration (1881–1924). German reformers already in America zealously pursued the western European liturgical emphasis on high art and emotional austerity, while erasing longstanding traditions like head covering for men. Its liturgical zenith was the 1894/95 publication of a Union Prayer Book. Staid and passive worshippers surrounded by architectural and cultural magnificence were expected to recognize the reality of a transcendent God. Conservative Judaism expressed the sentiment of eastern Europeans who found German Reform cold and 'churchy', but who eschewed equally Orthodoxy's unwillingness to change. It therefore adopted worship styles akin to those of eastern Europe, but modernized aesthetically and codified liturgically in an official prayer book of 1946. By then, eastern Europeans had joined Reform Temples too, reinstating some tradition.

Shocked above all by the extent of the Holocaust, post-war Jewry concentrated on supporting the new State of Israel and saving Jews still persecuted in Arab lands and behind the iron curtain. Movement to the suburbs by baby-boom parents prompted child-centredness which occasioned new children's liturgies, but froze adult worship in atrophied forms that adults attended rarely, usually for their children, or for ethnic nostalgia – a North American version of western European aesthetic for Reform, an equivalent eastern European version for Conservatives. Orthodox Jews, relatively few in number, scattered among modernist and traditionalist camps. Reconstructionism, a fourth movement founded in 1922, developed a traditional worship style with a 1945 liturgy devoid of certain traditional Jewish beliefs, such as the chosenness of Israel.

By the 1970s, as women were admitted to the clergy (in all movements but Orthodoxy), gender consciousness made extant liberal prayer books virtually unusable. Further, Jews sought ritual expression of the loss of the six million, and the miracle of a modern Jewish state. Finally, Jews were caught up in the era of worship renewal worldwide following the RC Vatican II – a phenomenon akin to a Third Great Awakening in American history or even a Second Reformation in the West, generally. Abetted by enhanced liturgical scholarship and the technological capacity to mass-market inexpensively, a plethora of new liturgies followed. An example is the ultra-Orthodox Artscroll liturgy that has virtually replaced every other Orthodox prayer book worldwide, including the venerable Singer *Prayer Book* which had dominated British Orthodoxy since 1890. Artscroll combines theological ultraconservatism with comprehensive traditional commentary.

4.2. *The Current Situation*. Worldwide, new liturgies have multiplied. Artscroll dominates Orthodoxy. Most liberal prayer books feature: (a) modern vernacular translations and altogether new creations alongside Hebrew originals; (b) poetry from the gamut of Jewish tradition, especially by Hebrew poets who exemplify a new cultural consciousness occasioned by Israel's rebirth; (c) ritual for the new Jewish holy days of *Yom Hashoah* (Holocaust Day) and *Yom Ha'atsma'ut* (Israel Independence Day); (d) lengthy sets of meditations from ancient, medieval and modern Jewish literature; and (e) gender-inclusive language. In a post-ethnic era, worship re-emphasizes spirituality, tradition is being reclaimed, and the home is re-emerging as liturgically central.

Though too early to predict their long-term viability, the most current innovations include special services like New Moon (*Rosh Chodesh*) liturgies for women's spirituality groups, innovative life-cycle ritual (again, especially for women) and 'healing services', where small groups pray for healing of body and soul. Of long-term interest is the estimate that some 20% of all North American congregations use liturgies of their own creation, not those of their movements – a trend supported by computer technology and the weakening of centralized authority in general. We may be witnessing a temporary or long-term abandonment of official denominational liturgies, and, instead, an accent on religious diversity where liturgical identity is formed locally.

Selected texts: *Forms of Prayer*, London 1977 (current liturgy for Reform Movement of Great Britain); *Hasiddur Hashalem: Daily Prayer Book*, ed. Philip Birnbaum, New York 1949, reprinted 1995 (text and translation of the traditional Siddur); *Minhag Ami: My People's Prayer Book*, ed. Lawrence A. Hoffman, Woodstock, VT 1997– (multi-volume treatment of the liturgy combining traditional text with new translation and marginal commentaries by scholars across the ideological spectrum of Jewish life); *Siddur Lev Chadash*, London 1995 (current liturgy for Liberal Movement of Great Britain).

Studies: Two Liturgical Traditions, a six-volume series ed. Paul F. Bradshaw and Lawrence A. Hoffman, Notre Dame 1991–9; Jack J. Cohen, *Major Philosophers of Jewish Prayer in the Twentieth Century*, New York 2000; Ismar Elbogen, *Jewish Liturgy: A Comprehensive History*, Philadelphia 1993 (English translation of 1913 classic); Joseph Heinemann, *Prayer in the Talmud: Forms and Patterns*, Berlin 1977; Lawrence A. Hoffman, *The Canonization of the Synagogue Service*, Notre Dame 1979; *Way Into Jewish Prayer*, Woodstock, VT 2000; Louis Jacobs, *Hasidic Prayer*, New York 1973; Ruth Langer, *To Worship God Properly*, Cincinnati 1998; Jakob J. Petuchowski, *Prayerbook Reform in Europe*, New York 1968; Stefan C. Reif, *Judaism and Hebrew Prayer*, Cambridge 1993; Leon J. Weinberger, *Jewish Hymnography: A Literary History*, London 1998; Chava Weissler, *Voices of the Matriarchs*, Boston 1998.

LAWRENCE A. HOFFMAN

Kiss, Ritual

The kiss functions in many religions, ancient and modern, as a sign of reverence for the gods: ancient religious art depicts persons 'blowing kisses' to the gods, and *icons and statues show wear from centuries of receiving kisses from devotees. Beginning with the NT church, however, Christians gave a ritual kiss to their fellow-worshippers rather than to the gods. Paul mentions the 'holy kiss' in four of his letters (Rom. 16.16; 1 Cor. 16.20; 2 Cor. 13.12; 1 Thess. 5.26). Prior to Paul, the phrase *philema hagion* ('holy kiss') is otherwise unattested in ancient literature, but may suggest that Paul is alluding to the kiss as a sharing of holy Spirit, similar to the pneumatic kiss in the Jewish novel, *Joseph and Asenath* (19.11), which dates from roughly the same period. Since kissing was restricted to family members in most ancient Mediterranean cultures, the holy kiss in the Pauline churches also indicates the radically altered social boundaries of Christian *koinonia* whereby unrelated persons become brothers and sisters and are members of one body.

While the Pauline letters predate the writing of the Gospels, there are indications that the holy kiss originated within the circle of Jesus' disciples. Thus, Judas' use of a kiss as a sign of betrayal hints that a kiss was the expected greeting among Jesus' followers. Furthermore, the account of the giving of the Holy Spirit in John 20.21–22, in which Jesus greets his disciples with the words, 'Peace be with you,' and then breathes on them, may allude to a ritual kiss. Similarly, 1 Peter 5.14 connects the kiss with the greeting of peace.

In the second and third centuries, the kiss of peace finds a place in the liturgy as a conclusion to prayer, witnessed as early as 150 CE by Justin Martyr in his description of a post-baptismal *eucharist (*First Apology* 65). Tertullian describes the kiss of peace as a 'seal of prayer' (*On Prayer* 18), though it is not clear what he means by this designation, since he also notes the use of the kiss in the public greetings of Christians. In addition to the use of the kiss after prayer, the *Apostolic Tradition* (perhaps third century) records that the congregation kisses a newly ordained bishop, and that the bishop gives the first kiss to the newly baptized at the conclusion of post-baptismal *anointing, a practice which may have continued into the later Latin rites. Throughout the early period, the kiss is restricted within the Christian community, and *catechumens are not allowed to share the kiss even among themselves. Since the early witnesses indicate that the kiss was performed mouth to mouth, this segregation may indicate fear of spiritual contamination through contact with the unclean *pneuma* ('spirit') of non-Christians.

During the fourth and fifth centuries, in the Eastern liturgies the kiss gradually became separated from the prayer of the faithful, and was placed among other pre-eucharistic rites, such as the *Lavabo* or the transfer of gifts. In the liturgies of Rome and North Africa, however, the kiss shifted to a place after the *eucharistic prayer. This change occurred either when the *Lord's Prayer was placed after the eucharistic prayer, or when the intercessions were incorporated into the prayer.

By the end of the first millennium in both the East and the West, the kiss of peace had declined as a congregational act, and was restricted to the clergy, or was diffused into the kissing of various objects (*altars, statues, church doors, etc.). In some Eastern liturgies, a double handclasp, sometimes accompanied with the kissing of one's own hands, replaced the kiss of peace. In the thirteenth century, some dioceses of the church in Europe used an *oscularium* or *pax brede*, a small tablet with a picture of Christ, which was brought down from the chancel and passed among the congregation for the each worshipper to kiss. By the sixteenth century, however, the kiss of peace had virtually disappeared from Latin liturgies, and none of the Protestant Reformers continued the practice.

The twentieth century has witnessed a revival of the kiss of peace, beginning with the rite of the Church of South India in 1950, and subsequently by the RC *General Instruction* for the mass in 1970. Other Western churches have followed suit, though typically inserting a 'sign' of peace following intercessory prayer before the eucharist, in the pattern of the pre-Nicene church, rather than before *communion, as in the Roman rite. It should be noted, however, that this sign of peace is rarely an actual kiss as in the ancient practice.

Stephen Benko, 'The Kiss', *Pagan Rome and the Early Christians*, Bloomington, IN 1984, 79–102; Colin Buchanan, *The Kiss of Peace*, Nottingham 1982; William Klassen, 'The Sacred Kiss in the New Testament: An Example of Social Boundary Lines', *New Testament Studies* XXXIX, 1993, 122–35; Nicolas J. Perella, *The Kiss Sacred and Profane*, Berkeley, CA 1969; L. Edward Phillips, *The Ritual Kiss in Early Christian Worship*, Cambridge 1996; Robert F. Taft, *The Great Entrance*, Rome 1978, 35–52.

L. EDWARD PHILLIPS

Kneeling *see* Posture 2

Kyrie

The Greek invocation Kyrie eleison ('Lord, have mercy') is found in nearly all the historic liturgies, in many of them in the original Greek, whatever the language of the rest of the service, and appears to have been derived both from Jewish and from pagan liturgical formularies. The first definite evidence of its use as the response to the petitions of a *litany comes from fourth-century Jerusalem and Antioch, whence both the litany form itself and this response rapidly spread to all parts of the Christian world.

At Rome an intercessory litany of this type was inserted after the introit at the *eucharist in the fifth century, probably during the pontificate of Gelasius (492–6), who was responsible for considerable changes in the Roman liturgy. At the time of Gregory the Great (590–604), and possibly at his instigation, the petitions of this litany were omitted on ordinary days, the responses being sung alone, as precatory acclamations, the number of repetitions being at the discretion of the presiding minister. By the end of the eighth century the litany had disappeared altogether, and the pattern of the acclamation became fixed as 'Kyrie eleison' three times, the variant 'Christe eleison' three times, and finally 'Kyrie eleison' again three times. During the Middle Ages, many of the numerous local variants of the Roman rite took to 'farcing' the Kyries on feasts, phrases appropriate to the day being inserted between 'Kyrie' or 'Christe' and 'eleison'. In the revised RC *Ordo Missae* of 1969, the same order was retained, on those occasions when the Kyrie is directed to be used, but the threefold form has been replaced by a responsorial twofold one (although the threefold form may be used if the musical setting at a sung mass requires it). The Kyrie-Christe-Kyrie alternation has often been explained in a trinitarian way, the prayer being said to be addressed first to the Father, then to the Son, then to the Holy Spirit. This is historically incorrect: there is no question but that the whole prayer was originally addressed to the Son.

Kyrie eleison is still the most common response to litanies in the Eastern rites, although the acclamation alone, in variously numbered groups, is found in them also; the ninefold and sixfold Roman forms, with other variants, are found also in many reformed liturgies in the West.

J. A. Jungmann, *The Mass of the Roman Rite*, New York 1951, I, 333–46.

W. JARDINE GRISBROOKE

Laity and Worship

1. *New Testament Background.* In the world of the NT the *laos* (people of God) played an active part in worship. No divisions were anticipated between those who gathered together for worship although some inevitably did arise (1 Cor. 11.18) based on class differences rather than on the later division between clergy and laity. In the world of the house church it was easy to feel part of a community, worshipping and breaking bread together.

2. *The Division of Clergy and Laity after Constantine.* After the conversion of the emperor Constantine in the fourth century, Christianity became the official religion of the Roman Empire. Great *basilicas were quickly built as a symbol of Christianity's new power and influence and the clergy became a new class of professional elite. The size of the

basilicas coupled with the new status of *bishops and *presbyters meant that a divide was soon apparent between clergy and laity. Worship now became increasingly shrouded in mystery as something done by the priest on behalf of the people. This was made even more difficult by the language barrier in the West: the Latin of the *Western rite would have been inaccessible to many except for the educated few.

Lay attitudes soon began to confirm this shift concerning the ethos of worship. By the Middle Ages attendance at worship had become for the laity an occasion when they said their private prayers, aided in the East by *icons and in the West by images of the saints and by wall paintings of biblical and hagiographical scenes. While in the East such devotion became an integral part of the liturgy, in the West lay spirituality was in many ways exercised quite independently of the action of the priest. This remained true in much of RC spirituality until the 1960s. Whilst the priest celebrated the *eucharist in Latin with his back to the people, the congregation recited the *rosary or said their private prayers. The accent was on attendance at *mass, which the priest 'celebrated' on behalf of the people. This is quite different from the emphasis today. Now the congregation participate in and celebrate the eucharist. The priest meanwhile has become the 'president', facilitating the prayers and actions of the people rather than praying or acting on their behalf.

3. *The Reformation.* The intention of sixteenth-century Reformers such as Luther, Zwingli and Calvin was to make the worship of the church once more accessible to the laity. All over England and continental Europe where Protestantism triumphed, the liturgy and the Bible were translated into the vernacular. *Screens and other impediments were removed, and the *altar or table for the celebration of holy *communion was brought nearer the people. In the Church of England the Prayer Books of 1549 and 1552 were intended to provide a source of common prayer that could be used not only on Sunday but also *daily by the laity as well as by the clergy. This dream was never satisfactorily realized. Church of England worship remained in practice the preserve of the minister and *choir, with the congregation having little to say or do except perhaps sing a *metrical psalm, say the responses and listen attentively to the prayers.

This pattern of worship has in many respects been retained at morning and evening prayer as they are celebrated in the majority of English cathedrals today. The sermon, too, as it was preached in many Anglican churches from the seventeenth to the nineteenth century, was often both long and erudite and contained little to appeal to the labouring classes. It was such practices that led to a concern for religious freedom among the Puritans in the seventeenth century. It was also into this vacuum that the sermons of John Wesley, with their appeal to the heart rather than to the intellect, spoke in eighteenth-century England. So successful were these sermons that crowds of several hundred persons were not unusual. In America a similar success was enjoyed by the preaching of Jonathan Edwards.

4. *Hymnody and Nonconformist Worship.* Today one of the main ways in which the laity participate in worship is through the singing of hymns and worship songs. Yet until 1872 the rubrics of the *BCP* contained no provision for hymnody, although a hymn was often inserted between the sermon and the state prayers at the end of morning or evening prayer. Within *Methodism and Nonconformist worship, however, the singing of hymns was central to the act of worship and this added to the popularity of the chapel over the church in the eighteenth and nineteenth centuries.

5. *The Role of the Laity in Twentieth-Century Worship.* In the twentieth century, as part of the *Liturgical Movement there has been a real desire across the churches to involve the laity more fully in the worship of the church and also to make that worship more relevant to the concerns of daily life. Since the 1970s in some churches, including the RC and Anglican traditions, there have also developed new *lay ministries, such as *readers, musicians, intercessors and ministers of communion at the eucharist. In Protestant churches there has also been increasing lay participation in the organization and design of services of the *word through the appointment of worship committees.

See also **Charismatic Worship.**

C. N. L. and R. B. Brooke, *Popular Religion in the Middle Ages*, London 1984; Barrie W. Tabraham, *The Making of Methodism*, London 1995.

ANNE DAWTRY

Lammas *see* **Harvest Thanksgiving**

Lamps *see* **Candles, Lamps and Lights**

Language, Inclusive
see **Inclusive Language**

Language, Liturgical

Liturgical language is the category used to designate the vocabulary, imagery, syntax and tone of the speech of worshipping assemblies. Historically the Christian churches of the East and those of the West have had markedly different liturgical languages. The Eastern speech has been more metaphoric and incantatory, and the Western speech more objective and terse, having taken as its model the curt formal rhetoric of Roman court address. The Western churches that publish prescribed language of public worship are marked by more grammatically controlled and succinct speech, while those churches that maintain an oral tradition relish more florid and repetitive speech. An example of the options in vocabulary in the English-language worship of Christians is whether 'thee' and 'thou' are retained; in imagery, whether God is commonly called 'King'; in syntax, whether sentences are complex or simple; and in tone, whether the speech is heard as elevated or colloquial. Especially in the UK, inspired by the work of Ludwig Wittgenstein, liturgical scholars have analysed liturgical language with the help of the categories of linguistic philosophy. Especially in the USA, inspired by the work of Paul Ricoeur, liturgical scholars have discussed the metaphoric nature of liturgical language.

During the second half of the twentieth century, many Christian worshipping communities wholly revised their liturgical language. *RCs and some immigrant *Orthodox churches began to use the local vernacular, and many Protestant denominations replaced their sixteenth-century style with one of the twentieth century. Early revisions, usually edited by committee, tended toward minimalist speech with simple vocabulary and elementary sentence structure. The revision process has continued, with churches in each decade publishing liturgical rites that utilized a larger vocabulary, more metaphoric biblical imagery, more complex syntax, and more resonant tone. Christian communities do not agree whether, taking its cue from the incarnation, liturgical language should closely resemble everyday speech, or whether, hoping to transform the profane by the sacred, liturgical language should be extraordinary speech.

Several cultural phenomena continue to influence decisions concerning liturgical language. The apparent intimacy of television speech has brought classical rhetoric into decline. The move toward inclusive language has altered traditional vocabulary about the assembly and about God. Recent biblical and linguistic studies of metaphor have influenced those who draft liturgical language to include speech far more metaphoric than was the speech of mid-century. Currently two opposite tendencies can be noted: some churches that publish liturgical texts have been influenced by the elaborate style of the oral traditions, such as those in the historically *Black churches; while, on the other hand, other churches have moved toward even simpler liturgical language than characterized the speech of the mid-century, in an attempt to keep the speech of the assembly available to visitors and to the uncatechized.

Ian T. Ramsey, *Religious Language: An Empirical Placing of Theological Phrases*, London 1967; Gail Ramshaw, *Liturgical Language: Keeping It Metaphoric, Making It Inclusive*, Collegeville 1996; A. C. Thiselton, *Language, Liturgy and Meaning*, Nottingham 1975; John D. Witvliet, 'Metaphor in Liturgical Studies: Lessons from Philosophical and Theological Theories of Language', *Liturgy Digest* IV, 1997, 7–45.

GAIL RAMSHAW

Last Gospel

The reading of the Johannine prologue (John 1.1–14) at the end of the *eucharist in the RC Church was general from the *Missale Romanum* of 1570 up to the reform of the rite in 1964, when it was discontinued. From the eleventh century the text was popular as a form of *blessing. In this role it is found in the visitation of the *sick in the *Rituale Romanum*, and in the medieval Sarum Manual it concluded the *baptism service, along with the reading of the curing of the epileptic (Mark 9.17–29), which was considered efficacious against this disease. In this respect the text was treated much as a holy object. It was even to be found as a blessing for fine weather. As the last gospel at *mass it was first found in the *Ordinarium* of the Dominicans in 1256, recited while the priest removed his *vestments. It spread to the Armenian mission and thence to the *Armenian liturgy. But the custom was not general in the West even in the sixteenth century. As time went by the role of the text as a means of blessing receded, and there was a greater interest in the content of the reading. Other texts might also be used. In the later Middle Ages it might be the gospel of a later celebration in the day (based on the custom of the 'dry mass' [*missa sicca*] in which the celebrant read the formulae without the *eucharistic prayer, or just the readings, of a later mass as an appendix to the first mass). The Jesuit rite of 1558 prescribed a last gospel, but it was an optional choice of John 1 or Luke 11.27f. The use of John 1 in the Tridentine rite was justified by it being seen as a kind of summary of the faith. But it was not proclaimed in the manner of a reading of scripture, being read quietly by the priest or perhaps recited by all.

J. A. Jungmann, *The Mass of the Roman Rite*, New York 1951, II, 447–51.

GORDON JEANES

Last Rites

The term used to refer to liturgical acts that are celebrated for the dying. These include: the *confession of sins (where the person is still able to speak) and *absolution; *anointing; and the reception of *communion, often known as the *viaticum.

EDITOR

Lauds *see* Daily Prayer

Lavabo

The ceremonial washing of the hands by the *celebrant after the preparation of the gifts in the RC *eucharist, so named from the first word of the Latin psalm-verse traditionally said, quietly, during the action: 'I will wash my hands in innocency, O Lord: and so will I go to thine altar' (Ps. 26.6). In 1969 the traditional text was replaced by Ps. 51.4. Although the custom of Christians washing their hands before praying is attested by the end of the second century, and probably goes back to earlier Jewish practice, the first explicit witness to the *Lavabo* in the eucharist is Cyril of Jerusalem in the fourth century (*Mystagogical Catechesis* 5.2).

Anglican Prayer Books have never contained any instructions about the *Lavabo*, but since the nineteenth-century Oxford Movement the custom has been widely followed. The Royal Commission on Ecclesiastical Discipline (1906) recognized it as an irregularity having significance, but did not list it as an 'illegal practice of a graver kind'.

J. A. Jungmann, *The Mass of the Roman Rite*, New York 1951, II, 76–82.

DONALD GRAY

Law and Worship

1. *Roman Catholic*. The RC Church consists of the Latin church, with about 95% of the membership, and twenty-one Eastern Catholic churches, each of which has its own liturgical discipline. The sources of liturgical law (*ius*) in the Latin church are legislation (*lex*), custom and administrative norms.

1.1. *Legislation*. The legislator for the universal church is the pope or an ecumenical council. Universal liturgical law is found principally in the liturgical books in the form of introductions and *rubrics, and the 1983 *Code of Canon Law* in Book IV, entitled 'The Sanctifying Function of the Church'. Book IV is divided into three parts: the *sacraments; other acts of divine worship (*sacramentals, liturgy of the hours, *funerals, the veneration of *saints, sacred images and relics, vows and oaths); and sacred places and times.

The introductions to the liturgical books go by several names: general instruction (*institutio generalis*), introduction (*praenotanda*), and general introduction (*praenotanda generalia*). Each begins with several theological paragraphs that concisely establish the doctrinal foundations of the rite, and these are followed by juridical norms that are true ecclesiastical laws equivalent in weight to the canons of the Code. These laws treat various disciplinary matters governing the rite: the ministers, the role of the assembly, requirements of the recipient of a sacrament or sacramental, matters governing the preparation for and celebration of the rite, adaptations, etc. Following the introductions, the liturgical books give the text of the rite itself, throughout which are rubrics, printed in red, directing the ministers on how they are to perform the rite correctly.

At the level of each nation or group of nations, the conference of bishops may issue liturgical laws governing certain matters as determined by the liturgical books or the *Code*, especially vernacular translations and adaptations of the Latin text of a rite, called the *editio typica*. Laws of the conferences of bishops must be approved by two-thirds of the bishops and submitted for approval to the Holy See.

At the level of the diocese, the diocesan *bishop is sole legislator, and he may freely make liturgical laws, provided none is contrary to higher law. Plenary councils (for a nation) and provincial councils (for an ecclesiastical province) may also make liturgical laws, but such councils rarely meet any more.

1.2. *Customs*. These are norms introduced by the community itself. Liturgical customs may develop in areas not regulated by law (*praeter legem*) or may even be contrary to the law (*contra legem*) if they are reasonable. After thirty years of continuous and peaceful observance, the custom itself achieves the force of law and may be abrogated only by a contrary law or custom, but not by a pastor or other administrative authority. The rules for formation of a legal custom are in canons 23–8 of the *Code of Canon Law*.

1.3. *Administrative norms*. These may be issued by executive authorities. At the universal level, these norms are found chiefly in documents of the Vatican Congregation for the Divine Worship and the Discipline of the Sacraments. Administrative norms enforce and implement the law and may even establish new discipline, but lack force if contrary to legislation.

John P. Beal, James A. Coriden and Thomas J. Green (eds), *A New Commentary on the Code of Canon Law*, New York 2000; John M. Huels, *More Disputed Questions in the Liturgy*, Chicago 1996; *The Pastoral Companion: A Canon Law Handbook for Catholic Ministry*, Quincy, IL 1995.

JOHN M. HUELS

2. *Church of England*. It is an agreed principle in English law that although the Church of England's liturgy and ceremony take specified forms prescribed by law in accordance with its doctrines and teachings, despite its position as the Established Church it is not for the judiciary to formulate those doctrines. In a classic nineteenth-century case (Gorham v. Bishop of Exeter 1850) the Privy Council laid down that 'This court has no jurisdiction or authority to settle matters of faith or to determine what ought in any case to be the doctrine of the

Church of England. Its duty extends only to a consideration of the articles and formularies.' However, for much of its history 'the High Court of Parliament' has exercised great influence over public worship in England. Acts of Uniformity accompanied the 1549 and 1552 Prayer Books, imposing penalties on those failing to use them, and when Prayer Book worship was resumed in 1662, a further Act made clear that modifications would require parliamentary approval (e.g. the Act of Uniformity Amendment Act 1872, generally known as 'the Shortened Services Act'). By the end of the nineteenth century the inadequacy of the *BCP* to supply all worship needs became obvious. One impetus for change was the activities of the Ritualists. An earlier attempt to 'legislate for belief' (Public Worship Regulation Act 1874) failed through its heavy-handedness: some offending clergy were jailed.

The report of the Royal Commission on Ecclesiastical Discipline (1906) declared that the law of public worship was 'too narrow for the religious life of the present generation, it needlessly condemns much which a great section of Church people, including many of her most devoted members, value'. The Commission proposed a reformed law admitting of great elasticity. Letters of Business were issued to the Convocations to frame modifications containing greater recognition of Anglican comprehensiveness. A Convocation-approved revised Prayer Book failed to gain parliamentary approval, both in 1927 and 1928, and in response the bishops took the technically illegal step of authorizing the book's contents for those who wished to use them.

The 1947 proposal to revise the Canon Law of the Church of England included a Canon which defined the term 'lawful authority' (who may determine what services can lawfully be used). It allowed experimentation, regulated by Convocations and the House of Laity, as a means of assuring Parliament that liturgical changes had been 'road-tested' at parochial level. The Prayer Book (Alternative and Other Services) Measure 1964 allowed such services to be authorized for use. By 1970 the Chadwick Church and State Report believed that the time had arrived for the Church of England to be freer from parliamentary control. The Church of England (Worship and Doctrine) Measure 1974 passed with large majorities in Synod but had a stormy parliamentary passage. It 'enables provision to be made by Canon with respect to worship in the Church of England', but guarantees the continuing availability of *BCP*. Under its provisions, the *Alternative Service Book 1980* and in 2000 its successor *Common Worship* were authorized for use.

———

James Bentley, *Ritualism and Politics in Victorian Britain*, Oxford 1978; Donald Gray, 'The Revision of Canon Law and its Application to Liturgical Revision in the Recent History of the Church of England', *The Jurist* XLVIII, 1988, 638–52; Mark Hill, *Ecclesiastical Law*, 2nd edn, Oxford 2001 (bib.); Robert E. Rodes, Jr, *Law and Modernisation in the Church of England*, Notre Dame 1991.

DONALD GRAY

Lay Ministries

In the World Council of Churches' document, *Baptism, Eucharist and Ministry* (1982), each of the participating churches recognized that ministry is a calling shared by the whole church, required as part of the proclamation and prefigurement of the kingdom of God here on earth (Ministry 1.6). Yet within this general understanding of ministry each church has also publicly endorsed certain individuals not only through *ordination but also through licensing to exercise particular gifts and ministries on behalf of the church, some of which have a liturgical dimension.

The idea of authorized lay ministries was first developed in the Calvinist churches and was particularly focused on the ministry of the *elder. Today many elders in the Free Churches have pastoral responsibility for a part of the community and may also sit or stand around the minister when he or she performs his or her liturgical functions. *Lay preachers are also common. In the Anglican tradition authorized lay ministry only made an appearance in the nineteenth century with the licensing in the Church of England of men as lay *readers from 1866. More recently women have also been admitted to this office.

In the RC Church lay ministries began to develop as a result of the Constitution on the Sacred Liturgy of Vatican II. The first to be recognized here were those of *acolyte and *lector. To these has subsequently been added a category of ministers known variously as special ministers, auxiliary ministers or extraordinary ministers of the sacrament. These are trained and authorized to assist in the administration of *communion at a celebration of the *eucharist, and also to take the sacrament to the *sick, the housebound and the dying. In places where there is no ordained priest the auxiliary minister may also lead the worship of the people and administer communion to them from the *reserved sacrament. This ministry has been particularly valuable in those parts of the world where there is a shortage of RC clergy as it enables the faithful to receive the sacrament more frequently than would otherwise be possible. Some or all of these provisions have also been developed in many parts of the Anglican Communion.

ANNE DAWTRY

Lay Preacher

As a third-century layman Origen preached for the bishops of Jerusalem and Antioch. Leo the Great forbade lay preaching but it was revived by men and women religious in the twelfth century and despite prohibitions flourished intermittently. RC laity now co-operate in the ministry of the word. In Orthodoxy lay theologians preach with a bishop's licence. Ancient British universities still claim the pre-Reformation right of lay fellows to preach in divine service. From the beginning Baptist, Reformed and Methodist Churches have permitted laymen to preach and (like Anglican *readers) to lead worship. All eventually opened this office to women.

———

Yngve Brilioth, *A Brief History of Preaching*, Philadelphia 1965; Patricia A. Parachini, *Lay Preaching: State of the Question*, Collegeville 1999.

C. NORMAN R. WALLWORK

Lay Reader *see* Reader

Laying-on of Hands *see* Gestures 3

Lectern

The development and place of the lectern, a stand for holding the Bible and other books for reading in church, significantly echoes theological and practical changes in the history of the church. Originally portable, it became solidified in the boat-shaped stone structure of the *ambo, at one or both sides of the church. The weight and number of early medieval books used by *deacon, *subdeacon and *lector meant that a substantial structure was needed.

The later medieval lectern held the lives of

the saints as well as the biblical *lectionary. It might be made of bronze or wood, a desk on a column with feet at the base. Occasionally it takes the shape of an eagle or phoenix (symbolizing resurrection and the strength and energy that comes from rising up refreshed after waiting on God). Wooden lecterns, often ornately carved, sometimes take the shape of a revolving double desk which in post-Reformation times had the OT on one side and the NT on the other. At the Reformation some European Continental re-orderings turned the *orientation of the church through ninety degrees and put lectern, holy table and *font in a line facing the people. In England the lectern was sometimes in the centre of the *chancel, guarding the way to the reception of *communion. Its incorporation as one of the stages of the three-decker *pulpit symbolized the unity of worship and proclamation. The modern provisions for the reading of the word to be done dramatically and visually, and often from within the congregation, have lessened the need for a major permanent reminder of the place of the word in the church building.

TREVOR LLOYD

Lectionaries

From the Latin word *lectio*, 'reading', a lectionary is either a list of the biblical references to, or the full text of, the readings (from canonical literature) appointed by a given ecclesiastical authority for a cycle of liturgical occasions, be that the weekly Lord's Day service (*see* **Readings, Eucharistic**), a *daily prayer or office pattern, or for 'ritual' or pastoral occasions.

1. Principles; 2. Recent History: Daily Lectionaries; 3. Recent History: The Roman Catholic Sunday Lectionary; 4. North American Ecumenical Efforts; 5. British Ecumenical Efforts; 6. International Efforts; 7. Function and Future.

1. *Principles*. The earliest lectionaries were simply a list, called in the West a *comes* or *capitulare*, and began to appear from the fifth century onwards. There might be separate lists of the different readings for a service, such as the epistle and the gospel, or less commonly, there might be a combined list of all the necessary readings. Similarly, the complete texts, when they later began to appear, might be in separate books, the 'epistolary' or the 'evangeliary', or be a complete lectionary. Thus in such traditions the readings were not proclaimed from a full Bible or Testament. Behind this seemingly simple distinction for the liturgical proclamation of the word of God – from lectionary or from Bible – there lurk significantly different ways of thinking of scripture by various traditions. At the time of the sixteenth-century Reformation and its technological ally, movable type, it did become practical publically to use a whole Bible. This crystallized a theological divide which roughly came to characterize Protestant and Catholic scriptural use and theology, and which the contemporary commentator on lectionary matters, Fritz West, has described as 'scripture' (the Protestant use of the whole Bible) and 'memory' (the Catholic use of a lectionary book).

The appearance of these two possibilities also revived a critical issue regarding the principle(s) of selection of texts to be proclaimed. That is the distinction known as *lectio continua* (continuous reading) or *lectio selecta* (selected reading). Whereas the use of ecclesiastically approved lectionary tables and books had over many centuries gravitated to the latter principle, wherein certain texts came to be traditionally selected for certain days, festivals or occasions, the use of an entire Bible revived the older practice of reading 'in course', that is, chapter by chapter. This for instance was the counsel of the seventeenth-century *Westminster Directory for Worship*. One speaks of this practice as older in that in all likelihood this was the synagogal tradition at the time of Jesus and the early church for the Sabbath reading of the Law, whether on a one-year or (as some have supposed) a three-year pattern. Early Christian lectionaries seem also to have used this system certainly for the gospels and one would think that such was the only reasonable way to read the epistles (Col. 4.16; 1 Thess. 5.27).

One might go so far as to say that the whole history of the liturgical use of scripture is a process whereby this course reading of the various books of the canon of scripture which the church inherited from its parental Judaism and its own apostolic writings gradually became dominated by the other 'selected' pattern, this having to do with the development of annual, weekly or local festivals which came to displace the ordinary courses of reading, to say nothing of Marian, hagiographical and theological cycles. At the same time, in a development which was certainly never carefully thought out if only because of local diversity of practice, the use of the OT at the principal service of the Lord's Day, though referred to by ancient writers (and the pericopes mentioned were preponderantly prophetic rather than Torah), had disappeared altogether by the time of the Reformation, perhaps in the period between the sixth and ninth centuries, having been relegated to the daily office as observed by parish clergy or monastic communities. Thus the Reformation became a movement to reintroduce the Bible to liturgical worship, both as book and in its entirety. This of course necessitated the drawing up of entirely new tables of readings.

2. *Recent History: Daily Lectionaries.* Lectionary systems, East and West, are primarily devoted to two cycles. One is the cycle of *daily prayer, encompassing two to seven or eight brief services of praise and prayer each day, characterized mainly by the use of the Psalter, 'course' reading of scripture (OT and NT), hagiographical readings and prayers. Although the Anglican Thomas Cranmer in the sixteenth century sought to make of this pattern a parish-wide experience, as apparently had been in the case of the early church's 'cathedral office', and Calvin and other Reformed leaders sought to transfer the practice into a domestic setting, neither option has prevailed very widely. Thus the daily office is still a discipline largely of clergy and intentional Christian residential communities. The importance of this cycle is at least twofold: (a) it provides a daily/weekly calendar for Christian worship, and (b) it has always included a full 'course' reading of the OT and a repetitive use of the Psalter. In our own time, with the development of a richer (three-year) cycle for the Lord's Day service, the parity or interplay of these two systems has taken on new significance, and certain ecumenical bodies such as the (North American) Consultation on Common Texts are seeking ways to interrelate these two cycles. At the same time the RC Church in the English-speaking world is engaged in an extensive project to reform the liturgy of the hours. The principal issue here is, of course, the comprehensive and comprehensible use of the canon of scripture.

3. *Recent History: The Roman Catholic Sunday Lectionary.* The other lectionary system, which has received considerable attention in the post-Vatican II era by the initiative of the Holy See but also by the enthusiastic response of many non-RC ecclesial bodies in English-, French- and German-speaking communities, is the weekly Lord's Day word-sacrament rite. The Council's formative document, The Constitution on the Sacred Liturgy, carefully defines the twin parts of this rite as being 'so closely connected with each other that they form but one single act of worship' (para. 56). In an earlier paragraph (51) the Council ruled that: 'The treasures of the Bible are to be opened up more lavishly, so that the richer fare may be provided for the faithful at the table of God's word. In this way a more representative portion of the holy scriptures will be read to the people in the course of a prescribed number of years.'

This sets the lectionary in a far more intimate relationship to the eucharist than much of post-Tridentine tradition gave it, notwithstanding the fact that the Council of Trent itself called on the Curia to revise the lectionary. Conversely, this reminds non-eucharistically orientated Protestantism to search its own soul as to the relationship of the two tables. As a direct result of the documents that emerged from the Council, the Roman Curia formed a working group to undertake a serious revision of the Sunday lectionary. The result of its work was published in 1969 as *Ordo lectionum missae* (*OLM*). This was to have a profound effect on the worship of the entire Western church, far beyond any expectations of the Roman authorities.

This RC production comprised a three-year cycle in order to read the entirety of the synoptic Gospels one year at a time (Matthew in Year A, Mark in Year B and Luke in Year C), the Fourth Gospel being read in the festival seasons of *Advent/*Christmas and *Lent/*Easter, and John 6 in Mark's year to fill out that shorter Gospel's sequence. The sequence of gospel readings was continuous or semi-continuous, beginning at Christmas but being interrupted by Lent-Easter. The Johannine and Pauline epistles were read continuously or semi-continuously during the Sundays which comprise '*Ordinary Time', namely the thirty-three or thirty-four Sundays following *Epiphany and *Pentecost. Thus there was no intended correlation with the gospel readings through that time (though many preachers never seem to have noticed this!). The OT selections were more or less typologically tied to the gospel for the day throughout the entire calendar year and the psalm was also thematically related to the OT passage.

4. *North American Ecumenical Efforts.* With the appearance of the RC lectionary (which received some minor additions in a second edition in 1981) an extraordinary *ecumenical development opened up in North America. Immediately following Vatican II, conferences of RC bishops in the English-speaking world created a secretariat to co-ordinate the vast work of translation of the Roman liturgical books into a common English. This was known as the International Commission on English in the Liturgy (ICEL). Some far-sighted and even prophetic individuals in ICEL and certain Protestant bodies quickly moved (in 1965) to create a parallel ecumenical agency, the Consultation on Common Texts (CCT), representing churches in both the United States and Canada and including ICEL, which became CCT's own secretariat in a most generous fashion for almost thirty-five years. Although CCT worked principally with liturgical texts at the outset, it provided the venue for consideration of lectionary matters. This was done in parallel with another ecumenical liturgical body, the Worship Commission of the (United States) Consultation on Church Union (COCU) whose membership significantly overlapped CCT's. As early as 1970 the United Presbyterian Church in the USA and the Presbyterian Church, US (Southern), published a dramatically new service book and hymnal, *The Worshipbook* (1970 and 1972), which at the very last moment before printing decided to include an edition of the 1969 RC lectionary. In very short order other Protestant bodies undertook their own editions and revisions of the *OLM*, such that by 1974 the COCU Worship Commission had to publish a consensus version, which turned out to be a surprisingly popular pamphlet.

Thus in 1978 CCT assembled a consultation which set up a task force to produce an ecumenically acceptable version of the Roman table. This work was done and published in 1983 as the *Common Lectionary (CL)*. It was understood at the time that this was a 'proposal' to be used experimentally for a period of nine years (three cycles) and then revised. It adopted virtually unchanged the gospel and epistle choices of the RC model. Its major divergence was in the OT set of readings for Ordinary Time. Although the Episcopal and Lutheran constituencies were fairly content with the Roman choices, the more Calvinist groups were unhappy with the so-called 'typological' principle of selection, on a Sunday-by-Sunday

basis. Reaction had also been registered from Afro-American churches, which missed the lengthy Patriarchal and Mosaic narratives and much of the more pungent prophetic literature. CCT's solution was to abandon, in Ordinary Time after Pentecost, a close thematic connection between gospel and OT lections in favour of a more broadly conceived typology and semi-continuous readings from the Hebrew Bible. Thus during the post-Pentecost time in Year A the core of the Patriarchal and Mosaic narratives were inserted; for the same period in Year B the Davidic narrative was excerpted; and for Year C the Elijah-Elisha narrative was read together with one passage from each of the Twelve Prophets (with the exception of Obadiah). Toward Advent the OT pericopes were drawn largely from Wisdom literature, which the RC table had barely touched.

5. *British Ecumenical Efforts.* At about the same time as the RC lectionary was being created, however, an ecumenical liturgical body in Great Britain had embarked upon a revision of the various one- or two-year systems then in use there. Thus in 1968 the Joint Liturgical Group produced a two-year cycle, which rather radically re-cast the annual calendar along trinitarian lines, devoting a greatly lengthened Advent season to the Father, the season from Christmas to Pentecost to the Son and from Pentecost to Advent to the Holy Spirit. The pericopes were selected on the basis of theological themes throughout and included three readings and a Psalm for each Sunday. For the season of the Father the OT pericope was the controlling lesson; for the season of the Son the gospel was the controlling lesson; and for the season of the Holy Spirit the epistle was the controlling lesson. This lectionary became widely used even by Free Churches which had not heretofore employed any lectionary.

6. *International Efforts.* As the CCT contemplated its further work of revision at the end of the 1980s, it determined that the rapidly growing convergence in lectionary usage between *CL* and *OLM* in North America needed a more international basis, especially if Roman authorities would ever consider giving permission to use *CL* in RC circles and if other linguistic groups were to be drawn in, perhaps through the World Council of Churches. CCT therefore invited ecumenical bodies in Australia, New Zealand, South Africa and Great Britain to create an international body as a successor

to the former International Consultation on English Texts (ICET), which had met last in 1974. This group, the English Language Liturgical Consultation (ELLC), immediately took over the stewardship of lectionary reform and revision. This made possible successive if not very successful visits to the World Council in Geneva (1993) and the Holy See in Rome (1994). At the same time the British group, JLG, was encouraged to participate in the revision of *CL* in anticipation of a published and final version in 1992. This process resulted in a refined form now known as the *Revised Common Lectionary*. This is now in widespread use not only in North America but elsewhere in the English-speaking world, including Great Britain. A vast literature of homiletical, catechetical, hymnic and euchological resources has appeared, making possible an entirely unprecedented set of possibilities for ecumenical fare.

But this narrative encompasses only the English-speaking, Western churches. ELLC has entered into conversations with RC German and French liturgical groups and is seeking connections with Protestant bodies as well. The German Protestant situation is still dominated by the classic Lutheran one-year multi-lesson lectionary together with its associated 'preaching texts' for each Sunday in a six-year cycle. And Eastern Orthodoxy is only tentatively entering into dialogue with CCT and ELLC, although it is expected that just as these ancient churches in English-speaking countries begin the painful process of translation out of their traditional tongues this sort of conversation will begin.

7. *Function and Future*. In conclusion it might be noted that the process of lectionary formation and reform subtly rests on a number of functions which various churches and traditions regard as essential in however different configurations. It is probably essential that this set of priorities be identified and employed, in that no lectionary system can possibly be flawless or perfect. As other linguistic groups enter upon these questions, and particularly as Eastern Orthodoxy and the Oriental churches undertake the same process of reform, these functions will have to be debated and given relative weight. This writer has in another place (*Studia Liturgica* XXII) delineated six such functions, roughly in order of historical incidence and possibly importance, as follows: (a) full and catechetical; (b) homiletical;

(c) feasts, festivals and seasons; (d) cultural, climatic, seasonal and ethnic; (e) liturgical and doxological; (f) historical and ecumenical.

No doubt other functions could be discerned by careful analysis but these seem to account for most extant or historic systems. The relative weight given each by any church's lectionary is probably a fairly good indicator of that community's ecclesiology, implicit or explicit. And beneath all of these criteria there rests the bedrock issue, which the RC lectionary directly addressed, but which any of the Protestant versions could only indirectly approach, namely, the assumption that the principal service of worship for the Lord's Day at which the lectionary will be employed is a word-sacrament rite. For Protestants the issue remains as to what sort of homiletical hermeneutic can govern preaching in the context of a sacramental service. For Catholics the issue arises as to how other euchological texts such as the opening prayer at mass and the form of the prayers of the people can be governed by the scriptural pericopes, to say nothing of the corporate sung portions of the liturgy.

For historical lectionaries: Eric Palazzo, *A History of Liturgical Books*, Collegeville 1998, 83–105, 149–60. Selected modern lectionaries: *Ordo Lectionum Missae*, Vatican City 1969; English translation: *Lectionary for Mass*, Collegeville 1970; *Revised Common Lectionary*, (USA) Nashville 1992; (Canada) Winfield, BC 1992; (UK) Norwich 1992.

Studies: Horace T. Allen, Jr, 'Lectionaries – Principles and Problems: A Comparative Analysis', *Studia Liturgica* XXII, 1992, 68–83; Horace T. Allen, Jr and Joseph Russell, *On Common Ground: The Story of the Revised Common Lectionary*, Norwich 1998; Norman Bonneau, *The Sunday Lectionary: Ritual Word, Paschal Shape*, Collegeville 1998; Peter C. Bower (ed.), *Handbook for the Revised Common Lectionary*, Louisville 1996; Arland J. Hultgren, 'Hermeneutical Tendencies in the Three-Year Lectionary', *Studies in Lutheran Hermeneutics*, ed. John Reumann, Philadelphia 1979, 145–73; Gail Ramshaw, 'The First Testament in Christian Lectionaries', *Worship* LXIV, 1990, 484–510; Gerard Stephen Sloyan, 'Some Suggestions for a Biblical Three-Year Lectionary', *Worship* LXIII, 1989, 521–35; Fritz West, *Scripture and Memory – The Ecumenical Hermeneutic of the Three-Year Lectionaries*, Collegeville 1997.

HORACE T. ALLEN, JR

Lector

One of the *minor orders in the West, whose function was originally to read liturgical lections at the *eucharist and other rites. There is no clear evidence for the existence of the office before the third century. Justin Martyr speaks of 'the one who reads' (*First Apology* 67.4), as does the *Second Letter of Clement* (19.1), usually dated mid-second century; but neither may have had an appointed official in mind: the function could have been exercised by different members of the congregation in turn, as was the Jewish practice, where the individual was handed the scroll from which to read (see Luke 4.16, where Jesus reads in the synagogue). However, in the third century Tertullian implies that he did know a formal office of this kind, Cyprian makes frequent reference to lectors in his correspondence, and they are also mentioned at Rome.

In Eastern traditions, a lector was appointed by being handed the book from which he was to read, a custom also later copied in parts of the West. Later Eastern rites add to this an imposition of hands and prayer, in imitation of the *ordination of other clergy. At Rome, on the other hand, there is no trace of any ritual of appointment to the office in the early evidence, and later it was usually conferred on adolescents whose parents wished them to embark upon an ecclesiastical career rather than upon those intended primarily to exercise the liturgical function. The office continues to exist in Eastern traditions, and also as one of two 'ministries' in the RC Church (the *acolyte being the other) which have replaced the minor orders since 1972 and are conferred not by 'ordination' but by 'institution'. This institution takes place after the ministry of the word in the eucharist, or during a service of the word, and consists of a bidding, a prayer and the giving of the Bible.

See also **Reader**.

EDITOR

Lent

The origins of Lent, the forty-day period (Latin *Quadragesima*, Greek *Tessarakoste*) for the preparation of *catechumens for Easter *baptism, penitents for reconciliation, and the faithful for the annual celebration of *Easter, are complex. Although all liturgical traditions refer to this period as the 'forty days', its actual length has varied according to how the days were counted and whether Saturdays and/or Sundays were to be included, with the result that today it is a total of six weeks in the West and seven in the East.

Traditional scholarship held that the season developed as a gradual backwards extension of the short preparatory and purificatory fast held before Easter. That is, that a one- or two-day fast became extended to include, first the entire week (later known as *Holy Week in the West and 'Great Week' in the East), then a three-week period (at least in Rome) including this final week, and finally, a six- or seven-week, forty-day preparation period (sometimes including, sometimes excluding Holy Week) assimilating those preparing for Easter baptism to the forty-day temptation of Jesus in the desert, the gospel account of which is still read on the First Sunday in Lent in the Western tradition. As it was an ascetical period, the public *penance of those undergoing canonical penance was also attached, with their reconciliation on *Maundy Thursday (at least in the Roman tradition).

While not discounting the development of the pre-paschal fast, modern scholarship has argued that what became Lent had its origins in an ancient post-Epiphany pre-baptismal fast in the Alexandrian church, where a forty-day period of fasting and baptismal preparation, already associated with Jesus' temptation, appears to have begun with the celebration of *Epiphany (the Baptism of Jesus) on January 6, with baptism conferred at some point in mid-February at its conclusion. In some places, such as Rome and Jerusalem, three weeks of preparation for Easter, with a possible Jewish precedent in terms of Passover preparation, may have been the practice; and three weeks of preparation for baptism whenever it was to be conferred seems to have been a practice elsewhere. Since a forty-day pre-paschal Lent makes its sudden and almost universal appearance in the aftermath of the Council of Nicaea (325), it is becoming common to see the forty days themselves as the contribution of the post-Epiphany pre-baptismal practice of the Alexandrian church, but now shifted to *before* Pascha and in synthesis with other pre-paschal or pre-baptismal preparation practices. It is also possible that this happened in continuity with a similar shift towards accepting a universal ideal of Easter baptism, a practice not well documented before this. Still, however, the precise organization of these forty days varied considerably in terms of geography and church, and the Alexandrian church itself, as witnessed in the *Festal Letters* of Athanasius, seems never to have embraced Easter baptism and only reluctantly accepted Lent itself as a pre-paschal period.

By the time of Pope Leo I (d. 461), the synthesis was complete and Lent had emerged as the season that it still is theoretically. With the demise of both the adult catechumenate and the system of canonical penance, however, Lent was ultimately limited to general and ascetic pre-paschal preparation for the Christian community as a whole, and the content of Lent tended to focus on the passion of Christ, together with various devotions (e.g. the *Stations of the Cross or the Seven Last Words of Christ), to the exclusion of baptismal themes. The Western Middle Ages witnessed a further 'pre-Lent' development, in which the three Sundays before Lent constituted an anticipatory season, with *Ash Wednesday itself developing to ensure that a literal forty days of possible fasting, excluding Sundays, might be counted. A parallel extension took place in the Byzantine tradition (*see* **Quinquagesima**).

Today, in light of modern liturgical reform, the season of Lent in the RC Church officially begins on the First Sunday of Lent (*Quadragesima*) and concludes on the evening of Maundy Thursday at the beginning of the Triduum of Easter. The period from Ash Wednesday through to the Saturday before *Quadragesima*, although still the popular beginning of Lent, is probably best seen as reflecting the remains of 'pre-Lent'. The restoration of the adult catechumenate and Easter baptism in the RC *Rites of Christian Initiation of Adults* and in other traditions, together with *scrutiny rites on the Third, Fourth and Fifth Sundays, closely reflects early Roman liturgical practice.

See also **Passiontide.**

Maxwell E. Johnson, 'From Three Weeks to Forty Days: Baptismal Preparation and the Origins of Lent', *Living Water, Sealing Spirit: Readings on Christian Initiation*, ed. Maxwell E. Johnson, Collegeville 1995, 118–36; Thomas J. Talley, *The Origins of the Liturgical Year*, 2nd edn, Collegeville 1991, 1–77, 163–225.

MAXWELL E. JOHNSON

Lesson *see* **Lectionaries**

Liberation and Worship

It is to be hoped that the expression 'worship which liberates' is redundant: all authentic Christian worship remembers our liberation to God, through Christ, in the Holy Spirit, and all authentic worship calls us and transforms us to continue that liberation in the world. Beyond that fundamental connection, the issues and concerns of theological approaches known as liberation theology, feminist theology, eco-theology and inculturation all should and do have an impact on the shaping and meaning of liturgical ritual. These varied approaches are all ways of articulating contextual and relational practices, and are also part of liturgical *theology, which increasingly finds itself concerned with issues of inculturation, justice and liberation.

1. *Theology and Liberation.* Liberation theology in the twentieth century can be characterized as the process and product of voices from the margins, rather than the centre. It is not a new way of doing theology, in spite of descriptions in some textbooks, because it is in continuity with the gospel and Christian history, throughout which the border regions of the church or the voices of liminal individuals have proved to be the inspired ground of renewal and insight. At times the breadth of liberation theology is obscured by too sharp a focus on political controversies, but the voices of liberation theologians as well as others speak across a wide range of insights and experiences. Their reminder of the present reign of God already and not yet, their application of the cost of discipleship to individual and corporate actions in everyday life, their faithfulness to gospel values, and their advocacy for the universality of God's presence in all people have challenged and changed the doing of theology for good. The liberation of theology itself, enabling greater dialogue with other religious systems, has been essential to the development of the field of comparative theology. The influence on worship is also profound. The balance of the implications of incarnational theology with the paschal mystery has contributed to the articulation of embodied worship as authentic worship in liturgical theology. The integral relationship of social justice and liturgy, especially in the *eucharist, has benefited from the insights of liberation theology by reminding us of the dynamic movement of the eucharist as the means to the end through multiple transforma-

tions. *Sacramental theology has assisted and been assisted in re-articulating a sacramental world view in which creation and this world are not stumbling blocks to salvation but the very vehicles of sacramental encounter because of insights from liberation theology. Overall, liturgical theology has been called to give meaning and expression to the radical inclusivity of the Christian message that liberating theology voices, to ask: 'How is this worship for *all* people, regardless of gender, race, culture or other differences, and how does authentic worship call us into a more profound relationship with God and all of creation?' If worship, because it is of God, both expresses what we believe and creates or forms us anew, it is always reflecting the insights of liberating theology and through expression of those insights leading people to live in the ways of justice and peace.

2. *Culture and Liberation.* One of the primary intersecting points between liberating theology and worship has been the creative tension between culture and liturgy. *Inculturation of the liturgy has become the preferred term in the decades-long development from liturgical indigenization, to incarnational liturgy, to acculturated liturgy to adaptation of the liturgy and now inculturation. The key difference with the latter is that inculturation presumes that both the liturgical text, the official worship of a church, and culture, defined as not only the customs and mores of a people but the social construction of reality as understood from a particular perspective, will change. True inculturation, then, calls both the liturgical text and practice and the culture to see with new eyes, to be engaged in liberation.

One of the most difficult modern challenges to inculturation, both theologically and ritually, is multicultural reality. It is patent to see how worship in one's own language, with one's own music, with leaders who are called out of one's own culture, and with corporate actions and relationships expressed in familiar cultural terms can be liberating. The de-colonization of theology and liturgy for many people in the world has been the beginning of real identification with the gospel of Christ and the subsequent living into that relationship, but multiculturalism, in worship particularly, has become a practical challenge to liberation and inclusivity. Inculturated liturgy is liberating for those whose culture it is, but in modern urban life particularly, this inculturation can be exclusive

and particular, rather than inclusive and universal, and therefore un-liberating. Theologically it raises serious questions regarding our ecclesiology: how is the whole body of Christ, in all of its necessary diversity of charism and rank, expressed in homogeneous worship gatherings of any type? Multicultural liturgy is a practical and theological necessity, therefore, and can be liberating worship based on liberating theology, but requires much catechesis and practice in the context of local Christian communities.

3. *Ritual and Liberation.* How do our rituals liberate, these actions which both outwardly express what we believe and lead us to new ways of understanding how God works in us and in the world? In light of the tenets of liberation theology, which call for radical inclusivity and hospitality, a preferential option for the poor, particular attention to the marginalized of society, a care for the earth and all of creation, and above all, a challenge to live the reign of God into fulfilment now by advocating for social and political systems to change, the role of ritual and worship can either seem inconsequential or unrelated. The reality is that worship is central to the entire project of liberating theology because it is both expression and creation, both 'source and summit' of what we believe and what we are called to believe in action. Three examples of the areas in which ritual and worship can function may be helpful.

(a) Liberating rituals and the Christian community. At the heart of the worship of the church stands the eucharist, and it is in that corporate action of God and the assembled body of Christ that liberation is most grounded. The central dynamic of the eucharist is the duality of remembering and invocation, and both act as liberating forces within the community and in the fruits of the eucharist in the world. To remember the saving death and resurrection of Christ, to remember the stories, especially those whose stories are in danger of being obscured, to remember what will be, is to be always reminded of the suffering of the world, the forgotten of the world and the hopefulness of God's faithfulness to draw all things to Godself. To invoke the presence of the Spirit on our community is to remember the importance of interceding for others, liberating in its ability to move our concerns outward. Throughout the eucharistic liturgy the church reminds itself, in the preaching of the just word and in the drinking of the cup poured out for us, of who the church is and where it is going –

strength for the journey of bringing about the reign of God. In addition, the eucharist, when celebrated as the ritual of the priesthood of all believers, each of whom is equally made in the image of God, is itself a liberating paradigm for how we are to live in the world.

(b) Liberating rituals and individuals. For individuals, rituals can also be occasions and expressions of liberation. Experience has shown that one of the most powerful ways to connect the liturgy of the church to the real lives of individuals is to use familiar rituals to mark important turning points in the lives of individuals. Life-cycle rituals which outwardly mark moments in individual lives can help people join in times which may have formally been occasions of shame, as well as confirm the necessary beginnings and endings of parts of each human life. When these ritual affirmations in the lives of individuals are rooted in cultural contexts, the result can often be a healing – literally a making whole – of the individual and the familial context, certainly a necessary prerequisite to creating healthy and whole communities.

(c) Liberating rituals and the world. Within the context of the wider world, recent developments in worship and liberation have pointed in two different directions. First is the growing consciousness of eco-theology, eco-feminist theology and creation spirituality. The focus of these developments in theology and their concretizing in worship is to look for more extensive relationships between humans, biblically confirmed as made in the image of God, and all of creation. This has required a shift in the concept of stewardship for the environment, and a recognition of the links between poverty and environmental abuse, and of creation as the means of encountering the sacred. The liberation of theology from the narrower concept of human domination of all other forms of life to the possibilities of partnership and conservation has impacted worship in a number of ways. Among these are the return to evening and morning prayer as authentic hours related to the temporal cycle, the more conscious alignment of the liturgical *year to the natural cycles, the composition and celebration of eucharistic liturgies in praise of the earth, the involvement of churches in 'earth day' celebrations, and the placing of environmental issues at the forefront of denominational concerns. The second area is in the modern reality of religious pluriformity. Ritual has played an important part in the growing area of comparative theology, as many

involved in *inter-faith dialogue have realized that often the only way to express the reality of the pluriformity of the world's people and their faith is to do ritual together, particularly in conjunction with making common cause in social action. This consciously moves the interaction from the realm of pure theory to the contextualized reality of local dialogue, and has been a place of restoring the relationship between liturgy and social justice in new ways.

Robert V. Andelson, *From Wasteland to Promised Land: Liberation Theology for a Post-Marxist World*, Maryknoll, NY 1990; Tissa Balasuriya, *The Eucharist and Human Liberation*, Maryknoll, NY 1979; James H. Cone, *A Black Theology of Liberation*, Maryknoll, NY 1990; Marc H. Ellis and Otto Maduro (eds), *The Future of Liberation Theology: Essays in Honor of Gustavo Gutiérrez*, Maryknoll, NY 1989; James L. Empereur and Christopher G. Kiesling, *The Liturgy That Does Justice*, Collegeville 1990; Monika K. Hellwig, *The Eucharist and the Hunger of the World*, Kansas City 1992; Lisa Isherwood, *Liberating Christ: Exploring the Christologies of Contemporary Liberation Movements*, Cleveland, OH 1999; Catherine Mowry LaCugna (ed.), *Freeing Theology: The Essentials of Theology in Feminist Perspective*, New York 1993; Sallie McFague, *The Body of God: An Ecological Theology*, Minneapolis 1993 (bib.); Mark Searle (ed.), *Liturgy and Social Justice*, Collegeville 1980.

LIZETTE LARSON-MILLER

Lights *see* Candles, Lamps and Lights

Litany

From the Greek *litaneuein*, and its noun, *litaneia*; a term found in the Septuagint, meaning entreaty (e.g. 2 Macc. 3.20; 10.16). The original classical Greek meaning of the term is to pray, entreat or supplicate. In Christianity a litany is a series of petitions, traditionally said by the *deacon, that precede a prayer. The response is fixed and is often *Kyrie eleison ('Lord have mercy'). In the early church the verb *litaneuein* was not used in connection with a specific form of supplication; rather, it referred to supplications made during a *procession, and the noun *litaneia* was Latinized to refer to processions in the Roman stational liturgy. In the Roman usage, the term can also refer to supplications performed inside the church, a usage attested in the Byzantine tradition only after the tenth century. In the Byzantine tradition the supplications are referred to as either *synapte* or *ektene*.

1. *Early Liturgy*. The roots of the litany lie in an ancient pattern of prayer in which the deacon said 'Let us pray', the people prayed in silence, and the *presbyter or *bishop then said a *collect. In at least some places, it was customary for the people to kneel during the silent prayer, and rise at the collect. In the Roman usage (and in the Byzantine, such as at vespers of the Holy Spirit) this was sometimes made explicit through diaconal commands. The litany is an expansion of this primitive unit of call to prayer and collect. In other words, the diaconal petitions of the litany replace and fill in what in the original core was a period of silent prayer. There is evidence that people knelt during the petitions of the litany. In a litany the deacon addresses the people (in first person plural), but the people in their response address God, as does the presbyter or bishop in the concluding prayer. Our first textual evidence of a litany comes from the fourth century (*Apostolic Constitutions* VIII.6; Egeria, *Itinerarium* 24.5).

2. *Byzantine Liturgy*. Because of the stational character of the liturgy in Constantinople, the Byzantine rite makes abundant use of litanies. There are three basic forms of the litany: the *synapte*, the *ektene*, and the *synapte meta ton aiteseon*. The *synapte*, or greater litany, consists of a series of invitations to pray for specific intentions coupled with response by the people (Kyrie eleison) and concluding prayer by the priest. In present usage the *synapte* is found at the beginning of services, a position acquired rather late in the Byzantine rite. The *mikra synapte*, or lesser litany, consisting of the first and the two last petitions of the *synapte*, is the normal introduction to any formal prayer by the celebrant and is used both in the *synaxis (preceding the prayers of the second and third antiphon respectively) and the hours of *daily prayer. The *ektene*, or fervent litany, consists not only of diaconal invitations but also of direct addresses to God, which are completed by the people's response. It is also characterized by the accumulation of intercessory verbs at the end of each prayer, and a triple repetition of the Kyrie eleison as the response of the people. The *ektene* is the main intercessory litany after the readings in the *eucharist

and at morning and evening prayer. It was originally used in stational processions, called *lite* at Constantinople. The *synapte meta ton aiteseon*, called in English the 'Angel of Peace litany', is a litany that traditionally precedes the final *blessing or inclination prayer in the Byzantine and other Eastern daily offices. Within the eucharist in present usage this litany appears in two places. The first instance is after the completion of the transfer of the bread and wine. It starts with the phrase *Plerosomen* ('let us complete'), betraying its *dismissal character, and is composed of the 'angel of peace' petitions with the reference to morning or evening omitted and a petition relevant to the gifts added, together with two additional petitions of the *synapte*. The second instance is before the recitation of the *Lord's Prayer, where the Angel of Peace litany has been appended to the primitive nucleus of the precommunion litany. Other litanies include those for *catechumens after the readings and those for candidates for *baptism at the *Presanctified Liturgy. Generally speaking, litanies in all services build upon the aforementioned types, adding petitions adapted to each liturgical context.

3. *Roman Liturgy*. Borrowed from Eastern liturgical use, the litany was probably introduced in the Roman rite by Pope Gelasius (492–6), and is known as the *Deprecatio Gelasii*, or the prayer/*intercession of Gelasius. This imported litany replaced the Roman *orationes solemnes* or solemn prayers, an ancient form of intercession used until the fifth century in the eucharist following the readings; after the fifth century their use was restricted to *Holy Week. Although the two forms are different in structure, subjects of intercession and language, a comparison between them reveals that they cover the same ground. By the eighth century the petitions of the litany were suppressed, and only the responses were used, hence the chanting of Kyrie eleison and Christe eleison without their petitions. The successor of the *Deprecatio Gelasii* in the Roman rite was the *litania*, a term which signifies either a penitential observance, or a procession, or, ultimately, a penitential procession. This type of litany was used on the three days preceding the feast of *Ascension, known as *Rogation Days. The rogation litany, also called the litany of the saints, is made up of the following parts: (a) the introductory Kyrie and the invocations of the persons of the Trinity; (b) the invocation of the saints; (c) the

supplications for deliverance; (d) the appeals for deliverance by virtue of events in Christ's redemptive life; (e) the intercessions; (f) a concluding invocation of Christ as the Lamb of God. To the last element various prayers of different origin, the Lord's Prayer, and a concluding collect were appended when the litany was used on other occasions.

4. *Other Litanies.* Several litanies in the vernacular were produced at the time of the Reformation, including those by Martin Luther in 1529 and by Thomas Cranmer in England in 1544, the latter being later included (with the omission of the invocation of the saints) in the *BCP*. Litanies have continued to be a widely used form of intercession in subsequent centuries, and a variety of forms can be found in the modern service books of many churches.

John Baldovin, *The Urban Character of Christian Worship*, Rome 1987, 169–226; Anton Baumstark, *Comparative Liturgy*, London 1958, 74–80; Edmund Bishop, *Liturgica Historica*, Oxford 1918, 116–64; Peter Jeffery, 'Litany', *Dictionary of the Middle Ages*, ed. Joseph R. Strayer, New York 1982–89, VII, 588–93; Juan Mateos, *La célébration de la parole dans la liturgie byzantine*, Rome 1971, 29–33, 148–73; Robert F. Taft, *The Great Entrance*, Rome 1978, 311–49; 'The Structural Analysis of Liturgical Units: An Essay in Methodology' in *Beyond East and West: Problems in Liturgical Understanding*, 2nd edn, Rome 1997, 187–202; *A History of the Liturgy of St John Chrysostom, Volume V: The Precommunion Rites*, Rome 2000, 74–103; G. G. Willis, *Essays in Early Roman Liturgy*, London 1964, 19–28.

STEFANOS ALEXOPOULOS

Little Entrance

Part of the *enarxis in the Byzantine eucharistic liturgy, a solemn procession focused on the formal entrance of the gospel book into the bema (altar area). Once an actual entrance into the church building by clergy and laity, it has evolved into a short procession in which the *deacon (or priest) takes the gospel off the *altar table, exits by the north door of the icon screen, pauses before the Beautiful Gates (central opening in the *iconostasis) to chant a brief hymn, and enters the bema to replace the gospel on the altar. The title 'Little Entrance' is a relatively late development (most likely the twelfth

century), meant to distinguish it from the '*Great Entrance' with the bread and wine to be consecrated. Prior to this, it was called simply 'the Entrance', 'first entrance' or 'Entrance with the Gospel'.

In Constantinople the laity gathered outside in the *atrium. The clergy said the entrance prayer before the doors into the *nave, after which all actually entered the building. Palladius testifies to an organized entrance of clergy during the time of John Chrysostom (*Dialogus* 14). Maximos the Confessor clarifies the picture by writing around 630 that the laity enter with the clergy (*Mystagogy* 8–9). A century later Germanos provides evidence for chant covering the entrance activity (*Historia Ecclesiastica* 24). By the tenth century, for reasons still unknown, church architecture and ritual shifted dramatically; buildings became small, while the entrance became an abbreviated procession of clergy. In the fourteenth century Nicholas Cabasilas declined to call it an entrance, favouring 'Showing of the Gospel' (*Commentary on the Divine Liturgy* 20).

The Little Entrance was originally explained in cosmic terms, angels and humans entering together to glorify God. Beginning in the eighth century, probably because of 'ritual downsizing', it was presented allegorically as the entrance of the Son of God into the world.

Juan Mateos, *La célébration de la parole dans la liturgie byzantine*, Rome 1971, 62–90; Thomas F. Mathews, '"Private" Liturgy in Byzantine Architecture: Toward a Re-appraisal', *Cahiers archeologiques* XXX, 1982, 125–38; Robert F. Taft, 'The Liturgy of the Great Church: An Initial Synthesis of Structure and Interpretation on the Eve of Iconoclasm', *Dumbarton Oaks Papers* XXXIV–XXXV, 1980–81, 45–75.

JOHN KLENTOS

Liturgical Theology

see **Theology of Worship**

Liturgical Movement, The

A twentieth-century movement for the revitalization of the church through the renewal of its worship, which began in the RC Church and has affected to a greater or lesser extent nearly all Western mainstream Christian traditions.

General bibliography: John Fenwick and Bryan Spinks, *Worship in Transition: The Liturgi-

cal Movement in the Twentieth Century, Edinburgh/New York 1995; Keith F. Pecklers, *The Unread Vision: The Liturgical Movement in the United States of America 1926–1955*, Collegeville 1998.

1. Europe; 2. United Kingdom; 3. USA.

1. *Europe*. The founding of the Liturgical Movement in Europe is sometimes attributed to Prosper Guéranger (d. 1875), who refounded the French Benedictine monastery of Solesmes in 1833. More recent scholarship tends to name the Belgian Benedictine Lambert Beauduin as founder in 1909.

1.1. *The French Liturgical Movement*. It is curious that Guéranger should be called 'founder' of the Liturgical Movement in Europe. He was opposed to liturgical creativity and diversity and initiated his campaign of liturgical reform precisely as a way of 'romanizing' the French liturgy through a rigid uniformity, proposing the Middle Ages as the period of greatest liturgical development. Guéranger criticized French liturgical innovations as lacking in fidelity to tradition; ironically, some of those same innovations were later incorporated into the universal liturgical reforms of Pope Pius X at the beginning of the twentieth century. Guéranger developed his classic work *L'Année liturgique* (begun in Advent, 1841) as a pastoral commentary, finishing only nine of the twelve proposed volumes prior to his death. That same year, he founded a more scholarly journal, *Institutions liturgiques*. Gregorian chant was promoted; today, Solesmes remains the leading centre for chant research in the world.

Years after Guéranger's efforts, the French Liturgical Movement expanded with the founding of the Centre de Pastorale liturgique in Paris (1943) and the launching of the important periodical *La Maison-Dieu* (1945). French pioneers, e.g. A.-G. Martimort, Pierre-Marie Gy, Louis Bouyer and Joseph Gelineau, would each make significant contributions to liturgical renewal far beyond the borders of France.

1.2. *The German Liturgical Movement*. The movement in Germany first took hold at the Benedictine monastery of Beuron, refounded in 1863 under the influence of Solesmes. In 1884, Dom Anselm Schott published the first German-Latin missal, *Das Messbuch der Hl. Kirche*; the *Vesperbuch* followed in 1893. Excerpts from Guéranger's *L'Année liturgique* were included in each volume. Another

Beuronese monk, Desiderius Lenz, founded a famous art school at the monastery which would have significant influence on liturgical art both in Europe and the Americas.

Beuronese monks refounded the Benedictine abbey of Maria Laach in 1893. There, the efforts of Abbot Ildefons Herwegen assisted by two of his monks, Kunibert Mohlberg and Odo Casel, and by the young diocesan priest Romano Guardini, shifted the centre of the German movement from Beuron to Maria Laach. With the collaboration of two German professors, Fr J. Dölger and Anton Baumstark, they initiated a threefold series of publications in 1918: *Ecclesia Orans, Liturgiegeschichtliche Quellen* and *Liturgiegeschichtliche Forschungen*. Moreover, they started the well-known journal *Jarbuch für Liturgiewissenschaft* in 1921. Undoubtedly, Odo Casel (d. 1948) was the theologian of the German movement, writing hundreds of articles and books. In his classic work, *Das christliche Kultmysterium,* Casel argued that the pagan mystery cults were a preparation for the mysteries of the Christian sacraments. Despite the fact that Casel's theory is no longer held by sacramental theologians, his work promoted a rich understanding of the church as the mystical body of Christ expressed symbolically through sacramental participation.

The German movement also had a more obscure pastoral dimension. The first *Missa recitata* was celebrated in the crypt chapel of Maria Laach on 6 August 1921. The mass took place in Latin, but included the praying of the Gloria, Credo, *Sanctus and *Agnus Dei in common, along with other responses involving the whole assembly. University chaplaincies in Berlin, under the direction of Johannes Pinsk (d. 1957) and at Burg Rothenfels under the direction of Romano Guardini (d. 1968), promoted liturgical renewal among German students. Guardini and other pioneers were also involved in collaborating with leading secular architects to create a new liturgical architecture which would facilitate participative worship.

The founding of the Liturgical Institute at Trier after World War II saw other names emerging, like Balthasar Fischer and Johannes Wagner, who made significant contributions. The Austrian Jesuit liturgist Josef A. Jungmann (d. 1975) was a significant force in both Germany and Austria through his teaching and writing. Liturgical pioneering in Germany was not limited to men. Aemiliana Löhr (d. 1972), a Benedictine nun of the Abbey of Holy Cross at

Herstelle, inspired other women towards greater involvement in the German movement, with her more than three hundred articles and books.

1.3. *The Belgian Liturgical Movement.* The beginnings of the Belgian Liturgical Movement are traced to the Benedictine monastery of Maredsous, founded in 1872. In 1882, the first French-Latin missal, *Missel des fidéles,* was edited by Dom Gérard van Caloen. In 1884, he founded the review *Messager des fidéles* (later *Revue bénédictine*), the first Belgian publication intended to promote the Liturgical Movement. In 1899, the monks of Maredsous founded the monastery of Mont César, providing another centre of liturgical renewal. Benedictines of Mont César inaugurated the periodical *Les Questions liturgiques* in 1910. In the summer of 1912, the famous 'sémaines liturgiques' began as a series of annual liturgical conferences.

The Belgian movement is known most for its pastoral focus, thanks to the leadership of Lambert Beauduin, OSB (d.1960). Soon after entering Mont César in 1906, Beauduin became convinced of liturgy's transformative power within a secularized world and as the necessary grounding for Christian social activism. The date given for the founding of the Liturgical Movement is September of 1909, during the National Congress of Catholic Works held at Malines. There, Beauduin delivered a talk entitled 'La vraie prière de l'Eglise', in which he called for full and active participation in church life and worship. He based his remarks on the *Motu Proprio* of Pius X (22 November 1903) which described the liturgy as the true and indispensable source. At the Malines conference, Beauduin met the lay historian Godefroid Kurth, who shared his concerns for a participative liturgy; together they devised a plan to launch the Liturgical Movement. In 1914, Beauduin wrote *La piété de l'Eglise,* intended as a public declaration of the Liturgical Movement. Beauduin was joined by other collaborators, among them, his confrère, Eugéne Vandeur (d. 1968), Bernard Botte (d. 1980), and the Benedictine women at the monastery of Ancilla Domini at Wépion.

1.4. *The Austrian Liturgical Movement.* For the first time in the European Liturgical Movement, the leadership did not come from Benedictines. Rather, it was the Augustinian Pius Parsch (d. 1954) of Klosterneuburg who led the way, giving German liturgical scholarship a pastoral expression. Using the best

biblical, catechetical and liturgical resources available, Parsch succeeded in bringing about an integration on the pastoral level unmatched in Europe. In 1923, he initiated *Das Jahr des Heiles,* a pastoral commentary on the *eucharist and the liturgy of the hours for the entire church year. Even more significantly, his publication *Bibel und Liturgie,* founded in 1926, promoted the relationship between scripture and liturgy and encouraged wider readership of the Bible among RCs. Parsch argued that the eucharist is a sacrifice offered by the entire parish community and is a meal eaten in common; he also called for a proper and expanded use of the scripture within liturgy.

1.5. *Elsewhere in Europe.* While it is true that Italy and Spain did not register the same level of participation as we have seen above, the Liturgical Movement was present nonetheless. In northern Italy, the Benedictine monastery of Finalpia inaugurated the review *Rivista Liturgica* in 1914. In his text *La pietà liturgica* (Turin 1921), Abbot Emmanuele Caronti promoted an ecclesial piety grounded in the liturgy. Moreover, the Italian missal, *Messale festivo per i fedeli,* published there in the same year, assisted large numbers of Italian Catholics to better appreciate the liturgy's richness. The Catalonian Benedictine monastery of Montserrat became the principal centre for the Liturgical Movement in Spain, thanks to the formation received by many of the monks at Maria Laach during the years of persecution under Franco.

Bernard Botte, *From Silence to Participation: An Insider's View of Liturgical Renewal* Washington, DC 1988; Anabale Bugnini, *The Reform of the Liturgy,* Collegeville 1990; William R. Franklin, 'The Nineteenth Century Liturgical Movement', *Worship* LIII, 1979, 12–39; Cuthbert Johnson, *Prosper Guéranger, 1805–1875, a Liturgical Theologian,* Rome 1984; Ernest Benjamin Koenker, *The Liturgical Renaissance in the Roman Catholic Church,* Chicago 1966; Thomas F. O'Meara, 'The Origins of the Liturgical Movement and German Romanticism', *Worship* LIX, 1985, 326–53.

KEITH F. PECKLERS

2. *United Kingdom.* Just as the RC Liturgical Movement had nineteenth-century precursors, so also has the wider movement as it came to develop in the United Kingdom. Guéranger's concern for fidelity to *rubrics had a counter-

part with the Tractarians, Pusey and Keble particularly stressing loyalty to the Prayer Book rubrics. Second-generation Tractarianism as it developed into anglo-catholicism also concerned itself with rubrics, though in this case assimilating the Roman rubrics to Anglican usage. They also 'enriched' the Anglican rite from RC sources. Among Anglican evangelicals, interest was shown in more informal forms of worship and mission services, with outreach to the unchurched. This was made possible (or legal) by the 1855 Religious Worship Act, which allowed worship in buildings which were not consecrated. Some of this type of service took place in theatres and circus tents, and perhaps conveyed a concept of participation through entertainment. The study by Donald Gray, *Earth and Altar* (Norwich 1986), has highlighted the importance of the nineteenth-century Christian Socialist movement for the development of the Parish Communion movement, encouraging more frequency of the sacrament.

North of the border the Church Service Society was founded in 1863. This society was concerned to raise the standards of worship in the Church of *Scotland. Its leaders were influenced by the liturgical rite developed by the Catholic Apostolic Church, and the Society published editions of the *Euchologion*, which was to assist ministers in reaching the desired standards.

In English *Congregationalism we find certain fashionable congregations adopting a liturgy in order to attract a 'more respectable' class of person. John Hunter's *Devotional Services* (several editions from 1880 onwards) made a huge impact on the denomination. English *Presbyterians revised the *Directory of Worship*, and various *Methodist groups produced worship books for the minister. Yet all of these were but forerunners.

2.1. *The Roman Catholic Church*. In the early years of the twentieth century the English RC Church remained suspicious of the Liturgical Movement. In 1929 the Society of St Gregory had been founded to promote Gregorian chant, and in the 1930s summer schools were held in Oxford. However, it was not until after the Second World War, when English RC forces chaplains had experienced worship on the Continent, that the Movement began to have a larger impact. From 1962 an annual conference on pastoral liturgy was held at Spode House, Staffordshire. Leaders included J. D. Crichton, Clifford Howells and Dom Edmund

Jones. Following the new rites which resulted from Vatican II, the Bishops' Office on Liturgy commissioned a plan for liturgical formation, published as *Living Liturgy*, 1981. It was never implemented. Reservations on the 'stripping' of ceremonial and traditional texts in the new rites have been expressed recently by certain groups, such as the collection *Beyond the Prosaic*, Edinburgh 1998.

2.2. *The Church of England*. In terms of the spread of the ideas of twentieth-century pioneers such as Beauduin, Herwegen and Casel, it was the Anglicans Henry de Candole (1895–1971) and Gabriel Hebert (1886–1963) who played a key role in mediating them in England. As a young curate in the 1920s De Candole began reading *Questions liturgiques*, and was involved in developing the Parish Communion at St John's, Newcastle. When chaplain of Peterhouse, Cambridge, he wrote *The Church's Offering: A Brief Study of Eucharistic Worship*, and *The Sacraments and the Church: A Study of the Corporate Nature of the Church*, both published in 1935. In a pamphlet entitled *The Parish Communion* in 1936 he argued that the eucharist should be the main worship of the church, and should be a corporate action. Gabriel Hebert published *Liturgy and Society* (London 1935) and this also introduced English readers to the Continental RC Liturgical Movement, and offered ideas adapted for the Anglican Church. Two years later Hebert edited a symposium entitled *The Parish Communion* (London 1937), again stressing the corporate nature of eucharistic worship, and the concept of the church as a fellowship. After the Second World War, De Candole was instrumental in helping found Parish and People, which was concerned to disseminate the ideas of the Liturgical Movement in the Church of England.

Parish and People was one catalyst for liturgical revision. Another was scholarship, and here Gregory Dix's *The Shape of the Liturgy* (London 1945) had an enormous impact on Anglican liturgical thought. Calls for renewal of worship led to thoughts of new forms of worship, and in 1955 the Church of England Liturgical Commission was established. It made key reports for the 1958 Lambeth Conference, on the place of the *BCP* in the Anglican Communion, and of saints in the Anglican Communion. The result in the 1960s was new experimental rites. Influential persons included Ronald Jasper, Edward Ratcliff, Arthur Couratin, Geoffrey Willis, Geoffrey Cuming and Colin Buchanan. The early 1970s saw modern English-language services. Finally the experimental series and booklets gave way to the *The Alternative Service Book 1980*. Subsequently there was felt the need to enrich provisions, and material was produced for *Lent, *Holy Week, and *Easter (1985), for *Advent to *Candlemas (*The Promise of His Glory*, 1991), and for more flexible forms of '*word' services (*Patterns for Worship*, 1995). Most recently the 1980 book has itself been replaced by *Common Worship* (2000). Yet alongside the official services, some evangelical Anglican parishes have adopted worship styles from the American Church Growth churches; and certain groups, such as feminist groups, have written their own rites.

2.3. *Other Churches*. Among the Free Churches the influence was mainly indirect. In 1936 some Congregationalists at Mansfield College, Oxford published a collection entitled *Christian Worship*, which challenged the prevailing liberal Protestant suspicion of worship which had come to dominate the Congregationalist Union. A group of younger ministers formed the Church Order Group, which was concerned with ecclesiology and the Reformed tradition. They published their ideas in a journal called *The Presbyter*. Four of these – John Marsh, John Huxtable, James Todd and Nathaniel Micklem – compiled *A Book of Public Worship* (London 1948), which provided ministers with a worthy manual for worship. Reflecting current scholarly concerns, a remarkable eucharistic liturgy was published in 1967. When the Congregationalists merged with the Presbyterian Church of England in 1972 to form the *United Reformed Church, a Worship and Doctrine Committee produced rich resources in *A Book of Services 1980*, and *Service Book 1989*.

In Methodism leading names in liturgy in the 1960s and 1970s were Raymond George, Gordon Wakefield, David Tripp and J. C. Bowmer. Journals such as the *London Quarterly and Holborn Review* and *The Epworth Review* frequently carried articles adapting aims of the Liturgical Movement to a Methodist setting. New liturgies emerged. *The Methodist Service Book* was published in 1975, and most recently, *The Methodist Worship Book 1999*. Controversy was caused by the inclusion of one prayer addressed to God as Father and Mother.

In the Church of Scotland the work of the Church Service Society bore fruit in the 1940 *Book of Common Order*. A slimmer volume

appeared in 1979. Most recently, under the guidance of Charles Robertson, *Common Order 1994/6* has given the Church of Scotland a very flexible and full liturgical provision.

Many of the liturgists in the various churches were drawn together by the Joint Liturgical Group, an ecumenical group which since its inception in 1963 has produced a number of ecumenical services and guides (*see* **Ecumenical Co-operation in Liturgical Revision**).

BRYAN D. SPINKS

3. *USA*. The RC Liturgical Movement in the USA had two notable characteristics: (1) a strong concern for social justice, thus a strong link with social movements of the day; and (2) the involvement of large numbers of lay people, both women and men. The movement was founded by Virgil Michel, OSB (d. 1938), a German-American monk of St John's Abbey, Collegeville, Minnesota. During philosophy studies in Rome and Louvain (1924–5), Michel was greatly influenced by the Belgian liturgical pioneer Lambert Beauduin, who was then professor at the Benedictine school of Sant' Anselmo, Rome. He was also influenced by the great Benedictine monasteries of Maria Laach, Beuron, Montserrat, Solesmes and Mont César, which he visited during his European sojourn.

Returning to his monastery, Michel launched the Liturgical Movement in 1925, assisted by William Busch, Gerald Ellard, SJ and German-born Martin Hellriegel. Other Germans and German-Americans also became active pioneers, Hans Anscar Reinhold, Reynold Hillenbrand, Godfrey Diekmann, OSB and Bernard Laukemper among them. The movement was centred at St John's Abbey, Collegeville, with the founding of the periodical *Orate Fratres* (later *Worship*) and The Liturgical Press (both in 1926).

3.1. *Theological Foundations*. What united the Liturgical Movement both in Europe and North America was a common theological foundation in the doctrine of the mystical body of Christ. This was held in suspicion by more conservative Catholics of the time, because it was seen as an attempt to promote equality in the church, and undermine the hierarchy. Indeed, as late as 1942, only one year before the encyclical *Mystici Corporis*, the doctrine was attacked as 'new' even though its origins could be traced backed to St Paul. Thus, Michel and his collaborators often met with resistance when attempting to promote their agenda. Nonetheless, they remained convinced that it was precisely the mystical body of Christ which gave the necessary grounding for a liturgical renewal concerned about linking liturgy with life, occasioning new or recovered insights about Christology and ecclesiology.

3.2. *The Movement Grows*. Unlike its European counterpart, the US movement left the confines of Benedictine monasteries and registered strong levels of lay participation. Even before Virgil Michel returned from his European studies, Justine Ward (d. 1975) and Georgia Stevens, RSCJ, were busy in administering the Pius X School of Liturgical Music, founded in 1916 at the College of the Sacred Heart, Manhattanville, New York. Ward was schooled in liturgical chant at Solesmes and returned often. She was largely responsible for popularizing Solesmes chant in the USA and, by 1925, more than thirteen thousand teachers had learned her 'Ward Method'. The school became a leading force both in the restoration of chant and in liturgical renewal until it closed in 1969. A related development was the founding of the Liturgical Arts Society in 1928 by Maurice Lavanoux and several others, involving many artists and architects, among them Eric Gill. Their journal, *Liturgical Arts,* soon followed. With the exception of their Jesuit chaplain John LaFarge, the group was largely a lay association. The Society ended in 1972.

Perhaps the most significant example of lay participation in the US movement comes from the Liturgical Conference (founded 1940), famous for its annual liturgical weeks which drew up to twelve thousand people each year for the three-day meeting. Women pioneers like Sara Benedicta O'Neill, Elizabeth Johnson, Mary Perkins Ryan, and the artist Adé Bethune were involved, as well as Joseph Morrisey, Gerard Sloyan, William Leonard, SJ, Frederick McManus, Robert Hovda and Thomas Carroll. The published *Proceedings* of the annual Liturgical Weeks bear testimony to the movement's vitality throughout the USA, especially in the 1940s and 1950s. The Conference (now ecumenical) continues today with its publications *Liturgy* and *Homily Service* and is located in Silver Spring, Maryland. The St Jerome Society (later Vernacular Society) was founded in 1946 by H. A. Reinhold during the Liturgical Week in Denver, Colorado, to link up with the already established Vernacular Society of Great Britain (under the direction of Jesuits Clifford Howell

and C. C. Martindale, along with Donald Attwater) to promote English in the liturgy. At its peak, the organization had several thousand members (including eighty-four bishops). The US Vernacular Society merged with the Liturgical Conference in 1967. A number of social activists from the Catholic Worker, Catholic Action, Friendship House, the Grail, and the Christian Family Movement, most notably Dorothy Day (co-founder of the Catholic Worker) and the Baroness Catherine De Hueck Doherty (founder of Friendship House), joined Michel in becoming liturgical pioneers. Moreover, a number of women opened bookstores around the country to promote liturgical renewal, the most famous of which was the St Benet's Bookshop in Chicago, founded by Sara O'Neill.

3.3. *The Movement's Cultural Dimension*. The Liturgical Movement grew in the German midwest (St Louis, Chicago, Collegeville) and was less successful on the Irish east and west coasts of the USA. With a strong tradition of congregational participation in Germany, those immigrants took more easily to the Liturgical Movement and its message. Irish immigrants, on the other hand, were unaccustomed to such participation and often celebrated mass quietly and expeditiously. They saw congregational singing as a 'Protestant thing' and were content with the continuation of 'low masses' upon arrival in the USA.

3.4. *Ecumenical Dimensions and the Liturgical Movement in Other Churches*. As RC scholars in the USA were returning to early and patristic sources to discover the origins and foundation of Christian liturgical practice, the same phenomenon was taking place in other churches, bringing about parallel liturgical movements. The Liturgical Movement in the American Episcopal Church took shape in 1946 with the Associated Parishes for Liturgy and Mission, founded by John Patterson (d. 1988). Like its RC neighbour, the Episcopal Liturgical Movement emphasized the important link between liturgy and justice, greater congregational participation, annual liturgical weeks, and public celebrations of morning and evening prayer. US *Lutheran liturgical renewal grew in the 1950s, when *altars were turned towards the people for the *eucharist and greater liturgical participation was advocated. Similar developments can be noted in the *Reformed churches. All these parallel movements led to the publication of new service books beginning in the 1970s through the 1990s, where the eucharistic and non-eucharistic liturgical structures bear a remarkable resemblance, one to another.

3.5. *Academic Programmes.* *Ecumenical liturgical co-operation in the movement is perhaps best seen in the founding of academic programmes in liturgy and professional societies of liturgical scholars. In 1947, Michael Mathis, CSC founded the Summer School in Liturgy at the University of Notre Dame. In 1965, it was expanded into the graduate programme in liturgical studies, and has granted over fifty doctorates to date – an even number to RCs and to members of other churches. The programme continues to thrive along with a strong graduate programme in liturgics at the Catholic University of America in Washington, DC. In 1973, the ecumenical North American Academy of Liturgy (NAAL) was founded by John Gallen, SJ. NAAL has grown to over four hundred members from Canada and the USA. In recent years, the Academy has also become inter-faith, with a small but growing number of Jewish liturgical scholars. A number of US liturgiologists are also members of the ecumenical and international Societas Liturgica founded in 1965.

3.6. *Conclusion.* For RCs, it was not until papal documents like *Mystici corporis* (1943) or *Mediator Dei* (1947) that the movement gained respectability. The bilingual *Collectio rituum* of 1954 was another significant advance, allowing for greater use of the vernacular. The 1955 restoration of the *Holy Week rites to their proper place marked another milestone. But the greatest milestone of all took place on 4 December 1963, when the Bishops of the Second Vatican Council together with Pope Paul VI solemnly promulgated their first Conciliar document – the Liturgy Constitution, *Sacrosanctum concilium,* with a vote of 2,147 bishops in favour and 4 opposed. This was the crowning achievement of the Liturgical Movement and the fulfilment of a dream for those who had laboured so earnestly on its behalf. Whether one is speaking of liturgical renewal within the RC Church, or in the Episcopal or Lutheran churches, liturgical pioneers had their critics over the years. In some places, the criticism continues today as Episcopalians debate over the preference for Rite I of the eucharist reflecting the more traditional *BCP* language and style, or the more contemporary 1979 revision reflected in Rite II. Meanwhile, some US Catholics claim that the current post-Vatican II liturgy is not what the

pioneers were advocating, and they call for a return to the Latin mass and to the 1962 pre-Conciliar missal. What is clear is that the reformed liturgy and unity of liturgical practice now enjoyed by most of our churches is far healthier and more successful than what preceded it, and for that we can be very grateful indeed.

Primary Sources: Gerald Ellard, *Men at Work and Worship*, New York 1940; The Liturgical Conference, *Proceedings*, 1940–67; Virgil Michel, *The Mystical Body and Social Justice*, Collegeville 1938; H. A. Reinhold, *H.A.R.: The Autobiography of Father Reinhold*, New York 1968.

Studies: Kathleen Hughes, *How Firm a Foundation, Vol 1, Voices of the Early Liturgical Movement*, Chicago 1990; Paul Marx, *Virgil Michel and the Liturgical Movement*, Collegeville 1957; Robert L. Tuzik, *How Firm a Foundation, Vol. 2, Leaders of the Liturgical Movement*, Chicago 1990; Susan J. White, *Art, Architecture, and Liturgical Reform: The Liturgical Arts Society, 1928–1972*, New York 1990.

KEITH F. PECKLERS

Liturgy of the Hours *see* **Daily Prayer** 3

Local Preacher

A ministry recognized and owned by John Wesley from the earliest days of *Methodism. The itinerant preachers 'travelled' in connection with the Methodist Conference and evolved into the ordained ministry. The local preachers were paid expenses but exercised a ministry of leading non-eucharistic worship and preaching in their own or neighbouring circuits and usually continued in their secular employment. The office was originally and eventually open to both men and women. The designation 'local preacher' dates from the 1750s. Itinerant or travelling preachers were often drawn from the ranks of local preachers. Every accredited local preacher must undergo a nationally approved course of study and training before being commissioned. British candidates for ordination in the Methodist Church must already be accredited local preachers.

G. Milburn and M. Batty (eds), *Workaday Preachers*, Peterborough 1995.

C. NORMAN R. WALLWORK

Lord's Prayer, The

Not surprisingly, the Lord's Prayer has come to be used universally and frequently in liturgical worship. It was not always so, however. Although its use at the times of *daily prayer is prescribed by several ancient Christian writers, it is not found in the public daily services of the fourth century onwards, being instead only a feature of some monastic and individual patterns of prayer, whence it spread into later forms of the daily office.

Its use at the *eucharist does not seem to antedate the middle of the fourth century at the earliest, being first clearly attested in the *Mystagogical Catecheses* attributed to Cyril of Jerusalem. From then onwards, liturgical commentators in East and West witness to its use after the *eucharistic prayer as a preparation for *communion, stressing its suitability for this purpose by laying emphasis on the petitions for the forgiveness of sins and, above all, for daily – or rather (arguing from an alternative reading) heavenly – bread. It has subsequently been so used in all the historic liturgies, and in many others as well; it is only in some of the post-Reformation Protestant rites that it has been removed from this position and function, and placed elsewhere in the service. In most of the historic rites the Lord's Prayer is placed after the breaking of the bread which follows the eucharistic prayer; in the two most widespread of them, however, the Roman and the Byzantine, it precedes the breaking of the bread, the Roman usage in this respect being probably a Byzantine importation.

In English-speaking countries, efforts have been made in recent decades to substitute a modern translation of the Lord's Prayer for the 'traditional' one, which, with minor variations, has been universally used since the sixteenth century. The form produced by the International Consultation on English Texts (ICET) at one time seemed likely to win widespread support, but it fact its success has turned out to be very limited, even in those churches which have happily adopted other ICET texts: the RC Church has so far retained the 'traditional' text, albeit with the ICET doxology, an inconsistent and inelegant compromise; other churches (e.g. the Church of England) have adopted texts based on that of ICET, but differing from it in various ways, thus frustrating the aim of establishing a new common text; and often even where one of these has been provided, permission has had to be given to substitute the 'tradi-tional' text where it is desired. In so far as the latter is the one prayer-text known by heart by large numbers of those who still know any prayer at all by heart, there appear to be major difficulties in the way of establishing any alternative version.

W. JARDINE GRISBROOKE

Lord's Supper, The

St Paul's name for the Christian communal meal celebrated in memory of Jesus' death, mindful also of his return (1 Cor. 11.20). In that context, the supper (Greek, *deipnon*, perhaps better rendered 'banquet') is comparable in basic form to suppers supporting quite different religious and ethical assumptions, such as those of pagan guilds or Jewish associations. After Paul, the term is occasionally used by early Christian writers referring either to the Last Supper of Jesus or to the *eucharist, typically with some allusion to Paul's use in 1 Corinthians. A somewhat different communal meal is also given this title in the *Apostolic Tradition* (attributed to Hippolytus) 26.

Although 'Lord's supper' continued to be applied to the eucharist into the Middle Ages, it was rarely if ever the preferred name, but seen (e.g. in the Catechism of Trent) as one title or image among others. The sixteenth-century Reformers, however, preferred the term as obviously biblical in origin, unlike '*mass' or 'eucharist'. In that setting, the character of the event as a meal was often affirmed in ritual, as well as by this title.

In the English language, use of 'Lord's supper' as a primary term for the eucharist stems in particular from the 1549 *BCP*; the alternative 'holy *communion' has often been preferred in practice, however. With the rise of the *Liturgical Movement and the emphasis on the meal as 'eucharist', use of 'Lord's supper' as the primary name for the Christian meal has become more characteristic of evangelical and *Pentecostal practice.

David Broughton Knox, *The Lord's Supper from Wycliffe to Cranmer*, Exeter 1983; Hans Lietzmann, *Mass and Lord's Supper: A Study in the History of Liturgy*, Leiden 1979; Gary Macy, *The Banquet's Wisdom: A Short History of the Theologies of the Lord's Supper*, New York 1992; J. Murphy-O'Connor, 'Eucharist and Community in First Corinthians', *Living Bread, Saving Cup*, ed. R. Kevin Seasoltz, Collegeville 1982, 1–30.

ANDREW MCGOWAN

Love-Feast

Eighteenth-century recreation of early Christian *agape, looking to John 13 (fellowship in Christ, humble mutual service and joyful encouragement), among German *Baptists and related churches, *Moravians and *Methodists; recently adopted for *ecumenical fellowship where eucharistic *communion is precluded, invoked as an aid to development in pastoral liturgy and as a pointer to the ethical enrichment of worship.

1. *Anabaptist Love-Feasts.* Both in Germany and after their removal to America, the Brethren (Alexander Mack, Sr) and their successors, Old German Baptists, Church of the Brethren, Brethren Church, Dunkard Brethren and Grace Brethren, and also the Brethren in Christ (a Brethren-related tradition with *Mennonite and pietist/revivalist elements), observe the love-feast and *foot-washing as dominical ordinances integral to the celebration of the *Lord's supper. Traditionally, after examination of the congregation's spiritual condition, and reconciliation of disputes among members, the congregation gathered in the evening for a communal meal (lamb, as at the Passover, or beef, the Passover being no longer normative, according to differing convictions), with fraternal conversation. Then would follow exposition of 1 Cor. 11 and prayer. Next day, the love-feast proper then followed. Introductory prayer led into the foot-washing (by successive pairs, or by each for their neighbour, women and men seated separately), during the reading of John 13, and singing. Table grace then introduced a simple meal, with scripture reading and exposition, and the Lord's supper strictly so called – with unleavened bread and wine (more recently, unfermented grape-juice), collection for the needy, reading of the passion narrative and solemn proclamation of 1 Cor. 16.20 and *kiss of peace. Thanks over the bread prefaced distribution and eating, thanks over the cup preceded administration of the wine. One form of administration has been: 'Beloved brother/ sister, this bread which we break is the communion of the body of Christ. Beloved brother/sister, this cup of the New Testament is the communion of the blood of Christ.' Blessing and song concluded. Originally, this extended celebration was held once a year, in the spring, but more recently specifically on *Maundy Thursday; in the twentieth century, a service on World Communion Sunday (first in

October) has been added. Historically, admission has been limited to those baptized on profession. At least in the Church of the Brethren, ecumenical invitations are now possible. Though the proceedings have been simplified, the custom is vigorous. Christ's presence in the act of fellowship and in each participating Christian, rather than in the elements, is emphasized. Recent Brethren scholarship has noted how ancient liturgical patterns, especially *anamnesis and *epiclesis, are maintained in this tradition.

2. *Moravian Love-Feasts.* From 1727, early in its formation at Herrnhut in Germany, the Renewed Church of the United Brethren (Moravian Church) held fellowship meals for various occasions, religious, civic or domestic, in preparation for a new task or journey, or in readiness for the Lord's supper, or (especially in the beginning) immediately after it, to prolong the sense of familial unity experienced in communion. The researches of Christian Arnold into early Christian usage provided the rationale. The atmosphere was soberly convivial, sanctifying the natural instinct for sociability. At first, Herrnhut love-feasts received gifts of food from Count Zinzendorf's own kitchen. The meals were held in distinct groups ('choirs', gathered according to gender, age or special work) or for the whole church. Two main versions developed, which survive in Moravian provinces worldwide: (a) freely structured special celebrations for festival seasons of the Christian *year or of the local congregation or smaller group, and (b) on the eve of a Communion Sunday. There is a simple meal, with conversation, sharing of local or distant church news, song and prayer, aimed at strengthening fraternal unity and mutual encouragement.

3. *Methodist Love-Feasts.* John Wesley had witnessed these meals in Georgia and at Herrnhut and shared them in London, and in 1738 the London Methodists adopted the practice, though with a shift of emphasis. During (or before or after) a token meal of cake or bread and water (from a 'loving-cup'), participants testify to experience of God's grace, in their own words or those of hymns (particularly by Charles Wesley), to sharpen the quest for conversion and growth in grace. A collection is taken for the needy (in the early nineteenth century, these offerings were significantly larger than collections for the poor taken up at

the Lord's supper). Partly because the love-feast (like the Band Meeting) had an element of mutual *confession, with the necessary implications of modesty and confidentiality, and partly to avert charges of lascivious behaviour which were prompted by the name, love-feasts were at first held for men and women separately. Love-feasts for the general membership of local Methodist Societies were permitted later. Tickets of Methodist Society membership ('Class Tickets') were required for admission until late in the nineteenth century. For some young Methodists, exclusion from love-feasts caused a sudden self-examination and a consequent spiritual crisis. In at least one case (William Clowes, a founder of the Primitive Methodist Church), illicit attendance with another's ticket, together with the misapprehension that this service was the Lord's supper, precipitated a comparable crisis. Through the nineteenth century, discipline was relaxed, and frequency of the observance declined steadily. In the north of England, love-feasts were partly replaced by fellowship gatherings for groups of churches or circuits, at which local Wesley Guilds or other fellowship groups share their faith by singing, for the others, significant hymns of faith and discipleship. At these gatherings, light refreshments and conversation follow the service, but are not integral to it.

In American Methodism, love-feasts served to test and encourage the work of the preachers, and District Presiding Elders would only permit love-feasts at Quarterly Meeting Conferences if the harmony and general spiritual state of the local church seemed to justify it. Methodist observance of the love-feast has markedly declined, more in White than in Black denominations, but recent liturgical books (African Methodist Episcopal and A. M. E. Zion, Christian Methodist Episcopal, United Methodist) have encouraged its renewal and offered resources.

4. *Recent Developments*. In the late twentieth century, in the Netherlands, Britain and the USA, the love-feast, under the tradition-claiming title of Agape, has generated ecumenical interest, used as a shared ritual acknowledgement of the pain of broken communion and petition for reconciliation, as a form of evangelistic service, and as an element in blessings of dwellings. Religious orders, such as the St Michael Brotherhood in the German Evangelical Church, have revived the agape, using prayers from the *Didache*. This interest has given new urgency to the debate about the early history of the agape and *refrigerium*. Even if the idea of an agape distinct from the *eucharist in NT times is untenable, the fellowship meal may win acceptance on its own merits. The concept of the love-feast has recently been used to illustrate aspects of the eucharist, and (in the light of patristic and monastic precedents) to develop pastoral liturgy suggestions for Maundy Thursday.

'Love Feast,' *Brethren Encyclopedia*, Philadelphia 1983, II, 762–5; Julius Friedrich Sachse, *The German Sectarians of Pennsylvania 1708–1742*, Philadelphia 1899, reprinted New York 1971; D. F. Durnbaugh, *A History of the Brethren 1708–1995*, Elgin, IL 1997; Jonathan R. Stayer, 'An Interpretation of Some Ritual and Food Elements of the Brethren Love Feast', *Brethren Life and Thought* XXX, 1985, 199–208; *Brethren in Christ, History and Life*, esp. IX, XII, XVIII; J. T. Hamilton and H. G. Hamilton, *History of the Moravian Church: The Renewed Unitas Fratrum 1722–1957*, Bethlehem, PA 1967; H.-C. Hahn and H. Reichel (eds), *Zinzendorf und die Herrnhuter Bruder: Quellen . . . 1722 bis 1760*, Hamburg 1977; F. Baker, *Methodism and the Lovefeast*, London 1957; R. O. Johnson, 'The Development of the Love Feast in Early American Methodism', *Methodist History* XIX, 1981, 67–83; W. Parkes, 'Love-Feast, Watch-Night, and Covenant Service in Early British Methodism', *Wesleyan Theological Journal* XXXII, 1997, 35–58; Benjamin Gregory, *The Holy Catholic Church, the Communion of Saints*, London 1873; V. M. Eller, *In Place of Sacraments*, 1972; Arthur C. Cochrane, *Eating and Drinking with Jesus: An Ethical and Biblical Inquiry*, Philadelphia 1974 (anti-sacramental view).

DAVID TRIPP

Low Sunday

The name given to the Sunday one week after *Easter Day in the medieval English tradition, and continued in later English usage, though not in the *BCP* itself. Its meaning is obscure, but it perhaps refers to the contrast between the elaborate rites of Easter and the return to more normal liturgical practice at the end of the *octave. In the Latin tradition this Sunday was called instead *Dominica post albas* or *Dominica in albis depositis*, and later simply *Dominica in albis*, a reference to the ancient custom of the newly baptized continuing to wear the white robes put on at their *baptism at Easter for seven days afterwards, ending on this day.

EDITOR

Lucernarium

'The bringing-in of the lamp', a ceremony originally observed in Christian homes and at congregational meals in ancient times as darkness fell. Thanksgiving would be offered for the light of the day, for the gift of light to illuminate the darkness of the night and for Christ the light of the world. It is often thought to have originated from the Jewish custom of the Sabbath lamp, though some have suggested pagan roots instead. In the fourth century it was incorporated into *daily prayer in church each evening in many places, by which time the use at it of the hymn *Phos hilaron* ('Hail, gladdening light') had already become traditional. Retained in Eastern liturgical practice down to the present day, the *Lucernarium* later became extinct in the West, except for the annual lighting of the *Easter candle. However, the custom has begun to be restored, at least on an occasional basis, in a number of ecclesiastical traditions in recent years.

EDITOR

Lutheran Worship

1. *Origins.* Lutherans confess 'the mass is retained among us and is celebrated with the greatest reverence' (*Augsburg Confession* 24). Though that confession does not yet establish a liturgy, it does give important background to a characteristic approach to liturgy among Lutherans, which has been marked by principles which must be regarded as critically conservative. The sixteenth-century liturgies which established these principles were not new creations, nor were they, for example, Renaissance attempts to enact the *Lord's supper in some manner regarded as the way it was done in NT times. Rather, these liturgies were varying receptions of the Western liturgical tradition, critically reworked to become evangelical and congregational services, accessible to the cultures and languages of late-medieval and early-modern northern Europe, and noted especially for their inclusion of hymnody and popular liturgical chant. These characteristics – reverence for liturgical tradition, criticism and reworking of the tradition according to a Lutheran conception of the

'gospel', and interest in vernacular language, popular participation and a communally sung rite – have continued to mark an authentic Lutheran approach to liturgy since the sixteenth century.

Thus medieval liturgical books and prevailing piety were the starting places for the Lutheran reform of worship. Luther produced reforms of the mass as he knew it in both Latin, *Formula Missae et Communionis* (1523), and German, *Deutsche Messe und Gottesdienstes* (1526). He also prepared revisions of the liturgy of *baptism (first in 1523 and again in 1526). They were especially central because of the affirmation of two sacraments instituted by Christ in the NT. These reforms had widespread influence among Lutheran churches and with other Protestants. Luther also provided directions on the form of *daily prayer. The liturgies of morning prayer (matins) and evening prayer (vespers) were used to replace daily mass in parish churches and especially in schools.

With the vernacular translation of the scriptures, Lutherans could hear and understand the readings at mass as never before. Sermons became expository, doctrinal and catechetical in nature rather than moralistic. Luther's own sermons were widely copied. A strong emphasis on *confession in both public and to a lesser extent private forms has also been retained in Lutheranism. The weekly use of a brief or longer form of public confession is common, often as preparation for receiving *communion.

Lutheran worship is characterized theologically by an emphasis on worship as an encounter with a gracious God. God is the primary actor in worship offering justifying grace to the worshipper through external means. These external means are the word of God and the sacraments. Lutheran worship is characterized by a repudiation of any understanding or practice which suggests that human beings act in worship to satisfy God. Word and *sacrament give and strengthen faith as a gift from God. They do not earn God's favour for those who worship. This theological emphasis led Luther to remove sections of the canon of the Roman mass, a distinguishing mark of Lutheran *eucharistic rites until recently. Insistence on the real presence or bodily presence of Christ in the eucharist is also an important mark of Lutheran worship.

Among the features which have given Lutheran worship a distinctive flavour have been its desire to conserve features of catholic practice which other reform movements abandoned. Luther retained the elevation of the *host. Lutheran churches retained the use of *vestments for clergy, an *altar with crucifix or *cross and *candles as well as paintings or statues, and liturgical texts chanted by the ministers, *choir and congregation. Lutherans have continued to use the liturgical *year and *lectionaries.

Congregational singing of hymns continues as a strong tradition. Luther himself was a writer of hymns. The form of the *chorale* is an important contribution of Lutheranism. Today many forms of hymnody and congregational song are found in practice.

*Confirmation, though not a sacrament, has assumed a special importance among Lutherans. It marks, liturgically, the conclusion of an intense period of catechesis that often focuses on Luther's *Small Catechism* and celebrates the beginning of adult responsibility in the church. In European Lutheran churches and their missions it marks the occasion of first communion. For most Lutherans in North America first communion happens well before confirmation.

2. *Phases of Development*. Following Luther's reforms, there were three phases of development in Lutheran practice: Orthodoxy (1550–1650), Enlightenment (1700–1800) and Pietism (1650–1800). Lutheran orthodoxy was a time of codification for theology and practice. Many national and territorial churches produced church orders (*Kirchenordnungen*) which regulated worship practices and church government. Luther had been content to allow considerable liberty in matters of worship so long as certain theological principles were clear. Subsequent generations found this impossible to manage in an orderly and practical way. The Lutheran musical tradition was exemplified by composers such as Michael Praetorius (d. 1621) and Heinrich Schütz (d. 1672).

The Enlightenment attempted to rationalize and intellectualize Christianity and had a significant effect on Lutheran worship in northern Europe and also North America. The frequency of celebrating the eucharist declined. Baptism was often administered in private. An emphasis on morality as a chief expression of Christian life undercut many of Lutheranism's original insights and altered the character of its preaching.

Pietism was an attempt to revive an intensely personal experience of Christian faith. Leaders such as Spener and Francke turned interest from the formal liturgies of the church in congregational settings to intimate groups of believers who gathered for prayer and study of the scriptures. This movement, which was not especially sacramental or liturgical in its sensibilities, was especially powerful in North America. The first great wave of immigration among Lutherans occurred during this period, and its church leaders and pastors were formed in the Pietist tradition. Among the gifts of Pietism to Lutheran worship were a flowering of new hymnody by Francke and others such as Paul Gerhard. Musical development continued in the work of Buxtehude (d. 1707), Pachelbel (d. 1706) and Johann Sebastian Bach (d. 1750).

3. *Liturgical Recovery*. The period from 1800 to the present has been a time of recovery of elements of the Lutheran tradition such as the centrality of the sacraments which the Enlightenment and Pietism had undervalued. Liturgies were reformed with an eye to recovering sixteenth-century models and insights. This was accompanied by a renewed appreciation for the centrality of the Lutheran Confessions.

In the twentieth century Lutheran worship, especially in North America, has contributed to and benefited from aspects of *ecumenical liturgical renewal. Frequent (even weekly) celebration of the eucharist and its reception is one example. Recovery of the *catechumenate for un-evangelized adults is another.

Lutheran practice continues a strong use of congregational song in hymns but also in the singing of the liturgical texts. The use of through-composed mass settings by the congregation is especially common in North American Lutheranism. In the late twentieth century a vigorous movement to supplement European traditions of congregational song and hymnody with global forms was evident.

Though more common in North America than Europe, the use of the three-year ecumenical *lectionary, enriched calendar, especially in the sanctoral cycle, and newly translated or composed *eucharistic prayers and *collects are all present today.

———

For bibliography, *see* **Books, Liturgical** 8.

PAUL R. NELSON

Magnificat *see* **Canticles**

Maniple *see* **Vestments** 3(c)

Mar Thoma Church Worship

During the second quarter of the nineteenth century, a section of the Syrian church in Kerala, the southernmost state of India, underwent a certain degree of reformation in its doctrine and practice through the influence of the Church Missionary Society of the Church of England. This church was later known as the Mar Thoma Syrian Church, and claims historical continuity with the ancient church which is traditionally believed to have been founded by the Apostle Thomas in 52 CE. It is in full communion with worldwide Anglicanism, the Church of *North India and the Church of *South India. It is unique in its position as at once an Eastern and Reformed church. It is oriental in that it still follows the patterns of the Antiochene (*West Syrian) liturgical tradition, but with a reformed doctrine. The aim of the reformers was to bring the church, which had been corrupted by Latin and Jacobite influence, back to the original purity of the early church, and part of that was that the liturgy should be celebrated in the language of the people, although in the beginning there was opposition to this from conservatives, and that it should be revised to eliminate certain wrong teachings that had crept into the church.

1. *The Eucharist*. The *eucharistic liturgy (*Qurbana*) was first revised and translated from Syriac into the Malayalam vernacular on the basis of the reformed doctrines in 1836, but afterwards the practice was that each member of the clergy used his own translation for the Holy *Qurbana* when celebrating the eucharist, with the result that a number of different translations existed in the church. It was only during the time of Titus II, Mar Thoma Metropolitan, that the liturgy was unified and printed. Among the changes made in the eucharistic texts were that all prayers for the departed and to the Blessed Virgin Mary and the saints were omitted, since Christ is the only mediator; all elements in the prayers which overemphasized the sacrificial aspect in the eucharist were eliminated; and prayers which had some kind of reference to the transubstantiation of the bread and wine were revised. With regard to practice, certain changes were also made: *communion had to be administered in both kinds separately, and the eucharist was not to be celebrated when there was no one to receive

it. Auricular *confession to a priest was also abolished. The Mar Thoma Church remains Eastern by not adding the *Filioque* clause in the *creed, and worship is conducted in standing posture. The Holy *Qurbana* is celebrated on each Sunday and on special feast days

Lay participation is very much emphasized in worship. Lay men assist in the service, read the biblical lections and preach, and lead the worship on Sundays when a priest is not available. Women are not allowed to lead the worship or to assist the priest during the eucharist, but they can preach and read the lections. The church has not yet made any decision to ordain women.

2. *Liturgical Texts*. Currently the anaphora of St James, and the anaphoras of Mar Dionysius Metropolitan, of Xystus Patriarch, of St Peter the Apostle, Mar Yuhannon Patriarch, of Thomas the Harclean Episcopa, Mar Ivanios Metropolitan are in use for the eucharist. There is also a *eucharistic prayer for the sick to be conducted at home. English, Hindi and other South Indian versions are used as well. The book of occasional offices was translated from Syriac in 1945 and contains the *baptism, *marriage and *funeral liturgies, thanksgiving after childbirth, prayer for the *sick, and the order for the dedication of a house. The first English version was printed in 1988, and a special order of service for the burial of those who have committed suicide was prepared in 1996. The seven canonical hours of *daily prayer were reduced to two, especially for laypeople, and the text was published in 1942.

The texts of services conducted only by *bishops (*ordination rites, admission to the monastic order, and the *dedication of a church) are still in manuscript form and no English translation is available. There is also a special order for the consecration of *muroon* (chrism), which is used for the dedication of a church and post-baptismal *anointing.

The Mar Thoma Church uses the *lectionary of the West Syrian tradition with certain adaptations, and a theme is provided for preaching and meditation on each Sunday. The liturgical *year begins with the festival of the 'Sanctification of the Church' (*Kudash Eetho*), which falls on the last Sunday of October or first Sunday in November. Then comes 'the Renewal of the Church', the period of the *Annunciation, the feast of Birth of our Lord (*Eldho*), the Baptism (*Danha*), the Presentation of the Lord, the three days' Fast of Nineveh, Great *Lent (fifty days), *Palm Sunday, *Holy Week, *Easter (*Kemtha*), *Ascension (*Suloko*) and *Pentecost. The *Transfiguration is kept on 6 August, and 21 December, the feast of St Thomas, is celebrated as the church day, and there is a special liturgy for the occasion. In addition various fasts are observed. None of the services for the festivals are yet translated into English, but that is in preparation.

3. *Inculturation.* The church believes that, because of its long existence in the land, a certain degree of *inculturation of worship has already taken place. But the search for a more authentic and contextual liturgy has to be continued. This is essential especially for the people who embrace Christianity from other faiths and for the migrant diaspora. The church uses both indigenous and Western hymns in worship. They are non-liturgical songs but are quite often used during worship.

Alexander Mar Thoma, *Mar Thoma Church, Heritage and Mission*, Tiruvalla 1985; Juhanon Mar Thoma, *Christianity in India and a Brief History of the Mar Thoma Syrian Church*, Madras 1968; K. K. Kuruvilla, *A History of the Mar Thoma Church and Its Doctrines*, Madras 1951; George Mathew, 'A Historical Introduction to the Liturgies of the Mar Thoma Syrian Church', *Mar Thoma Messenger*, October 1999, 19–21; 'Liturgy for the Twenty-First Century', *The Mar Thoma Church, Tradition and Modernity*, ed. P. J. Alexander, Tiruvalla 2000, 112–18.

GEORGE MATHEW

Maronite Rite *see* West Syrian Worship

Marian Feasts

1. *Mary in the Liturgy and in the Church.* That Mary, the mother of Jesus, holds a special place in the spirituality and liturgical practice of many Christians is indicated not just by the number of feasts devoted to her (some fifteen at present in the RC calendar, with numerous local additions) but also by their solemnity and historical importance.

The significance of Mary is that she shows Christians the true path to God and the way in which God's plan is achieved through the full co-operation of human beings. Her relationship to her son, her purity and her symbolic value as a fundamental sign of the decision of God

to achieve salvation for all through the co-operation of humanity also comprise significant parts of the content of Marian feasts: as *Theotokos* (literally, 'God-bearer', i.e., Mother of God), she ensured the full humanity of the Word made flesh, and continues to intercede for us. Mary represents the possibility for all Christians of asking 'How can this be?' (Luke 1.34), of questioning our beliefs and the frequent juxtapositions between what faith tells us and our experience in the context of a world in need of God's grace. She shows the attitude of wonder and prayer with which all liturgical ceremonies should be infused. Mary's decision to fulfil the will of God shows us the importance of witness and vocation in the presence of doubt and fear. The bishops of the Second Vatican Council place Mary in their decree on the Church, *Lumen Gentium,* in order to show her significance and the relationship between Mary and the body of Christ: she is the bearer of God's Word and also the outstanding example of discipleship for the church. Frequent references to these two key roles are made in the prayers of the feasts of Mary celebrated throughout the year. Mary also serves as the best example of Christian living to all who follow Christ: she exhibits the charisms of sincere, mature questioning (as in the story of the Annunciation, Luke 1.26–38), of greeting others with kindness (for example, in the story of the Visitation in Luke 1.41–45), of care and protection for those dear to her (the flight into Egypt in Matt. 2.13–18), of profound contemplation (Luke 2.19), and of appreciation of the centrality of the cross of Christ for salvation (John 19.25–27, where she does not abandon her son). Mary also reminds Christians that they are called to live their lives in the context of faith-filled communities whose members gather to pray and celebrate together.

2. *Feasts of Mary.* The cult of Mary is an ancient phenomenon. Devotion began in Jerusalem in the early years of Christianity, with the feasts both of Mary *Theotokos*, originally on August 15 and transferred to January 1, and later, of Mary *Kathisma* (resting) on August 15. This latter day became the feast of the Dormition by the end of the fifth century, as it remains in the East, and of the Assumption in the West during the eighth century. Although not defined as a dogma in the RC Church until 1950, this feast was one of the most ancient, celebrating the possibility of divinity for human beings, not just for Christ. Hope in the

resurrection for all is reflected in the readings for the feast.

The Birthday of Our Lady (September 8) was one of the four Roman feasts of the Virgin Mary (the others being the *Annunciation, the Dormition and the Meeting or *Hypapante*, which became the feast of the Purification and then of the Presentation of the Lord: *see* **Candlemas**) and may originate from the dedication of a church in Mary's honour in Jerusalem at the beginning of the sixth century.

The Immaculate Conception (December 8) may have originated in Jerusalem as a feast of her conception, with the idea of Mary's purity and holiness being introduced some time during the eleventh century, though it was not until 1708 that the feast became a required celebration in the Roman rite. It acquired its present title after the issuing of the dogmatic definition in 1854.

The Visitation (originally July 2 and now May 31) originated in Byzantium and became part of the calendar of the universal church in 1389 during attempts to heal the Great Schism.

There are many other additional feasts and commemorations celebrated in local churches according to popular devotion, for example, Our Lady of Lourdes, Our Lady of Mount Carmel, Our Lady of the Rosary, and Our Lady of Guadalupe, celebrated in many Latino churches, which originated in 1531 with the miracle of the apparition of Mary to Juan Diego near Mexico City.

————

Brian Daley, 'Mary, Feasts of', *New Dictionary of Liturgy and Sacramental Worship*, ed. Peter Fink, Collegeville 1990, 818–25; Paul A. Janowiak, 'Mary and the Liturgy', *Liturgical Ministry* VI, 1997, 21–7; A. G. Martimort et al., *The Church at Prayer* IV, Collegeville 1986, 130–50 (bib.).

ANDREW CAMERON-MOWAT

Marriage

The blessing of a marriage is practised in nearly all Christian traditions, and many of them also officiate at the (civilly recognized) exchange of vows.

————

General bibliography: Kenneth W. Stevenson, *Nuptial Blessing: A Study of Christian Marriage Rites*, London 1982; *To Join Together: The Rite of Marriage*, New York 1987; Mark Searle and Kenneth W. Stevenson, *Documents of the Marriage Liturgy*, Collegeville 1992.

1. Early Christianity; 2. Eastern Churches; 3. Medieval and Roman Catholic; 4. Anglican; 5. Baptist; 6. Christian Church; 7. Congregationalist; 8. Lutheran; 9. Methodist; 10. Old Catholic; 11. Pentecostal; 12. Reformed.

1. *Early Christianity*. How did early Christians marry? There has been a tendency in the past to accept that they did, but to be reticent about how they did it. The NT assumes that marriage happens, and, indeed, the first of Jesus' 'signs' in the Fourth Gospel takes place at the marriage of an unknown couple at Cana (John 2.1–11). Long-established Jewish practice involved the two stages of betrothal and marriage, the former being legally binding, with a contract, as we learn from the case of Mary and Joseph, where Joseph decides not to exercise his right by setting it aside (Matt. 1.18–25). The marriage rite took place at a feast in the bridegroom's house, when he recited the 'Seven Benedictions', which are still used to this day, and though their precise age is not certain, they were taken over by the rabbis, who presided over the rite, the nuptial canopy in the open air replacing the domestic context. The tension between the domestic and public characters of marriage persists through into Christian practice, as also the drawing together of betrothal and marriage, so that the consent of the couple, implicit in the betrothal, and explicit in the contract, becomes an essential part of the marriage rite itself. Roman imperial law permitted local religious customs, as long as the consent of the partners was secured, a ruling that was taken over into medieval canon law.

The evidence of patristic authors indicates an increasing interest by church authorities in who marries whom. Ignatius of Antioch in his *Letter to Polycarp* declares that marriage should be contracted 'with the advice of the bishop, so that their marriage is made in the Lord'. Clement of Alexandria, who refers to the use of a ring at betrothal, advises brides not to wear wigs, since it is their real hair which is blessed during the marriage rite. In the apocryphal *Acts of Thomas*, which probably originates in third-century Syria, the apostle Thomas comes across a wedding, and he is asked to give a blessing, a lengthy prayer which ends with him laying his hands on the couple. The wearing of crowns, alluded to in Isa. 61.10, was widespread in other religions, and, while Tertullian attacks their use, they become standard in all later Eastern rites. Basil of Caesarea in the fourth century insists that marriage must take place in church, not at home, that it consists of two stages, betrothal and marriage, and that the blessing is an echo of Jesus at Cana, his presence with the couple. Augustine refers repeatedly to the marriage contract, in which the church is directly involved, quoting Gen. 1.28 (God blessing Adam and Eve and telling them to multiply), thereby teaching, like other early writers, that marriage is about procreation, as well as fidelity; he also alludes to the veiling of the bride, another ancient custom. From the evidence, there is no standard liturgy, rather hints of a gradual christianization of betrothal (contract and ring) and marriage customs (blessing, with crowning in the East) by the Christian community.

Selected texts in David G. Hunter, *Marriage in the Early Church*, Minneapolis 1992.

KENNETH W. STEVENSON

2. *Eastern Churches.* In all the liturgical rites of the Christian East the sacrament of matrimony is known as 'Crowning' or 'The Blessing of the Crown(s)', designating the central ritual of the ceremony. In their richness of symbol and ritual, and in the unabashed theological exuberance of their prayers and hymnology, the Eastern rites of matrimony stand out from the more restrained, sober nuptial rites of the West.

2.1. *Early Development.* Unlike other sacraments, matrimony was a purely civil affair in the early Christian centuries. In the Byzantine empire clerical participation at weddings was at first frowned upon, but then gradually met with increasing acceptance. The earliest surviving Byzantine euchology, ms. Barberini gr. 336 (mid-eighth century), contains a series of prayers that appear to frame a complete marriage ceremony including betrothal, nuptial crowning and joining of right hands, drinking from the 'common cup', and holy *communion. A rite of Christian marriage was therefore at least available, and possibly encouraged at this time. The church's blessing of marriage did not become obligatory in the Empire until the late ninth or early tenth centuries with the *Novella* of Emperor Leo VI (866–912). Almost two centuries earlier compulsory ecclesiastical marriage was legislated in Armenia, where Canon 15 of the Synod of Duin (719 CE) required that 'the priest . . . lead those who are to be crowned into the church and . . . conduct over them the order and canon according to Christian regulations'.

2.2. *General Characteristics.* All Eastern rites except the *East Syrian at one time distinguished a betrothal ceremony from the marriage or crowning service, though they all gradually fused the two into one joint ceremony. For the Byzantine rite this conjunction was completed by the eleventh century. Throughout the Christian East the rite of marriage is inscribed within the shape of the eucharistic liturgy of the *word. This substantiates other evidence suggesting that originally marriage found its liturgical context in either the full or *pre-sanctified eucharistic liturgy. Today, only the *Ethiopians consistently celebrate matrimony within the *eucharist.

2.3. *The Byzantine Rite.* Marriage in the Byzantine rite begins, as noted above, with the betrothal ceremony, which should take place in the *narthex of the church, and is marked by the exchange of engagement rings accompanied by a lengthy prayer of late composition. A declaration of nuptial consent is found in some late Greek euchologies, but only became universal in Slavic traditions as a result of the seventeenth-century Westernizing reforms of the Metropolitan of Kiev, Peter Moghila (d. 1647). The crowning itself takes place in the church, accompanied by three magnificent prayers that narrate salvation history from the perspective of the blessed unions through which it unfolded in time: Abraham and Sarah, Isaac and Rebecca, Jacob and Rachel, Joseph and Asenath, Zechariah and Elizabeth. By naming the bride and groom at the end of this sacred lineage, the couple is effectively grafted into salvation history as its most recent heirs and perpetuators. Thus the Byzantine rite, like the other Eastern rites, offers a decidedly soteriological dimension that is far less explicit in Western marriage rites. The principal nuptial prayers of the Armenian and Coptic rites are strikingly similar to the Byzantine.

A liturgy of the word follows (Eph. 5.20–33; John 2.1–11). Next come a presbyteral prayer and the *Lord's Prayer, sandwiched between two diaconal *litanies, all remnants of the preparatory rites that once led to holy communion. The eucharistic *chalice was originally the only one offered in the Byzantine marriage rite. By the tenth century, a second chalice was offered to the couple at the end of the service, this one a cup of ordinary wine. In time holy communion was suppressed, perhaps, among other factors, because of complications raised by inter-confessional marriages. It was replaced by the 'common' (*koinon*) cup of wine, now integrated into the service. The common cup is usually interpreted as a symbol of the couple's common life and the indissolubility of the marriage bond.

The *celebrant then leads the couple on a ritualized *procession three times around the *analogion* or *tetrapodion*, a small table placed in the *chancel. Although sometimes characterized as a 'liturgical dance' based on an allusion in the accompanying troparion and some manuscript *rubrics, this ritual actually seems to be a fairly late reduction of what was originally a procession to the home of the newly crowned couple for additional prayers and the wedding festivities. Traditionally the marriage crowns were removed at the home of the newly crowned eight days after the marriage ceremony, marking the end of a period of continence imposed out of reverence for the sacramental blessing of matrimony. This rite has also become fused to the marriage rite, accompanied by a prayer for fertility. A *dismissal *blessing concludes the ceremony.

Byzantine rites for second, and even third marriages developed after the tenth century, when the so-called *Henotikon* (920 CE) limited the number of times one can marry to three at most. The prayers contained in these rites have an unmistakable penitential tone.

2.4. *The Armenian Rite.* The *Armenian rite of crowning is characteristically eclectic, blending indigenous elements with usages from the Byzantine, East Syrian and Latin rites. As in all non-Byzantine Eastern rites, betrothal consists of the blessing of the bride's garments and jewellery, and the joining of the right hands of the bride and groom. In addition, the groom presents a ring to the bride, or perhaps originally, as in the East and West Syrian rites, a cross, as a sign of her betrothal. These rituals originally took place at the bride's home, but now occur in the church narthex. The crowning, still in the narthex, is followed by an admonitory oration by the priest and by a threefold interrogation concerning freedom of consent, presumably received, like other Latin usages, during Cilician Armenia's creative encounter with the Crusaders. Distinctive of the Armenian rite are the unusually generous OT lections in the liturgy of the word, which takes place in the chancel before the elevated bema. The sharing of a common cup of wine was appended under Byzantine influence after the tenth century.

2.5. *Coptic and Ethiopian Rites.* The *Coptic rite once included a nuptial *anointing of the bride and groom with olive oil before the crowning. The accompanying prayer is essentially apotropaic, but also asks for sanctification, purification, health and the fruit of good works. Bride and groom are draped in a white veil prior to crowning. The Ethiopian rite conforms substantially with the Coptic except that it preserves the eucharist as an essential component of the marriage rite.

2.6. *Greater Syria.* The Syrian rites are unparalleled in their exquisite elaboration, in prayers and opulent hymnography, of the Pauline 'mystery' of marriage as symbolic of the union of Christ and his church. The concept inspires sophisticated imagery, including a surprisingly graphic celebration of sexuality. The West Syrian rite prefaces the exchange of rings and crowning with an office for the Mother of God. The more concise and sober Maronite rite resembles the West Syrian, but displays late Latin influence, especially in the prominence given to questions of consent. It also underwent a certain Coptic influence through the *Nomocanon* of Ibn-al-Assal in the thirteenth century, adopting a rite of unction for the bride, groom and bridal party. The unction long ago fell out of use.

The expansive East Syrian rite boasts extensive psalmody and rich hymnody of diverse genres. Betrothal concludes with the *Hnana* ('mercy'), a chalice of water mixed with ashes or martyrs' relics that is blessed and consumed by the couple as a sort of nourishment for their nuptial union. Most interesting are the elaborate East Syrian rites for blessing the marriage bed and preparing the bridal chamber, which take place at the couple's home following the marriage. The hymns, diaconal proclamations and presbyteral prayers ask that God make the couple worthy to consummate their union, entreating God to 'surround them with the wall of your solicitude and the rampart of your mysterious love'.

O. H. E. Burmester, *The Egyptian or Coptic Church: A Detailed Description of her Liturgical Services and the Rites and Ceremonies Observed in the Administration of her Sacraments*, Cairo 1967, 128–42; Michael Findikyan, 'Old Testament Readings in the Liturgy of Matrimony of the Armenian Apostolic Orthodox Church', *St Vladimir's Theological Quarterly* XXXI, 1989, 86–93. John Meyendorff, *Marriage: An Orthodox Perspective*, Crestwood, NY 1975; Stefano Parenti, 'The Christian Rite of Marriage in the East', *Hand-*

book for Liturgical Studies, ed. Anscar J. Chupungco, IV, Collegeville 2000, 255–74.

M. DANIEL FINDIKYAN

3. *Medieval and Roman Catholic*. The evolution of the marriage liturgy through medieval Catholicism can be described as the Roman nuptial *mass with two types of additions; first of all, the blessing of the ring at the end of the *eucharist, and second, the displacement of that rite by the consent of the couple at the door of the church before the eucharist, which became the standard form after the Council of Trent, and which also lies behind the Anglican *BCP* tradition, albeit in simplified form. As always, there are other significant variants; the Visigothic rites of Spain in many respects resemble the East more than the West, with their elaborate forms for betrothal and marriage, and some of the late medieval German rites are non-eucharistic, and provide the inspiration for Luther's reforms.

The Roman Sacramentaries provide forms of nuptial mass, that is to say, a set of mass-prayers which includes a lengthy blessing of the bride between the *eucharistic prayer and the Peace. The standard form, in the Gregorian Sacramentary, calls the rite the 'veiling of the bride', even though there is no mention of veiling in the prayers; and whereas the actual mass-prayers pray for both the bride and the bridegroom, the blessing is exclusively for her, although there are some texts which pluralize the conclusion of the nuptial blessing. This Roman tradition contrasts with the Eastern rites where the prayers are for both partners, both of whom are crowned. There is a tendency to supplement the nuptial blessing with other blessings, of both partners, in local books. The gospel reading is usually Matt. 19.3–6, Jesus' teaching on the indissoluble nature of marriage.

Alongside the Sacramentaries there are local books which reflect a less formal, non-eucharistic context. One example is a tenth-century Pontifical attributed to Egbert of York, but probably Norman in origin and possibly reflecting practice from two centuries earlier. There are two rites, which consist of a series of short blessings, one of which also includes a blessing of the ring, now here definitely part of the marriage service. This rite was often added to the end of the nuptial mass, either to take place in church as its conclusion, or else, with other prayers, to take place at home afterwards. Sometimes there were blessings of the feast itself, as well as of the couple in the bedchamber afterwards.

From the twelfth century onwards, there is a rite of consent at the church door, the earliest example of which is to be found in the Bury St Edmunds rite (1125–35). Here, the priest asks the couple in the mother tongue if they want to be married, and the ring is blessed and given as part of this necessary preliminary. The need to accommodate the wedding party may be one of the reasons behind building church porches. After the procession into church to the accompaniment of Ps. 128, the nuptial mass followed, as well as the prayers at home afterwards. Two further additions to this basic shape come soon afterwards. One is to add further prayers for the couple after the rite of consent and the ring-giving, including such themes as angelic protection, a favourite in the later Middle Ages. The other is to expand the consent, from the fourteenth century onwards, so that in addition to being given passively ('I will'), it is also given actively ('I take thee . . .'); in this way, the marriage vow was born, the vernacular versions of which, whether in various forms of English or French, have their own rhythms. The Sarum Manual provided the version for the *BCP*, and much later, in the twentieth century, and in Latin translation, for the Roman *Ordo celebrandi matrimonium* (1969). These forms of consent and vow frequently included the promise by the bride to obey her husband, as in Sarum.

Many different strands come together in this process. For example, during the Romanization of the liturgy in the Empire of the Franks from the ninth century onwards, Visigothic customs persisted. These included prayers absorbed into the new composite rite before the mass, the giving of coins rather than the ring, and the practice of the priest, as *paterfamilias*, binding the couple together with a cord, and of giving the bride over to the man. And sometimes local rites include a short form of betrothal modelled on the rite of consent at the marriage itself, reflecting older practice (betrothal at engagement) but falling in line with wider developments (public consent immediately before the service). Moreover, the proper prayers at the nuptial mass are frequently those of the votive mass of the Trinity, an indication of a popular and festive occasion. Another north European custom in some places was to place a canopy over the couple during the nuptial blessing, an echo of Jewish practice. And, as if to add further variety to the theology of the rite in practice, various different formulas appear for the priest to say at the joining of the couple's hands; in England he says nothing, in Normandy he says 'I join you together', in Germany he 'solemnizes' the marriage.

After the Council of Trent, the two principal parts of the rite appear in a form more simple and austere than many of the services of the previous era. The Missal of 1570 provides the nuptial mass, with only one additional prayer at the end. The Ritual of 1614 provides a basic form of consent and ring-blessing, with the 'I join you together' formula. This was intended as an irreducible minimum, so that local customs could prevail. This they certainly did, in the most surprising ways; the Visigothic binding of the couple was taken by the Spanish into their imperial domains, including Mexico, where it was replaced by the lasso. But it highlighted too an inherent ambiguity in the rite: the consent of the partners is essential for the legality of the marriage, but the priest must also be there to recite the ratifying formula. Marriage is thus seen to be both a public and a private reality.

KENNETH W. STEVENSON

4. *Anglican.* There are three main eras in Anglican history. The first and initial period is marked by the English Prayer Books of 1549, 1552 and 1662; the second is the period of 'exporting' and adaptation, characterized by the American Prayer Books of 1789 and 1928; and the third is the period of ferment and creativity in the second part of the twentieth century, of which, not least for the marriage service, the American Prayer Book of 1979 is exemplary. The 1549 marriage rite is by far the most conservative of the Reformation; the Sarum Manual, on which it is based, was among the richest in medieval Europe, from which were extracted the essential ingredients, simplified and supplemented with new material from Germany. The three Prayer Books provide in essence the same rite, though (as one would expect) 1552 simplified 1549, in turn to be slightly enriched in 1662. The rite opens with a lengthy address, with the 'three reasons' for marriage (children, sexual union, companionship), leading into the consent, given, like Sarum, both passively ('I will') and actively, in the form of the vow (nearly all of which is Sarum). This whole section of address (with or without abbreviation), consent and vow was to prove of lasting influence outside Anglicanism. The ring-giving (without blessing) follows,

together with the declaration of marriage (using Matt. 19.6, from Luther), and prayers, based on medieval texts. The couple then process to the *altar during Ps. 128, and there follows an elaborate series of prayers, which are also based on the medieval rite, although the long prayer inspired by the Gregorian Sacramentary nuptial blessing is directed to both partners unambiguously throughout. The 1549 book intended that the *eucharist would immediately follow, but by 1662 this is a suggestion only.

The American Prayer Book of 1789 shortens the rite. The opening address omits the 'three reasons', concludes the service before the psalm, perhaps because there were no medieval *chancels to process through in North America, and the whole service can take place in the open air, reflecting a more mobile context than England. This simple version remained in use among American Episcopalians until 1928, when extra prayers were added from the old service, and a *collect and readings given for when a nuptial eucharist was celebrated, which was a mark of other revisions at the time. By this time, the promise of the bride to obey her husband, which had survived the Reformation into the *BCP*'s consent and vow, was coming under scrutiny; the American 1928 form omits it altogether, but it was to linger on in England, becoming optional in the revisions of 1980 and 2000. The American Prayer Book of 1979, following the lead taken by the RC Church in 1969, restructured the rite in a eucharistic shape. The collect and readings come between the consent and vows, thus making the latter more poignant, and the prayers for the couple and their blessing are distinguished from each other. A new feature is the question to the congregation for their support. Other revisions followed these new paths, including the Church of England's in *Common Worship* (2000).

KENNETH W. STEVENSON

5. *Baptist.* The Baptist insistence on separation from the state in matters of religion means that their marriage rites have legal effect only in so far as the state delegates powers to local congregations or ministers for the civil contract. Where this permission is not granted or sought, Baptists will offer a religious form of marriage only. Where the necessary powers are granted (or simply are not required) the rite of marriage will effect the legality of the marriage.

Of all services in which Baptists are involved, marriage rites are probably the ones they think of most sacramentally. They would see a clear transition in the celebrating partners from one status to another, and they would understand that transition to effect entry into sacred mysteries which are not properly legitimate to those who have not passed through the rite. Some Baptists, influenced by the Ecumenical Movement, would be willing to express the sacramental nature of marriage by the celebration of holy *communion. This is far from common, but it is not at all unknown. Marriage is also one of the services at which Baptists are most likely to use a liturgical *book, offering either a fully prescribed text or a pattern of service with any legally required formulae. Such texts are frequently derived from those of other Christian traditions.

The central elements of the marriage service remain as they have always been. Bride and groom declare that they are free to marry and promise to take one another as husband and wife, sealing their promises by the giving and receiving of rings. Hymns of praise for the gift of love are sung and prayers made for the couple and their families. But there are changes which reflect shifting social values. The old promise by the bride to obey her husband is less and less a preferred option. Many brides (and ministers, if not the brides' fathers!) now challenge the notion of being 'given away'. They argue that it is a relic of an age when a single woman was her father's (or other male guardian's) chattel to be passed as a piece of property into the care of another man.

While Baptists assert the Christian ideal of marriage as dissoluble only by death, they are prepared to marry those whose previous marriage has ended in divorce. This ambivalence is seen as showing both the covenantal nature of the marriage (an incarnated sign of Christ's covenant love for the church) and the willingness to offer a new start to those who have failed to meet that ideal in the past. Baptist willingness to permit the marriage of divorced persons is not to be understood as uncritical. Most congregations will leave the matter to the minister's discretion, while some will not countenance such remarriage at all. Where it is permitted, it inevitably means that those who would otherwise be married in other (more rigorist) churches approach the local Baptist minister on an ad hoc basis. This can introduce strains on ecumenical relationships and lead to accusations of schism.

Marriage is understood as the partnership of man and woman exclusively committed to one another in faith and love expressed in the joy of sexual intimacy and the stability of companionship. The solemnization of same-sex partnerships is not understood as marriage, and very few (if any) congregations indeed would expect or allow their ministers to officiate at same-sex weddings.

As sexual mores and social practices change, it can no longer be assumed that even those coming to their first marriage will not already be sexually active, if not cohabiting. The white wedding (a comparatively modern tradition) may become less common as couples choose less traditional services, or white may come to express not chastity but the *vestis candida* of *baptism.

In some parts of the world, Baptists (in common with others) are having to adapt marriage services to meet sociological and ecclesiological changes. Despite the existence of some well-documented super-congregations with many thousands attending, Baptists are predominantly a denomination of small churches. In many congregations there are few younger people of marriageable age. There is increased mobility of population. Such factors lead to young people looking beyond the congregation for their potential partners. Often young couples come from different religious traditions. Denominational allegiance can no longer be taken for granted; nor can a shared faith. Inter-church and inter-faith marriages are far more common than they were fifty years ago. Indeed, it is no longer certain that a couple coming to a Baptist minister will share any formal belief in God at all. In part this difficulty is eased where marriage is not seen as a church monopoly. Nonetheless, the old certainties can no longer be assumed. This entry began with a reference to Baptist understanding about the separation of church and state. Alongside this principle stands another – freedom of religious belief and practice. These tenets were formulated in a Europe where Muslims, Jews and Christians (not to mention Hindus, Buddhists and others) were unlikely to be commonly living on the same street. The regular possibility, indeed likelihood, of intermarriage was not then a practical consideration. Not the least of the changes facing Baptist understandings of marriage is to see how the lofty ideals of which our ancestors spoke translate into daily reality in the homes and lives of our contemporary people.

PAUL SHEPPY

6. *Christian Church*. The Christian Church

(Disciples of Christ) does not have an officially prescribed *book of worship. Local communities may develop their own theologies of marriage and their own marriage services. However, the theologies of marriage in congregations tend to reflect the dominant emphases of the churches participating in the Ecumenical Movement, including the liturgical renewal prompted by the Second Vatican Council. Local communities of the Christian Church (Disciples of Christ) hold few unusual beliefs with respect to marriage, nor do they engage in unusual Christian marriage practices.

Members of the Christian Church (Disciples of Christ) tend to think of marriage as a covenant. Divorce and remarriage do not interfere with lay participation in ecclesial community. The same is generally true for clergy, though occasional congregations are reluctant to call or continue a divorced pastor. This church has informally assumed that marriage between a man and woman would be the typical human state. However, congregations now typically honour the single life. Occasional congregations are exploring the theological appropriateness of unions between persons of the same gender.

Although the Christian Church (Disciples of Christ) does not authorize an official service book, the denominational publishing house makes available *Chalice Worship*, edited by Colbert Cartwright and O. I. Harrison (St Louis 1997), a book of services used in many congregations. This book contains two services of Christian marriage. The first is somewhat more formal. It begins when the congregation is seated in the worship space, and includes entrance, sentences of scripture, prayer, declaration of intent, affirmation of children, affirmation of the families, affirmation of the congregation, readings from the Bible, sermon, vows, exchange of rings, prayer, the *Lord's Prayer, candle lighting, announcement of marriage, charge, blessing, the breaking of the loaf, and blessing.

The second service is somewhat more informal. It begins in a gathering area outside the worship space as people mingle, hopefully establishing and re-establishing relationships. A call to worship takes place in the gathering area, with the congregation processing together into the worship space during a hymn of praise. After an opening statement, the service continues with three main parts: (a) celebration of the word through Bible reading, musical response, and sermon; (b) the making of

the covenant (involving the couple, families, the community), the rings, prayer, and the announcement of marriage; (c) the breaking of the loaf. The service concludes with a hymn of dedication and a blessing.

Chalice Worship also contains materials for an engaged couple, a wedding anniversary and the blessing of friendship. The volume does not contain liturgical materials specifically designed for the occasions of separation or divorce, nor for solemnizing the union of persons of the same gender.

_____

David M. Greenhaw and Ronald J. Allen (eds), *Preaching in the Context of Worship*, St Louis 2000, 103–7; Clark M. Williamson and Ronald J. Allen, *Adventures of the Spirit: A Guide to Worship from the Perspective of Process Theology*, St Louis 1997, 229–40.

RONALD J. ALLEN

7. *Congregationalist*. The Congregational view of marriage owes, in its origin, something to the Puritan and Separatist inclination to regard marriage as a civil ceremony. The Separatist John Greenwood, for example, is recorded as saying at his trial (1589), 'Neither is marriage a part of the minister's office.' This is not to say that marriage was without religious significance. Greenwood certainly prayed at a wedding, conducted in a private home, where the couple signified their consent, on which grounds they were considered married. What is more, the Congregational emphasis on the Covenant was reflected in both engagement (betrothal) and marriage wherein the couple gave themselves to each other. Robert Browne, for example, wrote in 1582, 'Betrothing is a covenant between the parties to be married, whereby they give their troth that they will and shall marry together . . . Espousing is a covenant between them, whereby they are pronounced before witnesses, to give themselves, and to be given each to other to become husband and wife.' There was, though, no inclination to devise wedding services, and indeed there was opposition to set forms of service, and in particular to the giving of a ring, which was held to be unscriptural and to reflect an RC understanding of the ring as the sign of a sacrament. The words 'with my body I thee worship' were held to be idolatrous.

After the Marriage Act in 1754, it was not possible to conduct a wedding in a Dissenting chapel, and indeed only the church wedding, not the verbal espousals in front of witnesses, was legally binding. By 1835, the Board of Congregational Ministers was arguing for a civil contract for those who desired it and a religious ceremony appropriate to the convictions of Dissenters, alongside one for Anglicans. Following the repeal of the Act in 1836, Congregational ministers, being now allowed to conduct weddings in chapels, for want of any other form, tended to adapt the order and words of the *BCP*.

Such liturgical borrowing has continued to the present day, both in the UK and in the USA, where the *Congregational Worshipbook* by Henry David Gray (Phoenix, AZ 1978) included three orders for marriage and an order for an engagement service. One of the orders for marriage offers the possibility of a 'charge' to the couple after the ceremony itself. In the UK, the service books of 1920 (*Book of Congregational Worship*) and 1936 (*Manual for Ministers*) described 'marriage as ordained of God as the sacrament of human society'. This reflected a liberal interpretation of the term *sacrament, rather than a particularly high view of marriage. The separation of marriage from the sacraments of *baptism and *communion was made clear in the 1959 *Book of Services and Prayers*, which was in some ways a reaction against liberalizing tendencies.

Throughout the twentieth century Congregationalists retained a pattern which included the following elements: a statement of the purposes of marriage, particularly emphasizing companionship and explaining that in marriage God adds his seal to the relationship; scripture reading; a declaration of no impediment; an exchange of promises and the vow of marriage; giving of a ring or rings if desired, as a sign of the promises; the declaration of marriage; prayers for the couple and intercession for the world; and the singing of hymns. It has become increasingly common to include a sermon in the wedding service, and one of the two orders in the Congregational Federation's *Patterns for Worship* by Richard Cleaves and Michael Durber (Nottingham 1992) places the marriage after a service of the *word.

R. Tudur Jones, *Congregationalism in England, 1662–1962*, London 1962.

MICHAEL DURBER

8. *Lutheran*. For Luther and for the emerging church that came to bear his name, marriage was a universal human institution, an 'order of creation', and therefore not an exclusively ecclesiastical concern. Luther wrote in 1529, 'Since marriage and the married estate are worldly matters, it behooves us pastors or ministers of the church not to attempt to order or govern anything connected with it, but to permit every city and land to continue its own use and custom . . .' Moreover, in the sixteenth century marriage rites and laws were still developing. Increasingly, however, church authorities, both catholic and evangelical, resisted secret marriages and insisted on the free consent of both partners in the marriage. Such a declaration had become a central element of church marriage since the seventh century.

8.1. *Early Rites*. Showing the secular understanding of marriage, the practice of the marriage taking place in the church porch, where legal contracts were ratified (first reported in the early twelfth century in Normandy), was still the custom in Germany at the Reformation. The presiding officer was often a layman, sometimes with the priest as a witness. This location at the door of the principal public building of the town, usually facing the town square, indicated the dual audience for what was taking place: in the sight of God and in view of the community.

Evangelical marriage rites frequently adapted the use of the local RC diocese. The oldest evangelical marriage rite, attributed to Bugenhagen, comes from 1524 at Wittenberg. After an address based on Gen. 1—3, which ever after serve as a kind of words of institution of marriage comparable to the *institution narrative of the *eucharist, the free consent is elicited ('N., will you have N. to be your wedded wife/husband according to God's ordinance?'), rings are exchanged, and the pastor, following a use common in various parts of Germany before the Reformation, pronounces them husband and wife in the name of the Holy Trinity. A form developed in Strasbourg, printed in 1525, regarded the blessing of marriage as a confirmation of the exchange of vows the couple had made.

Luther reluctantly provided a marriage order in 1529. He followed the Wittenberg order but also incorporated medieval forms and early church traditions. The rite consisted of three parts: (a) the banns, a public announcement primarily to request prayers and secondarily to discover impediments; (b) the betrothal at the church door (declaration of consent is elicited, rings are exchanged, and the pastor pronounces them married using Matt. 19.6); and (c) a day or more after the betrothal and after the consummation of the marriage, the blessing before the *altar in the church involving scripture readings (Gen. 2.18, 21–24; Eph. 5.25–29, 22–24; Gen 3.16–19; 17.27–28, 31; Prov. 18.33) and a prayer of blessing with hands outstretched over the bride and groom.

By the end of the sixteenth century there was a clear tendency to regard the church ceremony, rather than the betrothal, as the constitutive act by which the marriage was accomplished. By the seventeenth century the questions had become more imperative, and the couple promised love, fidelity and support for each other 'until death parts us'. In the eighteenth century church marriage became a legal act which the church performed on behalf of the state. In the nineteenth century in Europe an obligatory civil ceremony was introduced.

8.2. *Modern Practice*. In North America as in Europe, marriage rites of recent centuries have built upon Luther's order and have consistently declared by scripture and liturgical text God's institution of marriage, the cross of adversity which falls upon those joined in marriage, and God's abundant grace and support. Lutheran rites generally preserved both the betrothal questions and the more recent addition of the marriage vows, often in language modelled on the *BCP*.

Pastors have for some generations been careful to teach that marriage in a church is a service of worship in which the congregation ought to participate. Thus, it is significant that in the present North American rite (1978), composed with RC practice as well as that of the Episcopal Church in view, the marriage rite follows the pattern of the eucharist. The apostolic greeting (2 Cor. 13.14) begins the service; lessons and sermon are optional but almost invariably at least the lessons are included; an address to the couple and congregation follows setting forth the traditional themes. The declaration of intent has been folded into the promise of fidelity, the question 'Do you intend . . . ?' already having been implicitly answered in the joint appearance of the bride and groom. Rings are exchanged, and the pastor 'announces' (not 'pronounces') the marriage, since the bride and groom by the exchange of their vows have accomplished the marriage. A brief nuptial blessing and three prayers (of thanksgiving for God's gifts, for the couple in their life together, and for all the families of the world) follow. Provision is made, for the first time in a North American Lutheran rite, for the celebration of the eucharist, continuing with the peace and the *offertory. The long-standing objections to medieval distortions of the mass have faded, and the drafters of the *Lutheran Book of Worship* discovered and understood how marriage and the eucharist mutually enrich the imagery of the other and accepted what had become the practice in many parishes even in the absence of official liturgical provision. A newly composed proper *preface and postcommunion prayer are provided. Opening to other traditions of the human family, rubrics allow for the use of garlands or, as in Eastern Orthodox churches, crowns as signs of the gladness of marriage.

———

Martin Luther, 'The Order of Marriage for Common Pastors' (1529), *Luther's Works* LIII, Philadelphia 1965, 110–15; Philip H. Pfatteicher, *Commentary on the Lutheran Book of Worship*, Minneapolis 1990 (bib.); *Commentary on the Occasional Services*, Philadelphia 1983.

PHILIP H. PFATTEICHER

9. *Methodist*. Among the rites included in John Wesley's *Sunday Service of the Methodists in North America* (1784) was a 'Form of Solemnization of Matrimony' based upon the marriage liturgy in the Church of England's 1662 *BCP*. Wesley eliminated *rubrics that assumed an established church and the performance of the rite in a church building. The psalms and the concluding exhortation on marital duties disappeared (probably for brevity's sake), as did the concluding rubric on receiving *communion along with references to the Lord's table; the latter omissions effectively dealt with concerns about unprepared reception and indiscriminate distribution of the *sacrament. All references to the ring are gone, as is the giving away of the bride – two changes not commonly shared with other eighteenth-century proposals for revision of the *BCP*, and unfortunately Wesley provides no explanation for their deletion. Removal of the ring did address the perennial Puritan nervousness about the wedding band as an object of superstition, and complied with Methodist scruples regarding needless ornamentation. Because he vehemently objected to slavery, Wesley may have disapproved of the ring and the 'giving' as traditional signs of bride purchase.

Instructions about matrimony were also found among the rules and regulations of the

Minutes or the *Discipline* authorized in Britain and in America during the eighteenth century. Methodist marriages with unbelievers were prohibited, as were marriages undertaken without the consent of the woman's parents. The duration of these two restrictions through the nineteenth century and beyond varied among members of the Methodist family, with some Holiness and African-American Methodists retaining them into the twenty-first century. As cultural attitudes toward divorce gradually relaxed, Methodists added new regulations recognizing only 'scriptural divorce' (in cases of adultery). The Methodist branches in subsequent generations dealt in different ways with the issue of divorce, though none of them has ever condoned it.

In 1792, the American Methodists excised the three stated purposes of marriage (including the 'indelicate' subject of procreation) from the opening address. The *Kyrie, versicles, and prayer for childbearing vanished. The exchange of 'these thy servants' in the prayers for a more general 'this man and this woman' attests that the rite was used for couples whose depth of Christian faith and practice could not easily be verified by an itinerating minister. With subsequent revisions, Wesley's text was pared back further as prayers were dropped or altered. After several attempts at removal, the reference to Isaac and Rebecca was eventually deleted from the prayer 'O Eternal God' because of questions whether theirs was truly an exemplary marriage; British Methodists, for similar reasons, substituted Zachariah and Elisabeth for the patriarchal pair. Both long-time customs and new perspectives from the ambient culture influenced changes in some American Methodist denominations. Rubrics and actions with the ring became, in the 1860s, part of the official texts of the largest Methodist episcopal churches; a double ring ceremony was later approved. Even though the woman's promise to 'obey' and 'serve' fell out as early as 1864 from a Methodist rite, in the early twentieth century the giving of the bride (now understood solely as a 'traditional' practice) came into Methodist ritual texts.

Marriage ceremonies among the larger Methodist denominations in Britain were celebrated according to the *BCP* rite or from Wesley's *Sunday Service* (or a conservative revision of the 1792 text) with the text and performance modified to conform to legal requirements. Smaller denominations composed new rites with little connection to the Anglican text

and in a style more characteristic of extemporary prayer. The rite of the Wesleyan Conference produced in 1882 restored many of the components deleted by Wesley – giving away the bride, rings, psalms, and concluding exhortation – and also added legally necessary declarative and contracting words, and rubrics for hymn singing. The prayer for childbearing was, however, absent.

British and American marriage services from the first half of the twentieth century contained new prayers that emphasized family and the 'hallowing of the home', undoubtedly in response to escalating divorce rates. The covenantal aspects of marriage were stressed in the revisions undertaken in the 1960s and 1970s. For the first time in an approved Methodist marriage rite, the Methodist Church in Britain in 1975 presented a full service of the *word and an option for the *eucharist. Some Methodist worship books in use at the turn into the twenty-first century provide orders based on a Sunday-morning model that locate the marriage covenant within the context of the baptismal covenant. Texts for the blessing of a marriage previously solemnized are also available.

Karen B. Westerfield Tucker, *American Methodist Worship*, New York 2000, 176–98.

KAREN B. WESTERFIELD TUCKER

10. *Old Catholic*. In the Old Catholic churches, marriage is regarded as one of the sacraments. There are two different concepts prevalent among these churches. Some, in particular those in German-speaking countries (Germany, Switzerland, to a lesser degree Austria) and in the Czech Republic, used to follow exclusively the notion of the secular Roman law, that it is the couple themselves who bestow the sacrament upon themselves by exchanging the vows. Others, in particular the church in the Netherlands and the Polish National Catholic Church in the USA and Canada, teach that the sacrament is established by the presiding minister (*bishop, priest, [*deacon]) invoking God's blessing upon the couple, in this way more closely following the tradition of early Christianity and the Eastern churches. In the churches that used to see marriage established exclusively through the exchange of the consent, a rethinking has taken place to the effect that the blessing of the couple by praising God's grace in creation and redemption and by asking God to bless the lives of the wife and

husband together is at least as important for marriage as the exchange of the vows. This is a move away from the static understanding of the sacrament as being irrevocably established at the moment of the exchange to a view in which marriage is seen as a lifelong process of husband and wife trying to live together as a Christian couple should.

Consequently, modern revisions of the liturgy of marriage have intensified the *epicletic character of the celebration. *Collects and forms of blessing pray that the Holy Spirit may be at work in the life of the couple and be with them for strength and witness. The Dutch and German liturgies provide for the *Veni creator Spiritus* or another hymn to the Holy Spirit to be sung prior to the exchange of the vows. The blessing forms have been much inspired by (or even been translated from) Anglican texts (e.g. the Episcopal Church in the USA and the Church of Aotearoa/New Zealand and Polynesia). The hitherto prevalent notion of the life of the couple as reflecting the relationship between Christ as head and the church as his bride has not received as much attention in the latest revisions as was the case before.

The different forms of the marriage liturgy are composed of the same elements in all the churches: address to the couple or invitatory prayer, exchange of the vows (either by saying the word 'Yes' or by using the forms common in the Anglophone countries), blessing and giving of the rings, mutual joining of the hands, blessing of the couple. Often, but not exclusively, the marriage is part of the celebration of the *eucharist. All the Old Catholic churches recognize a civil marriage as a legitimate contract of marriage but do not regard it as having the same sacramental dimension as a marriage (established and) blessed in church.

Although not regarding it in any respect as a marriage liturgy, the celebration of the blessing of same-sex couples has been officially established in the Austrian Old Catholic Church and is being done in the Dutch and German churches as well; official liturgical forms have been, or are being, established in those churches.

THADDEUS A. SCHNITKER

11. *Pentecostal.* Pentecostal marriage services tend to be diverse. However, upon close inspection, one can identify several common theological concerns that are influenced by an understanding of the divine will for marriage. These concerns find expression in the homily that occurs at the heart of most Pentecostal wedding ceremonies. This message allows the Pentecostal preacher to bear witness to Christ to the general audience and to impress on the wedding party final words of instruction or encouragement about Christian marriage. In addition to the homily, Pentecostals tend to be eclectic in their order of service, though, as we will see, certain common characteristics in the typical order of service may be noted.

The ministers' manuals for the Assemblies of God, Church of God, Cleveland, Tennessee and the Church of God in Christ (*see* **Books, Liturgical** 11) reveal that Pentecostal wedding homilies tend to emphasize the following theological concerns. First, they emphasize the sacredness of marriage. They base this belief on what they hold to be three scriptural truths.

(a) The Genesis creation of man and woman as one flesh (Gen. 2.24) embodies one such truth. This text implies that God instituted the rite of marriage as something holy which would serve as the basis for the stability of family and society. A Pentecostal wedding service will usually include some statement alluding to God's institution of marriage in the Genesis creation story. According to one example service, marriage 'is the first and oldest rite of the world, celebrated in the worlds beginning before God, the Creator, himself, sole witness, guest and priest' (Zeno C. Tharp, *The Ministers' Guide for Special Occasions*, Cleveland, TN 1953, 20).

(b) Pentecostals will usually mention that Jesus blessed the rite of marriage with his participation in the wedding celebration at Cana (John 2.1–2). They find it 'not without significance that he chose this occasion to begin his miracles when he turned the water into wine' (William Pickthorn, *Minister's Manual*, Springfield, MO 1965, II, 16). Jesus' participation reached beyond his mere presence at the celebration. His miracle ensured the continuance of the celebration and symbolized his blessing on the rite of marriage.

(c) Pentecostals believe that the sacredness of marriage is set forth in the writings of Paul. Accordingly, they find it significant that, in Eph. 5.22–33, Paul would select 'the symbol of husband and wife as an apt emblem of the union that binds together Christ himself and his own blood-bought, ransomed church' (*Minister's Manual*). According to the Pentecostals, all of the above texts serve to undergird the sacredness of marriage as a God-ordained institution at the base of family and society.

Second, Pentecostals are concerned about the authority structure within marriage as a significant factor in its stability. For Pentecostals, the texts discussed above not only imply the sacredness of the rite of marriage, but also describe the order of authority in the relationship between the husband and wife within the marriage. For them, the Ephesians passage and the Genesis creation story set forth the social position of the man and the woman, in the home, the church and the society. Among most Pentecostals, the man is created by God to have authority over the woman. In the context of marriage, the husband is the head of the family as Christ is head of the church. Marriage founded in the teaching of scripture thus models the hierarchical order of creation as well as the subordination of the church to Christ. There are Pentecostals, however, who would call male authority into question and would seek a partnership model of marriage as opposed to a hierarchical understanding.

Third, Pentecostals will commonly seek to inspire couples in the wedding ceremony to guard against the dangers of divorce. Because Pentecostals believe in the divine institution of marriage, they also believe that divorce is contrary to the will of God. Most Pentecostal denominations base this position on scripture and a concern for society. Because divorce breaks up the family, the most basic unit of society, it damages society. Pentecostals see divorce and same-sex marriages as contributing to the moral failure of society. As for the church itself, most Pentecostal denominations would discourage divorce. Ministers are discouraged from divorcing their spouses or even performing wedding ceremonies where one or both parties are divorced. In the Assemblies of God, a divorced clergyperson may continue to hold papers unless she/he decides to remarry. Upon remarrying, the church will revoke the minister's papers because they will consider the divorce and remarriage as possibly damaging to the minister's witness to the moral ideal of remaining faithful to only one spouse for the life of that spouse. There is also the possibility of the minister committing adultery by remarrying if the divorce is not due to the unfaithfulness of the spouse (Matt. 19.2). Such restrictions apply to *deacons as well. Pentecostal denominations, like the Church of God, Cleveland, Tennessee, and the United Pentecostal Church, consider divorced and remarried ministers who want to hold papers on a case-by-case basis. Although some Pentecostal denominations make this exception, divorce is still considered to be contrary to the will of God, and damaging to society.

Pentecostal ministers do not follow any specific order when planning a wedding service. According to Tharp, 'the minister has the right to use his own arrangement and often uses portions of several to form one of his own liking' (12). Although Pentecostals tend to be eclectic in their service planning, drawing from sample services, tradition and local custom, various ministers' manuals suggest that their order of service tends to include certain common characteristics. All of the manuals include examples from Episcopal wedding ceremonies. With the exception of the manual for the Church of God in Christ, they also include sample services written either by the editor or by other ministers. That manual recommends the following service order: special music (bridal procession), the introduction to the marriage ceremony, a prayer, the scripture reading (Ps. 128), the vows, the ring service, the declaration of marriage, a prayer, the *Lord's Prayer (congregation and minister), the blessings and the special music (bridal recession). Tharp includes a simple ceremony which may be committed to memory. It begins with a brief introductory statement explaining why the guests have gathered together, followed by the homily, the vows, the declaration of marriage and the final blessing. A more recent manual by Clyne W. Buxton, *Minister's Service Manual* (Cleveland, TN 1999) includes sample ceremonies for informal weddings, home weddings and the renewal of vows. The sample services included in all these manuals are diverse in order, and only serve as recommendations for the pastor to follow.

MICHAEL D. MACCHIA

12. *Reformed*. By the time of the Reformation, marriage had made its way from what was formerly a civic ceremony firmly into the liturgical and sacramental life of the medieval church. The early Reformed churches did not reject churchly marriage ceremonies but sought to correct and purify them according to their own theological ideas

12.1. *Calvin's Rite*. Not surprisingly, it is Calvin's Genevan marriage service (found in *The Form of Prayers*, 1542) that has most influenced the practice of the Reformed churches, although Calvin's service was by no means original with him. It borrowed heavily from several sources, most notably from

Farel's *La manière et fasson* (1533). Calvin's service followed established custom in calling for the proclamation of the banns of marriage to be made in public worship several times before the day of the ceremony. The banns, an announcement of the couple's intent to marry, allowed persons in the community to challenge the upcoming marriage should there be cause (Were either party already married? Of low moral character?). The service itself was conducted as a part of regular Lord's Day worship (though probably not on *Communion Sundays) and was inserted in the service just before the sermon.

The service opened with a long scripturally based exhortation, drawn largely from Gen. 1 and 1 Cor. 7, on the nature of marriage as ordained by God in creation and on the moral virtues and responsibilities of marriage. The exhortation was followed by the first of two sets of vows, the betrothal vows, in which the bride and groom declared their willingness, freedom and intent to be married. Then, after the congregation was given one last challenge to state any lawful impediments to the marriage, the couple exchanged their marriage vows. The man promised to love, protect and to be loyal and faithful to his wife. The woman promised to be loyal, faithful, obedient, and to live in subjection to her husband. Both vows were made 'according to the Word of God and the holy gospel'. The ceremony concluded with the minister giving a brief charge to the couple, based upon the reading of Matt. 19.3–6 (' . . . what God has joined together let no one separate'), a marriage prayer, and a blessing.

Several features of Calvin's service demonstrate the impact of Reformed theology on the marriage rite. Marriage was described as a sign of grace, a gift from a bountiful God, but not as a *sacrament. The presiding minister did not 'perform the marriage' or execute any sacramental action, but rather 'confirmed' the action of the Holy Spirit forming the marriage bond. The service was governed by scripture, conducted within the context of the church's public worship, and it was spare and simple, shorn of any word or action (such as the exchange of rings) that could connect it to what Calvin viewed as the superstitions of the priesthood and the medieval mass.

12.2. *Later Rites*. At one level, the basic pattern and themes of Calvin's service have endured in subsequent Reformed marriage rites. At another level, however, three forces have worked to reshape those services: cultural accommodation, the Ecumenical Movement, and new theological understandings of marriage. In terms of cultural accommodation, from the very beginning the simple, biblically focused impulses of the Reformed service have always been in tension with cultural fashion. For example, Calvin's service was to be held on the Lord's Day, but an early trend toward un-Sabbath-like post-nuptial parties meant that, only a century after Calvin, *The Westminster Directory for Worship* (1645) was forced to advise that weddings be held on any day *but* Sunday! Reformed weddings today often feature processions, unity candles, secular songs and poems, and other ornaments that were hardly countenanced in Calvin's day and that sometimes clash with the central theological themes of the service. Moreover, in a time when marriage licences are routinely issued by the state, the charge to the congregation to announce any legal impediments to the marriage has all but disappeared from the marriage service.

Ecumenical conversation has encouraged heavy borrowing from other Christian liturgical traditions. The marriage service in John Knox's *Genevan Service Book* (1556), while closely following the Calvin predecessor, already showed some dependence upon the Anglican *BCP*, and modern Reformed marriage rites include elements from numerous sources – Protestant, RC, and Orthodox.

New theological understandings of marriage have resulted in a number of changes in current Reformed marriage rites. There is now a greater focus on the idea of marriage as a covenant between the partners and on the concept of marriage as an expression of a Christian's baptismal vocation. The theme of childbearing, often present in older marriage services, has been softened in favour of an emphasis upon the loving relationship, mutual accountability and forgiveness needed in marriage, and marriage as the environment for the expression of justice and compassion. The man and the woman are now understood as equal partners, and the older asymmetrical vows with language calling for the woman to obey and to be subject to her husband have been replaced with vows having the same wording for the bride and the groom. A late medieval addition to the marriage service, the 'giving away' of the bride by her father, has now mainly been eliminated from current Reformed practice, often replaced by a mutual pledge of support for the couple by their families and the whole congregation. The language of many modern Reformed services has been adjusted to acknowledge the fact that Christians often marry persons outside their own faith tradition.

THOMAS G. LONG

Martyrium

A site that is evidence of ('bears witness' to) the Christian faith especially through the suffering and death of the martyrs. The multiplicity of martyrial forms had a considerable later architectural influence. Following pagan heroes' shrines, open-air (sometimes underground) martyrial enclosures were developed before the Edict of Milan (313), the earliest probably being that of St Peter on Vatican Hill. During the fourth century monumental structures were built, notably the cemetery *basilicas on roads out of Rome and Constantine's basilica over Peter's tomb. Fourth-century and later building at the Palestinian holy places accommodated to the realities of each site, though a complex of *atrium, *aedicule* and basilican *catholicon* were often provided at what were, from the outset, pilgrim churches. Sites in Asia Minor, northern Africa and central Europe were also developed.

A. Grabar, *Martyrium*, 2 vols, Paris 1943–6; Richard Krautheimer, *Early Christian and Byzantine Architecture*, London 1965, 4th edn, 1986; *Rome: Profile of a City 312–1308*, London 1980; P. Walker, *Holy City, Holy Places?* Oxford 1990 (bib.).

JONATHAN GOODALL

Mass

The Latin word *missa* was first used by Western Christians to refer to the *dismissal of a group of people within an act of worship (see, e.g., Augustine, *Serm.* 49.8; John Cassian, *Inst.* 11.16), but it was later extended to refer to other liturgical units. In the monastic traditions of Gaul and Spain, it could denote an element that was repeated a number of times within a rite: thus Caesarius of Arles in his monastic rules speaks of a variable number of *missae* in the course of the night, each made up of three readings, three prayers and three psalms. It was also used to describe a complete liturgical rite, as occasionally in the *Pilgrimage of Egeria* (42; 43.3); and later, in the sixth century, it developed in the West into a technical term specifically for the *eucharist.

Distinctions came to be made between 'high' and 'low' mass. The term 'high mass', which translates the Latin *missa sollemnis*, denoted a sung celebration of the eucharist at which the presiding minister (*bishop or *presbyter) was assisted by other ministers, including a *deacon and a *subdeacon, who fulfil the liturgical functions proper to their orders, and at which *incense was also used. By contrast, a 'low mass' was the simpler form of celebration adopted when other ministers, except perhaps for a *server, were unable to be present and the *celebrant was therefore obliged to fulfil their functions as well as his own. It was said and not sung, and was in practice the form of service most familiar to Western congregations for hundreds of years. A 'private mass' was, as its name implies, a low mass celebrated without the presence of a congregation. These distinctions have largely disappeared in modern RC practice, where the office of subdeacon has been abolished, where singing may, and should, take place at every kind of mass, and incense may or may not be used according to choice.

EDITOR

Matins, Mattins *see* Daily Prayer

Maundy Thursday

The Thursday before *Easter is referred to as either Holy Thursday or Maundy Thursday in the Christian tradition. In late antiquity, there were several elements that shaped the liturgical celebrations of that day, some of which originated in fourth-century Jerusalem. The final preparation of *catechumens for *baptism and the reconciliation of those enrolled in the 'order' of penitents in the public rite of canonical *penance before the great feast of Easter were two important factors. Others included the afternoon celebration of the *eucharist to close the pre-paschal *fast of the day, and a second eucharist in the evening to commemorate the Last Supper in the upper room. In Rome, the eucharist to close the fast was celebrated in the smaller presbyteral *tituli* as was the later eucharist commemorating the Last Supper. The *papal liturgy of Thursday included the rites for the reconciliation of public penitents, as well as the papal blessing of holy oils, including chrism for baptism, at the evening eucharist of the Last Supper. From this complex of liturgies, the medieval Western church came to mark Maundy Thursday with one eucharistic celebration, that of the *Lord's supper, during which the consecration of oils could be added by the presiding *bishop.

By the seventh century, this evening mass was also marked by a characteristic ritual action: the *foot-washing, or *mandatum* ('commandment'; see John 13.34) as it is sometimes called. During the medieval period, the presiding bishop, abbot or priest, in imitation of Christ's humble service of his disciples at the Last Supper (John 13.3–20), would wash the feet of a number of clerics or paupers; frequently, a gift of *alms was also distributed. In England, this came to be known as Maundy money, and Thursday itself as Maundy Thursday (Maundy being a corruption of *mandatum*).

In antiquity, the celebration of the afternoon eucharist of Thursday marked the end of *Lent, while the evening eucharist, celebrated after sundown, was considered to be a part of the Easter Triduum. Through the medieval period and in Western churches today, this evening mass is the last celebration of the eucharist before that of the *Easter vigil. Since the medieval liturgy of *Good Friday called for the distribution of *communion from the reserved sacrament, other ceremonies developed to mark the action of removing these consecrated *hosts from the main church to a place of *reservation or reposition for Friday and Saturday. One was a formal procession to this special *altar or repository, often allegorized as Christ's tomb. This procession is still part of the Holy Thursday liturgy of some Western churches, e.g. Roman Catholicism. Another medieval practice, the ritual burial or entombment of consecrated hosts or a special *cross in a special location or vessel, has fallen into disuse. Yet another practice, which endures in the RC tradition to this day, is the adoration of the reserved sacrament at its place of reservation for the period of Christ's burial in the tomb (the Forty Hours' Devotion). Finally, this set of ritual actions was completed by the ritual stripping of the altars of the church, including removal of the altar linens, altar *candles and any other decoration, combined with the ritual washing of the main altar of the church with water and wine. The stripping of the altar remains part of RC practice, although the washing of the altar has been dropped (*see* **Altar, Stripping of; Altar, Washing of**).

The final liturgy of Holy Thursday, which also developed in the medieval period and can still be found in the RC tradition today, is that of *tenebrae, held later on Thursday night. It is not a eucharistic service, but rather is based on the morning office of matins. The psalmody of the service, accompanied by the gradual extinguishing of several candles, expresses the emotions of sorrow and mourning, emotions that will mark the services of Good Friday and the silence of *Holy Saturday until the beginning of the Easter vigil.

Today in the RC tradition, a separate chrism mass is celebrated, often during the mid-afternoon in cathedral churches, while the evening mass of the Lord's supper is held in all parishes, including the *mandatum* and the renewal of priestly vows.

For bibliography, *see* **Holy Week**.

JOANNE M. PIERCE

Media, Worship on the

Broadcast worship is the longest running strand of continuous programming in the history of radio and television. Two distinct approaches have characterized the transmission of acts of worship.

1. *Broadcast Technology as a Simple Conduit of Communication.* This allows listeners and viewers access to a church service that would in any case be taking place in the usual way. The first experimental broadcast service was conducted by the Revd Dick Sheppard from the church of St Martin-in-the-Fields in London in January 1924. Televising the funeral service of a head of state such as President John F. Kennedy or the broadcast of a royal wedding in the UK can command huge audiences around the world, but essentially the liturgy is independent of the vicarious involvement of the listener and viewer. To a degree this is also true of the regular weekly transmission of church services. In the case of a celebration of the *eucharist there is clearly a point where the listener and viewer are excluded from the act of 'holy communion' which has led some critics to contend that broadcast worship utterly distorts the religious experience.

What is taken for granted today as a regular broadcast act of worship was met in its infancy by suspicion and resistance on the part of some churches. The Dean and Chapter of St Paul's Cathedral in London refused a request in 1926 to broadcast choral evensong on the grounds that it would deplete Sunday congregations throughout the land. Today choral evensong, transmitted every week on BBC Radio Three, is among the most popular programmes of that classical music network in the UK.

Regular weekly broadcasts of church services continue to feature in the Sunday schedules of both Independent Television and BBC Radio channels in the UK. They were originally conceived to meet the spiritual needs of the housebound, the sick and elderly people. As such they had a strong pastoral motivation which is now used to justify their place in the schedules as part of the public-service responsibility of broadcasters even in a multicultural society. By contrast, church services in the USA and in other parts of the world might be broadcast by overtly Christian radio and television stations dedicated to explicit evangelism which can create a virtual church with no existence outside the air waves.

Broadcast worship, even in multi-faith societies, has been largely Christian. It may not always be so but some religions see no reason for their worship to be broadcast. The Jewish faith, for example, regards the proper focus of worship to be either in the home with the family or in the synagogue with the gathered community. In terms of legitimate worship anything else is simply private prayer and personal devotion.

2. *An Act of Worship Devised Solely for the Benefit of the Listener or Viewer*. Particularly in the UK, this evolved independently of the church. On 2 January 1928 the BBC broadcast the first of an experimental series of 'short religious services'. The public response was over seven thousand letters of appreciation and the fifteen-minute *Daily Service* has been a feature of BBC network radio ever since. Broadcast originally from a radio studio, it was devised as a simple daily office comprising a sentence of scripture, a hymn, a prayer, a Bible reading, psalmody, *intercessions and thanksgivings, a closing hymn and blessing. In the course of time this simple broadcast service pioneered many developments in the wider church. From the outset it was non-denominational and established *ecumenical worship. It introduced new hymns and music to a wider audience and explored more flexible forms of prayer. Women as well as men led the service at a time when liturgical ministry was largely the domain of the male gender. It gave rise to a service book of prayers, *New Every Morning*, which sold eight thousand copies within three weeks of publication in 1936. To accompany the service the *BBC Hymn Book* was published

in 1950 and a supplement of new hymns was included in *Broadcast Praise* published in 1981.

Radio is an intimate medium of communication. Though the presenter may in fact be addressing many thousands of people, in truth the speaker is talking to only one, be that a man in his garden or a woman driving to work. Radio has the potential capacity to draw the individual into that very personal experience of reflection and prayer. The *Daily Service* is no longer intended just for the housebound sick and elderly but has become an accessible oasis of reflection for a broad spectrum of people.

Television does not have the same capacity for intimacy. The sense of being a spectator looking in on pre-determined images mitigates against the immediacy of the imagination. Worship programmes on television which courageously attempted to involve the viewer in some shared act of breaking bread or lighting a candle have not stood the test of time. Nonetheless, programmes of hymn-singing, testimony and a blessing can still convey something of shared worship and attract large audiences to watch them. *Songs of Praise* transmitted on BBC Television and *Sunday Half Hour* broadcast on BBC network radio both reflect the continued popularity of hymn-singing and bear witness to the evolution of this genre by introducing new music and styles of singing.

Broadcast worship is made available in most countries where religion is not restricted and is transmitted as a public service even on state-controlled networks. In addition there are some ten dedicated Christian television channels in the USA, ten in Europe, five in Africa and two in Australia. There are eleven Christian radio channels in the USA, thirteen in South America, eight in Africa, twenty in Europe, one in the Far East and nine in the Pacific region. Other Christian groups buy air time from commercial channels.

The reputation of 'electronic churches' or so-called 'churches of the air' has been somewhat tarnished by personal scandal and in the USA by the flaunting of lavish wealth. Critics have accused some such broadcasters of exploiting the fears and anxieties of a vulnerable section of society by peddling a fraudulent and distorted version of the gospel which promises much but delivers nothing.

This is not to deny that there are religious broadcasters with great skill and integrity. Despite the clear limitations of the media when it comes to conveying the sense of God's mystery and the experience of the numinous, nonetheless there is in Christian worship an understanding of being surrounded by angels and archangels in the communion of saints with all the invisible host of heaven united in a single chorus of praise. Many individuals have testified to the powerful feeling of being united with a vast throng of unseen worshippers by means of radio and television. Churches quite rightly affirm the gathered community in a single place as the defining characteristic of what it means to be the church. But on occasion and for many different reasons broadcast worship has provided individuals with the opportunity to worship when they would not otherwise have felt able to do so. Churches can be intimidating places to enter for the uninitiated and the stranger and yet over the years broadcast worship has continued to allow huge numbers of people to hear the scriptures read, the *sacraments celebrated and the word of God preached. Some have testified to transforming moments and occasions when their own inarticulate prayers found expression in a broadcast prayer and elicited from them a surprising and profound 'Amen'.

The potential of mass media communication has had an effect on churches exposed to its revealing glare. To see yourself as others see you is a salutary experience. The explosion of local radio in the UK during the last quarter of the twentieth century allowed many more churches access to the airwaves. Opportunities for relayed church services were never very great but devised services or simple acts of worship especially during the religious seasons of *Christmas and *Easter remain surprisingly common. Many clergy have had their presentational skills developed and their more unfortunate eccentricities modified by simple training in media skills and personal awareness.

The churchgoing population may be declining but broadcast worship at times of national crises or personal need can provide a valued focus for the hesitant and unspoken prayers of many people. However ethereal it may be, at its best and sometimes at surprising moments, broadcast worship can channel what Isaac Watts in 1707 described as 'The breathings of our piety according to the variety of our passions, our wonder and our joy as they are refined into devotion and act under the influence of the Spirit!'

Wesley Carr, *Ministry and the Media*, London 1990; Charles Moore and Roger Mills, *Faith in*

the Media, Newcastle-upon-Tyne 1998; Colin Morris, *Wrestling with an Angel*, London 1990.

STEPHEN OLIVER

Melchite Rite *see* Orthodox Worship

Mennonite Worship

1. *Introduction*. Anabaptism, the sixteenth-century movement from which Mennonitism emerged, began in a liturgical act. Radical followers of the Zurich reformer, Ulrich Zwingli, became convinced that the ultimate goal of renewal was the restoration of the church as a community of believers outside the sphere of the state. *Baptism upon profession of faith was for them the act by which one entered the church. Similarly, the *Lord's supper was the event by means of which believers were united with Christ and one another. Both of these were spontaneously carried out in a farm kitchen near Zurich in January of 1525 and constitute the beginning of what was to become the Mennonite Church.

For Anabaptists the church was a visible community constituted by outward signs, and also a charismatic society whose members, individually and collectively, were bearers of the Holy Spirit. When they gathered for worship, study and decision-making believers relied on the immediate promptings of the Spirit in any member to reveal truth from God. The goal remained to hold the outwardness of the church's existence in the world and the inwardness of the Spirit's work together. This is illustrated by the work of the most liturgical of first generation Anabaptist leaders, Balthasar Hubmaier. In his 'A Form for Christ's Supper' he severely alters but retains the form of the medieval *mass. Within this form he provides, after the sermon, for any worshipper with an insight into the preaching text to contribute it, after the manner of 1 Cor. 14.

However, with the exception of Hubmaier, only fragmentary attempts were made to fashion worship forms out of pre-Reformation tradition. At the same time, these ancient forms were engraved on the people's souls. For example, the enquiry by the priest into the holiness of life of *Easter communicants at a late medieval preparatory service during *Holy Week is carried over with little change into Mennonite eucharistic practice. For the most part, liturgy emerged from below: prayers which a presider had led extemporaneously became normative as they were repeated by himself and others and then were set down in handwritten manuscripts. At the same time, there is a pattern of evidence that these orders were altered and even discarded from one generation to the next. In many Mennonite communities across the centuries order and inspiration were reconciled by having members, and especially leaders, internalize concepts and turns of phrase so that a predictable liturgical vocabulary was established. Yet, because these were not written down the fiction was preserved that worship was *extemporaneous.

Two other background comments are necessary: one of them is that Mennonitism remained a marginal movement whose adherents repeatedly migrated. Its published records are scant, and as much of the story of Mennonite worship is told by diary entries and the perseverance of ancient customs as by books of worship. The other is that Mennonites have remained astonishingly diverse and factional. In brief, there are three tendencies in historic Mennonitism in North America. The majority are moderates, who try to marry tradition and innovation in worship as well as in theology and lifestyle. The minority at one end are 'old order' movements, which arose at the close of the seventeenth century and again at the close of the nineteenth to preserve old ways. The form of their worship comes from Mennonite practice of the eighteenth and early nineteenth centuries. The minority at the other end are generic evangelicals, increasingly *charismatic in nature. The form of their worship is a mixture of revivalistic and contemporary Christian styles.

2. *Historical Developments*. The central rhythm of Anabaptist communities was their gathering to worship and dispersing to witness. When they met the heart of the matter was interpreting the scriptures and building one another up for mission. Singing, preaching, praying and prophesying according to the pattern of 1 Cor. 14 provided an organic pattern for worship. Some early exceptions aside, congregational singing was and is the most profound form of self-expression for the congregation. Two widely used hymnals were issued in Dutch and two in German in the 1560s alone. The texts were a mixture, some borrowed from Catholic and Protestant tradition and some written by Anabaptists. Proclamation of biblical texts by preachers, and initially by all with a gift of prophecy, was central to worship but was not set in opposition to the Lord's supper. Gradually the 'unsung' parts of the service were more and more assigned to the *elder or *bishop (preaching and presiding at ceremonies), minister (preaching), and *deacon (reading and praying).

At its origins the Sunday assembly often climaxed in the breaking of bread. In late medieval Catholicism the priest communicated without a congregation; in sixteenth-century Anabaptism the congregation communicated without a priest. The whole priesthood of believers was to be the actor in the service of the word and of the table. But like other Protestants, Mennonites were unable to overcome the medieval dread of unworthy *communion and so, as their life became routinized, they lapsed into the medieval practice of communicating once or twice a year. The form of the Lord's supper varied from region to region but by the beginning of the seventeenth century it exhibited a recognizable pattern. *Confession happened the week before communion. The sermon set forth the suffering and sacrifice of Christ. This theme was continued in a general communion prayer. Sometimes the Spirit was invoked to make the breaking of bread into a 'communion of the body and blood of Christ'. This phrase from 1 Cor. 10.17 as well as the *institution narrative from that epistle were preferred to the language of the Synoptics. Interestingly, concepts derived from John 6 are common, although their interpretation is more mystical than realist. The prayers of thanks Jesus offered before the bread and cup were imitated as simple acts of gratitude for his body and blood before each of the elements was received. A prayer of thanksgiving followed the communion. Only gradually did the rite of *foot-washing become the normative conclusion to the service. The breaking of bread was an act of covenant renewal, in which believers pledged to lay down their lives for others as Christ had laid down his life for them.

Baptism was offered to people, according to the Schleitheim Confession of 1527, 'who have been taught repentance and the amendment of life and believe truly that their sins are taken away through Christ and to all those who desire to walk in the resurrection . . .'. Initially, baptisms took place wherever believers met, in private homes, at village wells, in forests. As settled congregations developed, baptism was preceded by instruction (initially based on the

Apostles' *Creed, later on articles of faith, like the Dordrecht Confession of 1632, as these were composed). In some cases a personal testimony of faith as well as a willingness to give and receive counsel in the congregation were asked for in addition to assent to doctrine. Surprisingly, the form of baptism seems simply to have followed traditional local practice. Sprinkling and pouring, once or three times, were most common but immersion was also practised. The form of baptism did not become a matter of polemics until renewal movements among Mennonites in the seventeenth and nineteenth centuries associated immersion with a crisis conversion and an intensity of faith lacking in the Mennonite Church of the day. Baptism was and remains a highlight of Mennonite church life in all branches; the service often culminates in the celebration of the Lord's supper.

Church discipline was thought of as the necessary complement to baptism: one entered the church with a promise to live a holy life; one was excommunicated if one persistently violated that promise. Matt. 18.15–22 was held up as the model of charitable admonition. Although the motivation was to be one of mutual correction, the process often descended into self-righteousness. There was usually a public declaration of excommunication. Some formularies include a rite for the reception of penitents.

Conversion and baptism made women and men equal as heirs of grace, as set forth in parts of Paul's ecclesiology. Both possessed the Spirit, so both were called to witness to Christ at home and work. Almost as many women as men endured martyrdom. In some settings witnessing by women opened a space for them as interpreters of biblical texts. As congregations braced themselves for battle with the world, the setting apart of leaders became more formalized. Only men were chosen for these roles, which generally perpetuated the threefold ministry on the basis of biblical precedent. Initially, provision was made for prophets who received a direct call from God and had only to be acknowledged by the congregation. Mention of this role ceases after the second generation. Otherwise, choosing leaders seems to have happened by congregational or regional church discernment or by lot. Elders or bishops were always ordained, ministers usually, and deacons often not. Because of the importance of singing for worship, song leaders were elected by the congregation.

*Anointing for healing is but rarely mentioned in early Mennonite lore. It is not part of prayer formularies or minister's manuals until the twentieth century but it has a firm basis in oral tradition: everyone assumes it has always been done. It was customary for a minister, deacon and representatives of the congregation to visit a member privately at his or her sickbed. Today anointing is increasingly practised on an occasional basis in public worship.

Like anointing, celibacy is rarely mentioned but provided for as an honourable estate. By common prejudice, marriage was the preferred state but in some settings older women of stature were set aside as *deaconesses. With the institutionalization of church life in the nineteenth century celibate women were permitted to undertake missionary service at home and abroad and a few deaconess orders, whose ministry was nursing, emerged with rites for the consecration of their members.

Records of *marriage services tell us that the vows were most often celebrated as an appendix to the regular Sunday assembly. The couple came forward to sit in chairs set out for them to hear an admonition by the minister concerning the joys and pitfalls of conjugal life. His text was often Tobit 8. The vows for the woman and the man were usually identical. Later on weddings were more and more often solemnized domestically in a separate service, in the bride's home or (elaborately decorated) barn. In the course of the twentieth century church weddings have become the norm in mainstream Mennonitism.

Again, there is sparse documention of *funeral practices until the nineteenth century when collections of funeral sermons appear. Congregational singing accompanied the service and the cortège, as well as the burial. The order was that of a regular preaching service, with prayers for the occasion. In some records the weight of the sermon was placed on gratitude for the work of grace in the deceased's life, in others it was an occasion to warn mourners against the wrath to come.

For the most part, aside from the Lord's Day, the church *year and the *lectionary were discarded by Anabaptists as part and parcel of their rejection of clericalism and, in their view, religion imprisoned by its outer forms. Gradually anecdotal references appear, e.g. to the breaking of bread on *Good Friday and meeting for worship on *Ascension Day. Bit by bit the liturgical calendar from *Advent through *Pentecost made its way into Mennonite custom. In the 1767 Prussian hymnal, for example, the Lutheran lectionary was included. New Year's eve and day were almost universally observed. In the early nineteenth century Eternity Sunday, the European Protestant alternative to *All Souls' and *All Saints' Days, was taken up in some circles.

3. *Modern Practice*. Apart from the old order groups, the face of Mennonitism has changed markedly in the course of the twentieth century. Between 1850 and 1900 most Mennonite bodies experienced revival, and with it, the recovery of a missionary vision they had lost in the seventeenth century. Often the tension between tradition and innovation, preservation and outreach, burst the bounds of communal life and new Mennonite bodies came into being. Missionary activity led to the encounter with other cultures, both in the North Atlantic world and beyond it. Direct reliance on the Holy Spirit in worship and long-standing marginality to mainstream culture should have freed Mennonites to inculturate their faith and life in other societies. It was, in fact, the evangelical rather than the Anabaptist impulse that inspired Mennonites to sit lightly on their historical forms of worship in missionary settings. Sometimes the translation never moved beyond the transitional phase of Western generic evangelicalism. But gradually new Mennonite churches took ownership of their life and created worship forms which expressed their soul. Written documents are limited to the informal copying of resources passed on from congregation to congregation. The ecstatic dimension of many non-White societies drew Mennonites in such cultures to passages like 1 Cor. 14, much as it had drawn the Anabaptists. At the same time, these cultures are also more at home with elaborate ritual than is rationalistic White culture in the West. This richness of expression leads to elaborate services in which many gifts of the Spirit are exercised. 'Third world' Mennonite communities borrow music from their national and popular western culture as well as composing their own songs. The hymnal produced for the Mennonite World Conference of 1978 (Lombard 1978) illustrates how widely this is the case.

In North America, home missions among Native Americans, African Americans, Hispanic Americans and immigrants from around the world has led to similar inculturation. During the past thirty years the moderate White Mennonite majority has worked prodigiously to renew worship by judicious borrowing from two sources, church growth/*charismatic worship and the *Liturgical Movement. Churches attracted to the former have taken music and an oral style from it. The conferences have sought to recast the riches of the Liturgical Movement for a Mennonite ecclesiology. An abundance of pamphlets, many of them based on the church year and the *Revised Common Lectionary*, hymnals and minister's manuals have been issued. Along with these forms has come an encouragement to improvise on basic patterns in ways that make these resources accessible to people who lift up the charismatic dimension of worship.

Primary texts: W. Bakker and G. G. Hoekema (eds), *De Gemeente komt samen*, Amsterdam 1998; H. Wayne Pipkin and John H. Yoder (eds), *Balthasar Hubmaier*, Scottdale, PA 1989, esp. 393–408; Leonard Gross (ed.), *An Earnest Christian's Handbook*, Scottdale, PA 1996; John Rempel (ed.), *Minister's Manual*, Scottdale, PA 1998.

Studies: Ross Bender, 'Glimpses of Mennonite Worship on Five Continents', *Courier* VI, 1991, no. 2; 'Worship', *The Mennonite Encyclopedia* V, Scottdale, PA 1990, 943–8; John Rempel, *The Lord's Supper in Anabaptism*, Scottdale, PA 1993 (bib.).

JOHN REMPEL

Methodist Worship

1. *United Kingdom*. Original Wesleyan Methodism inherited two traditions of Sunday worship from John Wesley. The first was the morning service from the Anglican *BCP* consisting of morning prayer, *litany, *antecommunion and sermon. In practice the Methodist *chapels in the Prayer Book tradition used only morning prayer with hymns and sermon. Some of these survived late into the twentieth century. Despite Wesley's 1784 revision of the Prayer Book entitled *The Sunday Service of the Methodists*, the Prayer Book chapels continued to use the *BCP* for morning prayer until the 1882 Wesleyan Conference revision of the Anglican office. The majority of Wesleyan Methodists and those in the other branches of Methodism adapted Wesley's weekday preaching service as their main diet of Sunday morning and evening worship. The original preaching service of hymn, *bidding prayer, text, *collect, hymn and blessing was expanded as first one

and then a second Bible reading was added. Later still the long bidding or *extempore prayer was subdivided with the shorter prayer near the beginning and the 'long prayer' prior to the sermon and final hymn. When *choirs appeared in the larger chapels, introits, *anthems, psalms and *canticles were added to give a 'churchy' flavour and the preaching service became 'morning and evening worship' but still keeping its classical four or five hymns with a strong staple diet of Charles Wesley. Methodist Sunday morning worship has also proved an adaptable form for *family and all-age worship.

Although all the major non-Wesleyan bodies had their own service books for the guidance of the minister at *communion services, only the Wesleyans adhered to the Prayer Book communion office. Communion was celebrated twice or three times a quarter in the larger chapels and usually quarterly in the country. Until the late 1960s even most of the ex-Wesleyan chapels used only the second part of the communion office added to the end of the morning or evening preaching service. In *The Methodist Service Book* (1975) the preaching service was adapted to the eucharistic ministry of the word with the readings and sermon forming a unit and coming before the *intercessions. This was also when Methodists moved to contemporary language, began to give up extempore prayer and began to abandon the Prayer Book communion office. With the publication of the 1999 *Methodist Worship Book* there has been an enormous emphasis on the liturgical *year reflected in the eucharistic orders, the preaching services and daily prayer. New also is the service for healing and the rich provision of prayers and services surrounding a death.

Weekday worship consisted of private or family devotion using the hymnbook and daily Bible reading notes and often a 'prayer manual' of intercession for the world church. In mid-week fellowship meetings and where Methodists gathered overnight there was a tradition of 'prayers' consisting of hymn-singing, Bible reading, prayer and a short devotional address. Of the original 'prudential' means of grace the *love-feast, the *watch-night and the quarterly fast have all but disappeared leaving only the annual *covenant service as the one unique liturgical custom from Wesley's time.

C. NORMAN R. WALLWORK

2. *USA*. Prior to 1784, Methodist worship in America technically was meant to supplement Anglican worship. In reality, because of geographical, social and theological factors, most Methodists instead preferred lay-led and informal worship consisting of fervent hymn-singing, *extemporary prayer, scripture reading, and evangelical preaching; they also hungered for the *Lord's supper administered by their own preachers. Methodists worshipped in small groups and in the private meetings of the wider Society, but also in large public assemblies held out of doors or in any available building.

When the Methodist Episcopal Church was established in December 1784, the organizing Conference adopted John Wesley's revision of the 1662 *BCP* published as the *Sunday Service of the Methodists in North America. With other Occasional Services* (1784). Eight years later, the Methodists put aside 'Wesley's Prayer Book' in the belief that they prayed better with their eyes closed than open. Although Wesley's texts for Sunday were abandoned in favour of a more familiar informal service, revisions of his orders for holy *communion, infant and adult *baptism, *marriage, *funeral and *ordination were preserved. All American Methodist denominations directly or indirectly share the revised rites of 1792 as a common ancestor, but the degree to which those texts were kept unchanged varies; the African Methodist Episcopal Church has been among the most conservative in its revisions. Methodist churches have always had authorized texts for their worship, and by the late nineteenth century these would include explicit orders for Sunday morning. But no text has ever been strictly mandated; any order of worship is judged flexible enough to allow for expansion, abbreviation or alteration. However, at various times and in particular branches of Methodism, ministers have been strongly advised to follow the forms, especially for the sacraments and for ordination. Both ordered worship and the freedom of local expression thus have characterized Methodist worship, and this tension has been addressed in different ways and by different means.

Hymnbooks for Methodists have functioned in much the same way as prayer books for other Christians. Congregational singing is an integral part of Methodist worship; use of choirs in worship was strongly discouraged in some denominations even into the twentieth century. Authorized hymnals testify to the theological and liturgical emphases of a particular denomination, and include hymns of Charles Wesley and from the broader Christian tradition as well as new hymns reflective of contemporary experience. At the turn into the twenty-first century, Methodists in their worship often sing texts and tunes representative of ethnic and global Christianity.

From the mid-nineteenth century to the present, Methodists expanded their repertoire of authorized liturgical texts. Methodist worship gradually became more formal; in reaction, certain denominations (particularly the Holiness churches) and congregations advocated their 'birthright' of liturgical simplicity. Rites for 'church membership' were introduced, as were services for the *consecration of church buildings. Written forms were supplied for the historic Methodist services of *love-feast and *watch-night, and resources were developed for the festivals and fasts of the liturgical *year. Many of the authorized worship books from the latter third of the twentieth century contain services inspired by the Ecumenical and *Liturgical Movements. New liturgies have been published that ritualize events in the life of the local congregation and at times of crisis or change.

Karen B. Westerfield Tucker, *American Methodist Worship*, New York 2000; (ed.), *The Sunday Service of the Methodists*, Nashville 1996.

KAREN B. WESTERFIELD TUCKER

Metrical Psalms

The strength of vernacular lay devotion, the interest of the Reformers in the vernacular and the scriptures, and the spread of printing with movable type in the early sixteenth century provided the basis for the composition and wide circulation of translations of the psalms in versified form in the mid-sixteenth century. The recitation of the psalms of the office of the Blessed Virgin Mary and the office of the dead was commonplace in the later Middle Ages, as exemplified by the many Books of Hours (*see* **Daily Prayer** 3). In the early sixteenth century more of these texts appeared in the vernacular, in functional print rather than decorated manuscript.

The tide of reform in religious thinking not only favoured the vernacular as a means of ensuring better comprehension, but also the use of scriptural text. Central to both medieval and Reformation prayer and worship are the psalms, sacred poetry for singing. Some translators reshaped the psalm texts within the lyrical verse tradition of Western Europe, a tradition which uses regular metrical patterns and is often rhyming. Some used metres common to the medieval Latin hymns (e.g. Ps. 100 in Long Metre in Dutch, Genevan and English metrical translations, each with the melody known as Old 100th), but more often they adopted the metre of contemporary popular song. Most prevalent was the ballad metre of the fourteener or Poulter's Metre, known in hymn books as Common Metre (e.g. Old 107th, a melody imported from the Genevan Psalter).

Early examples of metrical psalms are found in German (Martin Luther, 1524), French (Clément Marot, 1537), English (Miles Coverdale, c. 1537) and Dutch (*Souterliedekens*, 1540). One of the most influential collections was the Calvinist psalter of 1551, published in French, a collection with which English Protestant exiles gained familiarity during the reign of Mary I. This Genevan Psalter was finally completed (150 psalms and 2 canticles) in 1562. The earliest English collection was begun by Thomas Sternhold, a courtier of Edward VI; this was enlarged by stages, mostly by John Hopkins, and then published as a complete psalter by John Day (1562), making use of some Genevan translations and melodies. Later collections based on this text, intended principally for domestic use and sung to the lute or in four-part harmony, included those published by Thomas Este (1592) and Thomas Ravenscroft (1621). Until the late seventeenth century the text of the English metrical psalter was that based on Sternhold and Hopkins. In 1696, Nahum Tate and Nicholas Brady produced *The New Version of the Psalms*, a translation which coexisted with 'The Old Version' until the nineteenth century, when it gained greater popularity. It was 'The Old Version' that formed the basis of American metrical psalm collections, although French translations had been used earlier by Huguenot settlers. Metrical psalms were known in Scotland from the 1540s, and included in the early Reformed prayer book of 1564, but the final complete and official text of the Scottish metrical psalter was not established until 1650.

While metrical psalmody could be included in Lutheran, Calvinist and other reformed patterns of worship, the texts were not authorized for use in Church of England services where the psalms were recited from the *BCP*. However, singing of psalms before and after the service was permitted, and many copies of the metrical psalter are bound in with the Prayer Book. In cathedrals a metrical psalm was sung before and after the sermon, for which those in *choir often moved to the *nave. It was customary in the late seventeenth and eighteenth centuries for organists to improvise before and between the verses of the psalm. The norm in parish churches was for psalms to be sung unaccompanied and in unison, led by the parish clerk. However, from the late seventeenth century until the early nineteenth century, many parishes made use of amateur groups of voices and/or instruments to provide settings of metrical psalms, often referred to as 'psalmody', some based on the old tunes, some new and some closer to *anthems. Some settings included independent organ accompaniment. Three categories of such psalmody can be identified: that associated with country parish choirs, with town parish choirs, and with the Dissenters. In this repertory the borderlines between music for Christian education, devotions in the home and music intended for public worship can be blurred, and this is also true of the American tradition.

Poets and musicians have continued to versify and set the psalms over the centuries. However, new impetus emerged in the late twentieth century to make the psalms more accessible, fuelled by liturgical reform, and particularly by the pastoral emphasis on the active participation of all present. Among the collections published in Britain are *Psalm Praise* (London 1973) and *Psalms for Today* (London 1990) from the Anglican evangelical tradition, *Psalm Songs* (London 1998) from the RC tradition, and John L. Bell's *Psalms of Patience, Protest and Praise* (Glasgow 1993) informed by the Iona Community's work and the Church of Scotland. In all these, directness of text and music are characteristic, though their ethos and theology are each distinct.

_____

'Psalms, Metrical' and 'Psalmody', *NG2*, XX, 472–518; Nicholas Temperley, *The Music of the English Parish Church*, Cambridge 1979.

JOHN HARPER

Minor Orders

A term which came to be used in the medieval West to designate the orders of doorkeeper (*ostarius*), reader (*lector*), exorcist and *acolyte, to distinguish them from what were known as the major or 'sacred' orders of *subdeacon, *deacon, *presbyter and *bishop. Eventually it was expected that all candidates for sacred orders would pass through each of the minor orders in turn, however briefly, since they were now viewed as a ladder of ascent rather than as distinctive ministries in their own right. The RC Church abolished the minor orders in 1972, replacing them with two 'ministries', acolyte and lector, which are conferred by 'institution' rather than 'ordination'.

_____

John St H. Gibaut, *The Cursus Honorum: A Study of the Origins and Evolution of Sequential Ordination*, New York 2000.

EDITOR

Missal *see* **Books, Liturgical** 3.1.1.e

Mission and Worship

The 1988 Anglican Lambeth Conference, which called for a decade of evangelism, set that call in the context of a prosaic but demanding definition of mission as (1) to proclaim the good news; (2) to teach, baptize and nurture; (3) to respond to human need; (4) to transform the unjust structures of society. Peter Cotterell in *Mission and Meaninglessness* (London 1990) describes mission as 'the people of God speaking and acting on behalf of God to explain and to resolve the apparent meaninglessness of life wherever that meaninglessness appears and however it is experienced'. This means not only grappling with the ultimate meaning of life and the universe, but focusing on the most incomprehensible bits: disease and death, poverty and natural disaster. The worship of God is the only context in which such things can be confronted, and yet what the church asks of people seems equally meaningless. Lesslie Newbigin wrote: 'How can this strange story of God made man, of a crucified saviour, or resurrection and new creation become credible for those whose entire mental training has conditioned them to believe that the real world is the world which can be satisfactorily explained and managed without the hypothesis of God?' It is as if the whole puzzling jigsaw of life, seemingly unrelated bits and questions, can only fall into place in the light of another kaleidoscopic jigsaw of God's revelation and our appreciation of the nature of God in Christ – and that is the work of the Spirit. But the Spirit uses tools, one of which is the liturgy. Newbigin answers his question 'I know of only one clue to the answering of that question, only one real hermeneutic of the gospel: a congregation which believes it . . .'

The chief purpose of the church is to worship Almighty God, to glorify him, and in doing that other purposes are met – the proclamation of the gospel and the meeting of the community in its need. Worship continually re-forms the church so that it becomes the hermeneutic of the gospel. It is the worship of the church which brings together proclamation and prayer, contemplation, reflection and social action, forcing the people of God to reconsider the question, 'What kind of church should we be?'

When the church and its worship are working properly (Eph. 4.16), there are two effects. The first is on those who come into church, perhaps as casual visitors, for whom the church's worship is a shop window, drawing them in to the point where they engage with the transforming presence of God. 'If everyone is proclaiming God's message when some unbeliever comes in, he will be convinced of his sin by what he hears . . . and he will bow down and worship God, confessing "Truly God is here among you!"' The sixteenth-century English Archbishop, Thomas Cranmer, used this argument of St Paul's (1 Cor. 14.23–25) against the Devon rebels – 'We will have the mass in Latin' – about the need for the *language of worship to be understood, 'otherwise you will answer Amen you wot not whereto'. The missionary church will want to examine issues of accessibility, both in language and culture. Some modern services deliberately allow for cultural variations with phrases such as 'in these or similar words', or are set out in outline form only, so that most of the service can be *inculturated.

How people hear is crucial. 'Everyone who calls on the name of the Lord will be saved. How can they call on him without having faith in him? How can they have faith without having heard of him? How can they hear without someone preaching to them?' (Rom. 11.13–14). Richard Hooker in his *Ecclesiastical Polity* stresses the importance of preaching for getting people to eternal life: 'For the instruction therefore of all sorts of men to eternal life it is necessary that the sacred and saving truth of God be openly published unto them which open publication of heavenly mysteries is by an excellency termed preaching.' He links this with the public reading of scripture as part of the liturgy. Cranmer (*Confutation of Unwritten Verities*) argues strongly that nothing but holy

scripture can prove or promote faith: 'No oracles of angels, apparitions of the dead, miracles, or custom. Without faith it is not possible to please God. Faith cometh by hearing of God's word; therefore where God's word lacketh there can be no faith.' So he filled the *BCP* full of scripture: quotations, allusions, pictures, as well as a *lectionary based on the principle of the semi-continuous reading of the Bible, a principle to which churches are returning today in the ecumenical *Revised Common Lectionary*.

This pattern is true of many of the liturgies of churches today; one of the tasks of those planning worship is to ensure that in the readings, *preaching, prayers, responses and songs there is sufficient of the scriptures to lead people to God. This does not mean that *sacrament, symbol and the visual are excluded. Cranmer uses rich language about the personal appropriation of Christ in the sacrament, speaking of 'the cup of the most holy blood wherewith you were redeemed and washed from your sins'. The Church of England has recently redefined the word 'sermon' to include less formal exposition, the use of drama, interviews, discussion, audio-visuals, and the insertion of hymns or other sections of the service between parts of the sermon. And in lectionary revisions there is a recovery of storytelling. Stories are important because they are memorable, people identify with them and enter into them. As we hear the Christian story rehearsed in church, so we enter into it, it becomes our story, and we make links between that and the story of our own personal faith. In the Church of England's new *baptism and *funeral services, for instance, there are opportunities for stories of personal faith to be heard.

But proclamation, inculturation, storytelling are not enough to ensure that everyone hears. The missionary church will look at ways of applying the message to individuals. The group and family preparation envisaged in the RC Rite for the Christian Initiation of Adults, the growth of the adult *catechumenate, and Christian foundations courses such as Alpha all provide for enquirers and others to go on an accompanied journey of faith. This is reflected in new liturgies for initiation – and even for funerals and other pastoral rites, where the encouragement to see staged liturgy as an accompanied journey enables people other than the church leader to minister at the crisis times of faith.

So the missionary church uses all the means

at its disposal to ensure that its worship leads people to faith in Christ, and becomes the place where in the presence of God and in community with other Christians the jigsaw of apparent meaninglessness fits together. But the mission of the church is not primarily centripetal, drawing people into the life of the church, but centrifugal, expelling people, presence and message out into the world. If one effect of the church's self-understanding in worship is on those who come into the church, a far greater effect should be on those outside the church.

If the church's self-understanding is that it is a refuge from the storms of the world outside, a haven of peace or even a hallowed enclave of the past, to which the battered Christian retreats for comfort and strength before venturing out into the nasty world again for another week, then the agenda and language of the church will be determined by that. It will not matter if a specialized hieratic language is used, or if the concerns addressed in preaching and prayers are internal ones to do with whether women can be priests or the precise wording of the creeds.

But the concerns of the world outside come into church in the minds and hearts of the worshippers. Unless they are invited to leave them in a box by the door because church is not the place for thoughts like that, and they can pick them up again, undisturbed, on the way out, worshippers will spend the service grappling with how what they are engaged in relates to and makes sense of their everyday lives. These matters of the world, the community, work and family life need to be brought into the presence of God, into worship where the word, preaching, prayers, interviews and the sharing of fellowship help worshippers to make sense of life and give them the vision, motivation and energy to go out and transform the world. So the preaching might be a prophetic word about the effect of structures of society on the local community, and the morality discussed will not always be that of personal sexual ethics.

Those preparing worship should look at the beginning and ending of services. Does the gathering of the Christian community acknowledge realistically the different situations from which people have come? Is the ending likely to send people out in the power of the Spirit to live and work to God's praise and glory? Some services, such as the Church of England's new initiation services, have a 'missio' section at the end, in which people can think about exactly what it is that they take

out into the world. The giving of the candle at this point symbolizes going out into the world with the light of Christ. Moving the giving of symbols to new ministers to the end of an ordination service has a similar effect.

The missionary church will also want to consider whether being sent out involves taking the worship of the church outside, not just into services in people's homes, but into the streets and parks, perhaps on the great festival occasions of the church's *year. Some places do this on *Palm Sunday or *Good Friday, but there are other opportunities too – depending on the climate.

––––––

J. G. Davies, *Worship and Mission*, London 1966.

TREVOR LLOYD

Mitre *see* **Vestments** 3(d), 4(h)

Mixed Chalice

This expression is used to denote the mingling of water and wine in the cup at the *eucharist. It is usually explained as a continuation of the normal watering down of wine for consumption in the ancient Middle East, which would have been the usual custom of Jesus and his disciples. However, there is also evidence that some early Christian communities used water only and not wine in their eucharistic practice, and it has even been suggested that the rather odd reference in Justin, *First Apology* 66, to 'water and wine mixed with water' may be a later interpolation into a text that had originally only mentioned water. Since many early Christian writers inveigh strongly against the use of water alone, the nearly universal insistence on the addition of water to wine in later Christian practice may have originated as a deliberate compromise between these two traditions.

Various symbolic interpretations became attached to the custom: it was viewed as symbolizing the union of Christ with his people, or the water and blood which is said to have flowed from his side on the cross (John 19.34), or the union of the two natures of Christ, human and divine. The sixteenth-century Reformation rejected the practice as an unedifying ceremony, but many later Anglicans from the eighteenth-century Nonjurors onwards have restored its use, and it was declared to be legal in the Church of England in a bitter late-nineteenth-century dispute over various rituals and ceremonies.

Only the Byzantine rite mixes the chalice twice during the eucharist, adding hot water at the *commixture. Although the original reason for this is unknown, it is said to symbolize the fervency of faith and the descent of the Holy Spirit and goes back to at least the sixth century.

Robert F. Taft, 'Water into Wine: The Twice-Mixed Chalice in the Byzantine Eucharist', *Le Muséon* C, 1987, 323–42.

EDITOR

Monstrance

Taking its name from the Latin verb *monstrare*, 'to show', the vessel used to contain the consecrated *host and to reveal it to those present for the purpose of veneration in the Western Catholic tradition. The institution of the feast of *Corpus Christi in 1264 was directly related to the Cathar heresies permeating Christendom at that time, which rejected the flesh and material creation as inherently evil, and denied the possibility of the divinity of the human person of Jesus Christ. In thus promoting such a feast, the church developed differing forms of cultus in various parts of Europe, leading directly to the veneration of the blessed sacrament in its own right, not simply as a response to the dominical command to 'take, eat'. To facilitate one particular aspect of the cultus, *exposition, the monstrance was created: it developed into a shape like a long-stemmed daisy, with the addition of a base, which enabled it to be free-standing. The stem is used by the priest to hold it high and to make with it, in the sign of the cross, a blessing over the faithful who are present. At the top, it contains a lunette or small, round window, in which the blessed sacrament is held. From the lunette, what appear to be petals or rays of sunlight project outwards, in various degrees of elaboration.

TRISTAM HOLLAND

Moravian Worship

The Moravian Church (*Herrnhuter Brüder-gemeine*) grew, under the leadership of Count Nikolaus Ludwig von Zinzendorf (1700–60), out of the settlement of Herrnhut (Saxony), founded by Moravian exiles in 1722. It continues the tradition and orders of their ancestral church, the *Unitas Fratrum* (Church of the *Bohemian Brethren), and has congregations in Europe, North and South America, the Caribbean, Africa and North India. Zinzendorf, a Lutheran of Pietist upbringing, created a unique and original Christ-centred worship tradition, emphasizing experience, simplicity and community, which is reflected to varying degrees in the worship of today's nineteen provinces, but which remains the source of its distinctive common features.

1. *The General Tradition*. The pattern of worship was designed for congregational settlements. For Zinzendorf, the whole of life was *Gottesdienst* (the worship or service of God), and each day was punctuated with *Versammlungen* (meetings), following daily, weekly and monthly cycles.

The chief setting was the rectangular *Saal* (hall), initially in a communal house. Zinzendorf called it the congregation's 'front room' (*gute Stube*). It had no *pulpit or *altar; the *Liturgus* sat behind a table in the middle of one of the long sides, flanked by the 'labourers'. The congregation sat, closed up as a community, on benches, men on one side, women on the other. The ministers and *acolytes wore albs (recalling the white robes of Rev. 7.14 and also Christ's graveclothes) for *ordination, holy communion (*eucharist) and *baptism, but otherwise smart, sober dress.

Each element of worship formed a separate service. Public prayer was confined largely to free-standing *litany services (Zinzendorf opposed public *extempore prayer), Bible reading to the Bible hour (in which a long, continuous passage was read and allowed to have effect without exposition), addresses to the preaching (aimed chiefly at non-Moravians) and daily quarter-hours (brief homilies from the heart to the heart). The unifying factor was song, since at least a few verses were sung at all services; the eighteenth-century Moravians were prodigious hymn-writers.

2. *Particular Practices*. In the *Singstunde* (singing hour), a series of verses from different hymns expound a text or develop a theme. For Zinzendorf, who believed that religious truth was perceived best by the heart and could be expressed most directly in song, this service was second in importance only to holy communion (which was itself encompassed in what was essentially a singing hour on the *sacrament).

In Continental Europe holy communion has

changed little. The singing of hymn verses remains the main element, supplemented only by an initial prayer of *confession, a thanksgiving prayer, a minimum of liturgical exchange and the *institution narrative. There is no Bible reading or address, and the liturgy proceeds uninterrupted by announcement or comment. Only intending communicants attend. During appropriate verses they shake hands with their neighbours on either side after the confession (as a sign of forgiveness) and towards the end (the right hand of fellowship). The elements are distributed to them standing in their places after the respective words of institution. Each wafer is broken before two communicants; the congregation consumes the bread simultaneously. The congregation no longer prostrate themselves after receiving *communion, but still kneel in adoration (as also for confession). In other provinces the liturgy varies. In America holy communion normally concludes a Sunday morning service; in Britain it follows another service or a *love-feast.

Hymns are also the liturgical component of the love-feast. Dating from 1727, this is a symbolic fellowship meal – tea (in America, usually coffee) and a bun – with music, conversation and reports of Moravian work locally, nationally and internationally. It is held to celebrate festivals or other events in the congregation's life, or in preparation for communion.

Another expression of fellowship, for example as a corporate act of rededication, is the sharing of wine in the cup of *covenant. *Footwashing (often performed at a love-feast prior to communion to symbolize absolution) is no longer practised. Except at episcopal consecrations and communion services for the congregation's married couples, the right hand of fellowship has replaced the *kiss of peace.

In addition to song, a second unifying factor are the *Losungen* (watchwords or daily texts), drawn by lot for each year from a collection of *c.* 1,830 OT texts, to which an NT 'doctrinal text' and a hymn verse or devotional text are added. They are now published in forty-six languages. The German edition, with a print run of around one million, is widely used by non-Moravians.

Zinzendorf's chief liturgical compositions were litanies. In addition to the church litany (developed from that of Luther) there were litanies to the persons of the Trinity, including the *Te Patrem*, the *Te Matrem* to the Holy Spirit and the 'Litany of the wounds of the husband'

(to Christ and his wounds). Originally, baptisms, marriages and ordinations were performed at the appropriate point in the church litany. Only the church litany and the Easter litany survive (in amended forms) today. Elements derived from the litanies are also found in other services.

3. *Seasons and Festivals.* On the first Sunday in *Advent, as on *Palm Sunday, Christian Gregor's 'Hosanna Anthem' (1784) is sung antiphonally. Homes and churches are decorated with *advent stars. Christmas Eve sees the *candle service, at which, in Britain and Ireland, *Christingles are distributed. In some congregations the *Putz* (an extended nativity scene consisting of a miniature village and landscape) is displayed. At New Year's Eve *watch-night services, held since 1732, the Memorabilia from the congregation's life in the previous year are read.

During *Lent and *Holy Week there are special liturgies and meditations on the passion. In Holy Week a harmonization of the gospel accounts of the week leading up to the crucifixion is read on successive days, interspersed with hymn verses but without an address. Holy communion is celebrated on *Maundy Thursday and a liturgy on *Good Friday. (A Good Friday evening liturgy commemorating the laying of Christ in the grave and a *Holy Saturday love-feast are traditionally celebratory in tone.) The distinctive *Easter celebration began in 1732. The congregation assembles before dawn for the Easter greeting and a great confession of faith, and then processes, led by trombones, to the burial ground, to celebrate the resurrection with the Easter litany, in which those who have died in the preceding year are named.

Ten memorial days mark important events in Moravian history, and the 'choirs' (divisions of the congregation by age, sex and marital status) have their own festival days.

4. *Change and Diversity.* Worship eventually came to be concentrated on Sundays, though in some provinces the Saturday evening *Singstunde* also survives. Everywhere, worship and its setting are influenced to varying extents by the ecumenical and cultural context.

In Continental Europe the liturgical and homiletic elements were combined from 1873 into a single Sunday morning service, to which preaching is central. Initially this began with a shortened church litany; in the twentieth cen-

tury additional liturgical forms were composed.

The American 1876 hymnal established a
new pattern for worship there. This soon resembled that of many other American Protestant denominations; the sermon became central
and free prayer replaced the liturgies. The
American Moravian Church has been described as 'not so much a liturgical church as
. . . a free church with a long and rich tradition
of liturgical prayer'. The *Moravian Book of
Worship* (Bethlehem, PA 1995) shows the influence of both the *Liturgical Movement and
the Church Growth Movement.

The British *Moravian Liturgy* (Oxford
1960), also used in the West Indies, draws on a
number of British liturgical sources; the influence of the Church of England's *BCP* (1662)
and the Church of Scotland's *Book of Common
Order* (1940) is strong. It is supplemented by
*The Moravian Church, Alternative Orders of
Worship*, London 1987. British Moravian worship is also influenced by non-liturgical Free
Church worship.

In the four Tanzanian provinces, forms of
worship developed in the last fifty years express in a free yet structured way the rhythmic
music and dance of Africa. Songs, often composed by the choir leaders and choirs themselves, are accompanied by guitars and drums,
and biblical stories are acted out in dance form.
In Nicaragua, Honduras and Costa Rica, folk
hymns and songs in Spanish and Miskito are
sung. In all these provinces, more traditional
liturgical orders continue to be used for the
sacraments and ordinations.

Otto Uttendörfer, *Zinzendorfs Gedanken über
den Gottesdienst*, Herrnhut 1931; Wilhelm
Lütjeharms, 'Gemeindeleben im Zeichen der
Liturgie (Gottesdienste – Liturgische Bräuche
– Sitte)', *Die Brüder-Unität*, ed. Heinz
Renkewitz, Stuttgart 1967, 134–47; *Handbuch
für die Versammlungen in der Brüdergemeine*,
Herrnhut/Bad Boll 1990; Adelaide L. Fries,
*Customs and Practices of the Moravian
Church*, 3rd edn, Winston-Salem 1973; Fred
Linyard and Phillip Tovey, *Moravian Worship*,
Nottingham 1994; Colin Podmore, *The Morav-
ian Church in England, 1728–1760*, Oxford
1998 (bib.).

COLIN PODMORE

Mormon Worship

see **Church of Jesus Christ of Latter-day
Saints Worship**

Motet

The motet (from the French *mot*, 'word') arising as a trope, or insertion, in the liturgy of
the thirteenth century, was one of the most
significant forms of *polyphonic music. The
medieval motet and its allied forms cover a
huge area of music, little of which is still sung
in church, but they can be heard in the concert
hall, on the radio and on CDs, performed by
specialist vocal groups. The characteristic
features of the early motet may be summarized
as follows : the lowest voice (the tenor) carried
the chant melody, usually cut up and arranged
as a series of recurring rhythmic patterns;
above this voice were added one, two or three
extra parts with texts that normally paraphrased
the text of the tenor, as in the following
example:

1. In saeculum saeculi, Artifex saeculi, etc.
2. In saeculum saeculi, supra mulieres, etc.
3. IN SAECULUM (this was the chant
   itself, known as the *cantus firmus*).

The added parts normally moved more quickly
than the *cantus firmus*. Each part was independent, so that if one upper part was omitted, or
sung alone, the music still made sense; but the
fragmented chant in the tenor, deprived of its
original flowing context, would not. Poly-
textuality enabled the clerical poet-musicians
to create a kind of musical mosaic which could
only be appreciated to the full by the singers.
This inherently attractive art became corrupted
by the use of polylingual texts, sometimes of
purely secular origin; thus, a French *chanson*
might be chosen for the top part with the Latin
liturgical text beneath it. Among the many subsequent developments, the most important, in
the early fifteenth century, was the replacement
of the chant by a freely composed melodic line,
combined with a contrapuntal treatment in
which all the parts were equally dependent
on one another, often imitating each other's
phrases and none being primus inter pares.

The motet had no necessary place in the
services. The liturgy required that if a motet
used the full text (or a part) of an *offertory
chant, for example, the latter had still to be sung
complete in its usual place in the *eucharist
before the motet was performed. However,
during the fifteenth century a more strictly liturgical practice was adopted, with texts drawn
from the *ordinary, or from the divine office
(*see* **Daily Prayer** 3).

One distinguished composer of motets in the late fifteenth century and early sixteenth was Josquin des Prez. He was followed by a pleiad of outstanding composers: Gombert, de Monte, Lassus, Palestrina, Giovanni Gabrieli, Morales and Victoria. In England the genre was magnificently represented by Power and Dunstable, the Eton Choirbook, and later by William Byrd, Thomas Tallis (with his forty-part *Spem in alium*) and Peter Philips. The subsequent history of the motet includes the works of Alessandro Grandi in Italy; of Du Mont, Lalande, Nivers and Clérambault in France; the classical motets of Michael Haydn and Mozart; Gounod's *Motets solennels*; the *20 Motets* of Saint-Saens; and in England compositions by Edmund Rubbra and Bernard Naylor.

Anselm Hughes and Gerald Abraham (eds), *Ars Nova and the Renaissance, 1300–1540*, Oxford 1960; H. B. Lincoln, *The Latin Motet: Indexes to Printed Collections, 1500–1600*, Ottawa 1993; D. Leech-Wilkinson, 'The Emergence of *ars nova*', *Journal of Musicology* XIII, 1995, 285–317; 'Motet', *The New Grove Dictionary of Music and Musicians*, 2nd edn, ed. Stanley Sadie and John Tyrrell, London 2001.

MARY BERRY

Movements in Worship

Worship involves the body as well as the mind and spirit. The liturgy includes a repertoire of *postures and movements which, in addition to being practical, often have symbolic importance. Each act or movement draws its significance from a symbolic matrix defined by a particular liturgical tradition which defines both meaning and acceptability. That which is normal practice in one tradition may be considered irreverent or offensive to another. Liturgical movement has often been borrowed from secular practice, and a number of reverential acts in the post-Constantinian church were derived from the Roman law courts and in Baroque Europe from the elaborate ceremonial of royal palaces. Liturgical *inculturation outside Europe and North America has seen the introduction into worship of those indications of authority and acts of reverence that belong to particular cultures (e.g., in certain African cultures, the reader of the gospel at the *eucharist holding a staff indicative of the authority of a messenger).

The repertoire of liturgical posture and movement includes walking, standing, sitting, kneeling, bowing (of the head and of the upper body), genuflection, prostration, kissing (of persons, books and objects), the joining, extending and lifting of the hands, the laying-on of hands, and the making of the sign of the cross on oneself and over other people or objects (*see* **Gestures**). It also includes intentional movement of people, and of objects carried by them, from one place to another, e.g. *processions, moving the missal from one end of the *altar to the other. Acts of washing, *anointing, sprinkling, and presentation (of *books, *candles, vessels, etc.) are frequent in liturgy. In the past liturgy has also included *insufflation (in the sense of breathing on something), standing on someone's foot, and slapping the face! Changing clothes, undressing and dressing (ritual *vesting) have also been included in liturgical acts. Certain groups of actions are unique to particular liturgical days. One of the most notable in the Western tradition is the complex group previously associated with the *Easter vigil, involving the *new fire, the handling of the *Easter candle, and the blessing of the water in the *font, which included actions not used at other times of year.

In the same way that liturgical texts can be rewritten, so the repertoire of movements can be redefined. The twentieth-century *Liturgical Movement has on the whole reduced rather than expanded the repertoire (e.g. in abandoning many reverential acts towards persons). This reduction also happened during the 1960s and 1970s in the RC Church when many of the practices common to worship before Vatican II (e.g. kissing of hands) were abolished or replaced by different ones (standing to receive *communion rather than kneeling). The complexities of certain liturgies, including the Easter vigil, were much reduced. *Charismatic revival has produced a new repertoire of movements (the raising of the single hand above the head, 'laying-on' of hands without physical contact), and liturgical *dance, formerly practised in a number of greater Spanish and Italian churches, has returned to frequent though not universal use.

MARTIN DUDLEY

Mozarabic Rite *see* **Western Rites**

Mozetta *see* **Vestments** 3(d)

Music

see **Anthem; Antiphon; Byzantine Chant; Canticles; Carol; Chants; Chants of the Proper of the Mass; Choir (Musical); Church Modes; Gregorian Chant; Hymns; Metrical Psalms; Motet; Music in the Mass of the Roman Rite; Music as Worship; Notation and Rhythm; Office Hymn; Organ; Polyphony; Psalmody; Psalm-Tones; Responsorial Chant; Responsorial Psalm; Responsory; Spirituals**

Music as Worship

Theological reflection on music as worship depends on an interlocking set of assumptions about what music, worship and theology are, how they relate, and what procedures would most fruitfully bring them into correlation. For example, if one assumes that music consists of ordered sound and silence without reference to human intention or perception, birdcalls, whale-songs, gurgling brooks and rustling trees are all musical phenomena and not simply acoustic events. If one also assumes (1) that non-rational living beings do not bring themselves into existence but owe their existence to a divine creator and (2) that these creatures, being incapable of actual sin, exist in a redeemed creation, their music-making would reflect their divine creator's intention without contamination. Their wordless 'pure' music might then be held up as an example of 'pure' worship and humans would be encouraged to follow their example. On the other hand, if one assumes that non-rational living beings produce ordered sounds and silences, but only human beings by intention and/or perception produce music, the categorization of musical phenomena changes. If one further assumes (1) that human beings do not bring themselves into existence but owe their existence to a divine creator and (2) that humans, capable of and fated to actual sin, exist in a sin-corrupted yet redeemed creation, their music-making would respond ambiguously to their divine creator's intention. Wordless 'pure' music might then be forbidden at worship since one could not guarantee that it is not demonically inspired; texted music (especially employing texts perceived to be divinely sanctioned) would be preferred, but even texted music might be suspect since the music might contradict or subvert rather than adorn and embellish an otherwise acceptable text. One's experience

and understanding of music, engagement with and conceptualization of worship, and theological convictions will all have a role to play in assessing music as worship.

This essay will assume: (1) that music is a humanly perceptible ordering of sonic events, with the boundaries between speech, music and noise varying from culture to culture; (2) that worship involves both divine initiative and – through Christ by the power of the Spirit in the church – divinely enabled human response; (3) that theology is the attempt to articulate in an adequate and coherent way knowledge gained from disciplined reflection on divine revelation. Founding itself on biblical insight and the historical tradition of the church, it will inquire about music's origin and status as part of the divinely created order, music's meaning and purpose in the divinely redeemed order, and music's use and misuse in Christian worship.

1. *Music in the Order of Creation.* Christian theology holds that God alone may be considered Absolute, Self-Subsisting, Necessary Being; all other beings, distinct from yet related to God, are contingent and are brought into and sustained in being by divine initiative. As part of the contingent creation, music finds its ultimate origin in God, as do all other beings. (This assertion holds even if one holds that music is generated only by humans; in so far as humans are also part of the created order, their activity must be referred back to their creator.)

Endowed by their Creator with the ability to encounter the world of space and time by means of their senses, human beings gain insight into aspects of reality through their sense of hearing. Edward Foley notes five characteristics of human sound-sensing that both give particular knowledge of the empirical created order and provide metaphors for a distinctive understanding of God. Hearing sound makes time audible for humans in so far as all perception of sound involves an experience of impermanence, acoustic events that come into and go out of existence; this characteristic correlates with the theological claim of the historical character of the created order and the eternal God who really relates to it. Hearing sound confronts humans with the intangible and elusive, since the vibrations that constitute sound do not permanently transform the medium through which they pass; this characteristic correlates with the notion of God as an elusive presence. Hearing sound engages humans in an experience of activity, in contrast to the relatively more static engagement of, e.g., seeing a painting; this characteristic correlates with the concept of God as dynamically initiating contact with humans and seeking their response. Hearing sound invites humans to unitive engagement, especially when they generate sound-events or receive other humanly generated sound-events which unite producer with sound, listener with sound, producer with listener, listener with other listeners, and producer with self; this characteristic correlates with the understanding of a God who seeks unitive engagement with humans. Finally, hearing sound conveys an experience of the personal to humans, in so far as it creates an acoustic space in which personal events unfold; this characteristic correlates with the idea of a God who chooses to address human beings in revealing Godself.

While music belongs to the world of sound, it is a particularly complex structuring of that world, going beyond the fundamental necessities of acoustic communication. In so far as music moves beyond basic sound events to engender beauty and delight, it reveals itself not only as *creatura* like all contingent beings but as gracious gift, an unexpected blessing from a God whose stance toward the created order is not that of reluctant supplier of necessities but of lovingly benevolent philanthropist.

Sound makes time audible but music both reveals and creates a further ordering of time. The Priestly creation narrative in Genesis presents God bringing order to the *tohu wabohu* in a complex construction of light/darkness, firmament/waters, above-earth/earth/under-earth, sun/moon/stars, flying/swimming creatures, domesticated/wild animals, and humanity. This divine creative ordering finds an auditory correlate in music's complex construction of pitches, volumes, durations and timbres. Composers and performers of music demonstrate the unique status of human beings in the created order as *imago Dei* by exercising their creativity in musical structuring of sound, fulfilling the divine mandate to steward the gifts of the created order (including sound) that they have received from the hand of God.

Music not only makes time audible in beauty, it functions as a model and metaphor for creation. In the relationship between composer and performer, with the latter constrained by the score provided by the former yet empowered to actualize the given musical patterns by exercise of creative ingenuity, one discovers

a model for the relationship between God and humanity. Music operates in a realm between total chaos (perhaps exemplified by the aleatory compositional techniques of a John Cage) and mechanistic structure (perhaps exemplified by the 'total serialism' of a Pierre Boulez or computer-generated compositions), providing a metaphor for the mix of determinisms and novelties that mark the created order.

Music may even provide an image for the personal relations of the Triune God. While a dance image *(perichoresis)* has traditionally been applied to the processions of the divine persons, polyphonic compositions give auditory expression to this metaphor. Just as each of the voices in a fugue maintains its own identity yet is derived from an initial motif and just as the music of a fugue consists of the interplay of voices and would cease to be a fugue if only individual voices were sounded separately, so the Son is begotten of the Father and the Spirit proceeds from the Father [and the Son], and yet they form one Godhead with the Father.

Finally, music considered in the order of creation reveals the tension devolving upon the rest of the created order between contemplation and action. In contrast to any Gnostic system which views material creation as evil, orthodox Christianity affirms creation as good, participating in the goodness of its creator. As part of that creation, music is likewise affirmed as good. It needs no further justification: music may be enjoyed for its own sake, like other high pursuits of the human spirit. But creation may also be ordered to proximate and ultimate ends, and music, as part of that creation, may be used for various purposes: stirring emotion, engendering group solidarity, inculcating messages, etc. Worship itself exhibits the same tension between its contemplative dimensions (the 'disinterested' praise and adoration of God) and its pragmatic dimensions (evangelization, catechesis, moral conversion, building community, etc.). But it must be admitted that just as creation's primary purpose is to praise God, so worship is fundamentally adoration of the living God with its other functions ordered to that primary end. Music as worship will share this ordering.

2. *Music in the Order of Redemption.* Many religious systems would share elements of the insights recounted above, modifying them in so far as they conceptualize a single God or multiple gods/goddesses, a personal God or an impersonal Force as ultimate reality, the space-

time world as real or illusory, etc. Thus it is not surprising that music plays a role in most religions' worship.

A distinct perspective on music as worship, however, arises from Christianity's unique understanding of how God has interacted with creation, especially with humanity. Along with many religious and some philosophical systems, Christianity affirms that it is possible to gain some notion of God from examining the empirical universe, 'logic-ing' back from effects to cause. With Judaism and Islam, Christianity affirms that the one, true God has revealed Godself in distinctive interventions in history: in privileged encounters with individuals, in mystical experiences, in written scriptures. But uniquely Christianity affirms that God has ultimately revealed Godself in the life, deeds, death and destiny of Jesus of Nazareth, whose presence and action in the world not only makes God present from 'within' history but transforms that history, creating new possibilities for human encounter and union with God, a transformation with implications for the whole created order.

In contrast to the order of creation that does not need explicit proclamation (since every human being is potentially able to affirm the existence of a creator from the evidence of their own existence and that of the world around them), the order of redemption presumes proclamation. Witnesses testify to what God has done in history and, while such testimony is not limited to worship services, they provide a privileged place for this testimony. The very fact that some human beings gather bodily to worship under Christian auspices establishes them as a witnessing group. During the service they hear narratives of how God has acted in history according to their religious world view. In the light of these narratives liturgical *preaching declares how God is continuing to work in their midst and in their world. Prayer for the needs of the church and the created order is a primary exercise of the priesthood of Christian believers at worship, witnessing to their conscious alignment of themselves with the divine will for working out the effects of redemption in Christ. The faithful are sent from worship into service with blessing and commission. Music can play a role in each of these segments of worship, enhancing the proclamation made to and by Christian believers.

Music in the order of creation might be considered ontologically symbolic; unlike formalists who claim that music's meaning has no reference outside its own sonic structure, those who believe that music is part of a contingent created order declare that it refers beyond itself: to non-human, human and divine spheres of experience. But music in the order of redemption might be considered functionally symbolic, i.e., as a means of communication, especially a medium to present and elucidate a text. Contrary to the view of some theologians who have reduced music to a simple bearer of words, however, music's role in the order of redemption is more complex.

In another context I have suggested that traditional marks of the church announced in the Second Testament all have their musical correlate. To *kerygma*, the effective proclamation of the gospel to those who have not heard the good news of Christ, corresponds 'evangelical' music; its proper venue is not so much the worship service as situations in which non-Christians may be open to the Christian message (radio, television, films, coffee-houses, concerts, etc.). To *didache*, the process by which believers think through the implications of the kerygma for their daily living, corresponds 'catechetical' music; its proper venue is also not so much the worship service as Christian educational venues and teachable moments. To *koinonia*, the communion established among believers by the Holy Spirit, corresponds 'fellowship' music; its proper venue may include the worship service but could extend to situations in which Christians simply rejoice to be together (hymn sings; skits; common meals, etc.). To *diakonia*, the service of church and world in works of charity and action for justice, corresponds 'healing' music, whether of the therapeutic variety found in music therapy or of the confrontational variety found in protest movements and public marches. Note that in so far as *leitourgeia* subsumes and organizes the other functions into a well-ordered whole, worship music will sustain evangelical, catechetical, fellowship and healing characteristics in the context of explicit praise and thanksgiving of the God who makes them possible.

Jeremy Begbie suggests that the Christian narrative of creation/fall/redemption is mirrored in music exhibiting both honesty and hope: honesty at the reality of a disordered world and human complicity in that disorder, yet hope that chaotic meaninglessness will ultimately give way to ordered meaning. This perspective provides criteria for evaluating music: that which balances honesty and hope in creative tension is valuable; that which either, in the name of honesty, embodies unmitigated despair at the disorder of the world or, in the name of hope, enshrines a superficial optimism, is less valuable.

3. *The Use and Misuse of Music in Christian Worship.* Over the twenty centuries of Christian history, three fundamental models regarding music in worship have appeared. The first, represented by figures such as Ambrose of Milan and Martin Luther, regards music as a gift of God, bearing God's word, enabling human praise of God and bold proclamation of God's deeds. The second, represented by thinkers such as Abbot Pambo of Egypt and Ulrich Zwingli, sees no place for music in worship since it pertains to a world of sensuality opposed to pure spiritual worship. The third, represented by individuals such as Augustine of Hippo and John Calvin, admits music into worship, but seeks to restrain its penchant for distracting the faithful from genuine worship by strategies such as restricting its texts to those found in the scriptures and promoting austere musical styles removed from those used for entertainment and enchantment in the wider culture. Once again one's assumptions about what constitutes music and worship determine in large part one's theological judgements about what constitutes proper and improper Christian worship music.

A document entitled *Musicam sacram*, issued in 1967 by the Sacred Congregation for Divine Worship implementing the liturgical music directives of the Constitution on the Sacred Liturgy, adumbrates five functions for Christian worship music from an RC perspective. It may be, first of all, alluring in its effect on worshippers, its beauty adorning worship ceremonies and making worship texts more memorable. Second, it has the potential to unify the assembly of worshippers, the unity of their voices in song symbolizing the unity of their hearts and minds. Third, by distinguishing the various chants performed by clergy, *cantor, *choir and congregation, music differentiates the various roles operative in worship. Fourth, music may serve as a bridge to contemplation, revealing transcendental dimensions in the mundane speech and action of worship. Finally, by employing a variety of styles from many eras and cultures, music may hint at an eschatological dimension in worship, where no single human artefact can capture the fullness of the mystery and where ultimately all sound will find its transfigured fulfilment in God's eternal silence.

Ultimately, choosing proper music for Christian worship will be a matter of making prudential judgements by keeping three aspects in creative tension for each choice: musical (i.e., does the music chosen exhibit characteristics of authentic crafting within particular genres and styles?), liturgical (i.e., does the music chosen serve and illuminate the proper textual-ceremonial ritual unit involved?), and pastoral (i.e., does the music chosen enable gathered believers to receive God's presence and message to them and to offer God their presence, praise, and petition in return?).

———

Jeremy Begbie, *Music in God's Purposes*, Edinburgh 1989; Q. Faulkner, *Wiser than Despair: The Evolution of Ideas in the Relationship of Music and the Christian Church*, Westport, CT 1996; Edward Foley, *Ritual Music: Studies in Liturgical Musicology*, Beltsville, MD 1995; Joseph Gelineau, *Voices and Instruments in Christian Worship: Principles, Laws, Applications*, Collegeville 1964; Jan Michael Joncas, 'Christian Mission and Pastoral Music: Biblical Foundations for Contemporary Practice', *Church Music and Mission*, ed. Stephen Dean, Mildenhall 1996, 53–66; *From Sacred Song to Ritual Music: Twentieth-Century Understandings of Roman Catholic Worship Music*, Collegeville 1997; D. B. Pass, *Music and the Church: A Theology of Church Music*, Nashville 1989; Erik Routley, *The Church and Music*, London 1950; *Church Music and the Christian Faith*, Carol Stream, IL 1978; O. Soehngen, 'Fundamental Considerations for a Theology of Music', *The Musical Heritage of the Church*, ed. T. Hoelty-Nickel, VI, St Louis 1963, 7–16; J. M. Spencer, *Theological Music: Introduction to Theomusicology*. New York 1991; P. Westermeyer, *Te Deum: The Church and Music*, Minneapolis 1998.

JAN MICHAEL JONCAS

Music in the Mass of the Roman Rite

The *mass of the Roman rite is derived structurally from the *papal mass of the early seventh century. Apart from chanted readings and the *celebrant's prayers, the music of the mass falls into two categories, the *proper and the *ordinary. Full musical settings of the texts of these in *Gregorian chant may be found in the *Graduale Romanum*. The *chants of the proper of the mass have texts drawn mainly from the Psalms, differing from day to day. The ordinary chants have fixed texts, the same for all masses, the *Kyrie, Gloria in excelsis, Credo, *Sanctus (with Benedictus) and *Agnus Dei. The Gloria and the Credo are sung on Sundays and feast days. From medieval times to the present day countless settings of the ordinary have been composed, both for voices and for the organ. Certain pieces of the proper have also been set: Byrd's *Gradualia* is a collection of mass propers, Some of the finest music for the mass was composed by the great European masters of the Renaissance.

The Tridentine *Missale Romanum* of 1570 is frequently thought to be a creation of the Council of Trent, under the presidency of Pius V. It was, however, in all essentials a replica of the Roman missal of 1474, which, in its turn, followed the church's practice under Innocent II, itself derived from the usage of Gregory the Great and his successors in the seventh century. The 1570 missal was therefore essentially traditional, indeed more so than the reformed missal of 1971. The modern *Missa normativa* of Pope Paul VI, now the official mass of the RC Church, is usually celebrated in the vernacular. Special permission may be obtained for the occasional celebration of the old so-called 'Tridentine' mass. But the new *Missa normativa* was first formulated in Latin and may therefore be freely and legitimately celebrated in that ancient and universal tongue. When celebrated in Latin, the Church's 'treasury of sacred music', dating from the earliest centuries to the present day, is always available to choirs and congregations. Indeed, it would be a major loss if a repertoire of such momentous cultural and spiritual value were to be permanently deprived of its raison d'être and merely relegated to the concert hall. Latin chants and Latin *polyphony may be successfully combined with readings and prayers in the vernacular during a single celebration. Furthermore, the permission, widely interpreted as an injunction, to celebrate in the vernacular has opened up endless possibilities for the composition of new musical settings of the texts of both proper and ordinary, in English and in other modern languages.

'The Constitution on the Sacred Liturgy' and 'Instruction on Music in the Liturgy', *Vatican Council II: The Conciliar and Post Conciliar Documents*, ed. Austin Flannery, Leominster

1981; Richard L. Crocker, *An Introduction to Gregorian Chant*, New Haven, CT 2000; Thrasybulos Giorgiades, *Music and Language: The Rise of Western Music as Exemplified in Settings of the Mass*, Cambridge 1982; Ferdinand Haberl, *Das Graduale Romanum, liturgische und musikalische Aspekte*, Bonn 1976; *Das Kyriale Romanum, liturgische und musikalische Aspekte*, Bonn 1975; Guy Oury, *La Messe de S. Pie V à Paul VI*, Solesmes 1975; *La Messe Romaine et le Peuple de Dieu dans l'Histoire*, Solesmes 1981; Susan Rankin and David Hiley (eds), *Music in Medieval English Liturgy*, Oxford 1993.

MARY BERRY

Mystagogical Catechesis

If pre-baptismal catechesis in the early church focused on moral formation and Christian lifestyle, and, eventually, on the contents of the *creed, post-baptismal catechesis during Easter Week, called 'Mystagogy' or 'mystagogical catechesis' (i.e., 'explanation of the mysteries'), focused on the unfolding of the meaning of the 'mysteries' or *sacraments of Christian initiation and *eucharist which the neophytes had just received and experienced at the *Easter vigil. Hints of some post-baptismal catechesis appear already in the *Apostolic Tradition*, but the use of the term itself, perhaps borrowed from the Graeco-Roman mystery religions, appears to have become common only in the late fourth century and Cyril (or John) of Jerusalem may well be the first to have employed it to describe the process at Jerusalem. With the *De sacramentis* and *De mysteriis* of Ambrose of Milan, Cyril's own *Catecheses mystagogicae* share a common pedagogical approach, namely, that the experience of Christian initiation and eucharist precedes extended reflection and step-by-step explication of these sacramental liturgies. As such, it is primarily from these and similar extant mystagogical homilies that we are able to reconstruct liturgical practice at Milan, Jerusalem and elsewhere during this time period.

With the demise of the adult *catechumenate and the rise of infant *baptism, so mystagogy in the classic sense of the word also ceased. Nevertheless, even in the early Middle Ages at Rome (e.g. the Gelasian Sacramentary and other documents) it appears that parents and *godparents still brought their infant neophytes to daily eucharist and vespers during Easter

Week. And, in the case of infants, with catechesis ultimately and necessarily postponed until after baptism, there is a sense in which all catechesis became, essentially, post-baptismal, or lifelong mystagogy.

The publication of the RC *Rites of Christian Initiation of Adults* (1972), often adapted in several other Christian traditions today, restored the period of mystagogy as the final period of the adult catechumenate. In modern RC practice, this period begins at *Easter and culminates at *Pentecost, although it is to continue with at least monthly gatherings of the neophytes until the following Easter. Today, the focus of mystagogy includes continued formation and integration into the life and mission of the Christian community as the result and implication of initiation and eucharist.

Enrico Mazza, *Mystagogy: A Theology of Liturgy in the Patristic Age*, Collegeville1989; Edward Yarnold, *The Awe-Inspiring Rites of Initiation: The Origins of the R.C.I.A.*, 2nd edn Edinburgh/Collegeville 1994.

MAXWELL E. JOHNSON

Mystery

One can see the search for mystery in the earliest indications of humanity, in the diverse mythological art and writings of yet more advanced human civilizations, in philosophical studies, both East and West, and in the reflections which one finds in all religions. Both the term and the realities of 'mystery' are tensive, i.e., they have a large range of referents. The spectrum of these referents is diverse. Major scholars have studied the mystery: of the divine, of God, of the transcendent, of the universe, of life, of the unconscious, but they have also studied the mystery of the occult, of evil and of sin. It is a very complex undertaking to speak of the mystery of the Christian sacraments, of Christian liturgy and Christian spirituality.

In Christian sacramental and liturgical rituals and theological discourse various interpretations of 'mystery' have played major roles throughout history. Early Christian writers frequently describe their liturgical rites as being 'mysteries' (Greek, *mysterion*; Latin, *mysterium*), and in the Eastern churches the celebration of the *eucharist is still called a celebration of the sacred mysteries. In Western theological writings and in liturgical celebrations both

baptism and eucharist have also been called the holy mysteries, although the term *sacrament has been more commonly employed. Mystery and sacrament are profoundly interconnected. Mystery and sacramental spirituality are also deeply intertwined.

RC theology of the sacraments began to undergo a significant renewal in the first half of the twentieth century, in large part as a consequence of the *Liturgical Movement. The Benedictine Odo Casel's 'Mysterienlehre', for example, helped move *eucharistic theology away from its reliance on traditional scholastic analysis (matter and form, substance and accident). For Casel (as for Leo the Great), the mysteries of Christ's life have passed over into the sacraments of the church, where they are enacted, embodied, and 're-presented'. Casel's thought, though controversial, was to have considerable influence on Vatican Council II's notion of the 'paschal mystery' as the efficacious centre and source of the church's sacramental life.

Modern liturgical and sacramental thinking centres profoundly on human experience in the presence of the divine. Perhaps the term 'experience' indicates best where both Protestant and Catholic have moved in a central way. *Mystagogy is a major term in baptismal and eucharistic initiation. Sacraments centre on the mystery of our faith, a faith which is not academic, but lived in human experience. The mystery of the word is indispensable for an understanding of the mystery of the sacraments, especially the eucharist. Protestants have celebrated the word far more than Catholics, but third-millennium Catholics have united both word and sacrament in an intrinsic way. Not only is this done in theological explanation, but in the experiential celebration of sacramental life.

A central issue on this current focus of mystery is this: Protestant thought has long emphasized that one is saved by faith alone, that good works do not bring about salvation. Catholics, since the Reformation, have struggled to balance faith alone and good works. Mystery needs to be appreciated in a similar way. In the mystery of faith God is always prior to human response. In the mystery of the liturgy God acts and only then do we respond.

David Brown (ed.), *Christ the Sacramental Word*, London 1996; Odo Casel, *The Mystery of Christian Worship*, Westminster, MD 1962 (originally published in German, 1932);

Michael Lawler, *Symbol and Sacrament*, New York 1995; David Power, *Sacrament: The Language of God's Giving*, New York 1999.

KENAN B. OSBORNE

Narthex

An entry porch that can be exterior or interior. An interior narthex of a church can extend the entire width of the building and is usually separated from the main body of the church by a wall with doors, or by an arcade. The narthex serves as a gathering place for processions, as a funerary wake space, or as a place for introductory rites. It is occasionally called a *Galilee* or *Paradise*.

MARCHITA B. MAUCK

Nave

The central part of a church between the entrance and the crossing of the *transept. The nave is usually flanked by aisles, and is characteristically taller than the adjacent aisle or aisles. The nave arcades that separate the nave from the aisles support the clerestory (walls taller than the roofs of the aisles, pierced with windows to allow light directly into the nave).

MARCHITA B. MAUCK

Nestorian Church

see **East Syrian Worship**

New Fire

The ceremony of the new fire takes place at the Church of the Holy Sepulchre in Jerusalem during the *Easter vigil. From the early Middle Ages it has been the practice to bring a candle, lit from the 'eternal flame' which burns at the Sepulchre, and to distribute the fire to the pilgrims assembled there for Easter. The newly produced fire is thought by many pilgrims to be a miracle of spontaneous ignition, and is seen as a powerful symbol of the resurrection. The ceremony was imitated in other Eastern churches, and was transported to the churches of the West and adapted to local situations. At Leon, Milan and Beneventum the fire was brought out of the sacristy; at Rome a flame was reserved in a remote part of the Cathedral of St John Lateran, in readiness for Easter. The ceremonial varied from church to church, and became modified and subsequently replaced by alternative new-fire rites adopted from the pre-Christian religious rituals of northern Europe.

From at least the ninth century it became the practice in a number of Gallican churches for the new fire to be kindled annually on *Maundy Thursday and reserved until the Easter vigil, or at the vigil itself, either by friction (flint against steel) or by the refraction of the sun's rays (using a lens or translucent stone). Evidence for the former means is more plentiful in view of the vagaries of the European weather and the use of an interior location for the kindling in many churches. Medieval symbolism saw in the leaping of a spark from the stone to ignite the tinder a symbolic re-enactment of the resurrection, and the lens was seen as the 'clear resurrection body of Christ' bringing new life to the world. In the Roman rite firm evidence for the kindling, as opposed to the reservation, of new fire dates from the tenth century.

In view of the ease with which fire can be kindled today, the ceremony has lost much of its former importance and significance. In pre-Christian Europe fires were lit annually for a number of different religious reasons. The church adopted rather than suppressed the ceremonies for evangelistic purposes. For the carrying of fire, blessed by the church, to every home both placed those homes under the protection of the church and also gave the church potential spiritual authority over them. Moreover, it was a widely held belief that the person who kindled the fire possessed authority over the ground on which the ceremony took place.

From its first appearance in Christian ceremonial over eleven hundred years ago the new fire has been honoured with a *procession. In northern Europe it was formerly conveyed by means of a candle, sometimes shaped like a serpent, whilst Prudentius' hymn *Inventor rutili* was sung as the procession moved into church prior to the lighting of the *Easter candle. The practice of chanting *Lumen Christi*, 'The Light of Christ', three times seems to be an Italian innovation, as was the now-superseded triple candle which bore the new fire.

Adrian Fortescue and J. B. O'Connell (eds), *The Ceremonies of the Roman Rite*, 1st and 11th editions, London 1917 and 1960; A. J. MacGregor, *Fire and Light in the Western Triduum*, Collegeville 1992.

A. J. MACGREGOR

New Testament Worship

Modern English translations of the NT use

'worship' for a number of Greek words suggesting piety, service and obeisance, referring not only to cultic activities or to acts of homage or adoration, but also to general dispositions such as faith and religious allegiance. In this broad sense, 'worship' includes pagan (1 Cor. 10.14) as well as Jewish (Heb. 8.5) practices, and continuous heavenly praise (Rev. 5.14) as well as specific personal actions (John 9.38). What now appears as 'worship' then involved not only public or communal processes such as sacrifice or prayer, but meals, education and other things besides. The more specific (and later) sense of worship as Christian communal prayer and ritual will be the main concern here.

1. *Using the Evidence of the New Testament.* The NT offers important evidence for the earliest Christian actions that we might now gather under the title 'worship', but often assumes or alludes to basic practices rather than fully prescribing or describing orders of proceedings. The gospels are likely to reflect early Christian liturgical practice even where referring to the ministry of Jesus, but it is difficult to be sure where and how. Likely sources of evidence in the Gospels and Acts might include references to prayer, meals and other practices common to the Jesus movement and the early church, where some retrojection of later uses may be involved. Paul's and other letters provide theological underpinnings for worship, refer to some elements of practice in criticizing excesses or misunderstandings, and may also include hymns and other liturgical formulae.

Careful attention to the various genres of the NT literature, the cultural background of Jewish and other Graeco-Roman settings, and to our own presuppositions, are all necessary. We should probably assume a basic diversity of practice regarding prayer and ritual, similar to the obvious theological diversity of the documents. Hence there is no single picture to be reconstructed from behind the texts, beyond the common assertion of the early Christians and their literature that worship (in the broadest sense) belongs to Jesus Christ.

2. *Jewish Practice and Early Christian Worship.* NT worship is often Jewish worship of one kind or another. Early NT traditions assume Christian participation in various forms of Jewish practice, including the liturgies of the Temple, as well as (or including) distinctive gatherings of the Christian community. The ministry of Jesus is linked to the Temple (not

without tension: Mark 11.15–19) and the early Christians who were Jews seem to have continued to participate in its life (Acts 2.46), including the sacrifices (Matt. 5.23–24; Acts 21.26; cf. Num. 6.1–21). The destruction of the Temple in 70 CE may have encouraged use of sacrificial imagery and thought elsewhere, such as for the eucharistic meal.

The synagogue was also an important setting for worship, especially away from Jerusalem (Luke 4.16–27), but its practices were probably quite fluid through the first few centuries; reading of scripture and instruction are all that can be assumed in NT references. Both Jesus (Mark 1.39; Luke 4.16) and the earliest Christians (Acts 13.5) seem to have participated in the synagogue and used it as a base for preaching. It is less likely than previously assumed that there was some general 'expulsion' of Christians from synagogues (see John 9.22), even late in the first century; in any case, breaches of relationship did not preclude continuing mutual influence between Christianity and (other) forms of Judaism.

Christians may nevertheless have formed distinct gatherings for prayer well prior to formal and definitive separation from Judaism (cf. the Qumran community). In some cases, a specifically Christian assembly might be referred to as a 'synagogue' (James 2.2). This does not mean the synagogue was the only or even main source of Jewish religious influence on Christian worship. Domestic settings for prayer (at meals and at various times of day) and instruction may also be assumed. When a gathered community (Acts 2.46) rather than the household is involved, *chavuroth* or associations such as were formed by the Pharisees may have been models.

3. *Initiation.* *Baptism is certainly one element retained by the Christian community from its Jewish setting, although the exact origins of the practice cannot clearly be traced past the figure of John the Baptist. Jesus' own baptism (Mark 1.9–11, etc) seems to stand in the synoptic Gospels as a model; John's Gospel has him baptizing, rather than baptized (John 3.22). The Matthean command to baptize (28.16–20) is clear and could suggest a triadic formula or ritual, although in the Pauline and Lucan documents baptism 'in the name of Jesus' seems to have been the expected form (Acts 2.38, 8.16, etc.; 1 Cor 6.11). In neither case should a specific form of words be assumed. Understandings of baptism vary, including emphasis on repent-

ance and purification, participation in Jesus' messianic identity, incorporation into his death and resurrection, reception of the Holy Spirit, and others besides.

Further ritual elements are not especially clear. Imagery evocative of *anointing and/or sealing (e.g. 2 Cor. 1.21–22), or of stripping and/or reclothing (Gal. 3.27), may be the inspiration for later ceremonial elaboration, rather than evidence for such early use of these practices. Laying-on of hands does seem to have occurred early and widely (Heb. 6.2), but a clear ritual pattern is hard to discern; the Acts of the Apostles provides much data, but varying as far as the order of ritual and meaning of this gesture is concerned (8.14–17; 19.1–7).

4. *Eucharistic Meals*. Communal meals with ritual dimensions are a distinctive and common tradition in the earliest Christian practice. The prominence of the Last Supper as a basis for the meal (1 Cor. 11.23–26; cf. Mark 14.22–25) is clear, although it can be exaggerated. In various ways the synoptic Gospels, Paul and the Gospel of John all connect that final meal with Passover (Mark 14.12–16 and parallels; 1 Cor. 5.7; John 13.1; 18.28; cf. 6.1–59). None, however, describe a recognizable Jewish *seder*; regardless of the historical problems concerning the original event, these texts are now presented in some relation to the ongoing Christian meal.

For Paul, the meal commemorating Jesus' death is the '*Lord's supper' (1 Cor. 11.20). Other names and motifs reflect a diversity of early eucharistic theory and practice. The Lucan phrase 'breaking of the bread' (Luke 24.30–35; Acts 2.42, etc.) also describes the *eucharist, but evokes the resurrection appearances and the ministry of Jesus (Luke 9.12–17). Numerous stories of Jesus' meals, including the miraculous feedings, seem to have elements that reflect Christian liturgy. Others call the meal (or the gathering that includes it) *agape, 'love(-feast)' (Jude 12). A diversity of meal traditions broadly linked with the practice of Jesus therefore seems more likely than a sole (or dual, i.e., eucharist and agape) meal-model.

5. *Other Elements*. Meal gatherings also included other elements; in Acts, the 'breaking of the bread' is associated with teaching (20.7f.; cf. 2.42). Paul's instructions on spiritual gifts (1 Cor. 12) immediately after those on the Lord's supper may imply that instruction,

prophecy and other forms of inspired speech took place in that setting (cf. *Didache* 10.7), but not that they only occurred there. The prominence of ecstatic and other charismatic elements in gatherings at Corinth (1 Cor. 14) should not be taken as evidence for all communities (cf. Matt. 6.7–13), or even as prescribing these elements for worship in Pauline churches. Paul indicates concern for an orderly and edifying communal gathering, but no particular structure linking 'word' and 'table' is apparent.

Not all gatherings were eucharistic. Christians seem often to have observed set times of prayer during the day, in some continuity with Judaism (Acts 3.1), although the precise times, as well as the form and content, were variable at this point.

The use of 'psalms and hymns and spiritual songs' (Eph. 5.19; Col. 3.16), at meal gatherings and elsewhere, is clear. While the biblical Psalms were included in Christian worship, new compositions may be preserved in narratives (Luke 1.46–55, etc.) as well as cited in letters (Phil 2.6–11, etc.). Not all poetic compositions, however, can be assumed to have been used in worship prior to their appearance in NT literature. Less clear again is the exact use or setting of formulaic statements often regarded as connected to baptism (Gal. 3.28) or eucharist (1 Cor. 11.23–25). While these could be pronouncements accompanying ritual actions, they might also have been catechetical formulae.

Although some have suggested the structure of the Pauline writings reflects a liturgical process, the *kiss (Rom. 16.16) found at the end of five letters may simply indicate the form of greeting common in the Christian communities. Such attempts to see whole liturgies or ritual processes reflected in the structure of NT documents have generally been more valiant than convincing, and the increasing acknowledgement of early liturgical diversity makes reading one document in terms of other evidence less plausible than ever.

David E. Aune, 'Worship, Early Christian', *Anchor Bible Dictionary*, New York 1992, VI, 973–8 (bib.); Paul F. Bradshaw, *Daily Prayer in the Early Church*, London 1981/New York 1982; *The Search for the Origins of Christian Worship*, London/New York 2002 (bib.); Larry Hurtado, *At the Origins of Christian Worship*, Carlisle 1999 (bib.); Ralph P. Martin, *Worship in the Early Church*, London 1974.

ANDREW MCGOWAN

Nocturns *see* **Daily Prayer**

None *see* **Daily Prayer**

Noonday Prayer *see* **Daily Prayer**

North India, Worship in the Church of

The Church of North India was the result of a multilateral union of churches of diverse ecclesiastical and confessional traditions – the (Anglican) Church of India, the Methodist Church of British and Australian provenance, the Congregationalist, Baptist and Presbyterian Churches, the Church of the Brethren and the Disciples of Christ Church – which united on 29 November 1970 at the Indian city of Nagpur. In addition to acceptance of the Nicene and the Apostles' *Creeds as authoritative summaries of the true faith, the Church of North India upholds the canonical scriptures of the OT and NT, it affirms the accustomed worship and rites of the church universal, pre-eminent among them the two sacraments of *baptism and the *Lord's supper, and it perpetuates the time-honoured ministry of *bishops, *presbyters and *deacons. Regarding the form and nature of worship, the Constitution and by-laws lay down that the Church of North India aims at conserving for the common benefit whatever spiritual riches were gained by the uniting churches in their pre-union existence and separate experience. Forms of worship which were generally accepted prior to the union and were still used in any of the uniting churches are allowed to continue, and no form of worship or ritual to which any member may conscientiously object may be imposed on any congregation.

The task of developing new forms of worship was assigned to the Liturgical Commission, which began its work by making available alternative forms of worship on experimental basis. From 1976 onwards it prepared and distributed separate orders of worship in booklets. The 'Lima' eucharistic liturgy of the World Council of Churches was also used. All these experimental resources, along with a three-year *lectionary for Sundays and major festivals and liturgies for *ordination, were constantly reviewed and revised, and eventually culminated in the production of a single volume, the *Book of Worship*, which was released on the occasion of the twenty-fifth anniversary of the Church in 1995. One advantage of having the forms within a single cover is that it has encouraged members of the church to avail themselves more fully of what is now the common property of the church but of which previously they might not have been aware. The Liturgical Commission drew upon the different traditions of the uniting churches to produce forms of worship acceptable to all, and the Preface to the *Book of Worship* invites its users to point out any valuable liturgical element in any tradition that has been overlooked or neglected. The work of the Commission has also been ecumenical. It has tried to keep in touch with the *Liturgical Movement of the wider church, particularly regarding the use of cultural motifs, symbolism and idiom, and it has endeavoured to ensure that the language of the worship resources combines simplicity with dignity and is gender-*inclusive.

The release of the *Book of Worship* marked only an initial step in an ongoing process of evolution of worship and was not an attempt to impose uniformity. It is obvious from the number of alternatives which are offered that many decisions are left to local congregations, and there is ample allowance for the presbyter and the worshippers to adapt or even alter the contents according to local needs and priorities. So, far from calling a halt to the spirit of experimenting, its use has encouraged the worship to be more open to the guidance of the Holy Spirit in discovering new forms to express devotion to God. Worship in the Church of North India has been governed by the twin principles of freedom and of order. It had been found from experience that different church traditions had tended sometimes to stress one principle at the expense of the other. But it is increasingly being realized that genuine worship in spirit and truth has to be both ordered and free. The Liturgical Commission has sought to give expression to this dialectical principle of 'ordered freedom'. So the basic structure of liturgies is clearly indicated in order that the purpose and direction of worship may be easily understood. At the same time the content of the worship is open to be adapted with greater freedom.

The territorial jurisdiction of the Church is spread over an area of more than two-thirds of the Indian subcontinent. This geographical expanse contains and exhibits a rich diversity of culture and lifestyle, and during its existence for the last three decades the church has been seeking to develop bold experimentation with local culture to evolve new forms and experiences of worship in its pluralistic context. One of its nine projected priorities is 'indigenisation and contextualisation of life, work and worship of the Church'. This indicates that meeting the challenge of *inculturation and evolving meaningful, relevant and vibrant forms of worship will be an ongoing preoccupation. The task also presupposes translations in future into various regional languages of India. As it is natural for the members of the church to express their worship in terms of their own culture, presbyters are encouraged to have a truly indigenous setting for worship in keeping with the local culture, which will differ from region to region. This aspect includes such details as the arrangements of the place, the use of such accessories as lamps, *incense or *bells, *vestments and *music, and also on appropriate occasions the introduction of cultural elements such as *rangoli* (symbolic and decorative designs worked out in powdered colours usually on the floor of a shrine) and similar visual motifs, and even *dance and *drama. The posture of worshippers is another aspect which has been given serious attention. In the Indian context, with the exception of urban churches, worshippers usually sit on the floor because in rural congregations benches, chairs and pews are not available. For literate congregations changes in posture are indicated in the rubrics of the liturgy, but in the rural congregations this is done through announcements made by the presbyter.

The experience of worship is a complex phenomenon variously defined. In the Indian context it is seen as a response of adoration or an attitude of *bhakti* or loving devotion invoked in the believers who encounter the presence of the divine. It has also been described as grateful rejoicing of those who experience the divine hand guiding their lives. However, it is possible for the use of set forms of prayers and liturgies to degenerate into a mechanical and shallow exercise without any meaningful, imaginative and inspirational dimensions. At a number of points in the liturgies of the Church of North India, therefore, a *rubric prescribes an interval of silence. Nowadays in the rush of busy life, the use of silence in prayer can be quite difficult and even trying for many of the worshippers. In the tradition of Indian spirituality, it is in moments of silent submission of prayer that the Holy Spirit may communicate most vividly to the heart of the worshippers.

See also **South India, Worship in the Church of.**

GODWIN R. SINGH

Notation and Rhythm

Isidore of Seville (*c*. 560–636) claimed that in his day music was taught and passed on orally, for there was no way of setting down audible sounds on the parchment. The invention of a system of neume notation was therefore a major event. The term 'neume' appears to be derived from a Greek word meaning 'sign'. If a singer traces in the air with his hand the movement of his voice, so too the pen of a scribe might trace on parchment the movement of the singer's hand, following the flow of the melody. Some form of sign notation was possibly already known to the Synod of Cloveshoe (747), and certainly to Charlemagne (747–814), legislating for the programme of studies in his schools. Even punctuation is itself a rudimentary written notation. The earliest surviving musical notation, however, is probably that of Engyldeo of St Emmeram, Regensburg (*c*. 817–34).

Fully notated manuscripts appear shortly before 900. Various schools of neume notation arose, in centres like St Gall or Laon, each devising ways of showing pitch, rhythm, and occasionally dynamics. Before staff-lines were invented notation was written *in campo aperto* ('in an open field'), without precise indications of pitch. Later, heighted neums placed relatively higher or lower foreshadowed an invisible stave. Pitch imprecision presented no inconvenience, since the whole repertoire was still memorized: the notated books were probably intended for reference purposes, not for sight-reading.

The earliest rhythmic indications are today revealing their secrets. Sometimes the shape of a sign is modified to show length or brevity. Sometimes a different sign is used – a dot replacing a stroke, for example, indicating extreme brevity. Sometimes an extra sign is attached to a note to show length. Letters indicate pitch, rhythm or dynamics: 'l', *levate*, indicates higher pitch, 'c', *celeriter*, fast, 't', *trahere*, hold back. Another principle, that of *coupure*, first described by Cardine in 1957, was an ingenious way of showing length by separating the notational elements.

The four-lined stave came into general use in the twelfth century when the detailed indications of earlier manuscripts were fast disappearing. Traditional performance practice was losing ground with the rise of measured music, resulting in a slowing down of the chant. Notation became thicker and heavier, developing into 'square notation' similar to that of modern service books. Scholars dispute possible interpretations of the chant rhythm, which depends upon many factors: evidence demonstrates that the chant was performed differently at different periods of its long existence.

From c. 1250 various systems of mensural notation for *polyphony arose, in which note-shapes borrowed from chant notation were gradually developed, added to, and allotted values of duration. Chant manuscripts copied during the next few hundred years are generally faithful to tradition, as were early printed service books, although under the influence of mensural notation they sometimes exhibit a degree of rhythmic ambiguity. In polyphonic music, at first a 'mensuration sign' ruled the relationship between the different note-shapes. When, from c. 1450, the so-called white or void, mensural notation took over from the black, musicians were already well on their way to developing our modern western system of fixed note-values.

Eugene Cardine, *Gregorian Semiology*, Solesmes 1982; Solange Corbin, *Die Neumen*, Cologne 1977; Leo Treitler, 'Reading and Singing: On the Genesis of Occidental Music-Writing', *Early Music History* IV, 1984, 135'208. See also the series produced by the monks of Solesmes, *Paléographie musicale*, in particular II (2e séries), *Cantatorium, IXe siècle, MS St Gall 359*, Solesmes 1924 (revised edn), and X (1e série), *Antiphonale Missarum Sancti Gregorii Ixe–Xe siècle, Codex 259 de la Bibliothèque de Laon*, Solesmes 1909.

MARY BERRY

Nunc dimittis *see* Canticles

Octave

The celebration of a feast again on the eighth day after the feast itself (the day itself being reckoned as the first day) or continuously throughout the eight-day period. It became a significant feature of the medieval Latin rite, and continued as such in the RC rite until largely abolished by the liturgical reforms that followed the Second Vatican Council. As a consequence of this it is a custom that has virtually disappeared from modern liturgy. It

could be argued that major feasts merit the additional emphasis that this custom gave them, and no doubt the practice originated in the first place for this reason, but with the passage of time the increasing number of feasts that were granted octaves devalued the whole idea. It now seems extremely unlikely that any serious attempt will ever be made to revive the custom.

RICHARD F. BUXTON

Offertory

By its title, offertory refers to the presentation of something in the liturgy. Essentially Western as a term, in the RC rite it has for centuries meant the preparation of the bread and wine at the *eucharist. Simple enough in principle, it has had a controverted history. In the East, there is no such rite during the liturgy, since the gifts are prepared beforehand, and the bread and wine are transferred from the *prothesis to the *altar at the *great entrance. In the early Anglican rites, however, the offertory was replaced by the presentation of the collection of money, deliberately positioned in order to de-emphasize the possible sacrificial overtones of the eucharist.

The early Roman Sacramentaries contain prayers for use *super oblata, 'over the oblations', to be recited by the president at the conclusion of the preparation of the gifts, which was often a lengthy process. The choir would sing a chant while the bread and wine were carried forward by members of the congregation, and the vessels filled from them, sufficient for the distribution of *communion. The eighth-century *Ordo Romanus Primus*, probably reflecting earlier usage, describes the fuller version of this process, but it would obviously be considerably simpler, involve fewer people – and vessels – in a more modest context. With the growth of the side-altar *mass in the Carolingian monasteries, the priest himself took over all the responsibilities of others, with the exception of the presentation of the wine and water *cruets. At these celebrations, the chant became recited instead by the priest, who then said a number of prayers to accompany each of the actions involved in preparing the paten with the *host, mixing the *chalice and placing it on the altar, and washing his hands. The offertory prayers became a devotional backdrop for the priest, along with other devotional prayers at the start of the mass and before and after making his communion.

They were sometimes called 'the little canon', demonstrating their importance, as well as the fact that they were laden with sacrificial imagery. Through the Middle Ages, different regions and religious orders developed their own repertoire, and though a few of these were allowed to be retained, most disappeared when the Missal of the Council of Trent was introduced in 1570.

The Reformers swept aside this offertory, and because of their insistence on the congregation's part in the service, not least as communicants in both kinds, the preparation of the gifts was seen as functional rather than symbolic, let alone allegorical. The 1549 and 1552 Prayer Books in England step by step threw the eucharistic spotlight away from being a preparation, consecration and communion of the bread and wine, to being a preparation of the congregation so that they could faithfully receive the elements. Accordingly, at the point where the offertory of the bread and wine used to take place, there was instead an offering of money, a new action for congregations to perform in the liturgy; and as if to underline the fact, *sentences from scripture were to be read out by the priest while this was going on. The large *alms dish used to gather the collection sometimes had eucharistic symbolism on it. In time, the new style offertory migrated into nearly all services other than the eucharist, as a witness to the intrinsic connection between worship and service. But the solemn presentation of the eucharistic gifts at the holy table did not die away, as seventeenth-century Anglican writers make clear, and later Anglican revisions, e.g. the Scottish Liturgy of 1637, refer to this action as if it were just as much symbolic as functional.

In the 1930s, liturgical renewal, usually in the context of loyal adherence to the authorized rites, saw the introduction of the 'offertory procession' in the Anglican Communion. Viewed as a revival of the kind of ceremonial described on the grand scale in the *Ordo Romanus primus*, this custom gained popularity easily, as members of the congregation would bring up the bread and wine, and the money, at the offertory, and the prayer often used, inspired by 1 Chron. 29.11ff. ('Thine, O Lord, is the greatness and the power . . .') was taken to refer to all that was being presented. Thus, the Anglican reaction at the Reformation provided its own way for the reintroduction of the offertory, whether or not the precise means was as ancient as some of its enthusiasts believed; and it

served to engender a sense of the eucharist being a people's liturgy, especially if the bread and wine had been literally prepared at home. Later liturgical revisions have sought to regularize some of these developments.

In the RC Church, offertory processions, with the eucharistic gifts (only), also began to appear, paving the way for the liturgical revisions after the Second Vatican Council. The 1970 RC Missal encouraged such processions, in the context of a liturgy in which the offertory prayers were considerably simplified. The Jewish-style *berakoth* prayers that were then introduced ('Blessed are you . . .') were only intended to be recited aloud at a said eucharist (and to be whispered during the offertory chant at sung celebrations), but they have proved so popular that they have even spilled over into Anglican usage, albeit optional.

The offertory marks a complex web of history, in which the church's ambivalent relationship with the created order is played out in terms of how far the redemption it heralds is enacted in ritual – or sacramental – terms. There is an inescapable sense in which the eucharist is about relinquishing the things of this world, so that God may bless them to his use on his own, without the human race getting in the way. But the church needs ritual actions and words in order to express this with appropriate reticence. As far as the collection is concerned, a consumer society is rightly fascinated by the reality of its own dependence on others for its sustenance and appropriate, wider responsibilities.

See also **Chants of the Proper of the Mass; Music in the Mass of the Roman Rite**.

Colin O. Buchanan, *The End of the Offertory – An Anglican Study*, Nottingham 1978; Kenneth W. Stevenson, *Eucharist and Offering*, New York 1986.

KENNETH W. STEVENSON

Office, Divine *see* Daily Prayer

Office Hymn

Metrical hymns emerged in the West in the fourth century, but were at first looked on with suspicion and only very gradually found their way into regular services in the succeeding centuries, usually being accepted in monastic offices before they were admitted into wider ecclesiastical practice. Monastic rules assigned particular hymns for regular use at specific hours of *daily prayer for which they were deemed appropriate, and it is these to which the designation 'office hymn' is given.

EDITOR

Old Catholic Worship

In order to understand Old Catholic worship, it is essential to comprehend that the Old Catholic churches of the Union of Utrecht are autonomous local churches. The Union of Utrecht itself, established in 1889, is 'a union of churches and bishops governing them who are determined to maintain and pass on the faith, worship, and essential structure of the undivided Church of the first millennium' (*Statute of the Bishops United in the Union of Utrecht, Ecclesiological Foundations*). Unlike the RC and other churches, the Old Catholic churches are not a centralized church body; and unlike the churches of the Anglican Communion with which the Old Catholic churches have been in full communion since 1931/32, they are not metropolitically organized. The bishop-in-synod governs the church, without any interference from outside the diocese. The liturgy of each church is set by the implementation of the *ius liturgicum* of the *bishop governing that church.

Old Catholic churches of the Union of Utrecht governed by a bishop exist in the Netherlands, Germany, Switzerland, Austria, the Czech Republic, the USA, Canada and Poland. There are also parishes and communities in France, Italy, Scandinavia, Slovakia and Croatia. Since 1965 the Old Catholic churches of the Union of Utrecht have been in full communion with the Philippine Independent Church. Old Catholics consider themselves to be the Catholics in that particular country in continuity with the catholic church prior to the First Vatican Council (contrary to the 'New Catholics' adopting the papal dogmas of infallibility and supreme jurisdiction). Thus, they have common liturgical roots with RCs, Anglicans and Lutherans.

The Old Catholic Church of the Netherlands is the continuing church for which Willibrord was consecrated Archbishop of Utrecht in 695. In 1723 Cornelius Steenoven was elected and consecrated archbishop but was refused recognition by Rome and excommunicated. Since that time the church has officially existed as the 'Roman Catholic Church of the old episcopal clergy'. Worship life continued in Latin, following the Roman post-Tridentine liturgy almost completely. This church began to call itself 'Old Catholic' after 1870. In the first decade of the twentieth century, liturgical books in Dutch were issued.

Catholics in Germany, Switzerland and the Austro-Hungarian Empire unwilling to accept the papal dogmas of 1870 were forced, after their excommunication by their bishops, to establish parishes of their own. The Old Catholics, as they came to be known, since they intended to adhere to the old faith of the catholic church, established synods in whom the laity had the majority and elected bishops (Germany in 1873, Switzerland in 1876, Austria [a diocesan administrator] in 1886). The bishops of these three countries, together with the Dutch bishops, linked up in 1889 to form the Union of Utrecht which was later joined by other duly elected and consecrated bishops.

Worship in these German- (and French-) speaking countries was soon celebrated according to adaptations of the then RC texts and ritual. But there were radical departures from RC usage as well as theology: the assembled congregation played an integral part, the liturgy was celebrated in the vernacular, private *masses were rejected, the character of the *eucharist as both memorial and sacrificial meal was emphasized. Many devotions found in other catholic churches like shrines, *pilgrimages, the veneration of images, the *Sacred Heart, an abundance of *Marian feasts, were rejected. Indulgences, surplice fees and other RC peculiarities were abandoned. Considerable influence was exercised in the establishment of a genuine Old Catholic worship life by Eduard Herzog (1841–1924), who from 1876 until his death was the first bishop of the Christian Catholic (i.e., Old Catholic) Church of Switzerland, and Adolf Thürlings (1844–1915), professor of liturgy at the university in Bern and eminent expert in patristics and musicologist.

The Polish National Catholic Church in the USA and Canada, founded in 1897, and the Polish Catholic Church in Poland, established after the First World War, translated the Roman rite into Polish (without deviations).

From the mid-twentieth century onwards, the Old Catholic churches in western Europe, like most other churches, began to revise their liturgies, following the impact of the *Liturgical Movement. Although each church retains some local colour, the patterns (official as well as private 'adaptations') have become identical to those of the other Western catholic churches. Full communion with the Anglican Communion has had considerable effect in this process in that theological views and various Anglican texts have been incorporated into revised Old Catholic liturgies. The most 'productive' churches have been those in the Netherlands, Germany and – since the late 1990s – the Czech Republic. English (and even Spanish) has increasingly replaced Polish as the liturgical language in the USA and Canada.

The International Bishops' Conference of the Union of Utrecht established the International Old Catholic Liturgical Commission in the 1970s as the standing commission to advise in matters liturgical and to draft common rites and liturgical texts, when desired (eucharist, *ordination). A representative of the Archbishop of Canterbury is a full voting member of that commission. All Old Catholic churches have reacted positively to the World Council of Churches' *Baptism, Eucharist and Ministry*, trying through their individual liturgical commissions or through the International Liturgical Commission to include the theology expressed in that document in their own liturgical life. The churches in the Netherlands, Germany, Switzerland and Austria have ordained women to the diaconate and presbyterate and have opened the way to the episcopate to them as well, a course strictly rejected by the Polish National Catholic Church as not in accordance with the catholic faith.

Antonius Jan Glazemaker, 'Eucharistie und Amt', *Christus Spes: Liturgie und Glaube im ökumenischen Kontext*, ed. Angela Berlis and Klaus-Dieter Gerth, Frankfurt 1994, 157–61 (English summary); Petrus Maan, 'The Old Catholic Liturgies', *Old Catholics and Anglicans 1931–1981*, ed. Gordon Huelin, Oxford 1983, 86–95; Thaddeus A. Schnitker, 'The New Altar Book of the Old Catholic Church in Germany', *Studia Liturgica* XXXI, 2001, 119–24.

THADDEUS A. SCHNITKER

Old Testament Worship

A wide variety of modes and styles of worship are recorded in the long and varied literature of the OT. They range from the simple sacrifices and prayers of the patriarchs to the elaborate national rituals of the Temple in Jerusalem. Much was borrowed from neighbouring cultures, but this took place alongside a critical adaptation in the light of key historical and theological affirmations. In particular, worship had to be directed only to Yahweh, the God of Israel; and the canonical texts encourage their readers to eliminate all traces of syncretism and devotion to other gods. The historical study of the development of worship is difficult, because the dating and setting of the various sources are disputed. Nevertheless, the final canonical text sets out a number of guidelines and perspectives that will inform any Christian theology and practice of worship.

Worship is first of all humanity's grateful response to the gracious God who created the world (Gen. 4.3–4). But the focus of the OT is on the worship of Israel, whom God has called and saved, and who now gratefully responds to the Lord through worship. The first purpose of the Exodus was that Israel worship the Lord on his holy mountain (Ex. 3.12; 5.3), and at Sinai instructions about worship are a substantial proportion of the legislation (Ex. 25—Num. 10). The Tabernacle is a movable Sinai, the means given by God to his people to enable them to continue the blessing and enjoyment of his presence. The Temple is at the heart of the prayer and worship of individual, nation and king (1 Kings 8).

Israel's worship affirms God both as creator and saviour, sovereign and merciful. The pattern of seven that structures the creation narrative of Gen. 1 is at the heart of Israel's distinctive observance of the Sabbath. The three great annual pilgrimage festivals (Passover-Unleavened Bread, Weeks, Booths/Tabernacles) originally marked stages of the agricultural year, but were then transformed to become celebrations of the Exodus story (Ex. 12—13; 19.1; Lev. 23.43). The offering of first-fruits included a response that recalled Israel's origins (Deut. 26).

Three general goals of worship may be identified. A ritual may strengthen the relationship between God and the individual or the people (e.g. the burnt offering, Lev. 1; the peace offering, Lev. 3). Ritual may also restore that relationship if there is fault on the human side, whether because of impurity or sin (the sin or purification offering, Lev. 4) or economic fraud (the guilt offering, Lev. 5). A third purpose of ritual is to effect the transition of a person or group from one state to another in a rite of passage (e.g. ordination, Lev. 8—9). The primary ritual in the ancient world was sacrifice, but sacrifice is a flexible language that can say and perform many different things. The purpose of a ritual determined the types of sacrifice offered, and the details of the performance allowed significant features to be highlighted while others were left in the background. Thus any sacrifice requires the shedding of blood, but the focus of the peace offering was on the eating of meat and the strengthening of the corporate bonds between worshippers and God. On the other hand, the atoning effect of blood was the primary feature of the sin or purification offering and the offerer gained no benefit from it.

In its fullest expression worship was a bodily experience that took place in a corporate context in a holy place at a holy time, facilitated by the holy priests. One common word for worship indicates bowing down to the ground, and a person often stood to pray (1 Sam. 1.26). It engaged the senses of smell (incense), touch (hands were laid on a sacrifice), taste (sacrificial meat was eaten) and eye (the architecture and materials of the sanctuary were richly symbolic). The verbal dimension of worship is represented by the Psalter, which provides for both individual lament and communal praise. The Temple service eventually included singing, dancing and the use of musical instruments (Ps. 150). The Temple defined the stage on which the priests, the Levites and the non-priests enacted their variegated roles. Detailed guidelines for the performance of the rituals had to be carefully observed in order to allow safe and appropriate access to the holy God. Only those who were clean could enter the Temple precincts, and the more dangerous tasks in the holy inner spaces could only be carried out by the priests. The high priest embodied the greatest degree of holiness. Only he could enter the holy of holies, and that once a year on the Day of Atonement (Lev. 16).

Although priestly texts make sharp distinctions between the roles of various groups, the starting point is that the entire covenant people is a holy priesthood (Ex. 19.6), called to serve or worship the Lord (Ex. 7.16). The majority of texts assume it is possible for the ordinary Israelite to approach God as fully as is humanly possible or desirable (Ps. 84). Worship could be (and was) all too easily misunderstood as an external act by which the well-being of worshippers could be guaranteed. The prophets make it clear that, if a choice has to be made, covenant loyalty was to be preferred to sacrifice (Hos. 6.6). But the ideal worshipper was not only generous and faithful in his or her religious devotion, but was also exemplary in

generosity to others and compassion for the poor (Job 1; 31). The descriptive ritual texts have to be read in conjunction with the strong personal exhortations of Deuteronomy (e.g. Deut. 16), as well as the prayers and praises of the Psalter. Holiness includes external obedience as well as internal attitude (Ps. 15; 51.18–19 [20–21 in Hebrew]).

Lively connections were made between worship in the Temple and the rest of life. Offerings and sacrifices were the fruit of God's blessing in home and field (Prov. 3.9–10). The experience of salvation was not complete until it was celebrated and proclaimed in the context of the covenant community (Ps. 40.9–10 [10–11 in Hebrew]). The prophet-priest Ezekiel announced the destruction of the Temple because of idol worship and injustice (Ezek. 8—9), but he also set out a vision of renewed worship that remained an ideal and inspiration for later generations (Ezek. 40—48; Rev. 21—22). The fate of the people of God has always been bound up with the quality and integrity of its worship.

Reiner Albertz, *A History of Israelite Religion in the Old Testament Period*, London 1994; Samuel E. Balentine, *The Torah's Vision of Worship*, Minneapolis 1999; Walter Brueggemann, *Israel's Praise: Doxology against Idolatry and Ideology*, Philadelphia 1988; Frank H. Gorman, *The Ideology of Ritual: Space, Time and Status in the Priestly Theology*, Sheffield 1990; Philip P. Jenson, *Graded Holiness: A Key to the Priestly Conception of the World*, Sheffield 1992; Jacob Milgrom, *Leviticus*, New York 1991, 2001; Richard D. Nelson, *Raising Up a Faithful Priest: Community and Priesthood in Biblical Theology*, Louisville 1993; Roland de Vaux, *Ancient Israel*, London 1961.

PHILIP JENSON

Orarion, Orarium

see **Vestments** 3(c), 4(c)

Ordinary

A term with three different, though related, liturgical meanings: (1) the unvarying parts of the *eucharistic rite, as distinct from the *proper; (2) those unvarying parts of the rite which are rendered chorally, and which compose the 'mass' as a musical work, namely, the *Kyrie, Gloria in excelsis, Credo, *Sanctus (with Benedictus) and *Agnus Dei (*see* **Chants of the Proper of the Mass**); (3) the unvarying parts of the eucharist up to the secret prayer or *super oblata*, a usage followed in the page headings of the Roman Missal of 1570, but abandoned in the RC *Ordo Missae* of 1969.

W. JARDINE GRISBROOKE

Ordinary Time

A modern expression, originating in the RC Church, to denote the periods of the liturgical *year which lie outside principal seasons, a shorter span from the end of the *Christmas or *Epiphany season to the beginning of *Lent and a considerably longer one from *Pentecost to the beginning of *Advent.

EDITOR

Ordination

The act of appointing a person to a specific ministry of leadership. In most traditions within Christianity, all (or nearly all) ordained ministries have usually been restricted to men alone, but the *ordination of women is being increasingly practised.

General bibliography: Paul F. Bradshaw, *Ordination Rites of the Ancient Churches of East and West*, New York 1990 (bib.); James F. Puglisi, *The Process of Admission to Ordained Ministry: A Comparative Study*, Collegeville 1996–2001; Wiebe Vos and Geoffrey Wainwright (eds), *Ordination Rites Past and Present*, Rotterdam 1980 (*Studia Liturgica* XIII).

1. Early Christianity; 2. Eastern Churches; 3. Medieval and Roman Catholic; 4. Anglican; 5. Baptist; 6. Christian Church; 7. Congregationalist; 8. Lutheran; 9. Methodist; 10. Old Catholic; 11. Pentecostal; 12. Reformed.

1. *Early Christianity*. The NT does not provide evidence for the existence of a standard pattern of Christian leadership but rather for a diversity of forms of ministry in different places, nor does it make clear how a person came to occupy a position of leadership in a local Christian community. By the beginning of the second century, however, it is apparent that Christian congregations were increasingly under the leadership of a group of *presbyters or *bishops and *deacons, with the monepiscopate gradually emerging as normative in the middle of that century. Other ministries either came under the direction of the bishop or were

eventually completely subsumed into his office, as in the case of prophets and teachers. That ministers were selected by the local Christian community is recorded in a number of sources (among the earliest, *Didache* 15.1; *1 Clement* 44.3), but with little indication of the process involved. The oldest extant ordination rites as such appear to be those in the so-called *Apostolic Tradition* conventionally attributed to Hippolytus of Rome in the early third century, but the identity, date and provenance of this document have been questioned, and it displays some features not otherwise attested in ancient sources. Apart from this work, and the church orders derived from it, the Sacramentary of Sarapion in the middle of the fourth century provides the earliest examples of ordination prayers for bishops, presbyters and deacons, but this does not include any directions as to how ordinations were to be performed. Thus reconstruction of early ordination practice therefore relies heavily on sparse references in late-fourth-century writings and on attempts to discern the oldest strata in later ordination rites of East and West.

Ordinations to the episcopate, presbyterate and diaconate in early Christianity were conducted within the congregation in which the ministry was to be exercised, not simply so that the people might witness the proceedings, but because ordination was understood as an action which involved the active participation of the whole local church. 'Absolute' ordinations were originally unknown: a person could not be ordained simply as a bishop, presbyter or deacon in the universal church, but had to be appointed to a specific, vacant ministerial role by and within a particular Christian congregation. It is for the same reason that the ordination normally took place on Sunday, the day of the community's regular assembly for worship, and the ordinand usually exercised the liturgical role of his new order in the *eucharist which followed. The evidence suggests that the process comprised two distinct but related parts: first, the selection of the candidate by the local Christian community; and second, prayer by the community for the bestowal on the person chosen of the gifts needed to fulfil the particular ministry.

The selection by the community was not an expression of a belief in democracy, but was seen as the way in which God's call and choice was made manifest, and the election of bishops in this way continued to be the standard practice throughout the Christian church for several centuries, although from the middle of the third century onwards (Cyprian *Ep*. 55.8; 67.5) a local church begins to be expected to obtain from neighbouring bishops approval of the candidate chosen as its bishop. It was this requirement, rather than any theory of sacramental transmission, which led to their presence at the ordination itself. The practice became the universal rule in the fourth century and the number of bishops requisite for a valid ordination was formalized. Canon 4 of the Council of Nicaea directed that all the bishops of the province should be involved, but if that were not possible, then there should be a minimum of three, with the rest sending their approval in writing. Canon 6 permitted a majority verdict to suffice where unanimity could not be reached. Presbyters and deacons, on the other hand, were often simply nominated by their bishops and the congregation asked to voice their approval of his choice, or alternatively given opportunity to object to them (the practice at Rome).

The second half of the process, prayer for the chosen minister, included both an act of congregational prayer (in silence or in the form of a *litany) and a prayer said by the presiding minister (the bishop in the case of deacons and presbyters, and one of the neighbouring bishops in the case of a bishop). During this prayer, the bishop would lay his right hand on the person being ordained, and at the end of the prayer the new minister would be greeted with a *kiss by all present. The increased importance given to the gesture of the imposition of hands as ordination rites evolved seems to be due at least in part to the ambivalence of the Greek term *cheirotonia*, 'the lifting up of hands'. In classical Greek this word signified the act of election, but early Christianity extended it to designate the whole ordination – both election and prayer with the laying-on of hands. By the late fourth century, however, the word seems to have been understood as referring primarily to the lifting up/laying-on of hands in prayer rather than to the election. In the case of the episcopate, at least from the late fourth century onwards, the book of the Gospels was also held over the candidate during the prayer in most traditions. Although it is given a variety of interpretations by ancient writers, this ceremony was probably originally intended to express the belief that it was Christ who was the true ordainer, and may at one time have been practised in place of the imposition of human hands rather than in addition to it. A

new bishop would also be ritually seated in his chair (*cathedra*) at the conclusion of the rite.

EDITOR

2. *Eastern Churches*. Like all other Eastern liturgies, ordination rites in the various traditions have undergone development and expansion in the course of their history. Because in no case is the earliest manuscript older than the eighth century (and in some traditions it is very much later), recovering the details of that evolutionary process is not easy. Nevertheless, although extant texts tend to display considerable variation in *rubrics between one manuscript and another, there is a high degree of stability in the form of the prayers themselves (which in any case are likely to be older than the rubrics), and this suggests that they may have undergone relatively little alteration from earlier times. Furthermore, in spite of many differences in detail from one another, the rites of the various churches also display a considerable number of similarities. While some of these are the consequence of the later influence of one tradition upon another, and especially the spread of Antiochene and/or Byzantine features to other churches (which can sometimes be detected by the fact that they duplicate the equivalent indigenous liturgical units), other similarities must be attributed to a common root that probably goes back to the late fourth century.

2.1. *General Characteristics*. The older manuscripts tend to provide only for the ordination of *bishops, *presbyters, *deacons, *subdeacons and *lectors, although some lack those for a bishop and some also include forms for *deaconesses and *chorepiscopoi* (rural bishops). Later pontificals often add rites for appointment to other offices, among them *cantors, archdeacons, abbots and abbesses, metropolitans and patriarchs. Some traditions reserve the term 'ordination' for the higher orders alone, while others extend it more widely.

The principal common features that seem to underlie all rites for bishops, presbyters and deacons are: an introductory proclamation/ bidding formula; the prayer of the people, usually in the form of a *litany; an imposition of hands, nearly always performed by the presiding bishop alone; the ordination prayer; and a concluding *kiss. Rites for the episcopate include the imposition of the gospel book on the ordinand and usually end with the ritual seating of the newly ordained bishop. All ordinations originally seem to have taken place on a Sunday within the context of the *eucharist (although the later Byzantine tradition allows the diaconate to be conferred on a day when only the Liturgy of the *Presanctified is celebrated, and the East Syrian tradition permits both the presbyterate and the diaconate to be conferred outside the context of a eucharist).

2.2. *The Byzantine Rite.* The oldest manuscripts reveal a simple structure, and even later ones add only very minor ceremonial embellishments to the earlier texts. In the case of the subdeacon and lector there is merely a single prayer accompanied by the imposition of the bishop's hand, while the rites for bishop, presbyter, deacon and deaconess have a proclamation/bidding formula and two ordination prayers separated by a litany (although there are reasons to suppose that the first prayer is a later insertion). Except for the names of the particular offices, the proclamation/bidding formulary is virtually identical for each order, and is typical of those in other traditions. For a bishop it reads as follows: 'The divine grace, which always heals that which is infirm and supplies what is lacking, appoints the presbyter N., beloved by God, as bishop. Let us pray therefore that the grace of the holy Spirit may come upon him.' Its original function seems to have been as a sort of bridge between the two parts of the ordination process, proclaiming the result of the election of the ordinand and inviting the congregation to pray for him; and there is evidence to suggest that an early version of it was already current in Antioch before the end of the fourth century. Later, however, the imposition of hands became attached to it, with the result that it tends to be regarded by many as the vital formulary which effects the ordination.

The substance of the second of the prayers for a bishop is also found in most other Eastern rites for bishops, suggesting that again it derives from fourth-century Antiochene use. The two images of the episcopal office which seemingly constitute part of its original nucleus are those of the imitator of Christ the true shepherd and the teacher/guardian of the truth, utilizing a quotation from Rom. 2.19–20. Cultic/liturgical imagery seems to have had no place at all in the earliest stratum, but to have been gradually introduced at a later stage in the various traditions.

The second prayer for a presbyter asks that the ordinand may be worthy to stand at the altar, to proclaim the gospel and exercise the sacred ministry of the word, to offer gifts and spiritual sacrifices, and to renew the people by the bath of regeneration. The substance of this prayer recurs in some other Eastern rites, while others which have independent prayers also tend to give a prominent place to the ministry of the word in their description of the presbyteral office. Some later versions, however, modify the references to that ministry (since it later ceased to be a function normally exercised by presbyters) and introduce the term 'priest' or 'priesthood' into the prayers.

The prayers for a deacon, both of which are also found in some other Eastern rites, say nothing about any functions which belong to the order apart from assistance at the celebration of the eucharist, but they speak instead of the virtues which God is being asked to bestow upon the ordinand. While one of them draws upon the typology of Stephen (Acts 7) to define the office, the other does not. This same variation, and also a similar tendency to reticence with regard to the actual functions of the diaconate, can also be seen in the independent prayers of other Eastern traditions. The prayers for a deaconess, both in this and in the other Eastern traditions where such rites survive (the Armenian, East Syrian and Georgian), are no more explicit about what it is that deaconesses do.

2.3. *Other Eastern Churches.* The present form of the pontifical of the Syrian Orthodox Church is attributed to Michael the Great, patriarch 1166–99 CE, and the ordination rites show evidence of considerable accretion: several preparatory and supplementary prayers have grown up around the principal ordination prayer for each order, and elaborate ceremonial has been added. The manuscripts of the ordination rites of the Coptic Orthodox Church are also late, dating from the fourteenth century onward, and again the rites are very lengthy and elaborate. The principal ordination prayers here closely parallel those found in the fourth-century *Apostolic Constitutions*, and are supplemented by material derived chiefly from the West Syrian rites. The Ethiopian Orthodox Church, being until this present century under the jurisdiction of the Alexandrian patriarch, has no ordination rites of its own, but uses a translation of the Coptic rites.

The Maronite ordination rites are the most complex of all the Eastern rites, containing a multiplicity of prayers and other formularies for each order, which suggests a long process of accretion. It is difficult to establish their early history as the oldest manuscript of the pontifical dates only from 1296 CE. The closest parallels are, not surprisingly, with the West Syrian tradition, but there are also some resemblances to other rites. A number of the prayers have no known parallels, but it is not easy to decide whether they represent an ancient and independent euchological tradition, or are later compositions.

Because of the geographical, political, and eventually ecclesiastical isolation of the East Syrians, their ordination rites display relatively little Antiochene influence. The oldest extant manuscript dates from 1496 CE and the rites include many prayers of an obviously secondary character, but their principal elements can still easily be discerned. The ancient Armenian ordination prayers too were independent creations. The earliest extant manuscript appears to date from the ninth or tenth century. The rites are relatively simple in form, and their structure – though not the contents of most of the texts – seems to have been influenced by the Byzantine rites. This shape was abandoned in later manuscripts, where the rites become more elaborate. The Armenian Apostolic Church was in some degree of union with Rome in the late Middle Ages and so its ordination rites then became subject to Western influences.

Two other ancient Eastern forms are also worth noting. A manuscript from the Georgian tradition, which is thought to have been copied in the tenth or eleventh century but may reflect usage of the seventh century, contains virtually no rubrics and so is little more than a collection of prayers for each order. The episcopate, presbyterate and diaconate are here each provided with three prayers, one copied from the *Testamentum Domini* (a fourth-century church order), one resembling the East Syrian prayers, and the third possibly being derived from Jersualem. There is also a manuscript originating from the Melkite tradition, written in a mixture of Christian Palestinian Aramaic and Greek, which contains quite complex ordination services. Several prayers are provided for each order: some closely resemble the Georgian texts thought to derive from Jerusalem; others are similar to certain of the Byzantine prayers; versions of others are found in the Maronite rites; while the rest have no clear parallels with any other known texts.

EDITOR

3. *Medieval and Roman Catholic.*
    3.1. *Medieval.* The ancient ordination prac-

tices of Rome are known to us from prayer texts in the sacramentaries and the *ordines* which give directions on how the rites are to be performed. The ordination of *bishops, *presbyters and *deacons each consisted primarily of a bidding inviting the people to pray for the candidate, the prayer of the people in the form of a *litany with a concluding *collect, and an appropriate ordination prayer, during which apparently the pope alone laid his hand on the ordinand, although the *ordines* are not very explicit about this. The candidates were brought in at the beginning already *vested in the robes of their new order, and at the end they exchanged a *kiss with the other ministers. There were similar practices in other parts of the West. However, in the earliest form in which ordination prayer texts from the Gallican churches are extant in the eighth century, they have already been fused with Roman texts to produce the composite rite that would characterize medieval practice. Also, as a first step in the process of combining *rubrics with texts, which would lead in time to the emergence of complete pontificals, at the head of the collection of formularies for each order in some sacramentaries were inserted directions concerning the laying-on of hands taken from a document known as the *Statuta ecclesiae antiqua*, perhaps written by Gennadius of Marseilles at the end of the fifth century. The ultimate source of these directions appears to have been the so-called *Apostolic Tradition*, and in this way the custom of all bishops laying hands on a candidate for the episcopate, and of presbyters joining the bishop in laying hands on a presbyter, was introduced into the Western tradition.

Later medieval ordination rites develop many secondary or explanatory texts and ceremonies, embellishing the fundamental rite while giving symbolic expression to the understanding of ordained ministry current at the time of the introduction of these rituals. *Anointings, vestings, formal presentations of objects employed in ministry, etc. all find a place in the Latin ordination rites of the Middle Ages. Manuscript sources by which the development of these later rites may be traced include the Romano-Germanic Pontifical of the tenth century, the Roman Pontificals of the twelfth and thirteenth centuries, and the Pontifical of William Durand of Mende in the thirteenth century; printed sources include the *Pontificalis liber* of 1485, the Pontifical of Julius II of 1511, and the Castellani Pontifical of 1520, culminating in the *Pontificale Romanum* of Clement VIII published in 1595, which officially codified the developments in the earlier liturgical books and served as the basis for RC ordination rites until 1968.

The rites as they appear in this last-named book are as follows. After the rite of 'making a cleric' (the tonsure), texts and ceremonies for accession to four *minor orders (doorkeeper, *lector, *exorcist and *acolyte) are provided. The minor orders had by this time become purely ceremonial stages on a candidate's journey to the priesthood. They were conferred during the multiple readings and chants of *Ember Day *eucharists. Their ritual structure was identical. Dressed in surplices and carrying candles, candidates were called by name to kneel before the bishop, who offered them short allocutions on the duties of their order. He then presented them with an object appropriate to their office (keys to the church for door-keepers, a *lectionary for lectors, a book of exorcisms or a missal for exorcists, and an unlit candle and an empty *cruet for acolytes) with a short admonitory text. The ordinations concluded with prayers offered by the bishop for the new members of the minor orders.

The book then provides texts and ceremonies for the ordination of three major orders: *sub-deacon, deacon and presbyter (since the consecration of bishops is conceptualized as distinct from these ordinations). These ceremonies were positioned, like those of the minor orders, during the liturgy of the word at the eucharist. The candidates for all three orders first prostrated themselves during the chanting of the litany of the saints. Then the bishop instructed the candidates for the subdiaconate on their duties, and presented them with objects associated with their order – an empty *chalice and paten – with a short admonition. The archdeacon presented them with cruets containing wine and water and a basin with a towel, and the bishop offered prayers for them. The subdeacons were then vested, blessed by the bishop, and presented with the epistle book, and one of their number exercised his ministry by reading the epistle.

The ordinations of deacons and presbyters were structurally similar. The candidates were presented by the archdeacon, the bishop inquired if they were worthy, the archdeacon testified that they were, and the bishop formally elected them. The bishop then instructed them on the duties of their office, and in the case of the deacons immediately recited or sang the ordination prayer. This prayer had been modified from its ancient form by an insertion in the midst of the prayer ('Receive the Holy Spirit for strengthening, and for resisting the devil and his temptations: in the name of the Lord') during which the bishop imposed his right hand on the head of each candidate. The bishop then vested the new deacons and presented them with a gospel book. He prayed a second set of ordination prayers stemming from the Gallican tradition, and one of their number immediately exercised his ministry by reading the gospel.

In the case of the presbyterate, with the candidates kneeling before him, the bishop imposed his hands on their heads in silence and the presbyters who were present did likewise. Then the bishop and presbyters stood with hands extended toward the candidates while the bishop pronounced two invitational texts that had been turned into prayers, and recited or sang the ordination prayer. He then vested the newly ordained and recited a second ordination prayer stemming from the Gallican tradition. After the *Veni, Creator Spiritus* was sung, he anointed and blessed the new presbyters' hands and presented them with a paten containing bread and a chalice containing wine and water. They joined the bishop in *concelebrating the rest of the eucharist, and after *communion the bishop again imposed hands on them while reciting a text conferring the power to forgive and retain sins.

The consecration of a bishop began with a formal election and examination of the candidate. The ordination proper again took place during the liturgy of the word before the gospel. The consecrating bishop gave a short statement on the duties of a bishop and invited the candidate to prostrate himself while the litany of saints was sung, during which the consecrating bishop interrupted the chant to bless the candidate three times. An open gospel book was held over the candidate, and the consecrating bishop and two assisting bishops imposed hands on the candidate's head while saying, 'Receive the Holy Spirit.' After pronouncing an invitational prayer, the principal consecrating bishop sang or recited the prayer of ordination. This prayer had been modified from its ancient form by having the singing of the *Veni, Creator Spiritus*, an anointing of the candidate's head, and a kiss inserted into the midst of it. Then the principal consecrating bishop anointed the new bishop's hands, and presented him with crozier, ring and gospel book. The mitre and gloves were not given until the conclusion of the ordination eucharist, when the new bishop was also enthroned and received a kiss from the other bishops present.

3.2. *Ordination in De Ordinatione Diaconi, Presbyteri et Episopi (1968)*. Responding to the mandate in the Second Vatican Council's Constitution on the Sacred Liturgy that both texts and ceremonies were to be revised, the Congregation of Rites issued the *editio typica* of rites for the orders of deacon, presbyter and bishop on 15 August 1968. The minor orders were either suppressed (porter, exorcist) or revised as 'installations' (lector, acolyte); the major order of subdeacon was also suppressed.

Among the more important ritual changes for all three orders were: (a) celebrating ordinations on Sundays or feasts so that more of the faithful might attend; (b) providing an expanded set of scriptural readings for the liturgy of the word; (c) positioning the ordination between the liturgy of the word and the liturgy of the eucharist; (d) standardizing the ritual structure to initial ordination rites (call and acceptance of the candidates, address on their duties, statements of commitment by the candidates, and the litany of the saints); the essential rite (laying-on of hands with ordination prayer); and explanatory rites (vesting and *traditio instrumentorum* – the delivery of symbols of office); and (e) changes in the eucharistic euchology. While the ordination prayers for deacons and presbyters have been only lightly revised from the ancient Roman forms, the ordination prayer for the bishop has been replaced by a prayer modelled on that found in the *Apostolic Tradition*. The explanatory rites are much simplified from their medieval predecessors.

3.3. *Ordination in De Ordinatione Episcopi, Presbyterorum, et Diaconorum (1990)*. On 29 June 1989 an *editio typica altera* of the ordination rites was promulgated, the Latin text appearing in printed form in 1990. Although the fundamental revision of the ordination rites in the 1968 edition is confirmed, aspects of the revision are modified or supplemented in the light of nearly two decades' experience. Among the major changes appearing in the second edition are: (a) a change in title and sequence of chapters to highlight the bishop's status as one possessing the fullness of the *sacrament of holy orders, and the roles of presbyters as co-workers with the episcopal order and deacons as those ordained to service; (b) *praenotanda* containing not only rubrical requirements for the celebration but a concise statement of the liturgical theology underlying holy orders; (c) changes in the ordination prayers – extensive for presbyters, less so for deacons – so that the ancient Roman texts might be enriched with NT perspectives; (d) additions to the presbyters' statements of commitment, highlighting their ministry of sacramental reconciliation and celebrating the eucharist; (e) a rite of commitment to celibacy added in the ordination of deacons to apply even to those who have pronounced perpetual vows in a religious institute before being ordained; (f) statements of respect and obedience to the Ordinary and his successors to be made also by members of institutes of consecrated life when being ordained; (g) a rite of admission to candidacy for holy orders included as an appendix.

J. Bligh, *Ordination to the Priesthood*, New York 1956; D. N. Power, *Ministers of Christ and His Church*, London 1969; M. M. Schaefer and J. Frank Henderson, *The Catholic Priesthood: A Liturgically Based Theology of the Presbyteral Office*, Ottawa 1990.

JAN MICHAEL JONCAS

4. *Anglican*. The first Anglican ordination rites for *deacons, priests and *bishops were drawn up in 1550, using a rite composed by the German reformer Martin Bucer as their main source supplemented with material adapted from the medieval ordination services. The accompanying preface directed that ordinations were to be performed on a Sunday 'in the face of the Church', and insisted, among other things, that candidates needed to be 'first called, tried, and examined', and following medieval precedent, the services for deacons and priests included a formal presentation of the candidates by the archdeacon in which he vouched for their suitability, and following the common practice of other Reformation churches, all three rites included a series of questions to the candidates concerning their beliefs and intentions.

The preface to the Ordinal also declared the essentials of ordination to be 'public prayer with imposition of hands', and the rites themselves confirm this. In the service for the diaconate, the regular *litany used in other services, but with a special suffrage and final *collect for the ordinands, is the only prayer that precedes the imposition of hands by the bishop, that action being accompanied by an imperative formula, 'Take thou authority to execute the office of a Deacon in the Church of God . . .' The rite for priests does in addition include the ordination prayer from Bucer's rite immediately before the imposition of hands by the bishop and other priests, but with the petition for the ordinands completely excised from it. The formula accompanying the laying-on of hands in this case is based in part on John 20.22–23 ('Receive the Holy Ghost . . .'), which had been used in this way is some medieval rites. Only in the case of the episcopate is there an ordination prayer as such before the imposition of hands, forming by fusing part of Bucer's prayer with material drawn from the medieval rite, the imposition of hands in this case being accompanied by a formula based on 2 Tim.1.6–7, 'Take the Holy Ghost, and remember that thou stir up the grace of God, which is in thee . . .'

When the *BCP* was revised in 1552, the ordination rites were also revised and then bound up with the Prayer Book, although retaining their own title page. In response to protests from extreme Protestants, at this time all directions about *vesture were removed from the services and the delivery of symbols of office was modified. In 1550, adapting medieval custom, the NT had been delivered to deacons, a Bible and a *chalice and paten to priests, and a Bible laid on a new bishop's neck after the imposition of hands, and then a pastoral staff delivered to him. In the 1552 revision, deacons continued to receive the NT, both priests and bishops were simply given the Bible.

Several further changes were made at the 1662 revision of the *BCP*. Some vague directives about vesture were restored, and the wording of the imperatives formulas for priests and bishops was modified: they had been criticized by RCs for failing to name explicitly the particular order being conferred, and this was now rectified. A few other alterations were made to clarify the distinction between priests and bishops, in reaction to Puritan claims that they did not constitute separate orders; and the preface to the rites was amended so as explicitly to require all ministers to have received episcopal ordination, in order to exclude those ordained without bishops during the years after the Civil War.

Other provinces of the Anglican Communion at first adopted the English ordination rites with only minor modifications, but in the twentieth century they began to introduce other changes, especially the insertion of an ordination prayer before the imposition of hands. After the appearance of ordination rites in the Church of *South India in 1958, however, which reverted to the more primitive Christian pattern whereby the ordination prayer rather than an imperative formula was said while hands were laid on the candidates, this arrangement was adopted in many parts of the Anglican Communion when new rites were drawn up in the second half of the twentieth century. Provision is also usually made for a variety of symbols of office to be presented to the newly ordained.

Paul F. Bradshaw, *The Anglican Ordinal*, London 1971; 'Ordinals', *The Study of Anglicanism*, ed. Stephen Sykes and John Booty, London/Philadelphia 1988, 143–53; Colin O. Buchanan, *Modern Anglican Ordination Rites*, Nottingham 1987; E. P. Echlin, *The Story of Anglican Ministry*, Slough 1974.

EDITOR

5. *Baptist*. Baptists, both in history and in the present, have expressed differing views on ordination. On the one hand, early seventeenth-century General Baptists took a high view of the office of pastor and ordained them at a solemn service with the laying-on of hands, an act shared only by other ordained persons. On the other hand, there have also been Baptists who have resisted the concept of ordination, arguing that any form of separation in ministry risks compromising the one vocation in baptism and the priesthood of all believers. Nevertheless, most Baptists have recognized the significance of ordination and have sought to express their conviction that the ministry of word and *sacraments is a calling and gift of Christ to the church. The report *The Meaning and Practice of Ordination among Baptists* defines ordination as 'the act, wherein the Church, under the guidance of the Holy Spirit, publicly recognises and confirms that a Christian believer has been gifted, called and set apart by God for the work of the ministry and in the name of Christ commissions him for this work' (Baptist Union of Great Britain, 1957).

Given their ecclesiology, most Baptists hold services of ordination in local churches. The call to ministry is tested in various ways. For example, in the USA, an Ordination Council might be called by the church seeking the ordination of one who has already been through theological college and has had their calling tested in local ministry. The Council would be composed of local churches in association, who would hear the testimony of the candidate and would question them on issues of faith and practice. Others would be invited to speak to the Council about the candidate. After a time of prayer, the Council, whose membership would include ministers and local church representatives, would then decide upon the suitability of the candidate for ordination.

Another approach, more common in Britain, involves a local church and the Association of Churches interviewing and examining candidates before they are accepted by a recognized college for preparation for ministry. Such a candidate is known as an ordinand. Ordination would only follow after a successful course of study, commendation by the college staff and, crucially, the invitation of a local church to the pastorate. In either approach the essential elements are the personal sense of the call of God, the testing of the call by local churches, the intellectual, practical and spiritual preparation and the invitation by a church to ministry.

The service of ordination might be held at the 'home' church or the 'calling' church. Only in some Baptist Unions are candidates ever ordained at a local Assembly. The service would include the usual elements of praise, prayer, *confession and declaration of forgiveness, the reading of scripture and a sermon. The ordination would usually be presided over by a denominational official, for example, a *superintendent minister. Representatives of the home church, the Association, the college and the calling church would tell the story of the call. Questions would than be put to the candidate concerning their faith in the triune God, their trust in Christ as Saviour and Lord and their conviction that they are called to the ministry. Following a suitable response the candidate would solemnly be given a copy of the Bible and, kneeling, receive the laying-on of hands from the superintendent, other ministers and church members. Care is usually taken to ensure that those laying on hands are representative of the wider church. Often ecumenical colleagues are present by direct invitation. Following the ordination prayer, the candidate stands for the declaration of ordination. If the service includes the *eucharist, the new minister would be invited to preside before declaring the final *blessing.

Such ordination is traditionally understood to be to the ministry of word and sacraments. The candidate's name would be placed on the list of ministers accredited by that Union of Churches. Thus, although, ordination is related to the call to a particular pastorate it is not confined there and the new minister is a minister of the whole church of Christ. Upon moving to another pastorate the minister would be inducted to the new charge. Ministry is exercised at the call and in the name of Christ, and thus ordination is more than the declaring of the church's representative.

Although the pattern has changed in history, it is not normal to ordain *deacons who are chosen for a ministry only in the local church. Both men and women are ordained in many Baptist Unions but some large groupings of Baptists, particularly in the USA, do not ordain women. There is no separate order of *bishops. Those who are appointed to national tasks, if they are ordained, are commissioned.

Alec Gilmore (ed.), *The Pattern of the Church*, London 1963; Roger Hayden, *Baptist Union Documents 1948–1977*, London 1980; Ernest Payne, *Free Churchmen, Repentant and Unrepentant*, London 1965; Robert Torbet, *Baptist Ministry: Then and Now*, Philadelphia, PA 1953; Edward Hiscox, *The New Directory for Baptist Churches*, Grand Rapids 1970.
                                                    BRIAN HAYMES

6. *Christian Church.* For the Christian Church (Disciples of Christ) ordination is a public rite of the church through which persons, having received from God a special calling to ministry, are set apart for tasks of servant leadership. The ordained ministry is representative in nature, setting before the church the one ministry of Jesus Christ shared by all. Ordination is to the ministry of the church rather than a specific congregational or other assignment. Combining functions of service, proclamation and oversight, it is most commonly exercised within local congregations through leadership in worship, theological reflection and teaching, fostering growth in the faith, and administering the life of the community. The same ministry is exercised in other forms in other contexts, e.g. in church administration at regional and national levels or in institutional chaplaincies.

In the earliest Disciples' congregations, ministerial offices included (a) *elders, persons with secular employment but ordained by a local congregation to oversee its life, including administering the *Lord's supper and *baptism (and preaching, if they were suited); (b) *deacons, also chosen locally and charged with practical service; and (c) evangelists, whose work lay in itinerant preaching and planting churches. A professionally trained, salaried ministry emerged in the latter decades of the nineteenth century. This has become the norm for congregational leadership, it now being the minister who preaches and presides at worship (though, significantly, leadership at the Lord's table is still shared with elders).

Ordination follows a process of discernment to ensure the candidate's suitability for ministry. Especially since the 1960s this has involved local, regional and national levels of the church. The rite of ordination normally occurs within a special service which includes preaching, and involves local and regional church authorities. The elders and ministers present lay their hands on the candidate's head and prayers are offered, invoking the Spirit and dedicating the ordinand to a life of servant leadership.

Until the mid-twentieth century only men were ordained as ministers, elders or deacons. This restriction was more a reflection of current cultural – and apparent NT – patterns than the result of theological reflection. The situation has changed radically in the past fifty years, and women in substantial numbers are now being ordained to ministry and are serving as elders and deacons.

Differences of opinion and practice remain, but the trend is to restrict the term 'ordination' to the professional, (normally) full-time ministry. Elders are now usually installed rather than ordained; in the case of deacons installation is the norm. The Commission on Theology has recommended that the current office of licensed ministry (persons preparing for ordination, or serving as ministers under special circumstances) be more clearly distinguished from that of the ordained ministry. The Commission has also suggested that the church should establish a single order of ministry with three offices, seeking to align its ministry with the classic threefold pattern of deacon, *presbyter and *bishop. This proposal would raise significant questions in some parts of the church, but will certainly receive serious consideration in the years ahead.

'A Word to the Church on Ministry (1985), A Report of the Committee on Theology', *The Church for Disciples of Christ: Seeking to be Truly Church Today*, ed. Paul A. Crow, Jr and James O. Duke, St Louis 1998, 109–20; D. Newell Williams (ed.), *Ministry among*

Disciples: Past, Present, and Future, St Louis 1985.

THOMAS F. BEST

7. *Congregationalist*. One of the most controversial aspects of the Reformation in England was the governance of churches. The Congregational view was based on the unit of the gathered, or 'embodied', congregation. Henry Barrowe wrote, 'all the affairs of the Church belong to that body together. All the actions of the Church – as prayers, censures, sacraments, faith – be actions of them all jointly, and of every one of them severally: although the body, unto divers actions, use such members as it knoweth most fit to the same.' This teaching was part of the accusation against the martyrs, Barrowe, Penry and Greenwood, in the trial that condemned them to hang in 1595.

A resolution of the Houses of Parliament on 1 September 1642 cancelled the Church of England orders of archbishop, *bishop, priest and *deacon, and established the Westminster Assembly, consisting mostly of Presbyterian divines, with a smattering of Congregationalists, to devise a new pattern of governance. Because of the urgent need of congregations for leadership, Parliament pressed the question for early resolution.

The Congregational view was that a congregation may be organized into a church before any recognizable pattern of leadership has emerged. Such leadership would most suitably take the form of pastors and teachers, that is, at least two leaders, working together. Though the Congregational view was repressed, John Owen continued in the Dissenting tradition, arguing that a congregation may 'become a Church essentially before they have any Ordinary Pastor or Teacher', though without a minister, they 'cannot come to that Perfection and Compleatness which is designed unto them. That which renders a Church completely Organical' is the 'Gift of Christ in the Ministry'. Nevertheless churches often existed and practised for some time before they had any settled leadership. Some congregations, for example the settlements established in New England in the seventeenth century, held ordained ministry to be essential for the *Lord's supper. However, the tradition in England was that the sacramental life of a congregation could be carried out through any member authorized by the congregation. Some ministers of Congregational churches renounced their earlier Anglican or Presbyterian ordination. John Owen, for example, eschewed the use of the title 'Reverend'.

The Savoy Declaration of 1658 locates the recognition of ministry in the local church. Ministers are 'solemnly set apart by Fasting and Prayer, with imposition of hands of the Eldership of that church'. Alternatively, because the practice of laying-on hands was felt by some to be tainted by sacerdotal associations, 'those chosen and separated by Fasting and Prayer . . . though not set apart by Imposition of Hands, are rightly constituted Ministers of Jesus Christ.' The principle continued to be argued strongly. R. W. Dale argued that the use of titles such as bishop, *elder and deacon in the Acts and epistles was fluid and sometimes interchangeable. The Congregational pattern of recognizing gifts of leadership was, he held, nearer to that of the NT churches. The fact that ministers were recognized by local congregations led to the Congregational churches being among the first to ordain women. Constance Coltman was ordained in 1917.

However, ordination services, in the service books that appeared in the nineteenth and twentieth centuries, show a decline in this Congregational understanding. *The Manual for Ministers of Congregational Churches* (London 1936) explicitly states that 'it is necessary that this service shall have the concurrence and approval of the County Union expressed by the presence of one or more appointed representatives, and it is highly desirable that some representative of the denomination (e.g., the Moderator) should preside'. The prayers and laying-on of hands recognize the essential presence of authority outside the local church. This pattern persisted in later books.

The Congregational Federation recognizes that a local church has the full authority to call its own minister and elect its own leadership, though generally there is still a recognition of the fellowship of churches. Some churches are experimenting with a pattern of pastoral, teaching and preaching ministry shared among more than one recognized leader. In any case, no exclusive rights are conferred by any act of ordination and Congregational churches continue to permit lay presidency at the eucharist.

The practice and importance of ordination differs from country to country, and many national fellowships recognize a variety of ministries. Congregational churches have found great blessing in the rediscovery of historic freedoms and in the authority of the local church to seek and recognize the gifts of God's Spirit necessary to the completeness of church life.

———

Richard Cleaves and Michael Durber, *Patterns for Worship*, Nottingham 1992; R. W. Dale, *History of English Congregationalism*, London 1907; *Manual of Congregational Principles*, London 1884; R. Tudur Jones, *Congregationalism in England, 1662–1962*, London 1962; Janet H. Wootton, *Ordination*, Savoy Paper no. 4, Nottingham 1994.

JANET H. WOOTTON

8. *Lutheran.* Ordination among Lutherans began in controversy and ambiguity. Luther himself vacillated on the theological foundations for ordained ministry. He strongly objected to late medieval understandings of ordination to a sacrificing priesthood (though priests like himself, who had received ordination to such a priesthood, were not forced to renounce such ordination nor were they reordained using an evangelical rite). In its place he spoke of a ministry of the word of God. Priests were understood to have an office bestowed upon them which gave them a legitimate ministry of word and *sacraments in the church – not a special sacramental power or personal status before God.

Where particular churches were unable to find evangelical priests and where the *bishops refused to ordain evangelical candidates, Luther argued in 1523 that congregations could call and ordain ministers themselves. Luther also ordained priests himself, such as George Rörer in 1525. By 1535 Elector John Frederick mandated a more regular system of examination, call and ordination. Luther prepared the 'Ordination for Ministers of the Word' (1539) during this period. Luther continued to serve as primary ordinator under this mandate and the theological faculty at Wittenberg had the responsibility to examine candidates. Luther ordained both priests and bishops to evangelical ministry. The well-known example is Nicholas von Amsdorf, who was ordained bishop for Naumburg in 1542. Other ordained persons were designated to serve as ordinators in some circumstances. Johannes Bugenhagen served in this capacity when the church in Denmark was reformed.

Lutheran ordination in the sixteenth century focused on what the Reformers took to be the scriptural sign associated with setting apart for ministry: prayer and the laying-on of hands. Absent from the Reformed rites is all language of power to offer sacrifice for the living and the dead. The explicatory rites of the medieval ordinal – the *anointings and *traditio instrumentorum*, the handing over of symbols of office (e.g. *chalice and paten) – were abandoned. Luther's 1539 rite follows the theological examination and call that took place the day before or earlier in the day. Call here is understood as an invitation or assignment to serve in a particular setting. The rite itself begins with the singing of *Veni, Sancte Spiritus* and the *collect for Pentecost. Then come the reading of 1 Tim. 3.1–7 and Acts 20.28–31, an exhortation, and the consent of the candidate. The laying-on of hands by 'the whole presbytery' follows while the ordinator prays the *Lord's Prayer aloud and an optional ordination prayer, which Luther describes as an exposition of the three chief parts of the Lord's Prayer and includes Matt. 9.37–38. The rite concludes with a second exhortation based on 1 Peter 5.2–4, blessing with the sign of the cross, and the singing of 'Now let us pray to the Holy Ghost' as a congregational hymn. The *eucharist followed. This rite made no provision for the public assent of the congregation to the ordination. This function may have been part of the call which had already taken place. It may be that because many ordinations were taking place in Wittenberg, and not in the location where the new priest would serve, such an element was regarded as inappropriate.

Luther's ordination rite was enormously influential in all the territorial churches of the Lutheran Reformation even down to modern times. Modern Lutheran practice includes: call (generally attested by a document); examination of the candidate (which now often includes a pledge to teach in conformity with the Lutheran Confessions); the singing of a hymn to the Holy Spirit; exhortation (often in the form of several scripture passages); the laying-on of hands and prayer (in most Lutheran churches this is done by a bishop with other ordained pastors joining; in others that have no bishops, the designated ordinator is an already ordained pastor); a blessing of the newly ordained pastor; and sometimes an opportunity for acclamation by the congregation. The congregation's assent to the candidate and the ordination may take place as a part of the presentation of the call or after the laying-on of hands.

Lutherans have been divided on the theological foundations and meaning of ordination. Some have argued that the 'call' and not the ordination rite is sufficient. Others have argued that when the confessions speak of *rite vocatus* (Augsburg Confession XIV) an ordination rite is demanded. Whatever position is taken, Lutherans do not ordinarily repeat ordination, even for pastors who have left the pastoral office for a time. Offices and forms of ministry also vary from one Lutheran church to another. Most embrace a threefold office of bishop, pastor or priest, and *deacon. Others have adopted other patterns of supervision and other forms of diaconal ministry. The office of pastor or priest is universal among Lutherans.

———

For texts, *see* **Books, Liturgical** 8. Studies: Frieder Schultz, 'Evangelische Ordination', *Jahrbuch für Liturgik und Hymnologie* XVII, 1972, 1–54; Ralph F. Smith, *Luther, Ministry, and Ordination Rites in the Early Reformation Church*, New York 1996.

PAUL R. NELSON

9. *Methodist*. Throughout most of his ministry, John Wesley insisted that the Methodists should not separate from the Church of England. However in 1784, after unsuccessful appeals to the Bishop of London to consecrate a *bishop for America, he took matters into his own hands. Believing himself to be a scriptural *episkopos*, Wesley formed a presbytery with Anglican priests Thomas Coke and James Creighton and ordained two men *deacon and, the next day, *presbyter. Dr Coke was 'set apart' as 'superintendant' (sic): Wesley's private diary indicates Coke was 'ordained', but the word is not used in Wesley's published *Journal*; Wesley's choice of terms would be a subject of ongoing debate among Methodists.

The new presbyters and Coke took with them to America Wesley's relatively conservative revision of the Anglican ordinal. Wesley's rites published in the *Sunday Service of the Methodists* (1784) contain a few significant alterations, among them: deacons were not restricted to a single parish, priests were designated '*elders' and no longer charged with the binding and loosing of sins, and the 'superintendant' (not 'bishop') was ordained rather than consecrated. The oath to the sovereign necessarily was removed from all the rites, but the *litany was kept, as was John Cosin's version of *Veni, Creator Spiritus*, though the latter was to be said, not sung.

Much to Wesley's dismay, the Methodist Episcopal Church began using the title 'bishop' in their polity by 1787. In 1792, the 'superintendant' rite was adjusted for a 'bishop' and other revisions were made, including the dropping of the litany from all three services. The introductory phrase at the imposition of hands in the elders' rite was altered from the imperative, 'Receive the Holy Ghost . . .', to a somewhat precatory, 'The Lord pour upon thee the Holy Ghost . . .', a formulation which, though still addressed to the candidate, recognized both divine and human action. This revised formulation was placed into the rite for bishop of some episcopal Methodist branches in the mid-nineteenth century at around the same time as the rite was modified to be one of 'consecration'. The three rites in the ordinal of episcopal Methodists retained a close connection to Wesley's orders at least to the late twentieth century; the United Methodist Church's 1980 ordinal and its subsequent revisions departed somewhat from the historic Methodist texts, especially after the creation of a permanent diaconate in 1996. Original orders for the consecration of *deaconesses emerged in the late nineteenth century, with the first authorized service of the Methodist Episcopal Church in 1908 borrowing the deaconess prayer from the fourth-century *Apostolic Constitutions*.

Some Methodists in America objected to the episcopal form of government, preferring instead a more democratic form in which eligible elders elected a 'President of Conference'; they thus abandoned the rite for bishops. A few non-episcopal denominations also dropped the diaconate from their orders of ministry in the belief that the single order of elder was sufficient and theologically justifiable. One such denomination, the Methodist Protestant Church (founded in 1830, it abandoned the order of deacon in 1874), slightly revised the inherited words at the imposition of hands in a manner that articulated more fully the widespread Methodist understanding about ministerial orders: they were given through 'the election of thy brethren' just prior to or days before the ordination service, and by the liturgical 'imposition of our hands'. In laying on hands and presenting a Bible, the president (or the bishop, in episcopal denominations) acted on behalf of the Conference that had duly elected candidates to the *ministerium*. There is thus in Methodism historically and at present some ambiguity about precisely when orders are given: at the election (where Conference membership is bestowed) or in the ordination rite.

In British Methodism, the representative

ministry comprised only one order, since superintendents were not distinguished from other ministers. Admission to Full Connexion at a public service after the Conference election came to be equated with ordination and distinct ordination services with the laying-on of hands were generally not held until 1836 (except for overseas missionaries). Yet all three ordination rites from 1784 continued to be reprinted in subsequent editions of the *Sunday Service* until 1846. Then the Wesleyan Methodist Connexion introduced a single 'Form of Ordaining Candidates for the Ministry' which blended features from the three separate rites. This text was kept relatively unchanged even after the 1932 union and the revision of the rite for the 1936 *Book of Offices*, though the smaller denominations had brought to union much simpler services. The ordination rite in the 1975 *Methodist Service Book* was heavily influenced by the Church of *South India rite, which had already inspired the ordinal proposed by the abortive Anglican–Methodist Unity Scheme. The 1999 *Methodist Worship Book* contained a revised service for the 'Ordination of Presbyters, usually called Ministers' and authorized a service for 'Ordination of Deacons' that had few ties to the historic Wesley text.

A. Raymond George, 'Ordination', *A History of The Methodist Church in Great Britain*, ed. Rupert Davies, A. Raymond George and Gordon Rupp, London 1978, 143–60; John D. Grabner, 'A Commentary on the Rites of *An Ordinal, The United Methodist Church*', Ph.D. dissertation, University of Notre Dame 1983 (bib.).

KAREN B. WESTERFIELD TUCKER

10. *Old Catholic*. The Old Catholic churches have always maintained that their ministry is an expression of the catholicity and apostolicity of the church and shares in the apostolic succession, even in the narrow definition of RC canon law. The essential words, as defined by Rome, were until the 1980s the same as in the RC liturgy so as not to jeopardize the canonical validity of the order. The threefold ministry of *bishop, *presbyter (commonly called priest) and *deacon has been maintained; the so-called *minor orders have been abolished.

In 1899 a German translation of the Roman pontifical was produced by order of the International Bishops' Conference of the Union of Utrecht (IBC) and then translated into the other languages. This version was closely followed. In 1975 the IBC charged the International Liturgical Commission to draft new ordination forms for the churches of the Union of Utrecht. In 1985 these rites were confirmed by the IBC and made official for all the member churches of the Union, although they have not yet been adopted by each Old Catholic church. The rites have been officially approved in German, but an English translation has been provided for use in the Polish National Catholic Church in the USA and Canada. Although strongly shaped by RC practice, the texts themselves – and therefore the theological patterns – of the ordination rites have also been greatly influenced by modern Anglican rites, even to the point of adopting some texts verbatim.

The ordination is structured in the same way for the three orders of the ministry and always takes place within a celebration of the *eucharist. A bishop or priest is ordained after the gospel and sermon, a deacon is ordained after the second reading. The preparatory rites include: (a) the presentation of the candidate, leading up to the consent of the people, 'He (She) is to be bishop/priest/deacon: to the glory of God, for the ministry in the Church of the Lord'; (b) the invocation of the Holy Spirit (hymn *Veni, Creator Spiritus* in the vernacular); (c) the commission and examination of the candidate(s). The central rites, the consecration, include: (a) the *litany (an adaptation of the litany of the saints in the RC rite); (b) the laying-on of hands and prayer of consecration; (c) in the case of the ordination of a bishop, the *anointing of the head. The explanatory rites include, in the case of the ordination of a bishop, the presentation of the book of Gospels and the episcopal insignia; in the case of the ordination of a priest or deacon, the vesting with the appropriate liturgical *vestments (and, for new priests, the anointing of the hands). The Peace concludes the ordination liturgy proper. A newly ordained bishop then presides at the eucharist; a new priest joins the bishop at the *altar; a new deacon proclaims the gospel.

A new prayer of consecration has been drafted for the ordination to each order of the threefold ministry with both a strong *anamnetic part and an explicit *epiclesis. It is sung after the imposition of hands by the bishop on the candidate(s) and, in the case of the ordination to the episcopate and presbyterate, the imposition of hands by all the other bishops present and all the priests present, respectively. In the case of the ordination of a presbyter, the text makes clear that the bishop 'will, in the Name of our Lord Jesus Christ, together with the presbyterium ordain the Deacon N. a priest'; the laying-on of hands by all the priests present is constitutive for the ordination, not merely a sign of accepting the ordinand into the college of presbyters.

Old Catholic theology stresses that it is the church, not the bishop, who calls to the ministry and ordains to it; the ordination forms make clear that the church is more than the hierarchy – it is the entire community of the baptized. Clandestine ordinations are therefore impossible for the Old Catholic churches. Old Catholics also emphasize that a person is ordained a bishop/priest/deacon in the [whole] church of God, carrying out the ministry in a particular local church (i.e., diocese).

The IBC approved the ordination of women to the diaconate in 1985, making clear that they would be included in the apostolic ministry as well. The western European Old Catholic churches have in the meantime also ordained women to the presbyterate, adapting the biblical references in the prayer of consecration accordingly (for instance, by alluding to Matt. 28.8–10 and John 20.11–18 instead of pointing to the selection of apostles from the disciples). Their synods have likewise opened up the episcopate to women, although none has been elected and ordained so far.

THADDEUS A. SCHNITKER

11. *Pentecostal*. Ordination for ministry in the Pentecostal churches is generally understood as a preparation for preaching in the context of the pastorate or other forms of church leadership. Ordination to the ministry always begins with a call to preach, akin to what one may term a prophetic call. The call to preach is usually understood as an experience of the Holy Spirit designated as an anointing by God. An ordained minister is expected to remain conscious of and obedient to his or her prophetic call and the anointing of the Spirit that supports the gift of preaching. The call implies a clear break with ways of life deemed ungodly by the Pentecostal community and a new beginning of exemplary loyalty to God. Walter Hollenweger's description of this call and its effect on the life of the ordained minister is illuminating: 'In the Pentecostal movement, the call to be a pastor must be an experience which in the eyes of the person who is called and of his future followers allows a break with previous loyalties, and indeed demands and gives a positive

interpretation to such a break. It can be brought about by visions, dreams, voices, prophecies on the part of another person, the reading of the Bible, or doubts about the established church. The final step is usually brought about by a combination of factors.'

Connected to the call to ordained ministry is a testimony of conversion to Christ and an experience, equally available to all Christians called a baptism in the Holy Spirit, evidenced according to most Pentecostals by speaking in tongues (Acts 2.4). Spirit baptism signals for Pentecostal ministers a life of service devoted to the preaching of God's word that resembles the adventures of the Apostles depicted in the book of Acts. Such an expectation has drawn people to ordination in Pentecostal churches who seek a fresh experience of the empowering and sanctifying presence of the Holy Spirit. Of four hundred Pentecostal pastors interviewed, approximately one-quarter came to Pentecostal ministry from other church traditions in order to find a 'more lively and missionary-minded group, closer to other people and closer to the Bible, of Christians whose talents were both intellectual and intuitive, both rational and emotional'. They sought 'a church which did not carry on its institutions for their own sake and was ready to give up or replace parts of an institution which had lost their function' (Hollenweger).

It is important to emphasize that the experiences of conversion and Spirit baptism that provide the framework for the prophetic call for ordained ministers is to be shared by all Christians, according to the Pentecostals. All Christians have a call to serve and are bearers of the Spirit. Pentecostals definitely tend to view ordained ministers within the broader notion of the charismatic structure of the church in which, ideally, all Christians are gifted to participate in the ministry of the church. All are called to function prophetically and have a prophetic call of sorts, though not all will be ordained to preach. And though not all will have the gift of prophecy as described in 1 Cor. 14, all are meant by the empowerment of the Holy Spirit to join the general 'prophethood of believers' (Roger Stronstad) in order to minister the gospel to the world.

The general Pentecostal devotion to the charismatic nature of the church and its ordained clergy does not mean that Pentecostal ministers are never authoritarian, which they tend to be in various places, especially in parts of Asia and Latin America, since the minister can claim to function as a 'man of God' or 'woman of God' with unique prophetic insights that may be invoked to dominate the decision-making of the community of faith. Nor does it mean that there has not been an institutionalization of Pentecostal churches which has tended to cause female leadership and cultural diversity to wane over time. Furthermore, though many Pentecostal churches have ordained women to preach from the beginning of the Pentecostal movement, not many of these women have found placement historically in senior pastorates. And the large African-American Pentecostal denomination, the Church of God in Christ, does not ordain women to the ministry, though women in that church still function in a broad spectrum of ministerial activities.

The level of education required of candidates for the ordained ministry in most Pentecostal churches rarely exceeds a two-year correspondence course. However, there is a trend, especially in the USA, for potential candidates for ordination to seek a college or even a graduate seminary education, though such is never expected by governing ecclesiastical bodies (and may even be discouraged by them). The lack of education required is due to the accent that is placed on one's prophetic call, and has encouraged an ordained clergy that would tend to be viewed by those of historic churches as consisting of lay ministers, especially since many of them carry on secular employment while they pastor congregations too small and/or poor to adequately support them financially. Though often lacking theological depth, these ministers tend to be close to the life concerns of their congregations and often serve as effective leaders of their churches. One hopes that the gradually increasing level of institutional complexity and educational achievement in Pentecostal churches will deepen theological awareness while not causing a decline of the inclusiveness of Pentecostal ministry and the closeness to the lives of the non-ordained laity characteristic of Pentecostal church life at its best.

Charles Barfoot and Gerald Sheppard, 'Prophetic vs Priestly Religion: The Changing Role of Women Clergy in Classical Pentecostal Churches', *Review of Religious Research* XXII, 1980, 2–17; Sheri Benvenuti, 'Anointed, Gifted, and Called: Pentecostal Women in Ministry', *Pneuma: The Journal of the Society for Pentecostal Studies* XVII, 1995, 229–35;

Roger Heuser and Byron Klaus, 'Charismatic Worship Theory: A Shadow Side Confessed', *Pneuma* XX, 1998, 161–74; Walter Hollenweger, *The Pentecostals*, reprinted Peabody, MA 1988, 477–83; Margaret Poloma, 'Charisma, Institutionalization, and Social Change', *Pneuma* XVII, 1995, 245–52; Roger Stronstad, 'The Prophethood of Believers: A Study in Luke's Charismatic Theology', *Pentecostalism in Context: Essays in Honor of William W. Menzies*, ed. Wonsuk Ma and Robert P. Menzies, Sheffield 1997, 60–77.

FRANK D. MACCHIA

12. *Reformed*. Reformed thought-patterns in the context of ordination, while making a departure from many aspects of medieval teaching, are from Calvin onwards for the most part given positive and confident expression. The Reformed Church is part of the universal church. Guidelines are to be sought in scripture and in apostolic practice. The Church of Scotland and others did not hesitate to describe the living continuity of the church in faith and obedience to the apostolic teaching as the true Apostolic Succession, and in the middle years of the last century that was still the argument that was advanced in discussions with Anglicans on the subject of validity of orders. The Reformed Church has always refused to recognize an independent succession tied only to persons and isolated from the whole life of the church in Christ. An ordained ministry, of divine institution, within that continuum, has been treated by the majority of Reformed churches with great respect and seriousness.

Emphasis has been placed on 'lawful calling', an inward calling from God and an outward calling from the church in election and ordination. Calvin, while recognizing that ordination is not a 'sacrament of the gospel', nevertheless speaks of it in quasi-sacramental terms: God bestows a special gift or charism in ordination in answer to the prayer of the church, so that the sign of the laying-on of hands is 'not useless but a sure pledge of the grace received from God's own hand' (Commentary on 2 Tim. 1.6 and Eph. 4.11). Reformed teaching has, however, always stressed that this grace is not received magically or mechanically or *ex opere operato* but only through prayer and in accordance with divine promise.

Prayer with the laying-on of hands featured centrally in ordination rites in Zurich, in Strasbourg, in Frankfurt, in France and in the prescriptions of the First and Second Helvetic Confessions. The original situation in Geneva and in Holland is not clear. In Scotland, though writings seem to suggest a brief period of hesitation, there is no record of an actual ordination without laying-on of hands. Prayer and the laying-on of hands remained the central and basic feature of ordination services into modern times. And while in their day the *Euchologion* in Scotland, Osterwald in Switzerland, van Dyke in America, Bersier in France, van der Leeuw in Holland and Albertz in Germany made distinctive contributions in their respective churches, the various ordination rites display strong family links and follow a common pattern.

The ordination rite contained in the twentieth-century *Ordinal and Service Book* of the Church of Scotland was for much of the century fairly representative of developed rites in the Reformed Church. This book was first published in 1931 and revised in 1954 and again in 1962. In this book the liturgical setting for ordination is a service which follows a eucharistic pattern. A liturgy of the word, which includes a preamble concerning the faith of the church and questions to the ordinand, leads to the ordination. The ordination prayer is one of thanksgiving (introduced by *sursum corda*), *epiclesis and petitions for gifts and graces appropriate to the ministry of word and sacrament in all its aspects. A declaration and charges to minister and people follow.

The new Scottish *Ordinal and Service Book*, published in May 2001 and subtitled *Interim Edition*, retains many features of the earlier book but takes one important step forward in that it suggests in a *rubric that after ordination the *eucharist may be celebrated, the newly ordained minister presiding. An ancient practice in the church is thereby recovered. This has, however, been included in the rite of the Presbyterian Church of Canada since 1991 and is the form in the recent *Book of Occasional Services* of the Presbyterian Church (USA).

In the Reformed churches it was required that a number of ministers (in time, the presbytery) be involved in ordination, no man having the power of ordination in his own right. Views differed as to whether *elders should take part and the debate goes on at the present time. The 2001 Scottish Ordinal adheres to the ruling of the Westminster *Form of Presbyterian Church Government* of 1645, which stated that imposition of hands should be 'by those preaching presbyters to whom it doth belong'. The

Canadian rite and the new Dutch Reformed Rite likewise restrict laying-on of hands to ministers of word and sacrament. However, in the new American rite it would appear that the action is shared by elders, and in the rite in the 1996 Common Liturgy of the Reformed Church in France the action is shared by elders, *deacons, *catechists and members of the congregation. This church also decided in 1984 to abandon the use of the word 'ordination' and replace it with the term 'recognition of ministries', this in an attempt to avoid clericalism.

Besides accepting the Helvetic Confessions' prescription of laying-on of hands in ordination, most Reformed churches gave attention also to the other prescription about 'public prayer'. Unlike medieval ordinations, which often took place in private, Reformation ordinations were always public affairs and in the Reformed churches still arc, usually taking place in the context of the congregation among whom the ordinand will minister and, except in Scotland, usually on a Sunday at a time of public worship. The new American rite interprets public prayer generously: in two of three forms of the ordination prayer offered, a rubric states 'all present may pray together', and bold print indicates that the congregation is to pray audibly.

Increasingly in the Reformed churches, as in other churches, there is an emphasis on the understanding of the ordained ministry as a special function within the larger ministry and mission of the whole people of God, and *baptism as being the moment when all are enlisted, are in a sense ordained as priests, initiated into the royal priesthood of the church, which shares in the priesthood of Christ. The Scottish rite shows awareness of this in a brief allusion within a charge to the congregation, and the French in a change of terminology, as mentioned above. The concept permeates the prayer-language of the American rite and a 'Statement on Ordination' that is made after the sermon. It is also given expression in words and actions at the baptismal *font: 'Reaffirmation of the Baptismal Covenant, Renunciations and Thanksgiving for Baptism'. *Anointing of the candidate is also suggested. In all of this revision of ordination rites the Reformed Church is being true to its essential nature: *ecclesia reformata* but also *semper reformanda*.

Paul F. Bradshaw, 'Ordination: Reformation Churches: 2. Reformed', *The Study of Liturgy*, ed. Cheslyn Jones, Geoffrey Wainwright, Edward Yarnold and Paul Bradshaw, 2nd edn, London/New York 1992, 382–4 (bib.); T. F. Torrance, *Conflict and Agreement in the Church*, London 1960.

STEWART TODD

Ordination of Women

During the nineteenth and twentieth centuries, a growing number of churches of the Reformation began to ordain women to the same orders as men, using the same rites. These developments have been accompanied by reassessment of historical evidence and substantial theological reflection. Since the RC Church and the Orthodox churches do not ordain women and not all Reformation churches do so, debate continues.

1. *Apostolic and Patristic Evidence.* Women were certainly among Jesus' followers (Matt. 27.55; Mark 15.40f.; Luke 8.2f.) and were active in the mission of the apostolic church. Some women owned houses where churches met, a sponsorship which may have included leadership responsibilities (Acts 12.12; Col. 4.15). Prisca/Priscilla and her husband Aquila owned a house where Christians met, and she accompanied Paul on a missionary journey (Acts 18.1–3, 18, 24–28; Rom. 16.3–5; 1 Cor. 16.19); Junia is described as an 'apostle' (Rom. 16.7); and Phoebe is called by Paul a 'deacon' (*diakonos*) and a 'presiding officer' or 'leader' (*prostatis*: Rom. 16.1f.). Several texts indicate appointment of men to an office or ministry through prayer and laying-on of hands (Acts 6.6, 13.3: 1 Tim. 4.14), but the NT does not specify whether women were commissioned in a similar manner. However, women's roles seem to have been increasingly restricted in at least some communities. NT books from later decades, particularly the Pastoral Epistles, reflect this conservatism (1 Tim. 2.12–15).

As the orders of *bishop, *presbyter and *deacon emerged more formally in the second century, restrictions on women's leadership continued to develop. Montanists acknowledged two women, Priscilla and Maximilla, as prophets who received direct revelation from the Holy Spirit, and among the Montanists as well as some Gnostic groups, women presided at the *eucharist, preached and baptized. These ministries were vigorously condemned by theologians who sought to distinguish orthodox Christianity from schismatic or heretical sects. Nonetheless, some patristic evidence suggests that women may have been recognized and served as presbyters and bishops within orthodox Christianity.

During the third and fourth centuries, the office of *deaconess gradually developed to minister to women, chiefly by visiting sick women and assisting in the administration of *baptism to women. Ancient texts disagree as to whether deaconesses were ordained, but even if they were, their ministry was quite different from that of men who were deacons. The order gradually fell into disuse during the Middle Ages.

2. *The Ministry of Women during the Middle Ages and the Reformation.* Women were restricted from ordained ministry throughout the Middle Ages. Scholastic theologians developed theological justification for this practice: woman's 'natural' state of subjection would be contradictory to the priestly exercise of authority. Yet some women exercised considerable authority as leaders of monastic communities, having many of the same juridical powers as medieval bishops and in some cases hearing *confessions and attending church councils.

Limitations on women's ministry continued at the time of the Reformation. Luther and Calvin believed that women's place was in the home. Yet in some more radical sects, women began to exercise leadership. A seventeenth-century 'Declaration of Faith' by English *Baptists called for men and women to be deacons. *Quakers upheld the authority of women to preach, and many women did so despite considerable opposition, including beatings and imprisonment.

3. *Modern Developments.* During the nineteenth century, the office of deaconess was revived, first as a Protestant community in Kaiserworth, Germany, in 1836. From there it spread to other countries, including the Anglican and Methodist churches in England and the USA. The 1968 Lambeth Conference of Anglican bishops recommended that the diaconate be open to women and that those already made deaconesses by laying-on of hands and prayer be recognized as within the diaconate, and in the years following, churches of the Anglican Communion gradually implemented this recommendation.

Although women preached and exercised other leadership in the American revival movements of the eighteenth and nineteenth centuries, social norms and biblical injunctions kept women from being ordained in mainline denominations. But the nineteenth-century temperance and women's rights movements began to provide a context that supported the ordination of women. The first woman to be ordained was Antoinette Louise Brown, ordained in a Congregational Church in New York in 1853; in the decades following, a few other women were ordained in other Protestant churches in the USA. In Britain, Congregationalist and Baptist churches began to ordain women in the early twentieth century. Other Protestant churches have gradually admitted women to ordained ministries, although more conservative Protestant churches that emphasize a literal interpretation of scripture, such as the Southern Baptist Convention in the USA, have restricted women from ordained leadership.

In Anglicanism, Florence Li Tim Oi was ordained priest in 1944 by R. H. Hall, Bishop of Hong Kong, to serve Christians in China. When the Archbishop of Canterbury refused to support the bishop's decision, Li Tim Oi voluntarily agreed to refrain from serving as a priest. After the 1968 Lambeth Conference acknowledged the possibility of the ordination of women to the priesthood, two other women were ordained in the Diocese of Hong Kong and Macao in 1971. Since then, women have been ordained priest in several other provinces of the Anglican Communion, including the USA, where irregular ordinations in 1974 and 1975 were followed in 1976 by legislation enabling the ordination of women; Canada (1976); and the Church of England (1994).

Ordination of women to the episcopacy has proceeded more slowly. The 1988 Lambeth Conference agreed that each province could make its own decision in this matter, and in the USA the following year, Barbara Harris became the first woman to be ordained bishop in the Anglican Communion. A decade later, there was a total of eleven Anglican women bishops in the USA, Canada and New Zealand. Some Anglican churches, including the Church of England, which permit the ordination of women to the priesthood, do not currently allow their ordination to the episcopate. Women have been ordained bishop in some Lutheran churches, including those that retain the historic succession.

In 1994, the diocese of the Old Catholics in Germany removed barriers to the ordination of women in all three orders, and two years later the diocese ordained its first women as priests.

Some of the other member churches of the Union of Utrecht also have ordained women as priests.

4. *Theological Issues*. As churches have considered the possibility of the ordination of women, theological anthropology has been one important consideration. While medieval anthropology viewed women as naturally inferior to men and so unsuitable for ordination and the authority it conferred, proponents of the ordination of women have turned to scripture to support claims for the equal dignity and rights of women and men. Not only are women and men created in the image of God (Gen. 1.27), they are also equally called and redeemed by Christ (Gal. 3.28).

Another scriptural argument is the tradition that Jesus designated twelve men as apostles and did not include women among those to whom he gave his apostolic charge. Although it is difficult to establish a precise relation between the 'the twelve' and the threefold ordained ministry which took shape during the second century, some churches which oppose the ordination of women consider Jesus' choice of twelve men to be determinative for Christian tradition. Those favouring the ordination of women emphasize that Jesus included women as well as men among his followers and that there is no direct link between 'the twelve' and the ordained ministry which later developed.

The relation of the ordained priest to Christ and to the community is also a disputed matter. In some traditions, the priest acts sacramentally at the eucharist *in persona Christi*, representing Christ as head of the church. Because the incarnate Christ was male, only a man can adequately fill this role. However, some who understand the priest to represent Christ argue that it is the humanity of Christ, not the maleness, that is significant; hence both women and men can represent Christ sacramentally. Another perspective views the priest as representative of the church, embodying not only the faith of the people of God but also the unity of the local church with the church universal. Understood in this way, it is not only appropriate to ordain women as well as men, it is essential that both women and men are ordained to represent the faithful.

Modern movements to ordain women have taken place in the context of social and cultural changes in which women have challenged patriarchal assumptions and claimed equal status with men. Some Christians view this as consistent with scripture and thus a continuing unfolding of God's reign, in which the ordination of women is part of the development of tradition. Others argue that ordaining women is counter to the tradition and indicative of a damaging secularization of the church. The unwillingness of some churches to recognize the ordination of women by others has also created obstacles in ecumenical dialogue, making it more difficult to achieve mutual recognition of ministries.

Karen Armstrong, *The End of Silence: Women and Priesthood*, London 1993; Ute E. Eisen, *Women Officeholders in Early Christianity: Epigraphical and Literary Studies*, Collegeville 2000; Virgil Elizondo and Norbert Greinacher (eds), *Women in a Men's Church* [*Concilium* CXXXIV] Edinburgh/New York 1980; Paul K. Jewett, *The Ordination of Women*, Grand Rapids, 1980; J. Gordon Melton (ed.), *The Churches Speak on Women's Ordination: Official Statements from Religious Bodies and Ecumenical Organizations*, Detroit 1991; Joan Morris, *The Lady Was a Bishop: The Hidden History of Women with Clerical Ordination and the Jurisdiction of Bishops*, London/New York 1973; Constance F. Parvey (ed.), *Ordination of Women in Ecumenical Perspective: Workbook for the Church's Future*, Geneva 1980 (bib.); Rosemary Ruether and Eleanor McLaughlin (eds), *Women of Spirit: Female Leadership in the Jewish and Christian Traditions*, New York 1979; Carl J. Schneider and Dorothy Schneider, *In Their Own Right: The History of American Clergywomen*, New York 1997; Elisabeth Schüssler Fiorenza, *In Memory of Her: A Feminist Theological Reconstruction of Christian Origins*, New York 1984; Karen Jo Torjesen, *When Women Were Priests: Women's Leadership in the Early Church and the Scandal of Their Subordination in the Rise of Christianity*, San Francisco 1993; World Council of Churches, *Concerning the Ordination of Women*, Geneva 1964 (bib.).

RUTH A. MEYERS

Organ

A mechanical musical instrument, in which air, blown from bellows, is held under pressure in a wind chest, and a player using levers releases the air into tuned pipes standing on the windchest. The early history of the organ is far from clear. However, early survivals and representations suggest that it was a ceremonial, outdoor instrument, used in the Romano-Greek Byzantine Empire. This instrument is known as *hydraulis*, because of its use of water to sustain the air pressure. The term *organum* is found in the Vulgate (e.g. Ps. 150), but may not have been applied to the instrument until early medieval times, when it most often appears in the plural, *organa* (in English as 'a pair of organs'). The organ made its way into northwest European culture by the reign of Charlemagne. The organ at Charlemagne's imperial palace in Aachen may have been an outdoor instrument. Its use in church was established by the tenth century, as the famous account by Wulstan, monk of Winchester, confirms. The loudness of the Winchester instrument may indicate that the organ was still primarily intended to be heard outside, to sound out greeting to important visitors or to mark great occasions.

In the later Middle Ages, three kinds of organ are found throughout Europe: (1) portative – a small organ carried on the shoulder in procession, blown by one hand and played by the other, and frequently represented in painting, glass and sculpture, especially as played by angels; (2) positive – a semi-portable organ, blown by one person and played by another, which could stand in a palace room or a *chapel of a church, and could be moved semi-dismantled when required; (3) 'great' organ, a permanent fixture, which in medieval times might require several players and blowers, often erected on a *gallery in a church. By the fifteenth century, some organs in northern Continental Europe were sophisticated machines with several wind chests, each controlled by its own set of keys – manuals (played by the hands) – and in some countries by pedals played with the feet.

Both descriptions and repertory confirm that, up until the sixteenth century, the organ in church was used in two ways: played on its own, or played in alternation with voices at specific points in the liturgy. Most often the music was based on the melody of the liturgical chants, according to time and season, and part of the skill of the player was to be able to improvise on these melodies. The organ was used for three liturgical purposes: to add solemnity on great occasions and feasts (e.g. during the solemn singing of *Te Deum* either at matins or at the arrival of a prelate or prince), to embellish the liturgy according to the day or season (e.g. at the *offertory in the *mass, or in alter-

nation at the *office hymn), to relieve the strain of singing the chant of the daily services of the office and mass in small communities of secular priests or monks (such practice in England was formalized by Cardinal Wolsey). *Cathedrals, monasteries, colleges and wealthier parish churches owned organs by 1500. A church often installed several organs to serve the various functions in different parts of the building: for instance, an organ in the *choir (either on the floor or a gallery) for the daily services, an organ in the Lady Chapel for Lady mass and office, and a great organ (on the north side of the church, or on a pulpitum or west gallery) for special feasts and occasions. In the Roman rite it is normative for the organ to be silent during *Advent and *Lent, but this was not the case in the pre-Reformation church in Britain, where the surviving repertory includes liturgical organ music for both pentitential seasons.

The Reformation polarized the use of the organ in the liturgy. It was excluded in Calvinist worship, while it continued to be used in both mass and office in the RC Church. In the *Lutheran Church its use was linked to the chorale, with a new repertory of preludes and variations based on chorale melodies, not least those by J. S. Bach. In England it was used for the accompaniment of the new Anglican cathedral repertory of *anthems and services. Throughout Europe, where the organ was allowed in worship, it was often often used to improvise accompaniments for singers (solo and choral) from the later sixteenth century onwards, within the emerging conventions of basso continuo. The development of independent organ accompaniments in the English church music of Byrd, Weelkes, Gibbons, Tomkins and their early seventeenth-century contemporaries is unique.

The organ was played for public recitals in some Calvinist churches (e.g. Oude Kerk, Amsterdam, where Sweelinck was organist in the early seventeenth century), and the reputation of some organists and organs became legendary. From the sixteenth century onwards the art of 'fantasia', of writing or improvising freely composed music, extended throughout Europe, with a repertory of fantasias, preludes, toccatas, variations, ricercars, canzonas, capriccios and fugues. Different traditions of organ playing and organ design resulted in different styles and idioms, most particularly in the Netherlands and North Germany, in South Germany and Austria, in Italy, in Spain and in

France. In the nineteenth century the mechanical sophistication of organ construction, with pneumatic action, allowed the building of very large instruments of symphonic proportions, with expressive devices and orchestral colours. There was a reaction to this development in the twentieth century, when players and organ builders developed preferences for organs modelled on specific historical styles with mechanical action, notably the French and German organs of the earlier eighteenth century. With factory methods of building, cheap pipe organs became commonplace even in very small churches in the nineteenth century. Those without the resource for a pipe organ have often resorted to the reed organ (harmonium) or, since the 1930s, to an electronic organ – an instrument which has developed rapidly with advances in electrical and computer engineering, and can mimic the pipe organ with some success.

The tradition of liturgical organ-playing has survived most strongly in France, where generations of organists have improvised at mass and vespers: de Grigny and Couperin are well known from the eighteenth century; Widor, Franck, Vierne, Dupré, Langlais and Messiaen represent part of a continuous line from the nineteenth century which is continued by their contemporary successors (e.g. Olivier Latry). Messiaen did not intend his written organ music for the liturgy, but for recitals. Nevertheless, through his use of theology and Catholic spirituality in his composition, he has created some of the most powerful Christian musical statements of his time.

'Organ', *NG2*, XVIII, 565–650; Stephen Bicknell, *The History of the English Organ*, Cambridge 1996; Peter Williams, *A New History of the Organ*, London 1980.

                                    JOHN HARPER

Orientation

The deliberate alignment of Christian worship, and the construction of places designed specifically for Christian worship, on an eastward, oriental, axis. Though pagan practice of facing the sunrise no doubt played a part, Christian liturgical prayer is directed to Christ, the rising sun, whose return is looked for. Later, burials were often oriented in the same manner.

The *basilican form adopted for church building in the fourth century was dominated by an axial arcaded *nave, culminating in an eastern *apse. Although it was no longer the ubiquitous form after the sixth century, its strong sense of orientation (both in worship and in architectural construction) had a profound controlling influence on the various later patterns of development, which were in turn shaped by a variety of regional and ritual innovations, and orientation was maintained as a norm throughout the Middle Ages. However, in Continental Reformation (especially Calvinist) churches, the dominance of the *pulpit often prompted a ninety-degree turn in the liturgical arrangement. In Anglican eighteenth- and early-nineteenth-century church furnishing, an elevated *lectern/pulpit often obscured the eastern *altar, a pattern that was maintained in the internal arrangements of Nonconformist churches, even where the building was not formally oriented. Recent reform in the RC Church and less formal developments in other Western churches have concentrated on a restoration of 'the image of the gathered assembly' (*General Instruction on the Roman Missal* 257). The resulting centralized churches are not normally orientated, as many Byzantine or Baroque examples are, but are often arranged in the round, focused on an altar in the middle.

Richard Krautheimer, *Early Christian and Byzantine Architecture*, London 1965, 4th edn 1986; Cyril Mango, *Byzantine Architecture*, London 1979; 'Church', I and IV, *The Grove Dictionary of Art*, London 1996 (bib.).

                               JONATHAN GOODALL

Orthodox Worship

1. *Roots and Locations*. Most commonly associated with Byzantine liturgy, the phrase 'Orthodox worship' actually embraces a much wider array of worship traditions. During the fourth century the overwhelming variety of local rites began to coalesce into distinct liturgical families, each based in a major city or region. Over the course of time, local churches were affected by politics and cultural differences, resulting in doctrinal divergences and liturgical shifts both reflecting and influencing the theological environment. 'Orthodox worship' is celebrated by churches often indicated by geographic/cultural titles (*Armenian, *Coptic, Greek, *East Syrian) or by theological designation (Jacobite, Nestorian). This frequently results in any one rite being described by several different terms, revealing historical prejudice as well as liturgical heritage.

Strictly speaking, the term 'Orthodox' refers to two groups of churches: (a) 'Eastern Orthodox' churches rooted in the Eastern Roman Empire who affirm seven ecumenical councils and, as a point of unity, recognize the Patriarchate of Constantinople as 'first among equals', and (b) 'Oriental Orthodox' churches with their most influential regions beyond the borders of the historical Roman Empire, who refused to accept the Council of Chalcedon (451 CE) and its christological formulation. When discussing liturgical matters, however, two other groups must be added: (a) the Assyrian Church of the East, which rejected the christological formulation of the Council of Ephesus (431 CE), and (b) the various Catholic churches in communion with the Bishop of Rome while worshipping according to an Eastern rite.

The churches belonging to the five 'liturgical families' of Eastern Christianity are as follows († indicates Oriental Orthodox Churches):

(a) *Armenian family*: Armenian Apostolic Church†; Armenian Catholic Church;

(b) *Byzantine family*: Eastern Orthodox Churches; Byzantine Catholic Churches (including the Melchite Church);

(c) *East Syrian (or Persian) family*: Assyrian Church of the East (or Nestorian); Chaldean Catholic Church; Syro-Malabar Catholic Church;

(d) *West Syrian (or Antiochene) family*: Syrian Orthodox (or Jacobite) Church†; Syrian Catholic Church; Malankara Orthodox Syrian Church†; Syro-Malankara Catholic Church; Maronite (portions of their rites);

(e) *Alexandrian family*: Coptic Orthodox Church†; Coptic Catholic Church; *Ethiopian Orthodox Church†; Ethiopian Catholic Church; Eritrean Orthodox Church†.

2. *Theological Characteristics*. In Eastern traditions, liturgy is the primary environment for Christian education and formation. Liturgical compositions are saturated with scriptural phrases and images. Rather than employing direct quotations or systematic exegesis, they instruct by means of allusions, images and theological riffs. Prayers regularly introduce supplication with a lengthy *anamnetic preface which serves as both theological foundation and homiletical meditation. Hymns provide emotional elaboration and complementary perspectives on scriptural passages as well as perpetuating the memory of significant personalities and events. Continuing the tradition

begun in the days of christological controversies, hymnographers often use poetry and music to express doctrinal statements in memorable ways. The rich theological content of liturgical texts enabled the faithful of these churches to thrive even in the absence of educated teachers and during times of persecution.

Orthodox liturgy is characteristically popular and ecclesial: the good news proclaimed, received and celebrated by the Body of Christ. Services designed to be performed by only one person are very rare, usually developing within the context of a solitary monastic's daily prayer. Most liturgy requires the presence of several people: a priest, *deacon, *lector, *cantor (and/or *choir) and congregation. Within this context, ministers function primarily on behalf of the gathered faithful. The priest gives voice to their prayers, the vast majority of which are cast in the first person plural. In proclaiming *litanies, the deacon prompts the people to remember a wide range of concerns in their prayers; deacons also instruct the people in what posture to assume ('You who are seated, stand' or 'Look to the East'), sometimes offering a theological commentary ('How awful is this hour and how dreadful is this moment, my beloved, wherein the Holy Spirit from the topmost heights takes wing and descends and hovers and rests upon this eucharist here present and sanctifies it. Be in calm and awe, while standing and praying': Syriac Liturgy of St James).

Liturgy's ecclesial nature extends beyond the present, commemorating saints frequently and often at length. The usual *dismissal of Byzantine rite services asks for Christ's mercy and salvation through the *intercessions of a long list of saints. Similarly, in the Coptic *eucharistic liturgy the consecration is followed by several petitions on behalf of all hierarchs, clergy of all ranks, and all faithful people. This leads into an explicit commemoration of hundreds of saints; modern editions of the Coptic Liturgy of St Basil list thirty-six by name. Even though each particular service is limited by time and space, the sacred liturgy itself involves the whole church of all times and places.

3. *Ritual Characteristics*. Orthodox worship appeals to the senses through diverse elements: *incense, beeswax *candles, chant, percussive music and *dance (especially in the Ethiopian Church), *vestments, *anointing with perfumed oils, bread and wine (both eucharistic

and non-eucharistic), a variety of blessed foods, *icons and *processions. These function as more than simply entertainment or emotional stimuli; they are theological-cultural expressions of a physical world completely penetrated and transfigured by the divine.

Similar in many ways to the liturgy of Western Christianity, the worship of Eastern churches is distinct. The date of *Easter and annual commemorations, in many churches, follow the Julian calendar. Influenced by Scholastic theology, Orthodox Christians affirm seven *sacraments, but historically sacramental language was used to describe many other services (e.g. monastic profession, blessing of water, and *funerals).

For the most part, Orthodox worship has never undergone a comprehensive and studied reform. Its organic evolution involved the introduction of new elements and reduction or suppression of old elements, resulting in long, multi-layered services. Lacking a central authority regulating liturgy, local Orthodox churches (under the leadership of their hierarch) are free to introduce elements taken from the local culture or to adapt received traditions. Although relying on detailed ritual scripts, Eastern Christian liturgy is ultimately an action that can not be appreciated only through textual study.

See also **Books, Liturgical** 2.

Ephrem Carr, 'Liturgical Families in the East', *Handbook for Liturgical Studies*, ed. Anscar J. Chupungo, I, Collegeville 1997, 11–24; Irénée Henri Dalmais, 'The Eastern Liturgical Families', *The Church at Prayer*, ed. A. G. Martimort, I, Collegeville 1987, 27–43; Paul Meyendorff, 'Origins of the Eastern Liturgies', *St Nersess Theological Review* I, 1996, 213–21; Manel Nin, 'History of the Eastern Liturgies', *Handbook for Liturgical Studies*, ed. Anscar J. Chupungo, I, Collegeville 1997, 115–30; Paul Verghese, *The Joy of Freedom: Eastern Worship and Modern Man*, London/Richmond VA 1967.

JOHN KLENTOS

Pall

From the same root as pallium (*see* **Vestments** 3.c), pall has described various ecclesiastical cloth coverings over the years, but is now generally used of only two.

1. A stiffened cloth used to cover the *chalice from the *offertory to the *communion; as such, it probably developed out of a *purificator or *corporal, but is now quite distinct, being four or five inches square, and the stiffening being usually a removable piece of cardboard enveloped by the linen. Originally, it probably had the purely practical role of preventing falling plaster or other foreign bodies from contaminating the chalice, and still functions as a preventative to flying insects, but it now has various pseudo-liturgical actions associated with it.

2. A large cloth thrown over – and completely covering – the coffin at a *funeral, usually of white or black or purple. Christian *baptismal and funeral rites have always been closely linked (cf. Rom. 6.3–5), and thus the white cloth used to cover the newly baptized is reflected in the use of the white pall, directly linking death to new life in Christ. Such a cloth was the property of each parish and used at all funerals, bringing some sense of uniformity and disregarding the social status of the departed.

TRISTAM HOLLAND

Pallium *see* **Vestments** 3(c)

Palm Sunday

In the Western Christian tradition, this Sunday one week before *Easter Day begins the ritual activity of *Holy Week (in the East, the weekend of Lazarus Saturday and Palm Sunday mark an independent unit between *Lent and Holy Week). There are two key components in the distinctive ritual activity of Palm Sunday: the procession with palms, and the solemn reading of the Passion. The first and most striking commemoration was that of Christ's entry into Jerusalem and his acclamation by the townspeople with waving palm branches and a chant of praise ('Hosanna to the Son of David'). It is from this that the day takes its name of Palm Sunday (from the branches used in the celebration at that time, the day could also be called Willow or Olive Sunday in the medieval period). From the fourth-century practice in Jerusalem, a liturgical *procession with palms spread to other areas of Europe, and finally to Rome by the eleventh century. Throughout later medieval Europe, the congregation would assemble before the *eucharist outdoors or at another location (e.g. a town gate) for a ritual blessing of palm branches, accompanied by the relevant gospel reading (usually Matt. 21.1–12 or John 12.12–19). The palms would be blessed, and the entire congregation would participate in a liturgical procession around or to the main church building. In many areas, the procession included a central symbol of Christ: the *bishop himself, who in some areas would knock for admittance on the doors of the main church or *cathedral; the consecrated *host, with or without other relics or the saints; or the German wheeled statue of Christ on a donkey, called the *Palmesel*. The hymn *Gloria, laus et honor* ('All glory, laud and honour') was often sung during this procession.

The second ritual component, originally the main focus of the day in Rome, was the formal chanting of the Passion taken from Matthew (Matt. 26.1—27.61) at the time of the gospel reading (as on *Good Friday). This lengthy reading was usually sung by three ministers, each in a different vocal range, and each taking a different role or part. The tenor voice took the narration, while the bass voice chanted the words of Christ, and an alto sang other individual parts (e.g. Pilate, the crowd). The celebration of the eucharist then continued as usual.

The liturgy of Palm Sunday was part of the liturgical renewal in the RC Church mandated by the Second Vatican Council. The blessing of palms may now take place outside of the church itself, and the congregation may form a liturgical procession back into the church. The Passion is still formally chanted or read, with the presider usually taking the part of Christ, and other lay readers or singers taking the parts of narrator and other roles. Similar practices have also been adopted in Anglican and other churches.

For bibliography, *see* **Holy Week.**

JOANNE M. PIERCE

Papal Rites

With religious toleration established by Constantine's Edict of Milan (313 CE) the Christian church came into a new era characterized by development in its organization, theology and liturgy. In this atmosphere the solemn sacerdotal functions of the Bishop of Rome became possible. The popes officiated in the *basilicas of Rome until their exile to Avignon in the fourteenth century. Upon their return to the Vatican, they used the domestic chapels; eventually the Sistine Chapel was erected for this purpose. From the occupation of Rome in 1870 until the Concordat was signed in 1929,

solemn liturgical functions were considered incompatible with the situation as it existed. Papal high *masses prior to 1870 differed from those of other bishops in length (up to three hours or more) and solemnity. Additional *vestments reserved for the pope were worn at papal masses and the pope received *communion at his throne rather than the *altar.

Brought in to conformity with the liturgical reforms of the Second Vatican Council, today the papal mass does not differ from that at which any other *bishop presides. Moreover the *vestments that were peculiar to the pope (such as the *falda* or white skirt and the *fanon* or double cape of white silk, the *subcinctorium*, a girdle related to the maniple) are no longer worn. The *ferula*, the papal staff surmounted by a cross, has been retained in place of the episcopal crozier. The papal tiara has been replaced with the episcopal mitre. The last pope to have a coronation at his installation was Paul VI in 1963 and he subsequently gave away the papal tiara.

The ceremonies that are still proper to the pope are opening and closing of the holy door for a jubilee year, the opening and closing of ecumenical councils, the canonization of saints, the creation of cardinals, and the blessing of palliums – given to archbishops throughout the world on their appointment. The rites by which the pope is installed and buried have been simplified and are familiar on account of media coverage in recent years.

J. Nabuco, 'Papal Ceremony and Vesture', *New Catholic Encyclopedia*, ed. T. O'Brien, X, New York 1967, 972–3.

JOSEPH WEISS

Pasch, Pascha *see* Easter

Passiontide

The traditional English name for the period beginning on the fifth Sunday of *Lent, commonly called Passion Sunday, and extending for two weeks to *Holy Saturday. In the RC Church the sixth Sunday of Lent is now officially called Passion Sunday, though its popular title remains *Palm Sunday.

TRISTAM HOLLAND

Pastoral Care and Worship

The Christian ministry of pastoral care shares in the one ministry of Christ. The pastoral care of the church is formed and sustained by worship and prayers offered through Christ to the glory of the Father in the power of the Holy Spirit. It is by this channel of grace that the distinctive Christian pastoral ministry receives strength and stamina to stay with unimaginable human anguish and celebrate with integrity the joys of human life. To this source of grace the NT bears witness. It is through Jesus' own prayer of thanksgiving and the breaking of bread that the hungry were fed (Matt. 15.36). From prayer and preaching sprang the care of widows (Acts 6). Money for the relief of the poor was set aside on the first day of the week (1 Cor. 16.2), and the ministry of healing was exercised by the *elders with prayer and *anointing (James 5.13). Pastoral care is not restricted to the sole preserve of private practice but is properly the ministry of the whole church. Christian pastoral care even when it is necessarily to be exercised by individuals is still a ministry offered on behalf of the entire Christian community and in the name of Christ.

1. *Authorized Pastoral Liturgy*. Much pastoral practice does not revolve around an isolated event but is intimately involved with a personal process of illumination, growth or healing. Recent liturgical revisions have recognized this process by making provision for staged rites to be used at appropriate points on the journey. Liturgical provision for Christian initiation reflects the evolution of a growing relationship with God which moves from enquiry through the *catechumenate to *baptism, welcome and life in the body of Christ. The *funeral service is clearly a pivotal focus in the process of bereavement but in practice may well be preceded by the pastoral care of the dying, ministry at the time of death, preparation for the funeral, reception of the coffin into church and a *vigil. It may be followed by the burial of ashes, a memorial service and remembrance on the anniversary of death. In addition the funeral service of a Christian will mark the pilgrimage of faith from baptism through discipleship to the committal in faith that lays claim to the promises of God. Pastoral rites which support the *marriage service may provide for prayers at the time of engagement and a service of thanksgiving for use in later years. This inauguration of staged rites makes available flexible and comprehensive resources in order that sensitive liturgical provision might be responsive to pastoral need.

2. *Specialist Resources*. Authorized liturgical texts cannot cater for every pastoral situation that might be encountered. More specific prayers and liturgies can be provided by sector ministries and specialist institutions. Decades of work among the *deaf and hard of hearing have produced much creative material and helpful advice. Chaplains in hospitals, prisons and schools often maintain useful prayers and liturgies for particular occasions of pastoral need.

In some circumstances it is not wise to construct a pastoral liturgy without seeking experienced assistance. Ministry involving *exorcism or deliverance is fraught with potential difficulty for the innocent and inexperienced. In other situations much care and sensitivity is required. When ministering to a family where there has been the tragedy of a cot death, for example, it may appear appropriate to use the gospel words of Jesus, 'Let the children come to me. Do not try to stop them' (Matt. 19.14), but experience suggests that grieving parents in shock can 'hear' that Jesus has robbed them of their child.

Pastoral liturgy must be responsive to the vagaries of the human condition, but a skeleton structure is useful in meeting the needs of those situations which are described as 'endings and new beginnings'. Human beings are usually more concerned to celebrate a new start than to mark a formal conclusion, but to end well is to be better prepared for a new beginning. A liturgy which recognizes the end of a group or enterprise needs to convey an opportunity for: remembrance without fantasy; thanksgiving; a moment to let go; and a turning to the future with faith and trust in the purposes of God.

Pastoral liturgy which is sensitive to the needs of the moment can bear the truth of realities which lie beyond words and helps to discern the deep things of the Spirit. Often a simple symbolic action in a safe environment can speak more eloquently than a construction of words. This is particularly the case where fragile areas of human hurt involve grief, betrayal, guilt and failure.

3. *Collective Pastoral Care and Worship*. Individuals are not the sole focus of Christian pastoral care. It is sometimes forgotten that institutions also encounter times of threat and change which elicit anxiety, fear and loss of confidence. The church has a long tradition of ministering to institutions, civic societies and public services. Some services may be newcomers to the area providing opportunities for

employment and fresh involvement with the local community. Other societies may have achievements to celebrate. In many circumstances an appropriate pastoral liturgy and a ministry of encouragement and support are much appreciated.

4. *Conclusion*. Pastoral liturgy springs from the consistent prayer and worship of the church. Both worship and pastoral care share in the redemptive work of Christ. The *dismissal at the conclusion of an act of worship is intended to send out the restored and renewed people of God to be a blessing in the world. It is in the world that the profound theological themes of grace, forgiveness and reconciliation are worked out in practice. Pastoral liturgy strengthens the wider ministry of the church in evangelism, education, and marriage and bereavement support. At the heart of pastoral care is the pattern of Jesus' ministry to welcome the stranger, to celebrate new life, to hold those who are hurt and to stand with the victims of trauma and tragedy. Pastoral liturgy is the focus and expression of that ministry where human need lies open to the grace and healing power of God.

Wesley Carr, *Brief Encounters*, London 1994; Stephen Oliver (ed.), *Pastoral Prayers*, London 1996; Michael Perham, *New Handbook of Pastoral Liturgy*, London 2000; Elaine Ramshaw, *Ritual and Pastoral Care*, Philadelphia 1987; William Willimon, *Worship as Pastoral Care*, Nashville 1989.

STEPHEN OLIVER

Paten *see* **Chalice and Paten**

Patronal Festival *see* **Dedication**

Pax, Peace *see* **Kiss, Ritual**

Penance

Penance derives from the Latin *poenitentia*, used in the Vulgate to translate the NT Greek *metanoia* ('conversion' or 'repentance'). The term refers to practices furthering conversion (especially prayer, fasting, and works of charity and service) and to the sacramental process and liturgical ritual whereby the Christian church assists its members in pursuing conversion and obtaining forgiveness from God through reconciliation to the church.

1. *New Testament Roots*. Repentance and gracious forgiveness were central to Jesus' proclamation of God's reign in preaching, personal encounter and companionship at table. The paschal mystery of his dying, rising, ascension and sending the Spirit is likewise central to the NT understanding of sinful humanity's reconciliation with God sacramentalized in *baptism and *eucharist.

Several NT writers speak of the church's role and responsibility to maintain holiness through ongoing forgiveness of sins. Serious sinners are to be shunned in hope of repentance (1 Cor. 5) and reconciliation (2 Cor. 2.5–11). Using the rabbinic term for authority, 'binding and loosing', Matthew gives detailed procedures (18.15–20) in a context stressing forgiveness (18.1–14, 21–35). Peter and the disciples are singled out as having such authority (Matt. 16.19; cf. John 20.23 and its emphasis on the Spirit). Some authors are reluctant to offer forgiveness for some sin after baptism (1 John 5.14–17; Heb. 6.4–8; 10.26–31; 12.16–17; cf. Mark 3.29), but the overall spirit is one of welcome and forgiveness.

2. *Ancient Penance*. The post-apostolic church continued to call sinful members to repentance and reconciliation (*Shepherd of Hermas*). Worship included *confession of sin as praise of a merciful God (*Didache* 4.14, 14.1–2; cf. *1 Clement*). Ordinary sinners continued the process of baptismal conversion: sincere repentance, penitential practices to deepen conversion, and eucharist as sign of communion with the church and forgiveness from God.

A formal process for the most serious sinners developed in the second and third centuries as a 'second conversion' parallel to *catechumenal formation (first conversion) but more difficult. The order of penitents provided opportunity for reformation and rehabilitation for sinners excluded from the eucharist (Tertullian, *De paenitentia*; *De pudicitia*). Individuals entered penance in a community liturgy, with the central act the *bishop's laying-on of hands to *exorcize them and make them penitents. Penitents showed their repentance in public ritual (*exomologesis*) and through practices that expressed interior repentance in a bodily way. The bishop supervised the process and decided regarding reconciliation. Generally this was allowed only once. Initially reconciliation was often refused those guilty of certain offences. In some places liturgical rituals marked stages of development toward full conversion and reconciliation.

Controversy with Montanism and Novatianism led to affirming the church's authority to forgive all sinners (Cyprian; later, Ambrose and Pacian), but the principle of one baptism, one penance was maintained for centuries. Because of the controversy, the liturgy of reconciliation developed to show official forgiveness. After conversion was sufficiently complete, the penitents were given the church's peace and communion through the bishop's laying-on of hands. Reconciliation with the church was the sign and experience of reconciliation with God. Canonical legislation in the fourth and fifth centuries developed penance as an institution. As earlier, little is known of ministry beyond recommended penitential practices and the increasingly elaborate liturgy.

As penance became punitive, people were less willing to use the formal institution with its public stigma and lifelong consequences. The order of penitents practically disappeared in the sixth and seventh centuries except as a deathbed ritual. The pious sometimes became penitents (*conversi*) and lived much like members of later religious orders. *Lent shifted from a baptismal focus and gradually became a time for the whole community to enter penance.

3. *Penance in the East.* Penance in the East was less complicated and severe, probably because development was unaffected by puritanical controversies. The East tended to regard all sins as remissible (Clement of Alexandria; Origen; the *Didascalia*). It gave more place to healing through spiritual direction and less emphasis to a public process for supporting repentance. Overall, the East has not given as much attention to specific confession as the West and has changed less over time. It has also kept a clearer orientation to the eucharist as itself the *sacrament of reconciliation, although that understanding is now primarily expressed in the use of confession to prepare for (infrequent) *communion.

4. *Medieval Penance.* Like John Chrysostom in the East, Caesarius of Arles and others in Gaul sometimes permitted those unwilling to enter canonical penance to do penance privately and then return to the eucharist. From the sixth through the ninth centuries Celtic and Anglo-Saxon monks developed and then spread to the Continent of Europe a new form which fitted this individualism. Originally spiritual direction and counselling borrowed from Eastern monasticism, this became a reassuring means of post-baptismal formation when extended to the laity. A monk (not always ordained) listened to the confession of sins and, using books called penitentials, for each sin prescribed penitential deeds (especially fasting) as a remedy and a sort of tariff whereby to even accounts. After completing the penance (making satisfaction) the individual could return to the eucharist. Confession of sins and satisfaction were thus linked as the cause of forgiveness. To the average person this procedure seemed much like canonical penance. It was, however, more practical because it was private and repeatable. It differed primarily in the lack of a public liturgy of reconciliation. Also, certain religious practices could serve as a pardon (indulgence), shortening long periods of penance.

As tariff penance became popular in the eighth and ninth centuries, episcopal synods reacted against it and tried to restore canonical penance, at least for sins publicly known, or to require a public reconciliation after confession to a priest (not a lay person) and doing the penance assigned. Since penitents rarely came for public reconciliation, in the tenth century priests began to reconcile immediately after the confession and before penance was done. From the ninth to the fourteenth centuries *absolution was sometimes given publicly prior to communion without confession being required. Satisfaction postponed until after absolution began to diminish in importance. Oral confession absorbed satisfaction as the means of self-purgation, and absolution (originally the blessing at the end of doing penance) grew in importance as the cause of forgiveness through the priestly exercise of the power of the keys in official judgement. Confession and absolution thus replaced confession and satisfaction as the cause of forgiveness, and the sacrament came commonly to be called confession.

Before canonical penance faded, conversion had already begun to be reduced from a life-process in community to a ritual. As this continued, Scholastic theology individualized the phases of conversion as the acts of the penitent: contrition and confession (entry into penance), satisfaction or acts of penance (efforts to deepen conversion during the time spent in penance), followed by absolution (completion of conversion and consequent reconciliation).

From the twelfth century theologians debated the interrelation of the personal (conversion) and ecclesial (exercise of the power of the keys) elements of penance. Abelard saw contrition as decisive. Hugh of St Victor and others saw absolution as effective in removing guilt. Aquinas' synthesis balanced the two, regarding the penitent's acts as the matter of the sacrament and the priest's absolution as the form, with an intrinsic causal relationship between contrition and absolution. The Fourth Lateran Council (1215) obliged all who had attained the use of reason to make an annual confession to their own priest. By the fifteenth century confession with absolution was regarded as the only normal form of the sacrament.

5. *The Reformation Churches*. Protestant Reformers criticized the penitential discipline as semi-Pelagian because of its emphasis on human action and accomplishment and as giving too much control to priests. They rejected both confession and absolution, although Luther himself was ambivalent regarding penance as sacrament. Lutherans and Anglicans currently provide a rite for private confession – to reassure repentant sinners – but do not require it. Pastoral counselling in other churches serves a similar purpose. Most churches include a confession of sin and prayer for forgiveness (sometimes called absolution) as part of Sunday worship.

6. *Modern Penance*. The medieval system's defenders saw human weakness receiving consolation by submitting to the power of the keys. The Council of Trent regarded the priest's absolution as authoritative and effective, analogous to court judgement, and insisted on individual auricular confession of all mortal sins (integral confession) as required by divine law (*iure divino*) and necessary for the priest's judgement. Trent's defence of the system as consistent with Christ's will for the church, particularly these two dogmatic teachings, seems to rule out a development that does not include integral confession and juridical absolution, although the interpretation of Trent's meaning is still debated.

The Roman Ritual of 1614 had an abbreviated liturgy which highlighted confession and absolution. Confession became more frequent in Counter-Reformation Catholicism, not only for the forgiveness of mortal sins but also as an aid to spiritual growth and a means of purification in preparing for communion. The confessional booth was required in the sixteenth century to prevent solicitation or the accusation of it. Large numbers of penitents in the mid-twentieth century led to further streamlining of the ritual. This often reduced confession to a list, made the confessor's counsel a perfunctory *ferverino*, and removed the last pieces of prayer. Yet at the same time frequency of confession began to decline.

Early-twentieth-century RC theology rediscovered the communal and liturgical character of patristic penance. By mid century theologians reached consensus that reconciliation with the church (declared by the absolution) functioned as sacramental sign of reconciliation with God. Community liturgies supporting repentance began to develop in Europe in the 1950s and 1960s. These services centred on scripture and followed various formats: with individual confession and absolution; with a communal confession in general terms and public absolution; with a communal confession but without any absolution.

Vatican II's Constitution on the Liturgy called for a reform to highlight the social and communal character of conversion and its outcome, reconciliation with the church and God. The 1973 *Rite of Penance* provides three sacramental rituals: reconciling an individual penitent (private confession enriched with scripture and prayer); reconciling several penitents with individual confession and absolution (individual confession and absolution in community liturgy); reconciling several penitents with general confession and absolution (community liturgy with communal, non-specific confession and public proclamation of absolution). It also has a 'non-sacramental' penitential service for supporting conversion but without reconciliation.

The 1973 rites have been poorly implemented. The first is often simply confession with a new absolution formula. The second is unwieldy unless a proportionate number of priests is available; otherwise, the service is too long or the confession is hardly what Trent had in mind, even though judgement is clearly and individually expressed. The third official rite, which became popular where used, has since come to be heavily restricted by Rome and even prohibited by many bishops. The 'non-sacramental' penitential service is rarely used.

7. *Theological Reflection*. The history of penance shows an interplay of the personal and the ecclesial in challenging sinners and supporting

conversion. Sometimes the bodily expression of repentance has been emphasized and sometimes the verbal expression of sin. Sometimes individuals have entered penance voluntarily and other times they have been coerced. Sometimes the church's involvement has emphasized supporting conversion and sometimes re-establishing a relationship by welcoming back or authoritatively judging.

The varied shape of the sacramental ministry and ritual has generally resulted from a pastoral response to the cultural setting. A constant has been the church's responsibility to call sinful members to repentance and to support their conversion. It does so in order to fulfil its mission in service to God, God's reign, humanity and the individual: the church is to be holy and its members are to be holy. A missing element historically has been the church's own admission of wrongdoing and commitment to conversion.

Currently the sacrament is as marginal as in the fifth and sixth centuries, and new forms are needed. Conversion ministry can take many forms, including peer and mutual, though the priest's role in reconciliation parallels that in the eucharist, presiding at church worship. Liturgically, the service can take the form of lament for sin and commitment to justice as well as confession of individual weakness and need for purification. Congregations in conflict should experience the restoration of communion. Repentant sinners should find themselves reformed and transformed to share the church's ministry of reconciliation.

James Dallen, *The Reconciling Community: The Rite of Penance,* Collegeville 1986 (bib.); Joseph Favazza, *The Order of Penitents: Historical Roots and Pastoral Future,* Collegeville 1988 (bib.); Kenan Osborne, *Reconciliation and Justification: The Sacrament and Its Theology,* New York 1990 (bib.).

JAMES DALLEN

Pentecost

The celebration of Pentecost occurs on the seventh Sunday after *Easter, and is the day of the closing of the Easter season, traditionally known in England as *Whitsunday. The name Pentecost is derived from Greek for 'fiftieth', which was translated into Latin as *quinquagesima*, also meaning 'fiftieth', and in turn Pentecost also referred to the 'fifty-day' period spanning the seven weeks from Easter Day to Pentecost. From early times until now, there has been some degree of ambiguity in the tradition about whether 'Pentecost' refers to the span of fifty days or to the fiftieth day itself. Most presently regard Pentecost as the latter, the Sunday at the end of the fifty-day span that is the Easter season.

The day of Pentecost itself was originally observed by the Jews as a harvest festival, the Feast of Weeks (see the deutero-canonical texts, Tob. 2.1 and 2 Macc. 12.32), marked in the span following the annual observance of Passover. The evangelist Luke, who is most intent on establishing chronology in the life of Jesus in his Gospel and in the emergence of the church in the Acts of the Apostles, is the only NT witness to refer to Pentecost (Acts 2.2–4), which he describes as the occasion of the bestowal of the Holy Spirit on the Apostles.

The Christian observance of the fifty-day period following Easter as a festal season is first attested in a number of sources from a variety of regions at the end of the second century. It was regarded as a time of rejoicing, and every day was treated in the same way as Sunday, that is, with no kneeling for prayer, or fasting. It was inevitable that in the fourth century, along with the development of other festal days in the year, the fiftieth day itself should come to be celebrated in many places as the commemoration of the gift of the Spirit, although in other places – including Jerusalem – both the *ascension and the gift of the Spirit were at first celebrated together on that day. After the emergence of a separate feast of the Ascension on the fortieth day in a number of churches towards the end of the century, becoming almost universal early in the fifth century, some churches continued for a while to observe the whole fifty days as a festal season, but others resumed the regular weekly fasting after the fortieth day, while still others (at least according to Filastrius, bishop of Brescia in northern Italy in the late fourth century) fasted even before the Ascension. The emphasis given to the first week of the Easter season for the post-baptismal *mystagogy of the newly baptized also helped to erode the unity of the season, so that in the later tradition Pentecost came to be regarded as a separate feast from Easter, with its own *octave, and it is only in the past few decades that in many Christian denominations emphasis has once again been placed on the Easter season as a whole and on the unique character of Pentecost Sunday as its close.

Martin F. Connell, 'From Easter to Pentecost', *Passover and Easter: The Symbolic Structuring of Sacred Seasons*, ed. Paul F. Bradshaw and Lawrence A. Hoffman, Notre Dame 1999, 94–106.

MARTIN F. CONNELL

Pentecostal Worship

1. *The Past*. Historically, Pentecostal worship has been characterized by three things: spontaneity, emotion, and the operation of the gifts of the Spirit. It was spontaneous, in that little pre-planning was done (especially in the matters of music, prayer and, to some extent, preaching); and it was emotional, in that the aim of worship was the passionate arousal of feeling. Both of these traits combined to foster a climate believed to encourage the third, the operation of the *charismata* – the gifts of the Spirit. Taking their cue from NT accounts and believing that supernatural manifestations were meant for today's church as much as for the church of two thousand years ago, Pentecostals found speaking in tongues (with and without interpretation), words of knowledge, prophecies and healings normative. Physical manifestations such as being 'slain in the Spirit', trances, laughing and crying were also accepted.

Added to its Wesleyan theological base was what Pentecostals termed the baptism in the Holy Spirit. The initial evidence of this experience was believed to be speaking in tongues as recorded in Acts 2.4. This activity of tongues-speaking set Pentecostals apart from other evangelicals and gave Pentecostal worship its unique ambience. Since Spirit manifestations were seen as more spontaneous than planned, more emotional than rational, Pentecostal worship always emphasized things which provided the right atmosphere for the exercise of these manifestations. Key was emotion-driven believer participation. Music was boisterous, physically stimulating, emotionalistic, highly repetitious, and generally accompanied by hand-clapping. *Extemporaneous prayer with the people all praying aloud simultaneously and fiery sermons with Christians shouting verbal acclamations contributed to generating the sought-after atmosphere thought necessary for supernatural phenomena. Tongues and interpretation were deemed of particular importance because tongues was seen as a direct word from the Lord, although technically subservient to the written word.

One additional focus of Pentecostal worship was evangelistic outreach. In fact, Pentecostals routinely set aside Sunday morning for 'worship' and Sunday evening for 'evangelism'. The evening format was more free-wheeling than the morning service, with an informality which gave it an air of relaxation and good will. Such evangelistic emphases combined with the spontaneity, emotion and supernatural manifestations of Pentecostal worship have shaped Pentecostal liturgy into patterns which continue (variously to be sure) to the present.

From its inception, Pentecostalism accommodated the gospel to the popular culture of the day. Preaching was common oratory, church music stylistically that of popular music. In both instances what became normative did not stem from academic speech or high art, but the language of commoners and the music of entertainers. A popular style always took precedence over content considerations.

There was also a pragmatic approach to worship. If something effected what was envisioned, it was adopted. Pentecostals eschewed church tradition and took up new methods on the assumption that 'if they worked' they were acceptable. Pipe organs were rejected as too formal and liturgical. Piano, with orchestral or band instruments, became the accompaniment of choice. The rise of rock 'n' roll eventually initiated the widespread use of the drum set – a further musical inducement to physical activity such as hand-clapping, dancing, or other bodily movement. Amplification equipment for preaching and music was utilized as much for control of the congregation as for hearing clarity. Background music for prayers, altar services, and sometimes even for preaching, became common. These things were appropriated because they appeared to bring the desired results. Worship's philosophical governance was pragmatism.

2. *The Present*. Pentecostal worship continues in its historic pattern but with some major shifts. First, ostensibly spontaneous worship remains highly charged emotionally, perhaps even more so than previously. But there is a difference. Worship now is crafted to seem extemporaneous but is often highly scripted. Specifically, the singing of long strings of emotionalistic songs, accompanied by a band and prompted by words projected on a screen, is carefully orchestrated. Orders of songs, number of repetitions, keys and decibel levels require pre-planning and rehearsal. Since only

the leaders have the song menu, the appearance is that of singing which is unplanned and unrehearsed.

Second, the influence of the wider *charismatic renewal has been significant, Pentecostals having adopted their more narrow understanding of worship. Whereas worship was previously thought to comprise singing, praying, testifying, admonishing, operation of the gifts of the Spirit, offering, sermonizing and interceding, there is presently an almost universal shift toward fragmentation and compartmentalization in which *praise and worship has become an entity in its own right. Distinct and separate from other components of a church service, worship is primarily thought of as singing a repetitive series of mostly Christian contemporary songs (the hymnal largely having been dropped) for long periods of time, with the congregation standing, accompanied by a praise band and led by a microphoned praise team and worship leader. Congregants are often urged to raise their hands, worship God, and give verbal praise. People sway, hop, dance and clap to pop-style music of varying physical intensities. Congregational singing has waned as the amplified voices of the praise team have taken over. After the worship, the service continues with prayer, offering, sermon, and sometimes an altar service of *intercession.

Third, supernatural utterances in tongues with interpretation appear to be diminishing. With the advent of large worship spaces with dead acoustics which require the use of voice amplification, most in the congregation cannot hear another believer well (unless they are quite close together). Since it is impracticable to give every person a microphone, congregational body ministry is largely eliminated. In some places where hearing is unimpeded, the gifts of the Spirit continue unabated.

Fourth, accommodation of the gospel to culture is accelerating. The content of worship, especially in the music, is often patterned after the more radical idioms of the day. CCM (Christian Contemporary Music), the counterpart of secular pop, has largely replaced the gospel songs and choruses of yesteryear. The use of technology (projection screens, sound tracks, electronic keyboards, mega-amplification), rock/pop bands, with the ever-present drumset are now the *modus operandi* of the Pentecostal Church music scene.

And finally, the pragmatic philosophy of its forebears continues unabated. Marketing, psychology and business acumen are utilized in the drive to spread the gospel. Pastors are encouraged to be CEOs with staffs who work under them. Workshops, conferences and seminars aid the full-time ministry in reaching the 'unchurched'. Sunday morning and evening services have tended to lose their distinctive identities.

In conclusion, Pentecostal worship has maintained its subjective and emotional approach. To a considerable extent it has dropped true congregational spontaneity and a good share of congregational participation for the appearance of a 'spontaneity' which is highly planned and dominated by the worship leaders. Pragmatic and driven by popular culture, contemporary Pentecostal worship mirrors the changing values of society. Service style, sermon content, song texts, musical standards, and operation of the supernatural gifts have been adapted to our postmodern, pluralistic, and relativistic culture. Pentecostals, like many others, have separated theology from worship style. Believing they have retained their historic theological heritage, they have also retained their heritage of changing their worship to fit the times.

See also **Assemblies of God Churches' Worship**.

Edith L. Blumhofer and Joel A. Carpenter, *Evangelicalism in Twentieth-Century America: A Guide to the Sources*, New York 1990; Charles Edwin Jones, *A Guide to the Study of the Pentecostal Movement*, Metuchen, NJ 1983; Grant Wacker, 'Bibliography and Historiography of Pentecostalism (U.S.)', *Dictionary of Pentecostal and Charismatic Movements*, ed. Stanley M. Burgess, Gary B. McGee and Patrick H. Alexander, Grand Rapids MI 1988, 65–76 (bib.).

                                          CALVIN M. JOHANSSON

Pews

The word comes from the Latin *podia*, seats raised on a platform, a good description for the raised west-end platforms and *galleries from which people in the eighteenth century viewed the liturgy, sang and played their instruments in English churches.

Pews describe the shape and activities of the congregation. Until the late Middle Ages standing, walking and kneeling were the *postures for liturgical participation. Stone benches around the walls were a concession for those too infirm to stand: hence the expression 'the weakest go to the wall'. The islands of pews on platforms in medieval churches, often with beautifully carved bench ends telling the gospel story, left plenty of space for *processions. After the Reformation, the major activity of listening to sermons was reflected in packing churches with pews. Sometimes these were privately owned or rented box pews for a family, with cushions, even a fireplace, and seats facing in any direction. With the *pulpit often half way down the church, it did not matter if some had their backs to the *sanctuary. All this changed with the reforming zeal of the Ecclesiologists in the second half of the nineteenth century, ripping out the box pews and cramming churches with rows of pine benches facing the *chancel, which itself was filled for the first time with seats for the newly robed *choir. If the main activity of the congregation was going to return to the medieval pattern of observing the distant mysteries, the Victorians were going to do it in comfort.

Thus pews can reflect the theology as well as the activity and relationships of the congregation. It took a long time in the twentieth century before thinking of the church as the body of Christ, with the people of God celebrating the *eucharist together in a more interdependent mode, gathered around the holy table, began to have any effect on seating. There were some brave attempts at providing blocks of curved pews around a more central *altar, some good arrangements with short movable pews, and some disastrous replacements of traditional pews with contract upholstered seats on wall-to-wall carpeting. One consistory court judgement in England in the last year of the century listed the emotional (or spiritual?) and practical advantages of pews. They 'exude an air of tradition and permanence . . . provide an ordered appearance . . . are easier to clean, being of a much simpler geometry . . . are flexible in their capacity . . . more readily provide space for storing hats, coats and umbrellas . . . help to contain restless children . . . provide greater mechanical stability for the elderly . . . and where pews have been in place for many generations, there is felt by some to be value in worshipping in the same seats as those who have gone before us' (*Re Holy Cross, Pershore, Worcester Consistory Court, Mynors Ch.2000*). But the judge ordered that half the pews should go. It is a problem that pews define not only the seating area, but the area in which other things can be done – space for the gathering of the assembly (and for coffee and ministry afterwards), space for processions, space for groups of people to face one another in discussions or teaching groups, space for musicians in churches where there is no longer a gallery for this purpose. Despite its traditional advantages, immovable bench seating is culturally obsolete, and may hinder both the church's perception of itself and the flexibility of its worship.

TREVOR LLOYD

Phelonion *see* Vestments 4(d)

Pilgrimage

Pilgrimage describes a practice which is not unique to Christianity. The focal role of the Temple in pre-rabbinic Judaism and the significance of the oracle at Delphi in ancient Greece are just two examples of religious sites drawing people significant distances to worship. Even the 'song-lines' in Australian Aboriginal culture suggest a not dissimilar practice. The actual term 'pilgrimage', however, was coined early on within the Christian tradition. It is derived from the Latin word *peregrinus*, meaning 'stranger', and has come to mean journeying for religious reasons in a foreign land. In contemporary social anthropological terms, pilgrimage stands alongside 'rites of passage' as a liminal experience. This implies the crossing of a threshold into a strange land or strange territory by means of the journey. The effect of experiencing 'difference' is to change the religious consciousness of the pilgrim; through this liminal threshold experience the pilgrim returns home transformed.

In Christian history, pilgrimage can probably be traced to the origins of liturgical and spiritual practices in first-century Palestine. Many gospel critics now assume that the earliest traditions within the Gospels are the passion narratives. In turn, biblical scholars have argued that the passion narratives themselves may be the fruits of early pilgrimage practice. The events recorded in the passion narrative became linked together through the practice of early Christians following the path to Calvary. This practice was then later written down to form a continuous narrative of the passion. We cannot be absolutely certain of these facts but we can be certain that pilgrims were travelling to the Holy Land to walk the Via Dolorosa in Jerusalem in the early Christian centuries. The narrative of the journey of the devout woman, Egeria, throughout Asia Minor and the Middle

East describes a pilgrimage probably between the years 381 and 384; Egeria is believed to have been a nun from Gaul. This pattern of pilgrimage to Palestine, exemplified classically in Egeria's travels, continued and became more popular during the later Middle Ages; Margery Kempe, an English mystic of the late fourteenth and early fifteenth centuries, describes in her book journeys to the Holy Land and also to Assisi, Rome and Compostela.

In the Western church the practice of pilgrimage developed within two broad and differing patterns relating to the Irish-Celtic and the Roman traditions. The Irish-Celtic pattern related directly to distinctive approaches to mission and evangelization. For Irish monks travelling to foreign lands the motivation was as much missionary as ascetic. St Columba was thus a pilgrim for the gospel in his mission to the Pictish peoples; similarly St Fursey's journey from the skelligs on the west coast of Ireland to East Anglia was as a missionary pilgrim. Working most frequently in wild rural landscapes the Irish-Celtic pilgrim evangelists set up monasteries or minsters (the derivation of monastery and minster is cognate) which acted as missionary centres equipping them to take the gospel into the surrounding countryside. The monastic tradition here bears close similarities to the semi-eremitic patterns established by St Antony and the later desert fathers in the Egyptian desert.

The pattern of pilgrimage more familiar to us today is that which was established within the Western Roman tradition of Christianity. This is the pattern exemplified well in *The Book of Margery Kempe* and immortalized in Geoffrey Chaucer's *Canterbury Tales*. Here pilgrimage was often centred on the shrine of a local saint or on the site of a significant vision. People would often journey to such a shrine in the hope of receiving a cure for some sort of ailment or disease. Notable sites for pilgrimage in the Middle Ages, for example, included Hailes Abbey in Gloucestershire, where a local knight had enshrined a phial of the 'holy blood', or, rather differently, at Conques, on the edge of the Pyrenees, where the relics of St Faith had found their final resting place. Certain centres became particularly popular: in England thousands of pilgrims were attracted to Walsingham, where there had been a vision of the Blessed Virgin Mary; Durham, the final resting place of the mortal remains of St Cuthbert; and pre-eminently Canterbury, the shrine of St Thomas Becket. The classical centre for pil-grimage in mainland Europe was Santiago da Compostela, where it was believed the body of St James found its final resting place, following a tradition dating back to the ninth century; it was here that the cockle shell became the symbol of pilgrimage. The pilgrims journeyed on to Finisterre, which was then literally 'the end of the earth'; to mark their completion of the pilgrimage, they collected shells from the beach, which eventually became symbols of the journey to Santiago.

The motivation for pilgrimage in the Roman tradition varied. Realistically pilgrimage was the only form of holiday available in the medieval period. Nonetheless great courage and perseverance were required to complete the journey and so a pilgrimage would also be undertaken as either a sign of piety or as a penitential exercise. King Henry II of England made pilgrimage to Rome following the martyrdom of Becket, and St Lawrence O'Toole, the Irish warrior bishop, made similar penitential pilgrimages to both Canterbury and Rome. It was this association of pilgrimage with the system of *penance and indulgences which led to the unpopularity and condemnation of the practice by elements within the Protestant tradition following the Reformation. Although it was seen generally by Protestants as being associated with corrupt spiritual practices, nevertheless the images surrounding it lived on; John Bunyan's *Pilgrim's Progress* is the classical example of a Protestant use of the allegory of pilgrimage.

During the twentieth century pilgrimage has enjoyed a new popularity. This rediscovery of the tradition issues from a number of different sources. The combination of piety with leisure opportunities has led to an enormous increase in the number of pilgrimages to the Holy Land. Contemporary experience of visions has helped to establish modern pilgrim centres. The visions of St Bernadette at Lourdes, in the mid-nineteenth century, have issued in numerous pilgrimages to that town with a noted emphasis upon healing; visions at Medjugorje in the Balkans in 1981 have also established a tradition of pilgrimage there. In Ireland the village of Knock has also been a centre of visions and thus now of pilgrim activity. In England, both Glastonbury and Walsingham have been rediscovered as pilgrimage centres. Compostela now once again attracts thousands of pilgrims annually; the main route begins in central France and crosses the Pyrenees, but many earlier routes from other directions are being opened up and rediscovered, including the southern route from Seville. The ecumenical community at Taizé in Burgundy has become a very significant focus for pilgrimage among young people.

Part of the contemporary interest in pilgrimage relates to the use of the image of the journey or of pilgrimage as applied to people's lives as a whole. The work of analytical psychologists, which emphasizes the process of personality development throughout our lives, has been applied by theologians and spiritual writers to ascetic theology and linked with images of pilgrimage.

———

J. G. Davies, *Pilgrimages: Yesterday and Today – Why? Where? How?* London 1988; Nancy Louise Frey, *Pilgrim Stories On and Off the Road to Santiago*, Berkeley 1998; K. Hughes, 'The Changing Theory and Practice of Irish Pilgrimage', *Journal of Ecclesiastical History* II, 1960, 143–51; E. D. Hunt, *Holy Land Pilgrimage in the Later Roman Empire AD 312–460*, Oxford 1982; Stephen Platten, *Pilgrims*, London 1996; V. and E. Turner, *Image and Pilgrimage in Christian Culture*, New York 1978; John Wilkinson, *Egeria's Travels*, 3rd edn, Warminster 1999; Peter Yeoman, *Pilgrimage in Mediaeval Scotland*, London 1991.

STEPHEN PLATTEN

Piscina

A drain or *sacrarium* into the fabric of the church through which water used for the purification of the *celebrant's hands at the *eucharist (the *lavabo*) is poured. Generally they discharge into the wall; some, as in Notre Dame, Paris, end in spouts over the churchyard. Formerly the water used to cleanse the vessels during the eucharist was thus disposed. Increasing reverence for the sacred elements probably accounts for the mid-thirteenth-century development of the double piscina. Here two *sacraria* were found side by side, one for the *ablution of the vessels, the other for that of the hands. Ceremonial clearly varied from place to place: a triple piscina is sometimes found (Rothwell, Northamptonshire). The growing practice of consuming the water from the vessels obviated the need for the second piscina, which disappeared in the fifteenth century. When the celebrant ceased going to the piscina to wash his hands but used a bowl, that water was poured into the *sacrarium*. Simi-

larly that used after the eucharist to wash the ritually cleansed vessels was poured away. *Sacristies, a rarity in all but the largest churches, had piscinas. Modern RC liturgical law requires their use for the washing of cloths used to wipe spilled consecrated wine. The piscina is to be found to the right of most medieval *altars, often that of the high altar as a continuation of the *sedilia. A shelf above the drain within the retaining arch is common, very likely as a place for the *cruets.

———

Francis Bond, *The Chancel of English Churches*, Oxford 1916; W. Lockton, *The Treatment of the Remains at the Eucharist after Holy Communion and at the Time of the Ablutions*, Cambridge 1920; Gerald Randall, *Church Furnishings in England and Wales*, London 1980.

MICHAEL THOMPSON

Plymouth Brethren/Christian Brethren Worship

A religious community characterized by one of the Open Brethren as 'fundamentalist, evangelical, Calvinist, Baptist [true only of the "Open" branch], objectivist, congregational, non-clerical, futurist and separatist', the Brethren emerged in Dublin (Ireland) in 1826 and in Plymouth (England) in 1831, subsequently spreading worldwide. The popular name is derived from the latter city, in which one of the early major splits of the movement (into 'Exclusive' and 'Open' Brethren) occurred in 1848. In Canada, the Open Brethren are legally known as 'Christian Brethren'. The Brethren do not claim 'Brethren' as a distinctive name for themselves, but as properly descriptive of all true Christians. Two corollaries of this are their practice of social egalitarianism within the congregations, irrespective of class distinctions, and their denial of all distinction between clerical and lay members. Early central figures included John Nelson Darby (1800–82), who had been an Anglican assistant curate, of anglo-catholic persuasion, in Ireland, and who led the translation of a new English version (1885) – and new French, German, Dutch and Italian versions – of the Bible; George Müller (1805–98), who in Bristol founded extensive orphanages; Anthony Norris Groves (1795–1853), advocate of missions; and Samuel Prideaux Tregelles (1813–75), pioneer NT textual critic and hymn-writer. Much of the growth of the Brethren movement is later than and quite independent of these beginnings, being derived from the evangelical revival of the 1850s. Kindred associations, such as the '(Local) Church' movement of Watchman Nee (died in prison, 1972), Witness Lee and others, spreading from China, represent the same general tradition.

The 1848 division was doctrinal, on the subjects of Christology and eschatology, and on strict separation from the world and from existing denominations, and the two main branches differ also on modes of church government, but their liturgical life is essentially the same. Only men speak in the worship assembly, but any man may be led by the Spirit to speak from scripture or to pray, or to call for a hymn, on the model of 1 Cor. 14.26. 'This is . . . the mind of God concerning us, that we should come together in all simplicity as disciples, not waiting on any pulpit or minister, but trusting that the Lord would edify us together, by ministering as He pleased and saw good from the midst of ourselves' (Groves). 'True ministry is the gift and the power of God's Spirit, not man's appointment' (Darby). Preaching or mission services, on Free Church lines, with a stated preacher as worship leader, and often using hymns from non-denominational collections, have been added to the programme especially of Open Brethren churches.

'Open' Brethren require *baptism (by immersion) on profession of faith. 'Exclusive' Brethren require the same, after detailed doctrinal examination, except in the case of those baptized in infancy within 'Exclusive' families, by the head of the family ('household baptism'). The centrality of the 'Breaking of Bread' is distinctive of the Brethren: 'Worship is that for which Christians should meet, and I add, the *Lord's Supper is the centre of worship' (Darby). Brethren interpretation emphasizes thankfulness for the objective reality of redemption in Christ, obedience to Christ's command, the unity of the Body of Christ, purity through faith required of all members of the Body, and expectation of the Lord's return.

First-hand accounts of Brethren worship are few. An 'Exclusive Brethren' Breaking of Bread (more formal and uniform than among the Open or Independent Brethren) is described by an Anglican visitor (R. C. Walls): 'In the centre of the room was a table, three foot by two, spread with a linen cloth. On the table was a basket in which was half a loaf on a linen napkin. By its side was a glass of wine. The chairs were grouped in three rows round the sides of the table.

'The congregation . . . assembled in silence, which was maintained after all had arrived . . . Then one of the men in the front row suggested a hymn – a hymn to the Holy Spirit. Sitting still as we were we sang it slowly without any musical accompaniment. After the hymn we sat again in stillness for two or three minutes and then another brother led us in prayer. We still sat (not crouched). In fact we sat upright with eyes open or closed for the whole service. This induced a composed contemplative attitude accompanied by an intensity of prayer, silent or conducted, which was remarkable. The prayer thanked God the Spirit for this particular gathering on the Lord's Day, thanked him for the privileges we have as the people of God, for the gifts of unity and peace, for the love of God shed abroad in our hearts. Again two or three minutes' silence and then a reading from Ephesians and more silence. Then, in the Spirit and through thanks and prayer over the bread and wine which were passed from hand to hand round the circles, we approached the Son. At this point there was a long *anamnesis and thanksgiving for his birth, life, passion, death and resurrection, his heavenly priesthood and abiding presence, and a looking forward to his second coming. After another two or three minutes' silence there was a hymn of praise to Christ, sung still sitting, and after more silence another reading from the Bible, this time from the Gospels.

'The climax of the service came when in the Spirit, through the Son approached by the sacrament, we claimed access to the Father. The movement had been completed. Gathered in the Spirit, renewing the covenant in the sacrament, we now moved forward spiritually with our High Priest into the Holy of Holies, and a hymn to God the Father was sung and praise and thanksgivings for privileges in grace and hopes of glory were made by members of the congregation. The service, after more intervals of completely still silence, came to an end with a hymn to the Blessed Trinity . . . Things were conspicuous by their absence. First, there were no prayers of penitence . . . Unworthiness was expressed through deep thanksgiving. Secondly . . . there was no extended *intercession. The three elements of *eucharistic prayer were adoration, thanksgiving and contemplation; the rhythm of the *extempore service was maintained by the Trinitarian structure of the service' (R. C. Walls, 'A Visit to the Brethren –

A Lesson in Liturgy', *Theology* LX, 1957, 265–6).

The Brethren have produced a considerable number of hymn-writers, including J. N. Darby (*Spiritual Songs*); Sir Edward Denny (1796–1889, *Hymns and Poems*, definitive edition 1889; 'Light of the Lonely Pilgrim's Heart' has been widely current); G. V. Wigram (*Hymns for the Poor of the Flock*, 1828); Robert C. Chapman (*Hymns and Meditations*, 1871); S. P. Tregelles; J. G. Deck (*Psalms and Hymns and Spiritual Songs*, 1842); Carl Brockhaus (*Kleine Sammlung geistlicher Lieder*, Elberfeld 1853, and nine editions to 1909); Mary Jane Walker; Emma Frances Bevan (1827–1909; *Hymns of Ter Steegen, Suso and others*, and *Hymns of Ter Steegen and Others*, second series; her version of Erdmann Neumeister's 'Sinners Jesus will receive', from her *Songs of Eternal Life*, 1858, is widely used); Albert Midlane (1825–1909; 'Revive Thy Work, O God', and 'There's a Friend [originally, 'a rest'] for Little Children', have been included in numerous British denominational collections); and Stuart K. Hine ('How Great Thou Art'). Except at the Breaking of Bread, Open and Independent Brethren make considerable use of non-denominational hymnals. The Brethren view of hymnody is set out in the preface to the 1881 edition of *Hymns for the Little Flock*. 'Three things are needed for a hymn-book. A basis of truth and sound doctrine; something at least of the Spirit of Poetry, though not poetry itself, which is objectionable as merely the spirit and imagination of man; and thirdly, the most difficult to find at all, that experimental acquaintance with truth in the affections which enables a person to make his hymn (if led of God to compose one) the vehicle in sustained thought and language of practical grace and truth which sets the soul in communion with Christ and rises even to the Father, and yet this in such sort that it is not mere individual experience which for assembly worship is out of place.'

————

F. Roy Coad, *A History of the Brethren Movement*, Exeter 1968; H. L. Ellison, *The Household Church Apostolic Practice in a Modern Setting*, Exeter 1963; H. A. Ironside, *A Historical Sketch of the Brethren Movement*, Grand Rapids 1941; William Kelly (ed.), *The Collected Writings of J. N. Darby*, Kingston upon Thames (n.d.); Watchman Nee [Nee To-sheng], [Chinese original, 1938; English version, *Concerning Our Missions*, abridged as] *The Normal Christian Church Life*, Washington, DC 1969; Harold H. Rowdon, *The Origins of the Brethren 1825–1850*, London 1967; J. T. [James Taylor], *The Assembly: Readings and Addresses*, revised H. F. Nunnerley, Exeter (n.d.).

DAVID TRIPP

Polyphony

From Greek *polyphonia*, 'many-voices', the technical term for music having two or more individual parts intended to be heard simultaneously, as opposed to monophony, where one part only is sung by one or more voices. There are many theories about the invention of polyphony, which appeared in Western church music in about the ninth century. It might have been prompted by chants that lay too high for basses, or too low for tenors.

The earliest polyphony appears to have consisted in adding a part which moved in parallel fifths or more usually fourths with the given part, a chant phrase. Another ancient form of polyphony, still heard in the Eastern rites, was the accompaniment of the traditional chant by a bass drone. In the ninth century these two systems were combined in the West with the emergence of *organum*, a technique described in detail in a widely disseminated treatise *Musica enchiriadis*. It was only a step from this kind of musical parallelism to discover how to give greater independence to the parts by the systematic use of contrary motion.

These simple beginnings gave place to various innovations, such as the transference of the *cantus firmus* from the top to the lowest part, where it was known as the *tenor*, or 'holding' part, above which one or more voices indulged in long florid melismatic passages. The chant itself, in the lowest voice, came to be drawn out with long notes, completely losing its original freedom and flexibility. The increasing complexity of these developments, both rhythmically and melodically, made the notation of precise time values an urgent necessity, in order that several voices might sing together in a disciplined way. Measured music thus became totally distinct from the chant, which, when sung on its own, was characterized by its highly complex freedom and flow of phrase and rhythm. If *Gregorian chant found its architectural counterpart in the churches of the Romanesque period, the development of measured music in the Gothic era became the perfect counterpart of those rising edifices in stone and glass that, from about 1180 to 1250, were constructed by the genius of Germany, England, Spain, and pre-eminently France, with Notre Dame of Paris and Chartres as prime centres of highly sophisticated musical composition and performance. Two great masters have been associated with Paris: Léonin (*c.* 1162–90), whose *Magnus liber* left to posterity the most important musical legacy of the period, and his pupil Pérotin (fl. *c.* 1200), possibly the first composer to write for three and four voices in a truly contrapuntal style.

Succeeding generations were to witness the steady development of polyphony, with the evolution and perfection of harmonic techniques, until it reached its highest point in the hands of the Renaissance composers Palestrina, Lassus and Victoria. This greatest epoch of polyphonic liturgical music came to an end with the first decade of the seventeenth century. It was to witness the creation of ever more mighty musical colossi, those with polychoral structures, culminating in such crowning works as Tallis's forty-part motet *Spem in alium* or the large-scale motets of Giovanni Gabrieli.

John Caldwell, *Medieval Music*, London 1978; Sarah Fuller, 'Early Polyphony', *The Early Middle Ages to 1300*, ed. Richard Crocker and David Hiley, Oxford 1990, 485–556; Janet Knapp, 'Polyphony at Notre-Dame of Paris', *The Early Middle Ages to 1300*, 557–635; Richard Crocker, 'French Polyphony of the Thirteenth Century', *The Early Middle Ages to 1300*, 636–720; J. A. Owens, *Composers at Work: The Craft of Musical Composition, 1450–1600*, New York 1997; 'Latin Church Music on the Continent', *The Age of Humanism, 1540–1630*, ed. Gerald Abraham, Oxford 1968, reprinted 1998, chapters V, VI, and VII.

MARY BERRY

Polystavrion *see* **Vestments** 4(d)

Pontifical *see* **Books, Liturgical** 3.1.1.c

Posture

A liturgical posture is a position of the body for worship that is set by a deliberate preliminary *movement and then sustained for a determined period of time. Combined with interior disposition, it is a way of involving the whole person, mind and body, in the various activities that constitute worship. With gestures properly used and understood, the conscious adoption of a particular posture by the whole worshipping assembly for the different parts of the liturgy promotes unity and community of faith and practice and 'both fosters and expresses the attitude of those taking part' (*General Instruction on the Roman Missal*).

The basic postures for worship are standing, sitting, kneeling and prostration. To these might be added the adoption of a particular relational position, for example: *orientation – literally facing east, or, in the case of the posture of the presiding minister, facing the assembly or, with them, facing in the same direction. By adopting a different posture from the rest of the assembly, the president at the liturgy demonstrates his or her relationship to the worshipping community at that moment in the liturgy. Liturgical postures can also imply different attitudes or dispositions such as reverence, awe, supplication, penitence, attentiveness. They can convey the dignity of the human person in the eyes of God or our humility before the transcendent majesty of the divine. More practically, postures can be functional – sitting, for example, is the most comfortable position for listening to readings or sermons – or they may be but a prelude to a movement, activity or gesture.

1. *Standing*. Because by common consent this posture implies an attitude of respect between individuals (politely, one might stand when someone enters a room) and in most western cultures can define the relationship between persons (one stands in the presence of an authority figure or one of higher rank), it should be the normative posture for worship. To stand at the opening of an act of worship implies attentiveness, alertness and a readiness to begin. This custom is deeply rooted in the Bible: the whole assembly stands, for example, when Nehemiah opens the book of the Law to read it for the first time in generations (Neh. 8.5). Here the people stood to hear and obey and thus set the example for those who stand to hear the gospel proclaimed at the *eucharist. Standing for prayer is similarly attested in scripture, as when Hannah stands to pray before the Lord at Shiloh (1 Sam. 1.26). Following the Jewish tradition of standing to pray ((Luke 18.11–13), Jesus assumes his followers will continue so to do (Mark 11.25). With hands uplifted (*see* **Gestures** 5), the posture of standing for prayer continued to be normative in the early Christian centuries but

was reinterpreted in the light of the resurrection. Tertullian records that Christians stand on Sundays and throughout the *Easter season in joyful celebration of the resurrection (*De oratione* 23).

As, in the words of Augustine, 'an Easter people', counted worthy to stand in the presence of God through their baptismal incorporation into the resurrection of his Son, Christians stand in worship ready to greet the Lord Jesus when he comes again in glory. Today the revised eucharistic liturgies once again encourage the adoption of a standing posture for the principal parts of the service: for the gathering, from the prayers of penitence until after the *collect, for the reading of the gospel and its acclamation, for the *creed and the prayers of *intercession, and from the preparation of the table to the *dismissal.

2. *Kneeling.* 'O come let us worship and bow down, let us kneel before the Lord our maker!' Psalm 95.6 takes us directly into the primary reason for adopting this posture, for the position clearly signifies adoration through the difference in levels between the adored and the adoring. This spatial differential also gives the posture significance in prayer of supplication or contrition (Matt. 18.26). Practically, it has been found by many to be the most comfortable position for sustained private prayer at the same time as establishing a status relationship between the person who prays and the one prayed to. In the extremity of his psychological agony, Jesus used this posture for prayer at Gethsemane before his passion: 'Then he withdrew from them about a stone's throw, knelt down, and prayed, "Father, if you are willing, remove this cup from me; yet, not my will but yours be done"' (Luke 22.41f.).

The early Christian fathers made much of the contrast between the two postures of standing and kneeling. Kneeling was regarded as inappropriate for the celebration of the Sunday eucharist and all through the Easter season because of its association with penitence. It was actually forbidden to kneel during the Easter season by Canon 20 of the Council of Nicaea in 325. Jerome later explained: 'It is a time of joy and of victory when we do not kneel or bow to the earth, but risen with Christ, we are raised to the heavens' (*Ep. ad Ephes.*). On the other hand, times of penitence and *fasting were marked by kneeling for prayer, as Tertullian makes clear: 'As for other times, who would hesitate to bow before God, at least for the first prayer by which we begin the day. And on the days of fasting, all the prayers are made kneeling' (*De oratione* 23).

The change in the West from an almost universal standing position for liturgical prayer to the kneeling position adopted from the Middle Ages right up to the liturgical reforms of the last century seems to have accompanied or even resulted from a change in the worshipping community's self-understanding. Instead of seeing itself as the assembly of the redeemed, made worthy by the paschal mystery to stand proudly at the banquet of the Lamb, it saw itself as a penitential community, unworthy even to gaze upon the eucharistic elements let alone to gather up the crumbs under the Lord's table. The role of the congregation gradually diminished until their presence was totally peripheral to any liturgical event. Private prayer in an attitude of *penance and distant adoration became the only mode of participation open to the ordinary lay person at the eucharist and on the rare occasions that *communion was received, the communicants knelt at a rail. Even today, when Anglican congregations pray 'we thank you for counting us worthy to stand in your presence and serve you' (*Common Worship*, Order One, Eucharistic Prayer B) the majority still insists on kneeling.

With the recovered ecclesiological insights of today, there is much to be said for restricting kneeling to private prayer and acts of penitence and encouraging the assembly to stand or sit as appropriate for the rest of the liturgy. It would be good finally to put an end to the custom of so many congregations of falling to its collective knees at the words 'Let us pray'.

3. *Sitting.* The word 'president' actually means 'one who sits before', an indication that at one time the only one who ever sat in the liturgical assembly was the *bishop or the one who deputized for him. The bishop's seat is symbolically significant (*see* **Cathedra**), as Jesus himself often taught his followers from a seated position (Matt. 5.1; Luke 4.20). Seats were often provided for the college of *presbyters who flanked the bishop's seat, but the rest of the assembly were expected to stand throughout. A bench might be provided for the elderly or infirm but until the advent of monastic *choir stalls, seating was unknown in churches. In the NT, those who listen with attention adopt a sitting position (Luke 10.39) and it was the long sermon which was finally responsible for the demand for the provision of seating in church

(*see* **Pews**). What was originally a convenience became a necessity.

Today the posture has been reappraised in a more positive light. The eucharistic assembly is encouraged to sit for reflection and meditation 'during the readings before the gospel and during the responsorial psalm, for the homily and the presentation of the gifts, and, if this seems helpful, during the period of silence after communion' (*General Instruction on the Roman Missal* 21).

4. *Prostration*. Adoption of this posture is a dramatic act, to be used with care in the liturgy and infrequently. It is indicative of complete submission to a greater authority, 'flat out for God', as Abram felt compelled to be when God announced his new covenant relationship with him (Gen. 17.3). It was considered the appropriate posture for *catechumens and penitents in the early centuries but today, save in some monastic communities, it is usually reserved to the ministers at the beginning of the *Good Friday liturgy and in some traditions to those to be ordained during the singing of the *litany in the *ordination rite.

All these postures have been subject to review and reassessment in recent years as the role of the laity in the liturgical assembly has been revalued. The clergy have learned to sit down more frequently and God's holy people to stand uninhibitedly and joyfully in asserting their indispensable part in all that goes on around the table of the Lord.

Gestes et paroles dans les diverses familles liturgiques, Conferences Saint Serge, Paris 1978; R. D. H. Bursell, *Liturgy, Order and the Law*, Oxford 1996; P. J. Elliott, *Ceremonies of the Modern Roman Rite*, San Francisco 1995; Balthasar Fischer, *Signs, Words and Gestures*, New York 1981; M. R. Francis and K. F. Pecklers (eds), *Liturgy for the New Millennium*, Collegeville 2000; J. A. Jungmann, *The Mass of the Roman Rite*, New York 1951; Aidan Kavanagh, *Elements of Rite*, New York 1982; A. G. Martimort et al., *The Church at Prayer* I, Collegeville 1987; M. P. Perham, *New Handbook of Pastoral Liturgy*, London 2000.

JEREMY HASELOCK

Praise-and-Worship Movement

The Praise-and-Worship movement is a recent Protestant approach to worship renewal. Inter-

national in its scope, its roots are in the *Charismatic Movement and its influence extends to nearly all other Protestant groups and Roman Catholicism.

A Praise-and-Worship approach to corporate liturgy sequences the order of worship, using contemporary Christian music to lead participants through a series of affective states. This sequencing serves as a kind of long entrance rite, with worshippers ushered into an ever more strongly felt sense of God's presence. No physical movement through space is involved; the progression is inward and affective. Music is used sacramentally in that the worship created by the music enables the worshippers to experience God's presence.

Proponents of Praise-and-Worship often use a typology based on Israel's tabernacle or Temple to explain the desired progression. These structures had several thresholds leading to an area designated for a certain kind of liturgical experience. Praise-and-Worship advocates see these biblical structures as the template for liturgy. A typical application of this typology might result in the following order. The service begins with songs of thanksgiving as the initial threshold. Then follows an extended time of sung praise to represent the outer courts of the worship area. The next threshold may be songs of repentance or supplication to prepare worshippers for entrance into the inner sanctum of God's presence. There worshippers engage in songs of intimate worship with God. In some settings, this time of intimate fellowship with God culminates with singing in tongues under the Holy Spirit's inspiration. Some churches place their *eucharist at this point if it is administered. Preaching and other acts of worship follow the time of praise and worship. *Extemporaneous prayer is common throughout. In the time of praise and worship, these prayers often bridge the songs, although this type of prayer is not absolutely necessary. Frequently, one song immediately flows into the next under the direction of the worship leaders, whose task it is to discern the worshippers' progression into God's presence. The time of singing is often extensive: from thirty minutes to an hour or more.

The name itself, 'Praise-and-Worship', parallels the logic of this typology. Proponents make a distinction between praise – usually defined as extolling God by remembering or proclaiming God's character and activity – and worship – usually defined in more relational terms of direct communion with God. Within these broad definitions, proponents often use detailed studies of various biblical Hebrew and Greek words to support the distinction between praise and worship. They also use such studies to bring finer nuances of meaning to these fundamental terms. Thus various aspects of 'praise' might be explored, from biblical words suggesting physical actions and gestures in praise of God to those associated with adoring remembrances of God's activity.

The basic movement from praise to worship is achieved by adjusting certain characteristics of the music. At least three are standard. The first is a move in the types of personal pronouns used for God, from third person to second person. In Praise-and-Worship, for instance, the liturgy could begin with songs referring to God as 'he' (Praise-and-Worship churches are often unconcerned with *inclusive-language issues). As participants progress into worship, they begin to address God with the more intimate 'you'. The second common adjustment is in the tempo, tone and key of the music. Frequently, Praise-and-Worship services begin upbeat, utilizing songs in major keys to proclaim the goodness of God's character and activity. Somewhere in the progression, the tempo slows and repetition is more frequent and extended. The volume is diminished as worshippers enjoy communion with the living God. The third shift is in the songs' content. Frequently, the Praise-and-Worship progression moves from more objective remembrance of God to songs reflecting upon God's person and our relationship with God.

Beyond these adjustments, Praise-and-Worship music often shares certain common traits. Its style is contemporary, reflecting and derived from pop idioms, although classic hymns can be used. Its instrumentation, too, seems derived from pop genres, emphasizing acoustic and electronic guitars, pianos and synthesizers, and percussion instruments. Praise-and-Worship is typically led by a small team of vocalists placed in a prominent spot in the liturgical space. Electronic projection of the songs' words for worshippers' benefits is common. Much of the music is produced and distributed by large publishing houses such as Maranatha! Music, the Vineyard Music Group, and Integrity Music.

Paul Basden, *The Worship Maze: Finding a Style to Fit Your Church*, Downers Grove, IL 1999; Barry Liesch, *The New Worship:*

Straight Talk on Music and the Church, Grand Rapids, MI 1996; Robert E. Webber (ed.), *The Complete Library of Christian Worship*, 7 vols, Nashville, TN 1993.

LESTER RUTH

Prayer

The NT uses a variety of words translated in English as either 'prayer' or 'worship', understood as communication with God either by the individual alone or in public gatherings. In the Judaism of NT times prayer was rooted in *blessing and thanksgiving; it was pattern, gesture and form; sacrifice of animals, *incense and other elements of creation; singing and reciting of texts of scripture; holy places, practices and ministries; it was part of the Jewish genius that prayer should also be associated with ordinary actions in the flow of everyday life, part and parcel of righteous living, and articulated in the round of the calendar. No prayer would be considered as totally private, for prayer always had within it a consciousness of being Israel, God's people.

The Christian tradition continued this in varying ways. The ideal of seeing the whole of life as prayer is witnessed by the monastic tradition, but also in a wider understanding of Christian life as being a living sacrifice, whose every aspect is informed by the active presence of God. In this sense the whole of life is prayer. But time set aside for immediate attention to God has always been necessary in order to foster and sustain this Godward orientation, and its content and spirit has reflected the fact that each Christian prays 'in Christ', and within the united voice of the people of God.

1. *Prayer within Liturgy*. In patristic times *daily liturgy was an important part of the practice of prayer, within a wider range of public and private forms. There was no clear division between private and public. As well as taking their proper part in the liturgy, people tended to offer up their own prayers aloud while services were going on, and hence the diaconal biddings to be silent which survive in some ancient rites such as the Mozarabic. In the home the same patterns seem to be found. Domestic liturgical prayer is referred to by many writers: 'personal' prayer as we understand it must have been rare due to lack of privacy and the difficulty people had in praying silently in a world not used to such internalization. There are many references to the practice of at least

some Christians praying at specific set hours in the day. This situation continued through the Middle Ages, when there were similar problems with individuals praying aloud during services, while, partly as a result of people's alienation from full participation in worship, substitute forms of popular devotion grew up, and there began to develop the new phenomenon of systematic pursuit of silent, contemplative prayer in private.

The Reformation and Counter-Reformation both effected a split between public and private areas. In Protestantism in the most general terms the liturgy became a gathering designed to foster the individual's heartfelt communion with God in response to his word. The physical-spiritual approach inherited from Judaism and put in centre stage by the incarnation receded in importance, and so did the sense of worship as being the united voice of the church on earth and in heaven. In Roman Catholicism, on the other hand, liturgy came to be seen as an objective duty needing to be complemented by the entirely separate activity of personal, private prayer, and the notion of the prayer of the church was narrowed down to the clerical recitation of the breviary.

In the twentieth century there were growing attempts to bring the two dimensions back together, coming to a climax in the liturgical reforms of Vatican II and their counterparts in other churches. The ecumenical convergence reflected in documents such as the World Council of Churches' *Baptism, Eucharist and Ministry* (1982) came to acknowledge the *eucharist as the centre of the church's life and prayer, with a renewed highlighting of *baptism as a model for our discipleship and a source for reflection on it. Daily liturgical prayer is increasingly seen as an extension of these, supporting through the day and week this eucharistic life centred without ceasing on our relation with God as the body of Christ. It is now widely thought that this needs to be restored fully to the whole membership of the church, and numerous forms of daily office have been produced with laypeople or representative groups in the Christian community in mind.

2. *Two Facets of One Reality.* Prayer and liturgy are therefore two facets of one reality, which is the people of God walking with God. The recovery of the *eucharistic prayer as a prayer-form of prime importance has helped reconnect worship with Jewish origins, especially in the rehearsal of the great acts of God for our redemption.

Most of the prayer-forms found in the liturgy have been used in different ages for people's private prayers, and there is a return to encouraging this, including songs and *canticles, psalms and scripture readings, acclamations, *litanies and responsorial forms, words sung and spoken, *posture, place and movement; texts which are more straightforwardly understood as prayers, not least the *Lord's Prayer, petitionary prayers, *collects, blessings and thanksgivings. There has also been a slow recovery of the role of *gesture and symbol, and a realization that prayer is not confined to words alone.

3. *Praying the Liturgy.* If private prayer has to be related to the liturgy, the converse is also true. The common problem of inability to remain 'prayerful' during public worship is partly a reflection of modern difficulties in accepting the reality and sovereignty of God, but is also something natural to participation in worship. We have to accept that our minds will wander at intervals, and in some cultures this even takes the form of leaving the church building for a short break. A famous example of such distraction was St Anselm, who hit upon his ontological argument for the existence of God during morning prayer. The combined effect of Reformation and Enlightenment brought to the fore an assumption that real engagement can only take place at the mental level. This deep body–mind split in western culture is now being modified in a significant cultural shift, as we increasingly recognize that bodily participation or even simple presence at an act of worship sets up engagement and resultant memory at levels other than the merely conscious one, even when the mind seems totally distracted. Modern psychology acknowledges subliminal and unconscious communication, while the recent growth of *ritual studies adds further confirmation to the fact that objective physical actions can in themselves be prayer, providing an important key to understanding the nature of liturgy itself.

4. *Prayer and Liturgical Theology.* Prayer is often thought of as humanity reaching out to God, but this presupposes a degree of distance between heaven and earth which is sub-Christian: the gap has been for ever bridged through the incarnation, death and resurrection of Christ. Because we are in Christ, the subject

of our prayer is plural: the Holy Spirit within us cries 'Abba'; in prayer we are co-operating with an initiative which is God's alone, the action of the Spirit in us. A fundamental principle of the liturgy is that prayer is addressed to the Father. While from early times a practice of addressing prayers to Christ became increasingly common, this has always been subordinate to the prior practice of addressing the Father in the name of Christ, especially in certain key texts such as the eucharistic prayer.

Prayer in addition is always in the body of Christ, making it impossible for a Christian ever to pray utterly 'privately'. The liturgy in this way is the ultimate source of all our day-by-day prayer. One way of understanding this is as participation in the life of the Trinity, the mutual regard of the three persons, a *perichoresis* in which we ourselves are taken up. Orthodox liturgical theology sees liturgy as bringing about an ascent into the full life of the kingdom, earth raised to heaven. Odo Casel's *mystery-theology is important here in showing how the Jewish rehearsing of the saving events anchors our experience of worship, and the Christ whom we come to know in it, in history and the physical order. Knowledge of Christ while praying in the liturgy is not simply abstract knowledge of an imagined person, but a reliving of what is recounted in the scriptures. Casel is quick to add, however, that we are not necessarily talking here about experience. Prayer in the liturgy can have a very objective character, a corporal registering of the visible action in which we participate. Worship therefore can never adequately be either assessed or justified simply on the basis of personal experience – any worthwhile fruit at the level of interior knowledge and experience can normally be gained sight of only in the long term. Our prayer in the liturgy, therefore, may be of a very objective and physical nature, a truth that can only be grasped by giving due acknowledgement to the complexity of our levels of perception, intuition and memory. So St Ambrose could say, 'not by mirrors and enigmas, O God, but face to face have you revealed yourself to me, and I find you in your mysteries' (*Apol. David* 1.12.58).

Romano Guardini, *The Spirit of the Liturgy*, New York 1998; George Guiver, *Company of Voices: Daily Prayer and the People of God*, 2nd edn, London 2001; K. W. Irwin, *Liturgy, Prayer and Spirituality*, New York 1984.

GEORGE GUIVER

Prayer Meeting

The practice and the title came to the fore in the evangelical revival. Some *Methodist circuits not only produced 'Preaching Plans' indicating the time and place of Sunday worship but also a second plan or roster indicating the time and place of the Sunday and weekday prayer meetings and who would conduct them. There was a loose but predictable structure. The leader would decide if there was to be singing. If there was a specific theme or overall purpose this would be announced. The leader prayed once at the beginning and for a second time to indicate that the period of prayer was at an end.

The primary emphasis was petitionary or intercessory with an element of thanksgiving. If the prayer meeting took place immediately before divine service its purpose was to ask a blessing on the worship that it might be to God's glory and that lives would be touched in the service itself. If the prayer meeting or 'after meeting' took place at the close of worship it was often to confirm the message or the decisions of converts or those seeking holiness of life. Midweek prayer meetings were designed to deepen the spiritual life of the congregation. Although anyone could offer *extempore prayer in these gatherings they often relied on the gifts of the prayer leaders. Eventually the meetings suffered from lack of new blood and new approaches but at their peak they brought enthusiasm and renewal into many churches. In the nineteenth and twentieth century, annual Bible weeks, holiness conventions and university Christian Unions fostered well-attended prayer meetings.

While it would we wrong to designate *Quaker meetings and *Independent Evangelical Sunday worship as prayer meetings, it is hard to separate prayer meetings from services of prayer and praise that have become such a strong feature of *charismatic revival inside and outside the evangelical movements of the late twentieth century and on into the present one.

*Pentecostalism and the movement for charismatic renewal within the more formal churches have meant a rebirth of the prayer meeting, more often than not transcending all Christian traditions. Prayer meetings have regained a certain credibility in the guise of 'prayer breakfasts'. The clergy or the ecumenical leaders of a town, city or university mission for evangelism or renewal may have drawn many Christian traditions together and summoned them to prayer before, during and after the event.

In some churches the Sunday *intercessions within the *eucharist or the ministry of the *word have become a type of prayer meeting. Often within the familiar structure of the *bidding prayer or general intercessions for the universal church, for world justice and peace, for the suffering and the needy, for local needs and in the commemoration of the faithful departed there has been a time of guided or open prayer which is hard to distinguish from a prayer meeting. Some of these have been opportunities for speaking in tongues or 'prophecy' or ministries of healing and deliverance.

C. NORMAN R. WALLWORK

Preaching and Worship

1. *In the New Testament*. The term 'preaching' in Christian usage is the proclamation of the good news of salvation in Christ Jesus. The derivation is from the Latin *praedicare* (literally, to speak in front of, to announce). The Greek NT employs several different words, which nuance the meaning of the term 'preaching'. *Kerugma* (from *kerussein*, to proclaim) means an official and solemn proclamation of an event of God or Christ; it focuses clearly on the very act of proclaiming under the aegis of the Spirit, rather than solely on the message or messenger. It is distinguished from *katechesis* and *didache*, whose functions are to explain or expound Christian teaching, and from *parainesis*, ethical exhortation, and *didascalia*, a deeper understanding of faith. To announce the gospel (*euaggelizein*) is to bear witness to the experiential event of this saving grace; critical to both Paul and John's grasp of the ministry of preaching is this notion of being a witness (*marturein*) (e.g. 1 John 1.1–3). Broadly speaking, apostolic preaching, always a public event, served different functions: to win over non-Christian listeners to faith in the risen Lord, i.e., conversion (e.g. Acts 2.14–36; 10.34–8; 17.19–31); to strengthen faith within the gathered Christian community, i.e., edification (e.g. Acts 14.27; 15.3); to renew paschal faith at the divine service, i.e., ongoing conversion (e.g. Acts 2.42).

The ministry of Christian preaching rests on Jesus' own ministry and the commissioning of the apostolic church. Jesus' fundamental proclamation in both word and deed was the reign of God, announced not as an idea, but as an existential reality (see Matt. 11.5; Luke 7.22). Healing the ill, forgiving the sinner, and uplifting the poor were unmistakable signs of God's saving reign. Parable, teachings and exhortations revealed dimensions of living in the new age of grace. The very *kerugma* of Jesus brings about what is proclaimed through the power of God's Spirit. The prophetic message of Isaiah (61.1) 'today . . . has been fulfilled in your hearing' (Luke 4.21). Jesus' proclamation is itself an event and a realization. Through the human words and actions of Jesus, God reveals Godself and draws forth a response of faith from hearers. Christ's mission of gathering the scattered into a unity (John 11.52) is continued through disciples, commissioned to preach to the ends of the earth (Luke 9.16; 10.12; Matt. 28.19–20).

In and through the power of the Spirit, the apostolic community announced salvation in Christ Jesus. Sent to preach on rooftops and streets (Matt. 10.27; Luke 12.3) were the eleven and their companions (Matt. 28.16–20; Mark 16.14–20), Mary Magdalene (John 20.17) and Paul (Gal. 1.11–17). They announced the coming of God's reign (Mark 3.14; Matt. 10.7; Luke 9.2), called listeners to conversion (Mark 6.12), and told of seeing the risen Lord and his return to the Father (John 20.17–18). What was central to apostolic preaching was not a truth or a doctrine, but rather a person, the exalted and glorified Jesus. If Jesus announced the reign of God, his disciples proclaimed the risen Jesus, as the pre-eminent saving Word of God, made flesh. This *kerugma* encompassed the entire mystery of Christ: the cross (1 Cor. 1.23), the resurrection (Rom. 10.8–9), the second coming of Christ (Acts 10.42). The good news announced was that any who repent and believe in the risen Lord shall be saved.

Since in Christian preaching, it is really the risen Lord who speaks and acts through the proclaimed word, the preacher, messenger of salvation, is but a servant of the Word. The power of preaching is 'the power of God' (Rom. 1.16; 1 Cor. 1.18) which depends not on human strength (1 Cor. 1.25) or wisdom, but 'with a demonstration of the Spirit' (1 Cor. 2.4). When Christ is preached, the gift of faith is proffered (Rom. 10.17). It is Christ himself who preaches through the word of the human preacher. This preaching clearly does not happen apart from the Spirit's activity (1 Cor. 2.13). The truth of the word of faith is known and accepted only through faith itself, a form of earthly life in which Christ and the believer are united in the one same Spirit. The believer takes hold of the hidden Christ so that Christ becomes the principle of living (Gal. 2.19–20). In the Spirit, believers can understand the thought of the Spirit, which is conceived by that same Spirit (1 Cor. 2.11–12).

The preaching of Jesus in the synagogue (Luke 4.16–20) demonstrates the practice of allowing anyone gifted with the Spirit to address the congregation, a rather more informal and conversational message addressed to the situation of the hearers; it would be homily, rather than oratory. Acting in accord with tradition, Jesus preached an interpretation and contemporization of the scriptures, which was at the heart of Jewish preaching. The tone of Jesus' preaching was prophetic, that is, speaking to present reality with divine authority and transforming revelation into a dynamic reality. Prophetic preaching not only challenges the hearers, but also animates and energizes them. The Sabbath service included not only reading from the Pentateuch but other biblical books; it clearly was more than *mere* reading; it was thus a ritualized celebration of God's word as a present ongoing event.

2. *In the Early Church*. In the apostolic and post-apostolic periods, apostles, teachers and prophets exercised various ministries of preaching within varied local Christian communities. These ministries of the word – whether fundamentally kerygmatic, paraenetic or catechetical – exhibited in varying degrees homiletic, liturgical, exegetical and prophetic dimensions. That these ministries were exercised within liturgical functions is clear, but equally evident is preaching outside the liturgical setting, especially, but not exclusively, in missionary settings. Although the charismatic preaching of itinerant prophets and teachers is evidenced in the *Didache* (*c*. 90 CE) and *The Shepherd of Hermas* (*c*. 100–150 CE), gradually preaching became aligned with the teaching office of the *bishop and his delegates. Today, depending upon church order, the ministry of preaching may be either more or less charismatic and more of less regulated by denominational policy, guidelines or law.

The *First Apology* of Justin Martyr (*c*. 150) testifies to the Sunday practice of reading from the prophets or the 'memoirs of the apostles' (the Gospels). When the readings are completed, the president of the assembly verbally exhorts all present to live by the noble words

and examples proclaimed (ch. 67). Such preaching would 'situate' the lives of believing hearers. Contrasted with Justin's humble description of preaching as a familial exhortation, stands Melito of Sardis' sermon *On the Pascha* (*c*. 150) which shows clearly the influence of contemporary rhetoric on the Christian preacher.

Preaching in the fourth century often took on the character of thematic exposition, *catechetical explanation, or *mystagogy, that is, scriptural and liturgical reflection on the *sacramental *mysteries for the newly initiated. Likewise, homiletic theory developed under the influence of Greek and Roman rhetoric, significantly shaping Christian forms of preaching. The *De doctrina christiana* of Augustine (d. 430) explores rhetorical theory in relation to the Bible and its interpretation and stands as the first significant work on Christian homiletics. Earlier, Origen (d. 253) probed the exegetical dimension and noted three senses of scripture – the literal, moral and mystical; later commentators divided the mystical into the allegorical and anagogical. Both Augustine and Origen sought to probe the existential meaning of God's word.

The common teaching of the patristic writers is that God is actively present in the reading of scripture and the preaching of the word of God. Supported by the experience of the effect of preaching on the hearers, their teaching rested on a theology of preaching of the NT, as well as in the understanding of the consequences of the reception of the Spirit. Commissioned for the ministry of preaching the apostolic word, the authorized preacher could rely on the Spirit's guidance.

Patristic writers did not work out the relationship between preaching and sacramental worship in any systematic manner, apart from Origen. Typical of Origen's thought is the phrase: 'bread (drink) of the word; bread (drink) of the eucharist'. This phrase signals a systematic approach to the modes of communication of the soul with the divine Logos. Despite Origen's spiritualizing tendencies, deriving from Neoplatonism, his insight is nonetheless valuable. Hilary of Poitier in his *Tractatus in Ps. 127.10* speaks of the table of the Lord's word and the table of the Lord. This idea was taken up by the Second Vatican Council in the twentieth century, speaks of the 'two tables' in relation to the dignity of God's word, the ministry of the ordained and the relationship of the word and sacrament in *eucharistic celebration (*Dei Verbum* 21; *Presbyterorum ordinis* 18; *Sacrosanctum concilium* 48, 51). By the end of the patristic era, the dominant dimension of Christian preaching was clearly catechesis or doctrinal explanation, often with a view toward combating heresy, diminishing especially the prophetic dimension.

3. *In the Middle Ages.* The question of the relation between preaching and sacramental worship was not central to Scholastic systematic theology. Taken for granted was that preaching the word of God was a means of communication and strengthening the life of faith that was ordained by God. To the extent that the preacher announced a word of God in the sense of an authentic witness to the faith of the church, that preaching was viewed as an offer of saving grace for the hearers. Preaching the authentic faith, mostly viewed in terms of content, however, could not be presumed. Thus, preaching could not be called an infallible offer of divine grace. The high dignity of sacramental action placed it in a different category.

4. *In the Reformation.* In the wake of the Reformation, a theology of the word of God, solidly grounded in the scriptures, developed. It responded to Scholastic sacramental theology of that same period and while there were legitimate grounds for probing whether sacraments had devolved into a 'cheap means of grace', the Reformed theology tended to reduce the theology of the word of God to a theology of preaching. Such a reduction did not do justice to a theology of communication between God and humanity based on the reality of various modes of communication of faith. In particular the symbolic dimension of communication suffered.

5. *In Modern Roman Catholicism.* The teaching of Vatican II on the theology of the word is found in the dogmatic constitutions on the liturgy (*Sacrosanctum concilium* [SC]) and on divine revelation (*Dei Verbum*). These documents highlight that the service of God's word is the history of salvation; God is present in the word and its preaching; the word of God has the power to communicate salvation. Preaching is a call both to faith and conversion (*SC* 9). Explicitly claimed as an act of worship – 'part of the liturgy itself' (*SC* 35, 52) – the homily is described as 'the proclamation of God's won-

derful works in the history of salvation, that is, the mystery of Christ, which is ever made present and active within us, especially in the celebration of the liturgy' (*SC* 35). Drawn from the scriptural and liturgical texts (*SC* 35), the homily is an essential part of sacramental celebration and ought to 'apply to concrete circumstances of life and particular needs of hearers' (*Presbyterorum ordinis* 4).

6. *Conclusion.* The ultimate vocation of the Christian is the glorification of God. God is glorified through Christian living in obedience to God's salvific word. God is glorified and humanity is sanctified through the acceptance of God's free offer of salvation in and through Jesus, the Word, and in the power of the vivifying Spirit. Worship, sacramental and nonsacramental, and preaching are responses to God's saving actions on humanity's behalf. Both preaching and worship are acts of faith, acts of the Spirit and both upbuild the body of Christ. Preaching and worship both interpret human life in light of the gospel – both enlighten a 'neutral situation' or change an existing situation in one direction or another. Sacramental worship, however, cannot be reduced simply to 'preaching', for the dimension of symbolic gesture is of the nature of sacrament. Nevertheless, the proclamation and preaching of the word of God is more fully 'celebrated' when it is part of an act of worship.

Yngve Brilioth, *A Brief History of Preaching*, Philadelphia 1965; Thomas K. Carroll, *Preaching the Word*, Wilmington, DE 1984; Bernard Cooke, *Ministry to Word and Sacraments: History and Theology*, Philadelphia 1977; Gerhard Ebeling, *God and Word*, Philadelphia 1967; Domenico Grasso, *Proclaiming God's Message*, Notre Dame 1965; William J. Hill, 'Preaching as a "Moment" in Theology', *Homiletic and Pastoral Review* LXXVII, 1976, 10–19; Mary Catherine Hilkert, 'Preaching, Theology of', *The New Dictionary of Sacramental Worship*, ed. Peter Fink, Collegeville 1990, 996–1003; Edward J. Kilmartin, *Christian Liturgy: Theology and Practice I. Systematic Theology of Liturgy*, Kansas City 1988.

JOHN A. MELLOH

Preces *see* **Intercession**

Preface

The first part of a *eucharistic prayer, originally so called in the Roman tradition not because it was prefatory to what followed but because the Latin word *praefatio* was meant in the sense of proclamation: in ancient eucharistic prayers the preface usually proclaimed the mighty acts of God in creation and redemption. While this part of the prayer came to be unchanging in Eastern rites, in the West a distinction emerged between the 'common preface', which was used on ordinary occasions and offered only a brief thanksgiving for God's works, and 'proper prefaces', each of which developed a specific theme appropriate to a particular day or season in the liturgical *year, but did not attempt a full account of salvation history. Although praise and thanksgiving ended at the *Sanctus in the historic Roman rite, in other traditions it was usually continued in a post-Sanctus section, and this arrangement has also been adopted in a number of modern Western prayers.

EDITOR

Presanctified, Liturgy of the

A service of evening prayer (*see* **Daily Prayer** 2) at which *communion is distributed from eucharistic elements usually consecrated the previous Sunday, and in the East now largely confined to *Lenten weekdays when the normal *eucharist is not allowed. The service originated in the custom of people taking the consecrated elements home to communicate during the week. This became common practice in monasteries. A relic of the monastic custom is the Byzantine *Typica* that follows the ninth hour on fasting days. It comprises Pss. 103 and 146; the Beatitudes; the *creed; further prayers including the *Lord's Prayer; and Ps. 34. Communion was probably given after the Lord's Prayer.

2. *Eastern Practice.* In the great city churches (e.g. Hagia Sophia) communion came to be given at evening prayer, the normal order of which had the communion rite from the eucharistic liturgy appended. This was used on all days in Lent except Saturday and Sunday, in other *fasting periods, on such occasions as weddings, and also at first on *Good Friday. It was probably the replacement of the cathedral office of Hagia Sophia (after 1204) by the Palestinian monastic office that led to the disappearance of the presanctified liturgy from Good Friday. It is now normally celebrated on the Wednesdays and Fridays of Lent, some saints' days in Lent and on the first three days of *Holy Week.

In some places it has become once more an evening celebration. Preceded by the ninth hour (and in the Russian tradition by the *Typica*), vespers at first follows the normal weekday order. During the recitation of the Psalter the intincted 'Lamb' is taken and moved to the table of the *Prothesis. After the evening psalms and 'Hail gladdening light' there are readings, usually from Genesis and Proverbs. Between the two the congregation is blessed with a lighted candle (an ancient *lucernarium*). The readings are followed by a duplication of Ps. 141 with an offering of *incense (another relic of the sung vespers of Hagia Sophia). An epistle and gospel reading may follow, and then the *litanies. The 'Lamb' is transferred, with a *chalice of unconsecrated wine, during the singing of 'Now the heavenly powers invisibly worship with us'; then come the litany before the Lord's Prayer, the prayer over the people and the *fraction. Many deem the placing of the particle in the chalice at the *commixture as consecrating it. Communion follows as normal.

The Syrian Orthodox presanctified liturgy is now only used by Syrian Catholics on the Fridays of Lent, and Maronite Catholics on Good Friday. Known as 'The Signing of the Chalice', the rite follows vespers. After Ps. 51, the gospel, and incensation prayers, there follows the creed and a form of *eucharistic prayer. This last prays that the chalice be blessed by the reserved *host for the benefit of the communicants. The Chaldean presanctified liturgy has not been used for some centuries. The Coptic, Ethiopian and Armenian churches do not appear to have possessed one.

2. *Western Practice.* The practice only survived in the West on Good Friday. Until the late sixth century the *papal rite had only readings with prayer on that day, and people went to other churches in the city to receive communion. After the sixth century the papal liturgy still remained very simple, the elements being brought in without ceremony and communion being given in silence after the Lord's Prayer. More prayers and ceremony developed later, and with the decline of frequent communion a host was reserved for the priest alone. The Missal of Pius V in the sixteenth century required a *procession with incense, lights and canopy to convey the host from its altar of

repose and a chalice was prepared. After the Lord's Prayer, fraction and commixture, the *celebrant communicated as usual, but the contents of the chalice were no longer seen as consecrated by contact. The modern RC service has much of the original austerity. The hosts are brought in with lights only and all may receive communion. This modern structure has also been adapted to the needs of those Anglican churches that provide such a rite for Good Friday, where communion in both kinds (bread and wine) is sometimes practised. The Ambrosian rite (in Milan) keeps Good Friday and all the Fridays of Lent as non-eucharistic days with neither eucharist nor a liturgy of the presanctified.

A new form of the presanctified liturgy has developed in the late twentieth century in the RC Church, intended for use on Sundays because of lack of clergy and thus different from celebrations on penitential weekdays. It typically has the same structure as the modern eucharistic rite but with a thanksgiving song or prayer in place of the eucharistic prayer. Similar forms are also used in some parts of the Anglican Communion.

M. Arranz, 'La Liturgie des Présanctifiés de l'ancien Euchologe byzantin', *Orientalia Christiana Periodica* XLVII, 1981, 332–88; N. D. Uspensky, *Evening Worship in the Orthodox Church*, Crestwood, NY 1985; Archdale A. King, *Liturgy of the Roman Church*, London 1957, 193–4, 366, 371–2, 379; H. W. Codrington, 'The Syrian Liturgies of the Presanctified', *Journal of Theological Studies* IV, 1903, 69–82; V, 1904, 369–77, 535–45. For Anglican practice: Phillip Tovey, *Communion Outside of the Eucharist*, Nottingham 1993; 'The Development of Extended Communion in Anglicanism', *Studia Liturgica* XXX, 2000, 226–38.

GREGORY WOOLFENDEN

Presbyter

In origin a Latin word translating the Greek term, *presbyteros*, meaning '*elder*', which is used in parts of the NT to refer to certain individuals within some primitive Christian communities. But exactly who these people were is not clear. Were they simply those who were older in years, or those who were older in conversion, i.e., had been Christians for longer than others, or a specific group elected in some way to form a collegiate governing body of the

local church? At least in the later books of the NT the word certainly appears to have this last meaning, and this is the sense in which it continues to be used in post-apostolic writings. It must also be noted that *presbyteros* often seems to be used interchangeably with *episkopos*, '*bishop*', both within and outside the NT (see, e.g., Acts 20.28).

By the early second century many local churches seem to be governed by a body of presbyters/bishops, and only slowly did the office of bishop emerge everywhere as distinct from and superior to that of the presbyters, who become an advisory council to the bishop in his pastoral and administrative functions. In liturgical assemblies, the presbyters were also associated with the bishop, being physically seated around him in his presidential role, and by the third century there are signs that on occasion the bishop might delegate to a presbyter presidency at *baptisms, at *eucharists, and perhaps at other rites. Nevertheless, even in the fourth century many presbyters still simply assisted their bishop liturgically, and especially in the ministry of preaching, and it was not until later that presbyters were normally the sole pastor of a Christian community and hence its regular liturgical president. In the third century the designation 'priest' (*hiereus* in Greek, *sacerdos* in Latin) had at first been attached primarily to the episcopal office, and presbyters seem to have been thought of as priests then solely in the sense that they participated in the bishop's priesthood. It was only later, when presbyters had assumed most of the bishop's former liturgical functions, that they were described as priests in their own right, although it needs to be noted that the English word 'priest', like its equivalents in most Germanic languages, is actually derived from 'presbyter' and not from the Greek or Latin for 'priest'.

At the Reformation, the Church of England and some Lutheran churches continued to use the designation 'priest' for the presbyter, but most other churches rejected it as having acquired unacceptable sacerdotal connotations and returned to terms like 'presbyter', 'minister', or in some cases 'elder'. In the course of the twentieth century a growing tendency to substitute the more primitive word 'presbyter' could also be detected in churches in which the word 'priest' was still used, including the RC Church (which in Latin had always continued to use *presbyter* more often than *sacerdos*).

EDITOR

Presbyterian Worship

1. *United Kingdom.* Presbyterian Churches are found in all parts of the UK, and originated from the Reformations in Scotland and, to a lesser extent, in England. Presbyterian worship is not bound by a fixed liturgy and the role of the minister is thus of crucial importance. Worship can also vary according to the local customs of congregations. A service usually consists of praise, scripture lessons, prayers and a sermon. The *Lord's supper is often celebrated three or four times a year, although in some places it will be held on fewer occasions and in others more frequently.

After the Reformation in Scotland worship was governed by the use of John Knox's *Book of Common Order*, which contained prayers which the minister could use. Other elements included the use of the Apostles' *Creed, the saying of the *Lord's Prayer, and the singing of *canticles and the *doxology. While it was hoped that *communion might be celebrated monthly, for various practical reasons it became an infrequent occurrence. Sunday worship, however, was based on the pattern of word and *sacrament, even when communion was not celebrated, with the prayers of *intercession and the Lord's Prayer coming after the sermon.

The struggles of the mid-seventeenth century saw a reaction against the imposition of a Prayer Book by Charles I and, largely due to Puritan influences from England, against set forms of worship as well. Even the Lord's Prayer disappeared from use and the *Westminster Directory* became the official standard of worship. Psalms alone were sung unaccompanied, a line at a time, and worship took on a heavily didactic character. In addition to a lengthy sermon, the lecture, an exposition of scripture, was given instead of the readings.

As a result of the liturgical revival during the Victorian period, hymns were introduced, accompanied by the organ, sermons became shorter and prayers were read. The lecture disappeared and there was a move towards the more frequent celebration of communion along with the observance of the main festivals of the Christian *year, which had been abolished at the Reformation. The order of worship could also be changed, however, reflecting the pattern of Anglican morning prayer, with the sermon being placed at the end of the service. Similar developments could be found in Presbyterian worship in England, Wales and Ireland, but not all Presbyterians favoured such change, and some remained faithful to the traditions of the seventeenth century. Service books were also produced, and the various *Books of Common Order* of the Church of Scotland of 1940, 1979 and 1994, although not mandatory, have been widely influential.

During the twentieth century there has been a renewed emphasis by some on expository preaching while others have introduced greater participation by the congregation and use has been made of modern hymns, instrumental music, and of *drama and *dance. But the essence of Presbyterian worship continues to be the two elements identified by the Scots Confession of 1560: the true preaching of the word and the right administration of the sacraments.

See also **United Reformed Church Worship.**

John M. Barkley, *The Worship of the Reformed Church*, London 1966; Horton Davies, *WTE*; Duncan B. Forrester and Douglas M. Murray (eds), *Studies in the History of Worship in Scotland*, 2nd edn, Edinburgh 1996; R. Buick Knox, 'The Doctrine and Practice of Worship in the Irish Presbyterian Tradition', *The Church Service Society Record* XXVII, 1994, 9ff.; 'Presbyterian Worship in England in the Nineteenth Century', *Liturgical Review* XI/1, 1981, 23–33; XI/2, 79–89; W. D. Maxwell, *The Book of Common Prayer and the Worship of the Non-Anglican Churches*, London 1950.

DOUGLAS M. MURRAY

2. *USA.* Presbyterians brought to the North American colonies from Scotland and Ulster the *Directory for Public Worship* (1645) and *Directory for Family Worship* (1647), along with *metrical psalters. The *Directory* was affirmed by the first Synod in 1729, but its impact on worship is unclear. Preaching services with psalm-singing on Sundays, *daily worship in households, and the annual *Lord's supper were basic. As early as the 1740s and the First Awakening, hymns by Isaac Watts and the preaching of George Whitehead were both popular and controversial. In 1757 the Synod of New York settled for the freedom to sing hymns as well as psalms, and rarely thereafter acted to guide worship. The new General Assembly adopted a *Directory for Worship* (1788), with limited and permissive guidance for the minister. The Synod of the Associate-Reformed Church in 1799 adopted a conserva-

tive revision. Adaptation to the colonial and national context was from the first in tension with the principle of worship according to scripture.

Annual 'sacramental seasons' with regional gatherings for the Lord's supper contributed to the rise of '*camp meetings' (Cane Ridge, 1800), and 'protracted meetings' in the churches, at the origin of revivalism. The 'new measures' of revivalism engaged Presbyterian participation and also criticism. Liberal and conservative ministers alike treated worship in terms of edification and effect. The romanticism of the Victorian period, and the turbulence of national growth and Civil War, opened Presbyterians to improvement of worship and its aesthetic, first through architecture and then by initial efforts to recover or compose forms and liturgy. A Reformed liturgical heritage new to most Americans was rediscovered. Interest either in forms for the minister's guidance, or in full liturgical services and books, increased through the later nineteenth century. In 1897, the American 'Church Service Society' was formed.

The *Book of Common Worship* appeared in five editions and three basic stages. The 1906 and 1932 editions were structured by *Directory* rubrics and reflected concern for order, simplicity and the dignity of worship. The 1946 edition offered five orders for morning and evening on Sunday, a *eucharistic prayer, and a two-year *lectionary and calendar, all in tune with broader Reformed liturgical work at mid-century (particularly the 1940 Church of Scotland *Book of Common Order*). The two recent books, *The Worshipbook* (1970) and *Book of Common Worship* (1993) bracket a generation of ecumenical liturgical renewal. The former was too radical, too early, with the eucharist as normative and adoption of the RC lectionary. *The Worshipbook, Services and Hymns* (1972) provided wider variety and contemporary English usage in hymns, and was loved or hated. New directories in 1961 (northern church),1963 (southern church) and 1989 for the reunited Presbyterian Church (USA) provided theological guidance in far greater scope and detail than previous revisions.

Worship in Presbyterianism in the USA at the turn of the century does not present a uniform visage. Smaller denominations are more conservative or less directive than the Presbyterian Church (USA). That church is itself internally diverse in practice. A majority of congregations celebrate the Lord's supper monthly; less than 10% have a normative Sunday eucharist. The *Common Calendar* and *Revised Common Lectionary* are widely used, but so is *lectio continua* preaching with less regard for calendar. Growing experimentation with 'contemporary worship' raises questions of culture, music, the role of preaching, sacrament, and the purpose of worship itself in relation to the mission of the church.

———

Howard G. Hageman, *Pulpit and Table*, Richmond, VA 1962; Julius Melton, *Presbyterian Worship in America: Changing Patterns Since 1787*, Richmond, VA 1967.

STANLEY R. HALL

Presentation of the Lord
  see **Candlemas**

President *see* **Celebrant**

Priest *see* **Presbyter**

Prime *see* **Daily Prayer**

Procession

A procession is an ordered and meaningful progress of liturgical ministers and people from one sacred place to another. It may include, depending on the reason for the procession, the carrying of *crosses, relics, the Blessed Sacrament, banners, statues, branches of palm or other trees. *Incense may be used and blessed water sprinkled along the way. *Litanies, hymns and *anthems may be sung. Processions are found in the fourth to the sixth centuries for the same occasions as in the medieval and modern liturgy. The name 'procession', however, did not gain currency until the twelfth century and prior to that 'litany' meant a procession of prayer.

Processions were an important and recurrent feature of medieval liturgy. They invoked both the biblical exodus out of Egypt and the sojourn in the wilderness, and the entry of the blessed into the new Jerusalem. Doors and gates were a significant part of the exit and entry of processions from sacred and secular enclosures, and particular ceremonies (banging on the closed doors, sprinkling and censing) and chants (especially Ps. 24) were associated with them. Every Sunday in greater churches there was a procession and in monasteries and collegiate churches it passed through the cloister and even through the chapter house, refectory and dormitories. On some occasions the procession went to the graveyard.

Instructions for one English Augustinian house tell us that the bearer of holy water went first, then the cross and lights, the three sacred ministers for the *eucharist following, the members of the community in order from junior to senior concluding with the prior. The canons are to walk two and two, straight forward evenly and regularly, with a space of four feet (150 cm) indoors and six feet (225 cm) outdoors. The reliquary shrine and banners were carried on greater feasts. *Vesture varied according to the purpose of the procession: without shoes on penitential occasions, all the brethren in albs for the *Candlemas procession and *Palm Sunday, and all in copes for *Easter, *Ascension, *Pentecost and the Assumption. The cloister was an alternative to the outdoors in the event of wet weather.

The main processional occasions of the Western liturgy are Candlemas (the procession of blessed and lighted candles recalling Mary and Joseph taking Jesus to the Temple), Palm Sunday (with the use of green boughs from trees and the solemn entry into the church singing Theodulph of Orléans' hymn *Gloria, laus et honor*), *Rogation Days, Ascension Day and *Corpus Christi (with its procession of the Blessed Sacrament). Other significant processions included that of the *Easter candle at the *Easter vigil and to the font at Easter vespers.

Processions were also important for religious guilds and confraternities and for civic authorities. Gentile Bellini evokes the grandeur of the religio-civic procession in Venice in his portrayal of the procession of the true cross in the Piazza San Marco, painted in 1496. Such processions were an important part of life in medieval cities. The solemn procession for St John's Day in Florence involved all the city's clerks, priests, monks and friars – 512 of them (266 pairs) in 1394 – carrying the many relics of the saints beneath a canopy, as one witness tells us, and distinguished by the marvellous richness of their habits and the splendour of the vestments of gold and of silk and of embroidered figures. All the city's bells rang throughout the procession, the clergy chanted, and trumpets announced its coming with holy water, censings and blessings. As the Rogation procession sanctified the fields, the great civic processions sanctified the towns.

A number of lesser processions are included in the eucharistic liturgy. The entry of the choir and ministers is sometimes erroneously called the entrance procession. In the gospel procession the *deacon or other reader bears the book to the *ambo or *lectern accompanied by *acolytes and perhaps with incense. The bringing of the bread and wine (and other gifts) to the *altar by the laity, which had fallen into desuetude, was recovered by the twentieth-century *Liturgical Movement as the '*Offertory procession' and has become a popular feature of modern liturgy.

In the Orthodox Church processions – called *Lity* from the Greek word for prayer, from which litany is derived – are prescribed for vespers on the eve of Sundays and great feasts. There are also processions on *Good Friday, *Holy Saturday, and at the beginning of matins in the Easter vigil. In the liturgy the *little entrance and the *great entrance both have a processional character. Other processions with *icons and relics are a common feature of worship.

————

For the origin and development of medieval processions, Terence Bailey, *The Processions of Sarum and the Western Church*, Toronto 1971. On sacral-civic processions, P. Fortini Brown, *The Renaissance in Venice*, London 1997; R. C. Trexler, *Public Life in Renaissance Florence*, Ithaca/London 1991. On Corpus Christi, Miri Rubin, *Corpus Christi*, Cambridge 1991.

MARTIN DUDLEY

Prone *see* Bidding Prayer

Proper

A term with two different, though related, liturgical meanings: (1) those parts of the *eucharistic rite which vary according to the day or season, as distinct from the unchanging *ordinary; (2) those variable parts of the rite which are rendered chorally, principally composed of psalmody, and comprising the introit or entrance chant; the gradual or *responsorial psalm (sung after the first reading), the alleluia (sung between the epistle and the gospel), the *offertory chant, and the *communion chant. Derivatively, the term may be used of those parts of any service which vary according to the day or season.

See also **Chants of the Proper of the Mass**.

W. JARDINE GRISBROOKE

Prothesis

Literally 'placing before' or 'offering', this term refers to the universal Eastern ritual preparation of bread and wine before the *eucharist begins. In the Byzantine tradition it can also designate the area north of the *altar where the gifts are prepared or the table on which the gifts are prepared.

Originally a purely practical preparation of the bread and wine brought by the faithful, it eventually became an elaborate ritual usually restricted to clergy. Prior to the ninth century, *deacons stationed in the *skeuophylakion* (*sacristy) received whatever gifts the people brought and prepared the necessary quantity for that day's eucharist. Sometime in the late seventh or early eighth centuries a prayer over the gifts was added. Beginning in the ninth century each local church developed its own unique ritual preparation. Uniformity was imposed by Patriarch Philotheos (Kokkinos) of Constantinople (d. 1379), who required five loaves of bread: one from which the *Amnos* (Lamb representing Jesus) was to be cut, and four to provide smaller pieces commemorating the Mother of God, various saints, and the living and departed faithful.

As the eucharist came to be explained as a dramatic allegory of the life of Christ, the Prothesis was interpreted along these lines, first as recalling the passion and death (Germanos, *Historia ecclesiastica* 21–2) and later incorporating 'nativity' language (Nicholas of Andida, *Protheoria* 9–10; Nicholas Cabasilas, *Commentary on the Divine Liturgy* 6–11; Symeon of Thessalonike, *De sacra liturgia* 84).

Vitalien Laurent, 'Le rituel de la proscomidie et le métropolite de Crète Elie', *Revue des Études Byzantines* XVI, 1958, 116–42.

JOHN KLENTOS

Psalmody

The 150 psalms found in the OT, together with the *canticle texts in both OT and NT, have always dominated the public *daily prayer of the church, and have been the principal source of the *proper sung texts of the *eucharist. Taken over directly from Jewish traditions of worship, and adapted in a christological context, their musical treatment has been formalized and categorized by the churches according to the manner of singing, their formal treatment, and their place in the liturgy.

The regular recitation of the Psalms in the seven offices of the liturgical day and the night office was codified by the sixth century. It brings together two traditions: the recitation of the Psalms in their numerical order, a pattern of disciplined prayer first adopted by the early monks in the fourth century; and the recitation of specific psalms according to the time of day, the practice of the early church's so-called 'cathedral' worship witnessed by Egeria in Jerusalem in the fourth century. The numerical monastic scheme is most evident in the night and evening offices, the 'cathedral' scheme in the morning office (with the daily recitation of Pss. 148–150) and compline (where the psalms are unchanging). In the Western church two variant cycles of reciting the psalms were prevalent: the cycle specified in the Rule of St Benedict in the sixth century, and used in monasteries based on that rule (including Benedictine and Cistercian); and the so-called 'secular' cycle adopted by cathedral and diocesan clergy, though also based on monastic practice, probably that of sixth-century Rome. The wholesale recitation of Latin psalms uses a limited number of simple melodic formulae – the *psalm-tones.

It has been traditional to group the chant repertory related to psalmody into three main types: antiphonal, responsorial and direct psalmody. Each type is distinguished by its position in the liturgy, its formal and musical characteristics, and its manner of performance, all deriving from the practice of the early church. However, there are distinctive genres within these broad categories.

1. *Antiphonal Psalmody.* Monks adopted the practice of sitting on two sides of the choir facing one another, thereby effecting a division of the community into two groups. A number of extended texts were shared by the two groups singing alternately, or in antiphony, in particular psalms and canticles which dominated the daily Latin office. The practice was extended throughout the Western church by secular clergy and religious as well as monks. The chanting of the main text of the psalm was shared by the clergy or monks present in *choir, singing alternately – one side then the other – verse by verse, or half verse by half verse, to one of the psalm-tones, and a melodic refrain (*antiphon) was sung by all before the psalm and after each verse. *Cantors from the choir began the antiphon and the psalm. In the Latin *mass this was the way in which introit

and *communion chants were sung. However, by the tenth century these antiphonal psalms had been truncated, probably because the liturgical action was by then so much reduced. The introit of the medieval Latin and later Roman rites includes: antiphon, psalm verse, (antiphon in some instances,) Gloria Patri and antiphon. At the communion, only the antiphon survives. In the Latin office almost all psalms and canticles are sung with an antiphon at the beginning and end of each psalm (or group of psalms). The *ferial, seasonal, common and *proper cycles of the liturgy therefore include several thousands of antiphons to be sung with the psalms, and *Benedictus and Magnificat. In the invitatory (Venite) the use of all or part of the antiphon as a refrain between the verses persists. The mode (i.e., melodic characteristics) of the antiphon dictates the psalm-tone to which the related psalm is chanted.

2. *Responsorial Psalmody*. Psalmody sung in response to a reading; nowadays the psalm sung after the first reading at the eucharist, but in the medieval Latin and later Roman rites, the *responsory or respond after the lesson or chapter in the daily prayer office, the gradual and alleluia after the first reading in the mass. The verse sections of responsorial psalmody are delegated to specific soloists. These singers are normally distinguished from the cantors or rulers who lead the choir, and often sing the verses of the responsorial chant from a specified position in the church – either the *lectern at the choir step or the lectern on the *pulpitum. This practice derives from the very early tradition of 'cathedral' worship, where the verses of the psalm were delegated to a solo singer and the assembly sang a refrain after each verse. The vestiges of such a practice may be observed in the simple short responsory chanted after the chapter in the Latin daily prayer office. The responsories at the night office of matins and the graduals and alleluias in the mass include some of the most elaborate chant in the Western plainsong repertory. Such demanding melodies belonged to the skilled body of medieval clergy and monks. Only one or two verses of the psalm are included in a responsory, normally with the first part of Gloria Patri. The most simple pattern consists of: refrain; verse; refrain. More elaborate patterns may include: refrain; verse; part of refrain; verse; part of refrain; Gloria; refrain. There are several variant patterns. The modern *responsorial psalm, recited after the first read-

ing at the eucharist, belongs to this genre of response to reading, but is normally set with a simple chant and congregational refrain.

3. *Direct Psalmody*. This was intended to be sung by a small group of soloists. There is no refrain, and the psalm text is sung through to a melismatic melody, often using specific melodic features. In the Latin mass examples of direct psalmody survive in the tracts, sung after the gradual in place of the alleluia in the penitential season between Septuagesima and the end of *Holy Week and at the *requiem. Most of these chants are in mode 2 or mode 8.

Not all medieval psalmody fits neatly into these three categories, and modern plainsong scholarship tends to treat each individual genre on its own merits. For instance, the offertory in the Latin mass is often headed 'antiphon', and is sung within the choir (with cantors, rather than soloists, like other antiphonal chants), but the elaborate melodic characteristics of the chant and the inclusion in some offertories of melismatic verses are closer in style to responsorial chant.

In the Protestant denominations after the Reformation, psalmody continued to be sung both in the liturgy (especially in Lutheran, Calvinist and Anglican worship) and in the home. The treatment varied. In the Lutheran and Calvinist churches psalms were sung in vernacular *metrical translations. In the Anglican Church, the recitation of the psalms continued at morning and evening prayer in vernacular prose translation, though without antiphons. Where they were sung this was to an adapted form of the plainsong psalm-tones, from which were derived the harmonized and stylized convention of Anglican *chant. Metrical psalms were also used before and after the specified public orders of prayer in the Church of England. Psalmody was the term used to describe the choral and/or instrumental settings of metrical psalms that developed both in Britain and America in the late seventeenth and eighteenth centuries, and persisted into the nineteenth century.

The revision of vernacular liturgies in the second half of the twentieth century, and the new translations of the Bible as a whole and the Psalms in particular, have raised new issues of singing the psalms, especially in a pastoral liturgical setting. New methods of chanting and new metrical versions of the Psalms have been devised, though none has proved universally appealing. Nevertheless, they demonstrate the church's continued engagement in liturgical singing of the Psalms.

'Psalm', *NG2*, XX, 449–71; David Hiley, *Western Plainchant: A Handbook*, Oxford 1993.

JOHN HARPER

Psalm-Tones

The eight tones, or 'tunes', used for psalmody are related to the eight *church modes. A psalm-tone is a neat little musical form made up of two balancing phrases, as follows:

PHRASE ONE

intonation – recitation – mediant cadence

PHRASE TWO

more recitation – final cadence

The first half of each psalm-verse corresponds to phrase one and the second to phrase two. The *intonation* (two or three notes) leads to the *reciting note* – the dominant of the mode: this note carries the recitation, ending with the *mediant cadence*. If the first phrase is long, it is subdivided by an intermediary drop, called a *flex*, before proceeding to the mediant cadence. The second phrase starts on the reciting note with no intonation, and ends with the final cadence. There is usually a choice of final cadences, or '*differences*'; tone I has at least ten. The choice of difference depends on the melody of the *antiphon, sung before and after the psalm.

One constant feature of psalmody is a silent pause between the phrases, but not between consecutive verses. This *pausa conveniens*, which allows for the resonance of the building, also provides a moment to meditate and to link phrase 1 to phrase 2, following the Hebrew parallelism: 'Praise him, sun and moon,' (pause) 'praise him, all ye stars and light.' The intonation is only used for the first verse of a psalm, subsequent verses beginning immediately on the reciting note. However, in the *canticles (Benedictus, Magnificat and Nunc dimittis) every verse begins with the intona-

tion. On major festivals an elaborate version of the whole psalm-tone is sung with the canticles. A more elaborate one still is the norm for the psalm-verse of the introit and communion chants (*see* **Chants of the Proper of the Mass**).

In addition to the eight psalm-tones, several other tones are used in psalmody. They include the *tonus irregularis* and the *tonus in directum*. Another is the *tonus peregrinus* (the 'wandering tone'), which has two reciting notes, the second, after the mediant cadence, lying a tone below the first. It is traditionally associated with Ps. 114 ('When Israel came out of Egypt'). Bach uses this tone, in its Lutheran form, at a high pitch on the oboes in the sixth verse of his Latin Magnificat. In Monteverdi's 1610 *Vespers* other psalm-tones are used effectively, for example, combined with the introduction of chromatic notes in four of the five psalms. The psalm-tones exert a stabilizing influence, especially in the florid passages. Mozart makes effective quotations of tone I by the oboes in his *Masonic Funeral March* (K 477) for small orchestra. During the fifteenth and later centuries composers frequently set verses of the canticles, either for organ or for choral performance, to alternate with the other verses sung to chant.

Codification of the psalm-tones dates from about the eleventh century. The notable resemblance between the first psalm-tone and the *tonus peregrinus* discloses a far-off link with the practice of the synagogue.

Mary Berry, *Plainchant for Everyone*, 2nd edn, Croydon 1987; David Hiley, *Western Plainchant: A Handbook*, Oxford 1993; Alberto Turco, *Tracce di Strutture Modali originarie nella Salmodia del Temporale e del Santorale*, Milan 1972.

MARY BERRY

Psychology and Liturgy

see **Social Sciences and the Study of Liturgy**

Pulpit

From the Latin, *pulpitum*, 'platform', an elevated construction from which a preacher gives a sermon or exhortation. The height and scope of the enclosure is gained either by a pedestal base, or by fixture to a wall, pier or corbel, and it is approached by steps. It is proper to the *nave, the place of the congregation. The earliest examples (northern Italian, late twelfth century) combine the attributes of the evolving *ambo form and the needs of the new mendicant orders; some were portable. A rectangular enclosure on marble pillars (first seen in Pisa in 1162 by Gugliemo) became very popular. From the outset, the use of painted or sculpted panels (of biblical authors, events, doctors of the church, etc.), figurative carving and metal ornament – and increasingly polygonal outlines – made pulpits artistically much livelier structures than ambos. By the 1400s the Italian forms were strongly influencing designs in Spain and Portugal. A Gothic pattern was to dominate in northern and central Europe – Alsemberg (1480), Strasbourg (1486), Vienna (1515), Leiden (c. 1525) – though Renaissance style and manners were increasingly influential: see Delft (1548). Reformation and Counter-Reformation both placed increasing emphasis on the pulpit, becoming in Protestant churches (and later some Nonconformist churches) a formal and sober focus of worship. In the RC Church, by contrast, sculpture became the overriding skill of pulpit construction: first in Germany and then Flanders, in an ever more sophisticated tradition until the early nineteenth century.

The earliest pulpits in England date from the turn of the fifteenth century. The tradition normally combines panels, architectural features, and carved standing figures rather than Renaissance decorative features, and often on a 'wine-glass' Gothic pedestal. From the early seventeenth century there was a great rise in their number and quality, usually in oak; and two- and three-decker pulpits (adding a reading desk and then clerk's stall, below the topmost pulpit tier) were introduced into box-*pewed or *galleried churches. The impact of the Gothic revival on pulpit design was modest, even if a greater variety of materials was introduced.

P. Poscharsky, 'Kanzel', *Theologische Realenzyklopädie* XVII, Berlin/New York 1988, 588–604; G. Randall, *Church Furnishing and Decoration in England and Wales*, London 1980; 'Pulpit', *The Grove Dictionary of Art*, London 1996 (bib.).

JONATHAN GOODALL

Purification of the Blessed Virgin Mary

see **Candlemas**

Purificator

The piece of white linen cloth often used to cleanse the lip of the *chalice after each individual *communion and to cleanse the whole chalice at the *ablutions after communion. It measures sixteen inches by eight inches and is folded in thirds lengthwise, and hangs directly over the chalice (and under the paten) until the *offertory. It is also often carried by the minister administering the chalice to communicants, though its practical use as a contamination prophylactic is highly questionable. Its history is vague, and although there is mention of such in the Middle Ages, its regular use is probably as late as the sixteenth century.

TRISTAM HOLLAND

Pyx

From the Greek word meaning a wooden container, the pyx has been used, since the early church, as a receptacle for carrying the consecrated *host after the conclusion of the *eucharist. Generally, this would be for communicating the *sick but, in the early church, there was a practice of daily *communion in the home, using the consecrated bread from the previous Sunday. Individual Christians would carry this away in their own pyx, usually in a pyx-bag suspended from a cord around the neck. The pyx became more ornamented, though not substantially increasing in size, but more often made of a precious metal or ivory. Also, with clericalization, the transporting of consecrated elements became the exclusive prerogative of the clergy. The pyx is usually wrapped in a linen cloth, such as a *purificator or *corporal, itself being a portable altar-cloth. In the later Middle Ages, with the onset of the *reservation of the sacrament and its subsequent veneration, the pyx acquired a more permanent status within a church building as a receptacle for the consecrated host. Often a stem was added, by which it might be hand held, or it became a part of a 'hanging pyx', suspended from the ceiling of a *chapel, sometimes in the form of a dove or covered in hanging silks.

TRISTAM HOLLAND

Quadragesima *see* Lent

Quaker Worship

Worship after the manner of The Religious Society of Friends may have a variety of expressions, but mostly it is characterized as a time of attentive waiting upon God in which spoken and expressive ministries are welcome, but not the primary focus. The central concern is to open oneself to the transforming presence of God, believing that therein abides the well-spring and essence of spiritual vitality. At times this endeavour is referred to as silent worship, but silence is less of a goal than the facilitative setting within which the divine will can be attended, discerned and obeyed. Worship is the adoring response of the heart to God. Independent of place and form, authentic worship will always be 'in spirit and in truth' (John 4.21–24); and Friends affirm it is into such a reality that God seeks to draw all who are willing.

In addition to corporate worship, Friends have long emphasized a private life of personal devotion. It is said of George Fox that he could have reproduced the entirety of the scriptures from memory, and John Woolman's reading the Bible after 'First Day' meetings for worship as a six-year-old sensitized his heart to spiritual matters at a very early age. Likewise, the prayer-lives of Fox and other Friends have been legendary. William Penn said of George Fox, 'The most awful, living, reverent frame I ever felt or beheld, I must say, was his in prayer.' In adition, the religious writings of such Friends as Hannah Whitall Smith, William Penn, George Fox, John Woolman, Thomas Kelly and Richard Foster have been favourites among the classics of devotional literature, and Friends have long advocated the practice of setting a special time apart for prayer as a daily discipline. Friends seek to cultivate a spiritual awareness of God's presence and workings in the world, characterized as listening for the promptings of the Holy Spirit inwardly and discerning the voice of God coming through those around them. In so doing, the private life of devotion complements the corporate life of worship, and vice versa.

1. *Programmed and Unprogrammed Quaker Worship.* An attender of a Quaker meeting for worship may experience any number of approaches to worship, depending upon which group of Friends one joins. Within Friends' meetings and congregations in America, Africa and Latin America, the predominant form of worship has come to follow a 'low church' structure of worship, including the singing of hymns and worship choruses, the reading of scripture, the delivery of a sermon, and times of open worship, quiet waiting and prayer. This approach to worship has come to be known as 'programmed', and about 80% of the world's 350,000 Quakers use some form of this more expressive approach. Programmed Friends normally make use of pastoral leadership, although the distinction between the clergy and laity is minimized, from the belief that every Christian is called to ministry. Friends do not ordain their ministers; they believe that *God* ordains, and that humans simply 'record' that the exercise of giftedness in public ministry attests to the reality of divine ordination unto gospel ministry. On this matter, Friends believe that God calls women as well as men to proclamational service and pastoral ministry, and they seek to affirm the sense of God's calling on people's lives as befits their experiences. Friends also do not view subsidized ministry as 'paid' ministry; rather, they view subsidy as the practical means by which one is 'released' to pursue one's calling to serve the meeting in ministry.

Despite the growth of pastoral Friends over the last century, the traditional 'meeting for worship after the manner of Friends', however, is 'unprogrammed'. The typical unprogrammed meeting for worship in Britain, Europe, America or Australasia will last about an hour, and it is characterized as a largely silent time of corporate waiting upon God. *Elders and others are expected to come to meeting prepared to share if they feel led, and the elders of the meeting will often sit upon a 'facing bench' at the front of the room. Vocal ministry tends to be brief within such a meeting, with subsequent contributions developing an emerging concern, providing a brief time for reflection between the contributions. Rather than come to meeting with a speech to be delivered, or rather than starting in on a new theme, the goal of vocal ministry is to be a means of furthering the divine word and message to the community of faith. Distinguishing a sense of leading to speak over and against a good idea to share is a weighty concern for Friends. Historically, as early Friends felt moved to speak – sometimes smitten with a sense of awe regarding the message to be delivered – they trembled in the fear of the Lord, and hence were given the pejorative label, 'Quakers'. Vocal ministry within the unprogrammed tradition of Friends has varied in its characteristics from biblical homilies, to sing-song exhortations, to social-reform admonitions, to meditative reflections, and yet one common feature persists. Attenders view the meeting as a participatory gathering in which all have access to the living word of God, and they hold that all should be willing to speak if led to do so. Where it is felt that God has indeed led within the meeting – both in the silence and through the vocal ministry – this is called a 'gathered' meeting for worship. It cannot be manipulated or predicted; it is a spiritual reality, which can only be experienced and embraced when it happens.

At times, Friends have met together and have shared with each other from their respective traditions with much benefit extending in all directions. This has led in some instances to a 'semi-programmed' modification of either approach. Times of corporate singing, scripture reading, and prepared speaking at times are added to an unprogrammed meeting as is felt to be serviceable; and space is created for quiet waiting upon God within the programmed meeting for worship, often before or after the message, or both. Either way, it would be a mistake to regard silent worship as a 'formless form' to be implemented strategically. Silence creates the space within which to listen to God, and because it is fragile, it is respected among Friends. Worship is both expressive and impressive. In the meeting for worship we express our love for God and receive God's love for us. The priority of worship, therefore, is to open our lives to God's saving-revealing work – whether it comes to us in the spoken word, the music or the silence – and to respond faithfully to its transforming effect within.

2. *Historical Developments among Friends.* Historically, the Quaker approach to worship was anticipated by Christian contemplative traditions in north-west England in the mid-seventeenth century. Groups of people had begun to gather in silent waiting on the Lord, calling themselves 'Seekers', and it was among these gatherings that George Fox and other early Quaker leaders exercised their early ministries in the 1650s. As England had come through a bitter century and a half of civil struggle in which religion was wielded as a pawn by Roman Catholics, Anglicans and Puritans alike, emphasis upon the authentic and unmediated worship of God was a welcome balm for many. George Fox, Robert Barclay, William Penn and others proclaimed the recovery of primitive Christianity and, in that sense, the Quaker movement was inspired by restorationist concerns. Early Friends were critical of institutionalizing tendencies within

Christianity, and they sought to recover apostolic Christianity as a Spirit-based reality rather than an organizational one. In these respects, they saw themselves as challenging not only the established churches, but the Reformers as well. In the implementing of attentive waiting upon the Holy Spirit in worship, Fox sought to recover the experiential setting out of which the prophets of old produced the inspired scriptures, and the act of meeting together for worship marked aspirations of drinking from the spring-waters of the inspirational fountain rather than its collected pools.

Quakers grew rapidly, numbering as many as 10,000 by 1660 and 50,000 by 1700. The movement especially took root in America, where the granting of a large portion of land to William Penn (Pennsylvania) became a site in which Friends attempted to erect a society patterned after the kingdom of God and the teachings of Jesus, and it was known as 'the Holy Experiment'. Here the Quaker movement flourished, and Quaker worship developed into its classical form of quietism. With the American revivalist movement in the late-nineteenth century, however, Friends in the midwest assisted in the endeavour to bring spiritual renewal and social reform, and this led to the introduction of prepared messages, singing and the emergence of pastoral ministry among Friends. Where revivalist meetings in America served to heal the nation after the Civil War, Quaker revivalist preachers and travelling ministers eventually settled down as pastors and teachers within the new meetings that were springing up throughout Ohio, Indiana, Iowa, Kansas, Idaho, Oregon and California. These regions have since become centres of evangelical and pastoral Quakerism, and the fruit of their missions work in the twentieth century has been the primary factor in the doubling of the membership of Friends in the same period.

3. *Quaker Convictions about Worship.* In addition to the above convictions of Friends as to the spiritual and unmediated character of authentic worship, Friends also hold several other beliefs. The first regards the character of sacramentality, wherein it is seen not as a liturgical or an instrumentalistic act, but as an incarnational reality. A common misconception is that Friends do not believe in *baptism and *communion, but this is not the case. Friends believe that baptism is essential for Christian living, but they believe the baptism of Jesus –

by fire and by Spirit – is experienced as a factor of faithful abiding in Christ spiritually. Likewise, communion after the manner of Friends is central to the life of the Spirit, and the real presence of Christ is encountered wherever two or three are gathered in his name (Matt. 18.20) and where the faithful open themselves to God's transforming love in their lives (John 15.1–15). The true outward sign of the church is likewise the changed and changing lives of believers. The 'fruits of the Spirit' (Gal. 5.22–24) provide the most telling measure of authentic Christianity, and it is by persons' loving character and deeds that the authentic followers of Jesus are recognized (John 13.34). In these ways, Friends believe authentic sacramentality is incarnational rather than ritualistic, and that the truest outward sign of the authentic church will always be the incarnational measure.

A second conviction about worship is that human access to God is unmediated and apprehended by faith inwardly. Christ alone is the true priest, and while humans carry out a variety of ministries on behalf of Christ, the goal of ministry is always to draw people to the saving, revealing and healing work of Christ. For these reasons, Friends seek to diminish all else in order to heighten the sense of the divine presence within the meeting for worship. While room is made for expressions of worship, Friends resist tendencies to coerce or manipulate worship experiences by others, and for this reason consider even their structured approaches to worship non-liturgical. Such can lead to an individualistic approach to worship, but at the core of this testimony is the belief that it is God who gathers participants in worship, and the power of the corporate worship experience roots in transcending oneself and being open and responsive to the divine initiative. The simplicity of architecture and plain furnishings typifying Quaker meeting houses reflect this concern. All else is diminished in order to focus on the singular priority of the divine presence in the midst.

A third Quaker conviction about worship is that the Spirit of the risen Christ continues to lead the church (John 14—16) as the centre of normative NT Christianity, and this informs the meeting for worship in which business is conducted. The Quaker decision-making process roots in the proclamation of George Fox that 'Christ is come to teach his people Himself', and Friends have sought to take this conviction seriously. As well as seeking to live in faithful responsiveness to Christ's leadings personally, Friends have developed an impressively effective approach to corporate discernment in which the clerk of the business meeting will articulate the issue, invite contributions from all sectors of the membership (even dissenting ones), call for a time of threshing the chaff from the kernels and finally suggest a common 'sense of the meeting'. While critics of such a deliberative approach claim a voting system of judgement can be more expeditious, it should be made clear that there is nothing as inefficient as a divided group – especially over important matters. Further, the goal is not decision-making primarily; rather, the need to make corporate decisions is seen as an occasion wherein to come together and learn discernment, wisdom and prayerful searching within a community of faith. Neither is decision-making after the manner of Friends to be regarded simplistically as a 'consensus' process alone. The goal is to come together around a common sense of a divine leading, and such an aspiration is rooted squarely in seeing the endeavour as a worship event in which humans listen for God's present leadings.

Paul N. Anderson, 'Was the Fourth Evangelist a Quaker?' *Quaker Religious Thought* LXXVI, 1991, 27–43; Robert Barclay, *Barclay's Apology in Modern English*, ed. Dean Freiday, Newberg, OR 1967/1991; Francis B. Hall (ed.), *Quaker Worship in North America*, Richmond, IN 1978.

PAUL N. ANDERSON

Quinquagesima

The name denotes the Sunday preceding *Lent, being fifty days before *Easter. Similar names became attached to the Sunday before that, Sexagesima, and the one before that, Septuagesima, these names meaning 'sixtieth' and 'seventieth' respectively, even though they are clearly not these precise numbers of days before Easter. These three Sundays emerged as a preparatory cycle for Lent itself in the West from the middle of the fifth century onwards and were established at Rome before the end of the sixth century. The spread of the Roman rite ensured their eventual acceptance throughout the West and at the Reformation into the *BCP*. As Septuagesima was the Sunday that came to mark the beginning of the approach to Easter, it became the custom to celebrate the doctrine of the beginning of things, namely creation, on this day, with appropriate readings.

A parallel development took place in the Byzantine tradition, with the creation of a three-week period prior to the beginning of Lent. The Sundays in this period are known as the Sunday of the Publican and the Pharisee; the Sunday of the Prodigal Son; the Sunday of the Last Judgement (Meatfare Sunday); and the Sunday of Forgiveness (Cheesefare Sunday). The week between Meatfare and Cheesefare Sunday is a time of partial fasting, a compromise between the Constantinopolitan and Palestinian lengths of Lent. Lent officially begins on 'Clean Monday', the day after Cheesefare Sunday.

The 'Gesimas' have been abolished in the modern RC rite. The names were also abolished in the 1980 Alternative Service Book of the Church of England, though following the Joint Liturgical Group calendar which that book largely adopted, it still had a nine-Sunday pre-Easter period, naming these three Sundays prosaically as the ninth, eighth and seventh Sundays before Easter. More recent calendrical revisions in Britain do not use them. In North America and elsewhere it is clear that these names have largely fallen out of use. Quite apart from the philosophical question as to whether a period of preparation (i.e., Lent) should itself have a period of preparation, there seems little merit in continuing to name Sundays after inaccurate Latin calculations, and it seems very unlikely that anyone will wish to revive their use.

RICHARD F. BUXTON

Rastafarian Worship

1. *Background*. The attitudes and practices of today's Rastafarian worship developed out of 'Ethiopianism', an intense, global, black identity movement from the eighteenth to the early twentieth century, focusing on Africa as the true 'Bible land', where a black Christ and apostles lived out the passion account that provides the possibility of salvation. Revivalist in nature, it featured a number of charismatic preachers travelling between the UK, USA (sometimes Africa) and the Caribbean, claiming to have special appointment from God to illuminate the formerly enslaved Afro-Americans. Many of these preachers adopted African sounding titles like Royal Prince Thomas Makarooroo of Ceylon or Prince Mitcheline. The most famous was Prophet Alexander Bedward, who amassed a significant following by holding massive open-air preaching and healing meetings in Jamaica. Bedward baptized so many followers that a folk song saluted him, 'Dunk them, Bedward, Dunk them, Dunk them in the healing stream'. Other Jamaicans followed the trinitarian Christian Marcus Garvey, who encouraged worshipping the triune God 'through the spectacles of Ethiopia' to parallel the consciousness-raising work of his United Negro Improvement Association. Some embraced Masonic ritual with its strange rites to 'Juhbuhlon', a syncretistic composite name for God drawn from Jah (see Ps. 68.4) or Jehovah, Baal and On (or Osiris). Some followed the Anguillan Robert 'Shepherd Athlyi' Rogers of his Afro Athlican Constructive Church, whose 'black man's Bible', *The Holy Piby* (Woodbridge, New Jersey 1924), identified Marcus Garvey as a prophet and attempted to redirect worship from Jesus to Elijah, as a black incarnation of God.

Two years later, the Revd Fitz Balintine Pettersburgh attempted to win to himself all these competing movements. In his *The Royal Parchment Scroll of Black Supremacy* (Kingston, Jamaica *c*. 1926, reprinted 1996), he debunked the revelatory angelic visitation claimed by 'Professor Rogers' of 'The House of Athlyi' as actually demonic and 'Poor Rogers did not know, he was "The Principal of Hell"'. Next, he denounced 'The Pilot Marcus Garvey' as deluded by 'the fallen Angel, whose name is Lady Astonishment' and 'The Pilot Believed the Angle-Militant Upside Down Queen'. He also attacked 'PASTOR RUSSEL and Judge Rutherford' of the Jehovah's Witnesses movement for preaching 'the Lies' of 'Judge Lucifer the Devil' (31). In place of all these movements, while falling short of assuming supreme divinity, Pettersburgh offered himself and his wife as objects of reverence: 'His Majesty King Alpha and Queen Omega are not Our Creator HIMSELF . . . The Tri-Divinity, and Her Tri-Virginity King Alpha and Queen Omega, are Man and Wife, (commonly) called "Alpha and Omega" we are Black Peoples . . . Queen Lula May Fitz Balintine Pettersburgh, Owner of Money Mint and Bible House and Human Family. Supreme Judge of Creation, and Arch Bishop of Holy Time' (54–5). Though Pettersburgh refers to 'Christ' and 'Jesus', 'God Almighty' and 'The Holy Spirit' (12–13), he intended to replace the Bible with his own writings: 'I am The Holy Bible's Owner, therefore, I have taken away the Adamic, imperfect (version) that is (dated)

B.C. 4004 and closed A.D. 96. And give to Creation, my perfect Husband and Wife's Theocracy (dated) A.D. 1925 and 26' (84). Modelling worshipping communities on African 'balm yards', which gather around preachers/healers for healing from curses and illnesses, Pettersburgh extolled marriage, baptism, fasting and superstitious rituals. *The Parchment*, although failing to attract a sizeable following for the Pettersburghs, became seminal for shaping the growth of Rastafari.

2. *A Prince Comes Out of Egypt* . . . Eventually, each of the Ethiopianist movements began to disintegrate. The Prophet Bedward announced he would ascend to his heavenly Father. After an embarrassing failure to rise he was led off to an insane asylum. His disappointed followers scattered, their desire for an inclusive expression of God still intense and persistent. Marcus Garvey was jailed in the USA for fraud for overselling stock in his steamship line. Deported back to Jamaica, he exiled himself to England, dying disappointed. Pretenders like Thomas Makarooroo and Prince Mitcheline were exposed as frauds. Then, on 2 November 1930, a surprising event took place. A world away in the fabled land of Ethiopia, Ras ('prince' in Amharic) Tafari Makonnen was crowned with the titles 'King of Kings', 'Lord of Lords', 'Conquering Lion of the Tribe of Judah', 'Scion of David', Haile Selassie I ('Might of the Holy Trinity'). A theological shock wave raced across the Caribbean, electrifying preachers like the former follower of Bedward and Garvey, Robert Hinds, the reputed Masons Archibald Dunkley and Joseph Hibbert, and a healer named Leonard Howell, who had 'several meetings' with Fitz Balintine Pettersburgh, 'especially a meeting in October 1933 whereby they attacked "Ministers of the Gospel, also churches and white men"'.

Howell incorporated Pettersburgh's ideas nearly word for word into his own seminal book, *The Promised Key* (*c.* 1935), with a significant difference: Howell refocused from Petterburgh and his wife Lula May to the newly crowned monarch of Ethiopia and his empress, proclaiming these to be the real 'King Alpha and Queen Omega'. Further, the proponents of Ras Tafari Makonnen did not stop short of identifying him as either the return of Christ or the presence of Jah, the Living God the Father on earth.

Copying the open-air meetings of the revivalists and balm-yard gatherings recommended in the *Parchment*, and now the *Key*, early Rastas took to the streets, holding mass meetings in Jamaica's urban centres. These early gatherings involved singing Christian hymns and 'Sankeys' (gospel rousers named after D. L. Moody's song leader, but applying them to Selassie), testimonies and a challenging sermon presenting Selassie for worship. Some, like Hibbert, practised divination using the Bible, and Howell was known for having 'excellent hands with sickness'. By the mid-twentieth century, 'Prince' Edward Emmanuel had peeled off a segment revering himself as well as Selassie, Hibbert had established the Ethiopian Coptic Church and Howell had taken over an old planter's estate and amassed several hundred live-in followers. These 'balm-yard' communities became the predecessors of today's Rasta camps.

By the late 1950s, musician Count Ossie and his drumming corps, the Mystic Revelation of Rastafari, introduced drumming, building on the African burra rhythms that provided the basis for Jamaican slaves' work songs, and Howell championed ganja (cannabis) as a cash crop and a means to instigate 'revelations'. These elements remain in current camp worship, which includes daily drumming, chanting (singing) praises to the Most High, 'eating the chalice' (smoking ganja for revelations), and reasoning (talking theology). Periodically, camps become the focal point for huge gatherings called 'grounations', which celebrate major events in the life of the emperor or Rasta 'blackmystory' (history).

Despite its strong initial leaders and early communal nature, Rastafari maintained an emphasis on the autonomy of each believer. As a result, decentralization of authority became valued and no uniformity of belief exists about the proper theological place of the emperor or how he should be revered. While many adherents remain independent, Rastafari does have several major sub-movements within it, including the Twelve Tribes of Israel, Bobo Dreads, Niyabinghi, Ethiopian Coptic Church, and numerous adherents within the *Ethiopian Orthodox Church. Many of these still keep alive the seminal worship practices.

Some are baptized, as are the Rastas within the Ethiopian Orthodox Church, initially appalling priests – and the emperor himself – by seeking baptism in Selassie's, not Jesus' name. Some still live in camps and worship through long reasoning sessions, accompanied by drumming, and fuelled by ganja, as do the Bobo

Dreads. The Twelve Tribesmen 'chant a psalm' or read a chapter of the Bible each day. Some feel free to fluctuate between worshipping in Christian churches and Rastafarian gatherings. One prominent Rasta explained to the present writer: 'I can get up and say, "Hail! Hail this Selassie I!" because Selassie I is a Power of the Trinity. So I can hail Selassie I anytime. I can go down, say, "Jesus Christ Almighty!", you know, because I'm praising him the same way.'

In the UK the weekly worship style of the Birmingham Ethiopian World Federation was explained in a children's book, *I Am a Rastafarian* (London 1986). The ritual involved signing a 'security book' on entering the gathering, males removing hats, all singing the 'Ethiopian National Anthem' (a hymn associated with Marcus Garvey's United Negro Improvement Association), drumming, singing and praying with thumbs and index fingers touching in a pear-shaped form adapted from a photograph of the emperor.

3. *The Jesus Movement of Jah People*. Today an increasing number of Rastas in Jamaica are moving from worshipping Haile Selassie as God to worshipping Haile Selassie's own God, Jesus Christ. These are entering Christian churches but retaining their locks (from the Nazarite vows of Num. 6), ital (vegetarian) eating practices, and self-identity as Rastas, interpreting the term to mean those who follow the path of the emperor to Jesus Christ. These are responding to the emperor's own unswerving devotion to Jesus. While adjusting their doctrines to proclaim Jesus as the only name under heaven that gives salvation, they are in turn raising the consciousness of Christians to pursue less transplanted missionary and more Afro-Caribbean styles of self-identity and worship.

_____

Primary sources: Malcolm C. Duncan, *Duncan's Masonic Ritual and Monitor*, Chicago 1974; Marcus Garvey, *Philosophy and Opinions of Marcus Garvey*, New York 1968; G. G. Maragh [pseudonym of Leonard Howell], *The Promised Key*, Accra, Gold Coast [but probably Kingston, Jamaica], n.d. [*c.* 1935], now with commentary in Nathaniel Samuel Murrell, William David Spencer, Adrian Anthony McFarlane (eds), *Chanting Down Babylon: The Rastafari Reader*, Philadelphia 1998, 361–89 (bib.).

Studies: Robert Beckford, *Dread and Pentecostal*, London 2000; *Jesus Is Dread*, London 1998; Barry Chevannes, *Rastafari: Roots and Ideology*, Syracuse 1994; Aida Besançon Spencer, Donna F. G. Hailson, Catherine Clark Kroeger, William David Spencer, *The Goddess Revival*, Grand Rapids 1995; William David Spencer, *Dread Jesus*, London 1999; William David Spencer and Aida Besançon Spencer (eds), *God through the Looking Glass: Glimpses from the Arts*, Grand Rapids 1998; Abuna Yesehaq, *The Ethiopian Tewahedo Church*, New York 1989.

WILLIAM DAVID SPENCER

Reader

The word 'reader' is in one sense simply the translation of the Latin term '*lector', but the title has also been used in some Reformation churches. In the Church of Scotland, because of a shortage of qualified ordained ministers at the time of the Reformation, readers were appointed as their assistants, and in the absence of the minister they were authorized to *read* the Sunday service – the scriptural lessons, the prayers, and even a homily. This office continues to the present day. In the Church of England from 1866 onwards men could be designated as 'lay readers' to conduct morning and evening prayer and to preach. Subsequently women were also admitted to the office, and more recently the word 'lay' has been dropped from the title.

EDITOR

Readings, Eucharistic

While we do not know the process that led to the reading of scripture at every *eucharist, it is right that Christ is encountered in both word and *sacrament. The proclamation of scripture is not merely educational but a celebration of the presence of Christ the Word of God. Hence the reading of scripture is often accompanied by ritual action and words, mainly focused on the gospel (see below) as the symbol or *icon of Christ himself. By an almost universal rule only scripture may be read at services. The sole exception in the early church was the acts of martyrs read on their feast days. Liturgical reading is intimately connected with the development of the biblical canon.

The synagogue custom of reading passages of scripture was more than likely continued by the first Christians. The earliest description is in Justin Martyr's account of the Sunday assembly (150 CE), which begins with the reading of the records of the apostles and the writings of the prophets (he is too vague for us to discern any system), followed by the sermon preached by the president of the assembly. The fourth-century *Apostolic Constitutions* speak of readings from the law, the prophets, the NT and the gospel, but commentators differ as to whether this implies three or four readings, or even more. Nor do we know if this pattern was typical or exceptional at the time, but four readings after this pattern have been the practice of the *East Syrian Church to this day. A common pattern evolved of three readings, the OT, the NT reading from the epistles or from Acts or Revelation, and the gospel reading. This was the regular pattern in Constantinople in the seventh century, but the OT reading disappeared by the early eighth century. In Rome likewise the OT reading tended to disappear, leaving the epistle and gospel as the readings in the eucharist through the Middle Ages. But the Gallican rites in the West and the *Armenians in the East preserved three readings.

In the sixteenth century the *RC, *Lutheran and *Anglican rites continued the medieval pattern. The *Reformed rites preferred to have a single lengthy reading which was expounded in the sermon. The late twentieth century saw the reintroduction in the new RC *lectionary of the ancient pattern of three readings in the Sunday eucharist, while retaining a weekday pattern of one reading, from either the OT or NT, before the gospel. This has been widely followed by other Western churches, though in practice three readings have sometimes proved something of a burden and the two-reading system has often persisted.

1. *The Old Testament Reading*. Through the greater extent of the church, apart from a very few instances where it took the place of the epistle, a reading from the OT was not heard at the eucharist from the eighth to the mid-twentieth century. In the West the most important exception was the *Easter vigil, which was based around a series of OT readings. Thus the role of the OT reading in modern lectionaries has been something of a problem which is not yet resolved. It is either ignored or treated as purely prophetic: the promise of the OT fulfilled in the NT. This has several problems: theological, with the status of the OT; educational, with familiarity gained only through public reading at the eucharist (with the demise in many churches of services of the *word); and spiritual, with the religious experience of many, espe-

cially in *Black churches, solidly grounded in the OT.

The 1969 lectionary of the RC Church made three readings obligatory on Sundays and feast days, with the first reading being from the OT (except in the Easter season). This was in fulfilment of Vatican II's desire for a greater and wider reading of scripture in the liturgy. However, unlike the other readings, the OT was generally selected typologically for its relation to the gospel. The ecumenical *Common Lectionary*, based on the RC lectionary, added the alternative of *lectio continua* of the OT in *ordinary time in order to redress this balance, and this has been continued in the more recent *Revised Common Lectionary*.

2. *The New Testament Reading (Epistle)*. The reading from the NT normally comes after the OT in modern eucharistic lectionaries. (In the RC lectionary and the *Revised Common Lectionary* the first reading in the Easter season is also from the NT, from the Acts of the Apostles.) In the early church it was read by a specially appointed *lector, and in the Middle Ages by the *subdeacon. The demise of the separate OT reading from the eighth to the twentieth century led to the reading before the gospel being known generally as 'the epistle' or 'the apostle' even when, on occasions, it was taken from the OT. In the current RC lectionary and the *Revised Common Lectionary* the epistle is generally read by *lectio continua*. In the RC lectionary on weekdays, when only one reading precedes the gospel, it alternates every few weeks between OT and NT books.

3. *The Gospel*. The reading of the gospel is the last of the scripture readings and the climax of the series. In it is seen the presence of Christ the Word of God. Hence great honour is often accorded to the gospel book itself. In the East the *little entrance was originally the solemn entry of the congregation into the church, led by the clergy with the gospel book, and medieval commentaries emphasized the link with Christ. The reading of the gospel was reserved to the *deacon from the fourth century. The book is frequently carried in procession to the place of reading, accompanied by lights and *incense. Traditionally it was read from a *pulpit or *ambo, but often today in the middle of the congregation.

A. G. Martimort (ed.), *The Church at Prayer* II, Collegeville 1986, 59–68, 197–202.

GORDON JEANES

Reformed Worship

The origins of Reformed worship can be traced to the Reformation in Strasbourg under Martin Bucer, in Zurich under Ulrich Zwingli, and in Geneva under John Calvin. The Reformers inherited the worship of the medieval church, and for the most part kept the underlying structure of the *mass. Worship thus had two main elements, word and *sacrament, and it consisted of two movements, listening to the word of God and then responding in the sacrament. But while the pattern of the mass was kept, other features were changed.

In the first place worship was to be corporate in character. Worship was seen as the activity of the whole people of God, not just of the clergy. Instead of taking place in the *chancel of the church, at a distance from the congregation, worship was to be carried out in one part of the building, usually the *nave, where it was visible to all. Churches built after the Reformation would consist of one space, not two, and would often be rectangular in shape with *pulpit and table in a central position. The *eucharist was celebrated from behind the table with the people gathered round either sitting or standing. In some places the congregation sat at long tables which were set up for that purpose. *Communion was received in both bread and wine, and instead of the previous habit of communicating once or twice a year at *Christmas and *Easter, the Reformers wished there to be a much more frequent celebration. In Scotland this desire led to the abolition of Christmas and Easter, but most Reformed churches continued to observe the main festivals of the Christian *year.

In addition, whereas worship had been inaudible and in Latin, it was now to be clearly heard by all in their own language. Ministers led worship and were trained and authorized to preach and administer the sacraments, but participation by the congregation was to be encouraged by the singing of the psalms and other scriptural songs and by corporate prayer. To facilitate this participation service books were produced for use by the worshippers. Thus prayer books, which were rare in the medieval church, were introduced as a result of the Reformation. In some Reformed churches, however, their use was rejected in the seventeenth century when there was a reaction against 'set forms' in worship.

Another important principle of Reformed worship was that it be carried out according to

scripture – not that a strict literalism was enforced, but rather worship was to be based upon scriptural authority and biblical principles. According to Bucer, worship was to be founded on the clear and plain declarations of scripture. It is only the worship which God asks of us which really serves him. God directs us above all to worship him by the proclamation of the word, the celebration of communion, and by prayers and praises.

The systematic reading of scripture (*lectio continua*) was followed by its exposition in a sermon as the basis on which the sacraments were administered. The reformers wished to ensure that preaching did not become separated from the eucharist. The word was needed in order to explain the action which followed, otherwise the sacrament could become surrounded by superstition. Preaching was to be an essential feature of Sunday worship and would also be carried out at services during the week. In addition ministers met regularly for group Bible study and sermon preparation.

The Reformers wished the *Lord's supper to be the other main focus of worship, but they did not achieve the frequency of communion which they desired. The first Reformed service at Strasbourg was the German mass of Diebold Schwarz in 1524, which was simply the Latin eucharist translated into the vernacular with many of the ceremonial elements remaining, and the sacrificial language removed from the prayer of *consecration. Martin Bucer simplified the liturgy, introducing a greater degree of choice in the prayers and a rather didactic exhortation before the communion, which came to be a prominent characteristic of Reformed worship. His intention, however, was clearly to restore a weekly communion, although this was only achieved in the *cathedral. The services in the other churches, however, continued to be based on the pattern of word and sacrament with the prayers of *intercession and the *Lord's Prayer following the sermon.

In Zurich, Zwingli based Sunday worship on the medieval Prone, a service preparatory to high mass which emphasized the place of preaching. It was designed to lead into the celebration of the eucharist, and it may be that Zwingli's intention was that word and sacrament should be seen as complementary. With the establishment of the practice of quarterly communion at Zurich, however, Sunday worship mostly took the form of a preaching service.

John Calvin was influenced by the liturgical

reforms at Strasbourg rather than those at Zurich. At Geneva, however, he was unable to achieve his aim of a weekly communion and had to settle for a quarterly celebration. Yet when communion was not celebrated, the service was an *ante-communion. It consisted of the following elements: call to worship, *confession of sins, declaration of pardon, the commandments in metre with *Kyries, prayer of illumination, scripture reading and sermon, the offering, prayers of intercession and the Lord's Prayer, the Apostles' *Creed, a psalm and the blessing. *Metrical psalms would also be sung at different points during the service. When communion was celebrated, the creed was followed by the *institution narrative from 1 Cor. 11 (read as a warrant for what was to follow) and a lengthy exhortation, warning against unworthy participation and encouraging the faithful to communicate. This finished with a Sursum corda in which the worshippers were urged: 'let us lift our spirits and hearts on high where Jesus Christ is in the glory of his Father' so that our souls be 'nourished and vivified by his substance'. There then followed the breaking of the bread and the administration of the elements. The service concluded with a brief prayer of thanksgiving, the singing of the Nunc dimittis, and the Aaronic blessing. There was thus no prayer of consecration as such and Calvin's high eucharistic doctrine, of spiritual feeding on Christ by the Holy Spirit, was not given full liturgical expression. This has meant that at the popular level the tendency has been to view the sacrament in purely symbolic terms. In addition, the practical difficulties of achieving more frequent communion have resulted in Reformed worship being characterized by the sermon rather than by word and sacrament together.

Selected texts: William D. Maxwell, *The Liturgical Portions of the Genevan Service Book*, London 1931; Bard Thomson (ed.), *Liturgies of the Western Church*, Cleveland 1962.

Studies: John M. Barkley, *The Worship of the Reformed Church*, London 1966; Duncan B. Forrester and Douglas M. Murray (eds), *Studies in the History of Worship in Scotland*, 2nd edn, Edinburgh 1996; Howard G. Hageman, *Pulpit and Table*, London 1962; Alasdair Heron, *Table and Tradition*, Edinburgh 1983; Hughes Oliphant Old, *Worship That Is Reformed According to Scripture*, Atlanta 1984.

DOUGLAS M. MURRAY

Remembrance Sunday

The cessation of hostilities ending World War I took place at eleven o'clock on the eleventh day of the eleventh month in 1918. This memorable time and date immediately came to be observed annually in those countries which had been at war and was known as 'Armistice Day', even though the official peace treaty was not signed until a much later date. Local commemorations usually took place at the war memorials which became an architectural feature of most towns and villages, and involved the Royal British Legion and other ex-service organizations. In Britain the ceremony inevitably included the sounding of the Last Post and Reveille, the laying of poppy wreaths and a two-minute silence, the last first suggested by Sir Percy Fitzpatrick, a South African, as late in the day as October 1919. After World War II the commemoration of the fallen of both wars was transferred to a Sunday, in Britain the Sunday nearest to 11 November. But in recent years there has been a strong movement which has resulted in a return to some observance of the actual 1918 time and day in addition.

In 1968 one of the earliest ecumenically agreed forms of service commended by the Archbishops of Canterbury, Wales, Westminster and York together with the Moderator of the Free Church Federal Council was for use on Remembrance Sunday. A revision is being contemplated. It will need to reflect changing attitudes to remembrance, which wish to transform remembrance of the past into hope for the future.

In the United States 11 November is now known as 'Veterans' Day'. Memorial Day (the last Monday in May) together with Veterans' Day have now more prominence than Remembrance Day, while in Australia and New Zealand ANZAC Day (25 April) is more widely observed than the November day.

A Service for Remembrance Sunday, London 1968, 1984; Owen Chadwick, 'Armistice Day', *Theology* LXXIX, 1976, 322–9; Alan Wilkinson, *The Church of England and the First World War*, London 1978.

DONALD GRAY

Renewal of Baptismal Vows

see **Baptismal Vows, Renewal of**

Requiem Mass

In the Western Catholic tradition, a *mass

offered for the repose of the dead. The name is derived from the first words of the introit (*Requiem aeternam dona eis Domine*), which, until the liturgical reforms of Vatican II, was the *proper entrance *antiphon of all such masses. The requiem became the normative funeral mass for adults in the Tridentine *Missale Romanum* (1570) and characterized the RC *funeral liturgy until the revised missal of Paul VI (1970). The requiem mass is now called the 'funeral mass', or simply the 'mass for the dead' when celebrated apart from the 'Order of Christian Funerals' (1989).

The *Roman Missal* (1970), which contains a complete revision of 'masses for the dead', provides four formulas for the funeral mass and five formulas for the anniversary mass. Both categories include texts for use during and outside of the *Easter season. There are five formulas for various commemorations and fourteen formulas of various prayers for the dead, i.e., for a priest, a married couple, a young person, one who suffered a long illness, parents, etc. Finally, the missal contains five *prefaces for Christian death and a variety of scriptural readings in the *lectionary.

In accord with *General Instruction of the Roman Missal*, funeral masses may be celebrated on all days except solemnities which are holy days, Sundays of *Advent, *Lent or Easter, on *Maundy Thursday and the Easter Triduum. Masses on the occasion of news of death, final burial, or the first anniversary may be celebrated on days within the *Christmas *octave, on obligatory memorials, and on *ferias, except *Ash Wednesday and during *Holy Week. Daily mass for the dead is permitted on ferias and optional memorials whenever *votive masses are allowed. This mass should not be used frequently since every mass is offered for the living and dead, and the *eucharistic prayer makes the remembrance of the faithful departed clearly prominent.

J. A. Jungmann, *The Mass of the Roman Rite*, New York 1951, 219, 295, 488; Richard Rutherford, *The Death of a Christian: The Rite of Funerals*, New York 1980, 27ff., 56–9.

JOSEPH WEISS

Reredos

A decorative screen of stone or wood or a hanging of velvet or silk, covering the wall behind an *altar and extending the length of the altar or beyond it on each side. It is sometimes held that

a reredos rises from the floor behind the altar and differs from a retable, which is a shelf with ornaments or a frame with decorative panels behind and above the altar. An elaborately carved reredos or retable or one containing a painting may also be described as an altarpiece.

In medieval England reredoses in parish churches were not generally very high, rising to under a metre above the altar. They were frequently made of alabaster in five panels with a crucifixion in the central panel. Most were destroyed or badly damaged at the Reformation. They returned under the Stuarts, and post-Restoration examples, especially in London's City churches, are 'evocative of the confident splendour of triumphant Anglicanism'. Among Corinthian columns, broken pediments, cherubim and garlands they set above and behind the altars the texts of the *Lord's Prayer, Ten Commandments and Apostles' *Creed.

A different approach was taken on the Continent of Europe and the altarpiece became a significant artistic genre. In Italy the altarpieces progressed from Gothic multiple images framed together to Renaissance single scenes enclosed between classical pilasters. The section immediately above the altar had a series of small images and was known as the *predella*. In Germany and the Netherlands the late medieval altarpiece was frequently wooden, with carved images in niches, often portraying elaborate scenes from the life of Christ or of the Virgin Mary. Such altarpieces were often triptychs that could be folded in *Lent with the exterior depicting monochromatic saints. In the vast baroque structures of seventeenth-century Spain (and Spanish South America) and Italy the east wall is taken up by a towering architectural edifice with statues and cherubs and six or more tall candlesticks dwarfing the altar.

For European development: Eve Borsook and Fiorelli Superbi Gioffredi (eds), *Italian Altarpieces 1250–1550*, Oxford 1994; and Peter Humfrey and Martin Kemp (eds), *The Altarpiece in the Renaissance*, Cambridge 1990. For England: Gerald Randall, *Church Furnishings in England and Wales*, London 1980.

MARTIN DUDLEY

Reservation

1. *Origins.* In the earliest description of the *eucharist to come down to us, Justin Martyr (*c.* 155) tells how at the end of the Sunday celebration *deacons took the eucharistic ele-

ments to those who were unable to be present (presumably including the *sick). In the third century Tertullian, Hippolytus, Novatian and Cyprian all testify to the practice of taking the elements home from the Sunday liturgy to communicate oneself on weekdays when there was no liturgical assembly, and where no doubt they would be available for the use of the sick and the dying. The practice declined considerably after the fourth century as the eucharist came to be celebrated daily, at least in the cities, to meet the pastoral needs of an expanding urban community. But that it still survived into seventh-century England can be seen from the writings of Bede. It seems that the *sacrament must have been reserved in both kinds, at least in some places, since the sick were often given *communion by intinction. The practice is not heard of in the West after the twelfth century.

Alongside domestic reservation, the sacrament was also reserved in churches for *viaticum (and at Rome for inclusion in the next celebration of the pope's *mass, where it was known as the *sancta*). From the ninth century the practice became general. At first it had been in a simple box (*capsa*), then in a more elaborate *pyx, casket or 'propitiatory', usually kept in the *sacristy. But in the early Middle Ages the place of reservation came closer to the *altar. The Fourth Lateran Council (1215) required the sacrament to be kept in safe custody under lock and key, but did not specify a method. In England and France a hanging pyx (sometimes in the form of a dove) was often used; in Scotland, Scandinavia, Portugal and parts of Italy it was more often an *aumbry; in Germany and the Low Countries most commonly a sacrament-house (an elaborate freestanding tower).

2. *Western Cult*. There is little evidence of any devotional cult of the eucharistic elements outside the liturgy before Carolingian times. But within the celebration gestures of reverence and adoration began to appear at the invitation to communion ('Holy things for holy people') from the fourth century in the East, also in the Gallican and Ambrosian rites in the West, and at the elevation which concluded the *eucharistic prayer at Rome (seventh century). The eucharistic controversies of the ninth century in the West, and the triumph of the realist school of interpretation, did not lead immediately to the extra-liturgical veneration of the elements, but did hasten a number of developments which

indicated a new type of eucharistic piety and a shift of interest and emphasis from the dynamic to the static presence of Christ. Thus, alongside communion given directly into the mouth, unleavened bread, the progressive distancing of the laity from the *chalice, the giving of communion after or outside mass, private masses and the intrusion of private devotions into the mass liturgy, we also find instances of consecrated *hosts being sealed into altars in the manner of relics.

But it seems to have been in the communion of the sick that special signs of reverence to the reserved sacrament first appeared. In England, the tenth-century *Regularis concordia* describes a solemn *procession to the sick with the reserved sacrament, and a century later Lanfranc's *Monastic Constitutions* prescribe *incensations, genuflections and a perpetually burning lamp. The same two sources enable us to see the evolution of the traditional *Palm Sunday procession into a solemn procession with the sacrament, and the gestures of reverence previously accorded to cult objects like the *cross and the gospel-book are now transferred to the eucharistic elements. At the same time a comparable development took place all over Europe in the burial originally of a cross but now of the eucharistic host in the *Easter sepulchre on *Good Friday to be solemnly brought forth on Easter morning. In all these trends, the sacrament could be seen less as something to be eaten and drunk, more as a cult object to be venerated for its own sake outside the context of the mass.

Further theological controversies in the eleventh and twelfth centuries about the nature of eucharistic change and the moment of consecration seem to have led directly to the custom of elevating the elements after the *institution narrative in the eucharistic prayer (first decreed by Eudes de Sully, Archbishop of Paris, *c.* 1200). From this developed in turn the devotion of *exposition.

Devotional 'visits' to the reserved sacrament seem to have originated in the priest's private salutation of the elements before communion (eleventh century), which the people subsequently adopted as a greeting of the Lord after the introduction of the new elevation (early thirteenth century), and which was then extended to periods of adoration outside the liturgical celebration, probably by religious communities and contemplatives (thirteenth century, e.g. in England, the *Ancrene Riwle*).

After the Council of Trent (mid-sixteenth

century), the sacrament was increasingly reserved in a fixed *tabernacle placed on the altar itself. This innovation has been attributed to the reforming Italian bishops Matteo Giberti (d. 1543) and especially St Charles Borromeo (d. 1584). The Roman Ritual of 1614 encouraged this development, but at least in major churches the altar in question would not have been the principal altar. It was only Baroque piety and architecture which finally installed the tabernacle at the centre of the principal altar and made it the pre-eminent visual focus of the entire building. (So much did the tabernacle become wedded to the altar that from the seventeenth century onwards even side-altars were each designed with an integral tabernacle, even though few of them could ever have been used.)

3. *Current Roman Rite*. In the recently revised Roman rite it is stressed that 'the primary and original reason for the reservation of the eucharist outside mass is the administration of viaticum. The secondary reasons are the giving of communion and adoration of the Lord present in the sacrament.' Because of the nature and dynamics of the eucharistic celebration, the sacrament should no longer be reserved on an altar where mass is celebrated but elsewhere in the church in a worthy location suitable for private adoration and prayer. The tabernacle should be solid, fixed and opaque, and there should normally be only one in a church, covered by a *veil or otherwise suitably decorated, and indicated by a lamp.

While communion may be given outside mass for good reasons and according to a special rite, it should never normally be distributed from the tabernacle during mass. The Council of Trent had called for communion as the normal conclusion of the eucharistic sacrifice for all the faithful, and since the eighteenth century various popes, the Sacred Congregation of Rites, the Second Vatican Council and the revised liturgical books have all insisted that the congregation should receive elements consecrated during the same celebration and not on some previous occasion. Only a small quantity of consecrated elements, therefore, needs to be kept in the tabernacle as a reserve or 'float'. The one occasion in the year in the Roman rite when communion is universally and mandatorily given outside the celebration of mass is on Good Friday, when the solemn afternoon liturgy concludes with a communion service with bread consecrated at the mass of the *Lord's supper the previous evening and reserved overnight at a separate 'altar of repose' where the faithful watched in prayer until midnight.

4. *Other Traditions*. This practice, known as the 'liturgy of the *pre-sanctified', is much more widespread in the Byzantine, Maronite and Syrian Catholic traditions. It originated probably in Antioch, and is best known in the Byzantine rite where during *Lent the full eucharist is celebrated only on Saturdays and Sundays; on other days the reserved sacrament is brought in solemn procession to the altar during vespers and is distributed after veneration and after a portion has been mixed with a chalice of unconsecrated wine. But apart from the reverence shown to the reserved sacrament during this liturgy and during communion of the sick, the sacrament is otherwise kept without ceremony and inaccessible to the faithful in an annexe of the *sanctuary, usually in the care of deacons. The marks of reverence which in the West are shown to the reserved sacrament tend rather to be addressed to the altar itself and to the icons. The Copts and the Ethiopians generally do not practise reservation at all.

In many churches of the Anglican Communion, reservation (most often in an aumbry) is fairly widely practised, and in recently revised liturgical books it is increasingly provided for in rites and *rubrics. For *Maundy Thursday reservation, the English rubrics stipulate a 'safe and seemly place', the American a separate *chapel or place apart from the sanctuary. For communion of the sick, the revised English rite includes a declaration emphasizing its direct derivation from a celebration of the eucharist.

Archdale King and Cyril Pocknee, *Eucharistic Reservation in the Western Church*, London 1965; Nathan Mitchell, *Cult and Controversy: The Worship of the Eucharist outside Mass*, New York 1982.

CHRISTOPHER WALSH

Responsorial Psalm

In modern liturgies, a specified psalm (or extract of a psalm) recited or sung in response to the first reading at the *eucharist. It therefore occupies the place allocated in the Latin *mass by the gradual, and is sometimes known as the gradual psalm. When singing the psalm it is usual for the whole assembly to sing a refrain before the psalm and after each verse (or pair of verses), and for one or more *cantors to sing the text of the psalm. Such performance practice has erroneously led some to identify the refrain as the response to the psalm text, rather than the whole psalm as response to the reading.

See also **Chants of the Proper of the Mass; Psalmody**.

JOHN HARPER

Responsory or Respond

A text sung in response to a reading in the *daily prayer office. It may be *proper, seasonal, common or *ferial. There are several patterns, depending on the particular monastic or diocesan use and on the specific liturgical occasion, but a common pattern consists of: refrain; psalm verse; part of refrain; first half of the Gloria Patri; whole or part of refrain. In the Latin office the musical treatment of the responsory changed according to the service. Where there was only a short reading or 'chapter', there was a standard simple melodic formula. By contrast, the responsories sung after the lessons at the night office represent some of the richest and most elaborate chant in the whole Western repertory, including the famous *tenebrae responsories sung at matins in *Holy Week. *Polyphonic and solo settings of responsories were composed from the sixteenth century onwards. Some responsories became detached and were used in liturgical *processions. Responsories are included in the modern RC office, and in some of the new orders of daily prayer in the Lutheran and Anglican churches.

See also **Psalmody**.

'Responsory', *NG2*, XXI, 221–8; David Hiley, *Western Plainchant: A Handbook*, Oxford 1993.

JOHN HARPER

Retable see Reredos

Riddel (also Ridle, Ridel, Ridle or Riddell)

A curtain, from the medieval Latin *ridellus* or *redellus* and the French *rideau*. Riddels, part of the *altar hangings, are curtains hanging close to the ends of an altar on metal rods which either project at right angles from the wall behind the altar or are supported on two or four pillars (riddel posts) placed near the four corners of the altar. The ends of the rods fre-quently held prickets for candles. The posts were often surmounted by figures of angels holding candles. The architect Sir Ninian Comper reintroduced them in the twentieth century.

MARTIN DUDLEY

Rite, Ritual

1. *Definitions*. In classical Latin, *ritus* (ordinarily in the plural) means 'religious observances' or 'familiar forms of ceremonies'. Key connotations attached to *ritus* are custom, habit, repetition, tradition, the 'correct way of behaving' within ceremonial contexts. Thus the Latin adverb *rite* signifies religious acts that are done *properly*, according to the rules, in a manner that is right, just, fitting, suitable. From such roots come the common meanings of the English 'rite': (a) repeated, ceremonial activity governed by fixed rules; (b) the outward form that '*cult' (understood as service – of a human ruler, of God, of a religious sanctuary) takes. Rite is thus behaviour deliberately distinguished from 'ordinary deeds' by its normative, regulatory and repetitive character, while ritual is a more inclusive term that includes multiple genres (speech, song, movement, dance, drama, mime). In short, ritual is the 'general idea' of which rite is a specific instance.

2. *Distinctions: Rite, Decorum, Ceremony.* Rite must be distinguished, moreover, from related notions such as 'decorum' and 'ceremony'. Decorum is a conventionalized mode of ritual that comes into play whenever human beings engage in 'face-to-face' behaviour. Thus, decorum deals with socially sanctioned (hence, 'obligatory') forms of human interaction, but does not claim any 'cosmic' or 'ultimate' significance. Decorum, for example, requires one to bow or curtsy when greeting a monarch; it obliges spouses to kiss in the morning before parting for the day, partners to shake hands when concluding a business deal, strangers to avert their gaze when riding on the same elevator. Failure to honour decorum's obligatory observances results in social penalty, shunning and embarrassment – even if the effects are negligible and short-lived. Note, further, that decorum reflects specific cultural customs and mores. To belch loudly after eating dinner is considered indecorous in some cultures, but is expected as a sign of satisfaction and appreciation in others.

The ritual transactions of a liturgy, however, are usually freighted with meanings that transcend the immediate social or cultural order. A rite's rules (unlike the rules of decorum) imply sanctions based on cosmic meanings, ultimate reality, transcendent frames of reference. Still, it is true that remnants of the rules of decorum may continue forming a layer within complex ritual structures, long after the originating social or cultural context has disappeared. Thus, for example, many features of Byzantine court etiquette found their way into the liturgy of the Roman *eucharist (especially in the seventh and eighth centuries) – practices such as kissing ritual objects (the book, the *chalice and paten) before handing them to the presiding prelate. These regulating remnants (which once governed face-to-face behaviour in the imperial household) continued to form a sandwiched layer of 'decorum' within ecclesiastical rites well into modern times.

Similarly, ceremony has 'legal, tribal, or racial import; it includes gestures such as standing for a national anthem, wearing a tribal lip disc, or bearing a clan's coat of arms into battle. The distinction between decorum and ceremony hinges largely on the differences between face-to-face and large-group, political interaction' (Grimes, *Beginnings in Ritual Studies*, 41). Decorum's importance is historically fluid: its status is 'unofficial', its rules are defined by etiquette books, and its observance may become optional. In contrast, ceremony possesses imperative force; it asks participants to surrender a significant degree of personal preference and freedom for the sake of some 'greater cause' that commands allegiance, loyalty and homage. Central to ceremony, in most cases, is the display of power for the sake of its veneration by the public. Thus, for example, the ceremonies that surround the opening of Parliament or those that govern the raising and saluting of the nation's flag by a military unit are designed both to display and to reinforce socio-political (and sometimes, religious) power and those who possess it.

Because of its symbolic connection to power, ceremony may be understood as a ritual strategy aimed at social control. While it is true that virtually all forms of ritualization are strategies that construct limited (and limiting) power relationships between people, liturgy's connection to power is more comprehensive than ceremony's is. Liturgical power – the power of *rites* – is not about social control or coercion, but about *receptivity*. Liturgical rites create in participants an expectant 'waiting upon' power – power that comes from another (ultimately, a divine) source. In liturgy, worshippers speak in the 'passive voice'; they do not try to wield or wrest, seize or hold, power *for* themselves or *over* others.

3. *Rite and Myth*. The relationship between rite and myth has been reinterpreted by contemporary scholars. It was long assumed that myth is a 'sacred narrative' (words, story) that accompanies ritual deeds; but this view tends to reduce myth to *text*. Today, many scholars see myth as a 'sub-unit' of ritual performance itself. In short, myths are not texts divorced from ritual or social action. Anyone who has ever experienced a myth performed in its proper cultural context knows instantly that it is not only a pattern of words but a sequence of non-verbal codes as well: mime, gesture, singing, drawing, innuendo (cued by voice inflections), etc. Indeed, myth's multiple layers of meaning can be accessed only within a ritual context – as embodied performance rather than simple 'story'.

Moreover, myths deal not simply with 'sacred origins' but, more importantly, with *transitions*. Myths tell how one situation or state of affairs became another – how, for example, chaos became cosmos; how a barren couple became parents; how 'no' people became 'a' people. The context that interprets the significance of these mythic transitions is, however, cultic. Thus myth is not simply a linguistic or cognitive structure aimed at validating an existing social order (e.g. by explaining its origins or relating it to the will of the gods), it is also a ritual performance involving an interplay of language, imagery, music and gesture.

4. *Rite as a Limited, Technical Term*. Within Christianity, 'rite' has also acquired a more limited, technical meaning. It is used to designate the specific Christian liturgical tradition to which one belongs, e.g. the Roman (Latin) rite, the Byzantine rite, the Anglican rite, the Ethiopian rite, etc. Each 'rite' (or 'ritual family') is characterized by distinctive liturgical practices and variations, especially in the celebration of the eucharist. (In the Byzantine family of liturgical rites, for example, the *kiss of peace is exchanged before the beginning of the *eucharistic prayer; in the Roman rite, it follows the *Lord's Prayer and precedes the *communion.) Scholars some-

times further subdivide the Roman rite by noting distinctive forms practised by religious orders, such as the 'Dominican rite', the liturgy of the mendicant Order of Preachers, prescribed by Humbert de Romanis in 1259.

5. *Models*. In the twentieth century, particularly, 'rite' and 'ritual' came under close scrutiny by *social scientists. Anthropologists (e.g. Mary Douglas, Clifford Geertz, Victor Turner), sociologists (e.g. Robert Bellah) and psychologists (e.g. Erik Erikson) sought to identify the roots of ritual and to assess the ways it shapes human behaviour, religious ceremony and Christian liturgy. As a result, several models for ritual studies have emerged. These may be outlined as follows:

(a) The 'classical' model. This model sees religious ritual as communal action linked to socially mediated structures of authority, tradition and worship. Rites provide religious groups (like the Christian churches) with a cultic (liturgical) means of rehearsing, reviewing and renewing their traditions (beliefs, meanings, values) for the sake of insuring social cohesion and survival. Ritual, in this view, is normative, prescribed, formal, symbolic, invariable, repeated behaviour closely linked to the ontogenetic development of the human person; it is neither obsessive neurosis nor a spontaneous 'happening'. Individuals or groups may sometimes devise new rituals, but normative religious rites are best described as public, social and collective occasions rather than personal, private or solitary ones. Ritual's primary purpose is thus to transmit – through speech, song, symbol and gesture – the religious traditions embodied in creed and celebrated in cult. Rituals preserve and represent archaic acts, ancestral memories that give the community access to its own history; hence, a community without rites is a community without memory. In short, ritual is essentially a way to regulate the social life of religious groups, to shape personal and corporate identity, to review and renew values, to express and transmit meaning in symbolic word and deed, to preserve tradition, and to insure social cohesion and continuity.

(b) The 'process' model. In contrast to the classical view, this model holds that since ritual is precisely a cultural and historical *process*, it is characterized to a high degree by creativity and change, innovation and variability. Ritual is neither a cultural museum, nor a repository, passive and inert, of past traditions; it erupts spontaneously, especially on society's margins (rather than among its power-brokers). Seen in this light, rites serve not so much to reinforce and formalize tradition, but to revise, redefine or reinterpret a group's beliefs, meanings and values. Rites thus become potent agents of social and religious change; their goal is not the preservation of the past, but change – the critical re-evaluation of what and how a community believes. Rather than reinforcing 'social identity and cohesion', ritual promotes conversion, a new understanding of religious truths and tasks.

Because rituals are always embodied; because the body itself is cognitive (i.e., can gain, give and process knowledge); and because ritual's meanings unfold within the rites themselves (i.e., are not imposed or imported without), one must speak of ritual's inherent *inventiveness*. Hence, 'emerging rituals' – which often arise among politically, socially or religiously disenfranchised people – do not rely, for their power, on a set of 'codes' (authorized meanings, references) that lies beyond the ritual performance itself. Rituals are 'meaningful' not because of what they 'refer to' but because of what they *do*. A ritual is a score to be performed rather than a 'meaning' to be grasped and preserved.

(c) The 'technology' model. This model argues that ritual is *not* primarily a coded symbol system that produces religious meanings (transmitted through symbols and known only to initiates); instead, it is a technology (i.e., an acquired aptitude, an embodied skill) that seeks to produce a 'virtuous self'. The aim of a hospitality ritual, for example, is not to produce hospitable meanings or thoughts but hospitable people. Ritual is thus embodied practice, rehearsal, routine – an apt performance that does not require 'decoding'. Together, rituals form a 'technology of the self' whose aim is not the preservation of a past identity but the formation of a *new* one. What is 'produced' in ritual is not 'meaning', but a new self.

(d) The 'biogenetic' model. This model holds that ritual behaviour is genetically hardwired into the human species. Ritual is less technological 'practice' than 'meta-praxis', i.e., a way of doing which comments upon and assigns meaning to all other human ways of doing. Biogeneticists see rite as an attempt to resolve problems that myths (sacred stories, narratives in cultic context) pose to the analytical, verbalizing consciousness – an attempt, that is, to control the world of events and situations by means of *motor activity* (ritualizing) that involves repeated visual and auditory stimuli, kinetic rhythms, and other 'triggers' that reach far back into our phylogenetic past.

Talal Asad, *Genealogies of Religion*, Baltimore 1993; Catherine Bell, *Ritual: Perspectives and Dimensions*, New York 1997; Mary Douglas, *Natural Symbols: Explorations in Cosmology*, new edn, New York 1982; Ronald Grimes, *Beginnings in Ritual Studies*, New York 1982; Nathan D. Mitchell, *Liturgy and the Social Sciences*, Collegeville 1999; Victor Turner, *The Ritual Process: Structure and Anti-Structure*, Chicago 1969.

NATHAN MITCHELL

Rochet *see* Vestments 3(a)

Rogation Days

From the Latin *rogare*, to ask, days of prayer involving *processions and fasting associated with *intercession for agriculture. The Major Rogation was observed on 25 April and replaced a Roman agricultural procession honouring a deity invoked to protect the crops from mildew. The Minor Rogations on the three days before *Ascension Day derived from processional *litanies used in Gaul during a period of volcanic eruptions in the fifth century. In the Missal of 1570 the same texts were used for all Rogation Days with a *mass being said after the litanies of the saints had been sung in procession. In England Rogation Days were known as 'Gang Days' from the Old Norse *gangr,* meaning walking. On these days the clergy and people progressed through the fields carrying *crosses and green branches and making a number of stations at the parish boundaries with readings and prayers. Place names such as Gospel Oak and Amen Corner recall these stations. Abolished in 1547, the perambulation of the parish before Ascension Day was restored by Elizabeth I in 1559 both to define the parish boundaries and to give thanks to God for the fruits of the earth or, in times of dearth, to intercede with him. Rogation Days are maintained in the 1662 *BCP* and in *Common Worship* (2000) on the three days before Ascension Day 'when prayer is offered for God's blessing on the fruits of the earth and on human labour'. In the RC Church the days were replaced in 1969 by periods of prayer to be determined by the local bishops' conference.

MARTIN DUDLEY

Roman Catholic Worship

The phrase 'Roman Catholic Worship' is capable of several interpretations. For the purposes of this entry it will be understood as: first the origins and development of the Roman rite and second, more precisely as that branch of Western liturgy practised by RCs since the Reformation.

1. *Origins and Development of the Roman Rite*. A distinctive liturgical tradition in the Latin language at Rome appears only in the fourth century with references in the sermons of Ambrose of Milan. With the building of churches and the development of an annual calendar, what we know as the Roman rite begins to appear in the fifth and sixth centuries, especially with the collection of prayers for the *eucharist known as the Verona or Leonine Sacramentary, actually a collection of *libelli* (pamphlets) for use by *celebrants, as well as the 'Letter of John the Deacon' on *baptism. A letter of Pope Innocent I (to Decentius of Gubbio in 416) indicates that three types of liturgy were celebrated in the city of Rome. The first was the *papal liturgy that took place at various churches (*stationes*) in the liturgical cycle. The second was the liturgy presided over by *presbyters in the neighbourhood churches (*tituli*). The third type of liturgy took place in the shrine churches (tombs of the martyrs) outside the walls of the city. Innocent tells of the fragments of consecrated eucharistic bread (*fermentum*) being shared from the papal liturgy with the other churches within the city walls.

Other major documents of the Roman rite in late antiquity include the Gelasian Sacramentary, a book for the celebrant of the liturgy, much of which originated in the presbyteral churches of Rome as well as surrounding dioceses in the sixth century. Manuscripts from this tradition were imported north of the Alps in the seventh and eighth centuries and eventually helped to make up the Roman rite as it returned from the north in the tenth century. In addition to the Gelasian, the Roman rite also consisted of the Gregorian Sacramentary tradition, the celebrant's book for the papal liturgy. When the northerners wished to copy the Roman rite they ended up working with manuscripts from the various traditions and creating their own hybrids. A final source for the Roman rite consists of orders of service (*ordines*) which were collected north of the Alps but meant to describe the liturgy of Rome itself.

In the tenth century, with the Roman monasteries at a very low ebb, liturgical books were reimported from the north. But now they consisted of hybrid documents that contained material from elsewhere in medieval Europe, not simply from the tradition of the city of Rome. Thus what eventually became the Roman rite was the result of a considerable amount of the sharing of various Western European liturgical traditions.

In addition the medieval rite of the papal court, which represented the hybrid Romano-Frankish liturgy, became widespread through the agency of the Franciscans in the thirteenth century. It was this liturgy that served as the foundation for the first printed books of the Roman rite after the Council of Trent.

2. *Trent and After*. In the aftermath of the Council of Trent (1545–63) RC worship can be generally characterized by several factors: retention of the Latin language, withholding of the eucharistic cup from the laity, centrality of eucharistic devotion to the reserved sacrament (*exposition, *benediction), devotion to the *saints (novenas and other extra-liturgical devotions) and especially the Virgin Mary (the *rosary, many feast days), and a concern with *rubrical directions.

Florid *polyphonic music and elaborate architecture, meant to focus the eye on the *altar which housed a *tabernacle for the reserved sacrament, not to mention elaborate confessional boxes for sacramental *confession, were also characteristic of post-Tridentine worship. The invention of movable print in the fifteenth century now made it possible to make liturgical books uniform. Between 1568 (Breviary) and 1614 (Ritual), all the books of the Roman rite were revised. Only rites that had been in existence more than two hundred years were allowed to continue after the Council of Trent.

Some efforts were made, however, to reform RC worship prior to the reform of the late twentieth century. The eighteenth-century Enlightenment saw efforts in France (Neo-Gallicanism) and German-speaking areas to streamline and rationalize the Roman liturgy. Of particular note is the Synod of Pistoia, a Tuscan city, held under Bishop Scipione de'

Ricci in 1786. The reforms mandated by Pistoia (use of the people's language, one altar in each church and only one eucharist on a Sunday, etc.) were quickly condemned by the Roman authorities. Liturgically the most significant event in RC worship in the nineteenth century was the revival of monasticism in France by Prosper Guéranger (1805–75) at the Abbey of Solesmes. Guéranger's intent was to restore the liturgy of the Roman rite in the face of Neo-Gallicanism and especially to restore *Gregorian chant.

Biblical, patristic and other liturgical-historical studies combined to inspire a pastoral *Liturgical Movement in the twentieth century. Beginning with the encouragement of Gregorian chant (1903) and frequent *communion (1910) by Pope Pius X, the movement spread through Europe and eventually the USA. Pope Pius XII issued a significant encyclical letter, commending the Liturgical Movement in general in 1947 (*Mediator Dei*).

3. *Modern Liturgical Reforms*. The Second Vatican Council (1962–5) signalled a sea-change in RC worship. With its Constitution on the Liturgy (*Sacrosanctum concilium*) of 3 December 1963, the Council opened the way for widespread and thoroughgoing reform. Under the post-conciliar Consilium for the Implementation of the Constitution on the Liturgy every rite was revised in Latin and provisions were made for translation into the various modern languages. The first rite to be issued was that of *ordinations (1968) and the last were the Book of *Blessings and the Ceremonial of Bishops (1984). Most significant, of course, was the publication of the Roman Missal, in two books: Sacramentary and *Lectionary, in 1970.

Some RCs have reacted negatively to the reform and insist on the pre-conciliar rites (not to mention theology and piety). They have been granted permission by John Paul II in 1988 (*Ecclesia Dei*) to maintain these rites in Latin. Various groups have been organized to do so.

The reform has been characterized by several significant principles: intelligibility of the liturgy by means of language understood by the people, the removal of encumbrances caused by accidental historical accretions, appropriate cultural adaptation, and most of all the full, conscious and active participation of the people. Among the most significant changes in RC worship in the years of the post-Vatican II reform are the rearrangement of the architecture of churches to allow for free-standing altars and greater visual access to liturgical action as well as the composition of vernacular liturgical music.

With over thirty years of experience the various liturgical books are being issued in revised editions. The responsibility for the preparation of these books lies with the Vatican's Congregation for Divine Worship and the Discipline of the Sacraments. The various national conferences of RC bishops translate and prepare the texts for Vatican approval. In the case of English (International Commission on English in the Liturgy – ICEL), French (Commission Internationale Française pour la Traduction de la Liturgie – CIFTL) and German (Internationale Arbeitsgemeinschaft – IAG), a number of nations have formed mixed commissions to do this work. In addition the work of liturgical adaptation or *inculturation, especially with regard to neglected popular piety and devotion, proceeds apace.

See also **Books, Liturgical** 3.

For a comprehensive historical survey of the subject since the Reformation: James F. White, *Roman Catholic Worship: Trent to Today*, New York 1995. For the beginnings: Gordon Jeanes, *The Origins of the Roman Rite*, 2 vols, Nottingham 1991 and Cambridge 1998. For the medieval development: Cyrille Vogel, *Medieval Liturgy: Introduction to the Sources*, Washington, DC 1986; S. J. P. van Dijk and Joan Hazelden Walker, *The Origins of the Modern Roman Liturgy*, Westminster, MD 1960. For the story of the modern reform, Annibale Bugnini, *The Reform of the Liturgy 1948–1975*, Collegeville 1990. For the documentation of the modern reform: *Documents of the Liturgy 1963–1979*, Collegeville 1980; David Lysik (ed.), *The Liturgy Documents, Volume Two*, Chicago 1999.

JOHN F. BALDOVIN

Rosary

The name normally refers to a pious Christian exercise which involves bodily, vocal and mental prayer (fingers, lips, minds). It combines repetition of familiar prayers in mantra fashion with meditation on selected mysteries of salvation. The prayers used are fifteen 'decades' (tens) of 'Hail Mary', each decade preceded by an 'Our Father' and concluded by a 'Glory be'. The fifteen 'mysteries' or topics of meditation are grouped in series of five (which are usually prayed separately): the joyful mysteries (annunciation, visitation, nativity, presentation, finding in the Temple), the sorrowful mysteries (agony, scourging, crowning with thorns, carrying the cross, death on the cross), the glorious mysteries (resurrection, ascension, descent of the Spirit, assumption of the Virgin Mary, crowning of Mary and glory of all saints). The origin of the devotion has long been popularly associated with St Dominic (d. 1221), whose order has certainly done most to propagate it, but the attribution is unsustainable. The origins are in fact very obscure, but seem to involve a gradual coalescence of christological and Marian devotions from the twelfth century onwards.

In an effort to make the benefits of the liturgy more accessible, the laity were encouraged to resort to the 'poor man's psalter' propagated by Irish missionaries in the early Middle Ages, that is, the recitation of the *Lord's Prayer (Pater noster)* 150 times, often in blocks of fifty, as a substitute for the psalms. Strings of beads, known as 'paternosters', were used to count off these prayers. A slightly later development seems to have been the parallel practice of 'Our Lady's psalter'; in England there are examples from St Anselm and Stephen Langton consisting of 150 quatrains beginning with the word *Ave* and applying to Mary a theme from each psalm in turn. Elsewhere it consisted of 150 'Hail Marys' (only the first half of the present formula) recited in blocks of ten or fifty, often with a genuflection for each. St Louis, King of France, observed this devotion daily, and in 1440 the statutes of Eton College (England) required the pupils to recite it daily.

The first clear evidence for the association of specific meditations with the recitation of the rosary comes from the fifteenth-century Carthusian, Dominic of Prussia, who added short scriptural verses to the 'Jesus' of each 'Hail Mary' (a tradition which persists to this day in the German use of the rosary). In the same century the Breton Dominican, Alain de la Roche, recommended that the three groups of fifty 'Hail Marys' be said in honour of the incarnation, passion and glorification of Christ respectively. Through the establishment of rosary confraternities (1475 onwards) and the diffusion of books with methods of praying the rosary, he did perhaps more than anyone to propagate and popularize the devotion.

The precise subjects of the fifteen mysteries that have come down to us seem to have been popularized in a series of woodcuts from German Dominican circles in the late fifteenth century. They constitute a comprehensive digest of the main events of salvation history, and a summary of the liturgical *year. A bull of Pius V in 1569 confirming the devotion, and the introduction of a feast of Our Lady of the Rosary into the Roman calendar in 1573, both helped to establish and standardize its use. It was subsequently encouraged by a succession of popes. It was often prayed silently by individuals during the celebration of the Latin *eucharist, and recited publicly as a vernacular evening service. With the reform of the liturgy in the late twentieth century the public and private recitation of the rosary experienced a steep decline, though Paul VI in his document *Marialis cultus* of 1974 endorsed it as a gospel prayer, deriving from and leading to the liturgy.

Maisie Ward, *The Splendor of the Rosary*, New York 1945; Franz Willam, *The Rosary: Its History and Meaning*, New York 1953.

CHRISTOPHER WALSH

Rostrum

A platform or stage for public speaking. The name derives from the Latin *rosus*, 'beak', describing the projection on the prow of war galleys used to ram other ships. The speaker's platform in the Roman Forum was decorated with beaks from conquered ships. The term rostrum came to describe any public platform for speaking.

MARCHITA B. MAUCK

Rubrics

Derived from the Latin *ruber*, red, and *rubricare*, to write in red, the word denotes liturgical instructions, which were often printed in red in Western liturgical books to draw attention to them and distinguish them from the text of the service. They are not themselves part of the text but indicate the way in which it is to be celebrated. Rubrics enable the ministers of the liturgy to discharge their liturgical functions correctly with ease and grace. Early liturgical texts contained in the sacramentaries have no instructions at all and separate volumes called *ordines* contained the instructions (*ordo*) for the celebration of the rites (*see* **Books, Liturgical** 3). Even when the missal and other liturgical books developed, only very limited instructions could be included in the text if the books were not to become unwieldy. Fuller

directions were given in an *ordinale* (for the daily office) or *caeremoniale*, and the instructions for the whole liturgical *year were set out in the *customary* or *consuetudinary* of a *cathedral, collegiate church or monastery. 'Rubricism' refers to an exaggerated attention to the rules contained in the rubrics. The RC liturgy from the Council of Trent to the Second Vatican Council was marked by rigidity and rubricism. Modern rubrics have been described as 'much less prescriptive, much more indicative' and the reformed RC rites are preceded by general instructions of a pastoral nature.

MARTIN DUDLEY

Sacrament

1. *Historical*. Early Christian writers frequently describe their liturgical rites as being '*mysteries' (Greek, *mysterion*; Latin, *mysterium*), and Latin writers also adopt the term 'sacrament', *sacramentum* for the same purpose. Thus by the third century Cyprian had already begun to link the language of sacrament with the Christian *eucharist (*dominicae passionis et nostrae redemptionis sacramentum*). In the fourth-century *mystagogical catecheses of bishops East and West, this language attains special prominence. So, for example, Cyril of Jerusalem speaks of 'the divine mysteries' which Paul had taught the Corinthians, citing Christ's words, 'This is my body . . . this is my blood' (*Catechetical Lectures* 4.1); and Ambrose of Milan reminds the neophytes that they 'came to the altar, turned [their] gaze to the sacraments on the altar, and marvelled' (*De sacramentis* 4.8).

For centuries the language of sacrament remained fluid and was applied to a variety of liturgical rites as well as being used in other ways. Thus Leo the Great (d. 461) also spoke of *sacramentum dominicae passionis* – not, however, as limited to the paschal sacraments of *baptism and eucharist, but as *the* comprehensive 'sacrament to which, from the beginning, all other mysteries were directed' (*Sermon* 47.1, 3). But eventually the notion of sacrament grew more restricted in the medieval West, as the Scholastic theologians developed a sacramental theology that was a reflection, using many Aristotelian categories, on the liturgical praxis of the times. They defined the sacraments of the church as just seven: baptism, *confirmation, eucharist, *marriage, *ordination, *penance and extreme unction (*see* **Sick, Liturgical Ministry to the**). They also developed far narrower ideas about how and why eucharist should be considered a *sacramentum*. Thus, in his *Summa theologiae* (IIIa.73.1, ad 3), Thomas Aquinas explains that a reality is called 'sacrament' when it contains 'something sacred'. In the eucharist, what is contained is 'something sacred *absolutely*', i.e., Christ himself. Hence, the eucharist is properly a sacrament, fulfilled (*perficitur*) when, by consecration of the bread and wine, Christ becomes present in his body and blood. In contrast, according to Aquinas, other sacraments are fulfilled (*perficiuntur*) only when their material elements – e.g. water, oil – are directly applied to the persons receiving them. In Aquinas's view of the eucharist as *sacramentum*, note the separation between 'consecration' – the act that 'perfects' (completes, fulfils) the sacrament – and the church's 'offering' and *communion. For Thomas, the mere 'making present' of Christ's body and blood seems to 'perfect' the sacrament. Obscured by this formula, perhaps, is the ancient idea that sacrifice must be completed by meal, that consecration achieves its goal in communion.

The sixteenth-century Reformers did not repudiate the notion of sacraments, though they usually limited their number to the only two that they believed could be found in the NT (baptism and *Lord's supper) and sought to revise all liturgical rites in accordance with scripture and the 'ancient custom'. Thus, for example, John Calvin's 1542 Genevan liturgy was entitled 'The Form of Church Prayers and Hymns with the Manner of Administering the Sacraments and Consecrating Marriage According to the Custom of the Ancient Church'. The liturgy reminds communicants that Jesus 'addresses his word to us, to invite us to his table and to give us this holy sacrament', which is 'medicine for poor sick souls'. Similarly the 1549 and 1552 prayerbooks of Edward VI in England are called *The Book of Common Prayer and Administration of the Sacraments*, and the eucharist is spoken of as 'the moste comfortable Sacrament of the body and bloud of Christ'. The *Presbyterian Confession of Westminster (1647) calls sacraments 'holy signs and seals of the covenant of grace' whose efficacy depends not 'upon the piety or intention of him that doth administer it, but upon the work of the Spirit'.

As this last quotation implies, one of the great contributions of the Reformation was the reaffirmation that sacramental efficacy flows strictly from the divine initiative, and not from the minister's merit or from a quasi-magical *ex opere operato* that, as it were, 'obligates' God to dispense grace whenever the sacrament is validly enacted by an authorized agent. Calvin, for example, carefully derived his understanding of church and sacrament not from the doctrine of the incarnation (Christ as sacrament of God, the church as sacrament of Christ; individual sacraments as actions of God in Christ, acting through the efficacious ministry of the church); rather, he began with an emphasis on God's sovereign, unconditional power of election and predestination. This provided Calvin with a rationale for rejecting the idea of 'secondary causality' in the sacraments. Sacraments, he thought, are real and 'effective' through the power of the Holy Spirit, who unites believers to Christ. But he was hesitant to regard the Spirit's power as a permanent endowment immanent within church life, for that might seem either to compromise God's freedom or to 'divinize' the church as though it were simply 'identified' with God's own activity and power. On the other hand, more radical Reformers preferred to avoid the language of sacrament altogether as too bound up with connotations of the quasi-magical dispensation of grace, and opted instead for 'ordinance' to refer to the dominically instituted rites of baptism and the Lord's supper. Other groups, most notably the *Quakers, rejected all sacramental rites.

Louis-Marie Chauvet, *The Sacraments: The Word of God at the Mercy of the Body*, Collegeville 2001; Joseph Martos, *Doors to the Sacred*, Garden City, NY 1981; 2nd edn Liguori, MO 1991.

NATHAN MITCHELL

2. *Modern*. During the twentieth century both the theology and practice of Christian sacraments underwent enormous changes. These changes involved more than a renewal; they involved in many ways a radical revision. In the course of the first half of the century five key issues began to produce major changes in sacramental theology and even practice.

First, a critically correct historical research on the history of each sacrament both as regards its theology and its liturgical practice was produced. These detailed histories were unknown to scholars of earlier centuries, and their implication was that both sacramental theology and liturgy during the last two thousand years had varied considerably. Consequently what each church today accepts for its sacramental theology and liturgy involves considerable relativity and even the possibility of radical change.

Second, an emphasis on both Jesus as primordial sacrament and the church as a foundational sacrament expanded the very understanding of sacrament, particularly in the RC Church (e.g. Karl Rahner, *The Church and the Sacraments*, London 1963; Edward Schillebeeckx, *Christ the Sacrament of the Encounter with God*, New York 1963). In this perspective, sacramentality was envisioned as primarily and originally expressed in the human nature of Jesus, and in a secondary but still fundamental way in the church. Not only did this approach affect the question of the number of sacraments, but it also considered Jesus and church as the primary analogue for all other sacramental expression, i.e., *baptism can be considered a sacrament only on the basis that Jesus and church are primordially and foundationally sacraments. This theology was accepted by many RCs, including the bishops at Vatican II, at least as far as the church as sacrament is concerned. Some major RC scholars, however, were opposed to this way of thinking and maintained that only the ritual sacraments were truly sacraments and the presentation of Jesus and the church as sacraments was at best descriptive, not constitutive, of sacramentality (R. Schulte, 0. Semmelroth and, more importantly, *The Catechism of the Catholic Church*). By and large, Protestant theology remained rather reluctant to follow this RC approach.

Third, the *Liturgical Movement during the first part of the twentieth century began to revise the rather formal liturgical celebrations in all the mainstream churches.

Fourth, the theologians who represented *la nouvelle théologie* were key in the production of critical editions of the church fathers. This research opened horizons for a new understanding of sacramental theology and liturgical practice far beyond the theological and liturgical presentations of Scholastic, Reformation, and Tridentine theologies. Although rejected by the RC magisterium (*Humani generis*, 1950), most of the ideas and trends of these theologians were re-accepted by the bishops and scholars at Vatican II.

Fifth, contemporary western philosophy, particularly existentialism and phenomenology, began to reshape sacramental theology and liturgical practice. By the end of the twentieth century this philosophical influence had sub-

stantially affected church thinking. Rudolf Bultmann and Paul Tillich played major roles in Protestant churches, especially in the Lutheran Church. In England major existential leaders for existential thought were John Macquarrie and J. A. T. Robinson. In Catholicism Edward Schillebeeckx used many phenomenological elements in a foundational way, and Karl Rahner's theology cannot be understood without a solid grounding in the philosophy of Martin Heidegger.

Between 1959 and 1965 the Second Vatican Council was a watershed for the renewal of sacraments. The Constitution on the Liturgy, *Sacrosanctum concilium* (1963) contained a series of general norms for all liturgical theology and ritual (22–25), norms for the hierarchic and communal nature of the liturgy (26–32), didactic and pastoral liturgical norms (33–36), and norms for adapting liturgy in multicultural regions (37–40). Although these norms are still binding for RCs, there remains for a number of specific issues ambiguity as regards their specific clarity and particular applicability. They are general norms, not micro-managing norms. Some official Vatican statements have tried to clarify these ambiguities, but there remains in the RC Church diversity in the way these norms are viewed and applied. The constitution on the church, *Lumen gentium* (1964), the decree on ecumenism, *Unitatis redintigratio* (1964), the decree on biblical studies, *Dei Verbum* (1965) have also seriously contributed to the sacramental and liturgical renewal in the RC Church as well as in Anglican and Protestant churches.

During the years since Vatican II a number of factors have played a role in revising liturgies and in re-expressing sacramental theology. First, the revised rituals which were developed in all the major churches provided liturgical flexibility, even creativity. Theological reflection on this variability called for a more flexible and open-ended sacramental theology than the church sacramental theologies had formerly allowed. Among RCs the use of the vernacular rather than Latin made liturgies more understandable.

Second, the *liberation theology of South America called on the northern churches to stress the ethical dimension of sacramental theology and practice. In the USA Virgil Michel of St John's Abbey had already done this, as well as the Niebuhr brothers. James Cohn pointedly stressed the ethical basis in black theology, and feminist theologians called not only for an ethical dimension of sacramental thought and practice but also a feminist revision of sacramental theology itself. The roles of *women in liturgy have expanded but there continue to be glass ceilings in many church polities as regards this involvement of women in liturgy.

Third, *ecumenical dialogue has focused generously on sacramental theory and practice. The number of bilateral and multilateral dialogues have produced statements by church leaders in which theological agreement on such issues as baptism, *eucharist and ministry has taken place.

Fourth, *lay involvement in sacramental liturgy has mushroomed after Vatican II, particularly in the RC Church, but there has also been a growth of liturgical lay involvement in the Anglican and Protestant churches. In the Eastern church tradition lay people were at times the major theologians. In the Western tradition often only ordained men became theologians. Lay men and women are now major theologians in almost all of the churches and this has provided a certain lay reformulation of both sacramental and liturgical theologies. Ordained people often see the sacred only through ordained lenses, while lay men and women see the sacred through lay lenses.

Fifth, the renewal of the diaconate has been a major component of this sacramental renewal. In the RC Church not only are married men ordained at least as *deacons, but also in many RC communities baptisms, *marriages and *funerals are normally celebrated with a married deacon present as presider or official witness.

Sixth, sacramental theology is no longer the preserve of Euro-American theologians. Indian, Sri Lankan, Filipino, African and South American theologians have all made major contributions to sacramental theology which in many ways depart from the Euro-American systems. Even more evident is the inclusion in sacramental celebrations of cultural songs, dances and music. These cultural symbols are not in any way western symbols, and their actual symbolizations in liturgies are subtly but strongly new voices and new interpretations of sacramental liturgy. Just as the symbol system of language is so diverse that already any translation changes an original meaning to some degree, so also cultural non-verbal symbols connote and denote different meanings than their western counterparts.

Seventh, there are in almost all mainline churches in the West communities which can be called traditional. These communities are adverse to radical changes and at times even to less than radical changes. Their presence within the church catholic will remain and this presence, even if it is at times jarring, should not be dismissed. The presence of such traditional groups provides yet another variant of sacramental theology and liturgy, but a variant that calls all of us to question what we call 'tradition' and what we call 'Tradition', to use Yves Congar's terminology.

Eighth, the influence of postmodern philosophy has certainly become more pressing on sacramental theology. In postmodern philosophy all human knowledge is to some degree subjective, and subjectivity is not a theme appreciated in all the churches. A small amount of subjectivity might be sufferable, but that all knowledge is somewhat subjective raises the issue of objective truth in any theological presentation. What is objectively true in either sacramental theology or liturgy? Linguistics have also been applied to theological expression (Gadamer and Habermas) and a universal claim for any hermeneutics has been challenged. This raises the question: are all sacramental theologies hermeneutically different with no universality at all?

Conclusion. The inheritance we have from the twentieth century as regards sacramental theology and practice is indeed rich and multifaceted. It is also diverse and divisive. Sacramental traditions have been strongly challenged. Relativity in both thought and practice is omnipresent. Experience, rather than doctrine, is considered foundational. Since sacraments are only real when they are experientially celebrated and all theology is only a reflection on sacramental experiences, theologians are challenged not to develop overarching constructs. Rather, they are called on to be of help as individual Christian communities existentially celebrate a sacrament. These tensions will remain for a good part of the new millennium. One needs only to recall that liturgy changes only gradually, respecting the affectivities of Christian communities. Sacramental liturgies touch on deep areas of faith and prayer and, because of this, sudden change only causes pain and confusion. When we realize that in every liturgical celebration it is primarily God who is acting, then neither theology nor any liturgy should be seen as manipulating God's action. God's action is free and it is grace. How to understand God's free and grace-giving presence is a matter of hermeneutics, not manipulation. Whenever we are in God's presence we need to take our theological and liturgical shoes off, for we are in the presence of a mystery that is both overwhelming and still strongly and sweetly alluring.

See also **Sacramentals.**

Louis-Marie Chauvet, *Symbol and Sacrament*, Collegeville 1995; Peter Fink (ed.), *The New Dictionary of Sacramental Worship*, Collegeville 1993; Edward J. Kilmartin, 'Theology of the Sacraments: Toward a New Understanding of the Chief Rites of the Church of Jesus Christ', *Alternative Futures for Worship* I, ed. Regis Duffy, Collegeville 1987, 123–75; Jean-Luc Marion, *God without Being*, Chicago 1991; Kenan B. Osborne, *Christian Sacraments in a Postmodern World*, New York 1999; David Power, *Sacrament: The Language of God's Giving*, New York 1999; Michael Townsend, *The Sacraments*, London 1999; Geoffrey Wainwright, *Worship with One Accord: Where Liturgy and Ecumenism Embrace*, Oxford 1997; James F. White, *The Sacraments in Protestant Practice and Faith*, Nashville 1999; World Council of Churches, *Baptism, Eucharist and Ministry*, Geneva 1992; Maximilian Zitnik, *Sacramenta: Bibliographia Internationalis*, 3 vols, Rome 1992 (bib).

KENAN B. OSBORNE

Sacramentals

Today any theology of sacramentals must run parallel to an emerging theology of *sacraments, at times with no meaningful distinction between the two. Formerly, RCs had confined sacraments to seven, all of them 'instituted by Christ', while a large variety of sacramentals were 'instituted by the church'. The Vatican II Constitution on the Liturgy described sacramentals as signifying effects, particularly of a spiritual kind, that are obtained through the church's intercession. Some RC theologians, writing at the end of the twentieth century, have continued to present sacramentals basically in a traditional Catholic way but strongly renewing and adapting their presentation because of the Constitution on the Liturgy's description.

James White notes that current environmental concerns have reawakened Christians to a renewed view of creation as a symbol or sacrament of God. Edward Kilmartin has stressed the sacramentality of the world, and Louis-

Marie Chauvet stresses a sacramental dimension in human life itself, even 'in our most archaic and least recognizable drives'. Interfaith dialogues have shown an openness by Christians to the sacred 'sacraments' and 'sacramentals' within other religions. All of this indicates that today an understanding of sacramentals is very open-ended. No definition is possible and any single description fails to catch the multiple dimensions of human symbolism. Nonetheless, this current flux is providing the Protestant, Anglican and RC world with an ever richer and deeper understanding of both sacrament and sacramental.

Louis-Marie Chauvet, *Symbol and Sacrament*, Collegeville 1995; Joseph L. Cunningham, 'Sacramentals', *The New Dictionary of Theology*, ed. Joseph A. Komonchak, Mary Collins and Dermot A. Lane, Wilmington, DE 1987, 922; Edward J. Kilmartin, 'Theology of the Sacraments: Towards a New Understanding of the Chief Rites of the Church of Jesus Christ', *Alternative Futures for Worship* I, ed. Regis Duffy, Collegeville 1987, 123–75; Mark R. Francis, 'Sacramentals', *Encyclopedia of Catholicism*, ed. Richard P. McBrien, San Francisco 1995, 1148–9; James F. White, *The Sacraments in Protestant Practice and Faith*, Nashville 1999.

KENAN B. OSBORNE

Sacramentary

see **Books, Liturgical** 3.1.1.a

Sacrarium *see* **Piscina**

Sacred Heart

A form of devotion to the human and divine love of the incarnate Word expressed in the symbol of the physical heart of Jesus. Though the basic elements and themes of the devotion are indeed to be found in scripture and the fathers (see John 7.37; 19.34), as a devotion it can be traced back only to the more subjective piety of the Middle Ages, perhaps to the cult of the five wounds. St Bonaventure (d. 1274) and Dame Julian of Norwich (d. 1413?) wrote of it, and in the visions of St Mechtilde and St Gertrude of Helfta at the close of the thirteenth century it achieved great depth and intensity. In the later Middle Ages it was sustained by the Carthusians and the *devotio moderna*. In the seventeenth century in France the Jesuits and the Visitandine sisters (following St Francis de

Sales) propagated it as a popular devotion and campaigned for its recognition in the official liturgy. St John Eudes (d. 1680) elaborated the theology, but it was the visions of the Visitandine sister St Margaret Mary Alacoque at Paray-le-Monial (1673–5) which succeeded in popularizing the devotion and shaping its practices, particularly the emphasis on reparation for outrages against God's love and on more frequent reception of *communion. Devotion to the heart of Jesus also found eloquent expression in Protestant traditions, for instance in the seventeenth-century treatises of Thomas Goodwin and Richard Baxter and the eighteenth-century hymns of Charles Wesley. Twentieth-century theologians strove to deepen the doctrinal basis of the devotion while detaching the symbol from its more questionable cultural representations.

Despite its widespread popularity, it was not until 1765 that Rome authorized the *mass and office of the feast, which was later extended to the whole church by Pius IX in 1856. It is observed in the Roman calendar as a solemnity on the Friday of the week following *Corpus Christi.

———

Jan Bovenmars, *A Biblical Spirituality of the Heart*, New York 1991; J. A. Jungmann, *Pastoral Liturgy*, London/New York 1962, 314–21; K. Rahner, *Theological Investigations* III, London 1967; Josef Stierli (ed.), *Heart of the Saviour*, New York 1958; J. Weber, 'Devotion to the Sacred Heart: History, Theology, Liturgical Celebration', *Worship* LXXII, 1998, 236–54.

CHRISTOPHER WALSH

Sacrifice *see* Eucharistic Theologies

Sacristy

A room in a church where the sacred vessels, books, liturgical items and *vestments are kept. It can also be the room in which the clergy put on their vestments for services.

MARCHITA B. MAUCK

Saints, Cult of the

1. *History*. The early development of cults of saints is an example of the traditional and historical importance for Christianity of local manifestations of popular religiosity. Tombs and other places of burial became sites of *pilgrimage and popular burial sites for other Christians: the nearer to the holy remains that one could place the remains of a loved one, the greater the chance of the intercession of the saint or martyr on their behalf. As the cult and devotion to a particular martyr or person of distinguished sanctity became more popular, official church authorities tended to ratify the status of that person through some form of canonization. In some cases, a day was given over to the celebration of that saint or martyr's memory. *Eucharists were celebrated near the tomb of the saint, often on the birthday or on the date of martyrdom, providing an explicit link between the sacrifice of Christ on the cross and the sacrifice of the martyr or the life handed over to Christ by the saint. The ancient text of the *Martyrdom of Polycarp*, Bishop of Smyrna, provides an account of the event in the year 155, and indicates a devotion to the martyr which may have been typical: 'We did gather up his bones – more precious to us than jewels, and finer than pure gold – and we laid them to rest in a spot suitable for the purpose. There we shall assemble, as occasion allows, with glad rejoicing, and with the Lord's permission we shall celebrate the birthday of his martyrdom. It will serve both as a commemoration of all who have triumphed before, and as training and preparation for any whose crown may still be to come' (18).

The earliest stage of the cult of saints, in which the popular belief was that the martyr would intercede for the salvation of the dead, gradually evolved by the end of the second century into a belief that intercession could also be made for the living. Alongside this development we find the creation and use of sanctoral calendars: lists of saints' days to be held in devotion by local church communities, or by the whole church. On these days of commemoration, special prayers were offered to particular saints for their intercession, both for the dead and for the living. Cyril of Jerusalem states that 'we commemorate also those who have fallen asleep before us, first, patriarchs, prophets, apostles, martyrs, that at their prayers and intervention God would receive our petition' (*Mystagogical catechesis* 5.9).

Pope Gregory the Great declared at the end of the sixth century that the principal purpose of officials was the correct administration of the sanctoral calendar according to name, place of celebration and feast day, and to ensure the validity of the cult of the martyr or saint. Two important examples of the calendars are the *Almanac* of 354, containing lists of dates of the burials of *bishops (including a list of popes) and of martyrs, and the *Depositio martyrum*, which gives the date and place of burial of martyrs in Rome during the third century. Many of these saints are still to be found in the universal calendar of the RC Church: Sebastian, Agnes, the Chair of Peter, Perpetua and Felicity, Peter and Paul, Sixtus II and companions, Lawrence, Pontian and Hippolytus, Timothy, Cyprian and Callistus.

The cult of the saints developed still further during the fourth to eighth centuries when devotion evolved to include, not just the place of martyrdom or of burial, but also the actual remains themselves, and, where these were not available (the distribution of parts of saints' bodies was a later development in the West, but not in the East), any objects deemed to have come into contact with the remains or with the tombs of the saints. These became highly prized artefacts as trade in relics grew into an enormous money-making enterprise. This practice of devotion to the relics of saints also acted as a reminder that Christianity, while being a religion based on the resurrection of Christ from the dead, was also a non-gnostic religion: it was a *body* that was raised, and the relics acted as visual and spiritual witness to the possibility of such resurrection available to all those who believed.

Once the normal expectation of martyrdom as the preferred passage to and sign of sanctity began to recede during the fourth century, other manifestations of holiness took over to provide exemplars for the cult of the saints. So from this time onward we find examples of saints of profound charity, holiness, ascetical life, poverty and generosity, virginity and purity, wisdom and spiritual acumen, and leaders and founders of religious groups, who become subjects of sanctity. For most of these, the clue to their holiness would be numbers of miracles which could be directly attributed to their intervention, whether while still alive or once dead.

During the Middle Ages cults of saints took on widespread importance as one of the means whereby Christianity remained at the heart of civilization in many countries throughout Europe. Since the celebration of the liturgy was now becoming a 'closed book' for the vast majority of believers, spoken in an obscure language and with opaque signs and symbolic actions, often behind a rood *screen, it became essential to promote the popular cults of Christianity which kept the faith of most people alive. Pilgrimages to their tombs became a popular method of *penance for grave sins and as

walking 'ways of prayer' to greater holiness. It became commonplace to name churches after saints, and to develop devotions and prayers in their honour. More feast days were gradually added to the calendars of churches in order to celebrate particular local devotions. Popular lives of saints were written and became sources of legendary miracles and other stories about heroes and heroines of Christianity.

2. *Calendar Reform.* A long period of reform to the calendars and to the practice of the cults of the saints took place between the sixteenth and twentieth centuries, with major changes taking place as a result of the Reformation, the Council of Trent and the Second Vatican Council. Underpinning the changes was a theological understanding that the saints, devoted to Christ in their lives and now close to Christ after death, help us by leading us to Christ and to the salvation which his death on the cross gained for us. Therefore, cults of saints of legendary power and status, which seemed to bring those saints close to or surpassing the place of Christ, were to be shunned by the churches of the Reformation, and to varying degrees by the RC Church since the sixteenth century. The Council of Trent reminded the whole church that 'it is good and beneficial suppliantly to invoke [the saints] and to have recourse to their prayers, assistance and support in order to obtain favours from God through his Son, Jesus Christ our Lord, who alone is our redeemer and saviour.' Similarly, in *Lumen gentium*, the bishops of the Second Vatican Council reminded the church of the necessity to grow in love for Christ and one's neighbour, rather than in the number of external acts of piety that one could achieve. In *Sacrosanctum concilium* they stated that 'by celebrating their passage from earth to heaven the Church proclaims the paschal mystery achieved in the saints, who have suffered and been glorified with Christ; it proposes them to the faithful as examples drawing all to the Father through Christ, and pleads through their merits for God's favours' (104).

3. *Popular Devotion.* Current evidence shows signs of continuing devotion to popular saints around the Christian world, concentrating, in particular, on their perceived ability to intercede for the living and the dead. In addition, there have been signs of an earlier stratum of the cult returning, namely, the honour and adoration given to as yet uncanonized martyrs

for the Christian faith. This is found particularly in places where the oppression of the poor and the unvoiced has been challenged by men and women who have given their lives for the service of faith and the promotion of justice. Recent examples of martyrdom in Nicaragua and Guatemala show that the practice of the local people has preceded official statements of sanctity from church authorities. This is exactly what took place at the beginning of Christianity. Those who have suffered in the cause of right and according to the teaching of the gospel of Christ are now in a position to intercede and to provide comfort and hope to those who continue to suffer oppression as part of their sharing in the cross of Christ. Recent liturgical revision in the Anglican Communion has enabled a flexible variety between traditional and more recent examples of holy men and women (though not specifically canonized or recognized universally) to be included in the liturgical calendar; examples include George Herbert, Oscar Romero, Dietrich Bonhoeffer, Christina Rossetti, Josephine Butler, Evelyn Underhill and William Wilberforce. The Evangelical Lutheran Church in the USA has gone further and added to its calendar the names of those considered to have distinguished themselves in a variety of forms of conspicuous Christian service, even if only on the fringes of the church, including J. S. Bach, Copernicus, Albrecht Dürer, Dag Hammarskjöld, G. F. Handel, Michelangelo and Heinrich Schütz.

Peter Brown, *The Cult of the Saints*, Chicago 1981; Michael Driscoll, 'Saints, Cult of the', *New Dictionary of Liturgy and Sacramental Worship*, ed. Peter Fink, Collegeville 1990, 1137–43; A. G. Martimort et al., *The Church at Prayer* IV, Collegeville 1986, 108–29 (bib.); Michael Perham, *The Communion of Saints*, London 1980; Stephen Wilson, *Saints and Their Cults: Studies in Religious Sociology, Folklore, and History*, Cambridge 1983.

ANDREW CAMERON-MOWAT

Sakkos *see* Vestments 4(e)

Salvation Army Worship

'The Salvation Army, an international movement, is an evangelical part of the universal Christian church. Its message is based on the Bible. Its ministry is motivated by love for God. Its mission is to preach the gospel of Jesus Christ and meet human needs in his name

without discrimination' (International Mission Statement). Although distinctive in government and practice, the Army's doctrine follows the mainstream of Christian belief, and its articles of faith emphasize God's redemptive purposes.

1. *Historical Background.* The movement, founded in 1865 by William Booth in East London as the Christian Revival Association (subsequently named the Christian Mission), has since spread to over 107 countries (1999). The rapid deployment of the first Salvationists was aided by the adoption of a new name (Salvation Army) and a quasi-military command structure in 1878, thus reflecting its understanding of the church's mission as engagement in spiritual warfare.

From its earliest days, the Army's worship was influenced by its functional missiology. In order effectively to communicate the message of salvation to the unreached masses, the Army employed novel revivalistic techniques. Using a variety of means, Booth preached on themes of personal conversion and sanctification. Beginning with open-air meetings, the Army's worship services were moved inside to dance halls and theatres, employing music which combined popular tunes of the day with evangelistic words better to communicate the gospel. Worship emphasized simplicity, joyous spontaneity, personal experience and active congregational participation. It is noteworthy that from the start, women Salvationists had equal status with men as both participants and leaders in worship. Praise (which included lively singing and personal testimony), *extemporaneous prayer, scripture reading with exposition, and invitation to experience justifying or sanctifying grace at the mercy seat (penitent bench), were regular components of Salvation Army worship.

Principles of pragmatism and accommodation were especially evident within the Army's developing music ministry. Singing was to be congregational, joyful and of practical use. Simple songs were to be sung, with tunes that could be easily learned and remembered. Rather than calling them 'hymns', the Army chose to refer to them as 'songs' in order to avoid the stigma of ecclesiastical associations. The use of brass instruments beginning in 1877 had the express purpose of 'attracting the masses'. The employment of dramatic means to attract attention was not limited to musical expression, but included the use of banners, flags and uniforms. These means were more than attention-getting devices, serving a practical role in symbolizing Army doctrine and mission.

In 1879 Booth wrote concerning the soteriological priority of his movement: 'This is our speciality, getting saved, and then getting somebody else saved, and then getting saved ourselves more and more, until full salvation on earth makes the heaven within, which is finally perfected by the full salvation on the other side of the river.' In 1889 Booth expanded his message to include the social dimension of salvation, as reflected in his article, 'Salvation for Both Worlds'. Preaching to the poor had to be complemented by caring for their physical needs. *In Darkest England and the Way Out* (London 1890) was Booth's call for a two-front war, for the souls of people and a rightly ordered society. Thus from an early date, the Army sought to find effective ways to express in worship its dual priorities of evangelism and social action.

The Army's continuing mission is to express in word and deed the compassion of God for the lost. Worship, life in the Spirit, and the study of scripture are understood to be the basis of the movement's spiritual vitality, equipping its members for such evangelism and service. As a 'unique fellowship', the Army's freedom in Christ is evident in its flexible use of methods to accomplish its ministry to the unchurched through proclamation of the Wesleyan-holiness message of free salvation for all people and full salvation from all sin.

2. *Worship as Divine Encounter*. The recently released 'International Spiritual Life Commission Report' (1998) states that Salvationists are called 'to worship and proclaim the living God, and to seek in every meeting a vital encounter with the Lord of life, using relevant cultural forms and languages'. Thus, worship is understood as a celebration of the promised presence of Christ with his people. To respond in faith to the word of God preached, results in a 'decisive encounter' with the living Word. In response to the reconciling work of Christ, Salvationists 'offer worship to the Father, through the Son, in the Spirit'.

Influenced by the revivalistic methodology of Charles Finney, Booth adopted the use of the mercy seat, often referred to as the penitent form, altar, or mourner's bench. This was the central place for personal encounter with Christ, and symbolized God's continuous call to his people to meet with him. The mercy seat thus occupies an important place in Salvation Army worship as a place of prayer, functioning not only as 'a place for repentance and forgiveness', but also as a 'place for communion and commitment'. The mercy seat, as 'a means of grace', confirms God's presence and provides the place where God's 'boundless salvation' may be experienced. The use of the mercy seat in worship also provides a public witness. Not only do individuals receive benefit from their decisive encounter with Christ, but this public display serves to compel the attention of others to their need for the justifying and/or sanctifying grace of God.

Salvationists acknowledge that those who are in Christ are baptized into the one body by the Holy Spirit (1 Cor. 12.13). The Army understands that there are many ways of publicly witnessing to a life-changing encounter with Christ, one of which is the swearing in of a soldier (lay member) beneath the trinitarian sign of the Army's flag. This belief is based on the long-held conviction that God's grace is universally available, and that no particular outward rite is requisite to receive inward grace. The indwelling of the Spirit is the necessary component of soldiership, whereas the swearing-in ceremony is a means whereby a person professes new life in Christ, signs the Articles of War (a covenant-affirming agreement with Army doctrine and principles), and is formally initiated into the church as a member of the Salvation Army.

3. *Sacramental Living*. Proclaiming 'Jesus Christ is the one true sacrament', Salvationists experience his gracious presence through the indwelling of the Holy Spirit, 'recognizing the freedom to celebrate Christ's real presence at all meals and in all meetings'. Fundamental to this understanding of real presence is the belief that Christ's presence can be enjoyed 'anywhere, at any time, by anyone'. Salvation Army *love-feasts are opportunities to remember Christ's death within the context of a shared meal, serving as 'an anticipation of the feasts of eternity, and a participation in that fellowship which is the Body of Christ on earth'. Sacramental living, understood as Christ working in and through his people by the power of his Spirit, is what makes possible radical discipleship and holiness of life, in both personal and social dimensions. Thus, having experienced 'closer communion' with Christ, Salvationists are meant to communicate his presence to

others. This understanding of sacramental living is expressed in the words of a song written by General Albert Orsborn: 'My life must be Christ's broken bread, my love his outpoured wine; a cup o'erfilled, a table spread, beneath his name and sign; that other souls refreshed and fed, may share his life through mine.'

Although Salvation Army worship does not include *sacramental practice, emphasizing the inward presence and power of the Holy Spirit over outward rites of *baptism and the *Lord's supper, the Army does believe in the importance of ceremonies such as infant *dedication, the enrolment of soldiers, and the commissioning of officers (clergy). These events, which recognize and celebrate decisive moments in an individual's spiritual life, are not understood as replacements for traditional sacraments, since what is essential to the Christian life is baptism by the Holy Spirit and constant communion with God. The accessibility and immediacy of grace is thus emphasized, without the reliance on external rites.

4. *Militant Discipleship*. Radical obedience to the word of God is central to the Army's understanding of Christian discipleship. The function of worship thus also includes the cultivating of faith, the teaching of holiness, and the equipping for spiritual warfare. The missiological focus of the Army requires its soldiers to grow in spiritual maturity. Opportunities for such growth in faith are found within the context of worship and fellowship, and are experienced primarily by means of preaching and teaching. Salvationists are also called to lives of holiness, purity of heart understood as a gracious gift of God by means of the indwelling presence of the Spirit of Christ. Lives transformed by the presence and power of the Holy Spirit are thus enabled to serve as a means of grace to others, as well as engage in spiritual warfare. Called to join in a holy war against evil in all its forms, Salvationists fight 'in the power of the Spirit in the assurance of ultimate and absolute victory through Christ's redemptive work'.

The Salvation Army Year Book, London 1999; *Salvation Story* (Handbook of Doctrine), London 1998; R. Green, *War on Two Fronts*, Atlanta 1989; P. Needham, *Community in Mission*, Atlanta 1987; R. D. Rightmire, *Sacraments and the Salvation Army*, Metuchen, NJ 1990; R. Sandall, *History of the Salvation Army* I, London 1947; II, London 1955; R. Street, *Called to Be God's People*, London 1999.

R. DAVID RIGHTMIRE

Sanctification of Time, The

Our appreciation of time is the product of human experience. We perceive it as flowing in one direction only, 'the arrow of time', and the nature of the universe we live in is that we can relate time to observable physical phenomena in such a way as to provide ourselves with a quantitative measure of it by which to relate all the events of our lives and the history of our civilization, and all the rich variety of human cultures, past and present. Though not always the case on a cosmic or sub-atomic level, at a terrestrial and human level time is sensed as linear and constant in its passage, an essential component in the framework of all human activity, individual and corporate.

If God therefore is to involve himself with humanity in a way that is specific, historic and identifiable, then he must do it at a particular point in time, and this is precisely one of the facets of the doctrine of the incarnation, that the birth, life, death and resurrection of Jesus of Nazareth occurred at a specific time in human history. This point is in no way vitiated by the fact that we cannot now put a precise date to these events in terms of our modern calendrical chronology, though we can locate them to within a very few years. The same observations are true about the central event of the OT, the Exodus, even if its actual date can be determined with far less precision.

Christian liturgical celebration, like the Jewish celebration of the Passover before it, is therefore of events that happened in time, and has a triple relationship to those times. It celebrates them as they happened in history; it makes available the spiritual power of these past events in the celebration in the present; and, because of the eschatological doctrine of the ultimate consummation of all things in Christ, the celebration is seen as an anticipation of that consummation and as a pointer towards it. The early Christian acclamation, 'Maranatha' – 'Our Lord, Come' – points to this.

At different times and places, different individuals and groups have put more stress on one aspect or another of this triple relationship. Gregory Dix (*The Shape of the Liturgy*, London 1945, ch. 11) argued with his customary force that the predominant note of pre-Nicene celebration was eschatological expectation, and that only after the peace of the church did it settle down to a much more historically minded 'this-worldly' celebration of its redemption as it had happened in Christ Jesus. He accounted for the pre-Nicene calendrical simplicity and the post-Nicene tendency to historicization and elaboration in this way. More recent research has shown that this theory cannot be sustained in detail, and that all these outlooks were present in both pre- and post-Nicene worship. Nevertheless, there must have been a change in the psychology of worship between the period when Christians were an illegal and persecuted sect, being saved out of a world that had rejected them into the church, a foretaste of the heavenly bliss that awaited them and into which they could be catapulted through martyrdom at any time, and when Christianity was the approved religion of the empire, when the stress was on the making Christian of the order of this world. The tension between sanctification for the world to come and sanctification in this world, so that through the church the world might be sanctified, has inevitably always been there, and certainly no more so than throughout the twentieth century. It remains to be seen how the twenty-first century will respond to this issue.

In origin God sanctified time by being incarnate in the historical process; all liturgy therefore, being a memorial of the incarnation, continues the sanctification of time, the potential making holy of all temporal processes. But just as the incarnation makes all time holy by a specific focusing of the holy at a particular point in time, liturgy makes the whole of a Christian's life potentially holy, and that of the church, by setting aside certain times for itself. As a matter of history, the pre-Nicene focuses for this were the *Sunday *eucharist and the annual celebration of *Easter, and the whole of the development and evolution of the Christian *year over the centuries can be seen as a continuation and elaboration of this process. The variety of events celebrated during the church's year, with its rhythm of feast and fast, ensures that adequate attention is given to all aspects of the Christian *mystery in a balanced way.

Likewise the evolution of the combination of the times of individual *daily prayer and the communal non-eucharistic worship of the church of the early centuries into the elaborate pattern of daily worship of monastic communities is a way of sanctifying the whole day by prayer at particular times during it. And while there is a considerable contrast between the length and complexity of formal monastic prayer and the simplest lay observance, there is no fundamental difference in purpose between them. All Christian devotional life, be it monastic prayer, the daily office of the secular clergy (the appropriateness of the still essentially monastic pattern of much of this can be questioned) or any rule of life for anyone, lay or cleric, concerning corporate worship and private prayer has the same aim, making holy the passage of time that life itself may be made holy. Recent years have seen a wide variety of official and unofficial liturgical material produced to facilitate these ends, and certainly the feeling that past patterns will no longer serve is widespread. But it seems fair to say that no clear consensus has yet emerged as to what future patterns should be.

David Filkin, *Stephen Hawking's Universe*, London 1997; Sir Bernard Lovell, *In the Centre of Immensities*, Manchester 1979; Geoffrey Wainwright, *Eucharist and Eschatology*, London 1971.

RICHARD F. BUXTON

Sanctorale *see* **Saints, Cult of the**

Sanctuary

Also called *chancel or presbytery, traditionally all the area reserved for the clergy. The sanctuary included the space around the main *altar as well as the *choir. At times elevated above the floor of the *nave, it could be separated from the nave by steps, a railing, an arch or a *screen. It usually included all the space between the *transept and the *apse. In a few examples the *pulpit (also called *ambo) for the proclamation of the word was located on a raised platform or pathway (*solea*) extending from the sanctuary into the nave. The sanctuary represented a holy place separate from the worshipping assembly where the sacred mysteries were celebrated.

An ecclesiology of the gathered assembly, the people of God, as a primary locus of the presence of Christ, articulated in the Second Vatican Council's 1963 Constitution on the Liturgy, led to a shift in the definition of the sanctuary. No longer a place reserved exclusively for the clergy, but rather the holy place where a holy people with its presider and ministers celebrates its liturgy, in its widest sense the whole worship space is the sanctuary.

In practical terms, in contemporary church designs, the ritual area reserved for the altar, pulpit or ambo, *font and presider's chair thrust into the assembly, or surrounded by the assembly, is the sanctuary.

MARCHITA B. MAUCK

Sanctus

This Latin word for 'holy' denotes an anthem based on Isa. 6.3, 'Holy, holy, holy . . .', which is found in several Christian sources and then increasingly as a standard element in *eucharistic prayers from the middle of the fourth century onwards, usually followed by the Benedictus qui venit, 'Blessed is he who comes in the name of the Lord . . .' (Ps. 118.26a; Matt. 21.9; 23.39; Mark 11.9; Luke 19.38), both of them being sung or said by the whole congregation. It is generally thought to be derived from Jewish usage. While in the historic Roman rite it concludes the praise and thanksgiving of the eucharistic prayer, in other traditions it occurs in the middle of it. Those Reformation churches which retained the Sanctus generally omitted the Benedictus as suggestive of a doctrine of eucharistic presence which they rejected.

See also **Music in the Mass of the Roman Rite**; **Ordinary**.

Bryan D. Spinks, *The Sanctus in the Eucharistic Prayer*, Cambridge 1991; Robert F. Taft, 'The Interpolation of the Sanctus into the Anaphora: When and Where? A Review of the Dossier', *Orientalia Christiana Periodica* LVII, 1991, 281–308; LVIII, 1992, 83–121.

EDITOR

Sarum Rite *see* Western Rites

School Worship (England and Wales)

1. *Historical Background.* The origins of schooling in England and Wales lie in the church, and prior to 1870 (the Forster Education Act) nearly all schools were church schools. It was inevitable that when the 1870 Act established school boards in every local area, 'religious observances' should become part of the daily life of the school. These acts of worship, which consisted mainly of hymns, prayers, readings from the Bible and the recitation of the Ten Commandments and the *Lord's Prayer, were controlled by regulations

laid down by each local school board. They were permissive rather than mandatory, since the 1870 Act had stated that although neither religious instruction nor worship were to be required by law, where such teaching and worship did take place, it must not be in accordance with any 'formulary or catechism distinctive of a denomination'. The government enquiries carried out in the late 1870s revealed that religious observances were taking place in almost all of the 2,225 boards.

The Butler Education Act of 1944 made obligatory the worship which the schools had been performing voluntarily: 'the school day . . . shall begin with collective worship, on the part of all pupils in attendance at the school, and the arrangements made . . . shall provide for a single act of worship attended by all such pupils' (Sect. 25 [1]). No provision was made regarding the content of worship but the 1870 prohibition against denominational worship was maintained (Sect. 26 [1]). However, church-related schools were permitted to offer worship consistent with the church to which they were affiliated.

Another development in 1944 was the use, for the first time, of the expression 'collective worship'. There was to be a distinction between the corporate worship of a body of leaders in a church, and the collective worship of pupils in a school who would come from a range of backgrounds. Section 25 [4] of the Act provided for 'the parent of any pupil' to withdraw the child from the acts of school worship. These requirements applied not only to pupils who were within the statutory ages of school attendance, but continued to apply to all pupils whose names were registered on the roll of a school regardless of the age of a pupil.

2. *The Present Position.* The 1988 Education Reform Act not only maintained the legal requirements for collective worship in schools but strengthened them in several significant directions. Whereas the older Act required that there should be a single act of collective worship which should take place at the commencement of each school day, the new act does not specify the time at which the acts of collective worship should take place, and permits them to include all of the pupils in a single ceremony or to be arranged by classes or other groups of pupils (1988 Era 6 [1, 2]). However, worship could not be conducted on the basis of the faith or religious orientation of the pupil. The group for collective worship 'means any

group in which pupils are taught or take part in other school activities' (section 6 [7]). In other words, the secular, educational and collective character of these acts of worship was maintained.

Of far greater significance was the introduction of a required content for school worship. Section 7 of the Act is a new section, specifying that collective worship 'shall be wholly or mainly of a broadly Christian character'. This requirement is met 'if it reflects the broad traditions of Christian belief without being distinctive of any particular Christian denomination' (sect. 7 [2]). However, this situation need only occur on most (not all) of the days of the school term. The legislators were well aware of the fact that in thus requiring collective worship to take on a 'broadly Christian character', pupils from other religious traditions would be placed in an awkward position. In order to meet this need, provision was made for a school to make application to its local education authority to have the requirements for Christian worship lifted on behalf of the school as a whole or any group of pupils within the school, and here the pupils in question could be selected because of their religious faith. Thus it would be possible for pupils to meet in distinctive faith groups, and the school which had received such a 'determination' could be in the position of having to organize several acts of collective worship every day. If the school applied for the lifting of the Christian worship clauses from all pupils, then the situation reverted to that described in Section 6, i.e., collective worship would still be required in the normal way but need not be of a broadly Christian character. These determinations have to be reviewed by the local authority every five years.

3. *Current Professional Opinion and Practice*. Although at first the collective worship clauses of the 1988 Education Reform Act were widely interpreted as requiring distinctive collective worship, closer examination of the complex legislation revealed wide possibilities of interpretation and diverse practice. It was pointed out that the words 'wholly or mainly' (7[1]) meant that in no case was it required that the collective worship should ever be entirely and exclusively Christian. It need only be mainly Christian, and this led to the view that even on the days when the Christian requirement was in force (i.e., on most days) it was possible also to include material selected from other world religions provided they remained a minor aspect of

the worship for that day. One must remember that acts of collective worship seldom exceed fifteen or twenty minutes and may often be considerably less.

The situation was complicated rather than clarified by the publication on 31 January 1994 of the official guidance offered by the Department for Education (DFE circular 1/94 *Religious Education and Collective Worship*). Paragraph 57 declares that collective worship 'should be concerned with reverence or veneration paid to a divine being or power. However, worship in schools will necessarily be of a different character from worship amongst a group with beliefs in common.' Moreover, it must 'accord a special status to Jesus Christ'. Not only did the legislation begin to appear too complicated for practical school use, but these definitions seem to require subtle, theological judgement from governing bodies and headteachers, who on the whole began to feel that this went beyond their proper duties. School worship had been valued in the English and Welsh tradition for more than a century, because it provided an opportunity for an emphasis upon the values and ideals which lay behind the work of the school, and was a focus for the spiritual development of the pupils. This could only take place as long as a broad interpretation of worship was permitted. The detailed theological definition in the Act meant that the whole business began to appear implausible. Local education authorities, church and professional bodies produced many leaflets and statements on these problems.

In 1997 a number of professional and religious bodies conducted a review of opinion regarding collective worship. The twenty-nine participating organizations were invited to indicate their preference for three possible ways forward. The first option, described as a 'new way forward', would replace the present legislation with a requirement for regular assemblies of a spiritual and moral character. The second option was to maintain the present (i.e., 1988) situation. The third option was to withdraw the requirements for collective worship without replacing them with anything. Twenty-four bodies declared in favour of the first option. They included all of the professional religious education organizations, the teachers' unions together with the Free Church Federal Council and the Buddhists, Sikhs, Hindus and Jews. No single organization wanted the third option. However, the Catholic education service and the school governors elected option two, while the Evangelical Alliance and the Church of England failed to complete the form. On these grounds, the report of the review was inconclusive and the government declined any further action.

4. *Conclusions*. In many schools, both primary and secondary, collective worship remains a significant occasion, with pupils presenting their work on a range of value-laden and topical issues, accompanied by the use of *dance, *drama and other media. A range of religious points of view is often presented, and the various festivals of the religious traditions are celebrated. New songs suitable for collective worship are being composed and published in considerable quantity, and there is a substantial literature of guidance and resource material for the conduct of collective worship. If in-service training begins with the question 'How can assembly and worship contribute to the educational and spiritual life of the school?', there is usually a positive and creative response. When, however, in-service training commences from the legislation and its inspection, the result is often frustration. One suspects that the maintenance of a spiritual aspect of schooling in a pluralistic and money-based culture is not best served by a specification of religious content.

Alan Brown, *Between a Rock and a Hard Place: A Report on School Worship*, London 1996; Richard Cheetham, 'Collective Worship: A Window Into Contemporary Understandings of the Nature of Religious Belief?', *British Journal of Religious Education* XXII, 2000, 71–80; Terence Copley, *Worship Worries and Winners: Worship in the Secondary School After the 1988 Act*, London 1989; John M. Hull, *The Act Unpacked: The Meaning of the 1988 Education Reform Act for Religious Education*, Derby 1989; 'Can One Speak of God or to God in Education?', *Dare We Speak of God in Public?*, ed. Frances Young, London 1995, 22–34; 'Collective Worship: The Search for Spirituality', *Future Progress in Religious Education: The Templeton London Lectures*, London 1995, 27–38; *School Worship, An Obituary*, London 1975; The RE Council of England and Wales, *Collective Worship in Schools*, Abingdon 1996, and *Collective Worship Reviewed: Report of the 1997 Consultation*, Abingdon 1998; Derek Webster, *Collective Worship in Schools: Contemporary Approaches*, Cleethorpes 1995.

JOHN M. HULL

Scotland, Worship in the Church of

see **Presbyterian Worship** 1

Screen

A demarcation of areas within the church building, especially those associated with the *altar, *baptistery and place of the clergy. The parclose is a side screen; the *reredos the screen behind an altar. Low walls, *cancelli*, define the sanctuaries of early Roman churches and were widely used in the Gothic revival as chancel screens as in Cork Cathedral (Burgess) and Cleveland Episcopal Cathedral, Ohio (Schweinfurth).

The beam supporting the rood developed in Italy into the colonnade now rarely seen beyond the patriarchate of Venice. Elsewhere a rood screen was the principal division of *nave from *chancel. Shorn of their figures, many survived the Reformation in England, enclosing the space used by communicants at the *eucharist. The seventeenth century saw new chancel screens as at Cartmel Priory, Cumbria and Abbey Dore, Hereford.

The French term *jube*, from the petition of the *deacon, indicates the use of screens for the singing of the gospel. Though these are all but lost in France beyond Brittany, Abli Cathedral retains an important example. Trondhjem in Scandinavia has a open tracery screen filling the central chancel arch. Almost all Iberian cathedrals have screens; the *choir being entered from the east, there is no western door. In parts of Germany two doors pierce the screen, with the throne of a prelate in the midst. In Britain the greater churches often had two screens, the more westerly supporting the rood, with an altar beneath flanked by doors, and behind a solid pulpitum with central doorway as at St Albans.

The altar screen survives in the *iconostasis of the Eastern rites. Covered in *icons, it is solid with central royal doors and often two smaller doors at either side. In the medieval West curtain altar-screens might be suspended by beams from the vaults, especially the *Lenten veil. Occasional structural examples survive, as in St David's Cathedral.

Tractarian influence saw many open-work screens erected in Episcopalian and Anglican churches, for example the nineteenth-century Skidmore screen in Lichfield Cathedral and the twentieth-century screen by Irving Casson and A. H. Davenport in Washington Cathedral. Pugin failed to win a restoration of screens in the RC tradition. An engraved glass screen by Piper separates the old and new cathedrals at Coventry.

———

G. W. O. Addleshaw and F. Etchells, *The Architectural Setting of Anglican Worship*, London 1948; Francis Bond, *Screens and Galleries in English Churches*, Oxford 1908; Gerald Randall, *Church Furnishings in England and Wales*, London 1980.

MICHAEL THOMPSON

Scrutinies, Baptismal

Rites or ceremonies celebrated generally during *Lent as part of the final *catechumenal preparation of the 'elect' for *baptism at the *Easter vigil. Often accompanied by *exorcism and *insufflation, these rites were designed to 'scrutinize' or examine closely the elect in order to discern whether any aspects of their lives still needed to be set free from the influence of sin and evil. In some early Christian traditions, such as North Africa (see, e.g., Quodvultdeus of Carthage), scrutinies also appear to have included dramatic physical examinations. Generally speaking, however, the scrutinies were public examinations of the progress made by the elect in their process of conversion to Christ and the church. Testimony from sponsors or *godparents in support of the elect appears to have been a characteristic in some places as well.

Although the number and nature of the scrutinies varied in early Christianity (e.g., Egypt appears to have known only one, and its nature was not exorcistic), at Rome there were originally three, celebrated on the third, fourth and fifth Sundays in Lent, in close connection to the assigned gospel readings from John 4, John 9 and John 11, respectively. The Gelasian Sacramentary contains three *missae pro scrutiniis* ('masses for the scrutinies') on these Sundays but, together with *Ordo Romanus* XI, also indicates that by the Middle Ages the scrutinies at Rome had become *seven* in number and had been shifted from Sundays to weekdays during the last three weeks of Lent. With the demise of the adult catechumenate itself, these scrutinies became little more than solemn exorcisms of infant 'catechumens'. Ultimately, they were further reduced or compressed as part of the initial pre-baptismal rites taking place at the church door at the beginning of the baptismal rite for infants.

With the publication of the RC *Rite of Christian Initiation of Adults* (1972) and the revised rites for adult baptism in several other churches today, the three ancient scrutinies of the Roman tradition have been restored, together with the Johannine gospel readings on the three Sundays in Lent. Consistent with early Roman practice, these scrutinies include *intercessions, prayers of exorcism, and *dismissals from the liturgical assembly. They are followed during the week by the *traditio symboli* ('the handing over of the *creed', week three) and the presentation of the *Lord's Prayer (week five), with final rites of preparation on *Holy Saturday morning.

MAXWELL E. JOHNSON

Secret *see* Silent Prayer; Super Oblata

Secularization and Worship

The English word 'secularization' has been in use since at least the early eighteenth century. It refers, specifically, to the historical process by which church property passed from ecclesiastical to state control, possession and use (as, for example, when English monasteries were seized by the crown – in effect, 'secularized' – during the reign of King Henry VIII). Secularization could happen to persons as well as to property. Thus, the canonical process by which a religious (e.g., a monk or nun) was released from vows and returned to 'life in the world' came to be called 'secularization'. More broadly, however, secularization describes the modern social process by which, especially in western industrialized nations, ever larger portions of human life (work, education, health care, ethics and morality, art and science) are placed under secular (state, civil) control rather than assigned to sacred (religious) sponsorship. In sum, the term 'secularization' suggests the elevation of secular concerns, values and procedures over sacred ones.

As John Bossy's research revealed ('The Mass as a Social Institution, 1200–1700', *Past and Present* C, 1983, 29–61), this passage from a 'sacred universe' to a secular one had already begun in the late Middle Ages, when the socially unifying and integrative powers of Christian liturgy (especially the *eucharist) were slowly displaced by the rituals of monarchy and secular community. Primary responsibility for achieving unity in the 'body politic' was transferred from church to state, from bishop to monarch, from liturgical assembly to parliament, from cathedral chapter to secular court.

For centuries in the West, therefore, the movement toward secularization has been linked to worship.

1. *Positive Assessments of Secularization.* Although Christians have been counselled from earliest times to resist worldly ways and wisdom (see 1 Cor. 2.1–10), church leaders and theologians of the twentieth century began to reassess that advice. In his famous manifesto *The Secular City: Secularization and Urbanization in Theological Perspective* (London/ New York 1965), the Harvard University professor Harvey Cox distinguished *secularism* from secularization, defining the latter as an almost irreversible historical process 'in which society and culture are delivered from tutelage to religious control and closed metaphysical world-views' so that people can 'turn attention away from other worlds toward this one'. The roots of this secularization, Cox argued, are biblical. The Genesis account of creation, for example, was designed to teach that 'the magical vision, by which nature is seen as a semi-divine force, has no basis in fact'. God alone is creator, and God's being and action transcend all natural processes – thereby 'disenchanting' creation and freeing humanity to deal with nature in a matter-of-fact ('scientific') way.

Cox's ideas sparked vigorous debate and criticism in the USA during the mid-to-late-1960s, but the notion of secularization as a positive force had gained strength among European Christians even earlier. The world's renewal (*renovatio mundi*) is already, really and irrevocably, under way – and the church itself exists as a *sacrament of that renewal. So argued section 48 of *Lumen gentium*, the Constitution on the Church issued by the Second Vatican Council in November 1964. Indeed, the worship life and sacraments of the 'pilgrim church . . . belong to this present age', a time when believers are called to build up the city of God which will usher in the eschatological era of peace and justice. This positive assessment of the link between human progress, secularization and worship was expanded by the Council's pastoral constitution on the Church in the Modern World (*Gaudium et spes*, December 1965), and it was developed still further in the post-conciliar period by theologians such as Karl Rahner.

Rahner's notion of 'the liturgy of the world' suggested that the first and most fundamental liturgy is the one God always, already celebrates throughout the length and breadth of human history. That awesome liturgy of human life, 'smelling of birth, death and sacrifice', is the primordial act of worship through which human beings come to know, name and celebrate their creator and redeemer. Within this deep, pervasive liturgy of the world, God reveals, communicates and bestows the divine self, thereby revealing that humanity's vocation is an inclusive call to unity, to the shared experience of grace and salvation. It is thus the liturgy of the world to which the sacraments of the church – small, humble landmarks – always point. In short, the liturgy of the church exists for the sake of the liturgy of the world, not vice versa.

2. *Negative Assessments of Secularization.* More recently, however, adherents of a movement known as 'Radical Orthodoxy' have challenged these optimistic views of the relation between world and worship. Catherine Pickstock argues that (unlike today) the earlier medieval liturgy of the Latin West was well rooted within a culture that was ritual in character. Early medieval Christians saw life itself as a liturgical category. Thus, for example, the eucharistic gifts were not disconnected from the produce of everyday life; instead, communities saw their whole existence as 'flowing from eternity through the sacraments'. Organizations like the medieval guilds served to 'sacralize' the world of commerce, because they insured that work, worker and product were perpetually offered in worship and so returned to their source. There was no 'disconnect' between life and liturgy – and no absolutizing of power and sovereignty on a secular level. The 'sacred centre' was neither place nor (human) potentate, but God.

In the early modern and baroque eras, this situation changed drastically with the advent of absolutist political structures that, in effect, displaced the ancient 'sacred centre' (God, as worshipped both in human life and in the church's liturgy and sacraments). Once power was transferred to such absolute (secular) authorities, everything 'below' was effectively secularized, commodified, commercialized. Far from resisting such (negative) secularization – so this argument runs – the Christian liturgical reforms of the twentieth century unwittingly supported it. By rejecting as 'secular interpolations' many features of the medieval rites (e.g. multiple repetition, complexity of genre, constant interruptions of the ritual 'flow', frequent prayers of penitence and self-effacement), reformers actually reinforced the secularization of liturgy. The result is worship focused not on God but on the self seen in isolation from God.

Catherine Pickstock, *After Writing: On the Liturgical Consummation of Philosophy*, Oxford 1998; 'A Short Essay on the Reform of the Liturgy', *New Blackfriars* LXXVIII, 1997, 56–65; Karl Rahner, 'Considerations on the Active Role of the Person in the Sacramental Event', *Theological Investigations* XIV, New York 1976, 161–84; Michael Skelley, *The Liturgy of the World: Karl Rahner's Theology of Worship*, Collegeville 1991.

NATHAN MITCHELL

Sedilia

Fixed seats for the clergy when they are not presiding, located in the *chancel area. Sedilia were often set into the wall of the chancel and topped with elaborately carved canopies. They appeared by the twelfth century and were a particularly English convention.

MARCHITA B. MAUCK

Sentences

This term denotes individual verses of scripture that are read aloud during services. The practice arose in the Reformation churches and was derived from the medieval tendency to abbreviate to a single verse psalms that had been sung or said at key points of movement in liturgies (e.g. *offertory). The Reformers, however, drew from the whole of the Bible and not just the Psalter for their sentences, which were used to provide a biblical warrant or commentary in relation to the liturgical act that was taking place. Thus, for example, in the English *BCP* of 1552 scriptural verses concerning the need for penitence and the assurance of forgiveness preface the *confession and *absolution at morning and evening prayer. Especially in more recent service books, sentences have also been used to introduce into an act of worship scriptural theme(s) associated with the particular festival or season being celebrated.

EDITOR

Septuagesima *see* Quinquagesima

Sepulchre *see* Easter Garden

Sequence

see **Chants of the Proper of the Mass; Music in the Mass of the Roman Rite**

Sermon *see* Preaching and Worship

Server

The name given to a lay person who assists an ordained minister at a liturgical celebration, especially the *eucharist, fulfilling functions in earlier times chiefly performed by an *acolyte in bringing the eucharistic elements to the celebrant, assisting with the *ablutions, etc.

EDITOR

Seventh-Day Adventist Worship

1. *Beginnings*. Seventh-Day Adventists trace their roots to the Second Advent Movement of the 1830s and 1840s in America, led by the Baptist lay preacher, William Miller (1782–1849). The movement appealed to Christians of many denominations and spawned a powerful spiritual revival throughout America, accented by a fervent interest in the second coming of Christ.

Key Adventist pioneers – former followers of Miller – came to believe that while Miller had incorrectly predicted the date of the second coming of Jesus to the earth, he had uncovered an important prophecy in Dan. 8.14, highlighting the beginning of the final phase of Jesus' work as high priest in heaven, as described in Heb. 8 and 9. This involved a transition by the resurrected Christ from ministry in the heavenly temple's 'holy' place to its 'most holy' place, thus initiating a special work of 'mediation' and 'judgement' in preparation for his second coming (Heb. 8.1–2). It was believed that this second coming would be a key event in salvation history and would take place in the near future – but at an unspecified time.

Seventh-Day Adventism, then, actually came into being as a result of earnest Bible study regarding the liturgical work of Christ in heaven as priest and his preparation for return to earth as king. Christ's ministry in heaven, therefore, became a core doctrine of the Adventist movement and helped shape its early theological base and liturgical practice. These early Adventists continued to review the scriptures in order to establish a balanced and Bible-based authentic set of doctrines and formulate appropriate liturgical practices.

Early on, they came to the conviction that the Ten Commandments were still to be respected by Christians as an expression of love to God, even though commandment-keeping is not the basis for salvation. As a consequence, they came to recognize the seventh day, i.e., Saturday, as the true Bible Sabbath (Ex. 20.8). Worship on Saturday, rather than Sunday, became one of the most important distinguishing liturgical practices for early Adventists.

The revivalist branch of Methodism was a particularly strong influence on early Adventism, including its worship practices, owing to the fact that some of its key leaders had a Methodist connection. Other significant influences on early Adventism were the frontier and *camp-meeting traditions, which were characterized by evangelistic zeal, spontaneity, and the participation of the people. Adventist meetings included spirited singing, shouting, clapping, healing, weeping and visions.

Growth was slow at first, but by 1860 these loosely knit congregations of 'Sabbath-keeping' Adventists came together and chose the name, 'Seventh-Day Adventist', and then formally organized in 1863 with approximately 3,500 members. The name was – and still is – intended to be a prophetic call to other Christian churches to restore the seventh day Sabbath, which commemorates Christ's work as creator and saviour (Gen. 2.2; Ex. 20.11; 31.16–17; Col. 1.14–17), and the second coming of Christ, which points to the resurrection and the overthrow of sin (1 Thess. 4.13–18; 1 Cor. 15.51–54; John 14.1–3; John 5.28–29). The doctrines of the second coming, the Sabbath, and the high priestly ministry of Jesus in heaven – taken together – had a great impact on early Adventist liturgical practice. Adventism's day of worship, hymnody, preaching, scripture readings, prayers and worship art all sprang from these teachings.

2. *Historical Development.* Early Adventism, with its charismatic features and revivalistic religious services, was generally reflective of nineteenth-century culture. However, Adventism's unique pre-millennial message, belief in the objective authority of the Bible, and emphasis on a historical interpretation of biblical prophecy were counter to some of the major American trends of the 1850s and 1860s. Adventist worship, for example, did not follow the typical pattern in two areas: emotional expression and evangelistic zeal. While emotional expression was present in early Advent-

ist worship services, it was more restrained. And though Adventist worship was primarily evangelistic, it did not use common theatrical practices to convert people at any cost.

During the 1870s and 1880s, Adventist worship moderated even further as it became more solemn, more formal and less creative. By the 1890s, Adventism had become more of a religion of the 'mind' as seen in its emphasis on cognitive preaching, debate-style presentations of doctrine, and standardized worship. Reform-minded leaders called for revival of the Spirit, church reorganization, and fresh worship practices.

The first half of the twentieth century ushered in a period of respectability and conformity for Adventism. Starting in the 1920s, Adventists became more interested and more successful in being embraced by other Christians as a legitimate 'denomination', and being thought of less as a 'sect'. Adventist worship gradually muted or dropped the essential features of its formative period, thus becoming less participatory and less charismatic. Emphasis was placed on reverence and decorum in worship, and services were simple, uniform, sermon-centred, and governed by what was 'respectable' and 'sacred'. During this time there was a revival of Reformation-style hymnody and classical musical, especially during the 1930s and 1940s.

After 1951, a much greater concern was expressed about worship, as evidenced by an increase in articles in church publications on the nature and theology of worship. Biblical texts on worship were studied in order to inform current worship practices and to promote the importance of liturgical elements in worship, besides the sermon. The 1960s and 1970s were times of upheaval, re-evaluation, and doctrinal debate for Adventists as critical scholarship made an impact on the church. While these struggles tended to occupy the minds of Adventist scholars, at the expense of issues such as ecclesiology and worship, some Adventist leaders began a dialogue with leaders of the Ecumenical Movement that stimulated Adventist reflection on these issues. Also, new doctoral courses were offered at the Seventh-Day Adventist Theological Seminary to study the worship practices of other denominations.

In the belief that they were holding out for the worship pattern of the Protestant Reformation, Adventists of the post-World War II era consciously resisted key elements of the *Liturgical Movement. These elements included a move to make the *communion table the central element in worship rather than the sermon, use of the liturgical *year, and an increase in extravagant liturgical pageantry.

As the 1980s began, there were renewed signs of interest in enlivening church life and worship. Adventists adopted the motto of the 'caring church', which was intended to transform church life, including worship, and make it more vibrant. In 1984, Raymond Holmes, a seminary professor of preaching and worship, published the first book in Adventist history that articulated a complete Adventist theology of worship. This influential book called Adventists to bring about a 'worship revival' by embracing a 'liturgical mission', based on the central doctrines of the Adventist Church and the messages of the three angels of Rev. 14.

By the mid-1980s, an important new trend toward worship renewal was under way. This trend was brought about by church growth and small group movements, and by emerging mega-churches that focused on innovative, Spirit-filled worship. A number of Adventist pastors replicated these thriving congregations by shaping their own churches into joyful, nurturing and dynamic places of worship. They came to be known as 'celebration' centres, because worship was practised as celebratory praise to God. These centres of worship were identified as having visionary leadership; a warm, informal atmosphere; a participative, creative and emotional worship style; and active lay ministries. These churches incurred harsh criticism from some quarters and affirmation from others, especially because of their emphasis on a more *charismatic liturgy and use of contemporary music and instruments.

As the Adventist church moved into and through the 1990s the church was astir with discussions about celebration churches and worship-related issues. Numerous letters and articles began to appear in various Adventist publications showing an increasing interest in worship, but also a polarization over the trend toward celebration worship.

African-American Adventist worship services historically tended to resemble closely those in White Adventist churches, except for preaching style; African-American preaching generally was more dynamic and narrative in form, involved more participation, and was more vibrant and interactive. Since the 1960s, however, African-American Adventist churches, led by second- and third-generation Black leaders, have worked hard to launch out in establishing their own pattern of worship, which features both experimentation and the rediscovery of key elements of the rich African-American worship tradition, beyond denominational boundaries. The energy and expressiveness of African-American worship stands as a sharp contrast to the calm and sombre worship style of most North American White churches.

3. *Modern practice*. Today, Seventh-Day Adventism is a worldwide evangelical movement with approximately 85% of its over ten million members now living outside North America. While the worship patterns of the American church have had an important impact on how Adventists worship around the world, Adventist churches do not worship in a lock-step pattern. There is diversity, sometimes broad diversity, especially among ethnic and national groups around the world. And Adventist worshippers are increasingly encouraged to speak to, and reflect, their culture in worship. There is, however, a broad pattern offered to the world church regarding the primary worship service. According to the 2000 edition of the *Seventh-Day Adventist Church Manual* (Hagerstown 2000, 72, 88), the church's official policy book, the Sabbath worship service 'has two main divisions: the congregational response in praise and adoration, expressed in song, prayer, and gifts, and the message from the Word of God'.

Two things are clear about contemporary Adventist worship. First, the emphasis on 'participation' in the celebration movement has led to a positive revitalization of congregational hymn-singing, to an increase in the singing of contemporary praise songs, and to more frequent use of congregational readings and responses. Second, the increased interest in worship among Seventh-Day Adventists has sparked both a willingness to examine new worship forms, and a renewed appreciation for traditional Adventist worship.

In the Adventist tradition, the sermon is – and always has been – the high point of the service. The congregational hymn is one of Adventism's most cherished acts of worship and certainly the most significant 'musical' element. Adventist worship also includes the use of choirs, praise singers, soloists and a wide variety of musical instruments. Adventists are increasingly conscious of the use of arts in worship and the importance of architectural and acoustical designs to facilitate worship.

Adventists observe two *sacraments: *communion and *baptism. The communion service is generally conducted quarterly and includes the ordinance of *foot-washing and the *Lord's supper. Only unfermented grape juice and unleavened bread are used to represent the pure body and blood of Christ. Believer's baptism by immersion is a requirement for church membership and is normally conducted by an ordained minister during a regular worship service.

Malcolm Bull and Keith Lockhart, *Seeking a Sanctuary: Seventh-Day Adventism and the American Dream*, San Francisco 1989; Ronald D. Graybill, 'A Hymn of Joy: Enthusiasm and Celebration in Early Adventist Hymnody', *Adventist Heritage* XIV, 1991, 12–13; Viviane Haenni, 'The Cotton Celebration Congregation: A Case Study in American Adventist Worship Renewal', Ph.D. dissertation, Andrews University 1996, 38–61, 130–218 (bib.); Raymond C. Holmes, *Sing a New Song: Worship Renewal for Adventists Today*, Berrien Springs 1984.

KENNETH B. STOUT

Sexagesima *see* Quinquagesima

Sext *see* Daily Prayer

Shaker Worship

The worship patterns of the Shakers, or the United Society of Believers in Christ's Second Appearing, have evolved dramatically over the past two and a half centuries. When this sect first emerged in mid-eighteenth-century England on the religious fringe, its members were sometimes identified as 'Shaking *Quakers'. That name derived from Spirit-driven worship that included shaking and trembling. Frenzied screeching and singing often accompanied these actions, leaving Believers physically exhausted. The Shakers expressed their disapproval of other Christian worship by entering Anglican sanctuaries and disrupting services, for which actions they were on occasion jailed. Ann Lee (d. 1784), an uneducated visionary who became the leader of the Shakers, and a handful of her followers, brought this tradition of ecstatic worship and bold confrontation to America in 1774.

In 1780 when the Shakers entered the public arena near Albany, New York, their worship activities again attracted attention. Stories spread about uncommon occurrences in their meetings, including miracles, visions and prophecies. Reports spoke of unusual religious exercises, including whirling and dancing as well as solemn songs in unknown languages or unmeaning sounds. Ann Lee and her brother William presided over these meetings. The Believers construed these spontaneous activities as the return of apostolic signs.

Following the death of the English founders, the first generation of American converts began to regularize all aspects of Shaker life, including worship, as they gathered Believers into villages. Under the leadership of Joseph Meacham, the communities in eastern New York and New England ordered their worship activities, distinguishing and structuring public and church meetings. Organized dances and marches, with males and females carefully separated, overshadowed individual ecstatic expressions; songs and hymns with words and tunes accompanied physical exercises. The sense of spiritual labour and unity in the community pervaded this activity. Believers shared worship forms from village to village. They constructed meeting houses specially adapted to such exercises, buildings with separate entrances for males and females, who were also seated separately. Spectators 'from the world' frequently attended the public meetings as observers.

The 1830s and 1840s witnessed a burst of spiritualism among the Shakers with direct implications for worship, a period known as Mother Ann's Work. During these decades the villages were visited by spirits identified as Mother Ann Lee, Holy Mother Wisdom (the female aspect of God), biblical personalities, departed members of the Shaker hierarchy, former Believers, and secular figures such as Benjamin Franklin, as well as Native Americans. Mediums received messages of all kinds – some personal, some for the community, some conveying new worship forms, others communicating song texts and tunes. Ecstatic possession was again commonplace, ritual innovation astonishing. For example, 'mountain feasts' conducted in mime at special sites were spiritual moments of high intensity. But these activities were so controversial that the society closed its meetings to the public. Internal debate about these proceedings contributed to their gradual demise. The legacy of the period, however, was immense, including songs and hymns (for example, ''Tis the Gift to

Be Simple'), spirit drawings, and a sense of heightened spirituality.

Contact and conflict with the outside world inevitably affected Shaker life, including worship, especially in the years after the Civil War. Numerical decline and economic pressures led to greater interaction with non-Shakers. It was not uncommon, for example, for Believers to participate in evangelical *camp-meetings and revivals. At times the Shakers even invited Methodist, Baptist and Holiness clergy into their meeting houses and recorded 'mutual blessing'. As villages closed, Shaker worship practices at the remaining communities also changed, losing some of their most distinctive aspects. Yet memory of earlier patterns was not lost. The second half of the twentieth century witnessed a slow but steady renaissance of interest in traditional Shaker worship. The pioneering work of Edward Deming Andrews and the scholarship of Daniel W. Patterson accompanied the determination of Sister Mildred Barker in Maine to recover earlier Shaker traditions, especially the songs.

Today one Shaker community remains at Sabbathday Lake, Maine. The handful of Believers there is determined to carry on into the twenty-first century. Their meetings draw deeply on traditions recovered by Barker and others, but they have also been influenced by the ecumenical interests of Brother Theodore Johnson, who joined the community in the 1960s and rose to a position of leadership. Shaker meetings today include Bible readings, songs (a few accompanied by hand and body motions), periods of silence, testimonies, and a deep sense of continuity with former Believers. Gone are the dances and marches. Outsiders are welcome at these meetings, and often they take part enthusiastically.

Edward Deming Andrews, *The Gift to be Simple: Songs, Dances and Rituals of the American Shakers*, New York 1962; John T. Kirk, *The Shaker World: Art, Life, Belief*, New York 1997; Daniel W. Patterson, *The Shaker Spiritual*, Princeton 1979; Stephen J. Stein, *The Shaker Experience in America: A History of the United Society of Believers*, New Haven 1992.

STEPHEN J. STEIN

Shinto Worship

1. *General Character.* Shinto is much more than an ethnic religious tradition. It represents a world view and perspective so deeply rooted within Japan that its elements are frequently inseparable from the larger social, cultural and political fabrics of everyday life. As an orientation to the world that recognizes the potential for natural phenomena to become deities, that deifies ancestors and leaders of exceptional merit, and that has influenced through its rituals everything from rice planting to weddings to the construction of airports, its historical influence upon the development of Japanese society is enormous and long lasting.

Shinto's emphasis upon controlling and revitalizing powerful deities (*kami*) that are beneficial to society, as well as exorcizing those forces that are harmful, has made it a valuable and profoundly strategic resource, both for the common person as well as for ruling elites. In fact, the symbiotic nature of the state and those religious functions connected with the veneration of Shinto deities was encompassed by a single concept: *saisei-itchi*, or the union of ritual and rule. Most obviously, this has promoted and nurtured a fifteen-century tradition that has kept the emperor as the supreme Shinto priest. And yet, in contrast to conventional notions of ideology and institutions, shrine Shinto's lack of centralized dogma, charismatic leaders and sacred texts serves to promote both an institutional flexibility and a broad-based public participation. Neither doctrine nor institutional demand overshadows the socio-cultural gardens of practice, where an emphasis on ritual has promoted pragmatic benefits (*goriyaku*) for imperial, state, clan and communal petitioners.

A Shinto shrine embodies a set of dynamics and practices that serve to discipline activity and exact a kind of compliance for those entering into its arena. One of the key features of a shrine is the way in which its setting is organized both to embody and symbolize certain fundamental attitudes about the shrine's deity and power, and to provide gradations of physical access (mediated by rituals and priests the closer one gets) to this deity. The ubiquitous *torii* gateway serves as a point of demarcation between gradations of purity along this path.

Central to a shrine are its spatio-temporal practices (hand-rinsing, strolling, shaking out fortunes from a container, bowing, throwing coins into a coffer and so on) which provide modes of interaction between place and visitor. The layout of a shrine leads people into practices which have the potential to give expression to inner mental or emotional states that might approach what we call 'worship'. However, virtually no Japanese would use the term 'worship' to describe what they do when they go to a shrine; instead, *omairi suru* evokes 'paying a visit', 'dropping by' or participating in a ritual to which they were invited or which they contracted to address some concern. In a similar vein, the term 'Shinto' (literally 'the way of the *kami*') is a construct created by priests, shrine administrators and even politicians that is not shared by the common person. For the average person, a shrine (*jinja*) embodies a relationship between the community and its tutelary *kami* and is the locus of festivals, history and power.

Many but not all *kami* acquired names and specific powers from the third to the sixth century CE, which imbued them with personality traits not unlike those of human beings. *Kami* could be coarse and violent, causing earthquakes, typhoons or surprise attacks, but they could be beneficent and nurturing as well. As with one's neighbours or enemies, certain ritual strategies were required to control the temperament and influence of *kami*, thus maintaining a tenuous balance between human, phenomenal and trans-human worlds.

2. *Ritual Practice in Modern Shrine Shinto*. It is thought that rituals occurring before the sixth century in Japan were basically a two-part process: first an opening purification followed by a petition to the *kami*. However, as the more highly structured ritual practices of Buddhism made inroads with the aristocracy beginning in 538 CE, priestly clans specializing in *kami*-veneration (such as the Nakatomi) refined specific ritual actions and orientations better to fend off Buddhism and its appropriating tendencies. There are still many aspects of modern shrine-ritual practice which correspond to these early periods – elaborate food offerings, invocational prayers, priestly roles as life-enhancing ritual specialists – and because sacralization through ritual remains part of Japanese social and political practices, it may be said that modern-day shrine Shinto is still 'in immediate association with its own historical depth' (Pye, 188). One need only see a community come together in its annual festival or *matsuri* to see how shrines, through the public festivals they stage, serve to create a kind of short-term cosmos of community. Whether sanctifying the start of a new company, blessing a fire truck, honouring one of the shrine's *kami*, or purifying the entire nation, contemporary shrine rituals and festivals conducted by

priests proceed in orderly, predictable rhythms, moving from framing techniques at the start to sublime closures at the end.

Robert Ellwood has proposed a four-part structure for Shinto rituals that consists of purification, presentation, petition and participation. As a model 'good to think', it encompasses both the preliminary and concluding framing activities as well as those when the *kami* is thought to be present.

A variety of purifications helps to prepare an individual for closer contact with the place of the *kami*. Whether purification consists of simply rinsing one's hands and mouth with water, having a wand of white paper streamers (*haraigushi*) waved in the air over the heads of priests and lay participants, or readying a site for the *kami* to be summoned, these acts (*harae*) are essential first steps.

The next stage involves the presentation of offerings and entertainments, beginning after the participants move into the shrine buildings (occupying either the outer or lower Hall of Worship [*haiden*] or the inner/upper Hall of Offerings [*heiden*]). In their state of purity and readiness, the participants present themselves through the person of the head priest before the innermost sanctuary, the *honden*. Before the *honden* doors are opened by a senior priest, the head priest leads everyone in a single silent bow (*ippai*). Then, riding the eerie sound of a single drawn-out vowel (*keihitsu*) intoned by a nearby senior priest, the *kami* descends from its 'heavenly realm' to the shrine's *go-shintai*, a sacred object (such as a stone, a sword, a jewel or mirror) sequestered within the inner sanctuary.

The second presentational phase (*kensen*) consists of food and rice wine offerings (*osonaemono*). Their presentation is stately and labour-intensive, occupying most of the attending priests. Rice, thought to be a gift from the *kami*, is offered first, followed or accompanied by water, salt and sake. The offerings proceed to the *honden* along a chain of priests arranged according to rank, with the head priest supervising from his seat. Often accompanied by music, offerings may occasionally be more elaborate (silk, money or utensils) as in the case of gifts made from one shrine to another or those from the imperial household, but the presentation consistently follows the same general structure and pace regardless of the variables of season, circumstance or the numbers of participants.

After the offerings are in place, the *norito*-

sojo, or 'words spoken to the *kami*' (usually referred to simply as *norito*), is that place in the ritual where there is an intensification of attention directed towards the *kami* and is thus of paramount importance. Beautiful, correct words of petition, intoned with reverence and awe, are intended to bring about good influences through the power of *kotodama*, a spiritual power thought to reside in words. To make a mistake in the recitation or incantation of these vibrations bodes ill for the efficacy of the ritual (which of course parallels practices found all over the globe, from the ancient Vedic rites to the Catholic high *mass).

After the slow rhythms of the *norito*, a sudden movement to 'centre stage' of the female shrine attendants (or *miko*) marks the beginning of several participatory interactions regarding entertainment and offerings. While not all shrines utilize the *miko* tradition, they are easily the most dramatic and accessible part of the ritual. Dressed in vermilion slit-skirt bloomers, spotless long-sleeved white kimono, and white gossamer slippers, these young women perform a slow, circular dance (*urayasu-no-mai*) as entertainment for the *kami* while carrying bell wands in their outstretched arms.

The next phase of participation – where those in attendance rise to present offerings, bow and clap twice – is formally called *hairei*. Leafy sprigs (*tamagushi*) are distributed as emblems that are said to link the individual heart/mind to that of the *kami*. Each designated person (often one represents an entire group) follows the example of the head priest by slowly coming forward, bowing, and then presenting the little branch on a small table so that its stem, pointed first to the centre of the individual's body, is now turned to point towards the *honden*. Kneeling in some shrines and standing in others, the participants then bow twice before enacting the two hand-claps of the *kashiwade*, followed by a final, single bow. The participation phase is temporarily suspended while the food offerings are removed (*tessen*), the doors to the *honden* formally closed, and the *kami* sent back (*kami-age*) with another ascending yowl (*shoshin*).

The final but by no means unimportant aspect of participation occurs after the ritual has formally ended. In many shrines the lay participants receive a sip of sanctified sake (*omiki*) upon leaving the Hall of Worship, while the invited guests and the head and senior priests reassemble in an adjacent building's special banquet hall to partake of more substan-

tial fare. Called *naorai*, the eating and drinking are also thought to be efficacious means of incorporating the *kami* (which has permeated these offerings with its essence) into the communal and individual mind and body. A departing act might be to purchase a talisman or amulet (*ofuda*, *omamori*) from the information counter at the front of the shrine. This small object is said to connect the worshipper to the *kami* in ways more vast and potentially propitious than they could ever be aware of, as well as extending ritual access to the *kami* to secular areas where its influence is really needed.

It is no exaggeration to say that much of the socio-cultural identity of the Japanese people is broadly shaped by Shinto, ranging from its obvious impact on national holidays, community festivals and familial rites of passage, to less obvious areas such as national self-sufficiency in foodstuffs (especially the role of rice agriculture) and the influence of Shinto views of nature on Japanese behaviour in the global environment. If the nearly 80% of the Japanese population visiting shrines on or soon after New Year's Day is any indication, it is likely there is far more substance and reassurance in these activities than they either know or would ever admit. For those who participate in shrine rituals throughout the year, we can assume a complex interplay of associations and meanings that, at the very least, reinforce cultural identity and historical continuity, empower the individual or group in a variety of ways, and resonate with possibilities for renewal with and realignment to what it means to be human within Japanese society and culture.

———
Robert S. Ellwood, 'Harvest and Renewal at the Grand Shrine of Ise', *Readings on Religion from Inside and Outside*, ed. Robert S. Ellwood, New Jersey 1978; Allan Grapard, 'Shinto', *The Kodansha Encyclopedia of Japan*, Tokyo 1983; *Protocol of the Gods: A Study of the Kasuga Cult in Japanese History*, Berkeley 1992; Helen Hardacre, *Shinto and the State: 1868–1988*, Princeton 1989; Sakamoto Koremaru, 'The Structure of State Shinto: Its Creation, Development, and Demise', *Shinto in History: Ways of the Kami*, ed. John Breen and Mark Teeuwen, Honolulu 2000, 272–94; Toshio Kuroda, 'Shinto in the History of Japanese Religion', *Religion and Society in Modern Japan: Selected Readings*, ed. M. Mullins, S. Shimazono and P. Swanson, Berkeley 1993; Takeshi Matsumae, 'Early Kami Worship', *The Cambridge History of*

Japan, ed. Delmer Brown, Cambridge 1993, I, 317–58; John Nelson, *A Year in the Life of a Shinto Shrine*, Seattle 1996; *Enduring Identities: The Guise of Shinto in Contemporary Japan*. Honolulu 2000; Donald L. Philippi, *Norito: A New Translation of the Ancient Japanese Ritual Prayers*, Tokyo 1959; *Kojiki*, Tokyo 1968; Michael Pye, 'Shinto and the Typology of Religion', *Method and Theory in the Study of Religion* I–II, 1989, 186–95.

JOHN NELSON

Sick, Liturgical Ministry to the

Christian care for the sick imitates the healing ministry to the possessed and infirm performed by Jesus and his disciples. The gospel writers record that among the ritual actions employed were the *absolution of sins (Mark 2.5), laying-on hands (Mark 6.5; 16.18), *anointing with oil (Mark 6.13) and prayer (Mark 9.29). All but one of these actions, namely a direct reference to laying-on of hands, were brought together in James 5.14–16 as a summary of the church's work with the sick. Christians have understood these verses to provide a warrant for liturgical ministries to persons in sickness; thus the passage often appears in formal liturgical texts intended for use at sickbed or in corporate healing services. Yet different interpretations have resulted in a variety of ritual practices within the church.

1. *Early Practice*. Incidental references in the patristic writings – especially comments upon James 5 – point to what may have been practices with the sick. In his second homily on Leviticus, Origen in the third century interprets the prayer 'over' the sick person in James 5.14 to mean the laying-on of hands, and he ascribes a penitential function to the anointing. John Chrysostom in *De sacerdotio* in the fourth century likewise links the anointing of the sick with the forgiveness of their sins. Given the connection made between anointing and *penance, it is no surprise that among the oldest liturgical texts related to care for the sick are blessings of olive oil, usually said by the *bishop during the *eucharist. The so-called *Apostolic Tradition* (third century?) contains an oil blessing, but only hints that the oil may be applied to or consumed by the infirm. Two fourth-century documents derived from *Apostolic Tradition* specify that the oil is for the ailing: *Canons of Hippolytus* (canons 3 and 21 taken together) and *Apostolic Constitutions*

(8.29); a similar purpose of healing is stated in another derivative document, *Testamentum Domini* (1.24). The sacramentary ascribed to Sarapion of Thmuis (fourth century) has two general prayers for the sick (22, 30), and a prayer for the 'oil of the sick' (17) that describes the oil as 'a medicine of life and salvation'.

Until the fifth century, little is said about the application of the oil. A letter of Pope Innocent I to Bishop Decentius of Gubbio (*c.* 416) reveals that in Rome bishops had primary responsibility for preparing and administering the oil to the sick in the church or in their homes. Yet out of necessity priests, *deacons, the laity, and sometimes even the sick themselves could also handle the oil for either internal or the more common external usage. Only Christians in good standing were eligible to receive the blessed oil since it was regarded as a type of *sacrament (*genus sacramenti*). Eventually the privilege of anointing was reserved exclusively to the clergy, who in the West typically ministered singly with the afflicted. From at least the eight or ninth centuries in the East, the service of anointing (*euchelaion*), where the oil was both blessed and applied, had seven priests in attendance to fulfil the 'instruction' of James 5.14 that the church's '*presbyters' should attend the sick.

Around the sixth century, church leaders actively urged the Christian sick to receive not only anointing but also the eucharist for their health and for remission of sins. From the earliest time, arrangements had been made to distribute the sacrament to the infirm; the *First Apology* (65, 67) of Justin Martyr (second century) mentions this task to be a duty of the deacons. But now, as evident in the writings of Caesarius of Arles and others, explicit connections were made between anointing and the healing power of the body and blood of Christ. Anointing and *communion of the sick appear listed together within collections of orders and prayers, as evident in some of the oldest extant Western manuscripts (eighth or ninth centuries). The oldest full texts for anointing the sick that come from the West – dating from the early ninth century and incorporating prayers from earlier sources – place communion after the anointing and the accompanying prayers.

2. *Medieval Practice*. Western manuscripts from the ninth and later centuries indicate that the church's rites for the sick varied widely by

region and in their content and complexity. Prayers could be said in the context of the eucharist, or in an office for the sick. Special *masses for the sick could be offered. Rites with the infirm could take place in the home or in the church. The exorcistic sprinkling of salt and/or blessed water could begin the rite, and *incense might be used. Prayers of different lengths could emphasize *confession, absolution, petition, *intercession and *blessing. The healing stories from the Gospels and other readings from scripture could be declaimed. *Antiphons, hymns and psalms (especially the seven penitential psalms) might be said or sung. The laying-on of hands with prayer could accompany the anointing or be separate from it; in the Ambrosian liturgy of Milan, unction is called *impositio manuum*. The blessed oil could be applied in different places using special formulas: in addition to the five senses, oil might be placed on the location of pain and on the body parts associated with sin.

Gradually, the rite consisting of penance, anointing and communion that focused on the remission of sins became associated less with the sick who anticipated recovery of health and more with the deathbed reconciliation of penitents. Anointing came to be viewed as an unrepeatable sacrament, and the communion liturgy that followed was identified as *viaticum*. By the fifteenth century, ritual texts no longer directed unction for the sick, but extreme unction (*extrema unctio* or *unctio exeuntium*) for the dying. The Sarum 'Order for the Visitation of the Sick' exhibits this transition by including prayers that speak both of recovery and of looming death.

3. *The Reformation*. The Protestant Reformers reacted against Rome's forms of ministry to the sick based upon their exegesis of James 5: anointing was not a sacrament, nor was it to be restricted to the dying; and the 'prayer of faith' was the central component of care. Martin Luther saw anointing as a means of encouraging faith in the disheartened sick, yet he advocated a form of visitation consisting of prayer and laying-on of hands. Sixteenth- and seventeen-century Lutheran church orders for the sick often included prayer, confession and absolution, the reading of scripture with an exhortation, and communion; a few church orders permitted private communion, though preferred the sacrament shared from the congregation's communion on that same day. John Calvin and others of the Reformed tradition,

however, determined that anointing of the sick had been suitable only for the apostolic age, and that the content of a visit to the infirm was best determined by the attending minister. Communion might be celebrated, but only in the presence of several members from the church. The *Westminster Directory* of 1644 reflected previous practice and shaped subsequent Reformed approaches for generations: the minister was to examine, instruct, admonish and exhort the invalid and also those in attendance on matters of penitence and faith, and offer prayer for recovery, should it be God's will.

Although Thomas Cranmer substantially abbreviated the Sarum rite to create an 'Order for the Visitation of the Sick' for the 1549 *BCP*, the new order maintained much of the shape of its predecessor. Cranmer kept penitential elements and prayers with themes related to impending death, preserved the rehearsal of the *creed by the infirm (though now in interrogatory form), and retained an optional anointing upon the forehead or breast. By means of a newly scripted exhortation, the afflicted were encouraged to accept the ailment as a means of spiritual discipline. A communion rite designated for the sick permitted two options for administration: the priest could reserve the sacrament from the day's celebration, or celebrate a short form of the liturgy in the home. In light of the critique made by Martin Bucer, Peter Martyr and others, the 1552 *BCP* emended the visitation order by dropping unction entirely and the communion rite by removing the option of the reserved sacrament. The 1662 *BCP* revision saw some changes along a Puritan line and the addition of four new prayers, including one for a sick child. A few Anglicans in the seventeenth century experimented with services for the sick, among them Lancelot Andrewes and Jeremy Taylor; the latter's *The Rule and Exercises of Holy Dying* deeply influenced approaches to sickness taken by evangelical Anglicans and Nonconformists in the eighteenth century.

4. *Modern Practice*. Because the Council of Trent had not been rigid in defining extreme unction as a sacrament to be administered at the time of death, RCs in the post-Tridentine period began to reclaim the sacrament for use with the seriously ill not necessarily in immediate danger of death. The *Rituale Romanum* (1614) provided the text for the sacrament with its multiple locations for applying the blessed oil,

and also an order for communion of the sick, a form for the visitation of the sick, and additional prayers and blessings. The *Ordo unctionis infirmorum eorumque pastoralis curae* ('Order of the Anointing of the Sick and their Pastoral Care') promulgated in 1972 supplanted the older rites, and within its texts and instructions locates liturgical ministries to the sick in the broader context of the paschal *mystery. Brief and flexible visitation services are supplied that consist of scripture reading and prayer, and conclude with signation and laying-on of hands. There are two forms for communion of the sick, one for 'ordinary circumstances' that includes a penitential rite, and the other without the penitential rite for home or institution; two separate rites for viaticum are also available. The anointing of the sick, no longer a sacrament solely for the dying and now applied only on the forehead and hands, is set out in forms either for inside or outside of the eucharist. Exhibiting sensitivity to local cultures, the new instructions allow olive oil, when difficult to acquire, to be replaced with another vegetable oil.

For Eastern churches that observe the anointing of the sick, texts for the *euchelaion* are found in their respective *euchologia*. Although sometimes used as a penitential devotion even by those not ill, in its fullest the rite requires the gathering of the faithful who attend the readings, prayers and anointings usually done in multiples of seven. The rite, which is not equated with last rites, is understood to convey spiritual and physical healing upon the sick person. The sick may also participate in the solemn consecration of oil and anointing that is held during *Holy Week.

Except for English Nonjurors and Tractarians, the Church of the Brethren, some Seventh-Day Adventists, and certain Pentecostal communities, Protestants did not practise anointing of the sick until the twentieth century. Up to that time (and also afterward), Protestant visits to the sick generally included scripture reading, laying-on of hands and prayer, the latter being *extempore or taken from a minister's manual; communion might be offered if requested by the invalid or the family. Recovery of anointing coincided with advances in medical technology and recognition of medicine's limitations, as well as a growing theological conviction across the churches of God's will for wholeness and healing. Several Anglican provinces during the 1920s and 1930s led the way by approving rites

of anointing in addition to their stated services for the visitation of the sick. Many Protestant denominations since the 1960s have included formal rites or prayers for visitation of the sick and for healing in their service books, and some have also added anointing rites. *Uniting in Worship* (1988) of the Uniting Church in Australia furnishes a service of healing with laying-on of hands and anointing, as does the United Methodist Church's *Book of Worship* (1992). Finding anointing too far a step, the Church of Scotland's *Common Order* (1994) contains a healing service with laying-on of hands and no anointing, yet their Reformed cousins in the Presbyterian Church, USA allow anointing as an option in their *Book of Common Worship* (1993).

Temple of the Holy Spirit: Sickness and Death of the Christian in the Liturgy, New York 1983; Charles W. Gusmer, *And You Visited Me: Sacramental Ministry to the Sick and Dying*, New York 1984 (bib.).

KAREN B. WESTERFIELD TUCKER

Sign, Symbol

1. *The Structure of Signification.* Modern theorists generally agree that the principal aim of all human linguistic activity is to create and communicate messages, to 'say something to someone about something'. But this very aim reveals a series of structural dualities that lie at the heart of language: between 'sound' and 'sense'; between 'speech-as-system' (grammar, syntax, dictionary definitions) and 'speech-as-usage' (living communication between people); between expression and content; between 'signifier' and 'signified'. Nor is knowledge of such dualities new. Medieval thinkers like Thomas Aquinas could write, *Signa dantur hominibus, quorum est per nota ad ignota pervenire*, 'signs are directed toward human beings, who use them to proceed from what is known to what is unknown' (*Summa theologiae*, IIIa Pars, 60.2, corpus). Every act of language implies both presence (known) and absence (unknown), and so launches a human process of discovery. When Aquinas used the Latin word *signum*, he was thinking of a reality closer to what theologians today would call 'symbol'; still, his point highlights the ambiguous, dual character of semantic events, whether these are verbal, non-verbal, or some combination of the two.

It is thus not surprising that modern scholars

define 'signification' as a relation constituted by the difference between two semantic terms. This suggests that the meaning of linguistic signs is *constituted by their structural difference from other signs within a system.* Take the simple words 'son' and 'daughter', for example. What these two English words mean results, in part, from a pair of binary oppositions: 'son' is 'not-daughter'; 'daughter' is 'not-son'. This opposition, in turn, is based on a meta-linguistic difference between 'male' and 'female': thus, 'son' is 'not-daughter' (because not-female), while 'daughter' is 'not-son' (because not-male). Notice that the disjunctions (e.g. daughter = not-son, not-male) can be affirmed only because of a more fundamental resemblance among the terms. In this example, the resemblance is rooted in gender. Gender is a category common to siblings, whether they are male or female, sons or daughters.

In modern linguistic theory, therefore, a 'sign' consists of two related phases or 'planes': the *signifier* (the acoustical image; usually, a word, though more technically a *morpheme*, the smallest morphological unit of language) and the *signified*. During the 'language-act' (i.e., during speech, live communication), the signifier represents the 'expression plane' (the embodied utterance itself). In contrast, the signified is that to which the sign refers – which might be a person or object ('Mary' or 'the table'), but could also be the mere 'mental representation' of an object, person, place, event, etc. The signified represents the 'content plane' of the language-act. At one level, the relation between signifier and signified is arbitrary; one can call a large female bovine 'cow' in English or *vaca* in Spanish. There is thus no intrinsic and necessary connection between the fact of female bovine-ness and the English word 'cow'. At another level, however, the relation between signifier and signified is *not* arbitrary. Once the relation has become established within a particular language, it cannot be changed simply by whim of an individual speaker. The complex relation between sign-signifier-signified is part of the deeper social contract that constitutes speech, for ultimately languages belong to communities, cultures and societies.

Most speakers do not, of course, engage in such contortions before uttering words like 'cow', *vaca*, 'son' or 'daughter'. They grasp their significance directly and, as it were, intuitively. Still, modern linguistics can be useful in defining the differences between signs, signals and symbols as these impact Christian theology and worship.

2. *Definitions: Sign, Signal, Symbol.* The definitions which follow are thus linked to contemporary linguistic categories, but are not restricted to speech or verbal communication. For instance, signs (whether in Christian liturgy or human life) may be visual or acoustic without being verbal. Similarly, symbols cannot be confined to words, objects or things; they are transactions or processes (verbs rather than nouns).

(a) *Sign.* A chief function of a sign is to provide information, accumulate fact, and assemble accurate data. Signs thus stand for or point to specific objects, events, persons, conditions or circumstances. Signs do not open large new vistas of knowledge or insight; they are primarily functional and pragmatic. Signs say things like 'Stop', 'Silence', 'Caution: Wet Floor'. Because they are customary social conventions, signs are especially sensitive to the culture that creates them. In order to function effectively, signs – whether verbal or non-verbal – must be instantly recognizable. They invite simple recognition and response; they do not require a deep level of personal engagement and participation. In liturgical usage, however, signs may stretch and acquire an added surplus of meaning. For example, the presence of chairs near the *altar in the space where the *eucharist is celebrated signifies, functionally, that at some point in the service the ministers may be seated. At the same time, the chairs may acquire a surplus significance that is not merely utilitarian; their arrangement may reveal a pattern of precedence and authority among the ministers who use them.

(b) *Signal.* This potential for a 'surplus of meaning' indicates how some signs may become signals. A signal is a sign whose significance has been stretched by the presence of *additional information or insight not provided by the sign itself.* For example, to a person with no prior knowledge of Christian worship, the presence of table and chairs in church may simply signify 'furniture'. Such furniture would give the outside observer a very limited understanding of the Christian assembly and its liturgy. If, however, worshippers began to enter the church and ministers started to take their places near altar and *ambo, the same observer might then notice that some spots seem 'reserved', while others are available for 'open seating'. In short, as the presence of people and ministers 'redefines' space within the church, some signs (e.g. chairs) begin to stretch, becoming signals, i.e., stimuli which reveal something new about the community. The observer begins to see that the 'information' given by table and chairs is not simply utilitarian; the furniture signals patterns of power, authority and responsibility within the assembly. When a sign becomes a stimulus, triggering new responses by revealing a surplus of meaning beneath or beyond the sign itself, one is dealing with a signal.

(c) *Symbol*. If, moreover, a liturgical signal's surplus of meaning is experienced (i) as inexhaustible; (ii) as initiated by a source beyond the participants' power to control; and (iii) as doing (or giving) what it embodies, then one has moved beyond both sign and signal to symbol. A symbol is neither information (sign) nor triggering surplus/stimulus (signal); it is an action that discloses new and unexpected relationships. More precisely, a symbol is a transaction in which the apparent 'actors' become the 'acted upon'; the apparent 'initiators' become the 'initiated'; the 'possessors' become the 'possessed'. Entering into a symbolic transaction, participants find that their assumptions and expectations are subverted or thrown into reverse. Take, for example, the symbolic actions of eating and drinking in the eucharist. When humans ingest food and drink, they ordinarily metabolize what they have consumed into themselves. We become what we eat. But eating and drinking at eucharist leads to precisely the opposite outcome. As St Augustine said, participants symbolically become what they consume through a kind of 'reverse' metabolism (*Confessions* VII.16). A symbol is thus neither 'thing' nor 'object' but new and unanticipated outcome.

One can now understand why Aquinas thought *signa* (i.e., symbols) trigger movement from the 'known' to the 'unknown'. For within every symbol (the word's Greek root suggests putting together two halves that have been separated) lies a powerful ambivalence. Every symbol simultaneously affirms both absence and presence – some act, person or relationship that is at once 'missing' yet potently 'present'. Seen from this angle, symbols are not 'things' we invent or invest with power and significance; they are realities that discover *us*. A symbol is not an object to be manipulated through memory, mime and rite, but a 'world' that continues opening up out ahead of its inhabitants. Thus a symbol is open-ended

action rather than closed-off object. By initiating movement from 'known' to 'unknown', symbols open a new way of life the meanings of which cannot be exhausted and the potentialities of which are ever new. For this reason symbols are innately pliant, supple, flexible, ambiguous, multilayered. Their relation to people is reciprocal: symbols open new potential for human life, yet they are also shaped and refined by the changing circumstances of that life. This could be called the 'principle of symbolic reciprocity': symbols both influence and are influenced by the very interactions that evoke them. In sum, by presenting (embodying) the familiar (e.g. eating and drinking, bread and wine) a symbol triggers access to the sublime (the transcendent, holy mystery, God).

Louis-Marie Chauvet, *Symbol and Sacrament: A Sacramental Reinterpretation of Christian Existence*, Collegeville 1995; Thomas M. Greene, 'Ritual and Text in the Renaissance', *Canadian Review of Comparative Literature* XV, 1991, 179–97; David N. Power, *Unsearchable Riches: The Symbolic Nature of Liturgy*, New York 1984; Karl Rahner, 'The Theology of the Symbol', *Theological Investigations* IV, London 1966, 221–52.

NATHAN MITCHELL

Sikh Worship

Born out of the protest made by Guru Nanak (1469–1539) against the religiosity of both the Hinduism and Islam of his day, Sikhism evolved under the guidance of successive human Gurus until the tenth and final human Guru, Guru Gobind Singh, installed the scriptures as Guru and established the basis of Sikhism as it has developed today.

For Sikhs the purpose of worship is the praise of God and the development of the spirituality of both the individual and the community. God must be kept in mind in all one does, and thus any understanding that the sacred and the secular can be separated is anathema. Worship provides an opportunity to give thanks for the grace of God and is 'offered by those awesomely aware of God within creation and within hearts' (Cole, *The Sikhs*, 7). It is considered a foretaste of eternity, a glimpse of 'the divine court' (*Adi Granth* [*Guru Granth Sahib*], 26).

In the Sikh diaspora congregational worship takes place in the *diwan* room – a hall at one end of which the *Guru Granth Sahib* (scriptures) are placed on a raised dais surmounted by an awning. The scriptures are usually installed in the early morning. Behind the scriptures sits a *granthi* (reader) who waves a *chauri* (a fan made of yak hair) over the scriptures as a sign of respect. On entering the *gurdwara* the devotees remove their shoes, wash their hands, cover their heads and enter the *diwan* hall. There they normally prostrate themselves before the scriptures and then sit cross-legged on the floor in front of the holy book. The form of worship is simple, comprising *kirtan* – the singing of hymns from the *Guru Granth Sahib*; a series of addresses based on the scripture passages sung; prayers of intercession; the singing of hymns; and at the end of the service the distribution of *karah prasad* – literally 'food made in an iron pan'. This last element symbolizes the egalitarian nature of the Sikh faith, but it is also a reminder that none should leave the Guru's presence hungry.

On festival occasions, or when Sikh believers wish to offer thanksgiving for an event in their lives or as a form of intercession, a complete reading (*akhand path*) of the scriptures is held. This takes about forty-eight hours. In the Sikh diaspora this usually starts on a Friday morning so that the completion will be on Sunday morning when many worshippers will be in the *gurdwara*. No day is considered to be more auspicious than others but Sunday is taken to be an appropriate day of worship in the West since many people would not be working.

Worship is practised both individually and corporately. Many Sikhs simply visit the *gurdwara* first thing in the morning to 'pay their respects' to the *Guru Granth Sahib* and to pray for God's blessing for the work of the day. Sometimes they do this at the time when the scriptures are installed in the *gurdwara*; others come later on their way to work. As they enter the *gurdwara* many Sikhs take a little of the dust at the threshold to place on their forehead. Such dust is regarded as holy, for it is brought by the feet of fellow believers and is of a holy place.

Corporate worship, as described above, is of great importance, for it unites the believers in faith. It offers mutual support and a sense of there being something far greater than oneself, a unity with fellow human beings and with God. Wherever there is a group of believers God is present: 'Attuned to you, your devotees constantly sing your praises. You are their refuge in which they find their liberation. In

you they find unity . . . through grace one finds God . . . through the Lord's Name one finds the True Guru . . . through the Guru's Word one frees the mind, subdues the ego and merges in the Lord' (*Adi Granth*, 1068). Worship alone, however, is insufficient. It must be accompanied by *seva* – service to one's fellow human beings: 'the true servant is the one whom God enables through following the divine will' (*Adi Granth*, 471).

Central to worship is the *Guru Granth Sahib*. It provides not only the hymns which are the backbone of worship but also takes the place of the human Guru. Within its pages is to be found the word of God, that from which one finds guidance for daily life and through which the will of God who is Guru is discerned. The scriptures themselves are 1,430 pages long and consist of the hymns of five of the human Gurus together with works of other hymn-writers, many of whom were not Sikh but Hindu or Muslim, high or low of caste, or even without caste, people who, for example, were butchers or leather-workers. The whole scripture is set to music and was written in the common language of the people of the day. Whereas there are translations into a variety of languages, they do not carry the weight of authenticity or authority of versions in the original language. Thus, they are not installed as Guru in *gurdwaras*. This leads to difficulties in the Sikh diaspora, since many young people, even though they may be able to speak modern Panjabi, cannot read the script and are doubly disadvantaged by the fact that, even if they read *Gurmukhi* script, the language of the original is now some three hundred years old with an economy of style and a vocabulary little used in this present day and age. Nevertheless, such is the reverence for the word of God that the *Guru Granth Sahib* is still regarded as God's word by which the believer finds spiritual nourishment. Devout Sikhs, like their forebears who learnt the specially devised *Gurmukhi* script, now make considerable effort to familiarize themselves with God's word at the heart of their faith.

Worship can be led by anyone who is deemed to be worthy and of good standing within the community. The *granthi* is not a priest or ordained minister, since Sikhism is very much a lay movement, but someone who is well versed in the scriptures and who is able to explain their meaning and purpose. In India training for this post is available. Diaspora *gurdwara* committees often have the employment of a full-time *granthi* as an objective, but often Indian-trained *granthis* do not understand the nature of life in the West and are not able to address the needs of the younger generation. The *granthi* is basically a reader of the scriptures; thus women may undertake that duty, though not normally as paid functionaries. Worship is often enhanced by the presence of *ragis* – musicians/singers. They are usually three in number; often two play portable harmoniums and the third a drum (*tabla*). Usually one of the harmonium players is the lead singer, who often will explain the meaning of the passage of scripture which they are singing and speak of its relevance to present-day life. In recent years such groups from India have begun to visit diaspora *gurdwaras*, where they are the recipients of monetary gifts from the worshippers.

Visitors to *gurdwaras* will find that an integral part of the building is the *langar*. This is the kitchen from which, free of charge, all who come will be able to take a meal. Physical as well as spiritual nourishment is vital to the Sikh way of life. Meals served should be vegetarian so that none are excluded through dietary restrictions. Usually a vegetable curry, lentils and *chapatis* form the basis of the meal, with maybe fruit or sweetmeats in addition. Traditionally the food is served in the *langar* hall, where those who eat sit on the floor in rows and are served by fellow worshippers. Implied in this arrangement is the equality of all people before God. The *langar* is open to all irrespective of race or creed. The same requirements made for entry into the *gurdwara*, that is, the removal of shoes and something to cover one's head, equally apply.

W. Owen Cole and Piara Singh Sambhi, *The Sikhs: Their Religious Beliefs and Practices*, Brighton 1995 (bib.); S. S. Kohli, *A Conceptual Encyclopaedia of Guru Granth Sahib*, New Delhi 1992; Hew McLeod, *Sikhism*, Harmondsworth 1997 (bib.); Gopal Singh, *The Religion of the Sikhs*, New Delhi 1987.

JOHN M. PARRY

Silent Prayer

Silent prayer within worship falls into three categories.

1. Periods of silent prayer which are integral to the structure of the service. Among the possibilities for this are between a bidding or invitation to pray and the formal prayer which follows it; meditation after readings from scriptures and after *communion; and space for recollection between major sections of the service. Some of these provisions have been included in several reformed liturgies of recent years, and in an age of far too little silence they can be of great devotional and psychological value. The effective timing and 'control' of these silences, on which in practice not a little of their value depends, calls for sensitivity and good judgement on the part of the officiating minister.

2. The silent, or nearly silent (technically 'secret'), recitation of certain prescribed prayers of private devotion by one or other of the ministers. This category calls for little comment: such prayers are to be found in most of the historic liturgies, in which they were inserted in the Middle Ages.

3. The similar recitation of prayers which should properly be recited aloud, or at least were originally so recited. The most outstanding example of this category is the *eucharistic prayer itself, large parts of which are recited secretly in many of the historic liturgies. This custom appears to have arisen from the desire to express and evoke an attitude of awe and fear towards the eucharistic mystery, the use of the secret voice being psychologically effective to this end. Such an attitude certainly existed to some extent from the very beginnings of Christian worship, as is clear from 1 Cor. 11.26–33, but it was in fourth- and fifth-century Syria that it came to dominate the approach to the eucharist, and it is in a Syrian document of the end of the fifth century, *The Liturgical Homilies of Narsai*, that we have the first definite evidence for the largely silent recitation of the eucharistic prayer. By the second half of the sixth century the practice had become widespread, although it was as yet by no means universal: in 565 the Emperor Justinian found it necessary to legislate against it. His legislation produced no lasting effect, and by the end of the eighth century the practice had become the established usage in the Byzantine rite. The first definite evidence of it in the West is found in the second Roman *ordo* of almost exactly the same date. It became and remained the normal usage in the Roman rite until 1966, when the recitation of the canon aloud was again prescribed. The silent recitation of the eucharistic prayer is undoubtedly a corrupt practice, but however undesirable it may be liturgically, the spread and persistence of the practice bear witness to an evident devotional need for silence and for its psychological

fruits. This should, however, be provided for in other ways: see (1) above.

See also **Super Oblata**.

W. JARDINE GRISBROOKE

Sitting *see* **Posture** 3

Social Sciences and the Study of Liturgy

Models and methodologies from the social sciences have been drawn on by students of liturgy since the emergence of the social sciences in the middle of the nineteenth century. J. M. Neale claimed to be the first scholar to develop what he described as 'Comparative Liturgiology' (*Essays on Liturgiology and Church History*, London 1863). In doing this he drew on a scientific model for the comparative study of species, societies, languages and numerous other things which was widely used in the contemporary social scientific literature. Anton Baumstark's work on comparative liturgy, first published in German in 1902 and in book form in French in 1940 (English edn, London 1958), was even more explicit in its attempt to use a methodology that had been developed for the study of language to analyse the development of liturgy. This led Baumstark to develop a series of rules for liturgical development which matched clearly very similar rules which were being put forward in comparative linguistics, comparative sociology and comparative religion at about the same time.

Such clear and acknowledged borrowing of social science methods was actually quite rare in the early years of the twentieth century. This does not mean, however, that such borrowing did not take place. Even Gregory Dix's famous book, *The Shape of the Liturgy* (London 1945), shows clear evidence of an acquaintance with contemporary thinking in the social sciences. Dix's emphasis on shape, or structure, and the similarities between his 'shape' for the *eucharist and Arnold van Gennep's threefold structure for all rites of passage (*The Rites of Passage*, first published in French, 1909; English edn, Chicago 1960) is clear for anybody to see. Dix, however, never acknowledged the debt to this writing and it was not until the late 1960s and early 1970s that an open and clearly acknowledged borrowing of social scientific methodologies and theories began to appear in liturgical writing.

Some of the earliest writing by social scientists on questions of worship and liturgy began to appear in reaction to the radical changes and revisions in liturgy which were being undertaken following Vatican II in the late 1960s. In Britain J. G. Davies began to combine sociological methods and a concern for contemporary worship to show that the revisions had not gone far enough to meet the growing secularization of society (*Every Day God: Encountering the Holy in World and Worship*, London 1973). Harvey Cox developed a very similar argument in the USA, presenting a radical theory of festivity and the secular city (*The Feast of Fools: A Theological Essay on Festivity and Fantasy*, Cambridge, MA 1969). On the other side of the debate, well-known anthropologists such as Mary Douglas (*Natural Symbols: Explorations in Cosmology*, Harmondsworth 1973) and Victor Turner (*The Ritual Process: Structure and Anti-Structure*, Harmondsworth 1969; *Dramas, Fields and Metaphors: Symbolic Action in Human Society*, Ithaca, NY 1974) drew on their studies of religion in other cultures to critique the revisions as being too radical and not aware enough of the nature of symbolism, ritual and the liminal in worship. Victor Turner's work in particular began to be widely drawn upon by liturgists trying to bring an understanding of ritual and symbolism back into the study of worship that they felt had become too textual.

The work of Davies, Cox, Douglas and Turner was all focused on the contemporary practice of worship as it happened. They were concerned to draw on the methodologies used to study the worship of non-Christian religions to make a specific contribution to current debates within the Christian churches. Having become more acceptable as methodologies, it was not long before these same techniques were also being applied to questions relating to the history of Christian worship and the classical issues in the study of liturgy. David Power among others began to explore the anthropological and philosophical literature on symbolism and to apply it to the study of liturgy in general (*Unsearchable Riches: The Symbolic Nature of Liturgy*, New York 1984). In another direction Robert Taft drew on the work of Clifford Geertz and of anthropological structuralists to ask questions about the deep and surface structures of worship within early Eastern liturgy ('The Structural Analysis of Liturgical Units: An Essay in Methodology' in R. Taft, *Beyond East and West: Problems in Liturgical Understanding*, Washington, DC 1984, 151–64). Each of these authors, and others like them, were looking to the social sciences, and particularly to anthropology, for tools which they could develop for the study of liturgy in general and liturgical texts in particular.

As the 1980s drew on there were three areas where social-scientific models or methodologies have been very important to the study of Christian worship. The first area develops Dix's own similarities with van Gennep and follows Turner in focusing on rites of passage as a central ritual to many if not all societies. Many writers in the field of pastoral liturgy in particular, as well as those writing on *baptism, *marriage and *funerals have all had to give at least a passing comment to van Gennep and his theory. Very few liturgists, however, have really engaged with van Gennep's own work or with those anthropologists such as Maurice Bloch (*Prey into Hunter: The Politics of Religious Experience*, Cambridge 1992) who have critiqued and developed van Gennep in recent years. There is still a great deal of work to be done on the theoretical questions surrounding rites of passage in different Christian communities.

A second area of development has mirrored, and become involved with, the growing field of *ritual studies. Ritual studies as a distinct discipline of its own has grown out of a range of social sciences including sociology, anthropology, semiotics and the study of performance. Again Victor Turner is central to the early development of ritual studies as he developed his own interests in the direction of performance during the final years of his life. Other writers and performers such as Richard Shechner (*The Future of Ritual: Writings on Culture and Performance*, London 1993) and Catherine Bell (*Ritual: Perspective and Dimensions*, Oxford 1997) have developed these interests in different directions. There is now a *Journal of Ritual Studies*, and the study of Christian ritual, particularly *pilgrimage, plays a central role in the development of this new field.

Finally the 1980s saw a small but significant rise in the development of psychological studies of worship. The psychology of religion had long had an interest in religious experiences but these were traditionally seen as being distinct from the experience or context of worship. In the 1980s psychologists with an interest in religion began to focus on what might be called the more mundane elements of religious experience, including the experience of worship. In part this coincided with the development and study of the *Charismatic Movement, but it also developed a crossover interest with both rites of passage (through literature on the stages of faith) and ritual studies with the recognition that ritual may well induce, or even be defined by, a particular psychological state or approach to the world.

At about the same time three particular scholars, all of whom had an interest and training in both the social sciences and liturgy, were working on material which specifically aimed to apply a particular social scientific methodology to the study of Christian worship. Mark Searle, based at the University of Notre Dame in Indiana, began to work with sociologists from the university on a major study of RC parish life across the USA ('The Notre Dame Study of Catholic Parish Life', *Worship* LX, 1986, 312–33). This project was based on detailed questionnaires and observation in a very large number of different kinds of parishes and, unlike many other similar projects which were being undertaken at the time, Searle's involvement meant that worship was one of the principal areas which was studied. The Notre Dame Study of Catholic Parish Life therefore provided a considerable amount of quantitative and qualitative data on what RC parishes in the USA were actually doing within worship in the mid 1980s.

Where the Notre Dame study was very clearly on the empirical end of sociological research, Keiren Flanagan's important work on liturgy and sociology was far more on the theoretical end of the spectrum (*Sociology and Liturgy: Re-presentations of the Holy*, London 1991). Having recognized the very serious difficulties of undertaking empirical fieldwork on worship as it happens, Flanagan chose to draw on both his experiences as a practising RC and his training as a sociologist to reflect critically on the process of worship within the context of sociological theory. The results focus on elements of the worship such as the roles played by actors, the nature of performance and the desire to partake in the perfect act of worship. This is an important work in being the only real attempt to date to match sociological theory to liturgy.

Finally the work of Martin Stringer drew much more on anthropological methods and theories in an attempt to try and understand the nature of worship in contemporary mainstream churches (*On the Perception of Worship: The Ethnography of Worship in Four Christian*

Congregations in Manchester, Birmingham 1999). Stringer undertook fieldwork in the 1980s in four congregations from different Christian traditions in Manchester, England. From this fieldwork he developed the view that the meaning of worship cannot be read directly out of the texts and actions of the worship itself but rather is constructed, or negotiated, by each individual present in dialogue with other aspects of that individual's life. Stringer draws widely on various strands of anthropological theory in order to present a coherent view of how ordinary members of the congregation perceive and understand their worship.

In all these developments from the end of the twentieth century the emphasis once again moved on to the study of contemporary worship and the practice of worship as it happens in churches today. As there was some development of sociological methods in the study of the early church and the origins of Christianity, there was also a very marginal interest in the application of social science methodologies to historical contexts. This kind of application, however, is still in its infancy so far as the history of Christian worship is concerned. The other more traditional concern of liturgists, the study of texts, has probably fared slightly better. With the growth of hermeneutics and critical theory, which some would see as a product of the social sciences, there have been a small number of recent attempts to come back to the texts using these new and more challenging methodologies. Again such analysis probably has a long way to go before this is seen as a standard methodology in the study of liturgy. However, with the turn to hermeneutics and critical theory we can see liturgy beginning to turn back to the social science which first drew its attention, linguistics, and while we are a long way from the comparative methods of the nineteenth century there is probably still a great deal which liturgists can continue to learn from the dialogue.

MARTIN STRINGER

South India, Worship in the Church of

The Church of South India (CSI) came into existence on 27 September 1947 as an organic union of Anglican, (British) Methodist, Presbyterian and Congregationalist churches in South India. These four denominational streams had distinctive worship traditions and brought those into the life of the united church. Valuing the diversity of worship patterns, the Basis of Union, as outlined in the Constitution of the Church of South India, described the worship in the united church in this way: 'The uniting Churches recognize that they must aim at conserving for the common benefit whatever of good has been gained by each body in its separate history, and that in its public worship the united Church must retain for its congregations freedom either to use historic forms or not to do so as may best conduce to edification and to the worship of God in Spirit and in truth.' There were two other considerations as well. First, the forms of worship used in any of the uniting churches at the time of the union should not be forbidden in the united church. Second, new forms of worship might be introduced only with the agreement of the local pastor and congregation. With these in mind the first Synod appointed a Liturgy Committee to explore and prepare new forms of worship for the church, in collaboration with the liturgy committees of the various dioceses. The Committee began by working on the *eucharist. This liturgy was first used during the Synod session in 1950 and was later approved by the Synod in 1954. The Committee also created liturgies for other occasions of public worship, such as *daily prayer, *baptism and *confirmation. These efforts eventually led to the publication of the *Book of Common Worship* in English in 1963. It was later translated into local languages, and the liturgy is now said or sung in at least four different languages – Tamil, Telugu, Kannada, and Malayalam – in South India.

The eucharistic liturgy of the CSI is well known for its historic authenticity and its ecumenical inclusivity. While being Anglican in its basic structure, it incorporates elements from the other traditions within the CSI in a creative way. This is one of the reasons why it has been widely accepted and used in ecumenical settings throughout the world. It was first introduced to the ecumenical community during the Assembly of the World Council of Churches at Evanston in 1954. The liturgy has also maintained its historic connections with both Western and Eastern churches. For example, the *Trisagion* is used as one of the alternatives for Gloria in excelsis at the beginning of the eucharist.

Right from its beginnings, the CSI has been committed to efforts at *inculturation of worship patterns. The uniting churches had in their own denominational histories dealt with this issue in differing ways. As a united church, the

CSI committed itself to conscious incorporation of indigenous elements in public worship. Local customs and practices are woven into the liturgical practice of the church. For example, the passing of the peace during the eucharist is done by the giver placing his or her right hand against the right hand of the receiver and each closing the left over the other's right hand. The *celebrant first gives the peace to the *deacons and they in turn to the people. The CSI liturgy has been set to South Indian classical and popular music by several church musicians, and the congregations choose to use the music they are familiar with. In most of the non-urban congregations, people sit on the floor during worship, with men on one side of the aisle, women on the other, children in the front, and older folks further down the nave.

The most recent attempt at a truly Indian liturgy is exemplified in the alternative version of the eucharistic liturgy published in 1985. It 'attempts to express an understanding of worship that is more Indian than our traditional Christian worship forms', and it encourages people to conduct the service in as authentic an Indian style as possible. The liturgy is organized around five stages: entry (*pravesa*), awakening (*prabodha*), recalling and offering (*smarana-samarpana*), sharing in the body and blood of Christ (*darsana*), and blessing (*preshana*). The language of the liturgy is guided by the concerns of both inculturation and the liberation of the oppressed.

Indigenous elements are more conspicuously present in worship settings outside the church building. The prayer meetings held in people's homes, lyrical or musical preaching performed during festive occasions, prayer services at home related to rites of passage such as puberty, weddings and funerals, and other such home-based worship services bear clear marks of indigenous elements and influence. In addition to *Christmas and *Easter, CSI congregations celebrate occasions such as Church Anniversary Festival, and *Harvest Festival. These are opportunities for much more celebrative worship services. The form and nature of these worship services differ from region to region and according to earlier denominational links. Although there have been attempts, especially in theological seminaries, to celebrate the Hindu festivals, such as Diwali, Pongal, Onam and others, most Christians tend to see these as beyond the boundaries of Christian life and witness.

The hymnody of the CSI is shaped by four streams of hymnic traditions. First, the hymns from the West translated into local languages are still a vital part of the worship life of the CSI. Second, from the nineteenth century onwards South Indian hymn-writers have composed hymns in local languages set to local classical music. Third came a wave of modern popular hymns, especially from the Pentecostal and Evangelical churches in India. These hymns have also become a part of the hymnic tradition of the CSI. Fourth, there is a growing corpus of hymns written by Dalit Christians and hymn-writers. These are set to folk music. One might encounter all four of these streams of hymnody and music in many CSI congregations.

See also **North India, Worship in the Church of.**

The Book of Common Worship, London 1963; *The Book of Common Worship Supplement*, Madras 1986. T. S. Garrett, *Worship in the Church of South India*, London 1958; *The Liturgy of the Church of South India*, Oxford 1954; Bengt Sundkler, *Church of South India*, London 1965; Marcus Ward, *The Pilgrim Church*, London 1953.

M. THOMAS THANGARAJ

Spanish Rite *see* **Western Rites**

Spirituality, Liturgical

At the heart of Christian life and faith is love of God and neighbour. The term 'spirituality' refers to the lived experience of such a life in both its outward social and inward personal dimensions. For Christians, the liturgical assembly gathered around scripture, proclamation, prayer and the *sacraments is central to the formation of a distinctive way of life. 'Liturgical spirituality' thus refers to the pattern of interior piety and social holiness formed by participation in the rites of the church, animated by the Holy Spirit.

In the language of the Constitution on the Sacred Liturgy of Vatican II, liturgy is the 'source and summit' of Christian life. The liturgical action of the church engenders and aims at particular qualities of existence implied by participation of the faith community in public worship. Louis Bouyer and Alexander Schmemann both employed the expression 'liturgical piety' to speak of moral dispositions and the vision of goodness, truth and holiness revealed in the patterns of worship over time.

Bouyer's *Introduction to Spirituality* (London/ Collegeville 1961) contrasted the 'religious life', 'interior life' and the 'spiritual life'. The latter requires both religiousness and interiority. The community's repeated gathering about the book of memory, the ongoing prayer of the church for the world, the *font and the *altar, constitutes the chief practice whereby a determinate spirituality is given shape and sustained.

The history of Christianity is replete with many so-called 'schools of spirituality'. These are associated with particular ways of life named after founders and communities such as Ignatian, Salesian, Carmelite, Puritan and the like. Liturgical spirituality may be said to belong to the whole church. In *Liturgical Piety* (Notre Dame 1955), Bouyer defined liturgy as 'that system of prayers and rites traditionally canonized by the church as her own prayer and worship' (1). At the same time Schmemann's *Introduction to Liturgical Theology* (London 1966) warns that the liturgical piety of an epoch can 'fail to correspond to the liturgy or cult of which the piety is nevertheless the psychological perception or experience' (77).

The Christian assembly not only shapes the faith of its members, it also gives expression to the life of faith brought to the liturgy by its members. As the Body of Christ worships over time, so members of the body bring their hopes and fears, suffering and joy to the liturgy as well. To comprehend the range of such formation and expression of faith requires mention of the structures and defining elements of Christian liturgy, and the dynamics of experience involved in ritual participation in these structures and elements.

1. *Spirituality and the 'Canon' of Christian Liturgy*. Particular traditions of public worship display differences in structures and patterns. Christian public worship is always culturally embodied and embedded. The range of formative practices and expressive means available to a particular time and culture is determined by the history of liturgical practice and the social/cultural sensibility at hand. There are remarkable differences between Pentecostal and Calvinist traditions of prayer and proclamation, between Irish and German Catholicism, or between North African and East Syrian fourth-century Christianity. It is appropriate, therefore, to refer to distinctive 'spiritualities' belonging to particular historical periods, cultural sensibilities, and especially

to differences between 'liturgical' and 'non-liturgical' traditions. In the case of more 'left-wing' Protestant and sectarian churches, the term 'liturgical spirituality' may be less appropriate, especially where the accent falls strongly on personal faith expression and sacramental practices are minimal.

With these differences and exceptions noted, it is nevertheless true that the continuity of some basic structures and elements constitutes a broader sense of common Christian worship practices over time. These constitute a kind of normative 'canon': (a) rites of initiation (*see* **Baptism**), (b) the holy meal (*eucharist, *Lord's supper), (c) *daily prayer, (d) cycles of time (*see* **Year, Liturgical**), and (e) rites of passage or pastoral offices. While some Christian traditions have not practised all of these with equal weight, they have been fundamental to public worship in the major ecclesial traditions, both West and East. Each of these elements contributes to the formation and expression of a way of life grounded in the incarnation, words and deeds, suffering, death and resurrection of Jesus Christ. In one sense we may speak of the whole of Christian spirituality as 'baptismal', 'eucharistic', prayerful at all times, and comprehending all the experiences of human existence, while oriented toward the divine promises of eternal life. These central features of Christian worship over time are the means by which human beings participate in the divine life. In this way the glorification of God and the sanctification of all that is human are mutually bound together.

2. *Patterns of Affection, Virtue and Experience*. The Christian life may be described as a pattern of deep affections rooted and grounded in Christ. The term 'paschal *mystery' is characteristic of the more Catholic traditions, including most Anglicans and Lutherans. Living the liturgy over time nourishes particular dispositions, such as gratitude to God for all the gifts of life and grace, compassion and love of neighbour, a yearning for truth and justice, the capacity to repent and make amendment of life, and the joy and hope of life 'before God'. Seen in this light, liturgical spirituality is existential. Such deep affections are invited and nurtured by faithful public worship. At the same time, liturgical spirituality is not reducible merely to its affective subjectivity. There remains the question of the objective grace of God mediated by the liturgy.

Traditions have differed with respect to how the affective dimensions of human subjectivity should be the measure of faithfulness. Yet not even the most objectivist views of how liturgy conveys saving grace have neglected the 'fruitfulness' of participation in the rites. This reflects a creative tension between liturgical forms, elements, and the question of 'faithful participation'. Not everyone who attends the liturgical assembly is formed with equal depth. Participation in the eucharistic action may not always lead to a more profound gratitude or hopefulness in life. Much will depend upon the resistances to a mature spirituality present in the community and in the broader cultural context in which a particular worship tradition is found. Formation in the paschal mystery must also attend to and receive the pathos of life outside the rooms of Christian worship. This is why any renewal of the liturgy must always attend to the actual event of liturgical celebration, and not only to its texts and forms. Hence liturgical reform and renewal of the faith life of the churches go together.

3. *The Mystery of Grace in Liturgy and Life.* The mystery of Christian liturgy remains: the triune God acts in and through the practices of the church. The meeting and the singing, the reading, preaching, praying, offering, blessing, breaking and pouring out, the water bath and laying-on of hands, the being sent to serve God and neighbour – all these point beyond what meets the human senses. The public worship of God through such liturgical forms waits for humanity to open itself to the redeeming grace of God in Christ. If we regard liturgy as the ongoing word and action of Christ present in the common prayer of the Church, then liturgical spirituality is our co-joining in that Spirit-animated life together.

A healthy Christian life practises the inter-relationships between the public liturgy and more intimate devotions; but so also a graced Christian life exhibits the interrelatedness of liturgical prayer and God-centred dispositions and intentions in daily life. This is true of the worshipping community and thus also of the individual lives of its members. To acknowledge and to praise the creator of all things who is the one who redeems all things 'in, with, and through Jesus Christ in the unity of the Holy Spirit' is both true worship and true human being 'fully alive'.

***

Eleanor Bernstein (ed.), *Liturgy and Spiritual-*

ity in Context, Collegeville 1990; Jean Corbon, *The Wellspring of Worship*, New York 1988; Kevin W. Irwin, *Liturgy, Prayer and Spirituality*, New York 1984; Philip H. Pfatteicher, *Liturgical Spirituality*, Valley Forge, PA 1997; Don E. Saliers, *Worship and Spirituality*, 2nd edn, Akron 1996.

DON E. SALIERS

Spirituals

African American spirituals, identified historically as 'negro spirituals', represent a genre of spontaneous 'songs of the soul' of an enslaved people, created, re-created, and transmitted orally. The earliest (seventeenth/eighteenth-century) folk composers left no records of the name that they would give this category of songs. Those who continued this tradition, including *Black congregations and former slaves, identified them as 'sperichils' or 'spirituals'. Throughout history other names have been given this body of musical literature to reflect the communal folk-song origin, the wide range of subjects, and in some instances the manner of performance. Names attached include: slave song, plantation songs, 'cornfield ditties', jubilees, minstrel songs, religious folk songs and most recently African American spirituals.

Africans from a variety of linguistic cultures who were forced into a strange and alien land were able to devise a means of communication. Through song, people from a large geographical area of Africa bonded as Americans as they shared folk tales, expressed their desire to return to Africa, taught, scolded and released emotional tension about their current plight. In the spirituals they pondered their existential condition, communicated with the Almighty and talked among themselves about an immediate future that was free from bondage. Many of the texts document the shaping of theological beliefs and unswerving faith in a liberating God who 'is always on time'. Much like the songs of their African homeland, spirituals are filled with allusions, symbolisms and hidden meanings. Through songs, coded messages could be sent great distances while slaves worked in open fields and prayed in secret places. In addition to the ultimate freedom and survival of generations of African Americans, these songs of protest and praise became the foundation of new musical genres.

Although biblical terms and stories pervade the literature, there is evidence that some of the creators of the spirituals were not Christians. Out of convenience, some knowledge of the religious terminology of their Christian oppressors provided opportunities for working slaves to continue their artistic improvisatory heritage as musicians. Biblical terms were apparently used ambiguously to project dual meanings. 'Good News' and 'gospel message' often communicated an immediate plan to escape via the Underground Railroad. References to 'Moses' often meant a message from Harriet Tubman including time and place to 'board the freedom train'. 'Beulah Land' and Canaan were used to describe places of freedom in the North. References to rivers and streams were often clues to escape routes through water.

The nearly six thousand extant spirituals provide a broad spectrum of melodies, rhythms, forms and harmonies that result from the oral, unaccompanied transmission of songs. Their beauty, simplicity and emotional depth make them suitable for symphonic themes, congregational songs, and as foundational for new musical forms around the world.

MELVA WILSON COSTEN

Sponsors *see* Godparents

Sri Lanka, Worship in the Church in

Tradition holds that the church that was established by the Apostle Thomas in the south-western part of India also took roots in Sri Lanka. Archaeological evidence suggests that at one period in its history Sri Lanka also had thriving Nestorian and Armenian congregations in the western coastal areas of the country. The churches prevalent in the island today, however, are the result of the successive colonial powers that ruled Sri Lanka until its independence from British rule in 1948. The Portuguese brought in Roman Catholicism. The Dutch, who followed them, established the Reformed tradition. The Anglican, Methodist, Congregational and Baptist traditions were introduced during the British rule. The missions that accompanied the colonial rulers, with the exception of some individual missionaries, were deeply suspicious of the religion and culture of the local population. They were considered to be inconsistent with the Christian faith. The result was the introduction of the respective liturgies and worship practices that were current in the parent churches in the West. Thus the Sri Lanka church architecture, church order and worship were, and to a large extent

continue to be, the Western models that were introduced into the country by the missionaries.

The earliest attempt at *inculuration was in the field of music, where words rich in Christian content could be set to Sinhalese and Tamil music. Today these 'lyrics' are sung in worship alongside Western hymns translated into the local languages. A more significant attempt at the indigenization of worship was introduced within the Ashram Movement that flourished after the independence of the island. In the Tamil-speaking areas near the town of Chunnakam in the North and Kiran in the East, Sevak Selvaratnam began monastic communities, patterned after Hindu monastic life. Hindu architecture influenced the shape of the worship spaces in these ashrams. The singing of *thevarams* (intensely devotional songs sung by individuals within the liturgy) and *bhajans* (community singing led by an individual), also taken from Hinduism, became popular in the Tamil-speaking areas. They eventually found their way also into the regular Sunday worship of the churches.

Similar attempts at indigenization in the Buddhist-dominated South resulted in the building of the Anglican cathedral in Kurunagale in Buddhist architectural style. Buddhist religious practices of chanting, drumming and dancing were introduced into the liturgy on special liturgical occasions. Sevak Johan Devananda, who spearheaded the Ashram Movement in the South, introduced into Christian liturgical worship Buddhist practices of silence, contemplation, meditation and chanting. The movement produced the 'New World Liturgy', which incorporated into an essentially Christian liturgy elements from other religious and secular traditions that were consistent with Christian worship. After the Second Vatican Council the RC Church in Sri Lanka also entered a period of liturgical renewal, introducing widespread use of the local languages in the celebration of the *eucharist and incorporating elements from the Sinhalese and Tamil culture into liturgical celebrations. Yet another innovation in liturgy came from the Christian Workers' Fellowship. On the first day of the month of May each year (Labour Day) the Christian Workers' Fellowship organizes an ecumenical liturgical celebration called the 'Workers' Mass', attended also by people of other religious traditions. While maintaining the core of a Christian liturgical event, the Workers' Mass took greater liberty in introducing symbols, readings and prayers that were meaningful to workers of all religious traditions in Sri Lanka.

These innovations, however, are still marginal to the worship and liturgical life of the major denominations and to the Pentecostal and other smaller churches in the island. The predominant structure of worship and liturgy in all churches continues to be patterned after the denominational or confessional traditions that established these churches in the first instance. The reluctance for greater liturgical innovation and inculturation stems from three distinctive factors that have characterized Christian missions from the very beginning: (1) a theological approach that sees other religions and cultures as devoid of God's revelation and hence, at best, 'misguided' or in 'error'; (2) the fear of syncretism, that would eventually lead to the devitalization of the faith and absorption of the Christian community into the larger community; (3) the need to maintain a distinctively Christian identity of a group that had at one time left behind Buddhism or Hinduism to embrace the Christian faith. Worship and liturgy have traditionally been at the heart of this distinctive Christian identity. Therefore, a more genuine worship and liturgical life, which reflects more fully the culture and religious ethos of the island, could emerge only with a radical theological reassessment of the Christian attitude and approach to the culture and religions of the land.

S. WESLEY ARIARAJAH

Standing see Posture 1

Stations of the Cross

The name denotes both fourteen selected representations of incidents in the last journey of Christ and the devotion which consists in pausing at them in sequence for prayer and meditation. The devotion probably arose out of the practice recorded from early times of pilgrims to Jerusalem following the 'way of the cross' from Pilate's house to Calvary, and wishing to re-enact it when they returned home. Devotion to the holy places and to Christ's passion received an extra fillip with the return of the Crusaders, who often erected tableaux of the places they had visited in the Holy Land. And when the Franciscans were given custody of the holy places in 1342, they saw it as part of their mission to promote the devotion and to encourage the erection of series of such tableaux. From their own churches the practice spread widely into parish churches too.

The subjects of these 'stations' varied widely, as did the number (anything from five to over thirty). The number fourteen seems to have appeared first in the sixteenth century in the Low Countries, and when the devotion was regulated by Clement XII in 1731, it stabilized at this number, comprising nine gospel scenes and five from popular tradition. By the nineteenth century virtually all RC churches tended to have a set of fourteen ranged around the internal walls (or occasionally out of doors in the church grounds).

The devotion can be used privately by individual worshippers, silently and informally, with or without texts (of which dozens of unofficial collections exist). More public forms are celebrated with a vested minister, *acolytes and *crucifer doing the circuit, the congregation following or remaining in their *pews. In this case verses of the medieval hymn Stabat mater, in the vernacular, have often been sung between stations, and meditations such as those of St Alphonsus Liguori (d. 1787) were particularly popular in the nineteenth and twentieth centuries. With the liturgical revival in the mid-twentieth century, the devotion has probably waned somewhat, though it is still widely practised in *Lent and as a supplementary service on *Good Friday. With the recovered theology of the paschal mystery stressing the integral unity of Christ's death and resurrection, a fifteenth station representing the resurrection has frequently been added to the series, and more exclusively scriptural meditations composed. As the devotion has always been strictly extra-liturgical, no official texts have ever been provided in the RC Church, but the Episcopal Church in the United States provides full texts and *rubrics in its Book of Occasional Services (1979, 1988).

CHRISTOPHER WALSH

Sticharion see Vestments 4(a)

Stole see Vestments 3(c)

Stoup

A vessel at the entrance of churches made to contain holy water and used by the faithful in recognition of baptismal graces and promises. This usage continues the practices of ritual cleansing provided for in the *atria of early

Western churches. Some few examples are attached to the *font itself. Too often stoups are neglected, empty, dirty and innocent of water. Clearly the water of *baptism or that set aside for penitential sprinkling should be used in the stoup in preference to other blessed water.

MICHAEL THOMPSON

Subdeacon

Evidence for the existence of subdeacons is first found in the middle of the third century. They are mentioned frequently by Cyprian in his correspondence, and they are also listed first, after *deacons, in the letter of Cornelius of Rome in 251. The office seems to have emerged in order to provide assistance to the deacon, and the principal liturgical duty was to prepare the vessels for the *eucharist. Later, as the office of *lector declined, subdeacons would also proclaim the epistle and any other *readings at the eucharist, except for the gospel. In the East, where the subdiaconate is also regarded as a lower degree of the diaconate, they came to be appointed by prayer and the imposition of the hand, as the form of their *ordination was gradually assimilated to that of a deacon. In the West, the office was conferred by the handing over of a symbol of office: from at least the sixth century onwards subdeacons in Rome received a *chalice, and in other Western traditions a chalice and paten tended to be given. In the later Roman tradition the subdeacon had a rather curious liturgical duty: to hold the empty paten in a humeral veil (see **Veil** 5) during the eucharistic rite from the *offertory until the end of the *Lord's Prayer. This had its origin in the *papal liturgy, when the bread for the eucharist was brought up on large platters and held by subdeacons during the *eucharistic prayer.

From the thirteenth century onwards in the West the subdiaconate began to be regarded as the lowest of the major orders rather than one of the *minor orders, and those admitted to it were placed under the same obligation to celibacy as the higher orders. But by this time it had ceased to be a real ministry and was usually no more than a brief stage through which candidates for the priesthood were required to pass. The liturgical duties attached to the office came to be performed instead by a priest, a deacon, or even a layman. It was finally suppressed in the RC Church in 1972.

EDITOR

Suffrages

Suffrages (from the Latin *suffragia*, prayers seeking favour or support) are found in the divine office in the historic *Western rites (see **Daily Prayer** 3). They are always petitionary, sometimes intercessory; they are usually couched in general, but sometimes in particular terms; they are normally in the form of versicles and responses, commonly include the *Lord's Prayer, and usually conclude with a *collect or collects. The suffrages in the morning and evening offices of the *BCP*, comprising the material from the *creed to the third collect, are typical; they are largely derived from those found in the Sarum books. Those in modern versions of the Anglican daily offices, although different in detail, follow the same basic pattern.

Suffrages were not part of the original Roman offices, but were added to them when they were adopted in the Frankish lands, where they were part of the Gallican offices. There they had been known as *capitella*, 'verses' from scripture, and originally functioned as the responses to various biddings to pray. When those biddings eventually disappeared, the *capitellum* was divided into two halves to form both versicle and response.

In the latest reform of the RC daily offices, suffrages have been replaced by *preces* (translated into the English version as 'intercessions', which is somewhat misleading, as by no means all of them are intercessory in character), in the form of a *litany which varies according to the hour, day, feast and season.

W. JARDINE GRISBROOKE

Sunday

Sunday, or the Lord's Day as it came to be known in the Christian dispensation, is the foundation of the entire structure of the rhythm of Christian worship, and represented simultaneously a continuing of and a profound transformation of the Jewish pattern of worship. In the Jewish system, the days of the week were known simply as the first day, the second day and so on. The last day of the week was given a title, the Sabbath, which became a weekly day of worship. However in Christianity it was 'the first day of the week' which took this position. By the end of the first century that designation had given place to one which more adequately conveyed the day's significance – the Lord's Day. The use of the name Sunday dates from about the middle of the second century. In 321 the official recognition by the Roman state of Sunday as the day of Christian worship and as a day of public rest meant that the Sabbath had now been incorporated into and transformed by Christian tradition.

As the Sabbath provided the model of a weekly day of worship, so its general influence is demonstrated by the fact that for a considerable period the Christian Sunday began with sunset on the Saturday evening; this was formalized at about 6 p.m. Centuries passed before the old Semitic reckoning from the setting of the sun yielded completely to the Roman conception of the day as beginning at midnight. The 'eves' of the great festivals represent the survival of the beginning of the Semitic day, the 'eve' being part of the festival itself. When this reckoning disappeared from common use, it remained in connection with the important days of the Christian *year.

The relationship between the Lord's Day of the Christian dispensation and the Sabbath of the old covenant also emphasizes the immense difference between them. The gospel narratives of the resurrection furnish the significance of the designation 'the first day of the week' as a proper name for the Christian day of worship. The binding link between Sunday and the resurrection becomes more obvious when it is remembered that primitive worship took place at an early hour of the morning. The resurrection on the first day of the week made it particularly the Lord's Day for Christians. Its predominant themes were always to be joy, thanksgiving, victory. The early church never lost this conception of Sunday as a sign of the inbreaking of the eternal order of God, and it remains a day of praise and triumph. Fasting and penitential observance of kneeling in prayer were strictly forbidden.

The immense change which substituted the Christian Sunday for the Jewish Sabbath took place within the first generation of the church's life. Certainly by the middle of the sixth decade when Paul, writing to the Corinthian church, refers to 'the first day of the week' (1 Cor. 16.2), regarding this day as the Lord's Day must have already become very well established. As a celebration of the resurrection the first day of the week is a kind of weekly *Easter; and indeed it predates the evolution of the annual cycle of the Christian year, which only became fully developed well into the fourth century. Those Christians who observe the yearly calendar tend now to regard the annual cycle as primary, with the weekly rhythm fitting into it, but in terms of historical development it was the other way round; the week came first, the liturgical year second.

In later years the prime importance of Sunday in its own right, and as the controlling rhythm of the liturgical year, was perhaps overshadowed by other calendrical developments, in particular the cycle of *saints' days, whose very considerable growth tended to obscure both the importance of Sunday and the rest of the liturgical year. Recent liturgical and calendrical revision has restored Sunday to its proper importance, something Reformed and Free Churches had done from the Reformation onwards, both by the stress they put on it and by their suppression of other observances. In an age when weekday liturgical observance additional to regular Sunday worship is only followed by a tiny minority of people, this emphasis on Sunday liturgy is surely right for both practical as well as theological reasons. On the other hand, changing secular patterns of life, with Sunday becoming more and more an ordinary day for commercial activity and with much emphasis on other leisure pursuits, may mean that a considerable number of people will come to make attendance at a weekday service their main weekly act of worship and then not go on Sunday at all. The end result of all this is likely to be a situation of some difficulty and complexity for those who have to organize the provision of public worship. Writing on the verge of the twenty-first century, it is very difficult to see what the future pattern of worship will be, even a comparatively short time into the future.

Adolf Adam, *The Liturgical Year*, New York 1981, 35–56; Harry Boone Porter, *The Day of Light: The Biblical and Liturgical Meaning of Sunday*, London 1960; Willy Rordorf, *Sunday*, London 1968; Thomas J. Talley, *The Origins of the Liturgical Year*, 2nd edn, Collegeville 1991.

RICHARD F. BUXTON

Sunday School

see **Children and Worship**

Super Oblata

Since the mid-fifth century, the *offertory ceremony in the Roman *eucharist has been concluded with a prayer which was originally called the *oratio super oblata* ('prayer over the offerings'), but was later known as the *secreta* ('secret'). As the latter name first appears in France and Germany, where the custom of saying the prayer in a low voice (*secreto*) originated, it probably refers to this custom, although other meanings are possible. At Rome it was anciently sung, and the singing or saying aloud of it has been restored in the 1969 RC *Ordo missae* along with its original name.

The prayer, which varies according to the day, is in form a variant of the *collect type; its basic content is always a prayer for the divine acceptance of the gifts just placed on the *altar within the context of the eucharistic mystery about to be accomplished. A prayer parallel to the *oratio super oblata* in function and content is found in a corresponding place in most of the historic liturgies.

See also **Silent Prayer**.

J. A. Jungmann, *The Mass of the Roman Rite*, New York 1951, II, 90–97.

W. JARDINE GRISBROOKE

Superintendent

Many of the sixteenth-century Reformation churches wished to continue an office of *episkope*, 'oversight', but wanted to avoid the name '*bishop' because of its prelatical and hierarchical connotations. Hence 'superintendent' was the usual alternative choice. There were, for example, superintendents in German Lutheran churches, which have continued to the present day, and in the Church of Scotland, although in this case the office was later discontinued. John Wesley ordained Methodist 'superintendants' (sic) for the USA, but to his dismay, the title 'bishop' was preferred by the church there. British Methodists have superintendent ministers who are in charge of a circuit, and the office also exists among Baptists, but in neither case is there an *ordination for persons so appointed.

EDITOR

Surplice *see* **Vestments** 3(a)

Symbol *see* **Sign, Symbol**

Synapte see **Litany**

Synaxis

A Greek word meaning 'assembly' or 'gathering' and used in early Christianity as a general term to denote any liturgical rite but more especially an office (*see* **Daily Prayer** 1) or service of the *word.

EDITOR

Syrian Worship

see **East Syrian Worship**; **West Syrian Worship**

Tabernacle

In Christian liturgical use, the tabernacle houses vessels containing the blessed sacrament, usually only the consecrated bread but occasionally the consecrated wine as well. The Christian tabernacle takes its name from the Jewish tabernacle, or 'tent of meeting' ('tent' itself being an English medieval abbreviation for 'tenement'), the portable shrine used by Moses, containing the ark of the covenant (Ex. 25—31, 35—40), itself representing the presence of God. A lamp is normally kept burning before the tabernacle when the blessed sacrament is housed, though the colour of the lamp varies from country to country. Sometimes the tabernacle is covered with a cloth, ornamented or otherwise, though this is not a requirement. Despite the preference of the reforms following Vatican II, that the tabernacle should not reside upon the high *altar in a church, the removal of the high altar from the far east end of the *sanctuary into a more central position in the sanctuary or *chancel has meant that the tabernacle often retains its customary former position, elevated at the east end of the sanctuary, thus complying with RC canon law, which also requires it to be structurally secured and its door locked with a key. In some churches, the consecrated oils are also placed in the tabernacle, although they more properly belong in a separate *aumbry.

See also **Pyx**.

TRISTAM HOLLAND

Te Deum Laudamus see **Canticles**

Tenebrae

The service of tenebrae ('darkness') was held on the night of *Maundy Thursday in the medieval Western Christian tradition. It was based on the early morning office of matins, with three unique characteristics. The first were the special readings from Lamentations, expressing the sorrow and mourning which would mark the next two days of *Good Friday and *Holy Saturday. The second was the ritual extinguishing of a number of lit candles (15 in Roman tradition, 24 in England, and any number from 5 to 72 elsewhere) one by one, at the end of each psalm. Contemporary sources interpreted this action in a number of ways, including some with an anti-Semitic theme, e.g. as a symbol of the Jews' rejection/persecution of the prophets and the apostles. After the candles were extinguished, the church was left in darkness. Then came the third ritual: the symbolic banging of the *pews by the ministers and congregation, possibly as a ritual remembrance of Christ's scourging by the soldiers. The service is still observed in the RC and some other traditions, but the anti-Semitic interpretations of the ritual actions have been rejected and replaced.

For bibliography, *see* **Holy Week**.

JOANNE M. PIERCE

Terce *see* **Daily Prayer**

Thanksgiving (USA)

Thanksgiving Day is a national holiday, celebrated on the fourth Thursday of November, during which people gather in family, civic or religious groups to give thanks to God. In many towns and cities the day is commemorated with ecumenical or inter-religious services of worship. In addition to public worship, Thanksgiving Day traditions include a feast of turkey with stuffing or dressing, pumpkin pie, and other distinctively American foods. Since the early twentieth century, Thanksgiving Day parades marking the beginning of the Christmas shopping season, and college and professional American football games have also been features of the holiday.

The contemporary Thanksgiving Day is widely assumed to be a yearly commemoration of the Puritan Pilgrims who established the Plymouth settlement. The Pilgrims arrived at Plymouth on a small ship, the *Mayflower*, during the winter of 1620, and in the following months as many as half of the settlers died. With the help of some of the Native American tribes, the survivors managed to plant a successful crop of corn and barley. In the fall of 1621, the Plymouth governor William Bradford called for a season of thanksgiving for the abundant *harvest that enabled the survival of the colony, and he invited the local Wampanoag tribe to a feast that lasted for three days. Other colonies held similar days of general thanksgiving, although Puritan objections to a liturgical calendar prohibited the establishment of annual celebrations.

During the Revolutionary War (1775–83) the Continental Congress called for the first National Day of Thanksgiving on 18 December 1777. After the war, the first two US presidents, George Washington and John Adams, continued to proclaim national days of prayer, although this prerogative later fell to state governors. By the middle of the nineteenth century, most northern states and many southern states had established annual days of thanksgiving and prayer. In 1846 Sarah Josepha (sic) Hale, the editor of *Godey's Lady's Book,* used her popular magazine to begin a campaign to establish the last Thursday in November as a national day of thanksgiving. Each year, Hale wrote the US president and the governors of every state with her petition. In 1863, toward the end of the Civil War, President Abraham Lincoln finally declared a nationwide Thanksgiving Day on the last Thursday in November. Each US president since has continued the annual tradition of declaring a national Thanksgiving Day.

RCs were initially cool to the holiday, since it was a Protestant invention. In 1884, however, the American RC bishops approved prayers for the government at the daily *mass said on Thanksgiving Day. Other religious groups were also wary of this 'Christian' holiday, though by the early twentieth century the nonsectarian patriotic focus of the day allowed for wider acceptance. In 1939, President Franklin D. Roosevelt moved the holiday from the last Thursday of November (which fell on the 30th that year) to the fourth Thursday in November to allow for a longer holiday shopping season before Christmas. In 1941, the US Congress passed a resolution making the fourth Thursday in November the official day.

Diana Karter Appelbaum, *Thanksgiving: An American Holiday, An American History*, New York 1984 (bib.); Jane M. Hatch, *The American Book of Days*, New York 1978; William DeLoss Love, Jr, *The Fast and Thanksgiving Days of New England*, Cambridge, MA 1895.

L. EDWARD PHILLIPS

Theology of Worship

1. *The Nature of Worship*. The worship of God is a primary activity of the church, requiring no justification beyond itself. It accomplishes

indeed 'man's chief end', which according to the Westminster Catechism is 'to glorify God and enjoy him for ever'. Phenomenologically, worship takes place in cultic acts. Such rites are intended as the vehicle of an inward and total devotion; they both form and express the believers who carry them out. The apostle Paul used cultic terminology both of the ethical conduct expected of Christians (Rom. 12.1f.; 1 Cor. 6.18–20; 2 Cor. 6.16ff.) and of his own evangelistic activities (Rom. 1.9; 15.15f.; Phil. 2.17; 2 Tim. 4.6). Liturgists are interested specifically in rites, and more particularly in the corporate worship of the church.

Worship is a faithful human response to the revelation of God's being, character, beneficence and will. In worship, God is adored simply as God, God's character is praised, thanks are given for God's acts, and conformity to God's will is sought. Worship is the requital of God's love in a personal encounter, a communion which is reciprocal but asymmetrical, involving a 'sacrifice of praise' (Heb. 13.15) on the part of the created and redeemed. God precedes humanity not only in the mighty deeds of creation and redemption but also in calling for, and in some sense enabling, the ever renewed response of worship. German theologians like to pun on 'divine service' (*Gottesdienst*), saying that God serves us before we serve God. Finally worship is participation in the life of God in the mode appropriate to created being.

Characteristically, Christian worship is trinitarian in theme and structure. The *eucharistic prayer is normally offered to the Father (the 'Abba' of Jesus; in Cappadocian terms, the 'Fount of Deity') through Christ in the Holy Spirit (cf. Eph. 2.18). This is not felt to be in contradiction with *doxology addressed to all three divine persons: the Nicene-Constantinopolitan *Creed confesses as Lord not only the Son but also the Holy Spirit, 'who with the Father and the Son together is worshipped and glorified'. This praise is offered 'in the church' (Eph. 3.20f.) whose 'principal manifestation', *praecipua manifestatio*, is the liturgical assembly (Vatican II, Constitution on the Liturgy 41). The etymology of *leitourgia* has sometimes been exploited to stress that worship is 'the work of the whole people' in the sense that it calls for the 'active participation' of the whole assembly, each member in its role (Constitution on the Liturgy 14; 26–30). Another interpretation makes of the liturgy a 'public service' rendered by the church on behalf of a world which is no longer, or not yet, able or willing to worship God in agreement with the vocation of humanity (J. J. von Allmen, *Worship: Its Theology and Practice*, London 1965). The eschatological nature of worship is shown in its 'playfulness' (R. Guardini, *The Spirit of the Liturgy*, English translation, London 1930), its resolution of work and rest: the service of God is perfect freedom (*BCP*, second *collect at morning prayer).

2. *Worship and Doctrine*. At their most elementary, liturgy and doctrine coincide: 'Jesus is Lord' is both an acclamation and an assertion. But as each develops with its own functions and in its own circumstances, the two risk growing apart. In its loving address to God, worship tends towards exuberance and abandon; theology, on the other hand, operates in controversy and responds to intellectual challenge, making fine distinctions and drawing conclusions by argument. Yet worship and theology continue to interact, and church dogma mediates between them. The fourth century provides a classic case that has been decisive for Christian identity. Worship had very early been accorded to Christ: apart from the acts of obeisance (*proskunesis*) in the synoptic Gospels and the 'My Lord and my God' of Thomas (John 20.28), the NT contains hymns in praise of Christ's sovereignty (Phil. 2.5–11; Rev. 1.5f.; 5.13; cf. 2 Tim. 4.18; 2 Peter 3.18). Against the Arians the Nicenes argued that the reduction of Christ to a creature would turn Christians into idolaters (Athanasius, *Letter to Adelphius* 3f.; cf. Gregory Nazianzus, *Oration XL on Holy Baptism* 42; Gregory of Nyssa, *On the Holy Spirit against Macedonius*). Athanasius and the Cappadocians also appealed, in support of the Trinity, to the threefold name confessed in the saving mystery of *baptism (Athanasius, *Letter to Sarapion* I.29f.; Gregory of Nyssa, *Sermon on the Baptism of Christ*; Basil, *On the Holy Spirit* 24–6; cf. Theodore of Mopsuestia, *Catechetical Homily* XIV.14–21; Ambrose, *On the Mysteries* V.28). Against the Macedonians, Basil of Caesarea was able to point to an existing tradition of addressing doxologies to the Holy Spirit alongside the Father and the Son (*On the Holy Spirit* 71–5). Eventually the conciliar Creed of Nicaea and Constantinople served not only to regulate the bishops' teaching on God but also became adopted into the eucharistic liturgies of both Byzantium and the

West as a doxological text: liturgy and doctrine there coincide once more.

The familiar tag *lex orandi, lex credendi* ('the law of praying [sets] the law of believing') has its verbal origins in the fifth century, although the mode of argument is substantially earlier. Before even such argumentation in the Arian controversy, Irenaeus and Tertullian had invoked against the Gnostics' depreciation of matter the sacramental practice of the church with bodily gesture, water and oil, bread and wine. Between 435 and 442 the lay monk Prosper of Aquitaine, in a work that became associated with Pope Celestine I, argued against semi-Pelagianism that the apostolic injunction to *pray* for the whole human race (1 Tim. 2.1–4) – which the church obeys in its intercessions – proves the obligation to *believe* that all faith, even the beginnings of good will as well as growth and perseverance, is from start to finish a work of grace. To show the need for grace from the very beginning, Prosper appeals also to pre-baptismal *exorcisms and *insufflations, as Augustine had already done in establishing that children are born with original sin. While liturgy is thus claimed to establish doctrine, doctrine may also have a return effect on the liturgy. In the area of soteriology, many collects in the ancient Western sacramentaries appear to have been deliberately composed with an anti-Pelagian intent and yet a due acknowledgement of the place of works in the salvation of believers. That should not be thought of as an alien imposition on the liturgy, for in its profoundest structures worship shows Christians ascribing salvation to God's grace alone yet themselves engaged in the active response of faith.

Worship is a first-order theology. In the words of Evagrius of Pontus: 'If you are a theologian, you will truly pray; and if you truly pray, you are a theologian.' In the liturgies of St Mark and St Basil, the doxologies addressed to God at the *Sanctus are called 'theologies'. Yet the initial gift and act of faith already contain an element of understanding, the *intellectus fidei*. So there should be no discontinuity between primary theology and second-order, or reflective, theology, or faith seeking (further or self-) understanding (*fides quaerens intellectum*). Nevertheless, reflective theology may have to act critically upon particular manifestations of worship. Thus the Reformation intended to correct developed liturgical practices that were the outcrop of distorted views on God, humanity and salvation. The Reformers

acted in the name of the scriptures which, though they themselves were to a great extent liturgically composed, defined and transmitted, nevertheless had a special authority in view of their canonical status. Protestants have usually held, too, that the Catholic magisterium would have done better to nip *Marian devotion in the bud rather than allowing it into the liturgy and eventually appealing to liturgical practice when defining the Marian dogmas. At all times, reflective theology has the duty to advise the pastoral office in its regulation of the more or less spontaneous popular developments that seek expression in the official liturgy.

The Protestant Reformers issued their own orders for public worship. In the circumstances these understandably had a somewhat aggressive doctrinal thrust. As a result, Protestant services have tended to an undue stress on the didactic over the latreutic. Yet there is a properly formative role for the liturgy. At the beginning of the modern *Liturgical Movement, Dom Lambert Beauduin recognized the worship assembly as the primary place in which people learned and grew in the faith. That may be seen as an extension of the *mystagogical catechesis of the patristic church. Official liturgical compositions after Vatican II, both Catholic and Protestant, privileged the paschal theme of Christ's death and resurrection (see Irmgard Pahl, 'The Paschal Mystery in its Central Meaning for the Shape of Christian Liturgy', *Studia Liturgica* XXVI, 1996, 16–38), leading some to regret the failure to take up other strands from the early tradition also, such as the theme of filiation favoured in the Syrian churches (see Paul F. Bradshaw, 'The Homogenization of Christian Liturgy – Ancient and Modern', *Studia Liturgica* XXVI, 1996, 1–15). Theological issues of principle involved in the revision and renewal of liturgy are discussed in Maxwell E. Johnson, 'Can We Avoid Relativism in Worship? Liturgical Norms in the Light of Contemporary Liturgical Scholarship', *Worship* LXXIV, 2000, 135–55, and in Geoffrey Wainwright, 'La règle liturgique est-elle universelle?', *La Maison-Dieu* CCXXII, 2000, 37–60.

3. *Recent Literature.* Among recent theologians with a strong interest in worship, emphasis varies as to how far the liturgy itself should control not only the theme but also the structure and texture of their work. Alexander Schmemann's theology of baptism, *Of Water and the Spirit* (Crestwood, NY 1974), is a

direct commentary on the Byzantine rite of initiation, just as his eucharistic theology, *The Eucharist: Sacrament of the Kingdom* (Crestwood, NY 1988), follows the order of the Sunday liturgy. In his *Theological Dimensions of the Liturgy* (English translation, Collegeville 1976), Cipriano Vagaggini locates the rites and prayers within a framework of salvation history and the classical tractates of Catholic theology. D. W. Hardy and David Ford, in their *Jubilate: Theology in Praise* (London 1984), take no account of the ritual action and scarcely cite a liturgical text. Dietrich Ritschl, while recognizing that the Christian 'story' is liturgically transmitted, holds that worship is a 'last word' and should not become a starting point for further 'scholastic deductions' (*Zur Logik der Theologie*, Munich 1984; English translation, Philadelphia 1987). On the other hand, Gerhard Ebeling makes the fundamental act of prayer the basis of his whole relational ontology (*Dogmatik des christlichen Glaubens*, Tübingen 1979). It seems proper that systematic theology should draw on and serve the worship of the church, just as it has also other sources and responsibilities in the evangelistic enterprise, the ethical endeavours of Christians, and the engagement with the history of ideas and culture. When it reaches into silence, worship may remind theology of its own apophatic dimension.

After the secular reductionism of the 1960s, liturgical scholars since the 1970s have tended to maintain a stress on the humanity of worship but have regained the sense of rites and signs as vehicles of transcendence from and towards God. They find tools in phenomenology, cultural anthropology and semiotics, but recognize the divine component in the system, structure or pattern of 'communication' which is Christian liturgy. Names to be mentioned here include Roger Grainger (*The Language of the Rite*, London 1974), Werner Jetter (*Symbol und Ritual: Anthropologische Elemente im Gottesdienst*, Göttingen 1978), L. M. Chauvet (*Du symbolique au symbole*, Paris 1979; English translation, Collegeville 1995), George S. Worgul (*From Magic to Metaphor: A Validation of the Christian Sacraments*, New York 1980), David N. Power (*Unsearchable Riches: The Symbolic Nature of Liturgy*, New York 1984), M. Jossutis (*Der Weg in das Leben: Eine Einführung in den Gottesdienst auf verhaltenswissenschaftlicher Grundlage*, Munich 1991), Rainer Volp (*Liturgik: Die Kunst, Gott zu feiern*, 2 volumes, Gütersloh 1992–4),

Hans Otmar Meuffels (*Kommunikative Sakramententheologie*, Freiburg 1995), and E. E. Uzukwu (*Worship as Body Language: An African Orientation*, Collegeville 1997).

On the borders between worship and systematics, the last quarter of the twentieth century was also marked by a lively exploration and debate concerning the nature of 'liturgical theology'. Surveys can be found in David W. Fagerberg, *What is Liturgical Theology? A Study in Methodology* (Collegeville 1992) and in Kevin W. Irwin, *Context and Text: Method in Liturgical Theology* (Collegeville 1994).

T. F. Best and D. Heller (eds), *So We Believe, So We Pray*, Geneva 1995; Peter Brunner, *Worship in the Name of Jesus*, English translation, St Louis 1968; Karl Federer, *Liturgie und Glaube: Eine theologiegeschichtliche Untersuchung*, Freiburg 1950; Aidan Kavanagh, *On Liturgical Theology*, New York 1984; Gordon W. Lathrop, *Holy Things: A Liturgical Theology*, Minneapolis 1993; E. J. Lengeling, *Liturgie: Dialog zwischen Gott und Mensch*, Altenberge 1988; A. Schmemann, *For the Life of the World*, 2nd edn, Crestwood, NY 1973; *Introduction to Liturgical Theology*, London 1966; H. C. Schmidt-Lauber and K. H. Bieritz (eds), *Handbuch der Liturgik: Liturgiewissenschaft in Theologie und Praxis der Kirche*, Leipzig/Göttingen 1995, especially 72–95 (Geoffrey Wainwright, 'Systematische Grundlegung') and 96–127 (K. H. Bieritz, 'Anthropologische Grundlegung'); Ninian Smart, *The Concept of Worship*, London 1972; Geoffrey Wainwright, *Doxology*, London 1980; *Worship with One Accord: Where Liturgy and Ecumenism Embrace*, New York 1997.

GEOFFREY WAINWRIGHT

Three Hours Devotion

A devotion in honour of the passion of Christ held from noon to 3 o'clock on *Good Friday. It was first introduced by Fr Alphonsia Messia, SJ in Lima, Peru, probably in 1687, and spread rapidly across South America. Initially it consisted of a prolonged silent meditation with some short devotional readings, usually concerning the Seven Last Words from the Cross. It changed to become a series of short sermons with musical interludes, and Haydn's *Seven Last Words* were intended for use during it. In Spanish-speaking countries it took place in a church hung in black with a large crucifix displayed on the *altar and with all light excluded from the windows and could give rise to considerable displays of emotion. Fr Mackonochie is said to have introduced it to the Church of England at St Alban's, Holborn in London in the 1860s, and in 1876 the devotion was observed at St Paul's Cathedral, London. It was, however, more widely taken up in the Church of England by evangelicals and anglo-catholics alike. Bishop Ridgeway of Chichester produced a popular and widely used order. When it became clear that the 1928 *BCP* would not contain liturgical provision for *Holy Week, it was promoted as an alternative, especially by W. K. Lowther Clarke, who warned against emotionalism. Though now largely displaced in RC churches by the renewed Good Friday liturgy, it continues to be popular in Anglican churches, where a two-hour preaching service is often concluded with a liturgical hour.

MARTIN DUDLEY

Thurible

Deriving its name from the Latin word for frankincense (*t[h]us*), a portable *censer in Christian liturgy, used for carrying hot charcoal on which *incense is burned. It consists of a bowl suspended on three or more fixed chains with a lid hung on a single separate chain, which is drawn up by the *thurifer to allow incense to be placed on the charcoal. The lid is pierced with ornamental holes to enable the smoke from the incense to escape, thus surrounding the immediate vicinity in a sweet-scented ambience. Any original link with the burning of incense in the OT seems to be spurious: the practice of the thurible preceding the *bishop in *procession developed after the end of the Diocletian persecution, and seems to have been adopted from the similar practice in Rome of a thurifer swinging a censer before senators and judges, the practical aim being to envelop and contain the other less salubrious smells of the city.

TRISTAM HOLLAND

Thurifer

The thurifer is the *server or *acolyte who carries the *thurible processionally and hands it to the president of the liturgical rite being celebrated or to another minister, for their use.

TRISTAM HOLLAND

Tippet *see* **Vestments** 3(d)

Tower

A tall structure of any shape that is high relative to its width. A tower can simply be a tall cylinder, or rise from a larger diameter at the base to a narrower width at the top by a series of stages marked by different or alternating shapes (e.g. cylinders alternating with octagons). Towers can be attached to a church, or free-standing. Church bell towers (belfries) housing one or more bells do not appear prior to the eleventh century. Towers can be topped with a spire. Church towers began as stairwells to reach second-level *galleries as early as the sixth century and gradually became integrated into the porch facades to achieve the familiar twin tower facades of Gothic cathedrals.

MARCHITA B. MAUCK

Tract *see* **Chants of the Proper of the Mass**

Transept

A large *aisle that crosses the *nave of a church at a right angle, thus creating a cross-shaped plan. The first example of a transept introduced into a *basilican plan occurs at Old St Peter's. The fourth-century transept at St Peter's architecturally set apart the site believed to be the burial place of St Peter, providing space for ritual action around the tomb. At this early date it was not deemed appropriate to mark the tomb of St Peter with the same funerary structure that marked the tomb of Christ in Jerusalem, a domed rotunda. The central plan tomb, an imperial prerogative that could include an opening to the sky for the apotheosis of the emperor, was adopted for the tomb of Christ and reserved for the holy sites connected with Christ. In later centuries the transept separated the nave from the *apse even when the church was not a martyrial church. By the ninth century on there are examples of a second transept at the west end of the nave, and both transepts could carry towers over their crossings with the nave.

MARCHITA B. MAUCK

Transfiguration

This commemoration on 6 August, derives from the Eastern church, where it is one of the major feasts in the year. Because there was a tradition that the transfiguration of Jesus took place forty days before his crucifixion, some have thought that this date was chosen so that it would be forty days before the feast of the

Exaltation of the Cross (14 September), but it is possible that it happened the other way around, the location of the feast giving rise to the tradition. The date may have been chosen as the commemoration of the *dedication of the basilicas on Mount Tabor (the mount of the transfiguration), and it is also one of the days for offering the fruit of the grape *harvest in the Byzantine tradition. It first appeared in the West in about the ninth century, and gradually spread to become universal in the fifteenth century. It is independent of and not related to the rest of the liturgical *year, and no doubt its late origin accounts for this lack of integration. It did not survive into the *BCP*s of the sixteenth and seventeenth centuries, but was widely restored in the various provincial Prayer Books produced by the churches of the Anglican Communion in the first half of the twentieth century, and it has been retained in recent revisions.

No serious effort ever appears to have been made to move it from its August isolation, perhaps because of the difficulty of finding somewhere else suitable for it. But the gospel accounts of the transfiguration do sometimes occur elsewhere in the course of *lectionary provision: in the historic Roman rite the narrative was read on the second Sunday of *Lent, and in the Lutheran tradition it was placed on the last Sunday of the *Epiphany season, a usage which has since spread to other churches, chiefly through its adoption in the *Revised Common Lectionary*.

RICHARD F. BUXTON

Triduum *see* **Easter**

Trinity Sunday

This festival, celebrated one week after *Pentecost, is different in character from those which commemorate the historical events of salvation, being concerned with theological ideas concerning the ontology of God himself. It originated in the West in the tenth century and spread slowly. Late in the eleventh century Pope Alexander II was not persuaded that the festival was a valid development, but Rome finally adopted it in the fourteenth century, though continuing to name succeeding Sundays as 'after Pentecost'. In contrast, some other parts of the church came to name the Sundays following until *Advent as 'after Trinity' rather than 'after Pentecost'. The Sarum use was among these and this was

copied by the *BCP*. Some years ago it became fashionable to return to 'after Pentecost' (at least in those churches that did not adopt an 'ordinary Sundays of the year' system) in order to give proper emphasis to the place of the Spirit in the life of the church. Recently there has been something of a swing back to 'after Trinity'. Both systems have merits, but numbering Sundays 'after Trinity' does emphasize that the whole economy of salvation is encompassed in the triune God.

RICHARD F. BUXTON

Trisagion

A Greek word meaning 'thrice-holy', and referring to the hymn, 'Holy God, holy and strong, holy and immortal, have mercy upon us', which is sung in all the Eastern liturgies, usually immediately preceding the readings. In modern Byzantine Orthodox use it is sung three times, followed by 'Glory be . . .', 'Holy Immortal . . .' and one more repetition. When a *bishop celebrates, he chants Ps. 80.15b–16a while blessing those present (a possible relic of an entry psalm with the *Trisagion* as a response). It is replaced on ancient baptismal days by 'You who have been baptized into Christ have put on Christ', and on feasts of the cross by 'Your cross we adore, O Master'. The hymn is part of the fixed prayers that open all services. The Syrians insert the words 'who was crucified for us' before 'have mercy . . .', and a complex version is sung before the gospel in Coptic and Ethiopian use. The Armenian version has seasonal variants and the Chaldean is unadorned. The Oriental Orthodox see the *Trisagion* as addressed to Christ, while the Eastern Orthodox and the Christian West see it as addressed to the Trinity.

In the Roman rite the hymn is traditionally sung in Greek and Latin and associated with the (now optional) Reproaches of *Good Friday. The Gallican and Mozarabic liturgies used it before the readings. Modern use can be quite varied in Western churches. The word was also sometimes used to refer to the *Sanctus of the *eucharistic prayer.

———

Sebastian Brock, 'The Thrice-Holy Hymn in the Liturgy', *Sobornost* VII, 1985, 24–34; C. Kucharek, *The Byzantine-Slav Liturgy of St John Chrysostom*, Allendale, NJ 1971, 399–405; Juan Mateos, *La célébration de la parole dans la liturgie byzantine*, Rome 1971, 98–110.

GREGORY WOOLFENDEN

Troparion *see* **Byzantine Chant**

Tunicle *see* **Vestments** 3(a)

Unction *see* **Anointing**

Unitarian Worship

1. *Principles and Structure.* Unitarians have for many decades been described as those who maintain a sturdy devotion to freedom, reason and tolerance in religion. Their historic roots are in the Judaeo-Christian tradition, but successive phases of influence from elsewhere are discernible on thought, practice and worship. Congregations are at liberty to develop their own worship patterns, being mainly congregational in church polity. Exceptions are found in Northern Ireland, which remains firmly Presbyterian, and Transylvania where, though not really episcopal, they have been presided over by a succession of *bishops dating back to the Reformation, and have taught a *catechism. Uniquely, in Kings Chapel, Boston, Massachusetts, one of the oldest American congregations, a revised version of the *BCP* is still in regular use. Other American Unitarian congregations, merged since 1961 with the Universalists, manifest radical and free forms of worship, drawing from a range of sources including non-Christian and religious humanist.

2. *Liturgies and Rational Dissent.* In England, the tension between desires for a free form of worship and an attachment to liturgical traditions dates from the Presbyterians of the seventeenth century. Strongly influenced by Puritanism and suspicious both of formalism and unseemly 'enthusiasm', they also retained a certain nostalgia for the established church. Early Dissenters' meeting houses were plain, preaching stations, but the late eighteenth and early nineteenth centuries saw the building of a number of larger, neo-Gothic edifices, allowing greater formality and some ritual. Twentieth-century buildings have returned to more modest proportions, and Cross Street Chapel, Manchester (1997), has reverted to a meeting-house style.

Presbyterians of the eighteenth century became increasingly identified with the growth of Rational Dissent, a trend that did much to determine the subsequent development of Unitarianism. This prompted them to create forms of worship of their own. Notable among these was Joseph Priestley's *Forms of Prayer for the Use of Unitarian Societies* (1783), and later theological developments brought a steady flow of such publications, continuing up to the present day. They provide insights into the growth of Unitarian thought, since the majority of preachers and congregations have always preferred conceived rather than *extempore prayer. They also reveal such influences as the philosophy of John Locke, Hartley's psychology, Newton's mathematical cosmology (contrasted with conservative supernaturalism) and the social idealism of the Enlightenment. Largely biblical in language and thought form and conveying a dignity and devoutness, these services pointed frequently towards the prophetic tradition of scripture and the ethical teachings of Jesus, addressing human moral responsibilities. The services frequently contained *litanies and responses for minister and people, providing for effective congregational participation with an avoidance of 'enthusiasm'.

3. *Anglican Influence and James Martineau.* In 1774 Theophilus Lindsey opened the first avowedly Unitarian church in Britain. Having resigned from the parish of Catterick, he then quit the Church of England altogether. He originally hoped to inaugurate a reformed Anglican church with a revised *BCP*, but the church which he opened in Essex Street, London (on the site now occupied by the headquarters of the Unitarian denomination), in fact used what he called *The Book of Common Prayer Reformed According to the Plan of the Late Dr. Samuel Clarke*. This went through repeated editions and attained an enormous popularity among Presbyterians who were moving towards Bible-based Unitarianism. The attractions were the non-eucharistic sources of the worship material and Lindsey's impulse to follow Clarke in addressing all prayers only to God the Father. This became one of the strongest features of Unitarian worship in subsequent generations, along with growing ideas of a humanistic Christology. The virgin birth was eliminated as unhistorical, and references to Satan disappeared.

The nineteenth century brought the enormous influence of James Martineau, who combined a thoroughgoing scholarship with deep piety. His thought and worship practice saw a gradual displacing of the older, biblical Unitarianism with a new and deeper spirituality. In 1862 Thomas Sadler, with the support of Martineau, published *Common Prayer for*

Christian Worship. This is seen as a milestone publication, in particular Martineau's contribution of the last two services, which reveal his remarkable liturgical genius, a first among Nonconformists. There is unmistakable beauty and spirituality in the prayers and responses, combining a deep inner devotion with a prophetic challenge to personal and social responsibility. In 1879 Martineau published *Ten Services of Public Prayer*, which took Unitarian theology a stage further. The formula for ending prayers 'through Jesus Christ our Lord' was omitted, as were any suggestions of the redemptive and intercessory functions of Jesus. The possibility of direct, personal communion with God, as seen in the piety of Jesus himself, became a basic concept.

4. *Denominational Forms*. Soon after the organization of Unitarian congregations in Britain into a General Assembly (1928), a denominational service book, *Orders of Worship*, was published, showing the continuing influence both of Anglicanism and of Martineau. This was widely used, probably by the majority of congregations, both by those attracted to the use of liturgy and by those that preferred 'open' orders but were happy to use liturgical publications as source material. In each service, opening sentences, both scriptural and other, are followed by a *collect for morning or evening, then the *Lord's Prayer and an 'Open thou our lips' or 'Lift up your hearts' and a selection of psalms or chants and litanies, followed by a selection of prayers, different for each of the eight services. There are additional orders for Christmas Day and Easter Day. This impulse to offer variation in service content grew in importance in the nineteenth and early twentieth century, to meet the much-debated view that set orders could lead to tiresome or 'vain' repetition. *Orders of Worship* also includes a time for silent prayer, perhaps originating in Martineau's affection for some *Quaker practices. The use of pauses for silent prayer has grown considerably in the twentieth century. In 1976 Upper Chapel, Sheffield, and its minister Peter Godfrey produced *Unitarian Orders of Worship*, also used as a resource by other congregations, but by the end of the twentieth century the use of liturgies had largely disappeared, preference being given to freer forms. Personal computers have enabled the use of 'one-off' prepared services.

5. *Current Trends*. For modern usage in the matter of *sacraments and rites of passage, the General Assembly produced *A Book of Occasional Services* (1932, ed. Mortimer Rowe) and *In Life and Death* (1972, ed. Kenneth Twinn). Most commonly used in churches are forms for infant *baptism (despite the influence of the General Baptists in the formation of the Unitarian tradition and the rejection by Unitarians of the concept of original sin). It is usually regarded as a welcoming of a new life, and an act of dedication of the parents.

Holy *communion or the *Lord's supper was at one time widely celebrated as an essential element of Unitarian practice, being a commemoration of the life and teaching of Jesus. It has steadily declined in the twentieth century, though maintained by some, especially in Northern Ireland, and it remains part of the annual meetings of the General Assembly. A popular innovation has been the 'Flower Communion', devised by the Czech Norbert Čapek, a Unitarian martyr murdered in a Nazi concentration camp. This has no eucharistic meaning but is an imaginative celebration of natural beauty and a memorial to Čapek.

The tradition of Rational Dissent remains predominant, and preaching, sometimes followed by 'talk-back', is still a substantial feature of services. The General Assembly's Worship Committee has, however, been influential in deepening awareness of the spiritual nature of worship, with effective workshops, conferences and a steady output of contemporary devotional materials. Hymns remain an important feature. The Unitarian contribution to hymnody of the so-called Transcendentalists of the nineteenth century is still evident, even outside the Unitarian movement. New hymns are frequently written, notably by John Andrew Storey. A new production, *Hymns for Living* (1985), was a bold attempt at combining traditional piety and personal and social responsibility, with some contemporary issues addressed, notably environmental concerns and women's rights. The use of masculine and militaristic language in worship has been vigorously debated. This hymnal tries to avoid gender-exclusive terms and occasionally addresses God as 'our mother'. Though widely used, and with a supplement published as *Let Us Sing* (1994), it was seen as too radical for some and *Hymns of Faith and Freedom* (1991), a distinctly more christocentric and scriptural production, was published by the Chalice Press.

Also somewhat controversial was the publication of *Celebrating Life* (1993, ed. Andrew Hill), a handbook of orders for rites of passage and sacraments. It includes orders for the ending of a marriage and for the celebration of a same-sex union, a practice carried out by some ministers. It was given an award for 'best spiritual invention' by the Institute of Social Inventions in 1993.

In the past Unitarian worship has been criticized for being cold or too formal, and occasionally for being too intellectual, more like a discussion group. These criticisms seem to have declined, with a deepening of awareness of spirituality, influenced to some extent by so-called 'new age' perceptions. There is generally less formality nowadays and increased congregational participation in the use of spoken or sung responses as well as movement, very occasionally *dance and visual aids. Increasingly popular is candle-lighting, usually a flame in a symbolic *chalice (the Unitarian symbol) at the opening of worship.

Duncan McGuffie, *The Hymn Sandwich: A Brief History of Unitarian Worship*, London 1982; A. E. Peaston, *The Prayer Book Reform Movement in the Eighteenth Century*, London 1940; *The Prayer Book Tradition in the Free Churches*, London 1964; 'The Unitarian Liturgical Tradition: Table Indicating Relationship of [123] Unitarian Liturgies to the Prayer Book (1741–1974)', *Transactions of the Unitarian Historical Society* XVI/2, 1976, 63–81; and several other articles by same author in that periodical; D. G. Wigmore Beddoes, *Yesterday's Radicals*, Cambridge 1971.

JOHN A. MIDGLEY

United Church of Canada

see **Canada, Worship in the United Church of**

United Reformed Church Worship

In 1972 the *Congregational Church in England and Wales and the *Presbyterian Church of England united to form the United Reformed Church (URC), subsequently joined by the Reformed Association of the Churches of Christ in 1981 and the Congregational Church in Scotland in 2000. All of these denominations, while cherishing freedom in worship, had either provided or recommended service books for the orderly conduct of worship and to give normative orders of worship

for such occasions as *ordinations and inductions of ministers.

The two founding denominations had only recently produced new service books, the Congregationalists *An Order for Public Worship* (1970) and the Presbyterians *The Presbyterian Service Book* (1968; largely a revision of its 1948 service book), with cross-representation on the committees responsible for their production. However, at the URC General Assembly in 1973 the decision was taken to produce a service book for the new denomination. A new book had in fact been under preparation since 1972, drawing on the work of the Joint Liturgical Group of Great Britain (JLG) as well as the existing service books. Such was the debt to the work of the JLG that it was commented that the URC had simply taken the JLG outline for a *eucharist and clothed it, turning it into a liturgy. The *Book of Order for Worship* was published in 1974 containing two complete sets of prayers for a eucharistic service drawn from the Congregational and Presbyterian books (one traditional and the other modern in language), with a *lectionary produced by the JLG. Effectively this established for the URC the principle that the normative Sunday service was a service of holy *communion although most services continued in the Nonconformist tradition of a 'hymn sandwich'.

The 1973 General Assembly had also authorized the production of a hymnbook supplement to stand alongside the two major hymnbooks then in use, *Congregational Praise* and the *Church Hymnary* (3rd edition). This book was to include some traditional hymns but mainly new material. *New Church Praise* appeared in 1975 and included an order of worship for the *Lord's supper with some musical settings. The order of worship was based on the modern text in the *Book of Order for Worship* with some variations, and in 1980 it was incorporated into *A Book of Services* with a full range of orders for *baptism of both children and adults (and An Act of Thanksgiving for the Birth of a Child where baptism may not be felt to be appropriate, e.g. for reasons of belief), *marriage, *funerals, ordination and inductions, and an order for a healing service. This final form included two further *eucharistic prayers, that published by the JLG in 1978 and one taken from the work of the Dutch RC priest, Huub Oosterhuis. One other change was the inclusion of the *institution narrative in the new prayers, where previously it had been used either as a warrant or in the *fraction. Some of the orders were also produced as small booklets, which could be used to put the liturgy into the hands of the congregation, a novel step for a Reformed church in Britain, but one which followed on from *New Church Praise*.

In 1985 a decision was taken to produce a new book, which finally appeared in 1989 as the *Service Book*. Although it had been only five years since the previous book had appeared, there were now issues relating to the use of *inclusive language and the union with the Reformed Association of the Churches of Christ, who brought with them a tradition of weekly communion and believer's baptism. The principal order of worship in the new book retained as its second eucharistic prayer the one which had first appeared in the 1974 service, and added a new prayer by Charles Brock of Mansfield College, Oxford, and a third based on one from the French Reformed Church. A second order of worship, which allowed for separate prayers before the distribution of the bread and the distribution of the wine, was included, reflecting the usage of the Churches of Christ.

By 1985 the stocks of *Congregational Praise* were almost exhausted and the decision was made to produce a new hymnbook incorporating the traditions of the three uniting denominations. *Rejoice and Sing* (Oxford 1991) begins with an order of service based on the main order of the 1989 *Service Book* with liturgical settings for the common texts of the eucharist. The language of the hymns was made inclusive where possible, but with no major rewriting, and there is a rich eucharistic section. It is of note that more copies of this book have been sold than there are members of the URC and it has found a niche even among anglo-catholic congregations.

A decision has recently been made to produce a new service book, utilizing the printed book, the CD-ROM and the Internet. The principal order of worship (eucharistic) and the order for baptism and *confirmation were both issued in a draft form for comment in 2000. It is intended that the more normative material will be available in printed form, but the more ephemeral material, including more seasonal material than has previously been provided, will be made available on electronic media.

The service books of the United Reformed Church have been in the nature of directories, providing guidance and examples of services and prayers (although some sections such as The Statement Concerning the Nature, Faith and Order of the United Reformed Church, and the baptismal promises are laid down as mandatory in the church's Basis of Union). In respect of this the worship of the URC encompasses a wide variety of styles and patterns which will continue to change and develop to meet the needs of Christians into the twenty-first century.

Horton Davies, *WTE* VI; Bryan D. Spinks, *Freedom or Order? The Eucharistic Liturgy in English Congregationalism 1645–1980*, Allison Park, PA 1984: Gordon S. Wakefield, *An Outline of Christian Worship*, Edinburgh 1998, 177–80.

HUGH F. GRAHAM

Veil

In the liturgy, a cloth used to cover various objects or to indicate certain sacred moments or places.

1. From the fourth century onwards (as today during *Orthodox worship) a curtain was drawn before the *altar, sometimes across the *templon* (an open screen of columns separating nave and sanctuary), although whether during or between liturgies is unclear. In the Byzantine rite since the fifteenth century the full-height *iconastasis has served in its place.

2. In the West veiling was not developed to the same extent, though in medieval England and elsewhere during *Lent, the altar was shrouded by a Lenten veil, which was drawn aside at certain points in the *eucharist.

3. Also during Lent, other veils covered or hung before the three figures on the rood beam, the *reredos, and every *cross, crucifix, statue and picture. Most were of unbleached linen or brown holland, and formed part of a general shrouding from the beginning of Lent until Easter eve. This is known as the Lenten array, and it is maintained in a minority of churches today. The veils often carry stencilled emblems in red, black or blue. In the modern Roman rite it is customary in some places, without obligation, to veil with purple-toned fabric throughout *Passiontide until Easter eve.

4. A *chalice veil, usually corresponding in *colour to the *vestments, was introduced in the 1570 Roman missal to cover the sacred vessels when not in use. Since the 1970 missal (as before 1570) the chalice has been covered with a large *corporal, though the chalice veil survives in much Anglican use. In the East both

chalice and paten are veiled during various parts of the liturgy.

5. The humeral veil is a large shawl, often highly embroidered, worn over all other vestments when the *host in a *pyx or *monstrance is held or carried in *procession.

JONATHAN GOODALL

Veneration of the Cross

The service of the veneration of the cross became over time a standard part of the Western liturgy of *Good Friday, along with the reading of the Passion and the distribution of *communion. This veneration ceremony seems to have begun in Jerusalem during the fourth century, and from there to have spread throughout the Christian world, although not always on Good Friday: in the Byzantine tradition, for example, it occurs on the third Sunday of *Lent. It first appears as part of the Good Friday service in the West in the Roman *tituli* in the seventh century (where it was also in use on September 14, the feast of the Exaltation of the Cross), and in the solemn *papal liturgy in the eighth century. The veneration of the cross became an important part of the Good Friday liturgy in northern Europe as well in the following centuries, and in at least one eleventh-century German ordo *rubrics indicate that the ceremony could be used at other times as well.

This Western version consisted of several components. It took place after the solemn reading of the Passion, and before the distribution of communion. A cross, veiled, would be brought in procession into the church. As the procession moved down the central aisle, it stopped three times; each time, the *Trisagion* acclamation would be sung. The cross would be fully unveiled by the *bishop (or other presiding minister) when the procession reached the *sanctuary area. Those venerating the cross would 'approach' it ritually with three distinct genuflections, later elaborated by private prayers. The floor, the feet and the hands of the *corpus* of Christ on the cross would be venerated with a kiss; later, brief acclamations or versicles would be added to accompany these actions as well. A specific set of chanted texts, called the *Improperia* or 'Reproaches', were sung as first the clergy, then the congregation, individually venerated the cross. This series of verses and responses, interpreted in the Middle Ages as Christ reproaching the Jewish people (the main refrain is addressed to

'My people') who crucified him, added to the pronounced anti-Semitic tone of the full Good Friday service.

Today, the RC Good Friday service still includes the ceremonial veneration of the cross. The ritual placement and shape of the procession remains the same. However, the veneration itself no longer includes the triple veneration or four separate kisses; usually, only the feet of the *corpus* or the foot of a plain wooden cross are kissed. Several smaller crosses may also be used in addition to the large processional cross, allowing for several stations to facilitate the veneration of the congregation.

Lili Gjerløw, *Adoratio Crucis*, Oslo 1961; Patrick Regan, 'The Veneration of the Cross', *Worship* LII, 1978, 2–12. For additional bibliography, *see* **Holy Week**.

JOANNE M. PIERCE

Vernacular *see* **Language, Liturgical**

Vespers *see* **Daily Prayer**

Vestments

1. Introduction; 2. The Early Church; 3. Liturgical Vesture in the West; 4. Liturgical Vesture in the East.

1. *Introduction.* Other than for the purely functional purposes of protection from the elements and some maintenance of modesty, vesture plays a number of important social roles. Common vesture (like uniforms) forges a sense of identity within a group (e.g. the military) and can define a particular role or function played or authority held (the police, railway officials, postal workers, etc.). Clothing, as an extension of the body, reveals something about the persons within and their relation to institutions and society as a whole. Vesture is often used by institutions to depersonalize the wearer in order to emphasize the primacy of the institutional role over the personality. In most western societies this use of vesture can still be seen in the courts, the universities and the churches. In the courts, judges judge in the name of the crown/state and not in their own right; in universities, academics have the responsibility of transmitting a corpus of knowledge greater than their own opinions; and, in the church, the vested individual acts in the name of the church or community and not on their own authority.

The use of vesture or special clothing to mark particular events or social roles is a phenomenon that is virtually universal and appears to be inescapable (i.e., when one type of clothing is abandoned for a particular social function a new type of clothing soon takes on the ceremonial status attributed to the old). At times, vesture is imputed a symbolic character from its inception (e.g. the white garment of the newly baptized); at other times the symbolic value is imputed long after the garment first began to be worn and after any sense of the garment's more utilitarian origins have been lost. This latter symbolization was a practice common to medieval commentators on the liturgy (Amalarius of Metz, Innocent III, William Durandus and many others), who sought either to establish the (at best tenuous) relationship between eucharistic vesture and that of the Temple priests, or to give them a moral meaning or, most common of all, to relate the vesture to Christ's own vesture at the passion. These symbolic interpretations were perpetuated in the vesting prayers prescribed in some churches until the recent past and in Eastern churches to the present day.

Much ceremonial or institutional vesture has its origins in the common clothing of another era, which, because of a latent conservatism, the holders of public office are often reluctant to change even when popular fashion has changed and a particular style of dress has been long since abandoned. Often vesture reflects an earlier relationship between an office and a particular social stratum or institution. Most of the traditional eucharistic vestments of both the Western and Eastern churches have their origins in the formal secular dress of the Roman empire of the first six centuries of the Christian era, while those of most Reformation churches born in the sixteenth century are of academic origin. For the former group, this reflects the social rank the senior clergy held as civil administrators in the empire, and for the latter, the academic roots of most sixteenth-century Reformers.

During the second half of the twentieth century there was a renewed sense of liturgical vesture as garment rather than costume. This began a trend in which greater emphasis was placed on the inherent beauty of the fabric and its weave or cut over and above the medieval and baroque emphasis on its ornamentation. Various writers inveighed against the industrial manufacture of vestments (e.g. Percy Dearmer, Dom E. A. Roulin) as they believed that the pursuit of commercial profit had resulted in a cost-cutting that cheapened vestments so that they had become unworthy of the liturgy. Workshops (e.g. the Warham Guild and various monastic studios) did much to re-establish vestment-making as a craft and individuals (notably Sr M. Augustina Flüeler) helped break the rigid interpretation of historical models that had come to dominate vestment design.

As with so many things, Vatican II was a watershed for the fundamental conception of the nature and purpose of vestments for many churches in addition to the RC Church. The *General Instruction* of the Roman Missal is unequivocal in stating that the beauty and symbolic value of the vestment must derive from its material and form rather than from its ornamentation. Since the vestment is a garment, not a costume, its sacredness derives from the nature of the events in which it is worn. As such, vestments should make an important visual statement about the importance of the liturgical act itself – the worship of the creator of all things through the Son and in power of the Holy Spirit.

In recent years there has been an evolution in respect to liturgical vesture in general. This has followed a somewhat circular course. Despite the emphasis of the *General Instruction* on material and form rather than ornamentation, the 1960s and 1970s often saw vestments used as background for the appliqué of verbal messages or, in some places, a tendency to abandon clerical vesture as a whole. A concern that churches should not spend money on 'ceremonial show' led to a new low in the cheapness of commercial manufacture. The present generation appears to be reacting against these trends and paying greater heed to the spirit of the *General Instruction*. While worship is no less 'valid' if celebrated in cheap, ill-fitting or gaudy vesture, the use of such clothing makes a particularly strong statement about our care for the liturgy as a whole and our concern for offering the best of our human gifts and creativity to God.

*Inculturation is also playing an important role in the development of vesture. This is true both between and within nations. In 'non-European' cultures, there is an interplay between the shape and design of modern liturgical vesture and the sacred vesture that was historically a part of the local culture. There is a growing willingness to acknowledge that sacred vesture need not be the same everywhere, nor should it all appear as if it had been ordered from the same catalogue. These concerns are increasingly influencing both the form of the garments themselves and the manner in which they are decorated.

Presently, there are voices calling attention to the church's concern for God's creation and its implications for vesture. Just as Percy Dearmer chastised the Victorian church for its use of 'sweated altars' (*altars made in workshops in which the labourers were not paid a living wage), the church in our own age needs to raise its consciousness about the materials used in its vestments, i.e., whether they are made from natural fibres which are environmentally friendly rather than from synthetic fabrics which are known to be created through processes which are detrimental to the environment. A conscious effort to use natural fibres in vesture makes an important statement about the interplay between human activity, the created order, and the *eucharist as the locus at which all of creation is brought together and offered to God.

2. *The Early Church*. In the earliest representations of celebrations of the eucharist (e.g. the *capella greca* in the catacombs of Callistus) no distinction in vesture can be seen between the presider and the others present. While among the charges made by the Emperor Julian (the Apostate) against Christians was their practice of dressing in special clothes to worship God, there is no suggestion that this was other than 'best dress'. Jerome writes of the distinction between everyday clothing and a 'special suit of clean clothes' for use in church. As late as the second quarter of the fifth century there was no liturgical vesture distinct from ordinary lay clothing. When Celestine of Rome heard of the growing distinction between clerical and lay vesture that had begun to appear in the church in Gaul, he wrote to the bishops of Vienne and Narbonne criticizing them for introducing distinctions which gave them a different appearance from that of the faithful. 'The true distinction between a bishop and his flock is to be found in his doctrine, not in his vesture' (*Letter*, 26 July 428).

The earliest piece of clothing to be given special significance in the church is the white baptismal garment – the *tunica alba* or alb. Patristic commentators on the baptismal liturgy make special mention of this garment, giving it symbolic meaning as 'the garment of salvation and robe of gladness' (John [Cyril] of Jerusalem), the external sign of 'putting on

Christ' (John Chrysostom), the garments of the transfigured Christ (Ambrose), the wedding garment (John the Deacon) and the fleece of Christ (Zeno of Verona). It is significant that the garment was common to all and not one that created distinctions among the baptized. The early symbolic interpretations of the baptismal garment must be understood alongside the symbolic interpretation of the removal of all regular clothing by the candidates before entering the *font for *baptism and in the context of the penchant for symbolism that characterized this genre of literature.

From the fourth century onwards, two phenomena characterize the evolution of vesture in church use. Among the many precious objects bestowed upon the church by the wealthy were gifts of clothing for use on special occasions. The Emperor Constantine gave a 'sacred robe of gold tissue' to be used at baptisms and the *Easter vigil (Theodoret, *Ecclesiastical History* II.27). As the church moved from private dwellings into larger spaces for worship, vesture began to appear in some churches, serving both to denote a particular role within the liturgical assembly and to create an atmosphere of dignity or splendour. When explaining the baptismal liturgy, Theodore of Mopsuestia draws attention on several occasions to the importance of vesture for its properties of enhancing and interpreting the liturgical event: 'The bishop, wearing vestments of light and shining linen anoints you . . .'; 'Instead of his usual clothes or his ordinary outer garment, he is wearing a delicate, shining linen vestment. He is wearing new vestments which denote the new world you are entering; their dazzling appearance signifies that you will shine in the next life; its light texture symbolizes the delicacy and grace of that world.' Later, he describes how the *deacons vest for the eucharist: 'They wear vestments which are in keeping with their true role, for their garments give them a more impressive appearance than they possess on their own account . . . On their left shoulders they drape a stole, which hangs down at equal length on either side, that is to say, in front and in back' (*Baptismal Homilies* II.17; IV). Garments given to the church specifically for liturgical use along with a self-conscious use of vestments to impress and add splendour, combined with a general conservatism in clerical dress, played an important part in the gradual emergence and development of what was to become specifically 'ecclesiastical' vesture.

3. *Liturgical Vesture in the West*. The basic forms of historic Western liturgical vesture are developed from three types of Roman dress: (a) the indoor tunic (the alb and dalmatic, and later, the surplice), (b) the outdoor cloak (the chasuble and cope), and (c) the mark of office (the stole, maniple). To these can be added (d) a number of vestments which are of later, usually medieval, origin.

(a) Alb, surplice, dalmatic, tunicle. Other than being the baptismal garment common to all Christians (see above), the alb is the vestment common to all liturgical ministers. In its present form it is derived in a direct line from the long, sleeved garment worn by the Greeks and Romans. As a basic secular garment it existed in both short and long forms. The short, knee-length *chiton*, was worn by men – particularly soldiers and labourers – and could be either with or without sleeves. The long version (known by various names: *talaris* or *tunica talaris* because it reached to the feet, *tunica alba* because of its white colour, or *tunica linea* if made from linen) generally had tight-fitting sleeves and was worn by women, elderly men and those in positions of authority. These two forms of tunic constituted the equivalent of 'shirt sleeves' in modern western dress. Those who were of greater importance or wealthier would wear a second tunic with wider sleeves often made from Dalmatian wool (*tunica dalmatica* or dalmatic) on top of the tunic with tight-fitting sleeves. The tunic could be decorated with strips (or *clavi*) of purple or russet material which originally served to reinforce the seams and, in time, became intentionally decorative. The tunic when worn as the under-garment was usually belted at the waist with a cincture or girdle.

The alb remained the basic garment of all clergy until about the eleventh century, when a looser-fitting version of the garment was developed north of the Alps. This *tunica linea alba superpelliceum* or *surplice* was intended to fit over the fur-lined garments (*superpellices*) worn for warmth during the winter by the secular clergy while singing the office in *choir. Thus, from its origins, the surplice was a very full garment which began to be truncated on the European Continent during the Renaissance and in England only in the nineteenth century.

The rochet is a variant on the alb of medieval origin. Originally somewhat shorter than the alb and either sleeveless or with tight sleeves, it was in general use by all clerics until the thirteenth century, when its use became restricted to prelates. In modern use, it is worn by *bishops as a part of 'choir dress'. In sleeveless and 'winged' form the rochet is often worn by *servers and organists.

In recent years, the alb has undergone several changes in character and design. In many countries, it has become the standard 'ecumenical' garment and is worn by liturgical ministers of many different denominations, replacing liturgical vesture of sixteenth-century origin. The alb is now commonly made of coarser material than in the past, often with wide sleeves and is generally worn without cassock or amice and is left unbound at the waist.

Vestments traditionally associated with the alb are the amice and the cincture. The amice (from the Latin *amicio*, to wrap around) is a rectangular piece of material originally worn as a scarf or neckerchief with the intention of protecting other, more precious, garments from sweat. It rarely appears as a liturgical garment in the West until the eighth century and never became an ordinary vestment in the Eastern churches. The form and manner of wearing it has varied considerably according to region and fashion. At first it was donned after the alb (a tradition continued in the rites of Lyons and Milan) but in the tenth century it became the first vestment to be put on, after longer hair styles had made the protection of other vestments an important concern. The amice was then put on as a helmet and brought down around the neck when all other vestments had been donned. In some monastic uses it was worn in its helmet-like position at the times in the liturgy when secular clergy would have covered their heads with other headgear. In present use, the amice has been generally abandoned and other, simpler, means have been found to protect outer vestments from perspiration.

The girdle or cincture (Latin, *cingulum*) is the belt used to tie the *tunica* at the waist. It passed into liturgical use along with the long tunic as a matter of practicality. It has taken various forms over time and place varying from that of a long rope to that of a broad band of cloth. Its current form, if used, is usually that of a long cord tied around the waste leaving loops through which the stole is passed. With the spread of modern forms of the alb its use has been generally abandoned.

(b) The chasuble and cope are vestments that have their origins in the outer cloak (*burrhus, planeta, paenula* or *lacerna*) worn by all in the Graeco-Roman world regardless of class or gender. Made from a large semi-circle of woollen material, the garment was either sewn into a single piece which hung like a small tent or 'poncho' with a hole cut for the head, or was left open in cape-like fashion and was joined by a clasp. In its cone-like form, known as the *casula* or 'little house', the garment is the ancestor of the chasuble, while its cape-like variation is the ancestor of the cope. According to the Roman *ordines*, all ranks of the clergy from *acolyte to pope wore a tunic with a *planeta*. Gradually the use of the garment came to be restricted to *presbyters and bishops. The use of the 'folded chasuble' or 'broad stole' by deacons and *subdeacons during *Advent, *Lent and certain penitential seasons (generally discontinued after Vatican II) was a vestige of this ancient use.

The chasuble, since it passed into liturgical use, has gone through a long evolution in shape over the centuries. This has often been a by-product of the evolution of eucharistic theology and ritual practice. In the medieval period, there was an tendency to decorate the chasuble with embroidery often featuring the crucifix. Over time, this often took the form of padded appliqué of several centimetres thickness which was not only heavy but proved to be cumbersome with the introduction of the elevation of the *host in the thirteenth century and of the *chalice a century later. This resulted in the gradual paring away of the fullness of the conical-shaped garment until it assumed a 'fiddleback' shape during the baroque period. The nineteenth-century affection for things medieval saw a gradual return to a fuller 'gothic'-shaped vestment, which, however, was still skimpy by earlier standards. The twentieth century, with its renewed interest in the importance of material and form over ornamentation, has seen a general return to much more full chasubles and often to the classic conical shape.

The other, cape-like, type of outdoor cloak evolved into the cope. This garment, sometimes known as the *pluviale* (because it kept off the rain) or the *cappa* (because it was the upper-most garment or 'top' coat), was also known under the names *paenula* and *planeta*, like its 'poncho'-like homologue. It is, in fact, often difficult to distinguish between the garment that evolved into the chasuble and that which evolved into the cope. Early mosaics and frescos which depict the *pluviale/cappa* usually show it open at the side and covering the whole body rather than open at the front in the fashion

the cope has generally been worn. The well-known mosaic from San Vitale in Ravenna which shows the Emperor Justinian (wearing a ceremonial *cappa* fixed with an elaborate clasp over his right shoulder) standing beside Archbishop Maximianus (wearing a *casula* in a rather cape-like fashion) well illustrates the similarity between the two garments in function and appearance.

In liturgical use, the cape-like garment continued to be used in a plain form (the *cappa nigra*, great cloak) in choir and for outdoor use because of its properties of keeping out the cold and wet. In its rich or ceremonial form it came to be used in the Western church for *processions and at *sacraments other than the eucharist. In many of the Eastern and Oriental churches (Coptic, Syrian, Armenian, etc.) it came to be the principal eucharistic vestment. At the time of the English Reformation, the 1549 *BCP* directed that the priest wear 'a vestment [i.e., chasuble] or cope'. This rubric did not appear in the second *BCP*. Canon XXIV (1604) enjoined that the presider at the eucharist wore a coloured cope over a plain alb. This use remains common in many Anglican cathedrals and parish churches to this day. There have been times when using a cope rather than a chasuble was claimed to distance the wearer from any commitment to the doctrine of eucharistic sacrifice (*see* **Eucharistic Theologies**). This is a rather tenuous interpretation of what was essentially a Reformation simplification of medieval English cathedral use and is without any theological foundation in the nature of the vestments themselves.

Like other vestments, the shapes and styles of the cope have varied over the ages but not to the same extent as the chasuble. It is the choice of fabric and decoration that has made the greatest difference in the appearance of the vestment as a whole. The use of heavily embroidered and metallic fabrics (particularly in the baroque period) with wide orphreys and exaggeratedly large (false) hoods have often given the cope the appearance of a costume rather than a vestment.

The modern development of the cope has generally followed several different directions, all of which have tended to involve a commitment to artists and the crafts. In some traditions there is a widespread return to a more cape-like shape with a genuine hood that is clearly reminiscent of the *cappa* or *pluviale*. These copes are often woven and the 'visual' interest is in the weave of the fabric itself. In other traditions, notably within Anglicanism, the cope has been given particular attention as a festal and episcopal vestment. As such, it often receives the most creative attention of embroiderers, who perpetuate in a modern style the tradition of the *Opus anglicanum* in handiwork. The mass-produced cope is becoming a thing of the past much more quickly than its homologue, the chasuble.

(c) Vestments originating in emblems of civil office. The *stole* and *pallium* have their origin in the pall or scarf which was worn over the *tunica* and *paenula*. In Rome a long scarf of white wool worn around the shoulders, with one end hanging in the back, the other to the front, the pallium was initially an honour granted by the emperor to members of his court. In Spain and Gaul another vestment unknown in Rome, the *orarium* (called *stola* from the ninth century), was the only distinctive garment of the deacon and was worn in a different fashion by presbyters. In the Carolingian period, with the fusion of Gallican and Roman practices, the stole became a part of Roman dress for deacons and presbyters.

From mosaics and frescos it appears that the pallium and stole were originally white and sometimes ornamented at the end with a cross and coloured border. As with all vestments, style and ornamentation have changed considerably. During the medieval period stoles remained long but were made of coloured material (often that of the orphrey) contrasting with the chasuble. In the baroque period stoles, like baroque vesture in general, were considerably shortened and their ends broadened so as to accommodate more decoration. The 'pastoral' stole, used for preaching and other sacraments, had ends that assumed shovel-like proportions. During the Gothic Revival in the nineteenth century stoles once again assumed their earlier long, narrow shape. Since the 1970s and the widespread adoption of the 'modern' alb as the primary liturgical vestment, stoles have become wider and rely heavily on the intrinsic merit of the weave of the fabric for their aesthetic interest. Fleetingly (one hopes) the stole was used as a means of conveyance of religious slogans – a practice now largely discontinued.

The manner in which stoles are worn has also varied over time. As early as the sixth century, bishops also began to wear the stole after the fashion of presbyters, deacons and subdeacons (both ends hanging towards the feet), in addition to the pallium. In the medieval period, with its fascination with symbols of the passion, presbyters began to wear their stoles so that they formed a cross on their chest. The current Western custom is that bishops and presbyters wear the stole around the back of the neck with the ends hanging down towards the feet. Deacons generally wear the stole sash-like (over the left shoulder and drawn across the chest to the right side where it is fastened) although it is increasingly common to wear it 'Byzantine'-style (over the left shoulder with ends hanging straight down both back and front).

The maniple has its origins in the *mappa*, which was a badge of office of the Roman consul. Beginning as a ceremonial handkerchief carried in the right hand (there were no pockets), the *mappa* was waved to signal the beginning of the games. When it made its way into ecclesiastical use, we find it being waved by the bishop to signal the beginning of the liturgy in *Ordo Romanus* I. It long continued to be carried in the hand (e.g. Archbishop Stigand in the Bayeux tapestry). Its use was adopted by all clerics, but in time limited to those between the orders of subdeacon and bishop, at which time it came to be worn looped over the left wrist. In its most recent form, the maniple consisted of a strip of cloth matching the chasuble and stole, about 4–6 cm wide and up to a metre in length. As a vestment it has generally fallen into disuse and is not mentioned in the present *General Instruction* of the Roman Missal.

(d) Other clerical vestments. The origins of the cassock probably lie in the sleeved barbarian tunic which was introduced into the late Roman empire and became regular dress. As was often the case with other vestments, as secular styles changed and the garment became shorter, the clergy retained it in its longer ankle-length form. Cut (and colour) of material, width of sleeves, placement (and number) of buttons, coloured piping, colour and style of cincture or belt have all varied tremendously with time and place, and have been used as a means to distinguish between religious communities, ecclesiastical ranks and academic degrees. The cassock is technically street dress for the clergy (and remains as such in some countries) and is not a liturgical vestment, although it is often worn under other liturgical vestments (alb, surplice, rochet, etc.).

The 'preaching' or 'Geneva' gown is a development of the medieval gown worn by a variety of professions and particularly by members of universities. On Christmas Day

1521, in the castle church at Wittenberg, Professor Andreas Karlstadt celebrated the eucharist wearing his 'professional' (not clerical) clothing – his academic gown. The idea gained favour among many Reformers whose roots were in the academy. For some, it was a visible means of distancing themselves from medieval eucharistic doctrines with which they disagreed. Until the last quarter of the twentieth century it was standard liturgical dress in many Reformation churches. In recent years, it has been widely replaced by the alb.

The chimere is an outdoor cloak of medieval origin worn by bishops while riding horseback, which was adopted by them for both liturgical and civil occasions. In modern use it is worn by bishops and doctors of divinity over a rochet as a part of 'choir dress'.

The tippet and hood are also of medieval origin. The tippet is a broad scarf-like piece of (usually black) material which hangs around the back of the neck and down the front. Originally a part of the medieval hood, it appears to have become detached and was worn separately from the hood, which, as a distinct vestment, then underwent its own evolution, assuming different shapes and colours according to university and academic degree. Both became standard vesture for Anglican clergy along with cassock and surplice as a part of 'choir habit'.

The almuce and mozetta are both types of short capes. The almuce is a fur-lined hood with two ends which hang down the front and was worn over the surplice as 'choir dress'. Over time, it came to be a mark of ecclesiastical rank. The mozetta is a short hooded cape made of silk or fur worn over the rochet. Its colour and ornamentation may vary with order, rank and place. It is part of the choir dress of RC bishops, prelates and canons.

The word *mitre* was used to describe a variety of forms of secular headgear before it emerged the distinctive hat of (principally) the bishop. It has evolved though a variety of shapes over the centuries. Its first depiction in Christian use is as a soft cap with two lappets (bands of cloth) hanging down the back. By the twelfth century the shape had changed to that of a circle rising to two peaks. At first, the peaks were worn to the side of the head but in the thirteenth century they were worn back and front, as they are today. Over time the fabric of the mitre was stiffened, heightened and ornamented until in the baroque period it rose as a great tower above the wearer's head. In modern use, the mitre is usually of modest proportions.

In RC use it may be either 'plain' or 'ornate', depending on the character of the celebration. In Anglican and Lutheran use, it is often made to match the cope with which it is to be worn. While generally reserved to episcopal use, the mitre is also worn by some abbots and, in the RC tradition, can be given to priests as a 'personal privilege'.

4. *Liturgical Vesture in the East*. The vestments used in the Byzantine rite have origins similar to those of the Western church. Differences are attributable to different paths of evolution, different cultural influences and the different periods when a particular garment's style became 'fixed'. Unlike Western use, in which a clear distinction evolved between vestments used for the eucharist and those worn during the office, Byzantine use does not have vestments reserved specifically as 'choir dress'. While there are some eucharistic vestments that have no Western equivalent (or vice versa), most vestments used in the Byzantine rite have Western homologues.

(a) The *sticharion* and the alb have a common ancestor. The *sticharion*, however, is generally made of coloured fabric.

(b) The *zone* and cincture have the same origin, although the former is made of fabric rather than cord and its ends are usually joined by a clasp.

(c) The *orarion* and *epitrachelion* have the same origin as the stole. In Byzantine use their form has evolved according to order. The *orarion* is the vestment of the deacon, worn over the left shoulder with its ends hanging down in front and back as described by Theodore of Mopsuestia (see above). The *epitrachelion* is a broad stole joined together down the front with an opening at the top for the head and is the vestment of bishops and presbyters.

(d) The *phelonion* and chasuble have a common ancestor. The evolution of the *phelonion* has involved a gradual paring away of material from the front of the garment so that it looks rather cope-like with material covering the whole breast (unlike the Western chasuble where the paring took place at the sides). From the eleventh century the white *phelonion* worn by patriarchs was decorated with many crosses and called the *polystavrion*.

(e) In the later Byzantine period Byzantine patriarchs began to wear the imperial *sakkos*, which is a dalmatic-like tunic. Its use, at first restricted to the patriarch, gradually devolved to other senior bishops and, after the fall of Constantinople, to all bishops.

Some Byzantine vestments have no Western equivalent. These include:

(f) The *epigonaton*, a stiff square of material worn suspended lozenge-like from the right side of the *zone*. It can be seen worn by the Emperor Justinian and his courtiers in the Ravenna mosaic and likely had its origins in a ceremonial handkerchief. In current use, it is worn by bishops and bestowed as a dignity upon certain presbyters.

(g) The *epimanikia*, cuffs worn on the *sticharion*. Like the *sakkos*, these were first worn by the patriarch of Constantinople, but over time their use has devolved to all bishops as well as presbyters and deacons.

(h) As the patriarch of Constantinople adopted the imperial *sakkos* and *epimanikia*, so too the imperial crown-like mitre which, in time, became the headgear for all bishops and, as in the West, is bestowed (but with greater frequency) as a 'personal privilege' on some presbyters. In Armenian use, the Western mitre was adopted by bishops at the time of the Crusades, so that the crown-like Byzantine mitre devolved to deacons as well as presbyters.

In vesture, the Orthodox Church preserved much of the visible splendour of the Byzantine court after the time of its political disappearance. In the appearance of the vested bishop the appearance of the Byzantine emperor lives on.

Outdoor dress of Orthodox clergy has origins similar to those in the West. The basic garment is a cassock along with a gown and a hat (with a veil if the wearer is a priest-monk or a bishop). Shapes and colours of each vary tremendously between (and, often, within) churches and nations.

Archimandrite Chrysostomos, *Orthodox Liturgical Dress: An Historical Treatment*, Brookline, MA 1981; Beryl Dean, *Embroidery in Religion and Ceremonial*, London 1981; Janet Mayo, *A History of Ecclesiastical Dress*, London 1984; Herbert Norris, *Church Vestments: Their Origin and Development*, London 1949; E. A. Roulin, *Vestments and Vesture*, London/St Louis 1933.

DAVID R. HOLETON

Vestry

A room in a church in which *vestments for the clergy, ritual books, and vessels for services are stored. The clergy dress here in preparation for services. The vestry is usually located off the *chancel or *sanctuary. This room can also be called a *sacristy.

MARCHITA B. MAUCK

Viaticum

This Latin word means provision for a journey, and is used to refer to the administration of *communion to someone dying or in danger of death, so that the *sacrament may provide the necessary spiritual sustenance for the journey from this life to the next.

See also **Sick, Liturgical Ministry to the.**

EDITOR

Vigil

A vigil, from the Latin, *vigilia*, 'watch', 'wakefulness', was originally a practice of staying awake for part or all of a night, probably rooted in the belief that Christ would come 'like a thief in the night' and Christians therefore needed to be watchful for his return (see, e.g., Matt. 24.42–44; 1 Thess. 5.1–7). Several early sources mention the existence of vigils, but their frequency in the first three centuries is unknown. Best attested is the annual *Easter vigil, but vigils may have been held more often, at least in some places. In the fourth century, the practice spread, apparently from Jerusalem, of holding a weekly vigil from very early on a Sunday morning until daybreak in commemoration of the resurrection, at which psalms were sung and one of the gospel accounts of the resurrection read. This survives in Eastern traditions but in the West it left only slight traces in some monastic rules. Another fourth-century custom, chiefly observed in monastic communities, was a weekly all-night vigil, usually from Friday to Saturday, and this too features in some later monastic rules. Such vigils were composed of psalmody and Bible readings. Some early Western monastic rules also assign the name 'vigil' to the regular night office of the community, while others restrict the term to the occasions of prayer which lasted throughout the night. In addition, the word is used more broadly to denote the day preceding a religious festival, otherwise called its 'Eve', because at one time vigils were kept on such occasions.

See also **Watch-Night.**

EDITOR

Visigothic Rite *see* **Western Rites**

Visitation *see* **Marian Feasts**

Votive Mass

In Western liturgy this term denotes a *mass formulary provided for optional use, not to observe a feast or season of the liturgical *year but to celebrate a chosen devotional theme or to petition for a particular intention (*votum*).

As early as the third century, there appears to be evidence that, in addition to Sunday celebrations for the entire community, the *eucharist was also celebrated at least occasionally on weekdays for smaller groups and for particular intentions. The Gelasian Sacramentary (a sixth-century collection) already contains about sixty such formularies for various occasions and intentions such as epidemics, travellers, weddings and anniversaries, the dead, but also against slanderers and crooked judges. By the tenth century the Sacramentary of Fulda had over 130. It is clear that not all of these presumed the participation or presence of a congregation and that they are to be associated with the widespread multiplication of masses, ordained monks, *altars and stipends in the early Middle Ages. In late medieval times votive masses often came to displace even Sunday formularies, and besides those directed to spiritual needs many were concerned with quite gross material advantage. Successive reformers and synods attempted to restrain their growth, on the whole without success until the sixteenth-century Council of Trent severely restricted the number of celebrations permitted and suppressed a large number of inappropriate formularies.

The Roman Missal of 1570 contained a small collection of *missae votivae* (in honour of the Trinity, the Virgin Mary, the apostles, etc.) and a much larger collection of masses and prayers *ad diversa* for a variety of needs and intentions (e.g. peace, pilgrims, the sick, famine, good weather, harvest, etc.). The 1970 Roman Missal further rationalized these collections, eliminating many titles but adding others which address more contemporary needs and often derive their content from documents of the Second Vatican Council (e.g. progress of peoples, laity, civil leaders, human labour). They may be used on weekdays in *ordinary time when no feast or commemoration is mandated.

J. A. Jungmann, *The Mass of the Roman Rite*, New York 1951, I, 217–21.

CHRISTOPHER WALSH

Vows, Renewal of Baptismal
see **Baptismal Vows, Renewal of**

Watch-Night

Methodist equivalent of a *vigil service, since spread to other traditions, now usually restricted to New Year's Eve. Converted Kingswood (Bristol) miners replaced Saturday night carousing with nights of prayer, praise and thanksgiving. John Wesley, answering charges of novelty and suspicions of immorality, appealed to the ancient saints'-day eve and other vigils prescribed in *BCP*, regulated watch-nights, and introduced them elsewhere. He recommended Friday nights nearest the full moon (for safety in the streets), and sometimes linked days of fasting and prayer (cf. Prayer Book vigil fasts). Preaching themes included urgency of repentance, deepening dedication and love as readiness for judgement and caution against millenarian obsessions. Prayer included thanksgiving for God's patient preservation of individuals, church and nation; petition for more abundant blessings, for national emergencies, for the increase of the work of God, and for spiritual fidelity and watchfulness. Wesley's observance of the Christmas/New Year season settled down to: Christmas Day, 4 a.m. preaching; *communion on the twelve days of Christmas; New Year's Eve watch-night; and *Covenant Renewal on first Sunday in January. In USA Methodism, watch-night was held from 1770; itinerant and local preachers shared the preaching; Charles's 'Covenant Hymn' was often sung just after New Year struck. The arrival of 2000 CE revived the custom, probably only temporarily.

John Wesley, *Plain Account of the People called Methodists*, London 1748; Charles Wesley, *Hymns for the Watch-Night,* London 1744, and *Hymns for New Year's Day*, London 1750; W. Parkes, 'Watch-Night, Covenant Service, and the Love-Feast in Early British Methodism', *Wesleyan Theological Journal* XXXII/2, Fall 1997, 35–58.

DAVID TRIPP

West Syrian Worship

West Syrian liturgy belongs to the Antiochene family of liturgies, of which the *East Syrian, Byzantine, Maronite and *Armenian liturgies are the other members. The Syrian Orthodox (Antioch), Malankara Orthodox (India), Syrian

Catholic, Syro-Malankara and the Independent Syrian Church of Malabar are the churches that follow this rite. The *Mar Thoma Syrian Church and the Saint Thomas Evangelical Church use a reformed version of the West Syrian liturgy.

West Syrian Christians, known as Jacobites (after Jacob Baradeus, the sixth-century organizer of the church) and as 'Monophysites' or 'Non-Chalcedonians' (as they were opposed to the Council of Chalcedon in 451 CE), inherited the Antiochene liturgy in its fifth-century form. Following expulsion by the Emperor Justin I (518–27), the Non-Chalcedonians took refuge in the Syriac-speaking areas of Mesopotamia and organized their own liturgical tradition, maintaining early Antiochene features (e.g. *litanies) and incorporating several Mesopotamian elements (e.g. hymnody). In the Syrian Orthodox Church, there existed two liturgical centres: Turabdin (south-east Turkey) in the Patriarchate of Antioch and Mosul (northern Iraq), the former seat of the 'Maphrian' (the Syrian Orthodox counterpart of the Nestorian patriarch). Both centres produced liturgical texts with considerable diversity, in spite of the basic unity in the structure of the celebration. The Mosul tradition shared several original Mesopotamian features with the East Syrians, which gradually disappeared under the influence of Turabdin.

Almost all the liturgical rites, including the *daily prayer offices and the *lectionary, have several versions. There are, for example, about a dozen *baptism liturgies, but most of them are not in use and only exist in manuscript form. It was in fact printing that contributed to the fixation of the liturgical texts and the disuse of different versions.

1. *Eucharistic Rites*. In the first half of the fifth century, the Antiochene church seems to have adopted the St James Liturgy of Jerusalem, incorporating a few local features, such as a long christological thanksgiving and *anamnesis. The Non-Chalcedonians of Mesopotamia translated the anaphora of St James into Syriac, probably in the second half of the sixth century. Later Jacob of Edessa (d. 708) made a more accurate Syriac version on the basis of existing Greek texts. Jacob is also credited with the Syriac translation of the West Syrian baptismal ordo, the Greek original of which has been attributed to Severus of Antioch (d. 538). Jacob is believed to be the author or compiler of most of the West Syrian liturgical texts.

The eucharistic liturgy has the following structure: preparation rites; pre-anaphoral rites (entrance, liturgy of the word, censing, *creed and the *lavabo); *kiss of peace; trinitarian blessing and the dialogue; *Sanctus; *institution narrative; anamnesis; *epiclesis; commemorations; *fraction; *Lord's Prayer; *Sancta sanctis*; *communion; *dismissal; postcommunion. The structure of the anaphora was fixed in the seventh century, while the preparation rites and the post-communion as well as the order of communion and the *diaconale* were added later. The present form of the eucharistic celebration belongs to the sixteenth century.

West Syrians have the largest number of *eucharistic prayers. More than seventy are known and about a dozen are still in use. They have been attributed to the apostles, early church fathers, West Syrian doctors, patriarchs or famous prelates. All the anaphoras follow the structure of St James and retain the main themes of the prayers, though the wording varies considerably. The anaphora attributed to Thomas of Harkel (d. 616) has a curious formula which combines the words of institution and anamnesis: 'When he duly united with the form of a servant, as the one who has to accomplish the preparations of our salvation, he took bread and wine and blessed, sanctified, broke and gave to his disciples, saying: Take, share (it) and do likewise, and when you receive it, believe and be convinced that you eat my body and drink my blood for the memory of my death until I come.' A similar formula is found in the anaphora of John Bar Shusan.

The liturgy is now celebrated mostly in the vernacular (Malayalam in Kerala). The Syrian Orthodox Church of Antioch continues to use Syriac, which is not always understood by the congregation. In the course of evolution, litanies have been replaced with hymns to assure the participation of the community.

2. *Daily Prayer*. This exists in two main forms: common prayer (*Shhimo*) for the weekly cycle, and the festal office (*Penkito* or *Hudro*) for the annual cycle. Daily offices are divided into seven canonical hours, beginning with *ramso* (vespers), followed by *sutoro* (compline), *lilyo* (night prayer in four nocturns), *sapro* (morning), and the third, sixth and ninth hours. Each day and hour has a fixed main theme. The ninth hour and the office of Saturday have 'the departed' as their theme. The theme of Sunday is always the resurrection, and that of

Wednesday is the Mother of God and of Friday is the cross and the martyrs. The offices, especially those of the Great *Lent and *Holy Week, include a series of genuflections, symbolizing repentance.

The psalms take comparatively a small place in West Syrian liturgy and are replaced by songs in the form of *antiphons, known as *qolo* (hymn) and *bo'utho* (petition), the origin of which is traced back to poet-theologians like Saint Ephrem (fourth century) and Jacob of Serugh (fifth century). Shorter antiphons known as *eqbo* and *eniyono* also have their place in the offices. The most characteristic West Syrian prayer is the *sedro* (i.e., a row, order or series), a long prayer in the form of a series of expositions or meditations, usually preceded by a *promiun* (i.e., introduction). Often the *sedro* provides a summary of theology. Thus the *sedre* of the office of *Pentecost are an excellent summary of pneumatology.

3. *Liturgical Year.* The liturgical *year of the West Syrians begins with the 'Sunday of the Consecration of the Church' (First Sunday of November or 30/31 October if it falls on a Sunday), followed by the 'Sunday of the Renewal of the Church' and the Sundays of *Advent. The liturgical year can be divided into a cycle of seven periods (each consisting approximately of seven weeks), centred on the Nativity, *Epiphany, the Great Lent, *Easter, Pentecost, the Feast of the Apostles Peter and Paul (29 June) and the Feast of the Cross (14 September).

4. *Liturgical Commentaries.* Several liturgical commentaries exist on the eucharist, baptism and the consecration of chrism (*see* **Anointing**), including those by Jacob of Edessa (d. 708), George, bishop of the Arab tribes (d. 724), John of Dara (ninth century), Moses Bar Kepha (d. 903), Dionysius Bar Salibi (d. 1171) and Bar Hebraeus (d. 1286). Most of them have been published. The most influential model for the Syriac commentators was *The Ecclesiastical Hierarchy* of Pseudo-Dionysius the Areopagite, which was known to them in a sixth-century Syriac translation. However their *mystagogy was rather a blend of Alexandrine *theoria* (a word which occurs in most of the commentaries), the Antiochene *historia* and the original Mesopotamian exegesis, which was largely indebted to the Targumic tradition. In their commentaries, the West Syrians used literary genres such as mystagogical homilies,

metrical homilies (*memre*), epistles, letters and treatises. Metrical homilies, the most original contribution of the Syrian tradition in this domain, were originally destined to be sung during liturgical or sacramental celebrations.

5. *Liturgical Music.* The West Syrians follow the *octoechos*, a modal system in eight modes or tunes (attributed to Severus of Antioch), analogous to the Byzantine *octoechos* and the eight-mode Gregorian system. The chants are organized in an eight-weekly modal cycle in the following order (week number followed by that of mode): 1/5; 2/6; 3/7; 4/8; 5/1; 6/2; 7/3; 8/4.

See also **Books, Liturgical** 2.6.

Sebastian Brock, *Syriac Studies: A Classified Bibliography (1960–1990)*, Kaslik 1996 (bib.); J. M. Sauget, *Bibliographie des liturgies orientales (1900–1960)*, Rome 1962 (bib.).

Liturgical texts: A. Raes et al., *Anaphorae Syriacae*, Rome 1939 (Syriac and Latin); *Ma'de'dono: The Book of the Church Festivals*, ed. Athanasius Yeshue Samuel, New York 1984 (Syriac text and English translation); *The Book of Common Prayer of the Syrian Church*, trans. Bede Griffiths, Kerala (n.d.).

Liturgical commentaries: R. A. Aytoun, 'The Mystery of Baptism by Moses Bar Kepha compared with the Odes of Solomon', *Studies on Syrian Baptismal Rites*, ed. Jacob Vellian, Kottayam 1973, 1–15; Sebastian Brock, 'Jacob of Edessa's Discourse on the Myron', *Oriens Christianus* LXIII, 1979, 20–36; R. H. Connolly and H. W. Codrington (eds), *Two Commentaries on the Jacobite Liturgy by George, Bishop of the Arab Tribes and Moses Bar Kepha'*, London 1913; Baby Varghese (trans.), *Dionysius Bar Salibi: Commentary on the Eucharist*, Kottayam 1998; *John of Dara: De Oblatione*, Kottayam 1999.

Studies: Sebastian Brock, 'Studies in the Early History of the Syrian Orthodox Baptismal Liturgy', *JTS* XXIII, 1972, 16–64; 'Two Recent Editions of Syrian Orthodox Anaphoras', *Ephemerides Liturgicae* CII, 1988, 436–45; Christine Chaillot, *The Syrian Orthodox Church of Antioch and All the East*, Geneva 1998; H. W. Codrington, *Studies of the Syrian Liturgies*, London 1952; Archdale A. King, *Rites of Eastern Christendom* I, Rome 1947, 61–208; Baby Varghese, 'Canonical Fasts in the West Syrian Tradition', *The Harp* VII, 1994, 89–108; 'Early History of the

Preparation Rites in the Syrian Orthodox Anaphora', *Symposium Syriacum VII*, ed. R. Lavenant, Rome 1998, 127–38; 'Holy Week Celebrations in the West Syrian Tradition', *Hebdomadae Sanctae Celebratio*, ed. A. G. Kollamparampil, Rome 1997, 167–86; *Les onctions baptismales dans la tradition syrienne*, Louvain 1989.

BABY VARGHESE

Western Rites

The term 'Western rite' in the singular is often used to denote the dominant liturgical synthesis that developed in the Latin West during the Middle Ages. However, even this synthesis did not bring about complete liturgical uniformity – that had to wait until the invention of printing and the actions of the sixteenth-century RC Council of Trent – and so there were many diocesan variations as well as the particular traditions of individual religious orders. Some of these diocesan forms (like the Sarum rite in England, stemming from the diocese of Salisbury) had wider influence and were followed in a number of neighbouring dioceses. Prior to the emergence of this broad synthesis, there were a number of distinct Western families of liturgies, as well as many local variants within those families.

1. The Roman rite, which came to constitute the foundation of the later Western rite, was originally simply the liturgy of the city of Rome and, with local variants, of the surrounding churches of southern Italy. The major extant sources are sacramentaries, *ordines* and other texts dating from the seventh century onwards, and knowledge of its earlier forms is very incomplete, being based mainly on brief comments in ancient writers (*see* **Roman Catholic Worship** 1).

2. The North African rite. No liturgical texts as such have survived from this tradition because of the Arab conquest of the region at the end of the seventh century, but from the limited information provided by earlier witnesses, North African practices seem to have been very similar to the liturgical traditions of Rome.

3. The Ambrosian rite, the liturgical traditions of north Italy, named after the fourth-century bishop of Milan, Ambrose. He himself, however, claimed that the practices known to him were very close to those of Rome, and indeed he is our earliest witness to the form of the Roman *eucharistic prayer. On the other

hand, from indications in his writings and in those of other fourth-century north Italian bishops, it is clear that there were in fact some significant variations in that region from Roman practice, some of which show similarities to Gallican and Eastern traditions. Later liturgical texts from the region continue to show variation from the Roman rite, and when uniformity of practice was imposed by the Council of Trent in the sixteenth century on all traditions less than two hundred years old, the Ambrosian rite was able to escape this, and remains to the present day with some interesting variations from the standard liturgy practised elsewhere in the RC Church.

4. The Gallican rite, the liturgical practices of Gaul, known chiefly from texts that became combined with Roman liturgical formularies under the Carolingians in the eighth and ninth centuries. The language was more prolix and colourful and the ceremonies more elaborate than the sober character of the Roman rite. Many of its practices and theological concepts show greater affinity with traditions found in the East than with the Roman rite.

5. The Spanish rite, also known (inaccurately) as the Visigothic rite and, in the period after southern Spain was occupied by Islamic Arabs in the eighth century, as the Mozarabic rite. Like the Gallican rite, it was very different in character from the Roman rite and displays some resemblances both to Gallican and to Eastern traditions. It was supplanted by the Roman rite at the end of the eleventh century, and what survived subsequently in the use of a single chapel at Toledo should not be equated with the richness of the older Spanish traditions.

6. The Celtic rite practised in the churches of the British Isles before Roman influence gradually overwhelmed it in the period between the seventh and eleventh centuries and left only remnants in later liturgical books.

––––––

John K. Brooks-Leonard, 'Traditions, Liturgical, in the West: Pre-Reformation', *The New Dictionary of Sacramental Worship*, ed. Peter Fink, Collegeville 1990, 1282–93.

EDITOR

Whitsunday

The traditional English name for the feast of *Pentecost, usually thought to be a contraction of 'White Sunday' and a reference to the white robes worn by the newly baptized, since this was an ancient alternative occasion to *Easter for *baptisms to be regularly administered.

EDITOR

Women and Worship

The twentieth-century women's movement, like its predecessor of the nineteenth century, includes in its cultural critique challenges both to some religious attitudes towards women and to the position of women within contemporary religious traditions. Several issues have emerged as a result of this renewed recognition of the role that religion in general and the Christian tradition in particular has played and continues to play in the oppression of women as a group.

1. *Equal Access to Leadership Roles.* Historically continuous with the nineteenth-century struggle for women's rights is a concern for equal access for women into existing ecclesial structures. In relation to worship, this concern has focused especially on the presence of women as leaders of worship in general and as ordained or otherwise officially recognized clergy in particular. The struggle of women to gain official recognition of their ministry by the church has, in some cases, been successful, yielding data for assessing the impact of women in roles of recognized leadership in the churches and synagogues as well as a significant body of publications on the history and theology of women's leadership in churches. This struggle for access and recognition has been motivated not only by a concern for public recognition of the call to ministry of individual women, but also by the conviction that such a recognition itself constitutes a powerful witness to the equality of women and men in the sight of God. At the same time, the presence of women at *altar and *pulpit also challenges presuppositions about the nature of God and the adequacy of exclusively male language to speak of and address God as well as ideas of gender-based hierarchies.

2. *Inclusive Language.* A more contemporary concern has been the use of language in such a way that women are included, both implicitly and explicitly. The conventional English-language practice of using male referents as 'generic' (referring to the whole human race) has been sharply challenged. Critics have pointed out that such usage perpetuates the misconception that men are normative human beings and that women are secondary, derivative, or deviant. These issues come to the fore liturgically in connection with historic or traditional texts, whether from scripture, hymns or liturgical texts. Considerable effort has been expended in seeking appropriate contemporary language both in translated texts and in traditional texts written in an earlier form of English. Recent liturgical and hymnal revisions have taken up the challenge to produce texts that combine respect for transmission of traditions with attention to the contexts of modern worshipping communities. Although the issues are somewhat different in those languages which, unlike English, use grammatical gender, the use of the male generic form in reference to human beings both male and female is increasingly avoided in those contexts as well. Strategies for responding to the problem, whether in English or other languages, have generally fallen into three categories. *Nonsexist language* seeks to avoid gender-specific terms. *Inclusive language* seeks to balance gender references. *Emancipatory language* seeks to transform language use and to challenge stereotypical gender references. Although these different strategies can be distinguished in theory, in practice they are often used in combination with one another.

3. *God-Language and Images.* Although it is often treated as an aspect of 'inclusive language', the problem of male-oriented language about God is more usefully understood as a separate (though not unrelated) issue. The extent to which God is unrelievedly portrayed as male in traditional scriptural, liturgical and hymn texts as well as in iconic representations, raises theological questions about whether women are indeed created in God's image to the same extent as men. Furthermore, not only are exclusively male names and images for God androcentric, that is, they assume that the male is the normative model for divine as well as human being; these images are also patriarchal in their use of names associated with male hierarchs: King, Master, Lord and Ruler. Thus the traditional images, references and titles assigned to God not only reinforce the male as normative, but also support male supremacy and hierarchies. Liturgical practices that exclude women from positions of leadership and presume hierarchical relationships between humans often are defended on the basis of this image of God as male hierarch.

The feminist liturgical movement has been raising the question of gendered God-language in an increasingly urgent and articulate way since the beginnings of the movement. The critique itself is simple: exclusively or dominantly male language about God grants authority to men in a patriarchal culture and religion. This is particularly true when titles ascribed to God duplicate those also given exclusively to men, such as father, king or master. Such titles operate in a dual manner. That is, they suggest not only that God is like a father, or king or master, but also that fathers, kings and masters are somehow like God. This issue relates to questions of women's access and recognition in leadership roles, particularly to the extent that liturgical leadership roles assume the representation of divinity. Strategies for dealing with the male hierarchical image of God vary widely, with feminist theologians and practitioners often differing on what language is acceptable and what is not. For some, the terms 'God' and 'Lord' lack sufficient gender connotation to be viewed as problematic. For others, the implicit maleness of the terms makes them unacceptable, generating the creation or reconstruction of female names and titles for the deity. For Christian feminists, the image and function of Jesus has created unique problems. On the one hand, the historical Jesus is often viewed as sympathetic towards women, and as one who identifies with the oppressed of the world. On the other hand, some of the christological images of Jesus, particularly as (male) saviour and as king, raise problems of the glorification of suffering and the sanctification of hierarchies. Solutions to these problems are far from resolved, as in the case of God-language, with feminist critics differing not only on the scope of the problem but also on which strategies are effective and acceptable.

4. *Women and Tradition*. At the heart of critiques of language or access to recognized leadership roles is the question of the ability of traditional structures of Christian and Jewish liturgical practices to tolerate the inclusion of women in full equality with men. Feminist critics point to the forgetfulness of the Christian tradition regarding women's participation in the life of faith. For some, Christian theological beliefs and liturgical practices are so irrevocably androcentric and patriarchal that they are not worth the effort required to reform them. Some would argue that if all elements of androcentrism and patriarchy were removed

from Christianity and Judaism, little or nothing would remain. Others, however, view Christianity's history as complex and ambiguous, and work to recover and reclaim the silenced, forgotten and distorted stories, beliefs and practices of women, and thus to reshape and renew biblical religion. Liturgical tradition in particular is subject to this critique, since it draws heavily on biblical texts, which reflect androcentric and patriarchal world views.

5. *The Development of Feminist Liturgical Tradition*. The organized centres of Christianity have not always been hospitable to feminist critiques on these issues, and have been reluctant to admit changes in liturgical language or practice to include women's history and perspective, or to take seriously women's spiritual needs. Therefore many women have turned to the creation of alternative religious communities for mutual support, spiritual nurture and liturgical life. This movement has several different forms, but with considerable commonalities. In the 1970s in North America, RC women began organizing around the issue of the *ordination of women to the priesthood, with similar groups forming also in Great Britain and elsewhere. These groups confronted the problems of language and leadership in traditional liturgies, and eventually began to create their own liturgical practices. Similarly, as women in other Christian groups gathered to organize and strategize about access to ordination and other leadership roles, these gatherings too developed a liturgical component. Women who had moved out of traditional Christianity began gathering in spirituality groups to create rituals based on the creative reconstruction of Goddess-centred religion. The organization of local groups for worship and support, in some contexts named 'women-church' gatherings, became in the 1980s a locus for the development of a feminist liturgical practice, with considerable fluidity among these different groups as new symbols, new language and new ritual practices were generated. For some women these local liturgical groups have become their primary religious communities; but for many they offer a necessary supplement to androcentric and patriarchal practices of mainline religious traditions.

6. *The Characteristics of Feminist Liturgical Practice*. Out of the experience of these local liturgical groups a kind of consensus has

emerged about what constitutes feminist liturgical practice. The most basic and common characteristics cluster around issues of leadership and power. A strong commitment to shared power leads to practices such as shared or rotating leadership and communal participation in the liturgical event itself as well as in its planning and preparation. This commitment to shared power and communal leadership leads also to celebration of diversity and recognition of particularity of experience within any group. There is reluctance to universalize from one's own experience, and a desire to create a community that is not only tolerant of difference but celebrates it. Feminist liturgies tend to be critical of traditional sources of authority, regarding texts, practices and indeed the very idea of a monolithic tradition with suspicion. The authority of a text, practice, model of leadership, or doctrine rests not on its claim to be traditional (after all, the silencing of women is also traditional), but on its ability to offer liberation to women. In other words, any liturgical act, event, or symbol is evaluated on the basis of its moral authority for women. Thus the ability of a given liturgical event to express a prophetic vision of the world and the reign of God that includes the freedom and well-being of women is valued highly.

A second cluster of feminist liturgical principles focuses on communal issues. Women are central to feminist liturgies, rather than peripheral as in traditional liturgies. Relationships and interconnections between and among women are valued and sacralized, in contrast to traditional Christian liturgies' primary interest in relationships between men. This sense of interconnection among women is often broadened to include men and the natural world, expressing a non-hierarchical web-like relationship of mutual interdependence. Thus hierarchical language for God is eschewed in favour of images that emphasize interconnection and mutuality. God is rarely imaged as a ruler but more often as a parent, friend, or in non-anthropological but immanent terms. This emphasis on interconnection with the natural, physical world leads also to a positive evaluation of the human body, especially the female body. Where traditional Christianity has often regarded the body as dangerous and the female body as especially so, feminist liturgies prefer to see the female body as representing the image of God, and the physical functions of the female body (traditionally regarded in Christian teaching as polluted and polluting) as

sacred. Finally, the feminist suspicion of tradition and texts combined with a commitment to ever-expanding ideas of diversity leads feminist liturgical planners to value creativity and experimentalism over the creation of fixed texts and practices. It is commonplace for feminist liturgies to be created by a particular group of people for a particular group and event or occasion, with no expectation that the liturgical event will ever be repeated. Indeed, the unrepeatability of feminist liturgies is held as a value that not only honours the specificity of any liturgical gathering and event, but also guards against the creation of a new orthodoxy. Feminist liturgical groups value self-criticism and ongoing reform, in the belief that diversity and authenticity are thus best served.

7. *Global Diversity*. The feminist liturgical movement is often perceived to be a North American phenomenon. However, as recent collections of feminist liturgies attest, Christian feminist groups across the world are claiming ritual authority and creating liturgies that both critique and honour the Christian liturgical tradition. Drawing on liberating elements within Christianity as a resource for women's liberation in contexts of extreme suffering and oppression, feminist groups in such diverse settings as Korea, Chile, Mozambique, Iceland and Australia are contributing their unique voices to the development of a diverse feminist liturgical tradition.

Teresa Berger, *Women's Ways of Worship: Gender Analysis and Liturgical History*, Collegeville 1999 (bib.); Frank Henderson, *Remembering the Women: Women's Stories from Scripture for Sundays and Festivals*, Chicago 1999; Janet Morley, *All Desires Known*, expanded edn, London 1992; Leslie Northup, *Ritualizing Women: Patterns of Spirituality*, Cleveland, OH 1997; Marjorie Procter-Smith, *In Her Own Rite: Constructing Feminist Liturgical Tradition*, Nashville 1990/Akron, OH 2000; *Praying With Our Eyes Open: Engendering Feminist Liturgical Prayer*, Nashville 1995 (bib.); Marjorie Procter-Smith and Janet Walton (eds), *Women at Worship: Interpretations of North American Diversity*, Louisville, KY 1993.

MARJORIE PROCTER-SMITH

Women, Ordination of

see **Ordination of Women**

Word, Services of the

Acts of worship consisting chiefly or exclusively of scriptural readings and/or *preaching, together with prayer.

1. Early Christianity; 2. Eastern Churches; 3. Medieval and Roman Catholic; 4. Anglican; 5. Baptist; 6. Christian Church; 7. Congregationalist; 8. Lutheran; 9. Methodist; 10. Old Catholic; 11. Pentecostal; 12. Reformed.

1. *Early Christianity.* Early Christians seem to have known several different kinds of services of the word.

(a) From very early times their community meals (often referred to as an *agape) appear to have included some kind of informal ministry of the word, generally centring around the singing of a hymn or a psalm by individual participants in turn, to the verses of which the assembly might respond with a refrain of praise (see, e.g. 1 Cor. 14.26f.; Tertullian, *Apol.* 39; *Ap. Trad.* 25).

(b) In many places there were regular liturgies of the word on the weekly *fast days, Wednesdays and Fridays, as well as on Sundays. The Sunday service was apparently held in the morning and soon became attached to the celebration of the *eucharist. Our earliest detailed witness, Justin, *Apol.* 1.67, informs us that 'the memoirs of the apostles or the writings of the prophets are read for as long as time permits. When the reader has finished, the president urges and invites [us] to the imitation of these noble things. Then we all stand up together and offer prayers.' The Wednesday and Friday services, on the other hand, generally took place at the ninth hour (around 3 p.m.), a time apparently chosen to associate them with the death of Jesus and to mark the conclusion of fasting. The readings at these services seem to have usually been drawn from the OT and to have been followed by preaching. At first they were not joined to the eucharist, because at that time the eucharist was restricted to Sundays and festivals, but in later centuries in many places in the East the liturgy of the *presanctified was added to them, and in the West they were held in the morning in conjunction with a full celebration of the eucharist.

(c) Daily assemblies for teaching appear to have been held at least in some places, although not necessarily all year round. While some sources suggest that they were intended primarily for the instruction of *catechumens in the faith, baptized members of the church were also encouraged to be present. By the fourth century, they seem to have become restricted to the season of *Lent and to Easter week, in connection with the practice of *baptism at *Easter.

(d) There is evidence for *vigils, during which passages from the scriptures would be read, but the frequency of these in the first three centuries is uncertain.

(e) Some early sources also encourage daily private Bible reading by individuals, but because of the high cost of obtaining a copy of the text and the low level of literacy among many Christians, this can only have been the practice of a privileged few. Later monastic communities continued this tradition.

———

Paul F. Bradshaw, *Daily Prayer in the Early Church*, London 1981/New York 1982.

EDITOR

2. *Eastern Churches.* The primary celebration of the word in all Eastern rites is the liturgy of the catechumens (i.e., liturgy of the word) in the *eucharist. In the Byzantine tradition, there are normally two readings, from the Epistles or Acts of the Apostles and from the Gospels. The readings are preceded by the *Prokeimenon* (a response and a verse of a psalm that may once have been sung at greater length) and between the two there is an *Alleluia chant with two verses. There is a possible reference to an OT reading in the *Mystagogy* of St Maximus the Confessor (d. 662), but the present arrangement was in place by the eighth century. OT readings are used at evening prayer in *Lent and on the eves of many feasts. When the eucharist is combined with evening prayer, e.g., *Christmas, *Epiphany and the ancient *Easter vigil, there may be as many as fifteen OT readings which are structurally part of evening prayer, the NT being read after the *Trisagion* (or equivalent) as usual.

The *lectionary has three cycles. One for the Sundays of the year and major feasts was in place by the eighth century. The Saturday cycle was added soon after, and the cycle for the rest of the week came much later, after the tenth century. In the absence of a priest, a *deacon, *lector or any other person may lead the congregation in the *Typica* (*see* **Presanctified, Liturgy of the**) with the set readings and chants to follow the Beatitudes. Known as the *obednitza* or 'deprived' service, this is clearly celebrated only as a second best.

The Syrian Orthodox books expect there to

be three OT readings, two epistles and the gospel. The *Trisagion* is sung before the epistles and there is an Alleluia chant before the gospel. Modern practice in India is to read the OT during the preparatory service of the eucharist. The Copts read four lessons; from the Pauline epistles, the Catholic epistles, the Acts of the Apostles and the Gospels. There is also a reading from the *Synaxarion* (lives of the saints, etc.) after the Acts reading. The Ethiopians do something similar with longer chants between the readings. In both cases it is possible that the first two readings were originally from the OT. The Armenians retain the ancient order of OT, epistle and gospel, with psalm verses chanted before each (with Alleluia before the gospel). The Nestorian or Chaldean rite has two readings from the OT, psalm verses, the *turgama*, epistle reading, Alleluia chant, another *turgama* and the gospel, followed by an anthem. The *turgama* is an often lengthy poetic text on the theme of the reading it precedes – that before the epistle is often omitted and the Chaldean Catholics do not seem to use them at all.

On most days, the *daily prayer offices of the Eastern churches do not have readings of the scriptures. However, as seen above, there are exceptions to this rule, another being the reading of a resurrection gospel at Orthodox morning prayer on Sundays (*see* **Vigil**). Something similar is found in the Armenian and Syrian traditions.

Georges Barrois, *Scripture Reading in Orthodox Worship*, Crestwood, NY 1977; Casimir Kucharek, *The Byzantine-Slav Liturgy of St John Chrysostom*, Allendale, NJ 1971, 381–465 (bib.); Juan Mateos, *La célébration de la parole dans la liturgie byzantine*, Rome 1971; Varghese Pathikulangara, *Qurbana*, Kottayam 1998, 169–78.

GREGORY WOOLFENDEN

3. *Medieval and Roman Catholic*. By the early medieval period the ancient liturgy of the word was not everywhere well understood. In the West new languages were widely spoken, but the liturgy continued to be celebrated in Latin. Thus many increasingly found it difficult or impossible to understand and to respond to the scriptural word read publicly in assembly.

3.1. *Eucharist*. The liturgy of the word associated with the *eucharist continued to be celebrated throughout the medieval period

even if few understood what was proclaimed. As in many liturgies of the Eastern churches, there were in the early medieval period three readings in most Western Sunday liturgies, including the Roman. A reading from the OT preceded the two from the NT (epistle and gospel). The latter two were originally read in a semi-continuous manner, but as the liturgical *year developed, there was an attempt to harmonize the readings to correspond with the themes evident in certain seasons of the year, such as *Lent and *Easter, and to reduce the number of readings before that from the gospels. The system of readings in Rome in the seventh century prevailed until the reforms of the Second Vatican Council. That system allowed only one reading, either from the OT or NT, before the gospel.

Although exposure to the word of God through the liturgy became more limited as the medieval period progressed, new ways of proclaiming the content of the scriptures arose, such as allegorical explanations of the mass; mystery and morality plays developing out of the sequences, which previously had grown out of the extended vocal passage (*jubilus*) concluding the *Alleluia before the gospel; and the representation in art of scenes from biblical narratives (e.g. the windows of the cathedral at Chartres).

3.2. *Daily Prayer*. Another form of proclamation of the word of God that has endured since at least the sixth century is that which occurs in what once was known as *vigils, later as matins, and now as office of readings in the liturgy of the hours. The oldest redaction of *Ordo* XIV, which gives the order of readings used at St Peter's Basilica in Rome probably during the pontificate of Pope Gregory the Great (590–604), states that 'all of Scripture . . . is read from the beginning of the year to the end' in the celebration of this office. *Ordo* XIIIB, from the eighth century, suggests that the scriptural readings in the Roman office, probably in the Lateran Basilica, were lengthy. That pattern, however, did not hold. Hagiographical readings, which were part of vigil services or occasional offices at the tombs of martyrs or in churches containing their relics, entered the Roman office at the end of the eighth century if *Ordo* XII is correct. Because of the popularity of saints in the later medieval period, these readings became major and sometimes altogether eliminated the scriptural readings of matins.

3.3. *Modern Revision*. The Second Vatican

Council (1962–5) recognized the paucity of public proclamation of the word of God in the liturgy, both in the eucharist and in the divine office or liturgy of the hours. The Constitution on the Sacred Liturgy, promulgated by Pope Paul VI on 4 December 1963, declared that 'in sacred celebrations there is to be more reading from holy scripture, and it is to be more varied and suitable' (35.1). Furthermore, 'Bible services should be encouraged, especially on the vigils of the more solemn feasts, on some weekdays in Advent and Lent, and on Sundays and feast days' (35.4). In the reform of the rite of the eucharist 'the treasures of the bible are to be opened up more lavishly, so that richer fare may be provided for the faithful at the table of God's word. In this way a more representative portion of the holy scriptures will be read to the people in the course of a prescribed number of years' (51). For the liturgy of the hours, the Council prescribed that 'readings from sacred scripture shall be arranged so that the riches of God's word may be easily accessible in more abundant measure' (92a).

In the post-conciliar period, those responsible for carrying out the reform of the liturgy according to the norms established by the Council proposed for the eucharist a three-year cycle of scriptural readings for Sundays (*see* **Lectionary**) and a two-year weekday cycle. For the liturgy of the hours they proposed a two-year daily cycle. The use of both the weekday cycles for the eucharist and the daily cycles for the liturgy of the hours would ensure the reading of almost the entire Bible in the course of a year.

In the liturgy of the hours, a one-year cycle of readings was eventually substituted for the two-year cycle in the office of readings (formerly matins), and the two-year cycle was made optional because it was thought that a two-year cycle was not able to be conveniently printed in the four volumes of the liturgy of the hours. *The General Instruction on the Liturgy of the Hours* made provision for scriptural reading in all the hours, but expressly allowed the longer readings in the office of readings or in the eucharist to be used also at morning prayer or evening prayer (n. 46). *The General Instruction* also permitted the extension of the office of readings, especially in monastic communities, to form a vigil for Sundays and solemn feasts. This extension is accomplished by the addition of three *canticles from the Hebrew scriptures and a proclamation of an account from the gospel taken from a series of narratives regarding the resurrection or from the gospel assigned to the feast (n. 73).

Although the Constitution on the Sacred Liturgy did not prescribe that sacramental rites other than that of the eucharist contain a liturgy of the word, the post-conciliar reform of these rites provided that in each of them there be a liturgy of the word. Thus, *baptism, *confirmation, *penance, *ordination, *marriage, anointing of the *sick, and other rites such as those for religious profession and *funerals are now celebrated either with a full liturgy of the word (one or more scriptural readings with responsorial psalm after the first reading) or at least a short scriptural reading.

After a millennium or so of being increasingly deprived of the word of God in public prayer, RCs today are presented with an embarras de richesses with respect to the scriptures. Faced with this richness, they must learn again how to encounter this word as the living word of God enlightening and directing the events of their lives.

For the eucharist: Robert Cabié, 'The Liturgy of the Word', *The Church at Prayer*, ed. A. G. Martimort, II, Collegeville 1986, 59–69. For bibliography relating to the divine office, *see* **Daily Prayer** 3.

STANISLAUS CAMPBELL

4. *Anglican*. The first *BCP* in 1549 reinstated *daily prayer services focused on the reading of scripture, but without provision for a sermon (in contrast to Lutheran Germany or Calvin's Geneva), although the combination of morning prayer, *litany and *ante-communion, which became the staple Sunday morning diet of most English parish churches, was usually accompanied by a lengthy sermon, as also was evening prayer on Sundays. With the later addition of hymns, this basic Sunday pattern persisted well into the twentieth century, although eventually litany and ante-communion were generally dropped from the morning worship.

In the eighteenth century non-eucharistic worship focused on scripture reached new heights in England in the *Methodist preaching services, immensely popular among the urban poor. Yet in 1851 a census revealed that a large proportion of the population of the United Kingdom were still unchurched and that millions no longer counted themselves as belonging to any of the mainstream Christian denominations. In order to meet this gap, 'mission services' were established which were much simpler than the normal Sunday morning or evening services of any of the mainstream denominations. Provision was also made within the Church of England (1872 Act of Uniformity Amendment Act) for a third service to be held on a Sunday supplementary to the statutory services of morning and evening prayer. Another important development was that of Sunday school services in the late nineteenth and early twentieth centuries (*see* **Children and Worship**), and subsequently of *family services, as well as services for particular occasions (e.g. Christmas *carol services, *harvest festivals). Various unofficial publications appeared to assist in the compilation of all these types of service, but legally these acts of worship could only be used as a third service within the Church of England.

The need to amend this situation was clear. In 1985 The Report of the Archbishops' Commission on the Inner Cities, *Faith in the City*, pointed to a need for more informal and spontaneous acts of worship in 'Urban Priority Areas'. This same report also put in a plea for short functional service booklets and cards which could be easily understood by a variety of people, young and old alike, and pleaded for the language of worship to become more concrete and less philosophical with an appropriate use of meaningful symbols. In 1989 the work on informal worship structures suitable for use in Anglican churches came together in the report, *Patterns for Worship*, later published in a version 'commended for use' in 1995. These proposals represented a huge step forward, in which Anglican worship is seen as being based upon a recognizable shape, with some elements mandatory and others optional, rather than upon slavish following of set texts. This was later confirmed when *A Service of the Word*, born out of *Patterns for Worship*, was finally authorized in 1993 (and reauthorized in 1999 to take account of the provisions of *Common Worship*). It is unique as a Church of England service, since it consists principally of a menu of essential elements which must be included in any service of the word together with notes and directions which allow for a wide range of optional elements and local variation within a common structure. Thus the structure may be used to construct a variety of forms of service, from informal family or all-age worship to regular patterns of daily prayer.

In some other parts of the Anglican Communion, especially those where there is a shortage of ordained ministers, 'Bible services' (often led by lay people) have been a long established feature of Sunday worship.

Anne Dawtry and Carolyn Headley, 'A Service of the Word', *A Companion to Common Worship* I, ed. Paul Bradshaw, London 2001, 52–84; Trevor Lloyd, *A Service of the Word*, Cambridge, 1999; Bryan Spinks, 'Not so Common Prayer: The Development of the Third Service', *The Renewal of Common Prayer: Unity and Diversity in Church of England Worship*, ed. Michael Perham, London 1993, 55–67; David Stancliffe, 'Is There an Anglican Liturgical Shape?', *The Identity of Anglican Worship*, ed. Kenneth Stevenson and Bryan Spinks, London 1991, 124–34.

ANNE DAWTRY

5. *Baptist.* For Baptists, who from their beginnings in the early seventeenth century have held strongly to the Reformation doctrine of *sola scriptura*, the proclamation of the word is central to worship. Although the *Lord's supper is highly regarded, the greater part of *Baptist worship takes the shape of the non-eucharistic service of the word, which sets at its heart the reading and exposition of scripture.

There is no hierarchical body dictating the form and structure of services and freedom of expression under the guidance of the Spirit is highly valued. As the responsibility for worship lies with the gathered community, there is a wide variety of practice, ranging from austere formality in one church to informal exuberance or pietistic simplicity in another. However, E. A. Payne's comment still holds true: 'The general pattern of church services has remained the same from the seventeenth century to the present day: scripture, prayer and sermon, interspersed with hymns' (*The Fellowship of Believers: Baptist Thought and Practice Yesterday and Today*, enlarged edition, London 1952, 96).

Among modern Baptists, such a pattern is broadly speaking likely to follow one of two basic structures: (a) in which the reading of scripture, the sermon and hymn or prayer of commitment occur as the culmination of the service, following an opening section of approach, praise and *confession, and a central section of *offertory and prayers of thanksgiving, supplication and *intercession; (b) in which the reading of scripture and the sermon occupy the central part of the service, preceded by an opening section of approach, praise and confession, and followed by a section of response to the word through thanksgiving, intercession, offertory and dismissal.

As there is no required *lectionary, leaders of worship are free to devise their own pattern of readings following the pastoral and spiritual needs of the congregation or the particular demands of leadership. There is no limit to the number of chosen readings, although a service might usually include two, one from the OT and one from the NT, not necessarily a gospel reading. There is no obligation to follow the pattern of the church *year, although most churches would celebrate at the very least *Christmas and *Easter and probably mark other occasions such as the anniversary of the congregation's foundation, *harvest festival and civic occasions such as *Remembrance Day. As there is no mandatory prayer book, prayers may be *extempore, pre-composed or drawn from printed sources. These are offered by the worship leader or sometimes by the congregation in times of 'open prayer'.

Baptist emphasis on preaching has produced preachers of renown such as John Bunyan and Martin Luther King or Charles Haddon Spurgeon and Billy Graham. The sermon, usually very closely based on the scripture readings, is often seen as the sine qua non of the service of the word. The seventeenth-century Baptist church in Amsterdam, established under the leadership of the separatist John Smyth, might have heard as many as five sermons during one service, and while modern services would usually include only one, it might occupy up to half the total duration of the worship or more. The role of preacher is not necessarily confined to the pastor or ordained minister.

Baptist worship places great emphasis on the responsibility of the individual believer. As H. Wheeler Robinson declared, 'Faith must be individual if it is to be faith' (*Baptist Principles*, London 1926, 20). Just as the individual believer comes into the membership of the church through individual confession of faith and believer's *baptism, so each worshipper participates in the service of the word through personal response to the divine invitation. The proclamation and exposition of scripture is as much seen to address the life and faith of each believer as the life of the church as a whole.

Given the oral nature of the tradition, patterns of worship are easily open to variation and change. In recent decades the *Liturgical and *Charismatic Movements have exerted an important influence. The Liturgical Movement has brought an increased use of written liturgical text, a deeper awareness of the church year, and has encouraged the development and practice of pattern (b) above. It has equally led to a heightened regard for regular eucharistic worship, which has in its turn displaced in some churches the centrality of non-eucharistic services of the word. The influence of the Charismatic Movement has served to strengthen the existing emphasis on the worship of the heart. While the proclamation of the word still has great importance, the introduction of the extended time of devotional singing has led in some quarters to the increasing perception of praise as the primary feature of worship. Thus each movement, in its own way, has had the effect of tempering the traditional stress on the central role of scripture and preaching.

Baptist Union of Great Britain, *Patterns and Prayers for Christian Worship*, Oxford 1991; Christopher J. Ellis, *Baptist Worship Today*, Didcot 1999; E. A. Payne and S. F. Winward, *Orders and Prayers for Church Worship*, London 1960; B. R. White, *The English Baptists of the Seventeenth Century*, Didcot 1996.

MARY COTES

6. *Christian Church.* Throughout its history the norm for worship in Christian Church (Disciples of Christ) has been its encounter with its Lord at the Lord's table. In contrast to the *Reformed aspects of its heritage, the church has adhered to the NT pattern according to which the community gathers each and every Lord's Day (Sunday) at his table. And not only on Sunday: as the decisive and most intimate expression of Christ's coming to be with his people, the *Lord's supper is central to high moments in the church's life, so that it is typical for a range of church gatherings to conclude with a full *eucharist including, as on Sunday, both proclamation of the word and gathering at the table.

Thus Disciples are aware of the service of the word as the first part of the normal Sunday service, including typically an entrance (often with hymn and *confession), scripture reading, proclamation of the gospel and response (with a statement of faith and prayers of the people), and followed invariably by the service of the table. But they have no experience of a service of the word in the classic Reformed sense, that is, a regular Sunday service including the above elements but stopping short of the sharing of Christ's body and blood. Indeed a person born and bred in the Disciples' tradition is likely to feel that something is 'missing' after a Sunday service – however solemn – which does not culminate in the community's gathering at the table of the Lord.

There are of course times at which a non-eucharistic service is appropriate or necessary. These include worship occasions where the focus is on other aspects of the community's common life or when a simpler, shorter service is needed, for example *dedication or installation services, services in observance of special days in the life of the community or nation, or services in institutional settings such as hospitals or church camps. And a non-eucharistic service may be preferred for worship in an *ecumenical context, especially when not all those present are able for reasons of church discipline to gather at the Lord's table. Since for Disciples the encounter with scripture is the wellspring of their faith and life, the reading of scripture and proclamation of the word (or at least an invitation to reflect upon the scripture which has been read) would be a focal point of most if not all non-eucharistic worship.

Such services of the word in the broader sense are being influenced by ancient patterns of Christian worship. Through their engagement with the *Liturgical and Ecumenical Movements, Disciples have become more aware of the integrity of the service of the word, including the elements of entrance, scripture reading, proclamation of the gospel and response. The awareness that this is a pattern shared by Christians of many times and many places is having an increasing impact on the planning of non-eucharistic services within the church. For example, the service for *daily morning worship in the current Disciples' worship book includes, with some additions and variations, elements of such a service of the word. This is all the more striking since these are occasions that would not necessarily focus on scripture, and in which a lengthy sermon would be out of place. Yet the purpose of gathering includes hearing and proclaiming 'God's holy word', and the service includes silence for meditation on the scripture, and allows for the possibility of a spoken meditation on the scripture which has been read. This service of morning worship has the following elements: statement of purpose (including the affirmation that the community meets 'to hear and proclaim God's holy word'); call to worship; hymn; psalm; scripture reading; silence (a spoken meditation may be given at this point 'if the occasion requires it'); hymn/*spiritual/chorus/*canticle; invitation to prayer; prayers of thanksgiving and *intercession; the *Lord's Prayer; hymn/song/spiritual/chorus; *dismissal with blessing.

To be sure, the elements of a classic service of the word have long been present in Disciples' non-eucharistic worship. But there is now a clearer awareness among those planning and leading worship that they, and the congregation which they are leading, are standing within the long tradition of the church as a whole. Thus while the regular Sunday service of word and table remains very much the norm for Disciples' worship, there is a renewed interest in services of the word classically understood as an inspiration for the community when it gathers for non-eucharistic worship.

––––––

Colbert S. Cartwright and O. I. Cricket Harrison (eds), *Chalice Worship*, St Louis 1997; Keith Watkins, *The Great Thanksgiving*, St Louis 1995, 94–113.

THOMAS F. BEST

7. *Congregationalist*. Worship in Congregational churches has always given a strong emphasis to *preaching of a scholarly and evangelistic mould. John Marsh, writing the introduction to *A Book of Public Worship*, notes that the Congregational order of worship is not derived from a series of offices, to which sermons are a later addition, but has seen the sermon as central from the outset.

Towards the end of the sixteenth century, under the influence of the European Reformation, parish churches in England began to encourage preaching. Where the incumbent was not a preacher, congregations would go to another place to hear a preacher after the regular service in their own church. As well as preaching, public 'prophesyings' arose, in which preachers and scholars engaged in debate as the religious ferment of the day was argued out. These gatherings were suppressed, among other tendencies to free forms of worship, as counter to uniformity, by injunction of Queen Elizabeth I. Licence to preach was limited to officers in the Church of England. The trial of John Penry, following which he was hanged, records the Nonconformist view that office in the 'true' church was conferred by the local congregation.

Following the ejection of ministers in the 1660s, under the various repressive measures of the Clarendon Code, Nonconformist worship and, above all, preaching became a highly dangerous activity. Extraordinary measures were taken to protect the preacher, whose life and liberty might be endangered by his activity. The disabilities enforced on all Nonconformists led, in the case of Congregationalists, to the formation of Dissenting academies, with a powerful tradition of scholarship. Ministers of Congregational churches brought to their preaching great depth of learning. During this time, ministers and congregations sought to escape persecution in their pilgrimage to New England, and there sought to form colonies whose civil life was based on congregational principles. Preaching played an important part in the political development of seventeenth- and eighteenth-century American life. Sermons were used to inform political debate and the Revolution inspired preaching against oppression. Elsewhere, preachers addressed political issues. The Congregational minister John Smith ended his days in jail in Guyana, condemned to death because of his stand against slavery.

In England, the nineteenth century was the golden age of popular Nonconformist preaching. In the latter half of the century, great church buildings were erected, with *galleries, to accommodate the enormous crowds who flocked to hear the popular preachers of the day. They, in common with actors and barristers, adopted a florid and dramatic style. The crowds that came to hear were more in the nature of an audience than a congregation. They tended not to become members of the churches at which they attended, nor did they even attend for the whole service. The growth of popular preaching, therefore, had a detrimental effect on Congregational ecclesiology. The great congregations of this era were moving away from the ideal of a covenanted and committed membership in a gathered church. Preaching lost its prophetic edge, in the constant attempt to form and please a large audience. This style of preaching seems to have been deprecated even at its height, and was certainly despised by a later generation, which attempted to regain a plainer and more direct address to the hearers. Joseph Parker at City Temple, London, Robert William Dale at Carrs Lane, Birmingham, and Henry Allon at Union Chapel, Islington, not only drew crowds to hear their preaching, but also had a great effect on the development of worship. They were not just preachers, but shapers of worshipping practice.

In the twentieth century a slow decline in the numbers attending worship went with a dramatic fall in the status of the minister, and a consequent decline in the popularity and, sometimes, the standard of preaching. The Ecumenical Movement of the early twentieth century led to growing conformity of worship patterns, and the distinction between a liturgical form of worship and the largely oral tradition of the Congregational and other Free Churches was blurred. Length of sermons dropped from the two hours of some high Victorian preachers to a regular twenty minutes or less. Eventually, preaching itself fell out of favour, as a non-participatory form of worship which reduced all but the speaker to silence.

The turn of the twentieth/twenty-first century has seen a development of new and more participatory forms of proclaiming the gospel. There has been a rediscovery of oral practices such as storytelling and the use of dialogue in worship. These may replace or complement the traditional sermon. Current Congregational Federation training material on leading worship engages with many methods of proclamation, but, in common with long tradition, aims at a style of preaching that 'is informed by the mind, and bears fruit in action, but it comes from the heart' (Congregational Federation Integrated Training, Module L, Section 5).

———

Selected text: J. Huxtable, John Marsh, Romilly Micklem and James Todd, *A Book of Public Worship, Compiled for the use of Congregationalists*, Oxford 1948.

Studies: R. W. Dale, *History of English Congregationalism*, London 1907; R. Tudur Jones, *Congregationalism in England, 1662–1962*, London 1962; John Von Rohr, *The Shaping of American Congregationalism 1620–1957*, Cleveland 1992; B. Thorogood, *Gales of Change*, London 1994; M. R. Watts, *The Dissenters*, 2 vols, Oxford 1985–95.

JANET H. WOOTTON

8. *Lutheran*. Lutherans have very little tradition of a service crafted solely to be a 'service of the word'. This assertion must be made with some care, however. It is certainly true that the Lutheran reception of the Western tradition of the *eucharist placed a new accent on the reading and *preaching of the scriptures in the

midst of the celebration of the old 'word' part of the liturgy, the *missa catechumenorum* or *ante-communion as it is sometimes called. It is also true that early Lutheran practice placed a strong accent on preparation for *communion by catechization and by *confession and *absolution, and a similarly strong accent on the necessity of avoiding the celebration of *mass if there were no communicants except for the priest or pastor. As a result of these emphases, the regular Sunday mass in Lutheran congregations of the sixteenth and seventeenth centuries would sometimes not be able to proceed to its conclusion in communion and would be celebrated only as a 'service of the word'. This was a result which occurred more and more frequently during the period of the Enlightenment, with its undervaluing of *sacraments, and under the influence of Pietism, with its great interest in profound personal preparation for a worthy communion. The nineteenth- and twentieth-century consequence of this history was a use of the ante-communion (or *missa brevis* as it was also called) – replete with the *confiteor*, the introits and *collects, the *Kyrie, Gloria, and Credo, and the classic *lectionary of the Western mass tradition – as the principal Sunday service known by Lutherans. It follows that one major goal of twentieth-century Lutheran liturgical reform has been a quest to reunite word and sacrament by a restoration of the early Lutheran unity, centrality and every-Sunday frequency of the full mass.

The Lutheran interest in the preached word also spilled over into the observance of *daily prayer. In the *Deutsche Messe* of 1526, Martin Luther, reporting on the practice in the churches of Wittenberg, writes about preaching on the lectionary epistle reading at Sunday matins, on the gospel at Sunday mass, and on passages taken chapter by chapter from the OT at Sunday vespers. Furthermore, during the week there were sermons on the *catechism following Monday and Tuesday matins, a sermon on Matthew on Wednesday morning, sermons on the epistles on Thursday and Friday morning, and a sermon on John at Saturday vespers. 'Thus', he writes, 'enough lessons and sermons have been appointed to give the Word of God free course among us.'

It followed that orders for matins and vespers as they were outlined in the church orders (*Kirchenordnungen*) of the sixteenth and seventeenth centuries and as they were used in Lutheran congregations frequently included provision for a sermon. These offices often

became 'services of the word'. Preaching on the catechism or, during *Lent, on the 'passion history' (a harmonization of the four accounts of the passion) became a widespread practice at morning or evening prayer. The nineteenth-century movements for recovery of Lutheran liturgical tradition restored this practice. Both Löhe's *Agende* of 1844 and the *Common Service* of 1888, for example, include the possibility of preaching in their orders for matins and vespers. This tradition has also yielded an informal but widely used order for a preaching service: psalms or hymns followed by scripture, preaching, a further hymn and prayers.

More recent Lutheran liturgical practice, however, has found occasions when a service of the word, designed as such, has been useful. While Lutheran liturgists of the twentieth century have argued for the recovery of the full order of mass on Sundays – and thus argued against the use of the ante-communion as a self-standing service of the word – they have also sought to recover the integrity of daily prayer. The North American *Lutheran Book of Worship* (Philadelphia/Minneapolis 1978), for example, includes the possibility of preaching in its orders of matins and vespers, but only after the office itself is completed and only as an option. Instead, this same book presents a new rite called 'Service of the Word'. A supplementary volume to the *Lutheran Book of Worship*, published in 1995 and called *With One Voice* (Minneapolis 1995), has continued this practice in its 'Service of Word and Prayer'. Other late-twentieth-century Lutheran liturgical books have similar newly created orders.

As an example of these rites, the pattern followed in *With One Voice* is this: a gathering song; a greeting and a biblically based, seasonally appropriate dialogue; a *canticle based on Rev. 7 and 15; the prayer of the day (or *collect); one or two lectionary readings with psalms or hymns in response; an acclamation welcoming the gospel reading; the appointed gospel reading; a sermon; response to the word in hymn, *creed, communal confession and forgiveness and an exchange of peace; a collection together with a sung *offertory and an offertory prayer; *intercessions; the *Lord's Prayer; a *blessing, a sending song and the *dismissal. It is clear from this order that the eucharistic origins of 'services of the word' still form a strong undercurrent in new Lutheran liturgical creations. The future of these creations remains unclear.

Luther's Works LIII: 'Liturgy and Hymns', Philadelphia 1965.

GORDON LATHROP

9. *Methodist*. During the eighteenth century, when Methodism was defined as a society within the Church of England, Methodists were expected to attend services and receive the *sacrament in the parish church. The distinct and supplementary 'Methodist' occasions for worship were always services of the word – of *extemporary prayer, song, scripture reading, and sermon – whether they were morning, afternoon or evening gatherings for *preaching, or the 'peculiar' Methodist services of *love-feast, *watch-night or *covenant renewal.

When in 1784 John Wesley published orders of service in the *Sunday Service of the Methodists in North America*, he did not formalize with a text what Methodists were already practising in their preaching services. Instead, Wesley edited and abbreviated the 1662 *BCP*'s orders for morning and evening prayer, and specified that these were to be used 'every Lord's day' rather than daily. In those texts, among other changes, he deleted apocryphal readings and the Athanasian Creed, and reworked prayers for the King's Majesty to be for 'the Supreme Rulers' (editions for 'His Majesty's Dominions' kept the original form). Wesley also slightly modified the *ante-communion (which contained the sermon) in the 'Order for the Administration of the Lord's Supper' by removing the Nicene *Creed, thereby indicating his expectation, following current Anglican practice, that the 'Order for Morning Prayer' would immediately be followed by the ante-communion and *communion. Since the Apostles' Creed was already in morning prayer, elimination of the second creed avoided a perceived redundancy.

Despite Wesley's intention that the *eucharist should be administered every Sunday, geographic and ecclesiological circumstances did not allow it. Methodist Sunday worship in North America, Britain and elsewhere around the globe has primarily been a service of the word. By 1792, Methodists in the United States had thrown out the orders for morning and evening prayer, and had dropped the ante-communion from the *Lord's supper rite. In their place stood a set of directory-like rubrics that indicated content and not an order: the morning service of 'Public Worship' was to consist of 'singing, prayer, the reading of a chapter out of the Old Testament, and another out of the New, and preaching'. This list of worship components survived in the *Discipline* of the various American Methodist branches for more than a century, though some denominations amended the length of the lessons and added the *Lord's Prayer and the 'apostolic benediction' (2 Cor. 13.14). Even though the Methodist Protestant Church in 1830 configured the components into a specified pattern, the order was understood to be suggestive and not mandatory. Services were usually ordered according to the preferences of the minister, the expectations of the local congregation, and the anticipated outpouring of the Holy Spirit. The central focus was always the sermon as the principal means for enabling conversion and discipleship. Towards the end of the nineteenth century, more complex orders of worship began to be published by American Methodist denominations, though at different rates. To the basic components might be added – in diverse locations – choral anthems, readings of the Decalogue or the Beatitudes, responsive readings of the psalms with the Gloria Patri, and affirmations of faith. Although the Sunday morning service often became more formal, services on Sunday and Wednesday evenings typically kept their simple, evangelistic – even revivalistic – flavour.

In British Methodism and its offshoots throughout the Empire, some chapels on Sundays used morning prayer as revised by Wesley or as found in the *BCP*. More often a preaching service was employed, which was uniformly the case among the small denominations. The preaching service in Britain generally followed an evolutionary process similar to the one in the USA but, unlike the American orders, relied heavily upon the placement of four or five hymns for determining the overall shape and content of worship. Hymns from the Wesleys remained prominent in congregational use.

Throughout the Methodist world, the preaching service became more elaborate during the course of the twentieth century, and even the Holiness branches printed model services for their constituents. Methodists rediscovered the liturgical *year, though it had been partially preserved in the previous century by seasonal hymns in official and unofficial hymnals. *Lectionaries were more frequently deemed an acceptable alternative to personal inspiration. The second half of the century saw substantial changes made to the Sunday morning service in the larger denominations. Influenced by the wider *Liturgical and Ecumenical Movements, these bodies moved toward or adopted a normative Sunday pattern of a service of word and table, though in practice the preaching service still predominated in most congregations. The British *Methodist Service Book* (1975) abandoned the form for morning prayer in favour of an order that included thanksgiving as a standard component after the sermon, whether it be a *eucharistic prayer or another prayer. This pattern has been kept in the *Methodist Worship Book* (1999).

Adrian Burdon, *The Preaching Service – The Glory of the Methodists*, Nottingham 1991; Karen B. Westerfield Tucker, *American Methodist Worship*, New York 2000, 3–81; (ed.), *The Sunday Service of the Methodists*, Nashville 1996.

KAREN B. WESTERFIELD TUCKER

10. *Old Catholic*. All the Old Catholic churches know services of the word separate from the *eucharist, which come in four different shapes: (a) an *ante-communion service; (b) evening prayer (vespers) or other parts of the liturgy of the hours; (c) Taizé-inspired meditation services; (d) the liturgy on *Good Friday.

Those churches which had to organize themselves after the First Vatican Council saw the need for services of the word in those parishes which for lack of a priest could not assemble for the celebration of the eucharist (e.g. the decision of the fourth synod of the German Old Catholic Church, 1877). The weekly assembly of the parish members on Sundays for worshipping God was deemed so important that, in such a case, a lay member of the parish, with the consent of the *bishop, presided at a liturgy of the word. The actual service normally follows the pattern of the ante-communion part of the eucharist, which, after the *intercession and the Peace, concludes with the *Lord's Prayer and a final prayer. Some parishes who have to resort to this shape of the weekly liturgy also have previously consecrated bread (and wine) distributed, thereby making the celebration a liturgy of the *presanctified gifts. However, other parishes prefer a 'pure' service of the word.

Evening prayer (vespers) is an element of the liturgical life of a number of Old Catholic parishes, either on a regular basis on (individual, some or most) Sundays or on a week-day, in each case in addition to the regular Sunday eucharist. Only the Old Catholic Church of the Netherlands and the Swiss Old Catholic Church have incorporated a common form of vespers in their service book. In other Old Catholic churches the structure follows roughly that of the RC liturgy of the hours: hymn, psalmody, reading, gospel *canticle (Magnificat), prayers. In almost all cases, this structure is preceded by a *lucernarium* with a thanksgiving for the light, a version of *Phos hilaron* and Ps. 141. An unofficial office book from the Church of England, *Celebrating Common Prayer*, has begun to exercise some influence on the actual shape of morning or evening prayer.

Taizé-inspired meditation services have begun to be a regular feature of the liturgical life of particular parishes in Germany, Austria and the Czech Republic. They belong to the best-attended services and are commonly held on a weekday night.

The liturgy on *Good Friday used to be a celebration of the eucharist in some parishes but is normally nowadays a service of the word: readings, intercessions, *veneration of the cross, possibly also the distribution of the consecrated bread. The rites and texts are closely related to those of the RC Church.

Some Old Catholic dioceses require a lay person presiding at such a liturgy of the word to follow some theological training and to be licensed by the bishop, especially if they preside on a regular basis and give a homily; others trust the selection of the person within the parish itself.

THADDEUS A. SCHNITKER

11. *Pentecostal*. For Pentecostals, the service of the word involves *preaching from a biblical text under the empowerment or 'anointing' of the Holy Spirit. Pentecostals rarely read sermons from a prepared text, for this would limit the spontaneity and innovation involved in the preacher's interaction with the congregation that is expected to take place under the guidance of the Holy Spirit. Such interaction is most intense in African-American and Hispanic Pentecostal congregations in the USA and in many congregations in the two-thirds world, though Pentecostals in general tend to converse with the preacher by saying 'Amen' or offering other expressions of approval and enthusiasm aloud when they believe the preacher is offering an important insight. The preacher is expected to remain innovative with

the content of his or her message as the biblical text is preached.

Such openness to innovation does not necessarily preclude a disciplined study of scripture and sermon preparation in advance of the service, but what is decisive as to the content and expression of a sermon is what happens at the time of delivery. Only then does the sermon take final shape to engage the congregation prophetically with the world and message of the biblical text through the work of the Holy Spirit. The Spirit thus anoints the preacher and helps people 'read their lives into the biblical text and the biblical text into their lives' (Richard Israel). As Daniel Albrecht noted, the Pentecostal sermon is a 'prophetic pronouncement by the Holy Spirit' that helps believers 're-experience a biblical text', and Pentecostals consider worship to be our address to God, while the sermon represents a major part of God's address to us. The sermon thus serves to unite the initial address to God made in worship with the important prayer time after the sermon at the altar in which people respond in repentance and faith to what God has said to them in the sermon.

The sermon, then, represents the major part of the divine speaking in a worship service, though not the only part. The sermon is also preceded by personal testimonies and various 'word gifts', such as prophecy, word of wisdom (or counsel), word of knowledge, speaking in tongues, and interpretation of tongues (1 Cor. 12—14). Prophecy as described in 1 Cor. 14 is commonly understood by Pentecostals as spontaneous comfort or admonition given by a member of a congregation during the worship service. The distinction between prophecy narrowly defined in this way and preaching is not sharp for Pentecostals, owing to the prophetic nature of preaching. The same may be said of the distinction between the other word gifts and preaching. But the distinction does serve to illustrate the complementary relationship between the sermon and word gifts in a Pentecostal worship service. On the one hand, the word gifts imply a common participation of the laity in the sharing of divine revelation in the church, helping to test the truthfulness of the sermon and to place limits on the role of the sermon in the congregation's discernment of truth. On the other hand, since the word gifts often function to prepare for or to confirm a sermon in a Pentecostal service, the preached word tends to hold a very important place in Pentecostal church life.

The role of the sermon and the word gifts imply for Pentecostals that 'God has not confined himself to the written word. He still speaks direct to his children as the Bible plainly teaches he has done in the past' (Hollenweger). Pentecostals believe that not confining God's revelation to the Bible makes them true to biblical teaching, since the Bible is meant to occasion a present experience of the God to whom the text bears witness. Pentecostals imply a certain 'present-tenseness' to the revelation of scripture, especially as conveyed in preaching. They are devoted to the authority of the Bible as a written text or canon, and will defend its truthfulness as a faithful description of how God still speaks and acts today. In other words, the Pentecostal devotion to the authority and truthfulness of the biblical text is not primarily for the sake of scientifically guaranteeing an inerrant system of doctrine as is typical of fundamentalist hermeneutics (and its Pentecostal imitators), but rather for encouraging the faith necessary to experience the God of the Bible as this same God was experienced in 'Bible times'. The Bible is therefore the standard for judging all other words that are spoken to occasion the self-disclosure of the God to whom the biblical text bears witness.

The end result of anointed preaching and the response of obedient faith is the transformation of the individual and the congregation. Pentecostals believe that empowered preaching is typically followed by repentance, conversion experiences, deeper commitments to the holy life, divine healing, and other signs and wonders. Preaching as an event of the Holy Spirit can be said to encourage faith and the participation of many in the charismatic life of the church. Not every sermon will have widespread and dramatic results, but Pentecostals anticipate that preaching, if faithfully done, will occasion at times such deeply felt experiences of renewal in the Holy Spirit. Pentecostals wish to carry that expectation with them along with their Bibles to every service of the word.

Daniel Albrecht, *Rites in the Spirit: A Ritual Approach to Pentecostal/Charismatic Spirituality*, Sheffield 1999, 162–3, 228–9; James Forbes, *The Holy Spirit and Preaching*, Nashville 1989; Gerald T. Sheppard, 'Word and Spirit: Scripture in Pentecostal Tradition', *Agora*, Spring 1978, 4–5, 21–2; Summer 1978, 4–9; John Christopher Thomas, 'The Word and the Spirit', *Ministry and Theology*, Cleveland,

TN 1996, 13–20; Walter Hollenweger, *The Pentecostals*, reprint, Peabody, MA 1988, 291–310.

FRANK D. MACCHIA

12. *Reformed*. 'Service of the word' in the Reformed tradition may refer to the entire Lord's Day service or to the portion of the *eucharist that includes the scripture reading and sermon. In the sixteenth century, strong vernacular *preaching in the context of a simplified liturgy was the central liturgical experience for most Reformed worshippers. In Zurich, in 1519, Zwingli preached daily expository sermons at prone, a medieval vernacular devotional service which preceded the Latin *mass. He preached verse by verse through the Gospel of Matthew (*lectio continua*) rather than relying on the Roman *lectionary (*lectio selecta*). In 1525, he abolished the mass, providing a revised version of prone as the normal Sunday liturgy. The simple service began with *intercessory prayer, focused on scripture reading and preaching, and concluded with *confession of sin and a prayer for *absolution.

In Strasbourg, the word was read and preached either in a weekly *Lord's supper service derived from the mass or in a liturgy that consisted of everything except the *sacrament (*ante-communion). Worshippers heard several overlapping series of sermons, all following *lectio continua*: the Gospels on Sunday morning, the Epistles and OT texts on Sunday afternoon services and during weekday services. In Geneva, Calvin followed a similar approach, adopting ante-communion as the Lord's Day service and preaching through nearly the entire Bible during his ministry. His liturgy featured unison congregational singing of metrical psalms and an *epicletic prayer for illumination, a liturgical corollary to his emphasis on the 'inner testimony of the Holy Spirit' which made the word effective.

Other Reformed liturgies, including Knox's *The Forme of Prayers* (1556) in Scotland, the *Palatinate Liturgy* (1563) in Germany, and Dathenus' *Netherlands Liturgy* (1566), all retained congregational singing of psalms, a prayer for illumination prior to the sermon, a central place for scripture reading and preaching, and set prayers ('free' prayer would come later). Throughout, notable Reformed emphases included preaching expository sermons, *lectio continua*, without allegorical exegesis, on both OT and NT texts. Reformed pastors also developed catechetical preaching, often in Sunday afternoon services, which taught the rudiments of the faith based on Reformed *catechisms.

From the seventeenth to the nineteenth centuries, the emphasis on the service of the word grew even stronger, though liturgical practices diverged, reflecting the influence, in turn, of rationalism, Pietism, revivalism and romanticism. Generally, the tradition witnessed a movement away from set liturgies. The directory for worship, with general parameters for worship, replaced the service book as the primary liturgical document in parts of the tradition. The 1644 *Westminster Directory for Worship* is notable for separating the sermon and scripture reading, which was to be an independent liturgical act, and for calling for the reading of one chapter from each testament in course at each service. As the use of set prayers declined, other liturgical elements were sometimes called merely 'preliminaries' to the sermon.

In contrast, there have also been several efforts to enrich the liturgy of the word. Examples include new liturgies in the seventeenth century by Swiss pastor Jean Frédéric Ostervald, and in the nineteenth by the Scottish Service Society, French pastor Eugene Bersier, and the Mercersburg theologians. These services restored a word–table liturgy and the practice of set prayer.

Preaching practices also diverged. In the seventeenth century Puritans such as Thomas Manton and John Cotton were masters of expository preaching, while the Dutch preachers Gisbert Voetius and Johannes Cocceius preached doctrinal sermons. In the eighteenth century the first Great Awakening was spread through the experiential preaching of George Whitefield, Gilbert Tennant and Jonathan Edwards, while the Swiss pastor Jean Frédéric Ostervald restored liturgical preaching. In the nineteenth century Charles Hodge's sermons read like systematic theology, while the erstwhile Presbyterian Charles Grandison Finney's sermons were emotion-engaging and evangelistic.

In the twentieth century, services of the word have been invigorated by developments as divergent as the revival of catechetical preaching, the rhetorical flair of tall-steeple Presbyterian preachers such as Harry Emerson Fosdick, Karl Barth's high theology of the Word of God, post-Vatican II ecumenical liturgical reforms (including the adoption of the Common Lectionary and the Christian *year), and new emphasis on evangelistic preaching (especially in the church growth movement).

Overall, Presbyterian and Reformed services of the word have a reputation for being simple, solemn and cerebral. They have been supported by a high theology of the word of God, including the assertion of the Second Helvetic Confession that 'the preaching of the Word of God is the Word of God'. Traditional *vestments more closely resemble academic gowns than eucharistic garments, and the centrality of the word has often been underscored by a *pulpit-centred architecture. Often the sermon has comprised over half of the Lord's Day service. Reformed catechisms have called preaching a primary means of grace, always insisting that the word of God is a gift effected by the Holy Spirit, rather than the product of human ingenuity or rhetorical flair.

Hughes Oliphant Old, *The Reading and Preaching of the Scriptures in the Worship of the Christian Church*, 4 volumes, Grand Rapids, 1998– ; *Worship That Is Reformed According to Scripture*, Atlanta 1984; Harry S. Stout, *The New England Soul: Preaching and Religious Culture in Colonial New England*, Oxford 1986.

JOHN WITVLIET

Words of Administration

The usual form of words used at the distribution of *communion in the early church was 'The body of Christ', 'The blood of Christ', to which the communicant replied 'Amen' each time (e.g. Augustine, *Sermon* 272), though variants are also found: in the *Apostolic Tradition* the formula at the giving of the bread is, 'The bread of heaven in Jesus Christ', and in the *Apostolic Constitutions* (Book 8) the formula at the giving of the wine is 'The blood of Christ, the cup of life'. In the later liturgies of St John Chrysostom and St Basil a combined formula is used incorporating the name, and even ecclesiastical title, of the communicant: 'The servant of God N. partakes of the precious and holy body and blood of our Lord and God and Saviour Jesus Christ for the remission of his/her sins and unto eternal life.' By the eighth century the Roman form had become a blessing: 'May the body and blood of our Lord Jesus Christ preserve you unto life everlasting' was its most common form, although there were many verbal (but not doctrinal) variations. The RC *Ordo Missae* of 1970 returned to the

simplicity of 'The body of Christ' and the answer 'Amen'.

In the Church of England the words were a point of contention. The words in the 1549 *BCP*, reproducing those from the 'Order of Communion' of 1548, were close to the traditional Western form. At the bread the form was: 'The Body of Our Lord Jesus Christ which was given for thee, preserve thy body and soul unto everlasting life.' The 1552 book removed mention of the body and blood of Christ from both formulae and substituted words which were reminiscent of the reformer John à Lasco. For the bread they read: 'Take and eat this, in remembrance that Christ died for thee and feed on him in thy heart by faith, with thanksgiving.' The 1559 *BCP* compromised by combining the two forms, and 1662 followed suit. *The Alternative Service Book 1980* and *Common Worship* (2000) contain these longer texts as well as shorter options, including 'The body/blood of Christ', and similar provisions have been made in other provinces of the Anglican Communion.

DONALD GRAY

Year, Liturgical

The holy days, festivals and seasons of the Christian year constitute one of the principal ways through which most Christians celebrate their faith. The year is made up of two overlapping cycles, known as the *temporale*, the temporal cycle (derived from the Latin word *tempora*, meaning 'seasons') and the *sanctorale*, the sanctoral cycle, which as its name suggests is the cycle of individual saints' days. The *temporale* does not coincide with the civil year, but itself is a combination of two spans of time, one based around the festival of *Easter, the dates of which change each year depending upon when Easter is calculated to fall and are often therefore called 'moveable feasts', and the other based around the festivals of *Christmas and *Epiphany, which always occur on the same dates. Since the two annual cycles overlap, they affect both each other and the weekly *Sunday observance in different ways each year, and hence churches often have complex rules for ranking them according to their relative liturgical gravity in order to resolve situations when various holy days coincide. The *temporale* also has two 'in-between' spans, nowadays called '*Ordinary Time' by some churches, the shorter one from the end of the Christmas/Epiphany season to the beginning of

*Lent (or pre-Lent) and the considerably longer one from *Pentecost to the beginning of *Advent. Behind this annual pattern, however, lies the more fundamental Christian cycle of the week.

1. *The Week*. The seven-day Christian week was inherited from Judaism, but the Jewish observance of the seventh day of the week, the Sabbath, as its climax seems to have quickly waned among early Christians and was replaced by the first day, Sunday, as the regular occasion for communal worship, which they began to designate as 'the Lord's Day' (Rev. 1.10; *Didache* 14.1). The narratives of the discovery of the empty tomb of Jesus and the proclamation of the resurrection on the 'first day of the week' in all four Gospels mark this shift in time-keeping (Matt. 28.1; Mark 16.2; Luke 24.1; John 20.1). It is likely that the emergence of Sunday as the weekly day of celebration is also linked to the antipathy towards the Sabbath in the sayings of Jesus in the Gospels. For several centuries it was the only day of the week on which the *eucharist was normally celebrated, and in order to set the day apart from others in the week, both kneeling for prayer and fasting came to be forbidden on all Sundays. Two other days of the week were also marked out in a particular way. Wednesdays and Fridays were observed as regular *fast days, in contrast to the standard Jewish fast days of Monday and Thursday, and marked liturgically with a service of the *word. In later centuries in the West Wednesday tended to decline in importance, leaving only Friday as a weekly day of fasting, although in the Middle Ages particular 'themes' were often attached also to other days in the week.

2. *The Easter Cycle*. Similar to the move from Jewish Sabbath to Christian Sunday as the weekly liturgical keystone was the move from Jewish Passover to Christian Easter as the annual marker, but, unlike the move in the weekly cycle, this shift was much more gradual, and when and how it occurred varied from place to place throughout the first three centuries of Christianity. The earliest Christian name for Easter, *pascha*, is the same as the Greek word for Passover, and the earliest theologies of Easter, in the second century, draw from the Jewish theology of Passover. Those Christian communities which most tenaciously kept Jewish traditions – liturgical, theological and calendrical – maintained the Jewish date of celebration, but saw Christ as the fulfilment of the Passover hopes (cf. 1 Cor. 5.7). They were known as 'Quartodecimans', which might be translated as 'fourteeners', from the Jewish date for Passover, 14 Nisan. Their opponents were those who thought that the most esteemed day in the year should coincide with the most esteemed day of the week, and this dispute between those who wanted the church to keep the *date* of Easter and those who wanted Easter on a Sunday continued until it was settled by the Council of Nicaea in 325.

The celebration of Easter came to be preceded by days of fasting, which in some places had increased to a full week in the third century, and was also followed by a fifty-day period of rejoicing known as Pentecost. Further developments took place in the fourth century. The forty-day season of Lent came to be prefixed to the paschal celebration, and the week before Easter, known as *Holy Week in the West and 'Great Week' in the East, gradually attracted to itself special commemorations on particular days of events in the last week of Jesus' life, a practice apparently originating primarily in Jerusalem and then copied elsewhere. With the later addition of three pre-Lenten Sundays (*see* **Quinquagesima**) and of an *octave to the day of Pentecost, the Easter cycle came to cover around a third of the year.

3. *The Christmas/Epiphany Cycle*. By the early fourth century Christians in Rome and North Africa had begun to observe a festival of Christ's incarnation on 25 December, while Christians in other parts of the world observed 6 January as a feast of his *epiphaneia* (manifestation), the scriptural narratives of which varied from place to place but might include his nativity, the visit of the magi (Matt. 2.1–12), his baptism, and the wedding feast at Cana (John 2.1–12). By the end of the fourth century, churches throughout the ancient world began to adopt both of these feasts into their local calendars, and gradually other festivals were added to the cycle, the dates of which were calculated in relation to 25 December as the commemoration of Christ's birth. Thus, for example, the *Annunciation (Luke 1.26–38) was celebrated nine months before, on 25 March, and the commemoration of the presentation in the Temple (Luke 2.22–40), popularly known in the West as *Candlemas, was observed forty days after his birth, on 2 February. In the West, a preparatory season for Christmas known as Advent also emerged, at first of varying duration in dif-

ferent places but eventually fixed as beginning four Sundays before 25 December.

4. *The Calendar of the *Saints*. At first only local martyrs were commemorated by Christian communities, usually at the site of their burial and on the date of their death. But in later centuries, after major persecution ceased, the concept of sainthood was expanded to include other Christians judged to have outstanding virtue as well as many biblical figures, and also ceased to be purely local. Especially through the dissemination of relics, a large number of saints' days were adopted widely or even universally, and by the late Middle Ages the majority of days of the year had one or more such commemorations attached to them, and further feasts reflecting popular devotion (e.g. *Corpus Christi on the Thursday after the octave of Pentecost, established in the West in 1264) also found their way into calendars.

5. *Reformation and Modern Practice*. The sixteenth-century Reformers drastically curtailed the liturgical year. Some removed every observance except for Sunday. Others abolished the *sanctorale* entirely because of the association with relics and with invoking the prayers of the saints (except for the Church of England, which made liturgical provision for a small number of biblical saints) and retained just the principal annual feasts and seasons, though eliminating many of the 'superstitious' ceremonies that had previously accompanied them. The RC liturgical changes that followed the Council of Trent included a major pruning of the *sanctorale*, but it grew again with many new additions in subsequent centuries, and it was not until the Second Vatican Council that a major reform of the whole liturgical year, recovering a more primitive simplicity, was achieved. Similar reforms of the calendar have also taken place in other Western churches, often leading to the restoration of elements that were discarded at the Reformation.

While the liturgical year has sometimes been viewed merely as a succession of historical commemorations which provide a useful aid to teaching the Christian faith, many would see it as much more than that, as a *sacramental means of entering into the mysteries of the faith that are proclaimed and celebrated through the year and as a foretaste of their ultimate fulfilment at the end of time.

Adolf Adam, *The Liturgical Year*, New York 1981; A. G. Martimort et al., *The Church at Prayer* IV, Collegeville 1986; Thomas J. Talley, *The Origins of the Liturgical Year*, 2nd edn, Collegeville 1991.

MARTIN F. CONNELL

Zone *see* **Vestments** 4(b)